AMERICAN
HISTORY

PEARSON

Boston, Massachusetts
Chandler, Arizona
Glenview, Illinois
New York, New York

Social Studies Reimagined

To start, download the free **Pearson BouncePages** app on your smartphone or tablet. Simply search for the Pearson BouncePages app in your mobile app store. The app is available for Android and IOS (iPhone®/iPad®).

Make your book come alive!

Activate your digital course interactivities directly from the page.

To launch the myStory video look for this icon.

To activate more interactivities look for this icon. ▶ **Interactive**

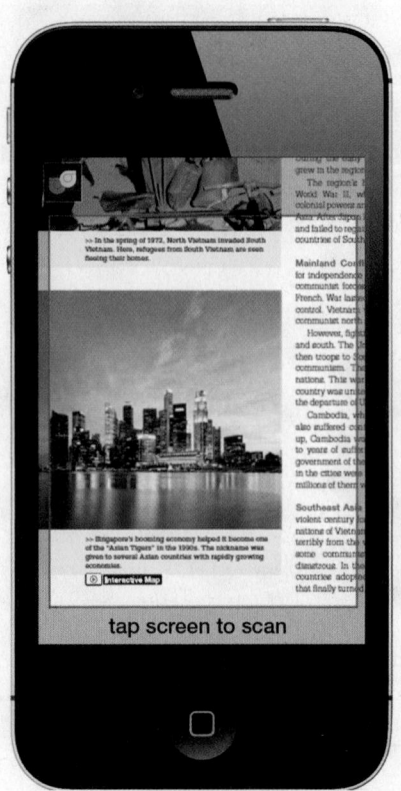

tap screen to scan

1. **AIM** the camera over the image so it is easily viewable on your screen.

2. **TAP** the screen to scan the page.

3. **BOUNCE** the page to life by clicking the icon.

Cover Image: South Dakota, Mount Rushmore with viewscope in foreground. Chris Cheadle/Alamy

Acknowledgments appear at the end of the book, which constitute an extension of this copyright page.

PEARSON

ISBN-13: 978-0-13-330701-6
ISBN-10:   0-13-330701-8

4 5 6 7 8 9 10 V011 18 17 16 15

Authors, Consultants, Partners

[Authors]

James West Davidson
Dr. James Davidson is coauthor of *After the Fact: The Art of Historical Detection* and *Nation of Nations: A Narrative History of the American Republic.* Dr. Davidson has taught at both the college and high school levels. He has also consulted on curriculum design for American history courses. Dr. Davidson is an avid canoeist and hiker. His published works on these subjects include *Great Heart,* the true story of a 1903 canoe trip in the Canadian wilderness.

Michael B. Stoff
Dr. Michael Stoff received his Ph.D. from Yale University and teaches history at the University of Texas at Austin. He is the author of *Oil, War, and American Security: The Search for a National Policy on Foreign Oil, 1941–1947,* coauthor of *Nation of Nations: A Narrative History of the American Republic,* and coeditor of *The Manhattan Project: A Documentary Introduction to the Atomic Age.* Dr. Stoff has won numerous grants, fellowships, and teaching awards.

[Contributing Author]

Jennifer L. Bertolet
Jennifer L. Bertolet is a Professorial Lecturer at George Washington University, where she teaches American history courses, among them Introduction to American History. She received her Ph.D. from George Washington University. In addition to teaching, she has served as an education consultant, a subject matter expert for online teaching and learning, and as an historian and policy consultant specializing in Indian policy and environmental issues.

[Program Consultant]

Dr. Kathy Swan is an Associate Professor of Curriculum and Instruction at the University of Kentucky. Her research focuses on standards-based technology integration, authentic intellectual work, and documentary-making in the social studies classroom. Swan has been a four-time recipient of the National Technology Leadership Award in Social Studies Education. She is also the advisor for the Social Studies Assessment, Curriculum, and Instruction Collaborative (SSACI) at CCSSO.

[Program Partners]

NBC Learn, the educational arm of NBC News, develops original stories for use in the classroom and makes archival NBC News stories, images, and primary source documents available on demand to teachers, students, and parents. NBC Learn partnered with Pearson to produce the myStory videos that support this program.

Constitutional Rights Foundation is a nonprofit, nonpartisan organization focused on educating students about the importance of civic participation in a democratic society. Constitutional Rights Foundation is the lead contributor to the development of the Civic Discussion Topic Inquiries for this program. Constitutional Rights Foundation is also the provider of the Civic A' Project (CAP) for the *Economics* and *Magruder's Government* programs. CAP is a project-base' model for civics, government, and econom'

Reviewers & Academic Consultants

Pearson American History was developed especially for you and your students. The story of its creation began with a three-day Innovation Lab in which teachers, historians, students, and authors came together to imagine our ideal Social Studies teaching and learning experiences. We refined the plan with a series of teacher roundtables that shaped this new approach to ensure your students' mastery of content and skills. A dedicated team, made up of Pearson authors, content experts, and social studies teachers, worked to bring our collective vision into reality. Kathy Swan, Professor of Education and architect of the new College, Career, and Civic Life (C3) Framework, served as our expert advisor on curriculum and instruction.

Pearson would like to extend a special thank you to all of the teachers who helped guide the development of this program. We gratefully acknowledge your efforts to realize Next Generation Social Studies teaching and learning that will prepare American students for college, careers, and active citizenship.

[Program Advisors]

Campaign for the Civic Mission of Schools is a coalition of over 70 national civic learning, education, civic engagement, and business groups committed to improving the quality and quantity of civic learning in American schools. The Campaign served as an advisor on this program.

Buck Institute for Education is a nonprofit organization dedicated to helping teachers implement the effective use of Project-Based Learning in their classrooms. Buck Institute staff consulted on the Project-Based Learning Topic Inquiries for this program.

[Program Academic Consultants]

Barbara Brown
Director of Outreach
College of Arts and Sciences
African Studies Center
Boston University
Boston, Massachusetts

William Childs
Professor of History Emeritus
The Ohio State University
Columbus, Ohio

Jennifer Giglielmo
Associate Professor of History
Smith College
Northhampton, Massachusetts

Joanne Connor Green
Professor, Department Chair
Political Science
Texas Christian University
Fort Worth, Texas

Ramdas Lamb, Ph.D.
Associate Professor of Religion
University of Hawaii at Manoa
Honolulu, Hawaii

Huping Ling
Changjiang Scholar Chair Professor
Professor of History
Truman State University
Kirksville, Missouri

Jeffery Long, Ph.D.
Professor of Religion and Asian Studies
Elizabethtown College
Elizabethtown, Pennsylvania

Gordon Newby
Professor of Islamic, Jewish and
    Comparative Studies
Department of Middle Eastern and
    South Asian Studies
Emory University
Atlanta, Georgia

Mark Peterson
Associate Professor
Department of Asian and Near Eastern
    Languages
Brigham Young University
Provo, Utah

William Pitts
Professor, Department of Religion
Baylor University
Waco, Texas

Benjamin Ravid
Professor Emeritus of Jewish History
Department of Near Eastern and
    Judaic Studies
Brandeis University
Waltham, Massachusetts

Harpreet Singh
College Fellow
Department of South Asian Studies
Harvard University
Cambridge, Massachusetts

Christopher E. Smith, J.D., Ph.D.
Professor
Michigan State University
MSU School of Criminal Justice
East Lansing, Michigan

John Voll
Professor of Islamic History
Georgetown University
Washington, D.C.

Michael R. Wolf
Associate Professor
Department of Political Science
Indiana University-Purdue University
    Fort Wayne
Fort Wayne, Indiana

Social studies is more than dots on a map or dates on a timeline. It's where we've been and where we're going. It's stories from the past and our stories today. And in today's fast-paced, interconnected world, it's essential.

Welcome to the next generation of social studies!

Pearson's new social studies program was created in collaboration with educators, social studies experts, and students. The program is based on Pearson's Mastery System. The System uses tested best practices, content expectations, technology, and a four-part framework—Connect, Investigate, Synthesize, and Demonstrate—to prepare students to be college-and-career ready.

The System includes:

- Higher-level content that gives support to access complex text, acquire core content knowledge, and tackle rigorous questions.

- Inquiry-focused Projects, Civic Discussions, and Document Analysis activities that develop content and skills mastery in preparation for real-world challenges.

- Digital content on Pearson Realize that is dynamic, flexible, and uses the power of technology to bring social studies to life.

- The program uses essential questions and stories to increase long-term understanding and retention of learning.

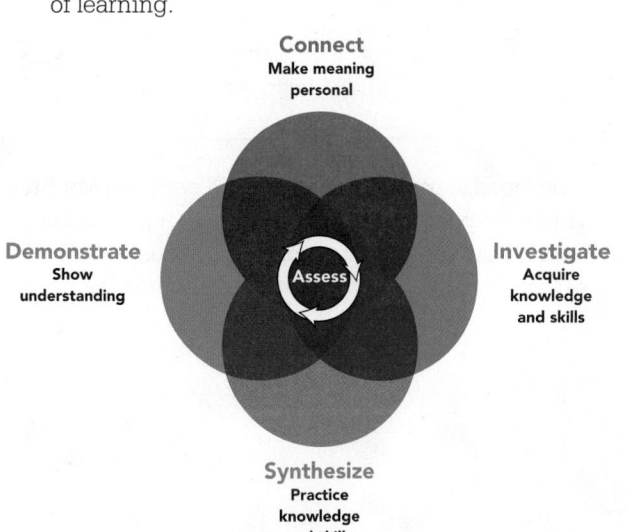

Connect
Make meaning personal

Demonstrate
Show understanding

Assess

Investigate
Acquire knowledge and skills

Synthesize
Practice knowledge and skills

» Go online to learn more and see the program overview video.

PEARSON
realize ™

The digital course on Realize!

The program's digital course on Realize puts rich and engaging content, embedded assessments with instant data, and flexible tools at your fingertips.

Connect: Make Meaning Personal

CONNECT! Begin the Pearson Mastery System by engaging in the topic story and connecting it to your own lives.

Preview—Each Topic opens with the Enduring Understandings section, allowing you to preview expected learning outcomes.

>> Instruction begins with an **Essential Question.** These thought-provoking questions engage students and introduce the Topic.

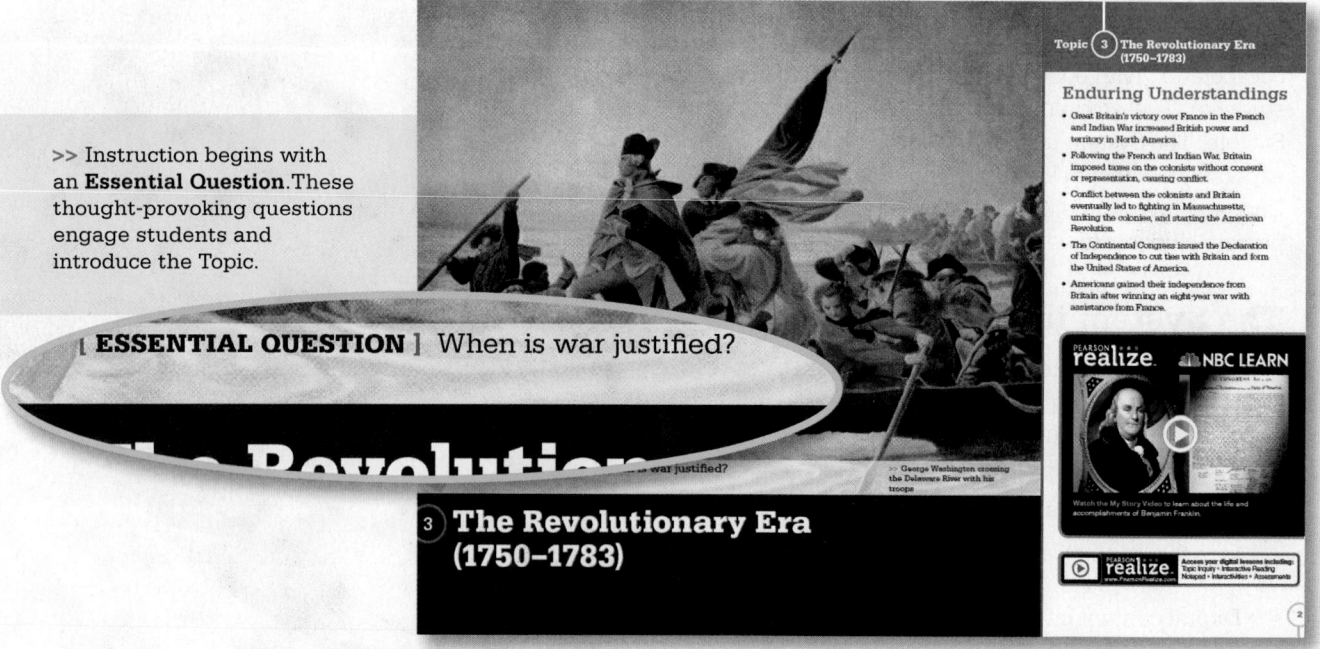

[ESSENTIAL QUESTION] When is war justified?

Topic **3** The Revolutionary Era (1750–1783)

Enduring Understandings

- Great Britain's victory over France in the French and Indian War increased British power and territory in North America.
- Following the French and Indian War, Britain imposed taxes on the colonists without consent or representation, causing conflict.
- Conflict between the colonists and Britain eventually led to fighting in Massachusetts, uniting the colonies, and starting the American Revolution.
- The Continental Congress issued the Declaration of Independence to cut ties with Britain and form the United States of America.
- Americans gained their independence from Britain after winning an eight-year war with assistance from France.

>> George Washington crossing the Delaware River with his troops

3 The Revolutionary Era (1750–1783)

Watch the My Story Video to learn about the life and accomplishments of Benjamin Franklin.

Developed in partnership with NBCLearn, the **My Story** videos help students connect to the Topic content by hearing the personal story of an individual whose life is related to the content students are about to learn.

Investigate: Acquire Knowledge and Skills

INVESTIGATE! Step two of the Mastery System allows you to investigate the topic story through a number of engaging features as you learn the content.

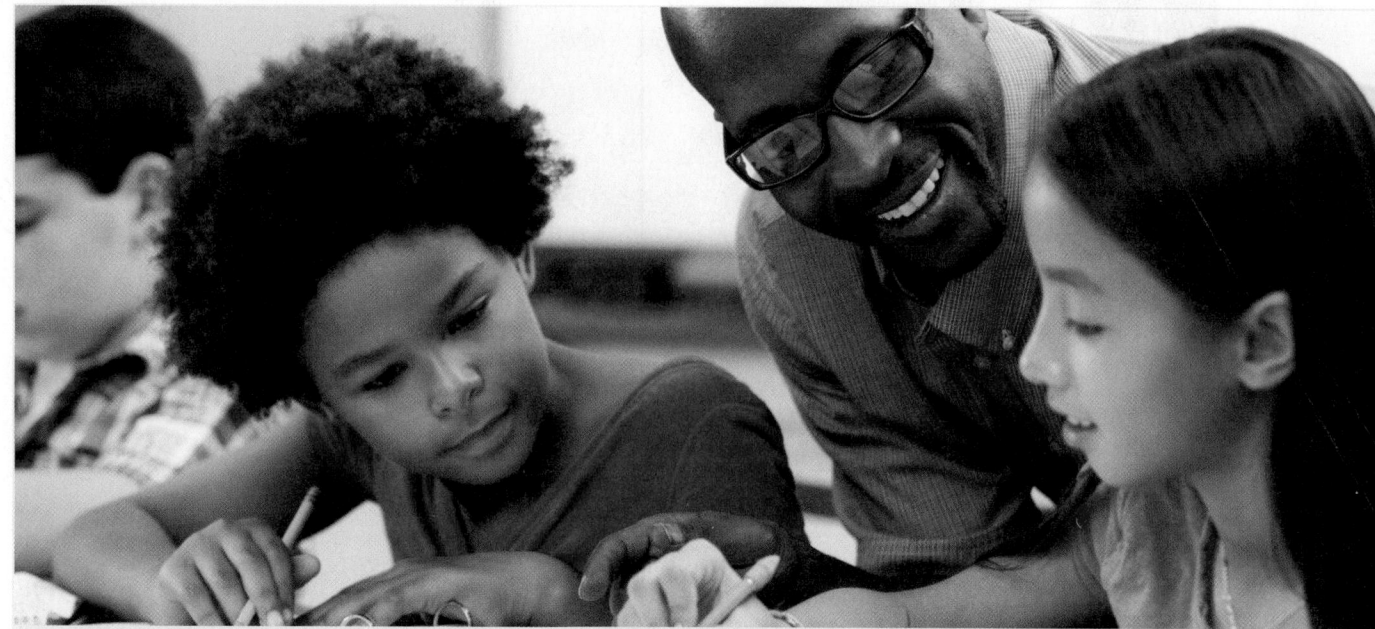

>> **Active Classroom Strategies** integrated in the daily lesson plans help to increase in-class participation, raise energy levels and attentiveness, all while engaging in the story. These 5-15 minute activities have you use what you have learned to draw, write, speak, and decide.

>> **Interactive Primary Source Galleries:** Use primary source image galleries throughout the lesson to see, analyze, and interact with images that tie to the topic story content.

Investigate

>> Feel like you are a part of the story with **interactive 3-D models**.

>> Continue to investigate the topic story through **dynamic interactive maps**. Build map skills while covering the essential standards.

>> Learn content by reading narrative text online or in a printed Student Edition.

Synthesize: Practice Knowledge and Skills

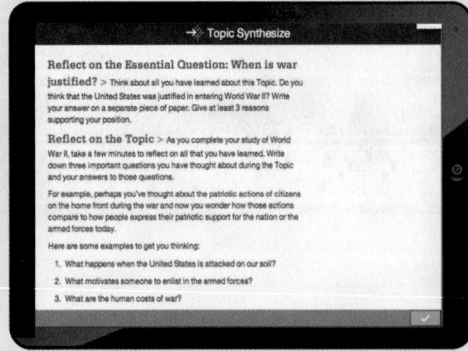

SYNTHESIZE!

In step three of the Mastery System, pause to reflect on what you learn and revisit an essential question.

Demonstrate: Show Understanding

DEMONSTRATE! The final step of the Mastery System is to demonstrate understanding of the text.

PEARSON realize™

>> The digital course on Realize!
The program's digital course on Realize puts engaging content, embedded assessments, instant data, and flexible tools at your fingertips.

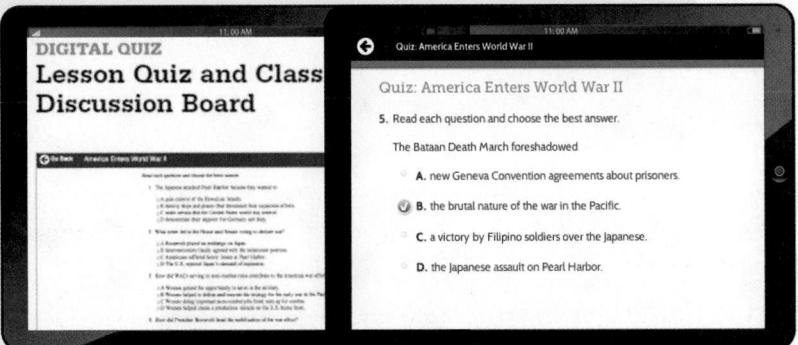

>> Assessment. At the end of each lesson and topic, demonstrate understanding through Lesson Quizzes, Topic Tests, and Topic Inquiry performance assessments. The System provides remediation and enrichment recommendations based on your individual performance towards mastery.

>> Class and Data features on Realize make it easy to see your mastery data.

Table of Contents

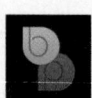

To activate your digital course interactivities download the free **Pearson BouncePages** app on your smartphone or tablet. Simply search for the Pearson BouncePages app in your mobile app store. The app is available for Android and IOS (iPhone®/iPad®).

Table of Contents

Table of Contents

Table of Contents

Table of Contents

TOPIC **10** **Industrial and Economic Growth (1865–1914)** **522**

Table of Contents

Table of Contents

Table of Contents

Table of Contents

PEARSON
realize™

www.PearsonRealize.com
Access your Digital Resources

Digital Resources

Many types of digital resources help you investigate the topics in this course. You'll find biographies, primary sources, maps, and more. These resources will help bring the topics to life.

Core Concepts

Culture

- What Is Culture?
- Families and Societies
- Language
- Religion
- The Arts
- Cultural Diffusion and Change
- Science and Technology

Economics

- Economics Basics
- Economic Process
- Economic Systems
- Economic Development
- Trade
- Money Management

Geography

- The Study of Earth
- Geography's Five Themes
- Ways to Show Earth's Surface
- Understanding Maps

- Earth in Space
- Time and Earth's Rotation
- Forces on Earth's Surface
- Forces Inside Earth
- Climate and Weather
- Temperature
- Water and Climate
- Air Circulation and Precipitation
- Types of Climate
- Ecosystems
- Environment and Resources
- Land Use
- People's Impact on the Environment
- Population
- Migration
- Urbanization

Government and Civics

- Foundations of Government
- Political Systems
- Political Structures
- Conflict and Cooperation
- Citizenship

History

- How Do Historians Study History?
- Measuring Time
- Historical Sources
- Archaeology and Other Sources
- Historical Maps

Personal Finance

- Your Fiscal Fitness: An Introduction
- Budgeting
- Checking
- Investments
- Savings and Retirement
- Credit and Debt
- Risk Management
- Consumer Smarts
- After High School
- Taxes and Income

Landmark Supreme Court Cases

- *Korematsu* v. *United States*
- *Marbury* v. *Madison*
- *McCulloch* v. *Maryland*
- *Gibbons* v. *Ogden*
- *Worcester* v. *Georgia*
- *Dred Scott* v. *Sandford*
- *Plessy* v. *Ferguson*
- *Schenck* v. *United States*
- *Brown* v. *Board of Education*
- *Engel* v. *Vitale*

- *Sweatt* v. *Painter*
- *Mapp* v. *Ohio*
- *Hernandez* v. *Texas*
- *Gideon* v. *Wainwright*
- *Wisconsin* v. *Yoder*
- *Miranda* v. *Arizona*
- *White* v. *Regester*
- *Tinker* v. *Des Moines School District*
- *Roe* v. *Wade*

- *Baker* v. *Carr*
- *Grutter* v. *Bollinger*
- *Edgewood* v. *Kirby*
- *Texas* v. *Johnson*
- *National Federation of Independent Businesses et al.* v. *Sebelius et al.*
- *Mendez* v. *Westminster* and *Delgado* v. *Bastrop*

Interactive Primary Sources

- Code of Hammurabi
- Psalm 23
- The Republic, Plato
- Politics, Aristotle
- Edicts, Asoka
- Analects, Confucius
- First Letter to the Corinthians, Paul
- The Quran
- The Magna Carta
- Travels, Ibn Battuta
- The Destruction of the Indies, Bartolomé de Las Casas
- Mayflower Compact
- English Petition of Right
- English Bill of Rights
- Two Treatises of Government, John Locke
- The Spirit of Laws, Baron de Montesquieu
- The Social Contract, Jean-Jacques Rousseau
- The Interesting Narrative of the Life of Olaudah Equiano
- "Give Me Liberty or Give Me Death," Patrick Henry
- "Remember the Ladies," Abigail Adams
- Common Sense, Thomas Paine
- Declaration of Independence
- Virginia Declaration of Rights
- Virginia Statute for Religious Freedom, Thomas Jefferson
- "To His Excellency, General Washington," Phillis Wheatley
- Articles of Confederation
- Anti-Federalist Papers
- The Federalist No. 10, James Madison
- The Federalist No. 39, James Madison
- The Federalist No. 51
- The Federalist No. 78, Alexander Hamilton
- Northwest Ordinance
- Iroquois Constitution
- Declaration of the Rights of Man and the Citizen
- Farewell Address, George Washington
- Mexican Federal Constitution of 1824
- State Colonization Law of 1825

- Law of April 6, 1830
- Debate Over Nullification, Webster and Calhoun
- Turtle Bayou Resolutions
- Democracy in America, Alexis de Tocqueville
- 1836 Victory or Death Letter from the Alamo, Travis
- Texas Declaration of Independence
- Declaration of Sentiments and Resolutions
- "Ain't I a Woman?," Sojourner Truth
- Uncle Tom's Cabin, Harriet Beecher Stowe
- "A House Divided," Abraham Lincoln
- First Inaugural Address, Abraham Lincoln
- Declaration of Causes: February 2, 1861
- Emancipation Proclamation, Abraham Lincoln
- Gettysburg Address, Abraham Lincoln
- Second Inaugural Address, Abraham Lincoln
- "I Will Fight No More Forever," Chief Joseph
- How the Other Half Lives, Jacob Riis
- The Pledge of Allegiance
- Preamble to the Platform of the Populist Party
- Atlanta Exposition Address, Booker T. Washington
- The Jungle, Upton Sinclair
- Hind Swaraj, Mohandas Gandhi
- The Fourteen Points, Woodrow Wilson
- Two Poems, Langston Hughes
- Four Freedoms, Franklin D. Roosevelt
- Anne Frank: The Diary of a Young Girl, Anne Frank
- Charter of the United Nations
- Universal Declaration of Human Rights
- Autobiography, Kwame Nkrumah
- Inaugural Address, John F. Kennedy
- Silent Spring, Rachel Carson
- "I Have a Dream," Martin Luther King, Jr.
- "Letter From Birmingham Jail," Martin Luther King, Jr.
- "Tear Down This Wall," Ronald Reagan
- "Freedom From Fear," Aung San Suu Kyi
- "Glory and Hope," Nelson Mandela

Biographies

- Abigail Adams
- John Adams
- John Quincy Adams
- Samuel Adams
- James Armistead
- Crispus Attucks
- Moses Austin
- Stephen F. Austin
- James A. Baker III
- William Blackstone
- Simón Bolívar
- Napoleon Bonaparte
- Chief Bowles
- Omar Bradley
- John C. Calhoun
- César Chávez
- Wentworth Cheswell
- George Childress
- Winston Churchill
- Henry Clay
- Bill Clinton
- Jefferson Davis
- Martin De León
- Green DeWitt
- Dwight Eisenhower
- James Fannin
- James L. Farmer, Jr.
- Benjamin Franklin
- Milton Friedman
- Betty Friedan
- Bernardo de Gálvez
- Hector P. Garcia
- John Nance Garner
- King George III
- Henry B. González
- Raul A. Gonzalez, Jr.
- Mikhail Gorbachev
- William Goyens

- Ulysses S. Grant
- José Gutiérrez de Lara
- Alexander Hamilton
- Hammurabi
- Warren Harding
- Friedrich Hayek
- Jack Coffee Hays
- Patrick Henry
- Adolf Hitler
- Oveta Culp Hobby
- James Hogg
- Sam Houston
- Kay Bailey Hutchison
- Andrew Jackson
- John Jay
- Thomas Jefferson
- Lyndon B. Johnson
- Anson Jones
- Barbara Jordan
- Justinian
- John F. Kennedy
- John Maynard Keynes
- Martin Luther King, Jr.
- Marquis de Lafayette
- Mirabeau B. Lamar
- Robert E. Lee
- Abraham Lincoln
- John Locke
- James Madison
- John Marshall
- George Marshall
- Karl Marx
- George Mason
- Mary Maverick
- Jane McCallum
- Joseph McCarthy
- James Monroe
- Charles de

- Montesquieu
- Edwin W. Moore
- Moses
- Benito Mussolini
- José Antonio Navarro
- Chester A. Nimitz
- Richard M. Nixon
- Barack Obama
- Sandra Day O'Connor
- Thomas Paine
- Quanah Parker
- Rosa Parks
- George Patton
- John J. Pershing
- John Paul II
- Sam Rayburn
- Ronald Reagan
- Hiram Rhodes Revels
- Franklin D. Roosevelt
- Theodore Roosevelt
- Lawrence Sullivan Ross
- Haym Soloman
- Antonio Lopez de Santa Anna
- Phyllis Schlafly
- Erasmo Seguín
- Juan N. Seguín
- Roger Sherman
- Adam Smith
- Joseph Stalin
- Raymond L. Telles
- Alexis de Tocqueville
- Hideki Tojo
- William B. Travis
- Harry Truman
- Lech Walesa
- Mercy Otis Warren
- George Washington

- Daniel Webster
- Lulu Belle Madison White
- William Wilberforce
- James Wilson
- Woodrow Wilson
- Lorenzo de Zavala
- Mao Zedong

21st Century Skills

- Identify Main Ideas and Details
- Set a Purpose for Reading
- Use Context Clues
- Analyze Cause and Effect
- Categorize
- Compare and Contrast
- Draw Conclusions
- Draw Inferences
- Generalize
- Make Decisions
- Make Predictions
- Sequence
- Solve Problems
- Summarize
- Analyze Media Content
- Analyze Primary and Secondary Sources
- Compare Viewpoints
- Distinguish Between Fact and Opinion
- Identify Bias
- Analyze Data and Models

- Analyze Images
- Analyze Political Cartoons
- Create Charts and Maps
- Create Databases
- Read Charts, Graphs, and Tables
- Read Physical Maps
- Read Political Maps
- Read Special-Purpose Maps
- Use Parts of a Map
- Ask Questions
- Avoid Plagiarism
- Create a Research Hypothesis
- Evaluate Web Sites
- Identify Evidence
- Identify Trends
- Interpret Sources
- Search for Information on the Internet
- Synthesize
- Take Effective Notes
- Develop a Clear Thesis
- Organize Your Ideas

- Support Ideas With Evidence
- Evaluate Existing Arguments
- Consider & Counter Opposing Arguments
- Give an Effective Presentation
- Participate in a Discussion or Debate
- Publish Your Work
- Write a Journal Entry
- Write an Essay
- Share Responsibility
- Compromise
- Develop Cultural Awareness
- Generate New Ideas
- Innovate
- Make a Difference
- Work in Teams
- Being an Informed Citizen
- Paying Taxes
- Political Participation
- Serving on a Jury
- Voting

Atlas

- United States: Political
- United States: Physical
- World Political
- World Physical
- World Climate
- World Ecosystems
- World Population Density
- World Land Use
- North Africa and Southwest Asia: Political
- North Africa and Southwest Asia: Physical
- Sub-Saharan Africa: Political
- Sub-Saharan Africa: Physical
- South Asia: Political
- South Asia: Physical
- East Asia: Political

- East Asia: Physical
- Southeast Asia: Political
- Southeast Asia: Physical
- Europe: Political
- Europe: Physical
- Russia, Central Asia, and the Caucasus: Political
- Russia, Central Asia, and the Caucasus: Physical
- North America: Political
- North America: Physical
- Central America and the Caribbean: Political
- Central America and the Caribbean: Physical
- South America: Political
- South America: Physical
- Australia and the Pacific: Political
- Australia and the Pacific: Physical

Celebrate Freedom

> "We hold these truths to be self-evident, that all men are created equal, that they are endowed by their Creator with certain unalienable Rights, that among these are Life, Liberty and the pursuit of Happiness. That to secure these rights, Governments are instituted among Men, deriving their just powers from the consent of the governed...."

Declaration of Independence

Every year, you and your classmates may participate in Celebrate Freedom Week activities. These activities are designed to remind you about some of the important ideas that make our country so special. In your school, you may have school-wide displays or an assembly. Maybe speakers come to share their thoughts or students write essays or make posters or develop presentations. Whatever happens in your school, you will likely take some time to think about America's founding documents, such as the Declaration of Independence.

The Declaration of Independence states some of America's most important ideas about society and government. It has played a key role in shaping America's constitutional republic. As you recite the words, think about why many students join in Celebrate Freedom Week.

Summarize According to the Declaration of Independence, who has rights? Who can take them away?

Paraphrase In your own words, restate the idea in the Declaration about the purpose of government.

Analyze Why do you think many students recite part of the Declaration of Independence when they celebrate Freedom Week?

self-evident, adj., obvious

endowed, v. given; provided

unalienable, adj., not to be taken away

deriving, v., getting from a source

consent, n., agreement

The Bill of Rights

One of the chief ways early American leaders tried to protect individual rights was by adding the first ten Amendments to the Constitution. This section is known as the Bill of Rights. The Bill of Rights guarantees certain legal rights, and it limits the power of the government to interfere with others.

Constructing an Argument Write an essay discussing one of the rights guaranteed in the Bill of Rights.

1. Review the Bill of Rights in the U.S. Constitution in the online Reference Center or at the back of your book. Notice that the Constitution has Commentary on the side of the actual document. This Commentary helps explain the language in the Constitution and can give you some background about each provision. Use the Commentary to help you review the first ten Amendments, or Bill of Rights.

2. Choose one basic right as the focus of your essay. Note that several of the Amendments—including the First, Fifth, and Sixth—are divided into different parts, each dealing with a specific right. You may choose to focus on one part of one of these Amendments rather than the entire Amendment.

3. Research a recent event or situation where the right you have chosen was protected or threatened. This might be an event or situation in your local community or a nearby community, in your state, or somewhere else in the nation. Be sure to use more than one source and to use reliable sources.

4. Begin your essay by naming the Amendment you have chosen, and restating in your own words what the right protects or guarantees.

5. Explain why you believe that right is important to guarantee liberty today.

>> The First Amendment protects the right to petition.

6. Describe what you think might happen if that right were not protected by the Constitution.

7. Support your opinion with facts you have learned from your research.

8. Don't forget to check and revise your essay, as needed. Be sure to use proper grammar, spelling, and sentence structure.

9. After you write your essay, your teacher may ask you and your classmates to share your views with the class. If so, remember to speak clearly and to present your views using the evidence you gathered for your essay. When listening to others, listen closely and be respectful of their views.

[**ESSENTIAL QUESTION**] How much does geography affect people's lives?

1 The Early Americas and European Exploration (Prehistory–1550)

>> The Cliff Palace, built in what is now Colorado during the 1200s

Enduring Understandings

- The physical geography of regions in the early Americas influenced the culture and societies of those regions.

- Physical geography also helped shape where early Native Americans lived.

- New ways of doing things from Asia, Africa, and Europe contributed to a growth of learning and exploration in Europe during the Renaissance.

- Europeans' desire for wealth and for the spread of Christianity brought them into contact with Native Americans.

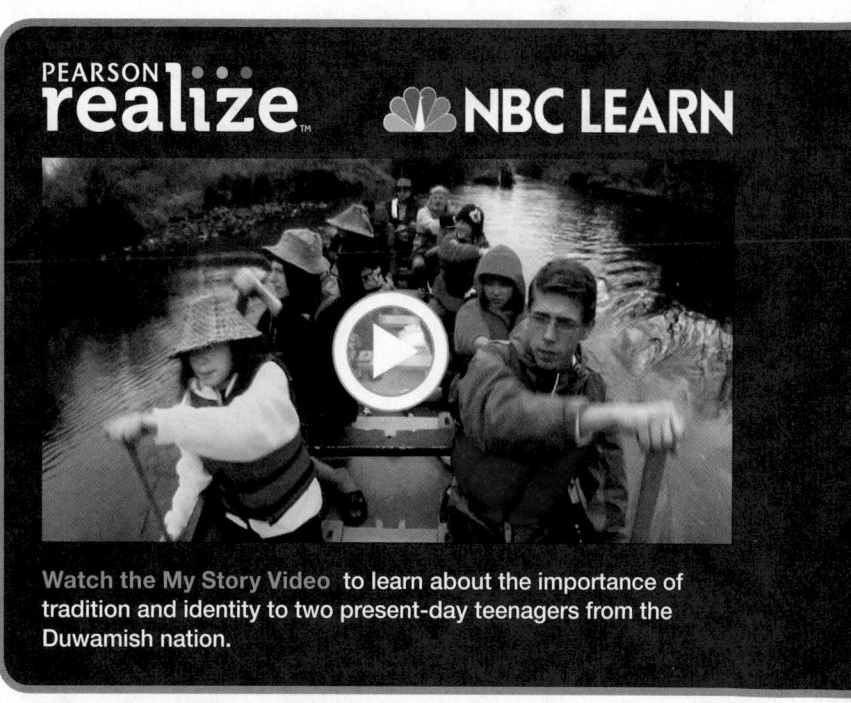

PEARSON realize **NBC LEARN**

Watch the My Story Video to learn about the importance of tradition and identity to two present-day teenagers from the Duwamish nation.

PEARSON realize
www.PearsonRealize.com

Access your digital lessons including: Topic Inquiry • Interactive Reading Notepad • Interactivities • Assessments

1.1 The Early Americas

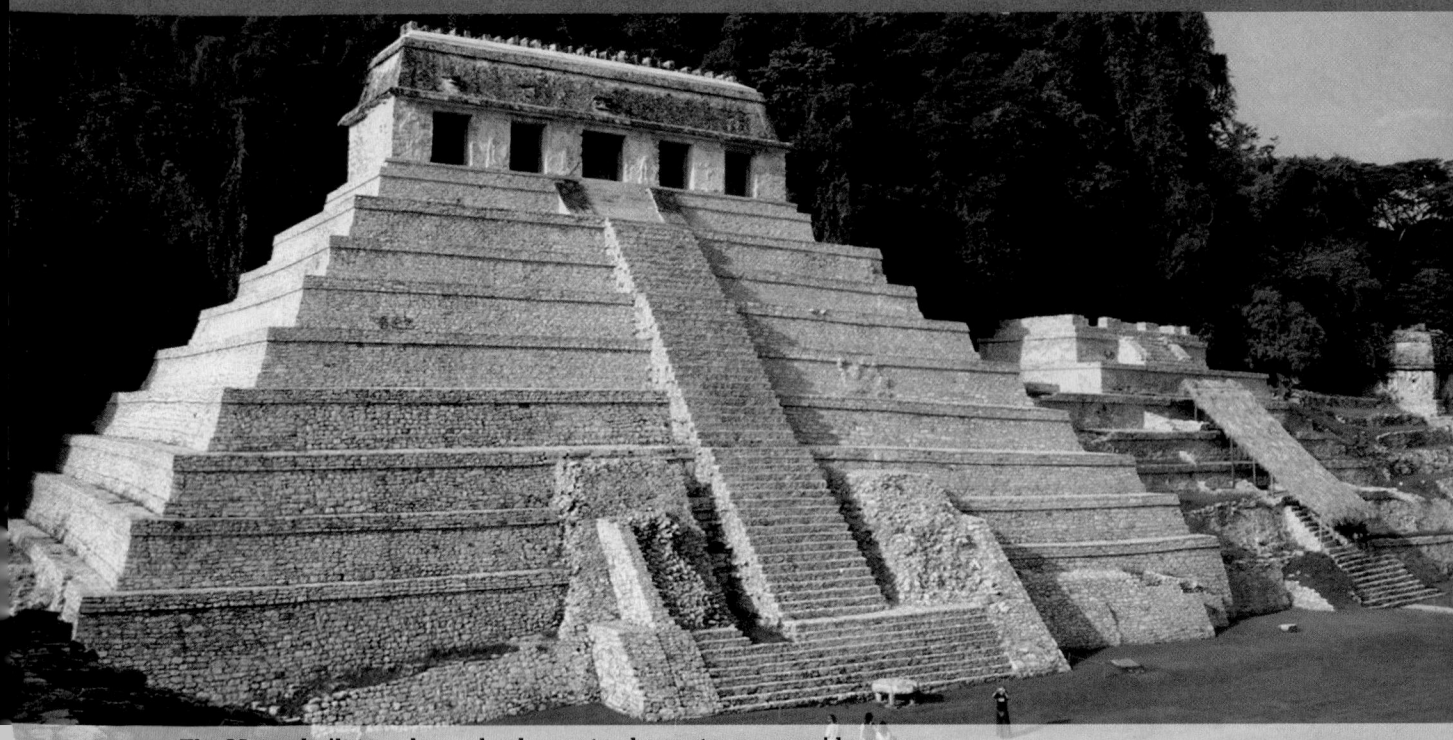

>> The Mayas built temples and palaces atop huge stone pyramids.

⏵ Interactive Flipped Video

>> Objectives

Explain how people first reached the Americas.

Describe early civilizations and cultures of the Americas.

Describe the human and physical geography of regions.

Analyze how the physical geography influenced where people lived.

>> Key Terms

glacier
surplus
causeway
quipu
terrace
culture
adobe
pueblo
Mound Builder
culture region
tribe
diffusion
pit house
potlatch
Kachina

clan
Iroquois League
sachem
settlement
city-state
civilization

Like other early people around the world, the first Americans left no written records to tell us where they came from or when they arrived. However, scientists have found evidence to suggest that the first people reached the Americas sometime during the last ice age.

The First Americans

According to geologists, the Earth has gone through several ice ages. The last ice age occurred between 100,000 and 10,000 years ago. During that time, thick sheets of ice, called **glaciers**, covered almost one third of the Earth. In North America, glaciers stretched across Canada and reached as far south as present-day Kentucky.

Populations Spread Glaciers locked up water from the oceans, causing sea levels to fall and uncovering land that had been under water. In the far north, a land bridge joined Siberia in northeastern Asia to present-day Alaska in North America.

Most scientists think that bands of hunters reached North America across this land bridge. These hunters tracked herds of grazing animals. Other scientists disagree. They think that the first Americans crossed the icy arctic waters by boat, reaching North America by sea.

Once these early hunters reached the Americas, they had to keep moving in search of food. Slowly, over thousands of years, they spread across North America, Central America, and South America. The physical environments where they settled varied widely. Native Americans adapted to the physical environments of mountain plateaus, dry deserts, fertile plains, lush woodlands, and thick rain forests. In adapting to these very different environments, Native American groups developed many different customs.

Adapting to and Modifying Environments About 12,000 years ago, the last ice age ended. As temperatures rose, the glaciers melted. The land bridge between Siberia and Alaska disappeared under the Bering Strait.

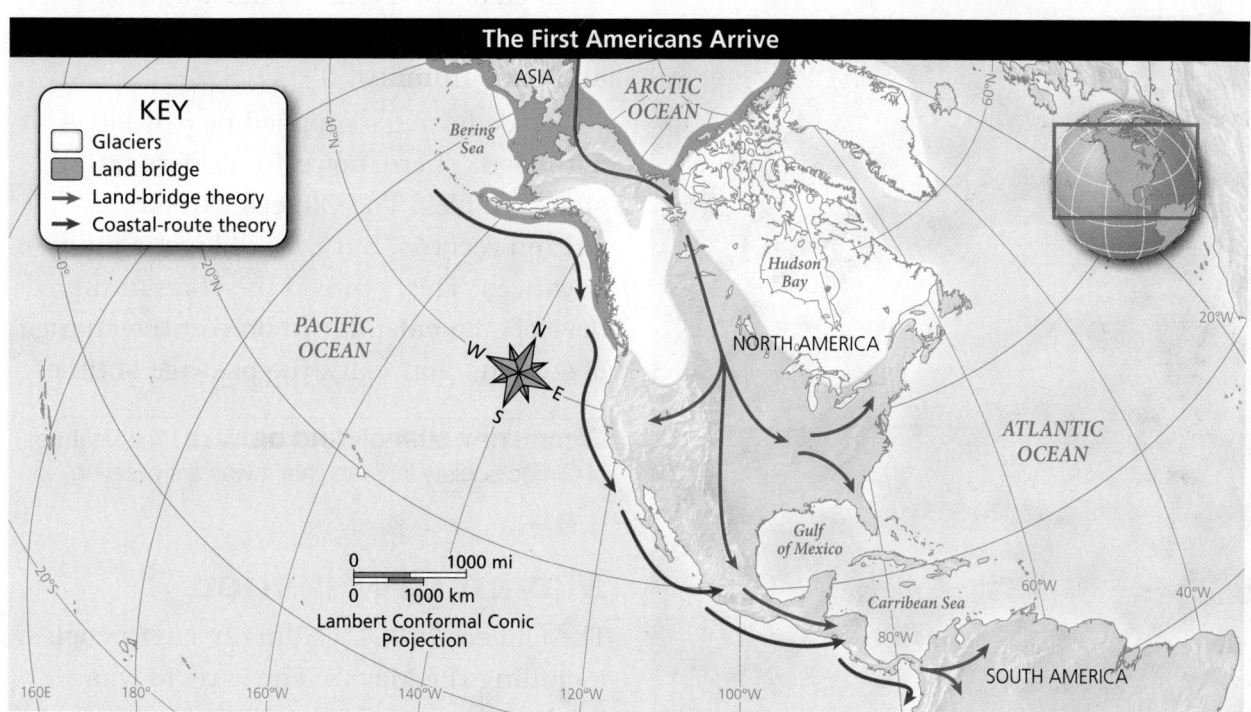

The First Americans Arrive

KEY
- Glaciers
- Land bridge
- → Land-bridge theory
- → Coastal-route theory

ASIA
Bering Sea
ARCTIC OCEAN
PACIFIC OCEAN
Hudson Bay
NORTH AMERICA
ATLANTIC OCEAN
Gulf of Mexico
Caribbean Sea
SOUTH AMERICA

0   1000 mi
0   1000 km
Lambert Conformal Conic Projection

>> This map depicts both the land-bridge and coastal-route theories of North American migration. **Analyze Maps** Why do some scientists disagree with the land-bridge migration theory?

About the same time, some kinds of large animals died out. This forced hunting bands to adapt to new conditions. Smaller animals, wild berries, nuts, grains, and fish became a larger part of their diets.

About 5,000 years ago, people in the Americas learned to grow crops such as corn, beans, and squash. Farming modified the environment and brought great changes to those who practiced it. Farmers no longer had to keep moving to find food. Instead, they stayed in one place and began to build permanent **settlements**, or small communities. As farming methods improved, people produced more food, which in turn allowed the population to grow.

? CHECK UNDERSTANDING How did farming affect communities in Central America?

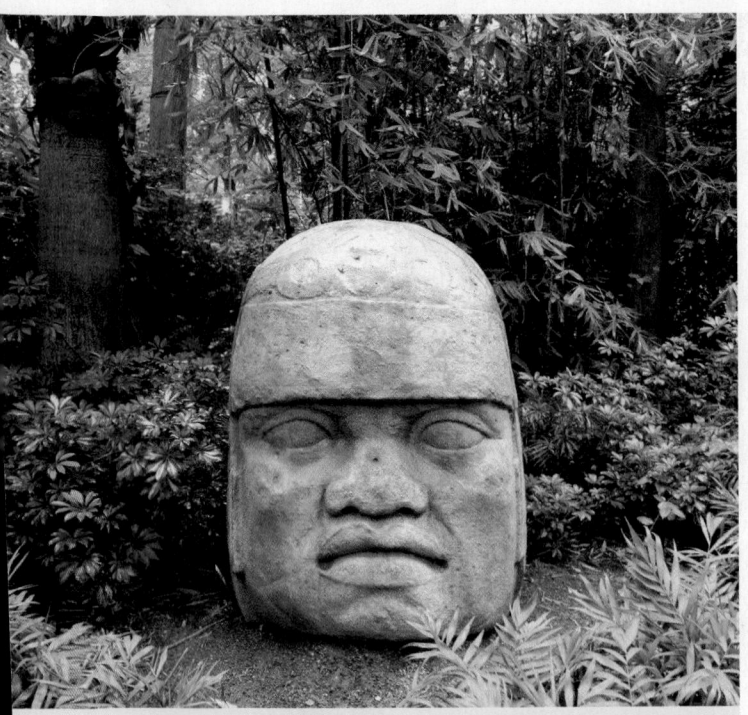
>> The Olmecs, a tropical civilization, left behind many carvings of giant stone heads. They are generally thought to be portraits of Olmec rulers

Olmecs Develop a Civilization

Farming was a key advance for early societies in the Americas. In time, some farming communities in the Americas grew enough **surplus**, or extra, food to support large populations, and the first cities emerged.

Cities marked the rise of the first civilization in the Americas. A **civilization** is a society—or a people sharing a language, territory, and economy—that has certain basic features. Among these are cities, an organized government, different social classes, a complex religion, and some method of record keeping.

The earliest known civilization in the Americas was that of the Olmecs in present-day Mexico. The Olmecs lived in the lowlands along the Gulf of Mexico about 3,500 years ago. Scientists have found huge stone heads carved by the Olmecs. Some were ten feet tall and weighed several tons. Smaller figures showed creatures that were part human and part animal.

Olmec farmers supplied nearby cities with food. There, powerful leaders built stone temples. The Olmecs left few written records, but they did make many advances. They studied the stars and developed a calendar to predict the change of seasons and mark the passage of time.

? IDENTIFY SUPPORTING DETAILS What features of Olmec society indicate that it was a civilization?

Mayan Civilization

The Olmecs influenced many later peoples, including the Mayas. The early Mayas lived in the rain forests of what are today Honduras, Belize, Guatemala, and southern Mexico. About 3,000 years ago, they began clearing the rain forest and draining swamps to create farmland.

Maya farmers were able to produce great harvests of corn, enough to feed large cities. As the Maya population grew, city-states began to spring up from Central America to southern Mexico. A **city-state** is a political unit that controls a city and its surrounding land. Trade flowed along a network of roads that linked inland city-states and the coast. City-states often waged war on one another for land, riches, and access to trade routes.

Mayan Social Classes Nobles also held great power in Maya society. The most powerful nobles were the kings, who also served as high priests. Other nobles also became priests. Priests held great power in Maya society. Only priests, the Mayas believed, could perform the ceremonies needed to bring good harvests or victory in battle. Priests conducted these ceremonies in temples built on top of huge stone pyramids.

Still other nobles served as warriors and government officials. Near the bottom of Maya society were laborers and farmers, who grew corn, squash, and many other crops. Below them were slaves, most of whom were prisoners of war or criminals.

Achievements in Mathematics and Astronomy Maya priests had to know exactly when to honor the many gods who were thought to control the natural world. Every day, priests anxiously studied the sun, moon, and stars. They learned much about the movement of these bodies.

Based on their observations, priests made great advances in astronomy and mathematics. They learned to predict eclipses and created a relatively accurate, 365-day calendar. They also developed a

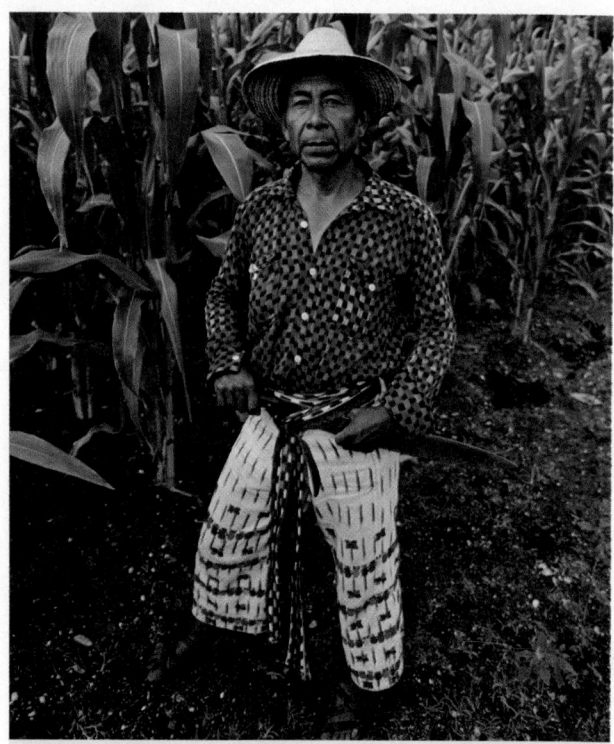

>> Farming techniques developed in ancient times by the Mayas are still used by Maya farmers today.

system of numbers that included the new concept of zero.

Then, around A.D. 900, the Mayas abandoned their cities. Historians are not sure why. Perhaps they did so because of warfare, a drought—or both. The rain forests swallowed up the great Maya temples and palaces. Although Maya cities decayed, the Maya people survived. Today, more than 2 million people in Guatemala and southern Mexico speak Mayan languages.

❓ **RECALL** What sort of scientific advances did the Mayas achieve?

Aztec Civilization

Long after the Maya cities were abandoned, a new civilization arose to the northwest. Its builders were the Aztecs. The early Aztecs were nomads, people who moved from place to place in search of food. In the 1300s, the Aztecs settled around Lake Texcoco (tays KOH koh) in central Mexico. From there, they built a powerful empire.

Tenochtitlán On an island in the middle of the lake, the Aztecs built their capital, Tenochtitlán (tay nawch tee TLAHN). They constructed a system of **causeways**, or raised roads made of packed earth. The causeways linked the capital to the mainland.

The Aztecs learned to farm the shallow swamps of Lake Texcoco. In some places, they dug canals, using the mud they removed to fill in parts of the lake. In other places, they attached floating reed mats to the lake bottom with long stakes. Then, they piled mud onto the mats to create farmland. Aztec farmers harvested several crops a year on these *chinampas*, or floating gardens.

With riches from trade and conquest, Tenochtitlán prospered. Its markets offered a wide variety of goods. "There are daily more than 60,000 people bartering and selling," wrote a Spanish visitor in the 1500s.

Religion Like the Mayas, Aztec priests studied the heavens and developed complex calendars. Such calendars gave them the ability to tell their people when to plant or harvest. Priests also performed rituals designed to please the many Aztec gods.

The Aztecs paid special attention to the god who controlled the sun. They believed that each day the sun battled its way across the heavens. They compared the sun's battle to their own, calling themselves "warriors of the sun." They believed that the sun required human sacrifices in order to rise each day. The Aztecs therefore killed thousands of captives each year to please this powerful god.

>> Aztecs adapted to life on an island in the middle of a lake with limited land area by using chinampas for agriculture, even planting trees to better anchor them to the lake bed.

Aztec Society

Emperor
Chosen by nobles and priests to lead in war

Priests
Performed rituals, gave advice, and ran schools

Nobles
Served as officials, judges, and governors

Warriors
Could become nobles by killing or capturing enemies

Merchants
Often acted as spies for the empire

Artisans
Passed skills on to their children

Farmers
Made up most of population

Serfs
Worked land owned by nobles

Servants
Worked for those in the higher classes

Slaves
Were mostly captives or criminals

>> **Analyze Charts** What does the organization of Aztec society tell us about the Aztecs' values?

A Powerful Empire By 1500, the Aztecs ruled a huge empire. It stretched from the Gulf of Mexico to the Pacific Ocean and included millions of people. The Aztecs took great pride in their empire and their capital. "Who could conquer Tenochtitlán?" boasted an Aztec poet. "Who could shake the foundation of heaven?"

The Aztec world was far from peaceful, however. Heavy taxes and the sacrifice of huge numbers of prisoners of war sparked many revolts. The Aztecs waged war in part to capture more prisoners for sacrifice. Across the empire, people conquered by the Aztecs were eager for revenge. Enemies of the Aztecs would eventually help outsiders from distant lands destroy the Aztec empire.

? IDENTIFY SUPPORTING DETAILS What is a physical characteristic of Lake Texcoco, and how did the Aztecs adapt to it to live there?

Inca Civilization

Far to the south of the Aztecs, the Incas built one of the largest empires in the Americas. By 1500, their empire stretched for almost 2,500 miles along the west coast of South America.

An Impressive Capital The center of the Inca empire was the magnificent capital at Cuzco (KOOS koh), located high in the Andes in present-day Peru. Cuzco was a holy city to the Incas. All nobles in the empire tried to visit it at least once in their lifetimes. The city had massive palaces and temples made of stone and decorated with gold ornaments. At the center was the palace of the emperor, who was known as the Sapa Inca. The emperor was regarded as a god who was descended from the sun god.

From Cuzco, the emperor ruled more than 10 million people. They lived in varied environments, from coastal deserts to lowland jungles to the highlands of the

Andes. The Incas conquered this land by waging war against surrounding peoples.

The Inca empire was very well organized. The emperor was kept well informed about affairs in all parts of his empire. He sent high officials out to act as governors of his domain. The governors made sure that every person worked at least part of the time on projects for the state, such as road building, mining, farming, and pottery making.

Inca Achievements To unite their empire, the Incas maintained a system of roads that covered more than 10,000 miles. Builders carved roads in rock cliffs and stretched rope bridges across deep gorges. Teams of runners quickly spread royal orders across the empire using these roads.

The runners carried with them a device known as a **quipu** (KEE poo). This was a cord or string with knots that stood for numbers or categories. The numbers might be bags of grain, numbers of soldiers, or other amounts of goods that the government ordered from different parts of the empire. The quipu was also used by government officials to keep records.

The Incas were skilled engineers. They built massive stone temples and forts. With only human labor, ropes, and wooden rollers, they moved stones weighing up to 200 tons. They used all their engineering skills to farm the dry, rugged mountain lands. They became experts at creating **terraces**—or wide, flat steps of land—out of the steep mountainsides. Sturdy stone walls kept rain from washing away the soil.

❓ **IDENTIFY CENTRAL IDEAS** Why was a system of roads so important to the Incas?

>> The Inca city of Machu Picchu shows how Inca engineering shaped and was shaped by the terrain of the Andes Mountains. Notice the terraces, or stepped strips of land, that allowed farming on steep slopes.

Early North American Societies

Scholars have found evidence of complex societies among some groups of people farther north. Traders and migrating people carried foods, goods, arts, and beliefs from Central America and Mexico to early peoples of North America. These peoples developed many distinct cultures in North America. A **culture** is the entire way of life of a people. It includes their homes, clothing, economy, arts, and government.

Land and People of the Southwest

At least 3,000 years ago, knowledge of farming spread northward. Gradually, farming societies emerged in what is today the American Southwest. Much of this region is desert, with little rainfall and hot summers. The early societies in this region included the Hohokams (hoh HOH kahmz) and Anasazis (ah nuh SAH zeez).

The Hohokams lived in present-day southern Arizona. About 2,000 years ago, they dug networks of irrigation ditches so that they could farm the desert land. The ditches carried water from the Salt and Gila (HEE luh) rivers to fields, where farmers produced corn, squash, and beans.

The Anasazis lived in the Four Corners region, where Colorado, Utah, New Mexico, and Arizona meet today. Like the Hohokams, the Anasazis irrigated the desert in order to farm. They also created a network of roads to link dozens of towns. Traders traveled these roads, carrying cotton, sandals, and blankets woven from turkey feathers.

Anasazi Houses
The Anasazis built large buildings with walls of stone and **adobe**, or sundried brick. When the Spanish later

>> The Anasazi made use of their environment by building dwellings along sheer cliffs as protection against intruders.

saw similar buildings in the early 1500s, they called them **pueblos** (PWEHB lohz), the Spanish word for "villages." (They also called the descendants of the Anasazis the Pueblo Indians.) About 1,000 years ago, some Anasazi villages faced attacks from warlike neighbors. To escape that threat, they built new homes along steep cliffs. Toeholds cut into the rock let people climb the cliff walls. Farmers planted their crops on land above the cliffs

Mound Builders
Far to the east, other farming cultures flourished in North America. Among them were the **Mound Builders**, various cultures that built large earth mounds beginning about 3,000 years ago. Thousands of these mounds dot the landscape from the Appalachian Mountains to the Mississippi Valley and from Wisconsin to Florida. What is now the eastern half of the United States had a

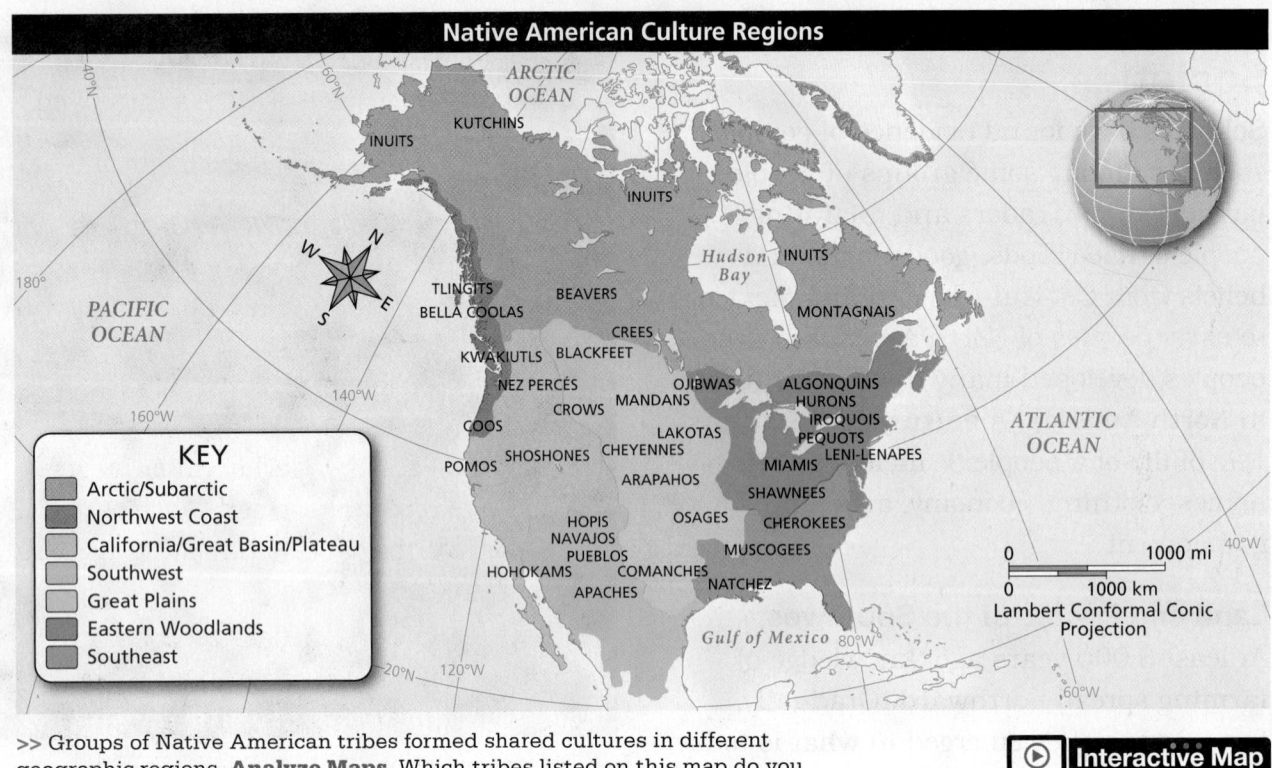

KEY

- Arctic/Subarctic
- Northwest Coast
- California/Great Basin/Plateau
- Southwest
- Great Plains
- Eastern Woodlands
- Southeast

>> Groups of Native American tribes formed shared cultures in different geographic regions. **Analyze Maps** Which tribes listed on this map do you know about?

Interactive Map

wetter climate than the Southwest, and the Mound Builders were able to farm without irrigation.

The first mounds were used for burials. Later mounds were used for religious ceremonies. They were similar in function to the pyramid temples of the Mayas.

The best-known groups of Mound Builders were the Hopewells and the Mississippians. The Mississippians took advantage of their moist climate to grow enough crops to feed large towns. BetweenA.D. 700 and 1500, the Mississippians built a city at Cahokia (kah HOH kee ah) in present-day Illinois. As many as 30,000 people may have lived there at one time.

? **IDENTIFY SUPPORTING DETAILS** How did the Hohokams adapt to living in a desert region?

Culture and the Physical Geography of North America

Native Americans did not belong to just one group. Instead, Native Americans included many different people with many distinct cultures. In North America alone, there were hundreds of Native American languages spoken. Native American cultures, too, varied greatly, much like the cultures of the people of Europe.

Native American cultures were adapted to the many different physical environments of North America. The physical geography in each region, as you will see below, influenced where Native Americans lived, right up to modern times.

A **culture region** is a region in which people share a similar way of life. Most culture regions shared similar physical environments. Each culture region was home to many different tribes. A **tribe** is a community of people who share common customs, language, and rituals. Members of a tribe saw themselves as a distinct people who shared a common origin. Tribal leaders often made decisions for the group.

Hunting, Gathering, and Fishing Native Americans developed a variety of ways to meet their basic needs for food, clothing, and shelter. In some culture regions, tribes hunted animals and gathered nuts, fruits, and vegetables that grew in the wild. Other tribes depended on the sea for food. They made boats out of animal skins or carved canoes out of trees. From their boats and canoes, they speared or netted fish or hunted marine animals such as seals, walrus, and whales.

Farming Other tribes lived mostly by farming, planting corn, beans, and squash. Native American tribes farmed in many parts of North America, from the American Southwest to the Eastern Woodlands. Over time, farmers improved their crops. For example, more than 5,000 years ago, wild corn was tiny, about the size of a human finger. Indian farmers developed dozens of varieties of corn including ones with larger ears.

Trade Indian tribes traded with one another for goods not found within their own region. Trade networks linked people across large distances. Goods sometimes traveled more than 1,000 miles from where they were made.

In the Northwest, traders met near the Dalles on the Columbia River. Local Indians caught and dried salmon, which they exchanged for goods and produce from other places. More than goods traveled from Indian group to group. New ideas and skills also spread.

Ways Native Americans Supported Themselves

	FORAGING	FARMING	HUNTING
FOOD SOURCE	Fruits, nuts, seeds, roots, stems, and leaves from wild plants	Cultivated plants such as maize, beans, and squash	Wild game and fish
TOOLS AND TECHNOLOGY	Grinding tools for crushing seeds	Tools for clearing and cultivating: axes, hoes made with bone, shells, or stone	Tools such as spears and sharp points; trapping and netting food
INNOVATIONS	Baskets for storage	Methods for storing and preserving foods over winter months, irrigation methods	Techniques for drying meat and fish to balance the food supply over the winter
CULTURAL CHANGES	Mobility needed to find new food sources	Cultivating land required more labor, but created settlements and communities	Mobility needed when food resources become depleted
ADVANTAGES	No need to work in fields and risk fatal encounters with wild animals	Control over the food supply when growing conditions were favorable	Hunted animals provided clothing and shelter in addition to food
DISADVANTAGES	Poor weather could lead to shortages	Poor weather conditions could wipe out a harvest	Required a plentiful supply of wild game

>> **Analyze Charts** How did the foods Native Americans ate influence their way of life?

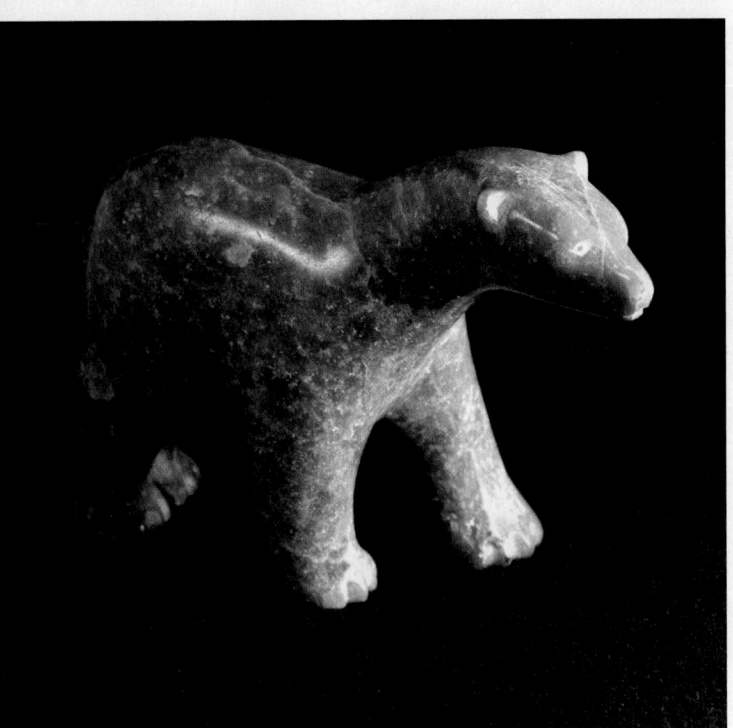

>> This Inuit sculpture of a bear is carved from soapstone, a type of rock mostly made up of the mineral talc.

>> The Inuit used caribou and seal fur to make warm clothing that would offer protection against extreme arctic weather.

This process of spreading ideas from one culture to another is known as **diffusion**. Through diffusion, skills such as farming spread from one Native American group to another.

Adapting to and Modifying Environments

Native American cultures adapted to the physical features of different regions. These features influenced the kinds of food people raised, collected, or caught. Climate determined people's needs for clothing and shelter. Resources provided the materials they were able to use.

Climate and resources also affected tribal organization. Where climates were harsh and resources limited, people struggled to find enough food and shelter. In such regions, people were often nomadic. They lived in small hunting bands. Each band included a number of families. In regions with more favorable climates and plentiful resources, people tended to live in larger groups and stay in one place for longer periods.

Cultures of the Arctic and Subarctic Regions

Frozen seas and icy, treeless plains made up the world of the Inuits, who lived in the Arctic region. The Inuits used all the limited resources of their environment. In the short summer season, they collected driftwood along the ocean shore, using it for tools and shelters. For most of the year, the Inuits lived in **pit houses**, houses dug into the ground and covered with wood and skins. Lamps filled with seal oil kept their homes warm even in the bitter cold. Women made warm clothing out of furs and waterproof boots out of sealskins.

The Subarctic culture region consisted of a belt of forest stretching across North

America south of the Arctic. This forest is made up mainly of conifers, or cone-bearing trees such as hemlock and spruce. People in the Subarctic lived where they could find food. Groups like the Chipewyan (chip uh WY un) were nomads, following large game like caribou. The physical geography influenced their settlement patterns. The Carrier, for example, settled near salmon streams, although they sometimes moved to other hunting sites.

Cultures of the California, Great Basin, and Plateau Regions

The California region offered more forgiving climates, with mainly hot, dry summers and mild, wet winters. The physical features included mountains, coastal lowland, and interior valleys and deserts.

Over 200 different tribes called this region home. Along the Colorado River, land was irrigated to grow corn, pumpkin, and beans. In the northwest, the Yoruk (YAWR uk) used redwood trees to build houses and canoes and caught the plentiful fish of that region. In central California, salmon and acorns were plentiful. People there hunted and gathered plant products instead of farming. With enough food nearby, people could spend time producing crafts. The Pomo wove watertight baskets out of grasses and reeds.

The Great Basin culture region consisted of mountains and valleys with a dry climate, with hot summers and cold winters. Many of the bands that lived here, like the Bannock, were small and nomadic. They traveled to find seeds, nuts, roots, and bulbs. The Northern Paiute (PY yoot) lived near lakes and marshes. Hunting, fishing, and farming often provided enough food for them to stay in one place.

The Plateau region, centered on the Columbia Plateau, has a cool and dry environment, but winter snows fed rivers flowing through the region. Surprisingly, numbers of hardy plants and animals thrive in the region. Among the people of the Plateau region were the Utes (YOOTZ) and Shoshones (shah SHOH neez). The Native Americans of the region had few possessions beyond digging sticks, baskets, and tools and weapons needed for hunting.

Cultures of the Northwest Coastal Region

Elsewhere in North America the climate was kinder, which helped more complex cultures emerge. The people of the mountainous Northwest Coast enjoyed milder temperatures and abundant rainfall and food supplies. They gathered rich harvests of fish from the sea.

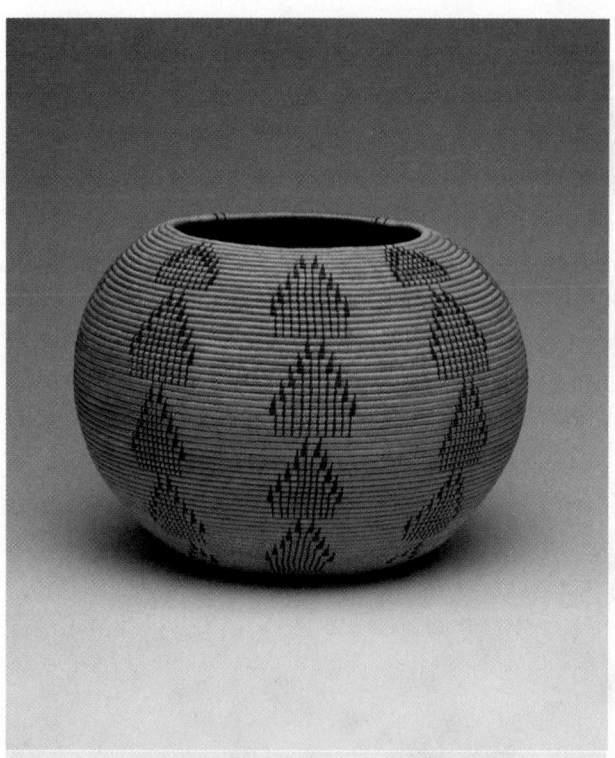

>> This early 20th century basket from Nevada is representative of Great Basin Native American artwork. It is made of willow, bracken fern, and red bud fibers.

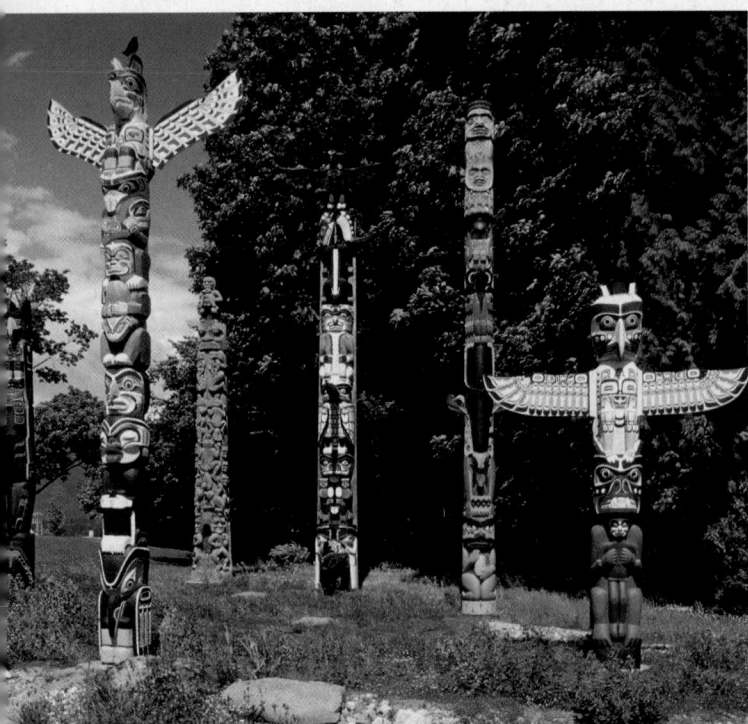

>> The abundant forests of the Pacific Northwest provide the cedar trees Native Americans use to carve totem poles. The images on the poles often tell stories from Native American legends.

>> Native American cultures of the Southwest built ball courts using stones they found in their desert environment.

From nearby forests, they cut down tall cedar trees and split the trunks into planks for houses and canoes. With plenty of food, the people of the Pacific Northwest stayed in one place. They built permanent villages and prospered from trade with nearby groups.

Within a village, a family gained status according to how much it owned and could give away. Families sometimes competed with one another. To improve its standing, a family might hold a **potlatch**, or ceremonial dinner, to show off its wealth. The potlatch could last for many days. The family invited many guests and gave everyone gifts. The more goods a family gave away, the more respect it earned. However, people who received gifts at a potlatch were then expected to hold their own potlatches and give gifts.

Cultures of the Southwest Region
The Southwest is a hot and dry region consisting of deserts, the southern Rocky Mountains, and the Colorado Plateau. People could survive only if they found water.

The Pueblo people used irrigation methods such as building dams and tanks to store water. They were able to grow corn and cotton on small farms. However, it wasn't all work in the desert. The Hohokams played games on ballcourts and made beautiful art with acid-etchings on shells.

Cultures of the Southeast Region
Many tribes inhabited the southeastern region of North America, which consisted of coastal plains, the southern Appalachian Mountains, and interior rolling hills and valleys. The region had hot summers, mild winters, and plenty of rainfall. Among the people of this region were the Natchez

(NACH ihz). They benefited from the region's warm, moist climate. They hunted, fished, and farmed in the fertile Mississippi Valley.

The Natchez calendar divided the year into 13 months. Each month was named after a food or an animal that the Natchez harvested or hunted. Their months included Strawberry, Little Corn, Mulberry, Deer, Turkey, and Bear.

The ruler of the Natchez was known as the Great Sun and was worshipped as a god. The Great Sun's feet never touched the ground. Either he was carried on a litter or he walked on mats. Below the Great Sun were members of his family, called Little Suns. Next came Nobles, then Honored People, and finally Stinkards, or commoners, who made up the majority of the people.

Marriage laws ensured that membership in each class kept changing. By law, Nobles had to marry Stinkards. Even the Great Sun chose a Stinkard as a wife. In this way, no one family could hold the position of Great Sun forever. In time, even descendants of a Great Sun became Stinkards.

Cultures of the Great Plains Region The Great Plains were dry, open grasslands in the center of North America with very few trees, hot summers, and cold winters. Tribes like the Sioux (SOO) hunted wild animals to survive. The Sioux were nomads who followed the buffalo. They ate buffalo meat and used the hide to build tents. These tents were easy to carry when they were on the move. No part of the buffalo was wasted. They made spoons and cups out of the horns and weapons from the bones.

Cultures of the Eastern Woodlands Region Like the peoples of the Southwest and Southeast, the peoples of the Eastern Woodlands were not nomads. Their culture region spanned what is today much of the Midwest and Northeast. This region includes coastal plains, the northern Appalachian Mountains, the Great Lakes region, and interior rolling hills and plains. The region receives plenty of rainfall, with warm summers and snowy winters.

The Iroquois (IHR uh kwoi) lived near lakes and streams. They cleared land for farming, which was mostly done by women. Their diet was based on the "Three Sisters": corn, squash, and beans. Algonquian (al GAHN kwee un) tribes lived near the ocean and along the Great Lakes. Many of them farmed as well. In some places it was too poor to farm. Instead, they built boats for fishing. Like

>> Before Europeans brought horses to the Americas, Great Plains tribes hunted buffalo on foot, dressed as wolves.

the Iroquois, they also used trees from the forests to make houses and tools.

? IDENTIFY SUPPORTING DETAILS Why were many people in central California able to settle in one place?

Religion

The many Native American groups had a wide variety of beliefs. Yet, they shared some basic ideas.

Close Ties to Nature Whether hunting, fishing, farming, or gathering wild plants, many Native Americans felt a close connection to the physical environment. Their prayers and ceremonies were designed to maintain a balance between people and the forces of nature. They believed that they must adapt their ways to the natural world in order to survive and prosper.

Many Native Americans believed that the world was full of powerful, unseen forces and spirits. They honored those spirits, which were thought to act and feel like humans.

In the Pacific Northwest, many tribes relied on fishing. One such group was the Kwakiutls (kwah kee OOT ulz). Each year when they caught their first fish of the season, they chanted this prayer:

> We have come to meet alive, Swimmer, do not feel wrong about what I have done to you, friend Swimmer, for that is the reason why you came, that I may spear you, that I may eat you, Supernatural One, you, Long-Life-Giver, you Swimmer. Now protect us, me and my wife.
>
> —Kwakiutl Prayer of Thanks

>> Pueblo Indians perform a religious harvest dance, part of the Green Corn Ceremony.

>> The Iroquois lived in wooden long houses that were built clustered together. The long houses were built of posts and poles covered with tree bark.

▶ Interactive Gallery

Special Ceremonies In farming regions, tribes held special ceremonies to ensure good rainfall. At midsummer, Pueblo villages in the Southwest rang with cries of: "The kachinas are coming!" **Kachinas** were spirits, who were represented by masked Native American dancers. The Pueblos believed that the kachinas had the power to bring good harvests.

At Pueblo festivals, the kachinas danced. Religious leaders prayed to the spirits and gave them gifts. Only if the spirits were treated well would they return each year with rain for the Pueblos' crops. In the Southwest and the Southeast, many tribes held a Green Corn Ceremony when the corn ripened in the fall.

The ceremony lasted for several days. It marked the end of the old year and the beginning of a new one. On the last day, a sacred fire was lighted. Dancers circled the flames, and the people enjoyed a great feast. Women then used coals from the sacred fire to make new fires in their own houses.

❓ **CHECK UNDERSTANDING** Why did many Native Americans in farming regions hold ceremonies?

The Iroquois League

The Iroquois (IHR uh kwoi) people of present-day New York State called themselves "The People of the Long House." They took great pride in their sturdy dwellings, called long houses. A typical long house was about 150 feet long and 20 feet wide. Twelve or more families lived in a long house.

Women had a special place in Iroquois society. They owned all the household property and were in charge of planting and harvesting. When a man married, he moved in with his wife's family.

Women also had political power. They chose clan leaders. A **clan** was a group of related families. If a clan leader did not do his job well, the women could remove him from his position.

The Iroquois included five nations that spoke similar languages: the Mohawk, Seneca, Onondaga (ahn un DAW guh), Oneida (oh NY duh), and Cayuga (kay YOO guh). Each nation had its own ruling council. Until the 1500s, the five nations were frequently at war with one another.

Then, in the 1500s, the five Iroquois nations formed an alliance to end the fighting. According to legend, a religious leader named Dekanawida (deh kan ah WEE dah) inspired Hiawatha (hy ah WAH thah) to organize the alliance. It became known as the **Iroquois League**.

A council of 50 specially chosen tribal leaders, called **sachems**, met once a year. The council made decisions for the League. Here, too, women had a political role because they chose the sachems and watched over their actions.

The Iroquois alliance did not end the fighting. The Iroquois spoke a different language from the Algonquian tribes, their neighbors to the east and west. The two groups fought many wars over land and trade.

? IDENTIFY SUPPORTING DETAILS What role did women play in Iroquois culture?

ASSESSMENT

1. **Identify Steps in a Process** Explain how scientists believe the first settlers arrived in the Americas.

2. **Support Ideas with Examples** What major impact did the development of farming have on the early settlers of the Americas?

3. **Identify Patterns** What effect did climate and the availability of natural resources have on the population distribution and settlement patterns of early Native American cultures?

4. **Make Predictions** How did the Aztecs' religious beliefs weaken their empire?

5. **Compare and Contrast** Compare and contrast how the Incas and Anasazi peoples used their engineering skills to adapt to their physical environment.

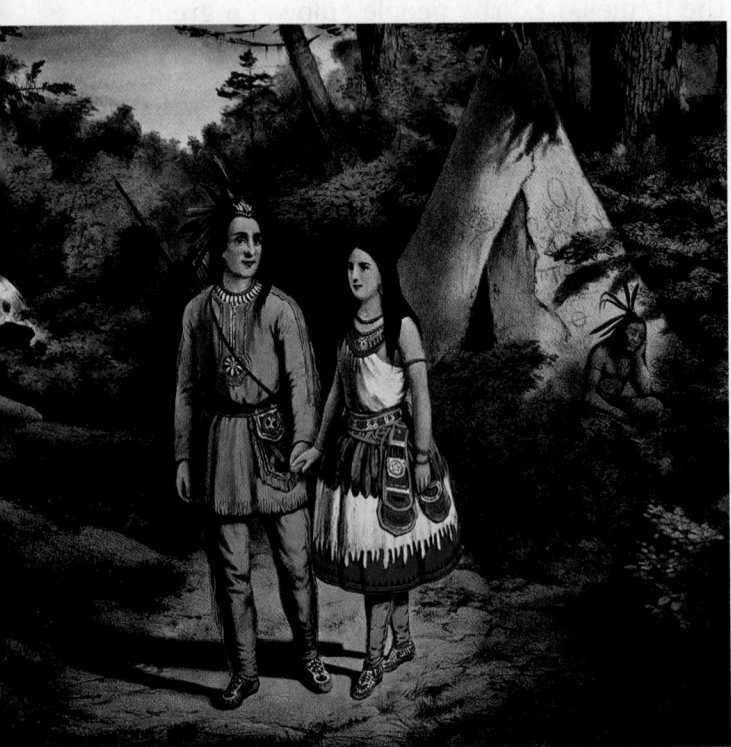

>> Stories were written in modern times about Hiawatha and his fictional wife, Minnehaha, shown in this artist's rendering.

Early Europe, Africa, and Asia

>> **Analyze Maps** What information does the image of Mansa Musa on his throne, holding a golden object, add to this medieval map?

▶ **Interactive Flipped Video**

The period from about A.D. 500 to around 1500 is known as the Middle Ages. During the early Middle Ages, invasion and war were common. People in Europe had to find new means of defending themselves.

>> **Objectives**

Describe how Europe changed in the Middle Ages, including through new ways of doing things.

Describe patterns of trade and new ways of doing things in the Muslim world, Africa, and East Asia.

Identify the impact of new ways of doing things on Renaissance Europe.

>> **Key Terms**

Renaissance
feudalism
manor
Crusades
innovation
astrolabe
Silk Road
caravan
savanna
extended family
kinship
Christianity
Islam

Europe in the Middle Ages

Feudalism A new kind of government evolved during the Middle Ages. Kings and queens divided their lands among warrior nobles. In return, nobles promised to fight for the ruler when asked. This system of rule by lords who ruled their lands but owed loyalty and military service to a monarch is called **feudalism** (FYOOD ul iz um).

At the top of feudal society stood the king and the most powerful lords. Next came the lesser nobles. Most people in feudal society were peasants who farmed the lord's lands and could not leave the land without the lord's permission.

Daily Life in Feudal Society Feudal life revolved around the **manor**, which included the lord's castle and the lands around it. Manor lands might include several villages. Each manor was self-sufficient. That is, people made almost everything they needed. Life for peasants was hard. Peasants were farmers who worked mostly by hand on small plots. They struggled to produce enough food just to survive.

By about A.D 900, life began to change. Peasants used new methods of farming to produce more food. Warfare declined and trade began to grow. Slowly, people began to look beyond their isolated villages.

Religion The most powerful force in medieval western Europe was the Roman Catholic Church. The Roman Catholic Church was the main branch of **Christianity** in western Europe. Like other branches of Christianity, it was based on the teachings of Jesus, who lived centuries earlier. During ancient and early medieval times, the religion spread across Europe.

The Church ruled more than religious life. The Church owned large amounts of

>> A typical medieval manor included a castle, a church, fields for agriculture and livestock, and dwellings for serfs.

>> Many medieval Christians joined the Crusades to fight for control of territory in the Middle East.

land and offered the only source of education. The clergy were often the only people who could read and write. Because of their efforts, much of the learning from the ancient world was preserved.

While Christianity was the main religion in western Europe, the region also had a strong Jewish community. Their religion was Judaism, a religion centuries older than Christianity. It, too, had spread across Europe in ancient and early medieval times. While Jewish people played an important role in medieval Europe, they often faced discrimination and persecution, or attacks because of their beliefs.

The Crusades The pace of change in Europe increased between 1100 and 1300 in part because of the Crusades. The **Crusades** were a series of wars fought by Christians to control the region then known as the Holy Land or Palestine, much of which is now Israel. This region included Jerusalem and the other places where Jesus had lived and taught. Muslims had controlled this region for centuries. During the Crusades, tens of thousands of Christians journeyed to the Middle East. Fighting between Christians and Muslims continued for almost 200 years. Christians won some victories, and they ruled kingdoms in the region for more than 100 years. But in the end, they failed to keep control of the Holy Land.

Growing Trade The Crusades had important effects on Europe, however. Crusaders traveled beyond their villages and came into contact with other civilizations. In the Middle East, they tasted new foods, such as rice, oranges, dates, and new spices. They saw beautiful silks and woven rugs.

Europe had traded with the Middle East for many years before the Crusades. However, returning Crusaders demanded

>> The magnetic compass greatly aided European nautical trade and exploration.

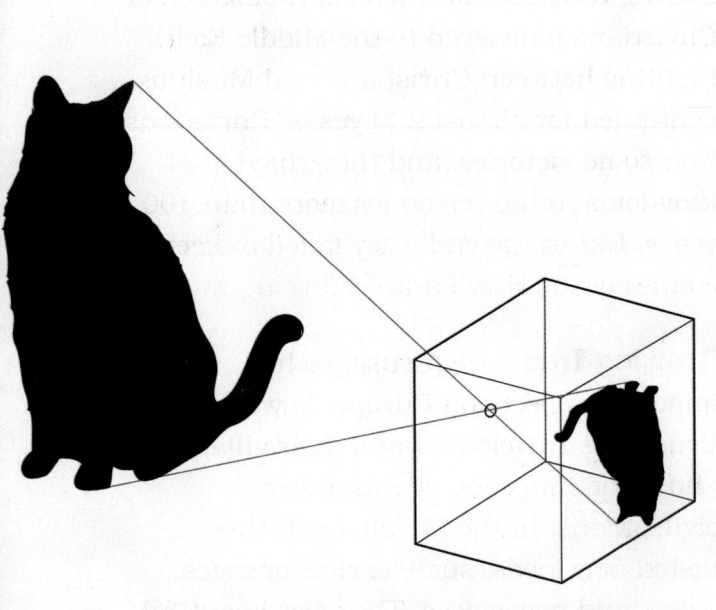

>> In a pinhole camera, light passes through a single point and projects an inverted image on the opposite side of the box.

more Asian foods, spices, silks, and rugs. Italian merchants realized that people would pay high prices for such goods. They outfitted ships and increased trade with the Muslim world.

Technological Innovations in Navigation
Trade brought new knowledge and with it, new technological **innovations**, or new methods and practical ideas. From the Muslim world, Europeans acquired sailing skills and the magnetic compass. Muslims had earlier adopted the magnetic compass from the Chinese. The magnetic needle of the compass always pointed north, which helped ships stay on course.

Another useful instrument was the **astrolabe** (AS troh layb), which helped sailors determine their latitude while at sea. These new instruments let Europeans sail far out to sea, beyond sight of land. By 1500, Portugal had taken the lead in this new overseas travel.

? IDENTIFY MAIN IDEAS How did the Crusades affect trade in the Middle Ages?

The Middle East
Middle Eastern merchants played a large role in this growing trade. Linking Europe, Africa, and Asia, the Middle East was a major crossroads of the world.

Muslim Conquests and Inventions The growth of trade was also linked to the spread of a new religion. In the early 600s, a new religion, **Islam**, emerged in Arabia. A people called the Arabs lived in Arabia, in the southern Middle East.

Islam won many followers among the Arabs. Beginning in the 600s, Islam spread rapidly. Devout followers conquered North Africa and much of Spain. They conquered lands to the east, too, from

KEY
— East African trade routes
— Trans-Saharan and Trans-Arabian trade routes

>> **Analyze Maps** How did the growth of trade in the Middle East influence the spread of Islam?

▶ **Interactive Map**

Persia to India and beyond. Eventually, the Muslim world spread from South Asia to what is now Portugal and Spain. In many countries ruled by Muslims, however, there were also communities of Christians and Jewish people.

Islam expanded through trade and conquest by sword. While some remained faithful to Christianity, Judaism, and other religions, many people in conquered lands chose to convert to the new religion. Others were converted by force, or under the threat of crippling taxes. Elsewhere, Muslim merchants carried the new faith to people living along the trade routes of Asia and Africa.

Islam united Muslims from many lands and fostered the growth of trade. Muslims had a basic duty to make a pilgrimage, or journey, to the holy city of Mecca at least once in their lives. Every year, people from across the Muslim world traveled to Mecca. Muslims from North Africa, Persia, Afghanistan, India, Spain, and West Africa crowded Mecca's dusty streets. They prayed in Arabic, the language of Islam. This regular travel encouraged trade among the Muslim lands.

People in the mainly Muslim Middle East developed many of the technologies we use today. Experiments with how light enters the eye led 10th century Muslim mathematician Ibn al-Haitham to invent the first pin-hole camera. A Muslim engineer invented the crankshaft, a key device in modern machinery, and the windmill was invented in Persia in the 600s to grind corn.

Navigating the Seas Middle Eastern merchants traded across a vast area. They sailed to ports around the Indian Ocean. Their ships used large, triangular sails that allowed captains to sail close to the direction the wind was blowing from.

Middle Eastern sailors had knowledge of wind and weather conditions in the Indian Ocean. As a result, merchants in ports around the region knew when the trading ships had to sail and when they would return. Middle Easterners made important technological innovations in the astrolabe, which, as you have learned, helped sailors find their way far from shore.

Middle Eastern merchants sold porcelains, perfumes, and fabrics from China. Jade and tea were popular, too. The Spice Islands of Indonesia offered nutmeg, clove, and mace. Cloth, indigo, and sugar came from East Africa, as well as spices, salt, and slaves. Goods like textiles and spices traveled well. They quickly spread across the globe.

Silk Road Some Middle Eastern traders traveled the overland routes that crossed the grasslands, mountains, and deserts of Central Asia and linked China and the Middle East. These routes had become known as the **Silk Road** because prized Chinese silks had been carried westward along them for more than 1,000 years.

Travel on the Silk Road was dangerous. Desert storms, hunger, and bandits were a constant threat. Traders formed **caravans**, or groups of people who traveled together for safety. Despite the dangers, trade along the Silk Road prospered.

By the 1400s, trade goods were flowing across a huge area. More than just silk was traded on the Silk Road. Everything from horses to spices and gems traveled along the route.

? DEFINE How would you define the Silk Road?

The Silk Road

KEY
— Silk Road

>> The trade routes between Europe and Asia became collectively known as the Silk Road. **Analyze Maps** What regions in Europe and Asia did the Silk Road connect?

▶ **Interactive Illustration**

African Cultures and Technologies

Trade routes played a large role in Africa, too. Long-distance trade routes crossed the vast Sahara, the desert linking West Africa and North Africa.

A peaceful afternoon in a West African village might be pierced by sounds of a horn. Children would shout, "Batafo! Batafo!" Traders! Soon, a long line of porters and camels arrived. Villagers watched as the tired travelers unloaded sacks of salt or dried fish. Gold, fabrics, jewelry, and slaves were also part of the caravan.

Sea traders also spread navigation technologies throughout Africa and eventually to Europe. The lateen sail, believed to have been invented first in Egypt, was a triangular sail that allowed ships to travel toward the wind. Although historians cannot be certain, it is likely that North Africans adapted the astrolabe for sea travel, too. It was used by African, Arab, and Indian sailors and then adopted by Europeans.

>> This instrument is an early astrolabe, which helped sailors determine their position at sea. North Africans helped to develop the astrolabe.

City-States of East Africa Trade had long flowed up and down the coast of East Africa. Small villages that had good natural harbors grew into busy trading centers.

Gold from Zimbabwe (zim BAH bweh), a powerful inland state, was carried to coastal cities such as Kilwa and Sofala. From there, ships carried the gold, and prized goods such as hardwoods and ivory, across the Indian Ocean to Arabia, India, and China.

Wealth from trade helped local East African rulers build strong city-states. East African city-states gained wealth and power by trading people as well as goods.

They traded enslaved people from the interior of East Africa to Arabs and other groups across the Indian Ocean.

Many rulers of these city-states became Muslims. In time, Muslim culture influenced East African traditions. The blend of cultures led to the rise of a new language, Swahili, which blended Arabic words and local African languages.

Trading Kingdoms of West Africa A region of grasslands, called the **savanna**, covers much of West Africa. Several rich trading kingdoms emerged there. Among the best known were Mali and Songhai (SAWNG hy). The city of Timbuktu was the major trading center for both kingdoms. These West African empires gained power through warfare. They conquered neighboring peoples and took control of surrounding lands.

The kingdom of Mali rose in about A.D. 1200 and flourished for about 200 years. Like the rulers of East Africa's city-states, many rulers in West African kingdoms adopted the religion of Islam.

Mali's most famous ruler, Mansa Musa, was a Muslim. In 1324, the emperor made a pilgrimage to Mecca. On the way, he and his caravan stopped in Cairo, Egypt. His wealth in gold amazed the Egyptians. In time, stories of Mansa Musa's immense wealth reached Europe. A Spanish map from that time shows Mansa Musa on his throne, holding a golden object.

> So abundant is the gold in his country that this lord is the richest and most noble king in all the land.
>
> —Catalan Atlas, 1375

In the 1400s, Songhai emerged as the most powerful empire in West Africa. Muslim emperors extended Songhai's power and made Timbuktu into a thriving city.

Ways of Life in Africa Ways of life varied greatly across the huge continent of Africa. While powerful trading states flourished in some regions, most people lived outside these kingdoms. Many lived in small villages. They made a living by herding, fishing, or farming.

Family relationships were important in African cultures. Although family patterns varied across Africa, many people lived within an extended family.

In an **extended family**, several generations live in one household. An extended family usually included grandparents, parents, children, and sometimes aunts, uncles, and cousins. The grandparents, or elders, received special respect for their wisdom and knowledge.

Ties of **kinship**, or sharing a common ancestor, linked families. People related by kinship owed loyalty to one another.

Trade in Africa and Eurasia

AFRICA		EURASIA	
Domesticated camels enabled North African merchants to cross the Sahara. Caravans could include merchants, missionaries, pilgrims, and scholars.		Improvements in land and sea travel enabled goods and ideas to travel between East Asia, South Asia, the Middle East, and Europe.	
RESOURCES AND GOODS	**TECHNOLOGY AND EDUCATION**	**RESOURCES AND GOODS**	**TECHNOLOGY AND EDUCATION**
• Gold, copper, and salt • Ivory for artistic carving • Kola nuts for medicine; coffee beans prized as a stimulant	• Advanced metal forging techniques for toolmaking • Weaving techniques for patterned textiles • Universities taught mathematics, medicine, law, geography, history, and art • Training in carpentry, fishing, and tailoring	• Spices for flavorings, perfumes, and medicines as well as European wines • Textiles including silk and wool • Copper, iron, and silver	• Techniques for making pottery, ceramics, glazes, glass, and lacquerware • Study in mathematics, medicine, and engineering, advances in agricultural and irrigation techniques • Architectural domes and arches used in building mosques, temples, and churches • Surgical instruments and techniques

>> **Analyze Charts** How did the exchange of goods and information between Africa and Eurasia benefit both regions?

Kinship ties encouraged a strong sense of community and cooperation.

Religious beliefs varied widely across Africa. Yet, African beliefs reflected some common threads. Links among family members lasted even after a person died. In their rituals and ceremonies, many Africans honored the spirits of their ancestors as well as the forces of nature. Powerful spirits, they believed, could harm or could help the living.

❓ **CHECK UNDERSTANDING** How would you explain what an extended family is to a friend?

Chinese Trade and Technology

Africa had many different cultures and kingdoms. By contrast, in China, power was centered on one emperor. Chinese rulers were often suspicious of outsiders. China was the most isolated civilization of the ancient world. Long distances and physical barriers separated it from Egypt, the Middle East, and India. This isolation contributed to the Chinese belief that China was the center of the Earth and the sole source of civilization. The ancient Chinese looked down on outsiders who did not speak Chinese or follow Chinese ways.

China Uses Technology to Increase Trade Chinese inventions changed shipbuilding around the globe. The Chinese invented the rudder, which made it easier to steer large ships. They created watertight compartments that went in the ship's hull to reduce the risk of sinking. They also probably invented the magnetic compass, which decreased the likelihood of getting lost on the open seas.

A young emperor who came to power in 1402 was eager to use these new

>> The rudder on this Chinese trading ship allowed the craft to be steered more easily.

technologies to increase trade. He ordered a huge fleet to be built and named Zheng He (JUNG HUH) to command it. Zheng He's fleet numbered more than 300 ships. It carried tons of trade goods. The largest ships were more than 400 feet long.

Between 1405 and 1433, Zheng He made seven long voyages. His fleet traded at ports in Southeast Asia, India, Arabia, and East Africa. At every port, Chinese traders carried on a brisk business. They expanded Chinese trade and influence across a wide region.

The Voyages End Zheng He's great fleet returned home with exotic goods and animals, such as giraffes, that the Chinese had never seen. However, China's overseas voyages soon ended. A new emperor decided that China had nothing to learn from the outside world. He outlawed most foreign trade. However, traders like Zheng

He had spread Chinese technological innovations around the world.

The Chinese first invented paper in A.D. 105. They also developed a printing press with movable type. The Chinese made advancements in timekeeping, developing several different kinds of clocks. They also invented gunpowder. Europeans later used gunpowder in handguns and cannons, which were based on Chinese designs.

? IDENTIFY SUPPORTING DETAILS How did new technologies improve Chinese ships?

Europe's Renaissance

Increased trade and travel made Europeans eager to learn more about the wider world. Scholars looked in monastery libraries for manuscripts of ancient Greek and Roman works. Some traveled to the Middle East, where many ancient works had been preserved.

>> The mechanical clock was one of ancient China's many technological innovations.

As scholars studied ancient learning, they began to make their own discoveries. They produced new books on art, medicine, astronomy, and chemistry. This great burst of learning and technological innovation was called the **Renaissance** (REN uh sahns), a French word meaning rebirth. It lasted from the late 1300s until the 1600s.

The Chinese had invented the printing press and movable type, or metal letters that could be used to print paper. However, the Chinese language required thousands of different letters, and movable type had little impact.

During the 1430s, a German printer named Johannes Gutenberg (GOOT un burg) is believed to have invented movable type without knowing that it had existed in China. Movable type was much more useful for printing in European languages, which used only 26 letters. Together, movable type and the printing press helped to spread Renaissance learning. Before movable type and the printing press, books were scarce and costly because each was copied by hand. With these technological innovations, large numbers of books could be produced quickly and at a low cost. Soon more people began to read, and learning spread more quickly.

Europeans Search for New Trade Routes
During the Renaissance, trade brought new prosperity. European rulers began to increase their power. In England and France, kings and queens worked to bring powerful feudal lords under their control. In Spain and Portugal, Christian monarchs drove out Muslim rulers, who had governed there for centuries.

Rulers in England, France, Spain, and Portugal were eager to increase their wealth. They saw the great profits that could be made through trade. However,

>> This painting of Renaissance nobles at a feast shows the wealth that Europe gained through trade.

Middle Eastern and Italian merchants controlled the trade routes across the Mediterranean Sea. So, Western Europe's leaders began hunting for other routes to Asia. European rulers also looked to Africa as a source of riches. Tales of Mansa Musa's wealth had created a stir in Europe, but no one knew the source of African gold.

Portuguese Voyages Portugal was an early leader in the search for a new trade route to Asia and for the source of African gold. In the early 1400s, Prince Henry, known as Henry the Navigator, encouraged sea captains to sail south along the coast of West Africa. Realizing that Portugal needed better navigators to accomplish the task, he set up an informal school to teach sailors techniques of navigation and the art of shipbuilding.

Under Henry's guidance, the Portuguese designed a new type of ship, the caravel

(KAR uh vel). With triangular sails and a steering rudder, caravels could be sailed closer to the direction the wind was blowing from. Portuguese caravels stopped at many places along the coast of West Africa. They traded cloth, silver, textiles, and grain for gold and ivory. They also bought Africans who had been forced into slavery and sold them in Europe and elsewhere.

Further Exploration Slowly, Portuguese explorers ventured farther south, hoping to find a sea route around Africa to the rich spice trade of Asia. In 1488, Bartolomeu Dias reached the southern tip of Africa.

Nine years later, in 1497, Vasco da Gama rounded the Cape of Good Hope at the southern tip of Africa. He then sailed up the coast of East Africa and across the Indian Ocean to India. The Portuguese pushed on to the East Indies, the islands of

Portuguese Routes of Exploration

KEY
→ Bartolomeu Dias, 1487–1488
→ Vasco da Gama, 1497–1499

>> This map shows the sea routes taken by Bartolomeu Dias and Vasco da Gama. **Analyze Maps** Which Portuguese explorer stayed closer to land?

Southeast Asia and the source of valuable spices.

? CHECK UNDERSTANDING What effect did movable type and the printing press have on learning?

ASSESSMENT

1. **Identify Cause and Effect** What advantages did Middle Eastern merchants possess that allowed them to take such a central role in the expansion of overseas trade?

2. **Identify Central Issues** What were the benefits of the feudal system in Europe in the Middle Ages?

3. **Identify Cause and Effect** What were some of the main causes that led to the great burst of learning known as the Renaissance?

4. **Draw Conclusions** How did trade between China and other civilizations have long term effects worldwide?

5. **Support Ideas with Examples** Explain how the Crusades set the stage for the Age of Exploration that followed.

1.3 European Exploration in the Americas

KEY
— Columbus, 1492–1493
— Cabot, 1497
— Vespucci, 1499
— Balboa, 1510–1513
— Magellan, 1519–1522
— Cortés, 1519–1521
— Pizarro, 1524–1533
— Hudson, 1609

>> **Analyze Maps** From which European country did most voyages of exploration originate?

▶ **Interactive Flipped Video**

Many stories exist about early people from Europe or Asia sailing to the Americas. Yet, real evidence has been hard to find. Most experts agree that such voyages were rare, if they occurred at all. Unlike other possible early voyagers to the Americas, the Vikings left behind a detailed record of their voyages.

>> **Objectives**

Identify reasons for European exploration of the Americas.

Describe the results of European exploration in the Americas.

Evaluate how exchanges between Europeans and Native Americans modified the physical environment .

>> **Key Terms**

colony
turning point
circumnavigate
Columbian
   Exchange
modification

PEARSON **realize** ™
www.PearsonRealize.com
Access your Digital Lesson.

>> This stone tablet shows warriors aboard a Viking ship. The Vikings were one of the first groups to travel from Europe to the Americas.

Early Contact With the Americas

In 1001, Viking sailors led by Leif Ericson reached the eastern tip of North America. Archaeologists have found evidence of the Viking settlement of Vinland in present-day Newfoundland, Canada. The Vikings did not stay in Vinland long and no one is sure why they left. However, Viking stories describe fierce battles with Skraelings, the Viking name for the Inuits.

Evidence suggests that Asians continued to cross the Bering Sea into North America after the last ice age ended. Some scholars believe that ancient seafarers from Polynesia may have traveled to the Americas using their knowledge of the stars and winds. Modern Polynesians have sailed canoes thousands of miles in this way. Still others think that fishing boats from China and Japan blew off

course and landed on the western coast of North or South America.

Perhaps such voyages occurred. If so, they were long forgotten. Before 1492, the peoples of Asia and Europe had no knowledge of the Americas and their remarkable civilizations.

? RECALL Why aren't we certain whether early people from Europe or Asia other than the Vikings sailed to America?

The Voyages of Columbus

Portuguese sailors had pioneered new routes around Africa toward Asia in the late 1400s. Spain, too, wanted a share of the riches. King Ferdinand and Queen Isabella hoped to keep their rival, Portugal, from controlling trade with India, China, and Japan. They therefore agreed to finance a voyage of exploration by Christopher Columbus. Columbus, an Italian sea captain, planned to reach the East Indies by sailing west across the Atlantic. Finding a sea route straight to Asia would give the Spanish direct access to the silks, spices, and precious metals of Asia. The spice trade was a major cause for European exploration and a reason the Spanish rulers supported Columbus's voyage. However, it was not the only reason. They hoped for wealth from any source. "Get gold," King Ferdinand said to Columbus. "Humanely if possible, but at all hazards—get gold."

Sailing Across the Atlantic In August 1492, Columbus set out with three ships and a crew of about 90 sailors. As captain, he commanded the largest vessel, the *Santa María*. The other ships were the *Niña* and the *Pinta*.

After a brief stop at the Canary Islands, the little fleet continued west into unknown seas. Fair winds sped them along, but a month passed without the sight of land. Some sailors began to grumble. They had never been away from land for so long and feared being lost at sea. Still, Columbus sailed on.

On October 7, sailors saw flocks of birds flying southwest. Columbus changed course to follow the birds. A few days later, crew members spotted tree branches and flowers floating in the water. At 2 A.M. on October 12, the lookout on the *Pinta* spotted white cliffs shining in the moonlight. *"Tierra! Tierra!"* he shouted. "Land! Land!"

At dawn, Columbus rowed ashore and planted the banner of Spain on the beach. He was convinced that he had reached the East Indies in Asia. He called the people he found there "Indians." In fact, he had reached islands off the coasts of North America and South America in the

>> Christopher Columbus sailed across the Atlantic Ocean in search of new trade routes for Spain.

>> This is a modern replica of the Santa María , the ship that Columbus sailed on the voyage that first brought him to the Americas.

Caribbean Sea. These islands later became known as the West Indies.

For three months, Columbus explored the West Indies. To his delight, he found signs of gold on the islands. Eager to report his success, he returned to Spain.

Spain Seeks Colonies In Spain, Columbus presented Queen Isabella and King Ferdinand with gifts of pink pearls and brilliantly colored parrots. The royal couple listened intently as Columbus brought with him several of many things that Europeans had never seen before: tobacco, pineapples, and hammocks used for sleeping. Columbus also described the "Indians" he had met, the Tainos (TY nohz). The Tainos, he promised, could easily be converted to Christianity and could also be used as slaves.

The Spanish monarchs were impressed. They gave Columbus the title Admiral of the Ocean Sea. They also agreed to finance future voyages. The promise of great wealth, and the chance to spread Christianity, gave them a reason to explore further.

Columbus made three more voyages across the Atlantic. In 1493, he founded the first Spanish colony in the Americas, Santo Domingo, on an island he called Hispaniola (present-day Haiti and the Dominican Republic). A **colony** is an area settled and ruled by the government of a distant land. Columbus also explored present-day Cuba and Jamaica and sailed along the coasts of Central America and northern South America. He claimed all of these lands for Spain.

Columbus proved to be a better explorer than governor. During his third expedition, settlers on Hispaniola complained of his harsh rule. Queen Isabella appointed an investigator, who sent Columbus back to Spain in chains. In the end, the queen pardoned Columbus, but he never regained the honors he had won earlier. He died in 1506, still convinced that he had reached Asia.

The Impact of Columbus's Voyages
Columbus has long been honored as the bold sea captain who "discovered America." Today, we recognize that Native Americans had discovered and settled these lands long before 1492. Still, in at least one sense, Columbus deserves the honors history has given him. Europeans knew nothing of the Americas until Columbus told them about this "new world." His daring voyages marked the beginning of lasting contact among the peoples of Europe, Africa, and the Americas.

>> This illustration shows Columbus meeting the Taino people of the West Indies. His voyages benefited Spain but brought much misery to the world of the Taino.

▶ **Interactive Chart**

The Life of Christopher Columbus

About 1451
Born in Genoa, Italy

1476
First sea voyage

1479
First marriage to Felipa Perestrello in Portugal

1485
Columbus moves to Spain and seeks support for a voyage west to Asia.

1492
Ferdinand and Isabella of Spain agree to fund Columbus after the rulers in Portugal and Venice reject him.

1492
First voyage to the West Indies

1493
Second voyage to the West Indies

1498
Third voyage to South America

1502
Fourth voyage to Central America; strandedon Jamaica by a storm

1506
Columbus dies without finding a shorter route to Asia.

1450 1460 1470 1480 1490 1500 1510

>> **Analyze Timelines** How many voyages did Columbus make to the Americas?

For a great many Native Americans, contact had tragic results. Columbus and those who followed were convinced that European culture was superior to that of the Indians. The Spanish claimed Taino lands and forced Tainos to work in gold mines, on ranches, or in Spanish households. Many Tainos died from harsh conditions or European diseases. Within 100 years of Columbus's arrival, the Taino population was virtually wiped out.

For better or worse, the voyages of Columbus signaled a turning point for the Americas. A **turning point** is a moment in history that marks a decisive change. Curious Europeans saw the new lands as a place where they could settle, trade, and grow rich.

❓ **IDENTIFY MAIN IDEAS** What reasons did Spain have for sending Columbus on his voyages?

Other Spanish Exploration

After the voyages of Columbus, the Spanish explored and settled other Caribbean islands. They wanted to take advantage of the land Columbus had found, seeking gold, crops, slaves, and converts to Christianity for the Spanish crown. By 1511, they had conquered Puerto Rico, Jamaica, and Cuba. They also explored the eastern coasts of North America and South America in search of a western route to Asia.

In 1513, Vasco Núñez de Balboa (bal BOH uh) plunged into the jungles of the Isthmus of Panama. Native Americans had told him that a large body of water lay to the west. With a party of Spanish soldiers and Indians, Balboa reached the Pacific Ocean after about 25 days. He stood in the crashing surf and claimed the ocean for Spain.

The Spanish had no idea how wide the Pacific was until a sea captain named Ferdinand Magellan (muh JEL un) sailed across it. The expedition—made up of five ships and about 250 crew members—left Spain in 1519. Fifteen months later, it rounded Cape Horn, the stormy southern tip of South America and entered the Pacific Ocean. Crossing the vast Pacific, the sailors ran out of food.

> We remained 3 months and 20 days without taking in provisions or other refreshments and ate only old biscuit reduced to powder, full of grubs and stinking from the dirt which rats had made on it. We drank water that was yellow and stinking.
>
> —Antonio Pigafetta, *The Diary of Antonio Pigafetta*

Magellan himself was killed in a battle with the local people of the Philippine Islands off the coast of Asia.

In 1522, only one ship and 18 sailors returned to Spain. They were the first people to **circumnavigate**, or sail completely around, the world. In doing so, they had found an all-water western route to Asia. Their voyage made Europeans aware of the true size of the Earth.

❓ **IDENTIFY** Identify the significance of Magellan"s voyage.

The Columbian Exchange

The encounter between the peoples of the Eastern and Western hemispheres sparked a global exchange of goods and ideas. Because it started with the voyages of Columbus, this transfer is known as the **Columbian Exchange**. The Columbian Exchange refers to a biological and cultural exchange of animals, plants, human populations, diseases, food, government, technology, the arts, and languages.

>> Horses and other domesticated animals were introduced to the Americas by Europeans. Horses soon became part of Native Americans' way of life.

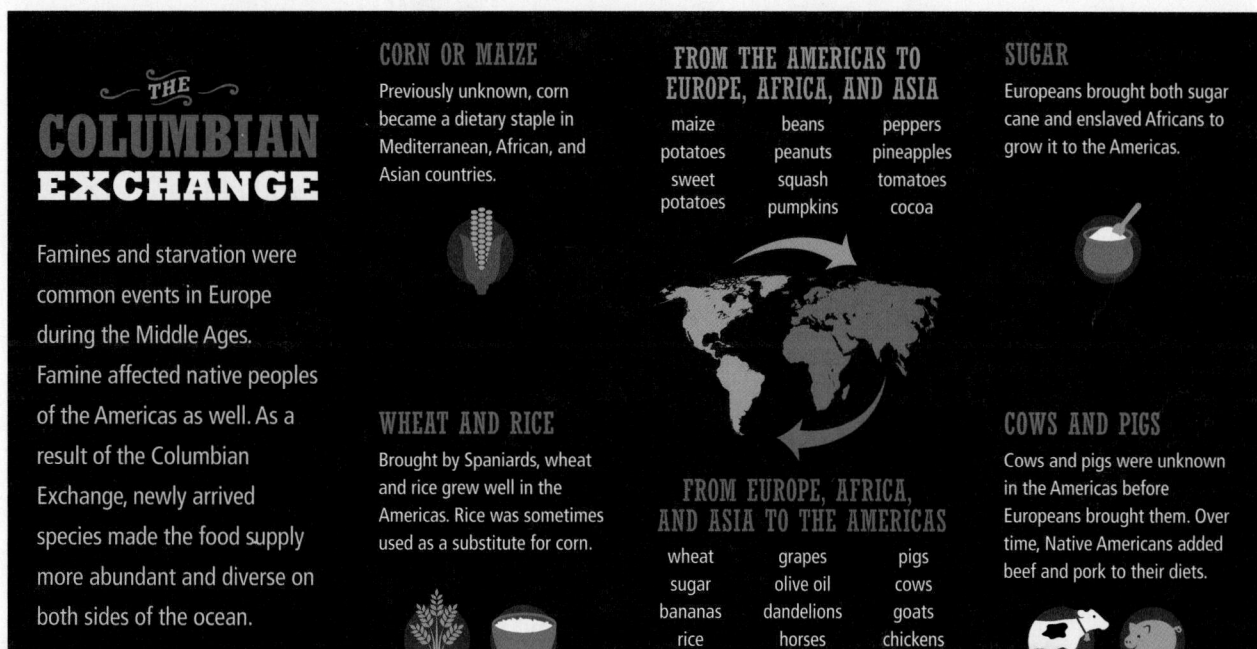

THE COLUMBIAN EXCHANGE

Famines and starvation were common events in Europe during the Middle Ages. Famine affected native peoples of the Americas as well. As a result of the Columbian Exchange, newly arrived species made the food supply more abundant and diverse on both sides of the ocean.

CORN OR MAIZE

Previously unknown, corn became a dietary staple in Mediterranean, African, and Asian countries.

WHEAT AND RICE

Brought by Spaniards, wheat and rice grew well in the Americas. Rice was sometimes used as a substitute for corn.

FROM THE AMERICAS TO EUROPE, AFRICA, AND ASIA

maize	beans	peppers
potatoes	peanuts	pineapples
sweet potatoes	squash	tomatoes
	pumpkins	cocoa

FROM EUROPE, AFRICA, AND ASIA TO THE AMERICAS

wheat	grapes	pigs
sugar	olive oil	cows
bananas	dandelions	goats
rice	horses	chickens

SUGAR

Europeans brought both sugar cane and enslaved Africans to grow it to the Americas.

COWS AND PIGS

Cows and pigs were unknown in the Americas before Europeans brought them. Over time, Native Americans added beef and pork to their diets.

>> **Analyze Graphs** What were some positive consequences of the Columbian Exchange?

The exchange went in both directions. Europeans learned much from Native Americans.

At the same time, Europeans contributed in many ways to the culture of the Americas. This exchange also brought about many **modifications**, or changes, to the physical environment of the Americas, with both positive and negative results.

Modifying Environments Europeans introduced domestic animals such as chickens from Europe and Africa. European pigs, cattle, and horses often escaped into the wild and multiplied rapidly. Forests and grasslands were converted to pastures. As horses spread through what would become the United States, Indians learned to ride them and used them to carry heavy loads.

Plants from Europe and Africa changed the way Native Americans lived. The first bananas came from the Canary Islands.

By 1520, one Spaniard reported that banana trees had spread "so greatly that it is marvelous to see the great abundance of them." Oranges, lemons, and figs were also new to the Americas. In North America, explorers also brought such plants as bluegrass, the daisy, and the dandelion. These plants spread quickly in American soil and modified American grasslands.

Tragically, Europeans also brought new diseases, such as smallpox and influenza. Native Americans had no resistance to these diseases. Historians estimate that within 75 years, diseases from Europe had killed almost 90 percent of the people in the Caribbean islands and in Mexico.

Native American Influences on Europe, Africa, and Asia For their part, Native Americans introduced Europeans, Africans, and Asians to new foods, customs, and ideas. After 1492, elements of Native American ways of life gradually spread around the world. Sadly, disease also spread from the Americas to Europe and other parts of the world.

Native Americans introduced Europeans to valuable food crops such as corn, potatoes, sweet potatoes, beans, tomatoes, manioc, squash, peanuts, pineapples, and blueberries. Today, almost half the world's food crops come from plants that were first grown in the Americas.

Europeans carried the new foods with them as they sailed around the world. Everywhere, people's diets changed and populations increased. In South Asia, people used American hot peppers and chilis to spice stews. Chinese peasants began growing corn and sweet potatoes. Italians made sauces from tomatoes. People in West Africa grew manioc and corn.

European settlers often adopted Native American skills. In the North, Indians showed Europeans how to use snowshoes and trap beavers and other fur-bearing animals. European explorers learned how to paddle Indian canoes. Some leaders studied Native American political structures. In the 1700s, Benjamin Franklin admired the Iroquois League and urged American colonists to unite in a similar way.

Positive and Negative Consequences

Through the Columbian Exchange, Europeans and Native Americans modified their environments and gained new resources and skills. At the same time, warfare and disease killed many on both sides. Europeans viewed expansion positively. They gained great wealth, explored trade routes, and spread Christianity. Yet their farming, mining, and diseases took a toll on the physical environment and left many Native Americans dead. Despite these negatives, the Columbian Exchange shaped the modern world, including what would become the United States.

? CHECK UNDERSTANDING How would you define the Columbian Exchange?

ASSESSMENT

1. **Support a Point of View with Evidence** How did European expansion in the Americas affect Native Americans?

2. **Compare** the expeditions of Vasco Núñez de Balboa and Ferdinand Magellan.

3. **Summarize** the career of Christopher Columbus.

4. **Identify Cause and Effect** Explain the causes and effects of the Columbian Exchange.

5. **Generate Explanations** Why were Native Americans so susceptible to European diseases such as influenza?

1. **Compare Culture Regions** Analyze the images above, which show settlements in two different Native American culture regions in North America. Then write a paragraph comparing the ways the two societies modified their environments. Identify the people and culture region shown in each image, explain how each society modified its environment, and discuss specific reasons why the two groups chose different ways to do so.

2. **Analyze Influence of Environment on Population** Write a paragraph analyzing how the physical geography of the Native American culture regions influenced whether the population was concentrated in specific areas or spread out across the region. Consider both the influence of climate and the availability of resources.

3. **Analyze Influence of Environment on Settlement** Write a paragraph analyzing how the environment influenced settlement patterns among the Chipewyan and Carrier. Identify in which region the Chipewyan and Carrier lived, describe the environment in that region, and describe how it affected settlement patterns.

4. **Compare Cultures** Write a paragraph comparing the cultures of the Plateau region with those of the Northwest Coastal region. Describe how the Utes and the Shoshones of the Plateau region lived and contrast the Plateau cultures with the more complex cultures found in the Northwest Coastal region.

5. **Evaluate Sources** Select an example of how human changes to the environment, such as the Columbian Exchange, can have negative consequences. Then locate a primary or secondary source that discusses similar negative consequences. Write a paragraph summarizing and evaluating the source. Answer these questions: What negative consequences does the author describe? Do other sources support the information in the source you chose? What information can you gather about the author and his or her knowledge of the subject?

TOPIC ① ASSESSMENT

6. **Describe the Drawbacks of the Columbian Exchange** Write a paragraph describing the drawbacks of the Columbian Exchange. Define the term *Columbian Exchange*. Describe how Native Americans were harmed by the Columbian Exchange and what harm the Columbian Exchange brought to other parts of the world.

7. **Locate and Use Valid Primary and Secondary Sources** Select two Native American culture regions that interest you. Then acquire information about both of these regions by locating a valid primary or secondary source from at least three of these categories: computer software, database, media or news service, biography, interview, and artifact. Be sure to select valid sources. Then use the information you have acquired to write a short essay comparing the two culture regions.

8. **Analyze the Environment's Influence on Settlement** Write a paragraph analyzing how the physical features of the Eastern Woodlands region influenced the location and structure of Iroquois settlements. Describe and analyze the region's climate and physical landscape, where the Iroquois settled, and the nature of Iroquois settlements.

9. **Compare the Effects of New Technologies on Daily Life** Write a paragraph comparing the effects of different technologies developed in the Middle East on daily life in the United States today. Consider the contributions of Middle Eastern engineers and inventors.

10. **Compare the Effects of New Technologies in Navigation** Write a paragraph discussing how advances in technology affected travel by sea for people in Europe, the Middle East, Africa, China, and later in the region that is now the United States. Consider what new technologies in navigation came from each area of the world and what effects these technologies had on navigation.

11. **Identify the Reasons for European Exploration** Write a paragraph identifying why the Spanish were interested in exploring North America. Include the political reasons for exploration, the religious reasons for exploration, and the economic reasons for exploration.

12. **Describe the Positive Consequences of the Columbian Exchange** Write a paragraph describing how people benefited from the Columbian Exchange. Define the term *Columbian Exchange* and describe how the Columbian Exchange changed the physical environment of North America, how Native Americans benefited from the results of these changes, and how the Columbian Exchange benefited other parts of the world.

13. **Compare Effects of New Technologies on Daily Life** Use the chart below and other sources to write about the effects of new ways of doing things on early Europe, Africa, Asia, and eventually on the region that became the United States. Write a paragraph comparing how these new technologies might have influenced daily life. Consider what information in the chart is relevant to the topic of your paragraph and how the technologies listed in the chart likely affected daily life.

Trade in Africa and Eurasia

AFRICA		EURASIA	
Domesticated camels enabled North African merchants to cross the Sahara. Caravans could include merchants, missionaries, pilgrims, and scholars.		Improvements in land and sea travel enabled goods and ideas to travel between East Asia, South Asia, the Middle East, and Europe.	
RESOURCES AND GOODS	**TECHNOLOGY AND EDUCATION**	**RESOURCES AND GOODS**	**TECHNOLOGY AND EDUCATION**
• Gold, copper, and salt • Ivory for artistic carving • Kola nuts for medicine; coffee beans prized as a stimulant	• Advanced metal forging techniques for toolmaking • Weaving techniques for patterned textiles • Universities taught mathematics, medicine, law, geography, history, and art • Training in carpentry, fishing, and tailoring	• Spices for flavorings, perfumes, and medicines as well as European wines • Textiles including silk and wool • Copper, iron, and silver	• Techniques for making pottery, ceramics, glazes, glass, and lacquerware • Study in mathematics, medicine, and engineering, advances in agricultural and irrigation techniques • Architectural domes and arches used in building mosques, temples, and churches • Surgical instruments and techniques

14. **Describe the Consequences of Environmental Changes** Write a paragraph describing the positive and negative consequences of the introduction of European pigs, cattle, and horses to North America. Describe the effect on the environment and the effect on Native Americans.

15. **Describe Environmental Change** Write a paragraph describing how the introduction of plants from Europe and Africa changed the environment in the Americas. Identify some of the new plants and describe how these plants changed the environment in the Americas.

16. **Differentiate Between Valid Primary and Secondary Sources** Differentiate between valid primary and secondary sources by analyzing and categorizing a list of sources related to reasons for European exploration of North America. The list of sources should include the European exploration article from *Encyclopedia Britannica* CD-ROM, the National Museum of American History online database, the Flipped Video on the Columbian Exchange, the news article about new archaeological evidence of Viking exploration, the interview with a boatbuilder who constructs replicas of caravels, and Christopher Columbus's autobiography. Write a paragraph categorizing the sources into two groups based on whether they are primary or secondary sources. Consider the following questions: What are the characteristics of a primary source? What are the characteristics of a secondary source? Which characteristics does the specific source reflect?

17. **Write about the Essential Question** **Write an essay on the Essential Question: How much does geography affect people's lives?** Use evidence from your study of this topic to support your answer.

2 European Colonization of North America

Enduring Understandings

- The Spanish were the first to colonize North America; they brought enslaved Africans as workers for their colonies.

- The French and Dutch also colonized North America, seeking to profit from the fur trade.

- English colonists settled along the east coast of North America.

- People seeking religious freedom founded New England's colonies, as well as Pennsylvania and Maryland.

- The slave trade brought enslaved Africans to the English colonies, especially in the South, which relied on slavery for plantation agriculture.

- The English colonies developed representative governments and inherited a tradition of legal rights from England.

>> The Mayflower, the ship that carried the English Pilgrims to America

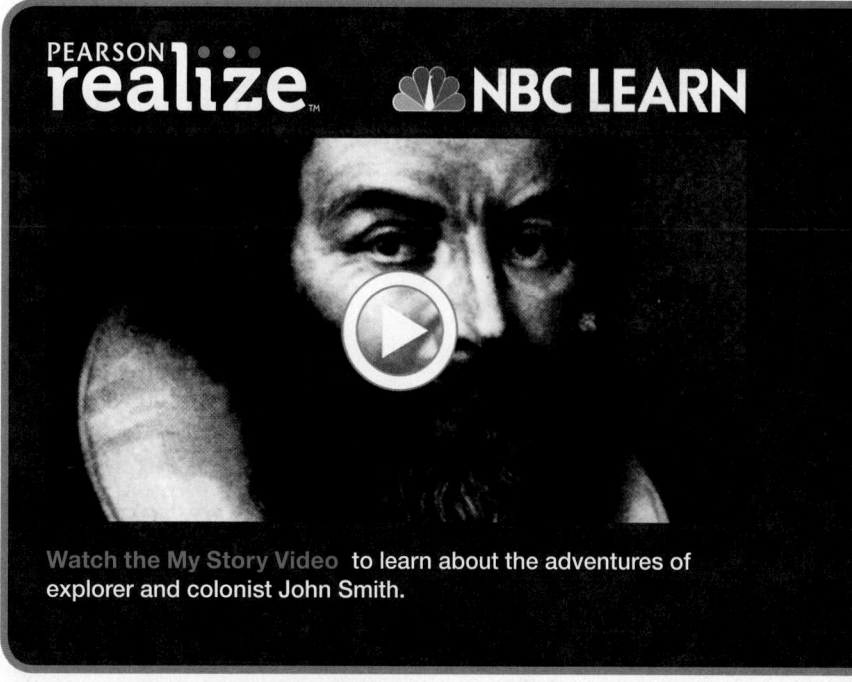

PEARSON realize. NBC LEARN

Watch the My Story Video to learn about the adventures of explorer and colonist John Smith.

PEARSON realize. www.PearsonRealize.com

Access your digital lessons including:
Topic Inquiry • Interactive Reading Notepad • Interactivities • Assessments

Spanish Colonization and New Spain

>> This illustration shows a Spanish conquistador frightening Incan soldiers. Conquistadors' superior military technology allowed them to defeat the Aztec and Incan empires.

▶ Interactive Flipped Video

>> **Objectives**

Describe how conquistadors defeated two Native American empires.

Explain why Spain settled its colonies.

Explain the causes and effects of the transatlantic slave trade.

>> **Key Terms**

conquistador
pueblo
presidio
mission
peninsulare
creole
mestizo
encomienda
plantation

" What a troublesome thing it is to discover new lands. The risks we took, it is hardly possible to exaggerate." Thus spoke Bernal Díaz del Castillo, one of the many Spanish **conquistadors** (kahn KEES tuh dorz), or conquerors, who marched into the Americas in the 1500s. When asked why they traveled to the Americas, Díaz responded, "We came here to serve God and the king and also to get rich."

Conquistadors Arrive in the Americas

In their search for glory and gold, the conquistadors made Spain one of the richest nations in Europe. Spanish colonists followed the conquistadors and created a vast new empire in the Americas.

The rulers of Spain gave conquistadors permission to establish settlements in the Americas. In return, conquistadors agreed to give Spain one fifth of any gold or treasure they captured.

Like other conquistadors, Hernando Cortés was eager to win riches and glory. He had heard rumors of a fabulously wealthy Native American empire in Mexico. With only about 600 soldiers and 16 horses, Cortés set sail for Mexico in 1519 in search of gold.

The Spanish Destroy an Empire

Moctezuma (mokt uh ZOO muh), the Aztec emperor who ruled over much of Mexico, heard disturbing reports of a large house floating on the sea. It was filled with white men with long, thick beards. Aztec sacred writings predicted that a powerful white-skinned god would come from the east to rule the Aztecs. The strangers were approaching Tenochtitlán (tay nawch teet LAHN), the Aztec capital, which is now Mexico City. Moctezuma decided to welcome them as his guests.

Cortés took advantage of Moctezuma's invitation. Shrewdly, Cortés had already begun to win the support of other Indians who resented Aztec rule.

One of his trusted advisers was an Indian woman the Spanish called Doña Marina. She gave Cortés valuable information about the Aztecs and acted as a translator and negotiator. On November 8, 1519, Cortés marched into Tenochtitlán.

The city was much larger than any Spanish city at that time. Thousands upon thousands of Aztecs turned out to see the astonishing newcomers riding horses. Díaz recalled:

> Who could count the multitude of men, women and children which had come out on the roofs, in their boats on the canals, or in the streets, to see us?

—Bernal Díaz del Castillo, *True History of the Conquest of New Spain*

At first, Cortés was friendly to Moctezuma. Soon, however, he made the emperor a prisoner in his own city. Tensions mounted in Tenochtitlán over the next half year.

Finally, the Aztecs drove out the Spanish. Their victory, however, was brief. Aided by people whom the Aztecs had conquered, Cortés recaptured the

>> Hernando Cortés kneels before the Aztec emperor Moctezuma. **Infer** What is the artist suggesting about this interaction between Moctezuma and Cortés?

city. In the end, the Spanish destroyed Tenochtitlán, and Moctezuma was killed. The Aztec empire had fallen.

The Inca Empire Falls Another conquistador, Francisco Pizarro (pee SAHR oh), set his sights on the Incan empire. Pizarro sailed down the Pacific coast of South America with fewer than 200 Spanish soldiers. In 1532, he captured the Incan emperor Atahualpa (ah tuh WAHL puh) and later executed him. Without the leadership of Atahualpa, Incan resistance collapsed. By 1535, Pizarro controlled much of the Incan empire.

Why the Spanish Won How were the Spanish able to conquer two great empires with only a handful of soldiers? First, the Spanish had superior military equipment. They were protected by steel armor and had guns. The Aztecs and Incas relied on clubs, bows and arrows, and spears. Also, the Native Americans had never seen horses. They were frightened by mounted Spanish soldiers.

In addition, the Native Americans did not fight as hard as they might have. The Aztecs hesitated to attack at first because they thought the Spanish might be gods.

The Incas were weak from fighting among themselves over control of their government.

Finally, many Indians died from European diseases, such as smallpox, measles, and influenza. Some historians believe that disease alone would have ensured Spanish victory over the Indians.

From the Spanish perspective, their interaction with the Aztecs and the Incas resulted in great victories that brought wealth and power. The Spanish also saw the conquests as further proof of their natural superiority. The Aztecs and Incas, of course, had a much different view of the same events. From their perspectives, the Spanish conquests were disasters that devastated their civilizations.

❓ IDENTIFY SUPPORTING DETAILS What reasons can you identify that help explain why the Spanish conquered the Aztecs and the Incas so easily?

Exploring Lands to the North

The Spanish search for treasure reached beyond the lands of the Aztecs and Incas. Moving north, conquistadors explored the Spanish borderlands. The borderlands spanned the present-day southern United States from Florida to California.

Juan Ponce de León (PAWN say day lay OHN) traveled through parts of Florida in 1513, looking for a legendary fountain of youth. Indians claimed that anyone who bathed in its magical water would remain

>> In 1532, Pizarro captured and executed Atahualpa, giving the Spanish forces control of much of the Inca empire.

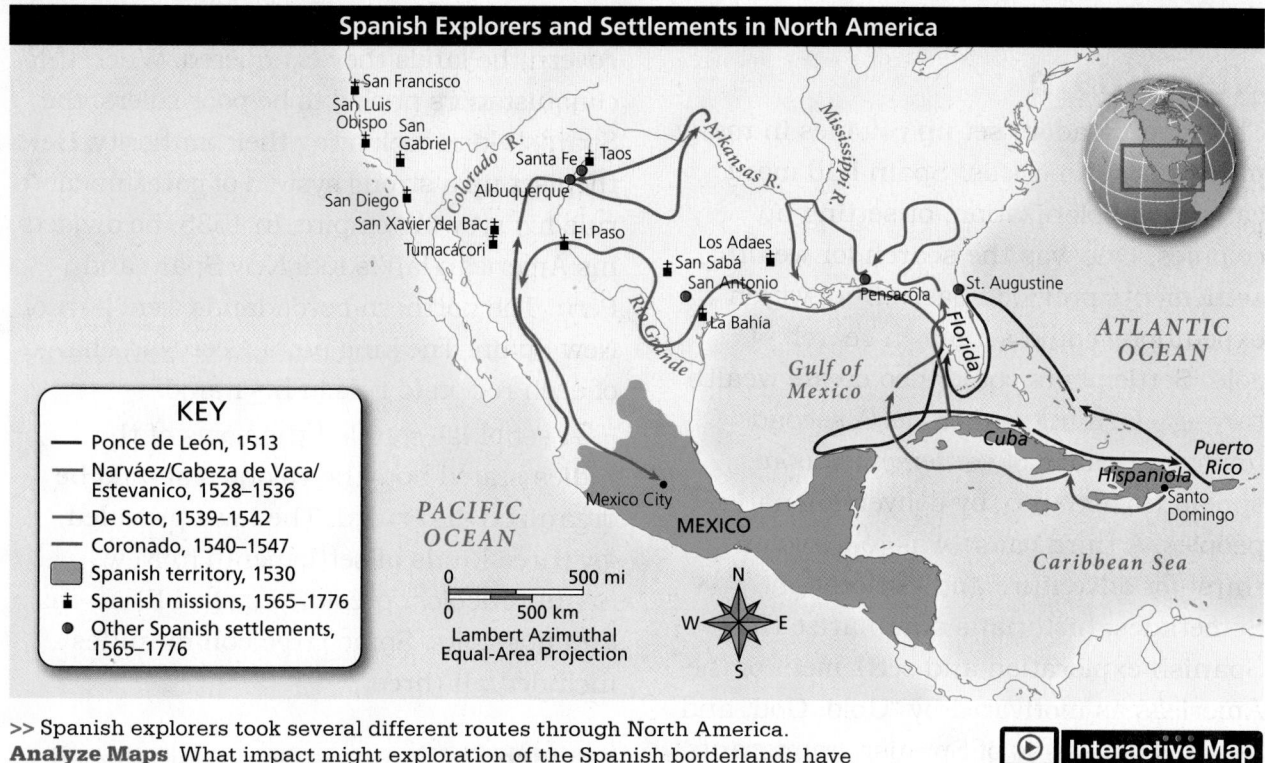

Spanish Explorers and Settlements in North America

KEY
— Ponce de León, 1513
— Narváez/Cabeza de Vaca/ Estevanico, 1528–1536
— De Soto, 1539–1542
— Coronado, 1540–1547
▨ Spanish territory, 1530
♰ Spanish missions, 1565–1776
● Other Spanish settlements, 1565–1776

>> Spanish explorers took several different routes through North America.
Analyze Maps What impact might exploration of the Spanish borderlands have had on the present-day United States?

▶ **Interactive Map**

young forever. Ponce de León found no such fountain.

An Expedition Proves Difficult Another explorer, Pánfilo Narváez (nahr VAH es), led an expedition that ended in disaster. In 1528, a storm struck his fleet in the Gulf of Mexico. Narváez and many others were lost at sea. The rest landed on an island in present-day Texas. Indians captured the few survivors and held them prisoner. Álvar Núñez Cabeza de Vaca (kah VAY suh day VAH kuh) assumed leadership of the small group.

Cabeza de Vaca, an enslaved African named Estevanico, and two others finally escaped their captors in 1533. The four walked across the plains of Texas, searching for a Spanish settlement. Finally, in 1536, they reached a town in Mexico. They had traveled by foot more than 1,000 miles through the Southwest.

The Search for Gold Continues From 1539 to 1542, Hernando De Soto explored Florida and other parts of the Southeast. In his search for gold, he reached the Mississippi River. De Soto died along the riverbank, without finding the riches he sought.

The conquistador Francisco Coronado (koh roh NAH doh) heard legends about "seven cities of gold." In 1540, he led an expedition into the southwestern borderlands. He traveled to present-day Arizona and New Mexico. Some of his party went as far as the Grand Canyon. Still, the Zuni (ZOO nee) villages he visited had no golden streets.

The Spanish expeditions into the borderlands met with little success. Faced with strong Indian resistance in the north, Spain focused instead on bringing order to its empire in the south.

❓ IDENTIFY What reasons did explorers have for traveling north?

The Colonization of New Spain

The conquistadors set up colonies in many parts of the Americas. Spain had many causes for colonization, or setting up colonies. One was the search for wealth: settlements provided bases from which expeditions could set out in search of gold. Settlements could also create wealth through farming and trade. A second important cause of settlement was to spread Christianity by converting native peoples. A third cause was to satisfy a thirst for adventure and exploration. Sometimes, historians summarize the Spanish exploration and settlement of the Americas as motivated by "Gold, God, and Glory." Thousands of Spanish immigrants moved to Spanish settlements looking for opportunities the colonies offered, especially farming.

At first, Spain let the conquistadors govern the lands they conquered. When the conquistadors proved to be poor rulers, the Spanish king took away their authority. He then set up a strong system of government to rule his growing empire. In 1535, he divided his American lands into New Spain and Peru. The northern borderlands were part of New Spain. The king put a viceroy in charge of each region to rule in his name.

A set of laws called the Laws of the Indies stated how the colonies should be organized and ruled. The laws provided for three kinds of settlements in New Spain: pueblos, presidios (prih SID ee ohz), and missions. Some large communities included all three.

Spanish Settlements Spain established many settlements in the Americas. Many of these Spanish settlements were built in a similar pattern. The **pueblos**, or towns, were

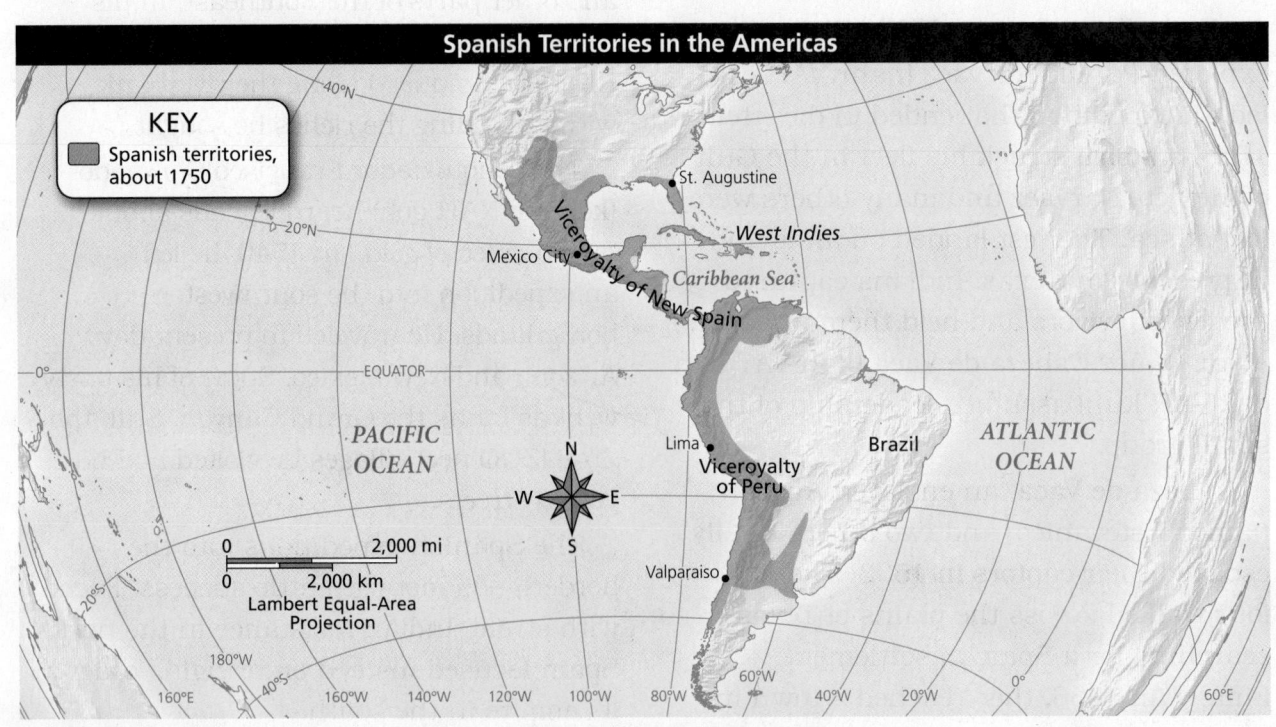

Spanish Territories in the Americas

KEY
Spanish territories, about 1750

40°N

St. Augustine

20°N

Mexico City

West Indies

Viceroyalty of New Spain

Caribbean Sea

0° EQUATOR

PACIFIC OCEAN

N
W — E
S

Lima
Viceroyalty of Peru

Brazil

ATLANTIC OCEAN

0   2,000 mi
0   2,000 km
Lambert Equal-Area Projection

Valparaiso

180°W
160°E   160°W   140°W   120°W   100°W   80°W   60°W   40°W   20°W   0°   60°E
40°S
60°W

>> Spanish territory covered Central America, part of North America, and much of the Caribbean Islands and South America. **Analyze Maps** How did the Spanish divide their territory into colonies?

centers of farming and trade. In the middle of the town was a plaza, or public square.

Here, townspeople and farmers came to do business or worship at the church. Shops and homes lined the four sides of the plaza.

The Spanish took control of Indian pueblos and built new towns as well. In 1598, Juan de Oñate (oh NYAH tay) founded the colony of New Mexico among the adobe villages of the Pueblo Indians. He used brutal force to conquer the Native Americans of the region. Don Pedro de Peralta later founded Santa Fe as the Spanish capital of New Mexico.

Presidios were forts where soldiers lived. Inside the high, thick walls were shops, stables, and storehouses for food. Soldiers protected the farmers who settled nearby. The first presidio in the borderlands was built in 1565 at St. Augustine, Florida. St. Augustine was the first permanent European settlement in what would become the United States. Its founding marked the beginning of the era of colonization in the future territory of the United States, which would continue until the United States declared independence in 1776.

The Legacy of Missions Like other Europeans in the Americas, the Spanish believed they had a duty to convert Indians to Christianity. They set up **missions**, settlements run by Catholic priests and friars whose goal was to convert Indians to Christianity. They often forced Indians to live and work on the missions. In New Mexico, the Spanish tried to destroy any trace of traditional Pueblo Indians' religious practices and subjected them to severe punishments. This resulted in the Pueblo Revolt of 1680. The Pueblo Indians rose up against Spanish rule. They killed

>> Settlers in St. Augustine, Florida, in New Spain came to town to do business, worship, and socialize.

about 400 Spaniards and drove the others out of the region. The Spanish recaptured the region in the mid-1690s.

Missions gradually spread across the Spanish borderlands. The first mission in Texas was founded in 1659 at El Paso.

In 1691, Father Eusebio Francisco Kino (KEE noh) crossed into present-day Arizona. He eventually set up 24 missions in the area. The missions were a direct result of early Spanish colonization efforts. Over time, they had a significant impact in the Americas. By the late 1700s, a string of missions dotted the California coast from San Diego to San Francisco, and Spanish language and culture gradually spread with them.

? RECALL What reasons did Spanish colonists have for coming to New Spain?

The Social Order in New Spain

The Laws of the Indies also set up a strict social system. People in Spanish colonies were divided into four social classes: peninsulares (puh NIN suh LAH rayz), creoles (KREE ohlz), mestizos (mes TEE sohz), and Indians.

Different Social Classes At the top of the social scale were the **peninsulares**. Born in Spain, peninsulares held the highest jobs in government and the Church. They also owned large tracts of land as well as rich gold and silver mines.

Below the peninsulares were the **creoles**, people born in the Americas to parents of Spanish origin. Many creoles were wealthy and well educated. They owned farms and ranches, taught at universities, and practiced law. However, they could not hold the jobs that were reserved for peninsulares.

Below the creoles were people of mixed Spanish and Indian background, known as **mestizos**. Mestizos worked on farms and ranches owned by peninsulares and creoles. In the cities, they worked as carpenters, shoemakers, tailors, and bakers. Over the course of Spanish colonization, mestizos came to be the largest class of people.

The lowest class in the colonies was the Indians. In the early years of Spanish colonization, Indians were the largest class. The Spanish treated them as a conquered people. Under New Spain's strict social system, Indians were kept in poverty for hundreds of years.

A Blend of Spanish and Indian Cultures The effects of colonization can be seen in the new way of life in New Spain that blended Spanish and Indian ways. Spanish settlers brought their own culture to the colonies. They introduced their language,

>> New Spain's society was divided into social classes based on birthplace and racial characteristics.

laws, religion, and learning. In 1551, the Spanish founded the University of Mexico.

Native Americans also influenced the culture of New Spain. Colonists adopted Indian foods, such as corn, tomatoes, potatoes, and squash. Indian workers used materials they knew well, such as adobe bricks, to build fine libraries, theaters, and churches. Sometimes, Indian artists decorated church walls with paintings of local traditions.

Harsh Treatment of Native Americans

Spanish colonists needed workers for their ranches, farms, and mines. To help them, the Spanish government gave settlers **encomiendas** (en koh mee EN dahz), land grants that included the right to demand labor or taxes from Native Americans.

Mines in Mexico, Peru, and other parts of the Americas made Spain rich. Treasure ships laden with thousands of tons of gold and silver sailed regularly across the Atlantic.

The Spanish forced Native Americans to work in the gold and silver mines. In flickering light, Indians hacked out rich ores in narrow, dark tunnels. Many died when tunnels caved in.

These harsh conditions led one priest, Bartolomé de Las Casas (day lahs KAH sahs), to seek reform. Traveling through New Spain, Las Casas witnessed firsthand the deaths of Indians due to hunger, disease, and mistreatment. What he saw horrified him:

> The Indians were totally deprived of their freedom. . . . Even beasts enjoy more freedom when they are allowed to graze in the field.
>
> —Bartolomé de Las Casas, *Tears of the Indians*

Many Spanish in New Spain did not share Las Casas' view or his values. So, he

>> Native Americans harvest maize. The Spanish government gave colonists the right to demand harsh labor from the Indians.

journeyed to Europe and asked the king of Spain to protect the Indians' civil rights. In the 1540s, the royal government passed laws prohibiting the enslavement of Native Americans. The laws also allowed Indians to own cattle and grow crops. However, few officials in New Spain enforced the new laws or took the time to think about Indians' basic human needs.

? **IDENTIFY SUPPORTING DETAILS** What were some ways in which peninsulares were powerful?

The Transatlantic Slave Trade

The death toll among Native Americans continued to rise. Faced with a severe shortage of workers, Spanish colonists looked across the Atlantic Ocean for a new source of labor.

Reasons for the Slave Trade Still seeking to protect Native Americans, Bartolomé de Las Casas made a suggestion that had a lasting, tragic impact. His idea was that Africans be brought as slaves to replace forced Indian laborers. Las Casas argued that Africans were less likely to die from European diseases. He also claimed that Africans would suffer less because they were used to doing hard farm work in their homelands.

Las Casas's arguments encouraged the Atlantic slave trade, or the trade of enslaved Africans across the Atlantic to the Americas. In many parts of Africa, slavery had existed for centuries. Often, war prisoners were enslaved. Eventually, these enslaved people or their children might gain freedom. After the Americas were colonized, though, some Africans began to capture and enslave people and sell them to European traders. The traders then shipped the enslaved men, women, and children to the Americas. Most Africans who settled in the Americas did so against their will.

By the time he died, Las Casas had come to regret his suggestion. He saw that enslaved Africans suffered as much as the Indians. By that time, however, it was too late to undo the damage. Slavery had become a key part of the colonial economy.

Slave Trade Expansion The European demand for African labor grew rapidly, mainly in Spain's colonies in the West Indies, including what are now Cuba, the Dominican Republic, and Puerto Rico, and in other parts of the Americas. Enslaved Africans were especially valued on sugar plantations in the West Indies and in the Portuguese colony of Brazil. A **plantation** is a large estate farmed by many workers. Sugar could not be grown on small estates

SLAVERY IN THE AMERICAS

DESTINATIONS OF ENSLAVED AFRICANS

4.5% BRITISH HELD LANDS IN NORTH AMERICA

2.5% EUROPE AND ASIA

37% BRAZIL

15% SPANISH HELD LANDS IN AMERICA

41% NON-SPANISH CARIBBEAN ISLANDS

Source: Albert M. Craig, World Civilizations

TOBACCO AND SLAVERY

Tobacco production rose in Virginia and Maryland as planters in those colonies imported more enslaved Africans to grow the crops.

Source: Encyclopaedia Britannica, Historical Statistics of the United States, Virginia Encyclopedia

MARYLAND AND VIRGINIA TOBACCO EXPORTS

ABOUT 20 MILLION POUNDS IN 1680

27 MILLION POUNDS IN 1700

35 MILLION POUNDS IN 1720

51 MILLION POUNDS BY 1750

MARYLAND AND VIRGINIA SLAVE POPULATION

4,000 IN 1680

17,000 IN 1700

35,000 BY 1720

140,000 BY 1750

>> Enslaved Africans were shipped to destinations in Europe, Asia, and the Americas. **Analyze Charts** Which region received the fewest enslaved Africans? Which received the most?

Atlantic Slave Trade

KEY
- Spanish America
- Non-Spanish Caribbean islands
- British North America
- Portuguese Brazil
- Europe and Asia
- ← Slave-trade route

NORTH AMERICA
FRENCH TERRITORY
EUROPE
ATLANTIC OCEAN
MEXICO
SENEGAMBIA
ASANTE GOLD COAST
AFRICA
KONGO
SOUTH AMERICA
ANGOLA
BRAZIL

0   2,000 mi
0   2,000 km
Miller Cylindrical Projection

>> Many Africans were captured and shipped to Europe and the Americas to work as slaves. **Analyze Maps** Most Africans enslaved in the Americas came from which coast of Africa?

because it required too much land and labor. Enslaved Africans often worked all through the night cutting sugar, which was then sold in Europe for a large profit.

Some scholars estimate that Europeans transported more than 10 million enslaved Africans across the Atlantic Ocean to the Americas between the 1500s and the 1800s. The vast majority came from West Africa.

? **IDENTIFY CENTRAL IDEAS** Why were plantations developed in the Americas?

ASSESSMENT

1. **Generate Explanations** Who helped Cortés destroy the Aztec empire and why?

2. **Identify Central Issues** What two reasons did the Spanish have for deciding not to focus on their northern borderlands?

3. **Analyze Information** What makes St. Augustine a particularly notable Spanish settlement?

4. **Identify Cause and Effect** What did the Spanish government's land grants include that caused hardship for Native Americans, and what hardship did it cause?

5. **Summarize** how Spanish and Native American cultures blended in New Spain.

The First French, Dutch, and English Colonies

>> Women from England arrive at the colony in Jamestown, where they are destined to become wives.

>> Objectives

Explain why Europeans explored North America's coast.

Identify the reasons for French and Dutch colonization in North America.

Identify the reasons for English colonization.

Explain how Virginia began a tradition of representative government.

Describe how different groups in Jamestown interacted with the environment.

>> Key Terms

northwest passage
Protestant
   Reformation
coureur de bois
charter
burgess
House of Burgesses
representative
   government
Magna Carta
Bacon's Rebellion
alliance
frontier
indentured servant

European nations began to compete for riches around the world. Religious differences heightened their rivalry. Until the 1500s, the Roman Catholic Church was the only church in Western Europe. That unity ended when a major religious reform movement sharply divided Christians.

European Rivalries

Religious Reform In 1517, a German monk named Martin Luther publicly challenged many practices of the Catholic Church. Soon after, he split with the Church entirely. Luther believed that the Church had become too worldly. He opposed the power of popes. He also objected to the Catholic teaching that believers could gain eternal life by performing good works. Luther argued that people could be saved only by faith in God.

Because of their protests against the Church, Luther's supporters became known as Protestants. The **Protestant Reformation**, as the new movement was known, divided Europe. Soon, the Protestants themselves split, forming many different churches.

By the late 1500s, religion divided the states of Western Europe. Roman Catholic monarchs ruled Spain and France. A Protestant queen, Elizabeth I, ruled England. In the Netherlands, the Dutch people were mostly Protestant.

Religious Difference Leads to Rivalries As Europeans settled in the Americas, they brought their religious conflicts with them. Queen Elizabeth encouraged English adventurers to raid Spanish colonies and capture Spanish treasure fleets. Protestant England also competed with Catholic France for lands in North America.

Not all rivalries were religious. Both the Netherlands and England were Protestant. Still, they competed for control of land in North America and for economic markets all over the world, including Asia.

Reasons for the Exploration of North America Like Columbus, Europeans continued during the 1500s to look for new ways to reach the riches of Asia. Magellan's route around South America seemed long and difficult. Europeans wanted to discover a shorter **northwest passage**, or waterway through or around North America.

Giovanni Caboto, an Italian sea captain who the English called John Cabot, set out to find a northwest passage for the English. He was confident he had found such a passage, but he was mistaken. The "new-found land" that he thought he had found off the Asian coast in fact lay off the coast of North America. Today, Newfoundland is part of the easternmost province of Canada.

French Exploration The French sent another Italian captain, Giovanni da Verrazano (vehr rah TSAH noh), in search of a northwest passage. Verrazano journeyed along the North American coast

>> Martin Luther, shown here preaching a sermon, led the Protestant Reformation in Germany. After the Reformation, rivalries between Catholic and Protestant countries led them to compete over territories in the Americas.

from the present-day Carolinas to Canada. During the 1530s, Jacques Cartier (kar tee YAY), also sailing for the French, traveled more than halfway up the St. Lawrence River.

Explorations of Henry Hudson In 1609, the English explorer Henry Hudson sailed for the Dutch. His ship, the *Half Moon*, entered present-day New York harbor. Hudson continued to sail some 150 miles up the river that now bears his name.

The following year, Hudson made a voyage into the far north—this time for the English. After spending a harsh winter in what is now called Hudson Bay, his crew rebelled. They set Hudson, his son, and seven loyal sailors adrift in a small boat. The boat and its crew were never seen again.

Mapping New Regions None of these explorers found a northwest passage to Asia. However, they did map and explore many parts of North America. The rulers of Western Europe began thinking about how to profit from the region's rich resources through colonization.

? CHECK UNDERSTANDING What factors contributed to rivalries between English and Spanish explorers?

New France Is Colonized

Samuel de Champlain (sham PLAYN) founded Port Royal, the first permanent French settlement in North America, in 1605. Three years later, he led another group of settlers along the route Cartier had pioneered. On a rocky cliff high above the St. Lawrence River, Champlain built a trading post known as Quebec (kwih BEK). The opportunity to create wealth through trade was one of the main reasons for French colonization in America. The

Exploring North America

KEY
— Cabot, 1497
— Verrazano, 1524
— Cartier, 1534–1536
— Hudson, 1609
— Hudson, 1610–1611
— Marquette and Joliet, 1673
— La Salle, 1678–1682

>> Explorers from England, France, and the Netherlands took different routes from Europe to North America. **Analyze Maps** Why might you expect conflict to develop between the English and French in North America?

French also wanted to surpass their rivals, the English. Many French settlers were looking for adventure and hoped to find their fortune in the New World.

Economic Activity in New France Unlike Spain's American empire, New France had little gold or silver. Instead, the French profited from fishing, trapping, and trading.

French colonists who lived and worked in Native American lands beyond the French settlements became known as *coureurs de bois* (koo RUHR duh BWAH), or "runners of the woods." The French brought knives, kettles, cloth, and other items for trade with Native Americans. In return, the Indians gave them beaver skins and other furs that sold for high prices in Europe.

Coureurs de bois established friendly relations with Native American groups. Unlike the Spanish, the French did not attempt to conquer the Indians. Also, because *coureurs de bois* did not establish farms, they did not interfere with Indian lands. Indians taught the French trapping and survival skills, such as how to make snowshoes and canoes. Many *coureurs* married Indian women.

Missionary Work Continues Catholic missionaries often traveled with fur traders. A missionary is a person who goes to another land to win converts for a religion. French missionaries tried to convert Native Americans to Christianity. They also drew maps and wrote about the lands they explored.

Life was difficult, especially in winter. One French priest recalled traveling on foot through deep snow:

If a thaw came, dear Lord, what pain! . . . I was marching on an icy path

>> Native Americans board a European trading ship to display their selection of furs. They will exchange the furs for the goods displayed at the feet of the seated European trader.

that broke with every step I took; as the snow softened . . . we often sunk [sank] in it up to our . . . waist.

—Paul Le Jeune, quoted in *The Jesuits in North America* (Parkman)

Colonization Along the Mississippi River French trappers followed the St. Lawrence deep into the heart of North America. Led by Indian guides, they reached the Great Lakes. Here, Indians spoke of a mighty river, which they called Mississippi, or "Father of the Waters."

A French missionary, Father Jacques Marquette (mar KET), and a fur trader, Louis Joliet (joh lee ET), set out to reach the Mississippi in 1673. Led by Indian guides, they followed the river for more than 700 miles before turning back. Nine years later, Robert de La Salle completed the journey to the Gulf of Mexico. La Salle named the region Louisiana in honor of the French king, Louis XIV.

To keep Spain and England out of Louisiana, the French built forts in the north along the Great Lakes. Among them was Fort Detroit, built by Antoine Cadillac near Lake Erie. The French also built New Orleans, a fort near the mouth of the river. New Orleans grew into a busy trading center. French control of the network of waterways at the heart of North America gave the French a strategic advantage over the Spanish and the English.

French colonists imported thousands of Africans to work as slaves on plantations around New Orleans. Some enslaved Africans, however, joined with the Natchez Indians in a revolt against the French. The French put down the Natchez Revolt in 1729. Some enslaved Africans who fought on the side of the French received their freedom. In Louisiana, free and enslaved Africans together made up the majority of settlers.

Government in New France New France was governed much like New Spain. The French king controlled the government directly, and people had little freedom. A council appointed by the king made all decisions.

Louis XIV worried that too few French were moving to New France. In the 1660s, therefore, he sent about a thousand people to the colony, including many young women. Despite the king's efforts to increase the population, New France grew slowly. Winters were harsh, and the short growing season made farming difficult. Only about 10,000 settlers lived in the colony by 1680. Of those, one third lived on farms along the St. Lawrence. Others chose to become *coureurs de bois*, living largely free of government control.

❓ IDENTIFY MAIN IDEAS Why was the Mississippi River important to the French?

The Dutch Establish New Netherland

Like the French, the Dutch hoped to profit from their discoveries in the Americas by colonizing. In 1626, Peter Minuit (MIN yoo wit) led a group of Dutch settlers to the mouth of the Hudson River. Other Dutch colonists had already settled on Manhattan Island and farther up the Hudson River. Minuit bought Manhattan Island from local Indians. Minuit called his settlement New Amsterdam. The entire colony was known as New Netherland (now known as New York).

New Netherland was privately funded by the Dutch West India Company. Many

>> The coureurs de bois, fishermen, and trappers who settled New France were mostly male. They gladly welcomed female settlers sent to the New World by the French king.

▶ **Interactive Map**

>> A canal to transport goods runs down the center of Broad Street in New Amsterdam, an early Dutch settlement. New Amsterdam later became New York City.

colonists immigrated to New Netherland hoping to profit from the region's active fur trade.

From a tiny group of 30 houses, New Amsterdam grew into a busy port. The Dutch welcomed people of many nations, ethnic groups, and religions to their colony. A Roman Catholic priest who visited New Netherland in 1643 reported:

> On the island of Manhattan, and in its environs, there may well be four or five hundred men of different sects and nations: the Director General told me that there were men of eighteen different languages; they are scattered here and there on the river, above and below, as the beauty and convenience of the spot has invited each to settle.
>
> —Father Isaac Jogues, quoted in *Narratives of New Netherland*, 1609–1664 (Jameson)

The Dutch also built trading posts along the Hudson River. The most important one was Fort Orange, today known as Albany. Dutch merchants became known for their good business sense.

The Dutch enlarged New Netherland in 1655 by taking over the colony of New Sweden. The Swedes had established New Sweden along the Delaware River some 15 years earlier.

Trade Rivalries in the Region Dutch traders sent furs to the Netherlands. The packing list for the first shipment included "the skins of 7,246 beaver, 853 otter, 81 mink, 36 cat lynx, and 34 small rats."

The Dutch and French became rivals in the fur trade. Both sought alliances with Native Americans. An **alliance** is an agreement between nations to aid and protect one another. The Dutch made friends with the Iroquois. The Hurons (HYOO rahnz) helped the French. Fighting raged for years among the Europeans and their Native American allies.

Dutch Culture Comes to North America

The Dutch brought many of their customs from Europe to New Netherland. They liked to ice skate, and in winter, the frozen rivers and ponds filled with skaters. Every year on Saint Nicholas's birthday, Dutch children put out their shoes to be filled with all sorts of presents. Known in Dutch as "Sinterklaas," Saint Nicholas came to be called Santa Claus.

Some Dutch words entered the English language. A Dutch master was a *boss*. The people of New Amsterdam sailed in *yachts*. Dutch children munched on *cookies* and rode through the snow on *sleighs*.

Interaction With Native Americans and the Environment
Dutch and French settlement on the east coast of North America brought major changes to Native Americans and the environment. As in New Spain, European diseases killed thousands of Indians, and rivalry over the fur trade increased between different European countries' Native American allies. The scramble for furs also led to overtrapping. By 1640, trappers had almost wiped out the beavers on Iroquois lands in upstate New York.

The arrival of Europeans affected Native Americans in other ways. Missionaries tried to convert Indians to Christianity. Indians eagerly adopted European trade goods, such as copper kettles and knives. They also bought muskets and gunpowder for hunting and warfare. Alcohol sold by European traders had a harsh effect on Native American life.

Europeans all waged warfare to seize Indian lands. As Indians were forced off their lands, they moved westward onto lands of other Indians, which sometimes led to violence between Native American groups. The conflict between Native Americans and Europeans would continue for many years.

? **IDENTIFY** What was one reason why the New Netherland colony was founded?

Roanoke and Jamestown

England watched with envy as other European countries gained riches from their colonies in the Americas. Several ambitious English gentlemen proposed that England settle the Americas as well. With Queen Elizabeth's permission, Sir Walter Raleigh raised money to outfit a colony in North America. In 1585, about 100 men set sail across the Atlantic. The colonists landed on Roanoke (ROH uh nohk), an island off the coast of present-day North

>> Native Americans trade goods with Dutch settlers on Manhattan Island.

Carolina. Within a year, however, the colonists had run short of food and were quarreling with neighboring Indians. When an English ship stopped in the harbor, the weary settlers sailed home.

The Lost Colony of Roanoke In 1587, Raleigh sent John White, one of the original colonists, back to Roanoke with a new group of settlers that included women and children. When supplies ran low, White returned to England, leaving behind 117 colonists. He planned to return in a few months. When he got back to England, however, he found the country was then preparing for war with Spain. It was three years before he was able to sail back to Roanoke.

When White arrived, he found the settlement strangely quiet. Houses stood empty. Vines twined through the windows and pumpkins sprouted from the earthen floors. On a tree, someone had carved the word CROATOAN, the name of a nearby island. No other trace of the colonists remained. White was eager to investigate, but a storm was blowing up and his crew refused to make the trip. To this day, the fate of the "Lost Colony" remains a mystery.

The Founding of Jamestown After the failure of Roanoke, nearly 20 years passed before England again tried to establish a colony in North America. In 1606, the Virginia Company of London, a private company, received a charter from King James I. A **charter** is a legal document giving certain rights to a person or company.

The royal charter gave the Virginia Company the right to settle lands along the east coast of North America. The charter also guaranteed that colonists of this land,

>> In the spring of 1607, English colonists began building a settlement at Jamestown, Virginia.

Interactive Gallery

>> Colonists in Jamestown hold religious services under a makeshift tent. The swampy land would prove challenging for the colonists.

called Virginia, would have the same rights as English citizens.

In the spring of 1607, a group of 105 colonists, funded by the Virginia Company, arrived in Virginia. They sailed into Chesapeake Bay and began building houses along the James River. They named their tiny outpost Jamestown after their king. Jamestown was the first permanent English settlement in what is now the United States.

Reasons for Colonization The settlers of Jamestown hoped to make a profit by finding gold or other riches. They also hoped to discover a water route to Asia. Furthermore, they wanted to claim the region for England.

The colonists soon discovered that Jamestown was located in a swampy area. The water was unhealthy, and mosquitoes spread malaria. Many settlers suffered or died from disease. Historians have long debated the reason why the settlers chose the location they did. One of the main reasons was security: they located their settlement in a place where Spanish ships would be unlikely to find them. If the Spanish did discover Jamestown, its location would make it more easily defensible against Spanish ships.

Governing the colony also proved difficult. The Virginia Company had chosen a council of 13 men to rule the settlement.

Members of the council quarreled with one another and did little to plan for the colony's future. By the summer of 1608, the colony was near failure.

The Colonists Face Further Difficulties Another major problem the Jamestown colonists faced was starvation. Their physical environment offered plenty of resources: fish to catch, plants to

>> Jamestown colonists constructed buildings such as this in the first permanent English settlement in what is now the United States.

gather, and animals to hunt. However, many colonists were not used to living in the wilderness and did not know how to take advantage of these resources. Furthermore, the colonists did not spend enough time producing food. Captain John Smith, a young soldier and explorer, observed that the colonists were not planting enough crops. He complained that people wanted only to "dig gold, wash gold, refine gold, load gold." As they searched in vain for gold, the colony ran out of food.

Smith helped to save the colony. He set up stern rules that forced colonists to work if they wished to eat.

He also visited nearby Indian villages. Powhatan (pow uh TAN), the most powerful chief in the area, agreed to supply corn to the English.

Peaceful relations with Native Americans did not last, however. Whenever the Indians failed to supply food, the colonists used force to seize what they needed. Once, Smith aimed a gun at Powhatan's brother until the Indians provided corn to buy his freedom. Such incidents led to frequent and bloody warfare. Peace was restored briefly when the colonist John Rolfe married Pocahontas, daughter of Powhatan.

However, problems arose soon after John Smith returned to England in 1609. Desperate settlers cooked "dogs, cats, snakes, [and] toadstools" to survive. To keep warm, they broke up houses to burn as firewood. The colonists gradually learned to use the sources available in their environment to survive.

Tobacco Crops Help Jamestown's economy finally improved after 1612, when colonists began growing tobacco.

>> Circumstances improved for the Jamestown colonists after they began cultivating tobacco, a profitable crop they exported back to England.

Europeans had learned about tobacco from Native Americans.

King James called pipe smoking "a vile custom." Still, the new fad caught on quickly. By 1620, England was importing more than 30,000 pounds of tobacco a year. At last, Virginians had found a way to make their colony succeed.

English immigrants to Virginia interacted with their environment by cutting down forests and planting the land with tobacco. Their interaction with the environment was different from that of other groups of immigrants to North America, such as the Dutch and the French, whose trading activity led to the near elimination of beaver populations in some areas.

? IDENTIFY What early difficulties did the Jamestown colonists face?

An Improved Form of Government

For a time, the governors sent by the Virginia Company ran the colony like a military outpost. Each morning, a drumbeat summoned settlers to work at assigned tasks. Harsh laws imposed the death penalty even for small offenses, like stealing an ear of corn. Such conditions were unlikely to attract new colonists. As John Smith commented after his return to England, "No Man will go . . . to have less freedom there than here."

The House of Burgesses To attract more settlers, the Virginia Company took steps to establish a more stable government. In 1619, it sent a new governor with orders to consult settlers on all important matters. Male settlers were allowed to elect **burgesses**, or representatives to the government.

>> The House of Burgesses in Jamestown, Virginia, was the first elected legislative assembly in the English colonies. **Infer** How was government in the English colonies different from that in the Spanish or French colonies?

The burgesses met in an assembly called the **House of Burgesses**. Together with the governor and his council, they made laws for the colony. The first session met in the Jamestown church in July and August 1619. In steamy weather, the burgesses sat in the church pews, while the governor and council took their places in the choir stalls.

The House of Burgesses marked the beginning of representative government in the English colonies. In a **representative government**, voters elect representatives to make laws for them.

Political Rights and Responsibilties The idea that people had political rights was deeply rooted in English history. In 1215, English nobles had forced King John to sign the **Magna Carta**, or Great Charter. This document said that the king could not raise taxes without first consulting a Great Council of nobles and church leaders. Over time, the rights won by nobles were extended to other people.

The Great Council grew into a representative assembly, called Parliament. Parliament was divided into the House of Lords, made up of nobles, and an elected House of Commons. Only rich men had the right to vote. Still, the English had established the principle that even monarchs had to obey the law.

Some Virginia Settlers Can Vote At first, free Virginians had even greater rights than citizens in England. They did not have to own property in order to vote. In 1670, however, the colony restricted the vote to free, white, male property owners.

Despite these limits, representative government remained important. The idea took root that settlers should have a say in the affairs of the colony. Colonists came to

COLONIAL SETTLERS' ORIGINS

ESTIMATED ETHNICITY OF AMERICAN COLONIES

1 IN 2 ENGLISH

1 IN 5 AFRICAN

1 IN 10 SCOTCH-IRISH

1 IN 10 GERMAN

1 IN 25 DUTCH

Sources: James T. Lemon, *Colonial America in the Eighteenth Century; Historical Statistics of the United States*

■ New England
■ Middle
■ Southern

ESTIMATED POPULATION IN 1700
89% WHITE 11% BLACK

SOUTHERN	MIDDLE	NEW ENGLAND
White: **81%**	White: **93%**	White: **98%**
Black: **11%**	Black: **7%**	Black: **2%**

ESTIMATED POPULATION IN 1770
78% WHITE 21% BLACK

SOUTHERN	MIDDLE	NEW ENGLAND
White: **59%**	White: **94%**	White: **97%**
Black: **41%**	Black: **6%**	Black: **3%**

>> The population of the English colonies in America included a variety of European ethnic groups. **Analyze Charts** What might account for the dramatic increase in the black population of the Southern Colonies between 1700 and 1775?

refer to the Virginia Company's 1619 frame of government as their own "Great Charter."

? IDENTIFY MAIN IDEAS Why was the House of Burgesses created in Virginia?

The Jamestown Colony Grows

During the early years of the Jamestown Colony, only a few women chose to make the journey from England. Nor did enough workers come to raise tobacco and other crops.

Women in Jamestown The colony's first women arrived in 1608—a "Mistress Forrest" and her maid, Anne Burras. Few others followed until 1619, when the Virginia Company sent about 100 women to help "make the men more settled." This shipload of women quickly found husbands. The Virginia Company profited from the

marriages because it charged each man who found a wife 150 pounds of tobacco.

Life for women was a daily struggle. Women had to make everything from scratch—food, clothing, even medicines. Many died young from hard work or childbirth. By 1624, there were still fewer than 300 women in the Jamestown colony, compared to more than 1,000 men.

Africans Arrive in Virginia Enslaved Africans were brought to Virginia early on. Recently discovered records show that at least 15 black men and 17 black women were already living there by 1619. That same year, a Dutch ship arrived with about 20 Africans. The Dutch sold the Africans to Virginians who needed laborers to grow tobacco. The colonists valued the agricultural skills that the Africans brought with them. From their perspective, the arrival of Africans meant the arrival of a labor force. From the enslaved Africans' perspective, this was a journey into a brutal life of forced labor.

About 300 Africans lived in Virginia by 1644. Some were slaves for life.

Others worked as **indentured servants**, or people who were pledged to work for a master for a period until they paid off the cost of their voyage, and expected one day to own their own farms. Some Africans did become free planters. Anthony Johnson owned 250 acres of land and employed five servants to help him work it. For a time, free Africans in Virginia also had the right to vote. These newcomers from Africa helped to transform the environment of Virginia by cutting down forests and planting tobacco fields.

Bacon's Rebellion Meanwhile, English settlers continued to arrive in Virginia, attracted by the promise of profits from tobacco. Wealthy planters, however, controlled the best lands near the coast. Many newcomers were indentured servants. When they finished their period of service, they looked for farmland. Because the best lands along the coast were taken, these and other newcomers had to push farther inland, onto Indian lands.

As in New England, conflicts over land led to fighting between some white settlers and Indians. After several bloody clashes, settlers called on the governor to take action against Native Americans. The governor refused. He was unwilling to act, in part because he profited from his own fur trade with Indians. Frontier settlers were furious.

Finally, in 1676, Nathaniel Bacon, an ambitious young planter, organized angry men and women on the frontier, including both black and white indentured servants. He raided Native American villages,

regardless of whether the Indians there had been friendly to the colonists or not. Then, he led his followers to Jamestown and burned the capital.

The uprising, known as **Bacon's Rebellion**, lasted only a short time. When Bacon died suddenly, the revolt fell apart. The governor hanged 23 of Bacon's followers. Still, he could not stop English settlers from moving onto Indian lands along the **frontier**, or the edge of the settlement.

Wealthy Virginians generally supported Governor Berkeley. They were alarmed that black and white indentured servants had joined together in a rebellion. In response, Virginia set up a system of laws replacing indentured servitude for Africans with a condition of lifelong slavery that would be passed on to enslaved Africans' children. As slavery expanded, free African Americans also lost rights. By the early 1700s, free African American property owners could no longer vote.

? IDENTIFY SUPPORTING DETAILS Why did many Africans come to Virginia?

ASSESSMENT

1. **Summarize** What did John Cabot, Giovanni da Verrazano, Jacques Cartier, and Henry Hudson all have in common?

2. **Support Ideas with Evidence** What evidence in this lesson supports the idea that Native Americans were not opposed to early interactions with French settlers?

3. **Support Ideas with Examples** What examples can you give to show that contacts between European colonists and Native Americans had negative consequences?

4. **Generate Explanations** Why did the Jamestown colony have so little food in its early years?

5. **Predict Consequences** What do you think happened after Virginia law established lifelong enslavement for people of African origin?

The New England Colonies

>> Male passengers on the Mayflower sign the Mayflower Compact, which established a government for the colony at Plymouth.

Interactive Flipped Video

After two hard months at sea, the colonists on board the small sailing ship were relieved to see the shores of New England. Still, there were no European colonies for hundreds of miles.

>> Objectives

Explain how the desire for religious freedom led to the settlement of the New England colonies.

Identify the significance of the Mayflower Compact.

Describe how conflicts over religion and politics were resolved in colonial New England.

Identify reasons for conflict between settlers and Native Americans.

>> Key Terms

Pilgrim
established church
persecution
Mayflower Compact
precedent
Thanksgiving
Puritans
General Court
Fundamental Orders
  of Connecticut
religious tolerance
Sabbath
town meeting

PEARSON realize. www.PearsonRealize.com
Access your Digital Lesson.

Seeking Religious Freedom

One of the voyagers, William Bradford, vividly remembered the situation:

> Being thus passed the vast ocean . . . they had now no friends to welcome them nor inns to entertain or refresh their weatherbeaten bodies; no houses or much less towns to repair to . . . And for the season it was winter, and they that know the winters of that country know them to be sharp and violent.
>
> —William Bradford, *Of Plymouth Plantation*

Unlike the Jamestown colonists or the Spanish, these newcomers sought neither gold nor silver nor great riches. What they wanted most was to practice their religion freely. Years later, the founders of Plymouth became known to history as the **Pilgrims**.

Religion in Europe It was not easy for people to practice religion freely in Europe during the 1500s. As you have read, after the Protestant Reformation, Christians in western Europe were divided into Protestants and Roman Catholics. This division led to fierce religious wars. In France, for example, Protestants and Catholics fought each other for nearly 40 years. Thousands upon thousands of people were killed because of their religious beliefs.

Most European rulers believed that they could not maintain order unless everyone followed the ruler's religion. The religion chosen by the ruler was known as the **established church**. In England, for example, the established church was the Anglican church, or Church of England. In the 1530s, Parliament passed laws making the English monarch the head of the Church of England.

In England and other nations, people who did not follow the established religion were often persecuted. **Persecution** is the mistreatment or punishment of certain people because of their beliefs. Sometimes, members of persecuted groups had to worship secretly. If they were discovered, they might be imprisoned or even executed by being burned at the stake.

The Pilgrims One religious group in England that faced persecution were the people we now call the Pilgrims. At the time, they were known as Separatists. They were called that because, although they were Protestant, they wanted to separate from the Church of England.

The English government bitterly opposed the Separatists. William Bradford remembered what some Separatists had suffered.

> They . . . were hunted and persecuted on every side. . . . For some were taken and clapped up in prison, others had their houses beset and

>> William Bradford was the governor of Plymouth colony.

watched night and day . . . and the most were [glad] to flee and leave their houses.

—William Bradford, *Of Plymouth Plantation*

In the early 1600s, a group of Separatists left England for Leyden, a city in the Netherlands. The Dutch allowed the newcomers to worship freely. Still, the Pilgrims missed their English way of life. They were also worried that their children were growing up more Dutch than English.

? **IDENTIFY MAIN IDEAS** Why did the Pilgrims want to establish their own colony?

Plymouth Colony

A group of Separatists decided to return to England. Along with some other English people who were not Separatists, they won a charter to set up a colony in the northern part of Virginia. Like the colonists who followed them, the Pilgrims' enterprise was started and funded privately in the hopes that it would earn a profit. In September 1620, more than 100 men, women, and children set sail aboard a small ship called the *Mayflower*. The journey was long and difficult.

At last, in November 1620, the *Mayflower* landed on the cold, bleak shore of Cape Cod, in present-day Massachusetts. The passengers had planned to settle farther south along the Hudson River, but the difficult sea voyage exhausted them. The colonists decided to travel no farther. They called their new settlement Plimoth, or Plymouth, because the *Mayflower* had sailed from the port of Plymouth, England.

A New Pledge to Govern the Colony
Before going ashore, the Pilgrims realized that they would not be settling within the

>> A Quaker in England stands trial for violating the religious practices of the Anglican Church. Quakers were also persecuted in New England for their religious beliefs

>> The pilgrims crossed the Atlantic in search of religious freedom in ships such as this.

boundaries of Virginia. As a result, the terms of their charter would not apply to their new colony. In that case, who would govern them? The question was important because not all colonists on the *Mayflower* were Pilgrims. Some of these "strangers," as the Pilgrims called them, said they were not bound to obey the Pilgrims, "for none had power to command them."

In response, the Pilgrims joined together to write a framework for governing their colony. On November 11, 1620, the 41 adult male passengers—both Pilgrims and non-Pilgrims—signed the **Mayflower Compact**. They pledged themselves to unite into a "civil body politic," or government. They agreed to make and abide by laws that insured "the general Good of the Colony."

The Mayflower Compact established an important tradition. When the Pilgrims found themselves without a government, they banded together themselves to make laws. In time, they set up a government in which adult male colonists elected a governor and council. Thus, like Virginia's Great Charter, the Mayflower Compact strengthened the English tradition of governing through elected representatives. These representatives were in turn expected to show the religious virtues that the Pilgrims valued and to make decisions for the common good. The colony at Plymouth thought that this type of representative government, rather than the monarchy that they knew in England, would best protect their religious freedom.

Creating a Tradition of Religious Freedom The Pilgrims were the first of many immigrants who came to North America in order to worship as they pleased. That did not mean that religious freedom spread quickly through England's colonies. Many settlers who wished to worship as they pleased still believed that only their own religious beliefs should be

>> Pilgrims enjoy the freedom to worship publicly in Plymouth Colony. The search for religious freedom was the motivation of many immigrants to what would become the United States.

observed. Most of the English colonies set up their own established churches.

Still, the Pilgrims' desire to worship freely set an important **precedent**, or example for others to follow in the future. In time, the idea of religious freedom for all would become a cornerstone of American democracy.

? **DESCRIBE** What was the Mayflower Compact?

Overcoming Hardships in Plymouth

The Pilgrims built their settlement on the site of a Native American village that had been abandoned because of disease. The colonists even found baskets filled with corn that they were able to eat.

A Cold Winter in Plymouth However, the corn was not enough to get the Pilgrims through their first winter. The Pilgrims had failed to bring enough food with them, and it was too late in the season to plant new crops.

The harsh season was also difficult to survive because the Pilgrims had not had enough time to build proper shelters. During the winter, the men worked to build houses onshore, while most spent nights aboard the Mayflower. Nearly half the settlers had perished of disease or starvation by spring.

Among those who died that winter was the colony's first governor. William Bradford was chosen to take his place. Bradford's able leadership helped the colony survive. Reelected many times, he would lead Plymouth for most of the next 36 years.

Despite the great suffering of that winter, the Pilgrims' religious faith remained strong. They believed that it was God's will for them

>> Faced with little time before the onset of winter, the Pilgrims built proper shelters as quickly as they could.

to remain in Plymouth. "What could now sustain them," wrote Bradford, "but the Spirit of God and His grace?"

Native Americans Offer Assistance In the spring, the Pilgrims began to clear land and plant crops. They also received help from neighboring Native Americans. A Pemaquid Indian, Samoset, had learned English from earlier explorers sailing along the coast. He introduced the Pilgrims to Massasoit (MAS uh soit), chief of the local Wampanoag (wahm puh NOH ahg) Indians.

The Wampanoag who helped the Pilgrims most was named Squanto. As a young man, Squanto had been captured by an English expedition led by John Smith. Squanto lived for a time in England, where he learned to speak the language. As a result, he could communicate easily with the Pilgrims.

Squanto brought the Pilgrims seeds of native plants—corn, beans, and pumpkins— and showed them how to plant them. He also taught the settlers how to catch eels from nearby rivers. By treading water, he stirred up eels from the mud at the river bottom and then snatched them up with his hands. The grateful Pilgrims called Squanto "a special instrument sent of God."

In the fall, the Pilgrims had a very good harvest. Because they believed that God had given them this harvest, they set aside a day for giving thanks.

In later years, the Pilgrims celebrated after each harvest season with a day of thanksgiving. Americans today celebrate **Thanksgiving** as a national holiday.

? IDENTIFY SUPPORTING DETAILS How did Native Americans help the Pilgrims?

>> Squanto teaches a group of Pilgrims how to plant corn, using dead fish as fertilizer.

Forming Massachusetts Bay Colony

The migration to Massachusetts Bay during the 1630s was led by a religious group known as the **Puritans**. Unlike the Pilgrims, the Puritans did not want to separate entirely from the Church of England. Instead, they hoped to reform the church by introducing simpler forms of worship. They wanted to do away with many practices inherited from the Roman Catholic Church, such as organ music, finely decorated houses of worship, and special clothing for priests.

Reasons for Immigration to Massachusetts The Puritans were a powerful group in England. Although some were small farmers, many were well-educated and successful merchants or landowners.

Charles I, who became king in 1625, disapproved of the Puritans and their ideas. He canceled Puritan business charters and even had a few Puritans jailed.

By 1629, some Puritan leaders were convinced that England had fallen on "evil and declining times." They persuaded royal officials to grant them a charter to form the Massachusetts Bay Company. The company's bold plan was to build a new society based on biblical laws and teachings. John Winthrop, a lawyer and a devout Puritan, believed that the new colony would set an example to the world.

Some settlers joined the Massachusetts colonists for economic rather than religious reasons. In wealthy English families, the oldest son usually inherited his father's estate. With little hope of owning land, younger sons sought opportunity elsewhere. They were attracted

THE NEW ENGLAND COLONIES

TIMELINE OF SETTLEMENT

1620 Plymouth Colony was settled by Pilgrims wishing to escape religious persecution in England.

1630 Massachusetts Bay Colony was settled by Puritans wishing to escape religious persecution in England.

1623 New Hampshire began as a group of coastal settlements.

1636 Connecticut was founded as a colony with strict limits on government power.

1636 Rhode Island was founded as a colony where church and state were separated.

PEOPLE

First settled by about 50 Pilgrims. Thousands came later.

Most were Puritans who wanted to reform the Church of England.

Persecution by King Charles I in the 1600s caused many to leave England.

ECONOMY

AGRICULTURE
80% OF POPULATION INVOLVED IN SUBSISTENCE FARMING

— NEW ENGLAND —
EXPORTS & IMPORTS

Imports

Exports

Pounds Sterling (thousands): 400, 300, 200, 100, 0

Year: 1710, 1730, 1750, 1770

>> This chart offers a snapshot of the people and economy of the New England Colonies. **Analyze Graphs** What does the graph of imports and exports tell you about the economy of the New England Colonies during the 1700s?

to Massachusetts Bay because it offered cheap land or a chance to start a business.

A Greater Say in Government In 1629, the Puritans sent a small advance party to North America. John Winthrop and a party of more than 1,000 arrived the following year. Winthrop was chosen as the first governor of the Massachusetts Bay Colony.

Once ashore, Winthrop set an example for others. Although he was governor, he worked hard to build a home, clear land, and plant crops. There was discontent among some colonists, though. Under the charter, only stockholders who had invested money in the Massachusetts Bay Company had the right to vote. Most settlers, however, were not stockholders. They resented taxes and laws passed by a government in which they had no say.

Winthrop and other stockholders saw that the colony would run more smoothly if a greater number of settlers could take part. At the same time, Puritan leaders wished to keep non-Puritans out of the government. As a result, they granted the right to vote for governor to all men who were church members. Later, male church members also elected representatives to an assembly called the **General Court**.

Under the leadership of Winthrop and other Puritans, the Massachusetts Bay Colony prospered. Between 1629 and 1640, some 15,000 men, women, and children journeyed from England to Massachusetts. This movement of people is known as the Great Migration. Many of the newcomers settled in Boston, which grew into the colony's largest town.

? CHECK UNDERSTANDING Why was the right to vote expanded in the Massachusetts Bay Colony?

>> In this artist's rendering, Puritans row to a ship off of the English shore that will carry them across the ocean. **Draw Conclusions** Look at each person on the boat. What is the artist suggesting about their motivations?

>> Thomas Hooker and his followers congregate at the spot in the forest they have chosen for the new settlement of Hartford in 1636.

▶ **Interactive Chart**

New Colonies Form Over Religious Differences

The Puritan leaders did not like anyone to question their religious beliefs or the way the colony was governed. Usually, discontented colonists were forced to leave. Some colonists who left Massachusetts founded other colonies in New England.

A New Colony with Limited Government

In May 1636, a Puritan minister named Thomas Hooker led about 100 settlers out of Massachusetts Bay. Pushing west, they drove their cattle, goats, and pigs along Indian trails that cut through the forests. When they reached the Connecticut River, they built a town, which they called Hartford.

Hooker left Massachusetts Bay because he believed that the governor and other officials had too much power. He wanted to set up a colony in Connecticut with strict limits on government.

The settlers wrote a plan of government called the **Fundamental Orders of Connecticut** in 1639. It created a government much like that of Massachusetts, which relied on the virtue of the people to obey the law and seek the common good. There were, however, two important differences. First, the Fundamental Orders gave the vote to all men who were property owners, including those who were not church members. Second, the Fundamental Orders limited the governor's power. In this way, the Fundamental Orders expanded the idea of representative government in the English colonies.

Connecticut became a separate colony in 1662, with a new charter granted by the king of England. By then, 15 towns were thriving along the Connecticut River.

A New Relationship Between Religion and Government Another Puritan who challenged the leaders of Massachusetts Bay was Roger Williams. A young minister in the village of Salem, Williams was gentle and good-natured. William Bradford described him as "zealous but very unsettled in judgment." Some Puritan leaders probably agreed with this. Most people, including Governor Winthrop, liked him.

Williams's ideas, however, alarmed Puritan leaders. Williams believed that the Puritan church in Massachusetts had too much power. In Williams's view, the business of church and state should be completely separate since concern with political affairs would corrupt the church. The role of the state, said Williams, was to maintain order and peace. It should not support a particular church. Finally, Williams did not believe that the Puritan leaders had the right to force people to attend religious services. Because of these political reasons, Williams sought to establish a new colony.

Williams also believed in religious tolerance. **Religious tolerance** means a willingness to let others practice their own beliefs. In Puritan Massachusetts, non-Puritans were not allowed to worship freely.

Puritan leaders viewed Williams as a dangerous troublemaker. In 1635, the General Court ordered him to leave Massachusetts. Fearing that the court would send him back to England, Williams fled to Narragansett Bay, where he spent the winter with Indians. In the spring of 1636, the Indians sold him land for a settlement. After a few years, the settlement became the English colony of Rhode Island.

In Rhode Island, Williams put into practice his ideas about tolerance. He

>> Roger Williams, shown here with Narragansett Indians, founded the colony later known as Rhode Island on land he bought from the Narragansetts. Rhode Island allowed religious freedom and expanded democratic rights.

allowed complete freedom of religion for all Protestants, Jews, and Catholics. He did not set up a state church or require settlers to attend church services. He also gave all white men the right to vote. Before long, settlers who disliked the strict Puritan rule of Massachusetts flocked to Providence and other towns in Rhode Island. The creation of a colony with freedom of religion thus offered a way to resolve conflicts between people from different religious groups.

A Woman's Voice Calls for Religious Freedom

Among those who fled to Rhode Island was Anne Hutchinson. A devout Puritan, Hutchinson regularly attended church services in Boston, where she first lived. After church, she and her friends gathered at her home to discuss the minister's sermon. Often, she seemed to question some of the minister's teachings. Hutchinson was very persuasive and neighbors flocked to hear her.

Puritan leaders grew angry. They believed that Hutchinson's opinions were full of religious errors. Even worse, they said, a woman did not have the right to explain God's law. In November 1637, Hutchinson was ordered to appear before the Massachusetts General Court.

At her trial, Hutchinson answered the questions put to her by Governor Winthrop and other members of the court. Each time, her answers revealed weaknesses in their arguments. They could not prove that she had broken any Puritan laws or that she had disobeyed any religious teachings.

Then, after two long days of hostile questioning, Hutchinson made a serious mistake. She told the court that God spoke directly to her, "By the voice of His own spirit to my soul." Members of the court were shocked. Puritans believed that God spoke only through the Bible, not directly to individuals. The court ordered her out of the colony.

In 1638, Hutchinson, along with her family and some friends, went to Rhode Island. The Puritan leaders had won their case. For later Americans, however, Hutchinson became an important symbol of the struggle for religious freedom.

? **CHECK UNDERSTANDING** What relationship did Roger Williams want to see between government and religion?

>> Anne Hutchinson was tried in Puritan Massachusetts for disagreeing with church teachings and forced to leave the colony. **Analyze Information** Why might the treatment of Hutchinson be seen as a violation of human rights today?

War Erupts Between Puritans and Native Americans

From Massachusetts Bay, settlers fanned out across New England. Some built trading and fishing villages along the

>> This illustration shows a battle between the forces of Wampanoag chief Metacom and New England colonists during King Phillip's War

coast north of Boston. Port towns with good harbors were ideal for the fishing industry and also lured trading ships, building the area's economy. In 1680, the king would make some of these coastal settlements into a separate colony called New Hampshire.

Mistrust and More Settlers Leads to Conflict

The first meetings between English settlers and Native Americans did not foreshadow the conflict that would eventually occur between them. Some colonial leaders such as Roger Williams tried to treat Native Americans fairly.

As more colonists settled in New England, they began to take over more Native American lands. By 1670, nearly 45,000 English settlers were living in the towns in New England. Land was a resource, but as more people lived in the region, it became increasingly scarce.

Fighting soon broke out between white settlers and Indian nations of the region.

King Phillip's War

The largest conflict came in 1675. Metacom, also known by his English name, King Phillip, was chief of the Wampanoag Indians. He watched for years as English towns were built on Wampanoag lands. "I am resolved not to see the day when I have no country," he told an English friend. Metacom's people attacked villages throughout New England.

Other Indian groups, from Rhode Island to Maine, soon allied themselves with the Wampanoags. They were determined to drive the English settlers off their land. Metacom and his allies destroyed 12 towns and killed more than 600 European settlers.

After more than a year of fighting, however, Metacom was captured and killed. The English sold his family and about 1,000 other Indians into slavery in the West Indies. Other Indians were forced from their homelands.

The pattern of English expansion followed by war was repeated between colonists and Indians throughout the colonies. It would continue for many years to come.

❓ IDENTIFY What was a significant cause of King Phillip's War?

The Towns of New England

Puritans believed that people should worship and tend to local matters as a community. As a result, New England became a land of tightly knit towns.

At the center of many towns was the common, an open field where cattle grazed. Nearby stood the meetinghouse, where Puritans worshiped and held town meetings.

Religious Practice The Puritans took their **Sabbath**, or holy day of religious observance and rest, very seriously. On Sundays, no one was allowed to play games or visit taverns to joke, talk, and drink. The law required all citizens to attend Sunday church services, which would last all day.

During the 1600s, women sat on one side of the church and men on the other. Blacks and Indians stood in a balcony at the back. Children had separate pews, where an adult watched over them.

The Importance of Local Government At **town meetings**, which were normally held in meeting houses where the settlers worshipped, settlers discussed and voted on many issues. What roads should be built? How much should the schoolmaster be paid? Town meetings gave New Englanders a chance to speak their minds.

Puritan congregations also discussed and voted on church issues. They chose their own ministers and members and answered to no other authority.

>> Puritans regularly held town meetings in meetinghouses such as this.

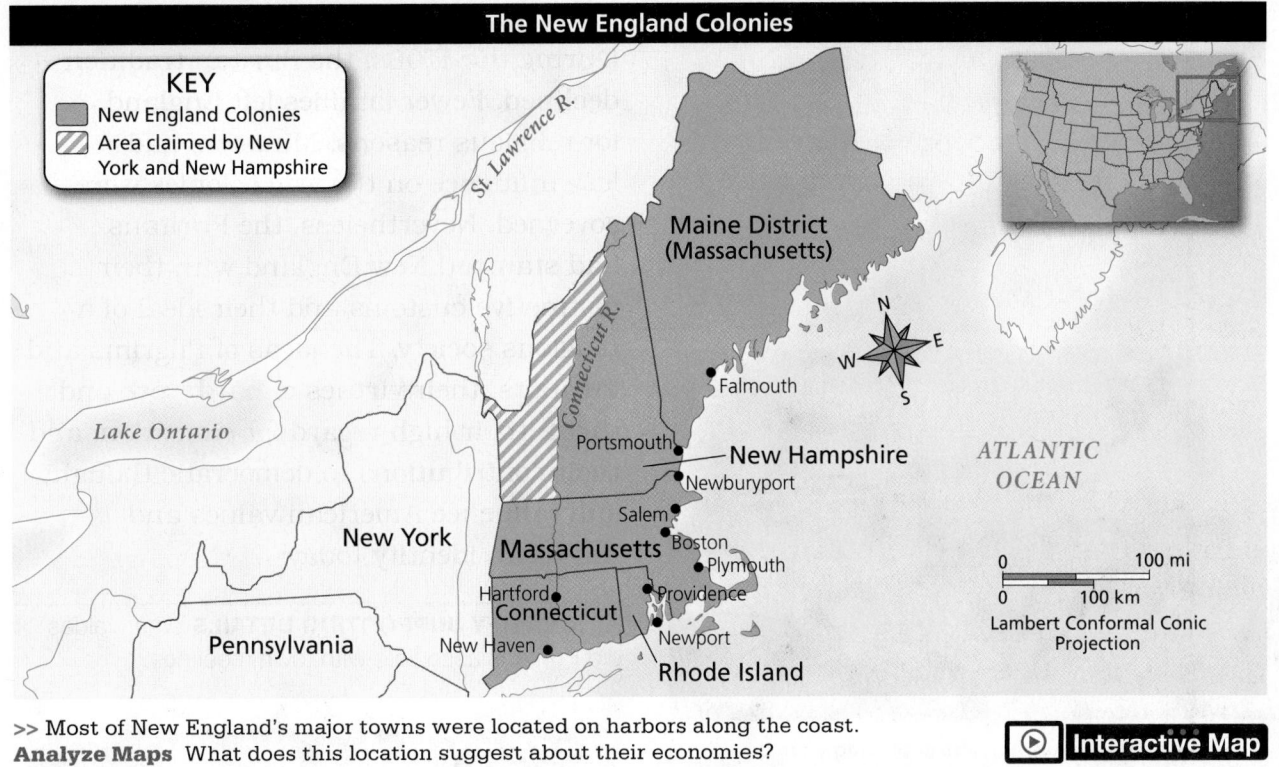

The New England Colonies

KEY
- New England Colonies
- Area claimed by New York and New Hampshire

St. Lawrence R.

Maine District (Massachusetts)

Lake Ontario

Falmouth

Portsmouth

New Hampshire

Newburyport

ATLANTIC OCEAN

New York

Salem

Massachusetts

Boston

Plymouth

Hartford

Providence

Connecticut

Pennsylvania

New Haven

Newport

Rhode Island

0   100 mi
0   100 km
Lambert Conformal Conic Projection

>> Most of New England's major towns were located on harbors along the coast. **Analyze Maps** What does this location suggest about their economies?

Interactive Map

These early experiences encouraged the growth of democratic ideas in New England. Values such as self-government, individual choice, and the common good took root and thrived.

Still, Puritan laws were strict. About 15 crimes carried the death penalty. One crime punishable by death was witchcraft. In 1692, Puritans in Salem Village executed 20 innocent men and women as witches.

The Environment Influences Economic Activity New England was a difficult land for colonists. The rocky soil was poor for farming and required much labor. After a time, however, Native Americans taught English settlers how to grow many crops, such as Indian corn, pumpkins, squash, and beans. Still, some communities relocated to take advantage of better lands. In the mid-1630s, cattle and dairy farmers who had settled in Dorchester,

Massachusetts, moved to the Connecticut River Valley. The rich river valley at Windsor, Connecticut, provided lush meadows and pastures better suited to their cattle than the sandy soils and rocky hills of Dorchester.

Although much of the soil was poor, the forests were full of riches. Settlers hunted wild turkey and deer. Settlers also cut down trees, floating them down rivers to sawmills near seaports such as Boston, Massachusetts, or Portsmouth, New Hampshire. With miles of coastline and nearby raw materials, these and other New England towns grew into major shipbuilding centers. Because abundant timber meant that ships could be built more cheaply in New England than in England, New England sold many ships to English buyers. New England's wooden ships and boats were used by a thriving fishing industry and for overseas trade.

>> This image shows whalers capturing a whale. Whaling grew into a big business in New England in the 1700s.

The Puritans Leave a Lasting Legacy

During the 1700s, the Puritan tradition declined. Fewer families left England for religious reasons. Ministers had less influence on the way colonies were governed. Nevertheless, the Puritans had stamped New England with their distinctive customs and their ideal of a religious society. The ideas of Pilgrims and Puritans, their virtues of hard work and thrift, their high regard for education, and their contributions to democratic thought still influence American values and American identity today.

❓ IDENTIFY SUPPORTING DETAILS What values did Puritans associate with town meetings?

New Englanders fished for cod and halibut. In the 1600s, people began to hunt whales. Whales supplied oil for lamps and other products. In the 1700s and 1800s, whaling grew into a big business.

Puritan communities and their governments often supported the development of important industries such as shipbuilding and ironworking. They found ways to work together for long-term goals that might benefit the general population. For example, sometimes they limited the sale of wood to make more available to shipbuilders.

ASSESSMENT

1. **Identify Central Issues** Why did settling in Plymouth in late 1620 pose significant problems for the Pilgrims?

2. **Compare and Contrast** the Pilgrims and the Puritans.

3. **Support Ideas with Examples** What examples from the text show that colonists adapted their local economy to the environment in which they lived?

4. **Identify Cause and Effect** What effect did population growth have on the conflict between colonists and Native Americans?

5. **Cite Evidence** to support the claim that the New England Colonies promoted the ideals of democracy and self-government.

The Middle Colonies

>> William Penn, shown on the banks of the Delaware River after his voyage from England in 1682, spread Quaker beliefs and founded the city of Philadelphia.

▶ Interactive Flipped Video

By 1700, England had four colonies in the region just south of New England. These colonies became known as the Middle Colonies because they were located between New England and the Southern Colonies. The Middle Colonies had a greater mix of people than either New England or the Southern Colonies.

>> **Objectives**

Explain the reasons for the establishment of the colonies of New York and New Jersey.

Explain the reasons for the establishment of the colonies of Pennsylvania and Delaware.

Describe the economy of the Middle Colonies, including the relationship between the economy and the physical environment.

>> **Key Terms**

patroon
proprietary colony
royal colony
Quakers
Pennsylvania Dutch
cash crop
William Penn

PEARSON realize. www.PearsonRealize.com Access your Digital Lesson.

A Dutch Colony Becomes English

Each of the colonies along the Atlantic coast had been established by different people for different purposes. Sometimes colonies were formed to escape political oppression or social tensions back home in Europe. The New England Colonies served as a refuge for people who faced religious persecution. Many were also created to profit a European company across the ocean, as many colonies to the south were. In the case of New Netherland, however, the conditions back home for the Dutch were stable and fairly prosperous. New Netherland was founded simply to take advantage of economic opportunities in North America.

New Amsterdam The Dutch set up the colony of New Netherland along the Hudson River. They developed the fur trade and built settlements where fur-bearing animals were abundant. In the colony's early years, settlers traded with Indians and built the settlement of New Amsterdam into a thriving port. Located near good farmland and with a safe harbor for ships, New Amsterdam quickly became a center for commerce and trading valuable beaver skins.

Although less interested in farming, Dutch officials did promote agriculture by granting some large parcels of land to a few rich families. A single land grant could stretch for miles. Indeed, one grant was as big as Rhode Island! Owners of these huge estates were called **patroons**. In return for the grant, each patroon promised to settle at least 50 European farm families on the land. Few farmers wanted to work for the patroons, however. Patroons had great power and could charge whatever rents they pleased.

The Middle Colonies

KEY
- Middle Colonies
- Area Claimed by New York and New Hampshire

0 — 150 mi
0 — 150 km
Lambert Conformal Conic Projection

>> The Middle Colonies lay between the New England Colonies and the Southern Colonies. **Analyze Maps** What geographic features of the Middle Colonies suggest that they were well placed for trade?

England Gains Control Many settlers lived in the trading center of New Amsterdam, which by 1664 had a population of about 1,500 people. They came from all over Europe. Most of them came for the economic opportunities, working as merchants or farmers, or in trades and crafts. Many were also attracted by the chance to practice their religion freely. African slaves were in demand as well. In the early years, they made up more than a quarter of the population of the town.

Dutch colonists were mainly Protestants who belonged to the Dutch Reformed Church. Still, they permitted members of other religions and ethnic groups—including Roman Catholics, French Protestants, and Jews—to buy land. "People do not seem concerned what religion their neighbor is" wrote a shocked visitor from Virginia. "Indeed, they do not seem to care if he has any religion at all."

In fact, Peter Stuyvesant (STY vuh sunt), the governor of New Netherland, had been ordered not to interfere with other religions as long as they did not disturb the peace or restrict commerce.

The relationship between the English and the Dutch was complicated by their common interest in creating new colonies and expanding trade. In North America, the Dutch wanted to continue benefiting from New Amsterdam's economic growth. However, the English wanted New Amsterdam for themselves.

By 1664, the rivalry between England and the Netherlands for trade and colonies was at its height. In August of that year, English warships entered New Amsterdam's harbor. Governor Stuyvesant swore to defend the city. However, he had few weapons and little gunpowder. Also, Stuyvesant had made himself so unpopular with his harsh rule and heavy

>> New Amsterdam became a thriving trade hub that attracted settlers from all over Europe who practiced many different religions.

taxes that the colonists refused to help him. In the end, he surrendered without firing a shot.

King Charles II of England then gave New Netherland to his brother, the Duke of York. He renamed the colony New York in the duke's honor.

? **DESCRIBE** Why did many people come to New Amsterdam?

New Jersey Forms Out of New York

At the time of the English takeover, New York stretched as far south as the Delaware River. The Duke of York decided that the colony was too big to govern easily. He gave some of the land to friends, Lord Berkeley and Sir George Carteret. They set up a proprietary (proh PRY uh tehr ee)

>> Ample farmland and fertile soil form the backdrop to the first Quaker meetinghouse built in Burlington, New Jersey, in 1683.

▶ Interactive Gallery

colony, which they called New Jersey, in 1664.

A Proprietary Colony and a Market Economy In setting up a **proprietary colony**, the king gave land to one or more people in return for a yearly payment. These proprietors were free to divide the land and rent it to others. They made laws for the colony but had to respect the rights of colonists under English law. This new system of colonization was different from most that had come before. Proprietary colonies placed vast lands and power in the hands of a few men loyal to the monarch. Earlier colonies had been financed by stock companies made up of a number of investors.

Like New York, New Jersey had fertile farmland and a wealth of other resources that attracted people from many lands. Thousands of European settlers immigrated to New Jersey as a haven from war and poverty. Settlers came from Finland, Ireland, Scotland, Germany, and Sweden. There were also English and Dutch settlers who moved there from the colony of New York. In addition, some New England colonists, hoping to find better farmland, chose to relocate to New Jersey.

The proprietors of the New Jersey encouraged a market economy, in which the government played a limited role in the economy. The market economy system benefited colonists. They could farm or run businesses without much control by the local government. Facing financial losses themselves, however, the proprietors eventually returned the colony of New Jersey to the English crown.

A Royal Colony In 1702, New Jersey became a **royal colony**, which is a colony under the direct control of the English king or queen. The colony's royal charter protected religious freedom and the rights of an assembly that voted on local matters. This charter could be viewed as a legal agreement between the monarch and settlers, binding to both. It was a step toward a more democratic form of government. Despite these improvements, direct English rule tended to be harsh toward colonists. New Jersey's independent-minded settlers struggled to gain more influence over decisions that affected them.

❓ DEFINE What was a proprietary colony?

Pennsylvania Becomes a Colony

West of New Jersey, **William Penn** founded the colony of Pennsylvania in 1681. Penn came from a wealthy English family and was a personal friend of King Charles II. At age 22, however, Penn shocked family and friends by joining the **Quakers**, one of the most despised religious groups in England.

The Quakers Seek Religious Freedom
Like Pilgrims and Puritans, Quakers were Protestant reformers. Their reforms went further than those of other groups, however.

Quakers believed that all people—men and women, nobles and commoners—were equal in God's sight. They allowed women to preach in public and refused to bow or remove their hats in the presence of nobles. Quakers spoke out against all war and refused to serve in the army.

To most English people, Quaker beliefs seemed wicked. In both England and New England, Quakers were arrested, fined, or even hanged for their ideas. Penn became convinced that the Quakers must leave England. He took steps to found a

>> A statue of William Penn stands atop Philadelphia's City Hall today

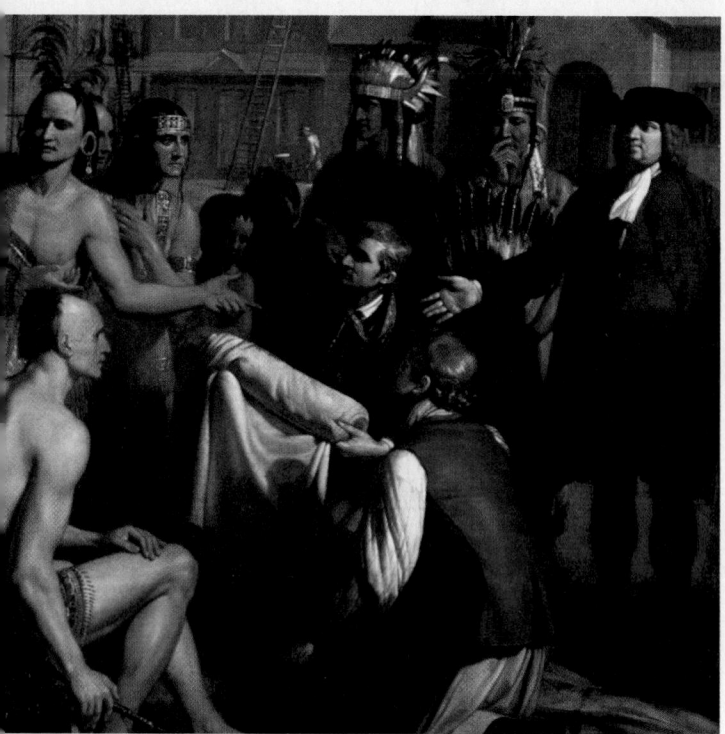

>> Penn's respect for the Native Americans living in and around Pennsylvania fostered good relations between the Indians and the colonists. This painting shows William Penn presenting a treaty to a group of Native Americans.

Protestants, Catholics, and Jews went to Pennsylvania to escape persecution. Later, English officials forced Penn to turn away Catholic and Jewish settlers.

Penn's Quaker beliefs led him to speak out for fair treatment of Native Americans. Penn believed that the land in North America belonged to the Indians. He insisted that settlers should pay for the land. Native Americans respected him for this policy. As a result, Pennsylvania colonists enjoyed many years of peace with their Indian neighbors. One settler remarked, "as Penn treated the Indians with extraordinary humanity, they became civil and loving to us."

Pennsylvania Expands Penn sent pamphlets describing his colony all over Europe. Soon, settlers from England, Scotland, Wales, the Netherlands, France, and Germany began to cross the Atlantic Ocean to Pennsylvania.

Among the new arrivals were large numbers of German-speaking Protestants. They became known as **Pennsylvania Dutch** because people could not pronounce the word Deutsch (doich), which means German. Many Pennsylvania Dutch had faced religious persecution in Europe, including the Amish and Mennonites. Because of their experiences in Europe, these German-speaking people were naturally attracted to the ideals of Penn's colony, in which people of different ethnicities and religions could live peaceably together. The ethnic diversity of Pennsylvania contributed to a developing American identity based on ethnic diversity.

Pennsylvania, like most other colonies, was created for a mix of political, economic, religious, and social reasons. Pennsylvania was like the New England colonies in the religious reasons for its creation.

new colony. Together with others, Penn purchased parts of New Jersey from their proprietors. Then he turned to the king for help.

Charles II issued a royal charter naming Penn proprietor of a large tract of land in North America. The king named the new colony Pennsylvania, or Penn's woodlands. During his time as proprietor, Penn took steps that aided the development of self-government in Pennsylvania. He proposed a constitution and a General Assembly. Later, he agreed to changes in the constitution and greater powers for the colonial assembly.

Showing Fairness to All Penn thought of his colony as a "holy experiment." He wanted it to be a model of religious freedom, peace, and Christian living.

Like New York, its political roots lay in a proprietor's ties to the king. Pennsylvania's social goals of harmony among different groups were similar to those of Rhode Island. Like most proprietors, Penn hoped to profit from his colony.

Enslaved Africans were also brought to the growing Pennsylvania colony. They made up about one third of all new arrivals between 1730 and 1750. Enslaved Africans were present in New York, New Jersey, and the New England Colonies as well, but in smaller numbers than in the Southern Colonies. Because of Philadelphia's location along the Delaware River, many worked as laborers in manufacturing and shipbuilding.

Delaware Is Born For a time, Pennsylvania included some lands along the lower Delaware River. The region was known as Pennsylvania's Lower Counties. Later, in 1704, the Lower Counties would break away to form the colony of Delaware.

? IDENTIFY CENTRAL IDEAS Why did Quakers want to establish their own colony?

Daily Life in the Middle Colonies

The majority of colonists made their living by farming. Farmers found more favorable conditions in the Middle Colonies than in New England. The broad Hudson and Delaware river valleys were rich and fertile. Winters were milder than in New England, and the growing season lasted longer.

A Thriving Economy On such promising land, farmers in the eastern counties of the Middle Colonies cleared their fields. They mostly chose to raise wheat, barley, and rye as a way to earn money. Wheat, barley, and rye were **cash crops**, or crops that were sold for money on the market

and not consumed by the farmer's family. In fact, the Middle Colonies exported so much grain that they became known as the Breadbasket Colonies.

The Pennsylvania Dutch tended to settle the fertile interior lands. They altered the environment by clearing land and starting farms, turning these regions into rich fields that are still productive today.

Farmers of the Middle Colonies also raised herds of cattle and pigs. Every year, they sent tons of beef, pork, and butter to the ports of New York and Philadelphia. From there, the goods went by ship to New England and the South or to the West Indies, England, and other parts of Europe.

Farms in the Middle Colonies were generally larger than those in New England. Landowners hired workers to

>> Settlers in the Middle Colonies altered the land to suit their physical and economic needs, chopping trees to build homes and plowing fields to farm.

▶ **Interactive Gallery**

help with the planting, harvesting, and other tasks. Enslaved African Americans worked on a few large farms. However, most workers were farmhands who worked alongside the families that owned the land.

Aside from farmers, there were also skilled artisans in the Middle Colonies. Encouraged by William Penn, skilled German crafts workers set up shop in Pennsylvania. In time, the colony became a center of manufacturing and crafts. One visitor reported that workshops turned out "hardware, clocks, watches, locks, guns, flints, glass, stoneware, nails, [and] paper."

Settlers in the Delaware River valley profited from the region's rich deposits of iron ore. Heating the ore in furnaces, they purified it and then hammered it into nails, tools, and parts for guns.

Home Life Because houses tended to be far apart in the Middle Colonies, towns were less important than in New England. Counties, rather than villages, became centers of local government.

The different groups who settled the Middle Colonies had their own favorite ways of building. Swedish settlers introduced log cabins to the Americas. The Dutch used red bricks to build narrow, high-walled houses. German settlers developed a wood-burning stove that heated a home better than a fireplace, which sent heat up the chimney and pulled cold air in through cracks in the walls.

Everyone in a household had a job to do. Households were largely self sufficient, which meant that most things needed for survival—food, clothing, soap, candles, and many other goods—were made at home. As one farmer said, "Nothing to wear, eat, or drink was purchased, as my farm provided all."

Expanding Beyond Philadelphia In the 1700s, thousands of German and Scotch-Irish settlers arrived in Philadelphia. From there, many traveled west into the backcountry, the area of land along the eastern slopes of the Appalachian Mountains. Settlers followed an old Indian trail that became known as the Great Wagon Road.

Although settlers planned to follow farming methods they had used in Europe, they found the challenge of farming the backcountry more difficult than they had thought it would be. To farm the backcountry, settlers had to clear thick forests. From Indians, settlers learned how to use knots from pine trees as candles to light their homes. They made wooden dishes from logs, gathered honey from hollows in trees, and hunted wild animals for food. German gunsmiths developed a lightweight rifle for use in

>> Blacksmithing was an important occupation in the Middle Colonies, where a significant part of the economy was based on farming.

Comparing the New England and Middle Colonies

	NEW ENGLAND	MIDDLE COLONIES
MAIN REASON FOR SETTLEMENT	Avoid religious persecution	Economic gain
BUSINESS AND TRADE	Shipbuilding, shipping, fishing, forestry	Agriculture, skilled trades, shipping
AGRICULTURE	Mostly limited to the needs of the colonies	Fertile farmland produced export crops
ETHNIC DIVERSITY	Mainly English	English, Dutch, German, and Scotch-Irish
SETTLEMENT STRUCTURE	Close-knit towns	More scattered settlements
CULTURE AND SOCIETY	Religious uniformity; small family farms and businesses with few servants or slaves	Ethnic and religious diversity; larger farms and businesses need indentured servants

>> Religious, economic, geographic, and ethnic differences distinguished the Middle Colonies from New England. **Analyze Charts** Which colonial region would you rather live in? Why?

forests. Sharpshooters boasted that the "Pennsylvania rifle" could hit a rattlesnake between the eyes at 100 yards.

Many of the settlers who arrived in the backcountry moved onto Indian lands. "The Indians . . . are alarmed at the swarm of strangers," one Pennsylvania official reported. "We are afraid of a [fight] between them for the [colonists] are very rough to them." However, officials did not step in to protect Indian rights. On more than one occasion, disputes between settlers and Indians resulted in violence.

? IDENTIFY MAIN IDEAS Why was so much of the Middle Colonies' economy based on farming?

ASSESSMENT

1. **Analyze Information** How did Dutch policies in New Netherland undermine support for Dutch rule?

2. **Compare and Contrast** New Jersey as a proprietary colony and as a royal colony.

3. **Apply Concepts** What did the market economy mean for New Jersey while it was a proprietary colony?

4. **Cite Evidence** that William Penn's Quaker beliefs were heartfelt and solid.

5. **Apply Concepts** How did a market economy encourage the cultivation of cash crops in the Middle Colonies?

The Southern Colonies

>> The settlement of Charleston was established where two rivers met the Atlantic Ocean.

>> Objectives

Explain the reasons for the establishment of Maryland.

Explain the reasons for the establishment of the Carolinas and Georgia.

Describe the relationship between different environments, different settlement patterns, and different economic systems in the Southern Colonies.

Explain the development of the slave trade and the spread of slavery in the Southern Colonies.

>> Key Terms

Act of Toleration
indigo
debtor
slave codes
racism

In 1632, Sir George Calvert persuaded King Charles I to grant him land for a colony in the Americas. Calvert had ruined his career in Protestant England by becoming a Roman Catholic. Now, he planned to build a colony where Catholics could practice their religion freely.

Lord Baltimore's Colony

He named the colony Maryland in honor of Queen Henrietta Maria, the king's wife. Calvert died before his colony could get underway. His son Cecil, Lord Baltimore, pushed on with the project.

Settlers Come to Maryland In the spring of 1634, about 200 colonists landed along the upper Chesapeake Bay, across the Potomac River from England's first southern colony, Virginia. Maryland was truly a land of plenty. Chesapeake Bay was full of fish, oysters, and crabs. Across the bay, Virginians were already growing tobacco for profit.

Maryland's new settlers hoped to do the same. Remembering the early problems at Jamestown, the newcomers avoided the swampy lowlands. They built their first town, St. Mary's, in a drier location.

As proprietor of the colony, Lord Baltimore owned Maryland. It was his responsibility, not that of a company, to start the colony. He used private funds to do it. He appointed a governor and a council of advisers. He gave colonists a role in government by creating an elected assembly. At first, settlers had to pay rent to Lord Baltimore. Few settlers came to Maryland, because most wanted to own their land. Eager to attract settlers, Lord Baltimore decided to make generous land grants to anyone who brought over servants, women, and children. Later he offered smaller farms, as well as great estates, to attract more settlers.

A few women took advantage of Lord Baltimore's offer of land. Two sisters, Margaret and Mary Brent, arrived in Maryland in 1638 with nine male servants. In time, they set up two plantations of about 1,000 acres each. Later, Margaret

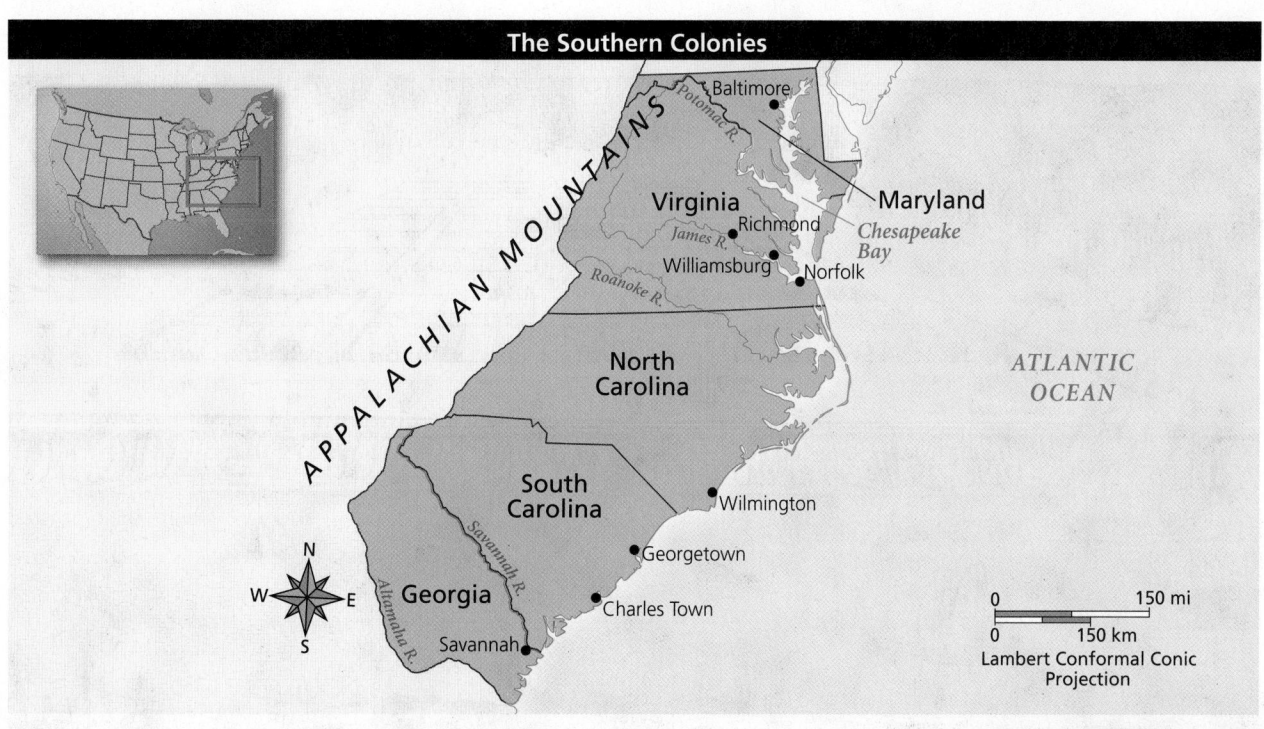

The Southern Colonies

>> The Southern Colonies were bordered on the west by the Appalachian Mountains and on the east by the Atlantic Ocean. **Analyze Maps** Which of the Southern Colonies is the southernmost? Which is the northernmost?

Brent helped prevent a rebellion among the governor's soldiers. The Maryland assembly praised her efforts, saying that "the colony's safety at any time [was better] in her hands than in any man's."

Acceptance of Other Religions To make sure Maryland continued to grow, Lord Baltimore welcomed Protestants as well as Catholics to the colony. Later, Lord Baltimore came to fear that Protestants might try to deprive Catholics of their right to worship freely. In 1649, he asked the assembly to pass an **Act of Toleration**. The law provided religious freedom for all Christians. As in many colonies, this freedom did not extend to Jews.

? **IDENTIFY** How did Lord Baltimore found the Maryland colony?

Settlement in the Carolinas and Georgia

South of Virginia and Maryland, English colonists settled in a region that they called the Carolinas. In 1663, a group of eight English nobles received a grant of land from King Charles II. Settlement took place in two separate areas, one in the north and the other in the south.

The Carolinas Develop Differently In the northern part of the Carolinas, settlers were mostly poor tobacco farmers who had spread south from Virginia. They tended to have small farms. Eventually, in 1712, the colony became known as North Carolina. Farther south, the group of eight English nobles set up a larger colony.

The largest settlement, Charles Town, sprang up where the Ashley and Cooper rivers met the Atlantic Ocean. Later, Charles Town's name was shortened to

>> The city of Savannah was founded in Georgia, a colony James Oglethorpe established with private funds.

Charleston. This colony became known as South Carolina in 1719.

Most early settlers in Charleston were English people who had been living in Barbados, a British colony in the Caribbean. Later, other immigrants arrived, including Germans, Swiss, French Protestants, and Spanish Jews.

Around 1685, a few planters discovered that rice grew well in the swampy lowlands along the coast. However, they were unable to grow rich crops until Africans from rice-growing areas of Africa were brought against their will to the colony. Before long, Carolina rice was a profitable crop traded around the world. Settlers farther inland in South Carolina later learned to raise **indigo**, a plant used to make a valuable blue dye.

Georgia Offers a Second Chance The last of England's Southern Colonies was carved out of the southern part of South Carolina. James Oglethorpe, a respected English soldier and energetic social reformer, helped to found Georgia in 1732. He and the other trustees started and funded the colony privately. They hoped it would solve an English social problem as well as defend the English colonies to the north from Spanish Florida to the south. Oglethorpe wanted the new colony to be a place where **debtors**, or people who owed money they could not pay back, could make a fresh start. Penn had established Pennsylvania as a refuge for people of different religions. Similarly, Oglethorpe established Georgia mainly for social reasons, as a refuge for debtors.

Under English law, the government could imprison debtors until they paid

>> Enslaved Africans, such as these unloading rice barges, made up the largest racial group in South Carolina.

▶ **Interactive Illustration**

what they owed. If they ever got out of jail, debtors often had no money and no place to live. Oglethorpe offered to pay for debtors and other poor people to travel to Georgia. "In America," he said, "there are enough fertile lands to feed all the poor of England."

In 1733, Oglethorpe and 120 colonists built the colony's first settlement at Savannah, along the Savannah River. Oglethorpe set strict rules for the colony. Farms could be no bigger than 500 acres, and slavery was forbidden.

At first, Georgia grew slowly. Later, however, Oglethorpe changed the rules to allow large plantations and slave labor. After that, the colony grew more quickly.

❓ **CHECK UNDERSTANDING** Why did South Carolina's economy come to depend on rice crops?

Two Regions Develop Differently

The plantation system developed in the Southern Colonies because of the headright. The headright was a grant of land for each settler who came to a colony, or for the person who paid to bring a settler. Wealthy settlers saw a chance to gain even more wealth by paying for farm workers and thus gaining ownership of large amounts of fertile, coastal farmland.

Although the plantation system developed first in Virginia, South Carolina planters turned to it as well. They wanted large numbers of workers for rice plantations. Few white settlers were willing to work in rice paddies. As in Virginia, planters turned to Africa for slave labor.

By 1700, most people coming to Charleston were African men and women brought against their will. Each time a planter bought an enslaved African, the planter gained more land. This system led to the expansion of slavery across the South.

Tidewater Plantations on the Coast

The Southern Colonies enjoyed warmer weather and a longer growing season than the colonies to the north. Parts of Virginia, Maryland, and North Carolina near the coast all became major tobacco-growing areas. Settlers in lowland South Carolina and Georgia raised rice, indigo, and cotton. In these regions, physical features, such as flat landscapes and fertile soils, resulted in a relatively dense population during the 1600s and 1700s.

Colonists soon found that it was most profitable to raise tobacco and rice on large plantations. As you recall, a plantation is a large estate farmed by many workers. The earliest planters settled along rivers and creeks of the coastal plain. Because these rivers and creeks rose and fell with ocean tides, the region was known as the Tidewater. The Tidewater's gentle slopes and rivers offered rich farmland for plantations.

Farther inland, planters settled along rivers. Rivers provided an easy way to move goods to market. Planters loaded crops onto ships bound for the West Indies and Europe. On the return trip, the ships carried English manufactured goods and other luxuries for planters and their families.

Most Tidewater plantations had their own docks along the river, and merchant ships picked up crops and delivered goods directly to them. For this reason, few large seaport cities developed in the Southern Colonies.

>> This print shows a Southern plantation during the 1700s, with enslaved workers assisting the lady of the house.

>> At a riverfront Tidewater plantation, ships could have tied up at pilings like this one and loaded goods to and from the plantation's dock.

Large Tidewater plantations often consisted of brick or framed mansions with nearby storehouses and quarters for enslaved workers. The mansions overlooked fields or paddies, and often, the nearest river. On these southern plantations, anywhere from 20 to 100 enslaved Africans and African Americans did most of the work. Most of these enslaved workers worked in the fields. Others were skilled workers, such as carpenters, barrel makers, or blacksmiths. Still other enslaved Africans and African Americans worked in the main house as cooks, servants, or housekeepers.

Only a small percentage of white southerners owned large plantations. Yet, planters set the style of southern living. Life centered around the planter's house, or the Great House. There, the planter's family lived in elegant quarters, including a parlor for visitors, a dining room, and guest bedrooms.

During the growing season, planters decided which fields to plant, what crops to grow, and when to harvest the crops. Planters' wives kept the household running smoothly. They directed enslaved cooks, maids, and butlers in the house and made sure daily tasks were done, such as milking cows.

In contrast to the lives of the planters, enslaved workers faced daily hardship. They were impoverished and denied basic rights. Their diets were often inadequate for the work they did. Their dwellings were rough and open to the weather. They faced diseases and other dangers.

Yet enslaved Africans played a crucial role on plantations. They used farming skills they had brought from West Africa. With their help, English settlers learned how to grow rice. Africans also knew how to use wild plants unfamiliar to the English. They made water buckets out of gourds, and they used palmetto leaves to make fans, brooms, and baskets.

The Backcountry Farther Inland West of the Tidewater, life, and the local economy, was very different. Here, at the base of the Appalachians, rolling hills and thick forests covered the land. These physical features would in turn influence where people lived and how they made a living in the region during the 1600s and 1700s. As in the Middle Colonies, this inland area was called the backcountry. Attracted by rich soil, settlers followed the Great Wagon Road into the backcountry of Maryland, Virginia, and the Carolinas.

Among the settlers who moved into the backcountry were Scotch-Irish and Germans, including German Moravians. The Scotch-Irish tended to be Presbyterian farmers and craftspeople. Many were escaping famine and harsh treatment under English rule in Northern Ireland, or were the children of such immigrants.

They built churches and started schools in their backcountry settlements. These immigrant groups transformed the environment by clearing the forests and creating fields where they grew crops such as wheat and fields and pens where they raised cattle and pigs.

The German immigrants to the backcountry, mostly Lutherans, sought good land at low cost. They often settled together in the same areas, speaking German and retaining German culture. The German Moravians were members of a Protestant group that sought to convert Indians to Christianity. They allowed women to preach and were pacifists. The Moravians kept careful records of backcountry life—including everything from the weather to fashions—that historians still use today.

The backcountry was more democratic than the Tidewater. Settlers there were more likely to treat one another as equals. Men tended smaller fields of tobacco or garden crops such as beans, corn, or peas. They also hunted game.

The distance of the backcountry from the coastline made trade difficult and prevented the development of a plantation economy. Instead, backcountry farmers had to be mostly self-sufficient. Surplus goods were sold at local markets. Women cooked meals and fashioned simple, rugged clothing out of wool or deerskins. Another major difference between the backcountry

Life in the Colonial Tidewater and Backcountry

	TIDEWATER	BACKCOUNTRY
LOCATION	Coastal plains	Appalachian mountains and their foothills
TERRAIN	Flat plain	Hilly, mountainous
POPULATION	Early English settlers and enslaved Africans	Scotch-Irish, poorer English migrants, Germans
ECONOMY	Large-scale plantation farming of cash crops for export	Small-scale subsistence farming, fur trade

>> The Tidewater and the backcountry differed greatly in terms of physical environment, population, government, economy, and culture. **Analyze Charts** How did the environment affect farming in each region?

and the Tidewater was slavery. Farms were smaller in the backcountry in part because of the hills and thick forests. Fewer enslaved Africans worked on these smaller farms, and most people were of European descent.

The hardships of backcountry life brought settlers closer together. Families gathered to husk corn or help one another build barns. Clustered in fertile valleys along the edge of the Appalachians, these hardy settlers felled trees and grew crops. By changing the environment for the better, they in turn encouraged further economic development in the region.

? IDENTIFY SUPPORTING DETAILS Why was there less slavery in the backcountry than the Tidewater region?

The Slave Trade Expands

In the early years, Africans in the English colonies included free people and indentured servants as well as enslaved persons. During the 1600s, even Africans who were enslaved enjoyed some privileges. The first enslaved Africans arrived in Virginia in 1619. For the next 50 years, since the African population was small, the status of Africans in the colony was not clearly established. Some enslaved Africans purchased their freedom. Several Africans during the 1600s, such as Anthony Johnson, became successful property owners. In South Carolina, some enslaved Africans worked without supervision as cowboys, herding cattle to market.

By 1700, plantations in the Southern Colonies had come to rely heavily on slave labor. Eventually, enslaved Africans made up the majority of the population in South Carolina and Georgia. They cleared the

>> Enslaved Africans were often crowded into extremely tight quarters during the Middle Passage across the Atlantic.

land, worked the crops, and tended the livestock. In order to maintain the supply of enslaved Africans, southern planters relied on a system of slave trading that stretched halfway across the globe.

Africans Are Enslaved In Africa, as you have learned, as elsewhere around the world, slavery had been part of the social and economic system since ancient times. Usually, slaves were people who had been captured in war. Muslim merchants sometimes brought enslaved Africans into Europe and the Middle East.

Over a period of about 300 years, as the transatlantic slave trade grew, millions of Africans were enslaved. Slave traders from European nations set up posts along the West African coast. They offered guns and other goods in exchange for enslaved Africans.

As the demand for cheap labor increased, Africans who lived along the coast made raids into the interior, seeking captives to sell to the Europeans. They marched their captives to the coast. There, the Africans were loaded aboard European ships headed for forced immigration to the Americas.

Sailing Across the Middle Passage In the 1700s, English sailors began referring to the passage of slave-trading ships west across the Atlantic Ocean as the Middle Passage. Below the decks of these ships, enslaved Africans were often crammed tightly together on shelves. One observer noted that they were "chained to each other hand and foot, and stowed so close, that they were not allowed above a foot and a half for each in breadth." The captives were allowed above deck to eat and exercise in the fresh air only once or twice a day.

Many enslaved Africans resisted, but only a few escaped. Some fought for their freedom during the trip. They would stage a mutiny or revolt. The slave traders lived in fear of this and were heavily armed. Other slaves resisted by refusing to eat or by committing suicide by jumping overboard to avoid a life of enslavement.

Records of slave-trading ships show that about 10 percent of Africans loaded aboard a ship for passage to the Americas died during the voyage. Many died of illnesses that spread rapidly in the filthy, crowded conditions inside a ship's hold. Others died of mistreatment. This slave trade lasted about 300 years. During that time, it may have caused the deaths of as many as 2 to 3 million Africans.

Human Rights Are Often Ignored As the importance of slavery increased during the 1600s, and particularly after Bacon's Rebellion in Virginia, greater limits were placed on the rights of enslaved Africans and African Americans. Colonists passed laws that set out rules for slaves' behavior and denied enslaved people basic human rights. These **slave codes** treated enslaved Africans and African Americans not as human beings but as property.

Most English colonists did not question the justice of owning enslaved Africans. They believed that black Africans, as a racial group, were inferior to white Europeans. The belief that one race is superior to another is called **racism**. Some colonists believed that they were helping enslaved Africans by teaching them Christianity.

A handful of colonists spoke out against the evils of slavery. In 1688, Quakers in Germantown, Pennsylvania, became the first group of colonists to call for an end to slavery.

? CHECK UNDERSTANDING Why did many colonists believe there was nothing wrong with slavery?

ASSESSMENT

1. **Contrast** the ownership of the colony of Maryland with the ownership of colonies that were founded earlier.

2. **Cite Evidence** What evidence supports the claim that the planters in the southern Carolinas could not make rice a profitable crop on their own?

3. **Analyze Information** How did Oglethorpe's idea to found Georgia help solve a social problem in England?

4. **Generate Explanations** Why was South Carolina the only English colony in 1700 where the majority of the population was made up of enslaved Africans?

5. **Summarize** what the Middle Passage was like for most enslaved Africans.

Colonial Society

A procession of singers heads for a church. Religious services played a central role in colonial culture.

▶ Interactive Flipped Video

For the most part, colonists enjoyed more social equality than people in England, where a person's opportunities in life were largely determined by birth. Still, class differences existed. Like Europeans, colonial Americans thought it was only natural that some people rank more highly than others. A person's birth and wealth still determined his or her social status.

>> Objectives

Outline the structure of colonial society.

Describe colonial art, music, and literature, and the impact of ideas on colonial society.

Describe the causes of the Great Awakening and its effects on colonial society.

Explain the growth of educational institutions.

>> Key Terms

gentry
middle class
Gullah
Great Awakening
apprentice
dame school
Enlightenment
libel

Society in Colonial Times

The Upper and Middle Social Classes

At the top of society stood the **gentry**. The gentry included wealthy planters, merchants, ministers, successful lawyers, and royal officials. They could afford to dress in the latest fashions from London.

Below the gentry were the **middle class**. The middle class included farmers who worked their own land, skilled craft workers, and some tradespeople. Nearly three quarters of all white colonists belonged to the middle class. They prospered because land in the colonies was plentiful and easy to buy and because skilled work was in high demand and paid relatively well.

The Lower Social Classes

The lower social classes included hired farmhands and indentured servants. Far below them in status were enslaved Africans and African Americans. Indentured servants signed contracts to work without wages for a period of four to seven years for anyone who would pay their ocean passage to the Americas. When their term of service was completed, indentured servants received "freedom dues": a set of clothes, tools, and 50 acres of land. Because there were so few European women in the colonies, female indentured servants often shortened their terms of service by marrying.

Thousands of men, women, and children came to North America as indentured servants. After completing their terms, some became successful and rose into the middle class.

Working Life in the Countryside

From New Hampshire to Georgia, most colonists survived by farming. Men worked long hours planting crops, tending the fields,

>> Wealthy members of the colonial gentry had money to buy such luxury goods as the fashionable clothing shown here.

>> Most colonists lived and worked on small family farms.

and raising livestock—pigs, cows, and other farm animals. Anything beyond what the family needed to live was taken to markets to sell. Families also traded crops and livestock with their neighbors for additional goods.

While men typically did much of the agricultural work, women often worked within the home. They worked hard taking care of the household and the family. By the kitchen fire, they cooked the family's meals. They milked cows, tended chickens and a vegetable garden, watched the children, cleaned, did laundry by hand, and made candles, cheese, and clothes.

Life was different in the backcountry, out beyond more settled lands. Life was difficult, and wives and husbands often worked side by side in the fields at harvest time. With so much to be done, no one worried whether harvesting was proper "woman's work." One surprised visitor described a backcountry woman's activities: "She will carry a gunn in the woods and kill deer, turkeys &c., shoot down wild cattle, catch and tye hoggs, knock down [cattle] with an ax, and perform the most manfull Exercises as well as most men."

Working Life in Cities In cities, women sometimes worked outside the home. A young single woman from a poorer family might work for one of the gentry as a maid, a cook, or a nurse. Other women were midwives, who delivered babies. Still others sewed fine hats or dresses to be sold to women who could afford them. Learning such skills often required years of training.

Some women learned trades from their fathers, brothers, or husbands. They worked as butchers, shoemakers, or silversmiths. Quite a few women became

>> In colonial cities and towns, men and women often worked together, as in this silk workshop in Jamestown, Virginia. **Draw Conclusions** What does this illustration suggest about the colonists' desire to succeed?

▶ **Interactive Gallery**

printers. A woman might take over her husband's business when he died.

Men often worked in trades, for example as coopers (who made and repaired wooden barrels), blacksmiths, and silversmiths. Most large towns in the colonies were seaports, where merchants and traders brought goods to and from Europe. As this trade grew, more men also took on jobs as bankers, lawyers, and businessmen.

Some educated men in the colonies became politicians. Others were pamphleteers, who wrote and distributed small booklets informing people on a subject. There were many doctors in the colonies, where illness was common. However, medical training varied. A surgeon might be a barber with little real medical training.

African Influences in the Colonies By the mid-1700s, the culture of Africans and African Americans in the colonies varied greatly. On rice plantations in South Carolina, enslaved Africans used methods from West Africa for growing and harvesting rice. For example, flat baskets holding the grains were shaken in the wind to separate the grains from leaves and other particles. Then a wooden mortar and pestle were used to clean the grains.

Language is another area where African influences were strong. In some coastal areas, enslaved Africans spoke a distinctive combination of English and West African languages known as **Gullah** (GULL uh). Parents often chose African names for their children, such as Quosh or Juba or Cuff.

In Charleston and other South Carolina port towns, some Africans worked along the dock, making rope or barrels or helping to build ships. Skilled craftsworkers made fine wooden cabinets or silver plates and utensils. Many of their designs reflected African artistic styles. Although most Africans in these towns were enslaved, many opened their own shops or stalls in the market. Some used their earnings to buy their own and their family's freedom.

In the Middle Colonies and New England, the African and African American population increased during the 1700s. Africans and African Americans in the northern colonies included both free and enslaved people. Their numbers were much lower than in the Southern Colonies. However, they were still an important part of the population.

In some of the Middle Colonies, such as New York, there were even plantations that relied on slave labor. Often, these plantations produced grains and meat for sale to feed enslaved workers in the Southern Colonies or the West Indies.

? **DEFINE** What was an indentured servant?

>> Enslaved African-Americans introduced new methods of harvesting and preparing different grains.

Colonial Art, Literature, and Music

Colonists brought with them the artistic traditions of their homelands. New artistic styles also developed that reflected colonial society. Wealthy gentry decorated their homes with paintings of landscapes and religious art. Furniture, houses, and clothing were often decorated with intricate carvings or designs.

Art Reflects Colonial Society Paintings that celebrated important people of the time were especially popular works of art. Those who could afford it hired artists to paint portraits of their family members.

>> Finely carved and painted pieces of furniture like this wooden chest were highly valued during the colonial era.

These portraits showed off the family's importance and provided a valuable keepsake to be passed on for generations to come. Portraits also honored famous individuals and key events. One of the oldest surviving colonial portraits is of New Netherland Governor Peter Stuyvesant, painted in the 1660s.

Prints were also popular in colonial families. These were small engravings scratched into metal or carved into wood. Printmakers used the metal or wood with ink, paper, and a press to make a picture that could be easily reproduced. Many people had prints of famous figures, such as politicians or clergymen.

Many artists were self-taught. Few became wealthy from their work. They often traveled from town to town in search of people who wanted portraits done. The paintings they left behind are like time capsules. Much like photographs do today, they show how people dressed, what their tastes were like, and how their families lived.

American Literature Emerges Literature also developed in the colonies. The first colonial printing press was built in Massachusetts in 1640. It printed religious books and books for Harvard College. With the spread of printing, more colonists began to read.

Colonists read reprints of European books and books by American writers. One of the most popular—and particularly American—types of stories was the captivity tale. In these stories, a white settler was captured by Native Americans and had to overcome hardships in order to escape.

Colonial Music Music was another popular art form in the colonies. Colonists brought popular folk music from Europe. They sang and danced at weddings and other celebrations. Enslaved Africans brought musical traditions with them from Africa. These traditions combined with European traditions in musical forms such as work songs and spirituals, or religious songs.

Music was closely tied to religious life for many colonists. New organs appeared in churches. The hymns people sang grew especially popular during the Great Awakening.

❓ **IDENTIFY SUPPORTING DETAILS** What clues can we find about colonial lives in artwork such as paintings?

A New Religious Movement

In the 1730s and 1740s, a religious revival, or movement, known as the **Great Awakening** swept through the colonies. It is sometimes also known as the First Great Awakening to distinguish it from later

>> With his fiery sermons, Jonathan Edwards, a New England preacher, helped spark the religious movement known as the Great Awakening.

religious revivals. Its drama and emotion touched women and men of all races, ethnic backgrounds, and classes.

Enthusiastic Preachers A New England preacher, Jonathan Edwards, helped set off the Great Awakening. In powerful sermons, Edwards called on colonists, especially young people, to examine their lives.

He preached of the sweetness and beauty of God. At the same time, he warned listeners to heed the Bible's teachings. Otherwise, they would be "sinners in the hands of an angry God," headed for the fiery torments of hell. The powerful sermons of preachers such as Edwards were one of the main causes of the Great Awakening.

In 1739, when an English minister named George Whitefield arrived in the colonies, the movement spread like wildfire. Whitefield drew huge crowds to outdoor meetings. An enthusiastic and energetic preacher, his voice would ring with feeling as he called on sinners to repent. After hearing Whitefield speak, Jonathan Edwards's wife reported, "I have seen upwards of a thousand people hang on his words with breathless silence, broken only by an occasional half-suppressed sob."

The Great Awakening's Impact The colonies were made up of many different religious groups. There were Quakers, Puritans, Catholics, Presbyterians, and more. Each group had its own ideas about the proper relationship with God.

Some groups, like the Anglicans, disagreed strongly with Whitefield. Others, like the Baptists and Methodists, found new opportunities to expand during the Great Awakening as people revisited their faith.

The Great Awakening aroused bitter debate. People who supported

>> Crowds of people gathered to hear sermons by English minister George Whitefield, as shown in a later print. **Infer** What does the artist suggest about the attitude of Whitefield's audience?

the movement often split away from their old churches to form new ones. Opponents warned that the movement was too emotional. Still, the growth of so many new churches forced colonists to become more tolerant of people with different beliefs. Also, because the Great Awakening appealed to people in all of the colonies, from different classes and ethnic backgrounds, it brought colonists together for the first time. Ties formed during the Great Awakening helped form the groundwork for future bonds among the colonies.

In the colonies, members of most churches controlled their parishes. The role parishes played in local communities made people think about the importance of self-rule—a key factor in the development of American democracy.

The Great Awakening contributed in another way to the spread of democratic feelings in the colonies. Many of the new preachers were not as well educated as most ministers. They argued that formal training was less important than a heart filled with the holy spirit. Such teachings encouraged a spirit of independence. Many believers felt more free to challenge authority when their liberties were at stake. People began to think differently about their political rights and their governments. They felt if they could figure out how to worship on their own and how to run their own churches, then they could govern themselves with those same virtues. Eventually, many of these colonists would challenge the authority of colonial governors and the English king.

? IDENTIFY CENTRAL IDEAS How did the Great Awakening change how people thought about themselves and their political rights?

Colonial Schools and Colleges

Among the colonists, New Englanders were the most concerned about education. Puritans taught that all people had a duty to study the Bible. If colonists did not learn to read, how would they fulfill this duty?

Public Schools in New England In 1642, the Massachusetts assembly passed a law ordering all parents to teach their children "to read and understand the principles of religion." They also required all towns with 50 or more families to hire a schoolteacher. Towns with 100 or more families also had to set up a grammar school to prepare boys for college.

In this way, Massachusetts set up the first public schools, or schools supported by taxes. Public schools allowed both rich and poor children to receive an education.

The first New England schools had only one room for students of all ages. Parents paid the schoolteacher with corn, peas, or other foods. Each child was expected to bring a share of wood to burn in the stove. Students who forgot would find themselves seated in the coldest corner of the room!

Private Education in Other Colonies

In the Middle Colonies, churches and individual families set up private schools. Because pupils paid to attend, only wealthy families could afford to educate their children.

In the Southern Colonies, people often lived too far from one another to bring children together in one school building. Some planters hired tutors, or private teachers. The wealthiest planters sent their sons to school in England. As a rule, enslaved African Americans were denied education of any kind.

Apprenticeships and Dame Schools

Boys whose parents wished them to learn a trade or craft served as **apprentices** (uh PREN tis ez). An apprentice worked for a master to learn a trade or a craft.

For example, when a boy reached the age of 12 or 13, his parents might apprentice him to a master glassmaker. The young apprentice lived in the glassmaker's home for six or seven years while learning the craft. The glassmaker gave the boy food and clothing. He was also supposed to teach his apprentice how to read and write and provide him with religious training.

In return, the apprentice worked without pay in the glassmaker's shop and learned the skills he needed to set up his own shop. Boys were apprenticed in many

>> In colonial New England, instructors taught students of all ages in a single classroom.

▶ **Interactive Chart**

>> Mothers and special girls' schools taught girls and young women the skills needed to run a household.

trades, including papermaking, printing, and tanning (making leather).

In New England, most schools accepted only boys. However, some girls attended **dame schools**, or private schools run by women in their own homes. Other girls, though, usually learned skills from their mothers, who taught them to cook, make soap and candles, spin wool, weave, sew, and embroider. A few learned to read and write.

The Growth of Colleges In 1633, Puritan John Eliot spoke of the need for Massachusetts to establish an official college. Institutions of higher learning were held up as a way to promote European culture in the Americas. As Eliot cautioned, "if we no[u]rish not L[e]arning both church & common wealth will sinke."

Harvard College opened in 1638 with 10 students. The goal of the college was to educate future ministers. It was modeled after English schools, where students studied six days a week in Latin and Greek. It was open only to men.

By the late 1600s, however, Harvard graduates were moving away from the ministry. Some became physicians, public servants, or teachers. The College of William and Mary opened in Virginia to prepare men for the Anglican ministry. Yale College in Connecticut aimed to educate clergymen. Gradually, however, nine colleges opened over the following century and expanded their areas of study. Students could learn other subjects, such as medicine and law.

? **RECALL** Why were there private schools in many colonies?

A New World of Ideas

During the 1600s, European scientists began to use reason and logic instead of superstition to understand the world. They developed theories, and then performed experiments to test them. In doing so, they discovered many of the laws of nature. The English scientist Isaac Newton, for example, explained the law of gravity.

The Ideas of the Enlightenment

European thinkers of the late 1600s and 1700s believed that reason and scientific methods could be applied to the study of society. They tried to discover the natural laws that governed human behavior. Because these thinkers believed in the light of human reason, the movement that they started is known as the **Enlightenment**. John Locke, an English philosopher, wrote works that were widely read in the colonies. He said people could gain knowledge of the world by observing and by experimenting.

In the English colonies, the Enlightenment spread among better educated colonists. They included wealthy merchants, lawyers, ministers, and others who had the leisure to read the latest books from Europe. Urban craftsmen also heard and discussed these ideas.

Benjamin Franklin Franklin's Thoughts and Inventions

The best example of the Enlightenment spirit in the English colonies was Benjamin Franklin. Franklin was born in 1706, the son of a poor Boston soap and candle maker. Although he had only two years of formal schooling, he used his spare time to study literature, mathematics, and foreign languages.

At age 17, Franklin made his way to Philadelphia. There, he built up a successful printing business. His most popular publication was *Poor Richard's Almanack*. Published yearly, it contained useful information and clever quotes, such as "Early to bed, early to rise, makes a man healthy, wealthy, and wise."

Like other Enlightenment thinkers, Franklin wanted to use reason to improve the world around him. He invented practical devices that helped improve daily life. For example, Franklin suffered from poor eyesight, so he invented bifocal glasses to help himself—and countless others—see better. Franklin also invented a new kind of iron stove. It was set in the middle of a room instead of in a wall, and it kept houses warmer without filling them with smoke. Another one of Franklin's inventions, the lightning rod, protected buildings from catching fire in a storm because of lightning strikes. As a community leader, Franklin persuaded Philadelphia officials to pave streets, organize a fire company, and set up the first lending library in the Americas. Franklin's inventions and his public service earned him worldwide fame.

>> Isaac Newton analyzes the colors in a ray of light shining through his door. Newton was an important figure in the Enlightenment, a movement that emphasized reason, logic, and individualism.

The Influence of Colonial Cities and Towns While most colonists lived on farms, towns and cities strongly influenced colonial life. Through the great ports of Philadelphia, New York, Boston, and Charleston, merchants shipped products overseas. Towns and cities also served as centers of a busy trade between the coast and the growing backcountry.

Culture flourished in the towns. By the mid-1700s, many colonial towns had their own theaters. Town dwellers found entertainment at singing societies, traveling circuses, carnivals, and horse races.

In 1704, John Campbell founded the *Boston News-Letter*, the first regular weekly newspaper in the English colonies. Within 50 years, each of the colonies, except New Jersey and Delaware, had at least one weekly paper.

John Peter Zenger's Libel Trial The growth of colonial newspapers led to a dispute over freedom of the press. John Peter Zenger published the *Weekly Journal* in New York City. In 1734, he was arrested for publishing stories that criticized the governor. Zenger was put on trial for **libel**—the act of publishing a statement that may unjustly damage a person's reputation. Zenger's lawyer argued that, since the stories were true, his client had not committed libel. The jury agreed and freed Zenger. At the time, the case did not attract a great deal of attention. However, freedom of the press would become recognized as a basic American right.

⁇ IDENTIFY How did some of Benjamin Franklin's inventions influence the daily lives of colonists?

>> This illustration shows the acquittal of John Peter Zenger on a charge of libel, which helped establish the American principle of freedom of the press.

ASSESSMENT

1. **Infer** Women did not have access to certain jobs in the colonies. How was women's access to employment was restricted?

2. **Analyze Information** How did the Great Awakening lead to greater religious tolerance?

3. **Support Ideas with Evidence** What evidence can you find in the reading to support the idea that educational opportunities were not equal between many of the colonies?

4. **Generate Explanations** Why do you think enslaved African Americans were generally denied an education?

5. **Make Generalizations** What generalization can you make about education in the 1700s based on the fact that newspapers were becoming increasingly popular throughout the colonies?

Colonial Trade and Government

>> This painting shows the busy Dutch colonial port of New Amsterdam. Under the policy of mercantilism, England was eager to capture the port and shift its trade to England.

▶ **Interactive Flipped Video**

>> Objectives

Explain the development of mercantilism and colonists' response to it.

Outline the relationship of the slave trade to other kinds of trade.

Describe the development of governments and legal systems in the colonies.

>> Key Terms

mercantilism
export
Navigation Acts
Yankees
triangular trade
legislature
Glorious Revolution
bill of rights
English Bill of Rights
imports
William Blackstone
legislature

Like other European nations at the time, England believed that its colonies should benefit the home country. This belief was part of an economic theory known as **mercantilism** (MUR kun til iz um). According to this theory, a nation could become strong by keeping strict control over its trade. As one English gentleman put it, "Whosoever commands the trade of the world commands the riches of the world."

Mercantilism and the English Colonies

Imports and Exports Mercantilists thought that a country should export more than it imported. **Exports** are goods sent to markets outside a country.

Imports are goods brought into a country. If England sold more goods than it bought abroad, gold would flow into the home country as payment for those exports.

The Navigation Acts Affect the Colonies Beginning in the 1650s, the English Parliament passed a series of **Navigation Acts** that regulated trade between England and its colonies. The purpose of these laws was to ensure that only England benefited from trade with its colonies.

Under the new laws, only colonial or English ships could carry goods to and from the colonies. Colonists were banned from trading directly with other European nations or their colonies. All trade had to go through England. The Navigation Acts also listed certain products, such as tobacco and cotton, that colonial merchants could ship only to England. In this way, Parliament created jobs for English workers who cut and rolled tobacco or spun cotton into cloth.

The Navigation Acts helped the colonies as well as England. For example, the law encouraged colonists to build ships for their own use and for sale to England. As a result, New England became a prosperous shipbuilding center. Also, because of the acts, colonial merchants did not have to compete with foreign merchants because they were sure of having a market for their goods in England.

Still, many colonists resented the Navigation Acts. In their view, the laws favored English merchants. Colonial merchants often ignored the Navigation Acts or found ways to get around them.

❓ IDENTIFY CENTRAL IDEAS Why did England pass the Navigation Acts?

Trading Across the Atlantic

The colonies produced a wide variety of goods, and merchant ships sailed up and down the Atlantic coast. Merchants from New England dominated colonial trade.

They were known as **Yankees**, a nickname, and had a reputation for being clever and hardworking. Yankee traders earned a reputation for profiting from any deal.

The Triangular Trade Colonial merchants developed many trade routes. One route was known as the **triangular trade**

>> Sugar cane grown by enslaved Africans in the West Indies, shown here, was used to make molasses, a key product for the triangular trade.

because the three legs of the route formed a triangle. On the first leg, ships from New England carried rum, guns, gunpowder, cloth, and tools from New England to West Africa. In Africa, Yankee merchants traded these goods for slaves.

On the second leg of the journey, ships carried enslaved Africans to the West Indies. It was because enslaved Africans traveled on the second leg of a three-leg voyage that this leg was known as the Middle Passage. With the profits from selling the enslaved Africans, Yankee traders bought molasses—a dark-brown syrup made from sugar cane—and sugar. On the final leg, ships then sailed back to New England, where colonists used the molasses and sugar to make rum for sale in Africa or Europe.

Merchants Disregard the Navigation Acts Many New England merchants grew wealthy from the triangular trade. In doing so, they often disobeyed the Navigation Acts. Traders were supposed to buy sugar and molasses only from English colonies in the West Indies. However, the demand for molasses was so high that New Englanders smuggled in cargoes from the Dutch, French, and Spanish West Indies, too. Bribes made customs officials look the other way.

❓ **CHECK UNDERSTANDING** Why did many traders ignore the Navigation Acts and buy sugar and molasses from non-English colonies in the West Indies?

The Foundations of Representative Government

Although each colony developed its own government, the governments had much in common. A governor directed the colony's affairs and enforced the laws. Most governors were appointed, either by the king or by the colony's proprietor. In Rhode Island and Connecticut, however, colonists

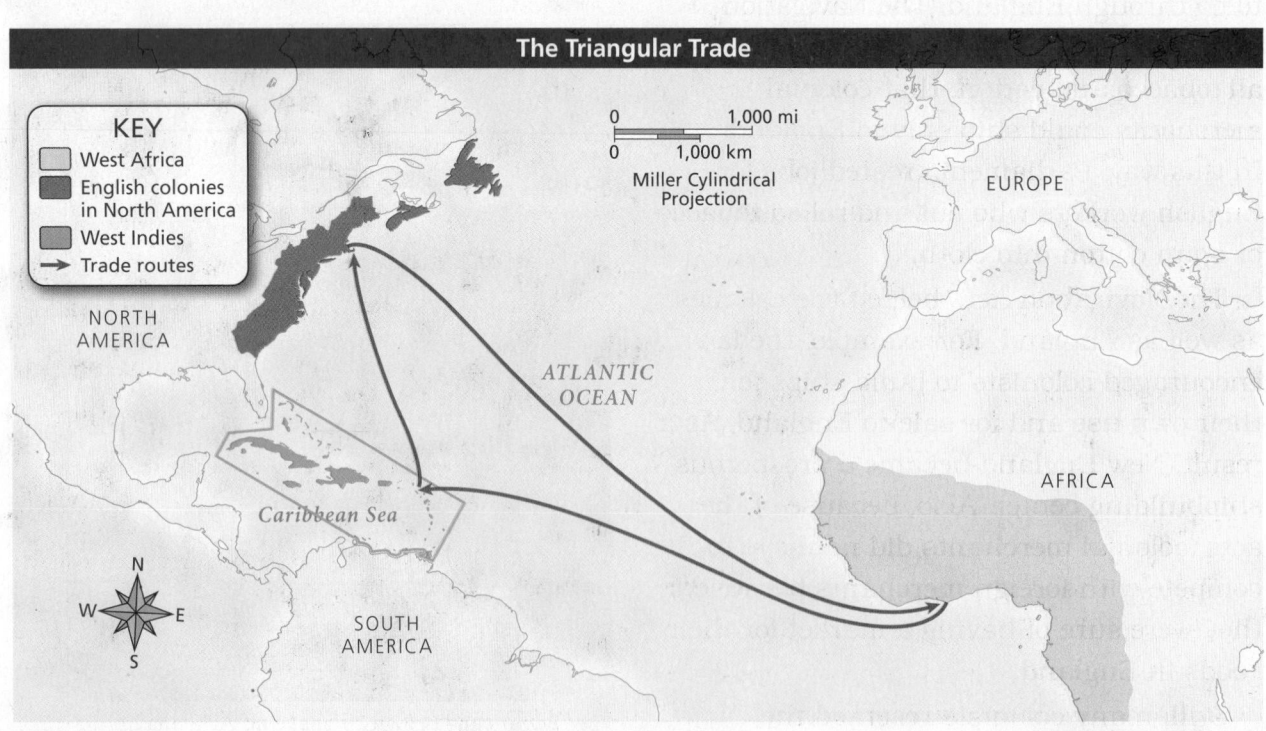

The Triangular Trade

KEY
- West Africa
- English colonies in North America
- West Indies
- → Trade routes

0   1,000 mi
0   1,000 km
Miller Cylindrical Projection

NORTH AMERICA

ATLANTIC OCEAN

Caribbean Sea

SOUTH AMERICA

EUROPE

AFRICA

>> This map shows the routes of the Triangular Trade. **Analyze Maps** Which region was the first destination for many enslaved Africans?

▶ **Interactive Map**

THE FOUNDATIONS OF AMERICAN DEMOCRACY

Founding Documents	Fundamental Principles	State constitutions, the United States Constitution and Bill of Rights
• Magna Carta • English Bill of Rights • Commentaries on the Laws of England	• Government authority comes from the consent of the governed • The power of government should be limited • Government exists to protect individual rights and freedoms	• Guarantee due process • Establish rule of law • Guarantee free elections and free speech • Establish checks on governmental authority

>> Colonial government in the English colonies was influenced by three important documents. **Analyze Charts** How did these documents influence the state and federal constitutions of the United States?

 Interactive Chart

elected their own governors. Representative government and institutions spread in the colonies for several reasons.

Elected Assemblies As you learned, the Virginia Company decided to establish an elected assembly to attract more settlers. For this reason, and inspired by the English tradition of representative government outlined in the Magna Carta, all of the colonies gained a **legislature** soon after they were founded.

A legislature is a group of people, usually elected, who have the power to make laws. In most colonies, the legislature had an upper house and a lower house. The upper house was made up of advisers appointed by the governor.

The lower house was an elected assembly. It approved laws and protected the rights of citizens. Just as important, it had the right to approve or reject any taxes or budget items the governor asked for. This "power of the purse," or right to raise or spend money, was an important check on the governor's power. Any governor who ignored the assembly risked losing his salary.

As colonial settlers spread inland and founded new cities and towns, representative government and institutions grew. Most colonial cities and towns had their own city and town councils.

The Right to Vote Each colony had its own rules about who could vote. By the 1720s, however, all of the colonies had laws that restricted the right to vote to white Christian men over the age of 21.

In some colonies, only Protestants or members of a particular church could vote. All colonies restricted the vote to men who owned a certain amount of property. Colonial leaders believed that only property owners knew what was best for a colony.

The Tradition of Common Law The colonies followed English common law. Under common law, laws develop from the past rulings of judges. In applying laws, courts followed the principle that "like cases should be tried alike."

Colonists brought the tradition of common law with them from England. In the 1760s, **William Blackstone** published a four-volume book, *Commentaries on the Laws of England*. In it, Blackstone reviewed the entire history of English law. As a member of Parliament and a judge in England, he believed common law was the highest and best form of law.

Blackstone supported Parliament and opposed colonists' moves toward self-rule. However, his ideas about common law took hold in the colonies. Common law was a body of laws that was valid independent of Parliament's acts. As such, it provided a basis for self-rule and an independent legal system once the colonies began to move toward independence.

The English Bill of Rights Supports Freedoms Colonists took great pride in their elected assemblies. They also valued the rights that the Magna Carta gave them as English subjects.

Colonists won still more rights as a result of the **Glorious Revolution** of 1688. Parliament removed King James II from the throne and asked William and Mary of the Netherlands to rule. In return for Parliament's support, William and Mary signed the English Bill of Rights in 1689. A **bill of rights** is a written list of freedoms the government promises to protect.

The **English Bill of Rights** protected the rights of individuals and gave anyone accused of a crime the right to a trial by jury. Just as important, the English Bill of Rights said that a ruler could not raise taxes or an army without the approval of Parliament. The Bill of Rights also strengthened the position of representative government and institutions in the colonies.

Liberties are Restricted English colonists in the Americas often enjoyed more freedoms than did the English themselves.

However, the rights of English citizens did not extend to all colonists. Women had more rights in the colonies than in England but far fewer rights than did free, white males. A woman's father or husband was supposed to protect her. A married woman could not start her own business or sign a contract unless her husband approved it.

In most colonies, unmarried women and widows had more rights than married women. They could make contracts and sue in court. In Maryland and the Carolinas, women settlers who headed families could buy land on the same terms as men.

African Americans and Native Americans in the colonies had almost no rights. While so many colonists enjoyed English liberties, most African Americans were bound in slavery. The conflict between liberty and slavery would not be resolved until the 1860s.

? DESCRIBE How did the English Bill of Rights promote freedom?

ASSESSMENT

1. **Compare Points of View** Compare how the English and the colonists viewed the Navigation Acts.

2. **Cite Evidence** What evidence is there in the reading to suggest that molasses was critical to the success of the triangular trade?

3. **Summarize** the rights of women in colonial America.

4. **Predict Consequences** Colonial traders profited greatly from the triangular trade, partly because they disregarded the Navigation Acts and traded with colonies of European nations other than England. How do you think they might have responded if England started to strictly enforce the Navigation Acts?

5. **Summarize** How did English laws contribute to the development of freedom and self-government in the American colonies?

TOPIC 2 ASSESSMENT

1. **Describe the Causes of Spanish Colonization** Write a paragraph about the reasons the Spanish had for colonizing New Spain. Explain the quotation below in relation to colonization. In your paragraph, consider what historians mean by gold, God, and glory.

   Sometimes, historians summarize the Spanish exploration and settlement of the Americas as motivated by "Gold, God, and Glory."

2. **Explain the Founding of Jamestown** Write a paragraph explaining the significance of the founding of Jamestown in 1607. Answer these questions: What is a charter? What rights did the royal charter give the Virginia Company and guarantee colonists? What were the goals of the colonists who arrived in 1607? What is the significance of the founding of Jamestown?

3. **Analyze the Importance of the Virginia House of Burgesses** Write a paragraph analyzing the importance of the Virginia House of Burgesses to the growth of representative government in the colonial period. Answer the following questions: What is a representative government? Why did the Virginia Company establish the House of Burgesses? Which settlers could be elected as burgesses? What was the purpose of the House of Burgesses? Why was the establishment of the House of Burgesses important?

4. **Describe Religious Reasons for Immigration** Write a paragraph describing the role that religion played in the Puritans' decision to immigrate to New England and establish the Massachusetts Bay Colony. Consider how the Puritans felt about the Church of England, why the Puritans persuaded royal officials to grant them a charter to form the Massachusetts Bay Company, and how religion influenced what the Puritans hoped to do in Massachusetts.

5. **Explain the Growth of Representative Government** Write a paragraph explaining how the colonial governments laid the foundations for representative government. Consider the role of governors, the role of assemblies, and the right to vote.

6. **Explain the Significance of the Mayflower Compact** Write a paragraph explaining why the Pilgrims signed the Mayflower Compact when they arrived in Plymouth in 1620 and analyzing why the document is important to the growth of representative government. Recount where the Pilgrims were headed and where they actually landed in 1620, explain why the Pilgrims believed they needed to write and sign the Mayflower Compact, summarize what the signers agreed to do, and analyze why the Mayflower Compact was an important step toward the U.S. system of representative government.

7. **Explain the Development of the Free-Market System** Write a paragraph describing why a free-market system developed in New Jersey when it was a proprietary colony. Explain why a free-market system was able to develop in New Jersey and why the system that developed is called a free-market system.

8. **Explain the Transatlantic Slave Trade** Write a paragraph explaining the reasons for the transatlantic slave trade. Consider reasons related to the Southern Colonies and reasons related to colonial trade.

9. **Analyze Mercantilism** Use the quotation below and other sources to write a paragraph analyzing how the theory of mercantilism influenced England's relationship with its colonies. Answer the following questions: How does the quotation below reflect the economic theory of mercantilism? What role did imports and exports play in mercantilism? How did the Navigation Acts support the theory of mercantilism? Why did many colonists resent the Navigation Acts?

   Whosoever commands the trade of the world commands the riches of the world.

   —Sir Walter Raleigh

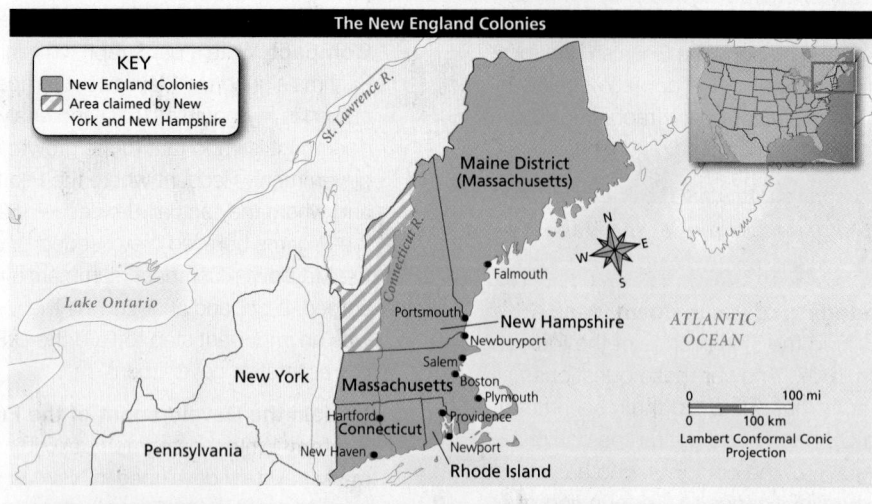

The New England Colonies

KEY
New England Colonies
Area claimed by New York and New Hampshire

The Middle Colonies

KEY
Middle Colonies
Area Claimed by New York and New Hampshire

10. **Pose and Answer Questions About Geographic Distributions and Patterns** Locate important regions in colonial American on the maps above and pose and answer questions about geographic patterns and distributions. Consider questions such as the following: Which region has the greatest number of coastal cities? What geographic factor might account for this pattern? What pattern is evident on both maps about the location of inland cities? What might explain this pattern?

11. **Explain William Penn's Role in the Development of Self-Government** Write a paragraph explaining the role William Penn played in the development of self-government in colonial America. Explain how Penn aided self-government in Pennsylvania and advanced self-government in the Lower Counties.

12. **Trace the Development of Religious Freedom** Write a paragraph describing how the Act of Toleration contributed to the development of religious freedom in colonial North America. Consider why Lord Baltimore welcomed Protestants to Maryland, why he asked the Maryland assembly to pass the Act of Toleration, what the act protected, and whom the act did not protect.

13. **Identify Economic Contributions of Women** Write a paragraph identifying the economic roles women played in colonial society. Identify the contributions of planters' wives, farmers' wives, backcountry wives, women in cities, and women in trades.

14. **Write about the Essential Question** Write an essay on the Essential Question: Why do people move? Use evidence from your study of this topic to support your answer.

Go online to PearsonRealize.com and use the texts, quizzes, interactivities, Interactive Reading Notepads, Flipped Videos, and other resources from this Topic to prepare for the Topic Test.

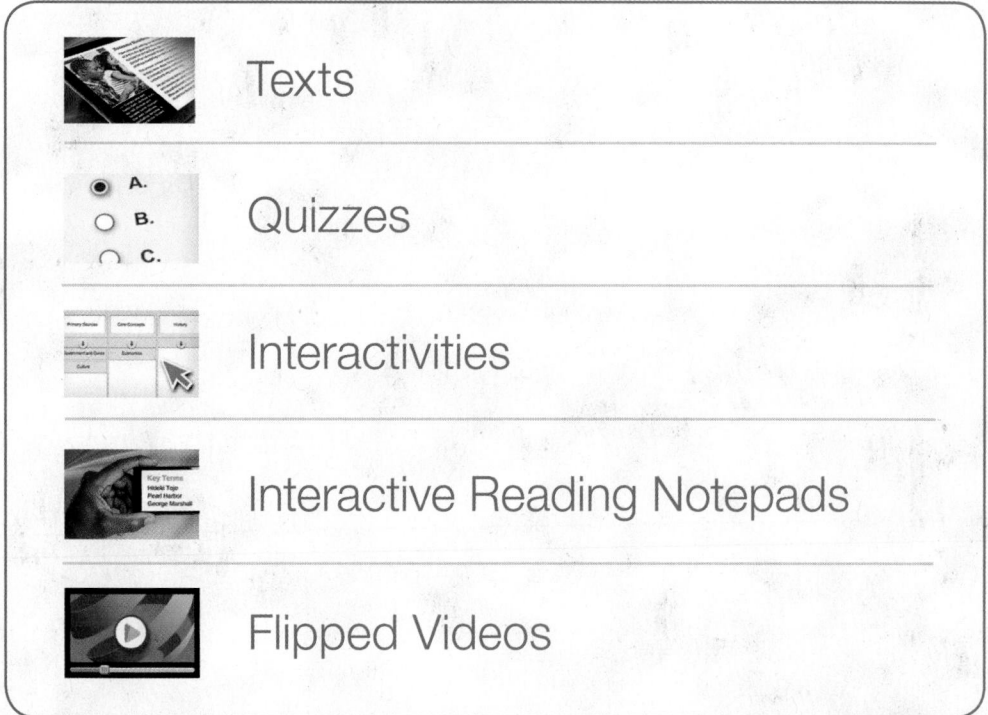

Texts

Quizzes

Interactivities

Interactive Reading Notepads

Flipped Videos

While online you can also check the progress you've made learning the topic and course content by viewing your grades, test scores, and assignment status.

3 **The Revolutionary Era (1750–1783)**

>> George Washington crossing
the Delaware River with his
troops

Enduring Understandings

- Great Britain's victory over France in the French and Indian War increased British power and territory in North America.

- Following the French and Indian War, Britain imposed taxes on the colonists without consent or representation, causing conflict.

- Conflict between the colonists and Britain eventually led to fighting in Massachusetts, uniting the colonies, and starting the American Revolution.

- The Continental Congress issued the Declaration of Independence to cut ties with Britain and form the United States of America.

- Americans gained their independence from Britain after winning an eight-year war with assistance from France.

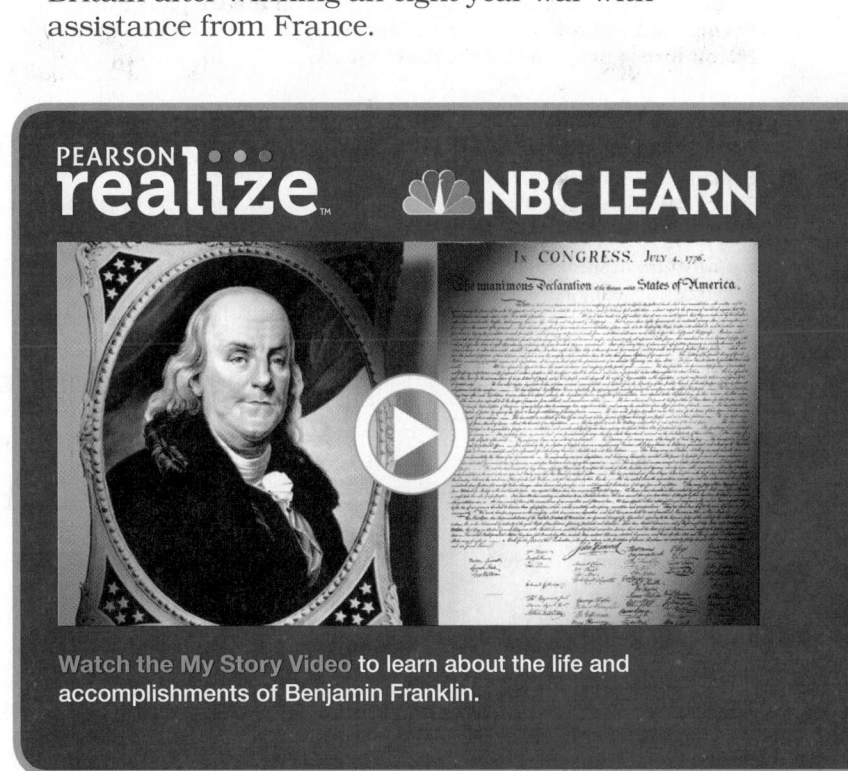

Watch the My Story Video to learn about the life and
accomplishments of Benjamin Franklin.

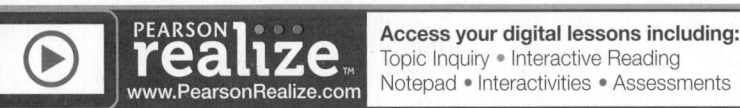

Access your digital lessons including:
Topic Inquiry • Interactive Reading
Notepad • Interactivities • Assessments

>> Both Hurons and Algonquins clashed with the Iroquois prior to the French and Indian War. In this illustration, the French and their allied Huron forces prepare to fight the Iroquois.

▶ **Interactive Flipped Video**

>> Objectives

Explain how the rivalry between Britain and France and conflict over the Ohio Valley led to the French and Indian War in North America.

Identify how mistakes and lack of unity led to British defeats early in the war.

Summarize how the tide of the war turned in Britain's favor.

Explain how the British won the war.

Describe the power shift that occurred after the war.

>> Key Terms

French and Indian
  War
Albany Plan of Union
Plains of Abraham
Treaty of Paris
George Washington

By the mid-1700s, the major powers of Europe were locked in a worldwide struggle for empire. Britain, France, Spain, and the Netherlands competed for trade and colonies in far-flung corners of the globe. The British colonies in North America soon became caught up in the contest.

Europeans Fight Over North American Land

The most serious threat came from France. It claimed a vast area that circled the English colonies from the St. Lawrence River west to the Great Lakes and south to the Gulf of Mexico. To protect their land claims, the French built an extensive system of forts. These forts blocked the British colonies from expanding to the west.

The Importance of the Ohio River Valley

At first, most settlers in the British colonies were content to remain along the Atlantic coast. By the 1740s, however, traders were crossing the Appalachian Mountains in search of furs. Pushing into the forests of the Ohio Valley, which supported an abundance of wildlife, settlers tried to take over the profitable French trade with the Indians.

France was determined to stop the British from expanding westward. The Ohio River was especially important to the French because it provided a vital link between their claims along the Great Lakes and their settlements along the Mississippi River.

Ohio Valley Native Americans Choose Allies

Native Americans had hunted animals and grown crops in the Ohio Valley for centuries. They did not want to give up the land to European settlers, French or British. One Native American protested to a British trader, "You and the French are like the two edges of a pair of shears. And we are the cloth which is to be cut to pieces between them."

Still, the growing conflict between Britain and France was too dangerous to ignore. Some Native Americans decided

North America in 1753

KEY
- Claimed by Britain
- Claimed by Spain
- Claimed by France
- ⌂ French fort

>> By 1753, the French had claimed a vast area of North America.
Analyze Maps Why were the French determined to prevent British colonies from expanding westward?

that the only way to protect their way of life was to take sides in the struggle.

The French expected the Indians to side with them. Most French in North America were trappers and traders. Generally, they did not destroy Indian hunting grounds by clearing forests for farms. Also, many French trappers married Native American women and adopted their ways. As a result, France had built strong alliances with such Native American groups as the Algonquins and the Hurons.

Many British settlers were farmers. These settlers usually ignored Indian rights by felling trees and clearing land for crops. However, an English trader and official, William Johnson, helped gain Iroquois support for Britain. The Iroquois respected Johnson. He was one of the few British settlers who had an Indian wife, Molly Brant. She was the sister of the Mohawk chief Thayendanegea, known to the British as Joseph Brant. Both Joseph and Molly Brant became valuable allies for the British. The British also won Native American allies in the Ohio Valley by charging lower prices than the French for trade goods.

In the end, Britain managed to convince the powerful Iroquois nations to join with them. The British alliance was attractive to the Iroquois because they were old enemies of the Algonquin and the Huron peoples. The war reignited old conflicts in the Ohio Valley between the Iroquois and the Algonquins and Hurons. Some tribes, like the Shawnees, Delawares, and Mingos, formed alliances to push Europeans off their lands. More often, however, the alliances Native Americans formed with the British and the French pitted tribes against each other in the fighting to come.

? IDENTIFY Which Native American groups sided with the British and which sided with the French as the war began?

The French and Indian War Begins in the Ohio Valley

Three times between 1689 and 1748, France and Great Britain fought for power in Europe and North America. Each war ended with an uneasy peace.

In 1754, fighting broke out for a fourth time. British settlers called the conflict the **French and Indian War** because it pitted them against France and its Native American allies. The French and Indian War was part of a larger war called the Seven Years' War that involved conflicts not just in North America but also in Europe and Asia. In North America, the Ohio River Valley was at the center of the

>> The Ohio Valley provided resources for settlers, such as fur-bearing animals that brought a profit from the fur trade. Both French and British fur traders competed for these resources.

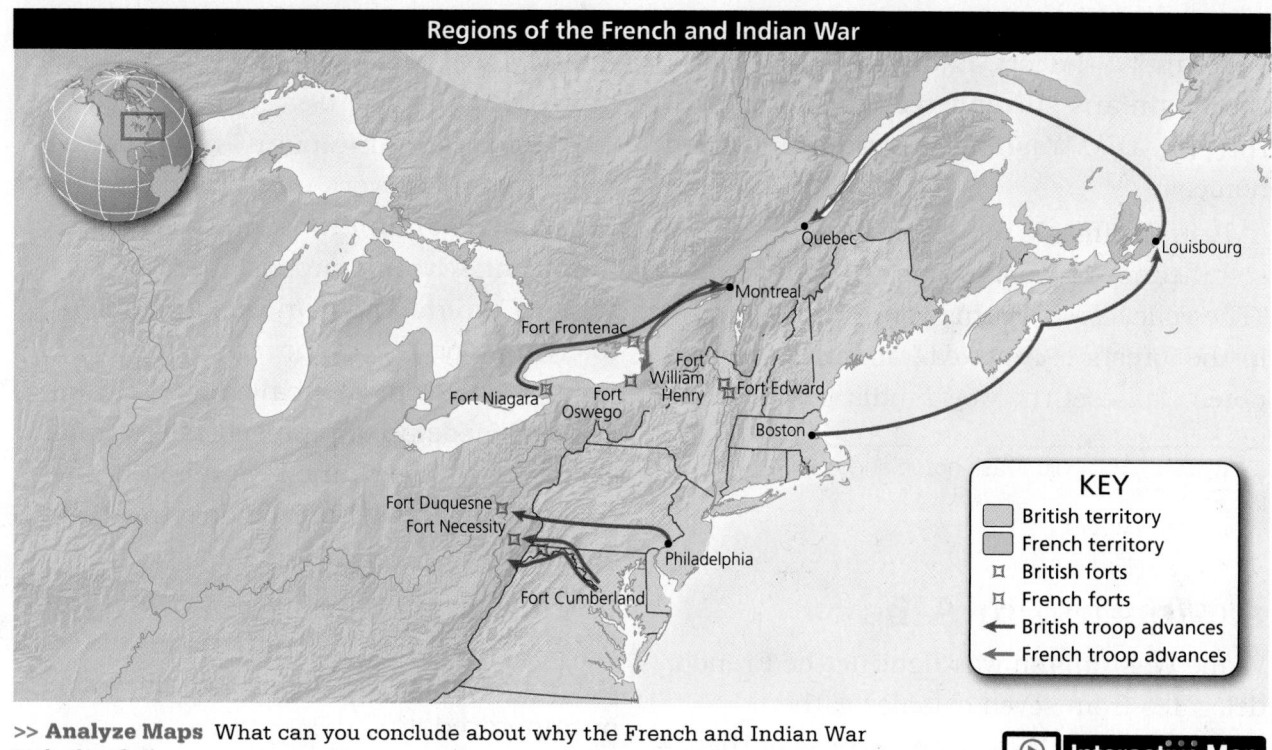

KEY
- British territory
- French territory
- ⊡ British forts
- ⊡ French forts
- ← British troop advances
- ← French troop advances

>> **Analyze Maps** What can you conclude about why the French and Indian War took place?

dispute. There, the opening shots of the war were fired by soldiers led by **George Washington**.

Washington Heads to Ohio When Washington took part in the Ohio Valley conflict he was only 22 years old. He had grown up on a plantation in Virginia, the son of wealthy parents.

Gifted at mathematics, he began working as a land surveyor at the age of 15. His job took him to frontier lands in western Virginia.

In 1753, the governor of Virginia sent Washington to deliver a letter to the French asking them to withdraw from the Ohio Valley. The French refused. After Washington returned from this mission, the governor of Virginia sent him west again. This time Washington's assignment was to build a fort where the Monongahela and Allegheny rivers meet to form the Ohio River (present-day Pittsburgh, Pennsylvania).

Washington led 150 men into the Ohio country in April 1754. Along the way, he heard that the French had just completed Fort Duquesne (doo KAYN) at the very spot where Washington hoped to build his fort.

Defeat at Fort Necessity Determined to carry out his orders, Washington hurried on. Indian allies revealed that French scouts were camped in the woods ahead. Marching quietly through the night, Washington launched a surprise attack and scattered the French. The Iroquois helped the British fight against the French, as well as the French allies, the Algonquins.

Washington's success was brief, however. Hearing that the French were about to counterattack, Washington and his men quickly built a makeshift stockade. They named it Fort Necessity.

A force of 700 French and Indians surrounded the fort. Badly outnumbered, the Virginians surrendered. The French then released Washington, and he returned home.

British officials recognized the significance of Washington's skirmish. "The volley fired by this young Virginian in the forests of America," a British writer noted, "has set the world in flames."

❓ **RECALL** Why did Washington and his men fight the French?

A Meeting in Albany

While Washington was fighting the French, delegates from seven colonies gathered in Albany, New York. One purpose of the meeting was to cement the alliance with the Iroquois, who were willing to defend the British claim to the Ohio Valley. This alliance would help the British fight the French and their Native American allies. Another goal of the meeting was to plan a united colonial defense.

The delegates in Albany knew that the colonists had to work together to defeat the French. Benjamin Franklin, the delegate from Pennsylvania, proposed the **Albany Plan of Union**. The plan was an attempt to create "one general government" for the British colonies. It called for a Grand Council made up of representatives from each colony. The council would make laws, raise taxes, and set up the defense of the colonies.

The delegates voted to accept the Plan of Union. However, when the plan was submitted to the colonial assemblies, not one approved it.

None of the colonies wanted to give up any of its powers to a central council. A disappointed Benjamin Franklin expressed his frustration at the failure of his plan:

Albany Plan of Union, 1754

Situation	Action	Plan
The British hoped to sign a treaty with the Iroquois and needed the cooperation of all colonies to enforce provisions of a Native American treaty.	Seven colonies sent representatives to an Albany Congress to consider the need for a central governing body within the colonies.	The colonies (with the exception of Georgia and Delaware) agreed to unite under a governing body that would manage Native American relations and conflicts between the colonies.

Outcome	Why It Failed
The Albany Congress adopted the plan, however individual colonial governments were unwilling to accept it.	With considerable competition among the individual colonies for power, territory, and trade, colonial governing bodies did not believe that a unified governing body would protect their interests.

>> The Albany Plan of Union proposed a single government for the 13 colonies to defeat the French. **Analyze Charts** Why would competition among the colonies keep them from supporting a central governing body?

> Everyone cries a union is necessary.
> But when they come to the manner
> and form of the union, their weak
> noodles are perfectly distracted.

—Benjamin Franklin, in a letter to Massachusetts Governor William Shirley, 1755

? IDENTIFY CENTRAL IDEAS Why did the delegates from the colonies want to form a union?

British Defeats in the Ohio Valley

In 1755, General Edward Braddock led British and colonial troops in an attack against Fort Duquesne. Braddock was a stubborn man who had little experience at fighting in the forests of North America. Still, the general boasted that he would sweep the French from the Ohio Valley.

Surprise Attacks in the Forests

Braddock's men moved slowly and noisily through the forests. Although warned of danger by Washington and by Indian scouts, Braddock pushed ahead.

As the British neared Fort Duquesne, the French and their Indian allies launched a surprise attack. Sharpshooters hid in the forest and picked off British soldiers, whose bright red uniforms made easy targets.

Braddock himself had five horses shot out from under him before he fell, fatally wounded. Almost half the British were killed or wounded. Washington, too, was nearly killed.

British Setbacks at Lake Ontario and Lake George

During the next two years, the war continued to go badly for the British. British attacks against several French forts failed. Meanwhile, the French won important victories, capturing

>> The French and their Indian allies had the advantage of familiarity with the forests of North America. General Braddock's forces were ambushed in the forests on their way to Fort Duquesne in 1755.

Fort Oswego on Lake Ontario and Fort William Henry on Lake George. (Both forts occupied land that is now part of New York state.) All these defeats put a serious strain on the alliances with the Iroquois who had been counting on the British to protect them from the French. The Iroquois faced increasing danger from enemy tribes, who fought them for prisoners and goods.

? IDENTIFY SUPPORTING DETAILS Why were French attacks in the forests successful?

Quebec and New France Fall

In 1757, William Pitt became prime minister, meaning he was the new head of the British government. Pitt made it his first job to win the war in North America. Once that goal was achieved, he argued, the British would be free to focus on victory in other parts of the world. So Pitt sent Britain's best generals to North America. To encourage the colonists to support the war, he promised large payments for military services and supplies.

Under Pitt's leadership, the tide of battle turned. In 1758, Major General Jeffrey Amherst captured Louisbourg, the most important fort in French Canada. That year, the British also seized Fort Duquesne, which they renamed Fort Pitt after the British leader. The city of Pittsburgh later grew up on the site of Fort Pitt.

The War Turns in Favor of the British

The British enjoyed even greater success in 1759. By summer, they had pushed the French from Fort Niagara, Crown Point,

and Fort Ticonderoga (ty kahn duh ROH guh). Next, Pitt sent General James Wolfe to take Quebec, capital of New France.

Climbing Cliffs to Attack Quebec

Quebec was vital to the defense of New France. Without Quebec, the French could not supply their forts farther up the St. Lawrence River. Quebec was well defended, though. The city sat on the edge of the **Plains of Abraham**, on top of a steep cliff high above the St. Lawrence. An able French general, the Marquis de Montcalm, was prepared to fight off any British attack.

General Wolfe devised a bold plan to capture Quebec. He knew that Montcalm had only a few soldiers guarding the cliff because the French thought that it was too steep to climb. Late at night, Wolfe ordered British troops to row quietly in small boats to the foot of the cliff. In the dark, the soldiers swarmed ashore, climbed up the cliff, and assembled at the top.

The next morning, Montcalm awakened to a surprise. A force of 4,000 British troops was drawn up and ready for battle on the Plains of Abraham.

Quickly, Montcalm marched his own troops out to join in battle. By the time the fierce fighting was over, both Montcalm and Wolfe lay dead. Moments before Wolfe died, a soldier gave him the news that the British had won. Wolfe is said to have whispered, "Now, God be praised, I will die in peace." On September 18, 1759, Quebec surrendered to the British.

British Make Huge Gains The fall of Quebec sealed the fate of New France, though fighting dragged on in Europe for several more years. Finally, in 1763, Britain and France signed the **Treaty of Paris**, bringing the long conflict to an end.

>> After sneaking up a steep cliff under the cover of darkness, the British defeated the French on the Plains of Abraham the next morning and captured the capital city of Quebec.

KEY
- Claimed by Britain
- Claimed by Spain
- Claimed by France
- Claimed by Russia
- 13 Colonies
- Territory boundary from the Proclamation of 1763

>> How did the balance of European power in North America change between 1753 and 1763? What role did Spain play in the war, and what effect did the Treaty of Paris have on New Spain?

▶ **Interactive Chart**

The Treaty of Paris marked the end of French power in North America. By its terms, Britain gained Canada and all French lands east of the Mississippi River except New Orleans. France was allowed to keep only two islands in the Gulf of St. Lawrence and its prosperous sugar-growing islands in the West Indies. Spain, which had entered the war on the French side in 1762, gave up Florida to Britain.

In return, Spain received all French land west of the Mississippi. In addition, Spain gained the vital port city of New Orleans. Spain retained control of its vast empire in Central America and South America.

After years of fighting, peace returned to North America. Yet, in a few short years, a new conflict would break out. This time, the struggle would pit Britain against its own 13 colonies.

❓ IDENTIFY SUPPORTING DETAILS How did Pitt persuade more colonists to support the war?

ASSESSMENT

1. **Interpret** Why did the Iroquois choose to side with the British?

2. **Make Predictions** about George Washington as a military leader based on what he did in the Ohio River Valley in 1754.

3. **Identify Central Issues** What choices did General Braddock make that endangered himself and his men?

4. **Draw Conclusions** Based on the text, how much of a priority do you think the French and Indian War was to Britain before William Pitt became head of the British government?

5. **Summarize** what the British gained in North America by defeating the French and signing the Treaty of Paris.

Tensions with Britain

>> Using a writ of assistance as legal authorization, British soldiers search a colonist's home for smuggled goods. Colonists claimed that writs of assistance violated their rights as British citizens.

Interactive Flipped Video

>> Objectives

Describe conflicts in the west after the French and Indian War.

Explain how Britain attempted to ease tensions with the Proclamation of 1763.

Explain why colonists opposed new British taxes such as the Stamp Act.

Describe new colonial leaders who emerged as conflicts with Britain escalated.

Summarize the significance of the Boston Massacre.

>> Key Terms

Pontiac's War
Proclamation of 1763
Stamp Act
petition
boycott
repeal
Townshend Acts
writ of assistance
Boston Massacre
committee of
    correspondence
Abigail Adams
Samuel Adams

Mercy Otis Warren
Crispus Attucks
Patrick Henry
John Adams
King George III
free-enterprise
    system

By 1760, the British and their Indian allies had driven France from the Ohio Valley. Their troubles in the region were not over, however. For many years, fur traders had sent back glowing reports of the land beyond the Appalachian Mountains. The dense forests of the Ohio Valley offered new resources that were in short supply in the East, and with the French gone, British colonists wanted to head west to claim the lands for themselves.

Conflict Over Land

Conflicts in the Ohio Valley Many Native American nations lived in the Ohio Valley. They included the Senecas, Delawares, Shawnees, Ottawas, Miamis, and Hurons. As British settlers moved into the valley, they often clashed with these Native Americans.

In 1760, the British made Lord Jeffrey Amherst military commander and governor general of its North American colonies. The British sent Amherst to the frontier to keep order. French traders had always treated Native Americans as friends, holding feasts for them and giving them presents. Amherst refused to do this. Instead, he raised the price of goods traded to Indians. Also, unlike the French, Amherst allowed settlers to build farms and forts on Indian lands.

Angry Native Americans found a leader in Pontiac, an Ottawa chief who had fought on the French side during the French and Indian War. An English trader remarked that Pontiac "commands more respect amongst these nations than any Indian I ever saw." In April 1763, Pontiac spoke out against the British, calling them "dogs dressed in red, who have come to rob [us] of [our] hunting grounds and drive away the game." Pontiac led violent raids against British forts. Hundreds of British were tortured and killed, leading some officials to fear for the safety of colonists near Native American land.

The British Secure the Frontier Later that year, Pontiac led an attack on British troops at Fort Detroit. A number of other Indian nations joined him. In a few short months, they captured most British forts in the Ohio country. British and colonial troops then struck back and regained much of what they had lost.

>> In April 1763, Chief Pontiac of the Ottawa addressed a gathering of Native Americans to rally them against the British. Soon after, Pontiac led an attack on British troops at Fort Detroit.

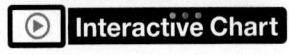

Pontiac's War, as it came to be called, did not last long. In October 1763, the French told Pontiac that they had signed the Treaty of Paris. Because the treaty marked the end of French power in North America, the Indians could no longer hope for French aid against the British. One by one, the Indian nations stopped fighting and returned home.

? **IDENTIFY SUPPORTING DETAILS** What arguments did Pontiac have against the British?

The Proclamation of 1763 Creates Tensions

Pontiac's violent raids against British troops convinced officials that they should prevent British subjects from settling beyond the western frontier for their own safety. To do this, the government issued the **Proclamation**

of 1763. The proclamation drew an imaginary line along the crest of the Appalachian Mountains. Colonists were forbidden to settle west of the line. All settlers already west of the line were "to remove themselves" at once.

The Purposes of the Proclamation

The proclamation was meant to protect Indians in the western lands. To enforce it, Britain sent 10,000 troops to the colonies. Few troops went to the frontier, however. Most stayed in cities along the Atlantic coast.

The proclamation also created four new places where colonists could settle. French Canada became part of the province of Quebec. Florida, once a Spanish colony, was divided into East and West Florida. British territories in the Caribbean became the province of Granada.

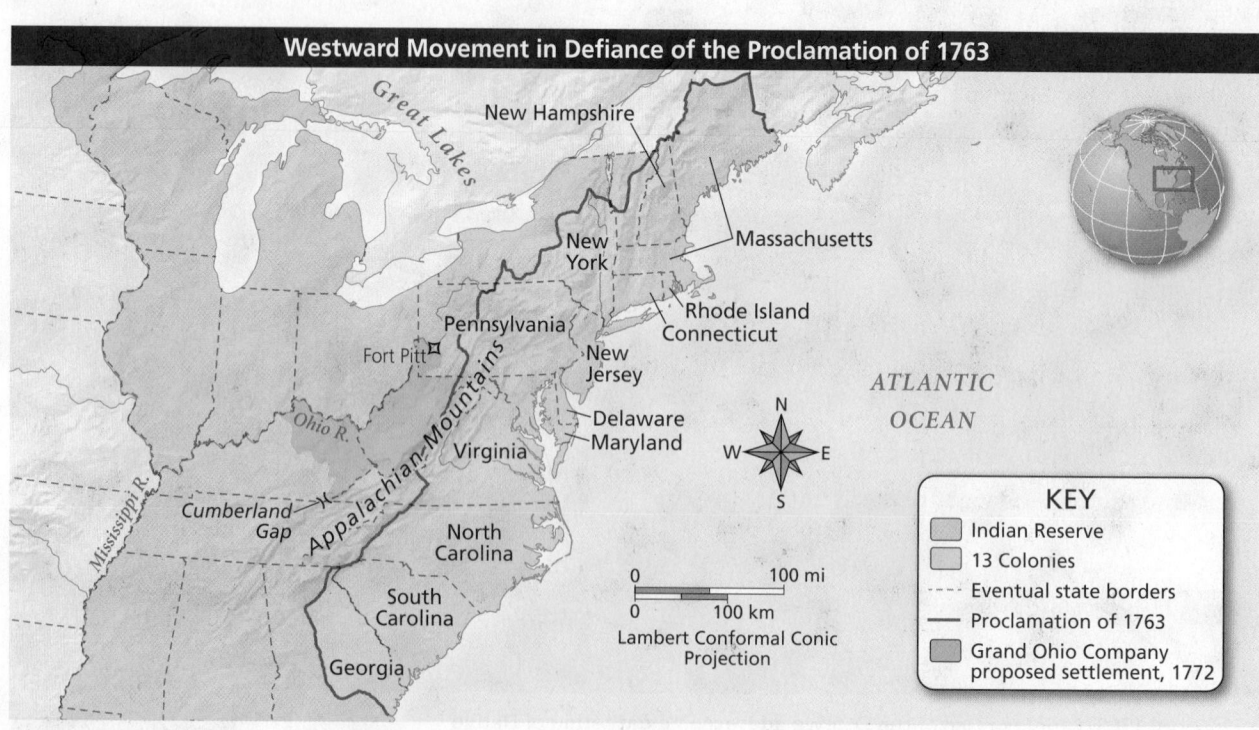

>> The Proclamation of 1763 prohibited colonial settlement west of the red line shown on the map.

Colonists Disagree with the Proclamation The proclamation angered many colonists. They thought it was unnecessary and unjust. They did not think the British government had the power to restrict state settlements. Nor were they concerned with the rights of Native Americans. After winning the French and Indian War, many colonists felt they had rights to the land.

Also, colonists now had to pay for the additional British troops that had been sent to enforce the proclamation. In the end, many settlers simply ignored the proclamation and moved west anyway. The proclamation remained most controversial in the west, where colonists clashed with Native Americans. Some colonies, including New York, Pennsylvania, and Virginia, claimed lands in the west. The Proclamation would continue to cause problems up to the American Revolution from the tension it caused between the colonists and Britain.

One colonist who defied the Proclamation of 1763 was Daniel Boone. In 1767, Boone visited Kentucky, west of the Appalachians. In 1769, he began what became a two-year journey of exploration through Kentucky. He traveled as far as the Falls of the Ohio, the site of the present-day city of Louisville. Later, he led settlers through the Cumberland Gap along an old Indian path. During his travels, Boone fought a number of battles against the Indians and was taken captive for a short period.

? CHECK UNDERSTANDING What was the reasoning behind the Proclamation of 1763?

>> British Prime Minister George Grenville wanted colonists to help share the burden of debt that Britain had incurred from the Seven Years' War.

Mercantilism and Taxation Cause Resentment

The Seven Years' War, which included the French and Indian War, plunged Britain deeply into debt. As a result, the taxes paid by citizens in Britain rose sharply. The British prime minister, George Grenville, decided that colonists in North America should help share the burden. In a mercantilist system, colonies were expected to serve the colonial power. Grenville reasoned that the colonists would not oppose small tax increases. The colonists, however, strongly resented these taxes. They argued that mercantilism was unfair because it limited trade and made goods more expensive. Many colonists also objected that the power to raise these new taxes was not granted by the English constitution. Grenville's policy led to the political and economic conflicts that would divide the colonies and England.

The Sugar Act Taxes the Colonies

In 1764, Grenville asked Parliament to approve the Sugar Act, which put a new tax on molasses. The Sugar Act replaced an earlier tax, which had been so high that any merchant who paid it would have been driven out of business. As a result, most colonial merchants simply avoided the tax by smuggling molasses into the colonies. Often, they bribed tax collectors to look the other way.

The Sugar Act of 1764 lowered the tax. At the same time, the law made it easier for British officials to bring colonial smugglers to trial. Grenville made it clear that he expected the new tax to be paid.

❓ IDENTIFY What arguments did the colonists have against more British taxes?

>> Though tarring and feathering was practiced in Britain as a form of punishment, tax collectors escaped this fate in the colonies. However, colonists imagined punishing tax collectors in this way as a protest of the Stamp Act.

The Stamp Act Provokes Resistance

Grenville also persuaded Parliament to pass the **Stamp Act** of 1765. The act placed new duties (taxes) on legal documents such as wills, diplomas, and marriage papers. It also taxed newspapers, almanacs, playing cards, and even dice.

All items named in the law had to carry a stamp showing that the tax had been paid. Stamp taxes were used in Britain and other countries to raise money. However, Britain had never required American colonists to pay such a tax.

Resistance to the Stamp Act When British officials tried to enforce the Stamp Act, they met with stormy protests from colonists. Lieutenant Governor Hutchinson's house in Massachusetts was looted by a mob. He was not the only official to feel the mob's anger. Some colonists threw rocks at agents trying to collect the unpopular tax.

In addition to riots in Boston, other disturbances broke out in New York City, Newport, and Charleston. In New York City, rioters destroyed the home of a British official who had said he would "cram the stamps down American throats" at the point of his sword.

The fury of the colonists shocked the British. After all, Britain had spent a great deal of money to protect the colonies against the French. The British at home were paying much higher taxes than the colonists. Why, British officials asked, were colonists so angry about the Stamp Act? As one English letter-writer commented,

Our Colonies must be the biggest Beggars in the World, if such small

>> Rioters in Boston protest against the Stamp Act. **Infer** What does the sign being carried through the street imply about the impact the Stamp Act might have on the colonies' relationship with Britain?

Duties appear to be intolerable Burdens in their Eyes.

—"Pacificus," *Maryland Gazette*, March 20, 1766

Lack of Representation in Parliament

Colonists replied that the Stamp Act taxes were unjust and unnecessary. "No taxation without representation!" they cried. That principle was rooted in English traditions dating back to the Magna Carta.

Colonists insisted that only they or their elected representatives had the right to pass taxes. Since the colonists did not elect representatives to Parliament, Parliament had no right to tax them. The colonists were willing to pay taxes—but only if the taxes were passed by their own colonial legislatures. They also felt that mercantilist policies like the Navigation Acts were unfair because they restricted their trade, which negatively affected colonists' income.

Peaceful Protests Lead Toward Revolution

The Stamp Act crisis united colonists from New Hampshire to Georgia. Critics of the law called for delegates from every colony to meet in New York City. There, a congress would form to consider actions against the hated Stamp Act.

In October 1765, nine colonies sent delegates to what became known as the Stamp Act Congress. The delegates drew up petitions to **King George III** and to Parliament. A **petition** is a formal written request to someone in authority, signed by a group of people. In these petitions, the delegates rejected the Stamp Act and asserted that Parliament had no right to tax the colonies. Parliament paid little attention.

The colonists took other steps to change the law. They joined together to boycott British goods. To **boycott** means to refuse to buy certain goods and services. The

>> British officials held a "funeral" for the Stamp Act, which Parliament repealed in 1766. **Analyze Political Cartoons** What does this cartoon say about the artist's opinion of the Stamp Act?

The Townshend Acts Spark Rebellion

In May 1767, Parliament reopened the debate over taxing the colonies. In a fierce exchange, George Grenville, now a member of Parliament, clashed with Charles Townshend, the official in charge of the British treasury.

"You are cowards, you are afraid of the Americans, you dare not tax America!" Grenville shouted.

"Fear? Cowards?" Townshend snapped back. "I dare tax America!"

The next month, Parliament passed the **Townshend Acts**, which taxed goods such as glass, paper, paint, lead, and tea. The taxes were low, but colonists still objected. The principle was the same: Parliament did not have the right to tax them without their consent.

Searches Without Reason Cause Unrest The Townshend Acts also set up new ways to collect taxes. Customs officials were sent to American ports with orders to stop smuggling. Using legal documents known as **writs of assistance**, the officers would be allowed to inspect a ship's cargo without giving a reason.

Colonists protested that the writs of assistance violated their rights as British citizens. Under British law, a government official could not search a person's property without a good reason for suspecting that the person had committed a crime. Yet the writs of assistance allowed persons and their property to be searched and even seized without reason in the colonies. Colonists angrily cited the words of James Otis of Massachusetts. Arguing against a British

boycott of British goods took its toll. Trade fell off by 14 percent. British merchants complained that they were facing ruin. So, too, did British workers who made goods for the colonies.

The colonists wanted the government to have less of a say over businesses and trade. They wanted a **free-enterprise system,** in which the market, rather than the government, determines what goods and services cost. British taxes, the colonists argued, unfairly restricted economic growth.

Finally, in 1766, Parliament **repealed**, or canceled, the Stamp Act. At the same time, however, it passed a law asserting that Parliament had the right to raise taxes in "all cases whatsoever."

? TRACE What events led to the repeal of the Stamp Act in 1766?

attempt to impose writs of assistance six years earlier, he had said:

> Now, one of the most essential branches of English liberty is the freedom of one's house. A man's house is his castle; and while he is quiet, he is as well guarded as a prince in his castle. This writ, if it should be declared legal, would totally destroy this privilege. Customhouse officers may enter our houses when they please . . . break locks, bars, and everything in their way. . . .
>
> —James Otis, February 24, 1761

Colonists Rebel Against British Economic Policies Colonists responded swiftly and strongly to the Townshend Acts. From north to south, colonial merchants and planters signed agreements promising to stop importing goods taxed by the Townshend Acts. The colonists hoped that the new boycott would win repeal of the Townshend Acts.

To protest British policies, some angry colonists formed the Sons of Liberty. From Boston to Charleston, Sons of Liberty staged mock hangings of cloth or straw effigies, or likenesses, dressed as British officials. The hangings were meant to show tax collectors what might happen to them if they tried to collect the unpopular taxes.

Some women joined the Daughters of Liberty. They paraded, signed petitions, and organized a boycott of fine British cloth. They urged colonial women to raise more sheep, prepare more wool, and spin and weave their own cloth. A slogan of the Daughters of Liberty declared, "It is better to wear a Homespun coat than to lose our Liberty."

Some Sons and Daughters of Liberty also used other methods to support their cause. They visited merchants and urged them to boycott British imports. A few even threatened people who continued to buy British goods.

? **DESCRIBE** How did many colonists respond to the Townshend Acts?

Colonists Provide Leadership in the Struggle With Britain

As the struggle over taxes continued, new leaders emerged in all the colonies. Men and women in New England and Virginia were especially active in the colonial cause.

Massachusetts Citizens Fight for Their Beliefs **Samuel Adams** of Boston stood firmly against Britain. Sam Adams seemed an unlikely leader. He was a failure in business and a poor public speaker. Often,

>> The Townshend Acts are named after Charles Townshend, the British statesman who passed measures through Parliament to tax colonists for goods such as glass, paper, paint, and tea.

he wore a red suit and a cheap gray wig for which people poked fun at him. Still, Adams loved politics. He always attended Boston town meetings and Sons of Liberty rallies. Adams's real talent was organizing people. He worked behind the scenes, arranging protests and stirring public support.

Sam's cousin John was another important Massachusetts leader. **John Adams** had been a schoolteacher before becoming a skilled lawyer. Adams longed for fame and could often be difficult. Still, he was more cautious than his cousin Sam. He weighed evidence carefully before taking any actions. His knowledge of British law earned him much respect.

Mercy Otis Warren also aided the colonial cause. Warren wrote plays that made fun of British officials. The plays were published in newspapers and widely read in the colonies. Warren formed a close friendship with **Abigail Adams**, the wife of John Adams. The two women used their pens to spur the colonists to action. They also called for greater rights for women in the colonies.

Virginians Join the Cause Virginia contributed many leaders to the struggle against taxes. In the House of Burgesses, George Washington joined other Virginians to protest the Townshend Acts.

A young lawyer, **Patrick Henry**, became well known as a vocal critic of British policies. His speeches in the House of Burgesses moved listeners to both tears and anger. Once, Henry attacked Britain with such fury that some listeners cried out, "Treason!" Henry boldly replied, "If this be treason, make the most of it!" Henry's words moved a young listener, Thomas Jefferson. At the time, Jefferson was a 22-year-old law student.

? **IDENTIFY** How did some colonists show leadership?

The Boston Massacre

Port cities such as Boston and New York were centers of protest. In New York, a dispute arose over the Quartering Act. Under that law, colonists had to provide housing, candles, bedding, and beverages to soldiers stationed in the colonies. The colonists did not want to house the soldiers. Many, including Sam Adams, did not think the soldiers should be stationed in the colonies at all during peacetime. When the New York assembly refused to obey the Quartering Act, Britain dismissed the assembly in 1767.

Britain also sent two regiments to Boston to protect customs officers from local citizens. To many Bostonians, the

>> Mercy Otis Warren's popular plays making fun of British officials motivated colonists to take action against Britain.

▶ **Interactive Gallery**

soldiers were a daily reminder that Britain was trying to bully them into paying unjust taxes. When British soldiers walked along the streets of Boston, they risked insults or even beatings. A serious clash was not long in coming.

A Crowd Challenges British Soldiers

On the night of March 5, 1770, a crowd gathered outside the Boston customs house. Colonists shouted insults at the "lobsterbacks," as they called the red-coated British who guarded the building. Then the Boston crowd began to throw snowballs, oyster shells, and chunks of ice at the soldiers.

The crowd grew larger and rowdier. Suddenly, the soldiers panicked. They fired into the crowd. When the smoke from the musket volley cleared, five people lay dead or dying. Among the first to die were Samuel Maverick, a 17-year-old white youth, and **Crispus Attucks**, a free black sailor.

Colonists were quick to protest the incident, which they called the **Boston Massacre**. A Boston silversmith named Paul Revere fanned anti-British feeling with an engraving that showed British soldiers firing on unarmed colonists. Sam Adams wrote letters to other colonists to build outrage about the shooting.

The soldiers were arrested and tried in court. John Adams agreed to defend them, saying that they deserved a fair trial. He wanted to show the world that the colonists believed in justice, even if the British government did not. At the trial, Adams argued that the crowd had provoked the soldiers. His arguments convinced the jury. In the end, the heaviest punishment any soldier received was a branding on the hand.

>> This engraving of the Boston Massacre by Paul Revere helped spread anti-British feeling among colonists.

Samuel Adams later expanded on the idea of a letter-writing campaign by forming a **committee of correspondence**. Members of the committee regularly wrote letters and pamphlets reporting to other colonies on events in Massachusetts. Within three months, there were 80 committees organized in Massachusetts. Before long, committees of correspondence became a major tool of protest in every colony.

The King Repeals Most Colonial Taxes

By chance, on the very day of the Boston Massacre, a bill was introduced into Parliament to repeal most of the Townshend Acts. British merchants, harmed by the American boycott of British goods, had again pressured Parliament to end the taxes. The Quartering Act was repealed and most of the taxes that had angered the Americans were ended. However, King George III asked Parliament

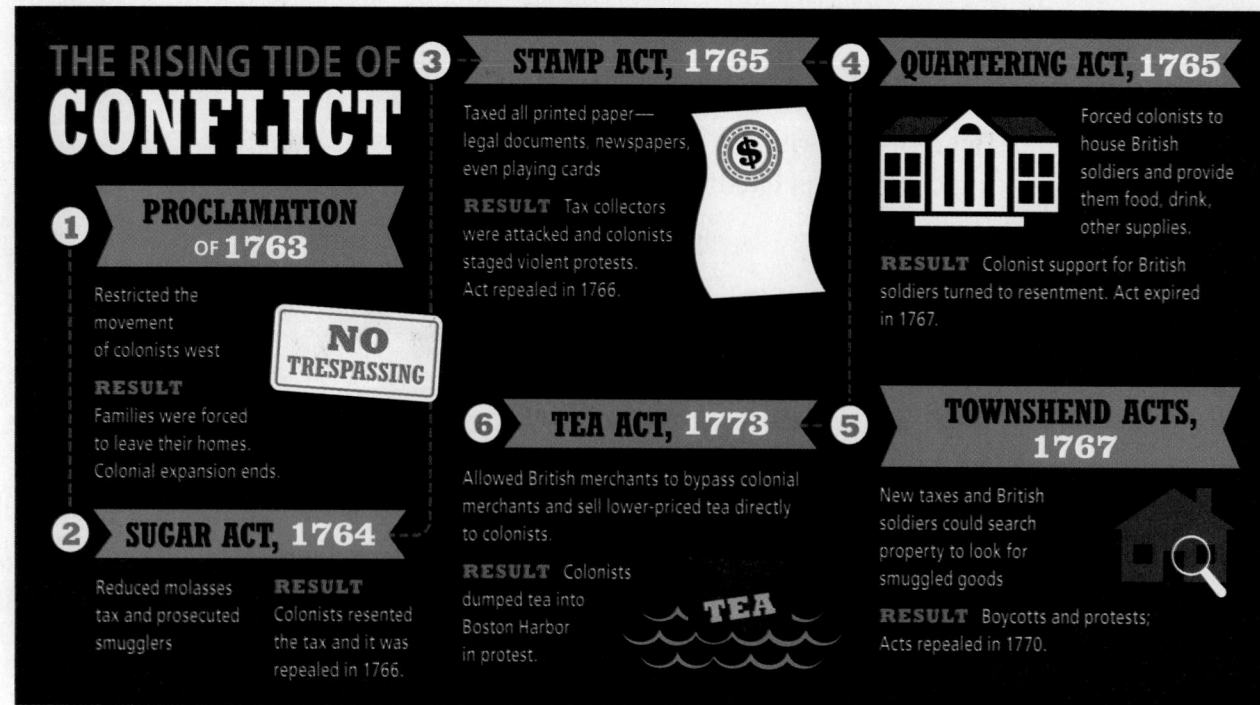

THE RISING TIDE OF CONFLICT

1 PROCLAMATION OF 1763

Restricted the movement of colonists west

RESULT Families were forced to leave their homes. Colonial expansion ends.

NO TRESPASSING

2 SUGAR ACT, 1764

Reduced molasses tax and prosecuted smugglers

RESULT Colonists resented the tax and it was repealed in 1766.

3 STAMP ACT, 1765

Taxed all printed paper—legal documents, newspapers, even playing cards

RESULT Tax collectors were attacked and colonists staged violent protests. Act repealed in 1766.

6 TEA ACT, 1773

Allowed British merchants to bypass colonial merchants and sell lower-priced tea directly to colonists.

RESULT Colonists dumped tea into Boston Harbor in protest.

TEA

4 QUARTERING ACT, 1765

Forced colonists to house British soldiers and provide them food, drink, other supplies.

RESULT Colonist support for British soldiers turned to resentment. Act expired in 1767.

5 TOWNSHEND ACTS, 1767

New taxes and British soldiers could search property to look for smuggled goods

RESULT Boycotts and protests; Acts repealed in 1770.

>> **Analyze Charts** In what way does the chart show a "rising tide" that would eventually lead to a conflict?

to retain the tax on tea. "There must always be one tax to keep up the right [to tax]," he argued. Parliament agreed.

News of the repeal delighted the colonists. Most people dismissed the remaining tax on tea as unimportant and ended their boycott of British goods. For a few years, calm returned. Yet the basic issue—Britain's power to tax the colonies—remained unsettled. The debate over taxes had forced the colonists to begin thinking more carefully about their political rights.

? CHECK UNDERSTANDING Why did John Adams choose to defend the British soldiers?

ASSESSMENT

1. **Contrast** the way the French had treated Native Americans in the Ohio Valley with the way the British did under Jeffrey Amherst.

2. **Cite Evidence** that shows Daniel Boone ignored the Proclamation of 1763.

3. **Identify Central Issues** What details about the colonial response to the Stamp Act tell you that it was a cause of the American Revolution?

4. **Infer** Based on James Otis's response to British writs of assistance, what concerns did the colonists have about British searches?

5. **Interpret** How did the Boston Massacre influence the colonists' feelings towards Britain?

Taking Up Arms

>> Eight colonists were killed in the skirmish between the minutemen and British soldiers at Lexington, Massachusetts, in 1775.

▶ **Interactive Flipped Video**

The calm between the colonies and England did not last long. Economic and political disputes continued, this time over a simple drink. Tea was tremendously popular in the colonies. By 1770, at least one million Americans brewed tea twice a day. People "would rather go without their dinners than without a dish of tea," a visitor to the colonies noted.

>> **Objectives**

Explain how a dispute over tea led to further tension between the colonists and Great Britain.

Describe ways that the British Parliament punished the colonists for the Boston Tea Party.

Explain how fighting broke out in Massachusetts, including battles in Lexington and Concord and Bunker Hill.

Explain actions the First and Second Continental Congress enacted to address the crisis with Britain.

>> **Key Terms**

Olive Branch Petition
Green Mountain
  Boys
Continental Army
Patriot
Loyalist
Battle of Bunker Hill
blockade
mercenary
Tea Act
Thomas Jefferson
Boston Tea Party
civil disobedience

Intolerable Acts
Quebec Act
First Continental
  Congress
militia
minutemen
Battles of Lexington
  and Concord

▶ **PEARSON realize**™ www.PearsonRealize.com
Access your Digital Lesson.

The Boston Tea Party

Mercantilist Policies Lead to the Tea Act Since the 1720s, Parliament had given the British East India Company exclusive rights to sell tea to the American colonies. Parliament protected this by mandating that tea sold to the colonies had to be shipped to England first so taxes could be paid. Then the tea was shipped to colonial tea merchants for sale in the American colonies.

This system met resistance due to the taxation of tea in the American colonies. Remember, to maintain its authority over the colonies, Parliament had kept a tax on tea when repealing the Townshend Acts. The tax was a small one, but colonists resented it. As a result, many colonists refused to buy British tea. Also, the colonists were able to get cheaper tea directly from Dutch and French traders who smuggled it to American merchants.

In the 1770s, the British East India Company found itself in deep financial trouble, due in part to dwindling tea sales in the American colonies. As a result, more than 15 million pounds of tea sat unsold in British warehouses.

Parliament tried to help the British East India Company by passing the **Tea Act** of 1773. The act let the company bypass colonial tea merchants and sell directly to colonists.

The Tea Act also gave the British East India Company a rebate on tea taxes. Although colonists would still have to pay the tea tax, they would not have to pay the higher price charged by colonial tea merchants. As a result, the tea itself would cost less than ever before. Parliament hoped this would encourage Americans to buy more British tea.

To the surprise of Parliament, colonists protested the Tea Act. Many colonists were opposed to British mercantilist policies that were supposed to generate wealth for England by taxing the colonies. However, American tea merchants were especially angry because they had been cut out of the tea trade. They believed that allowing the government-sponsored British East India Company to sell tea to Americans violated their right to conduct free enterprise.

Even tea drinkers, who would have benefited from the law, scorned the Tea Act. They believed that it was a British trick to make them accept Parliament's right to tax the colonies.

A Boycott Against Tea Once again, colonists responded to the new law with a boycott. A Philadelphia poet, Hannah Griffitts, urged American women to:

>> Many colonists were quite fond of tea. They opposed the Tea Act of 1773 because they did not believe the British had the right to tax them.

Stand firmly resolved and bid Grenville to see That rather than freedom we part with our tea, And well as we love the dear drink when a-dry, As American patriots our taste we deny.

—Hannah Griffitts in Milcah Martha Moore's *Commonplace Book*, 1773

Daughters of Liberty and women like Griffitts led the boycott. They served coffee or made "liberty tea" from raspberry leaves. At some ports, Sons of Liberty enforced the boycott by keeping the British East India Company from unloading cargoes of tea.

An Act of Civil Disobedience Three ships loaded with tea reached Boston Harbor in late November 1773. The colonial governor of Massachusetts, Thomas Hutchinson, insisted that they unload their cargo as usual.

Sam Adams and the Sons of Liberty had other plans. On the night of December 16, they met in Old South Meeting House. They sent a message to the governor, demanding that the ships leave the harbor. When the governor rejected the demand, Adams stood up and declared, "This meeting can do nothing further to save the country."

Adams's words seemed to be a signal. As if on cue, a group of men in Indian disguises burst into the meetinghouse. From the gallery above, voices cried, "Boston harbor a teapot tonight! The Mohawks are come!"

The disguised colonists left the meetinghouse and headed for the harbor. Others joined them along the way. Under a nearly full moon, the men boarded the ships, split open the tea chests, and dumped the tea into the harbor.

By 10 P.M., the **Boston Tea Party**, as it was later called, was over. The contents of

>> On December 16, 1773, a group of colonists emptied hundreds of tea chests into Boston Harbor to protest British taxation. **Infer** Why might this act of civil disobedience mark a turning point?

342 chests of tea floated in Boston Harbor. The next day, John Adams wrote about the event in his diary.

This destruction of the tea is so bold, so daring, so firm . . . it must have such important and lasting results that I can't help considering it a turning point in history.

—Diary of John Adams, December 17, 1773

The Boston Tea Party was an important act of **civil disobedience**. Civil disobedience is the non-violent refusal to obey laws that one considers unjust. The colonists had many reasons for this act of civil disobedience. They wanted to voice their discontent to the British without hurting anyone. They also wanted to stop the tea from entering Boston. The impact of their civil disobedience was perhaps greater than they had expected. Harsh punishment would come from Britain.

? IDENTIFY Why were many colonists dissatisfied with the Tea Act?

King George III Strikes Back at Boston

Colonists had mixed reactions to the Boston Tea Party. Some cheered it as a firm protest against unfair British laws. Others worried that it would encourage lawlessness in the colonies. Even those who condemned the Boston Tea Party, though, were shocked at Britain's harsh response to it. The unrest in Boston and the British reaction to the Tea Party would be yet another cause of the Revolution.

The Intolerable Acts Anger Massachusetts The British were outraged by what they saw as Boston's lawless behavior. In 1774, Parliament, encouraged by King George III, acted to punish Massachusetts.

Colonists called the four laws they passed the **Intolerable Acts** because they were so harsh. These Acts pushed the colonists closer to revolution.

First, Parliament shut down the port of Boston. No ship could enter or leave the harbor—not even a small boat. The harbor would remain closed until the colonists paid for the tea they had destroyed in the Boston Tea Party and repaid British officials, such as Thomas Hutchinson, for damage to personal property. Boston's harbor was central to the life of the city. With the closing of the port, merchants could not sell their goods and the colony's economy suffered.

Second, Parliament forbade Massachusetts colonists to hold town meetings more than once a year without

>> Following the Boston Tea Party, British warships closed the port of Boston. Parliament demanded that colonists repay the damages from the loss of tea before they would reopen the port.

Results of the Quebec Act

TERRITORIES GRANTED TO QUEBEC BY THE QUEBEC ACT
The area south of the Great Lakes, from the Appalachians to the Mississippi, which included:

southern Ontario	part of Minnesota
Illinois	Labrador
Indiana	Ile d'Anticosti
Michigan	Iles de la Madeleine
Ohio	Indian Reserve
Wisconsin	

>> All of these territories were awarded to Quebec as part of the Quebec Act.

the governor's permission. In the past, colonists had called town meetings whenever they wished. Public officials would now be selected by the king's governor rather than be elected by citizens.

Third, Parliament allowed customs officers and other officials who might be charged with major crimes to be tried in Britain or Canada instead of in Massachusetts. Colonists protested. They argued that a dishonest official could break the law in the colonies and avoid punishment by being tried before a sympathetic jury.

Fourth, Parliament passed a new Quartering Act. No longer would redcoats camp in tents on Boston Common. Instead, colonists would have to house British soldiers in their homes when no other housing was available. Colonists viewed this act as yet another tax, because they had to house and feed the soldiers. Many objected to having the British army stationed in the colonies at all.

The Quebec Act Redraws North American Borders About the same time, Parliament also passed the **Quebec Act**. It set up a government for Canada and gave complete religious freedom to French Catholics. The Quebec Act also extended the borders of Quebec to include the land between the Ohio and Missouri rivers. The act pleased French Canadians. The American colonists were angry, however, because some of the colonies claimed ownership of these lands.

The Intolerable Acts Draw Other Colonies into the Struggle The committees of correspondence spread news of the Intolerable Acts to other colonies. They warned that the people of Boston faced hunger while their port was closed. People from other colonies responded quickly. Carts rolled into the city with rice from South Carolina, corn from Virginia, and flour from Pennsylvania.

In the Virginia assembly, **Thomas Jefferson** suggested that a day be set aside to mark the shame of the Intolerable Acts. The royal governor of Virginia rejected the idea. The colonists went ahead anyway. On June 1, 1774, church bells tolled slowly.

Merchants closed their shops. Many colonists prayed and fasted all day.

In September 1774, colonial leaders called a meeting in Philadelphia. Delegates from 12 colonies gathered in what became known as the **First Continental Congress**. Only Georgia did not send delegates.

After much debate, the delegates passed a resolution backing Massachusetts in its struggle. They agreed to boycott all British goods and to stop exporting goods to Britain until the Intolerable Acts were repealed. The delegates also urged each colony to set up and train its own militia (mih LISH uh). A **militia** is an army of citizens who serve as soldiers during an emergency.

Before leaving Philadelphia, the delegates agreed to meet again in May 1775. Little did they suspect that before then, an incident in Massachusetts would change the fate of the colonies forever.

? IDENTIFY MAIN IDEAS How did other colonies respond to the Intolerable Acts?

The Battles of Lexington and Concord

In Massachusetts, colonists were already preparing to resist. Newspapers called on citizens to prevent what they called "the Massacre of American Liberty." Volunteers known as **minutemen** trained regularly. Minutemen got their name because they kept their muskets at hand and were prepared to fight at a minute's notice. In towns near Boston, minutemen collected weapons and gunpowder. Meanwhile, Britain built up its forces. More troops arrived in Boston, bringing the total number of British soldiers in that city to 4,000.

Early in 1775, General Thomas Gage, the British commander, sent scouts to towns near Boston. They reported that minutemen had a large store of arms in Concord, a village about 18 miles from Boston. Gage planned a surprise march to Concord to seize the arms.

The Redcoats Cross the Charles River
On April 18, about 700 British troops quietly left Boston in the darkness. Their goal was to seize the colonial arms. The Sons of Liberty were watching. As soon as the British set out, the Americans hung two lamps from the Old North Church in Boston. This signal meant that the redcoats were crossing the Charles River. The British had decided to cross the river rather than take a much longer route toward Concord by land.

>> On the night of April 18, 1775, Paul Revere rode to Lexington to warn the colonists that British troops were marching toward them on their way to seize rebel arms in Concord.

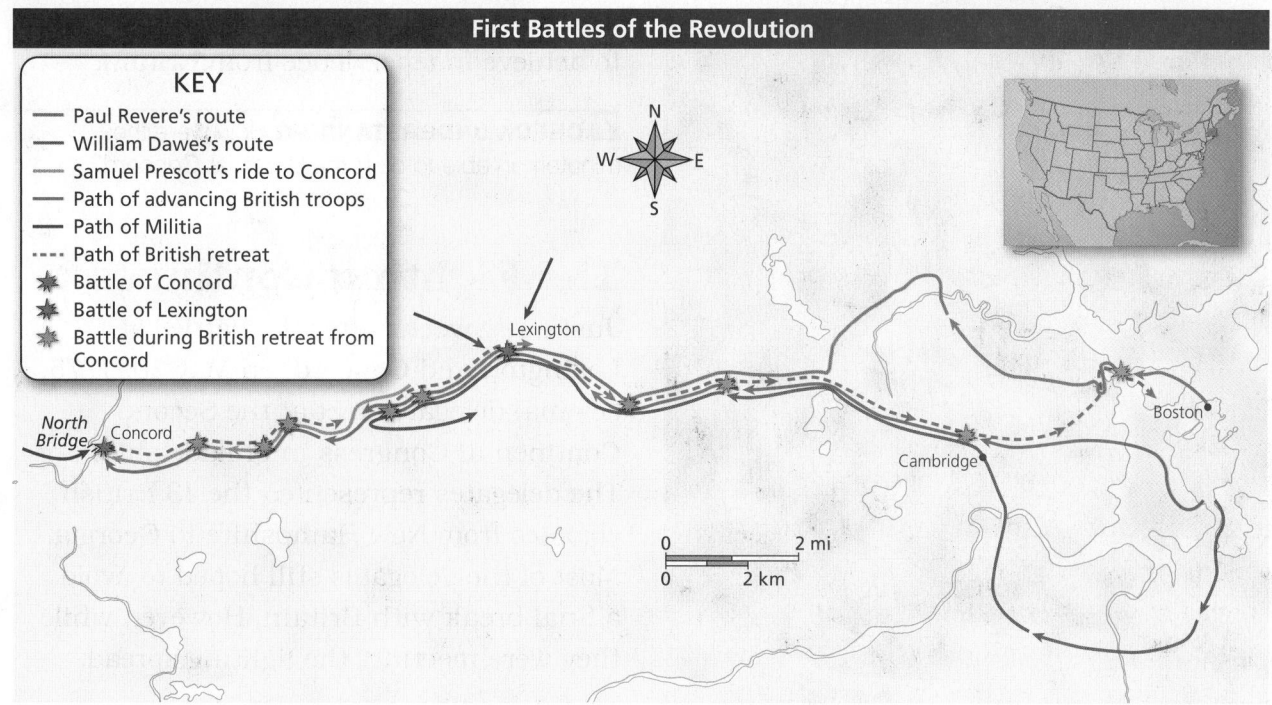

First Battles of the Revolution

KEY
- Paul Revere's route
- William Dawes's route
- Samuel Prescott's ride to Concord
- Path of advancing British troops
- Path of Militia
- --- Path of British retreat
- ★ Battle of Concord
- ★ Battle of Lexington
- ★ Battle during British retreat from Concord

North Bridge Concord Lexington Cambridge Boston

0   2 mi
0   2 km

>> **Analyze Maps** Why were colonial minutemen so prepared for the arrival of the redcoats near Concord?

Colonists who were waiting across the Charles River saw the signal. Messengers mounted their horses and galloped through the night toward Concord. One midnight rider was Paul Revere. "The redcoats are coming! The redcoats are coming!" shouted Revere as he passed through each sleepy village along the way.

Fighting in Lexington and Concord At daybreak on April 19, the redcoats reached Lexington, a town near Concord. On the village green, some 70 minutemen were waiting, commanded by Captain John Parker. The British ordered the minutemen to go home. Outnumbered, the colonists began to leave.

Suddenly, a shot rang out through the chill morning air. No one knows who fired it. In the brief struggle that followed, eight colonists were killed.

The British pushed on to Concord. Finding no arms in the village, they

turned back to Boston. On a bridge outside Concord, they met approximately 300 minutemen. Again, fighting broke out. This time, the British were forced to retreat because the minutemen used the geography of the region to their advantage. As the redcoats withdrew, colonial sharpshooters took deadly aim at them from the woods and fields and then took cover there, making it difficult for the British soldiers to fire back. Local women also fired at the British from the windows of their homes. By the time they reached Boston, the redcoats had lost 73 men. Another 200 British soldiers were wounded or missing.

News of the **battles of Lexington and Concord** spread swiftly. To many colonists, the fighting ended all hope of a peaceful settlement. Only war would decide the future of the 13 colonies.

More than 60 years after the battles of Lexington and Concord, a well-known New

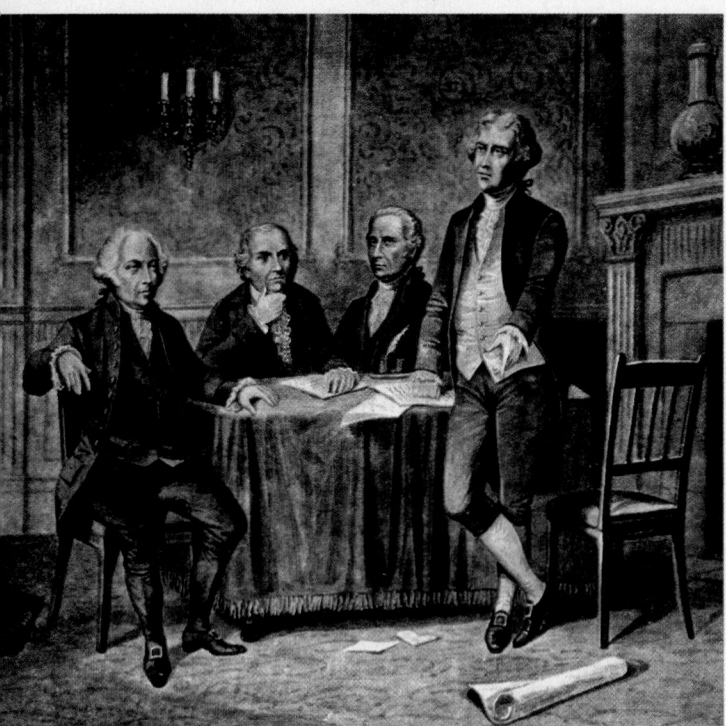

>> The Second Continental Congress met in the summer of 1775 to discuss how to respond to the British aggression at Lexington and Concord and the failure to rescind the Intolerable Acts.

England writer, Ralph Waldo Emerson, wrote a poem honoring the minutemen. Emerson's "Concord Hymn" created a vivid picture of the clash at Concord. It begins:

> By the rude bridge that arched the flood, Their flag to April's breeze unfurled, Here once the embattled farmers stood, And fired the shot heard round the world.
>
> —Ralph Waldo Emerson, "Concord Hymn," 1837

The "embattled farmers" would have years of difficult fighting in front of them. Lexington and Concord marked the beginning of the Revolutionary War.

The war and disagreements between the American colonists and the British prior to the war represent the era called the American Revolution, the period of struggle to achieve independence from Britain.

? CHECK UNDERSTANDING How were the minutemen able to beat the British at Concord?

The Fighting Continues

Just a few weeks after the battles at Lexington and Concord, on May 10, 1775, colonial delegates met at the Second Continental Congress in Philadelphia. The delegates represented the 13 British colonies from New Hampshire to Georgia. Most of the delegates still hoped to avoid a final break with Britain. However, while they were meeting, the fighting spread.

King George III Rejects Peace After much debate, the delegates sent a petition to King George. In the **Olive Branch Petition**, they declared their loyalty to the king and asked him to repeal the Intolerable Acts.

George III was furious when he heard about the petition. The colonists, he raged, were trying to begin a war "for the purpose of establishing an independent empire!" The king vowed to bring the rebels to justice. He ordered 20,000 more troops to the colonies to crush the revolt.

Congress did not learn of the king's response until months later. But even before the petition was sent, leaders like John and Sam Adams were convinced that war could not be avoided.

Vermont Rebels Gain a Route to Canada Ethan Allen, a Vermont blacksmith, did not wait for Congress to act. Allen decided to lead a band of Vermonters, known as the **Green Mountain Boys**, in a surprise attack on Fort Ticonderoga, located at the southern tip of Lake Champlain. Allen knew that the fort held cannons that the colonists could use, and its strategic location would help colonists control the region.

In early May, the Green Mountain Boys crept quietly through the morning mists to Fort Ticonderoga. They quickly overpowered the guard on duty and entered the fort. Allen rushed to the room where the British commander slept. "Come out, you old rat!" he shouted. The commander demanded to know by whose authority Allen acted. "In the name of the Great Jehovah and the Continental Congress!" Allen replied.

The British commander surrendered Ticonderoga. With the fort, the Green Mountain Boys won a valuable supply of cannons and gunpowder. Allen's success also gave Americans control of a key route into Canada.

>> Ethan Allen and the Green Mountain Boys from Vermont stormed Fort Ticonderoga, forcing the British commander there to surrender.

George Washington Takes Command

In the meantime, the Second Continental Congress had to decide what to do about the makeshift army gathering around Boston. In June, delegates took the bold step of setting up the **Continental Army**. They appointed George Washington of Virginia as commander.

Washington knew that he would be fighting against one of the world's toughest armies. Still, he was willing to do his best. He set off at once to take charge of the forces around Boston.

? **IDENTIFY SUPPORTING DETAILS** Why was Fort Ticonderoga important to the colonists?

Opposing Sides at War

The colonists who favored war against Britain called themselves **Patriots**. They thought British rule was harsh and unjust. About one third of the colonists were

>> The Second Continental Congress established the Continental Army and appointed George Washington of Virginia as its commander.

★ AMERICANS IN CONFLICT ★

The **Revolutionary War** was also a conflict between groups living in the colonies. During the Revolution, families fought each other. Communities were split apart.

1775-1783

80,000 to 100,000 **Loyalists** left the colonies during the war.

1760

Everyone is a Tory and supports the King.

1775

The War begins . . . relatives, friends, and neighbors take sides.

1776

Population of the United States is 2.5 million.

Source: United States Census Bureau

★ ★ ★ ★ ★ **PATRIOTS** ★ ★ ★ ★ ★
- Called **Rebels** by the Loyalists
- Felt oppressed by British rule and taxation
- Led by well-educated and wealthy individuals
- Supported Declaration of Independence and freedom from British rule

★ ★ ★ ★ ★ **LOYALISTS** ★ ★ ★ ★ ★
- Called **Tories** by the Patriots
- Mostly government officials, merchants, bankers, and tradesmen who had financial interests in maintaining British rule
- Felt it was morally wrong to oppose the King
- Started their own fighting regiments that were not part of the British Army

>> The Revolutionary War was largely a fight between the colonists and the British. Why was it also a fight between the colonists themselves?

▶ Interactive Chart

Patriots, one third sided with the British, and one third did not take sides.

Washington Leads the Patriots The Patriots entered the war with many disadvantages. Colonial forces were poorly organized and untrained. They had few cannons, little gunpowder, and no navy. Also, few colonists were willing to enlist in the Continental Army for long terms of service. They preferred to fight near home, as part of a local militia.

Yet, the Patriots also had advantages. Many Patriots owned rifles and were good shots. Their leader, George Washington, had experience and developed into an able commander. Furthermore, Patriots were determined to fight to defend their homes and property. Reuben Stebbins of Massachusetts was typical of many patriotic farmers. When the British approached, he rode off to battle. "We'll see who's going t'own this farm!" he cried.

British Advantages and Disadvantages The British were a powerful foe. They had highly trained, experienced troops. Their navy was the best in the world. In addition, many colonists supported the British.

Still, Britain faced problems. Its armies were 3,000 miles from home. News and supplies took months to travel from Britain to North America. Also, British soldiers risked attacks by colonists once they marched out of the cities into the countryside.

Loyalists Favor the King American colonists who remained loyal to Britain were known as **Loyalists**. They included wealthy merchants and former officials of the royal government. However, some farmers and craftsworkers were also Loyalists. There were more Loyalists in the Middle Colonies and the South than in New England.

Loyalists faced hard times during the war. Patriots tarred and feathered people known to favor the British. Many Loyalists fled to England or Canada. Others found shelter in cities controlled by the British. Those who fled lost their homes, stores, and farms.

IDENTIFY What positions did colonists take in regards to the war as it began?

The War Comes to Boston

During the first year of conflict, much of the fighting centered around Boston. About 6,000 British troops were stationed there. Colonial militia surrounded the city and prevented the British from marching out.

War Breaks Out Near Boston Harbor

Even before Washington reached Boston, the Patriots took action. On June 16, 1775, Colonel William Prescott led 1,200 minutemen up Bunker Hill, across the Charles River from Boston. From there, they could fire on British ships in Boston Harbor. Prescott, however, noticed that nearby Breed's Hill was an even better place to use the local geography to his advantage. A hilltop would be easier to defend, so he ordered his men to move there.

At sunrise, the British general, William Howe, spotted the Americans. He ferried about 2,400 redcoats across the river to attack the rebels' position. As the British approached, the Patriots held their fire.

When the Americans finally fired, the British were forced to retreat. A second British attack was also turned back. On the third try, the British pushed over the top. They took both Bunker Hill and Breed's Hill, but they paid a high price for their victory. More than 1,000 redcoats lay dead or wounded. American losses numbered only about 400.

The **Battle of Bunker Hill** was the first major battle of the Revolution. It proved that

>> Army recruits fortify Dorchester Heights in Boston. Washington quickly turned thousands of recruits from various colonies into a well-trained, unified army.

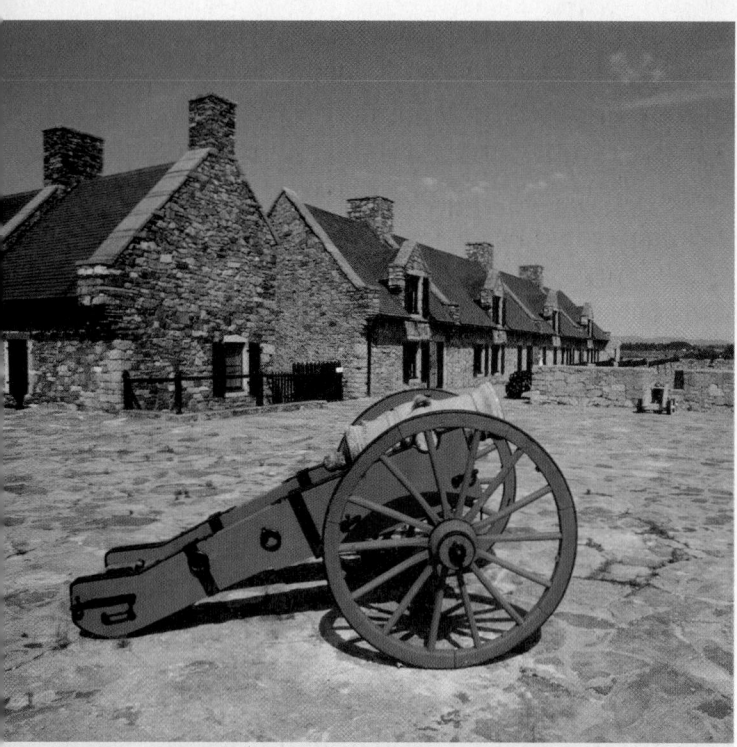

>> Soldiers transported the cannons captured at Fort Ticonderoga to Boston in order to force the British to leave New England.

the Americans could fight bravely. It also showed that the British would not be easy to defeat. Furthermore, it hinted that one effect of the Revolution would be continued bloodshed from a long and bitter war.

Washington Forces the British Out of Boston When Washington reached Boston a few weeks after the Battle of Bunker Hill, he found about 16,000 troops camped in huts and tents around the city.

General Washington quickly began to turn raw recruits into a trained army. His job was especially difficult because soldiers from different colonies mistrusted one another. "Connecticut wants no Massachusetts men in her corps," he wrote. And "Massachusetts thinks there is no necessity for a Rhode Islander to be introduced into her [ranks]." However, Washington won the loyalty of his troops.

They, in turn, learned to take orders and work together.

In January 1776, Washington had a stroke of good fortune. The cannons that the Green Mountain Boys had captured at Fort Ticonderoga arrived in Boston. Soldiers had dragged them across the mountains from Fort Ticonderoga. Washington had the cannons placed in a strategic location on Dorchester Heights, overlooking the harbor.

Once General Howe saw the American cannons in place, he knew that he could not hold Boston. In March 1776, he and his troops sailed from Boston to Halifax, Canada. About 1,000 American Loyalists went with them.

Although the British left New England, they did not give up. King George III ordered a blockade of all colonial ports. A **blockade** is the shutting of a port to keep people or supplies from moving in or out. The king also used **mercenaries**, or troops for hire, from Germany to help fight the colonists.

❓ **CHECK UNDERSTANDING** How did the colonists use the physical geography of the region to their advantage?

ASSESSMENT

1. **Summarize** Why did the colonists choose to throw British tea in Boston Harbor?

2. **Make Predictions** What would forming militias allow the colonies to do?

3. **Infer** why Ralph Waldo Emerson called the first shot fired in Lexington "the shot heard round the world."

4. **Analyze Information** Why do you think approximately one third of the colonists were Loyalists during the war?

5. **Summarize** the importance of the Battle of Bunker Hill.

3.4 Declaring Independence

>> Crowds in Philadelphia cheer during a public reading of the Declaration of Independence on the day of its adoption.

▶ **Interactive Flipped Video**

By 1776, many colonists had come to believe that Parliament did not have the right to make laws for the 13 colonies. After all, they argued, the colonists had their own elected legislatures. Some thought it was time for the colonies to become independent from Britain. At the same time, however, most colonists still felt a bond of loyalty to Britain. They especially felt that they owed allegiance to the king.

>> **Objectives**

Describe the impact of Thomas Paine's pamphlet, *Common Sense.*

Explain the steps Congress took to declare independence.

Summarize the main ideas of the Declaration of Independence.

>> **Key Terms**

traitor
Declaration of
  Independence
preamble
natural rights
unalienable rights
Richard Henry Lee
Robert Livingston
Roger Sherman
Common Sense
Thomas Paine
Benjamin Franklin

153

PEARSON realize
www.PearsonRealize.com
Access your Digital Lesson.

Thomas Paine's Common Sense

Thomas Paine was a British writer and editor who moved to Philadelphia in 1774. After Lexington and Concord, Paine wrote the pamphlet *Common Sense*, in which he set out to change the colonists' attitudes toward Britain and the king. Colonists, he said, did not owe loyalty to George III or any other monarch. The very idea of having kings and queens was wrong, he said.

> In England a King hath little more to do than to make war and give away [jobs]; which in plain terms, is to impoverish the nation. . . . Of more worth is one honest man to society and in the sight of God, than all the crowned ruffians that ever lived.
>
> —Thomas Paine, *Common Sense*, 1776

>> Thomas Paine's criticism of British rule in *Common Sense* prompted many colonists to consider the option of declaring full independence from Britain.

▶ **Interactive Gallery**

The colonists did not owe anything to Britain, either, Paine went on. If the British had helped the colonists, they had done so for their own profit. It could only hurt the colonists to remain under British rule. "Everything that is right or reasonable pleads for separation," he concluded. " 'Tis time to part." *Common Sense* was a great success, selling over 500,000 copies in six months. Paine's writing played an important role in moving toward revolution.

? **IDENTIFY CENTRAL IDEAS** What was the central idea of *Common Sense*?

Choosing Independence

Common Sense caused many colonial leaders to move toward declaring independence from Britain. It also deeply impressed many members of the Continental Congress. **Richard Henry Lee** of Virginia wrote to Washington, "I am now convinced . . . of the necessity for separation." In June 1776, Lee rose to his feet in Congress to introduce a resolution in favor of independence:

> *Resolved*, That these United Colonies are and of right ought to be, free and independent States, that they are absolved from all allegiance to the British Crown, and that all political connection between them and the State of Great Britain is, and ought to be, totally dissolved.
>
> —Richard Henry Lee, Resolution at the Second Continental Congress, June 7, 1776

Drafting the Declaration of Independence The delegates faced a difficult decision. There could be no turning back once they declared independence. If they fell into British hands, they would be hanged as traitors. A **traitor** is a person who betrays his or her country.

After long debate, the Congress took a fateful step. They appointed a committee to draft a formal declaration of independence. The committee included John Adams, **Benjamin Franklin**, Thomas Jefferson, **Robert Livingston**, and **Roger Sherman**. Their job was to tell the world why the colonies were breaking away from Britain.

The committee asked Thomas Jefferson to write the document. Jefferson was one of the youngest delegates. He was a quiet man who spoke little at formal meetings.

Among friends, however, he liked to sprawl in a chair with his long legs stretched out and talk for hours. His ability to write clearly and gracefully had earned him great respect.

Adopting the Declaration of Independence In late June, Jefferson completed the declaration, and it was read to the Congress. On July 2, the Continental Congress voted that the 13 colonies were "free and independent States." After polishing Jefferson's language, the delegates adopted the document on the night of July 4, 1776. They then ordered the **Declaration of Independence** to be printed.

John Hancock, president of the Continental Congress, signed the Declaration first. He penned his signature boldly, in large, clear letters. "There," he said, "I guess King George will be able to read that."

Copies of the Declaration were distributed throughout the colonies. Patriots greeted the news of independence with joyous—and sometimes rowdy—celebrations.

>> The Declaration of Independence, signed by the delegates to the Second Continental Congress, served notice to King George III that the 13 colonies had separated from Great Britain.

▶ **Interactive Gallery**

In New York, colonists tore down a statue of King George III. In Boston, the sound of cannons could be heard for hours.

❓ **IDENTIFY** What were the potential consequences for the delegates who chose to declare independence?

The Declaration of Independence

The Declaration of Independence consists of a **preamble**, or introduction, followed by three main parts.

Human Rights The first section of the Declaration stresses the idea of **natural rights**, or rights that belong to all people from birth. In bold, ringing words, Jefferson wrote:

>> The Declaration emphasized that natural rights belong to all people from birth. Colonists, such as this family, wanted to protect what they saw as their natural right to pursue life, liberty, and happiness.

>> The Declaration of Independence lists grievances against King George III, including the presence of British troops in the colonies during times of peace without the consent of colonial legislatures.

We hold these truths to be self-evident, that all men are created equal; that they are endowed by their Creator with certain unalienable rights; that among these are life, liberty, and the pursuit of happiness.

—The Declaration of Independence

According to the Declaration of Independence, people form governments in order to protect their natural rights and liberties.

These **unalienable rights**—including the rights to be free and to choose how to live—cannot be taken away by governments, for governments can exist only if they have the "consent of the governed." If a government fails to protect the rights of its citizens, then it is the people's "right [and] duty, to throw off such government, and to provide new guards for their future security." Ideas such as unalienable rights, adopted by the Founding Fathers (men such as George Washington, John Adams, Benjamin Franklin, and Thomas Jefferson), are good examples of the civic virtues that have since become the cornerstone of American government. These values continue to ensure that human rights are protected and human needs are met in our nation.

Colonial Grievances The second part of the Declaration lists the wrongs, or grievances, that led the Americans to break away from Britain. Jefferson condemned King George III for disbanding colonial legislatures and for sending troops to the colonies in peacetime. He complained about limits on trade and about taxes imposed without the consent of the people.

Jefferson listed many other grievances to show why the colonists had the right to rebel. He also pointed out that the colonies had petitioned the king to correct these injustices. Yet, the injustices remained. A ruler who treated his subjects in this manner, he boldly concluded, is a tyrant and not fit to rule:

> In every state of these oppressions, we have petitioned for redress in the most humble terms; our repeated petitions have been answered only by repeated injury. A prince whose character is thus marked by every act which may define a tyrant is unfit to be the ruler of a free people.
>
> —The Declaration of Independence

Independence The last part of the Declaration announces that the colonies are the United States of America. All political ties with Britain have been cut.

As a free and independent nation, the United States has the full power to "levy war, conclude peace, contract alliances, establish commerce, and to do all other acts and things which independent states may of right do."

The signers closed the declaration with a solemn pledge:

> And, for the support of this declaration, with a firm reliance on the protection of Divine Providence, we mutually pledge to each other our lives, our fortunes, and our sacred honor.
>
> —The Declaration of Independence

❓ LIST What are some of the grievances Jefferson included in the Declaration?

JOIN, or DIE.

>> Benjamin Franklin created this illustration encouraging colonists to band in 1754 during the French and Indian War. It was later used for the same purpose during the American Revolution.

ASSESSMENT

1. **Identify Central Issues** What was the main point of Thomas Paine's *Common Sense,* and how did he support this idea?

2. **Hypothesize** How do you think the Loyalists reacted when the Declaration of Independence was first distributed throughout the colonies?

3. **Make Generalizations** Why, to this day, do many people refer to their signatures as their "John Hancocks"?

4. **Cite Evidence** that the Second Continental Congress was acting like a governmental body.

5. **Evaluate Arguments** What justifications for separation were included in the Declaration of Independence?

Winning Independence

>> On Christmas night, 1776, Washington and his troops crossed the icy Delaware River to attack British forces at Trenton. Despite enduring the harshest conditions, Washington's forces were victorious.

Interactive Flipped Video

>> Objectives

Describe the war in the middle states, including how the battles at Trenton and Saratoga marked turning points.

Describe the roles of women and African Americans in the war.

Explain how the war was fought on the western frontier and at sea.

Describe the war in the south, including the American victory at Yorktown.

Summarize the reasons why the Americans won the war.

>> Key Terms

Battle of Long Island
Battle of Trenton
Battle of Saratoga
ally
cavalry
Valley Forge
Battle of Cowpens
guerrilla
siege
Battle of Yorktown
Treaty of Paris
ratify
Nathan Hale
Marquis de Lafayette

Friedrich von
    Steuben
Haym Salomon
Wentworth Cheswell
James Armistead
Bernardo de Gálvez
John Paul Jones

Through an odd coincidence, the British began landing troops in New York in the same month that the Continental Congress voted for independence, July 1776. General George Washington, expecting the attack, had led his forces south from Boston to New York City. His army, however, was no match for the British under the command of General Howe. Howe had about 34,000 troops and 10,000 sailors. He also had ships to ferry them ashore. Washington had fewer than 20,000 poorly trained troops, which he spread in various locations to defend New York. Worse, he had no navy.

Early Challenges for the Continental Army

In August, Howe's army landed on Long Island. In the **Battle of Long Island**, more than 1,400 Americans were killed, wounded, or captured. The rest retreated to Manhattan. The British pursued. To avoid capture, Washington hurried north.

Throughout the autumn, Washington fought a series of battles with Howe's army. In November, he crossed the Hudson River into New Jersey. Chased by the British, the Americans retreated across the Delaware River into Pennsylvania.

During the campaign for New York, Washington needed information about Howe's forces. **Nathan Hale**, a young Connecticut officer, volunteered to go behind British lines. On his way back with the information, Hale was seized by the British and searched. Hidden in the soles of his shoes was information about British troop movements.

There was no trial. Howe ordered Hale to be hanged the next morning. As Hale walked to the gallows, he is said to have declared: "I only regret that I have but one life to lose for my country."

Even as Washington's army retreated and the British took New York City, many people there remained as loyal to the American cause as Hale. **Haym Salomon** (HY um SAL uh mun), a Jewish immigrant from Poland, was arrested by the British in September of 1776 and thrown into prison. Salomon had supported the American cause from the start, helping the new government get loans. Salomon even gave his own money to soldiers and military units for equipment. He managed to escape to Philadelphia and continued to aid the fight for independence.

A Surprise Attack Leads to an American Victory Months of hard campaigning took a toll on the Continental Army. In December 1776, Washington described his troops as sick, dirty, and "so thinly clad as

Continental vs. British Forces

	CONTINENTAL	BRITISH
TOTAL FORCES	about 90,000 as a peak estimate	more than 70,000
COMPOSITION OF FORCES	Continental Army, State Militias	Army, Navy, hired mercenaries
ALLIES	France, Spain	Native Americans, Loyalists
QUALITY OF FORCES	untrained, unconventional	trained, disciplined
MOTIVATION	freedom from British control	regain British control
SUPPLIES	very limited weapons, food, and clothing	better availability of weapons, food, and clothing, but moving supplies was difficult

>> **Analyze Charts** Which forces, the Continental or the British, appear to be better prepared for battle? Why?

to be unfit for service." Every day, soldiers deserted. Washington wrote to his brother: "I am wearied to death. I think the game is pretty near up."

Washington decided on a bold move: a surprise attack on Trenton, New Jersey. The Delaware River separated the British in Trenton and the Americans, and the soldiers guarding Trenton would not expect American troops to cross it. On Christmas night, Washington secretly led his troops across the icy river. Soldiers shivered as spray from the river froze on their faces. Once ashore, they marched through swirling snow. Some had no shoes. They tied rags around their feet. "Soldiers, keep by your officers," Washington urged.

Early on December 26, the Americans surprised the Hessian troops guarding Trenton and took most of them prisoner. The Hessians were soldiers from Germany. An American summed up the **Battle of**

Trenton: "Hessian population of Trenton at 8 A.M.—1,408 men and 39 officers; Hessian population at 9 A.M.—0."

British General Charles Cornwallis set out at once to retake Trenton and to capture Washington. Late on January 2, 1777, he saw the lights of Washington's campfires. "At last we have run down the old fox," he said, "and we will bag him in the morning."

Washington fooled Cornwallis. He left the fires burning and slipped behind British lines to attack a British force that was marching toward Princeton. There, the Continental Army won another victory. From Princeton, Washington moved to Morristown, where the army would spend the winter. The victories at Trenton and Princeton gave the Americans new hope.

? RECALL What advantages did the British have in the Battle of Long Island?

The Tide Turns for the Americans

In London, British officials were dismayed by the army's failure to crush the rebels. Early in 1777, General John Burgoyne (bur GOIN) presented a new plan for victory. If British troops cut off New England from the other colonies, he argued, the war would soon be over.

The New England Strategy Burgoyne wanted three British armies to march on Albany, New York, from different directions. They would crush American forces there. Once they controlled the Hudson River, the British could stop the flow of soldiers and supplies from New England to Washington's army.

Burgoyne's plan called for General Howe to march on Albany from New York

>> The British hired Hessian mercenaries to compensate for a shortage of British troops. At the time, British troops were fighting in other wars.

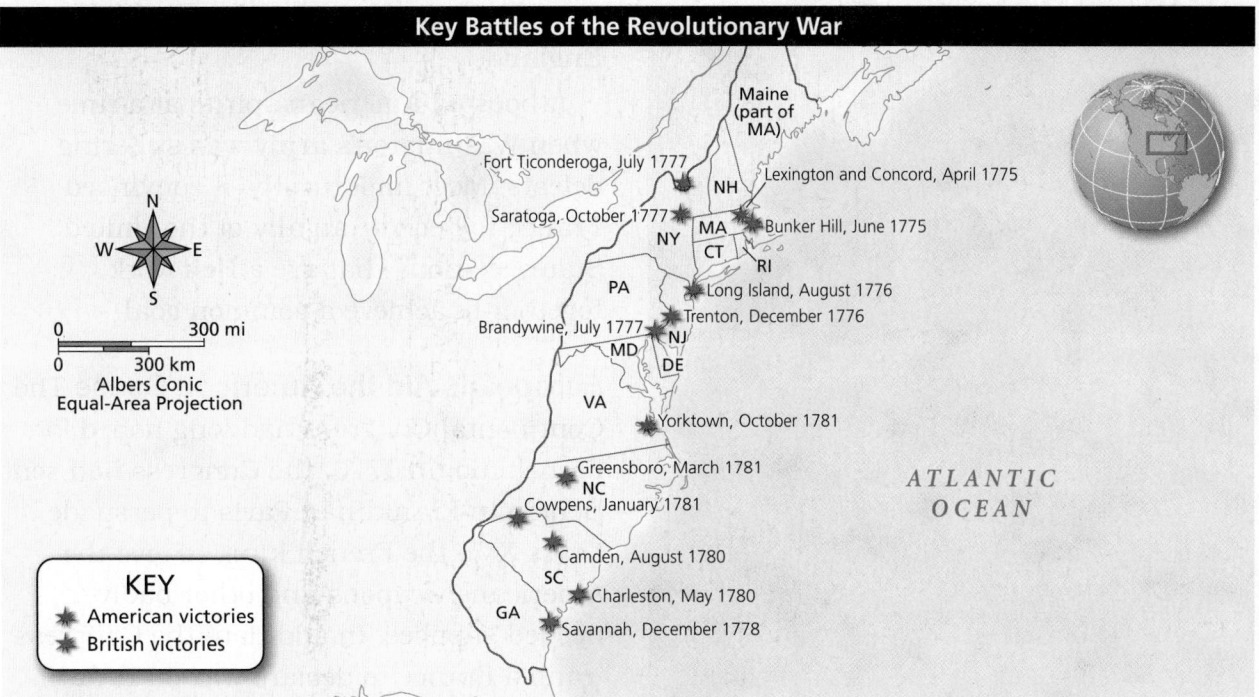

>> **Analyze Maps** What were the results of the battles in 1777 that were part of General Burgoyne's plan?

City. George III, however, wanted Howe to capture Philadelphia first.

In July 1777, Howe sailed from New York to the Chesapeake Bay, where he began his march on Philadelphia. Howe captured Philadelphia, defeating the Americans at the battles of Brandywine and Germantown. But instead of moving toward Albany to meet Burgoyne as planned, he retired to comfortable quarters in Philadelphia for the winter. For his part, Washington retreated to Valley Forge, Pennsylvania.

Meanwhile, British armies under Burgoyne and Barry St. Leger (lay ZHAIR) marched from Canada toward Albany. St. Leger tried to take Fort Stanwix. However, a strong American army, led by Benedict Arnold, drove him back.

American Troops Prevail at Saratoga

Only Burgoyne was left to march on Albany. His army moved slowly because it had many heavy baggage carts to drag through the woods. To slow Burgoyne further, Patriots cut down trees and dammed up streams to block the route.

Despite these obstacles, Burgoyne recaptured Fort Ticonderoga, shocking Americans. However, he delayed at the fort, giving American forces time to regroup. He also sent troops into Vermont to find food and horses. There, Patriots attacked the redcoats. At the Battle of Bennington, they wounded or captured nearly 1,000 British.

Burgoyne's troubles grew. The Green Mountain Boys hurried into New York to help American forces there. At the village of Saratoga, the Americans surrounded the British. When Burgoyne tried to break free, the Americans beat him back. Realizing that he was trapped, Burgoyne surrendered his entire army to the Americans on October 17, 1777.

The American victory at the **Battle of Saratoga** was a major turning point in

>> General John Burgoyne surrenders to General Horatio Gates after the British defeat at the Battle of Saratoga. This American victory ended the British threat to New England.

>> The Marquis de Lafayette (right), shown here with George Washington (left) at Valley Forge, commanded soldiers in support of the American cause.

▶ Interactive Timeline

the war. It ended the British threat to New England.

It boosted American spirits at a time when Washington's army was suffering defeats. Most importantly, it convinced France to become an ally of the United States. Nations that are **allies** work together to achieve a common goal.

Europeans Aid the American Cause The Continental Congress had long hoped for French aid. In 1776, the Congress had sent Benjamin Franklin to Paris to persuade Louis XVI, the French king, to give the Americans weapons and other badly needed supplies. In addition, the Congress wanted France to declare war on Britain.

The French were eager to defeat Britain, but they were also cautious. France was still angry about its defeat at British hands in the French and Indian War. However, Louis XVI did not want to help the Americans openly unless he was sure that they could win. The American victory at Saratoga convinced France that the United States could stand up to Britain.

In February 1778, France became the first nation to sign a treaty with the United States. It recognized the new nation and agreed to provide military aid. Later, the Netherlands and Spain also joined in the war against Britain. France, the Netherlands, and Spain all provided loans to the United States.

Even before European nations agreed to help the United States, individual volunteers had been coming from Europe to join the American cause. Some became leading officers in the American army.

The **Marquis de Lafayette** (mar KEE dah lah fay ET), a young French noble, convinced France to send several thousand trained soldiers to help the Patriot cause. Lafayette, who fought at Brandywine, became one of Washington's most trusted friends.

From the German state of Prussia came **Friedrich von Steuben** (STOO bun), who helped train Washington's troops to march and drill. Von Steuben had served in the Prussian army, which was considered the best in Europe.

Two Polish officers also joined the Americans. Thaddeus Kosciusko (kahs ee S koh), an engineer, helped build forts and other defenses. Casimir Pulaski trained **cavalry**, or troops on horseback.

? DESCRIBE In what ways did Europeans help the American war effort?

Winter at Valley Forge

The victory at Saratoga and the promise of help from Europe boosted American morale. Washington's Continental Army began preparing for the winter of 1777–1778 by building a makeshift camp at **Valley Forge**.

Conditions at Valley Forge were difficult, but the soldiers endured. About 2,000 huts were built as shelter. Several soldiers were improperly dressed, although many did have proper uniforms. As the winter wore on, soldiers also suffered from disease, a common problem in military camps. An army surgeon from Connecticut wrote about his hardships:

> I am sick—discontented—and out of humor. Poor food—hard lodging—cold weather—fatigue—nasty clothes—nasty cookery . . . a pox on my bad luck! There comes a bowl of beef soup, full of burnt leaves and dirt. . . . Away with it, boys!—I'll live like the chameleon upon air.

—Albigence Waldo, *Diary*, December 14, 1777

>> Martha Washington (in the red cloak) helped boost morale by visiting her husband and troops of the Continental Army at Valley Forge.

As news of the hardships at Valley Forge spread, Patriots from around the nation sent help. Women collected food, medicine, warm clothes, and ammunition for the army. Some women, like Martha Washington, wife of the commander, went to Valley Forge to help the sick and wounded.

The arrival of desperately needed supplies was soon followed by warmer weather. The drills of Baron von Steuben helped the Continentals to march and fight with a new skill. By the spring of 1778, the army at Valley Forge was more hopeful. Washington could not know it at the time, but the Patriots' bleakest hour had passed.

? IDENTIFY SUPPORTING DETAILS How did people help the soldiers at Valley Forge?

Women Contribute to the War Effort

When men went off to fight in the Revolution, women took on added work at home. Some planted and harvested the crops. Others made shoes and wove cloth for blankets and uniforms. One woman, called "Handy Betsy the Blacksmith," was known for making cannons and guns for the army. However, many historians point out that there is no proof she did this.

Supporting the Army Many women joined their husbands at the front. They cared for the wounded, washed clothes, and cooked. Martha Washington joined her husband whenever she could. Some women achieved lasting fame for their wartime service.

Betsy Ross of Philadelphia sewed flags for Washington's army. Legend claims that she made the first American flag of stars and stripes.

A few women even took part in battle. During the Battle of Monmouth in 1778, Mary Ludwig Hays carried water to her husband and other soldiers. The soldiers called her Molly Pitcher. When her husband was wounded, she took his place, loading and firing the cannon.

Women's Rights and the Revolution As women participated in the war, they began to think differently about their rights. Those women who had taken charge of farms or their husbands' businesses became more confident and willing to speak out.

Most men in Congress did not agree that women should be treated equally. Still, the Revolution established important ideals of liberty and equality. In later years, these ideals of the Revolution would encourage women to campaign for equal treatment—and eventually to win it.

❓ **DESCRIBE** How did many women assist the war effort?

>> Mary Ludwig Hays, known as Molly Pitcher, carried water to soldiers during battle. When needed, she even loaded and fired the cannon in support of the fight for independence.

▶ **Interactive Gallery**

African Americans in the War

By 1776, more than a half million African Americans lived in the colonies. This large racial group was quickly emerging as part of the American identity due to African American contributions during the Revolution. At first, the Continental Congress refused to let African Americans, whether free or enslaved, join the army. Some members doubted the loyalty of armed African Americans. The British, however, offered freedom to some male slaves who would serve the king. Washington feared that this would greatly increase the ranks of the British army. In response, Washington changed his policy and asked Congress to allow free African Americans to enlist.

Deciding to Fight About 5,000 African Americans from all the colonies, except South Carolina, served in the army. Another 2,000 served in the navy which, from the start, allowed African Americans to join. At least nine black minutemen saw action at Lexington and Concord.

Some African Americans formed special regiments. Others served in white regiments as drummers, fifers, spies, and guides. Saul Matthews and **James Armistead** were among those African Americans who served as spies. Whites recognized the courage of their African American comrades. As one eyewitness recalled, "Three times in succession, [African Americans] were attacked . . . by [British troops] and three times did they successfully repel the assault and . . . preserve our army from capture. . . ."

African Americans like **Wentworth Cheswell** served the Patriot cause from the start. A New Hampshire schoolmaster, Cheswell was an educated and free black man who was regularly elected to local and town positions.

Like Paul Revere, he rode all night from Boston to warn his community that the British were on the march. He later enlisted in the army to help fight at Saratoga.

Enslaved African Americans faced more difficult choices. If they joined the American army or continued to work on Patriot plantations, the British might capture and sell them. If they tried to flee to the British army to gain freedom, they risked being hanged by angry Patriots.

African Americans and the Revolution

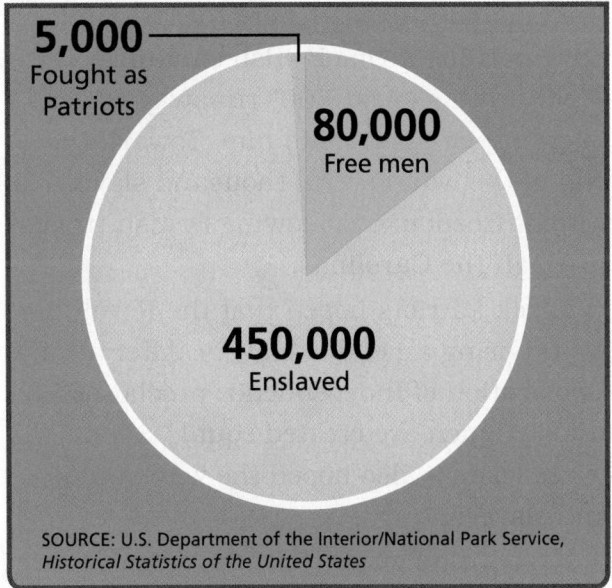

5,000 — Fought as Patriots

80,000 Free men

450,000 Enslaved

SOURCE: U.S. Department of the Interior/National Park Service, *Historical Statistics of the United States*

>> **Analyze Data** What does this data tell you about the status of African Americans during the Revolution?

>> James Lafayette Armistead was one of several African Americans who served the American cause as spies for the Continental Army.

Belief in Freedom Yet, many slaves did flee their masters, especially those who lived near the coast, where the British navy patrolled. One British captain reported that "near 500" runaway slaves offered their services to him. Toward the end of the war, several thousand slaves sought freedom by following British troops through the Carolinas.

Black Patriots hoped that the Revolution would bring an end to slavery. After all, the Declaration of Independence proclaimed that "all men are created equal." Some white leaders also hoped the war would end slavery.

James Otis wrote that "the colonists are by the law of nature free born, as indeed all men are, white or black." Quakers in particular spoke out strongly against slavery.

>> At the Battle of Wyoming in 1778, Loyalists and Native Americans, allied to the British, killed 360 colonial settlers in the Wyoming Valley of Pennsylvania.

By the 1770s, slavery was declining in the North, where a number of free African Americans lived. During the American Revolution, several states moved to make slavery illegal, including Massachusetts, New Hampshire, and Pennsylvania. Other states also began to debate the slavery issue.

? **IDENTIFY MAIN IDEAS** What difficult consequences did many slaves face when choosing sides in the American Revolution?

Native Americans and the Spanish Choose Sides

As the war spread to Indian lands in the West, the Americans and British both tried to win the support of Indian tribes. In the end, the British were more successful. They convinced many Native Americans that a Patriot victory would mean more white settlers crossing the Appalachians and taking Indian lands.

Loyalist Allies In the South, the British gained the support of the Cherokees, Creeks, Choctaws, and Chickasaws. The British encouraged the Cherokees to attack dozens of settlements on the southern frontier. Only after hard fighting were Patriot militia able to drive the Cherokees back into the mountains.

Fighting was equally fierce on the northern frontier. In 1778, Iroquois forces led by the Mohawk leader Joseph Brant joined with Loyalists in raiding settlements in Pennsylvania and New York. The next year, Patriots struck back by destroying dozens of Iroquois villages.

Other Tribes Choose to Help the Patriots Farther west, in 1778, George Rogers Clark led Virginia frontier fighters against the British in the Ohio Valley. With help from

Miami Indians, Clark captured the British forts at Kaskaskia and Cahokia near the Mississippi River.

Clark then plotted a surprise attack on the British fort at Vincennes. When Clark's small force reached the fort, they spread out through the woods to make their numbers appear greater than they really were. The British commander thought it was useless to fight so many Americans. He surrendered Vincennes in February 1779.

Spanish Assistance On the southwestern frontier, Americans received help from New Spain. In the early years of the war, Spain was neutral. However, **Bernardo de Gálvez** (bayr NARDO day GOLL vess), governor of Spanish Louisiana, favored the Patriots. He secretly supplied medicine, cloth, muskets, and gunpowder to the Americans.

When Spain entered the war against Britain in 1779, Gálvez took a more active role. He seized British forts along the Mississippi River and the Gulf of Mexico. He also drove the British out of West Florida. The city of Galveston, in Texas, is named after this courageous leader.

? RECALL Why were the British generally more successful at becoming allies with different Indian tribes?

Fighting for Independence in the Southern Colonies and at Sea

At sea, the Americans could do little against the powerful British navy. British ships blockaded American ports, which were oftentimes important supply routes for Patriot troops and towns. From time to time, however, a bold American captain captured a British ship.

>> Captain John Paul Jones shouts orders to his crew during battle aboard his ship *Bonhomme Richard*. Jones and his crew captured the British warship *Serapis*.

The greatest American sea victory took place in September 1779 in Britain's backyard, on the North Sea. After a hard-fought battle, Captain **John Paul Jones** captured the powerful British warship *Serapis*. Jones was one of many important military leaders who contributed to the American cause during the war.

Raids on the high seas and along the frontiers kept many Americans on the alert. However, the war between the Americans and Great Britain would be settled by battles in the South.

Battles in the South The South became the main battleground of the war in 1778. Sir Henry Clinton, the new British commander-in-chief, knew that many Loyalists lived in the southern backcountry. He hoped that if British troops marched through the South, Loyalists would join them.

At first, Clinton's plan seemed to work. In short order, beginning in December 1778, the British seized Savannah in Georgia and Charleston and Camden in South Carolina. "I have almost ceased to hope," wrote Washington when he learned of the defeats.

Patriots and Loyalists Clash In the Carolina backcountry, Patriots and Loyalists launched violent raids against one another. Both sides burned farms, killed civilians, and sometimes even tortured prisoners.

After 1780, attacks by British troops and Loyalist militia became especially cruel. As a result, more settlers began to side with the Patriots. As one Loyalist admitted,

"Great Britain has now a hundred enemies, where it had one before."

Momentum Shifts Toward the Patriots After the victory at Kings Mountain, two able American generals helped turn the tide against the main British army, led by General Charles Cornwallis. They were Nathanael Greene of Rhode Island and Daniel Morgan of Virginia.

General Greene's ability as a military leader was perhaps second only to Washington's. In 1780, Greene took command of the Continental Army in the South. Using his knowledge of local geography, Greene engaged the British only on ground that put them at a disadvantage. General Cornwallis wore out his soldiers trying to catch Greene's army.

In January 1781, General Morgan won an important victory at Cowpens, South Carolina. Morgan used a clever tactic to defeat the British. He divided his soldiers into a front line and a rear line. He ordered the front line to retreat after firing just two volleys. The British, thinking the Americans were retreating, charged forward—straight into the fire of Morgan's second rank. In this way, the Americans won the **Battle of Cowpens**.

Greene and Morgan combined their armies when they fought Cornwallis at Guilford Courthouse, near present-day Greensboro, North Carolina. The battle was one of the bloodiest of the war. Although the Americans retreated, the British sustained great losses.

Adapting Tactics to Geography Known as the Swamp Fox, Francis Marion of South Carolina added to British frustrations. He led a small band of militia, who often slept by day and traveled by

>> General Nathanael Greene's knowledge of local geography proved to be an important military advantage in defeating the British forces.

>> Yorktown was a stunning victory for the American and French armies. As troops gathered to accept the formal British surrender, Cornwallis, claiming illness, did not attend the ceremony.

night. His soldiers used **guerrilla**, or hit-and-run, tactics to harass the British.

Marion's band took advantage of the region's environment, appearing suddenly out of the swamps, attacking quickly, and retreating swiftly back into the swamps.

? **DESCRIBE** What did a superior navy allow the British to do?

A Decisive Win Brings the War to a Close

Cornwallis abandoned his plan to take the Carolinas. In the spring of 1781, he moved his troops north into Virginia. He planned to conquer Virginia and cut off the Americans' supply routes to the South.

Benedict Arnold's Betrayal The British had achieved some success in Virginia, even before the arrival of Cornwallis.

Benedict Arnold, formerly one of the Americans' best generals, was now leading British troops. Arnold captured and burned the capital city of Richmond. His forces also raided and burned other towns.

Arnold had turned traitor to the American cause in September 1780, while commanding West Point, a key fort in New York. The ambitious general was angry because he felt that he had not received enough credit for his victories. He also needed money. Arnold secretly agreed to turn over West Point to the British. The plot was uncovered by a Patriot patrol, but Arnold escaped to join the British.

Arnold's treason and his raids on towns in Connecticut and Virginia enraged the Patriots. Thomas Jefferson, governor of Virginia, offered a sizable reward for his capture. Washington ordered Arnold to be hanged. However, he was never captured.

The British Are Trapped at Yorktown

Cornwallis hoped to meet with the same kind of success in Virginia that Arnold had achieved. At first, things went well. Cornwallis sent Loyalist troops to attack Charlottesville, where the Virginia legislature was meeting. Governor Thomas Jefferson and other officials had to flee.

American troops under Lafayette fought back by staging raids against the British. Lafayette did not have enough troops to fight a major battle. Still, his strategy kept Cornwallis at bay.

Then, Cornwallis made a mistake. He disregarded an order from Sir Henry Clinton to send part of his army to New York. Instead, he retreated to Yorktown peninsula, a strip of land jutting into the Chesapeake Bay. He felt confident that British ships could supply his army from the sea.

Washington saw an opportunity to trap Cornwallis on the Yorktown peninsula. He marched his Continental troops south from New York. With the Americans were French soldiers under the Comte de Rochambeau (roh shahm BOH). The combined army rushed to join Lafayette in Virginia.

Meanwhile, a French fleet under Admiral de Grasse was also heading toward Virginia. Once in Chesapeake Bay, de Grasse's fleet closed the trap. Cornwallis was cut off. He could not get supplies. He could not escape by land or by sea.

The War Is Won By the end of September, more than 16,000 American and French troops laid siege to Cornwallis's army of fewer than 8,000. A **siege** occurs when an army surrounds and blockades an enemy position in an attempt to capture it. Day after day, American and French artillery pounded the British.

For several weeks, Cornwallis held out. Finally, with casualties mounting and his supplies running low, the general decided

Treaty of Paris, 1763

KEY
- Britain
- Spain
- United States

PACIFIC OCEAN

ATLANTIC OCEAN

Gulf of Mexico

Missouri R.

Mississippi R.

Ohio R.

Rio Grande

0   1,000 mi
0   1,000 km
Lambert Conformal Conic Projection

>> **Analyze Maps** How did the Treaty of Paris change the balance of power in North America?

that the situation was hopeless. The British had lost the **Battle of Yorktown**.

On October 19, 1781, the British surrendered their weapons. The French and the Americans lined up in two facing columns. As the defeated redcoats marched between the victorious troops, a British army band played the tune "The World Turned Upside Down."

The talks began in Paris in 1782. Congress sent Benjamin Franklin and John Adams, along with John Jay of New York and Henry Laurens of South Carolina, to work out a treaty. Because Britain was eager to end the war, the Americans got most of what they wanted.

Under the **Treaty of Paris**, the British recognized the United States as an independent nation. It extended from the Atlantic Ocean to the Mississippi River. The northern border of the United States stopped at the Great Lakes. The southern border stopped at Florida, which was returned to Spain.

For their part, the Americans agreed to ask the state legislatures to pay Loyalists for property they had lost in the war. In the end, however, most states ignored Loyalist claims.

On April 15, 1783, Congress **ratified**, or approved, the Treaty of Paris. It was almost eight years to the day since the battles of Lexington and Concord.

? IDENTIFY SUPPORTING DETAILS What were the results of the Treaty of Paris?

Explaining the American Victory

Geography played an important role in the American victory. The British had to send soldiers and supplies to a war that was several thousand miles from home.

>> American soldiers hoist the 13-star flag, a proud symbol of everything they fought for during the War for Independence.

They also had to fight an enemy that was spread over a wide area. For their part, the Americans were familiar with the local geography. They chose geographic features, like hilltops, that would provide an advantage in battle.

Assistance from Allies Help from other nations was crucial to the American cause. Spanish forces attacked the British along the Gulf of Mexico and in the Mississippi Valley. French money helped pay for supplies, and French military aid provided vital support to American troops. Without French soldiers and warships, for example, the Americans might not have won the Battle of Yorktown.

A Growing National Identity and Patriotism Throughout their struggles with Britain, the colonists benefited from their ability to unify for a shared

>> By war's end, Americans respected Washington's leadership and military skills. Here, Washington rides in triumph through the streets of Boston.

American cause. The American Revolution inspired people of many different racial and minority groups as well as social classes to fight for the same American ideals of freedom and rights. Debates about equality would continue long after independence was earned, but the ideals from the Revolution would further define a developing American identity.

Patriotism was another important factor in the American victory. Soldiers were fighting for their homes and their beliefs. Despite early setbacks, the Patriots continued to fight for their cause.

Gradually, Washington's inexperienced troops learned how to drill, how to march, and how to fight the British. Perhaps most important was Washington himself. By the end of the war, the general's leadership and military skills were respected by Americans and British alike.

Washington Leaves the Army In December 1783, General Washington, before resigning, bid farewell to his officers at Fraunces Tavern in New York City. Colonel Benjamin Tallmadge recalled the event:

> Such a scene of sorrow and weeping I had never before witnessed. . . . We were then about to part from the man who had conducted us through a long and bloody war, and under whose conduct the glory and independence of our country had been achieved.
> —Benjamin Tallmadge, *Memoir*

All along Washington's route home to Virginia, crowds cheered for their hero. The new nation faced difficult days ahead. In time, Americans would call on Washington to lead them once again.

? **RECALL** What were the main reasons for the American victory?

ASSESSMENT

1. **Identify Central Issues** Why was the American victory at Saratoga significant to the Patriots?

2. **Hypothesize** how surviving a long winter at Valley Forge with their commander affected the Continental Army.

3. **Draw Conclusions** Why did many people believe that the Declaration of Independence justified an end to slavery in the colonies?

4. **Generate Explanations** How was General Cornwallis defeated at the Battle of Yorktown?

5. **Summarize** Why did Benedict Arnold's name become synonymous with being a traitor?

North America in 1753

KEY
- Claimed by Britain
- Claimed by Spain
- Claimed by France
- ¤ French fort

1. **Locate Places of Importance** Use the map above to locate and describe French land claims in North America in 1753. First, use the key to locate French lands and forts and the lands claimed by Britain and Spain. Second, locate the major rivers in the French territory. Write a paragraph describing the French territory. Describe the location in relation to lands claimed by Britain and Spain, list the major rivers in the region, describe what you can infer about the location of French settlements from the location of the forts, and explain why controlling the Ohio River would be important to the French.

2. **Analyze the Effect of Human Geographic Factors** Write a paragraph analyzing why some Native American groups chose to form alliances with the French and others chose to form alliances with the British during the French and Indian War. Consider why the Algonquins and the Hurons sided with the French and why the Iroquois sided with the British.

3. **Analyze the Effects of Physical Geographic Factors** Write a paragraph analyzing how the physical geography of the area affected the British attack on Quebec during the French and Indian War. Describe what the physical geography was like and why the French felt protected, analyze how the British used physical geography to their advantage, and describe the consequences for the French.

4. **Analyze the Causes of the American Revolution** Write a paragraph analyzing how peaceful colonial protests against the Stamp Act led to revolution. Consider the Stamp Act Congress, boycotts, calls for free enterprise, and Parliament's actions.

5. **Create a Written Presentation Describing the Townshend Acts** Describe the Townshend Acts as a cause of the American Revolution by creating a written presentation using standard grammar, spelling, sentence structure, punctuation, and proper citation of sources. Describe what the Townshend Acts were as well as the role of boycotts, the Sons of Liberty, and the Daughters of Liberty in protesting the acts.

6. **Organize and Interpret Information from Reports** Analyze the excerpt below from a report about the Boston Massacre. Then write a paragraph organizing and interpreting the information in the report by explaining whether the report is a primary or secondary source and interpreting the report to determine whether it shows bias.

On the night of March 5, 1770, a crowd of colonial troublemakers gathered outside the Boston customs house in a massive display of civil disobedience. The angry mob shouted insults at the British troops guarding the building, even though the soldiers were showing no aggression toward the mob. Soon, the shouting turned to violence, as the crowd began to throw snowballs, oyster shells, and chunks of ice at the soldiers. As the mob grew larger and more menacing, the outnumbered British soldiers panicked and fired into the crowd. When the smoke from the musket volley cleared, five of the troublemakers lay dead or dying.

—*Civil Disobedience in the American Revolution*

7. Explain the Roles of Crispus Attucks, Samuel Adams, and John Adams in Boston Massacre Write a paragraph describing the roles played by Crispus Attucks, Samuel Adams, and John Adams in the Boston Massacre. Describe what led to the Boston Massacre; who Crispus Attucks was and what happened to him; who Samuel Adams was and how he reacted to the Boston Massacre; and who John Adams was, what he did after the Boston Massacre, and why.

8. Analyze the Reasons For and Impact of Civil Disobedience Write a paragraph analyzing the reasons for the Boston Tea Party and the consequences of this act of civil disobedience. Define the term *civil disobedience,* analyze why Sam Adams and the Sons of Liberty staged the Boston Tea Party, describe what the actual act of civil disobedience was, and analyze the impact of this act of civil disobedience.

9. Describe the Contributions of Military Leaders Write a paragraph describing how Ethan Allen contributed to the colonial war efforts in 1775 as the leader of the Green Mountain Boys. Describe who Ethan Allen was, what Allen and the Green Mountain Boys did in May 1775, and why the contribution was significant.

10. Use the Decision-Making Process Write a paragraph describing the decision-making process a colonist might have used to decide whether to support the Patriots, the British, or remain neutral in the war. Identify the situation that requires a decision, indicate what information the colonists would need to gather, identify the colonists' options, predict the consequences of the different options, and indicate what you would have done if the decision was yours to make.

11. Identify Major Events, Including Drafting the Declaration of Independence Write a paragraph describing the drafting and adoption of the Declaration of Independence. Explain why Congress drafted a formal declaration of independence, explain the role Thomas Jefferson played in the process, identify the date when the Continental Congress adopted the Declaration, and explain the effects of adopting the Declaration.

12. Define and Give Examples of Unalienable Rights Write a paragraph defining the term *unalienable rights* and giving examples of those rights. Define the term, give examples, and evaluate how the idea of unalienable rights adopted by the Founding Fathers represents good civic virtues.

13. Identify the Colonial Grievances in the Declaration of Independence Write a paragraph identifying the grievances that Thomas Jefferson outlined in the Declaration of Independence and describing his reasons for listing the grievances. Explain what is meant by *colonial grievances,* identify some of the grievances Jefferson listed, tell why Jefferson listed so many grievances and pointed out that the colonies had petitioned the king unsuccessfully to correct these injustices, and explain why the grievances caused the colonists to declare independence.

14. Explain the Issues Surrounding Declaring Independence Write a paragraph about the issues surrounding the decision to declare independence from Britain. Using the quotation below and other sources, explain what Richard Henry Lee risked by making the resolution below and what other delegates risked in supporting the resolution. Identify what Lee suggested in the resolution and explain why this course of action was risky.

Resolved, That these United Colonies are and of right ought to be, free and independent States, that they are absolved from all allegiance to the British Crown, and that all political connection between them and the State of Great Britain is, and ought to be, totally dissolved.

—Richard Henry Lee, Resolution at the Second Continental Congress, June 7, 1776

15. Identify a Colonial Grievance in the Declaration of Independence Write a paragraph drawing a connection between the Declaration of Independence's grievance that King George III had put limits on trade and the colonists' support for free enterprise over mercantilism. Consider how the Navigation Acts limited trade and how a free-enterprise system would benefit trade.

16. **Contributions of Women** Write a paragraph identifying the contributions of women to the war effort. Indicate how women helped economically, how women helped on the battlefield, and how their experiences in the Revolution encouraged women to campaign for equal treatment in later years.

17. **Contributions of African Americans** Use the graph below and other sources from this topic to write a paragraph analyzing the contributions of African Americans to the war effort. Use your mathematical skills to determine approximately what percentage of the African American population in the colonies was made up of free men, and what percentage of those free men fought in the Patriot army. Identify approximately how many African Americans served in the navy and what the enlistment policy was, and analyze how and why colonial views on African Americans serving in the army changed.

18. **Identify the American Revolution** Write a paragraph identifying the factors that contributed to the Americans winning the Revolutionary War and achieving independence during the revolutionary era. Identify the role played by geography, how the assistance from allies helped, and the effects of a growing national identity and patriotism during the revolutionary era.

19. **Write about the Essential Question** Write an essay on the Essential Question: **When is war justified?** Use evidence from your study of this topic to support your answer.

African Americans and the Revolution

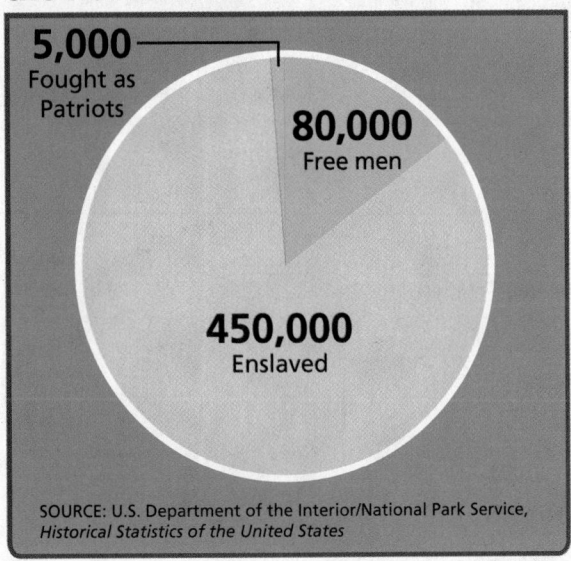

5,000
Fought as Patriots

80,000
Free men

450,000
Enslaved

SOURCE: U.S. Department of the Interior/National Park Service, *Historical Statistics of the United States*

[ESSENTIAL QUESTION] How much power should the government have?

4 **A Constitution for the United States (1776–Present)**

Enduring Understandings

- Weaknesses of the Articles of Confederation caused problems after the American Revolution.

- Enlightenment and Roman principles of government influenced the Constitution.

- After debate and ratification, the Constitution became the foundation of American government.

- The Bill of Rights (the first ten amendments) ensures protection of basic human rights.

- The Constitution established the executive, legislative, and judicial branches of government with a system of checks and balances to limit the power of each.

- People must meet criteria to be American citizens, and with citizenship comes rights and responsibilities.

>> Independence Hall in Philadelphia, Pennsylvania

PEARSON realize. NBC LEARN

Watch the My Story Video to learn how James Madison influenced the ratification of the Constitution.

PEARSON realize.
www.PearsonRealize.com

Access your digital lessons including:
Topic Inquiry • Interactive Reading
Notepad • Interactivities • Assessments

4.1 A Weak Confederation

>> The Second Continental Congress adopted the Articles of Confederation in 1777. The Articles spelled out the first constitution of American government.

▶ **Interactive Flipped Video**

>> Objectives

Explain why state governments wrote constitutions.

Identify the strengths and weaknesses of the Articles of Confederation.

Describe the process the Articles created for admitting new states.

Explain why many Americans called for changes to the Articles.

Summarize Shays' Rebellion and how it influenced leaders to change the Articles of Confederation.

>> Key Terms

constitution
bill of rights
Articles of
  Confederation
cede
currency
Land Ordinance of
  1785
Northwest
  Ordinance
depression
Shays' Rebellion

State governments vary from state to state. In forming a government, most states wrote constitutions. A **constitution** is a document that sets out the basic laws, principles, organization, and processes of a government. States wrote constitutions for two reasons. First, a written constitution would spell out the rights of all citizens. Second, it would limit the power of government.

Each State Creates a Constitution

People valued the rights that state governments protected. Virginia's constitution included a **bill of rights,** or list of freedoms that the government promises to protect. Virginia's bill of rights guaranteed trial by jury, freedom of religion, and freedom of the press. Several other states followed Virginia's lead. For example, the Massachusetts state constitution guaranteed people:

> . . . the right of enjoying and defending their lives and liberties; that of acquiring, possessing, and protecting property; in [short], that of seeking and obtaining their safety and happiness.

> —Massachusetts Constitution of 1780

The new state governments were somewhat similar to the colonial governments in structure. The states divided power between an executive and a legislature. The legislature was elected by the voters to pass laws. Every state but Pennsylvania had a governor to execute, or carry out, the laws.

Under the state constitutions, more people had the right to vote than in colonial times. To vote, a citizen had to be white, male, and over age 21. He had to own a certain amount of property or pay a certain amount of taxes. For a time, some women in New Jersey could vote. In a few states, free African American men who owned property could vote.

? IDENTIFY What sort of freedoms did many states agree to protect?

The Articles of Confederation

As citizens formed state governments, the Continental Congress was drafting a plan for the nation as a whole. Delegates believed that the colonies needed to be united by a national government in order to win independence.

It was hard to write a constitution that all states would approve. They were reluctant to give up power to a central government. Few Americans saw themselves as citizens of one nation. Instead, they felt loyal to their own states. Also, people feared replacing the "tyranny" of British rule with another strong government.

After much debate, the Continental Congress approved the first American constitution in 1777. The **Articles of Confederation** created a very loose alliance of 13 independent states.

>> The constitution of the state of Massachusetts declared that the primary purpose of the Massachusetts state government is to protect the natural rights of its inhabitants.

Strengths and Weaknesses Under the Articles of Confederation, the United States became a union of states with a weak central government. In a sense, the Articles simply put into law the existing reality of government in the colonies—a Congress with delegates acting on behalf of states that retained most of the power. The new nation was still at war, its revolution not yet won. It was not the time to discuss the political relationship between the states and Congress. The Articles of Confederation represented an effective compromise during a difficult time.

As a plan of government, the Articles of Confederation had strengths. It left states free to make decisions for themselves. It prevented the federal government from gaining too much power.

Under the Articles, each state sent one delegate to Congress. Thus each state, no matter its size or population, had one vote. Congress did have the power to declare war. It could appoint military officers, coin money, and operate post offices. It was also responsible for foreign affairs and could sign treaties.

However, the Articles of Confederation had weaknesses as well. Compared to the states, Congress had very limited powers. Congress could pass laws, but nine states had to approve a law before it could go into effect. Even then it was up to the states to enforce the laws passed by Congress. The Articles included no president to execute laws.

Congress could not regulate trade between states or between states and foreign countries. Nor did it have the power to tax. To raise money, Congress had to ask the states for funds or borrow them. No state could be forced to contribute funds. There was also no system of courts to settle conflicts between states.

Debates Over Western Lands One major dispute arose before the Articles of Confederation went into effect. Maryland refused to ratify the Articles unless

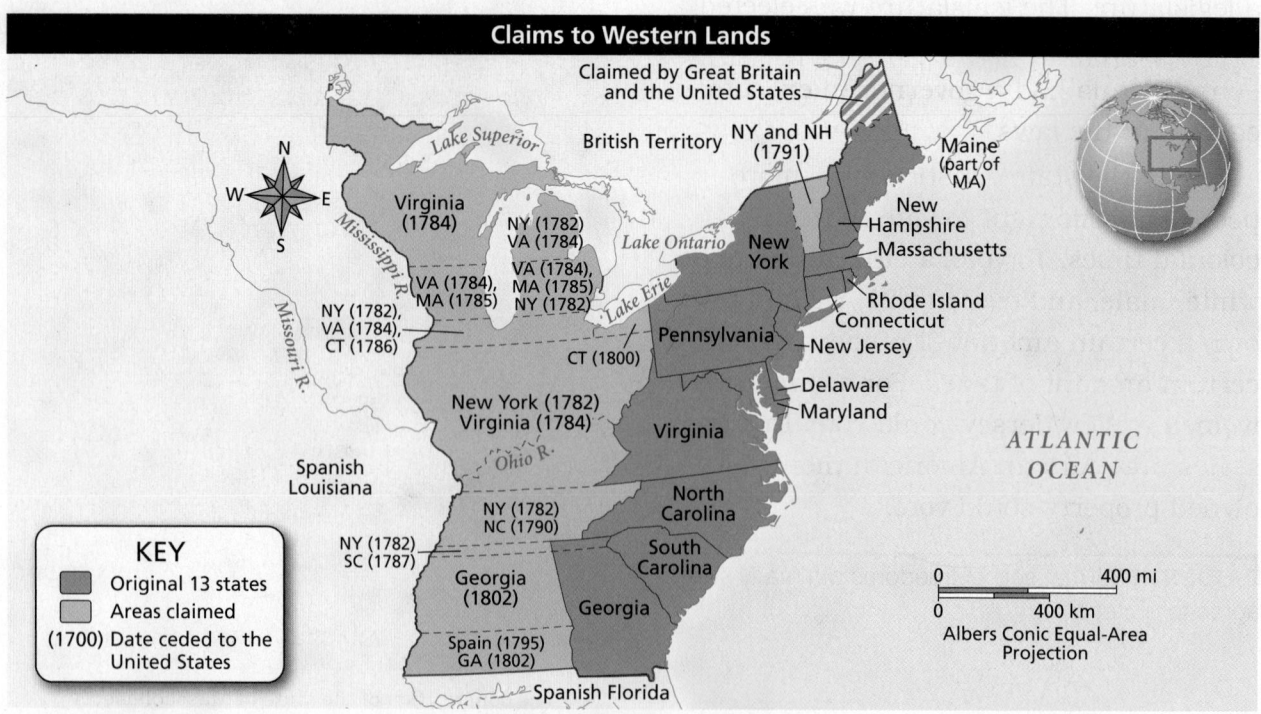

Claims to Western Lands

KEY
- Original 13 states
- Areas claimed
- (1700) Date ceded to the United States

>> **Analyze Maps** Based on the information in the map, what problems did the U.S. government face as the country expanded westward?

Virginia and other states **ceded,** or gave up, their claims to lands west of the Appalachian Mountains. Like other small states, Maryland feared that "landed" states would become too powerful.

One by one, the states agreed to cede their western claims to Congress. Finally, only Virginia held out. However, Thomas Jefferson and other leading Virginians recognized the great need to form a central government. They persuaded state lawmakers to give up Virginia's claims in the West.

With its demands met, Maryland ratified the Articles of Confederation in 1781. The new American government could at last go into effect.

? IDENTIFY SUPPORTING DETAILS What functions was Congress able to perform under the Articles of Confederation?

Weaknesses of the Confederation

By 1783, the United States had won its independence. Yet, the end of the American Revolution did not solve the confederation's troubles. Americans had reason to doubt whether "these United States" could survive.

Many States Have Disagreements

Disputes continued to arise among states. For example, both New Hampshire and New York claimed Vermont. The Articles did not give the central government power to resolve such conflicts. Noah Webster, a teacher from New England, saw the problem clearly:

> So long as any individual state has power to defeat the measures of the other twelve, our pretended union is

but a name, and our confederation, a cobweb.

—Noah Webster, *Sketches of American Policy*

Concerns Over Debt and Currency After the Revolution, the United States owed millions of dollars to individuals and foreign nations. Without the power to tax, Congress had no way to repay these debts. It asked the states for money, but the states often refused.

During the Revolution, the Continental Congress had solved the problem of raising funds by printing paper **currency,** or money. However, the Continental dollar had little value because it was not backed by gold or silver. Before long, Americans began to describe any useless thing as "not worth a Continental."

As Continental dollars became nearly worthless, states printed their own currency. This caused confusion. How

>> The currency issued by the Continental Congress lost value throughout the war. After the war, the United States owed millions of dollars to individuals and foreign nations.

▶ **Interactive Chart**

much was a North Carolina dollar worth? Was a Virginia dollar as valuable as a Maryland dollar? Most states refused to accept the money of others. As a result, trade became very difficult.

Foreign Countries Promote Their Own Interests Foreign countries took advantage of the confederation's weakness. Ignoring the Treaty of Paris, Britain refused to withdraw its troops from American territory on the Great Lakes. Spain closed its port in New Orleans to American shipping. This was a serious blow to western farmers, who depended on the port to ship their products to the East.

❓ CHECK UNDERSTANDING Why did trade between states become increasingly difficult?

An Orderly Expansion

Despite its troubles, Congress did pass important laws about how to govern the Northwest Territory. This was the U.S. territory west of Pennsylvania, north of the Ohio River, south of the Great Lakes, and east of the Mississippi. The laws established how territories would be governed and how they could become states.

The **Land Ordinance of 1785** set up a system for settling the Northwest Territory. The law called for the territory to be surveyed and divided into townships. Each township would then be further divided into 36 sections of one square mile each (640 acres).

Congress planned to sell sections to settlers for a minimum of $640 apiece. One section in every township was set aside to support public schools. Selling the land provided income for the government, which was significant because Congress did not

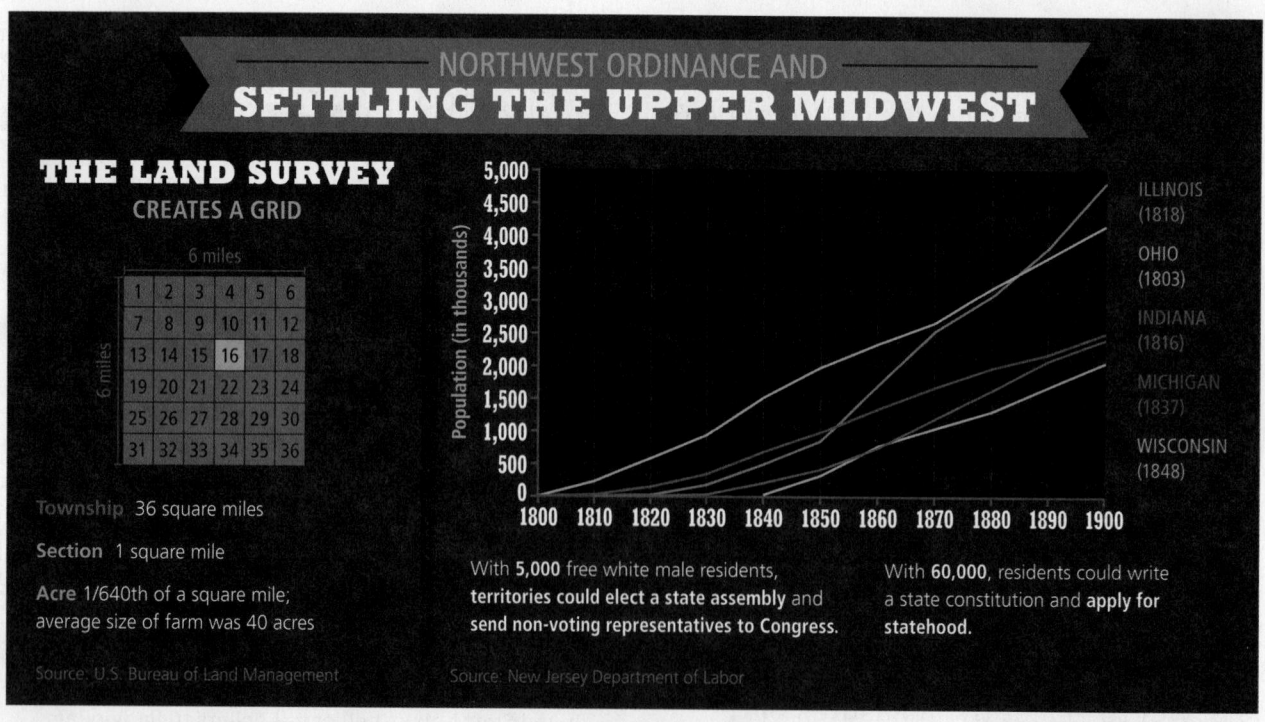

NORTHWEST ORDINANCE AND
SETTLING THE UPPER MIDWEST

THE LAND SURVEY
CREATES A GRID

6 miles

1	2	3	4	5	6
7	8	9	10	11	12
13	14	15	16	17	18
19	20	21	22	23	24
25	26	27	28	29	30
31	32	33	34	35	36

6 miles

Township 36 square miles

Section 1 square mile

Acre 1/640th of a square mile; average size of farm was 40 acres

Source: U.S. Bureau of Land Management

ILLINOIS (1818)
OHIO (1803)
INDIANA (1816)
MICHIGAN (1837)
WISCONSIN (1848)

Population (in thousands): 5,000 / 4,500 / 4,000 / 3,500 / 3,000 / 2,500 / 2,000 / 1,500 / 1,000 / 500 / 0
1800 1810 1820 1830 1840 1850 1860 1870 1880 1890 1900

With **5,000** free white male residents, **territories could elect a state assembly** and **send non-voting representatives to Congress.**

With **60,000**, residents could write a state constitution and **apply for statehood.**

Source: New Jersey Department of Labor

>> Analyze Information How did the Northwest Ordinance help to reduce conflict between the states as settlement expanded westward beyond traditional state boundaries?

 Interactive Map

>> A typical farm during the Revolutionary War could borrow the money it needed to continue producing goods because demand for them was high.

have the power to tax under the Articles of Confederation, yet the nation was in debt.

In 1787, Congress passed the **Northwest Ordinance**. It set up a government for the Northwest Territory, guaranteed basic rights to settlers, and outlawed slavery there. It also provided for the vast region to be divided into separate territories in the future.

The Northwest Ordinance established the principle that new territories should not become part of existing states but should be admitted as new states. It provided a procedure, or process, to admit new states to the nation. Once a territory had a population of 60,000 free settlers, it could ask Congress to be admitted as a new state. Each new state would be "on an equal footing with the original states in all respects whatsoever." In time, the states of Ohio, Indiana, Illinois, Michigan, and Wisconsin were created from the Northwest Territory.

Despite the drawbacks of the Articles of Confederation, the laws Congress created relating to the Northwest Territory proved to be a major success. These laws established principles defining the basic rights of settlers and served as a model for the rights citizens would expect to be protected. Trial by jury, freedom of religion, free use of waterways, fair treatment in the courts, and other rights were guaranteed. By providing that money from each township's land sales be used for schools, these laws also established federal support for education.

? **RECALL** What was the purpose of the Northwest Ordinance?

Economic Problems Lead to Change

The Northwest Ordinance was the finest achievement of the national government under the Articles. Still, the government was unable to solve its economic problems. After the Revolution, the nation suffered an economic depression. A **depression** is a period when business activity slows, prices and wages fall, and unemployment rises.

Farmers Demand Fair Treatment The depression hit farmers hard. The war had created a high demand for farm products. Farmers borrowed money for land, seed, animals, and tools. However, when the Revolution ended, demand for farm goods went down. As prices fell, many farmers could not repay their loans.

In Massachusetts, matters worsened when the state raised taxes. The courts seized the farms of those who could not pay their taxes or loans. Angry farmers felt they were being treated unfairly.

Daniel Shays, a Massachusetts farmer who had fought at Bunker Hill and Saratoga, organized an uprising in 1786. More than 1,000 farmers took part in **Shays' Rebellion.** They attacked courthouses and prevented the state from seizing farms when farmers could not pay their debts. Finally, the Massachusetts legislature sent the militia to drive them off.

A Call For Revision Many Americans saw Shays' Rebellion as a sign that the Articles of Confederation did not work. Warned George Washington, "I predict the worst consequences from a half starved, limping government, always moving upon crutches and tottering at every step."

To avert a crisis, leaders from several states called for a convention to revise the Articles of Confederation. They met in Philadelphia in May 1787. In the end, however, this convention would create an entirely new framework of government.

? CHECK UNDERSTANDING What did Shays' Rebellion show to many people?

ASSESSMENT

1. **Summarize** the voting rights in most states in the early 1780s.

2. **Identify Central Issues** What were three weaknesses of the central government under the Articles of Confederation?

3. **Generate Explanations** Why did people describe something without value as "not worth a Continental?"

4. **Hypothesize** about why slavery was outlawed in the Northwest Territories.

5. **Predict Consequences** How do you think the convention will improve upon the Articles of Confederation?

4.2 Drafting a Constitution

>> James Madison (standing) helped solve some of the most pressing problems delegates faced at the Constitutional Convention. **Infer** Why might Madison be considered a model of civic virtue?

▶ Interactive Flipped Video

The **Constitutional Convention** opened on May 25, 1787, in Philadelphia, Pennsylvania. Its goal was to revise the Articles of Confederation. Every state except Rhode Island sent representatives. The convention would prove historic because it did not revise the Articles of Confederation. Instead, it produced a new United States Constitution.

>> **Objectives**

Identify the leaders of the Constitutional Convention.

Compare the main differences between the two rival plans for the new Constitution.

Summarize compromises the delegates had to reach before the Constitution could be signed.

>> **Key Terms**

Constitutional
  Convention
Virginia Plan
legislative branch
executive branch
judicial branch
New Jersey Plan
compromise
Great Compromise
Three-Fifths
  Compromise

PEARSON realize www.PearsonRealize.com Access your Digital Lesson.

A Historic Convention

American Leaders Come Together

The convention's 55 delegates were a remarkable group. Eight of them had signed the Declaration of Independence, including the oldest, Benjamin Franklin. At age 81, Franklin was wise in the ways of government and human nature. George Washington was a representative from Virginia. Washington was so well respected that the delegates at once elected him president of the Convention.

Still, most of the delegates represented a new generation of American leaders. Nearly half were young men in their thirties, including Alexander Hamilton of New York. During the Revolution, Hamilton had served for a time as Washington's private secretary. Hamilton despised the Articles of Confederation. "The nation," he wrote,

>> Ben Franklin (with cane, center) and George Washington (raising hat, right) were among the delegates to the Constitutional Convention in 1787.

"is sick and wants powerful remedies." The powerful remedy he prescribed was a strong central government.

A Student of History and Politics Perhaps the best-prepared delegate was 36-year-old James Madison of Virginia. For months, he had been reading books on history, politics, and commerce. Madison set a model of civic virtue when he arrived in Philadelphia with a case bulging with volumes of research.

Madison was quiet and rather shy. Still, his keen intelligence and his ideas about how to structure a democratic government strongly influenced the other delegates. Today, Madison is often called the "Father of the Constitution."

Secret Conversations When the Convention began, the delegates decided to keep their talks secret. They wanted to speak their minds freely and be able to explore issues without pressures from outside.

The closed windows helped keep the debates secret, but they made the room very hot. New Englanders in their woolen suits suffered terribly in the summer heat. Southerners, with clothing more suited to warm temperatures, were less bothered.

? RECALL Why was James Madison considered the best prepared delegate at the Convention?

Disagreements Over a New Government

Soon after the meeting began, the delegates realized they would have to do more than simply revise the Articles of Confederation. They chose instead to write an entirely new constitution for the nation. They disagreed,

Virginia and New Jersey Plans

VIRGINIA PLAN

- Population as basis for house representation
- Two houses with seats based on population
- One house is elected by the people, the other house by state legislators
- Chief executive is chosen by the legislature
- Judicial branch is chosen by the legislature

- Three branches of government to prevent abuse of power
- Legislative branch consists of elected representatives

NEW JERSEY PLAN

- Drafted in response to Virginia Plan
- One house with one seat and one vote regardless of population as in the Articles of Confederation
- Executive branch consists of several executives
- Judicial branch is chosen by the executive branch

>> **Analyze Information** How did the New Jersey Plan and Virginia Plan differ in their approach to the executive branch of government?

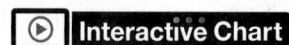 Interactive Chart

however, about what form the new national government should take.

Virginia Proposes a Plan Edmund Randolph and James Madison, both from Virginia, proposed a plan for the new government. This **Virginia Plan** called for a strong national government with three branches. The **legislative branch** would pass the laws.

The **executive branch** would carry out the laws. The **judicial branch,** or system of courts, would decide whether laws or the Constitution were violated.

According to the Virginia Plan, the legislature would consist of two houses. Seats would be awarded on the basis of population. Thus, in both houses, larger states would have more representatives than smaller ones. Under the Articles of Confederation, each state, regardless of population, only had one vote in Congress.

New Jersey Disagrees Small states opposed the Virginia Plan. They feared that the large states could easily outvote them in Congress. Supporters of the Virginia Plan replied that it was only fair for a state with more people to have more representatives.

After two weeks of debate, William Paterson of New Jersey presented a plan that had the support of the small states. Like the Virginia Plan, the **New Jersey Plan** called for three branches of government. However, it provided for a legislature that had only one house. Each state, regardless of its population, would have one vote in the legislature.

? IDENTIFY MAIN IDEAS What was the essential difference between the Virginia Plan and the New Jersey Plan?

The Great Compromise

For a while, no agreement could be reached. With tempers flaring, it seemed that the Convention would fall apart without adopting any plan. Finally, Roger Sherman of Connecticut worked out a compromise that he hoped would satisfy both the large and small states. A **compromise** is a settlement, or peaceful solution, in which each side gives up some of its demands in order to reach an agreement.

Sherman's compromise called for the creation of a two-house legislature. Members of the lower house, known as the House of Representatives, would be elected by popular vote. As the larger states wished, seats in the lower house would be awarded to each state according to its population.

Members of the upper house, called the Senate, would be chosen by state legislatures. Each state, no matter what its size, would have two senators. This part of Sherman's compromise appealed to the smaller states.

On July 16, the delegates narrowly approved Sherman's plan. It became known as the **Great Compromise.** Each side, in an admirable show of civic virtue, gave up some demands to achieve unity. With a margin of just one vote, the delegates had found a peaceful resolution to a problem that had threatened to bring the convention to a halt.

? IDENTIFY SUPPORTING DETAILS How did the Great Compromise address the concerns of small and large states?

>> Roger Sherman (right), mastermind of the Great Compromise, and fellow Connecticut delegate Oliver Ellsworth (left) draft a solution to the issue of representation in 1787.

[▶] Interactive Gallery

The Three-Fifths Compromise

Just as there were disagreements between large states and small states, there were also disagreements between northern states and southern states. The most serious disagreements concerned the issue of slavery. Would enslaved people be counted as part of a state's population? Would the slave trade continue to bring enslaved Africans into the United States?

The States Reach an Agreement

Southerners wanted to include enslaved African Americans in the population count even though they would not let those people vote. If enslaved African Americans were counted, southern states would have more representatives in the House of Representatives. Northerners objected. They argued that, since enslaved African Americans could not vote, they should not be counted when assigning representatives.

THE THREE-FIFTHS COMPROMISE

ISSUE AND COMPROMISE

THE NORTHERN VIEW
We'll be outvoted if we let them count slaves, and slaves are unable to vote.

THE COMPROMISE
Each slave counts as $\frac{3}{5}$ of a person.

THE SOUTHERN VIEW
Our slaves should be counted as part of our population and representation.

ESTIMATING THE EFFECT OF COMPROMISE

REPRESENTATION FOR VIRGINIA 1790

POPULATION
442,177 FREE WHITES
292,627 ENSLAVED

STEP **1**
$\frac{3}{5}$ OF **292,627** ENSLAVED POPULATION
= **175,576**

STEP **2**
175,576 ENSLAVED + **442,177** FREE
= **617,753** TOTAL

STEP **3**
Counting only the free population, Virginia would have **15 representatives**.

Counting the free + enslaved populations, Virginia would have **25 representatives**.

Counting free + $\frac{3}{5}$ enslaved populations, Virginia would have **20 representatives**.

Source: University of Delaware

EFFECT ON SOUTHERN REPRESENTATION

SOUTHERN REPRESENTATION IN THE HOUSE **1790**

31% NOT COUNTING THREE-FIFTHS OF SLAVES

43% COUNTING THREE-FIFTHS OF SLAVES

>> Based on the information presented, how did southern states benefit from the Three-Fifths Compromise?

Once again, the delegates compromised. They agreed that three fifths of the enslaved people in any state would be counted.

In other words, if a state had 5,000 enslaved residents, 3,000 of them would be included in the state's population count. This agreement became known as the **Three-Fifths Compromise**.

The fraction in the Three-Fifths Compromise had come from a rule in the Articles of Confederation. That rule tied taxes to population and counted only three fifths of enslaved residents when a state was being taxed. The new compromise balanced the concerns of Northerners and Southerners by using the three-fifths rule—which had already been agreed upon—as an acceptable way to assign both representatives and taxes to each state.

Further Disagreement Over Slavery

There was another disagreement over slavery. By 1787, some northern states had banned the slave trade within their borders. Delegates from these states urged that the slave trade be banned in the entire nation. Southerners argued that such a ban would ruin their economy.

In the end, northern and southern states compromised once more. Northerners agreed that Congress could not outlaw the slave trade for at least 20 years. After that, Congress could regulate the slave trade if it wished. Northerners also agreed that no state could stop a person fleeing slavery from being returned to an owner.

? IDENTIFY CENTRAL IDEAS Why did many of the northern states object to including enslaved people in population counts?

The Convention Comes to a Conclusion

As the long, hot summer drew to a close, the weary delegates struggled with one difficult question after another. How many

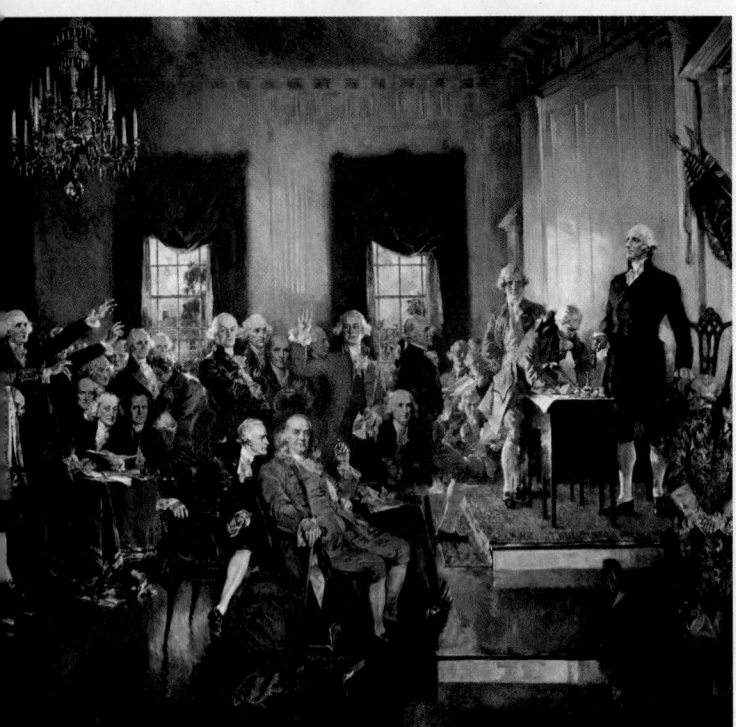

>> After the convention delegates returned to their home states where debate began about approving the Constitution. **Predict Consequences** How would the American public respond to the new Constitution?

years should the President, head of the executive branch, serve? How should the system of federal courts be organized? Would members of Congress be paid?

Finally, on September 17, 1787, the Constitution was ready to be signed. Its opening lines, or Preamble, expressed the goals of the framers: "We the People of the United States, in order to form a more perfect union . . . "

Gathering for the last time, delegates listened quietly as Benjamin Franklin rose to speak. He pleaded that the document be accepted:

I doubt . . . whether any other Convention . . . may be able to make a better Constitution. . . . I cannot help expressing a wish, that every member of the Convention who may still have

objections to it, would with me, on this occasion, doubt a little of his own infallibility, and . . . put his name to this instrument.

—Benjamin Franklin, *Records of the Federal Convention of 1787*

One by one, delegates came forward to sign the document. All but three of the delegates remaining in Philadelphia did so. Edmund Randolph and George Mason of Virginia, along with Elbridge Gerry of Massachusetts, refused to sign. They feared that the new Constitution gave too much power to the national government.

The main effect of the Constitution's creation was to set in motion a process in which states had to decide whether to approve the Constitution. The Constitution called upon each state to hold a convention to approve or reject the plan for the new government. Once nine states endorsed it, the Constitution would become the law of the land.

❓ IDENTIFY SUPPORTING DETAILS Why did some delegates choose not to sign the Constitution?

ASSESSMENT

1. **Contrast** the ideas of Alexander Hamilton with those of George Mason. Which one was more pleased with the final Constitution?

2. **Hypothesize** Why did New Jersey propose the plan that it did?

3. **Evaluate Arguments** The Great Compromise is so named because it was considered vital to the success of the Convention. What proof is there that it was a Great Compromise?

4. **Draw Conclusions** How did the agreement that no state could stop a fugitive slave from being returned to his or her owner affect slaves?

5. **Determine Relevance** What is so significant about the Preamble's opening words, "We the People of the United States . . ."?

>> The tradition of representative government in colonial history dates back to the Mayflower Compact, written and signed at sea in 1620 to provide rules for settling Plymouth.

▶ **Interactive Flipped Video**

Long before the Revolution, John Adams called on Americans to investigate how governments worked. The delegates to the Constitutional Convention followed this advice and borrowed many principles from the past to create the new government.

>> **Objectives**

Identify what American leaders learned about government from studying ancient Rome.

Summarize the traditions of freedom that Americans inherited from England and from their own colonial past.

Describe how the Enlightenment ideas shaped the development of the Constitution.

>> **Key Terms**

republic
dictatorship
Magna Carta
English Bill of Rights
habeas corpus
separation of
  powers
Founding Fathers

Principles from the Roman Republic

> Let us . . . search into the spirit of the British constitution; read the histories of ancient ages; contemplate the great examples of Greece and Rome; [and] set before us the conduct of our own British ancestors. . . .
>
> —John Adams, *Dissertation on the Canon and Feudal Law*

>> The Roman Republic, which lasted for over 400 years, provided an example to the framers of the United States Constitution of a representative government that was strong enough to survive over time.

The delegates wanted to create a **republic,** a government in which citizens rule themselves through elected representatives. Few republics in the history of the world survived very long. In order to create one that would last, American leaders looked first to the ancient examples of Greece and, especially, Rome.

The Virtues of a Republic Americans greatly admired the Roman Republic. General Charles Lee, one of George Washington's commanders, commented, "I used to regret not being thrown into the World in the glorious [era] of the Romans."

Independence and public service were virtues that the **Founding Fathers** saw in the citizens of Rome. Roman citizens were willing to serve in public office, not for money, but because they were devoted to their republic. The founders wrote the Constitution with these same civic virtues in mind and hoped Americans would live by the same principles.

Many American colonists admired Rome so much that when they debated politics in the newspapers, they often signed their opinions with Roman names such as Cincinnatus or Cicero.

A Belief in Independent Citizens At the same time, the Founding Fathers saw the collapse of Rome's republic as a warning

>> The Founders, including Thomas Jefferson shown here, looked to the Roman Republic for inspiration as they drafted the Constitution.

>> This illustration shows King John of England signing the Magna Carta in 1215. **Infer** How might the Magna Carta have influenced the ideas of the writers of the United States Constitution?

▶ **Interactive Timeline**

to the United States. No republic could survive unless its citizens remained independent and devoted to public service without the desire for personal or financial gains. Under the ruler Caesar Augustus, Rome eventually became a **dictatorship**, a government in which one person or a small group holds complete authority. The leaders of the American Revolution believed that Romans stumbled once they allowed corruption to take over.

Historians today admit that the Founding Fathers somewhat exaggerated the virtues of Rome's republic. Yet, the lessons they learned still have force. Republics do not always die because they are invaded from outside. Without educated and dedicated citizens who put the nation's needs above their own, republics can decay from within due to corruption.

❓ **LIST** What qualities of citizens in the Roman Republic did many early colonists admire?

English Influences

Greece and Rome were not the only examples of democratic government. Despite their quarrel with Britain, leaders of the Revolution valued British traditions of freedom.

The Magna Carta King John of England signed the **Magna Carta** in 1215. The Magna Carta contained two basic ideas that helped to shape both British and American government. First, it made it clear that English monarchs themselves had to obey the law.

Some Grievances Against the King

GRIEVANCE IN DECLARATION OF INDEPENDENCE	MODERN INTERPRETATION
He has forbidden his governors to pass laws of immediate and pressing importance, unless suspended in their operation till his assent should be obtained; and, when so suspended, he has utterly neglected to attend to them.	Colonial government in the colonies cannot function with the king's interference.
He has dissolved representative houses, repeatedly, for opposing, with manly firmness, his invasions on the rights of the people.	Colonial governments are not free to speak out against royal policies without fear of retribution.
He has kept among us, in time of peace, standing armies, without the consent of our legislatures.	The colonies have no representation in the British Parliament.
He has excited domestic insurrections amongst us and has endeavored to bring on the inhabitants of our frontiers, the merciless Indian savages, whose known rule of warfare is an undistinguished destruction of all ages, sexes and conditions.	The king's actions are causing conflicts between Loyalists and Patriots. He is also attempting to pit the Native Americans against the colonists by appearing as if he is protecting Native American lands from further western settlement.

>> **Summarize** How did Native Americans figure into the colonists' grievances against King George?

King John agreed not to raise taxes without first consulting the Great Council of nobles and church officials. Eventually, the Great Council grew into the British Parliament.

Just as important, the Magna Carta stated that English nobles had certain rights—rights that were later extended to other classes of people as well. These included rights to trial by jury and the right to private property. The idea of private property rights strongly influenced the beliefs of early Americans, which partly explains the development of a free-enterprise system throughout the nation.

The English Bill of Rights In 1689, the **English Bill of Rights** went further in protecting the rights of citizens. The document said that parliamentary elections should be held regularly.

It upheld the right to a trial by jury and allowed citizens to bear arms. It also affirmed the right of **habeas corpus,** the idea that no person could be held in prison without first being charged with a specific crime.

❓ **IDENTIFY CENTRAL ISSUES** What are some of the essential ideas found in the Magna Carta?

America Draws on Its Own Traditions

Americans enjoyed a long tradition of representative government. The Virginia colonists set up the House of Burgesses. Eventually, each colony elected its own legislature.

Self-Government Americans were also used to relying on written documents that clearly identified the powers and limits of government. The Mayflower Compact, written in 1620, was the first document of self-government in North America. Each of the 13 colonies had a written charter granted by the monarch or by Parliament.

Answerable to the People The framers of the Constitution also drew on their own experiences. The Founding Fathers bitterly remembered their grievances against the English king. In writing the Constitution, they sought to prevent such abuses.

For example, the Declaration of Independence accused the king of placing military power above civilian authority. The Constitution made the elected President "Commander in Chief of the Army and Navy . . . and of the militia of the several states." The Declaration protested that the king had made judges "dependent on his will alone." The Constitution set up a court system independent of the President and legislature.

The framers were very familiar with the workings of the Second Continental Congress, the Articles of Confederation, and their own state governments. Much that went into the Constitution came either from the Articles or from the state constitutions.

The Influence of the Enlightenment

The Constitution was also based on the ideas of the European Enlightenment. Enlightenment thinkers believed that people could improve society through the use of reason. Many of the Constitution's framers had read the works of Enlightenment thinkers.

John Locke The English writer John Locke published *Two Treatises of Government* in 1690. In it, he stated two important ideas. First, Locke declared that all people had natural rights to life, liberty, and property.

Second, he suggested that government is an agreement between the ruler and the ruled. The ruler must enforce the laws and protect the people. If a ruler violates the

people's natural rights, the people have a right to rebel.

Locke's ideas were popular among Americans. The framers of the Constitution wanted to protect people's natural rights and limit the power of government. They saw the Constitution as a contract between the people and their government.

Locke's principle of a natural right to property was established in the Constitution. Certain guarantees in the Constitution protect the rights of people to own private property, enforce contracts, and engage freely in business activities. These freedoms are essential to a market economy. Article I of the Constitution also gave Congress the power to regulate commerce and encourage the free flow of goods between states, creating an environment in which business could thrive.

>> John Locke's writings suggested the idea that governments exist to secure and protect the rights of their citizens.

Interactive Gallery

Baron de Montesquieu The French Enlightenment thinker Baron de Montesquieu (MAHN tus kyoo) influenced American ideas of how a government should be constructed. In his 1748 book *The Spirit of the Laws*, Montesquieu stressed the importance of the rule of law. The powers of government, he said, should be clearly defined and divided up. He suggested that three separate branches be created: the legislative, executive, and judicial. This idea, known as the **separation of powers**, was designed to keep any person or group from gaining too much power.

A New Tradition Emerges from Others

The Founding Fathers drew on many traditions. In the end, though, the new system of government was not quite like anything that came before it.

When John Adams received the news from Philadelphia while serving as an ambassador to Great Britain, he wrote, "As we say at sea, huzza for the new world and farewell to the old one!" He called the Constitution "the greatest single effort of national deliberation that the world has ever seen."

? RECALL What idea from Baron de Montesquieu influenced American government?

ASSESSMENT

1. **Support Ideas with Examples** The text says that the founders admired the Romans because they had successfully built a republic. What are some examples of the Roman ideas that the founders admired?

2. **Make Predictions** What do you think the Americans' attitude toward the English Bill of Rights would lead to?

3. **Draw Conclusions** Why is the right of habeas corpus so important in the U.S. criminal justice system?

4. **Draw Conclusions** Why do you think the founders learned to value written documents around the time they wrote the Constitution?

5. **Summarize** the influences of Enlightenment thinkers on the United States Constitution.

>> Baron de Montesquieu was a French Enlightenment thinker. **Summarize** How did French Enlightenment thinker Baron de Montesquieu's idea of the separation of powers affect the structure of the United States Constitution?

Federalists, Antifederalists, and the Bill of Rights

>> Patrick Henry's declaration, "...give me liberty or give me death," was both a cry for freedom from Britain and a statement of his Antifederalist views.

▶ **Interactive Flipped Video**

The framers of the Constitution sent the document to Congress, along with a letter from George Washington. Washington warmly approved the document, predicting that the Constitution would "promote the lasting welfare of that country so dear to us all."

>> **Objectives**

Identify the key issues in the constitutional debate.

Explain how the Constitution was finally ratified.

Describe how the Bill of Rights was added to the Constitution.

>> **Key Terms**

Federalist
Antifederalist
Federalist Papers
amend
Bill of Rights
ratify

>> Federalist Alexander Hamilton, shown here with his arms outstretched outside of King's College in New York City, favored ratification of the Constitution.

▶ **Interactive Chart**

The Federalists and the Antifederalists

The framers had set up a process for the states to approve, or **ratify**, the new government. The Constitution would go into effect when at least 9 of the 13 states had ratified it. In 1787 and 1788, voters in each state elected delegates to special state conventions. These delegates would decide whether or not to ratify the Constitution.

For Ratification: The Arguments of the Federalists In every state, heated debates took place. Supporters of the Constitution called themselves **Federalists** because they favored a strong federal, or national, government. They called people who opposed the Constitution **Antifederalists**.

Federalists argued that the Articles of Confederation left too much power with the individual states. This imbalance produced a dangerously weak central government. Disputes among the states, Federalists said, made it too difficult for the government to function.

Federalists believed that the Constitution gave the national government the authority it needed to function effectively. At the same time, they said, the Constitution still protected the rights and powers of the individual states.

Federalists James Madison, Alexander Hamilton, and John Jay wrote a series of essays, known today as the *Federalist Papers*. Their purpose was to explain and defend the Constitution. They used pen names, but most people knew who they were. Today, the *Federalist Papers* remain among the best discussions of the political theory behind the American system of government.

Courts still refer to the *Federalist Papers* in making decisions about the principles and role of government. In this way, they have had a lasting influence on the U.S. system of government.

Against Ratification: The Arguments of the Antifederalists Antifederalists felt that the Constitution made the national government too strong and left the states too weak. They also thought that the Constitution gave the President too much power. Patrick Henry of Virginia protested:

> This Constitution is said to have beautiful features, but . . . they appear to me horribly frightful. . . . Your President may become king . . . If your American chief be a man of ambition and abilities, how easy is it for him to render himself absolute!

—Patrick Henry, Speech to the Virginia Convention, June 1788

Most people expected George Washington to be elected President. Antifederalists admired Washington, but they warned that future Presidents might lack Washington's honor and skill. For this reason, they said, the office should not be too powerful.

? IDENTIFY MAIN IDEAS What was the Antifederalists' primary objection to the Constitution?

A Bill of Rights

The chief objection of Antifederalists was that the Constitution had no bill, or list, of rights. Federalists held that it was impossible to list all the natural rights of people. Besides, they said, the Constitution protected citizens well enough as it was.

Antifederalists responded that a bill of rights was needed to protect such basic liberties as freedom of speech and religion. Unless these rights were spelled out, they could be too easily ignored or denied by the government. Americans, after all, had just fought a revolution to protect their freedoms against a too-powerful government. Violations of those freedoms were the main grievances cited in the Declaration of Independence. Antifederalists argued that a bill of rights was needed to address those grievances. Under the new Constitution, the President would have veto power over Congress—the people's representatives. Surely placing so much power in one man's hands, the Antifederalists argued, likewise demanded the protection of a bill of rights.

One of the strongest supporters of a bill of rights was George Mason of Virginia. In 1776, Mason had written the bill of rights for Virginia's constitution. After the Constitutional Convention refused to include a bill of rights, Mason joined the Antifederalists. Mason wrote a pamphlet opposing the ratification of the Constitution. The pamphlet was titled, simply, "Objections to This Constitution of

>> A bronze statue of George Mason at George Mason University honors his role in supporting the addition of the Bill of Rights to the Constitution.

Government." Its opening words were equally direct: "There is no Declaration of Rights."

? CHECK UNDERSTANDING What was the purpose of George Mason's pamphlet?

The Ratification Process

One by one, the states voted. Delaware led the way, ratifying on December 7, 1787. Pennsylvania and New Jersey soon followed. In these states, as in the states that ratified later, the main cause behind ratification was that Federalists were able to convince a majority of delegates that the Constitution would bring an improved system of government.

The Debate in New England

Massachusetts was the first key battleground. There, the old patriots Sam Adams and John Hancock held back their support. The delay seemed "very ominous," wrote Madison. Finally, Adams and Hancock convinced the state convention to recommend adding a bill of rights to the Constitution.

Still the debate continued. "Some gentlemen say, don't be in a hurry . . . don't take a leap in the dark," a Federalist farmer told his fellow delegates. "I say . . . gather fruit when it is ripe." In February 1788, Massachusetts became the sixth state to ratify.

In June, New Hampshire joined ranks as the ninth state. The new government could now go into effect. Still, the nation's unity remained in doubt. New York and Virginia, two of the largest states, had not yet ratified the plan. In both states, Federalists and Antifederalists were closely matched.

A Vote to Ratify After Long Debates In Virginia, Patrick Henry, George Mason, and Governor Edmund Randolph led the opposition. Still a spellbinding speaker, Henry at one point spoke for seven hours. Soft-spoken, James Madison could not match Henry's dramatic style. Yet his arguments in favor of the Constitution were always clear, patient, and to the point.

The tide finally turned when Governor Randolph changed his mind. He gave

Voting for Ratification

- December 7, 1787 — Delaware
- December 18, 1787 — New Jersey
- January 9, 1788 — Connecticut
- April 26, 1788 — Maryland
- May 23, 1788 — South Carolina
- November 21, 1788 — North Carolina
- February 6, 1788 — Massachusetts
- January 2, 1788 — Georgia
- December 12, 1787 — Pennsylvania
- July 26, 1788 — New York
- June 25, 1788 — Virginia
- June 21, 1788 — New Hampshire
- May 29, 1789 — Rhode Island

Timeline: December 1787 — March 1788 — June 1788 — September 1788 — December 1788 — March 1789 — June 1789

>> Ratifying the Constitution was a long process, taking a year and a half. **Analyze Data** Which was the first state to vote for ratification? Which was the last?

▶ Interactive Map

his support only when the Federalists promised to support a bill of rights. Virginia voted to ratify in late June.

In New York, the struggle went on for another month. In July 1788, the state convention voted to ratify. North Carolina followed in November 1789. Only Rhode Island, which had refused to send delegates to the Constitutional Convention, remained. On May 29, 1790, Rhode Island became the last state to ratify the Constitution. The effect of ratification was to create a new system of government for the United States, the same basic system that remains in effect today.

Celebration of a New Constitution

Throughout the land, Americans celebrated the news that the Constitution was ratified. The city of Philadelphia set its festival for July 4, 1788.

A festive parade filed along Market Street, led by soldiers who had fought in the Revolution. Thousands cheered as six colorfully outfitted horses pulled a blue carriage shaped like an eagle. Thirteen stars and stripes were painted on the front, and the Constitution was raised proudly above it. Benjamin Rush, a Philadelphia doctor and strong supporter of the Constitution, wrote to a friend, "'Tis done. We have become a nation."

? RECALL What factor encouraged many states to vote for ratification?

New Amendments

Americans voted in the first election under the Constitution in January 1789. As expected, George Washington was elected President, while John Adams was chosen as Vice President.

The first Congress met in New York City, which was chosen as the nation's

>> A parade in New York City honoring Alexander Hamilton celebrates the ratification of the Constitution.

first capital. Congress quickly turned its attention to adding a bill of rights to the Constitution. Several states had agreed to ratify the Constitution only on the condition that a bill of rights be added.

Amending the Constitution The framers had established a way to **amend**, or change, the Constitution to modify the rules for the national government. They did not want people to make changes lightly, however. Thus, they made the process of amending the Constitution fairly difficult. In 1789, the first Congress proposed a set of 12 amendments, written by James Madison. As required by the Constitution, the amendments then went for ratification by the states, three fourths of which had to ratify an amendment for it to take effect. By December 1791, three fourths of the states had ratified 10 of the 12 amendments. These 10 amendments became known as the Bill of Rights.

>> George Washington was inaugurated as the first President of the United States on April 30, 1789.

The Bill of Rights James Madison insisted that the Bill of Rights does not *give* Americans any rights. The rights listed, he said, are natural rights that belong to all human beings. The Bill of Rights simply prevents the government from taking these rights away.

Some of the first 10 amendments were intended to prevent the kind of abuse Americans had suffered under English rule. For example, the Declaration of Independence had condemned the king for forcing colonists to quarter troops in their homes and for suspending trial by jury. The Third Amendment forbids the government to quarter troops in citizens' homes without their consent. The Sixth and Seventh Amendments guarantee the right to trial by jury.

Other amendments protected individual rights as many states had already done.

In 1786, the Virginia Statute of Religious Freedom stated that "No man shall be compelled to frequent or support any religious worship . . . or otherwise suffer, on account of his religious opinions or belief." Religious freedom became the very first right listed in the First Amendment. The First Amendment also emphasized a key element of the republic: freedom of speech, or the ability to express different points of view.

At first, individual state governments were not considered subject to the Bill of Rights. It was only after the ratification of the Fourteenth Amendment in 1868 and subsequent Supreme Court decisions that the Bill of Rights was applied to the states.

Still, with the Bill of Rights in place, the new framework of government was complete. Over time, the Constitution would grow and change along with the nation.

? IDENTIFY What amendments make up the Bill of Rights in the Constitution?

ASSESSMENT

1. **Summarize** the ratification procedure for the Constitution.

2. **Hypothesize** the reasons that the Anti-Federalists feared too much power resting with the central government.

3. **Support Ideas with Examples** What examples can you think of that support the idea that a bill of rights is a good idea?

4. **Draw Conclusions** What do you think is the most likely reason that Rhode Island was the last state to ratify the Constitution?

5. **Generate Explanations** Why do you suppose James Madison, a Federalist, was the person responsible for writing amendments to the Constitution, which became the Bill of Rights?

Understanding the Constitution

>> The original U.S. Constitution is on display at the National Archives in Washington, D.C.

▶ **Interactive Flipped Video**

The Constitution is divided into three main parts: the **Preamble**, or opening statement, the articles, and the amendments. The Preamble states goals of the Constitution. The details of the American government system appear within the articles. Changes to the Constitution are the amendments.

>> **Objectives**

Explain the basic goals of the Constitution as defined by the Preamble.

Identify the framework of government that the Constitution established.

Summarize the seven basic principles of American government.

Identify the powers and duties of the legislative branch, executive branch, and judicial branch of the American government.

>> **Key Terms**

preamble	bill
domestic tranquillity	electoral college
civilian	Supreme Court
general welfare	appeal
liberty	unconstitutional
article	veto
popular sovereignty	override
limited government	impeach
checks and balances	constitutional
federalism	initiative
House of	local government
Representatives	judicial review
Senate	infrastructure

The Preamble, the Articles, and the Amendments

The Preamble identifies six goals of the Constitution:

> We the people of the United States, in order to form a more perfect union, establish justice, insure domestic tranquility, provide for the common defense, promote the general welfare, and secure the blessings of liberty to ourselves and our posterity, do ordain and establish this Constitution for the United States of America.
>
> —Preamble to the Constitution

To Form a More Perfect Union When the Constitution was written, the states saw themselves almost as separate nations. The framers wanted to work together as a unified nation. Fortunately for us, they achieved this goal. Think of what it would be like if you had to exchange your money every time you visited another state!

To Establish Justice The framers knew the nation needed a uniform system to settle legal disputes. Today, the American justice system requires that the law be applied fairly to every American, regardless of race, religion, gender, or country of origin.

To Insure Domestic Tranquillity Under the Constitution, the national government has the power to insure **domestic tranquillity**, or peace and order at home. Have you seen reports of the National Guard providing assistance in a disaster area? By such actions, the government works to insure domestic tranquillity.

To Provide for the Common Defense Every country has a duty to protect its citizens against foreign attack. The framers of the Constitution gave the national government the power to raise armies and navies. At the same time, they placed the military under **civilian**, or nonmilitary, control.

To Promote the General Welfare The Constitution set out to give the national government the means to promote the **general welfare**, or the well-being of all its citizens. For example, today the National Institutes of Health leads the fight against many diseases.

To Secure the Blessings of Liberty During the Revolution, the colonists fought and died for **liberty**, or freedom. It is no surprise that the framers made liberty a

>> In order to ensure domestic tranquillity, the National Guard helps provide assistance during local and national crises.

>> As one of the three branches of the U.S. government, the U.S. Congress meets regularly to revise existing laws and make new ones.

major goal of the Constitution. Over the years, amendments to the Constitution have extended the "blessings of liberty" to all Americans.

The Articles and the Amendments The main body of the Constitution is a short document, divided into seven sections called **articles**. Together, they establish the framework for our government.

Seven Articles The first three articles describe the three branches of the national government: legislative, executive, and judicial. Article I establishes the powers of and limits on Congress. Articles II and III do the same for the President and the courts.

Article IV deals with relations among the states. It requires states to honor one another's laws and legal decisions. It also sets out a system for admitting new states. Article V provides a process to amend the Constitution.

Article VI states that the Constitution is the "supreme law of the land." This means that states may not make laws that violate the Constitution. If a state law conflicts with a federal law, the federal law prevails. The final article, Article VII, sets up a procedure for the states to ratify the Constitution.

Twenty-Seven Amendments In more than 200 years, only 27 formal changes have been made to the Constitution. The first 10 amendments, known as the Bill of Rights, were added in 1791.

? DEFINE What is each section of the Constitution called?

Seven Basic Principles

The Constitution reflects seven basic principles. They are popular sovereignty, limited government, separation of powers, checks and balances, federalism, republicanism, and individual rights.

Popular Sovereignty The framers of the Constitution lived at a time when monarchs claimed that their power came from God. The Preamble, with its phrase "We the people," reflects a revolutionary new idea: that a government gets its authority from the people. This principle, known as **popular sovereignty**, states that the people have the right to alter or abolish their government.

Limited Government The colonists had lived under a British government with nearly unlimited powers. To avoid giving too much power to their new government, the framers made limited government a

>> **Analyze Cartoons** What point do you think the cartoonist is trying to make about government?

principle of the Constitution. In a **limited government**, the government has only the powers that the Constitution gives it. Just as important, everyone from you to the President must obey the law.

Separation of Powers To further limit government power, the framers provided for separation of powers. The Constitution separates the government into three branches. Congress, or the legislative branch, makes the laws. The executive branch, headed by the President, carries out the laws. The judicial branch, composed of the courts, judges whether actions violate laws and whether laws violate the Constitution.

Checks and Balances A system of **checks and balances** safeguards against abuse of power. Each branch of government has the power to check, or limit, the actions of the other two. The separation of powers allows for this system of checks and balances.

Federalism The Constitution also reflects the principle of **federalism**, or the division of power between the federal government and the states. Among the powers the Constitution gives the federal government are the power to coin money, declare war, and regulate trade between the states. States regulate trade within their own borders, make rules for state elections, and establish schools. Some powers are shared between the federal government and the states. Powers not clearly given to the federal government belong to the states.

Republicanism The United States is a constitutional republic. This means that the Constitution provides the basis for its

Separation of Powers

Legislative Branch	Executive Branch	Judicial Branch
(Congress)	(President)	(Supreme Court and Other Federal Courts)
Passes Laws	**Carries Out Laws**	**Interprets Laws**
• Can override President's veto • Approves treaties and presidential appointments • Can impeach and remove President and other high officials • Creates lower federal courts • Appropriates money • Prints and coins money • Raises and supports armed forces • Can declare war • Regulates foreign and interstate trade	• Proposes laws • Can veto laws • Negotiates foreign treaties • Serves as commander in chief of the armed forces • Appoints federal judges, ambassadors, and other high officials • Can grant pardons to federal offenders	• Can declare laws unconstitutional • Can declare executive actions unconstitutional

>> **Analyze Charts** How is the power to make and enforce laws divided among the three branches of government?

▶ **Interactive Chart**

republican form of government. Instead of taking part directly in government, citizens elect representatives to carry out their will. Once in office, representatives vote according to their own judgment. However, they must remain open to the opinions of the people they represent. For that reason, members of Congress maintain websites and offices in their home districts.

Individual Rights The final principle the U.S. Constitution reflects is individual rights, such as freedom of speech, freedom of religion, and the right to trial by jury. You will read more about the rights protected by the Constitution later.

❓ **IDENTIFY SUPPORTING DETAILS** What is the principle of federalism?

The Legislative Branch— Congress

The first and longest article of the Constitution deals with the legislative, or lawmaking, branch. Article I sets up the Congress to make the nation's laws. Congress is made up of two bodies: the House of Representatives and the Senate.

The House of Representatives The larger of the two bodies is the **House of Representatives**, which currently has 435 members. Representation in the House is based on population, with larger states having more representatives than smaller states. Every state has at least one representative.

Representatives are elected by the people of their district for two-year terms. As a result, the entire House is up for election every other year. Representatives may run for reelection as many times as they want.

>> Congress meets at the U.S. Capitol in Washington D.C. The building is home to the Senate, the House of Representatives, and many congressional offices.

Interactive Gallery

The leader of the House is called the Speaker. The Speaker of the House is one of the most powerful people in the federal government. The Speaker regulates debates and controls the agenda. If the President dies or leaves office, the Speaker of the House is next in line after the Vice President to become President.

The Senate Unlike the House, the **Senate** is based on equal representation of the states, with two senators for each state. Senators are elected to six-year terms. Their terms overlap, however, so that one third of the members come up for election every two years. This way, there is always a majority of experienced senators.

Not all of the Founders trusted the judgment of the common people. As a result, they called for senators to be chosen by state legislatures. Over the years, the nation slowly became more democratic. The Seventeenth Amendment, ratified in 1913, provided that senators be directly elected

by the people of each state, like members of the House.

The Vice President of the United States is president of the Senate. The Vice President presides over the Senate and casts a vote when there is a tie.

The Vice President cannot, however, take part in Senate debates. When the Vice President is absent, the Senate's president pro tempore, or temporary president, presides.

Powers of Congress The most important power of Congress is the power to make the nation's laws. All laws start as proposals called **bills**. A new bill may be introduced in either the House or the Senate. However, an appropriations bill, which is a bill that sets aside money for government programs or operations, must be introduced in the House. After a bill is introduced, it is debated. If both houses vote to approve the bill, it is then sent to the President. If the President signs the bill, it becomes a law.

The Constitution gives Congress many other powers besides lawmaking. Article I, Section 8, lists most of the powers of Congress. They include the power to levy, or require people to pay, taxes and to borrow money. Congress also has the power to coin money, to establish post offices, to fix standard weights and measures, and to declare war.

The Elastic Clause Not all the powers of Congress are specifically listed. Article I, Section 8, Clause 18, states that Congress can "make all laws which shall be necessary and proper" for carrying out its specific duties. This clause is known as the elastic clause because it enables Congress to stretch its powers to deal with the changing needs of the nation.

Americans have long debated the true meaning of the elastic clause. What did the framers mean by the words *necessary* and *proper?* For example, early leaders debated whether the elastic clause gave Congress the right to set up a national bank, even though the Constitution does not specifically give Congress that power.

Today, political parties still have different points of view on how the elastic clause should be used. Some Americans continue to worry that Congress might use the elastic clause to abuse its powers. Sometimes, the terms *strict constructionists* and *loose constructionists* are used to refer to people with different views of the clause.

Strict constructionists think that Congress (and the courts that interpret laws) should strictly construe, or narrowly interpret, the elastic clause. They believe the elastic clause should be used to stretch the powers of government rarely, and only to a small degree. Partly because many members of the Republican Party today are strict constructionists, that party particularly believes in reducing or eliminating some government programs.

>> United States senators sit for a formal portrait in the Senate chamber of the Capitol.

In contrast, loose constructionists think that Congress (and the courts that interpret laws) should loosely construe, or broadly interpret, the elastic clause. They think the elastic clause should be used to stretch the powers of government as often as needed, and to a greater degree. Many members of the Democratic Party today are loose constructionists. Because they believe that the role of the federal government can and should expand as needed, they may support government programs opposed by members of the Republican Party.

The Committee System The First Congress, meeting from 1789 to 1791, considered a total of 31 new bills. Today, more than 10,000 bills are introduced in Congress each year. Clearly, it would be impossible for every member of Congress to give each new bill careful study. To

deal with this problem, Congress relies on committees.

Both the House and the Senate have permanent, or standing, committees. Each committee deals with a specific topic, such as agriculture, banking, business, defense, education, science, or transportation. Members who have served in Congress the longest are usually appointed to the most important committees.

Congress may sometimes create joint committees made up of both Senate and House members. One of the most important kinds of joint committees is the conference committee. Its task is to settle differences between House and Senate versions of the same bill.

? **IDENTIFY SUPPORTING DETAILS** How does a bill become a law?

The Executive Branch—The President

Article II of the Constitution sets up an executive branch to carry out the laws and run the affairs of the national government. The President is the head of the executive branch. Other members include the Vice President, and the executive departments. The heads of the executive departments, who advise the President, are called the Cabinet.

The Many Roles of the President You are probably more familiar with the President than with any other government leader. You see him on television climbing in and out of airplanes, greeting foreign leaders, or making speeches. Yet, many Americans do not know exactly what the President does.

The framers thought that Congress would be the most important branch of government. Thus, while the Constitution is very specific about the role of the

>> Congress forms committees to hear testimony from experts and other key witnesses. Here, witnesses testify before the Senate Homeland Security Committee.

legislature, it offers fewer details about the powers of the President. Beginning with George Washington, Presidents have often taken those actions they thought necessary to carry out the job. In this way, they have shaped the job of President to meet the nation's changing needs.

The President is our highest elected official and, along with the Vice President, the only one who represents all Americans. As head of the executive branch, the President has the duty to carry out the nation's laws. The President directs foreign policy and has the power to make treaties with other nations and to appoint ambassadors.

The President is commander in chief of the armed forces. (Only Congress, however, has the power to declare war.) As the nation's chief legislator, the President suggests new laws and works for their passage.

The President can grant pardons and call special sessions of Congress. The President is also the living symbol of the nation. Presidents welcome foreign leaders, make speeches to commemorate national holidays, and give medals to national heroes.

The Electoral College The President is elected for a four-year term. As a result of the Twenty-second Amendment, adopted in 1951, no President may be elected to more than two complete terms.

The framers set up a complex system for electing the President, known as the **electoral college**. When Americans vote for President, they do not vote directly for the candidate of their choice. Rather, they vote for a group of electors who are pledged to the candidate. The number of a state's electors equals the number of its Senators and Representatives. No state has fewer than three electors.

>> The White House in Washington, D.C., is where the President conducts daily business and meets with top officials.

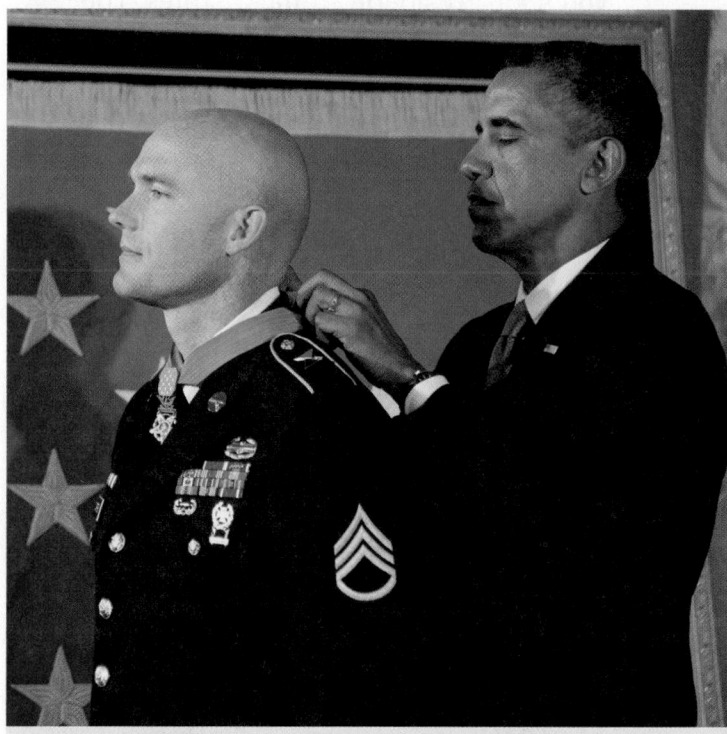

>> One presidential duty is to honor American soldiers. Here President Barack Obama awards a Medal of Honor to a member of the U.S. Armed Forces in the White House.

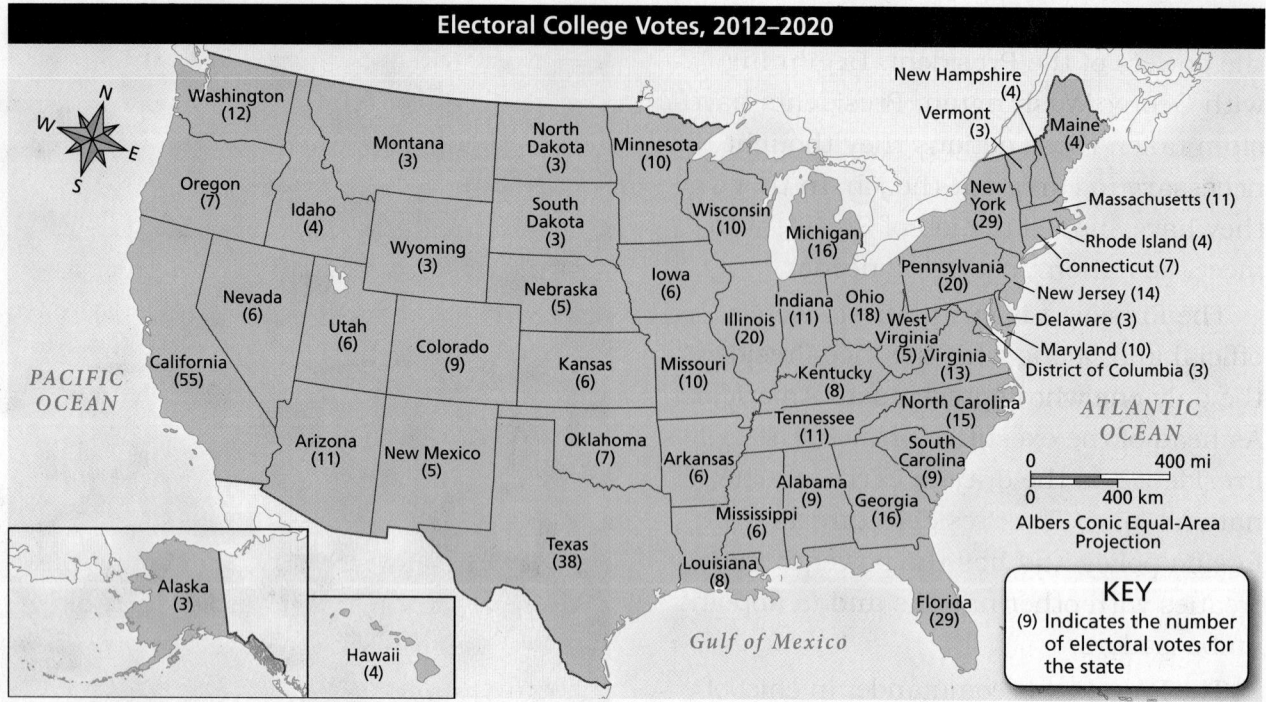

New Hampshire (4)
Vermont (3)
Maine (4)
Washington (12)
Montana (3)
North Dakota (3)
Minnesota (10)
Oregon (7)
Idaho (4)
Wyoming (3)
South Dakota (3)
Wisconsin (10)
Michigan (16)
New York (29)
Massachusetts (11)
Rhode Island (4)
Connecticut (7)
Nevada (6)
Utah (6)
Colorado (9)
Nebraska (5)
Iowa (6)
Illinois (20)
Indiana (11)
Ohio (18)
West Virginia (5)
Pennsylvania (20)
New Jersey (14)
Delaware (3)
Maryland (10)
District of Columbia (3)
California (55)
PACIFIC OCEAN
Arizona (11)
New Mexico (5)
Kansas (6)
Oklahoma (7)
Missouri (10)
Kentucky (8)
Virginia (13)
North Carolina (15)
ATLANTIC OCEAN
Tennessee (11)
Arkansas (6)
Alabama (9)
Mississippi (6)
Georgia (16)
South Carolina (9)
Texas (38)
Louisiana (8)
Florida (29)
Gulf of Mexico
Alaska (3)
Hawaii (4)

0 400 mi
0 400 km
Albers Conic Equal-Area Projection

KEY
(9) Indicates the number of electoral votes for the state

>> The number of electors each state has is based on the combined total of the state's Senators and Representatives. **Analyze Maps** Why might the number of a state's electors change?

A few weeks after Election Day, the electors meet in each state to cast their votes for President. In most states, the candidate with the majority of the popular vote in that state receives all that state's electoral votes. The candidate who receives a majority of the electoral votes nationwide becomes President.

Because of the "winner-take-all" nature of the electoral college, a candidate can lose the popular vote nationwide but still be elected President. This has happened four times. Today, some people favor replacing the electoral college with a system that directly elects the President by popular vote. Others oppose any change, pointing out that the electoral college has served the nation well for more than 200 years.

? **RECALL** How many terms is the President allowed to serve?

The Judicial Branch—The Supreme Court

Article III of the Constitution establishes a **Supreme Court** and authorizes Congress to establish any other courts that are needed. Under the Judiciary Act of 1789, Congress set up the system of federal courts that is still in place today.

Lower Courts Most federal cases begin in district courts. Evidence is presented during trials, and a jury or a judge decides the facts of the case. A party that disagrees with the decision of the judge or jury may **appeal** it, that is, ask that the decision be reviewed by a higher court. The next level of courts is the appellate courts, or courts of appeal.

Appellate court judges review decisions of district courts to decide whether the lower court judges interpreted and applied the law correctly.

Supreme Court At the top of the American judicial system is the Supreme Court. The Court is made up of a Chief Justice and eight Associate Justices. The President appoints the justices, but Congress must approve the appointments. Justices serve for life.

The main job of the Supreme Court is to serve as the nation's final court of appeals. It hears cases that have been tried and appealed in lower courts. Because its decisions are final, the Supreme Court is called "the court of last resort."

The Supreme Court hears and decides fewer than 100 cases each year. Most of the cases are appeals from lower courts that involve federal laws. After hearing oral arguments, the justices vote. Decisions require a majority vote of at least five justices.

Early on, the Court asserted the right to declare whether acts of the President or laws passed by Congress are **unconstitutional**, that is, not allowed under the Constitution. This power is called **judicial review**. The need for judicial review was first discussed in the *Federalist Papers*, and the Supreme Court has argued that the power is implicit in the Constitution, but it was not established until the 1803 case *Marbury* v. *Madison*, which gave the Supreme Court the power of judicial review.

Although powerful, the Supreme Court is limited by the system of checks and balances. One check on its power is that Congress can, in certain circumstances, remove Supreme Court justices from office. Also, the Supreme Court does not have the power to pass or enforce laws, it can only provide judicial review of laws.

? CHECK UNDERSTANDING What was the significant about the Supreme Court decision in the case *Marbury* v. *Madison* (1803)?

UNITED STATES SUPREME COURT

Reviews more than 7,000 petitions a year and selects 100–150 cases based on:	• National importance of the case • Need to eliminate conflicting court opinions related to a case	• Opportunity to set a precedent • Agreement among 4 of 9 Justices to accept a case

Original Jurisdiction	State Route	Federal Route
• Disputes between states or between a state and citizens of another state • Actions involving ambassadors or vice consuls of foreign nations • Actions between the U.S. and a state	State Supreme Court • Appeals of appellate court cases Appellate Court • Appeals of trial court cases Trial Court • Civil and criminal cases • Juries render verdicts • Judges enforce procedures	Court of Appeals • Appeals of cases originating in U.S. district courts • Reviews decisions by federal agencies District Court • Civil and criminal cases • Juries render verdicts • Judges ensure fair trial

>> A case can reach the Supreme Court through several paths. **Draw Conclusions** Why do you think so few cases reach the Supreme Court?

Preventing Abuse of Power

The framers hoped that the separation of powers among three branches would prevent the rise of an all-powerful leader who would rob the people of their liberty. But how could the framers prevent one of the branches from abusing its power? To answer this problem, they set up a system of checks and balances.

The system of checks and balances allows each of the three branches of government to check, or limit, the power of the other two. The President, for example, can check the actions of Congress by **vetoing**, or rejecting, bills that Congress has passed. Congress can check the President by **overriding**, or overruling, the veto, with a two-thirds vote in both houses. Congress must also approve presidential appointments and ratify treaties made by the President. The Supreme Court can check both the President and Congress by declaring laws unconstitutional through its power of judicial review.

Congress's most extreme check on the President is its power to remove the President from office. To do this, the House of Representatives must **impeach**, or bring charges of serious wrongdoing against, the President. The Senate then conducts a trial. If two thirds of the senators vote to convict, the President must leave office. Throughout our history, only two Presidents—Andrew Johnson and Bill Clinton—have been impeached by the House. Neither was convicted by the Senate.

The principle of checks and balances is based on the principle of separation of powers. Because the powers of government are separated into three branches, each branch can check the power of the other two. Like many principles in the Constitution, separation of powers and the system of checks and balances came from European philosophers of the Enlightenment.

One of these philosophers was Baron de Montesquieu, who wrote *The Spirit of Laws*. Montesquieu argued that the powers of government should be split among three equal branches: legislative, executive, and judicial. This would prevent any branch of government from becoming too powerful and protect individuals' rights. We can see many of Montesquieu's ideas reflected in the Constitution today.

? IDENTIFY SUPPORTING DETAILS What checks does Congress have over the President?

>> In this cartoon, each of the tree branches represents a branch of government—executive, legislative, and judicial. **Analyze Cartoons** How does the cartoon show that each branch can limit the power of the other two?

State Government

One principle of the Constitution is federalism, or the division of powers between the federal and state governments. The federal government deals with national issues. The states have the power to meet more local needs. There are also some powers that are shared. But state governments provide many basic services that Americans use each day.

The Question of States' Rights Many Americans originally opposed the Constitution because they thought it gave too much power to the federal government at the expense of the state governments. The Tenth Amendment was written to help ensure that the states keep powers not granted the federal government:

> The powers not delegated to the United States by the Constitution, nor prohibited by it to the states, are reserved to the states respectively, or to the people.
>
> —Tenth Amendment to the Constitution

Some Americans point to the Tenth Amendment as support for what is often called states' rights, or the idea that the federal government should not infringe on states' powers. A similar idea is that of state sovereignty, or the idea that, within a state, the state government is supreme.

The federal government has used the elastic clause to assume powers that some believe belong to the states. Thus, the debate over how power should be shared between the federal and state governments has been a matter of controversy through most of American history.

State Constitutions Each of the 50 states has a constitution that sets forth the principles and framework of its

>> The members of both houses of the Texas State Legislature, as well as the governor, carry out their duties at the State Capitol Building in Austin.

>> Arizona Governor Jan Brewer demonstrated state's powers by signing an appeal to the Obama administration over its denial of FEMA assistance for damage from wildfires.

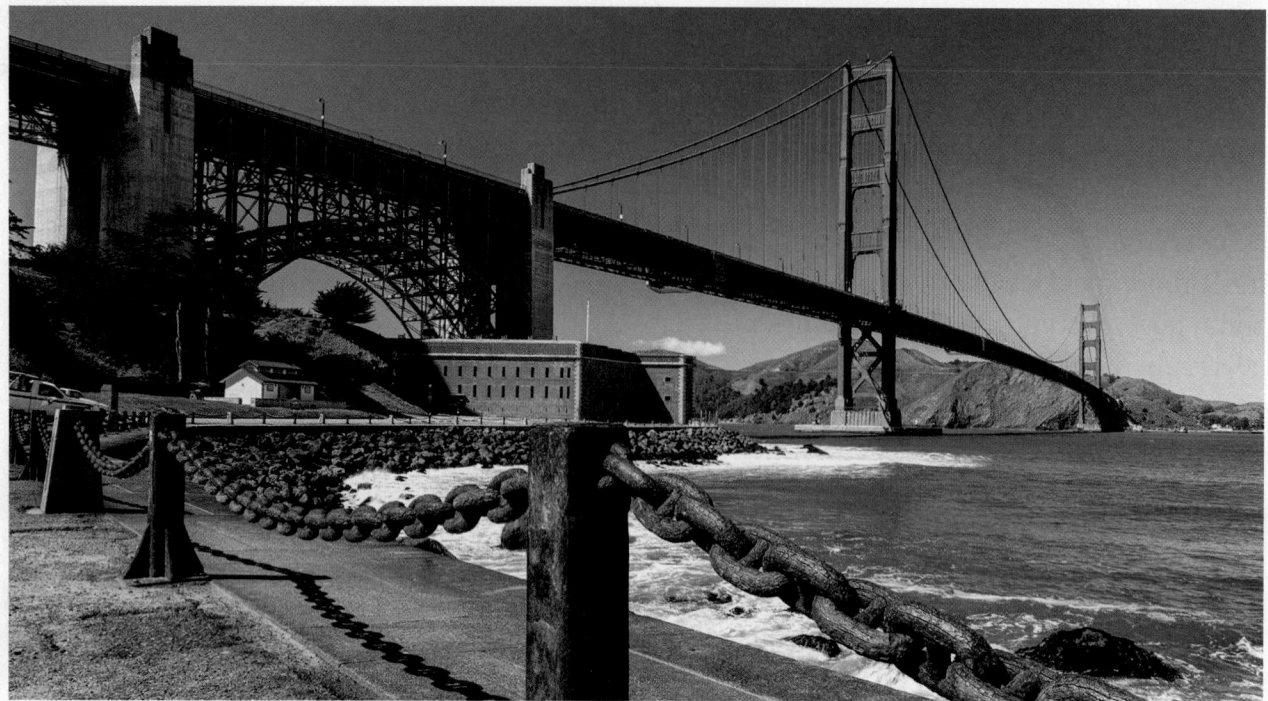

>> The California state government established the Golden Gate State Park in the 1870s, and ordered the construction of the Golden Gate Bridge, which opened to the public in 1937.

government. Although constitutions vary from state to state, they must all conform to the Constitution of the United States. If a conflict arises, the national Constitution—the "supreme law of the land"—prevails.

Most state constitutions resemble the national Constitution in form. They start with a preamble stating their goals and include a bill of rights guaranteeing individual liberties. State constitutions tend to be longer and more detailed than the national Constitution. Many include provisions on finance, education, and other matters.

State constitutions set up a government with three branches. The powers of the legislative, executive, and judicial branches on the state level are similar to those of the national government.

Changing State Constitutions State constitutions can be changed in several ways. In the most common method,

amendments are proposed by the state legislature and approved by the people in an election.

In almost one half of the states, citizens can act directly to change the constitution. In a process known as the **constitutional initiative**, sponsors of an amendment gather signatures on a petition. When the required number of signatures is attained, the petition goes to the legislature or to the voters for approval.

Finally, a state can rewrite its constitution. With the approval of the legislature or the people, the state may call a constitutional convention. The new constitution is then submitted to the people for official approval.

The States' Obligations to Citizens
State governments provide a wide range of services. They maintain law and order, enforce criminal law, protect property, and regulate business. They also supervise

public education, provide public health and welfare programs, build and maintain highways, operate state parks and forests, and regulate use of state-owned land.

The states, not the federal government, have the main responsibility for public education in the United States. Most students attend schools paid for and overseen by the state. The state sets general standards for schools and establishes a recommended course of study. It also sets requirements for promotion and graduation.

Each state must build and maintain its own **infrastructure**, or system of transit lines, roads, bridges, and tunnels. State departments or agencies manage more than 6,000 state parks and recreation areas. To help maintain high standards, state governments license the professionals who serve you, such as doctors, lawyers, and teachers.

When you are old enough to drive, the state will test you and, if you pass, give you a license. State police keep highways safe and protect us against criminal acts.

? IDENTIFY What are some examples of services that states provide to their citizens?

The Responsibilities of Local Government

The Constitution defines the powers of the federal and state governments. But it does not mention **local government**, that is, government on the county, parish, city, town, village, or district level. Local governments are created entirely by the states and have only those powers and functions that states give them.

Local governments have perhaps the greatest impact on our daily lives. At the same time, it is on the local level that citizens have the greatest opportunity to influence government.

Public Education The service that local governments spend the most money on

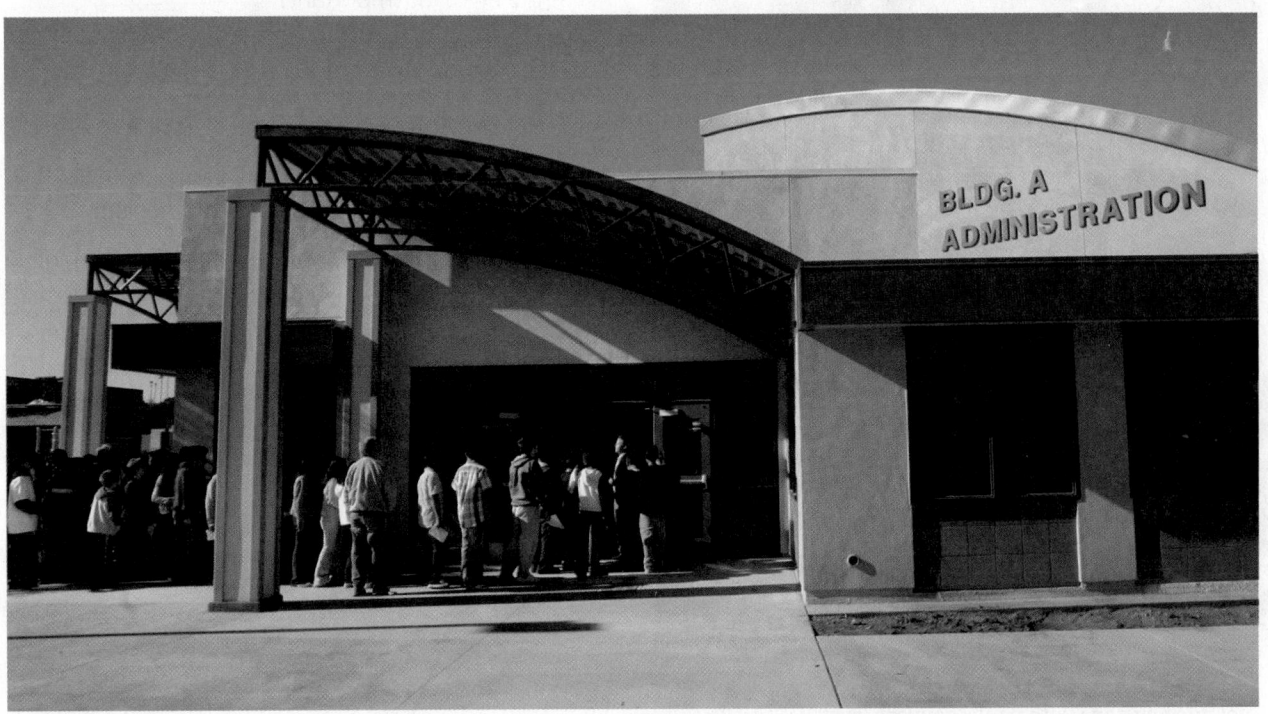

>> Locally-supported public education is important not only to the states, but also to the nation.

is education. While state governments set standards for schools, it is the cities, towns, or school districts that actually run them. Local school boards build schools and hire teachers and staff. They also have a strong say in which courses will be taught. However, school officials must make all decisions within the guidelines set by state law.

Education is one area of local government where citizens exert a great deal of control. Local residents may give up part of their time to serve on local school boards. In most communities, voters have the right to approve or turn down the annual school budget.

Many Other Services Local governments provide a variety of other services. They hire or support firefighters, police, and garbage collectors. Local governments provide sewers and water, maintain local roads and hospitals, and conduct safety inspections of buildings and restaurants. In many cases, water and sewage treatment plants are owned and run by local governments. Other communities hire private companies to supply local needs.

Over the years, Americans have looked to local government for more than basic services. Today, most local governments provide libraries and parks and other cultural and recreational facilities.

In larger cities, citizens expect their local governments to support airports, sports arenas, and civic centers. Public funding for such facilities is often the subject of debate in major cities.

? IDENTIFY On what service for citizens do local governments spend the most money?

ASSESSMENT

1. **Determine Relevance** What is the significance of the Preamble's opening words, "We the people of the United States"?

2. **Generate Explanations** Why is Article VI, which declares that the Constitution is the "supreme law of the land," so important?

3. **Analyze Information** What is meant by the statement that representatives "must remain open to the opinions of the people they represent."

4. **Compare and Contrast** the viewpoints of strict constructionists and loose constructionists.

5. **Support Ideas with Evidence** How would you use the Tenth Amendment of the Constitution to support the idea that the federal government should not assume more power than it already has?

>> Local governments take responsibility for providing citizens with public services, such as firefighters and police.

4.6 Amending the Constitution

>> The First Amendment protects freedom of speech and freedom of the press, or media. The media provide the public with a variety of perspectives on local, state, and national issues.

▶ **Interactive Flipped Video**

The framers foresaw that Americans might need to change the Constitution to address flaws or changed circumstances, However, they did not want to make it too easy to change the Constitution. As a result, they created a complex amendment process. The process may take months, or even years, to complete.

>> **Objectives**

Explain how the Constitution can be amended.

Identify the rights that the Bill of Rights protects.

Summarize how later amendments expanded democratic rights.

>> **Key Terms**

Bill of Rights
First Amendment
Second Amendment
incriminate
Civil War
   Amendments
Nineteenth
   Amendment
Twenty-sixth
   Amendment
civil

Methods of Amending the Constitution

PROPOSED

By Congress

by ⅔ vote of each house

OR

By national convention

called by Congress at request of ⅔ of state legislature

RATIFIED

By legislature

in ¾ of states

OR

By state convention

in ¾ of states

>> **Analyze Information** After an amendment to the Constitution has been proposed by both the Senate and the House of Representatives, what two options exist for the states to ratify the amendment?

 Interactive Chart

Constitutional Amendment

Article V outlines two ways to propose an amendment. An amendment may be proposed by two thirds of both the House and the Senate, or by a national convention called by Congress at the request of two thirds of the state legislatures. The second method has never been used.

An amendment may also be ratified in one of two ways. An amendment may be approved by the legislatures of three fourths of the states. Every amendment but the Twenty-first was ratified using this method. In the second method, an amendment may be approved by special conventions in three fourths of the states.

Not all amendments proposed by Congress have been ratified. In fact, Congress has proposed six amendments that the states refused to ratify.

? **IDENTIFY** Which article of the Constitution outlines the amendment process?

The Bill of Rights

As one of its first acts, the new Congress drafted a series of amendments in 1789 and sent them to the states for approval. In 1791, the **Bill of Rights**, the first ten amendments, became part of the Constitution.

Free Speech, Press, and Religious Freedom The **First Amendment** safeguards basic individual liberties. It protects freedom of religion, speech, and the press. It also guarantees the right to assemble peacefully and to petition the government to change its policies.

Because of the First Amendment, you cannot be arrested for criticizing a government official. You can attend the house of worship of your choice or none at all.

You can read newspapers that do not represent the views of an official political party. These freedoms are important in a constitutional republic because they allow citizens to make informed decisions and take part freely in political life. Still, there are limits on the First Amendment. For example, the government can limit free speech if there is "a clear and present danger," such as in time of war.

The First Amendment's guarantee of freedom of religion has a long history. Many colonists came to America to escape religious persecution. They wanted to be able to pray and worship freely. Today, Americans are allowed to practice religion as they please or not to practice religion, without fear of government interference. The guarantee of freedom of religion has remained a key American value.

Protection Against Abuse of Power

The **Second Amendment** states, "A well-regulated militia being necessary to the security of a free state, the right of the people to keep and bear arms shall not be infringed." Other amendments reflect the colonists' experiences under British rule. The Third Amendment says that Congress may not force citizens to put up troops in their homes. The Fourth Amendment protects Americans from unlawful searches of home or property.

Since early times, Americans have debated the exact meaning of the Second Amendment. Some believe that it guarantees individuals a basic right to bear arms. Others argue that it simply guarantees the individual states the right to maintain militias. The question of limits to gun ownership is one of the most complex and controversial constitutional issues facing Americans today.

Protecting the Rights of the Accused

The Fifth through Eighth amendments deal with the rights of people accused of crimes. The Fifth Amendment states that

>> Minutemen arm themselves before leaving for the Battle of Concord.

people cannot be forced to **incriminate**, or give evidence against, themselves. The Sixth Amendment guarantees the right to a speedy and public trial by an impartial, or fair, jury. It also states that people accused of crimes have the right to know the charges against them, as well as the right to confront the person making the charges. The Seventh Amendment provides for juries for **civil**, or noncriminal, trials. The Eighth Amendment forbids judges from ordering excessive bail or fines or "cruel and unusual punishments."

Upholding Individual Rights Some Americans had opposed adding a Bill of Rights. They argued that, if specific rights were listed in the Constitution, Americans might lose other rights that were not listed. The Ninth Amendment solved that problem. It makes clear that a citizen's individual rights are not limited to those listed in the Constitution.

The Tenth Amendment reaffirmed the framers' plan to create a limited federal government. It states that all powers not given to the national government or denied to the states are reserved for the states or for the people.

? RECALL Which amendments protect the rights of those accused of a crime?

Additional Amendments

Since the addition of the Bill of Rights, the Constitution has been amended only 17 times. Many later amendments reflect changing attitudes about equality and the expansion of democracy.

The Thirteenth, Fourteenth, and Fifteenth amendments are known as the **Civil War Amendments**. The Thirteenth Amendment abolished slavery. The Fourteenth Amendment guaranteed citizenship to former slaves. The Fifteenth

>> Although the police help to protect the public from criminals, the U.S. Constitution requires them to respect the rights of accused persons.

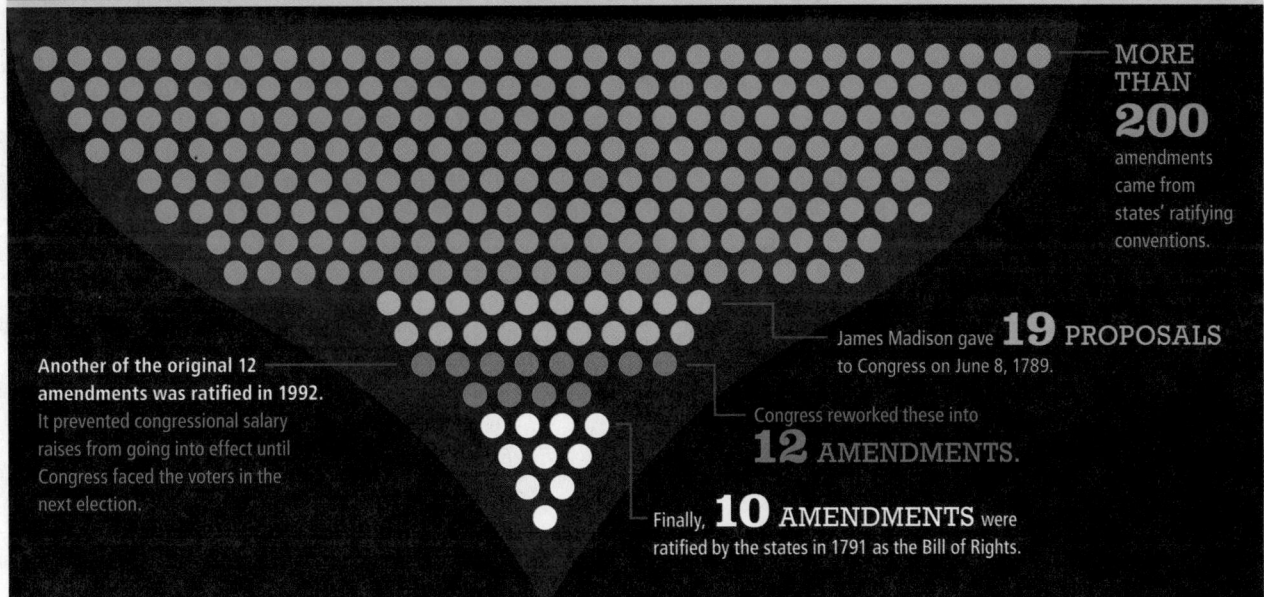

CHOOSING AMENDMENTS FOR THE BILL OF RIGHTS

MORE THAN **200** amendments came from states' ratifying conventions.

James Madison gave **19** PROPOSALS to Congress on June 8, 1789.

Congress reworked these into **12** AMENDMENTS.

Finally, **10** AMENDMENTS were ratified by the states in 1791 as the Bill of Rights.

Another of the original 12 amendments was ratified in 1992. It prevented congressional salary raises from going into effect until Congress faced the voters in the next election.

>> **Analyze Information** Approximately what percentage of the more than 200 amendments proposed by the states' ratifying conventions finally made it into the Bill of Rights?

Interactive Gallery

Amendment declared that states may not deny the vote to any citizen on the basis of "race, color, or previous condition of servitude." This guaranteed African American men the right to vote.

Other amendments further expanded voting rights. The **Nineteenth Amendment**, ratified in 1920, gave women the right to vote.

Women achieved this victory after more than 70 years of struggle. In 1971, changing attitudes toward the rights and responsibilities of young people gave birth to the **Twenty-sixth Amendment**. It lowered the minimum voting age from 21 to 18.

? IDENTIFY Which amendment gave women the right to vote?

ASSESSMENT

1. **Hypothesize** why the framers of the Constitution did not want to make it easy to amend the Constitution.

2. **Support Ideas with Examples** Give and explain an example of something that supports the idea that "In order to self-govern, people must be able to access information and make their own decisions"?

3. **Summarize** What fear did the Ninth Amendment address and how did it do so?

4. **Hypothesize** why the framers of the Constitution thought it was important to be able to change it with amendments, although they made it difficult to do so.

5. **Draw Conclusions** Why do you think the Constitution has been amended seventeen times in addition to the amendments called the Bill of Rights?

Citizens' Rights and Responsibilities

>> Spectators at a parade in Independence, Oregon celebrate Independence Day. **Generate Explanations** What does this day symbolize to the American people?

▶ **Interactive Flipped Video**

>> Objectives

Summarize what makes a person a citizen of the United States.

Identify how Americans can develop democratic values.

Describe the responsibilities of citizenship.

>> Key Terms

citizen
naturalize
immigrant
resident alien
civic virtue
patriotism
jury duty

A citizen is a person who owes loyalty to a particular nation and is entitled to all its rights and protections. Citizens must put the greater good ahead of their own desires when they follow the law, serve on juries, and make informed decisions about voting.

American Citizenship

To be a citizen of the United States, you must have fulfilled one of three requirements:

You were born in the United States, or at least one parent is a citizen of the United States.

You were **naturalized**, that is, you have completed the official legal process for becoming a citizen if you were born outside the United States.

You were 18 or younger when your parents were naturalized.

Becoming a Citizen Throughout American history, many millions of immigrants have become naturalized citizens. An **immigrant** is a person who enters another country in order to settle there.

To illustrate the naturalization process, we will look at one immigrant's story.

At age 15, Carla Rojas came to the United States from Argentina. Her mother returned home two years later, but Rojas decided to remain. After submitting numerous documents and photographs and attending several interviews, she received permission to remain in the country as a **resident alien**, or noncitizen living in the country.

After a required five-year waiting period, Carla submitted an application for citizenship. She had to take a test to show that she was comfortable with the English language and that she was familiar with American history and government. She also had to show that she was of "good moral character." Then, a naturalization examiner interviewed her about her reasons for becoming a citizen.

At last, Rojas stood before a judge and took the oath that confirmed her as an American citizen:

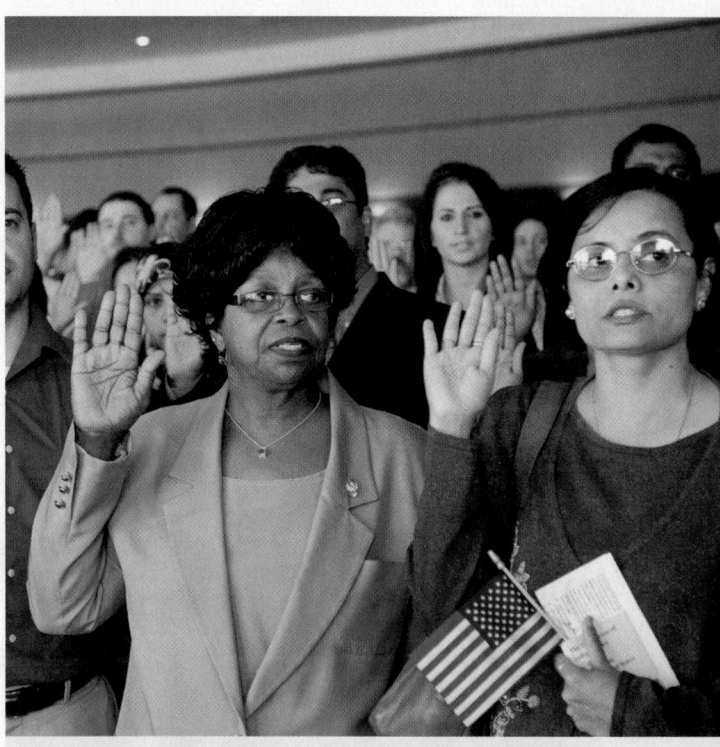

>> A group of immigrants swear the Oath of Allegiance to the United States in order to become citizens.

I hereby declare, on oath, that . . . I will support and defend the Constitution and laws of the United States against all enemies . . . that I will bear true faith and allegiance to the same . . . so help me God.

—Oath of Allegiance to the United States

A naturalized citizen enjoys every right of a natural-born citizen except one. Only natural-born citizens may serve as President or Vice President.

The Rights and Responsibilities of Citizens All American citizens have equal rights under the law. Americans have the right to speak freely, to worship as they choose, to vote, and to serve on juries. These rights are not based on inherited wealth or family connections. They are the rights of American citizens.

Still, nothing is free. As you will see, if we want to enjoy the rights of

>> One way students can express their civic virtue is by reciting the Pledge of Allegiance at school.

citizenship, we must also accept its responsibilities.

These rights and responsibilities reflect America's national identity—the common set of values that unites Americans. For example, citizens have both the right and the responsibility to vote. This reflects the principles of independence, liberty, and self-governance upheld in the Constitution and valued by the American people.

? DEFINE What is a citizen?

Citizenship and Democratic Values

The Founding Fathers admired **civic virtue**, that is, the willingness to work for the good of the nation or community even at great sacrifice. They looked to Roman models such as Cincinnatus, who, it was said, gave up a peaceful life on his farm when called upon to lead Rome. Again and again, leaders such as George Washington, Thomas Jefferson, and John Adams put the common good ahead of their own wishes. These three presidents maintained that democracy requires virtuous behavior by citizens.

The leaders feared that without this responsible behavior, American liberty would be at risk. How can a democracy run if individuals do not think about what is best for society and not just for themselves?

You do not have to go to great lengths to be a good citizen. At home, at school, and in the community, you can work to develop the values that are the foundation of our democratic system. Among these basic values are honesty and compassion. Others include patriotism, respect, responsibility, and courage.

A key democratic value is **patriotism**, or a feeling of love and devotion toward one's country. A sense of patriotism inspires Americans to serve their nation. It also encourages us to fulfill the ideals set forth in the Declaration of Independence, the Constitution, and the Bill of Rights.

As citizens, we must respect ourselves, our families, our neighbors, and the other members of our community. Respect may also involve objects or ideas. For example, a good citizen respects the property of others and the laws of the nation.

Responsibility may be both personal and public. We must accept responsibility for ourselves and the consequences of our actions and behaviors. In a democracy, individuals are expected to look out for themselves and for one another. For example, parents have a duty to support their families and teach their children. This is important because children depend on parents and families depend on one another. As a student, you have a responsibility to learn.

Courage may be either physical or moral. Soldiers, police, or firefighters display physical courage when they risk their lives for the good of others. Moral courage enables us to do the right thing even when it is unpopular, difficult, or dangerous. Americans such as George Washington, Abraham Lincoln, Susan B. Anthony, and Martin Luther King, Jr., faced risks in order to defend democratic values.

? DEFINE What is civic virtue?

>> Participating in community projects such as this clean-up activity strengthens the ties between community members and helps to ensure that public spaces remain usable.

 Interactive Chart

Responsible Citizenship

As citizens, we must accept our own civic responsibilities. Only if government and citizens work together can we meet our needs as a democratic society.

A Responsibility to Vote As citizens of a republic, we have the right to select the people who will represent us in government. But if that right is to have any meaning, then we must fulfill our responsibility to vote. A good citizen studies the candidates and the issues in order to make responsible choices.

The Obligation to Obey Laws and Rules In the Constitution, "we the people" give the government the power to make laws for us. Thus, we have a duty to obey the nation's laws. We have thousands of laws that keep us from hurting one another, regulate contracts, and protect citizens' rights. No one can know them all, but you must know and obey the laws that affect your life and actions.

You also have a responsibility to obey rules. You already have rules at home and rules at school—even rules to games you play. These rules are not enforced by the government as laws are. Like laws, however, they keep us safe, help us live together, and teach us to be accountable for our behavior. By learning to obey rules such as not to hit or cheat when we are young, we learn about responsible citizenship.

A Responsibility to Defend the Nation Americans have the duty to help defend the nation against threats to its peace or security. At age 18, all men must register for the draft. In time of war, the government may call them to serve in the armed forces. Many young citizens feel the duty to enlist in the military without being called.

Voter Turnout, 1900–2012

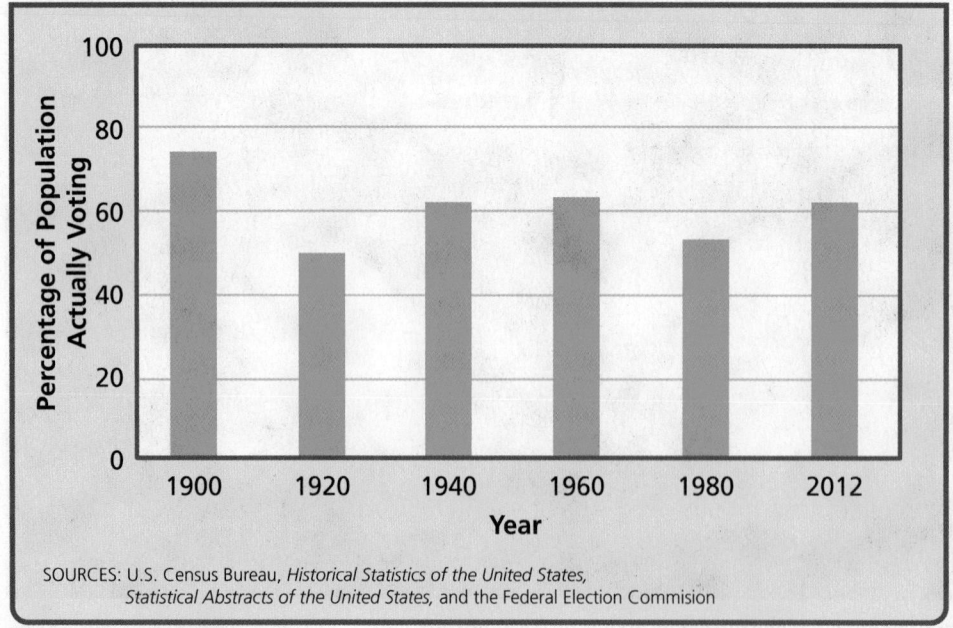

SOURCES: U.S. Census Bureau, *Historical Statistics of the United States,*
Statistical Abstracts of the United States, and the Federal Election Commision

>> **Analyze Data** Based on the information in the chart, what trend can you identify in the percentage of the population actually voting from 1960 to 2000?

 Interactive Chart

A Duty to Serve on Juries The Bill of Rights guarantees the right to trial by jury. In turn, every citizen has the responsibility to serve on a jury when called. **Jury duty** is a serious matter. Jurors must take time out from their work and personal lives to decide the fate of others.

Citizenship Means Participating in the Community Many Americans use their time and skills to improve their communities or to help others. As you read, David Levitt was in middle school when he started a program to help the needy in his Florida community. Many young people participate in walk-a-thons or bike-a-thons for charity. Others volunteer in hospitals or fire departments. When serious natural disasters damage cities and regions, millions of citizens aid in rescue efforts, donate blood, or contribute money and supplies.

A Responsibility to Stay Informed on Public Issues Thomas Jefferson observed, "If a nation expects to be ignorant and free . . . it expects what never was and never will be." You cannot protect your rights as a citizen unless you know what they are. You cannot choose elected officials who will make good decisions unless you know where they stand on the issues. It is your responsibility to be informed. You can watch television news programs and read newspapers, magazines, or government pamphlets. Your work in school will help you become educated about our history, our government, and the workings of our society.

❓ **IDENTIFY SUPPORTING DETAILS** What are some ways a citizen can stay informed about public issues?

>> Waiting to cross the street until the light is green illustrates one way that citizens observe their responsibility to obey the law.

ASSESSMENT

1. **Hypothesize** why someone who wants to become a citizen must take an oath of allegiance to the United States.

2. **Generate Explanations** Why is bullying an example of being an irresponsible citizen?

3. **Draw Conclusions** Why do you think the text says that, to be a good citizen, you have a responsibility to learn?

4. **Apply Concepts** Why do you think George Washington was a good role model for citizenship?

5. **Summarize** what you, as a student, should do to be a good citizen.

1. **Explain the Articles of Confederation** Write a paragraph explaining why the Continental Congress drafted the Articles of Confederation. Consider what the Articles of Confederation were, why the Continental Congress believed that it needed the Articles of Confederation, and what made the process of writing the Articles of Confederation difficult.

2. **Summarize the Weaknesses of the Articles of Confederation** Write a paragraph summarizing the weaknesses of the Articles of Confederation. Consider the limits placed on Congress and what the Articles of Confederation lacked.

3. **Analyze the Arguments For Ratification** Write a paragraph analyzing the arguments the Federalists put forward for ratifying the Constitution. Identify who the Federalists were, analyze why the Federalists thought the Articles of Confederation needed to be replaced, and analyze why the Federalists believed the Constitution should be ratified.

4. **Analyze the Great Compromise** Write a paragraph analyzing how the Great Compromise peacefully settled the debate over the Virginia and New Jersey Plans. Define the term *compromise,* describe the Great Compromise, and explain why it was a compromise.

5. **Analyze the Principle of Checks and Balances** Write a paragraph analyzing the principle of checks and balances. Identify what is meant by the term *checks and balances,* analyze why the framers made checks and balances a principle of the Constitution, and provide examples of how the different branches can check each other.

6. **Explain the Grievances Addressed in the U.S. Constitution** Write a paragraph explaining how the Founding Fathers sought to prevent the abuses that the Declaration of Independence accused King George of committing. Explain how the Constitution handled the grievances that the king placed military power above civilian authority and made judges "dependent on his will alone."

7. **Identify the Influence of the *Federalist Papers*** Write a paragraph identifying the role the *Federalist Papers* played in ratifying the Constitution and the influence of this document on the U.S. system of government. Identify the purpose of the *Federalist Papers,* identify who wrote the *Federalist Papers,* and identify the influence of the *Federalist Papers*.

8. **Explain the Northwest Ordinance** Write a paragraph explaining the principles and procedures the Northwest Ordinance established for how the Northwest Territory would be governed and how its territories could become states. Explain what the ordinance set up for the Northwest Territory, what the ordinance protected and banned, what could happen once a territory had 5,000 free white residents, and what could happen once a territory had 60,000 free residents.

9. **Explain How Rights and Responsibilities Reflect National Identity** Write a paragraph explaining how rights and responsibilities of citizens reflect our national identity. Explain how rights and responsibilities are tied together, define the term *national identity,* and provide an example of how the right to vote reflects our national identity.

10. **Analyze the Three-Fifths Compromise** Write a paragraph analyzing how the Three-Fifths Compromise peacefully settled disagreements between northern states and southern states. Describe the issue and the compromise, and analyze the effect of the compromise on representation in Congress in the North and South, using Virginia as an example.

Methods of Amending the Constitution

PROPOSED	RATIFIED
By Congress by ⅔ vote of each house	**By legislature** in ¾ of states
OR	OR
By national convention called by Congress at request of ⅔ of state legislature	**By state convention** in ¾ of states

11. Summarize Amending the U.S. Constitution Use the chart above and other sources to write a paragraph summarizing the amendment process. Describe the purpose of the amendment process and explain why the framers created a complex system for amending the Constitution. Describe the process for proposing and ratifying amendments.

12. Identify the Origin of Judicial Review Write a paragraph identifying what judicial review is and when it was established. Identify what is meant by *judicial review* and which Supreme Court case established judicial review.

13. Analyze the Impact of the First Amendment on Religious Freedom Write a paragraph describing how the First Amendment protects religious freedom. Indicate how the First Amendment protects religious freedom and how protecting religious freedom is important to the American way of life, both in colonial times and today.

14. Analyze the Principle of Individual Rights Write a paragraph summarizing how the Bill of Rights protects individual rights. Address each amendment in your paragraph.

15. Describe the Importance of Free Speech and Free Press Write a paragraph describing why free speech and a free press are important in a constitutional republic.

16. Summarize and Explain Becoming a Naturalized Citizen Write a paragraph about becoming a naturalized U.S. citizen. Summarize the criteria and explain the process.

17. Write about the Essential Question **Write an essay on the Essential Question: How much power should the government have?** Use evidence from your study of this topic to support your answer.

[**ESSENTIAL QUESTION**] What should governments do?

⑤ The Early Republic (1789–1825)

>> Washington's inauguration as President of the United States

Enduring Understandings

- Washington's presidency created the Cabinet, court system, and other government institutions that continue today.

- Under Washington, political parties developed over disagreements about policies.

- Washington, Adams, and Jefferson all worked to keep the early republic neutral in the face of war between Britain and France.

- The Louisiana Purchase greatly expanded the territory of the United States.

- The War of 1812 against Britain defended American interests but made little change in relations with Britain.

- The United States backed newly independent Latin American countries with the Monroe Doctrine.

PEARSON
realize. NBC LEARN

Watch the My Story Video to learn more about William Clark, an explorer of the American West.

PEARSON
realize.
www.PearsonRealize.com

Access your digital lessons including:
Topic Inquiry • Interactive Reading
Notepad • Interactivities • Assessments

233

>> President Washington reviewed his troops as they prepared to end the Whiskey Rebellion. His leadership helped to show the strength and resolve of the new national government.

▶ **Interactive Flipped Video**

>> Objectives

Describe the steps Washington took to set up the government of the new republic.

Explain how Hamilton aimed to create a stable economic system.

Explain Washington's foreign policy, including the goal of neutrality and the impact of his Farewell Address.

>> Key Terms

inauguration
precedent
Cabinet
Judiciary Act of 1789
national debt
bond
speculator
first Bank of the
   United States
tariff
Whiskey Rebellion
French Revolution
foreign policy
neutral
Neutrality
   Proclamation

Jay's Treaty
Farewell Address
early republic
George Washington
Thomas Jefferson
Alexander Hamilton

George Washington was inaugurated in New York City on April 30, 1789. A presidential **inauguration** is the ceremony in which the President officially takes the oath of office. A witness reported that the new President looked "grave, almost to sadness." Washington, no doubt, felt a great burden. He knew that Americans were looking to him to make the new government work.

The First American Presidency

Washington's presidency marked the beginning of what historians call the early republic. This period, between 1789 and about 1825, began when the first U.S. government was formed under the Constitution. Decisions made during the early republic had a lasting impact on the institutions and culture of the United States. As the first President, Washington showed strong leadership and set an example for future generations.

Although the Constitution provided a framework for the new government, it did not explain how the President should govern from day to day. "There is scarcely any part of my conduct," he said, "which may not hereafter be drawn into precedent." A **precedent** (PRES uh dent) is an act or a decision that sets an example for others to follow.

Washington set an important precedent at the end of his second term. In 1796, he decided not to run for a third term. Not until 1940 did any President seek a third term.

Washington's Cabinet The Constitution said little about how the executive branch should be organized. It was clear, however, that the President needed talented people to help him carry out his duties.

In 1789, the first Congress created five executive departments. They were the departments of State, Treasury, and War and the offices of Attorney General and Postmaster General. The heads of these departments made up the President's **Cabinet**. Members of the Cabinet gave Washington advice and were responsible for directing their departments.

As a proven leader himself, Washington knew he needed to appoint others with similar qualities to his Cabinet. He needed effective leaders who had the ability to persuade others to adopt new proposals and ideas.

Washington set a precedent by choosing well-known leaders to serve in his Cabinet. The two most influential were the Secretary of State, **Thomas Jefferson**, and the Secretary of the Treasury, **Alexander Hamilton**.

Setting Up the Court System The Constitution called for a Supreme Court. Congress, however, had to set up the federal court system. As one of its first actions, Congress passed the **Judiciary Act of 1789.** It called for the Supreme Court to consist of one Chief Justice and five Associate Justices. Today, the Supreme Court has eight Associate Justices because Congress later amended the Judiciary Act.

>> George Washington took the presidential oath of office on April 30, 1789. As the new nation's first President, Washington shaped the presidency for those who took office after him.

Washington named John Jay the first Chief Justice of the United States.

The Judiciary Act also set up a system of district courts and circuit courts across the nation. Decisions made in these lower courts could be appealed to the Supreme Court, the highest court in the land.

? LIST What positions were included in the first presidential Cabinet?

Alexander Hamilton and the National Debt

As Secretary of the Treasury, Alexander Hamilton faced many problems. Among the most pressing was the large national debt. The **national debt** is the total amount of money that a government owes to others.

During the Revolution, both the national government and individual states had desperately needed money. They had borrowed heavily from foreign countries and ordinary citizens to pay soldiers and buy supplies. Then, as now, governments borrowed money by issuing bonds. A **bond** is a certificate that promises to repay the money loaned, plus interest, on a certain date. For example, if a person pays $100 for a bond, the government agrees to pay back $100 plus interest (an additional sum of money) by a certain time.

A Plan to Reduce the Debt Hamilton wanted to pay off the government's debts and create a stable economic system for the United States. The plan he proposed showed that Cabinet members could provide strong leadership.

Hamilton called for the government to repay both federal and state debts. One of his first acts in government was to ask Congress to pass a tariff, or tax on imports, to pay for the government. Congress passed this tariff in 1789. Hamilton wanted the government to

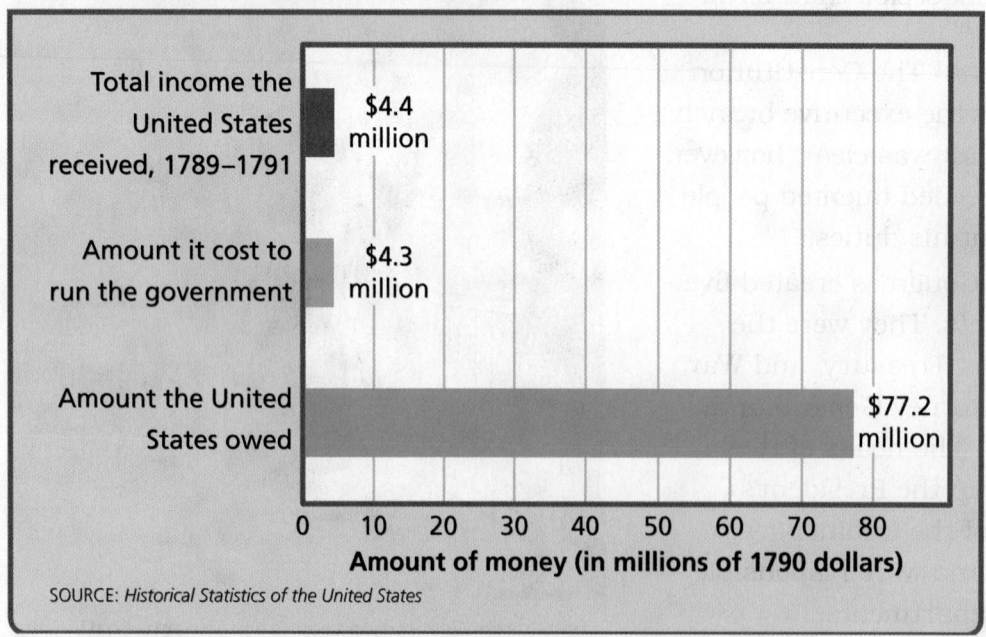

U.S. Financial Problems, 1789–1791

Total income the United States received, 1789–1791: **$4.4 million**

Amount it cost to run the government: **$4.3 million**

Amount the United States owed: **$77.2 million**

0   10   20   30   40   50   60   70   80
Amount of money (in millions of 1790 dollars)

SOURCE: *Historical Statistics of the United States*

>> **Analyze Data** Based on the information in the chart, what can you conclude about the economic situation of the federal government when Washington took office?

State Debt Assumed by the New Federal Government, 1790

STATE	ASSUMED DEBT (IN DOLLARS)	STATE	ASSUMED DEBT (IN DOLLARS)
New Hampshire	300,000	Delaware	200,000
Massachusetts	4,000,000	Maryland	800,000
Rhode Island	200,000	Virginia	3,500,000
Connecticut	1,600,000	North Carolina	2,400,000
New York	1,200,000	South Carolina	4,000,000
New Jersey	800,000	Georgia	300,000
Pennsylvania	2,200,000		

SOURCE: Library of Congress

>> **Analyze Data** Considering the differences among the states' debt levels, why might some states have objected to the federal government taking over every state's debts?

buy up all the bonds issued by both the national and state governments before 1789. He then planned to issue new bonds to pay off the old debts. As the economy improved and income from the tariff increased, the government would then be able to pay off the new bonds. Many people, including bankers and investors, welcomed Hamilton's plan. Others attacked it.

Arguments for and Against Hamilton's Plan
James Madison led the opposition. Madison argued that Hamilton's plan would reward speculators. A **speculator** is someone who invests in a risky venture in the hope of making a large profit.

During the Revolution, the government had issued bonds to soldiers and citizens who supplied goods. Many of these bondholders needed cash to survive. So, they sold their bonds to speculators. Speculators bought bonds worth one dollar for only 10 or 15 cents. If the government paid off the old bonds in full, speculators stood to make fortunes. Madison thought that speculators did not deserve to make such profits.

Hamilton replied that the United States must repay its debts in full. Otherwise, he said, it risked losing the trust of investors in the future. The support of investors, he argued, was crucial to building the new nation's economy. After much debate, Congress approved full repayment of the national debt.

As a southerner, Madison also led the fight against the other part of Hamilton's plan, the repaying of state debts. By 1789, most southern states had paid off their debts from the Revolution. They thought that other states should do the same. The New England states, for example, still owed a lot. Thus, some northern states stood to gain more than others from the plan. As a result, the southern states bitterly opposed Hamilton's plan.

This fight over how to use scarce capital resources fairly was only one of many in the **early republic**, the period from Washington's presidency until 1824.

A Compromise Is Reached In the end, Hamilton proposed a compromise. Many southerners wanted the nation's capital to be located in the South. Hamilton offered to support that goal if southerners agreed to his plan to repay state debts.

Madison and others accepted the compromise. In July 1790, Congress voted to repay state debts and to build a new capital city. The new capital would not be part of any state. Instead, it would be built on land along the Potomac River on land given up by two southern states, Virginia and Maryland. Congress called the area the District of Columbia. Washington, the new capital, would be located in the District. Today, it is known as Washington,

D.C., with *D.C.* standing for *District of Columbia*. Plans called for the new capital to be ready by 1800. Meanwhile, the nation's capital was moved from New York to Philadelphia.

? RECALL Why were federal and state debts so high?

Creating a Stable Economy

Hamilton's next challenge was to strengthen the faltering national economy. His economic plan was designed to help both agriculture and industry.

Hamilton called on Congress to set up a national bank. In 1791, Congress created the **first Bank of the United States**. The government deposited money from taxes in the Bank. In turn, the Bank issued paper money to pay the government's bills and to make loans to farmers and

>> Locating the nation's capital in what is now Washington was the result of a compromise in which southern states agreed for the federal government to take over state debts, mainly helping northern states. **Infer** What about Washington's location helped southern states accept the compromise?

businesses. Through these loans, the Bank encouraged economic growth and the development of a free-enterprise economic system.

To help American manufacturers, Hamilton asked Congress to pass a new **tariff**, or tax, on foreign goods brought into the country. He wanted a high tariff, to make imported goods more expensive than American-made goods. A tariff meant to protect local industry from foreign competition is called a protective tariff.

Hamilton's plan sparked arguments over taxation. In the North, where there were more and more factories, many people supported Hamilton's plan. Southern farmers, however, bought many imported goods. They opposed a protective tariff that would make imports more expensive.

In the end, Congress did pass a tariff, but it was much lower than the protective tariff Hamilton wanted. The tariff was also lower than American manufacturers would have liked in order to protect them from foreign competition. However, the tariff did help to pay off government debt, a central point in Hamilton's economic plan. The government needed to find a form of taxation that allowed it to pay off lenders, because attracting lenders is key to financing government in a free market economy.

>> This building in Philadelphia was the headquarters of the first Bank of the United States. It was founded in 1791 to bring stability to the nation's banking system.

❓ **CHECK UNDERSTANDING** What is the purpose of a protective tariff?

Taxation Sparks the Whiskey Rebellion

To help reduce the national debt, Congress approved a tax on all liquor made and sold in the United States. Hamilton wanted this tax to raise money for the Treasury. Instead, the new tax sparked a rebellion that tested the strength of the new government.

This tax was the first implemented by Congress under its new constitutional authority. Hamilton believed that reasonable taxes on alcohol would help to moderate consumption. He also hoped to gain a rich source of revenue for the federal government to pay its debts.

However, the new law varied the tax rate and often left smaller liquor manufacturers paying more than larger ones. Furthermore, the tax had to be paid in cash. This was often difficult for small distilleries. Large liquor enterprises in the East had less trouble with the tax than those on the frontier or in small towns.

Hamilton, though himself a man of humble origins, did not fully appreciate the economic concerns of Americans who

>> Frontiersmen tar and feather a government tax collector during the Whiskey Rebellion to protest a tax on liquor.

▶ **Interactive Chart**

lived on farms or in small towns. A large number of them opposed the new tax.

The Whiskey Rebellion Like many Americans, backcountry farmers grew corn. However, corn was bulky and expensive to haul long distances over rough roads. The cost of transport made western corn too expensive to sell in the East. Instead, farmers converted their corn into whiskey. Barrels of whiskey were worth much more and could be sold for a profit in the East despite the cost of transport.

Backcountry farmers hated the tax on whiskey because it sharply reduced their income. Many refused to pay it. They compared it to the taxes Britain had forced on the colonies.

In 1794, when officials in western Pennsylvania tried to collect the tax, farmers rebelled. During the **Whiskey Rebellion,** thousands marched in protest

through the streets of Pittsburgh. They sang Revolutionary songs and tarred and feathered the tax collectors.

A Show of Leadership President Washington responded quickly. He showed his abilities as a military leader once again. He called up the militia and dispatched them to Pennsylvania. When the rebels heard that thousands of troops were marching against them, they fled back to their farms. Hamilton wanted the leaders of the rebellion executed, but Washington disagreed and pardoned them. He believed that the government had shown its strength to all. Now, it was time to show mercy.

The Whiskey Rebellion tested the will of the new government. Washington's quick response proved to Americans that their new government would act firmly in times of crisis. The President also showed those who disagreed with the government that violence would not be tolerated.

❓ **CHECK UNDERSTANDING** What was the main cause of the Whiskey Rebellion?

Americans React to the French Revolution

Late in 1789, French ships arrived in American ports with startling news. On July 14, an angry mob in Paris, France, had destroyed the Bastille (bahs TEEL), an ancient fort that was used as a prison. The attack on the Bastille was an early event in the **French Revolution**. Before long, the revolution would topple the monarch and lead to the execution of thousands of ordinary French citizens.

The French Revolution broke out a few years after Americans had won their independence. Like Americans, the French fought for liberty and equality. As the French Revolution grew more violent, however, it deepened political divisions within the United States.

The French had many reasons to rebel against their king, Louis XVI. The peasants and the middle class paid heavy taxes, while nobles paid none. Reformers wanted a constitution to limit the king's power and protect basic rights, as the American Constitution did.

Supporting Liberty in France At first, most Americans supported the French Revolution. Americans knew what it meant to struggle for liberty. Also, during the American Revolution, France had been an important ally. Many Americans admired the Marquis de Lafayette, a leading French reformer who had fought with them in the American Revolution.

However, the French Revolution frightened most European rulers and nobles. They wanted to prevent revolutionary ideas from spreading to their lands. When two European countries, Austria and Prussia, appealed to other rulers to help the French king regain his throne in 1792, France declared war.

By 1793, the French Revolution was turning more and more violent. Radical reformers gained power. They beheaded the king and later the queen. During the Reign of Terror, tens of thousands of ordinary French citizens were executed.

Different Opinions Over Violence War and violence in France divided Americans. Some, like Thomas Jefferson, continued to support the French revolutionaries. He felt that the French had the right to use violence to win freedom, although he condemned the executions of the king and queen.

>> In this painting from the French Revolution, a mob in Paris burns symbols of the monarchy. The increasing violence of the revolution disturbed many Americans.

>> Alexander Hamilton not only influenced domestic affairs, but also played a key role in persuading President Washington to remain neutral toward France during its wars in Europe.

Alexander Hamilton, John Adams, and others strongly disagreed about the use of violence. One could no more create democracy through widespread violence, claimed Adams, "than a snowball can exist in the streets of Philadelphia under a burning sun."

President Washington's Foreign Policy

French armies' attack on Austria led Britain to declare war on France. Europe was soon plunged into a string of wars that lasted on and off for more than 20 years. The fight between France and Britain, Europe's two leading powers, threatened the economy of the United States. These countries were America's main trading partners.

Faced with war in Europe, President Washington had to decide on a foreign policy. **Foreign policy** is a nation's plan of action toward other nations. During the American Revolution, the United States and France had signed a treaty that made the two countries allies. Now, France wanted to use American ports to supply its ships and launch attacks on British ships. Allowing France to use American ports would expose the United States, still recovering from the Revolutionary War, to new British attacks. However, Washington worried that the United States could not honor its treaty with France and still remain neutral in the European conflict. **Neutral** means not taking sides in a conflict.

Washington also hoped to protect the American economy from the conflict between Britain and France. Merchants and farmers in the United States depended on American ports to maintain overseas trade with Britain and other countries. The British navy ensured the safety of American trading ships. Still, many Americans favored France. Staying neutral appeared to be Washington's best option.

>> **Analyze Information** Based on the information in the web, how did Washington deal with European powers? How did his actions reflect his foreign policy preferences?

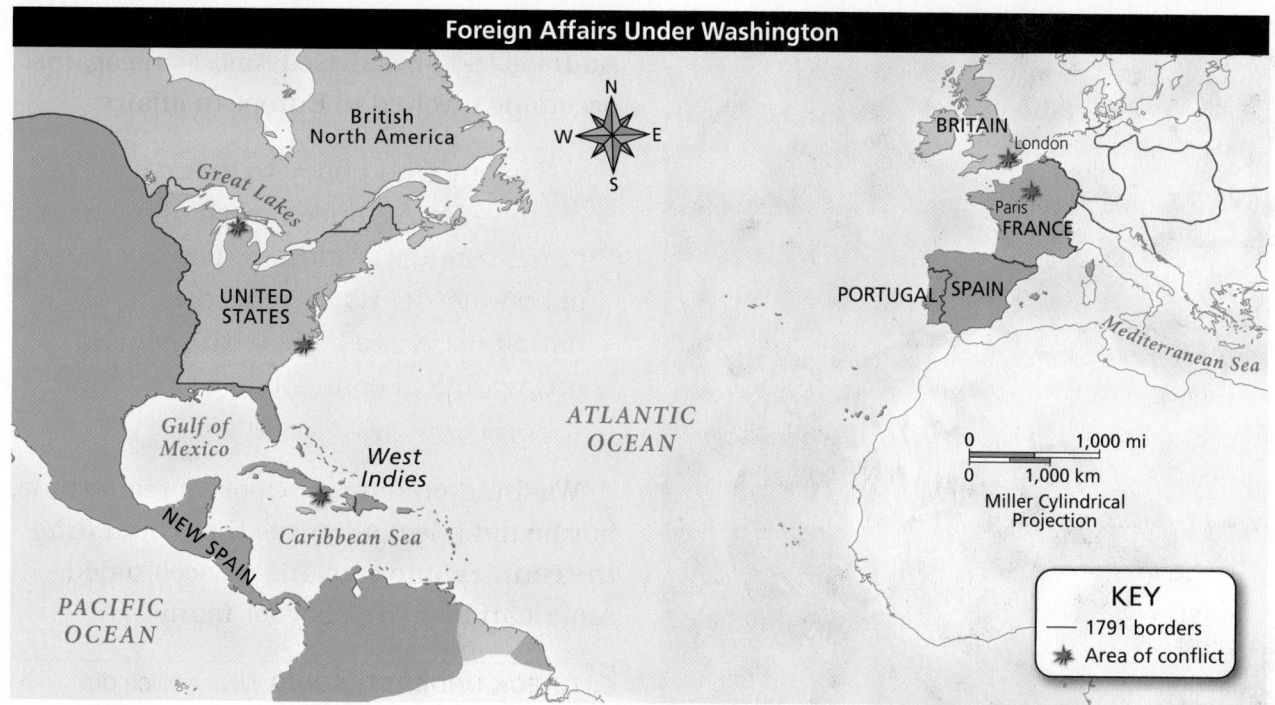

>> The map shows Paris, the site of the violent French Revolution, and places described in the text where the United States faced French and British aggression or hostility.

 Interactive Map

Protecting American Interests The issue of the treaty deepened the divisions within Washington's Cabinet. Hamilton pointed out that the United States had signed the treaty with Louis XVI. With the king dead, he argued, the treaty was no longer valid. Jefferson, a supporter of France, urged strict acceptance of the treaty.

After much debate, Washington issued the **Neutrality Proclamation** in April 1793. It stated that the United States would not support either side in the war. Further, it forbade Americans from aiding either Britain or France. The Neutrality Proclamation was a defeat for Jefferson. This and other defeats eventually led Jefferson to leave the Cabinet.

❓ DEFINE What is *foreign policy*?

Washington Defends Neutrality

Declaring neutrality was easier than enforcing it. Americans wanted to trade with both Britain and France. However, those warring nations seized American cargoes headed for each other's ports.

Jay's Treaty In 1793, the British captured more than 250 American ships trading in the French West Indies. Some Americans called for war. Washington, however, knew that the United States was too weak to fight. He sent Chief Justice John Jay to Britain for talks.

Jay negotiated an agreement that called for Britain to pay damages for the seized American ships. Britain also agreed to give up the forts it still held in the West. Meanwhile, Americans had to pay debts long owed to British merchants.

>> Frontiersmen tar and feather a government tax collector during the Whiskey Rebellion to protest a tax on liquor.

Jay's Treaty sparked loud protests because it did nothing to protect the rights of neutral American ships. After furious debate, the Senate finally approved the treaty in 1795.

The Impact of Washington's Farewell Address After serving two terms as President, George Washington refused to serve a third. Before retiring in 1796,

Washington published his **Farewell Address.** In it, he advised Americans against becoming involved in European affairs:

> Tis our true policy to steer clear of permanent Alliances, with any portion of the foreign World. . . . The great rule of conduct for us, in regard to foreign nations is . . . to have with them as little political connection as possible.
>
> —George Washington, Farewell Address, 1796

Washington did not oppose foreign trade, but he did reject alliances that could drag the country into war. His advice guided American foreign policy for many years.

? CHECK UNDERSTANDING What advice did Washington give in his final address?

ASSESSMENT

1. **Hypothesize** Why do you think Congress chose the five executive departments that it did?

2. **Generate Explanations** What did the Judiciary Act accomplish?

3. **Identify Central Issues** Explain Hamilton's argument in favor of paying the nation's debts in full.

4. **Generate Explanations** Why was the new nation's capital built as a new city in the South?

5. **Summarize** George Washington's response to the Whiskey Rebellion. What effect did this response have on the nation?

The Origin of Political Parties

>> The number of newspapers grew rapidly in the late 1700s. Infer How might newspapers have contributed to the development of political parties?

Interactive Flipped Video

When George Washington took office in 1789, the United States had no political parties. In fact, most American leaders disliked even the idea of parties. "If I could not go to heaven but with a party," said Thomas Jefferson, "I would not go at all."

>> **Objectives**

Contrast the views of Hamilton and Jefferson.

Explain the origin of political parties in the early republic.

Describe how the election of 1796 increased political tensions.

>> **Key Terms**

faction
unconstitutional
Democratic
  Republican
Federalist
John Adams

Americans Divide Over Politics

Early on, though, political disagreements divided Americans. "Men who have been [friends] all their lives," noted Jefferson, "cross streets to avoid meeting, and turn their heads another way, lest they should be obliged to touch their hats." Before Washington left office in 1797, two rival political parties had emerged to compete for power.

Americans also saw political parties as a threat to national unity. They agreed with George Washington, who warned Americans that parties would lead to "jealousies and false alarms."

Opposing Factions Grow in the Cabinet Despite the President's warning, **factions** grew up around two members of his Cabinet, Alexander Hamilton and Thomas Jefferson. The two men differed in background and in politics. Born in the West Indies, Hamilton had worked his way up from poverty. Hamilton believed that the wealthy and educated should control the government. He believed that supporting business and trade was the best way to improve the nation's economy. Hamilton also favored Britain over France.

Unlike Hamilton, Jefferson came from a wealthy family of Virginia planters. He owned large plantations and enslaved African Americans. Despite his wealth, Jefferson believed that the government should represent ordinary white people, not just the wealthy and educated. Jefferson supported policies that favored small farmers rather than businessmen. Jefferson favored France over Britain.

? **IDENTIFY MAIN IDEAS** Why did many Americans distrust political parties?

>> George Washington, shown here entering New York after his victory in the Revolutionary War, was a military hero who was able to unite Americans with different political beliefs. He opposed political parties.

>> This drawing shows the port of Boston in the early 1800s. Hamilton believed in supporting manufacturing and trade in cities such as Boston, while Jefferson favored agriculture.

Disagreements on Important Issues

The disagreements between Hamilton and Jefferson were not just differences of opinion. Their quarrels were rooted in their different views about what was best for the new nation.

Foundations of the American Economy

The two leaders differed on economic policy. Hamilton wanted the United States to model itself on Britain. The government, he thought, should encourage manufacturing and trade. He also favored the growth of cities and the merchant class.

Jefferson thought that farmers, rather than merchants, were the backbone of the new nation. "Cultivators of the earth," he wrote, "are the most valuable citizens." He feared that a manufacturing economy would corrupt the United States by concentrating power in the hands of a small group of wealthy Americans.

Federalism Hamilton and Jefferson also disagreed about the power of the federal government. Hamilton wanted the federal government to have greater power than state governments. A strong federal government, he argued, was needed to increase commerce. It would also be able to restrain mob violence like that of the Whiskey Rebellion.

In contrast, Jefferson wanted as small a federal government as possible, in order to protect individual freedom. He feared that a strong federal government might take over powers that the Constitution gave to the states.

Interpreting the Constitution Jefferson and Hamilton also clashed over the Bank of the United States. Jefferson worried that a national bank would give too much

Differing Views: Jefferson vs. Hamilton

JEFFERSON	HAMILTON
• Wanted strong state governments	• Wanted a strong central government
• Sympathetic to France	• Sympathetic to England
• Opposed a national bank	• Favored a national bank
• Thought the government should be controlled by ordinary Americans	• Thought the government should be controlled by the elite of society
• Wanted liberties to be protected by law	• Opposed to protecting individual liberties by law
• Believed the American government should not be modeled on the English government	• Wanted to model the American government after the English government

>> Thomas Jefferson and Alexander Hamilton held opposing views on many issues. **Compare and Contrast** How did Jefferson's views on civil liberties differ from Hamilton's?

 Interactive Gallery

power to the government and to wealthy investors who would help run the bank.

Jefferson opposed the law setting up the bank. He claimed that it was **unconstitutional**, or not permitted by the Constitution. Nowhere did the Constitution give Congress the power to create a Bank, he argued. For Jefferson, any power not specifically given to the federal government belonged to the states.

Hamilton did not agree with Jefferson's strict interpretation of the Constitution. He preferred a looser interpretation. The Constitution gave Congress the power to make all laws "necessary and proper" to carry out its duties. Hamilton argued that the Bank was necessary for the government to collect taxes and pay its bills.

Britain or France Finally, the two leaders disagreed over foreign policy. Hamilton wanted close ties with Britain, a major trading partner. Jefferson favored France, the first ally of the United States.

? IDENTIFY SUPPORTING DETAILS How did Hamilton feel about the division of power between the federal government and the states?

New Political Parties Take Shape

At first, Hamilton and Jefferson clashed in private. Then Congress began to pass many of Hamilton's programs. James Madison shared many of Jefferson's views, and the two men decided to organize supporters of their views.

Jefferson and Madison moved cautiously at first. In 1791, they went to New York, telling people that they wanted to study its wildlife. In fact, Jefferson was interested in nature. Their main goal, though, was to meet with leading New York politicians such as Governor George Clinton and Aaron Burr, a fierce critic of Hamilton. Jefferson asked them to help defeat Hamilton's program by convincing New Yorkers to vote for Jefferson's supporters.

Republicans and Federalists Soon, leaders in other states were organizing to support either Hamilton or Jefferson. Jefferson's supporters called themselves **Democratic Republicans**, often shortened to Republicans. Today's Republican Party is not related to Jefferson's party. The Jeffersonian Republicans included small farmers, artisans, and some wealthy planters in the South.

Hamilton and his supporters were called **Federalists** because they wanted a strong federal government. Federalists drew support mainly from merchants and manufacturers in such cities as Boston and New York. They also had the backing of some southern planters.

Newspapers Influence Public Opinion

In the late 1700s, the number of American newspapers more than doubled. This growth met a demand for information.

A European visitor was surprised that so many Americans could read. "The common people . . . all read and write, and understand arithmetic," he reported, and "almost every little town now furnishes a circulating library."

As party rivalry grew, newspapers took sides. In the *Gazette of the United States,* publisher John Fenno backed Hamilton and the Federalists. Jefferson's friend Philip Freneau (frih NOH) started a rival paper, the *National Gazette,* which supported Republicans.

Newspapers had great influence on public opinion. In stinging language, they raged against political opponents. Often, articles mixed rumor and opinion with facts. Emotional attacks and counterattacks fanned the flames of party rivalry.

Choosing Washington's Successor

Political parties played a large role in the election of George Washington's successor. In 1796, Democratic Republicans backed Thomas Jefferson for President and Aaron Burr for Vice President. Federalists supported **John Adams** for President and

>> In this cartoon, Congressman Matthew Lyon, a Democratic Republican, defends himself from Roger Griswold, a Federalist. **Analyze Political Cartoons** What does this cartoon suggest about the conflict between the parties?

Interactive Chart

★ THE ELECTION OF 1796 ★

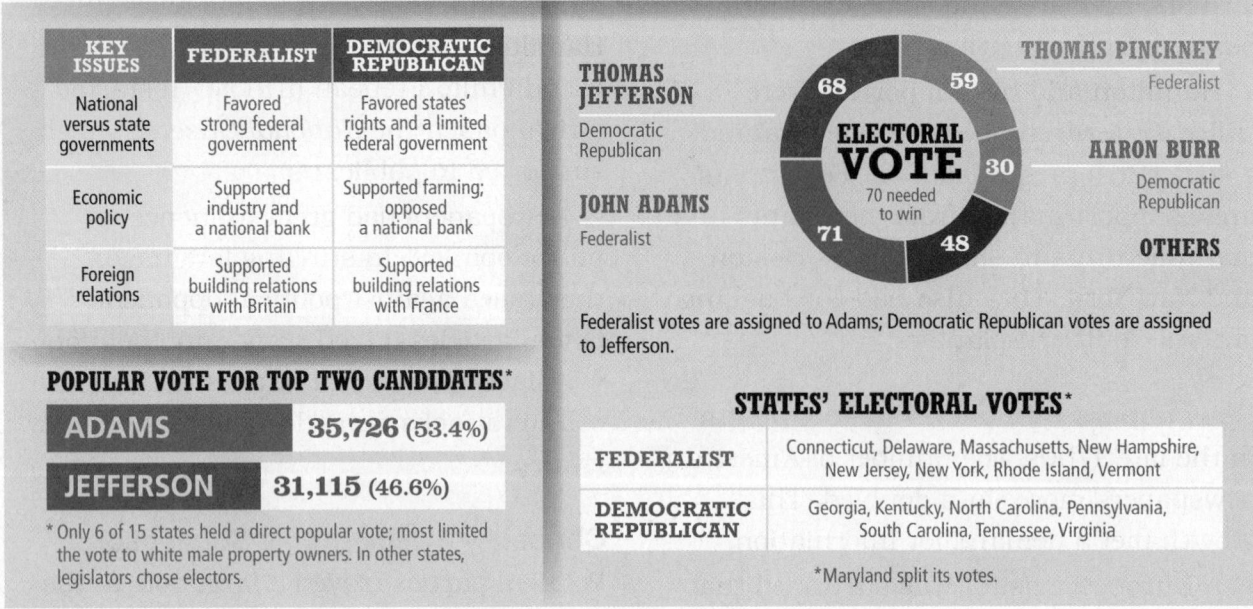

KEY ISSUES	FEDERALIST	DEMOCRATIC REPUBLICAN
National versus state governments	Favored strong federal government	Favored states' rights and a limited federal government
Economic policy	Supported industry and a national bank	Supported farming; opposed a national bank
Foreign relations	Supported building relations with Britain	Supported building relations with France

THOMAS JEFFERSON
Democratic Republican

JOHN ADAMS
Federalist

ELECTORAL VOTE
70 needed to win

68   59   30   71   48

THOMAS PINCKNEY
Federalist

AARON BURR
Democratic Republican

OTHERS

Federalist votes are assigned to Adams; Democratic Republican votes are assigned to Jefferson.

POPULAR VOTE FOR TOP TWO CANDIDATES*

ADAMS	35,726 (53.4%)
JEFFERSON	31,115 (46.6%)

* Only 6 of 15 states held a direct popular vote; most limited the vote to white male property owners. In other states, legislators chose electors.

STATES' ELECTORAL VOTES*

FEDERALIST	Connecticut, Delaware, Massachusetts, New Hampshire, New Jersey, New York, Rhode Island, Vermont
DEMOCRATIC REPUBLICAN	Georgia, Kentucky, North Carolina, Pennsylvania, South Carolina, Tennessee, Virginia

*Maryland split its votes.

>> **Analyze Charts** Which political party championed agriculture and campaigned against the establishment of a national bank? Which candidate finished third in the electoral vote tally?

Thomas Pinckney for Vice President. The election had an unexpected outcome.

Under the Constitution, the person with the most electoral votes became President. The candidate with the next highest total was made Vice President. John Adams, a Federalist, won office as President. The leader of the Democratic Republicans, Thomas Jefferson, came in second and became Vice President.

Having the President and Vice President from opposing parties further increased political tensions. John Adams took office in March 1797 as the nation's second President. Events soon deepened the distrust between him and Jefferson.

❓ **SUMMARIZE** How did political parties begin in the United States?

ASSESSMENT

1. **Hypothesize** Thomas Jefferson said that he disliked political parties. How might the United States government work today if there were no political parties?

2. **Summarize** Thomas Jefferson's views on the economy. What did he fear most about a manufacturing economy?

3. **Compare** Hamilton's and Jefferson's views on the power of the federal government.

4. **Identify Cause and Effect** In the late 1700s, the number of newspapers in the United States exploded. What effects did this have on the nation's politics?

5. **Generate Explanations** Why did Thomas Jefferson, who claimed to dislike political parties, lead the way in founding a party?

John Adams's Presidency

>> As President, John Adams faced a political crisis over whether to go to war with France.

▶ **Interactive Flipped Video**

No sooner had John Adams taken office than he faced a crisis with France. The French objected to Jay's Treaty because they felt that it put the United States on the side of Britain. In 1797, French ships began to seize American ships in the West Indies, as the British had done.

>> **Objectives**

Explain Adams's foreign policy.

Describe the controversy over the Alien and Sedition Acts.

Explain why Congress decided the election of 1800 and how that election set a precedent.

>> **Key Terms**

XYZ Affair
frigate
Alien and Sedition
    Acts
sedition
nullify
Kentucky and
    Virginia resolutions
states' rights

▶ **PEARSON realize** www.PearsonRealize.com
Access your Digital Lesson.

Escalating Conflict With France

Once again, Americans called for war, this time against France. To avoid war, Adams sent diplomats to Paris to discuss the rights of neutral nations.

The XYZ Affair The French foreign minister, Charles Maurice de Talleyrand, did not deal directly with the Americans. Instead, he sent three agents to offer the Americans a deal. Before Talleyrand would even begin talks, the agents said, he wanted $250,000 for himself and a $10 million loan to France. "Not a sixpence!" replied one of the Americans angrily. (A sixpence was a British coin worth six pennies.)

>> In this cartoon depicting the XYZ Affair, a five-headed monster demands a bribe from three Americans. **Analyze Political Cartoons** What details in the cartoon reflect the cartoonist's attitude toward the French?

▶ **Interactive Timeline**

The diplomats informed Adams about the offer. He then told Congress. Adams did not reveal the names of the French agents, referring to them only as X, Y, and Z.

Many Americans were outraged when news reached them about the **XYZ Affair** in 1798. (The affair had taken place in 1797, but it took time for news to cross the ocean by ship.) They took up the slogan, "Millions for defense, but not one cent for tribute!" They were willing to spend money to defend their country, but they would not pay a bribe to another nation.

The XYZ Affair ignited war fever in the United States. Despite strong pressure, Adams refused to ask Congress to declare war on France. Like Washington, he wanted to keep the country out of European affairs. However, he could not ignore French attacks on American ships, so he strengthened the navy by building **frigates**, fast-sailing ships with many guns. That move helped convince France to stop attacking American ships.

Adams's Foreign Policy Divides the Federalists Led by Hamilton, many Federalists criticized Adams. They hoped a war would weaken the Democratic Republicans, who supported France. War would also force the nation to build its military forces.

A strong military would increase federal power, a key Federalist goal. Many Federalists also favored Britain in its war against France.

Although Adams was a Federalist, he resisted Hamilton's pressure for war. Their disagreement created a split in the Federalist party.

Over Hamilton's opposition, Adams again sent diplomats to France. When they arrived, they found an ambitious young army officer, Napoleon Bonaparte, in charge. Napoleon was planning for war against several European powers. Thus, he had no time for a war with the United States. He signed an agreement to stop seizing American ships.

Like Washington, Adams kept the nation out of war. His actions showed qualities of leadership and courage. His success, however, cost him the support of many Federalists and weakened the party for the election of 1800.

? CHECK UNDERSTANDING Why did many Federalists support a war with France?

The Alien and Sedition Acts

In 1798, during the crisis with France, Federalists pushed several laws through Congress. These laws were known as the **Alien and Sedition Acts**.

Under the Alien Act, the President could expel any alien, or foreigner, thought to be dangerous to the country. Another law made it harder for immigrants to become citizens. Before 1798, white immigrants could become citizens after living in the United States for five years. The new law made immigrants wait 14 years. The Federalists passed this act because many recent immigrants supported Jefferson and the Democratic Republicans. The act would keep these immigrants from voting for years.

The Democratic Republicans grew even angrier when Congress passed the Sedition Act. **Sedition** means stirring up rebellion against a government. Under this law, citizens could be fined or jailed if they criticized the government or its officials. In fact, several Democratic Republican

>> Representative Albert Gallatin opposed Federalists in their attempts to fund the fighting with France. As a result, he was targeted by the Federalists. The Alien and Sedition Acts were believed by some to be written to remove Gallatin from power.

newspaper editors, and even members of Congress, were fined and jailed for expressing their opinions.

Democratic Republicans protested that the Sedition Act violated the Constitution. The First Amendment, they argued, protected freedom of speech and of the press. Jefferson warned that the new laws threatened American liberties:

They have brought into the lower house a sedition bill, which . . . undertakes to make printing certain matters criminal . . . Indeed this bill & the alien bill both are so [against] the Constitution as to show they mean to pay no respect to it.

—*The Writings of Thomas Jefferson*, 1798

States Challenge the Federal Government Vice President Jefferson bitterly opposed the Alien and Sedition Acts. He could not ask the courts for help because the Federalists controlled them. So, he urged the states to take strong action against the acts. He argued that the states had the right to **nullify**, or cancel, a law passed by the federal government. In this way, states could resist the power of the federal government.

With help from Jefferson and Madison, Kentucky and Virginia passed resolutions in 1798 and 1799. The **Kentucky and Virginia resolutions** claimed that each state "has an equal right to judge for itself" whether a law is constitutional. If a state decides a law is unconstitutional, said the resolutions, it has the power to nullify that law within its borders.

The Kentucky and Virginia resolutions raised the issue of **states' rights**. Did the federal government have only those powers that were listed in the Constitution? If so, did the states possess all other powers—for example, the power to declare a federal law unconstitutional? Within a few years, the Alien and Sedition Acts were changed or dropped. Still, the issue of a state's right to nullify federal laws would come up again.

❓ IDENTIFY CENTRAL IDEAS What did some states argue after the Alien and Sedition Acts became law?

An Important Presidential Election

By 1800, the war cry against France was fading. As the election neared, Democratic Republicans focused on two issues. First, they attacked the Federalists for raising taxes to prepare for war. Second, they opposed the unpopular Alien and Sedition Acts.

★ THE ELECTION OF 1800 ★

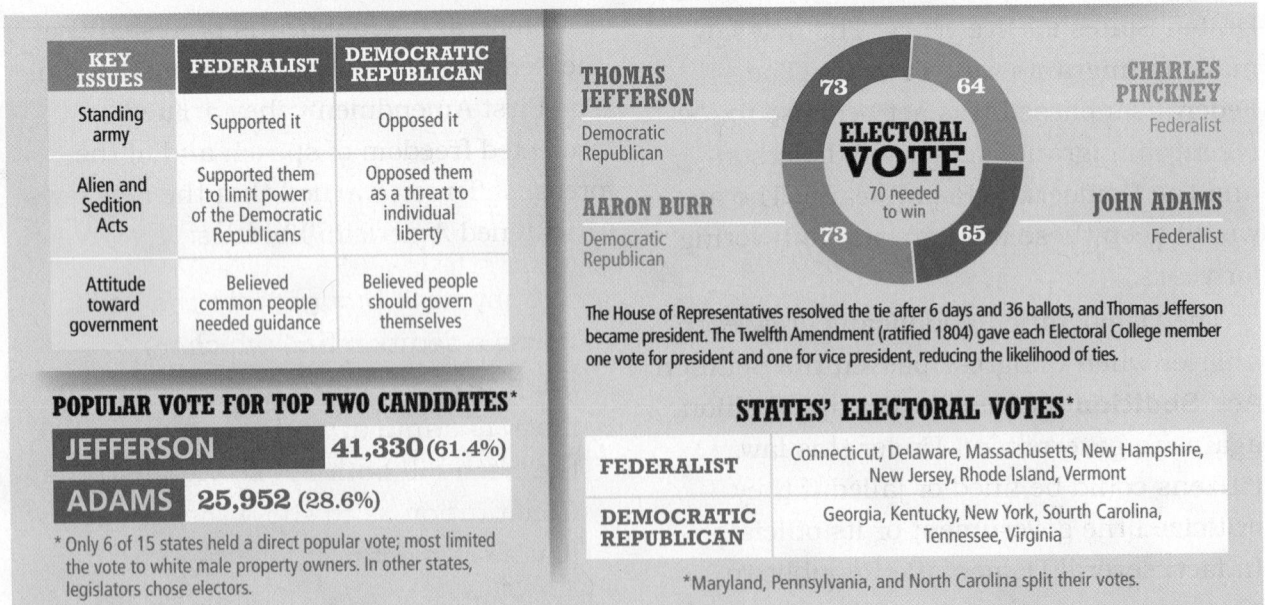

KEY ISSUES	FEDERALIST	DEMOCRATIC REPUBLICAN
Standing army	Supported it	Opposed it
Alien and Sedition Acts	Supported them to limit power of the Democratic Republicans	Opposed them as a threat to individual liberty
Attitude toward government	Believed common people needed guidance	Believed people should govern themselves

THOMAS JEFFERSON Democratic Republican

AARON BURR Democratic Republican

ELECTORAL VOTE 70 needed to win — 73 / 73 / 64 / 65

CHARLES PINCKNEY Federalist

JOHN ADAMS Federalist

The House of Representatives resolved the tie after 6 days and 36 ballots, and Thomas Jefferson became president. The Twelfth Amendment (ratified 1804) gave each Electoral College member one vote for president and one for vice president, reducing the likelihood of ties.

POPULAR VOTE FOR TOP TWO CANDIDATES*

JEFFERSON	41,330 (61.4%)
ADAMS	25,952 (28.6%)

* Only 6 of 15 states held a direct popular vote; most limited the vote to white male property owners. In other states, legislators chose electors.

STATES' ELECTORAL VOTES*

FEDERALIST	Connecticut, Delaware, Massachusetts, New Hampshire, New Jersey, Rhode Island, Vermont
DEMOCRATIC REPUBLICAN	Georgia, Kentucky, New York, South Carolina, Tennessee, Virginia

*Maryland, Pennsylvania, and North Carolina split their votes.

>> **Analyze Data** Based on the data shown, what explains the controversy over the electoral system that erupted after the 1800 presidential election?

 ▶ **Interactive Chart**

Democratic Republicans backed Thomas Jefferson for President and Aaron Burr for Vice President. Despite the bitter split in the Federalist party, John Adams was again named its candidate.

Political Power Goes to a Different Party In the race for the presidency, Democratic Republicans won the popular vote. However, when the electoral college voted, Jefferson and Burr each received 73 votes. At the time, the electoral college did not vote separately for President and Vice President. Instead, the college voted for each candidate. The candidate winning the most votes became President, and the runner-up became Vice President. However, each Democratic Republican elector cast one vote for Jefferson and one vote for Burr, so there was no clear winner.

Under the Constitution, if no candidate wins the electoral vote, the House of Representatives decides the election. Only after four days and 36 votes was the tie finally broken. The House chose Jefferson as President. Burr became Vice President. The election of 1800 set an important precedent. From then until today, power has passed peacefully from one party to another.

Soon after, Congress passed the Twelfth Amendment. It required electors to hold separate votes for President and Vice President. The states ratified the amendment in 1804.

The Federalist Era Comes to a Close

After 1800, the Federalist party slowly declined. Federalists won fewer seats in Congress. In 1804, the party was greatly weakened after its leader, Alexander Hamilton, was killed in a duel with Aaron Burr. Despite its early decline, the Federalist party did help shape the

>> This painting shows Alexander Hamilton, at the right, about to lose his life in a duel with Aaron Burr in 1804.

new nation. Even Democratic Republican Presidents kept most of Hamilton's economic programs.

? RECALL Why did the House of Representatives have to decide the 1800 election?

ASSESSMENT

1. **Summarize** the XYZ Affair.

2. **Generate Explanations** Why did Federalists pass the Alien Acts?

3. **Hypothesize** What likely would happen today if someone introduced a bill in Congress that was similar to the Sedition Act. Why?

4. **Support Ideas with Evidence** How did the Federalists contribute to shaping the United States as we know it today?

5. **Describe** the important change in the Constitution that was prompted by the results of the election of 1800.

>> The author of the Declaration of Independence, Thomas Jefferson supported limited government as President.

▶ **Interactive Flipped Video**

>> Objectives

Explain why Jefferson acted to limit the size of the federal government.

Describe the significance and effects of *Marbury* v. *Madison*.

Identify the causes and effects of the Louisiana Purchase.

Describe the discoveries of Lewis, Clark, and Pike.

>> Key Terms

laissez faire
Marbury v.
    Madison
judicial review
Pinckney Treaty
Louisiana Purchase
expedition
continental divide
tribute
impressment
embargo
Embargo Act
smuggling
Nonintercourse Act
John Marshall
James Madison

When Thomas Jefferson took office as the third President, some Federalists were worried about his political beliefs. They knew that he supported the French Revolution and they feared that he might bring revolutionary change to the United States. They were also afraid that he might punish Federalists who had used the Alien and Sedition Acts to jail Democratic Republicans.

Jefferson Redefines Government

In his inaugural address, Jefferson tried to calm Federalists' fears. He promised that, although the Democratic Republicans were in the majority, he would not treat the Federalists harshly. "The minority possess their equal rights, which equal laws must protect," he told the nation. He called for an end to the political disputes of the past few years. "We are all Republicans, we are all Federalists," the President concluded.

Jefferson had no plan to punish Federalists. He did, however, want to change their policies. In his view, the Federalists had made the national government too large and too powerful.

Promoting a Free Market Economy

One way Jefferson wanted to lessen government power was by reducing the federal budget. Such budget cuts would also keep the federal debt low. His Secretary of the Treasury, Albert Gallatin (GAL uh tin), helped him achieve this goal. A financial wizard, Gallatin reduced government spending through careful management.

Jefferson believed in an economic idea known as **laissez faire** (les ay FAYR), a French term meaning "let do," meaning letting people do as they please. The idea of laissez faire was promoted by the Scottish economist Adam Smith.

In his book *The Wealth of Nations*, Smith argued in favor of a system of free markets, where goods and services are exchanged between buyers and sellers with as little government interference as possible. Free competition, Smith said, would benefit everyone, not just the wealthy.

>> Thomas Jefferson rode a white horse into Washington, D.C., for his inauguration. Unlike Presidents before him, he walked from his hotel to his inauguration ceremony as the third President of the United States on March 4, 1801.

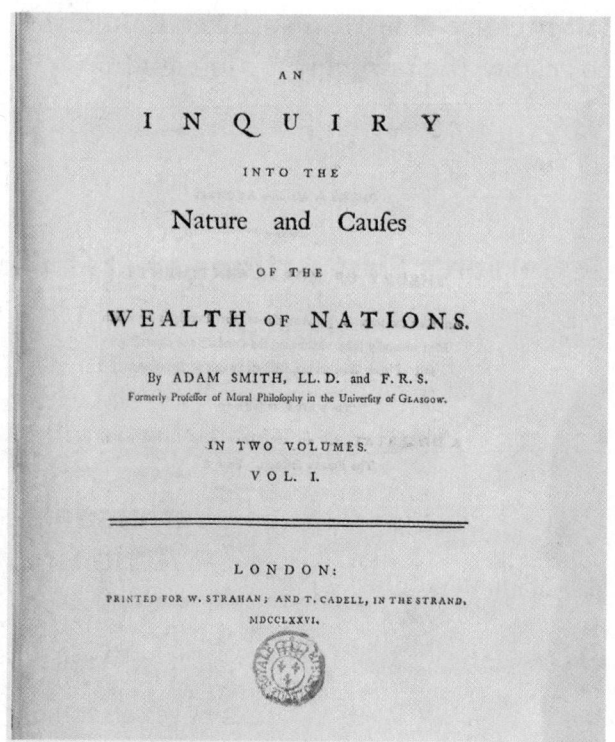

AN

INQUIRY

INTO THE

Nature and Caufes

OF THE

WEALTH OF NATIONS.

By ADAM SMITH, LL. D. and F. R. S.
Formerly Profeffor of Moral Philofophy in the Univerfity of GLASGOW.

IN TWO VOLUMES.
VOL. I.

LONDON:
PRINTED FOR W. STRAHAN; AND T. CADELL, IN THE STRAND.
MDCCLXXVI.

>> After becoming President, Jefferson pursued the free-enterprise economic policies suggested by Adam Smith's 1776 book, *The Wealth of Nations*.

Laissez faire economists believed that government should play as small a role as possible in economic affairs. Laissez faire was very different from the Federalist idea of government. Alexander Hamilton, you recall, wanted government to promote trade and manufacturing.

Jefferson Scales Back Government

Jefferson believed that the government should protect the rights of its citizens. Beyond that, he wanted the federal government to take a less active role in governing the nation. In addition to cutting the federal budget, he decreased the size of government departments. With the approval of Congress, he reduced the size of the army and navy. He also asked Congress to repeal the unpopular whiskey tax.

The Sedition Act expired the day before Jefferson took office. Jefferson hated the law, and he pardoned those who were in jail because of it. He also asked Congress to restore the law allowing foreign-born white people to become citizens after only a five-year waiting period.

Some Federalist Economic Policies Remain Jefferson did not discard all Federalist programs. On the advice of Albert Gallatin, he kept the Bank of the United States. The federal government also continued to pay off state debts, which it had taken over while Washington was President. In addition, Jefferson let many Federalists keep their government jobs.

❓ IDENTIFY MAIN IDEAS How would you define Jefferson's idea of government?

Landmark Supreme Court Cases

The election of 1800 gave Democratic Republicans control of Congress. Federalists, however, remained powerful in the courts.

Several months passed between Jefferson's election and his inauguration. In that time, Federalists in the old Congress passed the Judiciary Act of

Jefferson's First Actions as President

>> **Analyze Information** How do Jefferson's first actions as President reflect his political views?

▶ **Interactive Chart**

1801, increasing the number of federal judges. President Adams then appointed Federalists to fill these new judicial positions. When Jefferson took office, Jeffersonians repealed this part of the act, firing 16 Federalist judges by abolishing their offices.

One of the judges that Adams appointed was **John Marshall**, the Chief Justice of the United States. Like Jefferson, Marshall was a rich Virginia planter with a brilliant mind. Unlike Jefferson, however, Marshall was a staunch Federalist. He wanted to make the federal government stronger.

The framers of the Constitution expected the courts to balance the powers of the President and Congress. However, John Marshall found the courts to be much weaker than the other branches of government. In his view, it was not clear what powers the federal courts had.

>> Chief Justice John Marshall, a Federalist, helped to strengthen the U.S. Supreme Court by establishing its power to declare laws unconstitutional.

The Issues Behind *Marbury* v. *Madison*
In 1803, John Marshall showed courage and leadership by deciding a case that increased the power of the Supreme Court. The case involved William Marbury, one of the judges appointed by Adams. Adams made the appointment on his last night as President. The Republicans refused to accept this "midnight judge." They accused Federalists of using unfair tactics to keep control of the courts. Jefferson ordered Secretary of State James Madison not to deliver the official papers confirming Marbury's appointment.

Marbury sued Madison. According to the Judiciary Act of 1789, only the Supreme Court could decide a case that was brought against a federal official. Therefore, the case of ***Marbury* v. *Madison*** was tried before the Supreme Court.

The Significance of the *Marbury* v. *Madison* Decision The Supreme Court ruled against Marbury. Chief Justice Marshall wrote the decision, stating that the Judiciary Act was unconstitutional. The Constitution, Marshall argued, did not give the Supreme Court the right to decide cases brought against federal officials. Therefore, Congress could not give the Court that power simply by passing the Judiciary Act.

As a result of *Marbury* v. *Madison*, Congress had to amend, or change, the Judiciary Act to respond to the Supreme Court's objections. The part of the Judiciary Act of 1789 that the Supreme Court rejected could no longer be law.

The Supreme Court's decision in *Marbury* v. *Madison* set an important precedent. It gave the Supreme Court the power to decide whether laws passed by Congress were constitutional and to reject laws that it considered to be unconstitutional. This power of the Court is called **judicial review.**

The Reactions of Jefferson and Congress Jefferson was displeased with the decision. True, Marshall had ruled against Marbury, the Federalist judge.

But Marshall's decision gave more power to the Supreme Court, where Federalists were still strong. Jefferson also argued that the decision upset the balance of power among the three branches of government:

> The opinion which gives to the judges the right to decide what laws are constitutional and what not, not only for themselves . . . but for the Legislature and Executive also . . . would make the Judiciary a [tyrannical] branch.
>
> —Thomas Jefferson, letter to Abigail Adams, 1804

Jefferson did not want the judiciary to gain power over the executive branch. He refused the Court's order to testify at an important trial, saying it would upset the equality of the branches. He also used executive privilege to decide which government papers to show the Court and which to withhold.

In the end, the President and Congress accepted the right of the Court to overturn laws. Today, judicial review remains one of the most important powers of the Supreme Court.

❓ **IDENTIFY MAIN IDEAS** Why is the Supreme Court case *Marbury* v. *Madison* significant?

The Louisiana Purchase

The United States overcame a number of challenges in its early years, including creating a stable economic system, setting up the courts, and defining the authority

>> The Louisiana Purchase included the port of New Orleans, which controlled access to the North American West. As shown in this print from the mid-1800s, New Orleans became a busy American port.

of the central government. As the economy continued to grow, Americans needed to protect their economic interests. The Louisiana Territory became a key part of this effort.

Geography Shapes Domestic and Foreign Policy

A new development caused President Jefferson to pursue buying New Orleans in order to control this important port. By 1800, almost one million Americans lived between the Appalachian Mountains and the Mississippi River. Most were farmers. With few roads west of the Appalachians, western farmers relied on the Mississippi River to ship their wheat and corn. First, they sent their produce down the river to the city of New Orleans. From there, oceangoing ships carried the produce across the Gulf of Mexico, around Florida, and up to ports along the Atlantic coast.

Spain, which controlled New Orleans, sometimes threatened to close the port to Americans. In 1795, President Washington sent Thomas Pinckney to find a way to keep the vital port open. In the **Pinckney Treaty,** Spain agreed to let Americans ship their goods down the Mississippi and store them in New Orleans.

For a time, Americans shipped their goods through New Orleans peacefully. In 1800, however, Spain signed a new treaty giving Louisiana back to the French. President Jefferson was alarmed. He knew that the French ruler, Napoleon Bonaparte, had already set out to conquer Europe. Would he now try to build an empire in North America?

Jefferson had reason to worry. Napoleon wanted to grow food in Louisiana and ship it to French islands in the West Indies. However, events in Haiti, a French colony in the Caribbean, soon ruined Napoleon's

>> Toussaint L'Ouverture led a revolt by enslaved Africans to win independence from France for Haiti.

plan. Inspired by the French Revolution, enslaved Africans in Haiti decided to fight for their liberty. Toussaint L'Ouverture (too SAN loo vehr TYOOR) led the revolt. By 1801, Toussaint and his followers had nearly forced the French out of Haiti.

Napoleon sent troops to retake Haiti. Although the French captured Toussaint, they did not regain control of the island. In 1804, Haitians declared their independence.

Negotiations for Louisiana

Jefferson sent Robert Livingston and James Monroe to buy New Orleans and West Florida from Napoleon. Jefferson said they could offer as much as $10 million. Livingston and Monroe negotiated with Charles Maurice de Talleyrand, the French foreign minister. At first, Talleyrand showed little interest in their offer. However, losing Haiti caused Napoleon to give up his plan for an empire in the Americas. He also needed money to pay for his costly wars in Europe. Suddenly, Talleyrand asked Livingston if the United States wanted to buy all of Louisiana, not just New Orleans.

The question surprised Livingston. He offered $4 million. "Too low," replied Talleyrand. "Reflect and see me tomorrow."

Livingston and Monroe carefully debated the matter. They had no authority to buy all of Louisiana. However, they knew that Jefferson wanted control of the Mississippi.

They agreed to pay the French $15 million for Louisiana. "This is the noblest work of our whole lives," declared Livingston when he signed the treaty. "From this day the United States take their place among the powers of the first rank."

The Louisiana Purchase of 1803 Jefferson hailed the news from France. Still, he was not sure whether the President had the power to purchase Louisiana. He had always insisted that the federal government had only those powers spelled out in the Constitution. The document said nothing about a President having the power to buy land.

In the end, Jefferson decided that he did have the authority to buy Louisiana. The Constitution, he reasoned, allowed the President to make treaties, and buying the Louisiana territory was part of a treaty. Federalists opposed the purchase as unconstitutional and feared it would weaken the other states. But the Democratic Republicans supported it and the Senate approved the treaty. The **Louisiana Purchase** went into effect. In 1803, the United States took control of the vast lands west of the Mississippi. With one stroke, the size of the nation had almost doubled.

? RECALL Why was the port of New Orleans important to many Americans?

Louisiana Purchase, 1803

British North America

Oregon Country

New Hampshire
Vermont

Massachusetts

New York

Rhode Island
Connecticut
New Jersey

Pennsylvania

Missouri R.

Delaware
Maryland

Louisiana Purchase

Indiana Territory

Ohio

Washington, D.C.

Virginia

Kentucky

North Carolina

Tennessee

South Carolina

ATLANTIC OCEAN

PACIFIC OCEAN

Spanish Territory

Mississippi R.

Mississippi Territory

Georgia

0   400 mi

0   400 km

Albers Conic Equal-Area Projection

Spanish Florida

KEY
Louisiana Purchase
Disputed areas

Gulf of Mexico

>> **Analyze Maps** How did the Louisiana Purchase change the territory of the United States?

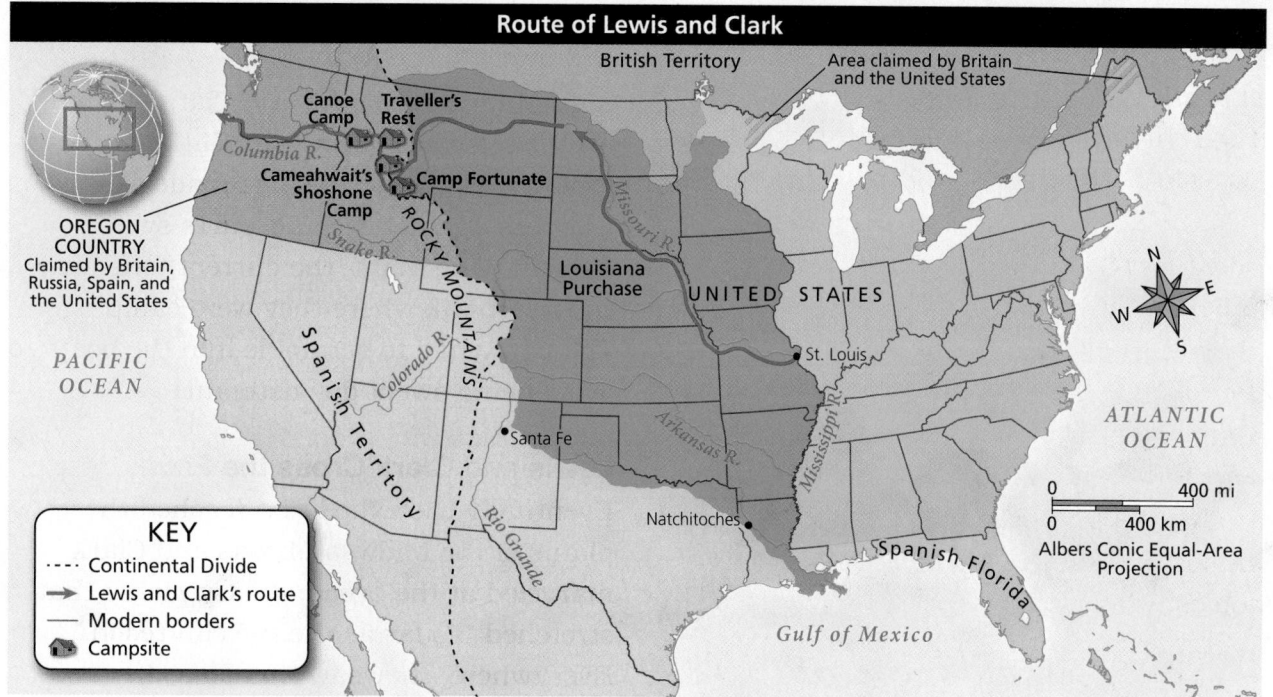

Route of Lewis and Clark

British Territory

Area claimed by Britain and the United States

Canoe Camp

Traveller's Rest

Cameahwait's Shoshone Camp

Camp Fortunate

Columbia R.

OREGON COUNTRY
Claimed by Britain, Russia, Spain, and the United States

PACIFIC OCEAN

Spanish Territory

Snake R.

Colorado R.

ROCKY MOUNTAINS

Louisiana Purchase

Missouri R.

UNITED STATES

St. Louis

Santa Fe

Arkansas R.

Mississippi R.

ATLANTIC OCEAN

Natchitoches

Spanish Florida

Rio Grande

Gulf of Mexico

KEY
- - - - Continental Divide
→ Lewis and Clark's route
— Modern borders
🏠 Campsite

0   400 mi
0   400 km
Albers Conic Equal-Area Projection

>> The Lewis and Clark expedition helped Americans learn more about the West. **Make Predictions** How might westward expansion lead to conflict with other nations?

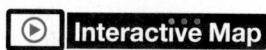 Interactive Map

Exploring the Louisiana Territory

Few Americans knew anything about the Louisiana territory. In 1803, Congress provided money for a team of explorers to study the new lands. Jefferson chose Meriwether Lewis, his private secretary, to head the **expedition,** or long voyage of exploration. Lewis asked William Clark to go with him.

Jefferson asked Lewis and Clark to map a route to the Pacific Ocean. He also told them to study the geography of the territory, including:

. . . climate as characterized by the thermometer, by the proportion of rainy, cloudy, and clear days, by lightning, hail, snow, ice . . . the dates at which particular plants put forth or lose their flower, or leaf, times of appearance of particular birds, reptiles, or insects.

—Thomas Jefferson, letter to Meriwether Lewis, 1803

Jefferson also instructed Lewis and Clark to learn about the Native American nations who lived in the Louisiana Purchase. These Native Americans carried on a busy trade with English, French, and Spanish merchants. Jefferson hoped that the Indians might trade with American merchants instead. Therefore, he urged Lewis and Clark to tell the Indians of "our wish to be neighborly, friendly, and useful to them."

The Expedition Begins Dozens of adventurous young men eagerly competed to join the expedition. Lewis and Clark judged volunteers on the basis of their character, strength, hunting skills, and ability to survive in the wilderness. In the

>> Lewis and Clark's expedition spent its first winter with the Mandan Indians, shown in this illustration crossing a stretch of ice with their sled dogs.

>> This painting shows Sacajawea interpreting for Lewis and Clark. Her help made communication much easier for the expedition.

end, about 50 men made up the "Corps of Discovery."

In May 1804, Lewis and Clark started up the Missouri River from St. Louis. At first, the expedition's boats made slow progress against the Missouri's swift current. One night, the current tore away the riverbank where they were camping. The party had to scramble into the boats to avoid being swept downstream.

Lewis and Clark Cross the Plains
Eventually the expedition reached the plains of the Midwest. Lewis and Clark marveled at the broad, grassy plains that stretched "as far as the eye can reach." Everywhere, they saw "immense herds of buffalo, deer, elk, and antelope."

As they traveled across the plains, the expedition met people of various Native American nations. Lewis and Clark had brought many gifts for Native Americans, such as "peace medals" stamped with the United States seal. They also brought mirrors, beads, knives, blankets, and thousands of sewing needles and fishhooks.

During the first winter, Lewis and Clark stayed with the Mandans in present-day North Dakota. The explorers planned to continue up the Missouri in the spring. The members of the expedition built a fort to live in over the winter. They took the opportunity to repair equipment in preparation for spring's new challenges.

The Mandans lived along the upper Missouri River. They grew corn, beans, and squash, and hunted buffalo. During the winter, they helped the explorers find food and hunt buffalo. They also traded with the expedition members.

Staying with the Mandans was a woman named Sacajawea (sak uh juh WEE uh). Sacajawea belonged to the Shoshone (shoh SHOH nee) people, who lived in the Rockies. She and her French Canadian husband agreed to accompany Lewis and Clark as translators. Sacajawea carried her baby with her on the journey.

Exploring the Rocky Mountains In early spring, the party set out again. In the foothills of the Rockies, the landscape and wildlife changed. Bighorn sheep ran along the high hills. The thorns of prickly pear cactus jabbed the explorers' moccasins. Once, a grizzly bear chased Lewis while he was exploring alone.

Crossing the Rocky Mountains meant crossing the Continental Divide. A **continental divide** is a ridge that separates river systems flowing toward opposite sides of a continent. In North America, some rivers flow east from the crest of the Rockies into the Mississippi, which drains into the Gulf of Mexico. Other rivers flow west from the Rockies and empty into the Pacific Ocean.

Past the Rockies, Lewis and Clark would be able to travel by river toward the Pacific. But to cross the Continental Divide, they needed horses. They began looking for the Shoshone, who had been using horses since Europeans brought them in the 1600s.

Finally, Lewis and Clark met some Shoshones. One of them was Sacajawea's brother, whom she had not seen for many years. Upon seeing her own people, wrote Clark, she began to "dance and show every mark of the most extravagant joy." The Shoshones supplied the expedition with the food and horses Lewis and Clark needed. They also advised them about the best route to take over the Rockies.

Lewis and Clark Reach the Pacific After building canoes, Lewis and Clark's party

>> Not only did Lewis and Clark record their observations in words, they also drew maps and illustrations of the new things they encountered.

floated toward the Columbia River into the Pacific Northwest. Finally, on November 7, 1805, Clark wrote in his journal, "Great joy in camp. We are in view of the ocean, this great Pacific Ocean which we have been so long anxious to see." Lewis and Clark had reached their goal. Viewing the Pacific from present-day Oregon, Lewis and Clark claimed the region for the United States by right of discovery.

The return trip to St. Louis took another year. In 1806, Americans celebrated the return of Lewis and Clark. Their journey had been difficult. Clark described some of the storms and high winds he faced as "the most disagreeable time I have experienced." But the explorers brought back much useful information about the Louisiana Territory, the land now part of the United States.

Pike's Expedition Before Lewis and Clark returned, another explorer set out from St. Louis. From 1805 to 1807, Zebulon Pike explored the upper Mississippi River, the Arkansas River, and parts of present-day Colorado and New Mexico. In November 1806, Pike viewed a mountain peak rising above the Colorado plains. Today, this mountain is known as Pikes Peak.

Continuing southward, Pike entered Spanish territory. Spanish troops soon arrested Pike and his men and took them into present-day Mexico. The Americans were later escorted through Texas back into the United States. The Spanish took Pike's maps and journals, but he was able to hide one map in the barrel of his gun. His report on the expedition greatly expanded Americans' knowledge about the Southwest.

The journeys of Pike and Lewis and Clark excited Americans. However, settlers did not move into the rugged western lands for a number of years. As you will read, they first settled the region closest to the Mississippi River. Soon, the territory around New Orleans had a large enough population of American citizens for the settlers to apply for statehood. In 1812, this territory entered the Union as the state of Louisiana.

? **IDENTIFY SUPPORTING DETAILS** Why did President Jefferson want Lewis and Clark to treat Native Americans fairly on their journey?

American Shipping Faces Challenges

After the Revolution, American overseas trade grew rapidly. Ships sailed from New England on voyages that sometimes lasted three years. President Jefferson's foreign policy during this time centered around protecting American shipping.

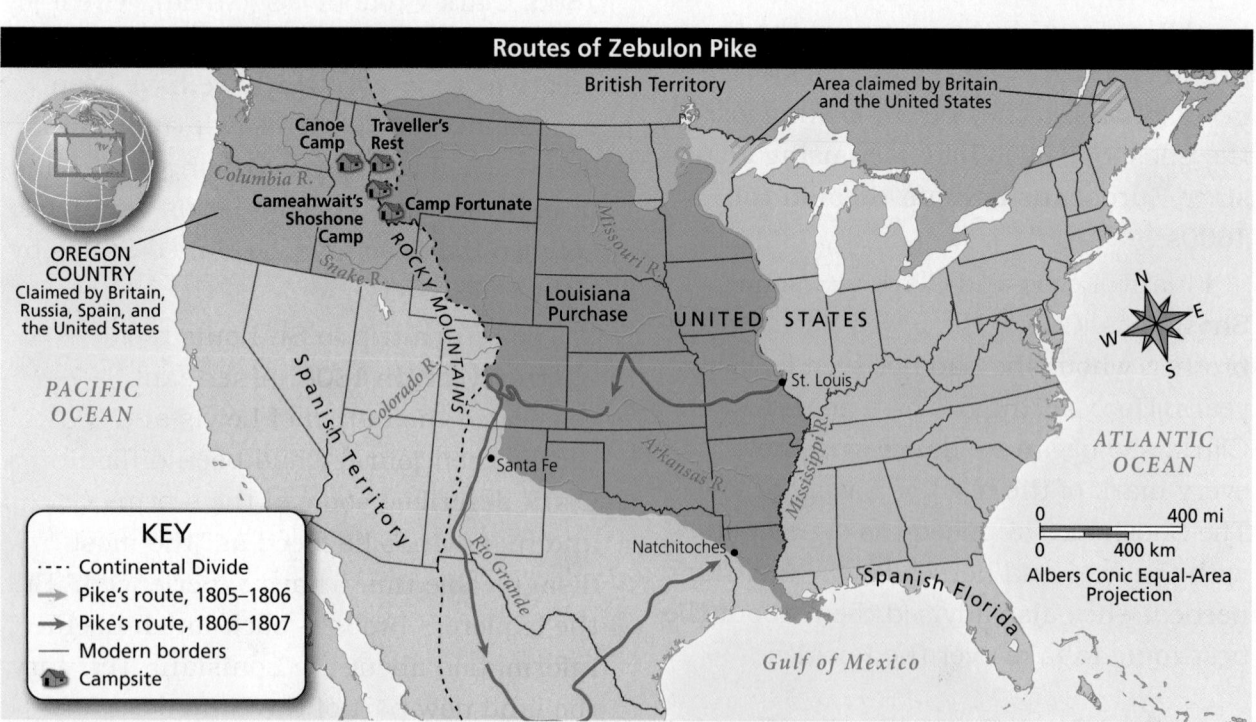

>> Zebulon Pike explored the Louisiana Purchase and Spanish territory. **Analyze Maps** What prominent geographic feature may have influenced Pike's route?

An Era of Trade Wherever they went, Yankee captains kept a sharp lookout for new goods and new markets. Clever traders sawed winter ice from New England ponds into blocks, packed it in sawdust, and carried it to India. There, they traded the ice for silk and spices. In 1784, the *Empress of China* became the first American ship to trade with China. New England merchants quickly built up a profitable China trade.

More than 10 years before Lewis and Clark, Yankee merchants sailed up the Pacific coast of North America. So many traders from Boston visited the Pacific Northwest that Native Americans there called every white man "Boston." Traders bought furs from Native Americans and sold them for large profits in China.

Jefferson Protects Trade Abroad

Traders ran great risks, especially in the Mediterranean Sea. Pirates from the Barbary States, countries along the coast of North Africa, attacked passing vessels. To protect American ships, the United States paid a yearly **tribute,** or bribe, to rulers of the Barbary States such as Tripoli.

In 1801, Tripoli increased its demands. When Jefferson refused to pay, Tripoli declared war on the United States. Jefferson then ordered the navy to blockade the port of Tripoli.

During the blockade, the American ship *Philadelphia* ran aground near Tripoli. Pirates boarded the ship and hauled the crew off to prison. The pirates planned to use the *Philadelphia* to attack other ships.

To prevent this, American naval officer Stephen Decatur and his crew quietly sailed into Tripoli harbor by night. They

>> These trading posts at Canton, China, were the site of early trade between China and other nations, including the United States.

then set the captured American ship on fire.

In the meantime, American marines landed on the coast of North Africa, marched 500 miles, and successfully captured, with the help of allies, the port of Derna. However, during the fight, the ruler of Tripoli signed a treaty promising not to interfere with American ships.

Caught Between France and Britain

American ships faced another problem. Britain and France went to war again in 1803. At first, Americans profited from the conflict. British and French ships were too busy fighting to engage in trade. American merchants eagerly traded with both sides. As profits increased, Americans hurried to build new ships.

Neither Britain nor France wanted the United States to sell supplies to its enemy.

As in the 1790s, they ignored American claims of neutrality. Napoleon seized American ships bound for England. At the same time, the British stopped Yankee traders on their way to France. Between 1805 and 1807, hundreds of American ships were captured.

Needing more sailors, the British navy stepped up **impressment,** the practice of forcing people into service. In Britain, impressment gangs raided English villages and took young men to serve in the navy. On the seas, British ships stopped American vessels, seizing any British sailors serving on American ships. Many American-born sailors were also impressed. Furious Americans clamored for war.

? IDENTIFY SUPPORTING DETAILS Why were Britain and France seizing American ships?

>> This illustration shows American sailors being impressed, or taken by force, into the British navy before the Revolution. Even after the Revolution, the British continued to impress American sailors at sea.

A Painful Embargo

Jefferson knew that the small American fleet was no match for the powerful British navy. Like Washington and Adams, he sought a foreign policy that would avoid war.

An Embargo on Foreign Trade Jefferson hoped that an American **embargo,** or ban on trade, would hurt France and Britain by cutting off needed supplies. "Our trade is the most powerful weapon we can use in our defense," one Democractic Republican newspaper wrote. In 1807, Jefferson persuaded Congress to impose a total embargo on foreign trade. This meant that American traders could not receive goods from European traders, and American traders could not ship their goods to Europe.

The **Embargo Act** did hurt Britain and France. But it hurt Americans even more. Supplies of imports such as sugar, tea, and molasses were cut off. Exports dropped by more than $80 million in one year. Docks in the South were piled high with cotton and tobacco. The Embargo Act hurt New England merchants most of all.

Merchants protested loudly against the embargo. Some turned to **smuggling,** importing or exporting goods in violation of trade laws. Jefferson began using the navy and federal troops to enforce the embargo. On the border between New York and Canada, some smugglers engaged in skirmishes with federal troops.

The two political parties had different points of view on the embargo. Democratic Republicans mostly supported the embargo as a way to protect the country and punish France and Britain. Most Federalists opposed the embargo as damaging to the economy.

AMERICA IMPOSES A TRADE EMBARGO

VALUE OF U.S. EXPORTS (IN MILLIONS)

$78 — 1804
$96 — 1805
$102 — 1806
$108 — 1807
$22 — 1808
$52 — 1809
$67 — 1810

JEFFERSON'S CONGRESSIONAL SUPPORT
128 DEMOCRATIC REPUBLICAN
48 FEDERALIST

JEFFERSON ASKS FOR AN EMBARGO
PASSING THE EMBARGO
82 YEA
45 NAY

PARTY MAJORITY INCREASES
144 DEMOCRATIC REPUBLICAN
32 FEDERALIST

CONGRESS REACTS TO THE LOSS IN TRADE
RETAINING THE EMBARGO
35 YEA
82 NAY

Sources: U.S. Senate and House of Representatives; Douglas A. Irwin, *Review of International Economics; Historical Statistics of the United States*

>> **Analyze Data** Cite data that explains why Congress canceled Jefferson's Embargo Act in 1809.

Jefferson Scales Back the Embargo

In 1809, Jefferson admitted that the Embargo Act had failed. Congress replaced it with the milder **Nonintercourse Act.** It allowed Americans to carry on trade with all nations except Britain and France. The Embargo Act had decreased support for the Democratic Republican party, as Americans hurt by the policy turned to the Federalists instead. Federalists favored maintaining closer relations with Britain.

They wanted to build ties with Britain because Britain was the main trading partner of the United States, and the powerful British navy could protect American merchants.

Although the embargo was the most unpopular measure of Jefferson's presidency, the Democratic Republicans still remained strong. Following President Washington's precedent, Jefferson refused to run for a third term. Democratic Republican **James Madison** easily won the 1808 presidential election. Madison hoped that Britain and France would soon agree to respect American neutrality.

? DEFINE Why did Americans turn against the Embargo Act?

ASSESSMENT

1. **Summarize** Jefferson's economic policies.

2. **Analyze Information** What might have been considered surprising about John Marshall's action in establishing judicial review?

3. **Draw Conclusions** Why do you think President Jefferson, who believed in a strict interpretation of the Constitution, decided that the President had the power to buy land when that was not mentioned in the Constitution?

4. **Compare** How were the Lewis and Clark expedition and the Pike expedition similar and different?

5. **Generate Explanations** Why was the Embargo Act so unpopular?

Madison and the War of 1812

>> The British burned the White House and other public buildings in Washington, D.C., in August 1814.

Interactive Flipped Video

>> **Objectives**

Explain the reasons for conflict between white settlers and Native Americans during the early 1800s.

Identify the causes of the War of 1812.

Explain the challenges that the United States faced in preparing for war.

Describe the important events and effects of the War of 1812.

>> **Key Terms**

Treaty of Greenville
confederation
Battle of Tippecanoe
War Hawks
nationalism
Battle of Lake Erie
Battle of New
   Orleans
Hartford Convention
Treaty of Ghent
Henry Clay
Andrew Jackson
John Quincy Adams

About 900,000 white settlers moved west of the Appalachians between 1790 and 1810. Some Native American groups resented these newcomers, who built farms on Indian lands and hunted the animals Indians needed for food. The settlers ignored treaties that the United States had signed with Native American nations of the region.

Conflict in Ohio

Fighting often broke out between these Native American groups and the settlers. Isolated acts of violence led to larger acts of revenge. As both sides killed innocent people, warfare spread. In Ohio, Little Turtle of the Miamis and Blue Jacket of the Shawnees organized a resistance movement in 1791. Armed with British muskets and gunpowder, the Miamis and Shawnees drove white settlers from the area.

President Washington had sent General Anthony Wayne into Ohio in 1794. Forces from the Delaware, Miami, Iroquois, Wabash, and others gathered at a place called Fallen Timbers.

They thought that Wayne would have trouble fighting there because fallen trees covered the land. But Wayne's well-trained army pushed through the tangle of logs and defeated the Indians.

In 1795, leaders of the Miamis and other Native American nations signed the **Treaty of Greenville.** They gave up land that would later become part of Ohio. In return, they received $20,000 and the promise of more money if they kept the peace.

Tecumseh's Confederation Confronts the New Republic Ohio joined the Union in 1803. By then, white settlers were pushing beyond Ohio into the Indiana Territory. Angry Shawnee, Kickapoo, and Ottawa vowed to keep settlers from taking more Indian land. They included two Shawnee leaders: Tecumseh and his brother Tenskwatawa (ten SKWAH tuh wuh), a religious leader also called the Prophet. The Kickapoo, Ottawa, Chippewa, and Piankashaw joined with the Shawnee leaders. The Miami initially remained neutral.

The Wyandot, Seneca, and Delaware stayed allied with the United States. So did

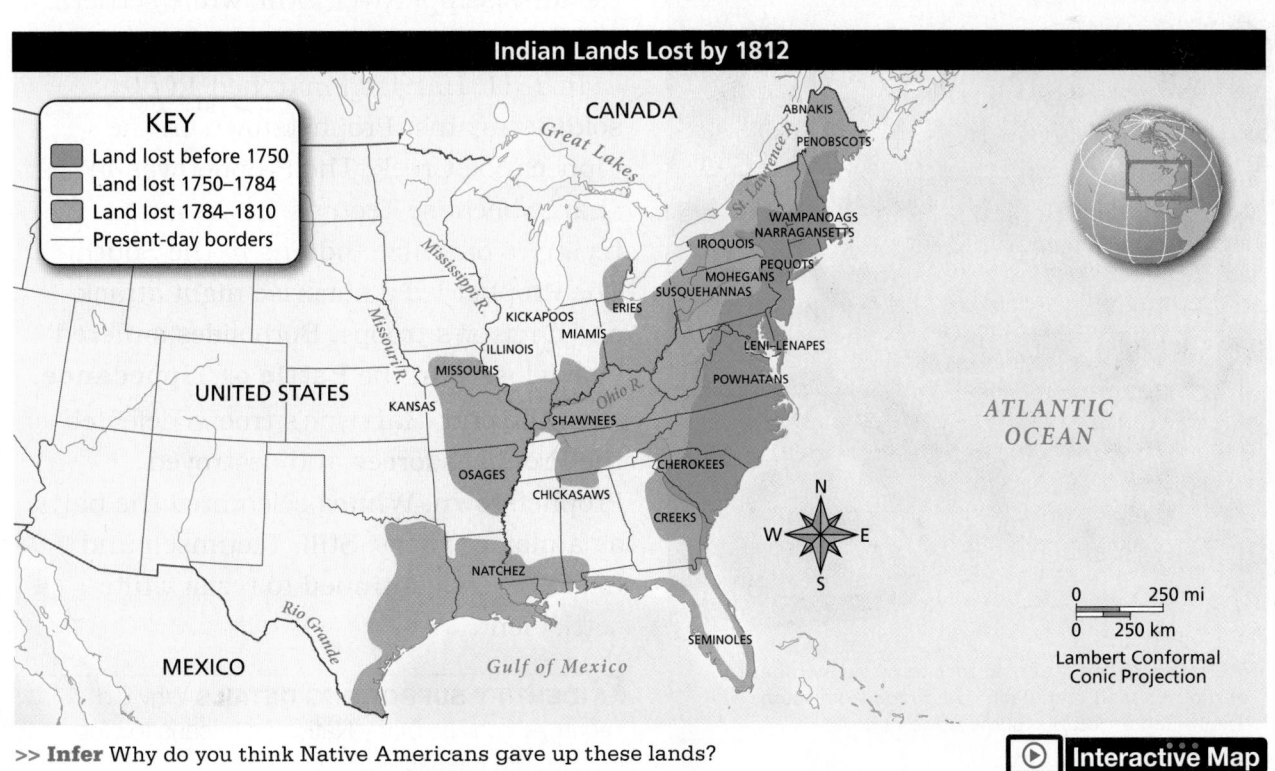

Indian Lands Lost by 1812

KEY
- Land lost before 1750
- Land lost 1750–1784
- Land lost 1784–1810
- Present-day borders

>> **Infer** Why do you think Native Americans gave up these lands?

▶ **Interactive Map**

the Chocktaw, Cherokee, Chickasaw, and some sections of the Creek.

The U.S. government had treaties with several of these Native American groups that said both sides would cease fighting. The treaties kept these groups from rallying together against the United States.

A New Settlement in Indiana Territory

The Prophet and Tecumseh taught that white customs corrupted the Indian way of life. They said that many Indians depended too much on white trade goods, such as muskets, cloth, cooking pots, and whiskey. They believed that by returning to their old ways, Native Americans could gain the power to resist the white invaders.

In 1808, the Prophet built a village for his followers along Tippecanoe Creek in Indiana Territory. Indians from lands as far away as Missouri, Iowa, and Minnesota

>> Native Americans sold furs to white merchants and purchased manufactured goods from them. Tecumseh urged his followers to end their dependence on whites.

traveled to Prophetstown to hear his message.

Tecumseh worked to organize the tribes of the Northwest into a **confederation,** or alliance with a shared military command. He called for unity against settlers:

> The whites have driven us from the great salt water, forced us over the mountains. . . . The way, the only way, to check and stop this evil is for all red men to unite in claiming a common equal right in the land.

> —Tecumseh, quoted in *Tecumseh: Vision of Glory* (Tucker)

Tecumseh impressed white leaders. Governor William Henry Harrison grudgingly admitted, "He is one of those uncommon geniuses which spring up occasionally to produce revolutions and overturn the established order of things."

A Major Battle at Tippecanoe
Rivalries among Native American nations kept Tecumseh from uniting all Indians east of the Mississippi River. Still, white settlers were alarmed at his success.

In 1811, Harrison marched 1,000 soldiers against Prophetstown on the Tippecanoe Creek. The Prophet was in charge because Tecumseh was away trying to organize Indians in the South. The Prophet led a surprise night attack on Harrison's troops. Both sides suffered heavy losses in the **Battle of Tippecanoe.**

In the end, Harrison's troops defeated the Prophet's forces and destroyed Prophetstown. Whites celebrated the battle as a major victory. Still, Tecumseh and his followers continued to resist white settlement.

? IDENTIFY SUPPORTING DETAILS Why did Tecumseh advise many Native Americans to stop trading with the settlers?

The Causes of the War of 1812

Fighting with Native Americans hurt relations between the United States and Britain. The British were supplying guns and ammunition to the Native Americans on the frontier. They also encouraged Indians to attack United States settlements.

Meanwhile, the ban on trade with Britain and France expired. Congress then authorized President Madison to make a tantalizing offer. If either the British or French stopped seizing American ships, the United States would reopen trade with that nation. Napoleon quickly announced that France would respect American neutrality. Britain did not respond to the offer. As promised, the United States resumed trade with France, but continued to ban all shipments to or from Britain.

The War Hawks Push for War While Madison did not want war, other Americans were not as cautious. In New England, antiwar feelings ran strong. However, members of Congress from the South and the West called for war. They were known as **War Hawks.**

War Hawks were stirred by a strong sense of **nationalism,** or devotion to one's country. War Hawks felt that Britain was treating the United States as if it were still a British colony. They were willing to fight a war to defend American rights.

The most outspoken War Hawk was **Henry Clay** of Kentucky. Clay wanted to punish Britain for seizing American ships. He also hoped to conquer Canada. "The militia of Kentucky are alone [able] to place Montreal and Upper Canada at your feet," Clay boasted to Congress.

>> Both sides suffered heavy losses, but General Henry Harrison's troops were able to destroy Prophetstown during the Battle of Tippecanoe in 1811.

>> British forts, like the one in Ontario pictured here, served as supply houses for the arms that the British supplied to the Native Americans living on the frontier.

>> As a War Hawk, Henry Clay seized the conflict with Britain as an opportunity to push his plan to conquer Canada from the British.

War Hawks saw other advantages of war with Britain. If Americans went to war with Britain, War Hawks said, the United States could seize Florida from Britain's ally, Spain. They also pointed out that Britain was arming Native Americans on the frontier and encouraging them to attack settlers.

The War Hawks felt that winning a war against Britain would bring lasting safety to settlers on the frontier.

War Is Declared The United States and Britain drifted closer to war as the security of American ships remained an issue. The British continued to board American ships and impress American seamen. To cut off American trade with France, British warships blockaded some American ports. In May 1811, near New York Harbor, a brief battle broke out between an American frigate and a British warship. The Americans crippled the British ship and left 32 British sailors dead or wounded.

The War Hawks urged Congress to prepare for war. Others in Congress disagreed. John Randolph of Virginia warned that the people of the United States would "not submit to be taxed for this war of conquest and dominion." Representatives of New England were especially concerned. They feared that the British navy would attack New England seaports.

At last, President Madison gave in to war fever. In June 1812, he asked Congress to declare war on Britain. The House and Senate both voted in favor of war. Americans would soon learn, though, that declaring war was easier than winning.

❓ **DEFINE** Who were the War Hawks?

>> **Identify Cause and Effect** How might events like this 1811 battle between a U.S. frigate and British battleship have led to war with Britain?

THE WAR OF 1812

CAUSES

- British interfere with American shipping.
- British kidnap American sailors.
- Americans believe British are persuading Native Americans to fight settlers.
- Some members of Congress ("War Hawks") want U.S. expansion into Canada.

CONGRESS IS DIVIDED OVER THE FIRST DECLARATION OF WAR

HOUSE
62% IN FAVOR   38% OPPOSED

SENATE
59%   41%

Source: Library of Congress

PREPAREDNESS FOR WAR

UNITED STATES	BRITAIN
12,000 TROOPS	**10,000** BRITISH & CANADIAN TROOPS
6 WARSHIPS	**584** WARSHIPS (2 WERE AVAILABLE)
4,000 SAILORS	**140,000** SAILORS (WORLDWIDE)
1,800 MARINES	**31,000** MARINES

Sources: Donald R. Hickey, *War of 1812*; U.S. Naval Institute

>> The United States faced the world's greatest power in the War of 1812.
Analyze Charts How does the graph on the right help to explain the graph on the left?

Early Events in the War of 1812

The American declaration of war took the British by surprise. They were locked in a bitter struggle with Napoleon and could not spare troops to fight the United States. As the war began, however, the United States faced difficulties of its own.

The Difficulties of Building a Military

The United States was not ready for war. Because Jefferson had reduced spending on defense, the navy had only 16 ships to meet the huge British fleet. The army was small and ill equipped, and many of the officers knew little about warfare. "The state of the army," said a member of Congress, "is enough to make any man who has the smallest love of country wish to get rid of it." These problems made it difficult to maintain national security.

Since there were few regular troops, the government relied on volunteers. Congress voted to give them a bounty of cash and land.

The money was equal to about a year's salary for most workers. Attracted by the high pay and the chance to own their own farms, young men eagerly enlisted. They were poorly trained, however, with little experience in battle. Many deserted after a few months.

Surprising Victories at Sea The British navy blockaded American ports to stop American trade. Though unable to break the blockade, several American sea captains won stunning victories.

One famous battle took place early in the war, in August 1812. As he was sailing near Newfoundland, Isaac Hull, captain of the USS *Constitution*, spotted the British ship HMS *Guerrière* (geh ree

AIR). For nearly an hour, the two ships jockeyed for position. At last, the guns of the *Constitution* roared into action. They tore holes in the sides of the *Guerrière* and shot off both masts. Stunned, the British captain had no choice but to surrender.

American sea captains won other victories at sea. These victories cheered Americans but did little to win the war.

? **DESCRIBE** What problems did the United States military face?

The War in Canada

One goal of the War Hawks was to conquer Canada. They were convinced that Canadians would welcome the chance to throw off British rule and join the United States.

>> After the British destroyed his flagship, the *Lawrence*, Captain Oliver Perry escaped to another American ship. Perry's fleet would regroup and eventually win the Battle of Lake Erie.

An Untested Force General William Hull moved American troops into Canada from Detroit. The Canadians had only a few untrained troops to ward off the invasion. However, they were led by a clever British general, Isaac Brock.

Brock paraded his soldiers in red coats to make it appear that experienced British troops were helping the Canadians. He also led Americans to think that a large number of Native Americans were fighting alongside the Canadians. Brock's scare tactics worked. Hull retreated from Canada. Other attempts to invade Canada also failed.

However, on April 27, 1813, U.S. soldiers crossed Lake Ontario and successfully captured York, present-day Toronto. The Americans seized British guns and supplies, and they set fire to public buildings.

American Victory on Lake Erie In 1813, the Americans, armed with the guns and supplies they had seized at York, set out to win control of Lake Erie. Captain Oliver Hazard Perry had no fleet, so he designed and built his own ships. In September 1813, he sailed his tiny fleet against the British.

During the **Battle of Lake Erie,** the British battered Perry's own ship and left it helpless. Perry rowed over to another American ship and continued to fight. Finally, the Americans won the battle. Captain Perry wrote his message of victory on the back of an envelope: "We have met the enemy and they are ours."

Native American Losses in the War of 1812 After losing control of Lake Erie, the British and their ally Tecumseh retreated from Detroit into Canada. General William Henry Harrison, veteran of Tippecanoe, pursued them. The Americans won a

>> This woodcut shows Fort McHenry's position at the entrance of Baltimore Harbor.

decisive victory at the Battle of the Thames (temz). Tecumseh died in the fighting. Without Tecumseh's leadership, the Indian confederation soon fell apart.

? CHECK UNDERSTANDING What became of the War Hawks' plan to conquer Canada?

The War's Conclusion

While Tecumseh was defeated in Canada, some sections of the Creeks continued their fight against U.S. settlers in the South. **Andrew Jackson**, a Tennessee officer, took command of American troops in the Creek War. In March 1814, with the help of Cherokees, Choctaws, and friendly Creeks, Jackson won a crushing victory at the Battle of Horseshoe Bend. The leader of the enemy Creeks walked alone into Jackson's camp to surrender. "Your people have destroyed my nation," he said.

The Burning of Washington and Victory in Baltimore In the spring of 1814, Britain and its allies defeated France. With the war in Europe over, Britain could send more troops and ships against the United States.

In August 1814, British ships sailed into Chesapeake Bay and landed an invasion force about 30 miles from Washington, D.C. American troops met the British at Bladensburg, Maryland. As President Madison watched, the battle-hardened British quickly scattered the untrained Americans. The British met little further resistance on their march to the capital.

In the White House, First Lady Dolley Madison waited for her husband to return. Hastily, she scrawled a note to her sister:

> Will you believe it, my sister? We have had a battle or skirmish near Bladensburg and here I am still within sound of the cannon! Mr. Madison comes not. May God protect us. Two

messengers covered with dust come bid me fly. But here I mean to wait for him.

—Dolley Madison, *Memoirs and Letters of Dolley Madison*

Soon after, British troops marched into the capital. Dolley Madison gathered up important papers of the President and a portrait of George Washington. Then, she fled south. She was not there to see the British set fire to the White House and other buildings. The British considered this an act of revenge for the burning of York.

From Washington, the British marched north toward the city of Baltimore. The key to Baltimore's defense was Fort McHenry on Baltimore Harbor. From the evening of September 13 until dawn on September 14 during the Battle of Baltimore, British rockets bombarded the harbor.

When the early morning fog lifted, the "broad stripes and bright stars" of the American flag still waved over Fort McHenry. American forces had won the Battle of Baltimore. The British withdrew and the threat to the nation's capital ended. Francis Scott Key, a young American lawyer who witnessed the battle, wrote a poem about it. Soon, his poem, "The Star-Spangled Banner," was published and set to music. Today, it is the national anthem of the United States.

Success in New Orleans Makes Jackson a Hero In late 1814, the British prepared to attack New Orleans. From there, they hoped to sail up the Mississippi. However, Andrew Jackson was waiting. Jackson had turned his frontier fighters into a strong army.

He took Pensacola in Spanish Florida to keep the British from using it as a base. He then marched through Mobile and set up camp in New Orleans.

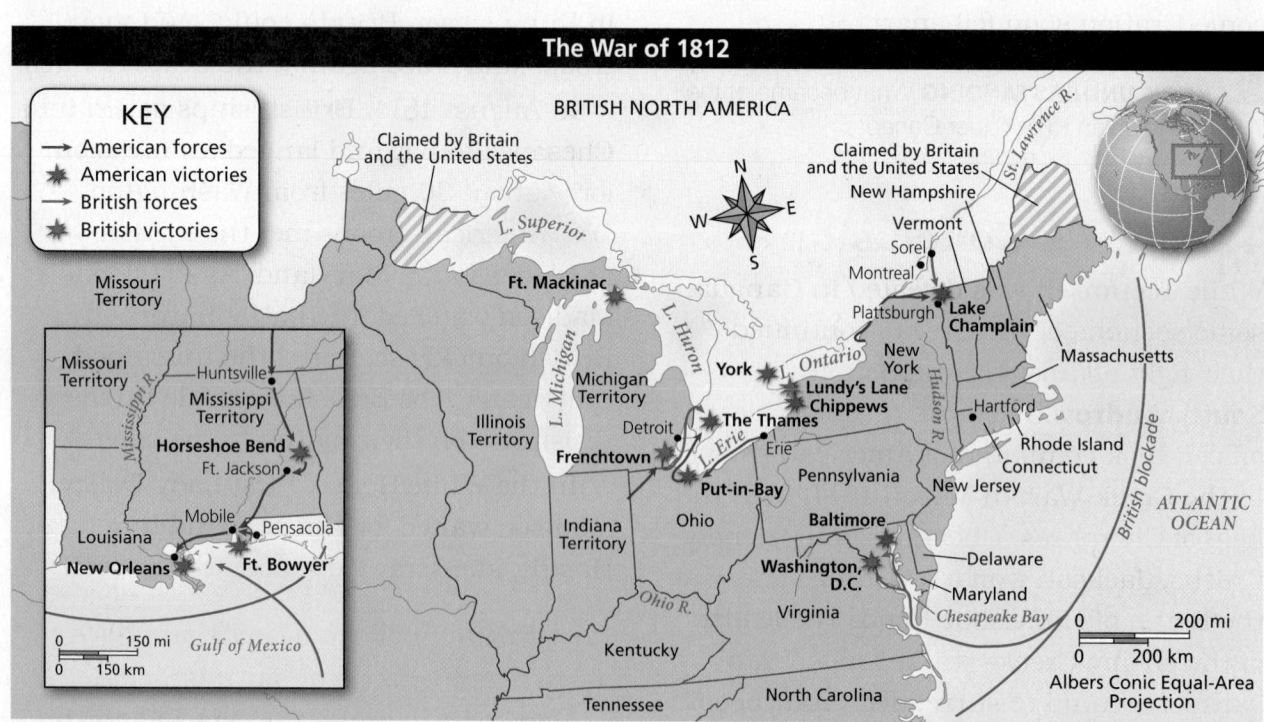

The War of 1812

KEY
→ American forces
✶ American victories
→ British forces
✶ British victories

>> Both sides won victories in the War of 1812, with no clear overall winner.
Analyze Maps Where did Andrew Jackson's forces win victories on their route to New Orleans?

▶ **Interactive Map**

Jackson's force included thousands of frontiersmen and Choctaws. The Choctaws were longtime rivals of the Indian nations who had been allied with the British. Many of Jackson's troops were expert riflemen. Citizens of New Orleans also joined the army to defend their city from the British. Among the volunteers were hundreds of African Americans.

The American soldiers dug trenches to defend themselves. On January 8, 1815, the British attacked. Again and again, British soldiers marched toward the American trenches. More than 2,000 British fell under the deadly fire of American sharpshooters and, especially, American cannons. Only seven Americans died.

Americans cheered the victory at the **Battle of New Orleans**. Overnight, Andrew Jackson became a national hero. His fame did not dim even when Americans learned that the battle had taken place two weeks after the war had ended.

The United States and Britain had already signed a treaty in Europe, but news took two months to cross the ocean by sail and had not yet reached the United States.

African Americans in the War The Battle of New Orleans was not the only place where black and white soldiers fought side by side. Throughout the War of 1812, African Americans joined in defending the nation against the British.

Following the British attacks on Washington and Baltimore, African American volunteers helped defend Philadelphia against a possible British attack. Bishop Richard Allen and the Reverend Absalom Jones recruited more than 2,000 men to help build

>> Cyrus Tiffany, an African American sailor shown here with his hand on the coat of Captain Oliver H. Perry, helped save the captain's life at the Battle of Lake Erie.

Philadelphia's fortifications. The state of New York organized two regiments of black volunteers to serve in the army.

African Americans also served with distinction in the United States Navy. They helped win the Battle of Lake Erie as well as other naval battles. Commander Nathaniel Shaler praised one particular black sailor who was killed in battle:

He fell near me, and several times requested to be thrown overboard, saying he was only in the way of others. When America has such [sailors], she has little to fear from the tyrants of the ocean.

—Nathaniel Shaler, letter to his agent, January 1, 1813

❓ **IDENTIFY** What achievement made Andrew Jackson well known throughout the country?

The Impact of the War of 1812

By late 1814, Americans knew that peace talks had begun, but they did not know if they would succeed or how long they would last. As Jackson was preparing to fight the British at New Orleans, New Englanders were meeting to protest "Mr. Madison's War."

New Englanders Protest Economic Instability The British blockade had hurt New England's sea trade. Also, many New Englanders feared that the United States might win land in Florida and Canada. If new states were carved out of these lands, the South and the West would become more influential than New England.

Delegates from around New England met in Hartford, Connecticut, in December 1814. Most were Federalists. They disliked the Democratic Republican President and the war.

Some delegates to the **Hartford Convention** threatened to nullify, or cancel, the state of war in their states if the war continued. Others threatened to leave the Union.

Then, while the delegates debated what to do, news of the peace treaty arrived. The Hartford Convention ended quickly. With the war over, the protest was meaningless. In the end, the threat of secession further weakened the dying Federalist party.

The Varied Effects of the War A peace treaty was signed in the city of Ghent, in present-day Belgium, on December 24, 1814. **John Quincy Adams**, son of John Adams and one of the American delegates,

>> In this cartoon, King George III offers New England politicians wealth and titles of nobility if they jump off the cliff to the British side. **Analyze Political Cartoons** What does this cartoon imply about some New Englanders' proposal to secede?

>> As the commander who won victory during the Battle of New Orleans, shown here, General Andrew Jackson became a military hero. His fame would later help him become President.

summed up the **Treaty of Ghent** in one sentence: "Nothing was adjusted, nothing was settled."

Britain and the United States agreed to restore prewar conditions. The treaty said nothing about impressment or neutrality. These issues had faded due to the end of the wars in Europe. Other issues were settled later. In 1818, for example, the two nations settled a dispute over the border between Canada and the United States.

Looking back, some Americans felt that the War of 1812 had been a mistake. Others argued that Europe would now treat the young republic with more respect. The victories of heroes like Oliver Hazard Perry, William Henry Harrison, and Andrew Jackson gave Americans new pride in their country. As one Democratic Republican leader remarked, "The people

are now more American. They feel and act more as a nation."

? RECALL What was the purpose of the Hartford Convention?

ASSESSMENT

1. **Draw Conclusions** Why were Native American groups resistant to white settlement west of the Appalachians?

2. **Generate Explanations** Why, when the Americans had already defeated a British ship near New York Harbor, were New England merchants fearful of British attacks on their seaports?

3. **Compare** the ability of the U.S. Army in 1812 with that of the Patriots at the beginning of the American Revolution.

4. **Summarize** what Andrew Jackson did that made him a national hero.

5. **Contrast** U.S. military might before and after the War of 1812.

Monroe's Presidency

>> President James Monroe faced little opposition as a Democratic Republican. **Infer** What does the lack of opposition imply about the the Federalist party at this time?

⊙ | **Interactive Flipped Video**

>> Objectives

Explain the significance of regional differences during the Era of Good Feelings.

Identify different points of view on tariffs.

Explain how the Supreme Court under John Marshall expanded federal power.

Explain U.S. foreign policy under Monroe, including the Monroe Doctrine and policies toward Florida.

>> Key Terms

sectionalism
American System
internal
    improvements
McCulloch v.
    Maryland
Gibbons v. Ogden
interstate commerce
creole
Republic of Great
    Colombia
United Provinces of
    Central America
Negro Fort
Monroe Doctrine

intervention
Adams-Onís Treaty
James Monroe
John C. Calhoun
Daniel Webster
Henry Clay

In 1816, the Democratic Republican candidate for President, **James Monroe**, easily defeated the Federalist, Senator Rufus King of New York. The election showed how seriously the Federalist party had declined in popularity. Many Federalists had joined the Democratic Republican party and voted for Monroe.

Sectionalism in the Era of Good Feelings

Monroe was the last Revolutionary War officer to become President. He was almost 60 years old when he took office, and he had old-fashioned manners.

Americans were fond of his old-fashioned ways. In 1817, he made a goodwill tour of the country. In Boston, crowds cheered Monroe enthusiastically. Boston newspapers expressed surprise at this warm welcome for a Democratic Republican from Virginia. After all, Boston had long been a Federalist stronghold.

An Era of Good Feelings Monroe hoped to create a new sense of national unity. One newspaper wrote that the United States was entering an "era of good feelings." By the time Monroe ran for a second term in 1820, no candidate opposed him. The Federalist party had disappeared.

While conflict between political parties declined, disputes between different sections of the nation sharpened. These disputes were a result of **sectionalism**, or loyalty to one's state or section rather than to the nation as a whole. In Congress, three ambitious young men took center stage in these disputes. All three would play key roles in Congress for more than 30 years, as well as serving in other offices. Each represented a different section of the country, and each had unique leadership qualities.

Calhoun Stands for the South Against Federal Power **John C. Calhoun** spoke for the South. He had grown up on a frontier farm in South Carolina. Calhoun's immense energy and striking features earned him the nickname "young Hercules."

He was slim and handsome, with deep-set eyes and a high forehead. His way of speaking was so intense that it sometimes made people uncomfortable to be in his presence.

Calhoun had supported the War of 1812. Like many southerners, he was a firm defender of slavery. In general, he opposed policies that would strengthen the power of the federal government.

Webster Speaks for the North Against Slavery and War **Daniel Webster** of New Hampshire was perhaps the most skillful public speaker of his time. With eyes flashing and shoulders thrown back, Webster was an impressive sight when he stood up to speak in Congress. An observer described him as a "great cannon loaded to the lips."

Like many New Englanders, Webster had opposed the War of 1812. He even

>> John C. Calhoun was the leading advocate for the interests of the South in Congress during Monroe's presidency.

Sectional Leaders: Calhoun, Webster, and Clay

JOHN C. CALHOUN	DANIEL WEBSTER	HENRY CLAY
• From South Carolina	• From New Hampshire	• From Kentucky
• Skilled orator, lawyer, and senator	• Skilled orator, lawyer, and senator	• Skilled orator, lawyer, and senator
• Sectional leader and spokesman for his region (South)	• Sectional leader and spokesman for his region (North)	• Sectional leader and spokesman for his region (West)
• Supported the War of 1812	• Against the War of 1812	• Supported the War of 1812
• Opposed the idea of a strong federal government	• Supported the idea of a strong federal government	• Supported the idea of a strong federal government
• Strong supporter of slavery	• Wanted slavery abolished	• Supported compromise over slavery
• Showed a concern for the country's economy	• Showed a concern for the country's economy	• Showed a concern for the country's economy
• Opposed the Compromise of 1850	• Defended the Compromise of 1850	• Defended the Compromise of 1850

>> **Analyze Information** Who supported the War of 1812 and the idea of a strong federal government?

 Interactive Chart

refused to vote for taxes to pay for the war effort. After the war, he wanted the federal government to take a larger role in building the nation's economy. Unlike Calhoun, Webster thought that slavery was evil.

Clay Speaks for the West in Favor of Active Government **Henry Clay** spoke for the West. You have already met Clay as a leader of the War Hawks, who pushed for war against Britain in 1812.

Clay was born in Virginia but moved to Kentucky when he was 20. As a young lawyer, he was once fined for brawling with an opponent. Usually, however, he charmed both friends and rivals. Supporters called him "Gallant Harry of the West." Like Webster, Clay strongly favored a more active role for the central government in promoting the country's growth.

? **RECALL** Which position did Webster share with Clay?

Creating a Stable Economy After the War

After the War of 1812, leaders such as Calhoun, Webster, and Clay had to deal with serious economic issues. Despite the nation's great physical growth and the soaring spirits of its people, the United States economy faced severe problems. This was due in part to the lack of a national bank.

The charter that had set up the first Bank of the United States ran out in 1811. Without the Bank to lend money and regulate the nation's money supply, the economy suffered. State banks made loans and issued money. However, they often put too much money into circulation. With so much money available to spend, prices rose rapidly.

In the nation's early years, Democratic Republicans such as Jefferson and

Madison had opposed a national bank because they saw it as unconstitutional.

They thought that the Constitution did not give the federal government the right to charter corporations, such as a national bank. By 1816, however, many Democratic Republicans believed that a bank was needed. They supported a law to charter the second Bank of the United States. By lending money and restoring order to the nation's money supply, the Bank helped American businesses grow.

Policies Protect Against Foreign Competition Another economic problem facing the nation was foreign competition, especially from Britain. In the early 1800s, the Embargo Act and then the War of 1812 kept most British goods out of the United States. In response, ambitious American business leaders such as Francis Cabot Lowell established their own mills and factories. As a result, American industry grew quickly until 1815.

Domestic Problems Caused by Foreign Goods With the end of the War of 1812, British goods again poured into the United States. Because the British had a head start in industrializing, they could make and sell goods more cheaply than Americans could. Most British factory buildings and machines were older and had already been paid for. In contrast, Americans still had to pay for their new factory buildings.

Sometimes, British manufacturers sold cloth in the United States for less than it cost to make so that they could capture the market. British manufacturers hoped to put American rivals out of business. Then, the British planned to raise prices.

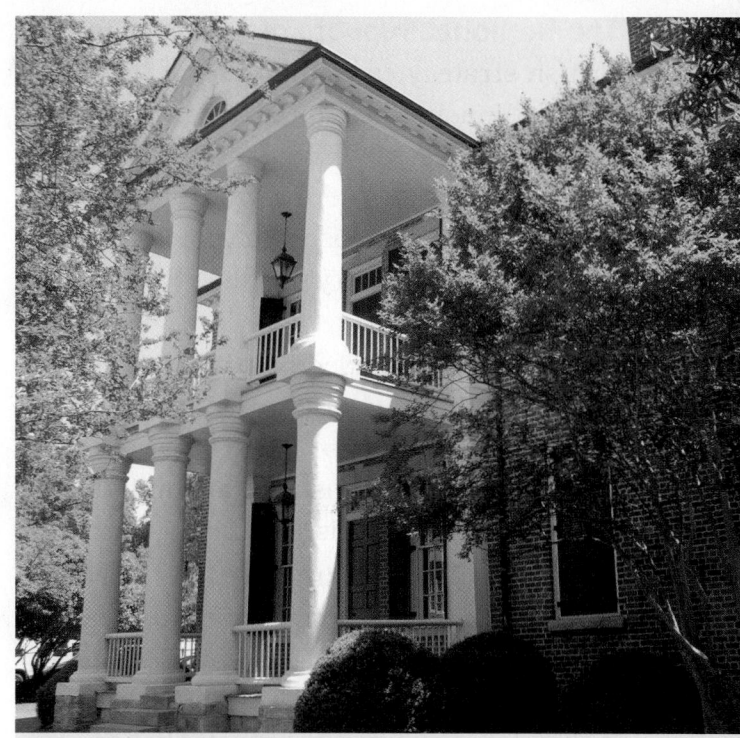

>> When the charter for the first Bank of the United States expired, state banks like this one in North Carolina began to make loans and print too much money, which caused prices to rise rapidly.

>> Inventions, such as the power loom shown here, helped propel American industry forward, making it more competitive with British manufacturing.

The Regional Impacts of Tariffs This British strategy caused dozens of New England businesses to fail. Angry owners asked Congress to place a protective tariff on all goods imported from Europe. As you have read, the purpose of a protective tariff is to protect a country's industries from foreign competition.

Congress responded by passing the Tariff of 1816. It greatly raised tariffs on imports. This increase made imported goods far more expensive than similar American-made goods.

The Tariff of 1816 impacted the North, West, and South differently because each region had a different economy. The North was the base of America's manufacturing. It therefore benefited the most. Higher prices on foreign goods made American goods more competitive. American factories sold more products, and businesses grew.

The economies of the South and West relied heavily on farming. They were not as financially invested in manufacturing and therefore did not experience the same benefits as the North. Goods like cloth and iron became more expensive to southern and western consumers. Northerners gained income as a result.

Higher tariffs led to angry protests. Lacking factories, southerners did not benefit from the tariff. Also, southerners bought many British goods. The new tariff drove up the price of British-made goods. Southerners complained that the tariff made northern manufacturers rich at the expense of the South.

Henry Clay Combats Sectionalism The bitter dispute over tariffs contributed to the growth of sectionalism. Americans identified themselves as southerners, northerners, or westerners. In Congress,

THE ROOTS OF AMERICAN INDUSTRIALIZATION

COTTON PRODUCTION (BALES)

178,000	1810	
209,000	1815	
335,000	1820	
533,000	1825	

COTTON TEXTILE FACTORIES

36	
153	
180	
258	

VALUE OF U.S. MANUFACTURES (IN MILLIONS)

1810	$128
1849	$464
1859	$854

NO RELIABLE INFORMATION EXISTS ON U.S. MANUFACTURES BETWEEN 1810 AND 1849.

Sources: *Historical Statistics of the United States;* "American Cotton Manufacture," *Quarterly Journal of Economics*

Source: U.S. Census Bureau

>> Cotton played a key role in the early U.S. economy, especially in the South. **Analyze Charts** As cotton production soared, what other features of the American economy also grew?

representatives from different sections often clashed.

Henry Clay wanted to promote economic growth for all sections. His program, known as the **American System**, called for high tariffs on imports, which would help northern factories. With wealth from industry, Clay believed, northerners would have the money to buy farm products from the West and the South. High tariffs would also reduce American dependence on foreign goods.

Clay also urged Congress to use money from tariffs to build roads, bridges, and canals. A better transportation system, he believed, would make it easier and cheaper for farmers in the West and the South to ship goods to city markets.

Clay's American System never fully went into effect. While tariffs remained high, Congress spent little on **internal improvements**—new roads, bridges, and canals. Southerners in particular disliked Clay's plan. The South had many fine rivers on which to transport goods. Many southerners opposed paying for roads and canals that brought them no direct benefits.

Some Americans also thought Clay's plan for developing transportation with federal support was unconstitutional. They did not believe the federal government had the authority to build such projects. They believed that by regulating industry and building roads and canals, the federal government would gain too much power.

? CHECK UNDERSTANDING Why did many states in the South and West oppose the Tariff of 1816?

>> Daniel Webster supported a tariff to help northern industry.

>> A slow freight wagon and a fast mail coach make their way down the National Road, built with federal support. Congress spent little on such roads, however.

Supreme Court Decisions Expand Federal Power

Under Chief Justice John Marshall, the Supreme Court strengthened the power of the federal government. The Court gave the federal government the power to regulate the economy.

A Broad Definition of "Necessary and Proper" After Congress chartered the second Bank of the United States, Maryland tried to tax the Bank in order to drive it out of the state. James McCulloch, the Bank cashier, refused to pay the tax.

In the case of *McCulloch* **v.** *Maryland* (1819), the Court ruled that states had no right to interfere with federal institutions within their borders. The ruling strengthened federal power. It also allowed the Bank of the United States to continue, which helped the economy to expand.

The Court decision addressed the issue of the meaning of the "necessary and proper" clause of the U.S. Constitution. It ruled that the federal government had the power to charter the Bank of the United States under the clause. This clause states that "The Congress shall have Power ... To make all Laws which shall be necessary and proper" for carrying out functions outlined elsewhere in the Constitution. Since the Constitution gave the federal government the power to tax and borrow money and to regulate business, the Court stated that creating a bank could be considered "necessary and proper" to carrying out these powers.

The Supreme Court took a "loose constructionist" view of the Constitution, believing that the "necessary and proper" clause should be interpreted loosely as circumstances changed. Many Americans disagreed with the Court.

>> Of all the capitols in the United States, the Maryland State Capitol building, built in 1784, has spent the most years in operation.

>> Robert Fulton built the first successful steamboats, shown here, and ran them as ferries from New York to New Jersey. In *Gibbons* v. *Ogden*, the Supreme Court ended the exclusive rights New York had given him to run these ferries.

▶ Interactive Gallery

Those who disagreed took a "strict constructionist" view that the "necessary and proper" clause permitted only actions absolutely necessary for performing the government's constitutional duties. Strict constructionists generally agreed that the Bank of the United States was not truly necessary for the government to function.

Broad Powers Over Interstate Trade In another case, ***Gibbons v. Ogden*** (1824), the Supreme Court upheld the power of the federal government to regulate trade between states. The Court struck down a New York law that tried to control steamboat travel between New York and New Jersey. The Court ruled that a state could regulate trade only within its own borders. Only the federal government had the power to regulate **interstate commerce,** or trade between different states. This decision helped the national economy by making it easier for the government to regulate trade.

These rulings not only affected the government. They also changed daily life for people in the United States. The New York law had given a monopoly, or exclusive rights, to Robert Fulton's steamboat company to run ferries to New Jersey. Fulton's company was the only one allowed to run ferries between the two states.

When the Supreme Court struck down this New York law, Fulton's monopoly on steamboat traffic ended. As a result, his company could not compete with companies that charged a lower fare, and people working for Fulton lost their jobs. However, the increased competition was good for consumers because it led to lower fares.

Many people also liked this ruling because it created a single national market for goods and services, regulated by the federal government. Having clear national laws to follow made it easier for people to do business and move goods and services nationwide.

? CHECK UNDERSTANDING How did the decision in *McCulloch* v. *Maryland* increase federal power?

Latin America Wins Independence

By 1810, many people in Spain's colonies in the Americas were eager for independence. They had many reasons to be unhappy. Most people, even wealthy creoles, had little or no say in government. In Latin America, the term **creole** described people born to Spanish parents there. They demanded a role in government. Opposition to Spain was also growing among Native Americans. Harsh rules kept Native Americans forever in debt. All over

>> Mexican priest and freedom fighter Miguel Hidalgo declares Mexico's independence from Spain.

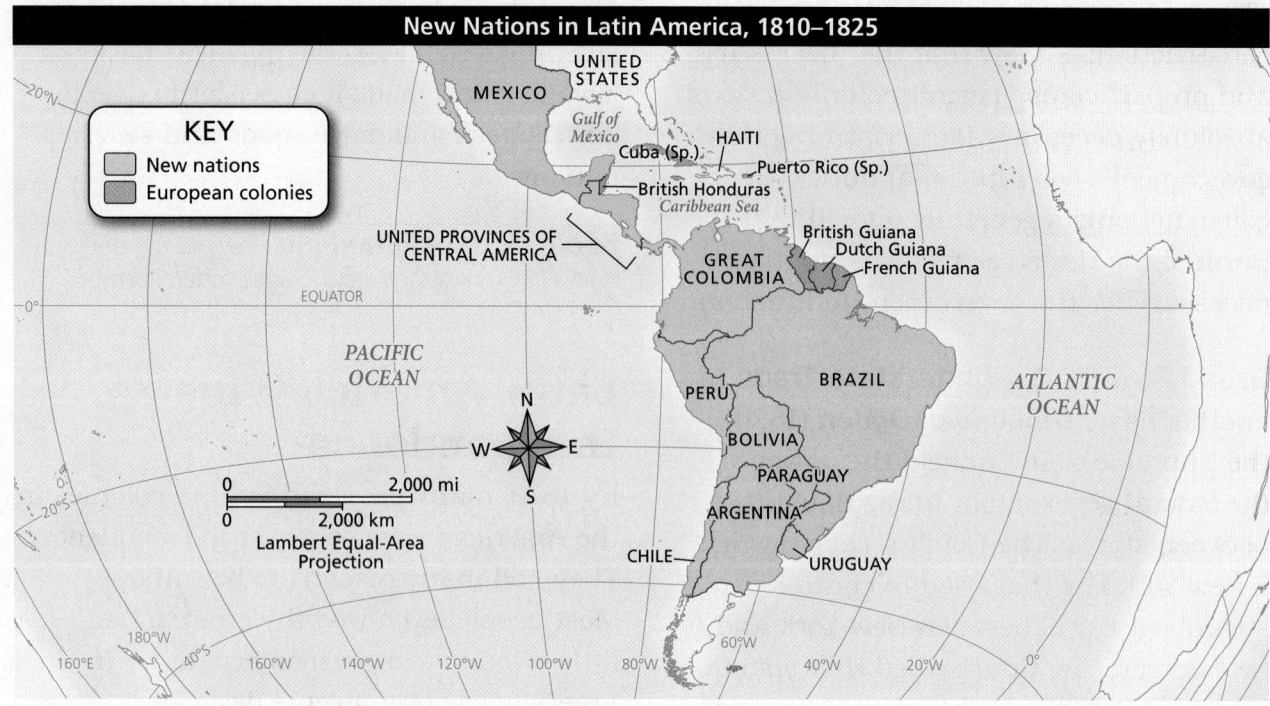

New Nations in Latin America, 1810–1825

KEY
New nations
European colonies

UNITED STATES
MEXICO
Gulf of Mexico
HAITI
Cuba (Sp.)
Puerto Rico (Sp.)
British Honduras
Caribbean Sea
UNITED PROVINCES OF CENTRAL AMERICA
British Guiana
Dutch Guiana
French Guiana
GREAT COLOMBIA
EQUATOR
PACIFIC OCEAN
BRAZIL
ATLANTIC OCEAN
PERU
BOLIVIA
PARAGUAY
ARGENTINA
CHILE
URUGUAY
0   2,000 mi
0   2,000 km
Lambert Equal-Area Projection

>> **Analyze Maps** In the early 1800s, colonies across South America were freed from Spanish rule as a result of revolution. Which European countries continued to exercise control on that continent?

Latin America, people were eager to be free of the Spanish.

Mexico Gains Independence A Mexican priest named Miguel Hidalgo (mee GEL ee DAHL goh) called on Mexicans to fight for independence from Spain in 1810. Many Mexicans answered his call. Rebel forces won control of several provinces before Father Hidalgo was captured. In 1811, Hidalgo was executed.

Another priest, José Morelos (hoh SAY moh RAY lohs), took up the fight. Because he called for a program to give land to peasants, wealthy creoles opposed him. Before long, Morelos, too, was captured and killed by the Spanish.

Slowly, though, creoles began to join the revolutionary movement. In 1821, revolutionary forces led by creoles won control of Mexico. A few years later,

Mexico became a republic with its own constitution.

Freedom From Spanish Rule in South America In South America, too, a series of revolutions freed colonies from Spanish rule. The best-known revolutionary leader was Simón Bolívar (see MOHN boh LEE vahr). He became known as the Liberator for his role in the Latin American wars of independence.

Bolívar came from a wealthy creole family in Venezuela. As a young man, he took up the cause of Venezuelan independence. Bolívar promised, "I will never allow my hands to be idle, nor my soul to rest until I have broken the shackles which chain us to Spain."

Bolívar rose to become a leader of the rebel forces. In a bold move, he led an army from Venezuela over the high Andes Mountains into Colombia. There, Bolívar took the Spanish forces by surprise and defeated them in 1819.

Soon after, Bolívar became president of the independent **Republic of Great Colombia**. It included the present-day nations of Venezuela, Colombia, Ecuador, and Panama.

Independence Movements Spread Other independent nations emerged in Latin America. José de San Martín (sahn mahr TEEN) led Argentina to freedom in 1816. He then helped the people of Chile and Peru win independence.

In 1821, the peoples of Central America declared independence from Spain. Two years later, they formed the **United Provinces of Central America.**

It included the present-day nations of Nicaragua, Costa Rica, El Salvador, Honduras, and Guatemala. By 1825, Spain had lost all its colonies in Latin America except Puerto Rico and Cuba.

The Portuguese colony of Brazil won independence peacefully. When Brazilian revolutionaries demanded independence, Prince Pedro, son of the Portuguese king, joined their cause. He became emperor of the new independent nation of Brazil in 1822.

The New Republics Spain's former colonies modeled their constitutions on that of the United States. Yet, their experience after independence was very different from that of their neighbor to the north. Unlike the people of the 13 British colonies, the peoples of Latin America did not unite into a single country. In part, geography made unity difficult. Latin America covered a much larger area than the British colonies. Thick rain forests and mountains such as the high, rugged Andes acted as barriers to travel and communication. Also, the Spanish colonies were spread out over a huge area. Therefore, several separate republics formed.

The new republics had a hard time setting up stable governments. Under Spanish rule, the colonists had gained little or no experience in self-government. Powerful leaders took advantage of the turmoil to seize control. As a result, the new nations were often unable to achieve democratic rule.

? IDENTIFY CENTRAL IDEAS What characteristics of physical geography made it more difficult for Latin American colonies to unite than it had been for the United States?

>> José de San Martín declared the independence of Peru in 1821. San Martín played a pivotal role in independence movements across South America during the early 1800s.

Gaining Florida

Spain lost another one of its colonies, Florida—not to independence, but to the United States. Many Americans wanted to gain possession of Florida. White southerners were especially worried about disturbances across the border. Creeks and Seminoles in Florida sometimes raided settlements in Georgia. Also, Florida was a refuge for many Africans and African Americans who escaped slavery.

Jackson Invades Spanish Florida Since the 1700s, Spanish officials had protected enslaved Africans who had fled from plantations in Georgia and South Carolina. Seminoles allowed Africans to live near their villages. In return, these "black Seminoles" gave the Seminoles a share of the crops they raised. The black Seminoles adopted many Seminole customs.

One settlement on the Apalachicola River known as the **Negro Fort** contained about 1,000 black Seminoles. General Andrew Jackson demanded that Spain demolish the Negro Fort. When the Spanish governor refused, the United States invaded Florida and destroyed the fort.

Adams Buys Florida In 1818, Jackson again headed to Florida with a force of more than 3,000 soldiers. Spain protested but did little else. It was busy fighting rebels in Latin America and could not risk war with the United States.

In the end, Spain agreed to peace talks. Secretary of State John Quincy Adams worked out a treaty with Spain's foreign minister, Luis de Onís (LOO ess day oh NEES). In it, Spain agreed to give Florida to the United States in exchange for $5 million. The **Adams-Onís Treaty** took effect in 1821.

? **DESCRIBE** What was the result of the Adams-Onís Treaty?

>> **Infer** Based on the illustration, what can you infer about the purpose of Negro Fort?

>> President Monroe met with his cabinet to discuss U.S. policy in the Americas.

The Monroe Doctrine

Americans cheered as Latin American nations won independence. The actions of European powers, however, worried Secretary of State Adams and President Monroe. In 1815, Prussia, France, Russia, and Austria formed an alliance aimed at crushing any revolution that sprang up in Europe. They seemed ready to help Spain regain its colonies in Latin America. In addition, Russia claimed lands on the Pacific coast of North America.

The British, too, worried about other European nations meddling in the Western Hemisphere. They feared that their profitable trade with the newly independent countries would be hurt if Spain regained control of its former colonies. Thus, they suggested that the United States and Britain issue a joint statement guaranteeing the freedom of the new nations of Latin America.

Monroe decided to act independently of Britain. In a message to Congress in 1823, he made a bold foreign policy statement, known as the **Monroe Doctrine**. Monroe declared that the United States would not interfere in the affairs of European nations or existing colonies of the European nations. At the same time, he warned European nations not to attempt to regain control of the newly independent nations of Latin America.

The Monroe Doctrine stated that the United States would oppose any attempt to reclaim old colonies or build new colonies in the Americas. Monroe's message showed that the United States was determined to keep European powers out of the Western Hemisphere.

The United States did not have the military power to enforce the Monroe Doctrine. Britain, however, supported the statement. With its strong navy, it could

>> In this political cartoon, Uncle Sam brandishes a big stick, labeled "Monroe Doctrine," as a warning to European nations not to attempt to re-colonize territory in the Americas.

stop Europeans from building new colonies in the Americas.

As the United States became stronger, the Monroe Doctrine grew in importance. On several occasions, the United States successfully challenged European

intervention, or direct involvement, in Latin America. In the 1900s, Presidents also used the Monroe Doctrine to justify sending troops to Caribbean nations. Thus, Monroe's bold statement helped shape United States foreign policy for more than 100 years.

❓ **IDENTIFY MAIN IDEAS** What was the purpose of the Monroe Doctrine?

ASSESSMENT

1. **Generate Explanations** After the War of 1812, British goods were again available in the United States. Why were these imported British goods less expensive than similar American goods?

2. **Identify** the principal reason the South rejected the American System, Henry Clay's plan to promote economic growth in all regions of the United States.

3. **Compare** In what ways were the outcomes in *McCulloch* v. *Maryland* and *Gibbons* v. *Ogden* similar?

4. **Evaluate Arguments** Evaluate the argument that a lack of experience in self-government affected the ability of Spain's former colonies in Latin America to form stable democratic governments.

5. **Infer** Why might southern slave states have supported the acquisition of Florida by the United States?

TOPIC (5) ASSESSMENT

1. **Analyze the Leadership of George Washington** Using the quotation below and other sources, write a paragraph analyzing George Washington's leadership and his role as the first President of the United States. Define the word *precedent,* analyze what the quotation shows about Washington's leadership, analyze what about the U.S. Constitution makes the point expressed in the quotation important, and describe what precedents Washington set when he established his cabinet and at the end of his second term as president.

   There is scarcely any part of my conduct which may not hereafter be drawn into precedent.

   —President George Washington

2. **Summarize Taxation and the Whiskey Rebellion** Write a paragraph describing how the tax on liquor sparked the Whiskey Rebellion. Explain what the tax was meant to do and why the tax presented special difficulties for small distilleries, particularly those on the frontier, and summarize why frontier farmers opposed the tax and how the opposition turned to rebellion.

3. **Explain the Origin of Political Parties** Write a paragraph explaining how Thomas Jefferson's and Alexander Hamilton's clashes over policies led to the formation of the first political parties. Consider what caused Thomas Jefferson and James Madison to start organizing their supporters, who Jefferson's supporters were and what they called themselves, and who Hamilton's supporters were and what they called themselves.

4. **Explain the Development of the Free-Market System** Write a paragraph explaining Jefferson's support for laissez-faire economics and the free-market system and how it represented a break with the Federalist policies of Alexander Hamilton. Define *laissez faire* and explain what it means in economic terms. Explain the influence of Adam Smith on Jefferson's economic ideas and why Jefferson's support of laissez faire marked a change from the Federalist approach to the economy.

5. **Analyze the Responses of Congress and the President** Write a paragraph analyzing how President Jefferson and Congress responded to John Marshall's decision in *Marbury* v. *Madison* and the precedent it set. Consider why Jefferson was displeased with the Court's ruling, what Jefferson believed judicial review did to the balance of power among the branches of government, and how Jefferson and Congress finally responded to the establishment of judicial review and why that is important.

6. **Summarize *McCulloch* v. *Maryland*** Write a paragraph summarizing the arguments regarding banking involved in *McCulloch* v. *Maryland*. Summarize the issues leading to the case being heard by the Supreme Court, the Supreme Court decision, and the significance of the decision.

7. **Locate Regions in History** Write a paragraph describing how the United States gained Florida. Describe why white southerners wanted Florida, the role General Andrew Jackson played in acquiring Florida, and the role Secretary of State John Quincy Adams played in acquiring Florida.

8. **Explain the Monroe Doctrine** Write a paragraph identifying what the Monroe Doctrine was and explaining its significance. Identify what concerns led President Monroe to issue the Monroe Doctrine and explain what the Monroe Doctrine stated and its short- and long-term impact.

9. **Identify the Era of Sectionalism** Write a paragraph describing what the era of sectionalism was and identifying the roles John C. Calhoun, Daniel Webster, and Henry Clay played in it. Define *sectionalism,* identify what area of the nation Calhoun spoke for and what his views were, identify what area of the nation Webster spoke for and what his views were, and identify what area of the nation Clay spoke for and what his views were.

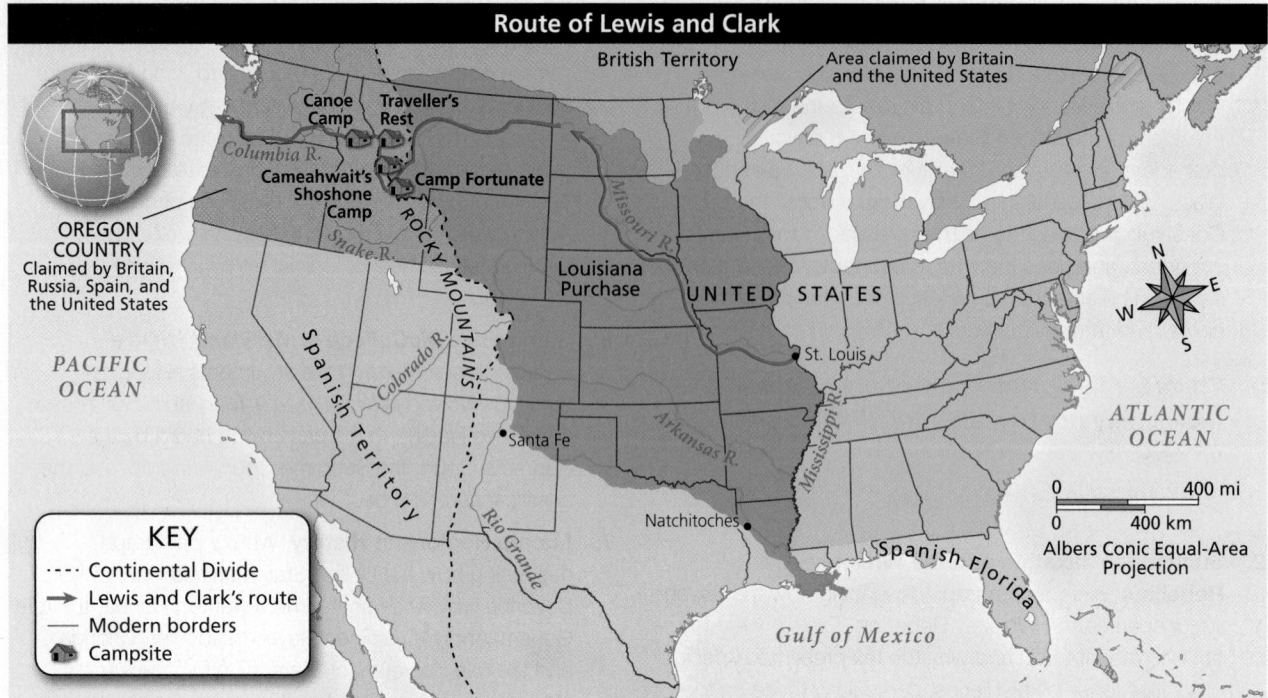

Route of Lewis and Clark

10. Identify and Locate the Louisiana Purchase Using the map above and other sources, write a paragraph identifying the area of the Louisiana Purchase and the route that Lewis and Clark took on their expedition. Use the map to locate and identify the eastern and western borders of the Louisiana Purchase, and explain and identify the Continental Divide. Use the map and text to describe the route that the Lewis and Clark expedition took, and indicate what additional land Lewis and Clark claimed for the United States.

11. Explain the Significance of the Louisiana Purchase Write a paragraph explaining the events leading to the Louisiana Purchase and why the purchase was significant. Explain why the Louisiana Territory was important to the economic interests of the United States, especially western farmers, why that access was in jeopardy in 1800, how the United States ended up acquiring Louisiana, including James Monroe's role, and why the purchase was significant.

12. Analyze the Effects of Geographic Features Write a paragraph analyzing how physical geography affected the Lewis and Clark expedition. Consider river currents, weather, landforms, plants, and animals.

13. Use Problem Solving Write a short essay identifying a problem related to human or physical geography encountered on the Lewis and Clark expedition and propose possible solutions. Identify the problem, gather information, list and consider options, consider advantages and disadvantages, and propose and evaluate possible solutions.

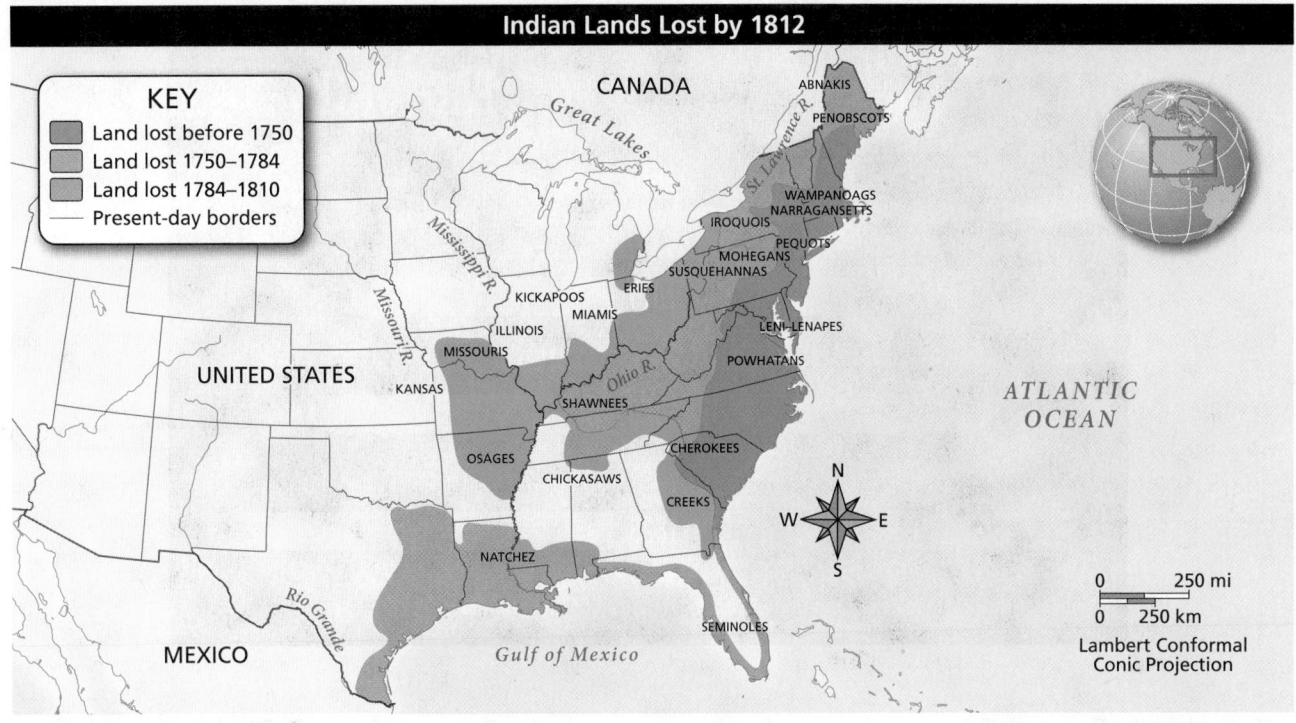

Indian Lands Lost by 1812

KEY
- Land lost before 1750
- Land lost 1750–1784
- Land lost 1784–1810
- Present-day borders

CANADA

ABNAKIS
PENOBSCOTS
Great Lakes
St. Lawrence R.
WAMPANOAGS
NARRAGANSETTS
IROQUOIS
PEQUOTS
MOHEGANS
SUSQUEHANNAS
ERIES
LENI-LENAPES
KICKAPOOS
MIAMIS
ILLINOIS
MISSOURIS
POWHATANS
Mississippi R.
Missouri R.
Ohio R.
UNITED STATES
KANSAS
SHAWNEES
OSAGES
CHEROKEES
CHICKASAWS
CREEKS
NATCHEZ
Rio Grande
SEMINOLES
MEXICO
Gulf of Mexico

ATLANTIC OCEAN

0   250 mi
0   250 km

Lambert Conformal Conic Projection

---

14. Describe National Security Problems Write a paragraph describing how the war between Britain and France that began in 1803 affected the United States and led to calls for the United States to go to war. Describe how American merchants responded to the war, how France and Britain responded to the American merchants' actions, and how Britain's need for sailors led to calls for war.

15. Analyze Conflict Resolution Using the map above and other sources, write a paragraph analyzing how migration and cultural differences led to conflict between Native Americans and white settlers west of the Appalachians and how these conflicts were resolved. Answer the following questions: What conflicts resulted from large numbers of white settlers moving west of the Appalachians beginning in 1790? What actions did Little Turtle of the Miamis and Blue Jacket of the Shawnees take, and how did the United States respond? What actions did Tecumseh and the Prophet take? What was the outcome of the Battle of Tippecanoe?

16. Explain the Cause of the War of 1812 Write a paragraph explaining the factors that led to the War of 1812. Explain why fighting with Native Americans hurt relations between the United States and Britain; what foreign-policy deal Congress authorized President Madison to offer to France and Britain, and how each reacted; and what reasons the War Hawks gave in support of declaring war on Britain.

17. Describe the Contributions of Andrew Jackson Write a paragraph explaining the events surrounding the battles of Horseshoe Bend and New Orleans and Andrew Jackson's contributions to the American victories. Explain how Jackson won the battles of Horseshoe Bend and New Orleans, and why the Battle of New Orleans was fought after the war officially ended.

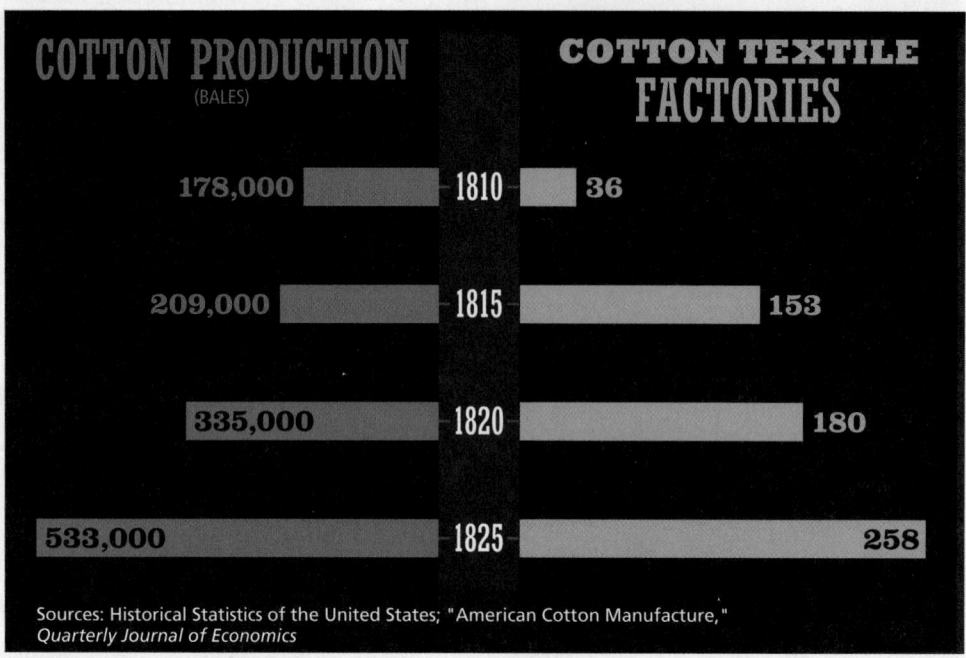

COTTON PRODUCTION (BALES)

COTTON TEXTILE FACTORIES

Production	Year	Factories
178,000	1810	36
209,000	1815	153
335,000	1820	180
533,000	1825	258

Sources: Historical Statistics of the United States; "American Cotton Manufacture," *Quarterly Journal of Economics*

18. Explain the Economic Effects of the War of 1812 Using the graph above and other sources, write a paragraph explaining how the War of 1812 contributed to economic growth and American industrialization. Explain how the Embargo Act and then the War of 1812 helped spark the growth of factories in the United States, what the graph indicates about the growth of factories, and how American businesses were affected by the end of the War of 1812.

19. Analyze the Sectional Impact of Tariffs Write a paragraph analyzing how the Tariff of 1816 affected the North, South, and West in different ways. Consider why Congress passed the Tariff of 1816 and what the tariff did, how the regional economies differed, how and why the North benefited from the tariff, and how and why the tariff did not benefit the West and South.

20. Describe the Causes and Effects of Sectionalism Write a paragraph describing how the Tariff of 1816 increased sectionalism and how Henry Clay tried to combat this sectionalism through his American System. Describe how Clay thought his American System would promote economic growth in all sections, why Clay wanted Congress to use tariff money for internal improvements and how Congress responded, and why southerners and others opposed Clay's ideas.

21. Identify Points of View of Political Parties Using the quotation below and other sources, write a paragraph identifying the Federalist and Democratic Republican points of view concerning the Alien and Sedition Acts. Identify the effects of the acts and the Federalist point of view about the acts, and use the quotation to identify the point of view of Democratic Republicans, such as Jefferson, about the acts.

They have brought into the lower house a sedition bill, which . . . undertakes to make printing certain matters criminal . . . Indeed this bill & the alien bill both are so [against] the Constitution as to show they mean to pay no respect to it.

—*The Writings of Thomas Jefferson*, 1798

22. Write about the Essential Question **Write an essay on the Essential Question: What should governments do?** Use evidence from your study of this topic to support your answer.

Go online to PearsonRealize.com and use the texts, quizzes, interactivities, Interactive Reading Notepads, Flipped Videos, and other resources from this Topic to prepare for the Topic Test.

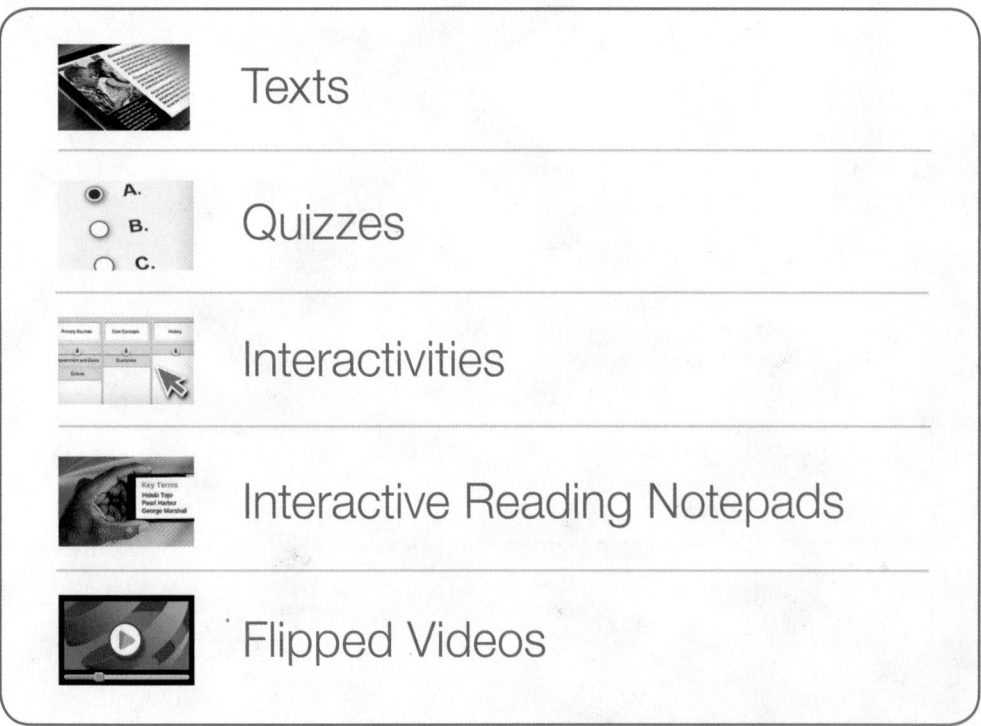

Texts

Quizzes

Interactivities

Interactive Reading Notepads

Flipped Videos

While online you can also check the progress you've made learning the topic and course content by viewing your grades, test scores, and assignment status.

[**ESSENTIAL QUESTION**] Why do people move?

6 The Age of Jackson and Westward Expansion (1824–1860)

>> Statue of gold miner Claude Chana, Auburn, California

Enduring Understandings

- During the Jacksonian era, American democracy expanded, and the political party system developed.

- Jacksonian Democrats wanted limited government, while Whigs wanted the government to support the economy.

- The United States forced Native Americans to leave the Southeast to make way for settlers.

- Seeking economic opportunity and religious freedom, Americans moved west, reshaping the landscape in the process.

- The United States expanded its borders from the Atlantic to the Pacific through compromise and conflict, including the Mexican-American War.

- People from many cultures shaped the American West.

Watch the My Story Video to learn about pioneer Narcissa Whitman.

Access your digital lessons including:
Topic Inquiry • Interactive Reading Notepad • Interactivities • Assessments

Jackson Wins the Presidency

>> This portrait of Andrew Jackson was painted during his first year in office. It is the model for his image on the $20 bill.

▶ Interactive Flipped Video

>> Objectives

Describe who gained suffrage by the 1820s.

Identify compromises made after the 1824 election, including the roles of Henry Clay and John Quincy Adams.

Explain the origin and development of new political parties under John Quincy Adams.

Describe the changes that helped shape Jacksonian democracy and the impact of the election of Andrew Jackson.

Explain the spoils system.

>> Key Terms

Andrew Jackson
Alexis de Tocqueville
suffrage
John Quincy Adams
Henry Clay
majority
Whig Party
Democratic Party
spoils system

During the early 1800s, a growing spirit of democracy changed the political system and affected American ideas about social classes. The main cause stemmed from the influence of **Andrew Jackson**. He was an American politician during this time who supported expanding democratic rights. From the time of his first campaign for president in 1824 until his death in 1845, he dominated American politics. Jackson's policies had a significant effect on issues such as voting rights and the ways in which government functions. This period is often known as the Age of Jackson.

Democracy Expands

Alexis de Tocqueville Most Americans did not feel that the rich deserved special respect. Wealthy European visitors to the United States were surprised that American servants expected to be treated as equals. Others were amazed that butlers and maids refused to be summoned with bells, as in Europe.

A visitor from France, **Alexis de Tocqueville** became especially well known for his observations on American democracy. He arrived in the United States in 1831. The French government had sent him to study the American prison system. For several months, Tocqueville toured much of the United States. However, he observed much more than prisons. He observed a society that was becoming more and more democratic.

After his return to France, Tocqueville recorded his experiences and observations in a book titled *Democracy in America*. In it, he admired the American democratic spirit and the American goals of equality and freedom. He found that the results of the social "revolution taking place" in America, while "still far from coming to an end," were "already incomparably greater than anything which has taken place in the world before."

Increased Suffrage During the 1820s, or the early years of the Age of Jackson, more Americans gained **suffrage**, or the right to vote. Others, however, were denied full participation in the growing democracy.

The United States was growing rapidly. New states were joining the Union, and there were many citizens eager to participate in elections. Some of the first states to give voting privileges to white males who did not own property were in the West. In these states, any white man over age 21 could vote.

Reformers in the East worked to expand suffrage in that region. By the 1830s, most eastern states had dropped the requirement that voters had to own

Class in America and Europe

QUESTION	SITUATION IN AMERICA	SITUATION IN EUROPE
Who had voting rights?	Almost all white men	Wealthy men in countries with elections; not all countries had elections.
Who had power?	White men of all incomes	Depending on the country, the king or queen, the nobility, and in some countries, wealthy male voters
How did people act toward those with more wealth?	They treated them the same as those without wealth.	They gave them special recognition.
How did ordinary people expect to be treated by those with more wealth?	They expected respect.	They expected to be looked down upon.

>> Attitudes toward social class privilege in the United States and Europe differed during the Age of Jackson. **Interpret** Based on what you've learned, what explains these differences?

 Interactive Timeline

land. In this way, many craft workers and shopkeepers won the right to vote.

Throughout the country, growing numbers of Americans exercised their newly acquired right to vote. Before 1828, the turnout of eligible voters was never more than 27 percent. That low percentage rose to nearly 58 percent in the election of 1828. By 1840, voter turnout was nearly 80 percent.

Limits on Suffrage Despite the nation's growing democratic spirit, a great many Americans did not have the right to vote. They included women, Native Americans, and the vast majority of African Americans. Slaves had no political rights at all. Meanwhile, the few states that still required white men to own property to vote failed to remove that barrier during Jackson's presidency.

Although most white men had won suffrage, free African Americans had lost it. In the early years of the nation, most northern states and a few southern states allowed free African American men to vote. By the 1820s, however, many of these states had taken away that right. By 1830, only a few New England states permitted free African American men to vote on equal terms with white men. In New York, African American men had to own property in order to vote while white men did not. No state allowed enslaved African Americans to vote.

? RECALL How did democracy expand during the Age of Jackson?

The Election of 1824 Leads to a "Bargain"

There were four candidates for president in 1824. All four were members of the old Republican Party. However, each had support in different parts of the country. **John Quincy Adams** was strong in New England. **Henry Clay** and Andrew Jackson had support in the West. William H. Crawford was favored in the South, but became too ill to campaign.

The Candidates John Quincy Adams of Massachusetts was the son of Abigail and John Adams, the second president. A graduate of Harvard University, the younger Adams had served as Secretary of State and helped end the War of 1812. People admired Adams for his intelligence and high morals. Adams, however, was uncomfortable campaigning among the common people. In fact, to most people he seemed hard and cold.

A Kentuckian, Henry Clay was a shrewd politician who became Speaker of the House of Representatives. In

>> Nearly all white men gained the right to vote during the Age of Jackson, but still most adults, including the enslaved African American men shown here, were not allowed to vote.

The Election of 1824

CANDIDATE	Andrew Jackson	John Quincy Adams	William Crawford	Henry Clay
HOME STATE	Tennessee	Massachusetts	Georgia	Kentucky
MAIN POSITIONS	Presents himself as the champion of the common man	Supports tariffs and spending on roads and canals to promote business	Supports states' rights	Supports tariffs and spending on roads and canals to promote business, compromise between North and South
POPULAR VOTE*	151,271	113,122	40,856	47,531
ELECTORAL VOTE	99	84	41	37
HOUSE VOTE BY STATE	7	13	4	Not on ballot

*The popular vote does not accurately measure candidates' popular support, because in several states there was no popular vote, and electors were chosen by state legislatures.

>> This chart shows information about the four candidates in the presidential election of 1824. **Compare** Which two candidates' positions were most similar, and how were they similar?

Congress, Clay was a skillful negotiator who had worked out several important compromises. Despite his abilities, Clay was less popular than the other candidate from the West, Andrew Jackson.

William H. Crawford had served as Treasury Secretary, War Secretary, Ambassador to France after the War of 1812, and as a senator from Georgia. Crawford's support was concentrated in the Southeast.

To many Americans, especially on the western frontier, Andrew Jackson was a hero. A general during the War of 1812, he had defeated the British and a group of Creek Indians who were allied with the British. He had gone on to defeat the Seminoles and the Spanish in Florida, gaining that territory for the United States. He was known as the "Hero of New Orleans" for his victory in the War of 1812. He also earned the nickname

"Old Hickory" after a soldier said he was "tough as hickory." Jackson's fame as a general helped him launch a political career. Although he was a landowner and a slave owner, many saw him as a man of the people. Jackson had been born in a log cabin, and his parents had been poor farmers. He was admired by small farmers and others who felt left out of the growing economy in the United States. The expansion of the vote to white men without property helped account for Jackson's political popularity.

The "Corrupt Bargain" No clear winner emerged from the election of 1824. Jackson won the popular vote, but no candidate won a **majority**, or more than half, of the electoral votes. As a result, under the provisions of the Constitution, the House of Representatives had to choose the president from among the top three candidates.

Because he had finished fourth, Clay was out of the running. As Speaker of the House, though, he played an important role in influencing the results and reaching a compromise to settle the conflict.

Clay urged members of the House to vote for Adams. Clay's support was enough for Adams to win the vote in the House. After he became president, Adams named Clay his Secretary of State. In the past, Secretaries of State had gone on to become president. Jackson and his backers were furious. They accused Adams and Clay of making a "corrupt bargain" and stealing the election from Jackson. In fact, the election was decided based on provisions of the Constitution. Still, the anger of Jackson and his supporters seriously hampered President Adams's efforts to unify the nation.

? CHECK UNDERSTANDING Why did some people refer to the 1824 election result as a "corrupt bargain"?

The Presidency of John Quincy Adams

Adams knew that the outcome of the election had angered many Americans. To "bring the whole people together," he pushed for a program of economic growth through internal improvements. His plan backfired, however, and opposition to him grew.

Promoting Economic Growth Like Alexander Hamilton and Henry Clay, Adams thought that the federal government should promote economic growth. He called for the government to pay for new roads and canals. These internal improvements would help farmers to transport goods to market.

Adams also favored projects to promote the arts and the sciences. He suggested building a national university and an observatory from which astronomers could study the stars. Most Americans objected to spending money on such programs.

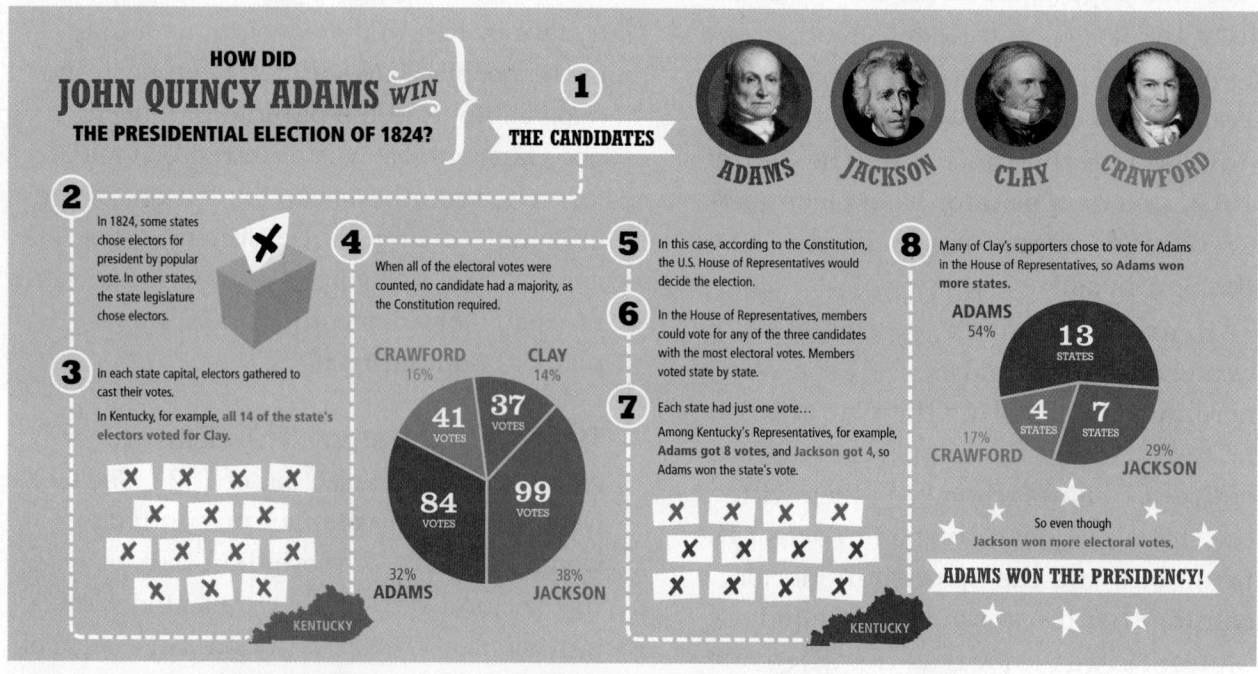

>> The election of 1824 was decided in the House of Representatives, according to the United States Constitution. **Cite Evidence** How was Adams able to win the vote in the House of Representatives?

They feared that the federal government would become too powerful. Congress approved money for a national road and some canals but turned down most of Adams's other programs.

Origin of New Political Parties During the 1820s, nearly all politicians were members of Jefferson's Democratic-Republican Party. In the 1830s, however, new political parties took shape. These parties grew out of the conflict between John Quincy Adams and Andrew Jackson.

The Whig Party Democratic-Republicans who supported Adams and his programs for national growth called themselves National Republicans. In 1834, many of them joined a new party, organized by Henry Clay and known as the **Whig Party**.

Whigs had very specific points of view. Whigs wanted the federal government to promote business by paying for roads and canals. Whigs believed that the federal government should oversee banks. They believed that a stable banking system would encourage business. Whigs also wanted higher tariffs.

The Whigs had their strongest support the Northeast, with some support in cities and towns in the South and West. People from these places backed the Whigs because these places relied on manufacturing and commerce, and Whig policies aimed to help those parts of the economy.

Tariffs are taxes or fees placed on imported goods. By making imports more expensive, they help domestic producers. However, they may prompt foreign governments to impose tariffs in response. So tariffs can threaten exporters. Those who supported the Whigs included eastern factory owners and other businessmen,

>> John Quincy Adams, the sixth President of the United States, thought that the federal government should adopt policies and pay for projects that would help the economy.

>> Henry Clay was a noted U.S. senator and a founder of the Whig Party. Like John Quincy Adams, he supported a strong federal government.

some southern planters, and many former Federalists. Whigs were often divided into factions, and not all of the party's members always followed the party's direction.

The Democratic Party Jackson and other Democratic-Republicans who supported him began to call themselves the **Democratic Party**. Today's Democratic Party traces its roots to Andrew Jackson's time. Like the Whig Party, Democrats also had a point of view. They called for more political power for ordinary white men and opposed privileges for the wealthy or educated. Democrats were opposed to tariffs and a federal government role in the economy.

Democrats opposed high tariffs, because farmers counted on being able to sell their goods overseas and did not want to risk retaliatory tariffs. They also did not want to pay more for imported goods. Democrats supported westward expansion to open up more land for frontier settlers.

Democrats were usually more tightly organized than Whigs. Members usually followed the direction set by party leaders. Democrats had strong support in the South and West, especially among small farmers and workers. These groups also supported Democrats in some parts of the Northeast. Small farmers and workers supported the Democrats because Democrats spoke up for small farmers, workers, and Westerners against bankers and Northeastern businessmen.

A Bitter Campaign In 1828, Adams faced an uphill battle for reelection. This time, Andrew Jackson was Adams's only opponent. The campaign was a bitter contest. The focus was not on issues, but on the candidates' personalities. Jackson supporters renewed charges that Adams

>> Andrew Jackson appealed to settlers on the western frontier because Jackson was a westerner himself, had grown up poor, and was seen as a self-reliant individualist.

Election of 1828

BRITISH TERRITORY

Claimed by Britain and the United States

Oregon Country (Claimed by Britain and the United States)

Unorganized territory

PACIFIC OCEAN

MEXICO

New Hampshire
Vermont
Maine
New York
Massachusetts
Rhode Island
Connecticut
Pennsylvania
New Jersey
Delaware
Maryland
Ohio
Indiana
Illinois
Virginia
Missouri
Kentucky
North Carolina
Tennessee
South Carolina
Arkansas Territory
Alabama
Georgia
Mississippi
Louisiana
Florida Territory

ATLANTIC OCEAN

Gulf of Mexico

L. Superior
L. Michigan
L. Huron
L. Ontario
L. Erie
Michigan Territory

0   400 mi
0   400 km
Albers Conic Equal-Area Projection

KEY
Andrew Jackson
John Quincy Adams

>> This map shows the results of the 1828 presidential election. **Synthesize** How was the vote in each region influenced by the region's economic interests?

 Interactive Chart

had made a "corrupt bargain" after the 1824 election. They also attacked Adams as an aristocrat, or member of the upper class.

Adams supporters replied with similar attacks. They called Jackson a dangerous "military chieftain." If Jackson became President, they warned, he could become a dictator like Napoleon Bonaparte of France.

Jackson won the election easily. His supporters cheered the outcome as a victory for the common people. By common people, they meant white people who worked for a living, including farmers and city workers. For the first time, the politics of the common people were important.

? SUMMARIZE Why did Andrew Jackson win the election of 1828?

Jacksonian Democracy

Like many who admired him, Jackson was born in a log cabin on the frontier. His parents had left Ireland to settle in the Carolinas. Both died before Jackson was 15. Jackson had to grow up quickly.

Although he was lean, he was a strong fighter. A friend who wrestled with him recalled, "I could throw him three times out of four, but he would never stay throwed."

Always determined, Jackson showed his toughness at 13 when he joined the Patriots during the American Revolution. He was captured by the British while carrying messages for the Patriots. When a British officer ordered the young prisoner to clean his boots, Jackson refused. The officer took a sword and slashed the boy's hand and face.

After the Revolution, Jackson studied law in North Carolina. He later moved to Tennessee and set up a successful law practice. Over time he became very wealthy by buying and selling land in Georgia and Alabama. While still in his twenties, he was elected to Congress. He served for just a few years before becoming a judge and a major general in the Tennessee militia.

Jackson won national fame for his achievements during the War of 1812. He led American forces to a major victory over the British at the Battle of New Orleans. He was also known for his leadership during the Creek War. A group of Creeks, angered in part by white settlers moving onto their land, began to attack settlers. These Creeks massacred at least 250 people, including soldiers and their families, at Fort Mims, in present-day Alabama. Commanding an army sent to stop the attacks, Jackson's victory at Horseshoe Bend forced the Creeks to give up vast

amounts of land in what are now Georgia and Alabama.

Andrew Jackson was a complex person. He had led a violent and adventurous life. He was quick to lose his temper, and he dealt with his enemies harshly. When he became president, his opponents sarcastically called him "King Andrew." Jackson intended to be a strong president by expanding the powers of the presidency. At the same time, Jackson's supporters admired his ability to inspire and lead others. They considered him a man of his word and a champion of the common people.

As Jackson traveled to Washington to be inaugurated, large crowds cheered him along the way. For the first time, thousands of ordinary people flooded the capital to watch the President take the oath of office. After Jackson was sworn in, the crowd followed the new president to a reception at the White House. One onlooker described the scene with amazement:

> Country men, farmers, gentlemen, mounted and dismounted, boys, women and children, black and white. Carriages, wagons, and carts all pursuing [Jackson] to the President's house.
>
> —Margaret Bayard Smith, *The First Forty Years of Washington Society*

The crowds were so huge, the observer continued, that the President was "almost suffocated and torn to pieces by the people in their eagerness to shake hands." Jackson's critics said the scene showed that "King Mob" was ruling the nation. Amos Kendall, a loyal Jackson supporter, viewed the inauguration celebration in a more positive way: "It was a proud day for the people. General Jackson is their own President."

>> An artist drew this cartoon to criticize what he saw as Andrew Jackson's hunger for power. **Cite Evidence** What features of this cartoon suggest that Jackson was hungry for power?

▶ **Interactive Chart**

>> Andrew Jackson's election as President made western settlers feel that one of their own was running the government. His election suggested that westerners and other ordinary citizens would have a voice.

The Rise of Jacksonian Democracy

Andrew Jackson was elected in 1828 largely because white men without property could now vote. He drew much of his support from these people. In return, he promised to help less wealthy white men, and especially small farmers on the western frontier. The spread of political power to more people was part of what became known as Jacksonian democracy.

The Impact of Jacksonian Democracy

Jackson was the first westerner to occupy the White House. His election marked a shift of political power to the West. He was seen as a daring individualist. His image helped shape an American consciousness focused on individual freedom and daring.

Another effect of Jacksonian democracy was the growth in political parties and in citizen participation in the political process. It was one thing to make it legal for nearly all white men to vote. It was another thing to convince them to vote.

Jackson's Democratic Party introduced political campaigns that appealed to common people and their concerns. These campaigns motivated white men to cast their vote for the Democrats.

? **DRAW CONCLUSIONS** Why was Andrew Jackson seen as a champion of the common people?

The Spoils System

One of the biggest effects of Jacksonian politics was the development of the spoils system. After taking office, Jackson fired many government employees. He replaced those employees with his supporters. Most other presidents had done the same, but Jackson did it on a much larger scale.

Critics accused Jackson of rewarding his supporters instead of choosing

>> A cartoonist drew this cartoon in 1877 to criticize the spoils system, which survived long after Jackson introduced it. **Interpret** How does the cartoon criticize the spoils system?

qualified men. Jackson replied that giving government jobs to ordinary men would prevent a small group of wealthy men from controlling the government. He felt that most Americans could fill government jobs.

"The duties of all public officers are . . . so plain and simple that men of intelligence may readily qualify themselves for their performance," he said.

A Jackson supporter explained the system another way. "To the victor belong the spoils," he declared. Spoils are loot. The practice of giving supporters government jobs became known as the **spoils system**.

? CHECK UNDERSTANDING Why did Jackson adopt the spoils system?

ASSESSMENT

1. **Hypothesize** about why expanding voting rights during the 1820s and 1830s also dramatically increased voter turnout.

2. **Identify Central Issues** What occurred that made Jackson's backers believe that John Quincy Adams won the presidency as the result of a "corrupt bargain"?

3. **Summarize** the views of the Whigs.

4. **Summarize** the views of the Democrats.

5. **Draw Conclusions** Today, it is illegal to fire a government worker because of whom he or she supported for the presidency, and government workers must take a civil service exam to be considered for a position. Why do you think these regulations became necessary?

Political Conflict and Economic Crisis

>> John Calhoun believed in nullification so strongly that he resigned as Andrew Jackson's Vice President when Jackson opposed it.

▶ **Interactive Flipped Video**

Although they had once been friends and allies, President Andrew Jackson and his Vice President, **John Calhoun**, were about to become fierce opponents. The issue that led them to quarrel was **states' rights**, or the rights of states to powers independent of the federal government.

>> Objectives

Explain the issues of nullification and states' rights.

Summarize arguments regarding the banking system.

Identify the economic problems Martin Van Buren faced.

Describe the election campaigns of 1840.

>> Key Terms

states' rights
nullification
Nullification Act
depression
Unemployment
caucus
nominating
  convention
John Calhoun
Daniel Webster
Martin Van Buren
William Henry
  Harrison
John Tyler

A Conflict Over States' Rights

The conflict over states' rights divided the country along regional lines. The United States at the time was made up of three regions. The North included the New England and Middle Atlantic states. Manufacturing and trade were very important to the economy of the North. The West was the region we now know as the Midwest. Its economy was based mainly on farming to raise livestock and food crops. Finally, the South consisted of today's Southeast and South Central states. The South's people relied heavily on farming to produce cash crops for export, such as cotton and tobacco.

Politically, northerners generally favored a strong federal government, which they saw as necessary to promote manufacturing and trade. Southerners feared the domination of the North and national policies that could hurt southern interests. Consequently, southerners tended to support stronger states' rights. These differences often made it hard for people from the North and South to agree on political issues.

Westerners sometimes sided with the North and sometimes with the South. For example, westerners wanted internal improvements for transportation, which most northerners supported. Westerners also wanted to be free to move into new territories, which southerners also wanted. Some westerners supported slavery, while others did not. In general, westerners agreed with northerners about tariffs.

Anger Over Tariffs In 1828, with the support of then President John Quincy Adams, Congress passed the highest tariff in the history of the nation. Southerners called it the Tariff of Abominations.

>> Wheat was an important crop in the West. The McCormick Reaper, which was invented in 1831, made the work of harvesting wheat much easier.

>> Trading ships brought southern cotton to England and finished goods back to the United States.

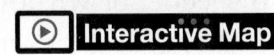

An abomination is something that is wrong and evil. Just like earlier tariffs, the new law, which was passed before Andrew Jackson's first term, protected manufacturers from foreign competition.

Most manufacturers lived in the North and were helped by the tariff. Southern planters, however, were hurt by it. Southerners sold much of their cotton to Britain and bought British manufactured goods in return. A high tariff would mean that southerners had to pay more for those British goods. Worse still, they feared that if the United States imposed a tariff on British manufactures, Britain could respond by imposing a tariff on American cotton. Many southerners thought the tariff was unconstitutional.

Debate Over Nullification A leader in the South's fight against the tariff was Vice President John Calhoun, whose home state was South Carolina. He claimed that a state had the right to nullify, or cancel,

a federal law that the state considered to be unconstitutional. This idea is called **nullification**. Calhoun believed that the states' rights gave them power over the provisions of the Constitution.

He argued that states could reject federal laws that they thought violated the constitution, because the states had joined together to form the federal government based on their understanding of the Constitution.

Daniel Webster, a Senator from Massachusetts, disagreed. He made a speech in 1830 to the Senate attacking the idea of nullification. The Constitution, he said, united the American people, not just the states, as a nation. If states had the right to nullify federal laws, the nation would fall apart. The U.S. Supreme Court had also ruled against earlier attempts at nullification, arguing that the provisions of Article III of the U.S. Constitution gave federal courts, not states, the right to decide on the constitutionality of federal laws. President Jackson agreed with the views of Webster and the Supreme Court. Because Calhoun strongly disagreed with Jackson, he resigned from the office of Vice President. He was then elected as a senator from South Carolina. The debate over nullification would continue for years.

The Nullification Act Leads to Crisis

Anger against the tariff increased in the South. Congress passed a new law in 1832 that lowered the tariff slightly. South Carolina was not satisfied. It passed the **Nullification Act**, declaring the new tariff illegal. It also threatened to secede, or withdraw, from the Union if challenged. Jackson was furious. He knew that nullification could lead to civil war.

To defuse the crisis, Henry Clay, now a senator from Kentucky, proposed a lower compromise tariff, which President Jackson supported. Jackson also asked Congress to pass the Force bill, which allowed him to use the army, if necessary, to enforce the tariff. Daniel Webster sided with Jackson on the Force bill but opposed Clay's compromise tariff. However, Congress passed both the compromise tariff and the Force bill.

Faced with Jackson's firm stand, no other state chose to support South Carolina. Calhoun supported the compromise tariff that Clay had proposed. South Carolina repealed its Nullification Act, and the Nullification Crisis passed. National identity had proven stronger than the claim of a single state.

However, tensions between the North and South would lead to increased sectionalism in the years ahead.

❓ **SUMMARIZE** Why did Webster and Jackson oppose nullification?

Milestones in the States' Rights Debate

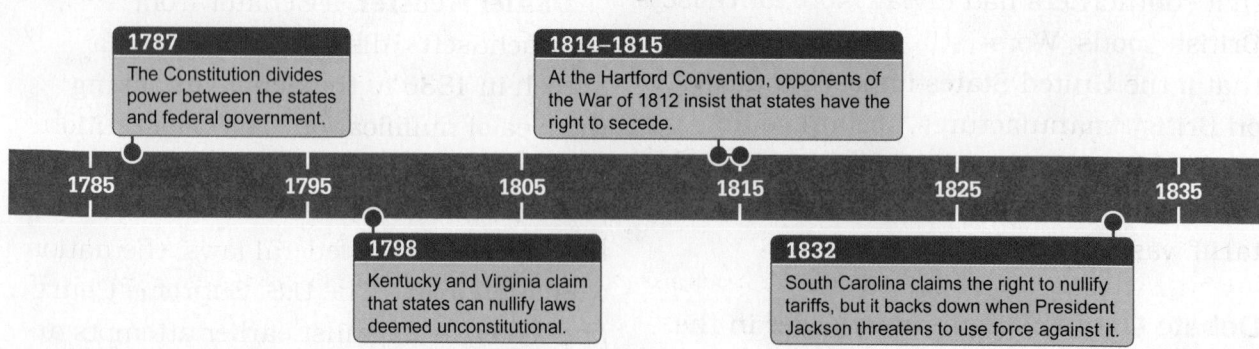

1787
The Constitution divides power between the states and federal government.

1814–1815
At the Hartford Convention, opponents of the War of 1812 insist that states have the right to secede.

1785   1795   1805   1815   1825   1835

1798
Kentucky and Virginia claim that states can nullify laws deemed unconstitutional.

1832
South Carolina claims the right to nullify tariffs, but it backs down when President Jackson threatens to use force against it.

>> **Analyze Timelines** Identify an instance of tension between a specific state and the federal government on the timeline. How might sectionalism have contributed to this tension?

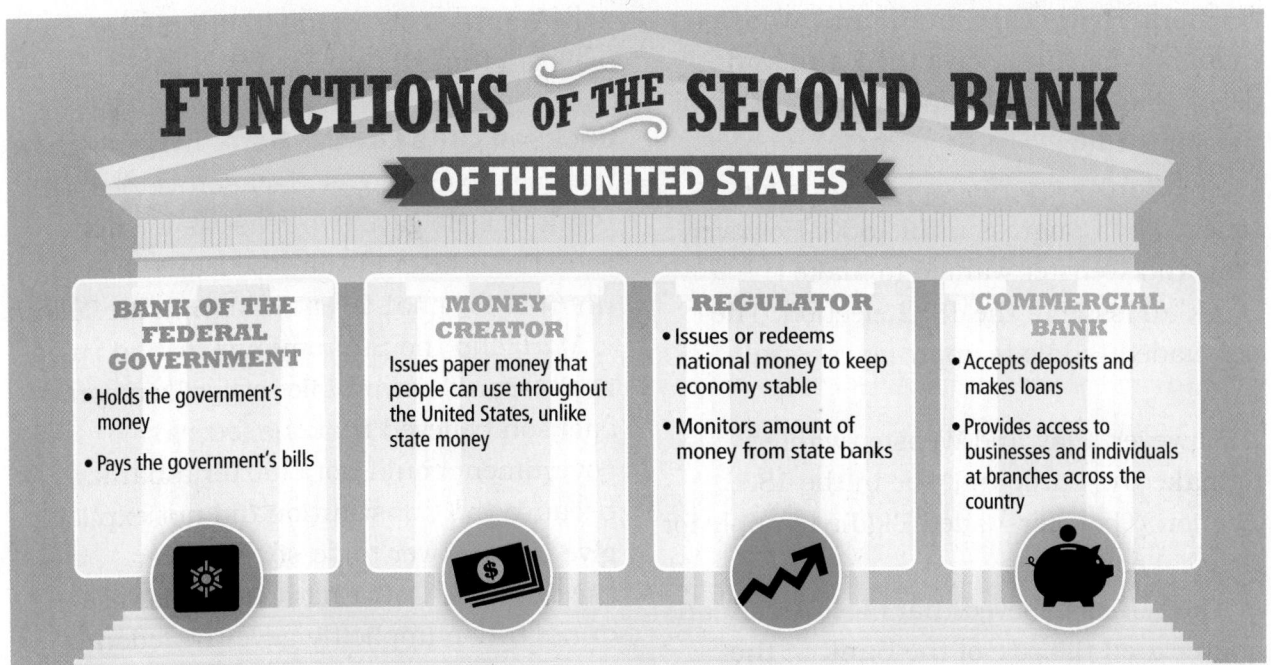

FUNCTIONS OF THE SECOND BANK OF THE UNITED STATES

BANK OF THE FEDERAL GOVERNMENT
- Holds the government's money
- Pays the government's bills

MONEY CREATOR
Issues paper money that people can use throughout the United States, unlike state money

REGULATOR
- Issues or redeems national money to keep economy stable
- Monitors amount of money from state banks

COMMERCIAL BANK
- Accepts deposits and makes loans
- Provides access to businesses and individuals at branches across the country

>> The second National Bank was founded to help the federal government manage its income and expenses. **Analyze Charts** How was the Bank involved in the nation's economy?

 Interactive Chart

The Bank War

Another political battle President Jackson waged during his first term as President was one against the Second Bank of the United States. Like many westerners, he thought that the Bank was too powerful and needed to be eliminated. Jackson's Democratic Party opposed the Bank. The Whig Party, however, supported the Bank. Whigs believed that the Bank was needed to regulate state banks' lending to prevent a buildup of debts that could not be repaid.

A Controversial Bank The Bank of the United States had been a subject of dispute since its early days. The Bank had great power over the nation's banking system because it controlled loans made by state banks. When the Bank's directors thought that state banks were making too many loans, they limited the amount these banks could lend. The cutbacks angered farmers and merchants who borrowed money to buy land or finance new businesses.

President Jackson and other leading Democrats saw the Bank as undemocratic. Although Congress created the Bank, it was run by private bankers. Jackson condemned these men as agents of "special privilege" who grew rich with public funds. He especially disliked Nicholas Biddle, president of the Bank since 1823.

Biddle came from a wealthy Philadelphia family. He was well qualified to run the bank. Under Biddle, the U.S. economy had experienced stability and prosperity. However, Biddle was arrogant and vain. Jackson felt that Biddle used the Bank to benefit the rich. He also resented Biddle's influence over certain members of Congress.

The Bank Applies for Renewal Biddle and other Whigs worried that the President might try to destroy the Bank. Two Whig senators, Henry Clay and Daniel Webster, thought of a way to save the Bank and defeat Jackson in the upcoming election at the same time.

The Bank's charter was not due for renewal by Congress until 1836. However, Clay and Webster wanted to make the Bank an issue in the 1832 election. They persuaded Biddle to apply for renewal early.

However, Clay and Webster wanted to make the Bank an issue in the 1832 election. They persuaded Biddle to apply for renewal early.

The Whigs believed that most Americans appreciated the role of the Bank in the nation's prosperity. If Jackson vetoed the bill to renew the charter, they felt sure that he would anger voters and lose the election. Clay pushed the charter renewal bill through Congress in 1832. Jackson was sick in bed when he heard that Congress had renewed the Bank's charter.

>> In this cartoon, President Jackson fights a snake representing the Bank and its branches. The largest head is Nicholas Biddle's. **Analyze Cartoons** How is Jackson trying to destroy the Bank?

"The Bank . . . is trying to kill me," Jackson fumed, "but I will kill it!"

Jackson Cuts Off the Bank In an angry message to Congress, Jackson vetoed the Bank bill. He gave two reasons for his veto. First, he said that the Bank was unconstitutional, even though in *McCulloch* v. *Maryland* the Supreme Court had ruled in the Bank's favor. Like other Democrats, Jackson believed that the federal government could not charter a bank, because the Constitution did not explicitly give it the power to do so. However, the Supreme Court had ruled that the Constitution implicitly gave the federal government this right in the "necessary and proper clause."

This clause states that the federal government has the power "To make all Laws which shall be necessary and proper for carrying into Execution the . . . Powers [already described], and all other Powers vested by this Constitution." The Supreme Court had decided that the "necessary and proper" clause gave the government the power to charter a national bank. Jackson believed that only states had the right to charter banks.

Jackson also felt that the Bank helped aristocrats at the expense of the common people. He warned:

> When the laws undertake . . . to make the rich richer and the potent more powerful, the humble members of the society—the farmers, mechanics, and laborers—who have neither the time nor the means of [getting] like favors for themselves . . . have a right to complain of the injustices of their government.

—Andrew Jackson, Veto Message, July 10, 1832

As planned, the Whigs made the Bank a major issue in the election of 1832. They chose Henry Clay as their candidate to run against Andrew Jackson.

When the votes were counted, however, they showed that Jackson had won a stunning election victory. The common people had surprised the Whigs by supporting Jackson and rejecting the Bank of the United States.

The Bank Loses Its National Role

Without a new charter, the Bank would have to close in 1836. Jackson refused to wait. He ordered Secretary of the Treasury Roger Taney to stop putting government money in the Bank. Instead, Taney deposited federal money in state banks. They became known as pet banks because Taney and his friends controlled many of them. The loss of federal money crippled the Bank of the United States. Its elimination as a national bank was another effect of Jackson's presidency. The end of the Bank's role in regulating lending contributed to an economic crisis that would have to be faced by the next President of the United States.

Without a national bank to regulate the country's financial system, responsibility for regulating banks fell to individual states. The period from the late 1830s until the 1860s is known as the state banking era. During this time, each state set its own rules for banks.

Many banks issued loans in the form of paper money, and promised to redeem it with silver or gold. Because federal law defined the value of dollars in terms of silver and gold, state banks sometimes failed when they did not have enough silver

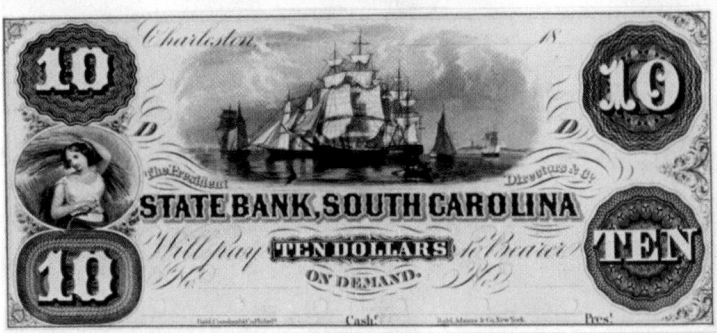

>> During the state banking era, Americans relied on currency issued by state or private banks. Money from banks with poor reputations might not be accepted by other banks or merchants. There were thousands of different kinds of money in circulation.

or gold on hand to redeem the paper money they had issued.

? RECALL What did Jackson do with the government's money after he ordered that it should no longer be deposited in the second National Bank?

Economic Crisis and Political Changes

Following tradition, Andrew Jackson left office after two terms. Americans then elected **Martin Van Buren** as President. Although Van Buren did not have Jackson's popularity, he was clever and intelligent. As President, however, Van Buren needed more than sharp political instincts.

>> A customer examines a store bill showing how much money he owes after the Panic of 1837.

The Panic of 1837 Two months after taking office, Van Buren faced the worst economic crisis the nation had known. After the Bank of the United States closed, state banks could lend money without limit. To meet the demand for loans, state banks printed more and more paper money. Often, they did not have enough gold or silver to back their paper money.

Before leaving office, Jackson was alarmed at wild speculation, or risky investment, in land. Speculators were borrowing more and more money to buy land and driving land prices up. To slow this process down, he ordered that anyone buying public land had to pay for it with gold or silver. Speculators and others rushed to state banks to exchange their paper money for gold and silver. Many banks had lent too much money. They did not have enough gold and silver and were forced to close.

The nation soon plunged into a deep economic **depression**, a period when the economy shrinks and many people lose their jobs. The depression lasted five years. During the worst period, 90 percent of the nation's factories were closed. **Unemployment** was widespread. Hundreds of thousands of people were out of work.

Many Americans blamed Van Buren and his policies for the economic depression. Van Buren believed in laissez-faire economics—the idea that government should play as small a role as possible in the economy. As the depression wore on, Van Buren became increasingly unpopular. His opponents called him "Martin Van Ruin."

>> President Martin Van Buren was blamed for the five-year economic depression America entered after the Panic of 1837.

Party Caucuses and Conventions By the time the next election for President occurred in 1840, Whigs and Democrats had developed more democratic ways to choose candidates for President. In the past, powerful members of each party held a **caucus**, or private meeting. There, they choose their candidate. Critics called the caucus system undemocratic because only a few powerful people were able to take part in it.

In the 1830s, each party began to hold a **nominating convention**, where delegates from all the states chose the party's candidate for President. Party leaders might still dominate a particular convention, but the people could now have some influence in the nominating process. Also, state nominating conventions encouraged citizen participation in elections. Once citizens learned about the events of the convention, they would work for their party's choices. Today, the major political parties still hold conventions.

Democrats Lose the Election of 1840
Although Van Buren had lost support, the Democrats chose him to run for reelection in 1840. The Whigs chose **William Henry Harrison** of Ohio as their presidential candidate and **John Tyler** of Virginia as their vice presidential candidate.

Harrison was known as the hero of the Battle of Tippecanoe, which was fought between the American military and a Shawnee-led alliance in 1811. To appeal to voters, the Whigs focused on Harrison's war record. "Tippecanoe and Tyler too" became their campaign slogan. The Whigs created an image for Harrison as a "man of the people" from the western frontier. They presented him as a humble farmer and boasted that he had been born in a log cabin. In fact, the Whigs' candidate,

>> State nominating conventions brought more people into the nominating process than earlier methods of choosing a presidential candidate.

▶ **Interactive Timeline**

>> At campaign events, the Whig party played the popular song "Tippecanoe and Tyler Too" to promote candidate William Henry Harrison.

Harrison, was a wealthy, educated man who, at the time of the campaign, lived in a large mansion.

The Whigs' policies included creating a new Bank of the United States, improving roads and canals, and demanding a high tariff. However, Whig hopes were dashed when, soon after taking office, President Harrison died of pneumonia. John Tyler then became President. President Tyler failed to live up to Whig expectations. He opposed many Whig policies. In response, the Whigs threw Tyler out of their party just months after he took office.

? RECALL How did President Jackson attempt to slow the land speculation that led to the Panic of 1837?

ASSESSMENT

1. **Generate Explanations** Why do you suppose Andrew Jackson supported Henry Clay's proposed compromise over nullification even though they had been enemies previously?

2. **Explain** why John Calhoun and Daniel Webster had directly opposite views about nullification.

3. **Draw Conclusions** What do you think happened to Secretary of the Treasury Taney and his friends who owned banks after the Bank of the United States was forced to close?

4. **Identify Central Issues** Why did certain banks have to close during the Panic of 1837?

5. **Express Problems Clearly** Why was it such a disaster for the nation when Andrew Jackson crippled the second National Bank?

Native Americans on the Frontier

>> Shawnee warriors and their allies fight Virginia troops in the Battle of Point Pleasant, 1774. Similar battles continued along the frontier during the early years of the United States.

▶ **Interactive Flipped Video**

Conflicts between people from different racial groups began in the early days of settlement in North America. Since the first European settlers arrived in North America and settled on lands that had belonged to Native American groups, repeated conflicts brought tension and mistrust. Often people used violence to attempt to settle these conflicts.

>> **Objectives**

Describe the cultures of Native Americans between the Appalachians and Mississippi.

Explain the conflict over land occupied by Native Americans between the Appalachians and Mississippi.

Discuss the forced removal of Native Americans.

>> **Key Terms**

frontier
Sequoyah
Worcester v.
  Georgia
John Marshall
Indian Removal Act
Indian Territory
Trail of Tears

Native Americans and the Frontier

Settlers, often greater in number and better armed, attacked Native Americans in efforts to force Native Americans to give up land or in response to Native American raids. Likewise, Native American groups attacked settlers who had taken their land or threatened their way of life.

A History of Conflict and Prejudice

On both sides, biases, stereotypes, and prejudices led to mistrust and hostility. White settlers saw Native Americans as dangerous and untrustworthy. Settlers, often greater in number and better armed, attacked Native Americans in efforts to force Native Americans to give up land or in response to Native American raids. Likewise, Native American groups attacked settlers who had taken their land or threatened their way of life.

Native Americans feared that settlers' hunger for land could never be satisfied and that settlers meant to kill them off. These fears fueled many bloody conflicts.

Before the Revolution, the British had made peace with Native American groups by drawing the Proclamation Line of 1763 through the Appalachian Mountains, roughly along the **frontier**, or edge, of white settlement. The British forbade whites to settle west of this line. The line gave Native Americans west of the line and east of the Mississippi River some protection.

Seeing the British as protectors, many Native Americans sided with them during the Revolutionary War. Native American fears were confirmed as more and more white settlers began moving into lands west of the Proclamation Line. After the war, Native Americans attacked white settlements in the new Northwest Territory. The Battle of Tippecanoe was a major defeat for Native American leader Tecumseh and his forces during this time of unrest.

When conflict between Britain and the United States broke out again in the War of 1812, many, but not all, Native American groups again sided with the British. A group of Creek Indians in present-day Georgia and Alabama formed an alliance with both Tecumseh and the British. Meanwhile, other Creeks and the neighboring Choctaw people sided with the United States. As you have learned, forces led by Andrew Jackson defeated the Creeks allied with the British.

>> A medal given by the British to Native American leaders who fought for the British during the Revolutionary War.

Tensions on the Frontier The Chickasaw, Choctaw, Creek, Seminole, and Cherokee nations lived in parts of what are now

Native American Groups, 1820

KEY
- Native American territory
- — Native American territory boundary
- — U.S. national boundary
- — U.S. state or territory boundary

>> This map shows the territories of several Native American groups in 1820.
Locate Describe the location of each group on the map.

▶ **Interactive Map**

Mississippi, Alabama, Florida, Georgia, North Carolina, and Tennessee. The Shawnee, Potawatomi, Sauk, and Fox nations lived in parts of present-day Michigan, Ohio, Indiana, Illinois, and Wisconsin. Many hoped to live in peace with their white neighbors on the frontier.

Some tribes, like the Cherokee nation, had adopted European customs hoping to preserve their land. They created a legal system and government that blended European and Cherokee traditions. Others, like the Choctaw, believed they would be allowed to keep their land because they had sided with the United States during the War of 1812.

In 1821, **Sequoyah** (suh KWOH yuh), a Cherokee man, created a writing system for his people. Using Sequoyah's letters, Cherokee children learned to read and write. The Cherokees also published a newspaper.

The efforts of Native Americans to adopt European ways failed to end the conflict with white settlers. The Native Americans' fertile land remained attractive to white settlers, and white settlers feared more violent conflict with Native Americans.

❓ **GENERATE EXPLANATIONS** Why did tensions exist between Native American groups and white settlers?

Indian Removal

In the eyes of government leaders, Native Americans east of the Mississippi River stood in the way of westward expansion of the United States. At first, they aimed to convince Native Americans to rely less on hunting. They wanted them to start farming cash crops such as tobacco and cotton in addition to food crops. Government leaders thought that Native Americans would then sell any land that they weren't farming to white settlers. While many Native Americans in the South did adopt cash-crop farming, they were not willing to sell their land. Meanwhile, prejudices on both sides stood in the way of white settlers and Native Americans living side by side.

Pressure on Native Americans Increases
In 1825, President James Monroe had suggested a plan to move all Native Americans living east of the Mississippi to land west of the river. At this time, nothing came of the plan. Yet, year by year, the pressure on the Native Americans living along the frontier grew. Those in the North occupied land good for growing corn and wheat and raising livestock. Native Americans in the South occupied land that was good for growing cotton.

>> John Ross was the principal chief, or highest leader, of the Cherokee people when they challenged Georgia in the Supreme Court and later when they were forced to move west.

Around them, more and more white settlers arrived, many with enslaved African Americans, seeking land to grow cotton. Many white southerners were demanding that Native Americans be removed by force.

In 1825 and 1827, the state of Georgia passed laws forcing the Creeks to give up most of their land. Georgia then claimed the right to make laws for the Cherokee nation in 1828.

Worcester* v. *Georgia* Decision Is Ignored** Georgia's actions were challenged in two suits that reached the Supreme Court. The decision in the first suit went against the Cherokees. In *Cherokee Nation* v. *Georgia* (1831), the Court refused to stop Georgia from enforcing its law. But in ***Worcester* v. *Georgia (1832), the Court ruled that Georgia had no right to enforce its laws within Cherokee territory.

Chief Justice **John Marshall** wrote the Court's majority opinion in *Worcester* v. *Georgia*. He quoted treaties that the United States had signed, guaranteeing certain territory to Native Americans. Under the Constitution, treaties are the supreme law of the land. Therefore, Marshall said, Georgia had no say over Cherokee territory, and Georgia's action was unconstitutional.

President Jackson's response to the ruling was stern. He wanted to remove Native Americans from their land, and was furious when he heard of the ruling in *Worcester* v. *Georgia*. "John Marshall has made his decision," he is reported to have said. "Now let him enforce it!"

In the Nullification Crisis, Jackson defended federal power. In the Cherokee case, however, he backed states' rights. He said that the federal government should not stop Georgia from controlling Cherokee lands, and he refused to enforce the Supreme Court's decision. This was a

>> At this gathering in 1833, the Potawatomi people signed a treaty with the United States agreeing to give up their lands and move west.

fateful step for the removal of Cherokees from their land.

The Indian Removal Act In 1830, more than 100,000 Native Americans still lived east of the Mississippi River. At Jackson's urging, the government set aside lands beyond the Mississippi River through the **Indian Removal Act**, which Congress passed in 1830. The law let the government give land west of the Mississippi to Native Americans in exchange for their lands to the east.

At the time of *Worcester* v. *Georgia*, Jackson was already applying this law. Jackson believed that moving Native Americans west would bring a permanent resolution to this conflict.

In the North, the Ottawa, Potawatomi, Sauk, and Fox peoples all signed treaties to move west to Indian Territories in what are now Kansas and Oklahoma. While most members of these groups moved west, a few stayed behind in what are now Michigan and Wisconsin.

The Indian Removal Act resulted in the forced migration of thousands of Native Americans from lands east of the Mississippi River. Among the groups affected included the Choctaw, Chickasaw, Cherokee, and Seminole. This human geographic factor from the 1800s has had an effect on contemporary events.

As a result of Jackson's policy, few Native Americans today live east of the Mississippi. Most live west of the Mississippi. As a result, that is where most events involving Native Americans take place in the contemporary United States.

? EXPLAIN Why did Congress pass the Indian Removal Act?

Southern Native Americans on the Trail of Tears

Faced with threats of military action, most Native American leaders in the South saw no choice but to sign new treaties giving up their lands. They agreed to move to what was called the **Indian Territory**. Today, most of that area is in the state of Oklahoma.

The Choctaw The Choctaw signed the first treaty in 1830. The Treaty of Dancing Rabbit Creek stated that

> the United States under a grant . . . shall cause to be conveyed to the Choctaw Nation a tract of country west of the Mississippi river . . .
>
> —Article II, Treaty of Dancing Rabbit Creek, 1830

The treaty allowed for Choctaw to remain in their homeland if they gave up their tribal organization and agreed to be governed as citizens of Mississippi. A few remained in Mississippi, but most agreed to leave to preserve their culture. Closely guarded by American soldiers, the Choctaw moved west between 1831 and 1833.

The federal government, however, did not provide enough tents, food, blankets, shoes, winter clothes, or other supplies. Heavy rain and snow caused enormous suffering. An army lieutenant wrote that one group "walked for 24 hours barefoot through the snow and ice" before reaching shelter.

The Chickasaw The Chickasaw people held out for payment for their lands east of the Mississippi before they would agree to move. Finally, in 1837, the United States government agreed to pay them $3 million for these lands.

Expecting to receive this money, the Chickasaw spent $500,000 to purchase land from the Choctaw in what is now Oklahoma.

Numbers Affected by Indian Removal

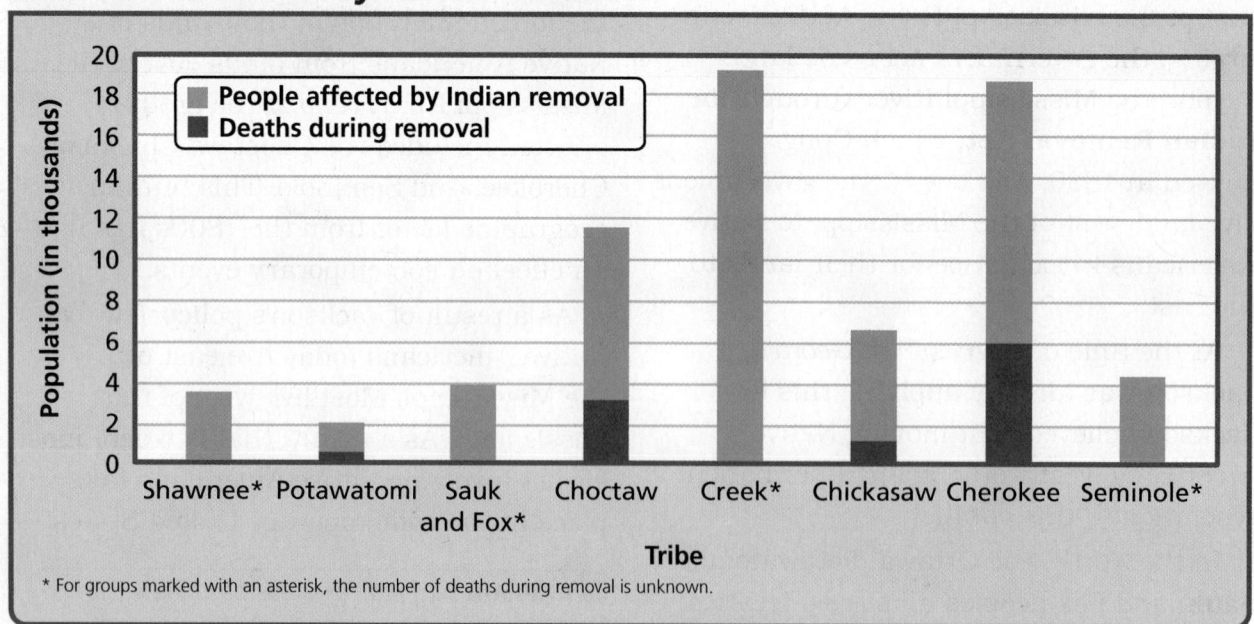

>> Several groups affected by Indian removal are shown here. **Identify Patterns** Look at the groups whose number of deaths is known. About what proportion of those groups died during removal?

In fact, the U.S. government failed to pay the Chickasaw the agreed amount for 30 years. The Chickasaw set out for their new land. Along the way, as a result of hardships, many became ill and died.

The Cherokee The Cherokee also tried to hold out. They were still on their land in 1836 when Jackson left office. A small group of Cherokee agreed to become citizens of North Carolina. As a result, they were allowed to stay. Other Cherokee hid in remote mountain camps.

Finally, in 1838, President Martin Van Buren forced the Cherokee who had not made agreements with North Carolina and those who were not in hiding to move. The United States Army forced more than 15,000 Cherokee to march westward. In the winter of 1838–39, they went to Indian Territory, patrolled by 7,000 soldiers. The Cherokee trekked hundreds of miles over a period of several months. Thousands perished during the march, mostly children and the elderly.

The Cherokee's long, sorrowful journey west became known as the **Trail of Tears**. A soldier's description helps explain why:

> On the morning of November 17th, we encountered a terrific sleet and snow storm with freezing temperatures, and from that day until we reached the end of the fateful journey on March the 27th, 1839, the sufferings of the Cherokee were awful. The trail of the exiles was a trail of death.
>
> —Memoirs of Private John G. Burnett, December 1890

The Seminole Resist In Florida, the Seminole Indians resisted the U.S. government. Led by Chief Osceola (ah see OH luh), they began fighting the United

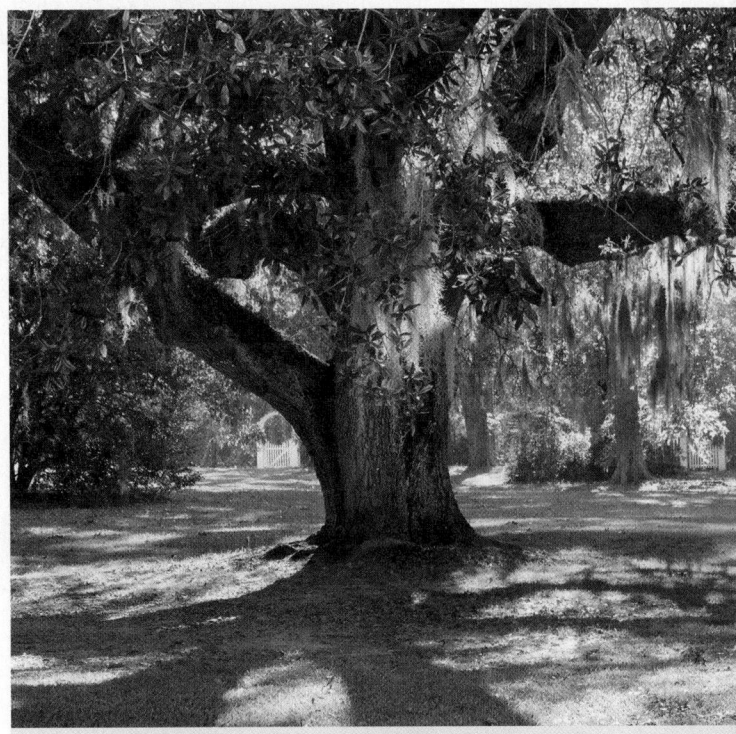

>> This photo shows the lush and fertile homeland of the Choctaw in present-day Mississippi. The Trail of Tears brought them to a drier and less fertile region in present-day Oklahoma.

>> This painting shows Cherokee people on the Trail of Tears being watched by U.S. troops. **Make Predictions** How might winter weather affect these people?

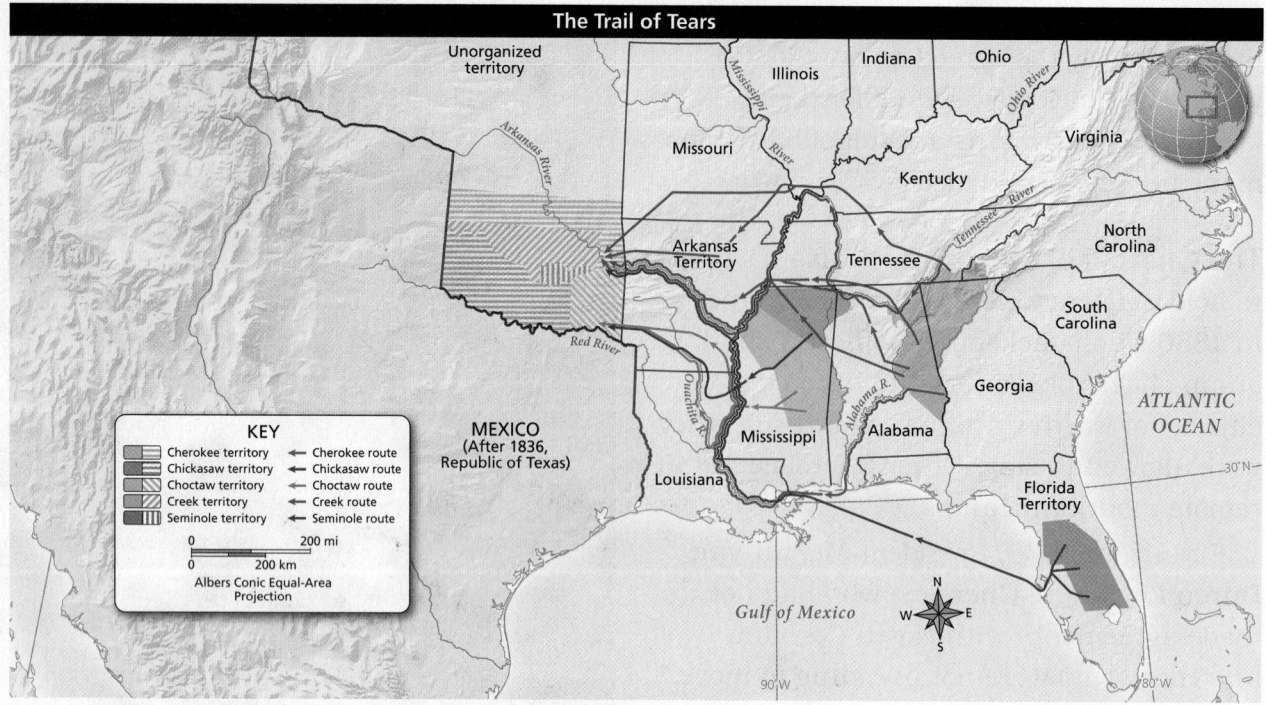

KEY

Cherokee territory	←	Cherokee route
Chickasaw territory	←	Chickasaw route
Choctaw territory	←	Choctaw route
Creek territory	←	Creek route
Seminole territory	←	Seminole route

0   200 mi
0   200 km
Albers Conic Equal-Area
Projection

>> This map shows the Trail of Tears and its outcome. **Interpret** Using the scale bar, find the distance the Cherokee walked. How might this explain why so many died on the journey?

States Army in 1817. This conflict, known as the first Seminole War, ended in 1818. The second Seminole War lasted from 1835 to 1842. It was the costliest war waged by the government to gain Indian lands. In the end, after a third war ending in 1858, the Seminoles were defeated. The government forced the Seminole leaders and most of their people to leave Florida.

In their new homes in the Indian Territory, Native Americans struggled to rebuild their lives under very difficult conditions. Meanwhile, white settlers moved quickly into lands given up by Native Americans. While Jackson's Indian removal cleared the area east of the Mississippi River for white settlement, settlers already had their eyes on lands west of the Mississippi.

? RECALL Where was the land known as Indian Territory located?

ASSESSMENT

1. **Summarize** the reaction of Native American groups who sided with the Patriots during the Revolution only to find that, after the Revolution, whites were settling their land.

2. **Generate Explanations** Explain why white settlers and Native Americans were typically unable to live peacefully in neighboring areas?

3. **Draw Conclusions** How does *Worcester* v. *Georgia* illustrate that much of the Supreme Court's power is based on the executive branch's willingness to enforce its decisions?

4. **Summarize** how Native Americans were removed from their land under the presidencies of Andrew Jackson and Martin Van Buren.

5. **Contrast** the land the Choctaw and other Native American nations had to leave with the land they were allowed to live on in Indian Territory.

Westward Movement

>> Entire families gathered up all their possessions, including furniture and livestock, and made the long journey westward in their quest for a better life on the frontier.

Interactive Flipped Video

Settlers had been moving steadily westward from the Atlantic coast since the 1600s. In the early 1800s, the promise of new farmland and other work opportunities brought a flood of new migrants to the lands west of the Appalachian Mountains.

>> **Objectives**

Describe how settlers traveled west.

List the steps Americans took to improve their roads.

Explain how steamboats and canals improved transportation for Americans.

>> **Key Terms**

flatboats
turnpikes
Lancaster Turnpike
corduroy roads
National Road
Erie Canal
Clermont

PEARSON **realize**™   www.PearsonRealize.com
Access your Digital Lesson.

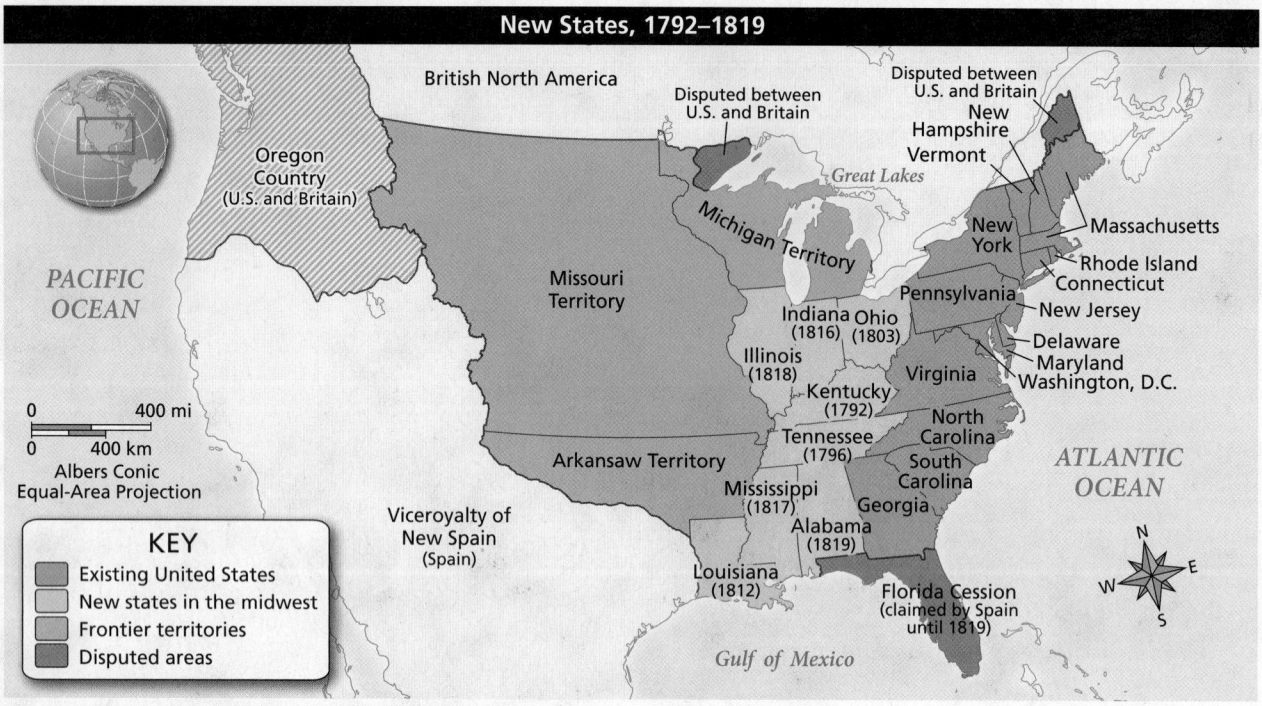

British North America

Oregon Country (U.S. and Britain)

PACIFIC OCEAN

Disputed between U.S. and Britain

Disputed between U.S. and Britain

New Hampshire

Vermont

Great Lakes

Michigan Territory

Missouri Territory

New York

Massachusetts

Rhode Island

Connecticut

Pennsylvania

New Jersey

Indiana (1816) Ohio (1803)

Delaware

Maryland

Washington, D.C.

Illinois (1818)

Virginia

Kentucky (1792)

North Carolina

Tennessee (1796)

South Carolina

Arkansaw Territory

Mississippi (1817)

Georgia

Alabama (1819)

Viceroyalty of New Spain (Spain)

Louisiana (1812)

Florida Cession (claimed by Spain until 1819)

ATLANTIC OCEAN

Gulf of Mexico

0   400 mi
0   400 km
Albers Conic Equal-Area Projection

KEY
- Existing United States
- New states in the midwest
- Frontier territories
- Disputed areas

>> By 1819, the United States had grown to 23 states. **Analyze Maps** What can the dates of statehood of the new states tell us about how settlers migrated into the western territories?

Heading Into the West

Settlers took a number of routes west. People from important regions and places like New England, New York, and Pennsylvania pushed into a region northwest of the Ohio River called the Northwest Territory. Some traveled west from Albany, New York, along the Mohawk River, through the Appalachians, and then west along the plains south of Lake Ontario. Many then sailed across Lake Erie into Ohio.

Another well-traveled path was the Great Valley Road that ran southward from Philadelphia, Pennsylvania, through Maryland and western Virginia. Some settlers would then continue south and west along the trail opened by Daniel Boone before the Revolution. Known as the Wilderness Road, it led through the Cumberland Gap into Kentucky.

Other settlers pushed west across the Appalachians to Pittsburgh, Pennsylvania. There, they loaded their animals and wagons onto **flatboats**, or flat-bottomed boats, and journeyed down the Ohio River into Ohio, Kentucky, Indiana, and Illinois. Flatboats were well suited to the shallow waters of the Ohio, which became known as the "Gateway to the West." Even when carrying heavy cargoes, these barges rode high in the water.

Pioneers from Georgia and South Carolina followed other trails west to Alabama, Mississippi, and Louisiana. Enslaved African Americans were forced to move with settlers or sold to new owners in these territories. There, enslaved workers cleared fields and built plantations in the rich, fertile soil.

Before long, some western territories had populations large enough to apply for statehood. Between 1792 and 1819, eight states joined the Union: Kentucky (1792), Tennessee (1796), Ohio (1803), Louisiana (1812), Indiana (1816), Mississippi (1817), Illinois (1818), and Alabama (1819).

? COMPARE How was travel during the early 1800s similar to and different from travel today?

Building Better Roads

Settlers faced difficult journeys as they traveled to the West. Many roads were narrow dirt trails, barely wide enough for a single wagon. Trails often plunged through muddy swamps. Tree stumps stuck up in the road and often broke the wagon axles of careless travelers. The nation badly needed better roads.

Paying Tolls In the United States, as in Europe, private companies built gravel and stone roads. To pay for these roads, the companies collected tolls from travelers. At various points along the road, a pike, or pole, blocked the road. After a wagon driver had paid a toll, the pike keeper turned the pole aside to let the wagon pass. As a result, these toll roads were called **turnpikes**.

Probably the best road in the United States was the **Lancaster Turnpike**. Built in the 1790s by a private company, the road linked Philadelphia and Lancaster, Pennsylvania.

Because the road was set on a bed of gravel, water drained off quickly. For a smooth ride, the road was topped with flat stones.

Other roads were more primitive. In swampy areas, roads were made of logs. These roads were known as **corduroy roads** because the lines of logs looked like corduroy cloth. Corduroy roads kept wagons from sinking into the mud, but they made for a very noisy and bumpy ride.

The First National Road Some states set aside money to improve roads or build new ones. Meanwhile, in 1806, Congress approved funds for the first national road-building project. The **National Road** was to run from Cumberland, Maryland, to Wheeling, on the Ohio River in western Virginia.

Work on the National Road began in 1811. Because of the War of 1812, it was not completed until 1818. Later, the road was extended into Illinois. As each new section of road was built, settlers eagerly used it to drive their wagons farther and farther west.

? SUMMARIZE How did turnpikes and corduroy roads make travel easier?

>> Many pike keepers lived by the gate they tended and could be awakened in the middle of the night by travelers seeking to pay the toll and pass through.

▶ **Interactive Gallery**

The Age of Steam

Whenever possible, travelers and freight haulers used river transportation. Floating downstream on a flatboat was both faster and more comfortable than bumping along rutted roads. It also cost a lot less.

Yet, river travel had its own problems. Moving upstream was difficult. People used paddles or long poles to push boats against the current. Sometimes, they hauled boats along the shore with ropes. Both methods were extremely slow. A boat could travel downstream from Pittsburgh to New Orleans in about six weeks. However, the return trip upstream took at least 17 weeks.

Steamboats Arrive Americans worked hard to develop new kinds of boats that would make river travel faster and cheaper. A new invention, the steam engine, started a new era in river travel. In 1787, John Fitch showed members of the Constitutional Convention how a steam engine could power a boat. He then opened a ferry service on the Delaware River. However, few people used the ferry, and Fitch eventually went out of business.

Inventor Robert Fulton may have seen Fitch's steamboat while in Philadelphia. In 1807, Fulton launched his own steamboat, the **Clermont**, on the Hudson River. On its first run, the *Clermont* carried passengers from New York City to Albany and back. The 300-mile trip took just 62 hours—a record at the time.

A Travel Revolution Fulton's success ushered in the age of steamboats. Soon, steamboats were ferrying passengers up and down the Atlantic coast. More important, steamboats revolutionized travel in the West. Besides carrying people, river steamboats gave farmers

>> Steamboats became more powerful when their engines were used to turn paddle wheels. These wheels allowed larger boats to be built that could carry more passengers and cargo.

 Interactive Gallery

and merchants a cheap means of moving goods.

Because western rivers were too shallow for larger boats, Henry Shreve designed a flat-bottomed steamboat. It could carry heavy loads without getting stuck on sandbars.

Still, steamboat travel could be dangerous. Sparks from smokestacks could cause fires. High-pressure boilers sometimes exploded as steamboat captains raced each other in an effort to get to their destination first. Between 1811 and 1851, 44 steamboats collided, 166 burned, and more than 200 exploded.

? IDENTIFY How did steamboats revolutionize travel in the West?

Canals Connect the Country

Steamboats and better roads brought many improvements to transportation. But they did not help western farmers get their goods directly to markets in the East. To meet this need, Americans needed to modify the physical environment in a whole new way: they dug canals. A canal is an artificial channel filled with water that allows boats to cross a stretch of land.

The earliest American canals were no more than a few miles long. Some canals provided routes around waterfalls on a river. Others linked rivers to nearby lakes. By the early 1800s, however, Americans were building longer canals.

The Erie Canal In 1805, some New Yorkers developed a bold idea. They wanted to build a canal linking the Great Lakes to the Mohawk and Hudson rivers. Later known as the **Erie Canal**, this artificial waterway would let western farmers ship their goods

>> Locks allow canal boats to rise in steps. When a boat enters a lock chamber, the lower gates close, the upper gates open, and water flows into the chamber, raising the boat.

▶ **Interactive Map**

to the port of New York. It would also bring business to towns along the route.

To many people, the idea of such a canal seemed far-fetched. When Thomas Jefferson heard of the plan, he exclaimed:

> Why, sir, you talk of making a canal 350 miles through the wilderness—it is little short of madness to think of it at this day!
>
> —Thomas Jefferson to Joshua Forman of New York, 1809

New York's governor DeWitt Clinton ignored such criticism. He persuaded state lawmakers to provide money for the Erie Canal. Critics referred to the project as "Clinton's Ditch."

Work on the Erie Canal began in 1817. At first, thousands of workers dug the waterway using hand tools. To speed up progress, inventors developed new

>> Early construction of the Erie Canal used teams of men working with hand tools, oxen, and horses. This was slow work. It took an entire year to complete a single mile.

fired a cannon. Town after town fired cannons, all the way to New York City. The thunderous salute took 80 minutes to complete.

The Erie Canal was an instant success. The cost of shipping goods dropped to about one tenth of what it had been before the canal was built. The canal also helped make New York City a center of commerce.

The success of the Erie Canal led other states to build canals. These canals created vital links between western farms and eastern cities, advancing the economic development of the United States. These links encouraged more growth, as people moved to the new cities in search of work.

? GENERATE EXPLANATIONS How did the Erie Canal make New York City a center of commerce?

ASSESSMENT

1. **Hypothesize** why the Northwest Territory was not in what we call the Northwest today.

2. **Summarize** the origin of the word turnpike.

3. **Compare** westward travel today with travel in the early 1800s.

4. **Draw Conclusions** The system of canals made it much easier to ship farm products to the East, which was beneficial to farmers in the West. How might this have affected westward expansion?

5. **Identify Central Issues** How did improvements in transportation affect the number of states admitted to the Union? Explain.

equipment. One machine, a stump-puller, could pull out nearly 40 tree stumps a day. In two places, the canal had to cross over rivers. Workers built stone bridges to carry the canal over the rivers.

An Instant Success By 1825, the immense job was finished. On opening day of the Erie Canal, a cannon fired in Buffalo, New York. When the sound got to the next town along the route, that town

Settling Oregon Country

>> Explorers found Oregon Country to be a wild region of tall mountains, rolling hills, lush forests, and fertile valleys.

Interactive Flipped Video

By the 1820s, white settlers had purchased and occupied much of the land between the Appalachians and the Mississippi River. Families in search of good farmland kept moving farther west. Many settlers, however, were not attracted to the Great Plains between the Mississippi and the Rockies. The plains were considered too dry to support farming. Instead, many of these settlers headed to lands in the Far West.

>> **Objectives**

Explain the appeal of Oregon and the Far West.

Summarize how mountain men helped explore the Far West.

Describe the role missionaries played in Oregon.

Identify the hardships faced on wagon trains to the West.

>> **Key Terms**

Oregon Country
mountain men
rugged individualists
Rendezvous
Oregon Trail

PEARSON
realize™
www.PearsonRealize.com
Access your Digital Lesson.

North America in 1830

>>By 1830, the United States had a claim to part of the Pacific Coast. **Analyze Maps** Considering the distance of states and organized territories from Oregon Country, why might it have been difficult for the United States to control that region?

In Search of New Territory

Americans first heard about the area known as Oregon Country in the early 1800s. Lewis and Clark had explored this area west of the Louisiana Purchase in 1805. **Oregon Country** was a huge region west of the Rocky Mountains. Today, it includes Oregon, Washington, Idaho, and parts of Wyoming, Montana, and western Canada.

Wild Country The geography of Oregon Country was varied. Along the Pacific coast, the soil was fertile.

Temperatures there were mild all year round, and rainfall was plentiful. Early white settlers found fine farmland in the valley of the Willamette River and the lowlands around Puget Sound.

Dense forest covered the Coastal Ranges and Cascade Mountains, which

surrounded these lowlands. Beavers and other fur-bearing animals roamed these forests and the Rocky Mountains to the east. For this reason, fur trappers were the first settlers to head into Oregon Country.

Not all of Oregon Country attracted Americans. Between the Cascade Mountains and the Rockies is a dry plateau. This region attracted neither fur trappers nor farmers.

Nations Compete In the early 1800s, four countries claimed Oregon. They were the United States, Great Britain, Spain, and Russia. Of course, Native American groups had lived there for centuries. However, the United States and European nations gave little thought to Indian rights.

In 1818, the United States and Britain agreed to occupy Oregon Country jointly. Citizens of each nation would have equal rights there. Spain and Russia had few settlers there, so they withdrew their claims to Oregon Country.

? PREDICT CONSEQUENCES How might the arrival of many U.S. settlers affect the agreement between Britain and the United States over Oregon Country?

The Far West Fur Trade

At first, only a handful of Europeans or Americans traveled to Oregon Country. Most were fur traders. Since furs could be sold for huge profits in China, merchants from New England stopped along the Oregon coast before crossing the Pacific. In fact, so many New England traders visited Oregon to buy furs that, in some areas, the Indian name for a white man was "Boston."

Only a few hardy fur trappers actually settled in Oregon. These adventurous men hiked throughout the region's vast forests, trapping animals and living off the land. They were known as **mountain men**.

Mountain men were admired as **rugged individualists**. Even their colorful appearance set them apart from ordinary society. Their shirts and trousers were made of animal hides and decorated with porcupine quills. Their hair reached to their shoulders. Pistols and tomahawks hung from their belts.

A Hard Life Mountain men could make fine profits selling their furs. They led dangerous lives, however. The long, cold winters demanded special survival skills. In the forests, mountain men had to watch out for bears, wildcats, or other animals that might attack.

In winter, food was scarce. Faced with starvation, a hungry trapper would eat almost anything. "I have held my hands in an anthill until they were covered with ants, then greedily licked them off," one mountain man recalled.

Trappers often spent winters in Native American villages. They learned trapping and hunting skills from Indians. Some mountain men married Indian women who helped the newcomers survive in the rugged mountains.

The Fur Trade During the fall and spring, mountain men tended their traps. Then in July, they tramped out of the wilderness to meet with fur traders. They headed to a place chosen the year before, called the rendezvous (RAHN day voo). **Rendezvous** is a French word meaning "get-together."

The first day of the rendezvous was a time for entertainment. A visitor to one rendezvous captured the excitement:

"[The mountain men] engaged in contests of skill at running, jumping, wrestling, shooting with the rifle, and running horses. . . . They sang, they

>> A rendezvous was a gathering for both business and pleasure. In the evening, trappers and traders would gather around camp fires and share stories.

▶ **Interactive Gallery**

laughed, they whooped; they tried to out-brag and out-lie each other in stories of their adventures."

—Washington Irving, *The Adventures of Captain Bonneville, U.S.A., in the Rocky Mountains and the Far West*, 1837

Soon enough, trappers and traders settled down to bargain. As long as beaver hats were in demand in the East and in Europe, mountain men got a good price for their furs. By the late 1830s, however, the fur trade was dying. Trappers had killed too many beavers, and the animals had become scarce. Also, beaver hats went out of style. Even so, mountain men found new uses for their skills. Some used their knowledge of the region to lead settlers along rugged mountain trails into Oregon Country.

>> James Beckwourth was a freed slave who became a fur trader and explorer. He guided settlers through the Sierra Nevada. Later, he worked for the army and ran his own hotel and store.

Guides to the West In their search for furs, mountain men explored many parts of the West. They followed Indian trails through passes in the Rocky Mountains. Later, they used these trails to help guide settlers heading west.

Jedediah Smith led settlers across the Rockies through South Pass, in present-day Wyoming. Manuel Lisa, a Latino fur trader, led a trip up the Missouri River. In 1807, he founded Fort Manuel, the first outpost on the upper Missouri, in what is now North Dakota.

James Beckwourth, an African American freed from slavery, traveled west from Missouri to seek a new life. He worked as a fur trader and lived among the Crow Indians, who later accepted him as a chief. In his work as a guide, Beckwourth discovered a mountain pass through the Sierra Nevada mountain range that later became a major route to California.

? INTERPRET How did mountain men help open up Oregon Country to white settlement?

The Oregon Trail

The first white Americans to settle permanently in Oregon Country were missionaries. In the 1830s, they began to travel west to bring their religious beliefs to Native Americans.

Missionaries Bring Settlers Among these early settlers were Marcus and Narcissa Whitman. In 1836, the couple married and set out for Oregon Country, where they planned to convert local Native Americans to Christianity.

The Whitmans built their mission near the Columbia River and began to work with Cayuse (kay-YOOS) people, setting up

>> The Whitman Mission was a major stopping point along the Oregon Trail during the 1840s. The mission ran a medical clinic and taught Bible classes to the local Native Americans.

a mission school and a clinic. Soon, other missionaries and settlers joined them.

Missionaries like the Whitmans helped stir up interest in Oregon Country. Eager to have others join them, the missionaries sent back glowing reports about the land. People throughout the nation read these reports. By 1840, more and more Americans were making the long and difficult journey to Oregon Country.

As settlers spread onto Cayuse lands, conflicts arose. Worse, the newcomers carried diseases that often killed the Cayuses. In 1847, tragedy struck. A measles outbreak among the settlers spread to the Cayuses. Many Cayuse children died. Blaming the settlers, a band of angry Indians attacked the mission, killing the Whitmans and 12 others.

Wagons Ho! Despite these and other killings, pioneers still boldly set out for Oregon Country. They were attracted by tales of wheat that grew taller than a man and turnips five feet around. Stories like these touched off a race to get to Oregon Country. Americans called it "Oregon fever." As Oregon fever spread, pioneers clogged the trails west.

Beginning in 1843, wagon trains left every spring for Oregon Country. They followed a route called the **Oregon Trail**. Families planning to go west met at Independence, Missouri, in the early spring.

By mid-April, the prairie outside Independence was packed with people and wagons. Somehow, the pioneers formed themselves into wagon trains. Each group elected leaders to make decisions along the way.

The Oregon-bound pioneers hurried to leave Independence in May. Timing was important. Travelers had to reach the Oregon lowlands by early October before the snow fell in the mountains. This meant that pioneers had to cover 2,000 miles in five months. In the 1840s, traveling 15 miles a day was considered making good time.

Life in a Wagon Train On the trail, families woke at dawn to a bugle blast. Everyone had a job to do. Girls helped their mothers prepare food. Men and boys harnessed the horses and oxen. By 6 A.M., the cry of "Wagons Ho!" rang across the plains.

The wagon train stopped for a brief noonday meal. Then, it returned to the trail until 6 or 7 P.M. At night, wagons drew into a circle to keep the cattle from wandering.

Most pioneer families started the journey with a large amount of gear. As they crossed rivers and scaled mountains, they discarded belongings to lighten their wagons.

The trail west held many dangers. During the spring, travelers risked drowning as they floated their wagons across rain-swollen rivers. In summer, they faced blistering heat on the treeless plains. Early snows could block passes through the mountains. Getting the heavy wagons past these obstacles was hard work. The biggest threat was sickness. Cholera and other diseases could wipe out whole wagon trains. Because the travelers lived so close together, diseases spread quickly.

Meeting the Locals As they moved toward the Rockies, pioneers often saw Indians. Often, they traded with the wagon trains. Hungry pioneers were grateful for the food

>> Settlers traveled in wagon trains for mutual assistance on their journey westward. A train would have about 20 to 40 wagons, although occasionally they could be much larger.

Interactive 3-D Model

>> The Oregon Trail was a 2,000-mile route that ran from the Missouri River to Oregon. **Analyze Maps** What were some of the difficulties that faced pioneers along the Trail?

that the Indians sold in return for clothing and tools. A traveler noted:

> "Whenever we camp near any Indian village, we are no sooner stopped than a whole crowd may be seen coming galloping into our camp. The [women] do all the swapping."
>
> —John S. Unruh, quoted in *The Plains Across: The Overland Emigrants and the Trans-Mississippi West, 1840–1860*

Journey's End Despite the many hardships, more than 50,000 people reached Oregon between 1840 and 1860. Their wagon wheels cut so deeply into the plains that the ruts can still be seen today.

By the 1840s, Americans outnumbered the British in Oregon Country. As you have read, the two nations had agreed to occupy Oregon Country jointly. Now many Americans wanted Oregon Country for the United States alone.

? IDENTIFY CAUSE AND EFFECT How did missionaries attract settlers?

ASSESSMENT

1. **Explain** why Britain and the United States agreed to occupy Oregon Country jointly.

2. **Generate Explanations** How do you suppose the arrival of white settlers changed the environment of the Oregon Country?

3. **Contrast** the lives of missionaries and mountain men in Oregon Country.

4. **Summarize** the reason for the Cayuse attack on the Whitman mission.

5. **Identify Central Ideas** Describe how settlers to Oregon Country made their trips from Independence, Missouri.

>> The Alamo in San Antonio, Texas, shown here, has come to symbolize courage, patriotism, and sacrifice for Texans and others in the United States.

▶ **Interactive Flipped Video**

>> **Objectives**

Summarize the cooperation and conflict between American settlers in Texas and the Mexican government.

Explain how Texas gained independence.

Describe how the events at the Alamo affected Texans.

Identify the challenges faced by the Lone Star Republic.

>> **Key Terms**

dictator
Tejanos
Alamo
siege
Battle of San Jacinto
annex
Stephen Austin
General Antonio
  López de Santa
  Anna
Sam Houston

In the early 1800s, Texas was part of a Spanish province in the colony of New Spain, or Mexico. Texas had very few Mexican settlers. As a result, Spain had difficulty keeping order in the province, where settlers faced frequent raids by Comanche Indians. In 1820, Spain gave Moses Austin a land grant and permission to colonize Texas with 300 Catholic families. Although Austin died before he could set up a colony, his son, Stephen, took over the grant.

Americans Colonize Mexican Texas

In 1821, before **Stephen Austin** could establish his colony, Mexico won independence from Spain. Austin went to Mexico City to make sure that the new government still supported his land grant. The new leaders agreed to let Austin bring settlers to Texas. As Spain had been, Mexico was eager for settlers to develop the land and help control Indian attacks. At the time, only about 4,000 Mexicans lived in Texas.

By the 1820s, most of the good land in the United States was already occupied, and land there could be expensive. There was a scarcity, or short supply, of affordable, fertile land, or land that is good for growing crops. In Texas, by contrast, there was a large supply of fertile land that settlers could buy very cheaply.

This pulled many Americans to settle beyond the frontier. The eastern portion of the Spanish province of Texas contained some very fertile soil. The physical features of the land, especially the fertile soil, increased settlement to Texas, and agriculture remains important in this region to this day.

Austin began to gather the 300 families who would settle his colony in Texas. Starting in late 1821, they began settling the colony. Many settlers came from the cotton country of the Southeast. Some built large cotton plantations and brought in slaves to work the land. Austin's land grant was located between the Colorado and Brazos rivers. He made sure to divide the grant so that each colonist purchased a parcel of land that bordered a river to allow access to water. Having access to water was vital for the settlers as well as their farms and livestock.

Average Annual Precipitation in the Southwest

KEY
Average Annual Precipitation (in inches)
- 60.1 – 80
- 40.1 – 60
- 30.1 – 40
- 20.1 – 30
- 10.1 – 20
- 10 and less

Azimuthal Equal-Area Projection

>>Americans were attracted to the northeast region of New Spain. **Analyze Maps** What details shown on the map explain why this region might attract settlers?

▶ Interactive Map

>> Often referred to as the "Father of Texas," Stephen Austin was a major figure in the early history of Texas.

>> Americans were not the only immigrants to settle in Texas. Mexico also encouraged Europeans, like these Germans, to settle there. **Infer** How might the presence of so many people with cultures from outside Mexico have contributed to conflict in Mexican Texas?

As Austin's colony grew and succeeded, Mexico gave Austin several more land grants. Grants were also given to other entrepreneurs like Austin to attract settlers to Texas. Some of these settlers were from Mexico, but the largest number came from the United States. By 1830, about 20,000 Americans had moved to Texas.

? RECALL What factors influenced where Americans settled in Texas?

Conflict With the Mexican Government

In return for land, Austin and the original American settlers agreed to become Mexican citizens and to worship in the Roman Catholic Church. Later American settlers, however, felt no loyalty to Mexico. They spoke little or no Spanish and most were Protestant. These and other differences led to conflicts between the settlers and the Mexican government.

Mexico Tightens Its Grip on Texas In 1830, Mexico barred any more Americans from settling in Texas. Mexico feared that the Americans would try to make Texas a part of the United States. It had good reason to fear this possibility. The United States had already tried twice to buy Texas from Mexico.

To assert its authority, Mexico began to enforce laws that had long been ignored. One was the law requiring Texans to promise to worship in the Catholic Church. Another law banned slavery in the region. American settlers resented these laws. The law against slavery was a serious problem for American settlers. Many American settlers had brought enslaved people with them and relied on enslaved workers to grow cotton. Settlers' anger grew when Mexico sent troops to enforce its will.

In 1833, **General Antonio López de Santa Anna** gained power in Mexico. Two years later, he threw out the Mexican constitution and began governing the nation as dictator. A **dictator** is a ruler with absolute power and authority. Rumors began to spread that Santa Anna intended to drive the Americans out of Texas.

Texans Rebel With Santa Anna in power, Americans in Texas felt that the time had come for action. They had the support of many **Tejanos** (teh HAH nohs), people of Mexican descent born in Texas. Tejanos did not necessarily want independence from Mexico. However, they did want to be rid of the dictator, Santa Anna.

In October 1835, Texan settlers in the town of Gonzales (gahn ZAH les) clashed with Mexican troops. They forced the troops to withdraw. Inspired by that victory, Stephen Austin vowed to "see Texas forever free from Mexican domination." Two months later, Texan settlers surrounded and then occupied the town of San Antonio. Determined to stamp out the rebellion, Santa Anna marched north with a large army.

❓ **EXPLAIN** Why were U.S. settlers opposed to Mexican laws?

Independence for Texas

While Santa Anna was on the move, a group of Texans declared independence for the Republic of Texas on March 2, 1836. **Sam Houston** was given command of its army. Volunteers from the United States and from other nations, along with African Americans and Tejanos, joined the fight for Texan independence from Mexico.

>> As a young officer in the Spanish army, Antonio López de Santa Anna fought against Mexican independence. Later, he became president of Mexico. He personally led the Mexican forces against the Texan rebels.

Siege at the Alamo By the time Santa Anna reached San Antonio, the Texans had taken up positions in an old Spanish mission called the **Alamo**. There they waited for the Mexican attack.

The Texans were poorly equipped. Their supplies of ammunition, food, water, and medicine were low. Only about 150 Texans faced a force of 6,000 Mexican troops. Inside the mission, a young lieutenant colonel, William B. Travis, was in command. Among the volunteers at the Alamo were the famous frontiersmen Jim Bowie and Davy Crockett as well as several Tejano families, two Texan women, and two enslaved young African American men.

On February 23, 1836, Mexican troops began the siege of the Alamo. In a **siege**, enemy forces try to capture a city or fort by surrounding and often bombarding it. The Texan defenders barely held out as cannons pounded the walls. Travis knew that without help the defenders were doomed. He sent a messenger through the Mexican lines with a letter addressed "to the people of Texas and all the Americans in the World":

> I shall never surrender or retreat. . . . I call on you in the name of Liberty, of patriotism and everything dear to the American character, to come to our aid, with all [speed]. . . . *Victory or Death.*
>
> —William B. Travis, Letter, February 24, 1836

Travis also sent scouts to find more volunteers and food. About 40 men also managed to slip through enemy lines and

>> Twelve feet high and two feet thick, the Alamo walls were good protection but unable to endure days of bombardment. **Hypothesize** How might the defenders' confidence have changed during the siege?

▶ **Interactive Gallery**

joined the Texans in their fight inside the Alamo. Still, no large force arrived to help the defenders of the Alamo. For 12 days, the Mexican bombardment continued.

At dawn on March 6, Mexican cannons shattered the mission walls. Santa Anna now launched an all-out attack. Thousands of Mexican soldiers poured over the broken walls, shouting *"Viva Santa Anna!"* ("Long live Santa Anna!"). Attackers and defenders battled in hand-to-hand combat. In the end, about 180 Texans and almost 1,500 Mexicans lay dead. Most of the few Texans who survived were executed.

The Battle of San Jacinto The fall of the Alamo sparked Texan cries for revenge. A few weeks later, Texan fury grew when Mexican troops killed several hundred soldiers fighting for the Texan cause after they had surrendered at Goliad. News of these events inspired new volunteers to join the Texan forces. Many came from the United States. Houston worked hard to turn the volunteers into an effective army. Even though the Texans were eager to attack, Houston held them back until the time was right.

Houston soon found the chance to attack Santa Anna. Scouts reported that the Mexican general and his army were camped near the San Jacinto (juh SIN toh) River. On the afternoon of April 21, 1836, the Texans caught their enemies by surprise. With cries of "Remember the Alamo!" and "Remember Goliad!" Texans charged into battle.

The **Battle of San Jacinto** lasted only 18 minutes. Although the Texans were outnumbered, the element of surprise was their greatest ally. They killed 630 Mexicans and captured 700 more. The next day, they captured Santa Anna,

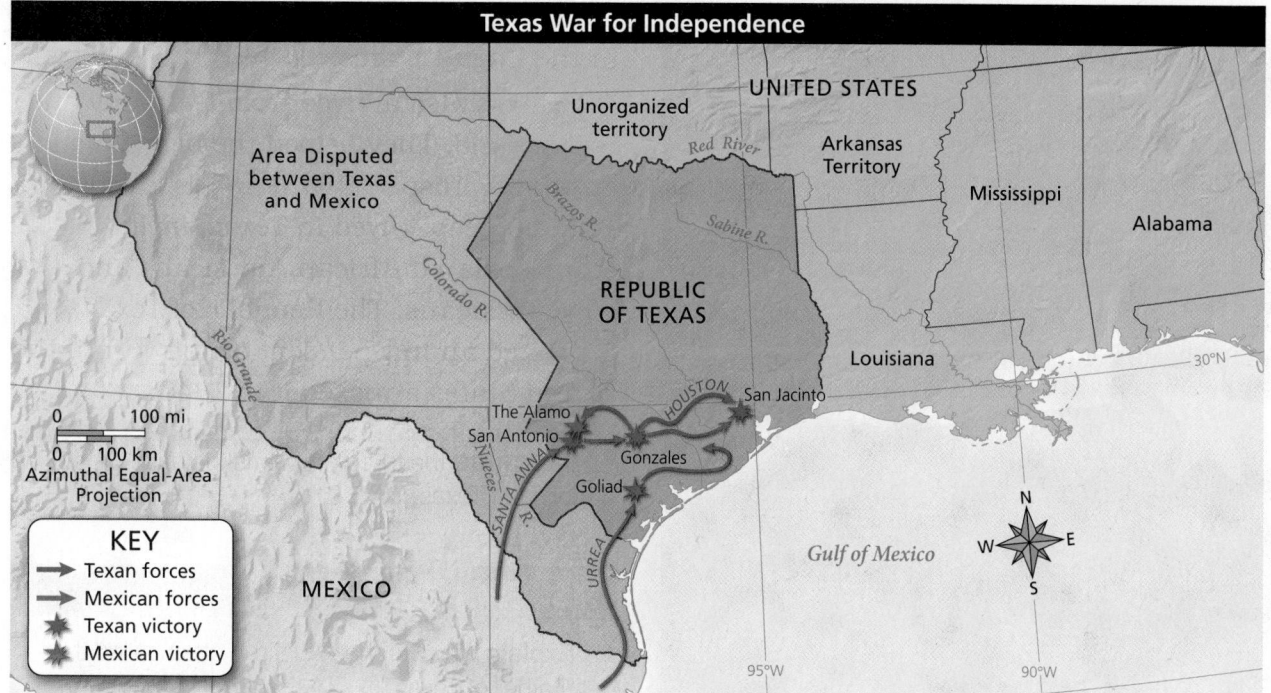

Texas War for Independence

UNITED STATES

Unorganized territory

Arkansas Territory

Mississippi

Alabama

Area Disputed between Texas and Mexico

Red River

Brazos R.

Sabine R.

REPUBLIC OF TEXAS

Colorado R.

Louisiana

30°N

Rio Grande

HOUSTON

San Jacinto

0   100 mi
0   100 km
Azimuthal Equal-Area
Projection

The Alamo
San Antonio

Gonzales

SANTA ANNA R.

Goliad

Nueces R.

URREA

Gulf of Mexico

N
W   E
S

95°W   90°W

KEY
→ Texan forces
→ Mexican forces
✦ Texan victory
✦ Mexican victory

MEXICO

>> After a brief yet bloody war, the Republic of Texas won its independence from Mexico. **Analyze Maps** Describe the movement of Mexican and Texan forces after the battle at the Alamo.

forcing him to sign a treaty granting Texas independence.

? RECALL What was the key to the Texan's victory at San Jacinto?

The Republic of Texas Is Born

In battle, Texans had carried a flag with a single star. After winning independence, they nicknamed their new nation the Lone Star Republic. A constitution was written using the United States Constitution as a model. In September 1836, voters elected Sam Houston president of the Republic of Texas.

The new country faced several serious problems, however. First, the government of Mexico refused to accept the treaty that Santa Anna had signed. Mexicans insisted that Texas was still part of Mexico. Second, Texas was nearly bankrupt.

Third, Comanche and other Indian groups threatened to attack small Texan communities. Most Texans thought that the best way to solve these problems was to become part of the United States.

In the United States, people were divided about whether to **annex,** or add on, Texas to the Union. The arguments reflected sectional divisions in the country. White southerners generally favored the idea. Many northerners opposed it. The main issue was slavery. By the 1830s, antislavery feeling was growing in the North. Because many Texans owned slaves, northerners feared that Texas would join the Union as a slave-owning state, strengthening support for slavery in the U.S. government. In addition, President Andrew Jackson worried that annexing Texas would lead to war with Mexico. As a result, Congress refused to annex the Republic of Texas.

>> The Lone Star flag was adopted by the Republic of Texas in 1839. It remains the Texas state flag to this day.

▶ **Interactive Timeline**

For the next nine years, leaders of the Republic of Texas worked to attract new settlers. The new Texas government encouraged immigration by offering settlers free land. During the Panic of 1837, thousands of Americans moved to Texas, where land was less expensive than in the United States.

Settlers also arrived from Germany and Switzerland. They helped the new nation grow and prosper. By the 1840s, about 140,000 people lived in Texas, including many enslaved African Americans and some Mexicans. The Republic of Texas remained an independent country until the United States annexed it in 1845.

❓ **DESCRIBE** the three problems that faced the new Republic of Texas.

ASSESSMENT

1. **Explain** why Stephen Austin is often called the "Father of Texas."

2. **Generate Explanations** Why did some U.S. settlers disagree with Mexico's insistence on enforcing the law banning slavery?

3. **Draw Conclusions** Why did U.S. settlers not come to the aid of the fighters under siege at the Alamo despite William Travis's plea for help?

4. **Identify Central Issues** Why did the Republic of Texas remain an independent country for 9 years?

5. **Draw Conclusions** Why do you suppose Texas is nicknamed "the Lone Star State"?

Manifest Destiny in California and the Southwest

>> Forty-niners came to California hoping to strike it rich in the gold fields.

▶ **Interactive Flipped Video**

In the 1840s, **New Mexico Territory** included present-day Arizona, New Mexico, Nevada, and Utah, and parts of Colorado. This huge region was ruled by Mexico. This land was southwest of the unorganized territory belonging to the United States from the Louisiana Purchase.

>> **Objectives**

Describe life for the Spanish and Native Americans on the missions and ranches of California and New Mexico.

Analyze the relationship between the concept of Manifest Destiny and the westward growth of the nation.

List the causes and effects of the Mexican-American War.

Explain why the Mormons moved to Utah.

Describe how the gold rush affected California.

>> **Key Terms**

New Mexico Territory
Santa Fe Trail
self-sufficient
vaqueros
Manifest Destiny
Bear Flag Republic
Chapultepec
Treaty of Guadalupe-
  Hidalgo
cede
Mexican Cession
Gadsden Purchase

forty-niners
James Polk
Joseph Smith
Brigham Young
Junípero Serra
mission

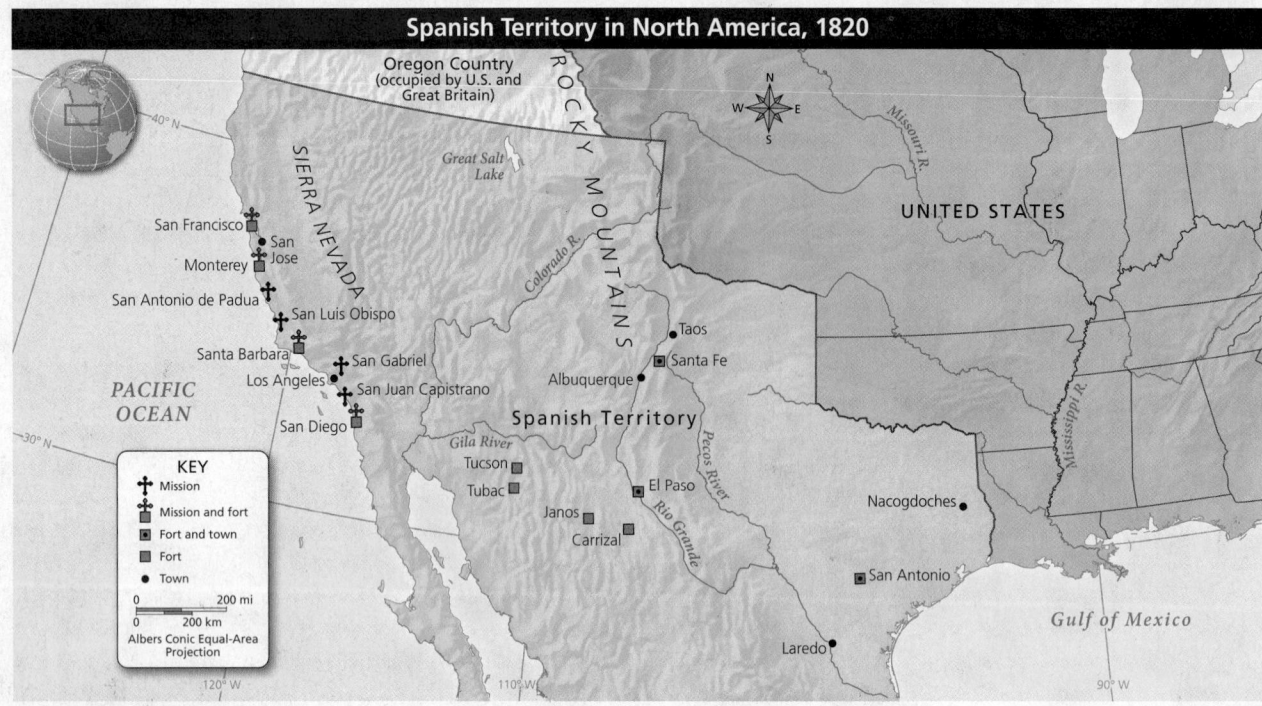

Spanish Territory in North America, 1820

>> Spain set up a series of missions, forts, and towns north of their earlier settlements in Mexico. **Analyze Maps** Why do you think Spain built these settlements in these locations?

New Mexico Territory and California

Spain and New Mexico Territory The physical features of this region vary depending on location. Much of this region is hot and dry desert. There are also forested mountains. In some areas, thick grasses grow. Before the Spanish arrived, the Zuñi (ZOON yee) and other Indians farmed here using irrigation, while other Native Americans lived mainly by hunting and gathering.

The Spanish explorer Juan de Oñate (ohn YAH tay) claimed the region for Spain in 1598. In the early 1600s, the Spanish built Santa Fe and made it the capital of the territory. By trading horses, fur, and wool, Santa Fe grew into a busy trading town.

Some Americans were eager to settle in New Mexico, which was thinly populated but had good physical features, including many natural resources. Spain, however, would not let Americans settle in Santa Fe or anywhere else in the territory. Only after Mexico became independent in 1821 were Americans welcome there. William Becknell, a merchant and adventurer, was the first American to head for Santa Fe. In 1821, he led some traders from Franklin, Missouri, across the plains to the New Mexico town. Other Americans soon followed Becknell's route, which became known as the **Santa Fe Trail**.

Spanish Settlements in California California, too, was ruled first by Spain and then by Mexico. In 1769, Captain Gaspar de Portolá led an expedition up the Pacific coast. With him was Father **Junípero Serra** (hoo NEE peh roh SEHR rah). Father Serra built his first **mission** at San Diego. Later he and other missionaries set up a string of 21 missions long the California coast.

Each mission complex included a church and the surrounding land. Each became **self-sufficient**, producing enough for its own needs. Spanish soldiers built forts nearby.

Before the Spanish arrived, California Indians lived in small, scattered groups. As a result, they had little success resisting the Spanish soldiers who made them work on mission lands. Native Americans were forced to herd sheep and cattle and raise crops for the missions. They were also forced to live at the missions and practice the Roman Catholic faith. Many missionaries were dedicated to converting the Indians to Christianity. However, mission life was harsh. Indians were forced to give up their culture. Families were often separated, and people faced great distress. Thousands of Native Americans died from overwork and disease.

Life on Mexican Ranches In the 1820s, newly independent Mexico decided that California's economy was growing too slowly. Hoping to speed up growth, the government took land from the missions and gave it to wealthy individuals. These new landowners set up huge cattle ranches in California.

Native Americans did most of the work on the ranches as well, tending cattle and other animals. A new culture developed on the ranches—the culture of the **vaqueros**. Vaqueros were the Indian and Mexican cowhands who worked on the ranches. They were excellent riders and ropers, and their traditions strongly influenced later cowhands.

? DESCRIBE Who were the vaqueros?

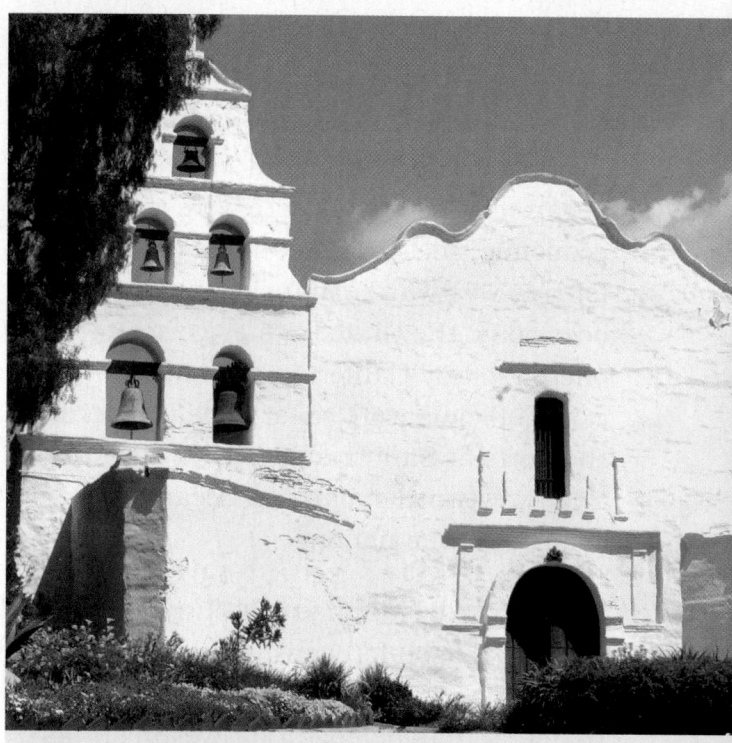

>> This mission in San Diego was the first one built in California. Father Serra established this and many other California missions in the late 1700s.

>> Native Americans did most of the labor on California missions, such as farming, cooking, and making everything the mission needed. Many Indians were overworked to the point of death.

Manifest Destiny

In the mid-1840s, only about 700 people from the United States lived in California. Every year, however, more Americans began moving west. There were many economic, social, and political causes for this westward expansion. On several occasions, the United States government offered to buy California from Mexico. Some officials were eager to gain control of the ports at San Francisco and San Diego. Soon westward expansion became a major priority for the nation.

The Roots of Manifest Destiny There was another reason for wanting to purchase California. Many Americans saw their nation and its democratic government as the best in the world.

In the 1840s, a newspaper created the term **Manifest Destiny** to mean that the United States had the right to spread across the continent. Manifest means clear or obvious. Destiny means something that is fated to happen. The social roots of Manifest Destiny lay in the belief that Americans had the right and the duty of westward expansion to spread their culture across the continent all the way to the Pacific Ocean.

Americans who believed in Manifest Destiny thought that westward expansion would also open new opportunities for the United States economy. To many Americans, the fertile farmland and natural resources in the West were prime opportunities for economic growth.

Manifest Destiny and westward expansion had some negative effects, however. Many white Americans believed that they were superior to Native Americans and Mexicans. They used this belief to justify taking lands belonging to people whom they considered inferior.

Polk and Westward Expansion The political roots of Manifest Destiny and westward expansion took hold during the election of 1844. The Whigs nominated the well-known national leader Henry Clay for President. Clay had opposed the annexation of Texas. The Democrats choose **James Polk**, a little-known candidate from Tennessee who wanted

Roots of Manifest Destiny

SOCIAL	POLITICAL	ECONOMIC
• Belief in America as an exceptional nation • Desire to spread American democracy and ideals • Belief that it was God's will for America to expand • View that white Americans were superior to Native Americans	• Monroe Doctrine warning against European colonization in the Western hemisphere • Desire to acquire Oregon from Britain • Desire to acquire Texas from Mexico • Success of Democrats, who supported expansion, over Whigs, who did not	• Farmland for settlers • Access to rich resources • Land for Southern crops such as cotton

>> People had different reasons for supporting Manifest Destiny. **Analyze Charts** How might people's values lead them to support Manifest Destiny?

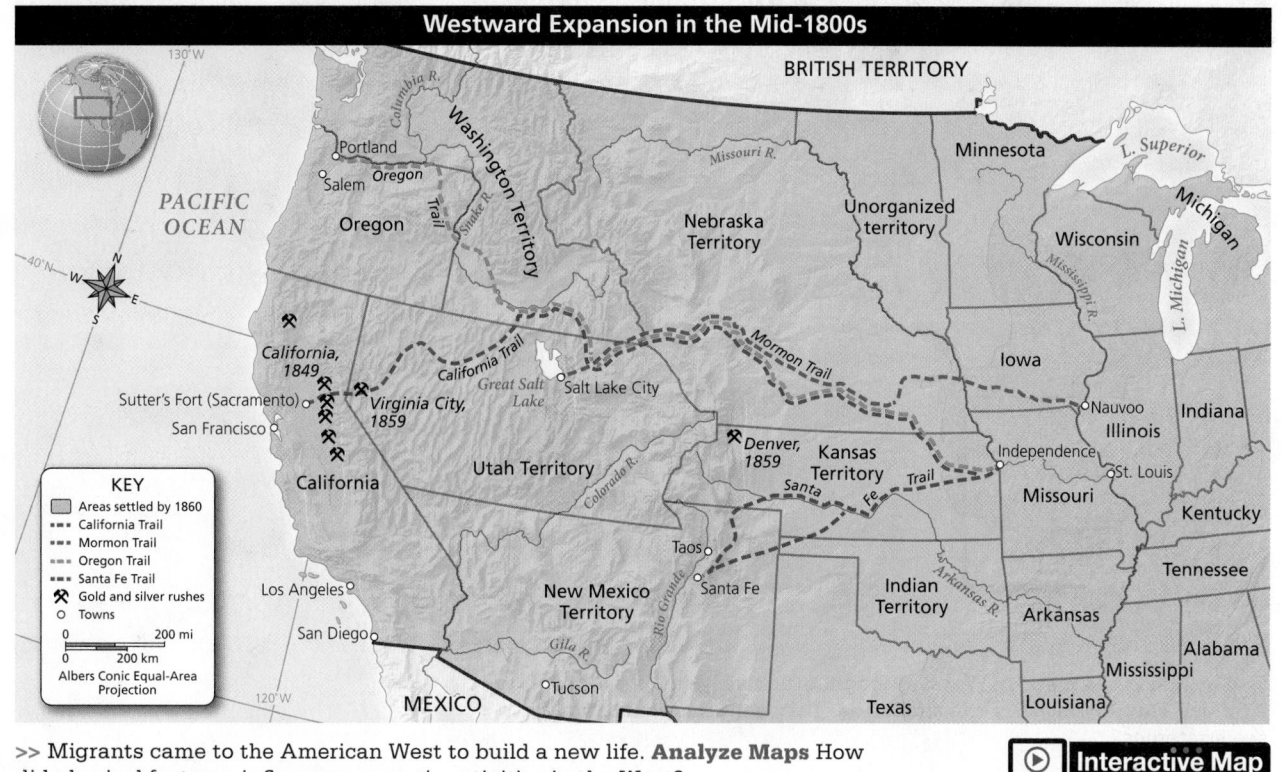

Westward Expansion in the Mid-1800s

KEY
- Areas settled by 1860
- California Trail
- Mormon Trail
- Oregon Trail
- Santa Fe Trail
- Gold and silver rushes
- Towns

0   200 mi
0   200 km
Albers Conic Equal-Area Projection

>> Migrants came to the American West to build a new life. **Analyze Maps** How did physical features influence economic activities in the West?

▶ **Interactive Map**

to add Texas and Oregon Country to the Union.

On Election Day, Americans showed their support for westward expansion by electing Polk president. He took office in March 1845 on a wave of support for expansion. Acting on his campaign promise, he took steps to gain control of Oregon Country. That move brought the possibility of war with Britain.

Polk did not really want to fight Britain, however. Instead, in 1846, he agreed to a compromise. Oregon Country was divided at latitude 49°N. Britain got the lands north of the line, and the United States got the lands south of the line. The United States named its lands the Oregon Territory. Later the states of Oregon (1859), Washington (1889), and Idaho (1890) were carved out of the Oregon Territory.

Texas proved a more difficult problem. The United States at first had refused to annex Texas. Then, in 1844, Texan president Sam Houston signed a treaty of annexation with the United States. However, the Senate again refused to ratify the treaty. Senators feared that annexing Texas would cause a war with Mexico.

Meanwhile, in a last effort to prevent annexation by the United States, Mexico offered to accept the independence of Texas if Texas rejected annexation. Sam Houston and other Texans who supported annexation would not give up, however. To pressure the United States to annex Texas, he pretended that Texas might ally itself with Britain. The trick worked. Americans did not want Britain to gain a foothold in Texas. In 1845, Congress passed a joint

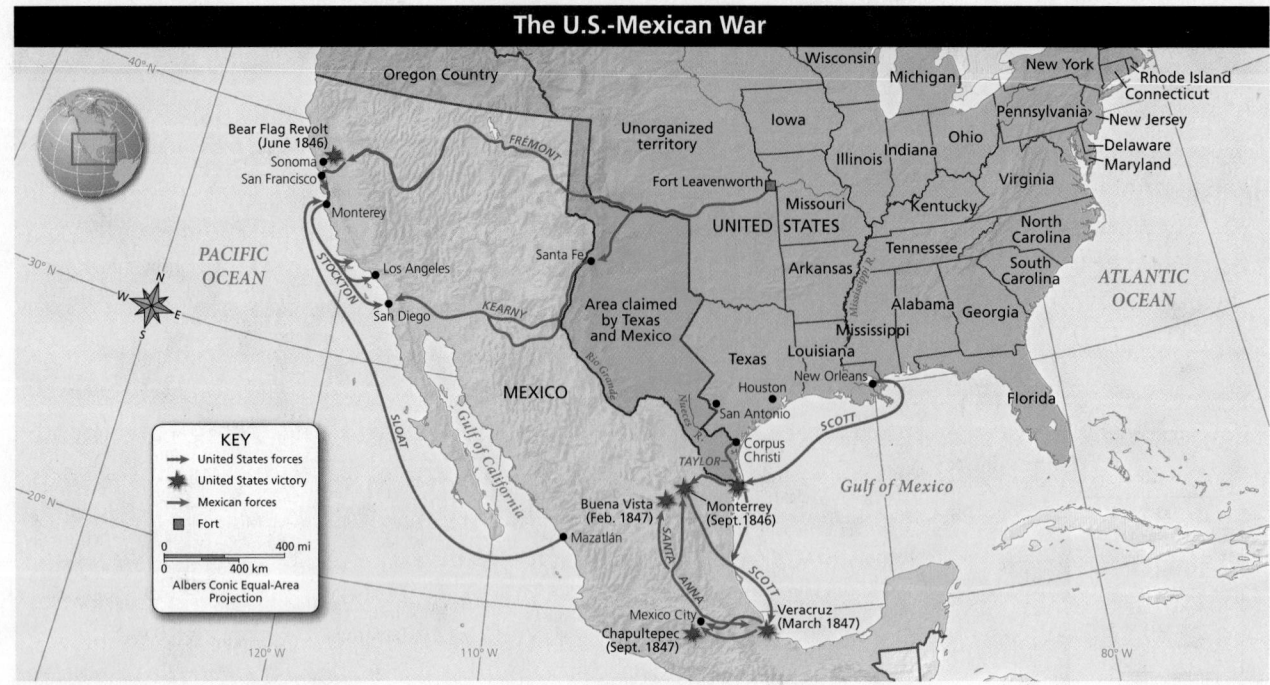

>> The Mexican-American War was fought over a vast amount of territory.
Analyze Maps What were the similarities between American land and sea strategies?

resolution admitting Texas to the Union. This set the stage for conflict with Mexico.

? RECALL Why did U.S. senators refuse to ratify the treaty to annex Texas?

The Mexican-American War

The annexation of Texas outraged Mexicans. They had not accepted Texan independence, much less annexation. They also worried that Americans might encourage rebellions in California and New Mexico as they had in Texas.

At the same time, Americans resented Mexico. They were annoyed when Mexico rejected President Polk's offer of $30 million to buy California and New Mexico. Many Americans felt that Mexico stood in the way of the Manifest Destiny of the United States.

The Clash Begins A border dispute finally caused a war. Both the United States and Mexico claimed control over the land between the Rio Grande and the Nueces (noo AY says) River. In January 1846, Polk ordered General Zachary Taylor to set up posts in the disputed area. Polk knew that the move might lead to war. In April 1846, Mexican troops crossed the Rio Grande and clashed with the Americans. At Polk's urging, Congress declared war on Mexico.

Americans were divided over the conflict. Many people in the South and West were eager to fight, hoping to win new lands. Some northerners, however, opposed the war. They saw it as a southern plot to add slave states to the Union. Still, the war was generally popular. When the army called for volunteers, thousands of young recruits flocked to the cause.

Fighting on Multiple Fronts During the Mexican-American War, the United

States attacked on several fronts at once. President Polk hoped that this strategy would win a quick victory.

General Taylor crossed the Rio Grande into northern Mexico. In February 1847, he met Mexican General Santa Anna at the Battle of Buena Vista. The Americans were outnumbered more than two to one, but they were better armed and better led. After fierce fighting and intense artillery fire, they forced Santa Anna to retreat. Meanwhile, a second army under General Winfield Scott landed at the Mexican port of Veracruz. After a long battle, the Americans took the city. Scott then headed toward Mexico City, the capital. A third army, led by General Stephen Kearny, captured Santa Fe without firing a shot.

Kearny then hurried on to San Diego. After several battles, he won control of southern California early in 1847.

Even before hearing of the war, Americans in northern California had begun a revolt against Mexican rule. The rebels declared California an independent republic on June 14, 1846. They nicknamed their new nation the **Bear Flag Republic**. Led by a young American officer, John C. Frémont (FREE mont), rebel forces then drove the Mexican troops out of northern California.

By 1847, the United States controlled all of New Mexico and California. General Scott, meanwhile, pushed closer to Mexico City. Blocking his way was the Mexican army in a well-protected position. At the Battle of Cerro Gordo, American troops went around this position to surprise the Mexican army. The Mexican army suffered heavy losses as it was forced to retreat. At the edge of Mexico City, Scott's forces faced one last obstacle. Teenage Mexican cadets, or soldiers in training, made a heroic stand at **Chapultepec** (chah POOL tuh pehk), a fort just outside the capital. Today, Mexicans honor those young cadets as heroes. At the battle's end, however, the capital city was overtaken by the American forces

When the American army captured Mexico City, the war was essentially over. Scott's Mexico City campaign remains one of the most successful in U.S. military history. The war was a crushing defeat for Mexico. An outnumbered American army had caused significantly more casualties than it had suffered.

The War Ends The Mexican government moved to make peace with the United States. In 1848, Mexico signed the **Treaty of Guadalupe-Hidalgo** (gwah duh LOOP ay hih DAHL goh). Mexico suffered the effects of losing the war. It had to **cede**, or give up, all of California and New Mexico to the United States. These lands were called

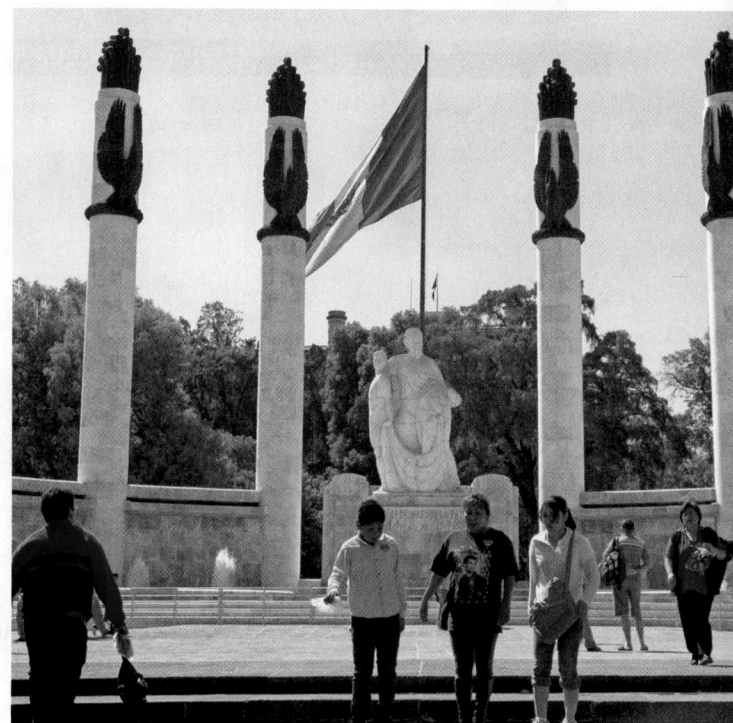

>> Mexicans today remember the six young cadets who stood against U.S. forces by visiting this monument in Chapultepec Park, Mexico City.

the **Mexican Cession**. In return, the United States paid Mexico $15 million and agreed to respect the rights of Spanish-speaking people in the Mexican Cession.

The war impacted the United States positively due to this new land. However, even more land was acquired later. In 1853, the United States paid Mexico an additional $10 million for a strip of land in present-day Arizona and New Mexico.

The Americans needed the land to complete a railroad. The land was called the **Gadsden Purchase**. With the Gadsden Purchase, many Americans felt that their dream of Manifest Destiny had been fulfilled.

? CHECK UNDERSTANDING Why were Mexicans worried about the annexation of Texas by the United States?

Settling the Mexican Cession

Winning the Mexican-American War had positive effects on westward expansion of the United States, which ushered in a whole new era of growth. New Mexico Territory, now the southwestern part of the United States, came to be known as the Southwest. After 1848, English-speaking settlers flocked to the Southwest. As the population of the country increased and affordable land in the east became scarce, more people decided to move. Americans migrated west for many reasons, from religious freedom to economic opportunities. The largest group of settlers to move into the Mexican Cession was the Mormons.

The Mormons Move West Mormons belonged to the Church of Jesus Christ of Latter-Day Saints. The church was founded by **Joseph Smith** in 1830. Smith, a farmer

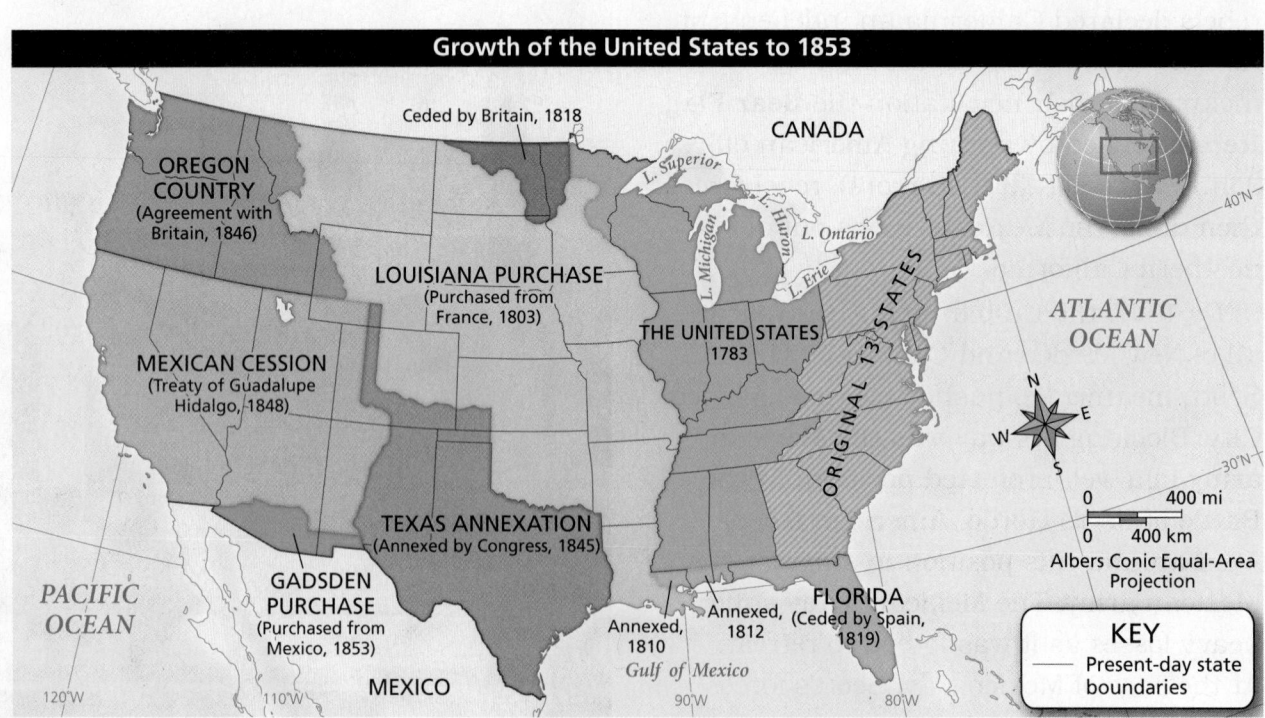

Growth of the United States to 1853

Ceded by Britain, 1818
CANADA
OREGON COUNTRY
(Agreement with Britain, 1846)
LOUISIANA PURCHASE
(Purchased from France, 1803)
THE UNITED STATES 1783
MEXICAN CESSION
(Treaty of Guadalupe Hidalgo, 1848)
ATLANTIC OCEAN
ORIGINAL 13 STATES
L. Superior
L. Michigan
L. Huron
L. Ontario
L. Erie
PACIFIC OCEAN
GADSDEN PURCHASE
(Purchased from Mexico, 1853)
TEXAS ANNEXATION
(Annexed by Congress, 1845)
MEXICO
Annexed, 1810
Annexed, 1812
FLORIDA
(Ceded by Spain, 1819)
Gulf of Mexico
120°W   110°W   90°W   80°W
40°N
30°N
0   400 mi
0   400 km
Albers Conic Equal-Area Projection

KEY
— Present-day state boundaries

>> By 1848, the United States extended from the Atlantic Ocean to the Pacific Ocean. **Analyze Maps** What was the impact of the Mexican-American War on the growth of the United States?

in upstate New York, attracted many followers to his new faith. Smith was an energetic, popular man.

Some of his teachings were different from other Christian churches' teachings. These new teachings angered many non-Mormons, who forced the Mormons to leave New York.

The Mormons moved west and, in the 1840s, built a community called Nauvoo on the banks of the Mississippi River in Illinois. Once again, the Mormons and their neighbors clashed. In 1844, an angry mob killed Joseph Smith, and **Brigham Young** was chosen as their new leader.

A New Home in Utah Young sought a place where Mormons would be safe from persecution. He had read about a valley between the Rocky Mountains and the Great Salt Lake in Utah. He hoped that this isolated valley might make a good home for the Mormons.

In 1847, Young led an advance party into the valley of the Great Salt Lake. Soon, waves of Mormon families followed. For several years, Mormon wagon trains struggled across the plains and over the Rockies to Utah. Once there, they had to learn how to survive in the desert climate. They transformed their environment by creating farmland in the desert. Young planned an irrigation system to bring water to farms.

He also drew up plans for a large city, called Salt Lake City, to be built in the desert. The Mormon settlements in Utah grew quickly. Congress recognized Brigham Young as governor of the Utah Territory in 1850. Eventually, in 1896, Utah became a state.

The California Gold Rush Begins While the Mormons were making the long trek

>> Mormon leader Brigham Young founded Salt Lake City and became the first governor of the state of Utah.

to what would become Utah, thousands of other Americans were racing even farther west to California. The great attraction there was gold, which offered settlers a chance to get rich.

In 1848, John Sutter was having a sawmill built on the American River, north of Sacramento, California. Sutter had hired James Marshall to supervise the job. Early on January 24, Marshall set out to inspect a ditch his crew was digging. He later recalled the events of that day:

> As I was taking my usual walk, . . . my eye was caught with the glimpse of something shining in the bottom of the ditch. . . . I reached my hand down and picked it up; it made my heart thump, for I was certain it was gold.

—James Marshall, quote in Hutchings' Illustrated California Magazine, 1857–1858

At first, Sutter tried to keep the news a secret. But within a few days, news reached San Francisco that gold had been found at Sutter's Mill. Carpenters threw down their saws. Bakers left bread in their ovens. Schools emptied as teachers and students joined the rush to the gold fields.

The news spread across the United States and around the globe. Thousands of Americans caught "gold fever." People from Europe, China, Australia, and South America joined in the great gold rush. More than 80,000 people made the long journey to California in 1849. They became know as **forty-niners** a nickname created in reference to the year they arrived.

Very few miners actually struck it rich. Many went broke trying to make their fortunes in the gold fields. Still, although many miners left the gold fields, they stayed in California. In time, they found jobs or took up farming.

Statehood for California The gold rush brought big changes to California. Almost overnight, San Francisco grew from a sleepy town to a bustling city, as newcomers poured in from all over the world. In the gold fields, towns sprang up just as quickly. Greed led some forty-niners into crime. Murders and robberies plagued many mining camps.

Californians soon realized that they needed a strong government to stop such lawlessness. In November of 1849, they drafted a state constitution. They then asked to be admitted to the Union. Their request caused an uproar in the United States. Many people wanted to know whether the new state would allow slavery. After a heated debate, California was admitted to the Union in 1850 as a free state. This was not the end of the issue. The question whether new states could

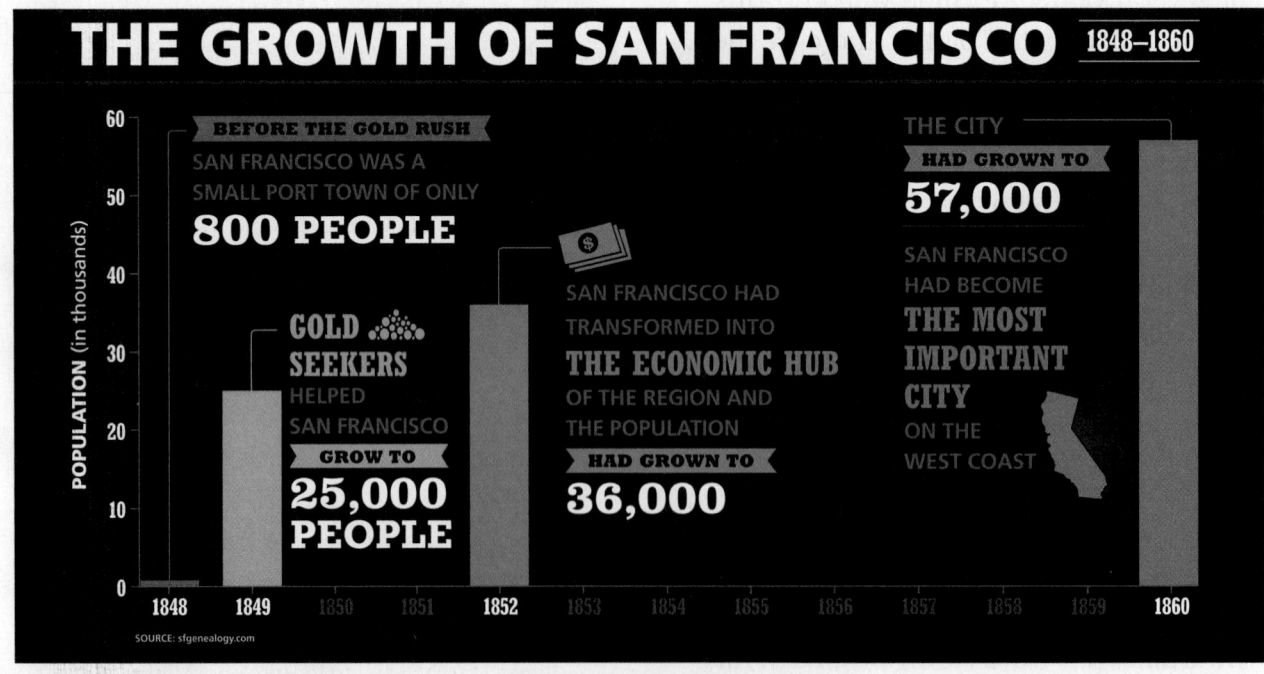

THE GROWTH OF SAN FRANCISCO 1848–1860

POPULATION (in thousands)

BEFORE THE GOLD RUSH
SAN FRANCISCO WAS A SMALL PORT TOWN OF ONLY
800 PEOPLE

GOLD SEEKERS HELPED SAN FRANCISCO
GROW TO
25,000 PEOPLE

SAN FRANCISCO HAD TRANSFORMED INTO
THE ECONOMIC HUB OF THE REGION AND THE POPULATION
HAD GROWN TO
36,000

THE CITY
HAD GROWN TO
57,000
SAN FRANCISCO HAD BECOME
THE MOST IMPORTANT CITY ON THE WEST COAST

SOURCE: sfgenealogy.com

>> The Gold Rush caused San Francisco to transform from a small port town into a major city. **Analyze Charts** How did immigration and migration impact the settlement of San Francisco?

>> People of all races came to California from across the country and around the world.

Interactive Gallery

allow slavery would end up causing bitter disagreements over the next ten years.

? **EXPLAIN** why the Mormons had to leave New York and were persecuted on their journey to Utah.

The Effects of Migration to California

Westward expansion had many effects on the cultures and peoples of California. The gold rush brought diverse groups of people to the West.

A Mix of Cultures Most of the newcomers were white Americans from the East. However, California's mining camps included African Americans who had run away from slavery in the South, free African Americans, and Native Americans. There were also people from Hawaii, China, Peru, Chile, France, Germany, Italy,

Ireland, and Australia. Not all groups fared well, however.

Before the gold rush, California's population had included large numbers of Mexicans. Mexican Americans faced serious hardships. During the 1850s and 1860s, many lost land that their families had owned for generations.

Native Americans fared even worse. Many were driven off the lands where they lived. Without any means to earn a living, large numbers died of starvation or disease brought by the newcomers. Still others were murdered. In 1850, about 100,000 Indians lived in California. By the 1870s, the state's Indian population had dropped to 17,000.

The physical features of California attracted the first settlers. Lured by the tales of a "mountain of gold," thousands of Chinese immigrants sailed across the Pacific to California. At first, the Chinese were welcomed because California needed workers. When the Chinese staked claims

>> By 1860, San Francisco was a well-established city, and California was a growing state.

African Americans faced discrimination and were denied certain rights.

Changes to the Region In spite of these problems, California continued to grow and prosper. Settlers from other states and immigrants from all over the world kept arriving. With their diverse backgrounds, the newcomers added to California's unique blend of cultures. That is, the mix of people added to the identity of California as a place. The economy grew as commerce and mining expanded, and farms grew to feed the settlers. Cities and roads grew to accommodate the increase in people and goods. By 1860, the state's population was about 300,000.

? CHECK UNDERSTANDING Why did so many Native Americans die of disease as newcomers moved westward?

in the gold fields, however, white miners often drove them off. Despite the harsh treatment, many Chinese Americans stayed in California. Their contributions helped the state to grow. They shaped the environment by draining swamplands and digging irrigation systems to turn dry land into fertile farmland.

Free blacks, too, joined the gold rush in California, hoping to strike it rich. Some became well-off by running businesses that contributed to the economy. In fact, by the 1850s, California had the richest African American population of any state. Yet,

ASSESSMENT

1. **Contrast** the treatment of Native Americans at most missions with how one would expect the missionaries to treat others.

2. **Summarize** the justifications Americans used to support the idea of Manifest Destiny.

3. **Generate Explanations** Briefly explain why and how the United States won the Mexican-American War.

4. **Draw Conclusions** Why do you suppose Brigham Young chose the isolated valley of the Great Salt Lake as a new home for the Mormons?

5. **Explain** why the Native American population in California decreases dramatically in the mid-1800s?

1. **Identify Congressional Conflicts and Compromises** Write a paragraph identifying the details of the conflict over tariffs that led to the Nullification Crisis and comparing the roles played by John C. Calhoun, Henry Clay, and Daniel Webster in this conflict. In a second paragraph, identify the provisions of the compromise that Congress reached to resolve the Nullification Crisis and the roles of these three men in that compromise. Explain what nullification is; explain how nullification was connected to conflict over the tariffs of 1828 and 1832; identify the details of that conflict and the provisions, or terms, of the compromise that Congress reached; and identify the roles that Calhoun, Webster, and Clay each played in the conflict and the compromise.

2. **Identify Political Party Points of View** Write a paragraph identifying the points of view the Whig Party and the Democratic Party held on major issues. Answer the following questions: What position did the Whigs take on internal improvements? How did the Whigs and the Democrats differ in their feelings about tariffs? What can you conclude from these positions about each party's point of view on the government's role in the nation's economy?

3. **Summarize Arguments About Tariffs** Write a speech about the tariff of 1828 that you will deliver in Congress as a senator from a Southern state. Express your state's strong opposition to the protective tariffs and explain the reasons for your state's position on this issue.

4. **Analyze the California Gold Rush** Write a paragraph describing the human geographic factor driving the California gold rush and the gold rush's effect on westward expansion. Consider why the event is significant, what human geographic factor caused people to rush to California, and the effect of the California gold rush on migration to California.

5. **Analyze Leadership** Write a paragraph analyzing President Andrew Jackson's and President Martin Van Buren's leadership before and during the Panic of 1837. Consider what Andrew Jackson did to contribute to the Panic of 1837 and why people blamed Martin Van Buren and his policies for the length and depth of the depression.

6. **Analyze the Indian Removal Act** Write a paragraph analyzing the impact of the Indian Removal Act. Consider the provisions of the Indian Removal Act, what effect the act had on Native Americans living east of the Mississippi River, and the effect Jackson hoped the act would have on the conflict over *Worcester* v. *Georgia*.

7. **Identify the Age of Jackson** Create an oral presentation that identifies events, issues, and other characteristics that made the Age of Jackson a distinct period in U.S. history. Consider political developments such as expanded suffrage and the growth of political parties, political conflicts such as the Nullification Crisis and the conflict over the Second Bank of the United States, and issues surrounding the forced migration of Native Americans living east of the Mississippi River.

8. **Explain the Causes of the Mexican-American War** Write a paragraph explaining the causes of the war between the United States and Mexico. Consider the long-term causes of the war and the immediate causes of the war.

Election of 1828

BRITISH TERRITORY

Claimed by Britain and the United States

Oregon Country (Claimed by Britain and the United States)

Unorganized territory

PACIFIC OCEAN

MEXICO

New Hampshire
Vermont
Maine
L. Superior
Michigan Territory
L. Michigan
L. Huron
L. Ontario
L. Erie
New York
Massachusetts
Rhode Island
Connecticut
Pennsylvania
New Jersey
Ohio
Delaware
Indiana
Maryland
Illinois
Virginia
Missouri
Kentucky
North Carolina
Tennessee
Arkansas Territory
South Carolina
Alabama
Georgia
ATLANTIC OCEAN
Mississippi
Louisiana
Florida Territory
Gulf of Mexico

0 ——— 400 mi
0 ——— 400 km
Albers Conic Equal-Area Projection

KEY
Andrew Jackson
John Quincy Adams

9. **Describe Expanded Suffrage** Use the map above and other sources to write a paragraph describing the role increased suffrage played in Andrew Jackson's victory in the presidential election of 1828 and how his election led to the growth of Jacksonian democracy during the Age of Jackson. Explain what the map indicates about which parts of the country supported Andrew Jackson in the election, describe how changes in suffrage help explain what the map shows about voting patterns, and describe the impact of Jackson's election on the spread of Jacksonian democracy.

10. **Analyze the Impact of Transportation Systems** Write a paragraph analyzing how the Erie Canal and other canal systems contributed to the growth and development of the United States. Consider how the Erie Canal influenced the building of more canals, how these canal systems contributed to economic development, and how these canal systems contributed to the population growth.

11. **Explain States' Rights** Write a paragraph explaining how the issue of states' rights affected the nation during the Age of Jackson. Define states' rights, explain

why many southerners supported states' rights, and summarize how and why the principle of states' rights divided the nation and threatened conflict.

12. **Explain the Constitutional Issues in the Nullification Crisis** Write a paragraph explaining the constitutional arguments for and against the idea that states' rights include nullification of federal laws. Explain John C. Calhoun's point of view on these issues and how Daniel Webster's point of view differed from Calhoun's.

13. **Explain the Roots of Manifest Destiny** Write a paragraph explaining the roots of Manifest Destiny. Explain what *Manifest Destiny* means and describe its social, economic, and political roots.

14. **Write about the Essential Question** Write an essay on the Essential Question: Why do people move? Use evidence from your study of this topic to support your answer.

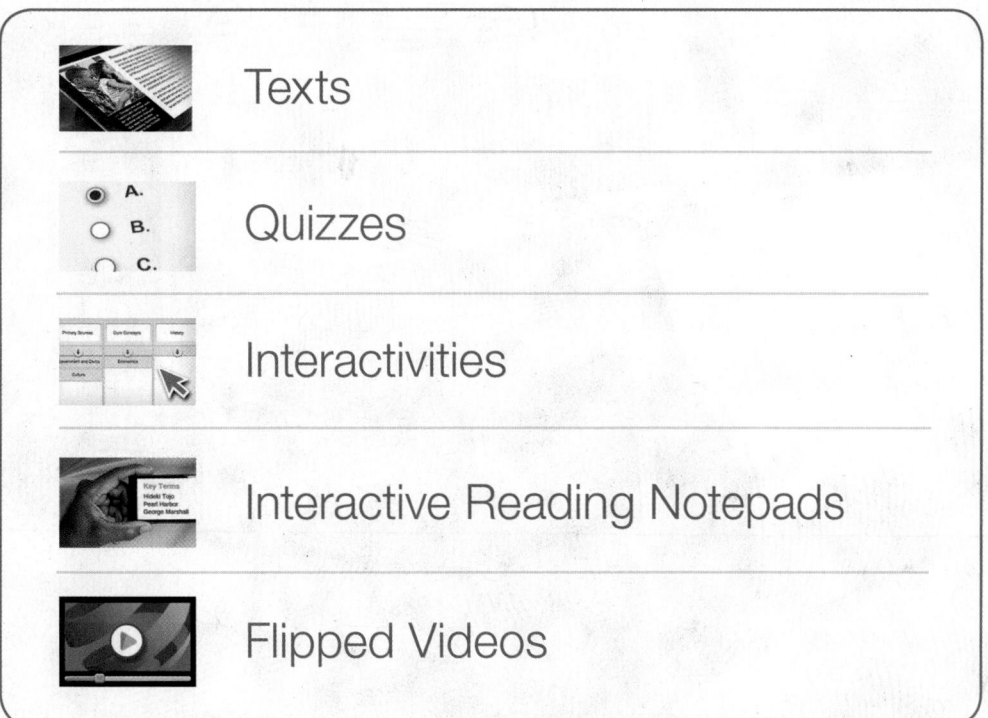

PEARSON
realize™

www.PearsonRealize.com
Access your Digital Lesson

Go online to PearsonRealize.com and use the texts, quizzes, interactivities, Interactive Reading Notepads, Flipped Videos, and other resources from this Topic to prepare for the Topic Test.

Texts

Quizzes

Interactivities

Interactive Reading Notepads

Flipped Videos

While online you can also check the progress you've made learning the topic and course content by viewing your grades, test scores, and assignment status.

[**ESSENTIAL QUESTION**] Why is culture important?

7 Society and Culture Before the Civil War (1820–1860)

>> Young women working in a Massachusetts textile mill in the mid-1800s

Enduring Understandings

- During the early 1800s, the Industrial Revolution brought urban and economic growth to the North.

- Plantation agriculture and slave labor dominated the economy of the South, with cotton the leading crop.

- Reform movements aimed to improve society.

- African Americans and some northern whites pushed for abolition, or an end to slavery.

- Women's rights leaders organized a movement calling for greater rights for women.

- American arts, music, and literature drew inspiration from the natural world and culture of the young United States.

PEARSON realize ® NBC LEARN

Watch the My Story Video to learn about the life of Lucy Larcom, a girl who went to work in a Massachusetts textile mill at the age of 11.

PEARSON realize
www.PearsonRealize.com

Access your digital lessons including:
Topic Inquiry • Interactive Reading
Notepad • Interactivities • Assessments

The Industrial Revolution and Life in the North

>> Work in the textile mills in the early 1800s, such as the one shown here, was hard and dangerous. Workers faced long hours on their feet amid noisy machines and a risk of being caught and injured by moving parts.

▶ Interactive Flipped Video

>> Objectives

Identify the Industrial Revolution and explain its effects.

Explain the impact of the Industrial Revolution on cities.

Describe how technological change affected the economy of the North.

Identify the impact of the Industrial Revolution on working conditions, social class, and daily life.

>> Key Terms

Industrial Revolution
spinning jenny
capital
capitalist
factory system
interchangeable
  parts
Lowell girls
urbanization
locomotive
clipper ship
trade union
strike
nativist

Know-Nothing party
demand
supply
scarcity
credit
profit

In the early 1800s, busy factories and whirring machinery were part of a revolution that was reaching the United States. Unlike the American Revolution, this one had no battles or fixed dates. The new revolution—the **Industrial Revolution**—was a long, slow process that completely changed the way goods were produced and where many people worked and lived.

The Industrial Revolution Begins

Before the 1800s, most Americans were farmers and most goods were produced by hand. As a result of the Industrial Revolution, this situation slowly changed. Machines replaced hand tools. New sources of power, such as steam, replaced human and animal power. While most Americans continued to farm for a living, the economy began a gradual shift toward manufacturing.

New Ways of Making Products The Industrial Revolution started in Britain in the mid-1700s. British inventors developed new machines that transformed the textile industry.

Since the Middle Ages, workers had used spinning wheels to make thread. A spinning wheel, however, could spin only one thread at a time. In 1764, James Hargreaves developed the **spinning jenny**, a machine that could spin several threads at once. Other inventions speeded up the process of weaving thread into cloth. In the 1780s, Edmund Cartwright built a loom powered by water. It allowed a worker to produce a great deal more cloth in a day than was possible before. These technological innovations would change how goods were made not only in Britain, but also in America and around the world.

The Factory System New inventions led to a new system of producing goods. Before the Industrial Revolution, most spinning and weaving took place in the home. Industrial production involved large machines, however, and these had to be housed in large mills near rivers. Water flowing downstream or over a waterfall turned a wheel that captured the power to run the machines.

To set up and operate a spinning mill required large amounts of **capital**, or invested money. Capitalists supplied this money. A **capitalist** is a person who invests in a business in order to make a **profit**, or the difference between the cost of a good and its selling price. Capitalists built factories and hired workers to run the machines.

The new **factory system** brought workers and machinery together in one place to produce goods. Factory workers earned daily or weekly wages. They had to work a set number of hours each day.

In Britain, investors saw an opportunity. Because a single worker could produce much more with a machine than by hand, the cost of goods made by machine was much lower.

As a result, more of those goods could be sold. If an investor built a factory that

>> Lucy Larcom wrote about her experience as a girl working in the textile mills in Lowell, Massachusetts. **Identify Cause and Effect** How did the Industrial Revolution affect women?

could produce cloth more cheaply, the investor could make a profit. Investors' desire to make a profit brought about rapid industrialization.

During the Industrial Revolution, the demand for factory-made products grew. In economics, **demand** is the readiness of people to purchase goods or services. The **supply**, or amount of goods available to sell, depended in part on the natural resources factories could get. To make products, factories needed raw materials, power, and laborers to run machinery. Some resources, such as cotton and iron, were in short supply. This **scarcity**, or limited supply, resulted in high prices. In response to high prices, farmers began to grow more cotton to supply spinning mills. Miners and others searched for new sources of iron and other materials used in machinery. The growing demand for products and for the supplies needed to make them led to a great change in standards of living.

❓ **GENERATE EXPLANATIONS** How did the Industrial Revolution affect the forces of supply and demand?

Factories Come to America

Britain wanted to keep its technological innovations, or new technologies, secret. It did not want rival nations to copy the new machines. Therefore, the British Parliament passed a law forbidding anyone to take plans of the new machinery out of the country.

Slater Emigrates to the United States

Samuel Slater soon proved that this law could not be enforced. Slater was a skilled mechanic in a British textile mill. He knew that his knowledge and skills would be in demand in the United States. In 1789, Slater boarded a ship bound for New York City. British officials searched the baggage of passengers sailing to the United States to make sure they were not carrying plans for machinery with them. Slater, however, did not need to carry any plans. Having worked in the British mills from an early age, Slater knew not only how to build the mills and machinery, but also how to operate them.

The First American Mill Slater soon visited Moses Brown, a Quaker capitalist who had a mill in Pawtucket, Rhode Island. The mill was not doing well because its machinery constantly broke down. Slater set to work on improving the machinery. By 1793, in Pawtucket, he built what became the first successful textile mill in the United States that was powered by water. Slater's wife, Hannah Slater, contributed to the success

>> Samuel Slater had to memorize plans for the design of water-powered factories in order to bring the plans to America without being stopped by British officials.

▶ **Interactive 3-D Model**

>> This diagram of a watch shows interchangeable parts. Using interchangeable parts made it possible to make goods much more quickly and easily than crafting each part separately for each watch.

of the mill. She discovered how to make thread stronger so that it would not snap on the spindles.

Slater's factory was a huge success. Before long, other American manufacturers began using his ideas.

Interchangeable Parts American manufacturers also benefited from the pioneering work of American inventor Eli Whitney. Earlier, skilled workers made goods by hand. For example, gunsmiths spent days making the barrel, stock, and trigger for a single musket. Because the parts were handmade, each musket differed a bit from every other musket. If a part broke, a gunsmith had to make a new part to fit that particular gun.

Whitney wanted to speed up the making of guns by having machines manufacture each part. All machine-made parts would

be alike—for example, one trigger would be identical to another. Identical parts would fit together with all other parts, and gunsmiths would not have build each gun from scratch. **Interchangeable parts** would save time and money.

Because the government bought many guns, Whitney went to Washington, D.C., to try to sell his idea. At first, officials laughed at his plan. Carefully, Whitney sorted parts for 10 muskets into separate piles. He then asked an official to choose one part from each pile. In minutes, the first musket was assembled. Whitney repeated the process until 10 muskets were complete.

The idea of interchangeable parts spread rapidly. Inventors designed machines to produce interchangeable parts for clocks, locks, and many other goods. With such machines, small workshops grew into factories.

The Spread of Factories The War of 1812 provided a boost to American industries. The British blockade cut Americans off from their supply of foreign goods. As a result, they had to produce more goods themselves. American merchants and bankers sought new ways to meet the increased demand. To profit from the efficiency provided by manufacturing, they built more factories. As American investors took advantage of new technologies and built more factories, the American economy grew.

Where Factories Were Built The first factories were built where physical features favored them. In Pennsylvania factories used charcoal, which could be made from abundant local timber, for power. These factories turned iron ore, which was mined and smelted locally, into machines, tools, and guns.

In New England, textile factories were built alongside the hilly region's numerous falling streams, which provided power for mills. Investors modified the environment by building dams and canals to power the mills. These modifications spurred economic growth. Local wool and cotton from the South provided the raw materials for thread, yarn, and fabric. In Lynn, Massachusetts, businesses systematized shoemaking, starting shoe factories in the early 19th century. The large factories attracted new workers to the town, and the economy grew rapidly. New England became the first region in the United States to develop manufacturing on a wide scale.

The Market Economy and the Industrial Revolution In the United States, the Industrial Revolution took place in a period marked by the growth of a laissez-faire market economy. British restrictions on trade had been lifted. Hamilton's reforms had strengthened the banking system, and banks were able to lend more money. New access to **credit**, or borrowed money, allowed people to start mills and factories in cities and in rural places where swift streams provided power.

These and other businesses operated, for the most part, without much government control. Nor did the government own factories or intervene heavily in the market. The government, however, protected contracts and property. People could buy, sell, or use property as they saw fit.

Most Americans wanted the freedom to try new things. They believed in competition, which encouraged new

>> On May 17, 1792, under a buttonwood tree at 68 Wall Street in New York City, investors signed the Buttonwood Agreement that started the New York Stock Exchange, as shown in this model.

>> As a market economy grew during the Industrial Revolution, investors responded to market forces. They built factories like this one in Pennsylvania to produce goods that were high in demand in the hope of making a profit.

inventions. In 1792, a group of 24 investors started the New York Stock Exchange. This stock market raised private capital to pay for new ventures. Success meant profits and brought new wealth to investors. Profits led to new investment and further economic growth.

Low taxes allowed businesses to hold onto large amounts of capital and use it to expand and create even more wealth. The desire for profit and accumulated wealth sparked new ventures under new investors.

The Role of Market Forces Investors looked to the market to decide where to invest or what businesses to start. In a market economy, goods are bought and sold, and wages are determined, by the market. If a product is in high demand and the supply is limited, the price will be high. Entrepreneurs started businesses to supply high-priced or high-demand products. They abandoned businesses where the demand and price were low.

Workers faced the same market forces. People with skills that were in demand in factories could expect higher wages than those whose skills had less value in the market.

? RECALL How did the British attempt to keep their technological innovations secret?

Daily Life in Factory Towns

Slater and Whitney's innovations were just the first steps in America's Industrial Revolution. During the early 1800s, entire cities began to emerge around factories.

The Lowell Mills During the War of 1812, Francis Cabot Lowell, a Boston merchant,

>> Organized child labor was common during the Industrial Revolution. Many American children worked in factories like the English factory shown here. **Draw Conclusions** Why did reformers begin to speak out against child labor?

found a way to improve on British textile mills. In Britain, one factory spun thread and a second factory wove it into cloth. Why not, Lowell wondered, combine spinning and weaving under one roof? The new mill that he built in Waltham, Massachusetts, had all the machines needed to turn raw cotton into finished cloth.

After Lowell's death, his partners took on a more ambitious project. They built an entire factory town and named it after him. In 1821, Lowell, Massachusetts, was a village of five farm families.

By 1836, it boasted more than 10,000 people. Visitors to Lowell described it as a model community composed of "small wooden houses, painted white, with green blinds, very neat, very snug, very nicely carpeted."

"Lowell Girls" To work in their new mills, the company hired young women from nearby farms. The **Lowell girls**, as they came to be called, usually worked for a few years in the mills before returning home to marry. These young women, and women like them in other mill towns, made an important economic contribution to American society by providing labor for the Industrial Revolution. Most sent their wages home to their families.

At first, parents hesitated to let their daughters work in the mills. To reassure parents, the company built boardinghouses, or buildings with many shared bedrooms and a kitchen that served meals. The company also made rules to protect the young women.

Although factory work was often tedious, hard, and dangerous, many women valued the economic freedom they got from working in the mills. One worker wrote her sister Sarah back on a farm in New Hampshire:

> Since I have wrote you, another pay day has come around. I earned 14 dollars and a half . . . I like it well as ever and Sarah don't I feel independent of everyone!

— from *Lowell Offering: Writings by New England Mill Women*

In Lowell and elsewhere, mill owners hired mostly women and children. They did this because they could pay women and children half of what they would have had to pay men.

Child Labor Boys and girls as young as seven worked in factories. Small children were especially useful in textile mills because they could squeeze around the large machines to change spindles.

Today, most Americans look upon child labor as cruel. Yet in the 1800s, farm children also worked hard.

Most people did not see much difference between children working in a factory or on a farm. Often, a child's wages were needed to help support the family.

Long Hours Working hours in the mills were long—12 hours a day, 6 days a week. True, farmers also put in long hours. However, farmers worked shorter hours in winter. Mill workers, in contrast, worked nearly the same hours all year round.

In the early 1800s, conditions in American mills were generally much better than in most factories in Europe. As industries grew, however, competition increased and employers took less interest in the welfare of their workers. This eventually led to worse working conditions.

Changes in Home Life The Industrial Revolution had a great impact on home life. As the factory system spread, more family members left the home to earn a living. These changes affected ideas about the role of women. In poorer families, women often had to go out to work. In wealthier families, husbands supported the family while wives stayed at home. For many husbands, having a wife who stayed at home became a sign of success.

? **DRAW CONCLUSIONS** How did competition change working conditions in American mills?

Cities Expand

In 1800, the vast majority of Americans lived in rural areas. During the Industrial Revolution, many people left farms for cities, attracted by the job opportunities to be found in factories. As investors

URBAN GROWTH & INDUSTRIALIZATION

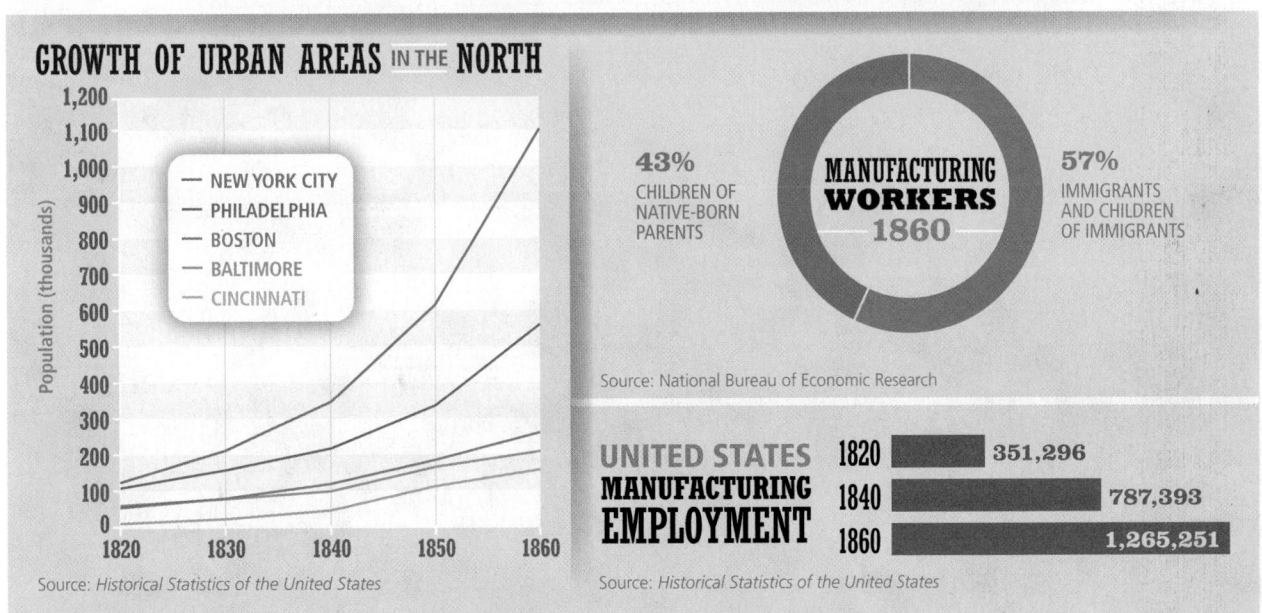

GROWTH OF URBAN AREAS IN THE **NORTH**

- NEW YORK CITY
- PHILADELPHIA
- BOSTON
- BALTIMORE
- CINCINNATI

Population (thousands) / 1820–1860

Source: *Historical Statistics of the United States*

43% CHILDREN OF NATIVE-BORN PARENTS

MANUFACTURING WORKERS 1860

57% IMMIGRANTS AND CHILDREN OF IMMIGRANTS

Source: National Bureau of Economic Research

UNITED STATES MANUFACTURING EMPLOYMENT
1820 — 351,296
1840 — 787,393
1860 — 1,265,251

Source: *Historical Statistics of the United States*

>> **Analyze Graphs** Based on the information in the graphs, what factor best explains the rapid rate of urbanization in northern cities during the mid-1800s?

found that factories produced a profit, they invested those profits in building more factories, which attracted still more workers from farms. Older cities expanded rapidly, while new cities sprang up around factories. This movement of the population from rural areas to cities is called **urbanization**. Urbanization increased as industry grew.

Urbanization was a steady but gradual process. In 1800, only 6 percent of the nation's population lived in urban areas. By 1850, the number had risen to 15 percent. Not until 1920 did more Americans live in cities than in rural areas.

By today's standards, these early cities were small. A person could walk from one end of any American city to the other in as little as 30 minutes. Buildings were only a few stories tall. As the factory system spread, the nation's cities grew.

Hazards of Urbanization Growing cities had many problems. Many of these were negative consequences of human modification of the environment. Dirt and gravel streets turned into mud-holes when it rained. Cities had no sewers, and people threw garbage into the streets. A visitor to New York reported that "The streets are filthy, and the stranger is not a little surprised to meet the hogs walking about in them, for the purpose of devouring the vegetables and trash thrown into the gutter."

Untreated sewage and garbage often seeped into wells or flowed into streams and rivers, polluting the water. The contaminated water spread disease. Epidemics of influenza and cholera (KAHL ur uh) raged through cities, killing thousands.

At about the same time, coal became an important source of industrial and

>> This drawing of New York City around 1850 shows the hustle and bustle of city life. The abundance of stores and places for entertainment contributed to the rapid urbanization of northern cities.

home heating power. The smoke and soot from burning coal seriously modified the environment, polluting the air and dirtying cities. It also caused health problems.

Attractions Cities had attractions besides work opportunities. Theaters, museums, and circuses created an air of excitement. In cities, people could shop in fine stores that sold the latest fashions from Europe. Some offered modern "ready-to-wear" clothing. While most women continued to sew their own clothes, many enjoyed visiting hat shops, china shops, shoe stores, and "fancy-goods" stores.

? DESCRIBE What were some drawbacks of urbanization?

New Technologies

Northern industry grew steadily in the mid-1800s. Most northerners still lived on farms. However, more and more of the northern economy began to depend on manufacturing and trade.

The 1800s brought a flood of new inventions in the North. "In Massachusetts and Connecticut," a European visitor exclaimed, "there is not a laborer who has not invented a machine or a tool." Americans of the period were a practical people. Americans, and especially northerners, looked to science for new and useful applications that could be put to work at once. They expected technology to bring economic development and to change the way people lived.

Technology refers to ways of doing things, sometimes involving advanced scientific knowledge, or tools that make use of advanced knowledge. Innovation is coming up with new ways of making or doing things.

>> During the Industrial Revolution, cooking shifted from fireplaces to wood-burning cast-iron stoves like this one. **Draw Conclusions** How did this invention affect the process of cooking food?

New technologies during the colonial period, such as Franklin's lightning rod, had brought limited and modest changes to daily life in America. By comparison, the new technologies of the 1800s transformed how Americans lived and worked.

In 1834, Philo Stewart developed a cast-iron stove small enough for use in an average kitchen. His factory-built wood-burning stove was a great success. About 90,000 were sold. The cast-iron stove was only one sign of the way northern factories were changing the lives of ordinary people.

Joseph Henry, a New Yorker, showed that electric current could be sent through a wire over long distances to ring a bell. His work paved the way for later inventions. Thomas Davenport, a blacksmith, invented a type of electric motor in 1834.

Both inventions were adapted and marketed. Competition among inventors brought about more innovation.

In 1846, Elias Howe patented a sewing machine. A few years later, Isaac Singer improved on Howe's machine. Soon, clothing makers bought hundreds of the new sewing machines. Workers could now make dozens of shirts in the time it took a tailor to sew one by hand.

Farm Machines Some new inventions made work easier for farmers. In 1825, Jethro Wood began the manufacture of an iron plow with replaceable parts. John Deere improved on the idea when he invented a lightweight steel plow. Earlier plows made of heavy iron or wood had to be pulled by slow-moving oxen. A horse could pull a steel plow through a field more quickly.

>> Singer's treadle sewing machine was powered by foot and allowed the seamstress or tailor to sew quickly and evenly.

▶ **Interactive Timeline**

In 1847, Cyrus McCormick opened a factory in Chicago that produced mechanical reapers. The reaper was a horse-drawn machine that mowed wheat and other grains. McCormick's reaper could do the work of five people using hand tools.

Other farm machines followed. There was a mechanical drill to plant grain, a threshing machine to beat grain from its husk, and a horse-drawn hay rake. These machines helped farmers raise more grain with fewer hands. As a result, thousands of farmworkers left the countryside. Some went west to start farms of their own. Others found jobs in new factories in northern cities.

A New Communications System, the Telegraph Samuel F. B. Morse received a patent for a "talking wire," or **telegraph**, in 1844. The telegraph was a device that sent electrical signals along a wire. It was a new technology that was made possible by scientific discoveries about electricity. The signals were based on a code of dots, dashes, and spaces. The dots stood for short tones, the dashes for long tones. Later, this system of dots and dashes became known as the Morse code.

Congress gave Morse funds to run wire from Washington, D.C., to Baltimore. On May 24, 1844, Morse set up his telegraph in the Supreme Court chamber in Washington.

As a crowd of onlookers watched, Morse tapped out a short message: "What hath God wrought!" A few seconds later, the operator in Baltimore tapped back the same message. The telegraph worked!

Morse's invention was an instant success. Telegraph companies sprang up everywhere. Thousands of miles of wire soon stretched across the country.

As a result of the telegraph, news could now travel long distances in a matter of minutes.

The telegraph helped many businesses to thrive. Merchants and farmers could have quick access to information about supply, demand, and prices of goods in different areas of the country. For example, western farmers might learn of a wheat shortage in New York and ship their grain east to meet the demand. The availability of instant information about markets changed the way goods were marketed across the country and contributed to the development of a nationwide market.

The quick and widespread use of the telegraph connected the nation in a completely new way. Almost every American town eventually had a telegraph, providing nearly instant communication from coast to coast. By the late 1850s, a telegraph cable connected the United States with Europe. Just as the telegraph transformed national marketing, it also helped change the way goods were marketed internationally.

Not only commerce and industry benefited from the telegraph, but ordinary people could communicate quickly with distant family and friends. The presence of telegraph offices in cities and towns was yet another of the many attractions that helped drive urbanization. The telegraph is an example of how scientific discoveries influenced daily life during the 1800s.

❓ **INFER** How did the invention of new farm machines contribute to urbanization in the North?

>> To send messages, Morse's telegraph required that distant locations be connected by wires, as shown in this illustration. **Identify Cause and Effect** How did the telegraph affect Americans' ability to communicate?

>> This telegraph key sent electrical impulses down a wire. Receivers at distant locations allowed operators to hear the impulses, which made up a message.

The Age of Steam Power

At first, railroads were used to provide transportation to canals. In time, however, the railroad became a more practical means of transportation than canals. The first railroads were built in the early 1800s. Horses or mules pulled cars along wooden rails covered with strips of iron. Then, in 1829, an English family developed a steam-powered **locomotive** engine to pull rail cars. The engine, called the Rocket, barreled along at 30 miles per hour.

Early Difficulties Not all Americans welcomed the new railroads. Workers who moved freight on horse-drawn wagons feared that they would lose their jobs. People who had invested in canals worried that competition from the railroads might cause them to lose their investments.

>> This engraving shows an early steam-powered locomotive. The steam-powered locomotive was the main way to travel and ship goods across America by the mid-1800s.

▶ **Interactive Gallery**

There were problems with the early railroads. They were not always safe or reliable. Soft roadbeds and weak bridges often led to accidents. Locomotives often broke down. Even when they worked, their smokestacks belched thick black smoke and hot embers. The embers sometimes burned holes in passengers' clothing or set nearby buildings on fire.

Part of the problem was the way in which railroads were built. Often, instead of two tracks being laid—one for each direction—only one was set. Signals to control traffic on a single track did not yet exist. This increased the likelihood of a collision.

Another problem with early railroads was that there was no standard gauge, or distance between the rails. As a result, different railroads often used different gauges. To transfer from one railroad line to another, people and goods had to be moved off one train and then loaded onto another.

A Railroad Boom Gradually, railroad builders overcame problems and removed obstacles. Engineers learned to build sturdier bridges and solid roadbeds. They replaced wooden rails with iron rails. Railroads developed signaling systems and agreed on a standard gauge. Such improvements made railroad travel safer and faster.

By the 1850s, railroads crisscrossed the nation. The major lines were concentrated in the North and West. New York, Chicago, and Cincinnati became major rail centers. The South had much less track than the North.

Railroads played an important role in urban growth. Cities with good rail connections attracted factories and other businesses. Railroads also made it possible

>> The broad sail area of clipper ships like the one shown here made them the fastest ships available for ocean transport until the development of steam-powered oceangoing ships in the 1850s.

for people to migrate more easily to new cities, increasing urban populations.

Yankee Clippers Railroads increased commerce within the United States. At the same time, trade also increased between the United States and other nations. At seaports in the Northeast, captains loaded their ships with cotton, fur, wheat, lumber, and tobacco. Then, they sailed to other parts of the world.

Speed was the key to successful trade at sea. In 1845, an American named John Griffiths launched the *Rainbow*, the first of the **clipper ships**. These sleek vessels had tall masts and huge sails that caught every gust of wind. Their narrow hulls clipped swiftly through the water. These new technologies gave up cargo space for speed, which gave American merchants an advantage.

In the 1840s, American clipper ships broke every speed record. One clipper ship sped from New York to Hong Kong in 81 days, flying past older ships that took many months to reach China. The speed of the clippers helped the United States win a large share of the world's sea trade in the 1840s and 1850s.

The golden age of clipper ships was brief. In the 1850s, Britain launched the first oceangoing iron steamships. These sturdy vessels carried more cargo and traveled even faster than clippers.

The Effects of New Technologies In the late 1700s and early 1800s, scientists and inventors had found ways to harness heat, in the form of steam, to power machines. By the 1830s, factories began to use steam power instead of water power. Machines that were driven by steam were powerful and cheap to run. Also, factories that

Expansion of U.S. Railroads, 1850–1860

KEY
— Railroads 1850
— Railroads 1850–1860

>> **Analyze Maps** Based on the information in the map, how might the growth of railroads between 1850 and 1860 have affected the development of industry in the United States?

used steam power could be built almost anywhere, not just along the banks of swift-flowing rivers. As a result, American industry expanded rapidly.

At the same time, new machines made it possible to produce more goods at a lower cost. These more affordable goods attracted eager buyers. Families no longer had to make clothing and other goods in their homes. Instead, they could buy factory-made products.

The Impact of Railroads Railroads allowed factory owners to transport large amounts of raw materials and finished goods cheaply and quickly. Also, as railroads stretched across the nation, they linked distant towns with cities and factories. These towns became new markets for factory goods. Railroads greatly increased the size of the American

marketplace and fueled even more factory production.

The growth of railroads also affected northern farming. Railroads brought cheap grain and other foods from the West to New England. New England farmers could not compete with this new source of cheap foods. Many left their farms to find new jobs in towns and cities as factory workers, store clerks, and sailors.

Rising Standards of Living The early rise of industrialization in the United States under a market economy brought striking economic and social benefits. Mass production lowered prices and raised Americans' purchasing power and standard of living. Wages increased for average workers. Food canned in factories improved peoples' year-round diets.

The use of stoves improved meals and home heating. Factory-made clothing was cheaper than homemade. Great numbers of newspapers and magazines reported regularly about the new inventions and advertised the new products. Along with these changes, though, there were also challenges.

? DRAW CONCLUSIONS What was the principal advantage of steam power over water power?

Workers Respond to Challenges

Factories of the 1840s and 1850s were very different from the mills of the early 1800s. As industrialization grew, life changed for workers. The factories were larger, and they used steam-powered machines. Laborers worked longer hours for lower wages. Usually, workers lived in dark, dingy houses in the shadow of the factory.

Changing Roles The emphasis on mass production changed the way workers felt about their jobs. Before the growth of factories, skilled workers, or **artisans**, were proud of the goods they made. The factory owner, however, was more interested in how much could be produced than in how well it was made. Workers could not be creative. Furthermore, unlike the artisan who could have his or her own business, the factory worker was not likely to rise to a management position.

Families in Factories As the need for workers increased, entire families labored in factories. In some cases, a family agreed to work for one year. If even one family member broke the contract, the entire family might be fired.

The factory day began when a whistle sounded at 4 A.M. The entire family—father, mother, and children—headed off to work.

Many factories, at that time, employed young children. The workday did not end until 7:30 P.M., when a final whistle sent the workers home.

Hazards at Work Factory workers faced discomfort and danger. Few factories had windows or heating systems. In summer, the heat and humidity inside the factory were stifling. In winter, the extreme cold contributed to frequent sickness.

Factory machines had no safety devices, and accidents were common. There were no laws regulating factory conditions, and injured workers often lost their jobs.

Trade Unions and Strikes Poor working conditions and low wages led workers to organize into groups to improve their conditions. The first workers to organize were artisans. In the 1820s and 1830s, artisans in each trade united to form **trade**

>> With the emphasis on mass production in the mid-1800s, workers like the ones in this rubber processing factory worked long hours for low wages.

unions. Trade unions were part of a labor reform movement.

The concentration of workers in cities helped the formation of unions by allowing people working in the same industry for different companies to organize together. Their trade unions called for a shorter workday, higher wages, and better working conditions. Sometimes, unions went on strike to gain their demands. In a **strike**, union workers refuse to do their jobs until managers agree to address their concerns.

In the early 1800s, strikes were illegal in many parts of the United States. Strikers faced fines or jail sentences. Employers often fired strike leaders. Employers were politically opposed to workers organizing.

Progress for Artisans Slowly, however, the labor reform movement made progress. In 1840, President Van Buren approved a ten-

>> As working conditions in factories worsened during the 1800s, workers, such as this group of women and their supporters in Lynn, Massachusetts, demanded reduced working hours and better pay.

hour workday for government employees. Workers celebrated another victory in 1842 when a Massachusetts court declared that they had the right to strike.

Artisans won better pay because factory owners needed their skills. Unskilled workers, however, were unable to bargain for better wages since their jobs required little or no training. Because these workers were easy to replace, employers did not listen to their demands.

During the Industrial Revolution, a new awareness of class differences began to emerge. As a farming people, Americans had long viewed labor with deep respect. The changing conditions of factory labor and the gaps between the wages of unskilled workers, managers, and business owners led to a sense of people grouped in classes with shared interests. The interests of these classes were often different. By bringing together workers and managers in the same factories and cities, urbanization led to a rise in conflicts resulting from differences in social class.

Women Workers Organize The success of trade unions encouraged other workers to organize. Workers in New England textile mills were especially eager to protest cuts in wages and unfair work rules. Many of these workers were women.

Women workers faced special problems. First, they had always earned less money than men did. Second, most union leaders did not want women in their ranks. Like many people at the time, they believed that women should not work outside the home. In fact, the goal of many unions was to raise men's wages so that their wives could leave their factory jobs.

Despite these problems, women workers organized. They staged several strikes at Lowell, Massachusetts, in the 1830s. In the

>> This scene shows immigrants landing in New York City in the 1850s. Many immigrants had little money when they first arrived in the United States and had to remain in the cities where they disembarked.

1840s, Sarah Bagley organized the Lowell Female Labor Reform Association. The group petitioned the state legislature for a ten-hour workday.

? **DRAW CONCLUSIONS** Why could artisans command higher wages while other workers could not?

Ethnic Minorities in the North

By the late 1840s, many factory workers in the North were immigrants. An immigrant is a person who enters a new country in order to settle there. In the 1840s and 1850s, about 4 million immigrants arrived in the United States. They were attracted, in large part, by the opportunities for farming the land or working in the cities. Among them were immigrants from Britain who came to

earn higher wages. There was a greater demand in the United States for skilled machinists, carpenters, and miners.

From Ireland and Germany In the 1840s, a disease destroyed the potato crop in Ireland, which was the main food of the poor people. Other crops, such as wheat and oats, were not affected. At the time, Ireland was under British rule and most Irish crops were exported to England. When a large part of the potato crop was lost to disease, British landowners continued to ship the wheat and oats to England. There was little left for the Irish to eat. This situation caused a **famine**, or severe food shortage. Thousands of people died of starvation. Nearly as many died from disease. Between 1845 and 1860, over 1.5 million Irish fled to the United States seeking freedom from hunger and British rule.

Meanwhile, many Germans were also arriving in the United States. Harsh weather conditions from 1829 to 1830 resulted in severe food shortages in Germany. By 1832, more than 10,000 Germans were coming to the United States in a single year seeking fertile land to farm and a better life. In 1848, revolutions had broken out in several parts of Germany. The rebels fought for democratic reforms. When the revolts failed, thousands had to flee. Attracted by its democratic political system, many came to the United States.

Many other German immigrants came simply to make a better life for themselves. Between 1848 and 1860, nearly one million Germans arrived in the United States.

Enriching the Nation Immigrants supplied much of the labor that helped the nation's economy grow. Although most of the Irish

immigrants had been farmers, few had money to buy farmland. Many settled in the northern cities where low-paying factory jobs were available. Other Irish workers transformed the environment by helping to build many new canals and railroads. Irish women often worked as servants in private homes.

Immigrants from Germany often had enough money to move west and buy good farmland. These immigrants transfomed the environment by turning prairie into farmland. Others were artisans and merchants. Cities of the Midwest such as St. Louis, Milwaukee, and Cincinnati had German grocers, butchers, and bakers.

A small minority of the immigrants from Germany were Jewish. German Jews began immigrating to the United States in the 1820s. By the early 1860s, there were about 150 communities in the United States with substantial Jewish populations.

Most Irish immigrants and many German immigrants were Catholic. By contrast, most Americans in the early 1800s were Protestant. Because many immigrants, especially from Ireland, were drawn to America's growing cities, the process of urbanization led to an increase in both ethnic and religious diversity.

A Reaction Against Immigrants
Not everyone welcomed the flood of immigrants. One group of Americans, called **nativists**, wanted to preserve the country for native-born, white citizens. Using the slogan "Americans must rule America," they called for laws to limit immigration. They also wanted to keep immigrants from voting until they had lived in the United States for 21 years. At the time, newcomers could vote after only 5 years in the country.

>> Millard Fillmore, a former President who had been a member of the Whig Party, ran for President again in 1856 as a member of the Know-Nothing Party, supporting an "Americans First" policy that opposed Catholics and immigrants.

Some nativists protested that newcomers "stole" jobs from native-born Americans because they worked for lower pay. Furthermore, when workers went out on strike, factory owners often hired immigrant workers to replace them. Many distrusted the different language, customs, and dress of the immigrants. Others blamed immigrants for the rise in crime in the growing cities. Still others mistrusted Irish newcomers because many of them were Catholics. Until the 1840s, the majority of immigrants from Europe had been Protestants. As American cities attracted Catholic immigrants, these cities became centers of conflicts over religion.

By the 1850s, hostility to immigrants was so strong that nativists formed a new political party. Members of the party were anti-Catholic and anti-immigrant. Many meetings and rituals of the party were kept secret. It was called the **Know-Nothing party** because members answered, "I know nothing," when asked about the party. The message of the party did gain supporters, but its support was limited to the North, where most immigrants settled. In 1856, Millard Fillmore, the Know-Nothing candidate for President won 21 percent of the popular vote. Soon after, however, the party died out.

In time, conflicts between ethnic groups were resolved as immigrants or their children became part of American society. Also, different ethnic groups became incorporated into the nation's political fabric as political parties, particularly the Democratic Party, began to speak for their interests.

African Americans Face Discrimination

During the nation's early years, slavery was legal in the North. By the early 1800s, however, all of the northern states had

>> The African Meeting House on Beacon Hill in Boston is the oldest standing black church in the United States.

passed laws to bring an end to slavery. In some states, only the children of slaves gained freedom at first. Many did not completely abolish slavery until the mid-1800s. Still, thousands of free African Americans lived in the North, and their number grew steadily during the early 1800s.

Free African Americans in the North faced discrimination. **Discrimination** is a policy or an attitude that denies equal rights to certain groups of people. As one writer pointed out, African Americans were denied "the ballot-box, the jury box, the halls of the legislature, the army, the public lands, the school, and the church."

Even skilled African Americans had trouble finding good jobs. One black woodworker was turned away by every furniture maker in Cincinnati. At last, a shop owner hired him. However, when he

>>Despite discrimination, some free African Americans such as William Whipper beat the odds to become successful. He used his wealth to fight slavery.

fact, some northern African Americans achieved notable success in business. William Whipper grew wealthy as the owner of a lumberyard in Pennsylvania. He devoted much of his time and money to fighting slavery. Henry Boyd operated a profitable furniture company in Cincinnati.

African Americans made strides in other areas as well. Henry Blair invented a corn planter and a cottonseed planter.

In 1845, Macon Allen became the first African American licensed to practice law in the United States. After graduating from Bowdoin College in Maine, John Russwurm became one of the editors of *Freedom's Journal*, the first African American newspaper.

? RECALL Why did skilled African Americans have trouble finding jobs in the North?

ASSESSMENT

1. **Identify Cause and Effect** How did the War of 1812 affect American manufacturing?

2. **Describe** the workers and working conditions in factories in the mid-1800s.

3. **Generate Explanations** Why did many farmhands leave the countryside to start their own farms or to work in factories?

4. **Summarize** the ways in which the invention of the telegraph changed life in America.

5. **Draw Conclusions** What do the conditions in factories in the mid-1800s suggest about the pros and cons of a laissez-faire market economy?

entered the shop, the other woodworkers dropped their tools. Either he must leave or they would, they declared. Similar experiences occurred throughout the North. In addition, African Americans faced competition from immigrants who settled in northern cities.

Yet Some Find Success Despite such obstacles, free blacks in North had some choice over where they lived and worked, unlike enslaved blacks in the South. In

King Cotton and Life in the South

>>These reconstructed slave cabins in Louisiana, which would have housed up to two families of enslaved African Americans each, appear as they would have on plantations in the mid-1800s.

▶ Interactive Flipped Video

During the 1800s, cotton continued to grow in importance in the South. It was so profitable, southerners did not even feel a need to invest in factories. Even though southerners grew other crops, cotton remained the region's leading export. Cotton plantations—and the slave system on which they depended—shaped the way of life in the South.

>> **Objectives**

Identify how the development of the cotton gin affected the South.

Describe the agricultural economy of the South.

Describe southern society.

Compare the economic, social, and political conditions of free and enslaved African Americans.

Explain the impact of slavery.

>> **Key Terms**

boom
cultivate
cottonocracy
slave codes
extended family

>> This photograph shows a boll of cotton on a cotton plant. Before the invention of the cotton gin, workers had to separate the seeds of picked cotton from the fibers by hand. This work was very time consuming.

The Cotton Kingdom

The Industrial Revolution greatly increased the demand for southern cotton. Textile mills in the North and in Britain needed more and more cotton to make cloth. At first, southern planters could not meet the demand. They could grow plenty of cotton because the South's soil and climate were ideal. However, removing the seeds from the cotton by hand was a slow process. Planters needed a better way to clean cotton.

Eli Whitney Invents the Cotton Gin

Eli Whitney, a young Connecticut schoolteacher, was traveling to Georgia in 1793. He was going to be a tutor on a plantation. At that time, there were few public schools in the South. When Whitney learned of the planters' problem, he decided to build a machine to clean cotton.

In only 10 days, Whitney came up with a model. His cotton engine, or gin, had two rollers with thin wire teeth. When cotton was swept between the rollers, the teeth separated the seeds from the fibers.

This machine had an enormous effect on the southern economy. A single worker using a cotton gin could do the work of 50 people cleaning cotton by hand. Because of the gin, planters could now grow cotton at a huge profit. As a result, this new technology brought economic growth.

Cotton Kingdom and Slavery The cotton gin led to a **boom**, or swift growth, in cotton production. In 1792, planters grew only 6,000 bales of cotton a year. By 1850, the figure was over 2 million bales.

There was not enough farmland suitable for growing cotton in the original southern states along the Atlantic coast to meet the demand. Cotton farmers needed new land to **cultivate**, or prepare for planting.

>> Workers fed cotton bolls through the gin's teeth and barbed roller to separate out the seeds and straighten the fibers. Using the gin, workers could produce much more cotton in a day. **Predict Consequences** How would this invention affect the demand for slaves?

▶ **Interactive 3-D Model**

After the War of 1812, cotton planters began to move west. They brought enslaved African Americans with them. The huge demand for cotton, the efficiency offered by cotton gins, and southern planters reliance on slave labor led to the growth of large plantations, each with many enslaved workers.

By the 1850s, there were cotton plantations extending in a belt from South Carolina to Texas. This area of the South became known as the Cotton Kingdom. Physical aspects of the environment in this part of the South, including rich soils, warm temperatures, and abundant rainfall, encouraged an economy focused on cotton farming.

Tragically, as the Cotton Kingdom spread, so did slavery. Even though cotton could now be cleaned by machine, it still had to be planted and picked by hand. The result was a cruel cycle in which slave labor brought profits to planters, who then used the profits to buy more land and more enslaved workers.

? GENERATE EXPLANATIONS How did the invention of the cotton gin lead to an increase in slavery in the South?

Reliance on Agriculture

Cotton was the South's most profitable cash crop. However, the best soils and climate for growing cotton could be found mostly in a belt stretching across inland South Carolina, Georgia, Alabama, Mississippi, Louisiana, and Texas. In other areas of the South, rice, sugar cane, and tobacco were major crops. In addition, southerners raised much of the nation's livestock. The physical geography in different regions of the South influenced what farmers in those regions produced.

Rice was an important crop along the coasts of South Carolina and Georgia. Sugar cane was important in Louisiana and Texas. Growing rice and sugar cane required expensive irrigation and drainage systems and a warm, moist climate, all found mainly along the coasts.

Cane growers also needed costly machinery to grind their harvest. Small-scale farmers could not afford such expensive equipment, however. As a result, rice and sugar farmers relied on the plantation system just as cotton farmers did.

Tobacco had been an export of the South since 1619, and it continued to be planted in Virginia, North Carolina, Tennessee, and Kentucky. However, in the early 1800s, the large tobacco plantations of colonial days had given way to small tobacco farms. On these farms, a few field hands tended five or six acres of tobacco.

>> This print from the 1800s shows the intense physical labor involved in harvesting sugar cane.

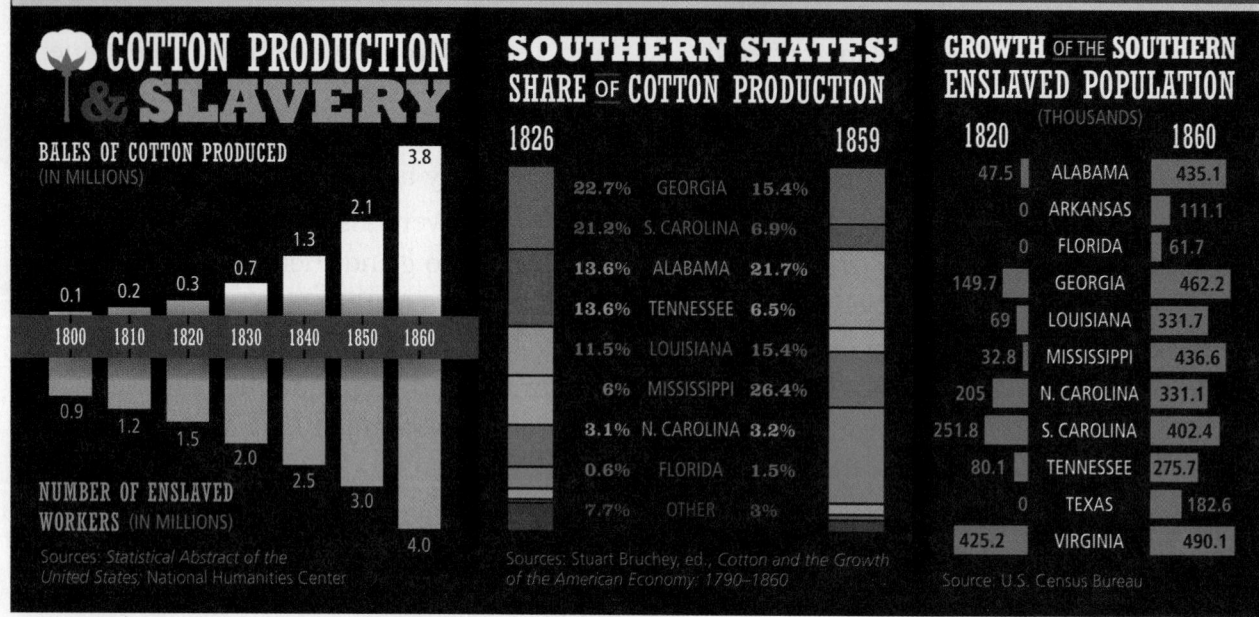

SOUTHERN DEPENDENCE ON AGRICULTURE

COTTON PRODUCTION & SLAVERY

BALES OF COTTON PRODUCED (IN MILLIONS)

1800	1810	1820	1830	1840	1850	1860
0.1	0.2	0.3	0.7	1.3	2.1	3.8

NUMBER OF ENSLAVED WORKERS (IN MILLIONS)

1800	1810	1820	1830	1840	1850	1860
0.9	1.2	1.5	2.0	2.5	3.0	4.0

Sources: *Statistical Abstract of the United States*; National Humanities Center

SOUTHERN STATES' SHARE OF COTTON PRODUCTION

1826	STATE	1859
22.7%	GEORGIA	15.4%
21.2%	S. CAROLINA	6.9%
13.6%	ALABAMA	21.7%
13.6%	TENNESSEE	6.5%
11.5%	LOUISIANA	15.4%
6%	MISSISSIPPI	26.4%
3.1%	N. CAROLINA	3.2%
0.6%	FLORIDA	1.5%
7.7%	OTHER	3%

Sources: Stuart Bruchey, ed., *Cotton and the Growth of the American Economy: 1790–1860*

GROWTH OF THE SOUTHERN ENSLAVED POPULATION (THOUSANDS)

1820	STATE	1860
47.5	ALABAMA	435.1
0	ARKANSAS	111.1
0	FLORIDA	61.7
149.7	GEORGIA	462.2
69	LOUISIANA	331.7
32.8	MISSISSIPPI	436.6
205	N. CAROLINA	331.1
251.8	S. CAROLINA	402.4
80.1	TENNESSEE	275.7
0	TEXAS	182.6
425.2	VIRGINIA	490.1

Source: U.S. Census Bureau

>> **Analyze Data** Based on the information in the graphs and chart, why did the number of slaves in South Carolina increase even though its share of cotton production declined?

In addition to the major cash crops of cotton, rice, sugar, and tobacco, the South also led the nation in livestock production. Southern livestock owners profited from hogs, oxen, horses, mules, and beef cattle. Much of this livestock was raised in areas that were unsuitable for growing crops, such as the pine woods of North Carolina and hilly regions of Georgia, western Virginia, Kentucky, Tennessee, and Arkansas. Kentucky developed a rural economy that included the breeding of horses.

Limited Southern Industry Because the South relied on agriculture, most of the industry in the South remained small and existed only to meet the needs of a farming society. This contrasted with the North, with its increasingly urban society and large and diverse industries. Agricultural tools such as cotton gins, planters, and

plows were manufactured. Factories also made goods such as ironware, hoes, and jute, or hemp cloth, which was used to make bags for holding bales of cotton. Cheap cotton cloth was made for use in enslaved workers' clothing. Some southerners wanted to encourage the growth of industry in the South. William Gregg, for example, modeled his cotton mill in South Carolina on the mills in Lowell, Massachusetts. Gregg built houses and gardens for his paid workers and schools for their children.

The South also developed a few other successful industries. In Richmond, Virginia, for example, the Tredegar Iron Works turned out railroad equipment, machinery, tools, and cannons. Flour milling was another important southern industry.

Even so, the South lagged behind the North in manufacturing. This difference had several causes. Rich planters invested their money in land and in purchasing enslaved African Americans rather than in factories.

Slavery also reduced the need for southern industry. In the North, most people had enough money to buy factory goods. In the South, however, millions of enslaved African Americans could not buy anything. As a result, the demand for manufactured goods in the South was not as great as it was in the North.

Southern Cities Although the South was mainly rural, there were some cities. The major ones were New Orleans, Louisiana; Charleston, South Carolina; and Richmond, Virginia. These cities had the same problems as northern cities, including poor housing and poor sanitation.

Fewer than 8 percent of white southerners lived in towns of more than 4,000 people. However, many free African Americans lived in towns and cities.

Economically Dependent The South's lack of industry had a number of effects on the South. Because there were few industrial jobs, small farmers in the South had few ways to escape the poverty of life on a small farm, whereas northern farmers could move to cities and take factory jobs. With little industry of its own, the South also came to depend more and more on the North and on Europe. Southern planters often borrowed money from northern banks in order to expand their plantations. They also purchased much of their furniture, farm tools, and machines from northern or European factories.

Many southerners resented this situation. One southerner described a burial to show how the South depended on the North for many goods in the 1850s:

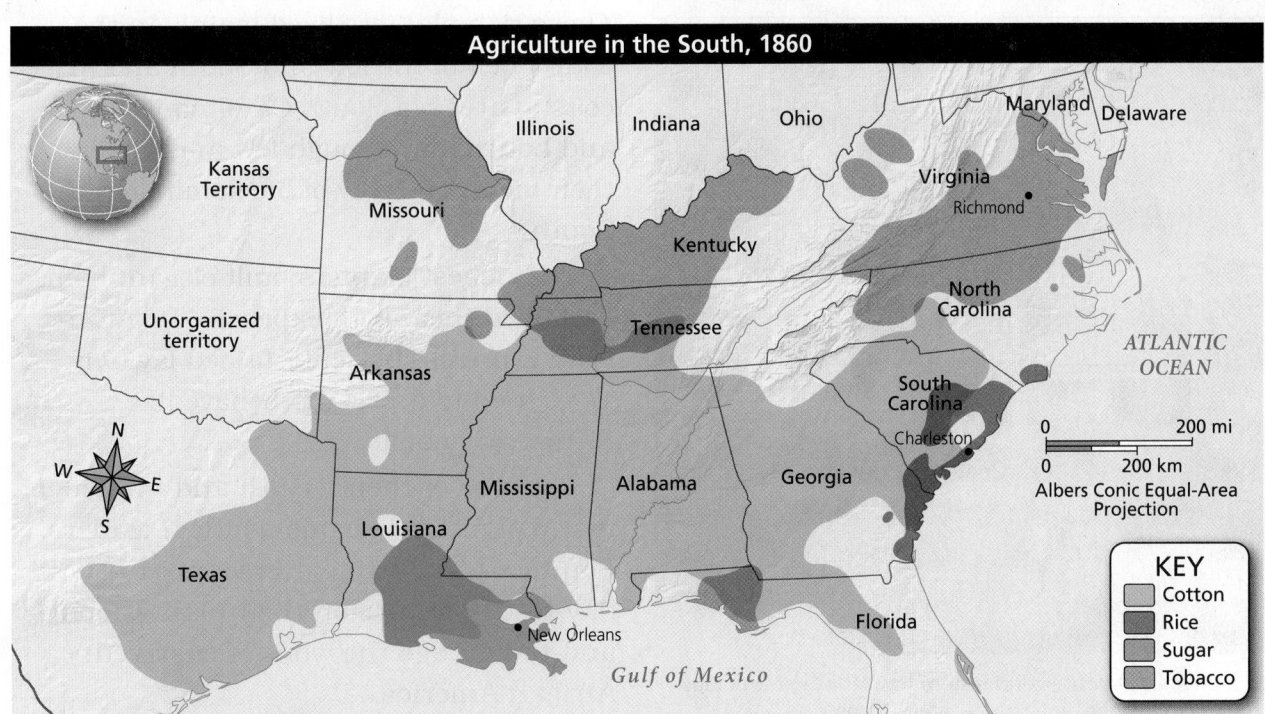

Agriculture in the South, 1860

KEY
Cotton
Rice
Sugar
Tobacco

>> **Analyze Maps** Based on the information in the map, what would you expect to be true about the economies of major Southern cities?

The grave was dug through solid marble, but the marble headstone came from Vermont. It was in a pine wilderness but the pine coffin came from Cincinnati. An iron mountain overshadowed it but the coffin nails and the screws and the shovel came from Pittsburgh. . . . A hickory grove grew nearby, but the pick and shovel handles came from New York. . . . That country, so rich in underdeveloped resources, furnished nothing for the funeral except the corpse and the hole in the ground.

—Henry Grady, Speech to the Bay Street Club, Boston, 1889

Still, most southerners were proud of the booming cotton economy in their region. As long as cotton remained king, southerners

>> Wealthy white southerners lived in elegant homes on plantations, like this plantation home in Mississippi.

▶ **Interactive Chart**

believed, they could look to the future with confidence.

? DRAW CONCLUSIONS Why was the South dependent on the North and Europe for non-agricultural goods?

Southern Whites

The Old South is often pictured as a land of vast plantations worked by hundreds of enslaved African Americans. Such grand estates did exist in the South. However, most white southerners were not rich planters. In fact, most whites owned no enslaved African Americans at all.

The "Cottonocracy" A planter was someone who owned at least 20 enslaved workers. In 1860, only one white southerner in 30 belonged to a planter family. An even smaller number—less than 1 percent— owned 50 or more enslaved workers. These wealthy families were called the **"cottonocracy"** because they made huge amounts of money from cotton. These rich planters lived mainly in the cotton belt of the lowland South and in coastal areas of South Carolina, Georgia, and Louisiana. Though few in number, their views and way of life dominated the South.

The richest planters built elegant homes and filled them with expensive furniture from Europe. They entertained lavishly. They tried to dress and behave like European nobility.

Because of their wealth and influence, many planters became political leaders. Planters hired white overseers to run day-to-day affairs on their plantations and to manage the work of enslaved African Americans.

Small Farmers About 75 percent of southern whites were small farmers. These "plain folk" owned the land they farmed. They might also own one or two enslaved African Americans. Unlike planters, plain folk worked with their enslaved workers in the fields. Small farmers could be found in most parts of the South, but their numbers were fewer in the cotton belt and in coastal regions where plantation agriculture was dominant.

Among small farmers, helping one another was an important duty. "People who lived miles apart counted themselves as neighbors," wrote a farmer in Mississippi. "And in case of sorrow or sickness, there was no limit to the service neighbors provided."

>> Many poor whites in the South, such as the farmer shown in this photo, did not own the land they farmed.

Poor Whites Lower on the social ladder were poor whites. These whites did not own enslaved African Americans. Many did not own the land they farmed. Instead, they rented it, often paying the owner with part of their crop. Many barely made a living.

Poor whites often lived in the hilly, wooded areas of the upland South, north and west of the cotton belt. They planted crops such as corn, potatoes, and other vegetables. They also herded cattle and pigs. Poor whites had hard lives, but they enjoyed rights that were denied to all black people, enslaved or free.

Comparing Northern and Southern Whites Like northern whites, most southern whites were farmers. Most white farmers in both regions were small farmers. However, there were important differences in the white populations of the two regions. In the South, the wealthiest whites were planters who made their money from the work of enslaved African Americans. In the North, the wealthiest whites were capitalists who made their money from investing in industry. There were many white industrial workers and middle class people living in cities in the North. Relatively few southerners of any class lived in cities.

? RECALL Who made up the "cottonocracy" in the Old South?

Southern African Americans

Both free and enslaved African Americans lived in the South. Their legal and political conditions were different. Although free under the law and with certain legal rights, free African Americans faced harsh discrimination. Enslaved African Americans had no rights at all.

>> In the early 1800s, free African Americans in the South often worked as farmers and skilled workers.

Free African Americans Most free African Americans were descendants of enslaved people who were freed during and after the American Revolution. Others had bought their freedom. In 1860, over 200,000 free blacks lived in the South. Most lived in Maryland and Delaware, where slavery was in decline. Others lived in cities such as New Orleans, Richmond, and Charleston.

Many free African Americans reached an impressive level of success. Working as farmers, laborers, and artisans, such as blacksmiths, carpenters, and cobblers, they contributed to and influenced southern life. Some owned and operated businesses, such as inns and barbershops. A few became large plantation owners, growing cotton and owning enslaved workers.

White slave owners did not like free African Americans living in the South. They feared that free African Americans set a dangerous example, encouraging enslaved African Americans to rebel. Also, slave owners justified slavery by claiming that African Americans could not take care of themselves. Free African Americans proved this idea wrong.

To discourage free African Americans, southern states passed laws that made life even harder for them. Free African Americans were not allowed to vote or travel. In some southern states, they had to move out of the state or risk the chance of being kidnapped and enslaved.

Despite these limits, free African Americans were able to make a life for themselves and make valuable contributions to southern life. For example, Norbert Rillieux (RIHL yoo) invented a machine that revolutionized the way sugar was refined. Another inventor, Henry Blair, patented a seed planter.

Enslaved African Americans By 1860, enslaved African Americans made up one third of the South's population. Most worked as field hands on cotton plantations. Both men and women cleared new land and planted and harvested crops. Children helped by pulling weeds, collecting wood, and carrying water to the field hands. By the time they were teenagers, they worked between 12 and 14 hours a day. Daily labor in the fields bound enslaved workers into a community of people who tried to help and protect one another.

On large plantations, some enslaved African Americans had better positions. They might work as household servants or as skilled artisans, such as carpenters and blacksmiths. Such jobs might entitle workers to better food or clothing than field hands. A few enslaved people worked in cities. Their earnings, however, belonged to their owners. Unlike free African Americans, enslaved African Americans could not easily start businesses of their own.

Another major difference between the social circumstances of free and enslaved African Americans was that enslaved African American families could be broken up by their owners, with family members sold separately. While they faced discriminations, free African American families were not forced to separate.

? **COMPARE AND CONTRAST** How was life in the South similar and different for free and enslaved African Americans?

Slavery in the South

The life of enslaved African Americans was determined by strict laws and the practices of individual slave owners. Conditions varied from plantation to plantation. Some owners made sure their enslaved workers had clean cabins, decent food, and warm

>> African Americans enslaved on a plantation load rice onto a barge for transport on the Savannah River.

clothes. Other planters spent as little as possible on their enslaved workers.

Slave Codes Southern states passed laws known as **slave codes** to keep enslaved African Americans from either running away or rebelling. These codes applied to enslaved blacks but not to free blacks. Under the codes, enslaved African Americans were forbidden to gather in groups of more than three.

They could not leave their owner's land without a written pass from their owner. They were not allowed to own guns.

Slave codes also made it a crime for enslaved African Americans to learn how to read and write. Owners hoped that this law would make it hard for African Americans to escape slavery. They reasoned that uneducated enslaved African Americans who escaped their owners would not be able to use maps or read train schedules. They would not be able to find their way north.

Some laws were meant to protect enslaved African Americans, but only from the worst forms of abuse. However, enslaved African Americans did not have the right to testify in court. As a result, they were not able to bring charges against owners who abused them.

Enslaved African Americans had only one real protection against mistreatment. Owners looked on their enslaved workers as valuable property. Most slave owners wanted to keep this human property healthy and productive.

Hard Work Even the kindest owners insisted that their enslaved workers work long, hard days. Enslaved African Americans worked from "can see to can't see," or from dawn to dusk, up to 16 hours a day. Frederick Douglass, who escaped slavery, recalled his life under one harsh master:

> We were worked in all weathers. It was never too hot or too cold; it could never rain, blow, hail, or snow too hard for us to work in the field. Work, work, work. . . . The longest days were too short for him and the shortest nights too long for him.
>
> —Frederick Douglass, *Narrative of the Life of Frederick Douglass, An American Slave*

Family Life It was hard for enslaved African Americans to keep their families together. Southern laws did not recognize slave marriages or slave families. As a result, owners could sell a husband and wife to different buyers. Children were often taken from their parents and sold.

>> Slave owners expected enslaved children to work alongside their parents, such as these children working on a cotton field in Georgia.

▶ **Interactive Chart**

>> Music served as a source of solace and hope for enslaved African Americans. The spiritual is closely associated with the culture of slavery.

On large plantations, many enslaved families did manage to stay together. For those African Americans, the family was a source of strength, pride, and love. Grandparents, parents, children, aunts, uncles, and cousins formed a close-knit group. This idea of an **extended family** had its roots in Africa.

Enslaved African Americans preserved other traditions as well. Parents taught their children traditional African stories and songs. They used folk tales to pass on African history and moral beliefs.

Religion Offers Hope By the 1800s, many enslaved African Americans were devout Christians. Planters often allowed white ministers to preach to their slaves. African Americans also had their own preachers and beliefs.

Religion helped African Americans cope with the harshness of slave life. Bible stories about how the ancient Hebrews had escaped from slavery inspired a new type of religious song called a spiritual. As they worked in the fields, enslaved workers would often sing about a coming day of freedom.

Enslaved African Americans had to be cautious even in their religious practice. While they sang of freedom in spirituals, the words of the spirituals suggested that this freedom would come after death, so as not to alarm slave owners.

? RECALL Why was it difficult for enslaved African Americans to keep their families together?

Resisting Slavery

Enslaved African Americans struck back against the system that denied them both freedom and wages. Some broke tools, destroyed crops, and stole food.

Many enslaved African Americans tried to escape to the North. Because the

>> In 1831, Nat Turner led other enslaved African Americans on a violent campaign against slave owners. In this image, Nat Turner is being captured. **Predict Consequences** How would Turner's rebellion affect the lives of enslaved African Americans who did not rebel?

In 1831, an African American preacher named Nat Turner led a major revolt. An enslaved worker on a plantation in Southampton County, Virginia, Turner believed his mission was to take revenge on plantation owners.

Turner led his followers through Virginia, killing more than 57 whites. For nearly two months terrified whites hunted the countryside looking for Turner. They killed many innocent African Americans before catching and hanging him.

Nat Turner's revolt increased southern fears of an uprising of enslaved African Americans. Revolts were rare, however. Since southern whites were well armed and kept careful track of African Americans, a revolt by African Americans had almost no chance of success.

❓ **DRAW CONCLUSIONS** What do the actions of Denmark Vesey and Nat Turner reveal about the conditions under which enslaved Africans were forced to live?

journey was long and dangerous, very few made it to freedom. Every county had slave patrols and sheriffs ready to question an unknown black person.

In the North, as you will learn, African Americans were able to fight slavery with peaceful means. Because southern laws offered no means to resist slavery, a few African Americans turned to violence to resist the brutal slave system. Denmark Vesey, a free African American, planned a revolt in 1822. Vesey was betrayed before the revolt began. He and 35 other people were executed.

ASSESSMENT

1. **Summarize** the effects of the cotton gin

2. **Identify Central Issues** How did the economy in the South encourage a dependence on slavery that the economy in the North did not?

3. **Generate Explanations** What worried white slave owners about free African Americans living in the South, and what stereotypes did successful African Americans disprove?

4. **Draw Conclusions** Why were so many enslaved African Americans devout Christians?

5. **Check Understanding** Why were slave revolts so dangerous for the slaves who rebelled?

Reform Movements

>> Dorothea Dix's efforts led to growing public awareness of the need to provide services for the mentally disabled, who often spent their lives in badly kept poorhouses or prisons.

Interactive Flipped Video

The period between 1815 and 1860 is sometimes known as the Reform Era in the United States, because there were so many movements for social reform during this period. **Social reform** is an organized attempt to improve what is unjust or imperfect in society. The impulse toward social reform had political, social, and religious causes.

>> **Objectives**

Explain how political and religious trends, including the Second Great Awakening, inspired reform movements.

Describe the impact of movements for temperance and for the reform of mental health care and prisons.

Explain the impact of movements for the reform of education and care for the disabled.

>> **Key Terms**

debtor
temperance
   movement
social reform
predestination
Second Great
   Awakening
revival

PEARSON realize™   www.PearsonRealize.com
Access your Digital Lesson.

An Era of Reform

Political Ideals Lead to Reform As you have read, during the Jacksonian era, politics was becoming more democratic. More people could vote and take part in government than ever before.

Still, some critics said American society was not living up to its ideals. They pointed to the promise of liberty and equality expressed in the Declaration of Independence. A society based on these ideals, they argued, would not allow slavery. Others asked why women had fewer rights than men. By changing such injustices, reformers hoped to move the nation closer to its political ideals.

Social Conditions Call for Reform As you have learned, the Industrial Revolution was changing the American economy and working conditions, especially in the North, and cities were growing rapidly. Crowded cities created new challenges for social well being. At the same time, there was a growing need for an educated workforce. As American society changed, it required new institutions to meet its changing needs.

The Second Great Awakening and Its Causes During the colonial era, many American Protestant Christians believed in **predestination**. According to this idea, God decided in advance which people would attain salvation after death. This belief led many people to worry that they could do nothing to be saved.

During the 1700s, Protestant thinkers in England and the colonies began to argue that salvation depended on a person's actions in this life. Its leaders stressed free will rather than predestination. They taught that individuals could choose to save their souls by their own actions. In the early 1800s, a dynamic religious movement known as the **Second Great Awakening** swept the nation. Arguments by religious thinkers were the main cause

The Reform Movement

Political Origins

- The ideals of liberty and equality in the Declaration of Independence inspire people to try to improve society
- During Jackson era, more people can vote than ever before
- Critics say slavery and other injustices violate democratic ideals

Religious Influences

- Second Great Awakening stresses free will rather than predestination
- Revivals encourage people to reform their lives
- Finney teaches that individual salvation is the first step to the reform of a society

>> **Analyze Charts** Based on the information in the chart, how did the reform movement reflect American culture in the early 1800s?

>> During the Second Great Awakening, preachers like the one at this camp meeting stressed the ability to save one's soul through action. **Identify Central Ideas** How did this teaching influence reform movements in the 1800s?

of this movement. Another cause was the democratic spirit of the Jacksonian era, which encouraged people to think independently and not blindly obey established religious authorities.

To stir religious feelings, preachers held **revivals**, huge outdoor meetings. Revivals might last for days and attract thousands of people. A witness recalled the excitement of a revival at Cane Ridge, Kentucky:

> The vast sea of human beings seemed to be agitated as if by storm. I counted seven ministers all preaching at once. . . . Some of the people were singing, others praying, some crying for mercy.
>
> —James B. Finley, *Autobiography*

One leader of the Second Great Awakening was a minister named Charles Grandison Finney. A powerful speaker,

Finney taught that individual salvation was the first step toward "the complete reformation of the whole world." Such teachings had effects that changed the country, inspiring a number of new social reform movements. Inspired by religion, these social reformers began a lasting tradition in American culture of working to improve society.

? IDENTIFY CENTRAL IDEAS What was the central premise on which the Second Great Awakening rested?

Social Reform Movements

The emphasis the Second Great Awakening placed on improving society inspired many Americans. Women often played a leading role in these reform movements. These Americans launched a number of reform movements, with far-reaching effects on prisons, care of the disabled, education, and attitudes toward slavery.

One of the most vigorous social reformers was Dorothea Dix, a Boston schoolteacher whose strong religious beliefs spurred her to care for those less fortunate. She turned her attention to what one minister called the "outsiders" in society: criminals and the mentally ill.

Reforming Care of the Disabled In 1841, Dix visited a jail for women near Boston. She was outraged to discover that some of the prisoners were not criminals, but mentally ill.

Dix demanded to know why these women were locked in small, dark, unheated cells. The jailer replied that "lunatics" did not feel the cold.

During the next 18 months, Dix visited every jail, poorhouse, and hospital in Massachusetts. Her shocking reports helped persuade state legislators to fund a new mental hospital:

I proceed, gentlemen, briefly to call your attention to the present state of Insane Persons confined . . . in cages, closets, cellars, stalls, pens! Chained, naked, beaten with rods, and lashed into obedience.

—Dorothea Dix, "Memorial to the State Legislators of Massachusetts"

Dix went on to inspect jails as far away as Louisiana and Illinois. Her reports persuaded most legislatures to treat the mentally ill as patients, not criminals.

The Impact of Prison Reform Dix also joined a growing movement to improve conditions in prisons. Men, women, and children were often crammed together in cold, damp rooms. When food supplies were low, prisoners went hungry—unless they had money to buy meals from jailers.

Five out of six people in northern jails were **debtors**, or people who could not pay money they owed. While behind bars, debtors had no way to earn money to pay back their debts. As a result, many debtors remained in prison for years.

Dix and others called for changes in the prison system. As a result, some states built prisons with only one or two inmates to a cell. Cruel punishments were banned, and people convicted of minor crimes received shorter sentences. Slowly, states stopped treating debtors as criminals.

The Impact of the Temperance Movement Alcohol abuse was widespread in the early 1800s. At political rallies, weddings, and funerals, men, women, and

>> **Analyze Political Cartoons** This cartoon shows a tree growing fruits with labels such as "Goodness," "Knowledge," "Morality," and "Patience." How did these "fruits" reflect reformers' hopes for the temperance movement?

sometimes even children drank heavily. Men could buy whiskey in candy stores or barbershops.

The **temperance movement**, a campaign against alcohol abuse, took shape in the late 1820s. Women often took a leading role in the battle. They knew that "demon rum" could lead to the physical abuse of wives and children and the breakup of families.

Some temperance groups urged people to drink less. Others sought to end drinking altogether. They won a major victory in 1851, when Maine banned the sale of alcohol. Eight other states passed "Maine laws." Most states later repealed the laws, but the temperance crusade would gain new strength in the late 1800s.

❓ **DESCRIBE** Dorothea's Dix's legacy as a social reformer.

>> In this engraving from the mid-1800s, students in a one-room schoolhouse recite poetry as their teacher listens.

The Impact of Educational Reform

In 1800, few American children attended school. Massachusetts was the only state that required free public schools supported by the community. Teachers were poorly trained and ill paid. Students of all ages crowded together in a single room.

As more men won the right to vote, reformers acted to improve education. They argued that a republic required educated citizens.

Education Reform Gives Rise to Public Schools Horace Mann became head of the Massachusetts board of education in 1837. A Unitarian inspired by the Second Great Awakening, Mann believed that education would help citizens become better Christians. He hounded legislators to provide more money for education.

Under his leadership, Massachusetts built new schools, extended the school year, and raised teachers' pay. The state also opened three colleges to train teachers.

Other states followed the lead of Massachusetts. By the 1850s, most northern states had set up free tax-supported elementary schools. Schools in the South improved more slowly. In both the North and the South, schooling usually ended in the eighth grade. There were few public high schools.

Expanding Education for African Americans In most areas, African Americans had little chance to attend school. A few cities, like Boston and New York, set up separate schools for black students. However, these schools received less money than schools for white students did. In the North, African American men

>> As part of the social and educational reform movements, Thomas Gallaudet opened this school in Connecticut to serve deaf children.

▶ Interactive Gallery

and women often opened their own schools to educate their children.

Some attempts to educate African Americans met with hostility. In the 1830s, Prudence Crandall, a Connecticut Quaker, began a school for African American girls. Crandall continued to teach even as rocks smashed through the window. Finally, a mob broke in one night and destroyed the school.

Despite such obstacles, some African Americans went on to attend private colleges such as Harvard, Dartmouth, and Oberlin. In 1854, Pennsylvania chartered the first college for African American men.

Reforming Education for People With Disabilities Some reformers improved education for people with disabilities. In 1817, a Christian evangelical Thomas Gallaudet (gal uh DEHT) set up a school for the deaf in Hartford, Connecticut.

Samuel Gridley Howe founded the first American school for the blind in 1832. Howe was active in many reform movements spurred by the Second Great Awakening, working for improvements in public schools, prisons, and treatment of the disabled. Howe used a system of raised letters to enable students to read with their fingers. One of Howe's pupils, Laura Bridgman, was the first deaf and blind student to receive a formal education.

? GENERATE EXPLANATIONS Why did reformers insist that states set up publicly funded schools for their residents?

ASSESSMENT

1. **Identify Central Issues** What did critics of American society feel was unjust about it?

2. **Analyze Information** What was the Second Great Awakening, and why did it have the effects it had?

3. **Summarize** Dorothea Dix's efforts to improve society.

4. **Hypothesize** why women so often took a leading role in the temperance movement.

5. **Contrast** the educational opportunities available for white children and African American children in the North while educational reform was going on.

7.4 Abolitionism

> Some abolitionists, such as William Lloyd Garrison, took a hard line on the issue of slavery by demanding that it be ended immediately. Here, Garrison makes an anti-slavery speech in Boston.

▶ **Interactive Flipped Video**

In the Declaration of Independence, Thomas Jefferson had written that "all men are created equal." Yet many Americans, including Jefferson himself, did not believe that this statement applied to enslaved African Americans. A growing number of reformers began to think differently.

>> Objectives

Describe the historical development of the abolitionist movement.

Explain the roles of Frederick Douglass and others in the abolitionist movement.

Identify the Underground Railroad and the role that civil disobedience played in it.

Describe the different points of view of interest groups on abolition.

>> Key Terms

American
 Colonization
 Society
abolitionist
The Liberator
Underground
 Railroad
Frederick Douglass
civil disobedience

407

▶ **PEARSON realize**™   www.PearsonRealize.com
Access your Digital Lesson.

Early Opposition to Slavery

Early Reforms in the North Religious beliefs led some Americans to oppose slavery. Since colonial times, Quakers had taught that it was a sin for one human being to own another. All people, they said, were equal in the sight of God. Later, during the Second Great Awakening, ministers such as Charles Grandison Finney called on Christians to join a crusade to stamp out slavery. A movement to abolish slavery developed in response to religious teachings in England in the late 1700s.

In the North, slavery was not important to the economy. As growing numbers of northerners opposed it, slavery gradually came to an end in the North. By 1804, all the states from Pennsylvania through New England had ended slavery or promised to free their enslaved African Americans over time. The Northwest Ordinance of 1787 had banned slavery in the Northwest Territories, which became the Midwestern states north of the Ohio River and east of the Mississippi River. Efforts to end slavery had little effect in the South. There were only 50,000 enslaved African Americans in the North in 1800, compared with nearly one million in the South.

At the same time as northern leaders were ending slavery in their states, the South was growing ever more dependent on slavery. As you have learned, plantation agriculture was growing rapidly in the South in the early 1800s. As a result, there was little support in the South for ending slavery.

The Colonization Movement The **American Colonization Society** proposed to end slavery by setting up an independent colony in Africa for Africans and African Americans who had gained freedom from slavery. In 1822, President Monroe helped the society found a colony in western Africa. This colony gained control over a territory that later became the nation of Liberia.

Some African Americans favored colonization, believing that they would never have equal rights in the United States. Most, however, opposed the movement. Nearly all, enslaved or free, had been born in the United States. They wanted to stay in their homeland. In the end, only a few thousand African Americans settled in Liberia.

? **RECALL** Why did the colonization movement fail?

>> This image of an enslaved African in chains was originally adopted as the seal of the Society for the Abolition of Slavery in England in the 1780s.

Abolitionism Gains Momentum

A growing number of reformers, known as **abolitionists**, wanted to end slavery completely in the United States. Some abolitionists favored a gradual end to slavery. They expected slavery to die out if it was kept out of the western territories. Other abolitionists demanded that slavery end everywhere, at once. Almost all abolitionists were northerners. The abolitionist movement gradually gained strength from the 1820s through the 1840s. It grew more rapidly during the 1850s.

African American Abolitionists Free African Americans played a key role in the abolitionist movement. Some tried to end slavery through lawsuits and petitions. In the 1820s, Samuel Cornish and John Russwurm set up an abolitionist newspaper, *Freedom's Journal.* They hoped to turn public opinion against slavery by printing stories about the brutal treatment of enslaved African Americans.

Other African American abolitionists called for stronger measures. In *An Appeal to the Colored Citizens of the World*, David Walker encouraged enslaved African Americans to free themselves by any means necessary. Walker's friend Maria Stewart also spoke out against slavery. Stewart was the first American woman to make public political speeches.

The Contributions of Frederick Douglass

The best-known African American abolitionist was **Frederick Douglass**. Douglass was born into slavery in Maryland. As a child, he defied the slave codes by learning to read.

Douglass escaped in 1838 and made his way to New England. One day at an antislavery meeting, he felt a powerful

>> Samuel Cornish published stories revealing the harsh treatment of enslaved African Americans. **Identify Cause and Effect** How did Cornish's stories affect American public opinion on slavery?

>> African American abolitionist Frederick Douglass, who escaped from slavery, gave speeches across the United States about the hardship of slavery.

The Underground Railroad

>> The Underground Railroad offered a network of routes African Americans fleeing slavery could take to reach free states in the North or Canada.

▶ **Interactive Map**

urge to speak. Rising to his feet, he talked about the sorrows of slavery and the meaning of freedom. The audience was moved to tears. Soon, Douglass was lecturing across the United States and Britain. In 1847, he began publishing an antislavery newspaper, the *North Star*.

William Lloyd Garrison Speaks Out The most outspoken white abolitionist was a fiery young man named William Lloyd Garrison. To Garrison, slavery was an evil to be ended immediately. In 1831, Garrison launched **The Liberator**, the most influential antislavery newspaper. On the first page of the first issue, Garrison revealed his commitment:

I will be as harsh as truth, and as uncompromising as justice. . . . I am in earnest. . . . I will not excuse—I will

not retreat a single inch—and I WILL BE HEARD.

—William Lloyd Garrison, *The Liberator,* January 1831

A year later, Garrison helped to found the New England AntiSlavery Society. Members included Theodore Weld, a young minister and follower of Charles Grandison Finney. Weld brought the energy of a religious revival to antislavery meetings.

The Grimké Sisters Contribute to Reform Angelina and Sarah Grimké were the daughters of a South Carolina slaveholder. Hating slavery, they moved to Philadelphia to work for abolition. Their lectures drew large crowds.

Some people, including other abolitionists, objected to women speaking out in public. "Whatsoever it is morally right for a man to do," replied Sarah Grimké, "it is morally right for a woman to do." As you will see, this belief helped spark a crusade for women's rights.

Civil Disobedience and the Underground Railroad Some abolitionists formed the **Underground Railroad**. It was not a real railroad, but a network of black and white abolitionists who secretly helped enslaved African Americans escape to freedom in the North or Canada.

"Conductors" guided runaways to "stations" where they could spend the night. Some stations were homes of abolitionists. Others were churches or even caves. Conductors sometimes hid runaways under loads of hay in wagons with false bottoms. It was illegal to help enslaved African Americans to escape, but these conductors felt strongly about disobeying laws they considered unjust. Such acts of **civil disobedience** led thousands of enslaved people to freedom.

One daring conductor, Harriet Tubman, had escaped slavery herself. She felt deeply committed to freeing others from slavery. Risking her freedom and her life, Tubman returned to the South 19 times. She led more than 300 enslaved African Americans, including her parents, to freedom. Those who admired Tubman's civil disobedience called her the "Black Moses" after the biblical leader who led the Israelites out of slavery in Egypt. Slave owners offered a $40,000 reward for her capture.

A Novel Promotes Abolitionism In 1852, a writer named Harriet Beecher Stowe published *Uncle Tom's Cabin*, a novel describing the suffering of enslaved African Americans.

The novel's characters were often unrealistic and stereotyped, or based on inaccurate assumptions and beliefs about supposed characteristics of African

Americans. However, the novel sold widely and convinced many northerners during the 1850s that slavery was evil and should be outlawed.

As abolitionism spread during the 1850s, it had a powerful impact on the United States. It increased tensions between the North and the South and helped set the stage for the Civil War.

? **GENERATE EXPLANATIONS** Explain the role of the press in the abolition movement.

Abolitionism Faces Opposition

By the mid-1800s, slavery existed only in the South. Still, abolitionists like Douglass and Garrison made enemies in the North as well.

>> This engraving shows the burning of the print shop of Elijah P. Lovejoy, an abolitionist who published a newspaper opposed to slavery in Illinois. Anti-abolition rioters murdered Lovejoy during their attack on his shop. **Identify Central Ideas** Why did some northerners resist abolition?

▶ **Interactive Chart**

Northerners Against Abolition As you have learned, abolitionists were one interest group in the controversy over slavery. Their view was that slavery had to end.

However, northern mill owners, bankers, and merchants depended on cotton from the South. Some saw attacks on slavery as a threat to their livelihood. Some northern workers also opposed abolition. They feared that African Americans might come north and take their jobs by working for low pay.

These groups in the North took the view that slavery should be left up to individual states. Because few southerners opposed slavery, their view was that slavery should be allowed to continue.

In northern cities, mobs sometimes broke up antislavery meetings or attacked homes of abolitionists. At times, the attacks backfired and won support for the abolitionists. One night, a Boston mob dragged William Lloyd Garrison through the streets at the end of a rope. A witness wrote, "I am an abolitionist from this very moment."

Southerners Defend Slavery Against the North Most white southerners were disturbed by the growing abolitionist movement. Because the southern economy depended on slavery, southerners strongly supported slavery, even if they were not slave owners personally. They accused abolitionists of preaching violence. Many southerners blamed Nat Turner's rebellion on William Lloyd Garrison, who had founded *The Liberator* only a few months earlier. David Walker's call for a slave revolt seemed to confirm the worst fears of southerners.

Slave owners responded to the abolitionist crusade by defending slavery even more. If enslaved African Americans were treated well, wrote one slave owner, they would "love their master and serve him . . . faithfully." Others argued that enslaved African Americans were better off than northern workers who labored long hours in dusty, airless factories.

Even some southerners who owned no enslaved African Americans defended slavery. To them, slavery was essential to the southern economy. Many southerners believed northern support for the antislavery movement was stronger than it really was. They began to fear that northerners wanted to destroy their way of life.

? **SUMMARIZE** the reasons many Northerners oppose abolition.

ASSESSMENT

1. **Generate Explanations** Why did so many free African Americans oppose the American Colonization Society's movement?

2. **Hypothesize** Why did William Lloyd Harrison, a white man, devote his professional life to the abolitionist movement?

3. **Identify Central Issues** What was the connection between civil disobedience and the abolition movement?

4. **Draw Conclusions** What can you tell about Harriet Tubman from her actions?

5. **Summarize** the reaction of southerners to abolitionists.

Women's Rights

>> Elizabeth Cady Stanton spoke publicly across the United States in support of women's rights. Here, she speaks at the Seneca Falls Convention.

Interactive Flipped Video

Women had few political or legal rights in the mid-1800s. They could not vote or hold office. When a woman married, her husband became owner of all her property. If a woman worked outside the home, her wages belonged to her husband. A husband also had the right to hit his wife as long as he did not seriously injure her.

>> **Objectives**

Describe the origins of the women's rights movement.

Explain the impact of the Seneca Falls Convention, including the roles of Elizabeth Cady Stanton and Susan B. Anthony.

Describe the impact of the women's rights movement on opportunities for women.

>> **Key Terms**

Seneca Falls
   Convention
women's rights
   movement
Elizabeth Cady
   Stanton
Susan B. Anthony

Early Calls for Women's Rights

Many women, such as Angelina and Sarah Grimké, had joined the abolitionist movement. As these women worked to end slavery, they became aware that they lacked full social and political rights themselves. Both black and white abolitionists, men and women, joined the struggle for women's rights.

Sojourner Truth Declares Equality

One of the most effective women's rights leaders was born into slavery in New York. Her original name was Isabella. After gaining freedom, she came to believe that God wanted her to fight slavery. Vowing to sojourn, or travel, across the land speaking the truth, she took the name Sojourner Truth.

>> Born into slavery but later freed, Isabella Van Wagener took the name "Sojourner Truth" because she believed God wanted her to travel, or sojourn, across the nation preaching abolition.

Truth was a spellbinding speaker. Her exact words were rarely written down. However, her message spread by word of mouth. According to one witness, Truth ridiculed the idea that women were inferior to men by nature:

> I have as much muscle as any man, and can do as much work as any man. I have plowed and reaped and husked and chopped and mowed, and can any man do more than that?

> —Sojourner Truth, speech at Akron Women's Rights Convention, 1851

Lucretia Mott and Elizabeth Cady Stanton Shape a Movement Other abolitionists also turned to the cause of women's rights. The two most influential were Lucretia Mott and **Elizabeth Cady Stanton**. Lucretia Mott was a Quaker and the mother of five children. A quiet speaker, she won the respect of many listeners with her persuasive logic. Mott also used her organizing skills to set up petition drives across the North.

Elizabeth Cady Stanton was the daughter of a New York judge. As a child, she was an excellent student and an athlete. However, her father gave her little encouragement. Stanton later remarked that her "father would have felt a proper pride had I been a man."

In 1840, Stanton and Mott joined a group of Americans at a World Antislavery Convention in London. However, convention officials refused to let women take an active part in the proceedings. Female delegates were even forced to sit behind a curtain, hidden from view. After returning home, Mott and Stanton took up the cause of women's rights with new energy.

? INFER What is surprising about women being forced to sit behind a curtain, hidden from view, at the World Antislavery Convention?

A Women's Movement Organizes

Even in London, Mott and Stanton had begun thinking about holding a convention to draw attention to the problems women faced. "The men . . . had [shown] a great need for some education on that question," Stanton later recalled. The meeting finally took place in 1848 in Seneca Falls, New York.

Different Views of Suffrage at the Seneca Falls Convention About 200 women and 40 men attended the **Seneca Falls Convention**. Stanton's greatest contribution to the convention was the *Declaration of Sentiments*, which she had modeled on the Declaration of Independence. The delegates approved the declaration. It proclaimed, "We hold these truths to be self-evident: that all men and women are created equal."

The women and men at Seneca Falls voted for resolutions that demanded equality for women at work, at school, and at church. Only one resolution met with any opposition at the convention. It demanded that women be allowed to vote. Even the bold reformers at Seneca Falls hesitated to take this step. In the end, the resolution narrowly passed.

Women Struggle for Justice The Seneca Falls Convention marked the start of an organized campaign for equal rights, or the **women's rights movement**. This

>> Susan B. Anthony was probably the most powerful and influential leader of the women's rights movement during the 1800s.

▶ **Interactive Timeline**

movement was one of the most important reform movements of the Reform Era. New leaders took up the struggle. **Susan B. Anthony** built a close working partnership with Elizabeth Cady Stanton. While Stanton usually had to stay at home with her seven children, Anthony was free to travel across the country. Anthony's contribution to the movement was her lifelong work convincing people that women deserved equal rights. Anthony was a tireless speaker. Even when audiences heckled her and threw eggs, she always finished her speech.

Around the country, Anthony campaigned for women's suffrage. She petitioned Congress repeatedly, and was even arrested in 1872 for trying to vote. Anthony did not live to see the passage of the 19th Amendment in 1920 granting women the right to vote, but the

>> This Currier and Ives print shows Mount Holyoke Female Seminary in Massachusetts, founded by Mary Lyon in 1837.

amendment is also called the Susan B. Anthony Amendment in her honor.

In the years after 1848, women worked for change in many areas. They won additional legal rights in some states. For example, New York passed laws allowing married women to keep their own property and wages. Still, many men and women opposed the women's rights movement. The struggle for equal rights would last many years.

? RECALL For what act of civil disobedience was Susan B. Anthony arrested in 1872?

Women Gain New Opportunities

The women at Seneca Falls believed that education was a key to equality. Elizabeth Cady Stanton said:

"The girl must be allowed to romp and play, climb, skate, and swim. Her clothing must be more like those of the boy—strong, loose-fitting garments, thick boots... She must be taught to look forward to life of self-dependence and, like the boy, prepare herself for some [profitable] trade profession."

—Elizabeth Cady Stanton, Letter, 1851

Such an idea was startling in the early 1800s. Women from poor families had little hope of learning even to read. Middle-class girls who went to school learned dancing and drawing rather than science or mathematics. After all, people argued, women were expected to care for their families. Why did they need an education?

Opportunities for Women's Education

Possibly the greatest impact of the women's movement in the mid-1800s was the creation of greater opportunities for women in education. Emma Willard opened a high school for girls in Troy, New York. Here, young women studied "men's" subjects, such as mathematics and physics.

Mary Lyon opened Mount Holyoke Female Seminary in Massachusetts in 1837. She did not call the school a college because many people thought it was wrong for women to attend college. In fact, however, Mount Holyoke was one of the first women's colleges in the United States.

New Employment Opportunities for Women

At about this time, a few men's colleges began to admit women. As their education improved, women found jobs teaching, especially in grade schools.

A few women entered fields such as medicine. Elizabeth Blackwell attended medical school at Geneva College in New York. To the surprise of school officials, she graduated first in her class. Women had provided medical care since colonial times, but Blackwell was the first woman in the United States to earn a medical degree. She later helped found the nation's first medical school for women.

Women made their mark in other fields as well. Maria Mitchell was a noted astronomer. Sarah Josepha Hale edited *Godey's Lady's Book*, an influential magazine for women. Antoinette Blackwell became the first American woman ordained a minister. She also campaigned for abolitionism, temperance, and women's right to vote.

NEW OPPORTUNITIES FOR WOMEN

COLLEGES OR UNIVERSITIES ADMITTING WOMEN FOR THE FIRST TIME

Before 1800	2
1800-1819	0
1820-1829	2
1830-1839	7
1840-1849	17
1850-1859	35

Source: Compiled from a variety of sources

FEMALE LABOR FORCE 1800–1860

Source: U.S. Bureau of Labor Statistics

STATES SLOWLY GRANT MARRIED WOMEN FULL PROPERTY RIGHTS

1844 Maine	1852 New Jersey
1845 Massachusetts	1855 Michigan Florida
1848 New York Pennsylvania Rhode Island	1860 Maryland
1850 Wisconsin	The remaining states gradually gave married women property rights between 1860 and 1980.

Source: *Journal of Economic History*, 1996; Law Library of Congress

>> Analyze Graphs What details in the graphs support the conclusion that women's educational opportunities expanded during the mid-1800s?

▶ **Interactive Gallery**

>> Antoinette Blackwell served as a role model for women seeking career opportunities when she became the first ordained female minister in the United States.

Different Points of View on Contemporary Women's Issues The struggle for women's rights continues today. As in the 19th century, different groups have differing points of view.

One issue on which women's groups differ today is whether companies or the government should be required to pay women on maternity leave, or a period away from their jobs to give birth and take care of babies. Some women's groups today, such as the National Organization for Women, believe that employers, including the government, should be required to pay women during maternity leave. They argue that women need this support. Other groups, such as the Independent Women's Forum, argue that requiring employers to pay for maternity leave might make them less willing to hire women.

? DRAW CONCLUSIONS What effects did the women's movement have during the 1800s?

ASSESSMENT

1. **Generate Explanations** What made Sojourner Truth an effective women's rights leader?

2. **Draw Conclusions** What would you conclude about the 40 men who attended the Seneca Falls Convention?

3. **Generate Explanations** Why was it fitting that the 19th Amendment was named the Susan B. Anthony Amendment?

4. **Hypothesize** Why do women have different opinions on issues of women's rights today?

5. **Summarize** the results of the women's rights movement of the mid-1800s.

Arts and Literature

>> In his 1849 painting *Kindred Spirits*, Hudson River School painter Asher Durand depicts the grandeur of New York's Catskill Mountains. The painting shows nature poet William Cullen Bryant and Durand's fellow painter Thomas Cole.

▶ **Interactive Flipped Video**

Before 1800, most American painters studied in Europe. Benjamin West of Philadelphia was appointed historical painter to King George III. Many American painters journeyed to London to study with West. Two of them, Charles Wilson Peale and Gilbert Stuart, later painted famous portraits of George Washington.

>> **Objectives**

Describe American painting in the early to mid-1800s, including the Hudson River School and the work of John James Audubon.

Analyze American literature and music during the early to mid-1800s.

Describe transcendentalism.

>> **Key Terms**

Hudson River
  School
transcendentalist
individualism
Henry David
  Thoreau
John James
  Audubon

A New American Art Style

By the mid-1800s, American artists began to develop their own style. The first group to do so became known as the **Hudson River School**. Artists such as Thomas Cole and Asher B. Durand painted vivid landscapes of New York's Hudson River region and other parts of the Northeast. African American artist Robert S. Duncanson reflected the style of the Hudson River School.

Other artists painted scenes of hard-working country people. George Caleb Bingham of Missouri created a timeless picture of frontier life along the rivers that feed the great Mississippi. George Catlin and Alfred Jacob Miller traveled to the Far West to record the daily life of Indians on the Great Plains and in the Rockies.

John James Audubon was a wildlife artist who traveled across the country painting birds and mammals. His collection of 435 life-size prints, entitled *The Birds of America*, portrayed every bird known in the United States at the time.

American artists in the early and mid-1800s showed that the American landscape and people were worthy subjects of art. They portrayed continuity in the American way of life. Their paintings reflected continuity in the timelessness of the country's geography and in the patterns of farm work. The y also reflected the great changes that were underway in this new era. Artists depicted the effects of westward movement and the settlement of the frontier, capturing the nation's expansion and growth. In their attention to these themes, the work of these painters reflected American society in their day.

? IDENTIFY common themes found in the works of American artists during the early to mid-1800s.

>> John James Audubon's painting of mourning doves shows his effort to capture the character of birds and his attention to detail.

▶ **Interactive Gallery**

A New Nation Finds a Voice

Like painters, early American writers also depended on Europe for their ideas and inspiration. In the 1820s, however, a new crop of poets and fiction writers began to write about American themes. At the same time, uniquely American forms of music began to emerge. These new forms of literature and music reflected American society in the early and mid-1800s.

A New American Poetry Henry Wadsworth Longfellow was the favorite poet of Americans in the mid-1800s. Longfellow based many poems on events from the past. "Paul Revere's Ride" honored the Revolutionary War hero. "The Song of Hiawatha" idealized Native American life.

Other poets spoke out on social issues. John Greenleaf Whittier, a Quaker from Massachusetts, and Frances Watkins Harper, an African American woman from Maryland, reflected change in American society as abolitionism gained supporters. They used their pens to make readers aware of the evils of slavery.

Walt Whitman's greatest work was a book of poems titled *Leaves of Grass*. He added to this collection over a period of 27 years. Like Longfellow, Whittier, and Harper, Whitman focused on themes that are unique to American culture. Whitman had great faith in the common people. His poetry celebrated democracy. He wrote proudly of being part of a "nation of many nations":

>> Walt Whitman, shown here in a colorized photo, wrote *Leaves of Grass* entirely in free verse, which did not apply a set meter or rhyming pattern.

> At home on the hills of Vermont or in the woods of Maine, or the Texan ranch, comrade of Californians, comrade of free North-Westerners. . . . of every hue and caste am I, of every rank and religion.
>
> —Walt Whitman, *Song of Myself*

Only seven of Emily Dickinson's more than 1,700 poems were published in her lifetime. A shy woman who rarely left her home, Dickinson called her poetry "my letter to the world / That never wrote to me." Today, she is recognized as one of the nation's greatest poets.

American Writers Begin to Tell American Stories One of the most popular American writers was Washington Irving, a New Yorker. Irving first became known for *The Sketch Book*, a collection of tales published in 1820. Two of his bestloved tales are "Rip Van Winkle" and "The Legend of Sleepy Hollow."

The exciting novels of James Fenimore Cooper were also set in the American

>> Emily Dickinson, shown here in an early photograph, wrote poems that reflected the loneliness of her life. She is still considered one of the greatest American poets.

▶ **Interactive Map**

>> Whalers face the angry whale Moby Dick in a scene from Herman Melville's epic tale *Moby-Dick*, considered one of the greatest American novels.

>> The works of Catherine Sedgwick, shown here, often used patriotic heroines to indirectly criticize what she viewed as an oppressive heritage of Puritan values in America.

past. In *The Deerslayer* and *The Last of the Mohicans*, Cooper created Natty Bumppo, a heroic model of a strong, solitary frontiersman. The novels gave an idealized view of relations between whites and Native Americans on the frontier.

The stories of Cooper and Irving gave Americans a sense of the richness of their past. Their appeal went beyond the United States, however. Washington Irving was the first American writer to enjoy fame in Europe.

Later Writers In 1851, Herman Melville published *Moby-Dick*. The novel tells the story of Ahab, the crazed captain of a whaling ship. Ahab vows revenge on the white whale that years earlier bit off his leg. *Moby-Dick* had only limited success when it was first published. Today, however, critics rank it among the finest American novels.

Nathaniel Hawthorne often drew on the history of New England in his novels and short stories. In *The Scarlet Letter*, published in 1850, Hawthorne explored Puritan notions of sin and salvation. The novel shows how a young man is consumed by guilt when he tries to hide his wrongdoing from the world.

Edgar Allan Poe became famous for his many tales of horror. His short story "The Tell-Tale Heart" is about a murderer, driven mad by guilt, who imagines he can hear his victim's heartbeat. Poe is also known as the "father of the detective story" for his mystery stories, such as "The Murders in the Rue Morgue."

William Wells Brown was the first African American to earn his living as a writer. He published *Clotel*, a novel about slave life, in 1853. Brown also wrote a play inspired by his own experiences as a fugitive slave and a conductor on the Underground Railroad. His lectures and readings drew large audiences in Europe as well as throughout the North.

Women Writers Flourish in the 1800s

Many best-selling novels of the period were written by women. Some novels told about young women who gained wealth and happiness through honesty and self-sacrifice. Others showed the hardships faced by widows and orphans.

Few of these novels are read today. However, writers like Catherine Sedgwick and Fanny Fern earned far more than Hawthorne or Melville. Hawthorne complained about the success of a "mob of scribbling women."

American Music American classical music in the 1800s continued to follow European traditions. Yet as American society changed and grew and different groups of people came into contact with one another, distinctly American musical forms began to emerge. Early songs were often patriotic or religious, such as "My Country Tis of Thee," written by Samuel Francis Smith in 1831, or "Amazing Grace," published in 1835.

The 1800s saw the rise of a middle class interested in music that was entertaining and emotionally stirring. The songs of Stephen Foster, which drew on American themes, were especially popular. Although Foster was a northerner, many of his songs, such as "Dixie," referred to southern traditions and were popular in the South. Western expansion, immigration, and migration mingled musical traditions together, creating new American sounds.

African American music in particular had a strong influence on the new forms that were developing. African American spirituals and work songs combined African and European musical traditions. During the 1800s, a new style of music now

>> The banjo, originally made from a gourd and thick strings, can be traced back to sub-Saharan Africa in the 1200s.

known as gospel music began to develop in African American religious congregations. These styles would later combine with European and American folk traditions to shape blues, jazz, country, and rock music.

? DRAW CONCLUSIONS What do many of the works of American literature of the early to mid-1800s have in common?

The Development of Transcendentalism

In New England, a small but influential group of writers and thinkers emerged. They called themselves **transcendentalists** because they believed that the most important truths in life transcended, or went beyond, human reason. They produced a unique body of literature reflecting transcendentalist thought. Transcendentalists valued the spark of deeply felt insights more than reason. They believed that each individual should live up to the divine possibilities within. This belief influenced many transcendentalists to support social reform.

Emerson's Lectures Emphasize the Individual The leading transcendentalist was Ralph Waldo Emerson. Emerson was the most popular essayist and lecturer of his day. Audiences flocked to hear him talk on subjects such as self-reliance and character. Emerson believed that the human spirit was reflected in nature. Civilization might provide material wealth, he said, but nature exhibited higher values that came from God.

In his essays and lectures, Emerson stressed **individualism**, or the importance of each individual. In its individual focus, transcendentalism is unique to American culture. Individualism and individual responsibility are central to America's democracy. Each person, Emerson said, has an "inner light." He urged people to use this inner light to guide their lives and improve society. "Trust thyself," he wrote. "Every heart vibrates to that iron string."

Henry David Thoreau and Civil Disobedience Henry David Thoreau (thuh ROH), Emerson's friend and neighbor, believed that the growth of industry and the rise of cities were ruining the nation. He urged people to live as simply and as close to nature as possible. In *Walden,* his best-known work, Thoreau describes spending a year alone in a cabin on Walden Pond in Massachusetts.

Like Emerson, Thoreau believed that each individual must decide what is right or wrong. "If a man does not keep pace with his companions," he wrote, in *Walden,* "perhaps it is because he hears a different drummer. Let him step to the music he hears."

Thoreau's "different drummer" told him that slavery was wrong. He argued in favor of civil disobedience and once went to jail for refusing to pay taxes to support the U.S.-Mexican War, which he felt promoted

>> Ralph Waldo Emerson lectures before a large audience during a meeting of the Summer School of Philosophy in Concord, Massachusetts. The successful school drew participants from across the United States and Europe.

slavery. Thoreau wrote an essay titled "Civil Disobedience" that explained why an individual may feel the need to break laws that are unjust without resorting to violence.

He argued, though, that anyone who chooses this course has to be prepared to be imprisoned or otherwise punished. This essay had a great impact on future leaders. Thoreau's ideas on civil disobedience and nonviolence later influenced Mohandas Gandhi, who led a struggle in India for independence from Britain, and Martin Luther King, Jr., an American civil rights leader during the 1900s.

[?] **RECALL** What was the core belief of the transcendentalists?

>> This replica of Henry David Thoreau's cabin sits near the site of his original cabin beside Walden Pond in Concord, Massachusetts.

ASSESSMENT

1. **Draw Conclusions** How did American artists during the early 1800s contribute to the historical record?

2. **Hypothesize** why the works of a "mob of scribbling women," as Nathaniel Hawthorne described them, were more successful than the works of their male counterparts, such as Herman Melville, and Hawthorne.

3. **Support Ideas with Evidence** How might you cite evidence to support the argument that American music would not be the same without the contributions of African Americans?

4. **Compare and Contrast** transcendentalism with what had been taught by the leaders of the Second Great Awakening.

5. **Identify Central Ideas** Although Thoreau encouraged individuals to follow their consciences and disobey those laws they believed were unjust, he added one important caution. What was that caution?

1. **Explain the Effects of the War of 1812 on Manufacturing** Write a paragraph analyzing the effects of the War of 1812 on American manufacturing. Consider how the war affected American access to foreign goods, how American merchants and bankers responded to the situation, and what effect this response had on the nation's economy.

2. **Describe the Features of the Free-Market System** Write a paragraph describing features of the free-market system in the 1800s. Consider the effects of Alexander Hamilton's banking reforms, the role of the government in the economy, the role of the New York Stock Exchange in spurring economic growth, and the role of low taxes in spurring growth.

3. **Explain Technology and Economic Growth** Write a paragraph analyzing how the technologies of clipper ships and steam power led to economic growth in the 1800s. Explain what technological advantage clipper ships had over other ships, how clipper ships gave American merchants an advantage, what steam power is, and how steam power helped industry expand.

4. **Analyze How Fine Arts Depicted American Continuity and Change** Write a paragraph that analyzes how American artists painted what was timeless in America and also painted the great changes that were occurring in the young nation. Analyze the continuity and the changes that American artists recorded.

5. **Describe the Women's Rights Movement** Write a paragraph explaining why some reformers in the mid-1800s began calling for greater rights for women. Describe the limits on women's rights in the mid-1800s and explain how the abolitionist movement helped launch the women's rights movement.

6. **Describe Sectional Differences in Society and Culture** Write a paragraph describing the causes and effects of sectional differences between the North and South by comparing northern and southern whites. Consider differences in the basis of wealth and in city populations.

7. **Describe the Effects of the Second Great Awakening** Write a paragraph describing how the Second Great Awakening influenced reform movements in the 1800s. Identify Charles Grandison Finney, explain his views on personal salvation, and describe the effect of Finney's ideas on social reform and the national identity.

8. **Analyze Slavery's Impact** Write a paragraph analyzing the effects of slavery in the different areas of the United States. Explain the difference between the thinking of Thomas Jefferson and the Quakers, describe the importance of slavery in the North and in the South and explain the difference between the two regions, and describe the status of slavery in the Northwest Territories.

9. **Describe the Contributions of Frederick Douglass** Write a paragraph analyzing the role of Frederick Douglass in the abolition movement. Analyze why Frederick Douglass was an effective advocate of abolition and describe how he communicated his experiences.

URBAN GROWTH & INDUSTRIALIZATION

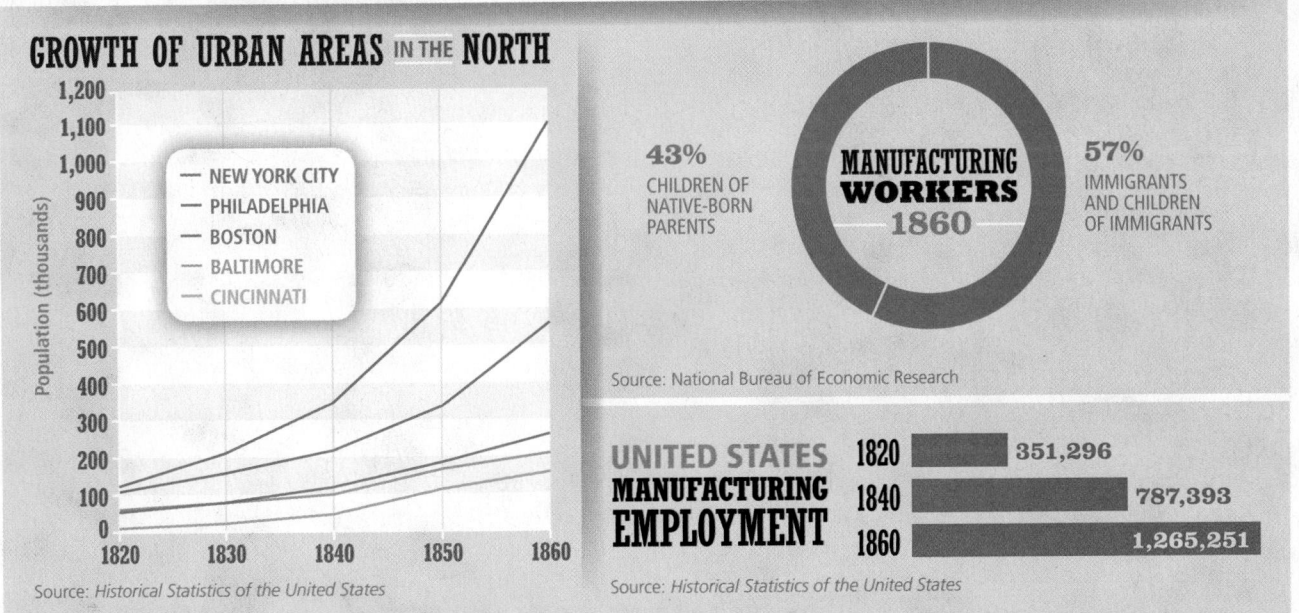

GROWTH OF URBAN AREAS IN THE NORTH

- NEW YORK CITY
- PHILADELPHIA
- BOSTON
- BALTIMORE
- CINCINNATI

Source: *Historical Statistics of the United States*

MANUFACTURING WORKERS 1860

43% CHILDREN OF NATIVE-BORN PARENTS

57% IMMIGRANTS AND CHILDREN OF IMMIGRANTS

Source: National Bureau of Economic Research

UNITED STATES MANUFACTURING EMPLOYMENT

1820 — 351,296
1840 — 787,393
1860 — 1,265,251

Source: *Historical Statistics of the United States*

10. **Explain the Reasons for Rapid Urbanization** Using the graphs above and other sources, write a paragraph explaining the relationship between industrialization and the growth of northern cities. Define *urbanization,* and explain the relationship between factory work and the movement of people from farms to cities, the relationship between the number of factories and the size of cities over time, and the speed of urbanization. Also analyze what the graphs show about the relationship between manufacturing and the growth of cities over time.

11. **Identify the Impact of Industrialization on Life** Write a paragraph identifying how life changed for workers as industrialization spread. Consider how the roles of workers changed; how the number of workers in families changed; and how wages, hours, and working conditions changed.

12. **Evaluate Educational Reform** Write a paragraph evaluating the educational reform efforts of Horace Mann. Explain why reform was needed and who Horace Mann was. Analyze the role religion played in his reform efforts and evaluate the effect of Mann's reform efforts.

13. **Identify the Colonization Movement** Write a paragraph that analyzes the point of view of the American Colonization Society toward slavery. Identify the society's proposal on how to end slavery and analyze the response of the President and of African Americans to the proposal.

14. **Identify Points of View and Frames of Reference** Write a paragraph identifying the points of view and frames of reference of those who supported the abolition of slavery prior to the Civil War and those who did not. Identify the points of view and frames of reference of both supporters and opponents of the abolitionist movement.

15. **Write about the Essential Question** **Write an essay on the Essential Question: Why is culture important?** Use evidence from your study of this topic to support your answer.

[ESSENTIAL QUESTION] When is war justified?

⑧ Sectionalism and Civil War (1820–1865)

Enduring Understandings

- Disputes over slavery led to shaky compromises and increased tensions between the North and South.

- Failed compromises over slavery led to outbreaks of violence.

- When Abraham Lincoln was elected president and promised to stop the spread of slavery, southern states seceded from the Union.

- The Civil War broke out as a result of secession, and the South won many early battles.

- President Lincoln's Emancipation Proclamation freed slaves in the Confederacy.

- Union victories eventually led to the defeat of the Confederacy and preservation of the Union.

>> President Abraham Lincoln

PEARSON **realize**™   **NBC LEARN**

Watch the My Story Video to learn about Robert E. Lee.

PEARSON **realize**™
www.PearsonRealize.com

Access your digital lessons including:
Topic Inquiry • Interactive Reading
Notepad • Interactivities • Assessments

>> The passage of the Fugitive Slave Act of 1850 pitted northerners against one another as some tried to assist African American fugitives, like this family, despite the law's requirement to return them.

[▶] **Interactive Flipped Video**

>> Objectives

Describe how the Missouri Compromise affected slavery.

Explain why conflict arose over the issue of slavery in western territories.

Identify why the Free-Soil party was founded.

Explain how the Compromise of 1850 tried to resolve the issue of slavery.

Summarize how Uncle Tom's Cabin affected attitudes toward slavery.

>> Key Terms

Missouri
  Compromise
Wilmot Proviso
popular sovereignty
Free-Soil Party
secede
fugitive
civil war
Compromise of 1850
Fugitive Slave Act
Uncle Tom's Cabin
John C. Calhoun
Daniel Webster
Henry Clay

There were 11 free states in the North and 11 slave states in the South in 1819. The era of sectionalism, or tension between people loyal to their section, or region, lasted from the 1810s to the 1860s. During this era, each of these two regions, or sections, had different economies, political views, and ideas about slavery. These differences were the main causes of sectionalism. The effects of sectionalism included political conflicts over issues important to each section, or region.

Henry Clay's Missouri Compromise

Before 1819, the equal number of slave and free states helped balance the sectional divide. That year, however, Congress considered Missouri's application to join the Union as a slave state. Immediately, a crisis erupted. Missouri's admission would give the South a majority in the Senate. Determined not to lose power, northerners opposed letting Missouri enter as a slave state.

The argument lasted many months. Finally, Senator **Henry Clay** made a proposal. During the long debate, Maine had also applied for statehood. Clay suggested admitting Missouri as a slave state and Maine as a free state. His plan, called the **Missouri Compromise**, kept the number of slave and free states equal.

Under the provisions of the Missouri Compromise, Congress drew an imaginary line extending the southern border of Missouri at latitude 36°30' N. Slavery was permitted in the part of the Louisiana Purchase south of that line. It was banned north of the Missouri Compromise line. The only exception to this was Missouri itself.

? CHECK UNDERSTANDING Why did Missouri's application to join the Union as a slave state spark a crisis in Congress?

Western Expansion Heightens Tension Over Slavery

The Missouri Compromise applied only to the Louisiana Purchase. In 1848, the Mexican War added vast western lands to the United States. Once again, the question of slavery in the territories arose.

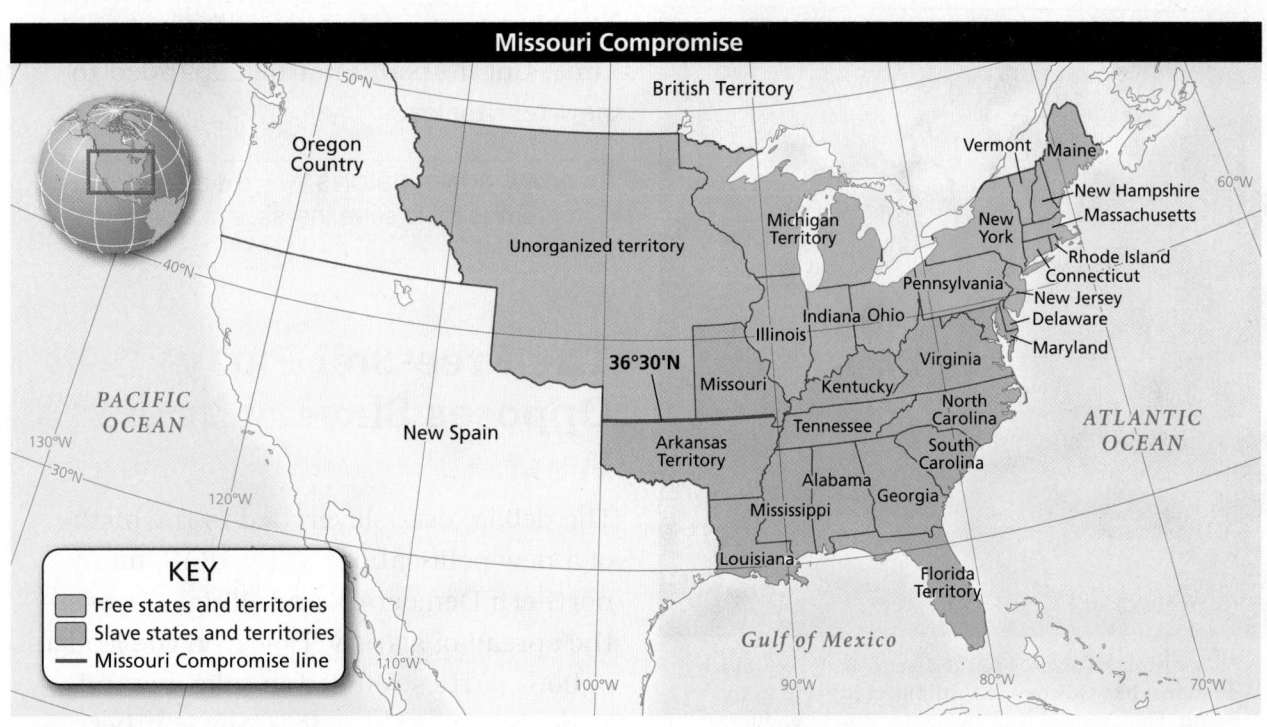

Missouri Compromise

KEY
- Free states and territories
- Slave states and territories
- Missouri Compromise line

>> **Analyze Maps** Based on the information in the map, how did the Missouri Compromise preserve a balance of power in the Senate?

The Wilmot Proviso Divides Congress

Many northerners feared that the South would extend slavery into the West. David Wilmot, a member of Congress from Pennsylvania, called for a law to ban slavery in any territories won from Mexico. Southern leaders angrily opposed this **Wilmot Proviso**. They said that Congress had no right to ban slavery in the West.

The House passed the Wilmot Proviso in 1846, but the Senate defeated it. As a result, Americans continued to argue about slavery in the West even while their army fought in Mexico.

Opposing Views Around the Country

As the debate heated up, people found it hard not to take sides. One of the effects of sectionalism was sharp division over the issue of expanding slavery. Abolitionists wanted slavery banned throughout the country. They insisted that slavery was morally wrong. Southern slaveholders thought that slavery should be allowed in any territory. They also demanded that enslaved African Americans who escaped to the North be returned to them. Even white southerners who did not own enslaved African Americans generally agreed with these ideas.

Between these two extreme views were more moderate positions. Some moderates argued that the Missouri Compromise line should be extended across the Mexican Cession to the Pacific. Any new state north of the line would be a free state. Any new state south of the line could allow slavery. Other moderates felt that the Missouri Compromise line should not be extended at all.

Still others supported the idea of **popular sovereignty**, or the right of people to create their government. Under popular sovereignty, voters in a new territory would decide for themselves whether or not to allow slavery. Some also felt that slavery should be allowed where it existed at the time, but it should not be expanded to new territories.

? DRAW CONCLUSIONS Why did the Missouri Compromise fail to solve the issue of slavery beyond 1848?

The Free-Soil Party Opposes Slavery in the West

The debate over slavery led to the birth of a new political party. By 1848, many northern Democrats and Whigs opposed the spread of slavery. However, the leaders of both parties refused to take a stand. They did not want to lose any southern

>> As Americans debated the issue of slavery, slave auctions, like this one in Virginia, continued in the South. Family members on auction had to endure the possibility of never seeing one another again.

▶ **Interactive Gallery**

Presidential Election of 1848

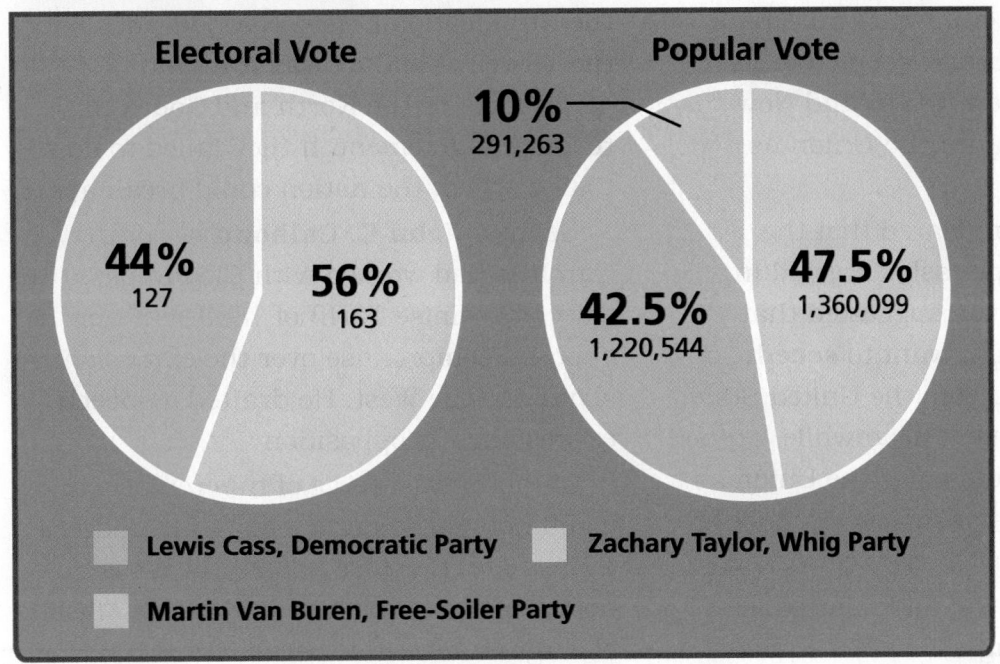

Electoral Vote

44%
127

56%
163

Popular Vote

10%
291,263

42.5%
1,220,544

47.5%
1,360,099

■ Lewis Cass, Democratic Party   ■ Zachary Taylor, Whig Party

■ Martin Van Buren, Free-Soiler Party

>> **Analyze Data** According to both pie graphs, what effect did Martin Van Buren's candidacy have on the other two candidates' electoral votes?

votes. Some also feared that the slavery issue would split the nation.

In 1848, antislavery members of both parties met in Buffalo, New York. There, they founded the **Free-Soil party**. The main goal of the Free-Soil party was to keep slavery out of the western territories. Only a few Free-Soilers were abolitionists who wanted to end slavery in the South.

In the 1848 presidential campaign, Free-Soilers named former President Martin Van Buren as their candidate. Democrats chose Lewis Cass of Michigan. The Whigs selected Zachary Taylor, a hero of the Mexican War.

For the first time, slavery was an important election issue. Van Buren called for a ban on slavery in the Mexican Cession. Cass supported popular sovereignty. Taylor did not speak on the issue. However, because he was a slave owner from Louisiana, many southern voters assumed that he supported slavery.

Zachary Taylor won the election. Still, Van Buren took 10 percent of the popular vote, and 13 other Free-Soil candidates won seats in Congress. The success of the new Free-Soil party showed that slavery had become a national issue.

? IDENTIFY CENTRAL ISSUES What was significant about the Free-Soil Party and the fact that slavery was a political issue for the first time?

California Reignites the Slavery Debate

For a time after the Missouri Compromise, both slave and free states entered the Union peacefully. However, when California requested admission to the Union as a free state in 1850, the balance of power in the Senate was once again threatened.

Conflict and Compromise Over California In 1849, there were 15 slave states and 15 free states in the Union.

If California entered the Union as a free state, the balance of power would be broken. Furthermore, it seemed quite possible that Oregon, Utah, and New Mexico might also join the Union as free states.

Many southerners feared that the South would be hopelessly outvoted in the Senate. Some even suggested that southern states might want to **secede**, or remove themselves, from the United States. Northern congressmen, meanwhile, argued that California should enter the Union as a free state because most of the territory lay north of the Missouri Compromise line.

It was clear that the nation faced a crisis. Many in Congress looked to Senator Henry Clay for a solution.

Conflicts Between Henry Clay and John C. Calhoun

Clay had won the nickname "the Great Compromiser" for working out the Missouri Compromise and the compromise Tariff of 1833, which resolved the Nullification Crisis. Now, decades later, the 73-year-old Clay was frail and ill. Still, he pleaded for the North and South to reach an agreement. If they failed to do so, Clay warned, the nation could break apart.

Senator **John C. Calhoun** of South Carolina had worked with Clay to pass the compromise Tariff of 1833, but now he opposed compromise over the extension of slavery to the West. He drafted a speech expressing his opposition.

Calhoun was dying of tuberculosis and could not speak loudly enough to address the Senate. He stared defiantly at his northern foes while Senator James Mason of Virginia read his speech.

Calhoun refused to compromise. He insisted that slavery be allowed in the western territories. In addition, Calhoun demanded that **fugitives**, or African Americans who had fled slavery, be returned to their owners. He wanted

Balance of Free and Slave States

Free States		Slave States	
Vermont (1791)	California (1850)	Tennessee (1796)	Texas (1845)
Rhode Island	Wisconsin (1848)	Kentucky (1792)	Florida (1845)
New York	Iowa (1846)	Virginia	Arkansas (1836)
New Hampshire	Michigan (1837)	North Carolina	Missouri (1821)
Massachusetts	Maine (1820)	South Carolina	Alabama (1819)
Connecticut	Illinois (1818)	Maryland	Mississippi (1817)
New Jersey	Indiana (1816)	Georgia	Louisiana (1812)
Pennsylvania	Ohio (1803)	Delaware	

■ Original 13 states

>> **Analyze Data** What effect did the admission of California to the Union as a free state in 1850 have on the balance of power in the Senate?

northerners to admit that southern slaveholders had the right to reclaim their "property."

If the North rejected the South's demands, Calhoun told the Senate, "let the states . . . agree to part in peace. If you are unwilling that we should part in peace, tell us so, and we shall know what to do." Everyone knew what Calhoun meant. If an agreement could not be reached, the South would use force to leave the Union.

Daniel Webster Offers Compromise

Daniel Webster of Massachusetts spoke next. He had opposed Clay's compromise Tariff of 1833. Now, he supported Clay's plea to save the Union. Webster stated his position clearly:

> "I speak today not as a Massachusetts man, nor as a northern man, but as an American. . . . I speak today for the preservation of the Union. . . . There can be no such thing as a peaceable secession."
>
> —Daniel Webster, Speech in the U.S. Senate, July 17, 1850

Webster feared that the states could not separate without starting a bloody civil war. A **civil war** is a war between people of the same country.

Like many northerners, Webster viewed slavery as evil. The breakup of the United States, however, he believed was worse. To save the Union, Webster was willing to compromise. He would support southern demands that northerners be forced to return fugitives from slavery.

? CHECK UNDERSTANDING Why did Daniel Webster, an avowed opponent of slavery, agree to support returning to their owners African Americans who had escaped slavery?

>> The admission of California to the Union threatened to upset the delicate balance of slave and free states. The issue led to a showdown in Congress between Henry Clay, Daniel Webster, and John C. Calhoun.

>> Daniel Webster (standing) addressed the Senate during the great debate on Clay's compromise plan in 1850. Webster feared the possibility of a civil war more than the spread of slavery.

Congress Reaches a Compromise

In 1850, as the debate raged, Calhoun died. His last words reportedly were "The South! The poor South! God knows what will become of her now!" President Taylor also died in 1850. The new President was Millard Fillmore. Unlike Taylor, he supported Clay's compromise plan.

The Compromise of 1850 Addresses Regional Concerns Henry Clay gave more than 70 speeches in favor of a compromise. At last, however, he became too sick to continue. Stephen Douglas, of Illinois, took up the fight for him and guided Clay's plan, the **Compromise of 1850**, through Congress.

The Compromise of 1850 had five main provisions. First, it allowed California to enter the Union as a free state. Second, it divided the rest of the Mexican Cession into the territories of New Mexico and Utah.

Voters in each would decide the slavery question according to popular sovereignty. Third, it ended the slave trade in Washington, D.C., the nation's capital. Congress, however, declared that it had no power to ban the slave trade between slave states. Fourth, it included a strict fugitive slave law. Fifth, it settled a border dispute between Texas and New Mexico.

The Fugitive Slave Act Helps the South The **Fugitive Slave Act** of 1850 required all citizens to help catch African Americans trying to escape slavery. People who let fugitives escape could be fined $1,000 and jailed. The new law also set up special courts to handle the cases of runaways. Suspects were not allowed a jury trial. Judges received $10 for sending an accused runaway to the South but only $5 for setting someone free. Lured by the

EFFECTS OF THE **COMPROMISE OF 1850**

CALIFORNIA JOINS THE UNION AS A FREE STATE

[ED: Can the pie graph title be shortened? It's much longer than the typical pie graph title, and it sounds a little redundant with the main title.]

HOUSE OF REPRESENTATIVES VOTES ON CALIFORNIA BECOMING A FREE STATE
1850

67% AYE
25% NAY
8% NOT VOTING

Source: GovTrack.us

SLAVERY DECLINES IN WASHINGTON, D.C.
Source: National Archives

1800
4 SLAVES TO 1 FREE BLACK

1860
1 SLAVE TO 3 FREE BLACKS

FUGITIVE SLAVE ACT
1850

11 RELEASED
332 RETURNED TO OWNERS

RUNAWAY SLAVES 1850–1860

20,000 Estimated number of blacks who fled to Canada

$500 fine & 6 months' imprisonment for any person aiding a fugitive slave

Source: *The Slave Catchers: The Enforcement of the Fugitive Slave Law*

>> **Analyze Information** Based on the information on the circle graph, what can you infer about the reason Congressional representatives from slave states agreed to the Compromise of 1850?

 Interactive Cartoon

extra money, some judges sent African Americans to the South whether or not they were runaways.

The Fugitive Slave Act Enrages the North The Fugitive Slave Act enraged antislavery northerners. By forcing them to catch runaways, the law made northerners feel as if they were part of the slave system. In several northern cities, crowds tried to rescue fugitives from their captors.

Despite the compromise, tensions remained high because neither side got everything that it wanted. The new Fugitive Slave Act was especially hard for northerners to accept. Each time the act was enforced, it convinced more northerners that slavery was immoral and evil.

To counter the Fugitive Slave Act, many northern states passed personal liberty laws. These laws made it harder to recapture those accused of running away. The laws brought suspects before judges, provided jury trials, and prohibited kidnapping.

Some laws also gave legal assistance. One state, Vermont, declared free any enslaved person who entered the state. Southerners were outraged by these laws and called any interference with the Fugitive Slave Act unconstitutional.

Effects of the Compromise of 1850
The Compromise of 1850 had the effect of holding the union together for a while longer and creating a peaceful solution to the threat of secession by the South and civil war. However, the conflict between the North and the South over the issues of slavery and its expansion remained. Many

$150 REWARD

RANAWAY from the subscriber, on the night of the 2d instant, a negro man, who calls himself *Henry May*, about 22 years old, 5 feet 6 or 8 inches high, ordinary color, rather chunky built, bushy head, and has it divided mostly on one side, and keeps it very nicely combed; has been raised in the house, and is a first rate dining-room servant, and was in a tavern in Louisville for 18 months. I expect he is now in Louisville trying to make his escape to a free state, (in all probability to Cincinnati, Ohio.) Perhaps he may try to get employment on a steamboat. He is a good cook, and is handy in any capacity as a house servant. Had on when he left, a dark cassinett coatee, and dark striped cassinett pantaloons, new—he had other clothing. I will give $50 reward if taken in Louisvill; 100 dollars if taken one hundred miles from Louisville in this State, and 150 dollars if taken out of this State, and delivered to me, or secured in any jail so that I can get him again. **WILLIAM BURKE.**
Bardstown, Ky., September 3d, 1838.

>> Slave owners often posted rewards for captured fugitives, as in this poster from 1838. **Hypothesize** How might the Fugitive Slave Act of 1850 have affected the practice of offering rewards for turning in African Americans who fled slavery?

▶ **Interactive Gallery**

in the North and in the South were not satisfied with the compromise.

Three great Congressional leaders' actions had an effect on the conflict over slavery and the Compromise of 1850, just as they had had on an earlier compromise, the compromise Tariff of 1833 that ended the Nullification Crisis. In 1833, the actions of Henry Clay and John C. Calhoun had brought the passage of the compromise tariff, while Daniel Webster stood in opposition. In 1850, Clay, the Great Compromiser, once again arranged the passage of a compromise, but this time with the support of Webster, as Calhoun tried to block the compromise. As they had in 1833, the compromisers of 1850 helped preserve the Union. In 1850, though, the opponents of compromise threatened to tear it apart.

? GENERATE EXPLANATIONS How did the Fugitive Slave Act cause tensions between northerners and southerners?

A Book Sways the North Against Slavery

An event in 1852 added to the growing antislavery mood of the North. Harriet Beecher Stowe, a New England woman, published a novel called *Uncle Tom's Cabin*. Stowe wrote the novel to show the evils of slavery and the injustice of the Fugitive Slave Act.

A Powerful Story Appeals to Northerners Stowe told the story of Uncle Tom, an enslaved African American noted for his kindness and piety. Tom's world is shattered when he is bought by the brutal Simon Legree. When Tom refuses to reveal the whereabouts of two runaways, Legree whips him to death. *Uncle Tom's Cabin* had wide appeal among northern readers.

The first printing, consisting of 5,000 copies, sold out in just two days. It quickly became a best seller, selling 300,000 copies the first year. Eventually, the book sold millions of copies and was translated into dozens of languages.

Nationwide Reaction Is Mixed Although *Uncle Tom's Cabin* was popular in the North, southerners objected to the book. They claimed that it did not give a true picture of slave life. Indeed, Stowe had seen little of slavery firsthand.

Despite such objections, *Uncle Tom's Cabin* helped to change the way northerners felt about slavery. No longer could they ignore slavery as a political problem for Congress to settle. More and more northerners now saw slavery as a moral problem facing every American. For this reason, *Uncle Tom's Cabin* was one of the most important books in American history.

? CHECK UNDERSTANDING What legitimate complaint did southerners have about *Uncle Tom's Cabin*?

ASSESSMENT

1. **Generate Explanations** What was the effect of the Missouri Compromise?

2. **Draw Conclusions** What could explain why the Wilmot Proviso passed in the House but did not pass in the Senate?

3. **Summarize** the South's reaction to California's request for admission to the Union.

4. **Compare** Vermont declared free any enslaved person who entered the state, an action in direct conflict with the Fugitive Slave Act. How was Vermont's declaration similar to that of South Carolina, which in 1832 declared a tariff passed by Congress, the so-called Tariff of Abominations, illegal?

5. **Draw Conclusions** Why was the Fugitive Slave Act advantageous to the southern states?

Growing Tensions

>> Border Ruffians from Missouri launched violent raids into the Kansas Territory to intimidate antislavery settlers. Here, the two sides clash at Fort Scott, Kansas.

⊡ **Interactive Flipped Video**

The Compromise of 1850 dealt mainly with lands that were part of the Mexican Cession. It did not change slavery policies of the Missouri Compromise for lands that had been part of the Louisiana Purchase. However, the Compromise of 1850 caused some people to question whether the Missouri Compromise needed changing.

>> Objectives

Identify the goals and outcomes of the Kansas-Nebraska Act.

Summarize the impact of the Dred Scott case on the nation.

Explain why the Republican Party was founded.

Explain the rapid emergence of Abraham Lincoln as a Republican Party leader.

Describe the reaction to John Brown's raid on Harpers Ferry.

>> Key Terms

Kansas-Nebraska Act
Border Ruffians
guerrilla warfare
lawsuit
arsenal
treason
martyr
Dred Scott v. Sandford
Republican Party

⊡ **PEARSON realize.** www.PearsonRealize.com
Access your Digital Lesson.

The Question of Slavery in Kansas and Nebraska

In January 1854, Senator Stephen Douglas introduced a bill to set up a government for the lands covering the northwestern part of the Louisiana Purchase. This territory stretched from present-day Oklahoma north to present-day Canada, and from Missouri west to the Rockies.

Douglas knew that white southerners did not want to add another free state to the Union. He proposed that this large region be divided into two territories, Kansas and Nebraska. The settlers living in each territory would then be able to decide the issue of slavery by popular sovereignty. Douglas's bill was known as the **Kansas-Nebraska Act.**

The Kansas-Nebraska Act Ignites Sectionalist Disputes The Kansas-Nebraska Act seemed fair to many people.

After all, the Compromise of 1850 had applied popular sovereignty in New Mexico and Utah. Southern leaders especially supported the Kansas-Nebraska Act. They were sure that slave owners from neighboring Missouri would move with their enslaved African Americans across the border into Kansas. In time, they hoped, Kansas would become a slave state.

President Franklin Pierce, a Democrat elected in 1852, also supported the bill. With the President's help, Douglas pushed the Kansas-Nebraska Act through Congress. He did not realize it at the time, but he had lit a fire under a powder keg. Sectionalist arguments over slavery once again erupted, this time bringing the nation closer to civil war.

Many northerners were unhappy with the new law. The Missouri Compromise had already banned slavery in Kansas and Nebraska, they insisted. In effect, the

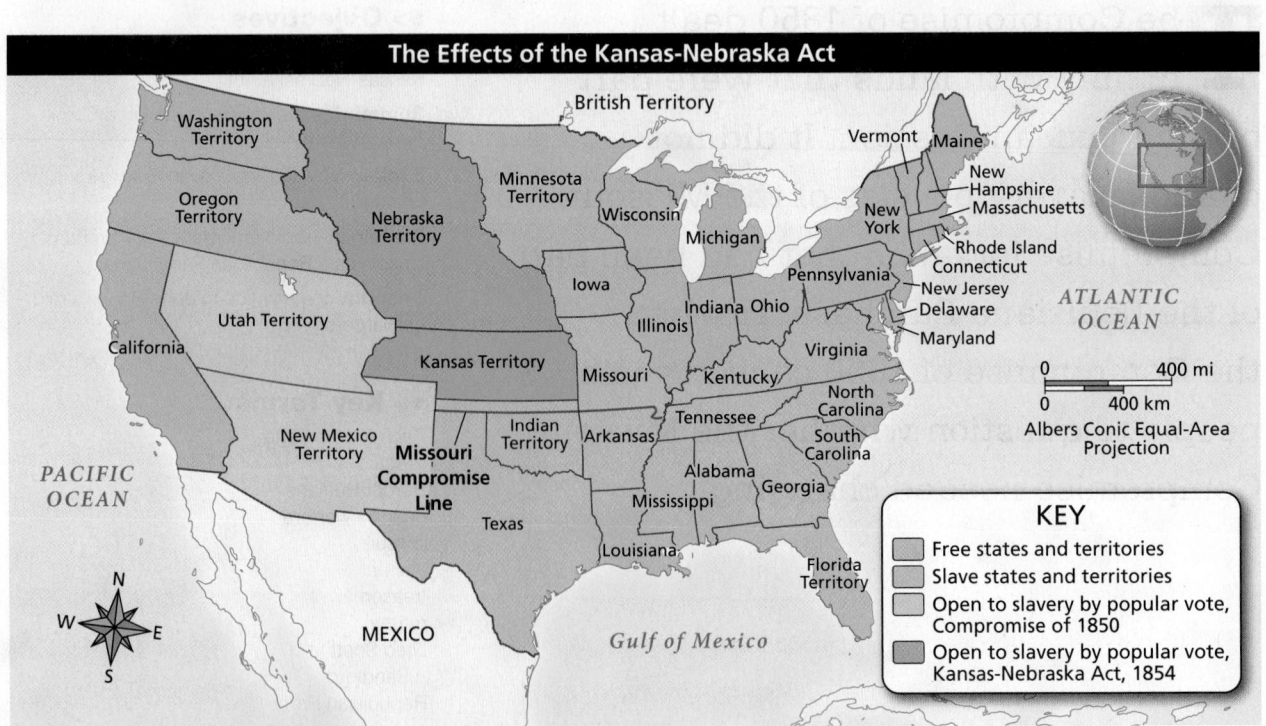

The Effects of the Kansas-Nebraska Act

KEY
- Free states and territories
- Slave states and territories
- Open to slavery by popular vote, Compromise of 1850
- Open to slavery by popular vote, Kansas-Nebraska Act, 1854

>> The Missouri Compromise of 1820 prohibited slavery in territory north of the 36' 30' parallel. **Analyze Maps** How did the Kansas-Nebraska Act of 1854 conflict with the Missouri Compromise of 1820?

Kansas-Nebraska Act would repeal the Missouri Compromise.

The northern reaction to the Kansas-Nebraska Act was swift and angry. Opponents of slavery called the act a "criminal betrayal of precious rights." Slavery could now spread to areas that had been free for more than 30 years. Some northerners protested by openly challenging the Fugitive Slave Act.

? CHECK UNDERSTANDING Why did northerners consider the Kansas-Nebraska Act a betrayal?

Violent Clashes Over Slavery in Kansas

Kansas now became a testing ground for popular sovereignty. Stephen Douglas hoped that settlers would decide the slavery issue peacefully on election day. Instead, proslavery and antislavery forces sent settlers to Kansas to fight for control of the territory.

Most of the new arrivals were farmers from neighboring states. Their main interest in moving to Kansas was to acquire cheap land. Few of these settlers owned enslaved African Americans. At the same time, abolitionists brought in more than 1,000 settlers from New England.

Proslavery settlers moved into Kansas as well. They wanted to make sure that antislavery forces did not overrun the territory. Proslavery bands from Missouri often rode across the border. These **Border Ruffians**, as they were called, battled the antislavery forces in Kansas.

Rival Governments in Kansas In 1855, Kansas held elections to choose lawmakers. Hundreds of Border Ruffians crossed into Kansas and voted illegally.

>> Angry citizens in Boston protested an 1854 court order to return Anthony Burns to slavery in Virginia. His return was in accordance with the Fugitive Slave Act. An army escort marched Burns to the Boston waterfront.

They helped to elect a proslavery legislature.

The new legislature quickly passed laws to support slavery. One law said that people could be put to death for helping enslaved African Americans escape. Another made speaking out against slavery a crime punishable by two years of hard labor. Antislavery settlers refused to accept these laws. They elected their own governor and legislature. With two rival governments, Kansas was in chaos. Armed gangs roamed the territory looking for trouble.

Pro- and Antislavery Forces Fight in Kansas A band of proslavery men raided the town of Lawrence, an antislavery stronghold, in 1856. The attackers

>> John Brown led fellow antislavery settlers on a murderous raid in Kansas against proslavery settlers in 1856. **Infer** What conditions led Brown to take this action?

destroyed homes and smashed the press of a Free-Soil newspaper.

John Brown, an abolitionist, decided to strike back. Brown had moved to Kansas to help make it a free state. He claimed that God had sent him to punish supporters of slavery.

Brown rode with his four sons and two other men to the town of Pottawatomie (paht uh WAHT uh mee) Creek. In the middle of the night, they dragged five proslavery settlers from their beds and murdered them.

The killings at Pottawatomie Creek led to even more violence. Both sides fought fiercely and engaged in **guerrilla warfare**, or warfare in which small military groups use surprise attacks and other methods. By late 1856, more than 200 people had been killed. Newspapers started calling the territory "Bleeding Kansas."

? GENERATE EXPLANATIONS How did events in Kansas foreshadow the looming Civil War?

Violence Over Slavery Breaks Out in the Senate

Even before John Brown's attack, the battle over Kansas had spilled into the Senate. Charles Sumner of Massachusetts was the leading abolitionist senator. In one speech, the sharp-tongued Sumner denounced the proslavery legislature of Kansas. He then viciously criticized his southern foes, singling out Andrew Butler, an elderly senator from South Carolina.

Butler was not in the Senate on the day Sumner spoke. A few days later, however, Butler's nephew, Congressman Preston Brooks, marched into the Senate chamber. Using a heavy cane, Brooks beat Sumner until he fell down, bloody and unconscious, to the floor. Sumner did not fully recover from the beating for three years.

Many southerners felt that Sumner got what he deserved for his verbal abuse of another senator. Hundreds of people sent canes to Brooks to show their support.

To northerners, however, the brutal act was more evidence that slavery led to violence. The violence in the Senate was another warning that the nation was veering toward a civil war over slavery.

? DRAW CONCLUSIONS What does the altercation in the Senate tell you about the mood of the country in the late-1850s?

>> Proslavery Representative Preston Brooks beat abolitionist Senator Charles Sumner on the Senate floor. **Analyze Political Cartoons** How does the cartoon portray northerners and southerners differently?

Interactive Gallery

The Impact of the Dred Scott Case

With Congress in an uproar, many Americans looked to the Supreme Court to settle the slavery issue and restore peace. In 1857, the Court ruled on a case that involved an enslaved man named Dred Scott. Instead of bringing harmony, however, the Court's decision further divided the North and the South.

Dred Scott had been enslaved for many years in Missouri. Later, he moved with his owner, who was an army surgeon, to Illinois and then to the Wisconsin Territory, where slavery was not allowed. After they returned to Missouri, Scott's owner died. The owner's wife took ownership of Scott, and eventually those rights transferred to her brother, John Sanford. Antislavery lawyers helped Scott

to file a **lawsuit**, a legal case brought to settle a dispute between people or groups. Scott's lawyers argued that, because Scott had lived in a free territory, he had become a free man.

The upreme Court Ruling on *Dred Scott v. Sandford* In time, the case reached the Supreme Court as ***Dred Scott v. Sandford.*** The Court's decision shocked and dismayed Americans who opposed slavery. First, the Court ruled that Scott could not file a lawsuit because, as an enslaved person, he was not a citizen. Also, the Court's written decision clearly stated that slaves were considered to be property.

The Court's ruling did not stop there. Instead, the Justices went on to make a sweeping decision about the larger issue of slavery in the territories. According to the Court, Congress did not have the power

>> Dred Scott, who had once lived in a free territory, appealed for his freedom after his owner died. **Predict Consequences** How did the Supreme Court ruling against Dred Scott challenge the Missouri Compromise?

▶ **Interactive Gallery**

>> An eloquent speaker, Frederick Douglass, who had once been enslaved, became a powerful spokesperson for the abolition of slavery. He also published an autobiography describing the brutality of slavery.

to outlaw slavery in any territory. The Court's ruling meant that the Missouri Compromise was unconstitutional.

The *Dred Scott v. Sandford* decision had a far-reaching impact on life in the United States. It meant that enslaved African Americans could not find freedom anywhere in the United States, and together with the Fugitive Slave Act, that no part of the United States could be completely free of slavery. The decision also further increased tensions between the North and South.

The Democratic Party began to divide over the issue of slavery. The decision also increased support for abolition in the North.

Reactions to *Dred Scott* v. *Sandford*
White southerners rejoiced at *Dred Scott v. Sandford.* It meant that slavery was legal in all the territories. This was just what white southerners had been demanding for years.

African Americans responded angrily to the Dred Scott decision. In the North, many held public meetings to condemn the ruling. At one meeting in Philadelphia, a speaker hoped that the ruling would lead more whites to "join with us in our efforts to recover the long lost boon of freedom."

White northerners were also shocked by the ruling. Many had hoped that slavery would eventually die out if it were restricted to the South. Now, however, slavery could spread throughout the West. Even northerners who disliked abolitionists felt that the ruling in *Dred Scott v. Sandford* was wrong. A newspaper in Cincinnati declared, "We are now one great . . . slaveholding community."

Abolitionist Frederick Douglass also spoke out against *Dred Scott v. Sandford:* "This infamous decision," he declared, "maintains that slaves . . . are property in the same sense that horses, sheep, and swine are property . . . that [people] of African descent are not and cannot be citizens of the United States." He told his listeners:

> "All I ask of the American people is that they live up to the Constitution, adopt its principles, [take in] its spirit, and enforce its provisions. When this is done . . . liberty . . . will become the inheritance of all the inhabitants of this highly favored country."
>
> —Frederick Douglass, *Collected Speeches, 1857*

❓ COMPARE the decision in *Dred Scott v. Sandford* with the Preamble to the Declaration of Independence which states ". . . all men are created equal; [and] are endowed by their creator with certain unalienable rights." How do the two differ?

The Republican Party Challenges Other Parties

By the mid-1850s, people who opposed slavery in the territories sought a new political voice. Neither Whigs nor Democrats, they argued, would take a strong stand against slavery. "We have submitted to slavery long enough," an Ohio Democrat declared.

A group of Free-Soilers, northern Democrats, and antislavery Whigs gathered in Michigan in 1854. There they formed the **Republican Party**. Its main goal was to keep slavery out of the western territories. Some Republicans were abolitionists. They hoped to end slavery in the South as well. Most Republicans, however, wanted only to stop the spread of slavery.

Growth of the Republican Party The new party grew quickly. By 1856, it was ready

to challenge the older parties for power. Republicans selected John C. Frémont to run for President.

Frémont was a frontiersman who had fought for California's independence. He had little political experience, but he opposed the spread of slavery.

Frémont's main opponent was Democrat James Buchanan of Pennsylvania. Many Democrats saw Buchanan as a "northern man with southern principles." They hoped that he would attract voters in both the North and the South. Former President Millard Fillmore also ran as the candidate of the American, or "Know-Nothing," party. A strong supporter of the Union, Fillmore feared that a Republican victory would split the nation apart.

Buchanan won the election with support from a large majority of southerners and

>> American Party candidate Millard Fillmore separates Republican John Frémont (left) and Democrat James Buchanan (right) before they can harm one another. **Analyze Political Cartoons** What can you infer about Fillmore's view on sectional tensions?

many northerners. Still, the Republicans made a strong showing in the election. Without the support of a single southern state, Frémont won one third of the popular vote. Southerners worried that their influence in the national government was fading.

? CHECK UNDERSTANDING Why was the Republican Party established in 1854?

Abraham Lincoln Leads the Republican Party

The next test for the Republican party came in 1858 in Illinois. Abraham Lincoln, a Republican, challenged Democrat Stephen Douglas for his seat in the Senate. Because most Americans expected Douglas to run for President in 1860, the race captured the attention of the whole nation.

>> Abraham Lincoln had only one year of formal education, so he taught himself to read by firelight in his Indiana home.

Lincoln Attacks Proslavery Positions

Abraham Lincoln was born on the Kentucky frontier. Like many frontier people, his parents moved often to find better land. The family lived in Indiana and later in Illinois. As a child, Lincoln spent only a year in school. Still, he taught himself to read, poring over his books by firelight.

After Lincoln left home, he opened a store in Illinois. There, he studied law on his own and launched a career in politics. He served eight years in the state legislature and one term in Congress. Bitterly opposed to the Kansas-Nebraska Act, he decided to run for the Senate in 1858.

When the race began, Lincoln was not a national figure. Still, people in Illinois knew him well and liked him. To them, he was "just folks"—someone who enjoyed picnics, wrestling contests, and all their favorite pastimes. His honesty, wit, and plain-spoken manner made him a good speaker. Lincoln strongly opposed the Dred Scott decision and used his political platform to speak against it. He voiced his opposition when he debated Stephen Douglas. He later spoke against it during his presidential campaign, rallying Republicans to oppose the Court's decision.

Lincoln and Douglas Debate Slavery

During the Senate campaign, Lincoln challenged Douglas to a series of debates. Douglas was not eager to accept, but he did. During the campaign, the two debated seven times. Slavery was the important issue.

Douglas wanted to settle the slavery question by popular sovereignty, or a popular vote in each territory. He personally disliked slavery, but stated that he did not care whether people in the territories voted "down or up" for it.

Lincoln, like nearly all whites of his day, did not believe in "perfect equality" between blacks and whites. He did, however, believe that slavery was wrong.

> "There is no reason in the world why the negro is not entitled to all the natural rights [listed] in the Declaration of Independence, the right to life, liberty, and the pursuit of happiness. . . . In the right to eat the bread, without the leave of anybody else, which his own hand earns, he is my equal and the equal of Judge Douglas, and the equal of every living man."
>
> —Abraham Lincoln, Speech at Ottawa, Illinois, August 21, 1858

Since slavery was a "moral, social, and political wrong," said Lincoln, Douglas and other Americans should not treat it as an unimportant question to be voted "down or up." Lincoln was totally opposed to slavery in the territories. Still, he was not an abolitionist. He had no wish to interfere with slavery in the states where it already existed.

Lincoln Emerges as a Leader Week after week, both men spoke nearly every day to large crowds. Newspapers reprinted their campaign speeches. The more northerners read Lincoln's words, the more they thought about the injustice of slavery.

In the end, Douglas won the election by a slim margin. Still, Lincoln was a winner, too. He was now known throughout the country. Two years later, the two rivals would again meet face to face—both seeking the office of President.

❓ **DESCRIBE** the contradiction in Lincoln's position on slavery.

>> In 1858, Abraham Lincoln and Stephen Douglas debated over the spread of slavery. Both men disliked slavery, but Lincoln opposed its spread, while Douglas favored settling the issue by a popular vote in each territory.

>> Although many northerners did not consider them equals, many African Americans in northern states were free.

THE CHANGING PERCEPTION OF SLAVERY

1854
SUPPORT FOR THE KANSAS-NEBRASKA ACT

HOUSE VOTE
100 AGAINST
113 FOR

SENATE VOTE
14 AGAINST
37 FOR

Source: Library of Congress

1855
KANSAS ELECTION FOR TERRITORIAL LEGISLATURE

2,905 LEGALLY-REGISTERED VOTERS

6,218 ACTUAL VOTES CAST

791 VOTES FOR ANTI-SLAVERY CANDIDATES

5,427 VOTES FOR PRO-SLAVERY CANDIDATES

Source: John Lalor, *Cyclopaedia of Political Science, Political Economy, and of the Political History of the United States* (1883)

1858
ILLINOIS SENATE ELECTION

54% DOUGLAS
(WON ALL DEMOCRATIC LEGISLATORS' VOTES)

46% LINCOLN
(WON ALL REPUBLICAN LEGISLATORS' VOTES)

Source: Northern Illinois University

>> **Analyze Data** How did the Kansas-Nebraska Act, which allowed states to decide if they would allow slavery, affect the outcome of the Kansas election for territorial legislature in 1855?

John Brown's Antislavery Campaign

In the meantime, more bloodshed inflamed divisions between the North and the South. In 1859, the radical abolitionist John Brown carried his antislavery campaign from Kansas to the East. He led a group of followers, including five African Americans, to the town of Harpers Ferry, Virginia.

There, Brown planned to raid a federal **arsenal**, or gun warehouse. He thought that enslaved African Americans would flock to him at the arsenal. He would then give them weapons and lead them in a revolt.

The Impact of John Brown's Raid Brown quickly gained control of the arsenal. No slave uprising took place, however. Instead, troops under the command of Robert E. Lee killed ten raiders and captured Brown.

Most people, in both the North and the South, thought that Brown's plan to lead a slave revolt was insane. After all, there were few enslaved African Americans in Harpers Ferry. Furthermore, after seizing the arsenal, Brown did nothing further to encourage a slave revolt. At his trial, however, Brown seemed perfectly sane. He sat quietly as the court found him guilty of murder and **treason**, or actions against one's country. Before hearing his sentence, he gave a moving defense of his actions. He showed no emotion as he was sentenced to death.

A Symbol of the Nation's Divisions

Because he conducted himself with such dignity during his trial, John Brown became a hero to many northerners. Some considered him a **martyr** because he was willing to give up his life for his beliefs. On the morning he was hanged, church bells rang solemnly throughout the North. In years to come, New Englanders would sing a popular song with the chorus: "John Brown's body lies a mold'ring in the grave, but his soul is marching on." When poet Julia Ward Howe heard the song, she was inspired to write the poem "The Battle Hymn of the Republic," which became a popular Civil War song set to the same tune, a piece of music that was unique to American culture.

To white southerners, the northern response to John Brown's death was outrageous. People were singing the praises of a man who had tried to lead a slave revolt! Many southerners became convinced that the North wanted to destroy slavery—and the South along with it. The nation was poised for a violent clash.

>> In this abolitionist painting, John Brown pauses on his way to his execution to kiss an enslaved woman's baby.

? **CHECK UNDERSTANDING** Why were southerners outraged at the northern response to John Brown's execution?

ASSESSMENT

1. **Draw Conclusions** Some northerners were outraged by the passage of the Kansas-Nebraska Act. What did that outrage have to do with the location of the Kansas Territory?

2. **Summarize** the issue that was brought to the Supreme Court in *Dred Scott* v. *Sandford*.

3. **Check Understanding** What worried southerners about the Republican Party victories in the election of 1856?

4. **Identify Central Issues** Neither Stephen Douglas nor Abraham Lincoln approved of slavery, so what disagreement did they have?

5. **Hypothesize** Why did John Brown's raid on a federal arsenal at Harpers Ferry fail?

Division and the Outbreak of War

>> Davis ordered Confederate troops to take control of federal buildings and forts in the South. Troops such as these soldiers began to join Confederate forces to respond to his order.

[▶] **Interactive Flipped Video**

>> Objectives

Identify how the 1860 election reflected sectional differences.

Explain why southern states seceded from the Union following the election of 1860.

Identify how the Civil War began in 1861.

Describe the strengths and weaknesses of the North and South as the war began.

Identify the leaders of each side in the war.

>> Key Terms

unamendable
border state
martial law
Robert E. Lee
Jefferson Davis

The Republican National Convention for the presidential election of 1860 took place in Chicago, Illinois. Abraham Lincoln faced William Seward for the nomination. Lincoln, whose fame had increased during the Lincoln-Douglas debates in 1858, won the nomination.

Abraham Lincoln and the Election of 1860

The Democrats held their convention in Charleston, South Carolina. Lack of unity proved costly for the Democratic party. Southerners wanted the party to call for slavery in all new territories. However, northern Democrats refused to do so. In the end, the party split in two. Northern Democrats chose Stephen Douglas to run for President. Southern Democrats picked John Breckinridge of Kentucky.

Some Americans tried to heal the split between the North and the South by forming a new party. The Constitutional Union party chose John Bell of Tennessee to run for President.

Bell was a moderate who wanted to keep the Union together. He got support only in a few southern states that were still seeking a compromise.

Douglas was sure that Lincoln would win. However, he believed that Democrats "must try to save the Union." He urged southerners to stay with the Union, no matter who was elected.

When the votes were counted, Lincoln had carried the North and won the election. He was able to take advantage of divisions in the Democratic party. Also, southern votes did not affect the outcome at all. Lincoln's name was not even on the ballot in 10 southern states. Northerners outnumbered southerners and outvoted them. The stage for civil war had been set.

? **GENERATE EXPLANATIONS** How did the split in the Democratic Party in the 1860 election reflect the split in the country?

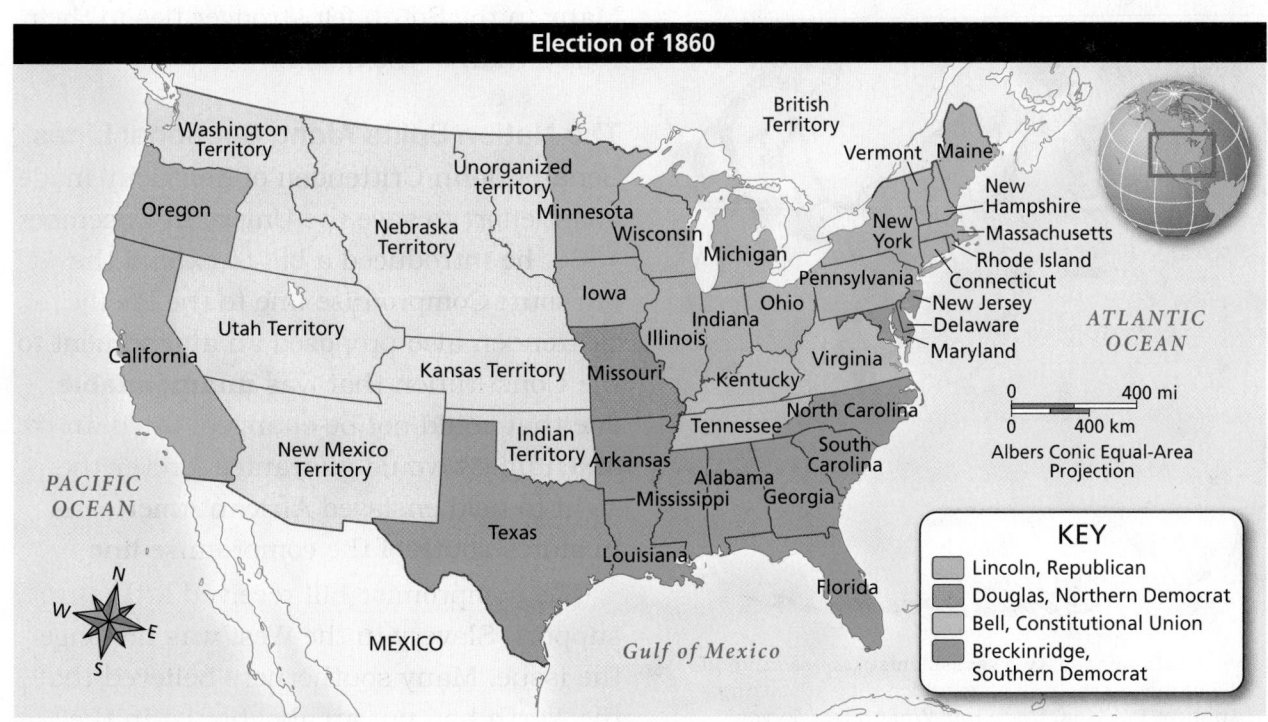

Election of 1860

KEY
- Lincoln, Republican
- Douglas, Northern Democrat
- Bell, Constitutional Union
- Breckinridge, Southern Democrat

>> The results of the 1860 election showed a nation deeply divided. **Analyze Maps** How did the electoral vote reflect sectional divisions?

>> A crowd in South Carolina gathered to learn that Lincoln had been elected President. **Infer** How was this crowd likely to have reacted to Lincoln's victory with only northern votes?

>> In this cartoon, two secessionists are sawing off the branch of the tree upon which they are sitting. **Analyze Political Cartoons** What effect do you think the artist believes secession would have on the South?

The Nation Moves Toward Civil War

Lincoln's election brought a strong reaction in the South. A South Carolina woman described how the news was received:

"The excitement was very great. Everybody was talking at the same time. One . . . more moved than the others, stood up saying . . . 'No more vain regrets—sad forebodings are useless. The stake is life or death.'"

—Mary Boykin Chesnut, *A Diary From Dixie*, 1860

To many southerners, Lincoln's election meant that the South no longer had a voice in national government. They believed that the President and Congress were now set against their interests—especially slavery. Even before the election, South Carolina's governor had written to other southern governors. If Lincoln won, he wrote, it would be their duty to leave the Union. This sentiment revealed the strong currents of sectionalism running through the country. Many in the South felt stronger ties to their region than to the nation.

The Nation Splits Along Sectional Lines

Senator John Crittenden of Kentucky made a last effort to save the Union. In December 1860, he introduced a bill to extend the Missouri Compromise line to the Pacific. Crittenden also proposed an amendment to the Constitution that was **unamendable**, one that could not be changed. Such an amendment would guarantee forever the right to hold enslaved African Americans in states south of the compromise line.

The compromise bill received little support. Slavery in the West was no longer the issue. Many southerners believed that the North had put an abolitionist in the White House. They felt that secession was their only choice. Most Republicans also were unwilling to surrender what they had won in the national election.

On December 20, 1860, South Carolina became the first state to secede. By late February 1861, Alabama, Florida, Georgia, Louisiana, Mississippi, and Texas had also seceded.

At a convention in Montgomery, Alabama, the seven states formed a new nation, the Confederate States of America. **Jefferson Davis** of Mississippi became the first president of the Confederacy.

Causes Leading to War Now a new issue emerged: whether southern states were allowed to secede under the Constitution. Most southerners believed that they had every right to secede. After all, the Declaration of Independence said that "it is the right of the people to alter or to abolish" a government that denies the rights of its citizens. Lincoln, they believed, would deny white southerners the right to own African Americans as slaves.

For many southerners, secession was an issue of states' rights and sovereignty, or independent control of an area. Many in the southern states believed that states had the sovereign right to secede. According to this view, states had the authority to make decisions without interference from the federal government, and the Constitution created a Union made up of states that could decide to leave the Union at any point. Those states also had the sovereign right to join together to form a new government, such as the Confederacy.

Lincoln disagreed. He maintained that the Constitution allowed for shared powers between national and state governments, but did not give states sovereignty that would allow them to secede. The causes of the looming Civil War thus

>> Jefferson Davis was sworn in as President of the Confederacy in Montgomery, Alabama, in 1861. He believed, as did most southerners, that Lincoln would violate southerners' rights.

included sectionalism, disagreement over the extension of slavery, claims of states' rights, and disagreement over the constitutionality of those claims.

? **COMPARE AND CONTRAST** the views of southerners and President Lincoln on the issues of state sovereignty and the right to secede from the Union.

War Breaks Out

When Lincoln took the oath of office on March 4, 1861, he faced a dangerous situation. Seven southern states had seceded from the United States and had joined together to form the Confederacy.

Lincoln's First Inaugural Address

When he took office, Lincoln delivered an inaugural address. In his inaugural

>> Just one month after Jefferson Davis became president of the Confederacy, Abraham Lincoln was sworn in as President of the United States at the Capitol. In his speech, Lincoln said that secession was unconstitutional.

required that the Union be preserved. On liberty, again, Lincoln emphasized that the states' liberty was constrained by their acceptance of the Constitution and did not include a right to secede.

Lincoln also addressed another aspect of liberty. He stated his willingness to enforce the Fugitive Slave Act, but only if the liberty of free African Americans from kidnapping and enslavement could be ensured. Regarding equality, Lincoln assured Americans that he would provide government services and enforce federal law equally in all states, whether they were slave or free states.

Finally, on government, Lincoln stated that government required acquiescence, or the willingness to accept laws whether or not a person agreed with those laws. The unwillingness of the South to accept his legal election under the Constitution, he implied, was a threat to government.

address, Lincoln warned that "no state . . . can lawfully get out of the Union." Still, he pledged that there would be no war unless the South started it:

"In YOUR hands, my dissatisfied fellow-countrymen, and not in MINE, is the momentous issue of civil war. . . . We are not enemies, but friends. We must not be enemies. Though passion may have strained, it must not break our bonds of affection."

— Abraham Lincoln, First Inaugural Address

Lincoln's First Inaugural Address expressed ideas about union, liberty, equality, and government. Regarding union, Lincoln emphasized that the Constitution set limits on the actions of states, and that there was no provision in the Constitution for secession. That is, the Constitution

The Inaugural Address of Jefferson Davis By the time Lincoln gave his address, the Confederate States of America had already sworn in Jefferson Davis as President. Davis had a role similar to that of the American President, being chief executive of the Confederate government. In his inaugural address, he said the Confederacy would adopt the same Constitution as the United States for its government

However, Davis's inaugural speech was very different from Lincoln's. Whereas Lincoln pledged to keep the Union together, Davis explained why the South had decided to secede from the Union. Davis said secession was based on "the desire to preserve our own rights and promote our own welfare."

He also said, "It is joyous, in the midst of perilous times, to look around upon a people united in heart, where one purpose of high resolve animates and actuates the whole—where the sacrifices to be made are not weighed in the balance against honor and right and liberty and equality." Lincoln, in contrast, described secession as "the essence of anarchy." He believed secession countered the principles of liberty and equality on which the nation was founded and its government was based. For Davis, liberty and equality existed only between white men. In a later speech, Lincoln would extend the idea of equality to all Americans.

Davis emphasized that government exists only with the consent of the governed. Since southerners could no longer consent to a government they considered opposed to their interests, they had to break away and form a government to which they could consent. This was in contrast to Lincoln's argument that government sometimes requires citizens to acquiesce to, or obey, laws with which they

disagree. Davis also argued that, under the U.S. Constitution, states had the right to reclaim powers that they had given to the federal government by seceding. Lincoln took the opposite view, that states had no such right.

1861—Lincoln Faces War Lincoln said in his inaugural address that he did not want war, but Jefferson Davis had already ordered Confederate forces to begin seizing federal forts in the South. Lincoln faced a difficult decision. Should he let the Confederates take over federal property? If he did, he would seem to be admitting that states had the right to leave the Union. On the other hand, if he sent troops to hold the forts, he might start a civil war. He might also lose the support of the eight slave states that had not seceded from the Union.

In April, the Confederacy forced Lincoln to make up his mind. By then, Confederate troops controlled nearly all forts, post

>> When Confederate troops fired across the Charleston Harbor at Fort Sumter, one of only four remaining federal forts in the South, they started the American Civil War.

offices, and other federal buildings in the South. The Union held only three forts off the Florida coast and Fort Sumter in South Carolina. Fort Sumter was important to the Confederacy because it guarded Charleston Harbor.

The Attack on Fort Sumter President Lincoln learned that food supplies at Fort Sumter were running low. He notified the governor of South Carolina that he was going to ship food to the fort. Lincoln promised not to send troops or weapons.

The Confederates, however, felt that they could not leave the fort in Union hands. On April 11, 1861, they demanded that Fort Sumter surrender. Major Robert Anderson, the Union commander, refused to give in until he had run out of food or was ordered to surrender by the United States government. Confederate guns then opened fire. The Union troops quickly ran out of ammunition. On April 13, Anderson surrendered the fort.

When Confederate troops shelled Fort Sumter, people in Charleston gathered on their rooftops to watch. To many, it was like a fireworks show. No one knew that the fireworks marked the start of the Civil War, which would last four terrible years, from 1861 to 1865. This deadly part of the Civil War era would have devastating effects to lives, property, and national unity.

? SUMMARIZE Lincoln's dilemma over southern states taking control of federal property.

Taking Sides

When the war began, each side was convinced that its cause was just. Southerners believed in states' rights, so they believed that states had the right to leave the Union. In fact, they called the conflict the War for Southern Independence. White southerners wanted independence so that they could keep their traditional way of life—including the institution of slavery. They also believed

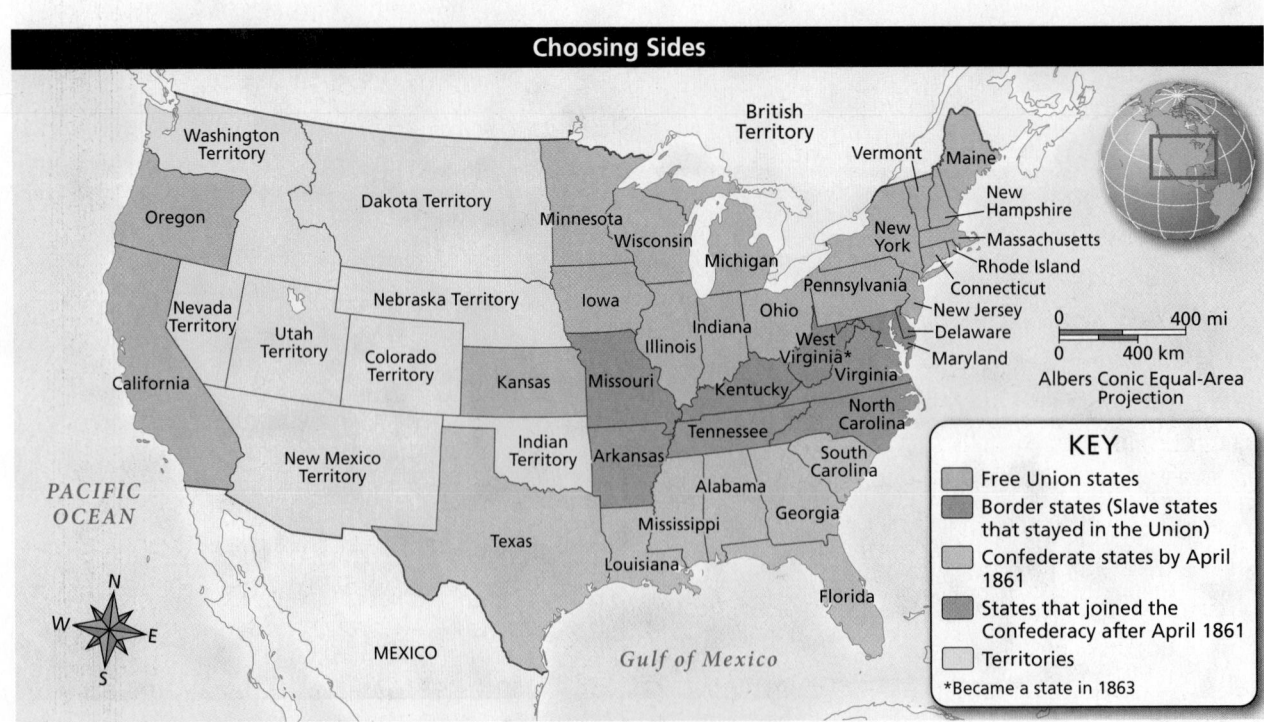

Choosing Sides

KEY
- Free Union states
- Border states (Slave states that stayed in the Union)
- Confederate states by April 1861
- States that joined the Confederacy after April 1861
- Territories

*Became a state in 1863

>> Analyze Maps Based on the information in the map, approximately what percentage of Union states were slave states during the Civil War?

the North had caused the war. Many southerners, therefore, also called it the War of Northern Aggression.

Northerners, meanwhile, believed that they had to fight to save the Union. At the outset of the war, abolishing slavery was not an official goal of the North. In fact, many northerners, guided by feelings of racism, approved of slavery. Racism is the belief that one race is by nature superior to another.

In April 1861, eight slave states were still in the Union. As the war began, they had to make the difficult decision of which side to join.

Their decision would greatly affect the outcome of the war. These states had more than half of the South's population and food crops. In addition, many of the South's factories were in these states.

Four of these states—Virginia, North Carolina, Tennessee, and Arkansas— quickly joined the Confederacy. However, after some wavering between the North and South, the four **border states**— Kentucky, Missouri, Maryland, and Delaware—decided to remain in the Union. Maryland was especially critical to the Union cause since it bordered the nation's capital at Washington, D.C.

Still, there were some citizens of the border states who supported the South. In April 1861, pro-Confederate mobs attacked Union troops in Baltimore, Maryland. In response, President Lincoln declared **martial law**, or rule by the army instead of the elected government. Many people who sided with the South were arrested. Sectionalism had led Americans to feel connected to their region, rather than to the country overall. Now they not only identified as northerners or southerners,

>> Recruitment of soldiers became major events in both the North and South, such as this parade in Philadelphia, Pennsylvania. Both sides needed soldiers quickly so that they could build their armies.

they had also officially split into two governments with military forces.

❓ **CHECK UNDERSTANDING** Why were both the North and South trying to attract slave states outside the Confederacy to join their cause?

Strengths and Weaknesses of the North and South

Both sides during the Civil War had strengths and weaknesses as the war began. The South had the strong advantage of fighting a defensive war. "We seek no conquest," said Confederate President Jefferson Davis. "All we ask is to be let alone." If the North did not move its forces into the South, the Confederacy would remain a separate country.

The South's Strengths at Home and Economic Limitations White southerners believed that they were fighting a war for

ECONOMIC DEVELOPMENT IN THE NORTH & SOUTH

POPULATION IN 1860

NORTH 27.71 MILLION

SOUTH 8.73 MILLION

50 U.S. CITIES WITH LARGEST POPULATIONS 1860

NORTH 38

5 BORDER STATES

SOUTH 7

Source: U.S. Census Bureau

TOTAL VALUE OF MANUFACTURED PRODUCTS 1860
TOP 5 NORTHERN & SOUTHERN STATES

Northern		Southern	
NY	$378,870,939	$50,652,124	VA
PA	$290,121,188	$17,987,225	TN
MA	$255,545,922	$16,925,564	GA
OH	$121,691,148	$16,678,698	NC
CT	$81,924,555	$15,587,473	LA

Source: Historical Census Browser, University of Virginia

UNION & CONFEDERATE RESOURCES 1861

	Union	Confederate
RAILROADS	71%	29%
FARM ACREAGE	65%	35%
MANUFACTURING WORKERS	92%	8%
FACTORIES (THOUSANDS)	110	18

Source: U.S. Census Bureau

>> **Analyze Data** Based on the information in the graphs, what advantages did the North have over the South at the start of the Civil War?

 Interactive Map

independence, similar to the American Revolution. Defending their homeland and their way of life gave them a strong reason to fight. "Our men must prevail in combat," one Confederate said, "or they will lose their property, country, freedom—in short, everything."

Confederate soldiers also enjoyed an advantage because they knew the southern countryside better. Friendly civilians often guided soldiers along obscure roads that did not appear on maps. Much of the South was wooded, too. Confederate forces used the woods for cover as they defended themselves against invading Union troops.

The South, however, had serious economic weaknesses. These weaknesses were the effects of economic differences between the North and the South. The South had few factories to produce weapons and other vital supplies. It also had few railroads to move troops and supplies. The railroads that it did have often did not

connect to one another. Tracks simply ran between two points and then stopped.

The South also had political problems. The Confederate constitution favored states' rights and limited the authority of the central government. As a result, the Confederate government often found it difficult to get things done. On one occasion, for example, the governor of Georgia insisted that only Georgian officers should command Georgian troops.

Finally, the South had a small population. Only about 9 million people lived in the Confederacy, compared with 22 million in the Union.

More than one third of the southern population were enslaved African Americans. As a result, the South did not have enough people to serve as soldiers and to support the war effort.

The North's Military Disadvantages and Financial Strengths The North had almost four times as many free citizens as the South. Thus, it had a large source of volunteers. It also had many people to grow food and to work in factories making supplies.

The North's biggest advantages reflected the effects of economic differences with the South. Industry was the North's greatest resource. Before the war, northern factories produced more than 90 percent of the nation's manufactured goods. Once the war began, these factories quickly began making guns, bullets, cannons, boots, uniforms, and other supplies for the Union army. In addition, the North had more than 70 percent of the nation's rail lines, which it used to transport both troops and supplies.

The North benefited from a strong navy and a large fleet of trading ships. With few warships and only a small merchant fleet, the South was unable to compete with the North at sea.

Despite these advantages, the North faced a difficult military challenge. To bring the South back into the Union, northern soldiers had to conquer a huge area. Instead of defending their homes, they were invading unfamiliar land. As Union armies marched into the South, their lines of supply would be much longer than those of the Confederates and thus more open to attack.

? **SUMMARIZE** how a weak economy and weak industry can be problematic during wartime.

The Leadership Roles of Lincoln and Davis

Leadership was a crucial factor in the Civil War. President Jefferson Davis of the Confederacy, President Abraham Lincoln of the Union, and military leaders on both sides played key roles in determining the war's outcome.

Jefferson Davis Leads the South Before the war, many people thought that Davis was a stronger leader than Lincoln. Davis's experience prepared him for the position. However, he did not want it. As one observer stated:

> "Mr. Davis's military instincts still predominate, and his eager wish was to have joined the army instead of being elected president."
>
> —Arthur James Freemantle, from *The Freemantle Diary*

Davis had attended the United States Military Academy at West Point. He had served as an officer in the Mexican War. Later, he served as Secretary of War under President Franklin Pierce.

>> A graduate of West Point and an accomplished military officer with experience in the Mexican War, Jefferson Davis wished to serve in the Confederate Army rather than become the Confederacy's president.

[▶] **Interactive Chart**

Furthermore, Davis was widely respected in the South as President of the Confederacy for his honesty and courage. Davis, however, did not like to turn over to others the details of military planning. As a result, he spent much time worrying about small matters and arguing with his advisers.

The Leadership Qualities of Abraham Lincoln

At first, some northerners had doubts about Abraham Lincoln's ability to lead as President of the United States. He did not have much experience in national politics or military matters. However, Lincoln proved to be a patient but strong leader and a fine war planner.

Day by day, Lincoln gained the respect of those around him. Many liked his sense of humor. They noted that Lincoln even accepted criticism with a smile. When Secretary of War Edwin Stanton called Lincoln a fool, Lincoln commented, "Did Stanton say I was a fool? Then I must be one, for Stanton is generally right and he always says what he means."

The Role of Robert E. Lee, Military Leader

As the war began, army officers in the South had to decide whether to stay in the Union army and fight against their home states, or join the Confederate forces.

Robert E. Lee of Virginia faced this dilemma when Lincoln asked him to command the Union army. He explained in a letter to a friend:

> "If Virginia stands by the old Union, so will I. But if she secedes . . . , then I will still follow my native State with my sword and, if need be, with my life."
>
> —Robert E. Lee, quoted in Carl Sandburg's *Abraham Lincoln*

Virginia did secede and Lee refused Lincoln's offer. Later, Lee became commander of the Confederate army. Many of the prewar United States Army's best officers served the Confederacy. As a result, President Lincoln had trouble finding generals to match those of the South.

? **CHECK UNDERSTANDING** What advantages in leadership did the South have over the North?

ASSESSMENT

1. **Draw Conclusions** Why did Senator Crittenden's proposed compromise receive little support?

2. **Check Understanding** Why did Lincoln make a point of telling the governor of South Carolina that he was sending food, but not troops or arms, to Fort Sumter?

3. **Identify Central Issues** What motivated the South to fight in the Civil War?

4. **Summarize** the principal disadvantages the North faced in fighting the Civil War.

5. **Express Problems Clearly** How did Jefferson Davis's reluctance to serve as President of the Confederacy affect his leadership?

>> At the start of his first term, President Lincoln gained the respect of those around him. He was admired for his leadership as well as his good nature and sense of humor.

8.4 The Course of War

>> General George B. McClellan's Union forces defeated the Confederates at the Battle of Antietam. This illustration shows Union soldiers advancing toward Dunker Church during the battle.

[▶] **Interactive Flipped Video**

The North and South had different strategies for victory. The Union planned an aggressive campaign against the South. The South, meanwhile, planned to hold tight until the North lost the will to fight.

>> **Objectives**

Describe the strategies the North and South adopted to win the war.

Explain how early battles dispelled hopes for a quick end to the war.

Identify the victories of the Confederates and the Union in the early years of the war.

>> **Key Terms**

Battle of Bull Run
Virginia
Monitor
Battle of Antietam
Battle of
  Fredericksburg
Battle of
  Chancellorsville
Battle of Shiloh

461

[▶] **PEARSON realize.** www.PearsonRealize.com
Access your Digital Lesson.

The Different Strategies of the North and South

Union Strategy First, the Union planned to use its navy to blockade southern ports. This would cut off the South's supply of manufactured goods from Europe and its ability to earn money from cotton exports.

In the East, Union generals aimed to seize Richmond, Virginia, the Confederate capital. They thought that they might end the war quickly by capturing the Confederate government.

In the West, the Union planned to seize control of the Mississippi River. This would prevent the South from using the river to supply its troops. It would also separate Arkansas, Texas, and Louisiana from the rest of the Confederacy.

>> Washington, D.C., became a staging area for Union troops such as these in 1861. Troops gathered and trained for invading the South, part of the Union's aggressive strategy to win the war.

Confederate Strategy The South's strategy was simpler: the Confederate army would fight a defensive war until northerners tired of fighting. If the war became unpopular in the North, President Lincoln would have to stop the war and recognize the South's independence.

The Confederacy counted on European money and supplies to help fight the war. Southern cotton was important to the textile mills of England and other countries. Southerners were confident that Europeans would recognize the Confederacy as an independent nation and that the South could continue to sell Europe cotton for its factories.

❓ DESCRIBE how the Union plan for victory was more aggressive than the southern plan.

The Beginnings of a Long War

"Forward to Richmond! Forward to Richmond!" Every day for more than a month, the influential *New York Tribune* blazed this war cry across its front page. At last, responding to popular pressure, President Lincoln ordered an attack.

Stonewall Jackson Makes a Stand at Bull Run On July 21, 1861, Union troops set out from Washington, D.C., to attack the Confederate army, which was camped 30 miles southwest of the capital. Hundreds of Washingtonians, in a festive mood, rode out along with them to watch the battle. Many northerners thought the Union army would crush the Confederates.

The Union troops had not gone far when they met up with Confederate soldiers. A battle quickly followed. It took place near a small Virginia stream known as Bull Run, which was also near the town of Manassas.

At first, Union forces succeeded in breaking up Confederate battle lines. "The war is over!" yelled some soldiers from Massachusetts. But General Thomas Jackson rallied the Virginia troops on a nearby hill. "Look!" cried a Confederate officer to his men, "There is Jackson standing like a stone wall! Rally behind the Virginians!" From that day on, the general was known as "Stonewall" Jackson. Historians consider him one of the most gifted tactical commanders in the Civil War, and he led many successful military campaigns for the Confederate army.

In the end, it was the Union troops who panicked and ran. "Off they went," reported one observer, "across fields, toward the woods, anywhere, everywhere, to escape." For most of the soldiers, the retreat did not stop until they reached Washington, D.C.

The **Battle of Bull Run** (also referred to as the Battle of Manassas by the Confederates) showed both the Union and the Confederacy that their soldiers needed training. It also showed that the Confederate army could stand up to the Union, meaning the war would be long and bloody.

George McClellan Takes Command of the Union Army After the shocking disaster at Bull Run, President Lincoln appointed General George McClellan as commander of the Union army of the East, known as the Army of the Potomac. McClellan, a superb organizer, transformed inexperienced recruits into an army of trained soldiers prepared for battle.

McClellan, however, was very cautious. He delayed leading his troops into battle. Newspapers reported "all quiet along the Potomac" so often that the phrase became a national joke. Finally, President Lincoln lost patience. "If General McClellan does not want to use the army," the President snapped, "I would like to borrow it."

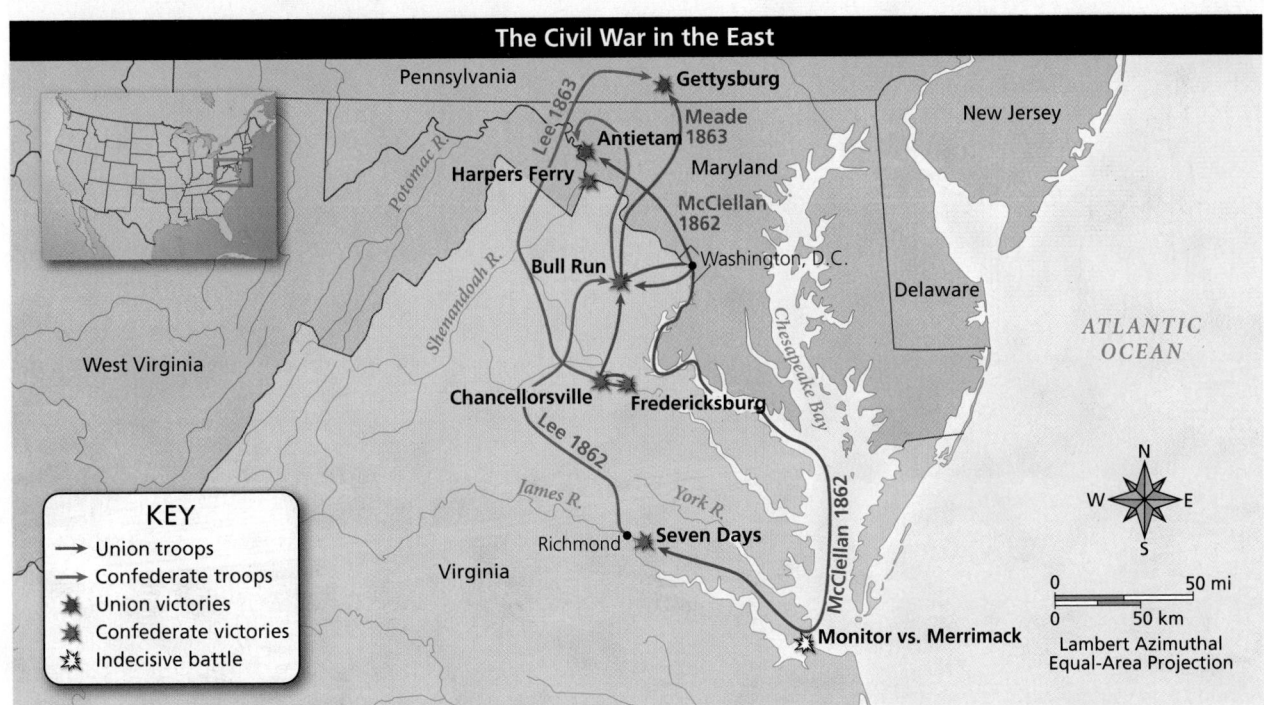

The Civil War in the East

KEY
→ Union troops
→ Confederate troops
✶ Union victories
✶ Confederate victories
✶ Indecisive battle

>> **Analyze Maps** Using the map key, measure the distance between the U.S. capital and the Confederate capital. How might the locations of the two capitals have influenced the battles and troop movements shown on the map?

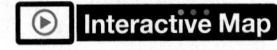
Interactive Map

At last, in March 1862, McClellan and most of his troops left Washington and sailed down the Potomac River and the Chesapeake Bay. After landing south of Richmond on the Virginia Peninsula, McClellan began inching slowly toward the Confederate capital.

Learning of the Union approach, General Robert E. Lee launched a series of counterattacks. At the same time, Lee sent General Stonewall Jackson north to threaten Washington. As a result, Lincoln was prevented from sending the rest of the Union army to help McClellan. Cautious as usual, McClellan abandoned the attack and retreated. The Peninsula Campaign, as it became known, had failed.

The Blockade and the Ironclads Early in the war, Union ships blockaded southern ports. At first, some small, fast ships slipped through the blockade. These "blockade runners" brought everything from matches to guns to the Confederacy.

In time, however, the blockade became more effective. Trade through southern ports dropped by more than 90 percent. The South desperately needed a way to break the Union blockade. One method it tried was the ironclad ship. *Clad* means *clothed*, or *covered*. Ironclad ships were covered with iron for protection.

Confederates took over an abandoned Union warship, the USS *Merrimack*. They covered it with iron plates and renamed it the **Virginia.** On its first day out in March 1862, the *Virginia* destroyed two Union ships and drove three more aground. Union cannonballs bounced harmlessly off the *Virginia's* metal skin.

The Union countered with its own ironclad, the **Monitor.** The two ships clashed in a body of water called Hampton Roads near the mouth of the Chesapeake Bay.

>> The Confederate ship *Virginia* battled the Union ship *Monitor* near Hampton Roads, Virginia, in 1862. This was the first engagement of ironclad warships in the Civil War.

Despite an exhausting battle, neither vessel seriously damaged the other, and both withdrew. Two months later, Confederates had to sink the *Virginia* when the Union captured Norfolk. The Union eventually built more than 50 ironclads.

Ironclad ships changed naval warfare. However, the South was never again able to mount a serious attack against the Union navy. The Union blockade held throughout the war.

The Battle of Antietam In September 1862, General Lee took the offensive and marched his troops north into Maryland. He believed that a southern victory on northern soil would be a great blow to northern morale.

Luck was against Lee, however. At an abandoned Confederate campsite, a Union officer found a copy of Lee's battle plan. It was wrapped around three cigars, left behind by a careless general. General McClellan was overjoyed to have the information. "If I cannot whip 'Bobbie Lee,' I will be willing to go home," he boasted.

However, McClellan was slow to act. Finally, after a few days, he attacked Lee's main force near a creek called Antietam (an TEE tuhm) in the town of Sharpsburg, Maryland, on September 17. In the battle that followed, more than 23,000 Union and Confederate soldiers were killed or wounded—in one day. September 17, 1862, remains the bloodiest day in American military history.

On the night of September 18, Lee ordered his troops to slip back into Virginia. The Confederates breathed a sigh of relief when they saw that McClellan was not pursuing them.

Neither side was a clear winner at the **Battle of Antietam** (also called the Battle of Sharpsburg by the Confederates). The

>> The crew of the Monitor is shown here on the ship's deck in 1862. During the battle with the Virginia , neither side suffered much damage.

battle was significant, however, because the North was able to claim victory, since Lee had ordered his forces to withdraw. As a result, northern morale improved. Still, President Lincoln was keenly disappointed. General McClellan had failed to follow up his victory by pursuing the Confederates. In November, Lincoln appointed General Ambrose Burnside to replace McClellan as commander of the Army of the Potomac.

? DRAW CONCLUSIONS What conclusions can you draw from the first battles of the Civil War?

Confederate Forces Win in the East

Two stunning victories for the Confederacy came in late 1862 and 1863. In December 1862, Union forces set out once again toward Richmond. General Robert E. Lee played a key role in both victories, part of

>> Union troops charged the Confederates at Fredericksburg. Confederate troops soundly defeated them and won the battle. **Predict Consequences** How might this defeat have affected Union strategy?

▶ Interactive Timeline

a record of success as the Confederacy's leading general.

Meeting General Ambrose Burnside's Union army outside Fredericksburg, Virginia, Lee's forces dug into the crest of a hill. There, in a strong defensive position, Confederate guns mowed down wave after wave of charging Union troops. The **Battle of Fredericksburg** was one of the Union's worst defeats.

Half a year later, in May 1863, Lee, aided by Stonewall Jackson, again outmaneuvered Union forces. The **Battle of Chancellorsville** took place on thickly wooded ground near Chancellorsville, Virginia. Lee and Jackson defeated the Union troops in three days.

Victory came at a high price for the South, however. During the battle, nervous Confederate sentries fired at what they thought was an approaching Union soldier. The "Union soldier" was General Stonewall

Jackson. Several days later, Jackson died as a result of his injuries. The Confederacy had lost one of its best generals.

❓ IDENTIFY How might the Confederates have felt after the Battles of Fredericksburg and Chancellorsville?

Union Forces Find Success in the West

In the West, Union forces met better results. As you have read, part of the Union strategy was to seize control of the Mississippi River. General Ulysses S. Grant began moving toward that goal. In February 1862, Grant attacked and captured Fort Henry and Fort Donelson in Tennessee. These Confederate forts guarded two important tributaries of the Mississippi.

Grant now pushed south to Shiloh, a village on the Tennessee River. There, on

April 6, he was surprised by Confederate forces. By the end of the day, the Confederates had driven the Union troops back to the banks of the river.

Grant now showed the toughness and determination that would enable him to win many battles in the future and made him the Union's most successful leading general. He rushed reinforcements to the battle. That night, one of Grant's generals approached him. The officer thought Union forces should retreat.

But, seeing Grant's stubborn face, the officer only said, "Well, Grant, we've had the devil's own day, haven't we?"

"Yes," Grant replied. "Lick 'em tomorrow, though."

And they did. With the aid of the reinforcements, Grant beat back the Confederates and won the **Battle of Shiloh**. It was, however, one of the bloodiest encounters of the Civil War.

While Grant was fighting at Shiloh, the Union navy moved to gain control of the Mississippi River. In April 1862, Union gunboats captured New Orleans, Louisiana. Other ships seized Memphis, Tennessee. By capturing these two cities, the Union controlled both ends of the southern Mississippi. The South could no longer use the river as a supply line.

? CHECK UNDERSTANDING Why was the capture of Fort Henry and Fort Donelson critical to the Union's overall war strategy?

>> General Grant's army was in Tennessee to capture the Mississippi River. However, the Confederates attacked at Shiloh and nearly destroyed his army before he could recover and claim victory.

ASSESSMENT

1. **Summarize** the problems that a successful blockade of southern ports would cause for the South.

2. **Identify Central Issues** What did the Battle of Bull Run reveal?

3. **Draw Conclusions** What can you conclude from the fact that hundreds of civilians went along with the Union troops on their march to Bull Run to watch the battle and the fact that they were in a festive mood?

4. **Analyze Information** How can you tell that General Robert E. Lee was an unusually good officer?

5. **Make Predictions** What do the battles and events that you have read about so far lead you to predict about the war?

>> This photo shows Union soldiers at mealtime. Lack of food led to malnutrition. Poor sanitation in army camps allowed disease to spread quickly.

[▶] **Interactive Flipped Video**

>> Objectives

Describe the purpose of the Emancipation Proclamation and its effects.

Explain African Americans' contributions to the war effort in the Union army and behind Confederate lines.

Describe conditions for Civil War soldiers.

Explain problems on the home front, including economic issues.

Identify the role women played in the war.

>> Key Terms

emancipate
Emancipation
  Proclamation
54th Massachusetts
  Regiment
Fort Wagner
Copperhead
draft
habeas corpus
income tax
inflation
profiteer
William Carney

The Civil War began as a war to restore the Union, not to end slavery. President Lincoln made this point clear in a letter that was widely distributed.

The Emancipation Proclamation

> "If I could save the Union without freeing any slave, I would do it; and if I could save it by freeing all the slaves, I would do it; and if I could do it by freeing some and leaving others alone, I would also do that."
>
> —Abraham Lincoln, August 22, 1862, quoted in Carl Sandburg's *Abraham Lincoln*

Lincoln had a reason for handling the slavery issue cautiously. As you have read, four slave states remained in the Union. The President did not want to do anything that might cause these states to shift their loyalty to the Confederacy. The resources of the border states might allow the South to turn the tide of the war.

By mid-1862, however, Lincoln came to believe that he could save the Union only by broadening the goals of the war. He decided to **emancipate**, or free, enslaved African Americans then living in Confederate territory. In the four loyal slave states, however, enslaved African Americans would not be freed. Nor would African Americans be freed in Confederate lands that had already been captured by the Union, such as the city of New Orleans, Tennessee, or parts of Virginia.

A Cautious Introduction Lincoln had practical reasons for his emancipation plan. At the start of the Civil War, more than 3 million enslaved African Americans labored for the Confederacy. They helped grow the food that fed Confederate soldiers. They also worked in iron and lead mines that were vital to the South's war effort. Some served as nurses and cooks for the army. Lincoln knew that emancipation would weaken the Confederacy's ability to carry on the war.

However, Lincoln did not want to anger slave owners in the Union. Also, he knew that many northerners opposed freedom for enslaved African Americans.

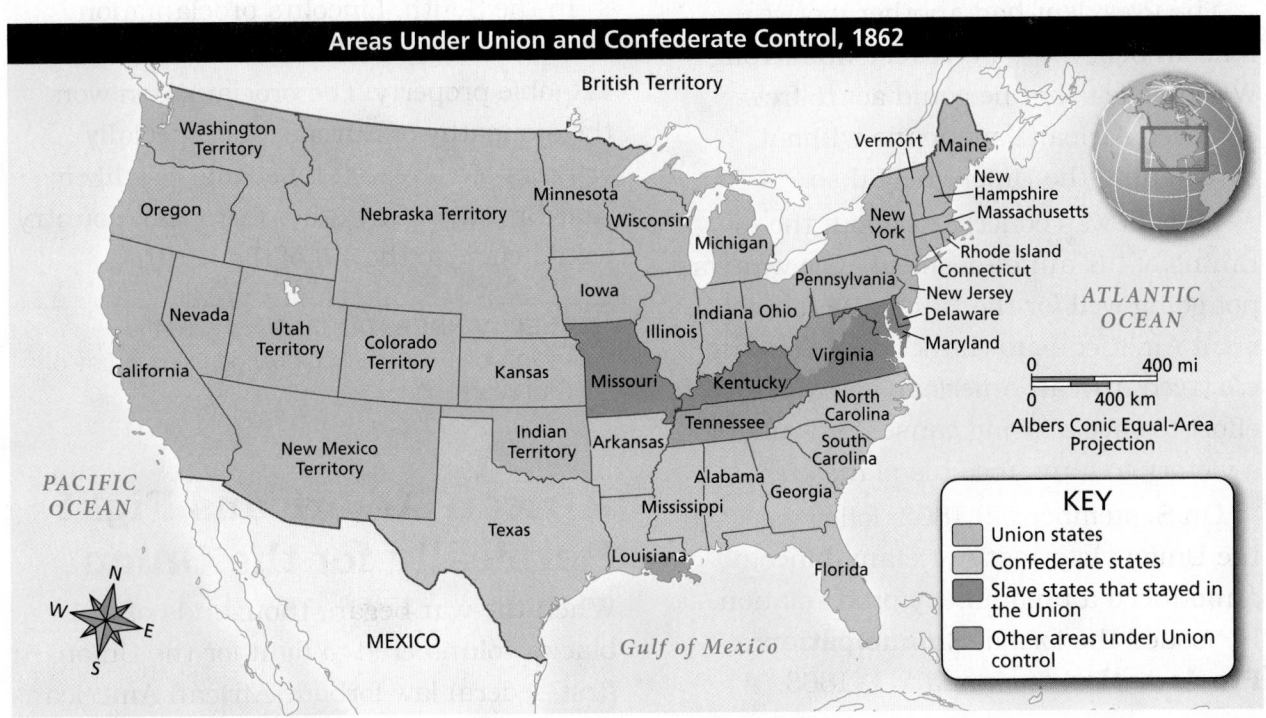

Areas Under Union and Confederate Control, 1862

KEY
- Union states
- Confederate states
- Slave states that stayed in the Union
- Other areas under Union control

>> **Analyze Maps** Why might some southern regions have been exempted from the Emancipation Proclamation?

>> President Lincoln told his Cabinet about the Emancipation Proclamation before he issued it. He wanted to wait for a Union victory before announcing it to the American people.

Lincoln hoped to introduce the idea of emancipation slowly, by limiting it to territory controlled by the Confederacy.

The President had another motive. Lincoln believed that slavery was wrong. When he felt that he could act to free enslaved African Americans without threatening the Union, he did so.

Lincoln was concerned about the timing of his announcement. The war was not going well for the Union. He did not want Americans to think he was freeing enslaved African Americans as a desperate effort to save a losing cause. He waited for a victory to announce his plan.

On September 22, 1862, following the Union victory at Antietam, Lincoln announced a preliminary proclamation. He issued the formal **Emancipation Proclamation** on January 1, 1863.

A Significant Proclamation Because the rebelling states were not under Union control, no African Americans actually gained their freedom on January 1, 1863. Still, the Emancipation Proclamation changed the purpose of the war. Now, Union troops were fighting to end slavery as well as to save the Union.

The opponents of slavery greeted the proclamation with joy. In Boston, African American abolitionist Frederick Douglass witnessed one of the many emotional celebrations that took place:

"The effect of this announcement was startling . . . and the scene was wild and grand. . . . My old friend Rue, a Negro preacher, . . . expressed the heartfelt emotion of the hour, when he led all voices in the anthem, 'Sound the loud timbrel o'er Egypt's dark sea, Jehovah hath triumphed, his people are free!'"

—Frederick Douglass, *Life and Times of Frederick Douglass*

In the South, Lincoln's proclamation was seen as a "fiend's act" that destroyed valuable property. The proclamation won the sympathy of Europeans, especially workers. As a result, it became less likely that Britain or any other European country would come to the aid of the South.

❓ CHECK UNDERSTANDING How did the Emancipation Proclamation change the purpose of the Civil War?

African Americans Fight Heroically for the Union

When the war began, thousands of free blacks volunteered to fight for the Union. At first, federal law forbade African Americans to serve as soldiers. When Congress repealed that law in 1862, however, both free African Americans and African Americans who had escaped from slavery enlisted in the Union army.

Military Service The army assigned African American volunteers to all-black units, commanded by white officers. At first, the black troops served only as laborers. They performed noncombat duties such as building roads and guarding supplies. Black troops received only half the pay of white soldiers.

African American soldiers protested against this policy of discrimination, which denied them the same treatment as other soldiers. Gradually, conditions changed. By 1863, African American troops were fighting in major battles against the Confederates. In 1864, the United States War Department announced that all soldiers would receive equal pay. By the end of the war, about 200,000 African Americans had fought for the Union. Nearly 40,000 lost their lives.

The Story of the 54th Regiment One of the most famous African American units in the Union army was the **54th Massachusetts Regiment.** The 54th accepted African Americans from all across the North. Frederick Douglass helped recruit troops for the regiment, and two of his sons served in it.

On July 18, 1863, the 54th Massachusetts Regiment led an attack on **Fort Wagner** near Charleston, South Carolina. Under heavy fire, troops fought their way into the fort before being forced to withdraw. In the desperate fighting, almost half the regiment was killed.

The courage and heroism of the 54th Massachusetts and other regiments helped to win respect for African American soldiers. Sergeant **William Carney** of the 54th Massachusetts was the first of 16 African American soldiers to win the Congressional Medal of Honor in the Civil War. Such Union heroes had "proved themselves among the bravest of the

>> Nearly half of the 54th Massachusetts Regiment died in the failed attack on Fort Wagner, South Carolina. Yet the regiment's bravery and heroism helped earn respect for African American soldiers in the Union army.

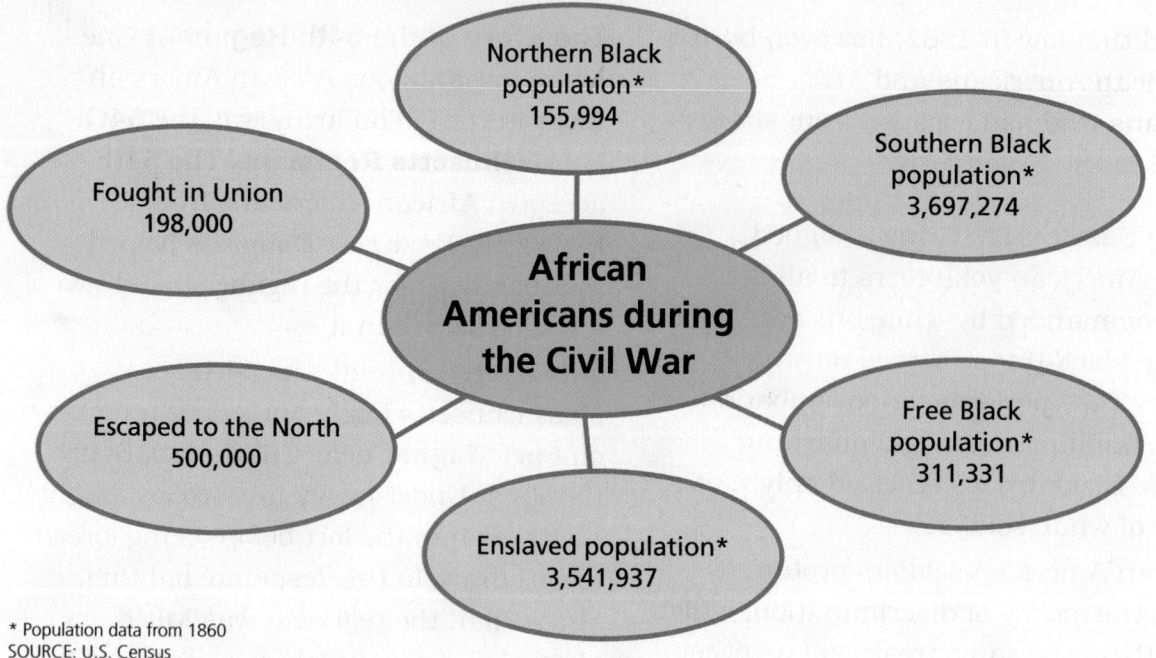

Northern Black population*
155,994

Southern Black population*
3,697,274

Fought in Union
198,000

African Americans during the Civil War

Free Black population*
311,331

Escaped to the North
500,000

Enslaved population*
3,541,937

* Population data from 1860
SOURCE: U.S. Census

>> **Analyze Data** Based on the information in the graphic organizer, approximately what percentage of enslaved African Americans from the South escaped to the North during the Civil War?

brave," Secretary of War Edwin Stanton told Lincoln.

An Opportunity for Freedom Despite the Emancipation Proclamation, African Americans still worked in the South as slaves on plantations. However, many enslaved African Americans slowed down their work or refused to work at all. In this way, they hoped to weaken the South's war effort. They knew that when victorious Union troops arrived in their area, they would be free.

Thousands of enslaved African Americans took direct action to free themselves. Whenever a Union army moved into a region, enslaved African Americans from all over the area would flee their former masters. They crossed the Union lines to freedom. By the end of the war, about one fourth of the South's enslaved population had escaped to freedom.

❓ **IDENTIFY SUPPORTING DETAILS** Why were many African Americans on plantations able to escape during the war?

Soldiers Face the Horrors of War

On both sides, most soldiers were under the age of 21. War, however, quickly turned gentle boys into tough men. Soldiers drilled and marched for long hours. They slept on the ground even in rain and snow. Often their clothing was inadequate and uncomfortable. Many soldiers had no shoes, especially in the Confederacy. In combat, boys of 18 learned to stand firm as cannon blasts shook the earth and bullets whizzed past their ears.

As the death toll rose, the age restrictions for soldiers were relaxed. The South drafted boys as young as 17 and men as old as 50.

New technology added to the horror of war. Cone-shaped bullets made rifles twice as accurate. Improved cannons hurled exploding shells several miles. The new weapons had deadly results. In most battles, one fourth or more of the soldiers were killed or wounded.

Sick and wounded soldiers faced other horrors. Medical care on the battlefield was crude. Surgeons routinely amputated injured arms and legs. At the time, doctors did not know how germs cause infection and disease. As a result, minor wounds often became infected. In addition, poor sanitary conditions in the army camps allowed disease to spread rapidly. Diseases such as pneumonia and malaria killed more men than guns or cannons did. Improper diet also caused sickness.

On both sides, prisoners of war faced horrifying conditions. At Andersonville, a prison camp in Georgia, many Union prisoners died of disease or starvation. The difficult life of soldiers led many to desert. One out of every seven Union soldiers and one out of every nine Confederate soldiers deserted.

? RECALL How did disease affect Civil War troops?

Political Challenges in the North and South

Many northerners opposed using force to keep the South in the Union. Supporters of the war called these people **Copperheads**, after the poisonous snake. Other northerners supported the war but opposed the way Lincoln was conducting it.

The Draft As the war dragged on, public support dwindled. When the war began, the North offered men money to enlist. However, some men abused the system. They would sign up, collect the money, and then desert. Soon, however, there was a shortage of volunteers to serve in the Union army.

Congress passed a **draft** law in 1863. It required all able-bodied males between the ages of 20 and 45 to serve in the military if they were called.

Under the law, a man could avoid the draft by paying the government $300 (about as much as an unskilled worker could earn in a year) or by hiring someone to serve in his place. This angered many people, who began to see the Civil War as "a rich man's war and a poor man's fight."

The Draft Riots Opposition to the draft law led to riots in several northern cities. The law had gone into effect soon after Lincoln issued the Emancipation Proclamation. Some white northerners, especially recent immigrants in the cities, believed that they were being forced to

>> The draft law of 1863 meant that if men wanted to avoid fighting in the war, they either paid the government $300 or hired others to fight in their place. Here, "bounty brokers" offer their services as potential substitutes.

▶ **Interactive Gallery**

fight to end slavery. Unlike abolitionists, many people in northern cities had little reason for wanting slavery abolished. Freed African Americans, they thought, would compete with them for jobs and drive down their wages. Essentially, they feared, the draft would force them to fight for something that was against their self-interest. The draft riots showed that urbanization could lead to violent unrest. With so many people gathered in northern cities, it was possible for large-scale unrest to develop over political issues such as the draft.

The worst riot took place in New York City during July 1863. For four days, white workers attacked free blacks. Rioters also attacked rich New Yorkers who had paid to avoid serving in the army. At least 74 people were killed during the riot.

PROVOST GUARD ATTACKING THE RIOTER'S

>> Rioters who opposed the draft law in New York City destroyed multiple buildings. In response, President Lincoln suspended the right not to be imprisoned without a court order and ordered Union troops to put down the riots.

President Lincoln moved to stop the riots and other "disloyal practices." Several times, he suspended **habeas corpus** (HAY bee uhs KOR puhs), the right to be charged or have a hearing before being jailed. Lincoln argued that the Constitution allowed him to deny people their rights "when in the cases of rebellion or invasion, the public safety may require it." The President also said that those arrested could be tried under the stricter rules of a military court. Eventually, nearly 14,000 people were arrested. However, most were never charged with a specific crime or brought to trial.

A Draft Comes to the South President Jefferson Davis struggled to create a strong federal government for the Confederacy. Many southerners firmly believed in states' rights. They resisted paying taxes to a central government. At one point, Georgia even threatened to secede from the Confederacy!

Like the North, the South was forced to pass a draft law to fill its army. However, men who owned or supervised more than 20 slaves did not have to serve. Southern farmers who had few or no slaves resented this law.

Near the end of the war, the South no longer had enough white men to fill the ranks. Robert E. Lee urged that enslaved African Americans be allowed to serve as soldiers. Desperate, the Confederate Congress finally agreed. The war ended, however, before more than a few thousand enslaved men fought for the Confederacy.

? IDENTIFY How were draft problems in the South different from those in the North?

CIVIL WAR

Causes of the Civil War	Effects of the Civil War
• The issue of slavery in the territories divides the North and South. • Abolitionists oppose slavery. • South fears northern domination. • Southern states secede after Lincoln's election. • Confederates bombard Fort Sumter.	• Lincoln issues the Emancipation Proclamation. • The northern economy booms. • The South loses its cotton trade with Britain. • Total war destroys the South's economy. • Hundreds of thousands of Americans die.

>> **Analyze Charts** Did the war's effects justify the South in its reasons for going to war?

War Challenges and Fuels the Northern Economy

The Civil War cost far more than any previous war. The Union had to use several strategies to raise money. In some ways, however, war helped the North's economy.

Taxation and Inflation To pay for the war, Congress established the nation's first **income tax,** or tax on people's earnings, in 1861. A new agency, the Internal Revenue Bureau, oversaw the collection process. The Union also issued bonds worth millions of dollars. Still, taxes and bonds did not raise enough money. To get the funds it needed, the North printed more than $400 million in paper money.

As the money supply increased, each dollar was worth less. In response, businesses charged more for their goods. The North was experiencing **inflation**, a rise in prices and a decrease in the value of money. During the war, prices for goods nearly doubled in the North.

Wartime Economic Advantages The war also helped the North's economy in several ways. Since many farmers went off to fight, there was a greater need for machines to plant and harvest crops. The purchase of reapers rose to nearly 165,000 during the war. As a result, farm production actually went up during the war.

The wartime demand for clothing, shoes, guns, and other goods helped many northern industries. Some manufacturers made fortunes by profiteering. **Profiteers** charged excessive prices for goods that the government desperately needed for the war.

❓ **CHECK UNDERSTANDING** How did the Civil War strengthen the North's economy?

War Devastates the Southern Economy

For the South, war brought economic ruin. The South had to struggle with the cost of the war, the loss of the cotton trade, and severe shortages brought on by the Union blockade.

A Weak Wartime Economy To raise money, the Confederacy imposed an income tax and a tax-in-kind. The tax-in-kind required farmers to turn over one tenth of their crops to the government. The government took crops because it knew that southern farmers had little money.

Like the North, the South printed paper money. It printed so much that wild inflation set in. By 1865, one Confederate dollar was worth only two cents in gold. Prices were especially high in Richmond, where a barrel of flour was $275 in early 1864, potatoes were $25 a bushel, and butter was $15 a pound.

The war did serious damage to the cotton trade, the South's main source of income. Early in the war, President Davis halted cotton shipments to Britain. He hoped to force Britain to side with the South in return for renewed shipments of cotton. The tactic backfired. Britain simply bought more cotton from Egypt and India. Davis succeeded only in cutting the South's income.

The Union Blockade Creates Shortages

The Union blockade created severe shortages in the South. Confederate armies sometimes had to wait weeks for supplies of food and clothing. With few factories of its own, the South bought many of its weapons in Europe. However, the blockade cut off most deliveries from across the Atlantic. To acquire goods, the government began building and running factories. Private manufacturers were offered contracts and draft exemptions for their workers if they started making war goods.

For civilians, the blockade brought food shortages. The production of food became critical to the economy. Many plantations switched from growing cotton to raising grain and livestock, or animals raised for food. In some states, cotton production was limited.

❓ **CHECK UNDERSTANDING** What happened when Jefferson Davis tried to use economic pressure to force the British to side with the South?

★ BLOCKADE OF SOUTHERN PORTS ★

$ PRICES $
FOR BASIC GOODS
IN THE SOUTH
DURING THE BLOCKADE
(IN CONFEDERATE DOLLARS)

Bacon	$8 a pound
Flour	$300 a barrel
Turkeys	$60 each
Milk	$4 a quart
Tea	$18 – $20 a pound
Sugar	$20 a pound

Source: *A Woman's Wartime Journal*

EXPENSES FOR AN
ARTILLERY OFFICER
TRAVELING FROM
RICHMOND TO ATLANTA,
1865

March 11	Meal on the road	$20
March 20	Eyeglasses	$135
March 23	Coat, vest, pants	$2,700
March 30	Cavalry boots (1 pr)	$450
April 24	Matches	$25
April 24	Penknife	$125

Source: *The Nation: A Weekly Journal Devoted to Politics, Literature, Science, and Art, Vol. 63*

COTTON PRODUCTION DURING THE WAR

(Line graph: Bales (in millions) on y-axis from 0 to 5, years 1860–1864 on x-axis. Values: 1860 ≈ 4, 1861 ≈ 4.5, 1862 ≈ 1.5, 1863 ≈ 0.5, 1864 ≈ 0.3)

COTTON PRICES

10 cents a pound → $1.89 a pound

>> **Analyze Graphs** Based on the information in the graph, what were the effects of the North blockading southern ports?

Contributions of Women to the War Effort

Women of both the North and the South played vital roles during the war. As men left for the battlefields, women took jobs in industry and on farms. While men fought in the war, many women took over responsibilities of family farms and businesses. They also had to raise their families on their own.

In rare instances, some women even disguised themselves as men and enlisted in the army to fight in the war. Others served as spies and provided valuable information to military commanders. Many served in army camps, some of them choosing to accompany their husbands to war.

Women's aid societies helped supply the troops with food, bedding, clothing, and medicine. Throughout the North, women held fairs and other fundraising events to pay for supplies.

Aid to the Wounded Women on both sides worked as nurses. At first, doctors were unwilling to permit even trained nurses to work in military hospitals. When wounded men began to swamp army hospitals, however, this attitude soon changed. In fact, women performed so well that nursing became an accepted occupation for women after the war.

Dorothea Dix, famous for her work reforming prisons and mental hospitals, and Clara Barton, who later founded the American Red Cross, both became nurses for the Union army. Sojourner Truth, the African American antislavery leader, worked in Union hospitals and in camps for African Americans freed from slavery.

>> During the Civil War, women helped by caring for the sick and wounded. They were so successful that nursing became an accepted profession for women following the war.

▶ **Interactive Gallery**

In the South, Sally Tompkins set up a hospital in Richmond, Virginia.

? **DESCRIBE** some ways in which women contributed to the war effort.

ASSESSMENT

1. **Draw Conclusions** What was the effect of the Emancipation Proclamation on the numbers of men choosing to join the Union army?

2. **Summarize** how the treatment of African American soldiers in the Union army changed as the war progressed.

3. **Check Understanding** Why did inflation become a problem in the North?

4. **Identify Central Issues** Why were urban areas the most frequent sites of draft riots?

5. **Draw Conclusions** Why do you suppose men who owned or supervised more than 20 enslaved African Americans did not have to serve in the Confederate army?

The War's End

>> Recognizing that any further fighting would be futile, General Lee (center, seated) surrendered to General Grant at Appomattox Court House on April 9, 1865.

▶ Interactive Flipped Video

>> **Objectives**

Explain why the Union victories at Vicksburg and Gettysburg helped turn the war in the Union's favor.

Describe Grant's plan for ending the war and the war's outcome.

Identify Lincoln's hopes for the Union after his reelection.

Summarize why the Civil War marked a turning point in American history.

>> **Key Terms**

siege
Battle of Gettysburg
Pickett's Charge
Gettysburg Address
total war
Appomattox Court
  House
Philip Bazaar

Confederate armies won major battles at Fredericksburg in December 1862 and at Chancellorsville in May 1863. These were gloomy days for the North. Then, in July 1863, the tide of war turned against the South as Union forces won major victories in both the East and the West.

The Siege of Vicksburg

General Grant Captures Vicksburg In the West, Union triumph came along the Mississippi River. The Union, which had captured New Orleans and Memphis, already controlled both ends of the southern Mississippi River. Still, the Confederates held Vicksburg, Mississippi. It controlled a crucial Mississippi River crossing linking the eastern and western Confederate states. Vicksburg sat on a cliff high above the river. Its physical geography made it difficult to attack from the river.

Early in 1863, Grant's forces tried again and again to seize Vicksburg. The Confederates held out bravely. At last, Grant devised a brilliant plan. Landing at an unguarded spot on the river and arching his troops inland, he launched a surprise attack on Jackson, Mississippi. Then, he turned west and attacked Vicksburg from the rear. On the side facing away from the river, no physical barriers protected Vicksburg.

For more than six weeks, Grant's forces laid siege to Vicksburg. A **siege** is a military encirclement of an enemy position and blockading or bombarding it in order to force it to surrender. Finally, on July 4, 1863, the Confederates surrendered Vicksburg.

On July 9, Union forces also captured Port Hudson, Louisiana. The entire Mississippi River was now under Union control. The Union took advantage of physical geography by using the Mississippi River to supply its troops.

The Confederacy was now split into two parts. Texas, Arkansas, and Louisiana were cut off from the rest of the Confederate states. This meant that the eastern Confederate states were no longer able to get supplies from the western

>> For more than six weeks, General Grant's forces circled Vicksburg, cutting off its supplies, and used siege cannons, like the one shown here, to bomb the city until its eventual surrender.

▶ **Interactive Map**

states. This was a devastating loss for the Confederacy.

? CHECK UNDERSTANDING Why was Union control of the Mississippi River a blow to the Confederacy?

The Battle of Gettysburg

Meanwhile, in the East, after his victory at Chancellorsville, General Lee moved his army north into Pennsylvania. He hoped to take the Yankees by surprise. If he succeeded in Pennsylvania, Lee planned to swing south and capture Washington, D.C. The Union army followed the Confederates, making sure to remain between the Confederates and Washington.

On June 30, 1863, the Union Army of the Potomac, now under command of General George C. Meade, met part of Lee's army at the small town of Gettysburg,

Pennsylvania. Both sides quickly sent in reinforcements. The three-day **Battle of Gettysburg** that followed was one of the most significant events of the Civil War.

On the first day of battle, July 1, the Confederates drove the Union forces out of Gettysburg. The Yankees, however, took up strong positions on Cemetery Ridge, overlooking the town. Union troops fortified these positions throughout that night.

The next day, Lee ordered an attack on both ends of the Union line, much of which was positioned on high ground, making the attacks difficult. Southern troops fought hard, but the Union army was well prepared for Lee's offensive. At the end of a day of savage fighting, Lee's forces had suffered heavy casualties but failed to dislodge the Union army from its strong position.

General Lee's Disastrous Decision

Despite his losses, Lee decided to attack again. He wanted to "create a panic and virtually destroy the [Union] army." On July 3, he ordered General George Pickett to lead 15,000 men in a daring charge against the center of the Union line. To reach their target, Pickett's men would have to march about 1,000 yards across sloping, open ground—all within clear view of the enemy.

This last attack led by Pickett is known as **Pickett's Charge**. Prior to the charge, Confederate cannons pounded the Union position on Cemetery Ridge, but the Union lines remained intact.

Pickett then gave the order to charge. As the Confederates marched forward, Union guns opened fire. Row after row of soldiers fell to the ground, dead or wounded. The battle noise, one soldier recalled, was "strange and terrible, a sound that came from thousands of human throats . . . like a vast mournful roar."

Pickett's Charge failed. The steady barrage of bullets and shells kept all but a handful of Confederate soldiers from

>> The Battle of Gettysburg involved three days of fighting with heavy casualties. The Confederates, like the prisoners shown here, hoped for a decisive victory that never came.

▶ Interactive 3-D Model

penetrating the Union lines. The next day, a Union officer trying to ride over the battlefield could not because "the dead and wounded lay too thick to guide a horse through them."

As the survivors limped back, Lee rode among them. "It's all my fault," he admitted humbly. Lee had no choice but to retreat with his weakened army. After they were defeated at Gettysburg, the Confederates would never invade the North again.

General Meade was proud of the victory. He had protected Pennsylvania and Washington, D.C. Lincoln, however, was disappointed. He felt that the Union army had once again allowed the Confederate troops to get away.

The Union victories at Vicksburg and Gettysburg marked the turning point of the Civil War. It seemed just a matter of time before the Confederacy would fall. However, the South was still determined to fight. The war would last another two years.

? IDENTIFY CENTRAL IDEAS Why was the Union victory at Gettysburg significant?

The Gettysburg Address

The Battle of Gettysburg left more than 50,000 dead or wounded. On November 19, 1863, there was a ceremony to dedicate a cemetery to the memory of those soldiers who died at Gettysburg. President Lincoln attended the ceremony. He delivered a speech now known as the **Gettysburg Address**. The speech expressed the purpose of the Civil War and exemplified Lincoln's leadership at a time of tremendous crisis. Lincoln said that the Civil War was a test of whether or not a democratic government could survive. This claim implied that the nation's survival

>> Describing the sacrifices made at the Battle of Gettysburg, President Lincoln proclaimed that, if the war preserved the Union and its principles of liberty and equality, "these dead shall not have died in vain."

depended on the integrity of the Union. He also addressed the theme of equality. He reminded Americans that their nation was founded on the belief that "all men are created equal." Lincoln told the audience:

"We here highly resolve that these dead shall not have died in vain—that this nation, under God, shall have a new birth of freedom—and that government of the people, by the people, for the people, shall not perish from the earth."

—Abraham Lincoln, Gettysburg Address, November 19, 1863

Lincoln's words, "all men are created equal," taken from the Declaration of Independence, and his mention of "a new birth of freedom" both express his ideas about liberty and equality. Coming so soon after the Emancipation Proclamation, made earlier that same year, Lincoln's words implied that "a new birth of freedom" for millions of African Americans had become not just one of the goals of the Civil War, but one of the nation's ideals. Lincoln's entire speech was only ten sentences long and took about three minutes to deliver, but it is honored as a profound statement of American ideals.

? RECALL Lincoln said that the Civil War was a test. What was that test?

Union Forces Move Southward

Since the beginning of the war, Lincoln had searched for a general who could lead the Union to victory. More and more, he thought of Ulysses S. Grant. After capturing Vicksburg, Grant continued to win battles in the West. In 1864, Lincoln appointed him commander of the Union forces. In this role, Grant would lead the final Union advance against the Confederacy.

Some questioned the choice, but President Lincoln felt that "Unconditional Surrender" Grant, as some called him, was the general who would end the war in the Union's favor. Even back when Grant had been criticized for near disaster at the Battle of Shiloh, Lincoln had defended Grant: "I can't spare this man," Lincoln said. "He fights."

Grant had a plan for ending the war. He wanted to destroy the South's ability to fight. To achieve this, Grant ordered his generals to wage **total war** against the South.

He wanted the Union army to destroy food, equipment, and anything else they found that might be useful to the enemy. In the past, most wars had been restricted to soldiers. Total war, however, did not make any distinctions. Civilians in the South, like the Confederate army, would suffer hardship.

The Civil War: Final Battles

KEY
→ Union troops
✳ Union victories
→ Confederate troops
✳ Confederate victories

>> **Analyze Maps** Based on the information in the map, what can you infer about the Union army's strategy toward the end of the Civil War?

▶ **Interactive Map**

Grant Sends Sheridan to the Shenandoah

To set his plan in motion, Grant sent General Philip Sheridan and his cavalry into the rich farmland of Virginia's Shenandoah Valley. He instructed Sheridan:

> "Leave nothing to invite the enemy to return. Destroy whatever cannot be consumed. Let the valley be left so that crows flying over it will have to carry their rations along with them."
>
> —Ulysses S. Grant, quoted in Bruce Catton's *Grant Takes Command*

Sheridan obeyed. In the summer and fall of 1864, he marched through the valley, destroying farms and livestock.

During the campaign, Sheridan's troops burned 2,000 barns filled with grain. There was nothing left for Lee's troops or for southern civilians.

Sherman's March to the Sea

Grant also ordered General William Tecumseh Sherman to capture Atlanta, Georgia, and then march to the Atlantic coast. Like Sheridan, Sherman had orders to destroy everything useful to the South.

Sherman's troops captured Atlanta in September 1864. They began their campaign by turning the people of Atlanta out of their homes and burning a large part of the city. Then, Sherman began his "march to the sea."

As they marched through Georgia, Sherman's troops ripped up railroad tracks, built bonfires from the ties, then heated and twisted the rails. (The now useless rails, often twisted around trees, were nicknamed "Sherman's neckties.") The soldiers killed livestock and tore up fields. They burned barns, homes, bridges, and factories.

? DESCRIBE Grant's concept of *total war*.

>> General William T. Sherman (using the telescope) led a campaign that cut a destructive path through the South. **Hypothesize** Why would Sherman order his troops to destroy all items of value?

Contrasting Ideas of Liberty and Union

Lincoln ran for reelection in 1864. At first, his defeat seemed, in his own words, "exceedingly probable." Before the capture of Atlanta, Union chances for a final victory looked bleak. Lincoln knew that many northerners were unhappy with his handling of the war. He thought that this might cost him the election.

The Democrats nominated General George McClellan to oppose Lincoln. They adopted a resolution demanding the immediate "cessation of hostilities" against the South. Although he had commanded the Union army, McClellan was willing to compromise with the Confederacy. If peace could be achieved, he was ready to restore slavery.

Then, in September, Sherman took Atlanta, and the North rallied around

Lincoln. Sheridan's smashing victories in the Shenandoah Valley in October further increased Lincoln's popular support. In the election in November, the vote was close, but Lincoln remained President.

In his Second Inaugural Address, Lincoln looked forward to the coming of peace:

> "With malice toward none, with charity for all . . . let us strive . . . to bind up the nation's wounds . . . to do all which may achieve a just and a lasting peace among ourselves and with all nations."
>
> —Abraham Lincoln, Second Inaugural Address

Two Inaugural Addresses Lincoln's Second Inaugural Address, along with his First Inaugural and Gettysburg Addresses, are landmark speeches in American history. Taken together, they present Lincoln's ideas about liberty, equality, union, and government.

In his First Inaugural, Lincoln emphasized the importance of the union of the states, which he viewed as "perpetual," or never-ending. Again, in the Gettysburg Address, he emphasized the importance of maintaining the union of the country, especially since the country was based on freedom and equality. Lincoln's Second Inaugural highlighted slavery as a violation of equality and liberty, yet emphasized, again, the preservation of unity by urging people to "bind up the nation's wounds."

In contrast, Confederate President Jefferson Davis had conveyed different views in his inaugural address, given shortly after Lincoln's inauguration. In his speech, Davis explained southerner's reasons for withdrawing from the Union and seceding. It was "a necessity, not a choice," he said. Quoting the Declaration of Independence, Davis stated this about government:

> "Our present condition . . . illustrates the American idea that governments rest upon the consent of the governed, and that it is the right of the people to alter or abolish governments whenever they become destructive of the ends for which they were established."
>
> —President Jefferson Davis, First Inaugural Address, February 18, 1861

Lincoln had insisted in his First Inaugural Address that the Constitution required union. In the Emancipation Proclamation and the Gettysburg Address, Lincoln had extended the idea of liberty to all Americans. While Lincoln's speeches called for equality and liberty for enslaved African Americans, Davis

>> By the election of 1864, as this photograph clearly shows, the war had taken an emotional and physical toll on President Lincoln.

>> Richmond, Virginia, shown here, was the capital of the Confederacy. It was in Richmond that Confederate President Jefferson Davis gave his inaugural address in 1861.

called for the equality and liberty only of southern whites.

In his commitment to principles of liberty, equality, and the preservation of the Union and the government, and in his decisions as President during the most difficult crisis the United States had ever faced, Lincoln demonstrated remarkable leadership qualities.

? **IDENTIFY CENTRAL IDEAS** How did Jefferson Davis use the Declaration of Independence to justify secession?

The Confederacy Surrenders at Appomattox

Grant had begun a drive to capture Richmond in May 1864. Throughout the spring and summer, he and Lee fought a series of costly battles.

Northerners read with horror that 60,000 men were killed or wounded

in a single month at the Battles of the Wilderness, Spotsylvania, and Cold Harbor, all in Virginia. Still, Grant pressed on. He knew that the Union could replace men and supplies. The South could not.

Lee dug in at Petersburg, near Richmond. Here, Grant kept Lee under siege for nine months. At last, with a fresh supply of troops, Grant took Petersburg on April 2, 1865. The same day, Richmond fell.

The War Ends Lee and his army withdrew to a small Virginia town called **Appomattox Court House**. There, a week later, they were trapped by Union troops. Lee knew that his men would be slaughtered if he kept fighting. On April 9, 1865, Lee surrendered.

At Appomattox Court House, Grant offered generous terms of surrender to the defeated Confederate army. Soldiers were required to turn over their rifles, but officers were allowed to keep their pistols. Soldiers who had horses could keep them. Grant knew that southerners would need the animals for spring plowing. Finally, ordered Grant, "each officer and man will be allowed to return to his home, not to be disturbed by the United States authorities."

As the Confederates surrendered, Union soldiers began to cheer. Grant ordered them to be silent. "The war is over," he said. "The rebels are our countrymen again."

Honoring Those Who Served The war was over, but for hundreds and thousands of men, women, and children, it would be remembered as the most important event of their lives. The men who fought on both sides were honored for their services with ceremonies up to 75 years after the war. During the war, President Lincoln had signed into law what would become the Medal of Honor, the highest honor in the American military. Over 1,500 soldiers were awarded the Medal of Honor for their heroic actions during the Civil War.

One Medal of Honor recipient was **Philip Bazaar**, an immigrant from Chile. He enlisted in the Navy at New Bedford, Massachusetts. Although his rank was low—"ordinary seaman"—his actions proved him a hero. He earned the Medal of Honor carrying vital messages between commanders while serving on the *U.S.S. Santiago de Cuba* during the assault on Fort Fisher, North Carolina, on January 15, 1865:

> "As one of a boat crew detailed to one of the generals on shore, O.S. Bazaar bravely entered the fort in the assault and accompanied his party in carrying dispatches at the height of the battle. He was 1 of 6 men who entered the fort in the assault from the fleet."
>
> —Medal of Honor Citation for Philip Bazaar, June 22, 1865

? RECALL What was significant about how General Grant treated Confederate soldiers after they surrendered?

The Nation Begins a New Chapter

The effect of the Civil War was immense. The Civil War years, 1861–1865, were significant on many levels. More than 360,000 Union soldiers and 250,000 Confederate soldiers lost their lives. No war has ever resulted in more American deaths. In dollars, the war's cost was about 20 billion. That was more than 11 times the entire amount spent by the federal government between 1789 and 1861.

The Civil War was a major turning point in American history. The balance of power was changed. The Democratic party lost its influence and the Republicans were

>> After four long years of battle, families on both sides were eager to see their loved ones return home, as was the case for this wounded Union soldier.

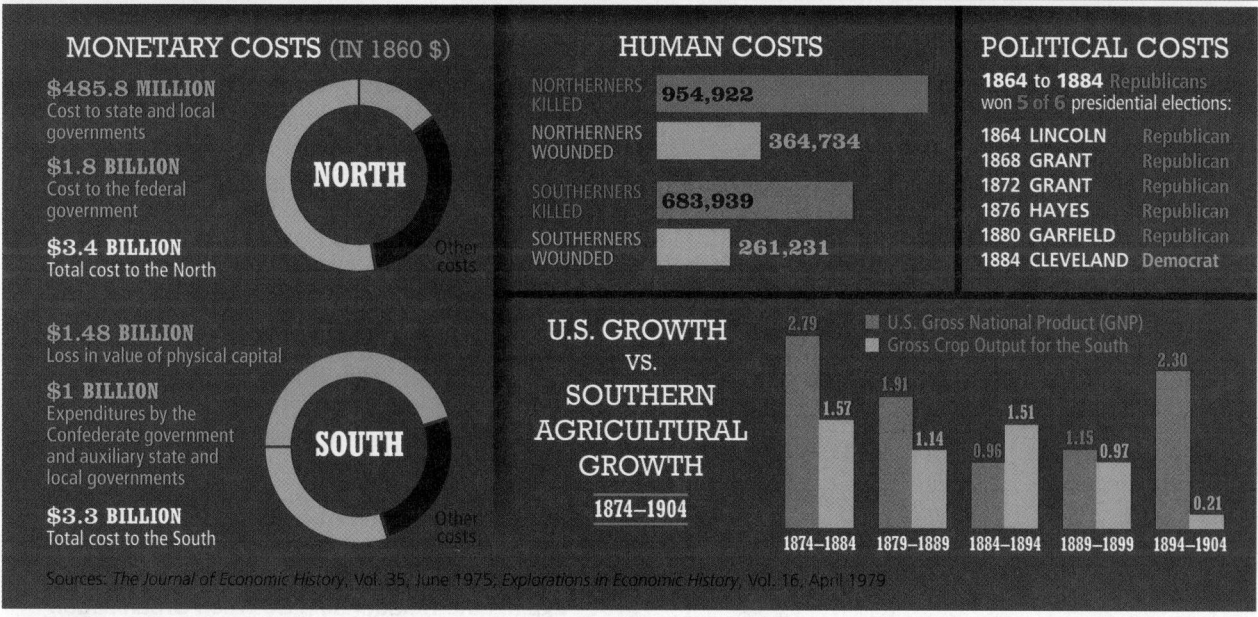

★ COSTS OF THE CIVIL WAR ★

MONETARY COSTS (IN 1860 $)

$485.8 MILLION
Cost to state and local governments

$1.8 BILLION
Cost to the federal government

$3.4 BILLION
Total cost to the North

NORTH

Other costs

$1.48 BILLION
Loss in value of physical capital

$1 BILLION
Expenditures by the Confederate government and auxiliary state and local governments

$3.3 BILLION
Total cost to the South

SOUTH

Other costs

HUMAN COSTS

NORTHERNERS KILLED	954,922
NORTHERNERS WOUNDED	364,734
SOUTHERNERS KILLED	683,939
SOUTHERNERS WOUNDED	261,231

POLITICAL COSTS

1864 to **1884** Republicans won 5 of 6 presidential elections:

1864 LINCOLN — Republican
1868 GRANT — Republican
1872 GRANT — Republican
1876 HAYES — Republican
1880 GARFIELD — Republican
1884 CLEVELAND — Democrat

U.S. GROWTH VS. SOUTHERN AGRICULTURAL GROWTH
1874–1904

■ U.S. Gross National Product (GNP)
■ Gross Crop Output for the South

	1874–1884	1879–1889	1884–1894	1889–1899	1894–1904
GNP	2.79	1.91	0.96	1.15	2.30
Crop Output	1.57	1.14	1.51	0.97	0.21

Sources: *The Journal of Economic History*, Vol. 35, June 1975; *Explorations in Economic History*, Vol. 16, April 1979

>> **Analyze Data** Based on the information about the human costs of the war, which side had more casualties during the war?

in a commanding position. No longer would Americans speak of the nation as a confederation of states. Before the war, Americans referred to "*these* United States." After, they began speaking of "*the* United States." The idea that each state might secede, if it chose, was dead. As a result, the power of the federal government grew.

The war also put an end to slavery in the United States. For years, Americans had debated whether slavery could exist in a nation dedicated to the ideals of liberty and equality. By the war's end, millions of African Americans had gained their freedom. Millions more Americans, both northern and southern, began to think about what it meant to be free and equal.

To be sure, a long and difficult struggle for equality lay ahead. Yet, Lincoln's words at Gettysburg were prophetic: "We here highly resolve . . . that this nation, under

God, shall have a new birth of freedom." From out of a cruel, bitter, often heart-rending war, the United States did indeed emerge a stronger, freer nation.

? **RECALL** Why was the Civil War significant?

ASSESSMENT

1. **Draw Conclusions** How might General Lee's goal of capturing Washington D.C. have led him to order Pickett's Charge at the Battle of Gettysburg?

2. **Interpret** What elements of total war do you see in General Sherman's "March to the Sea"?

3. **Address Central Issues** What was the major reason that Abraham Lincoln was reelected?

4. **Summarize** the terms of surrender that General Grant offered General Lee.

5. **Hypothesize** What was life like in the United States after the enormous loss of life and expenses of the war.

TOPIC 8 ASSESSMENT

1. **Identify Congressional Conflicts** Write a paragraph identifying and comparing the roles of John C. Calhoun and Henry Clay in the conflict over the extension of slavery that divided Congress in 1850. Explain how the slavery issue divided Congress in 1850, Calhoun's position on the issue, Clay's position in the conflict, and how the conflict was settled.

2. **Explain the Significance of the Civil War** Write a paragraph explaining the significant changes the Civil War brought to the United States. Explain how the war shifted the balance of power among political parties in the United States, how the war changed the way Americans perceived the nation, and how the end of slavery affected the nation's thoughts about liberty and equality.

3. **Analyze the Impact of the Fugitive Slave Act** Write a paragraph explaining why the Fugitive Slave Act increased tensions between the North and the South over slavery. Explain how northerners felt about the Fugitive Slave Act, how some northerners and northern states responded to the Fugitive Slave Act, and how southerners reacted to the northern response.

4. **Evaluate the Impact of Landmark Supreme Court Decisions** Write a paragraph evaluating the impact that the Supreme Court ruling in *Dred Scott* v. *Sandford* had on life in the United States. Describe the events that led to Dred Scott's filing a lawsuit that eventually reached the Supreme Court, explain the Court's ruling in *Dred Scott* v. *Sandford,* and evaluate the impact of the Court's decision.

5. **Explain How Sectionalism and States' Rights Caused the Civil War** Write a paragraph explaining how Lincoln's election as President split the nation along sectional lines and led some states to secede. Consider why Lincoln's election victory alarmed southerners, why Senator Crittenden's attempt at a compromise on slavery failed to gain support, and which states were the first to exercise what they saw as their states' right to secede.

6. **Explain the Role of Abraham Lincoln in the Civil War** Using Abraham Lincoln's quotation below and other sources, write a paragraph explaining President Lincoln's goal in fighting the Civil War and his decision to issue the Emancipation Proclamation. Explain President Lincoln's goal in fighting the Civil War, explain the purpose of the Emancipation Proclamation, and analyze why Lincoln did not free all enslaved African Americans.

If I could save the Union without freeing any slave, I would do it; and if I could save it by freeing all the slaves, I would do it; and if I could do it by freeing some and leaving others alone, I would also do that.

— *Abraham Lincoln, August 22, 1862, quoted in Carl Sandburg, Abraham Lincoln*

7. **Explain the Relationship Between Urbanization and Conflicts** Write a paragraph describing what led to the northern draft riots and what actions President Lincoln took to stop the riots. Answer the following questions: Why did many northerners see the Civil War as "a rich man's war and a poor man's fight"? How did the Emancipation Proclamation help trigger the draft riots? What steps did President Lincoln take to stop the riots?

8. **Identify the Social Contributions of Women to American Society** Write a paragraph describing the ways that women contributed to the Civil War effort. Describe the ways women contributed to the war effort on the home front and on the battlefield.

9. **Explain the Battle of Gettysburg and Robert E. Lee's Role in It** Write a paragraph analyzing how General Robert E. Lee's decisions affected the outcome of the Battle of Gettysburg. Explain General Lee's strategy for attacking in Pennsylvania and beyond, analyze how and why General Lee's decisions during the battle led to a Confederate defeat, and explain why the Battle of Gettysburg is considered a turning point in the Civil War.

10. **Explain the Constitutional Issues Regarding States' Rights in the Civil War** Write a paragraph explaining how southerners and President Lincoln differed in their views on whether southern states were allowed to secede under the Constitution. Consider how southerners used the Declaration of Independence, states' rights, and the Constitution to defend their right to secede, and how President Lincoln used the Constitution to argue against the right of states to secede.

11. **Explain the Effects of Physical Geography on the Battle of Vicksburg** Use the map above and other sources to write a paragraph explaining the Battle of Vicksburg. Explain why it was important for the Union to secure the city of Vicksburg. Look at the terrain and relief as shown on the map and analyze how the physical geography of Vicksburg affected the battle, and explain how General Grant took control of Vicksburg.

12. **Describe the Contributions of General George McClellan** Write a paragraph describing the contributions of General George McClellan to the Army of the Potomac and the Peninsula Campaign. Identify General George McClellan, describe McClellan's approach in leading the troops in the Peninsula Campaign, explain the results of the Peninsula Campaign, and draw a conclusion about General McClellan's leadership.

13. **Write about the Essential Question** Write an essay on the Essential Question: **When is war justified?** Use evidence from your study of this topic to support your answer.

HON. FREDERICK DOUGLASS

EX-SENATOR BRUCE

EX-SENA

[**ESSENTIAL QUESTION**] How should we handle conflict?

9 The Reconstruction Era (1865–1877)

>> African American heroes
Blanche Bruce, Frederick
Douglass, and Hiram Revels

Enduring Understandings

- Reconstruction was the era of rebuilding and political, economic, and social change in the South following the Civil War.

- Amendments passed during Reconstruction gave political rights to African Americans, but African Americans often were denied these rights in the South.

- Shifts in political power ended Reconstruction, followed by gradual economic recovery in the South.

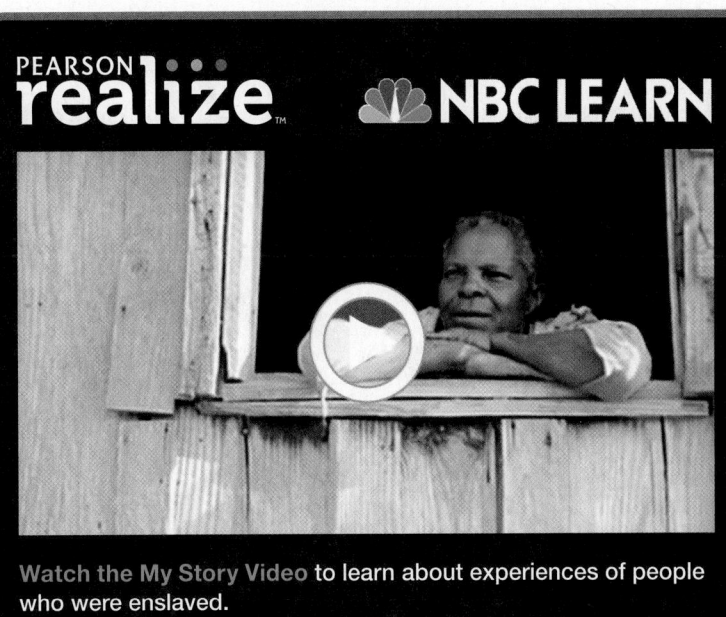

PEARSON realize.   **NBC LEARN**

Watch the My Story Video to learn about experiences of people who were enslaved.

PEARSON realize™
www.PearsonRealize.com

Access your digital lessons including:
Topic Inquiry • Interactive Reading
Notepad • Interactivities • Assessments

Early Reconstruction

>> Like other major southern cities, Atlanta lay in ruins after the Civil War. Much of the South needed to be rebuilt.

Interactive Flipped Video

>> Objectives

Describe the nation's economic, political, and social problems after the Civil War.

Identify the early steps that were taken during Reconstruction.

Explain how the assassination of Lincoln and the inauguration of a new President led to conflict.

>> Key Terms

freedmen
Reconstruction
Ten Percent Plan
amnesty
Wade-Davis Bill
Freedmen's Bureau
Thirteenth
  Amendment

At the end of the Civil War, the future looked bleak to many southerners. Across the South, cities and farms lay in ruins. All southerners, black or white, faced an unfamiliar new world. At the same time, a shattered nation had to find a way to become whole again.

Effects of the Civil War

After four years of war, both northerners and southerners had to adjust to a changed world. The adjustment was far more difficult in the South.

Political, Economic, and Social Problems in the North Despite their victory, northerners faced a number of economic problems. Some 800,000 returning Union soldiers needed jobs. The government was canceling its war orders, and factories were laying off workers. Still, the North's economic disruption was only temporary. Boom times quickly returned.

The North lost more soldiers in the war than the South did. However, only a few battles had taken place on northern soil.

Northern farms and cities were hardly touched. One returning Union soldier remarked, "It seemed . . . as if I had been away only a day or two, and had just taken up . . . where I had left off." However, thousands of soldiers suffered wounds from the war, many of which included missing limbs and other painful injuries.

The North faced political problems, too. There was disagreement about how to bring the South back into the Union and what to do with newly freed African Americans. Many wanted to punish southerners for what they had done, while others wanted a more moderate approach.

Political, Economic, and Social Problems in the South Economic conditions in the South were far worse than in the North. Confederate soldiers had little chance of taking up where they had left off. In some areas, every house, barn, and bridge had been destroyed.

Two thirds of the South's railroad tracks had been turned into twisted heaps of scrap. The cities of Columbia, Richmond, and Atlanta had been leveled.

The war wrecked the South's financial system. After the war, Confederate money was worthless. People who had loaned money to the Confederacy were never repaid. Many southern banks closed, and depositors lost their savings.

The war changed southern society forever. Almost overnight, there was a new class of nearly four million people known as **freedmen**—men and women who had been enslaved. Under slavery, they had been forbidden to own property and to learn to read or write. What would become of them? How could the South cope with this sudden, drastic change?

These economic and social problems combined with political problems. It was unclear how the southern states would run their governments. There were not yet

>> After the war, soldiers such as this Union officer returned to their homes. Despite the high loss of life, the North did not require as much rebuilding as did the South.

legal systems in place to protect African Americans, and many white southerners feared African Americans gaining political power. Also, many white politicians who had held office in the Confederacy were forbidden from politics.

Overall, the economic differences between the agrarian South and industrial North increased after the war. The northern economy picked up, while the South struggled to rebuild. Many southerners resented northerners coming in to "fix" southern problems, and the ruined economy made recovery especially hard.

? **DESCRIBE** the political, economic, and social difficulties faced by the South after the war.

The Causes and Effects of Reconstruction

When the Civil War ended, President Lincoln hoped to deal with the tremendous damage and turmoil the Civil War had caused. The era following the Civil War became known as **Reconstruction,** or the rebuilding of the South. Lincoln wanted to make it fairly easy for southerners to rejoin the Union. The sooner the nation was reunited, Lincoln believed, the faster the South would be able to rebuild.

Lincoln's Ten Percent Plan As early as 1863, Lincoln outlined his **Ten Percent Plan** for Reconstruction. Under this plan, a southern state could form a new government after 10 percent of its voters swore an oath of loyalty to the United States. The new government had to abolish slavery. Voters could then elect members

>> Registered enemies of the Union swear their allegiance to the United States at the office of General Bowen in New Orleans.

of Congress and take part in the national government once again.

Lincoln's plan also offered **amnesty,** or a government pardon, to Confederates who swore loyalty to the Union. Amnesty would not apply to the former leaders of the Confederacy, however.

Lincoln Rejects a Rival Proposal Many Republicans in Congress felt that the Ten Percent Plan was too generous toward the South. In 1864, they passed the **Wade-Davis Bill,** a rival plan for Reconstruction. It required a majority of white men in each southern state to swear loyalty to the Union. It also denied the right to vote or hold office to anyone who had volunteered to fight for the Confederacy. Lincoln refused to sign the Wade-Davis Bill because he felt it was too harsh.

The Freedmen's Bureau Addresses Economic and Social Needs There were many effects of the Reconstruction era. One such effect was Congress and the President agreed on a proposal to create a new agency. One month before Lee surrendered, Congress passed a bill creating the **Freedmen's Bureau,** a government agency to help former slaves. Lincoln signed the bill.

The Freedmen's Bureau gave food and clothing to former slaves. It also tried to find jobs for freedmen. The bureau helped poor whites as well. It provided medical care for more than one million people.

One of the bureau's most important tasks was to set up schools for freedmen. Most of the teachers were volunteers, often women from the North. Grandparents and grandchildren sat side by side in the classroom. Charlotte Forten, an African American volunteer from Philadelphia, wrote:

>> Southern freedmen attended schools set up by the Freedmen's Bureau to gain skills necessary for employment. In this engraving, African American children attend a school in South Carolina.

"It is wonderful how a people who have been so long crushed to the earth . . . can have so great a desire for knowledge, and such a capacity for attaining it."

—Charlotte Forten, article in the *Atlantic Monthly*

The Freedmen's Bureau laid the foundation for the South's public school system. It also created colleges for African Americans, including Howard, Morehouse, and Fisk. Many of the graduates of these schools became teachers themselves. By the 1870s, African Americans were teaching in grade schools throughout the South.

? **CHECK UNDERSTANDING** Why did President Lincoln want to make it easy for the South to rejoin the Union?

>> This present-day photo shows the box at Ford's Theatre where John Wilkes Booth assassinated Abraham Lincoln on April 14, 1865.

▶ **Interactive Gallery**

>> President Johnson's plan for Reconstruction did not place restrictions on southern candidates who could be elected to state legislatures or Congress. **Infer** Why might some Republicans reject this policy?

The Assassination of Abraham Lincoln

President Lincoln hoped to persuade Congress to accept his Reconstruction plan. However, he never got the chance.

On April 14, 1865, just five days after Lee's surrender, President Lincoln attended a play at Ford's Theatre in Washington, D.C. A popular actor who supported the Confederate cause, John Wilkes Booth, crept into the President's box and shot Lincoln in the head. Lincoln died the next morning. Booth was later caught and killed in a barn outside the city.

The nation was plunged into grief. The assassination was significant because Lincoln was the first American President to be assassinated. Also, millions who had been celebrating the war's end now mourned Lincoln's death. His body was transported by train for burial in his hometown, Springfield, Illinois. Millions of Americans came to pay their respects along the route. "Now he belongs to the ages," commented Secretary of War Edwin Stanton.

Booth was part of a group of ten conspirators who had long been plotting to kill Lincoln, Vice President Andrew Johnson, and Secretary of State William Seward. None of the other assassinations took place, although Seward was attacked by one of the conspirators. Four of Booth's co-conspirators were hanged for their crimes, including Mary Surratt, the first woman executed by the United States.

❓ **EXPLAIN** the meaning behind Secretary of War Edwin Stanton's statement about Lincoln.

>> Members of the House celebrated the passage of the Thirteenth Amendment, which permanently freed slaves and outlawed slavery. However, southern states still prohibited African Americans from voting.

President Johnson's Reconstruction Plan

Vice President Andrew Johnson was now President. Johnson had represented Tennessee in Congress. When his state seceded, Johnson had remained loyal to the Union.

The Impact of the Thirteenth Amendment Republicans in Congress believed Johnson would support a strict Reconstruction plan. But his plan was much milder than expected. It called for a majority of voters in each southern state to pledge loyalty to the United States. Each state also had to ratify the **Thirteenth Amendment,** which Congress had approved in January 1865. It banned slavery throughout the nation. (As you read, the Emancipation Proclamation did not free slaves in areas already under Union control.)

The Thirteenth Amendment had a significant impact on life in the United States. Without slavery, the South developed new social and economic systems. Many newly freed African Americans were hired on plantations. Others moved to towns or to the North to find work.

Politically, the amendment overturned previous state laws and Supreme Court decisions upholding slavery. Many people had argued that slavery was a state decision. The Thirteenth Amendment gave Congress the power to intervene, and later to pass additional legislation protecting civil rights.

Political Problems in Congress The southern states quickly met Johnson's conditions. As a result, the President approved their new state governments in late 1865. Voters in the South then elected

>> Republicans were outraged when southerners elected former Confederate leaders to Congress after the Civil War, such as former Confederate Vice President Alexander Stephens.

representatives to Congress. Many of those elected had held office in the Confederacy. For example, Alexander Stephens, the former vice president of the Confederacy, was elected senator from Georgia.

Republicans in Congress were outraged. The men who had led the South out of the Union were being elected to the House and Senate. Also, no southern state allowed African Americans to vote.

When the new Congress met, Republicans refused to let southern representatives take their seats. Instead, they set up a Joint Committee on Reconstruction to form a new plan for the South. The stage was set for a showdown between Congress and the President.

? **CHECK UNDERSTANDING** Which key difference between Lincoln's and Johnson's Reconstruction plans caused problems in 1865?

ASSESSMENT

1. **Identify Central Issues** What problems did the South face that the North did not after the Civil War?

2. **Summarize** what the Freedmen's Bureau accomplished.

3. **Describe** President Lincoln's Ten Percent Plan for Reconstruction.

4. **Compare** the Wade-Davis Bill to the Ten Percent Plan.

5. **Check Understanding** Why did Republicans in Congress refuse to let newly-elected southern representatives take their seats?

Radical Reconstruction

>> Voting rights for African Americans was a deeply contested issue in the South. This shows African American men voting in New Orleans in 1867.

▶ **Interactive Flipped Video**

Under Johnson's Reconstruction plan, most southern states promptly ratified the Thirteenth Amendment. However, southern legislatures also passed **black codes**, laws that severely limited the rights of freedmen.

>> **Objectives**

Describe how Congress reacted to the passage of black codes in the South.

Explain how Radical Republicans gained power in Congress.

Identify why President Johnson was impeached.

>> **Key Terms**

black codes
Radical Republican
Fourteenth
 Amendment
Radical
 Reconstruction
Reconstruction Act
impeach
Fifteenth
 Amendment

Reconstruction Difficulties Persist

Rights and Restrictions in the South

The black codes did grant some rights. For example, African Americans could marry legally and own some kinds of property. Still, the codes were clearly meant to keep freedmen from gaining political or economic power.

Black codes forbade freedmen to vote, own guns, or serve on juries. In some states, African Americans were permitted to work only as servants or farm laborers. In others, they had to sign contracts for a year's work. Those without contracts could be arrested and sentenced to work on a plantation.

Reconstruction Turns Radical

Republicans charged that, by placing too few restrictions on the South, Johnson's Reconstruction plan had encouraged southern legislatures to pass the black codes. Republicans were also outraged by reports of violence against freedmen. In 1866, white police officers in Memphis, Tennessee, attacked African American Union soldiers, who fired back at the officers. A protest against the police ended in violence, and rioting broke out. Angry whites burned homes and schools in a black section of the city. Similar riots broke out in New Orleans when freedmen met to support the right to vote.

A report by the Joint Committee on Reconstruction accused the South of trying to "preserve slavery . . . as long as possible." When President Johnson ignored the report, members of Congress

>> Plantations remained in the South after the war, but African Americans who worked on them, such as the ones shown here, were not enslaved. Black codes made it difficult for African Americans to break free from working in the plantation system.

called **Radical Republicans** vowed to take control of Reconstruction.

❓ **CHECK UNDERSTANDING** Why were Radical Republicans outraged at President Johnson's approach to Reconstruction?

Reforms of the Radical Reconstruction Congress

The Radicals were led by Thaddeus Stevens of Pennsylvania in the House and Charles Sumner of Massachusetts in the Senate. Radical Republicans had two main goals. First, they wanted to break the power of wealthy planters who had long ruled the South. Second, they wanted to ensure that freedmen received the right to vote. They used legislative reforms, or changes in laws, to achieve their goals.

Legislative Reform Radicals needed the support of moderate Republicans, the largest group in Congress. Moderates and Radicals disagreed on many issues, but they shared a strong political motive. Most southerners were Democrats. With southerners barred from Congress, Republicans could control both houses.

To combat the black codes, Congress passed the Civil Rights Act in April 1866. It gave citizenship to African Americans. When Johnson vetoed the bill, Congress overrode the veto.

The Impact of the Fourteenth Amendment Republicans feared that the Supreme Court might use its power of judicial review to declare the Civil Rights Act unconstitutional. In the Dred Scott decision of 1857, the Court had ruled that African Americans were not citizens. To avoid a similar ruling, Republicans proposed the **Fourteenth Amendment**. It defined citizens as "all persons born or

>> African Americans such as this laborer were granted citizenship with the Fourteenth Amendment. Yet during Reconstruction, African Americans still struggled to achieve basic rights, such as the right to vote.

naturalized in the United States." (The amendment did not apply to most Native Americans.) It guaranteed citizens "equal protection of the laws" and forbade states to "deprive any person of life, liberty, or property without due process of law." Thus, states could not legally discriminate against a citizen on unreasonable grounds, such as race.

The Fourteenth Amendment was proposed in 1866. As you will read, it was not ratified for another two years.

Under the Fourteenth Amendment, any state that denied any male citizen age 21 or older the right to vote would have its representation in Congress reduced. Republicans believed that freedmen would be able to defend their rights if they could vote.

>> This cartoon shows the terror of the New Orleans riots of 1866. **Analyze Political Cartoons** What meaning can you infer from the way President Johnson is portrayed in this cartoon?

▶ **Interactive Cartoon**

Republicans hoped the impact of the amendment on life in the United States would be to secure basic political rights for African Americans in the South. That goal would take a century to achieve. In the 1950s, the Fourteenth Amendment became a powerful tool in the struggle for citizenship rights.

? **EXPLAIN** why Republicans believed the Fourteenth Amendment was necessary.

Political and Social Problems During Reconstruction

President Johnson encouraged former Confederate states to reject the Fourteenth Amendment. He also decided to make the amendment an issue in the 1866 congressional elections.

A Republican Majority Across the North, Johnson urged voters to reject the Radicals. When a heckler yelled for Johnson to hang Jefferson Davis, Johnson shouted, "Why not hang Thad Stevens?" Many northerners criticized the President for losing his temper.

In July, riots in New Orleans killed 34 African Americans who had gathered in support of a convention backing voting rights. White mobs attacked the crowd and fired into the convention. The violence convinced many northerners that stronger measures were needed. In the end, the elections were a disaster for Johnson. Republicans won majorities in both houses of Congress.

Radical Reforms Impact the South In 1867, Republicans in Congress prepared to take charge of Reconstruction. With huge majorities in both houses, Congress could easily override vetoes. The period that followed is often called **Radical Reconstruction**.

Congress passed the first **Reconstruction Act** in March 1867. It threw out the state governments that had refused to ratify the Fourteenth Amendment—all the former Confederate states except Tennessee. The Military Reconstruction Acts of 1867 divided the southern states into five military districts, each governed by a military general. Army commanders were given broad permission to enforce Reconstruction.

Military rulers in these military districts had nearly unlimited power. They sometimes conducted trials without juries in the South. Many southerners bitterly resented the imposition of military rule. They argued that the military occupation violated their rights because it was done without their consent or representation.

Congress, however, continued to impose new rules. To rejoin the Union, former Confederate states had to write new constitutions and ratify the Fourteenth Amendment. The Reconstruction Act also required that southern states allow African Americans to vote.

With the new constitutions in place, reconstructed states held elections to set up new state governments. The Fourteenth Amendment barred former Confederate officials from voting. Many other white southerners stayed away from the polls in protest. Protected by the army, freedmen proudly exercised their new right to vote. Most favored the Republican party, since it had supported their rights. As a result, Republicans gained control of all of the new southern state governments.

? GENERATE EXPLANATIONS On what basis did the southern states argue against the Military Reconstruction Acts?

Political Problems and a New President

Congress passed other Reconstruction acts over Johnson's veto. As President, Johnson had a duty to execute the new laws. However, Johnson did what he could to limit their effect. He fired several military commanders who supported Radical Reconstruction. Republicans in Congress decided to try to remove Johnson from office.

The President on Trial On February 24, 1868, the House of Representatives voted to **impeach**, or bring formal charges against, Johnson. According to the Constitution, the House may impeach a President for "treason, bribery, or other high crimes and misdemeanors." The President is removed from office if found guilty by two thirds of the Senate.

RECONSTRUCTION POLITICS

CONGRESSIONAL VOTES ON KEY AMENDMENTS

14TH

KEY
- YAY
- NAY
- DID NOT VOTE

SENATE: 33, 11, 5
HOUSE: 120, 32, 32

15TH

SENATE: 39, 13, 14
HOUSE: 144, 44, 35

Sources: Library of Congress; Congressional Record

IMPEACHMENT OF PRESIDENT ANDREW JOHNSON

SENATE: 36, 19
HOUSE: 126, 47

Source: U.S. House and Senate

THE SENATE WAS ONE VOTE SHORT OF THE TWO-THIRDS MAJORITY NEEDED TO CONVICT PRESIDENT JOHNSON

ULYSSES S. GRANT **214**

ELECTION OF 1868
ELECTORAL VOTES EARNED

HORATIO SEYMOUR **80**

Source: The American Presidency Project

>> **Analyze Tables** How would you describe congressional support for the Fourteenth and Fifteenth Amendments?

During Johnson's trial, it became clear that he was not guilty of high crimes and misdemeanors. Even Charles Sumner, Johnson's bitter foe, admitted that the charges were "political in character." Despite intense pressure, seven Republican senators refused to vote for conviction. The Constitution, they said, did not allow Congress to remove a President just because they disagreed with him. In the end, the vote was 35 to 19—one vote shy of the two thirds needed to convict.

Grant Wins the Election of 1868 Johnson served out the few remaining months of his term. In May 1868, Republicans nominated the Union's greatest war hero, Ulysses S. Grant, for President.

In July 1868, the Fourteenth Amendment finally passed, granting citizenship to African Americans. Former Confederate states had to ratify the amendment as if they were in the Union—even though they had not yet been readmitted. On the other hand, states that had been loyal to the Union during the war felt that the Confederate states had lost their constitutional rights by rebelling. This rule did not affect Delaware, Maryland, Kentucky, or Missouri, slave states that did not secede.

By election day, most southern states had ratified the amendment and rejoined the Union. As Congress demanded, the southern states allowed African American men to vote. About 500,000 blacks voted— nearly all of them for Grant. With support from most northerners as well, he easily won the election.

The Impact of the Fifteenth Amendment In 1869, Congress proposed the **Fifteenth Amendment**. It forbade any state to deny any citizen the right to vote because

>> Thaddeus Stevens (standing) criticized President Johnson after Johnson fired military commanders who were in charge of enforcing Radical Reconstruction. **Summarize** How did Congress respond to Johnson's actions?

of "race, color, or previous condition of servitude."

Republicans had moral and political reasons for supporting the Fifteenth Amendment. They remembered the great sacrifices made by African American soldiers in the Civil War. They also felt it was wrong to let African Americans vote in the South but not in the North. In addition, Republicans knew that if African Americans could vote in the North, they would help Republicans win elections there.

The Fifteenth Amendment was ratified in 1870. At last, all African American men over age 21 had the right to vote.

The Fifteenth Amendment was a difficult amendment to enforce. The South soon found ways around it, as you will read. It was only in the mid-1900s that new legislation protected voting rights and the full impact of the amendment was felt.

>> This illustration shows African Americans voting for the first time in 1868. **Analyze** Why does the artist show different types of African American citizens?

[?] **CHECK UNDERSTANDING** Why did some Republican senators refuse to vote to convict Johnson after his impeachment?

ASSESSMENT

1. **Summarize** the rights allowed to freedmen by the black codes.

2. **Generate Explanations** Why were the black codes so restrictive?

3. **Draw Conclusions** With which political party did Andrew Johnson's sympathies seem to lie?

4. **Draw Conclusions** Why was the Republican plan for Reconstruction called "Radical Reconstruction"?

5. **Generate Explanations** Why did it take nearly a century for the full effect of the Fifteenth Amendment to be felt?

Reconstruction and Southern Society

>> After the Radical Reconstruction Act of 1867, southern states elected African Americans to state legislatures and both houses of Congress. Here African American legislators work on a bill in South Carolina.

▶ **Interactive Flipped Video**

>> **Objectives**

Identify new forces in southern politics.

Describe how southern conservatives resisted Reconstruction.

Analyze the economic, political, and social challenges facing Reconstruction governments.

Explain why sharecropping led to a cycle of poverty.

>> **Key Terms**

scalawag
carpetbagger
Ku Klux Klan
sharecropper
Hiram Rhodes
   Revels

Before the Civil War, a small group of rich planters had dominated southern politics. During Reconstruction, however, new groups tried to reshape southern politics. The state governments created during Radical Reconstruction were different from any governments the South had known before. The old leaders had lost much of their influence. Three groups stepped in to replace them.

New Political Groups in the South

White Southern Republicans One group to emerge consisted of white southerners who supported the new Republican governments. Many were businesspeople who had opposed secession in 1860. They wanted to forget the war and get on with rebuilding the South.

Many whites in the South felt that any southerner who helped the Republicans was a traitor. They called the white southern Republicans **scalawags**, a word used for small, scruffy horses.

Northerners in the South Northerners who came to the South after the war were another important force. White southerners accused the new arrivals of hoping to get rich from the South's misery. Southerners jested that these northerners were in such a hurry to move south that they had time only to fling a few clothes into cheap suitcases, or carpetbags. As a result, they became known as **carpetbaggers**.

In fact, northerners went south for various reasons. A few did hope to profit as the South was being rebuilt. Many more, however, were Union soldiers who had grown to love the South's rich land. Others, both white and black, were teachers, ministers, and reformers who sincerely wanted to help the freedmen.

African Americans African Americans were the third major new group in southern politics. Before the war, they had no voice in southern government. During Reconstruction, they not only voted in large numbers, but they also ran for and were elected to public office in the South. African Americans became

sheriffs, mayors, and legislators in the new state and local governments. Sixteen African Americans were elected to Congress between 1869 and 1880.

Two African Americans, both representing Mississippi, served in the Senate. **Hiram Rhodes Revels**, a clergyman and teacher, became the nation's first black senator in 1870. He completed the unfinished term of former Confederate president Jefferson Davis. In 1874, Blanche K. Bruce became the first African American to serve a full term in the Senate.

Revels's election had a powerful impact. It was an important victory for African American politicians. He served on the Committee on Education and Labor, where he opposed legislation that would segregate, or separate, schools for African Americans and whites. He

>> Hiram R. Revels became the first African American to serve in Congress in 1870. **Predict Consequences** How did gaining political representation affect most African Americans?

[▶] **Interactive Gallery**

also promoted opportunities for African American workers.

Freedmen had less political influence than many whites claimed, however. Only in South Carolina did African Americans win a majority in one house of the state legislature. No state elected a black governor.

❓ DESCRIBE how politics in the South changed during Reconstruction.

Conservatives Resist Reform

Most white southerners who had held power before the Civil War resisted Reconstruction. These Conservatives resented the changes imposed by Congress and enforced by the military. They wanted the South to change as little as possible. Conservatives were willing to let African Americans vote and hold a few offices. Still, they were determined that real power would remain in the hands of whites. This tension caused social problems in the South during Reconstruction that impacted free African Americans and Conservatives.

A few wealthy planters tried to force African Americans back onto plantations. Many small farmers and laborers wanted the government to take action against freedmen, who now competed with them for land and power.

Most of these white southerners were Democrats. They declared war on anyone who cooperated with the Republicans. "This is a white man's country," declared one southern senator, "and white men must govern it."

The Problem of the Ku Klux Klan Some white southerners formed secret societies

>> A representative of the Freedmen's Bureau stands between two angry and armed groups of whites and African Americans.

to help them regain power. The most dangerous was the **Ku Klux Klan**, or KKK. The Klan worked to keep African Americans and white Republicans out of office.

Dressed in white robes and hoods to hide their identities, Klansmen rode at night to the homes of African American voters, shouting threats and burning wooden crosses. When threats did not work, the Klan turned to violence. Klan members murdered hundreds of African Americans and their white allies.

The Social and Political Impact of the Klan Many moderate southerners condemned the violence of the Klan. Yet, they could do little to stop the Klan's reign of terror. Freedmen turned to the federal government for help. In Kentucky, African American voters wrote to Congress:

> "We believe you are not familiar with the Ku Klux Klan's riding nightly over the country spreading terror wherever they go by robbing, whipping, and killing our people without provocation."
>
> —Records of the U.S. Senate, April 11, 1871

In 1870, Congress made it a crime to use force to keep people from voting. Although Klan activities decreased, the threat of violence remained. Some African Americans continued to vote and hold office, but others were frightened away from the ballot box.

?EXPLAIN the social and political impact of southern conservatives during Reconstruction.

>> Both the KKK and White League used violence to try to prevent freedmen from voting. **Analyze Political Cartoons** What does the phrase "worse than slavery" suggest about the effect of this violence on African American families?

Political Problems and Legislative Reform

Reconstruction governments tried to rebuild the South. They built public schools for both black and white children. Many states gave women the right to own property. In addition, Reconstruction governments rebuilt railroads, telegraph lines, bridges, and roads. Between 1865 and 1879, the South laid 7,000 miles of railroad track. However, political problems due to controversial government policies and political corruption impacted southerners and hindered progress.

Taxation Without Representation Rebuilding cost money. Before the war, southerners paid low taxes. Reconstruction governments raised taxes sharply. This created discontent among many southern whites. Many former Confederate officers and officials were denied voting rights during Reconstruction and thus were being taxed without representation. The tax increases also caused some landowners to lose their land.

Corruption Plagues Reconstruction

Southerners were further angered by widespread corruption in the Reconstruction governments. One state legislature, for example, voted $1,000 to cover a member's bet on a horse race. Other items billed to the state included hams, perfume, and a coffin. Corruption was not limited to the South. After the Civil War, dishonesty plagued northern governments, as well. Most southern officeholders, however, served their states honestly.

Attempts at Legislative Reform

State legislative reform programs in the South met with mixed success. New state constitutions allowed all adult men to vote, removed restrictions for holding office, and made public officials elected rather than appointed. Executive branches were also given increased power to provide government services.

However, legislation to enroll voters was hindered by new voting restrictions that kept many African Americans from making use of their new voting rights. Many of the laws preventing former Confederates from voting and holding office did not last. In Georgia, African Americans were forced from the state legislature.

? SUMMARIZE the problems that faced Reconstruction governments trying to rebuild the South.

>> During Reconstruction, free African Americans emerged as an important political group. However, they faced difficulties securing political power and escaping poverty.

>> A visiting pastor joins an African American family for dinner in the South during Reconstruction.

Economic Problems During Reconstruction

In the first months after the war, freedmen left the plantations on which they had lived and worked. They found few opportunities, however.

Limited Opportunities for Freedmen

Some Radical Republicans talked about giving each freedman "40 acres and a mule" as a fresh start. This idea stemmed from a field order given by General William Tecumseh Sherman in 1865. Thaddeus Stevens suggested breaking up big plantations and distributing the land. Most Americans opposed the plan, however. In the end, former slaves received—in the words of a freedman—"nothing but freedom."

Through hard work or good luck, some freedmen were able to become landowners. Most, however, had little choice but to return to where they had lived in slavery. At the same time, some large planters found themselves with land but nobody to work it.

Economic Problems Confront the South

Before the Civil War, Southern planters enjoyed prosperity because of strong demand for cotton, tobacco, and other farm products in the North and in Britain. During the war, a Union blockade had prevented the South from selling most of its products in those markets. As a result, prices for those products rose, and suppliers in Latin America, India, and other parts of the world began producing more tobacco, cotton, sugarcane, and rice. When the war ended and southern farmers returned to the market, they faced much greater competition from foreign producers, resulting in lower prices according to the laws of supply and demand.

>> Sharecropping was a system in which poor African Americans and whites rented land from mostly white landowners in exchange for a portion of the harvest. **Predict Consequences** What impact did sharecropping have on African Americans' economic status?

▶ **Interactive Chart**

Meanwhile, the war had destroyed many of the South's cities and factories. Southern planters had lost their enslaved workers, who were often planters' main investment. The South had little money to invest in industry. As a result, it remained dependent on farming at a time when farming brought less income.

Poverty in the South During Reconstruction, many freedmen and poor whites went to work on the large plantations. These **sharecroppers** rented and farmed a plot of land. Planters provided seed, fertilizer, and tools in return for a share of the crop at harvest time. To many freedmen, sharecropping offered a measure of independence. Many hoped to own their own land one day.

In fact, this arrangement had a damaging impact on these groups. Most sharecroppers and small landowners became locked in a cycle of poverty. Each spring, they received supplies on credit. In the fall, they had to repay what they had borrowed. As you have read, southern farm products were worth less after the Civil War. If the harvest did not cover what they owed, they sank deeper into debt. Many farmers lost their land and became sharecroppers themselves.

? **EXPRESS PROBLEMS CLEARLY** What was the biggest problem with sharecropping?

ASSESSMENT

1. **Explain** why white southern conservatives resisted Reconstruction.

2. **Draw Conclusions** Why didn't any southern state elect an African American as governor?

3. **Summarize** the purpose and activities of the Ku Klux Klan.

4. **Identify Central Issues** What was the central challenge to rebuilding the South and how did the southern states meet this challenge?

5. **Explain** Why did freedmen have such difficulty finding work in the South after the war, and why did so many of them turn to sharecropping?

The Aftermath of Reconstruction

>> Workers process iron in a factory in Birmingham, Alabama, in the 1890s. Summarize How did the development of factories, such as this one, help to balance opportunities for workers in the southern economy?

▶ Interactive Flipped Video

By the 1870s, Radical Republicans were losing power. Many northerners grew weary of trying to reform the South. It was time to let southerners run their own governments, they said—even if it meant that African Americans in the South might lose their rights.

>> **Objectives**

Summarize the events that led to the end of Reconstruction.

Explain how the rights of African Americans were restricted in the South after Reconstruction.

Identify industries that flourished in the "New South."

>> **Key Terms**

poll tax
literacy test
grandfather clause
segregation
Jim Crow laws
"New South"
Plessy v. Ferguson
Compromise of
    1877

PEARSON
realize
www.PearsonRealize.com
Access your Digital Lesson.

Reconstruction Ends

Political Changes Impact the South

Disclosure of widespread corruption also hurt Republicans. President Grant appointed many friends to government offices. Some used their position to steal large sums of money from the government. Grant won reelection in 1872, but many northerners lost faith in Republicans and their policies.

Congress passed the Amnesty Act in 1872. It restored the right to vote to nearly all white southerners, including former Confederate officials who had lost voting rights due to the Fourteenth Amendment. White southerners voted solidly Democratic. At the same time, threats of violence kept many African Americans from voting. By 1876, only three southern states—South Carolina, Florida, and Tennessee—remained under Republican control.

Reconstruction Ends After Disputed Election of 1876

The end of Reconstruction came with the election of 1876. The Democrats nominated Samuel Tilden, governor of New York, for President. The Republicans chose Ohio governor Rutherford B. Hayes. Both candidates vowed to fight corruption.

Tilden won the popular vote. However, he had only 184 electoral votes, one short of the number needed to win. The outcome of the election hung on 20 votes from states where the election was disputed. All but one came from the three southern states still controlled by Republicans. The exception was Oregon, where a Democratic governor replaced a Republican elector with a Democratic one, even though his state had voted heavily Republican. In the three southern states, Republican election officials were accused of throwing out Democratic votes.

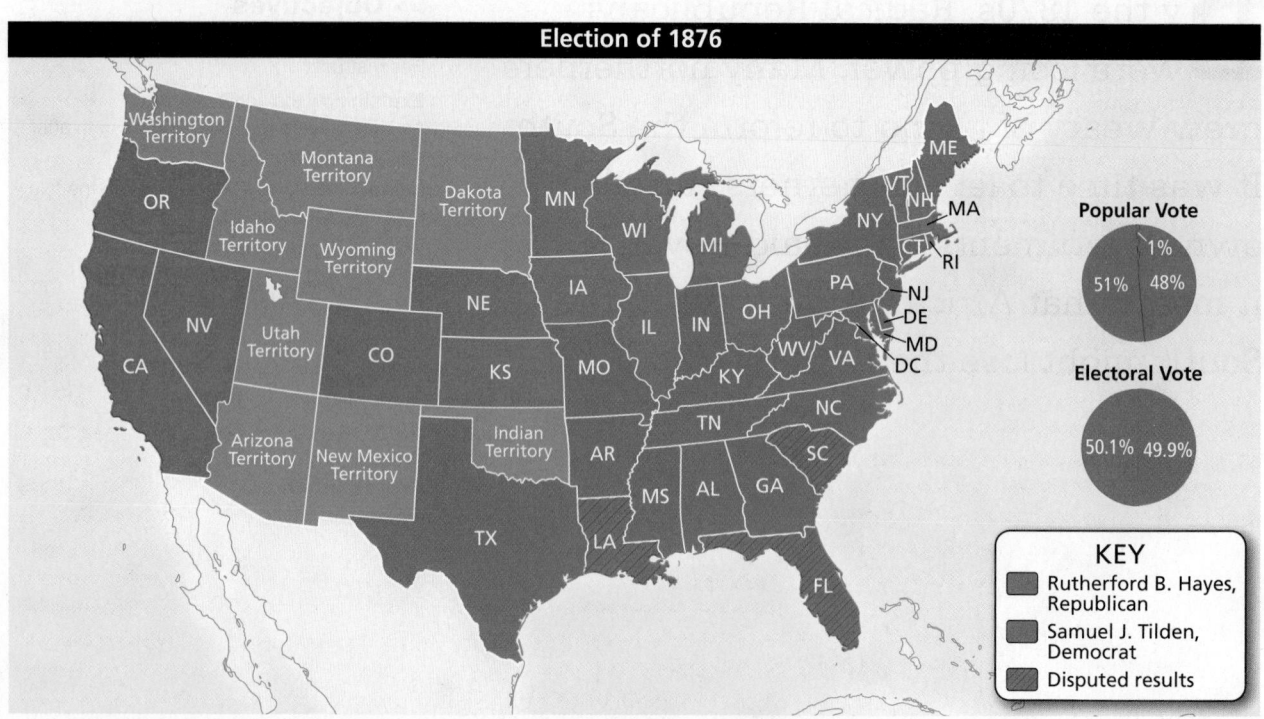

Election of 1876

Popular Vote: 51% / 48% / 1%

Electoral Vote: 50.1% / 49.9%

KEY
- Rutherford B. Hayes, Republican
- Samuel J. Tilden, Democrat
- Disputed results

>> **Analyze Maps** Based on the information in the map, why might Hayes's victory in the 1876 election have come as a surprise to some?

As inauguration day drew near, the nation still had no one to swear in as President. Congress set up a special commission to settle the crisis. The commission, made up mostly of Republicans, decided to give all the disputed electoral votes to Hayes.

Southern Democrats could have fought the decision. However, they agreed to support the commission's decision in return for a promise by Hayes to end Reconstruction. This agreement is known as the **Compromise of 1877**. Once in office, Hayes removed all remaining federal troops from Louisiana, South Carolina, and Florida. Reconstruction was over.

>> **Analyze Political Cartoons** How does this cartoon portray the literacy tests southern states used to prevent African Americans from voting?

The Political Impact of Reconstruction

Reconstruction had a deep and lasting impact on southern politics. White southerners had bitter memories of Radical Republican policies and military rule. For the next hundred years, the South remained a stronghold of the Democratic party. At the same time, black southerners steadily lost most of their political rights.

? EXPLAIN why southern Democrats did not fight the decision by the special commission to give the presidential election of 1876 to Rutherford B. Hayes?

New Legislation Restricts African American Rights

As federal troops withdrew from southern states, Conservative Democrats tightened their grip on southern governments. These Conservatives found new ways to keep African Americans from exercising their rights. Many of these were laws that restricted the right to vote.

Voting Restrictions Limit Political Participation Over time, many southern states passed **poll taxes**, requiring voters to pay a fee each time they voted. As a result, poor freedmen could rarely afford to vote.

States also imposed **literacy tests** that required voters to read and explain a section of the Constitution. Since most freedmen had little education, such tests kept them away from the polls. Election officials also applied different standards to black and white voters. Blacks who were able to read often had to answer much more difficult questions than whites on literacy tests.

Still, many poor whites could not pass the literacy test. To increase the number of white voters, states passed **grandfather clauses**. These laws stated that if a voter's father or grandfather had been eligible to vote on January 1, 1867, the voter did not have to take a literacy test. No African Americans in the South could vote before 1868, so grandfather clauses ensured that white men could vote.

Conservatives Implement Jim Crow Laws

After 1877, **segregation**, or legal separation of races, became the law of the South. **Jim Crow laws**, as they were known, separated blacks and whites in schools, restaurants, theaters, trains, streetcars, playgrounds, hospitals, and even cemeteries. Louisiana novelist George Washington Cable described segregation as:

"A system of oppression so rank that nothing could make it seem small except the fact that [African Americans] had already been ground under it for a century and a half."

—George Washington Cable, "The Freedman's Case in Equity"

African Americans brought lawsuits to challenge segregation. In 1896, in the case of *Plessy v. Ferguson,* the Supreme Court ruled that segregation was legal so long as facilities for blacks and whites were equal. In fact, facilities were rarely equal. For example, southern states spent much less on schools for blacks than for whites.

Despite such setbacks, the Constitution now recognized African Americans as citizens. Laws passed during Reconstruction—especially the Fourteenth Amendment—would become the basis of the civil rights movement almost 100 years later.

? **SUMMARIZE** the ways in which southern governments restricted the rights of freedmen.

>> Jim Crow laws made it legal to segregate nonwhites and whites in places such as this school. **Predict Consequences** What impact did these laws have on the equality of educational opportunities for whites and African Americans?

▶ Interactive Timeline

INDUSTRIAL GROWTH IN THE NEW SOUTH

COTTON MILLS IN THE SOUTH

Year	Cotton Mills
1860	165
1870	151
1880	161
1890	239
1900	400
1910	731

Source: National Park Service

COAL PRODUCTION IN THE SOUTH
(THOUSANDS OF TONS)

— ALABAMA
— TENNESSEE
— VIRGINIA

Source: National Bureau of Economic Research

LUMBER PRODUCTION IN THE NORTH & SOUTH

Year	North	South
1850	13.8%	54.5%
1860	16.5%	36.2%
1870	9.4%	36.8%
1880	11.9%	24.8%
1890	15.9%	18.4%
1900	25.2%	16.0%

Source: U.S. Census Bureau

>> **Analyze Charts** Cite evidence from the charts that the southern economy diversified following the Civil War.

 Interactive Map

The "New South" Moves Toward Industry

During Reconstruction, the South made some progress toward rebuilding its economy. Cotton production, long the basis of the South's economy, slowly recovered. By 1880, planters were growing as much cotton as they had in 1860.

After Reconstruction, a new generation of southern leaders worked to expand the economy. In stirring speeches, Atlanta journalist Henry Grady described a **"New South"** that used its vast natural resources to build up its own industry instead of depending on the North.

Agriculture Leads to New Industries in the South In 1880, the entire South still produced fewer finished textiles than Massachusetts. In the next decade, more and more communities started building textile mills to turn cotton into cloth.

The tobacco industry also grew. In North Carolina, James Duke used new machinery to revolutionize the manufacture of tobacco products. Duke's American Tobacco Company eventually controlled 90 percent of the nation's tobacco industry.

Developing the Environment to Shape New Industries The physical characteristics of the environment influenced many of the economic activities of the South. In addition to farming, abundant natural resources provided opportunities for new industries to emerge. In particular, the South tapped its mineral resources. With its large deposits of iron ore and coal, Alabama became a center of the steel industry. Oil refineries sprang up in Louisiana and Texas. Other states produced copper, granite, and marble.

By the 1890s, many northern forests had been cut down. The southern yellow

>> As southerners rebuilt their economy, they built manufacturing plants to process raw cotton into finished textiles, such as this mill in North Carolina.

use of natural resources provided jobs and opportunities for southerners who had been struggling economically after the Civil War. Its wood, steel, and other products were used in industry around the country.

The South had developed a more balanced economy by 1900. "We find a South wide awake with business," wrote a visitor, "eagerly laying lines of communication, rapidly opening mines, building furnaces, foundries, and all sorts of shops." Still, the South could not keep up with even more rapid growth in the North and the West.

? COMPARE the post-Reconstruction economy of the South with its pre-Civil War economy.

ASSESSMENT

1. **Infer** What was life like for African Americans in the South after Reconstruction ended?

2. **Draw Conclusions** Why did the South become a Democratic stronghold?

3. **Summarize** the effect of Jim Crow laws.

4. **Analyze Information** How was the decision in *Plessy* v. *Ferguson* inconsistent with reality?

5. **Identify Central Ideas** How did the South change to improve its economic situation?

pine competed with the northwestern white pine as a lumber source. Southern factories turned out cypress shingles and hardwood furniture.

Factories, farming, and mining modified the physical environment of the South. The work clearing land and making

1. **Analyze the Causes and Effects of Economic Differences Between the North and South** Write a paragraph analyzing the differences between the economies of the North and South after the Civil War and how these differences affected the two regions. Consider why the economies of the North and South were different after the Civil War and analyze what happened to the two regions as a result of the economic differences.

2. **Describe the Impact of the Fourteenth Amendment** Write a paragraph describing the impact the Fourteenth Amendment had on African Americans and the ongoing struggle for civil rights. Explain why Republicans proposed the Fourteenth Amendment and what guarantees the amendment granted. Describe the impact of the Fourteenth Amendment on the southern states, African Americans, and on the movement for citizenship rights.

3. **Identify the Impact of African Americans Elected to Public Office** Write a paragraph that evaluates the impact of the election of Hiram Rhodes Revels on freedmen during Reconstruction. Be sure to identify the role of African Americans in southern politics before the Civil War and during Reconstruction; identify Hiram Rhodes Revels, the office he held, and the positions he held on issues during Reconstruction; and explain the impact that Revels' election had on freedmen at the time.

4. **Evaluate Jim Crow Laws** Evaluate the impact of Jim Crow laws on African Americans in the South after the end of Reconstruction. In your answer, describe Jim Crow laws, explain what George Washington Cable meant in the quotation about Jim Crow below, explain the social problems these laws caused, and evaluate what effect these laws had on African Americans.

   A system of oppression so rank that nothing could make it seem small except the fact that [African Americans] had already been ground under it for a century and a half.

   —George Washington Cable, "The Freedman's Case in Equity"

5. **Describe the Effects of the Civil War on the South** Write a paragraph describing the problems the South faced as a result of the Civil War. In your paragraph, be sure to describe and explain the economic problems, the social problems, and the political problems.

6. **Evaluate the Impact of Economic and Social Problems on Freedmen** Using what you have learned about Reconstruction and the quotation below, write a paragraph evaluating the problems that freedmen faced during Reconstruction. In your paragraph, be sure to consider the economic and social problems that freedmen faced, what the Freedmen's Bureau was, and how the Freedmen's Bureau helped freedmen solve these problems.

   It is wonderful how a people who have been so long crushed to the earth . . . can have so great a desire for knowledge, and such a capacity for attaining it.

   —Charlotte Forten, article in the Atlantic Monthly

7. **Describe the Effects of Laws Passed During Reconstruction** Use the information from the lessons in this topic to write a paragraph explaining the problems freedmen faced in the South as a result of the passage of black codes and the reaction of the Radical Republicans to the actions of the southern legislatures. In your paragraph, be sure to describe the black codes and explain why southern lawmakers passed these laws; evaluate the impact of the black codes on freedmen in the South; and explain how these laws affected the Radical Republicans' reaction to President Johnson's Reconstruction plan.

8. **Evaluate Legislative Reform Programs** Use the information from the lessons in this topic to write a paragraph evaluating the actions of Radical Republicans as they took control of Reconstruction. In your paragraph, be sure to identify the Radical Republicans' two goals, explain how they planned to achieve these goals, and describe the purpose of the Civil Rights Act of 1866 and the Fourteenth Amendment.

9. **Describe the Effects of the Civil War** Use the information from the lessons in this topic to write a paragraph describing the problems the North faced as a result of the Civil War. In your paragraph, be sure to describe and explain the economic problems, the social problems, and the political problems.

10. Explain Political Problems During Reconstruction
Write a paragraph that describes the steps taken by the Radical Republicans to take charge of Reconstruction and evaluates the impact that Radical Reconstruction had on the South. Be sure to explain why Radical Republicans were able to take charge of Reconstruction in 1867, describe the provisions of the Military Reconstruction Act and explain why southern states opposed it, and analyze the impact of the Reconstruction Acts on the former Confederate states.

11. Analyze Thematic Maps Use the information from the map below and the lessons in this topic to write a paragraph analyzing the geographic distributions and patterns of the disputed election of 1876. In your paragraph, be sure to answer the following questions: In what areas of the country did Rutherford B. Hayes gain the most electoral votes? What pattern is evident from analyzing where Samuel J. Tilden won the electoral votes? What do the disputed states have in common?

12. Describe the Impact of the Election of 1868
Use information from the lessons in this topic to write a paragraph explaining how Radical Reconstruction affected the results of the 1868 presidential election. In your paragraph, be sure to explain what demands Congress made on the southern states regarding the election and explain why Ulysses S. Grant easily won the election.

13. Describe the Impact of the Fifteenth Amendment
Write a paragraph explaining the reasons Republicans supported the Fifteenth Amendment and describing the impact the Fifteenth Amendment had on African Americans. In your paragraph, be sure to explain what guarantees the Fifteenth Amendment granted, explain why Republicans supported the Fifteenth Amendment, explain the impact on African Americans, and explain why the amendment was difficult to enforce.

14. Describe the Effects of Reconstruction Use information from the lessons in this topic to write a paragraph that describes the rise, social impact, and political impact of the Ku Klux Klan. In your paragraph, be sure to explain the rise of the Ku Klux Klan (KKK) and the tactics they used to achieve their goals, describe the freedmen's efforts to oppose KKK activities, and evaluate the social and political impact of the KKK.

15. Analyze Economic Problems in the South During Reconstruction Explain the economic problems that arose in the South during Reconstruction and how they led to social problems. Be sure to describe problems faced by farmers and sharecroppers, and analyze social problems brought about by these problems.

16. Write About the Essential Question **Write an essay on the Essential Question: How should we handle conflict?** Use evidence from your study of this topic to support your answer.

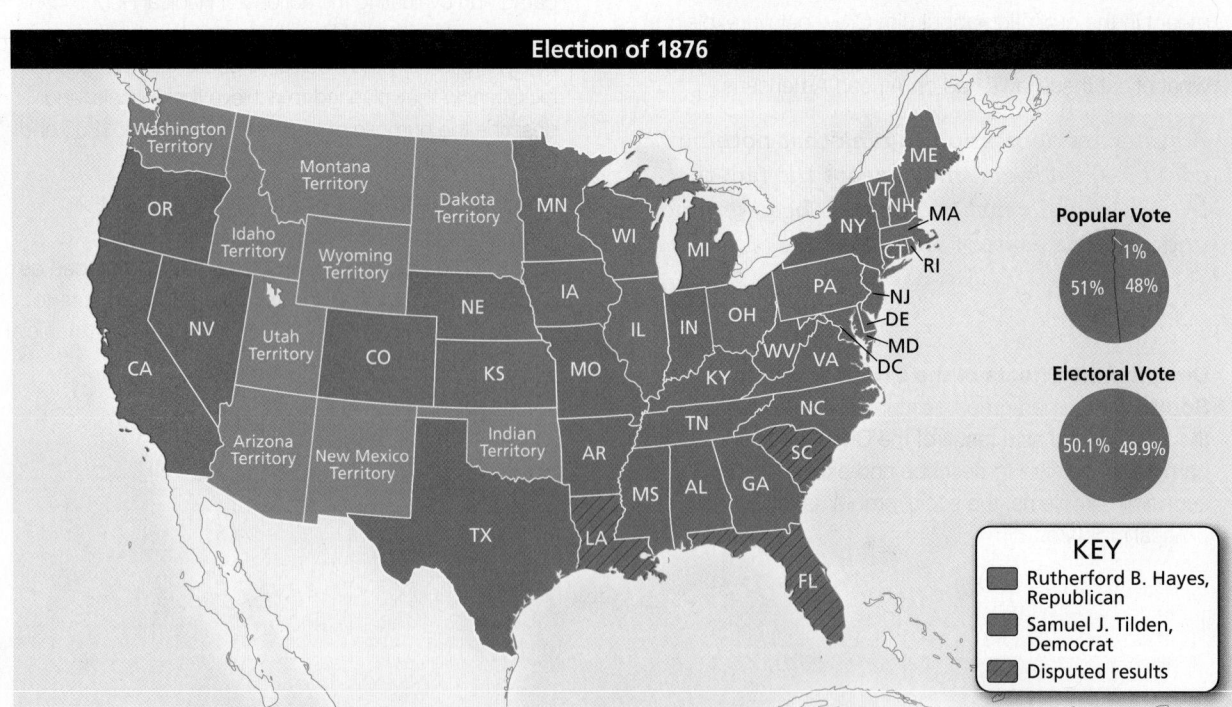

Election of 1876

Popular Vote
51% | 48% | 1%

Electoral Vote
50.1% | 49.9%

KEY
- Rutherford B. Hayes, Republican
- Samuel J. Tilden, Democrat
- Disputed results

Go online to PearsonRealize.com and use the texts, quizzes, interactivities, Interactive Reading Notepads, Flipped Videos, and other resources from this Topic to prepare for the Topic Test.

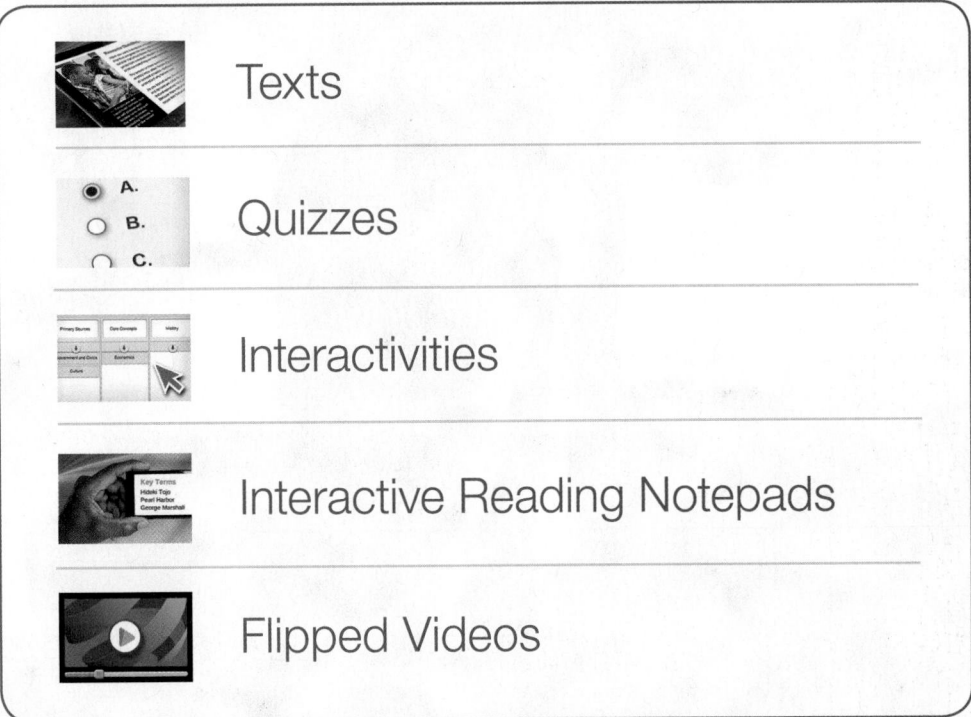

Texts

Quizzes

Interactivities

Interactive Reading Notepads

Flipped Videos

While online you can also check the progress you've made learning the topic and course content by viewing your grades, test scores, and assignment status.

[**ESSENTIAL QUESTION**] How should resources be distributed?

10 **Industrial and Economic Growth (1865–1914)**

Silver and Gold Mining

The Comstock Lode Two prospectors struck gold in Nevada in 1859. Then, another miner, Henry Comstock, appeared. "The land is mine," he cried, demanding to be made a partner. From then on, Comstock boasted about "his" mine. The strike became known as the Comstock Lode. A **lode** is a rich vein of gold or silver.

Comstock and his partners often complained about the heavy blue sand that was mixed in with the gold. It clogged the devices used for separating out the gold and made the gold hard to reach. When Mexican miners took the "danged blue stuff" to an expert in California, tests showed that it was loaded with silver. Comstock had stumbled onto one of the richest silver mines in the world.

Miners moved into many other areas of the West. Some found valuable ore in Montana and Idaho. Others struck it rich in Colorado. In the 1870s, miners discovered gold in the Black Hills of South Dakota. In the late 1890s, thousands rushed north to Alaska after major gold strikes were made there.

Boomtowns and Ghost Towns Gold and silver strikes attracted thousands of prospectors. Towns sprang up almost overnight near all the major mining sites.

First, miners built a tent city near the diggings. Then, people came to supply the miners' needs. Traders brought mule teams loaded with tools, food, and clothing. Merchants hauled in wagon-loads of supplies and set up stores.

Soon, wood-frame houses, hotels, restaurants, and stores replaced the tents. For example, it took less than a year for the mining camp at the Comstock Lode to become the boomtown of Virginia City, Nevada.

Most settlers in the boomtowns of the mining frontier were men. However, enterprising women also found ways to profit. Some women ran boardinghouses and laundries. Others opened restaurants, where miners gladly paid high prices for home-cooked meals.

Many boomtowns lasted for only a few years. When the gold or silver ore was gone, the miners moved away. Without the miners for customers, businesses often had to close. In this way, a boomtown could quickly go bust and turn into a ghost town.

Still, some boomtowns survived and prospered even after the mines shut down.

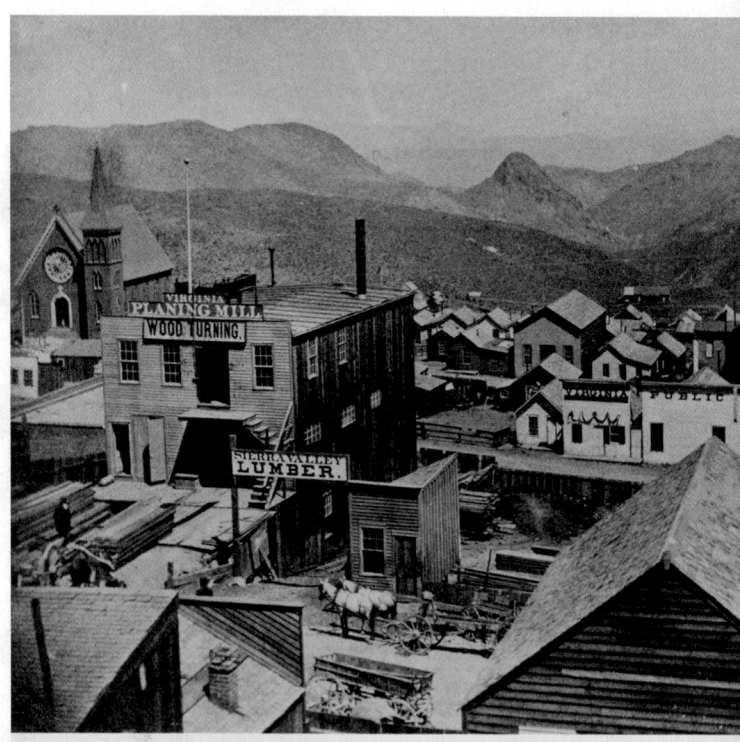

>> Virginia City, Nevada, became a boomtown due to mining activities from the Comstock Lode. **Identify Cause and Effect** How did silver and gold rushes affect settlement of the West?

▶ **Interactive Gallery**

In these towns, miners stayed and found new ways to make a living.

? IDENTIFY MAIN IDEAS Why did boomtowns spring up throughout the West?

The Costs of Mining

The surge of miners in the West created problems, as did the arrival of cattle ranchers and homesteaders. Mines and towns polluted clear mountain streams. Miners cut down forests to get wood for buildings. They also forced Native Americans from the land.

Foreign miners were often treated unfairly. In many camps, mobs drove Mexicans from their claims. Chinese miners were heavily taxed or forced to work claims abandoned by others.

Few miners ever got rich. Much of the gold and silver lay deep underground. It could be reached only with costly machinery. Eventually, most mining in the West was taken over by large companies that could afford to buy this equipment. Furthermore, independent prospectors like Henry Comstock largely disappeared. They were replaced by paid laborers who worked for the large companies.

Keeping the Law in Small Towns

Lawlessness and disorder often accompanied the rapid growth of a town. Stories have exaggerated the number of fights and killings that took place in these towns, but some towns actually were violent places. In response, miners sometimes resorted to organizing groups of **vigilantes**, or self-appointed law enforcers. Vigilantes tracked down outlaws and punished them, usually without trials. A common punishment was lynching.

Occasionally, vigilante groups did not form to fight crime. At least one San Francisco group organized to take political control of the city.

Informal methods of governing gradually gave way to more formal arrangements.

>> Prospectors, shown here with their equipment, prepare to head out for the gold and silver fields in hopes of striking it rich.

In 1861, Colorado, Dakota, and Nevada were organized into territories. Idaho and Arizona followed in 1863 and Montana in 1864. The process of permanent settlement and government had begun.

? RECALL How did informal methods of governance gradually become more formal?

The Railroad Encourages Economic Growth

To many Native Americans, the railroad was a terrifying monster, an "iron horse" belching black smoke and moving at stunning speeds. However, for the people of mining towns, railroads meant supplies, new townsfolk, and a rapid means of transporting their gold and silver. The West needed a transportation system that could carry heavy loads over great distances at a cost low enough to guarantee a profit. It is no wonder, then, that railroad companies raced to lay track to the mines and boomtowns. In time, the new technology of railroad transport opened the West and fostered economic growth for the nation.

The Transcontinental Railroad In 1863, two companies began a race to build the first transcontinental railroad. A **transcontinental railroad** is one that stretches across a continent from coast to coast. The Union Pacific Railroad started building a rail line westward from Omaha, Nebraska. The Central Pacific Railroad began in Sacramento, California, and built eastward. A local paper reported:

"With rites appropriate to the occasion . . . ground was formally broken at noon for the commencement of the Central Pacific Railroad—the California link of the continental chain

>> To build railroads, workers first had to lay wooden beams, or ties, then a layer of gravel to hold the ties in place. Finally, they used spikes to nail the rails to the ties.

that is to unite American communities now divided by thousands of miles of trackless wilderness."
—Sacramento *Union*, January 8, 1863

The federal government helped the railroad companies because it felt that rail lines in the West would benefit the entire nation. The government's aid came in the form of subsidies.

A **subsidy** is financial aid or a land grant from the government. Congress lent money to the railroad companies and gave them land. For every mile of track completed, the railroad companies received twenty sections of land in the states along the route and forty sections per mile in the territories. By the time the Central Pacific and Union Pacific railroads were completed, they had received about 45 million acres of land. Often, both business and government ignored the fact that Native Americans lived on the land.

Building the Transcontinental Railroad
Both companies had trouble getting workers. Labor was scarce during the Civil War. Also, the work was backbreaking and dangerous, and the pay was low.

The railroad companies hired immigrant workers, who accepted low wages. The Central Pacific brought in thousands of workers from China. The Union Pacific hired newcomers from Ireland. African Americans and Mexican Americans also worked for each line.

The railroad workers faced a daunting task. The Central Pacific had to carve a path across the rugged Sierra Nevada.

The Union Pacific had to cut through the towering Rocky Mountains. Snowstorms and avalanches killed workers and slowed

>> The completion of the transcontinental railroad was marked by the Golden Spike Ceremony, shown here. Rail travel was now possible from the shores of the Atlantic Ocean to the shores of the Pacific.

progress. At times, crews cutting tunnels through rock advanced only a few inches a day.

Building the railroad forced workers to adapt to or modify environments as varied as forests, deserts, and mountains. In some places, the railroad was built around mountains. In other places, however, workers blasted tunnels through mountains with new technologies such as specialized tools and explosives to achieve their goals.

Railroads Encourage Urban and Rural Growth The Central Pacific and Union Pacific met at Promontory, Utah, on May 10, 1869. Leland Stanford, president of the Central Pacific, dropped a solid-gold spike into a pre-drilled hole in the rail. In doing so, he joined the two tracks and united the country. The nation's first transcontinental railroad was complete.

With the Civil War fresh in their minds, people cheered this new symbol of unity. The words that were engraved on the golden spike expressed their feelings:

> "May God continue the unity of our Country as the Railroad unites the two great Oceans of the world."
> —Engraved on the Golden Spike

Before long, other major rail lines linked the West and the East. The railroads brought economic growth and new settlement all across the West. They enabled people, supplies, and mail to move quickly and cheaply across the plains and mountains. Wherever rail lines went, settlements—"railroad towns"—sprang up along the tracks. The largest towns and cities developed where major railroad lines met. Cities where sea and land transportation met, such as Seattle, San Francisco, and Los Angeles, experienced

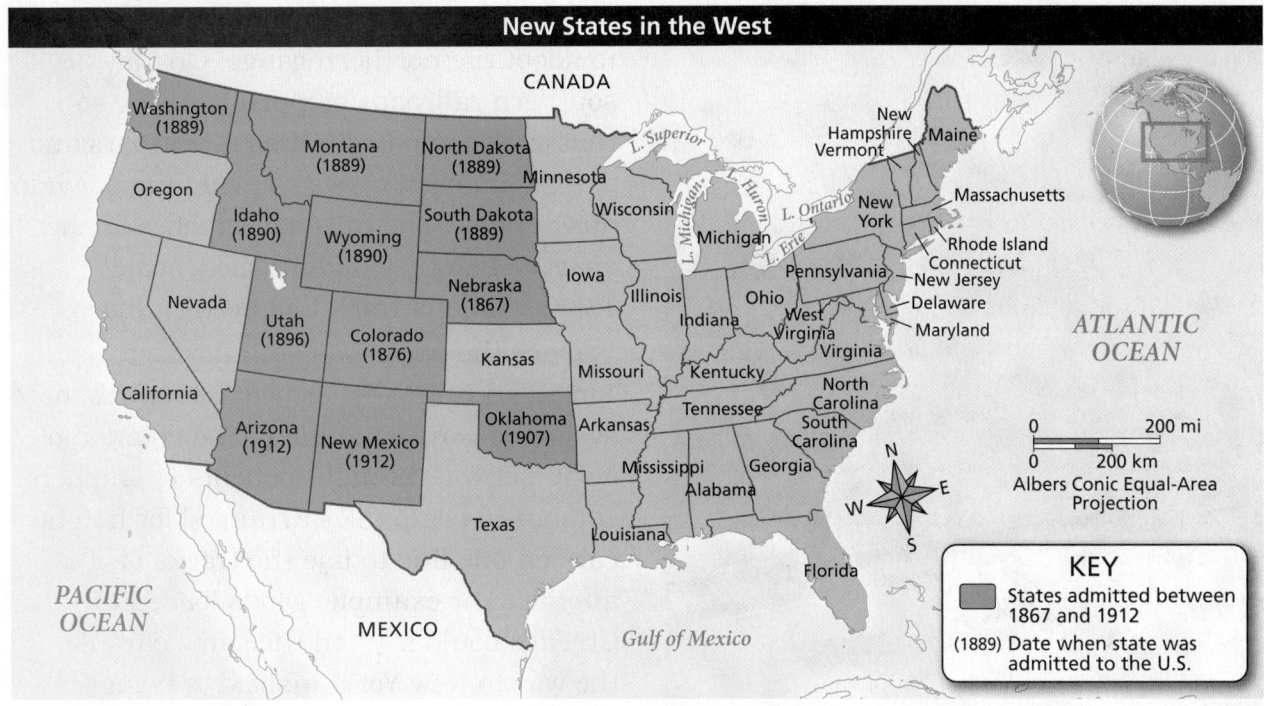

>> Based on the information in the map, what effect did migration to the West have by the end of 1912?

huge population growth with the coming of the railroads. Western cities, such as Denver, Cheyenne, and Wichita, grew when railroads were joined to the great cattle trails. Thus the railroad—the most advanced transportation system of its day—had a major impact on the urbanization of the United States.

Because of their rapid growth, western territories began to apply for statehood. Nevada became a state in 1864; Colorado, in 1876; North Dakota, South Dakota, Montana, and Washington, in 1889; Idaho and Wyoming, in 1890.

? SUMMARIZE Why was immigrant labor brought in to help build the railroads?

Building a National Network of Rails

The Civil War showed the importance of railroads. Railroads carried troops and supplies to the battlefields. They also moved raw materials to factories. After the war, railroad companies began to build new lines all over the country.

A Race to Construct New Lines Railroad builders raced to create thousands of miles of new tracks. In the years after completion of the first transcontinental rail line in 1869, Americans built three more. James Hill, a Canadian-born owner, finished the last major cross-country line in 1893. His Great Northern Railway wound from Duluth, Minnesota, to Everett, Washington.

Unlike other rail lines, the Great Northern was built without financial aid from Congress. To make his railroad succeed, Hill had to turn a profit from the start. He encouraged farmers and ranchers to move to the Northwest and settle near his railroad. He gave seed to farmers and helped them buy equipment. He imported special bulls in order to breed hardier cattle. Not only was Hill's policy generous,

>> Workers constructed what would become part of the Great Northern Railway in the 1880s. During this time, use of a standard line gauge helped link railroad lines.

▶ **Interactive Map**

it also made good business sense. In the end, Hill's railroad proved very successful even without government assistance, and it was a key to the development of the Northwest.

A National Transportation System Early railroads were short lines that served local communities. Many lines ran for no more than 50 miles. When passengers and freight reached the end of one line, they had to move to a train on a different line to continue their journey.

Even if the lines had been connected, the problem would not have been eliminated. Different lines used tracks of different **gauges**, or widths. As a result, the trains from one line could not run on the tracks of another line. In general, the tracks of northern lines used different gauges from those of southern lines.

In 1886, railroads in the South decided to adopt the northern gauge. On May 30, southern railroads stopped running so that work could begin. Using crowbars and sledgehammers, crews worked from dawn to dusk to move the rails a few inches farther apart. When they had finished, some 13,000 miles of track had been changed.

Once the track was standardized, American railroads formed a **network**, or system of connected lines. The creation of a rail network brought benefits to shippers. Often, rail companies arranged for freight cars on one line to use the tracks of another. For example, goods loaded in Chicago could stay on the same car all the way to New York, instead of being transferred from one car to another. As a result, the shipper had to pay only one fare for the whole distance.

New rails knit the sprawling nation together. By 1900, there were more miles of tracks in the United States than in Europe and Russia combined.

Westinghouse Brakes and Pullman Cars
New inventions helped make railway travel safer and faster. On early trains, each railroad car had its own brakes and its own brake operator.

If different cars stopped at different times, serious accidents could result. In 1869, George Westinghouse began selling his new air brake. Westinghouse's air brake allowed a locomotive engineer to stop all the railroad cars at once. The air brake increased safety and allowed for longer, faster trains.

Long distance travel also became more comfortable. In 1864, George Pullman designed a railroad sleeping car. Pullman cars had convertible berths for sleeping as well as lavatories. Rail lines also added dining cars. Porters (who carried baggage), conductors, and waiters attended to the needs of passengers.

The Railroads and Economic Growth

The growth of the railroads in the 1800s was one way in which a market economy led to greater prosperity. As William Vanderbilt pointed out, the railroads "are built for men who invest their money." That is, the railroads were built to make money for the people who invested in them. Yet the railroads benefited many other people: the workers who laid the tracks, the employees who ran the trains, the passengers who rode the rails, and the businesses that filled cars with cargo. People who lived in the towns that sprouted up along the rail lines also benefited. Ultimately, the railroads benefited the country as a whole.

The expansion of the railroads brought significant changes in ways of producing, distributing, and consuming goods. Businesses brought raw materials on railroads to factories. Finished goods from those factories could be shipped far and wide for a reasonable price. Consumers—especially those far from cities—could now have access to more goods than ever before. The same held true for farm goods: farmers had wider markets, and consumers had more food choices.

Consolidation Brings Efficiency As railroads grew, they looked for ways to operate more efficiently. Small lines were often costly to run, so many companies began to **consolidate**, or combine. Larger companies bought up smaller ones or forced them out of business. The Pennsylvania Railroad, for example, consolidated 73 companies into its system.

Tough-minded business people led the drive for consolidation. Cornelius Vanderbilt was among the most powerful of these leaders. The son of a poor farmer, Vanderbilt earned one fortune in steamship lines. He then began to buy up railroad lines in New York State.

Vanderbilt sometimes used ruthless tactics to force smaller owners to sell to him. In the early 1860s, he decided to buy the New York Central Railroad. The owners refused to sell. Vanderbilt then announced that New York Central passengers would not be allowed to transfer to his trains. With their passengers stranded and business dropping sharply, the New York Central owners gave in and sold their line to Vanderbilt.

Vanderbilt then bought up most of the lines between Chicago and Buffalo. By the time of his death in 1877, his companies controlled 4,500 miles of track and linked New York City to the Great Lakes region.

Other consolidations were soon underway. Before long, the major railroads

>> After making a fortune in the steamship business, Cornelius Vanderbilt turned his attention to railroads. He bought up most of the rail lines between Buffalo, New York, and Chicago, Illinois.

of the United States were organized into a number of systems directed by a handful of wealthy and powerful men.

❓ **IDENTIFY SUPPORTING DETAILS** What was significant about the way in which the Great Northern line was financed?

Railroads and Competition

With builders rushing to share in the profits of the railroad boom, overbuilding occurred. Soon, there were too many rail lines in some parts of the country. Between Atlanta and St. Louis, for example, 20 different lines competed for business. There was not nearly enough rail traffic to keep all these lines busy.

Owners Look for New Ways to Make Profits Especially in the West, there were too few people—and therefore not enough paying customers—for the railroads to make a profit. Competition was fierce. Rate wars broke out as rival railroads slashed their fares to win customers. Usually, all the companies lost money as a result.

Often, railroads were forced to grant secret **rebates**, or discounts, to their biggest customers. The railroads preferred big customers for two reasons. First, big customers were more likely to pay their bills and keep being customers in the future. Second, it was less expensive to deal with a few big customers than many small customers.

Fewer customers meant less paperwork and simpler loading and unloading. Unfortunately, the practice of giving rebates hurt small shippers, such as farmers, who still had to pay the full price. It even drove many small companies out of business.

Railroad owners soon realized that cutthroat competition was hurting even their large lines. They looked for ways to end the competition. One method was pooling. In a **pool**, several railroad companies agreed to divide up the

The Plight of Farmers and Small Businesses

Competition between railroad companies forces them to reduce rates.

↓

Railroad companies offer rebates and discounts to the biggest customers. Some railroad companies form pools and raise rates.

↓

Small farmers and shippers cannot afford to ship goods.

↓

Many small companies and farmers are forced out of business.

>> **Analyze Charts** What can you infer about why rebates and discounts caused many small companies and farmers to go out of business in the 1800s?

business in an area. They then fixed their prices at a high level.

Farmers React to High Railroad Prices

Railroad rebates and pools angered small farmers in the South and the West. Both practices kept shipping prices high for them. Indeed, rates were so high that at times farmers burned their crops for fuel rather than ship them to market.

Many farmers joined the Populist movement. Populists called for government regulation of rail rates. Some Populists even called for a government takeover of the railroads. Congress and several states passed laws regulating railroad companies. However, the laws did not end abuses. Railroad owners sometimes bribed officials to keep the laws from being enforced.

The Panic of 1893 In 1893, an economic panic hit the United States. The economy went through a drastic downsizing. About 15,000 businesses and 500 banks closed, leaving many American workers unemployed.

The railroads were both a cause and a victim of the economic downturn. Overbuilding in the 1860s meant that many railroad companies' finances were fragile—they were barely making money. In 1893, the Philadelphia and Reading Railroad went bankrupt, helping to start the panic. Many other leading railroads followed, including the Erie, the Northern Pacific, the Union Pacific, the Atchison, Topeka, and Santa Fe. Industries, like steel, and a wide variety of businesses that had come to depend on the railroad were hurt, as were businesses that depended on those businesses. Through a ripple effect, the whole economy suffered.

The economy would not recover for about four years. When it did, it was the

>> This cartoon shows congressmen looking like train engines. **Analyze Political Cartoons** What does this image suggest about the influence of the railroad industry in Congress?

railroad that once again provided the transportation the economy needed.

DESCRIBE How did railroad owners try to make profits in a competitive business environment?

Railroads Build a Nation

Although railroads caused certain problems, they also made possible the rapid growth of industry after 1865. Building rail lines created thousands of jobs. Steelworkers turned millions of tons of iron into steel for tracks and engines. Lumberjacks cut down whole forests to supply wood for railroad ties. Miners sweated in dusty mine shafts digging coal to fuel railroad engines. The railroad companies themselves employed thousands of workers. They laid tracks, built trestles across rivers, carved tunnels through

RAILROADS DRIVE INDUSTRIAL GROWTH

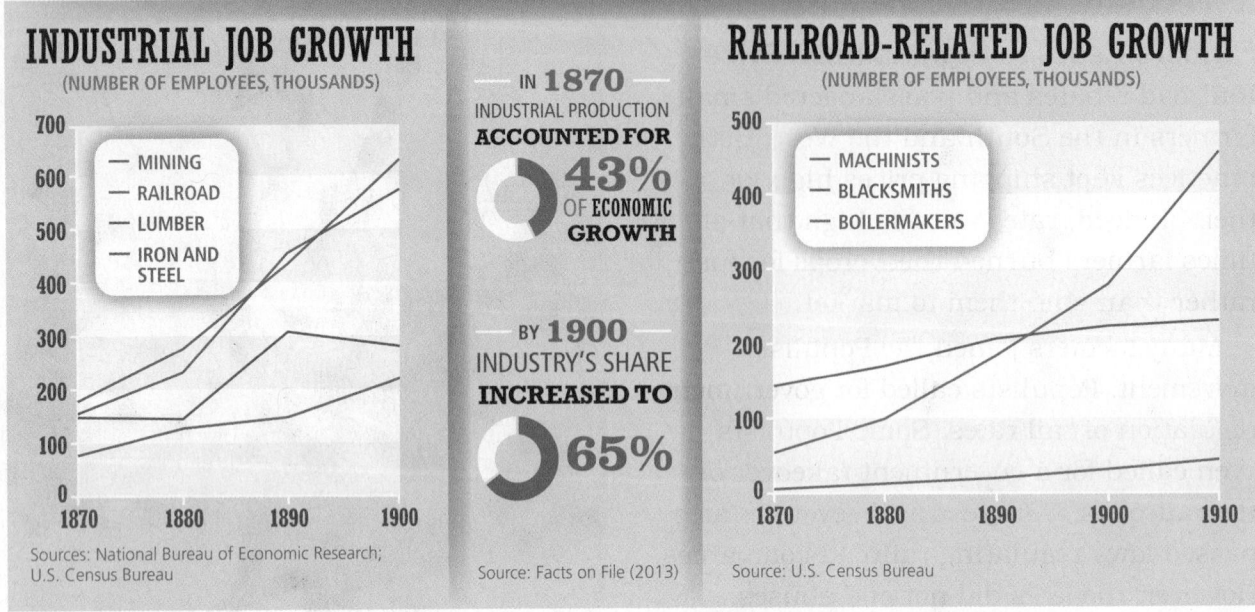

INDUSTRIAL JOB GROWTH
(NUMBER OF EMPLOYEES, THOUSANDS)

- MINING
- RAILROAD
- LUMBER
- IRON AND STEEL

Sources: National Bureau of Economic Research; U.S. Census Bureau

IN **1870**
INDUSTRIAL PRODUCTION
ACCOUNTED FOR
43%
OF **ECONOMIC**
GROWTH

BY **1900**
INDUSTRY'S SHARE
INCREASED TO
65%

Source: Facts on File (2013)

RAILROAD-RELATED JOB GROWTH
(NUMBER OF EMPLOYEES, THOUSANDS)

- MACHINISTS
- BLACKSMITHS
- BOILERMAKERS

Source: U.S. Census Bureau

>> **Analyze Graphs** What effect did the growth of the railroad industry have on the U.S. economy in the late 1800s?

mountains, and built countless railroad stations.

The large railroads also pioneered new ways of managing business. Rail companies created special departments for shipping and accounting and for servicing equipment. Expert managers headed each department, while chains of command ensured that the organization ran smoothly. Other big businesses soon copied these management techniques.

Railroads opened every corner of the country to settlement and growth. They brought people together, especially in the West. New businesses sprang up, and towns sprouted where rail lines crossed. With rail lines in place, the United States was ready to become the greatest industrial nation the world had ever seen.

? IDENTIFY MAIN IDEAS How did the growth of railroad companies change the management techniques of other large businesses?

ASSESSMENT

1. **Draw Conclusions** Why might a sudden surge of miners, ranchers, and farmers into an area cause problems other than environmental ones?

2. **Generate Explanations** Why were so many of the workers who built the first transcontinental railroad immigrants, African Americans, and Mexican Americans?

3. **Identify Central Issues** How did the development of the railroads affect business and travel in the United States?

4. **Express Problems Clearly** What problems did an excess of competition cause for the railroad companies and some of their customers?

5. **Summarize** how railroads helped the United States grow and prosper.

Western Agriculture

>> Cattle graze in a field in the West. **Infer** What clues in the painting suggest how the geography of the West contributed to the growth of ranching there?

▶ **Interactive Flipped Video**

While Reconstruction shaped the South following the Civil War, other events were occurring throughout the American West. In the 1860s, cattle ranching grew rapidly on the Great Plains.

>> **Objectives**

Identify the Cattle Kingdom.

Describe cowhands and cow towns during the cattle boom.

Summarize the massive westward migration following the Homestead Act.

Identify challenges western farmers faced and the alliances created to improve conditions.

Explain why the Populist Party was formed.

>> **Key Terms**

cattle drive
cow town
sod house
sodbuster
cooperative
wholesale
inflation
Morrill Acts
vaquero

PEARSON realize www.PearsonRealize.com Access your Digital Lesson.

A Cattle Kingdom on the Plains

Before this time, the Spanish, and then the Mexicans, had set up cattle ranches in the Southwest. Over the years, strays from these ranches, along with American breeds, grew into large herds of wild cattle. These wild cattle were known as longhorns. They roamed freely across the grassy plains of Texas.

After the Civil War, the demand for beef increased. People in the growing cities in the East were eating more meat. Miners, railroad crews, farmers, and growing communities in the West added to the demand. The Texas longhorns were perfect for the commercial market. They could travel far on little water, and they required no winter feeding.

In response, Texas ranchers began rounding up herds of longhorns. They drove the animals hundreds of miles north to railroad lines in Kansas and Missouri on trips called **cattle drives**.

Jesse Chisholm blazed one of the most famous cattle trails. Chisholm was half Scottish and half Cherokee. In the late 1860s, he began hauling goods by wagon between Texas and the Kansas Pacific Railroad. His route crossed rivers at the best places and passed by water holes. Ranchers began using the Chisholm Trail in 1867. Within five years, more than one million cattle had walked the road.

Tending Cattle in the West Ranchers employed cowhands to tend their cattle and drive herds to market. These hard workers rode alongside the huge herds in good and bad weather. They kept the cattle moving and rounded up strays. After the Civil War, veterans of the Confederate Army made up the majority of the cowhands who worked in Texas. However, it is estimated that

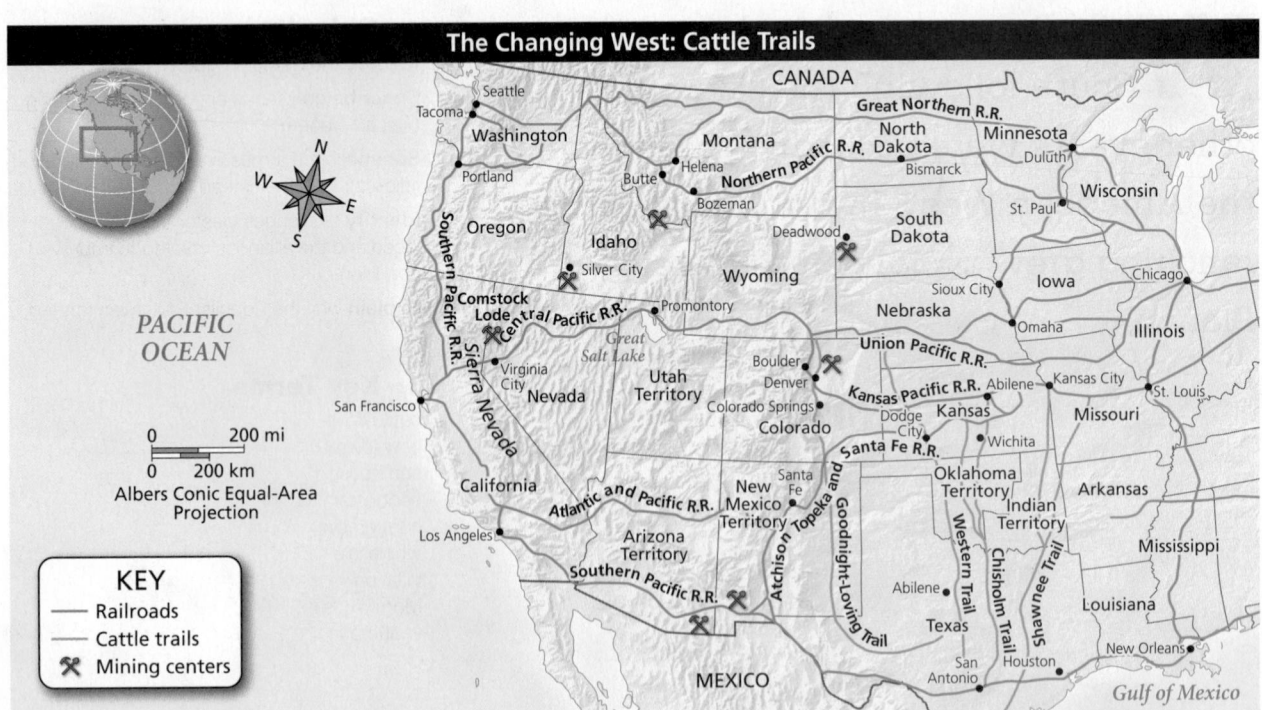

The Changing West: Cattle Trails

KEY
— Railroads
— Cattle trails
✗ Mining centers

>> After the end of the Civil War, cattle ranching boomed in the West. Cattle trails stretched from Wyoming and Nebraska in the North to beyond Houston, Texas, in the South.

nearly one in three cowhands was either Mexican American or African American. Some cowhands dreamed of setting aside enough money to start a herd of their own. Most, in the end, just worked to earn wages.

Spanish Influences American cowhands learned much about riding, roping, and branding from Spanish and Mexican vaqueros (vah KEHR ohs). **Vaqueros** were skilled riders who herded cattle on ranches in Mexico, California, and the Southwest.

The gear used by American cowhands was modeled on the tools of the vaquero. Cowhands used the leather lariat to catch cattle and horses. *Lariat* comes from the Spanish word for rope. Cowhands wore wide-brimmed hats like the Spanish *sombrero*.

Their leather leggings, called chaps, were modeled on Spanish *chaparreras* (chah pah REH rahs). Chaps protected a rider's legs from the thorny plants that grow in the Southwest.

The Physical Environment Shaped a Cowhand's Work A cattle drive was hot, dirty, tiring, and often boring work. A cowboy's days could last for nearly 18 hours.

The work was so strenuous that cowhands usually brought a number of horses so that each day a fresh one would be available. Cowhands worked in all kinds of weather and faced many dangers, including prairie dog holes, rattlesnakes, and fierce thunderstorms. They had to prevent nervous cattle from drowning while crossing fast-flowing rivers. They had to fight raging grass fires. They also faced

>> A young cowboy sits atop his horse in Texas. Ranchers employed cowhands to help them control their herds of cattle.

attacks from cattle thieves who roamed the countryside.

One of the cowhand's worst fears on a cattle drive was a stampede. A clap of thunder or a gunshot could set thousands of longhorns off at a run. Cowhands had to avoid the crush of hoofs and horns while attempting to turn the stampeding herd in a wide circle.

Most cowhands did not work for themselves. Instead, they were hired hands for the owners of large ranches. For all their hard work, cowhands were fed, housed, and lucky to earn $1 per day. Even in the 1870s, this was low pay.

? IDENTIFY SUPPORTING DETAILS What influences did the vaqueros have on cowhand culture in the United States?

Ranching Impacts Settlement Patterns

Before long, cattle drives began to influence the settlement of western towns. As more cattle were driven through these areas, businesses offering services to the cowhands began to form in towns. As a result, cattle drives ended in **cow towns** that had sprung up along the railroad lines. The Chisholm Trail, for example, ended in Abilene, Kansas. Other cow towns in Kansas were Wichita, Caldwell, and Dodge City. In cow towns, cattle were held in great pens until they could be loaded into railroad cars and shipped to markets in the East.

In Abilene and other busy cow towns, dance halls, saloons, hotels, and restaurants catered to the cowhands. Sheriffs often had a hard time keeping the peace. Some cowhands spent wild nights drinking, dancing, and gambling.

The main street of a town was where people conducted business. Almost every town had a general store that sold groceries, tools, clothing, and all sorts of other goods. The general store also served as a social center where people could talk and exchange the latest news. As a town grew, drugstores, hardware stores, and even ice cream parlors lined its main street.

Religion also played an important role for the townspeople. Throughout the West, places of worship grew in number and membership. They served as spiritual and social centers and as symbols of progress and stability. "A church does as much to build up a town as a school, a railroad, or a fair," noted one New Mexico newspaper.

? DESCRIBE How would you describe the settlement pattern of cow towns in the West?

>> Workers load cattle into a railway car in Kansas during the 1870s. **Identify Cause and Effect** What factors allowed cow towns to spread across the West?

▶ **Interactive Gallery**

The Spread of Farming

In the 1870s, ranching spread north from Texas and across the grassy Plains. Soon, cattle grazed from Kansas to present-day Montana. Ranchers had built a Cattle Kingdom in the West. They came to expect high profits. Millions of dollars poured into the West from people in the East and in foreign countries who wanted to earn money from the cattle boom. However, the boom did not last.

Conflicts Over Land Ranchers let their cattle run wild on the open range. To identify cattle, each ranch had its own brand that was burned into a cow's hide.

Sometimes, there were conflicts on the range. When sheepherders moved onto the Plains, ranchers tried to drive them out. The ranchers complained the sheep nibbled the grass so low that the cattle could not eat it. To protect the range, which they saw as their own, ranchers sometimes attacked sheepherders and their flocks.

New Settlements Encroach on Cattle Land In the 1870s, farmers began moving onto the range. They fenced their fields with barbed wire, which kept cattle and sheep from pushing over fences and trampling plowed fields. As more farmers bought land, the open range began to disappear. Large grants of land to the railroads also limited it. As a result, a more organized system began to develop in which ranchers bought and maintained private property. This protection of property rights further boosted settlement in the West.

Nature, however, imposed limits on the cattle boom. After a time, there just was not enough grass to feed all the cattle that lived on the plains. The need to buy feed and land pushed up the costs. Diseases

>> Ranchers used branding irons to brand their cattle, which helped ranchers keep track of their cattle on the open range where cattle ran wild.

such as "Texas fever" sometimes destroyed entire herds. Then, the bitterly cold winters of 1886 and 1887 killed entire herds of cattle. In the summer, severe heat and drought dried up water holes and scorched the grasslands.

Cattle owners began to buy land and fence it in. Soon, farmers and ranchers divided the open range into a patchwork of large fenced plots. The days of the Cattle Kingdom were over.

? RECALL What effect did the arrival of growing numbers of farmers have on the open range system?

Effects of the Homestead Act

Congress passed the Homestead Act in 1862. It was the centerpiece of the government's land policy. The law promised 160 acres of free land to anyone who was head of a household, who had not fought for

>> In exchange for farming the land for five years, this pioneer family gained ownership of their homestead in Custer County, Nebraska. **Summarize** What were settlers required to do in exchange for the free land on which they settled?

African Americans Settle in Kansas

African Americans joined the rush for land in the West. Some were able to take advantage of the Homestead Act. The largest group of black settlers moved west at the end of Reconstruction, when the freedoms African Americans had gained after the Civil War were slipping away.

In 1879, a group of African Americans moved to Kansas. They called themselves Exodusters, after Exodus, the book of the Bible that tells about the Jews escaping from slavery in Egypt. The Exodusters paid for their land rather than claim it under the Homestead Act. Between 40,000 and 70,000 African Americans had moved to Kansas by 1881, though only some of these were Exodusters.

Settlement Patterns of Anglos and Mexicanos

Easterners who moved to the Southwest found a large established Spanish-speaking population there. As you recall, the United States had gained much of the Southwest through the Mexican War. Many of its inhabitants were people of Spanish or Mexican origin who lived in the region before it became part of the United States.

Spanish-speaking southwesterners called themselves Mexicanos. White Americans who lived in the region were known as Anglos. Most Mexicanos lived in small villages, where they farmed and raised sheep. A few wealthy Mexicanos were large landowners and merchants.

As more Anglos settled in the Southwest, they acquired the best jobs and land. Often, Mexicanos found themselves working as low-paid laborers on Anglo farms. In New Mexico, in the 1880s, angry farmers known as *Las Gorras Blancas*, or "White Caps," demanded fair treatment. Other Mexicanos in Arizona founded the

the Confederacy, and who paid a small filing fee and improved the land over five years.

The Environment Impacts Western Settlement

The main effect of the Homestead Act was a stream of immigrants and easterners took up the offer of free land. Many planted their 160 acres with wheat and corn. By 1900, half a million Americans had set up farms under the Homestead Act. Under the Homestead Act the land was free, but setting up a farm required money and hard work. Many people did not have the money to move west and start a farm. Also, only about 20 percent of the homestead land went directly to small farmers. Land-owning companies took large areas of land illegally and resold it to farmers at a high price. As a result, many settlers struggled to make ends meet.

Hispanic-American Alliance in 1894 to protect and fight for their rights.

Settlements on Oklahoma Farmland As settlers spread across the West, free land began to disappear. The last major land rush took place in Oklahoma. Several Native American nations lived there, but the government forced them to sell their land. The government then announced that farmers could claim free homesteads in Oklahoma. They could not stake their claims, however, until noon on April 22, 1889.

On the appointed day, as many as 100,000 land seekers lined up at the Oklahoma border. At noon, a gunshot rang out. The "boomers" charged into Oklahoma, but they found that others were already there. "Sooners" had sneaked into Oklahoma before the official opening and had staked out much of the best land. The physical characteristics of the Oklahoma environment meant that farmers needed good land in order to succeed. Those who settled on fertile farmland had better chances than those who ended up with less fertile land.

? **ANALYZE INFORMATION** Who worked to get around the rules of the Homestead Act in order to profit from the land, and how did they profit?

Effects of the Morrill Acts

Agriculture was becoming more of a business as farmers increasingly grew food for the market at the same time as industry was growing. To train professionals for both agriculture and industry, there was a growing call for publicly supported agricultural and mechanical colleges. The Morrill Land-Grant Colleges Act of 1862, put forth during the Civil War by Justin Smith Morrill of Vermont, offered states a federal land grant to build schools that would teach and promote scientific farming and engineering.

>> On the first day of the Oklahoma land rush, nearly 100,000 set out to stake new claims, only to find other settlers already there.

>> Farmers like these in the Oklahoma Territory needed schooling and training. The Morrill Acts created colleges to support a scientific approach to agriculture.

States received 30,000 acres of public land per congressional representative, a policy that gave more land to more populous states. Colleges founded on this land had to teach science, classics, agriculture, mechanics, and military tactics.

In 1890, a second Morrill Act was passed to extend the benefits of land-grant funding to African American students. It required states either to admit students of all races to their land-grant colleges or to set up separate land-grant colleges for African Americans. Upholding segregation, the South created separate colleges for African American and white students. Many of these agricultural colleges grew into historically black colleges and universities serving African Americans in the South.

Both of the **Morrill Acts** had important effects on the country. Private colleges were expensive. The new public schools were more affordable. They made college more available to Americans and affirmed that the government would play a role in supporting higher education.

Private colleges also did not teach the practical skills that many Americans needed to find jobs. Land-grant colleges emphasized the training and skills needed in an agricultural and industrial society. The first land-grant college to open was the University of Massachusetts. Large universities also formed in the West and Midwest.

? DRAW CONCLUSIONS Why were the Morrill Acts important for the average American student?

Life on the Plains

Farmers on the western plains faced many hardships. The first problem was shelter. Because wood was scarce on the Great Plains, many farmers built houses of sod—soil held together by grass roots. Rain was a serious problem for **sod houses**. One pioneer woman complained that her sod roof "leaked two days before a rain and for three days after."

Sodbusting The fertile soil of the Great Plains was covered with a layer of thick sod that could crack wood or iron plows. A new sodbusting plow made of steel reached the market by 1877. It enabled **sodbusters**, as Plains farmers were called, to cut through the sod to the soil below.

Technology helped farmers in other ways. On the Great Plains, water often lay hundreds of feet underground. Farmers built windmills to pump the water to the surface. New reapers, threshing machines, and binders helped farmers to harvest crops.

Environmental Challenges The dry climate was a constant threat. When too little rain fell, the crops shriveled and died. Dry weather also brought the threat of fire. A grass fire traveled "as fast as a horse could run." The summers often brought swarms of grasshoppers that ate everything in their path—crops, food, tree bark, even clothing. Pioneers dreaded the winters most. With few trees or hills to block the wind, icy gusts built huge snowdrifts. The deep snow buried farm animals and trapped families inside their homes.

Women's Roles on the Plains Women had to be strong to survive the hardships of life on the Great Plains. Since there were few stores, women made clothing, soap, candles, and other goods by hand. They also cooked and preserved food needed for the long winter.

Women served their communities in many ways. Most schoolteachers were women. When there were no doctors nearby, women treated the sick and injured.

Pioneer families usually lived miles apart. They relaxed by visiting with neighbors and gathering for church services. Picnics, dances, and weddings were eagerly awaited events.

Dependence on the Physical Environment Homesteaders depended on the environment for their livelihood. They needed the right amounts of water, sunlight, rain, and soil for their crops. This made homesteading risky; there were many difficult harvests and lean years.

It also meant that homesteaders put a great deal of care into the land. Those who owned their farms worked hard to keep the land productive. They wanted to

>> Settlers built the roofs of sod houses using grass roots. **Predict Consequences** How would rain affect people living in sod houses?

 Interactive 3-D Model

>> Despite the challenges of the Great Plains' climate, homesteaders successfully grew wheat and corn there.

ensure that their property would continue to supply the resources they needed to survive.

Reliance on the land and distance from more populous eastern cities meant that homesteaders were extremely self-sufficient. They used resources from the environment to meet their needs. If something was broken, they fixed it themselves.

Economic Challenges Despite the harsh conditions, farmers began to thrive in the West. Before long, they were selling huge amounts of wheat and corn in the nation's growing cities and even in Europe. Then, farmers faced an unexpected problem. The more they harvested, the less they earned. In 1881, a bushel of wheat sold for $1.19. By 1894, the price had plunged to 49 cents. Western farmers were hurt most by low grain prices. They had borrowed money during good times to buy land and machinery. When wheat prices fell, they could not repay their debts.

❓ **IDENTIFY SUPPORTING DETAILS** What effects did the isolation of western farms have on the women of the Plains?

Farming and the Economy

As early as the 1860s, farmers began to work together. They learned that they could improve their condition through economic cooperation and political action.

The National Grange Supports Cooperation In 1867, farmers formed the National Grange. Grangers wanted to boost farm profits and reduce the rates that railroads charged for shipping grain.

Grangers helped farmers set up cooperatives. In a **cooperative** a group of farmers pooled their money to buy seeds and tools wholesale. **Wholesale** means buying or selling something in large

>> **Analyze Graphs** Based on the information in charts, why did farmers form Granges?

quantities at lower prices. Grangers built cooperative warehouses so that farmers could store grain cheaply while waiting for better selling prices.

Leaders of the Grange urged farmers to use their vote. In 1873, western and southern Grangers pledged to vote only for candidates who supported their aims. They elected officials who understood the farmers' problems.

As a result, several states passed laws limiting what could be charged for grain shipment and storage. Nevertheless, crop prices continued to drop. Farmers sank deeper into debt.

The Farmers' Alliance Spreads Another group, the Farmers' Alliance, joined the struggle in the 1870s. Like the Grange, the Alliance set up cooperatives and warehouses. The Farmers' Alliance spread from Texas through the South and into the Plains states. Alliance leaders also tried to join with factory workers and miners who were angry about their treatment by employers.

❓ IDENTIFY MAIN IDEAS What was the principle upon which the National Grange and the Farmers' Alliance were formed?

The Rise of the People's Party in the West

In 1892, farmers and labor unions joined together to form the People's Party, also known as the Populists. At their first national convention, the Populists demanded that the government help to raise farm prices and to regulate railroad rates. They also called for an income tax, an eight-hour workday, and limits on immigration.

The key Populist party demand was "free silver." Populists wanted all silver mined

>> **Analyze Political Cartoons** What does the object on which William McKinley is standing in this image suggest about his political views in the election of 1896?

in the West to be coined into money. They said that farm prices dropped because there was not enough money in circulation. Free silver would increase the money supply and make it easier for farmers to repay their debts.

Eastern bankers and factory owners opposed this. They argued that increasing the money supply would cause **inflation**, or increased prices. Business people feared that inflation would wreck the economy. They favored the gold standard with which the government backs every dollar with a certain amount of gold. Since the supply of gold is limited, there would be less money in circulation. Prices would drop.

Bryan Versus McKinley The Populist candidate for President in 1892 won one million votes. The next year, a severe depression brought the Populists new support. In 1894, they elected six senators and seven representatives to Congress.

The Populists looked toward the election of 1896 with high hopes. Their program had been endorsed by one of the great orators of the age: Democrat William Jennings Bryan.

A young Democratic congressman from Nebraska, Bryan was called the "Great Commoner" because he championed the cause of common people. Like the Populists, he believed that the nation needed to increase the supply of money. At the Democratic convention in 1896, Bryan made a powerful speech against the rich and for free silver. At the end of his speech, referring to the rich, Bryan proclaimed, "You shall not crucify mankind upon a cross of gold."

Both Democrats and Populists supported Bryan for President. However, bankers and business people feared that Bryan would ruin the economy. They supported William McKinley, the Republican candidate. McKinley and the Republican Party called for keeping the dollar tied to the gold standard.

Bryan narrowly lost the election of 1896. He carried the South and the West, but McKinley won the heavily populated states of the North and East.

The Populist Movement Ends With the Election of 1896 The People's Party broke up after 1896. One reason was that, with Bryan as a candidate, the Democrats adopted several Populist causes. Also, prosperity returned in the late 1890s. People worried less about railroad rates and the gold standard.

? **DESCRIBE** Why were eastern bankers opposed to the Populists' "free silver" demand?

ASSESSMENT

1. **Check Understanding** What were the benefits of driving cattle along a known trail, such as the Chisholm Trail?

2. **Draw Conclusions** Why did sheriffs often have a hard time keeping the peace in a cow town?

3. **Explain** why the second Morrill Act was passed.

4. **Summarize** What made farming on the western plains so difficult?

5. **Analyze Information** Why was the National Grange successful in meeting some of its goals?

Hardship for Native Americans

>> Plains Indians, like these Sioux, were skilled at riding horses. Introduced in the 1600s to the Great Plains, horses became central to the culture of Native Americans living there.

⊳ **Interactive Flipped Video**

Native Americans had been living for centuries on the Great Plains, the vast, gently sloping region west of the Mississippi River and east of the Rocky Mountains. Many different Native American nations lived on the Great Plains. A number of them, such as the Arikaras, had lived on the Plains for hundreds of years. Others, like the Lakotas, did not move to the Plains until the early 1700s.

>> **Objectives**

Describe the life of the Plains Indians and their uses of buffalo.

Summarize promises made to Native Americans.

Explain why the Plains Indian way of life ended.

Identify why reforms in favor of Native Americans failed.

>> **Key Terms**

tepee
travois
corral
jerky
reservation

The Plains Indians

Farming and Hunting Plains Indians had rich and varied cultures. They were skilled artists. They also had well-organized religions and warrior societies. Each nation had its own language. People from different nations used sign language to communicate with one another.

At one time, most Plains Indians were farmers who lived in semi-permanent villages. From there, they sent out hunting parties that pursued on foot herds of buffalo and other animals. Agriculture, however, was their main source of food.

The Introduction of Horses Proved Useful During the 1600s, the Plains Indians' way of life changed as they learned about horses from neighboring tribes.

Christopher Columbus had brought horses to the Americas in the late 1400s, and the Spanish brought them to the North American mainland in the 1500s. At first, Native Americans were not allowed to own horses, but they did learn how to care for them and ride them. After the Pueblo Indians revolted against the Spaniards in 1680, the Pueblos were left with thousands of horses. They started trading these horses to neighboring tribes. Eventually, the horses reached the tribes of the northern plains.

Plains Indians used horses while hunting. They also used horses when moving their villages and going on raids.

? **DESCRIBE** How did the practices of Plains Indians change after the Pueblo revolt of 1680?

Life on the Plains

The buffalo served as a living grocery store for Plains Indians. After acquiring horses, they followed the huge buffalo herds that had roamed their homeland for centuries. Plains Indians began to live in **tepees** (TEE peez), or tents made by stretching buffalo

>> Plains Indians developed a culture based on following and hunting buffalo. The introduction of the horse made this possible.

skins on tall poles. The tepees could easily be carried on a **travois** (truh VOI)—a sled pulled by a dog or a horse.

The migration of the Plains Indians mirrored the movement of the buffalo. In winter, small groups of buffalo moved to protected valleys and forests. In summer, huge buffalo herds gathered on the Plains where the grass was plentiful. In the same way, Plains Indians spent the winter in small bands and gathered in large groups during the summers.

Hunting the Buffalo There were different ways to hunt buffalo. Before horses came to the Plains, a group of hunters would shout and wave colored robes at the buffalo. The hunters would gradually drive a herd of buffalo into a **corral**, or enclosure.

There they killed the trapped buffalo. When the hunt was over, the women and children joined the hunters in cutting up the buffalo and taking it back to camp. Once they had horses, hunters would ride the horses right into the herd and kill the buffalo with bows and arrows.

The Buffalo Sustained a Way of Life
Although the Plains Indians also hunted deer and elk, they depended on the buffalo for food, clothing, and shelter. Buffalo meat, rich in protein, was a main item of the Plains Indians' diet. Women cut up and dried the meat on racks. The dried meat was called **jerky**.

Women also tanned buffalo hides to make sleeping robes and tepee covers. They wove buffalo fur into coarse, warm cloth. The cloth was used as an outer covering for a tepee.

>> Plains Indians lived in tepees. To build them, they wrapped buffalo skins around wooden poles. It was relatively easy to put up and take down these structures, so Plains Indians could move easily from place to place.

Councils and Ceremonies Many Native American groups met on the Plains. They hunted together and attended special events. Summer gatherings were the time for councils. At the councils, the elders were consulted about the problems that affected an entire Plains Indian nation.

The most important religious ceremony was the Sun Dance. Hundreds of people attended the four-day ceremony to thank the Great Spirit for blessings, good hunts, and help in times of trouble. Sun Dancers also asked the Great Spirit for good fortune in the coming year.

? **RECALL** How was the buffalo useful to the Plains Indians?

Gender Roles in Plains Indian Society

Women and men usually had specific roles in Plains Indian society. In some tribes, women helped men with the hunting and governing. A Blackfoot woman, Running Eagle, led many hunting parties herself.

Responsibilities at Home Women oversaw life in the home. They gathered food and prepared meals for their families. The women not only made the tepees, but they were also responsible for raising and taking down tepees. Women cared for the children and, along with the men, passed along the traditions of their people.

Women also engaged in many crafts. They made the baskets and blankets. Their work often showed great artistic skill and design. In fact, a woman's ability in crafts helped establish her rank in society.

Community Leadership The men of the Plains Indians had important responsibilities, too. They hunted to provide food and other materials they needed. They also protected the women, children, and the elders. They passed on their valuable skills and knowledge to the boys. They supervised the spiritual life of the community by leading religious ceremonies.

Another important responsibility of the men was to provide military leadership. They waged war to defend or extend territory, to gain horses and other riches, or to seek revenge. More than anything else, however, men waged war to protect their people and to prove their bravery and ability. The most successful warriors gained great respect from the members of their nation.

>> In Plains Indian societies, women were responsible for child rearing and also held many other roles. In some tribes, they took part in hunting and governing.

>> Two of the major roles for males in Plains Indian cultures were hunting and waging war.

? **DESCRIBE** the role women played in the household.

Broken Promises

Before Europeans and Americans began to settle on the Plains, the Plains Indians often fought with one another over territory or other resources. But as American settlers began to encroach on Plains Indians' lands, their attention turned toward this new threat. Conflict on the Plains began as early as the 1840s, when settlers and miners began to cross Plains Indian hunting grounds. The settlers and miners asked for government protection from the Native Americans.

A Treaty Quickly Forgotten The U.S. government built a string of forts to protect settlers and miners. In 1851, federal government officials met with Plains Indian nations near Fort Laramie in Wyoming. The officials asked each nation to keep to a limited area. In return, they promised money, domestic animals, agricultural tools, and other goods. Officials told the Native Americans that the lands that were reserved for them would be theirs forever.

Native American leaders agreed to the terms of the Fort Laramie Treaty. However, in 1858, gold was discovered at Pikes Peak in Colorado. A wave of miners rushed to land that the government had promised to the Cheyenne and Arapaho peoples. Federal officials forced Native American leaders to sign a new treaty giving up the land around Pikes Peak. Some Native Americans refused to accept the agreement. They attacked white settlers.

The Sand Creek Massacre The settlers struck back. In 1864, Colonel John Chivington led his militia against a Cheyenne village whose leaders had come to a fort asking for protection. When Chivington attacked, the Native Americans

>> Native American leaders met with government officials at Fort Laramie. The treaty they signed was part of a broader federal effort to create peace between native groups and western settlers.

raised both a white flag of surrender and the flag of the United States. Chivington had thought the Native Americans were hostile. He either ignored or did not see the flags. He ordered his men to destroy the village and take no prisoners. In what would become known as the Sand Creek Massacre, the militia slaughtered more than 150 men, women, and children.

After the massacre, soldiers said they found scalps of whites in the camp, indicating that there had been some hostile Native Americans there. A congressional committee that investigated the massacre condemned Chivington's actions, but Chivington had already left the army. As a result of the massacre, Plains Indians went to war. They attacked white settlers and U.S. troops. U.S. troops responded by attacking Indians.

>> Native American children were sent to boarding schools to be "Americanized." At these schools, authorities forbade Native American children from practicing their traditional ways..

Changing Traditional Ways of Life

In 1867, federal officials established a peace commission to end the wars on the Plains so that settlers would be safe. The commission urged Native Americans to settle down and live as white farmers did. It also urged them to send their children to white schools to learn "American" ways.

Agreeing to Resettle In 1867, the Kiowas, Comanches, and other southern Plains Indians signed a new treaty with the government. They promised to move to Indian Territory in present-day Oklahoma. The soil there was poor. Also, most Plains Indians were hunters, not farmers. The Native Americans did not like the treaty but knew they had no choice.

The Lakotas and Arapahos of the northern Plains also signed a second Fort Laramie Treaty in 1868. They agreed to

live on **reservations** in present-day South Dakota. A reservation is a limited area set aside for Native Americans.

Buffalo Populations Fall Dramatically

The Plains Indians suffered from lost battles and broken treaties. Even worse for them, however, was the destruction of the buffalo.

The decline of the buffalo began before the arrival of white settlers. Herds of buffalo lived in areas west of the Mississippi and east of the Rockies. However, with disease, drought, and destruction of the areas in which they lived, the herds were slowly growing smaller. As the market demand for buffalo robes increased during the 1830s and 1840s, professional buffalo hunters killed more buffalo. In addition, buffalo hunting became a pleasure sport when railroads cut through the areas in which buffalo lived. Native Americans themselves learned to hunt more efficiently. Some Plains Indian tribes, such as the Pawnees, continued to hunt buffalo even though they recognized that the number of buffalo was decreasing.

The buffalo hunt was a part of their culture that they did not want to give up. As the buffalo disappeared, so did the Plains Indians' way of life.

? CHECK UNDERSTANDING Why were the terms of the Fort Laramie treaty broken?

Conflict in the West Continues

Settlers and miners continued to move into the West. They wanted more and more land for themselves. Even on reservations, Native Americans were not left in peace.

The Battle of Little Bighorn In 1874, prospectors found gold in the Black Hills region of the Lakota, or Sioux, reservation. Thousands of miners rushed to the area.

In June 1876, Colonel George A. Custer led a column of soldiers into the Little Bighorn Valley. They were sent by the federal government to protect the miners, even though miners were violating the 1868 U.S. treaty with the Lakotas. A group of 600 men under Custer's command prepared to attack a Lakota hunting party, although the 1868 treaty gave the Lakota the right to hunt in the area. Indian scouts warned Custer that there were many Lakotas and Cheyennes camped ahead. Nearly 2,000 warriors awaited Custer and his men. Custer divided his troops and attacked with approximately 225 men.

Custer and all these men died in the Battle of Little Bighorn. This was the first battle of the Sioux War of 1876, in which the Lakotas, led by Sitting Bull, Crazy Horse, and other chiefs, fought U.S. forces.

The Native American victory at the Little Bighorn was short-lived. The army soon defeated the Lakotas and Cheyennes. Then, Congress ordered that no food rations be distributed to the Native Americans until they agreed to the government's demands. To avoid starvation, the Lakotas gave up most claims to the Black Hills and other territory. In this way, they surrendered about one third of the lands that the United States government had guaranteed them with the Fort Laramie Treaty of 1868.

Sitting Bull and Crazy Horse had taken their few remaining followers to Canada. Eventually, both men returned.

Chief Joseph Resists Further Settlement

The Nez Percé people lived in the Snake River valley, at the place where today Oregon, Washington, and Idaho meet. In 1855, some Nez Percé signed a treaty with the United States government in which they relinquished part of their land.

>> General George A. Custer (front, on horse) and his soldiers attacked a Lakota and Cheyenne camp at Little Bighorn. Far outnumbered, the U.S. soldiers were all killed, including Custer.

>> Chief Joseph of the Nez Percé resisted settlers' attempts to take over Nez Percé land. He fled to Canada with about 700 followers, until the U.S. Army forced him to surrender.

>> Geronimo was an Apache chief who fought U.S. expansion into Apache territory and resisted government attempts to force his people onto reservations.

In the 1860s, gold discoveries brought miners onto Nez Percé land. The government ordered the Nez Percés to move to a reservation in Idaho. Those who had not signed the treaty refused. Led by Chief Joseph, about 700 Nez Percés fled north toward Canada. Army troops followed close behind.

In the months that followed, the Nez Percés fought off or eluded pursuing army units. Finally, after a tragic journey of more than 1,000 miles, Chief Joseph decided that he must surrender. Of the approximately 700 Nez Percés who had set out with him, fewer than 450 remained.

Geronimo Surrenders in the Southwest

In the arid lands of the Southwest, the Apaches fiercely resisted the loss of their lands. One leader, Geronimo, continued fighting the longest. In 1876, he assumed leadership of a band of Apache warriors when the government tried to force his people onto a reservation.

Geronimo waged war off and on for the next 10 years. From Mexico, he led frequent raids into Arizona and New Mexico. His surrender in 1886 marked the end of formal warfare between Native Americans and whites.

? **IDENTIFY SUPPORTING DETAILS** Why did the Sioux War of 1876 begin?

Remembering a Lost Way of Life

Many Native Americans longed for their lost way of life. On the reservations, the Lakotas and other Plains Indians turned to a religious ceremony called the Ghost Dance. It celebrated the time when Native Americans lived freely on the Plains.

The Ghost Dance In 1889, word spread that a prophet named Wovoka (woh VOH kuh) had appeared among the Paiute people of the southern Plains. Wovoka said that the Great Spirit would make a new world for his people, free from whites and filled with plenty. To bring about this new world, all the Native Americans had to do was dance to the Ghost Dance.

In their ceremonies, Ghost Dancers joined hands in a large circle in which they danced, chanted, and prayed. As they danced, some felt a "growing happiness." Others saw a glowing vision of a new world.

Settlers Misinterpreted the Ghost Dance Many settlers grew alarmed. The Ghost Dancers, they said, were preparing for war. The settlers persuaded the government to outlaw the Ghost Dance.

In December 1890, police officers entered a Lakota reservation to arrest Sitting Bull, who had returned from Canada and was living on the reservation. They claimed that he was spreading the Ghost Dance among the Lakotas. In the struggle that followed, Sitting Bull was accidentally shot and killed.

Tragedy at Wounded Knee Upset by Sitting Bull's death, groups of Lakotas fled the reservations. Army troops pursued them to Wounded Knee Creek, in present-day South Dakota. On December 29, the Native Americans were preparing to surrender. As nervous troops watched, the Indians began to give up their guns.

Suddenly, a shot rang out. One account says a rifle went off by accident. The army opened fire. By the time the shooting stopped, nearly 300 Native American men, women, and children lay dead. About 25 soldiers had also died. The massacre at

>> This monument marks the spot of the Wounded Knee massacre and the mass grave of 300 Lakota men, women, and children.

Wounded Knee marked the end of the Ghost Dance religion.

? IDENTIFY What was the purpose of the Ghost Dance?

Calls to Reform Native American Policies

The Native Americans were no longer able to resist the government. During the late 1800s, more Native Americans were forced onto reservations.

Publicizing Native American Tragedies Many people, Native American and white, spoke out against the tragedy that was occurring. One reformer, Susette La Flesche, was the daughter of an Omaha chief. She wrote and lectured about the destruction of the Native American way of life.

>> Lakotas perform a traditional dance on the Rosebud Reservation in South Dakota. The reservation was created under the terms of the Fort Laramie Treaty of 1868.

Another reformer, Helen Hunt Jackson, published *A Century of Dishonor* in 1881. The book recounts the long history of broken treaties between the United States and the Native Americans.

The Dawes Act Calls for reform led Congress to pass the Dawes Act in 1887. The act encouraged Native Americans to become farmers. Some reservations were divided up and given to individual Native American families.

The Dawes Act was a major change in the government's policy toward Native Americans. Before the Act, Native Americans had been removed from their land and placed on reservations. There,

they were poorly provided for by the government. With the Dawes Act, the government hoped that Native Americans would adopt white ways and become farmers.

The Dawes Act did not have the desired effect, however. To Native Americans, land was an open space for riding and hunting. Moreover, much of the land they were given was not suitable for farming. As a result, Native Americans often sold their shares of land to whites for low prices.

Life on the reservations changed Native American culture. The federal government took away the power of Native American leaders. In their place, it appointed government agents to make most decisions.

? **IDENTIFY CENTRAL IDEAS** What was the purpose and effects of the Dawes Act?

ASSESSMENT

1. **Explain** the Plains Indians' dependence on the buffalo.

2. **Summarize** the roles men played in the Plains Indians' daily life.

3. **Analyze Information** Why couldn't the settlers and miners live in peace with the Plains Indians?

4. **Draw Conclusions** Given what you have learned about the treatment of Native Americans at the hands of the U.S. government, what best explains the reaction of Chief Joseph and some Nez Percé Indians when they were ordered to move to a reservation in Idaho after gold was discovered on their land?

5. **Support Ideas With Evidence** Using the Ghost Dance as an example, what evidence can you provide to support the idea that misunderstanding and fear can lead to tragedy?

Industry and Corporations

>> Steel mills were at the center of Pittsburgh's booming industrial economy in the late 1800s. As this illustration shows, however, the steel industry had a negative effect on the environment.

▶ **Interactive Flipped Video**

The growth of railroads after the Civil War spurred the growth of the steel industry. Early trains ran on iron rails that wore out quickly. Railroad owners knew that steel rails were much stronger and not as likely to rust as iron. Steel, however, was costly and difficult to make.

>> **Objectives**

Explain the growth of the steel industry.

Describe the economic contributions of corporations and bankers.

Explain how Rockefeller built a huge oil trust.

Identify arguments for and against trusts and monopolies.

>> **Key Terms**

Bessemer process
vertical integration
corporation
stock
dividends
trust
monopoly
capitalism
Sherman Antitrust
  Act
supply and demand
scarcity

The Steel Industry Expands

New Steel Production In the 1850s, William Kelly in the United States and Henry Bessemer in England each discovered a new way to make steel. The **Bessemer process**, as it came to be called, was a process that used oxygen and minerals from limestone or other sources to purify molten iron ore into steel. It enabled steel makers to produce strong steel at a lower cost than earlier methods. As a result, railroads began to lay steel rails.

Other industries also took advantage of the cheaper steel. Manufacturers made steel nails, screws, needles, and other items. Steel girders supported the great weight of the new "skyscrapers"—the new tall buildings going up in the cities.

>> The Bessemer process to change iron into steel used a large, fireproof converter (seen in the center). This process was one of several innovations in steel production during the 1800s.

Midwestern Steel Mills Steel mills sprang up in cities throughout the midwest. Pittsburgh became the steel-making capital of the nation. Nearby coal mines and good transportation helped Pittsburgh's steel mills to thrive.

The boom in steel making brought jobs and prosperity to Pittsburgh and other steel towns. It also caused problems. The yellow-colored river that Charles Trevelyan saw on his visit to Pittsburgh in 1898 was the result of years of pouring industrial waste into waterways. Steel mills belched thick black smoke that turned the air gray. Soot blanketed houses, trees, and streets.

? IDENTIFY How did the growth of the steel industry impact industrial cities?

Andrew Carnegie Builds an Empire

Many Americans made fortunes in the steel industry. Richest of all was a Scottish immigrant, Andrew Carnegie. Carnegie's ideas about how to make money—and how to spend it—had a wide influence.

Controlling Steel Production During a visit to Britain, Carnegie had seen the Bessemer process in action. Returning to the United States, he borrowed money and began his own steel mill. Within a short time, Carnegie was earning huge profits. He used the money to buy out rivals. He also bought iron mines, railroad and steamship lines, and warehouses.

Soon, Carnegie controlled all phases of the steel industry—from mining iron ore to shipping finished steel. Gaining control of all the steps used to change raw materials into finished products is called **vertical integration**.

CARNEGIE'S STEEL EMPIRE AND VERTICAL INTEGRATION

VERTICAL INTEGRATION IN THE STEEL INDUSTRY

COAL MINES
Supplied coal used to make coke

QUARRIES
Supplied iron ore and limestone to mills

COKE OVENS
Used coal to make coke (form of charcoal)

RAILWAYS, BARGES, AND PORTS
Used to transport raw materials to mills

STEEL MILLS
Created steel from raw materials

RAILWAYS, BARGES, AND PORTS
Used to transport finished steel to customers

Sources: *Western Pennsylvania History (Winter 2008); Making America: A History of the United States, Volume 2*

CARNEGIE INTEGRATES THE SUPPLY CHAIN

1861 ▸ Forms the Freedom Iron Company

1875 ▸ Opens nation's largest steel plant, employing 1,500 workers

1880s ▸ Expands interests in steel mills and iron ore production

1890s ▸ Creates a limestone company

1892 ▸ Merges with Frick Coke Company to form Carnegie Steel Company

1898 ▸ Builds the Union Railroad to transport steel

Sources: *Western Pennsylvania History (Winter 2008)*; PBS

THE ECONOMICS OF CARNEGIE STEEL

$445 MILLION INCREASE IN VALUE OF **CARNEGIE STEEL** FROM **1892** TO **1901**

2.5 MILLION TONS OF STEEL **PRODUCED BY CARNEGIE STEEL** IN LATE **1890s** APPROXIMATELY **25%** OF NATIONAL TOTAL

Sources: *Western Pennsylvania History (Winter 2008); Making America: A History of the United States, Volume 2*, History.com; *A Nation of Steel*

>> Andrew Carnegie dominated the steel industry by using the process of vertical integration in building his business. **Analyze Charts** How might vertical integration have given Carnegie's company an advantage?

 ▶ **Interactive Map**

Vertical integration gave Carnegie a great advantage over other steel producers. By 1900, Carnegie's steel mills were turning out more steel than was produced in all of Great Britain.

The "Gospel of Wealth" Like other business owners, Carnegie drove his workers hard. Still, he believed that the rich had a duty to help the poor and to improve society. He called this idea the "gospel of wealth." Carnegie gave millions of dollars to charities. After selling his steel empire in 1901, he spent his time and money helping people.

? RECALL Why did Andrew Carnegie have an advantage over other steel producers?

The Rise of Corporations and Banks

Before the railroad boom, nearly every American town had its own small factories. They produced goods for people in the area. By the late 1800s, however, big factories were producing goods more cheaply than small factories could. Railroads distributed these goods to nationwide markets. As demand for local goods fell, many small factories closed. Big factories then increased their output.

By increasing output, big factories were able to earn greater revenue, or income earned from a business after covering costs. Factories often used revenue to expand operations or buy out rivals. Revenues allowed them to grow.

Companies using revenues to expand increased their capital. Capital is money used to invest in the long-term health and success of a company.

However, sometimes companies borrowed money for capital investment. Other companies gave investors **stock**, or partial ownership of the company, in return for capital. Companies might use this capital to build factories, buy new equipment, or buy out other companies. To raise capital and invest in future growth, Americans adopted new ways of organizing their businesses.

Businesses Become Corporations

Many expanding businesses became corporations. A **corporation** is a business that is owned by investors. Laws and court rulings allow corporations to enjoy many of the rights of individuals.

Investors in stock, or stockholders, hope to receive **dividends**, or shares of a corporation's profit. Stockholders elect a board of directors to run the corporation.

Owners of stock in a corporation face fewer risks than owners of private businesses do. If a private business goes bankrupt, the owner must pay all the debts of the business. By law, stockholders cannot be held responsible for a corporation's debts.

Corporations and Banks In the years after the Civil War, corporations attracted large amounts of capital from American investors. Corporations also borrowed millions of dollars from banks. These loans helped American industry grow at a rapid pace. At the same time, bankers made huge profits.

The most powerful banker of the late 1800s was J. Pierpont Morgan. Morgan's influence was not limited to banking. He used his banking profits to gain control of major corporations.

During economic hard times in the 1890s, Morgan and other bankers bought up troubled corporations. They then adopted policies that reduced competition and ensured big profits. "I like a little competition, but I like combination more," Morgan used to say.

Morgan gained control of several major rail lines. He then began to buy up steel companies, including Carnegie Steel, and to merge them into a single large corporation. By 1901, Morgan had become head of the United States Steel Company. It was the first American business worth more than $1 billion.

? CHECK UNDERSTANDING Why did many businesses become corporations?

Rockefeller and the Oil Industry

Industry could not have expanded so quickly in the United States without the nation's rich supply of natural resources.

>> The New York Stock Exchange was a place where corporations sold and traded stocks, or shares in business.

Iron ore was plentiful, especially in the Mesabi Range of Minnesota. Pennsylvania, West Virginia, and the Rocky Mountains had large deposits of coal. The Rockies also contained minerals, such as gold, silver, and copper. Vast forests provided lumber for building.

In 1859, Americans discovered a valuable new resource: oil. Drillers near Titusville, Pennsylvania, made the nation's first oil strike. An oil boom quickly followed. Hundreds of prospectors rushed to western Pennsylvania ready to drill wells in search of oil.

The Standard Oil Empire Among those who came to the Pennsylvania oil fields was young John D. Rockefeller. Rockefeller, however, did not rush to drill for oil. He knew that oil had little value until it was refined, or purified, to make kerosene. Kerosene was used as a fuel in stoves and lamps. So Rockefeller built an oil refinery.

Rockefeller believed that competition was wasteful. He used the profits from his refinery to buy up other refineries. He then combined the companies into the Standard Oil Company of Ohio.

Rockefeller was a shrewd businessman. He was always trying to improve the quality of his oil. He also did whatever he could to get rid of competition. Standard Oil slashed its prices to drive rivals out of business. It pressured its customers not to deal with other oil companies. It forced railroad companies eager for its business to grant rebates to Standard Oil. Lower shipping costs gave Rockefeller an important advantage over his competitors.

The success of Rockefeller's empire reflects the economic principle of **supply and demand**. By lowering the price of oil, Rockefeller was able to attract the greater demand that existed at that lower

>> In 1859, the first oil well was built in Titusville, Pennsylvania. The oil industry used natural resources in the region to stimulate economic growth.

>> John D. Rockefeller made his fortune in the oil industry. He founded Standard Oil in 1870.

price and increase total sales. This would not have been possible without the rise of national markets. Railroads could distribute production nationally, not just locally. National corporations marketed products widely, and railroads delivered them to consumers across the country.

The Oil Monopoly To tighten his hold over the oil industry, Rockefeller formed the Standard Oil trust in 1882. A **trust** is a group of corporations run by a single board of directors.

Stockholders in dozens of smaller oil companies turned over their stock to Standard Oil. In return, they got stock in the newly created trust. The trust paid the stockholders high dividends. However, the board of Standard Oil, headed by Rockefeller, managed all the companies that had previously been rivals.

>> This 1906 photo shows a blacksmith in his shop in Chicago. Craftsmen and small business owners such as this blacksmith struggled to compete with large corporations involved in the same industry.

The Standard Oil trust created a monopoly of the oil industry. A **monopoly** controls all or nearly all the business of an industry. The Standard Oil trust controlled 95 percent of all oil refining in the United States.

Other businesses followed Rockefeller's lead. They set up trusts and tried to build monopolies. By the 1890s, monopolies and trusts controlled some of the nation's most important industries.

❓ IDENTIFY SUPPORTING DETAILS What detail from the text shows that Standard Oil was a monopoly?

The Debate Over Trusts

Some Americans charged that the leaders of giant corporations were abusing the free enterprise system. Under **capitalism**, businesses are owned by private citizens. Owners decide what products to make, how much to produce, where to sell products, and what prices to charge. Companies compete in a free market to win customers by making the best product at the lowest price.

All people in a free market system have to make choices about what products to buy. This is because there is a limited supply of resources. This principle is known as **scarcity**. Companies compete for scarce resources and for customers. Customers then make choices about what to buy to meet their needs, keeping in mind their scarce income or savings. When there are fewer companies competing, people have fewer options.

Arguments Against Trusts Critics argued that trusts and monopolies reduced competition. Without competition, companies had no reason to keep prices low or to improve their products. It was

>> This cartoon shows the Senate dominated by trusts, shown as oversized men watching over senators. **Interpret** Many people argued against trusts and monopolies. What message does the artist convey in this 1889 cartoon?

also hard for new companies to compete with trusts.

Critics were also upset about the political influence of trusts. Some people worried that millionaires were using their wealth to buy favors from elected officials. John Reagan, a member of Congress from Texas, said:

> There were no beggars till Vanderbilts . . . shaped the actions of Congress and molded the purposes of government. Then the few became fabulously wealthy, the many wretchedly poor.
>
> —John Reagan, *Austin Weekly Democratic Statesman*, 1877

Under pressure from the public, the government slowly moved toward controlling giant corporations. Congress approved the **Sherman Antitrust Act** in 1890, which banned the formation of trusts and monopolies. However, it was too weak to be effective. Some state governments passed laws to regulate business, but the corporations usually sidestepped them.

Arguments For Trusts Naturally, some business leaders defended trusts. Andrew Carnegie published articles arguing that too much competition ruined businesses and put people out of work. In an article titled "Wealth and Its Uses," he wrote:

> It will be a great mistake for the community to shoot the millionaires, for they are the bees that make the most honey, and contribute most to the hive even after they have gorged themselves full.
>
> —Andrew Carnegie, "Wealth and Its Uses"

Causes and Effects of Trusts

CAUSES	EVENTS	EFFECTS
Population growth and migration attract investment in railroads.	The Northern Securities Company controls three of the nation's railways by 1901.	The Supreme Court forces the Northern Securities Company to break apart in 1904.
Investors seek market control by forming trusts in the steel and oil industries.	Carnegie Steel Company produces 45.7% of U.S. steel output by 1900; The Standard Oil Company controls 90–95% of U.S. oil production by 1880	Conflicts with labor unions lead to violent strikes; The Supreme Court forces Standard Oil to break apart.
Investors seek market control over the coal and tobacco industries and face little or no government regulation to protect workers.	Pennsylvania coal companies control 96% of national output by 1900. American Tobacco controls 80% of the tobacco industry by 1904.	Strikes bring federal intervention. Factory workers face harsh conditions. Children are used as a source of cheap labor.

SOURCE: *Industrial Genius: The Working Life of Charles Michael Schwab; E.H. Harriman: Master Railroader; Big Steel: The First Century of the United States Steel Corporation 1901–2001; Encyclopædia Britannica*

>> The rise of trusts brought economic growth, but their concentrated power sometimes led to tensions with workers or government. **Analyze Chart** Using evidence from the chart, identify drawbacks to the rise of trusts.

 Interactive Chart

Defenders of big business argued that the growth of giant corporations brought lower production costs, lower prices, higher wages, and a better quality of life for millions of Americans. They pointed out that by 1900 Americans enjoyed the highest standard of living in the world.

? CHECK UNDERSTANDING Why was Andrew Carnegie in favor of trusts?

ASSESSMENT

1. **Describe** both the positive and negative effects of the growth of the steel industry during the mid-nineteenth century.

2. **Identify Steps in a Process** Describe the process of vertical integration, and explain how it affected Andrew Carnegie's business.

3. **Identify Patterns** Explain how factories changed toward the end of the nineteenth century.

4. **Generate Explanations** Explain the difference between private businesses and corporations, and describe how corporations work.

5. **Compare Points of View** Explain why some people supported trusts and others opposed them during the nineteenth century.

10.5 The Labor Movement

>> Members of the International Ladies' Garment Workers Union went on strike in 1909 to demand higher pay and shorter working hours. They were successful.

▶ **Interactive Flipped Video**

Workers had to adjust to the new kinds of factories of the late 1800s. Before the Civil War, most factories were small and family-run. Bosses knew their workers by name and chatted with them about their families. Because most workers had skills that the factory needed, they could bargain with the boss for wages.

>> **Objectives**

Explain how changes in the workplace led to the rise of labor organizations.

Identify the issues that women faced in the workplace during the late 1800s.

Explain the challenges that the labor movement faced during the late 1800s.

>> **Key Terms**

sweatshop
Knights of Labor
strikebreaker
anarchist
Haymarket Riot
AFL (American
    Federation of
    Labor)
trade union
collective bargaining
ILGWU (International
    Ladies' Garment
    Workers Union)
Triangle Fire

Changing Working Conditions

By the 1880s, the relationship between worker and boss had changed. People worked all day tending machines in a large, crowded, noisy room. Because their skills were easily replaced, many workers were forced to work for low wages. In the garment trade and other industries, sweatshops became common. A **sweatshop** is a workplace where people labor long hours in poor conditions for low pay. Most sweatshop workers were young women or children.

Child Labor The 1900 census reported nearly 2 million children under age 15 at work throughout the country. Boys and girls labored in hazardous textile mills, tobacco factories, and garment sweatshops. In coal mines, they picked stones out of the coal for 12 hours a day, 6 days a week. Working children had little time for schooling. Lack of education reduced their chance of building a better life as adults.

A Dangerous Workplace Factories were filled with hazards. Lung-damaging dust filled the air of textile mills. Cave-ins and gas explosions plagued mines. In steel mills, vats of molten metal spilled without warning. Some workers had their health destroyed. Others were severely injured or killed in industrial accidents. In one year, 195 workers died in the steel mills of Pittsburgh.

? DESCRIBE the working conditions of sweatshops.

Workers Organize Unions

Many workers found ways to fight back. Some workers slowed their work pace. Others went on strike. Strikes were usually informal, organized by workers in individual factories.

Sometimes workers banded together to win better conditions. However, most early efforts to form unions failed.

Knights of Labor In 1869, workers formed the **Knights of Labor**. At first, the union was open to skilled workers only. The members held meetings in secret because employers fired workers who joined unions.

In 1879, the Knights of Labor elected Terence Powderly as their president. Powderly worked to strengthen the union by opening its membership to immigrants, African Americans, women, and unskilled workers.

Powderly did not believe in strikes. Rather, he relied on rallies and meetings to win public support. Goals of the Knights included a shorter workday, an end to child labor, and equal pay for men and women. Most important, Powderly wanted workers

>> Many children, such as this one, had little choice but to work in sweatshops and factories.

▶ **Interactive Gallery**

>> In 1886, a bomb exploded during a workers' rights protest in Haymarket Square in Chicago. The Haymarket Riot damaged the labor movement's image.

and employers to share ownership and profits.

In 1885, some members of the Knights of Labor launched a strike that forced the Missouri Pacific Railroad to restore wages that it had previously cut. The Knights did not officially support the strike. Still, workers everywhere saw the strike as a victory for the union. Membership soared to 700,000, including 60,000 African Americans.

The Haymarket Riot The following year, the Knights of Labor ran into serious trouble. Workers at the McCormick Harvester Company in Chicago went on strike. Again, the Knights did not endorse the strike.

Like many companies at the time, the McCormick company hired **strikebreakers**, or replacements for striking workers. On May 3, 1886, workers clashed with strikebreakers outside the factory. Police opened fire, and four workers were killed.

The next day, thousands of workers gathered in Haymarket Square to protest the killings. The rally was led by **anarchists**, people who oppose all forms of organized government. Suddenly, a bomb exploded, killing seven police officers.

Eight anarchists were arrested for their part in the **Haymarket Riot** as the incident was called. No real evidence linked these men to the bombing, but four were tried, convicted, and hanged. A wave of antilabor feeling swept the nation. Many Americans thought that the unions were controlled by anarchists. As a result, membership in the Knights of Labor dropped sharply.

>> Samuel Gompers was the head of the American Federation of Labor, a union that fought for improved working conditions, higher pay, and shorter hours for skilled workers.

>> Women often worked in textile factories, and some formed their own unions. Most women, however, never joined a union. **Hypothesize** Why did so few women join unions?

A New Union Forms Despite the failure of the Knights of Labor, the labor movement continued to grow. In 1886, an immigrant cigar maker named Samuel Gompers organized a new union in Columbus, Ohio. The American Federation of Labor (**AFL**) was open to skilled workers only.

Workers did not join the AFL directly. Rather, they joined a **trade union**, a union of persons working in the same trade. For example, a typesetter joined a typesetter's union. The union then joined the AFL. Thus, the AFL was a large organization made up of many different unions.

Unlike the Knights of Labor, the AFL stressed practical goals. It focused on higher wages, shorter hours, and improved working conditions. It led the fight for **collective bargaining**, the right of unions to negotiate with management for workers as a group. The AFL also supported the use of strikes to achieve its goals.

Its practical approach helped the AFL become the most powerful labor organization in the nation. Between 1886 and 1910, membership in the AFL swelled from 150,000 to more than one and a half million. However, because African Americans, immigrants, and unskilled workers were barred from most trade unions, they could not join the AFL.

? **RECALL** What were the goals of the Knights of Labor?

Women in the Workplace

By 1890, one million women worked in American factories. In the textile mills of New England and the tobacco factories of the South, women formed the majority of workers. In New York City, women outnumbered men in the garment industry.

During the 1800s, some women formed their own unions. A few, like the all-black Washerwomen's Association of Atlanta, struck for higher wages. None of these unions succeeded, however.

Mother Jones The best-known woman in the labor movement was Irish-born Mary Harris Jones, known as Mother Jones. Jones devoted much of her adult life to the cause of workers.

Jones spoke out about the hard lives of children in textile mills, "barefoot . . . reaching thin little hands into the machinery." By calling attention to such abuses, Mother Jones helped pave the way for reform.

Organizing Garment Workers In 1900, garment workers organized the International Ladies' Garment Workers Union (**ILGWU**). More than 20,000 women and men in the ILGWU walked off their jobs in 1909. After a few weeks, employers met union demands for better pay and shorter hours. The ILGWU became a key member of the AFL.

Despite the efforts of the ILGWU and other labor groups, most women with factory jobs did not join unions. They continued to work long hours for low pay. Many labored under unsafe conditions. Then, a tragic event focused attention on the dangers faced by women workers.

The Triangle Fire The workday was just ending on a cool March day in 1911, when a fire broke out in the Triangle Shirtwaist Factory, a sweatshop in New York City. Within minutes, the upper stories were ablaze. Hundreds of workers raced for the exits, only to find them locked. The

>> Despite the efforts of firefighters, many people lost their lives in the Triangle Fire. **Infer** How did the public react to the event?

company had locked the doors to keep workers at their jobs. In their panic, workers ran headlong into the doors, blocking them with their bodies.

Fire trucks arrived almost immediately, but their ladders could not reach the upper floors. One after another, workers trying to escape the flames leapt to their deaths.

As I looked up . . . there, at a window, a young man was helping girls to leap out. Suddenly one of them put her arms around him and kiss[ed] him. Then he held her into space and dropped her. He jumped next. Thud . . . dead. Thud . . . dead.
—*The New York Times*, March 26, 1911

Nearly 150 people, mostly young women, lost their lives in the **Triangle Fire**. The deaths shocked the public. As a result,

New York and other states approved new safety laws to help protect factory workers.

? **CHECK UNDERSTANDING** How did the Triangle Fire affect labor reform in New York and other states?

Labor Faces Challenges

The new era of industry led to vast economic growth. At the same time, it created economic strains. In the rush for profits, many industries expanded too fast. As goods flooded the market, prices dropped. To cut their losses, factory owners often fired workers. As the supply of goods fell, prices rose again. In turn, factories geared up again, and the cycle was repeated.

The economy swung wildly between good times and bad. Between 1870 and 1900, two major depressions and three smaller recessions rocked the country. In such hard times, workers lost their jobs or faced pay cuts.

>> Federal troops guard a train against striking workers during the 1894 Pullman Strike.

▶ **Interactive Timeline**

Violent Strikes During a severe depression in the 1870s, railroad workers were forced to take several cuts in pay. In July 1877, workers went on strike, shutting down rail lines across the country. Riots erupted in many cities as workers burned rail yards and ripped up track.

Violent strikes also broke out in the West. In the 1870s, miners in Idaho tried to shut down two large mines. In 1893, after another bitter strike, miners formed the Western Federation of Miners. This union gained great strength in the Rocky Mountain states. Between 1894 and 1904, it organized strike after strike.

Rulings Against Unions The federal government usually sided with factory owners. Several Presidents sent in troops to end strikes. Courts usually ruled against strikers, too.

In 1894, a Chicago court dealt a serious blow to unions. A year earlier, George Pullman had cut the pay of workers at his railroad car factory. Yet, he did not reduce the rents he charged them for company-owned houses. Workers walked off the job in protest.

A federal judge ordered the Pullman workers to stop their strike. Leaders of the strike were jailed for violating the Sherman Antitrust Act. This act had been meant to keep trusts from limiting free trade. The courts, however, said that the strikers were limiting free trade.

Gains and Losses Union workers staged thousands of strikes during the late 1800s. However, many Americans opposed the strikes. Some were afraid that unions were run by foreign-born radicals. Because unions were unpopular, owners felt free to try to crush them.

POPULATION AND WORKFORCE DEMOGRAPHICS 1890–1910

POPULATION GROWTH

Population (in millions)
- 1890: 62.9
- 1900: 76
- 1910: 92

683,000 Average number of immigrants to the United States from 1890–1910

Source: Bureau of Labor Statistics

UNION MEMBERSHIP

Members (in millions)
- 1890: 0.8
- 1900: 1.2
- 1910: 2.3

Source: *Historical Statistics of the United States*

EMPLOYMENT TRENDS

- Agriculture
- Manufacturing
- Other
- Trade
- Services

1890: 42.7%, 17.7%, 8.2%, 12.6%, 18.8%

1900: 40.1%, 18.5%, 7.6%, 13.6%, 20.2%

1910: 31.4%, 25.2%, 7.1%, 14.1%, 22.2%

Source: *Historical Statistics of the United States*

>> Industrialization led to profound changes in the American workforce around the year 1900. **Analyze Graphs** Why might manufacturing jobs and union membership have risen at the same time?

Workers did make some gains. Overall, wages rose slightly between 1870 and 1900. Still, union growth was slow. In 1910, only one worker in 20 belonged to a union. Some 30 years would pass before large numbers of unskilled workers were able to join unions.

? RECALL Why were unions unpopular with many Americans?

ASSESSMENT

1. **Identify Cause and Effect** Explain how the employer-worker relationship changed over the course of the 1800s, and discuss the effects of this change.

2. **Compare and Contrast** the Knights of Labor with the American Federation of Labor.

3. **Generate Explanations** Describe the conditions of women in the workplace in the late 1800s, and explain how the Triangle Fire changed public opinion about workers' rights generally.

4. **Identify Patterns** Explain how economic depressions affected workers during the 1870s, and discuss the workers' responses to these conditions.

5. **Identify Central Issues** Discuss the federal government's involvement in the labor issues of the 1800s.

10.6 | New Technologies

>> Orville and Wilbur Wright's first flight lasted just 12 seconds, but the brothers quickly made longer flights and continued developing the airplane.

▶ Interactive Flipped Video

>> Objectives

Explain how new devices sped up communication during the late 1800s.

Describe how inventions by Thomas Edison and others transformed life for Americans.

Explain how automobiles and airplanes came to transform transportation.

>> Key Terms

patent
transatlantic
moving assembly
  line
mass production

The Patent Office had never seen a year like 1897. An average of nearly 60 **patents**, or licenses for new inventions, were being granted every day. By year's end, Americans had registered some 21,000 patents. This was more than the total recorded in the entire 1850s.

New Communication Technologies

The United States had become a land of invention. Between 1870 and 1900, patent officers issued more than 500,000 new patents. A flood of invention swept the United States in the late 1800s. Some inventions helped industry to grow and become more efficient. Others made daily life easier in many American homes.

Better communication was vital to growing American businesses. Some remarkable new devices filled the need for faster communication. The telegraph, which had been in use since 1844, helped people around the nation stay in touch. For example, a steel maker in Pittsburgh could instantly order iron ore from a mine in Minnesota.

Transatlantic Communication The telegraph sped up communication within the United States. It still took weeks, however, for news from Europe to arrive by ship.

Cyrus Field had the idea of laying a cable under the ocean so that telegraph messages could go back and forth between North America and Europe. He began working in 1854, making five attempts to lay the cable. Each time, the cable snapped. In 1858, two American ships managed to lay a cable between Ireland and Newfoundland, linking Europe and North America. Field then arranged for Britain's Queen Victoria in London to send the first **transatlantic**, or across-the-Atlantic, message to President James Buchanan in Washington, D.C. For three weeks, Field was a hero. Then, the cable broke. But Field would not give up. In 1866, the ship *Great Eastern* succeeded in laying a more durable cable. Field's transatlantic cable brought the United

>> The Patent Office in Washington, D.C., shown here, issued thousands of patents to inventors in the late 1800s. Many of these inventions raised the American standard of living.

>> The American ship *Niagara* unspooled the final lengths of the first transatlantic cable in August 1858. **Describe** the importance of creating a direct communications link between North America and Europe.

States and Europe closer together and made him famous.

> In five months . . . the cable had been manufactured, shipped . . . stretched across the Atlantic, and was sending messages . . . swift as lightning from continent to continent.
>
> —Cyrus Field, speech, 1866

The Bell Telephone Company The telegraph sent only dots and dashes over the wire. Several inventors were looking for a way to transmit voices. One of them was Alexander Graham Bell, a Scottish-born teacher of the deaf.

Bell had been working on his invention since 1865. In March 1876, he was ready to test his "talking machine." Bell sat in one room and spoke into his machine. His assistant, Thomas Watson, sat in another room with the receiver. "Mr. Watson, come here. I want to see you," Bell said. Watson heard the words faintly and rushed to Bell's side. "Mr. Bell," he cried, "I heard every word you said!" The telephone worked.

Bell's telephone aroused little interest at first. Scientists praised the invention. Most people, however, saw it as a toy. Bell offered to sell the telephone to the Western Union Telegraph Company for $100,000. The company refused—a costly mistake. In the end, the telephone earned Bell millions.

Bell formed the Bell Telephone Company in 1877. By 1885, he had sold more than 300,000 phones, mostly to businesses. With the telephone, the pace of business sped up even more. People no longer had to go to a telegraph office to send messages. Business people could find out about prices or supplies by picking up the telephone.

? CHECK UNDERSTANDING How did new communication devices help American businesses?

Thomas Edison, American Inventor

In an age of invention, Thomas Edison was right at home. In 1876, he opened a research laboratory in Menlo Park, New Jersey. There, Edison boasted that he and his co-workers created a "minor" invention every 10 days and "a big thing every six months or so." By the end of his career, Edison had earned worldwide fame as the greatest inventor of the age.

The "Wizard of Menlo Park" The key to Edison's success lay in his approach. He turned inventing into a system. Teams of experts refined Edison's ideas and translated them into practical inventions. The work was long and grueling. "Genius," Edison said, "is one percent inspiration and ninety-nine percent perspiration."

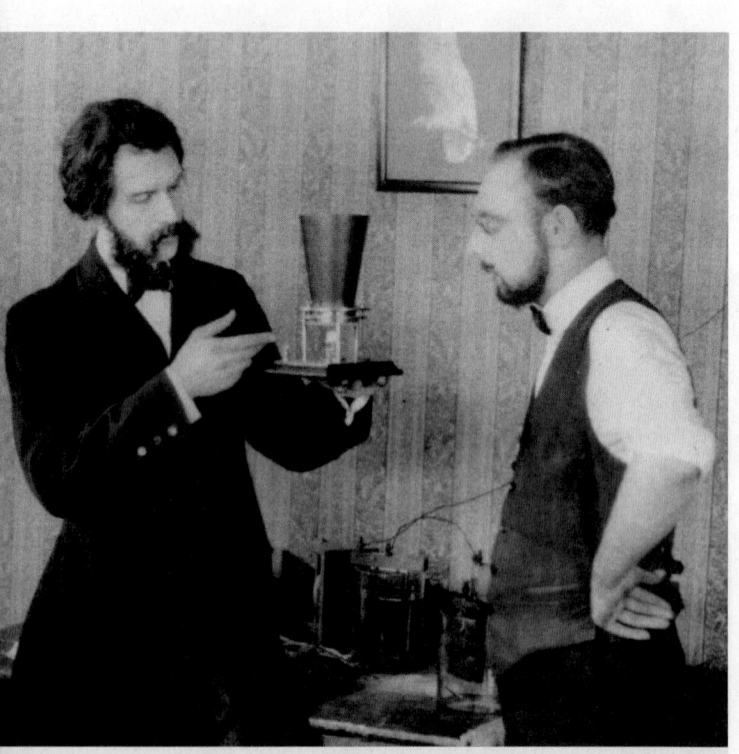

>> In 1876, Alexander Graham Bell (standing on the left) invented the telephone, a device that would revolutionize communication.

Interactive Chart

The results were amazing. Edison became known as the "Wizard of Menlo Park" for inventing the light bulb, the phonograph, and hundreds of other devices.

One invention from Edison's laboratory launched a new industry: the movies. In 1893, Edison introduced his first machine for showing moving pictures. Viewers watched short films by looking through a peephole in a cabinet. Later, Edison developed a motion picture projector, making it possible for many people to watch a film at the same time. By 1908, thousands of silent-movie houses had opened in cities across the United States.

The Age of Electricity One of Edison's most important creations was the electric power plant. He built the first power plant in New York City in 1882. He wired the business district first in hopes of attracting investors. With the flip of a switch, Edison set the district ablaze with light.

Within a year, Edison's power plant was supplying electricity to homes as well as businesses. Soon, more power plants were built. Factories replaced steam-powered engines with safer, quieter, electric engines. Electric energy powered streetcars in cities and lighted countless homes. The modern age of electricity had begun.

? **DESCRIBE** the impact of electricity on American homes and businesses.

Technology in Everyday Life

Almost every day, it seemed, American inventors were creating new devices. As technology spread, businesses became more efficient, and life became easier and more pleasant.

>> This photo was taken after Edison had worked tirelessly to find a way to record and play sounds. He heard his own voice reciting "Mary Had a Little Lamb."

▶ **Interactive Timeline**

>> The Edison Electric Lighting Station supplied electricity to homes and businesses in the late 1800s. Identify ways that electricity improved the standard of living in many homes.

Refrigeration In the 1880s, Gustavus Swift came up with an idea that transformed the American diet. Swift introduced refrigeration to the meatpacking industry. In the past, cattle, pigs, and chickens had been raised and sold locally. Meat spoiled quickly, so it could not be shipped over long distances.

Swift set up a meatpacking plant in Chicago, a railroad hub midway between the cattle ranches of the West and the cities of the East. Cattle were shipped by train to Chicago. At Swift's plant, the animals were slaughtered and carved up into sides of beef. The fresh beef was quickly loaded onto refrigerated railroad cars and carried to market. Even in summer, Swift sent fresh meat to eastern cities.

Improvements in Offices and Homes
New inventions also affected life at home and in the office. Christopher Sholes perfected the typewriter in 1868. This invention sped up communication between businesses.

In 1888, George Eastman introduced the lightweight Kodak camera. No longer did photography require bulky equipment and chemicals. After 100 snaps of the shutter, the owner returned the camera to Kodak. The company developed the pictures and sent them back, along with a reloaded camera. Taking pictures became a popular pastime.

African American Inventors African Americans contributed to the flood of inventions. In 1872, Elijah McCoy created a special device that oiled engines automatically. It was widely used on railroad engines and in factories. Another inventor, Granville T. Woods, found a way to send telegraph messages between moving railroad trains.

Jan Matzeliger invented a machine that could perform almost all the steps in shoemaking that had previously been done by hand. Patented in 1883, Matzeliger's machine was eventually used in shoe factories across the country.

Many African-American inventors had trouble getting patents for their inventions. Even so, in 1900, an assistant in the patent office compiled a list of patents issued to African-American inventors. The list, together with drawings and plans of all the inventions, filled four huge volumes.

❓ **RECALL** How did new technology affect the American diet in the late 1800s?

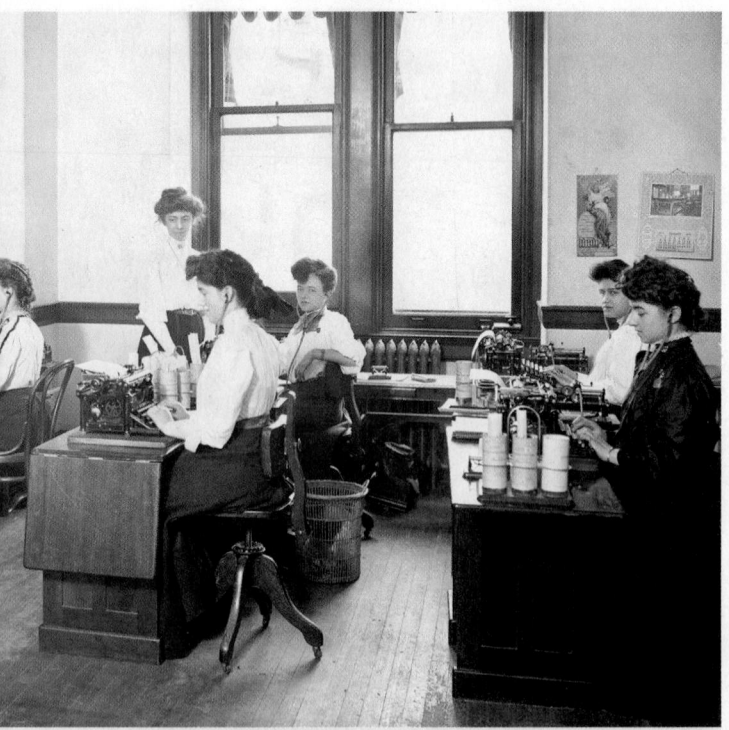

>> This photo from 1910 shows office workers using the typewriter, an invention from 1868 that made written business communications quicker and clearer.

Automobile Production

No single person invented the automobile. Europeans had produced motorized vehicles as early as the 1860s. By 1890,

France led the world in automaking. In the 1890s, several Americans began building cars. Still, only the wealthy could afford them.

Henry Ford's Assembly Line It was Henry Ford who made the auto a part of everyday American life. In 1913, Ford introduced the **moving assembly line**. With this method of production, workers stay in one place as products move along on a track or belt. At Ford's auto plant, one group of workers would bolt seats onto a passing car frame, the next would add the roof, and so on. The assembly line greatly reduced the time needed to build a car. Other industries soon adopted the method.

Ford's assembly line allowed the mass production of cars. **Mass production** means making large quantities of a product quickly and cheaply. Because of mass production, Ford could sell his cars at a lower price than other automakers.

"Horseless Carriages" Catch On It took a number of years for the automobile to catch on. At first, most people laughed at it. Some thought the "horseless carriage" was a nuisance. Others thought it was dangerous. A backfiring auto engine could scare a horse right off the road. Towns and villages across the nation posted signs: "No horseless carriages allowed." In Tennessee, a person planning to drive a car had to advertise the fact a week ahead of time. This warning gave others time to prepare for the danger!

Over time, attitudes toward the automobile changed. No other means of travel offered such freedom. As prices dropped, more people could afford to buy cars. In 1900, only 8,000 Americans owned cars. By 1917, more than 4.5 million autos were chugging along American roads.

Automobiles were at first regarded as machines for men only. Automakers soon realized, however, that women could drive—and buy—cars. Companies began to

>> On an assembly line, such as this one at the Ford Motor Company, cars were built piece by piece as they moved along a track.

direct advertisements to women, stressing the comfort and usefulness of automobiles. Driving gave women greater independence.

? IDENTIFY MAIN IDEAS How did the introduction of the moving assembly line lead to the increased popularity of automobiles?

The Wright Brothers Take Flight

Meanwhile, two Ohio bicycle mechanics, Orville and Wilbur Wright, were experimenting with another new method of transportation: flying. The Wright brothers owned a bicycle shop in Dayton, Ohio. During the 1890s, they read about Europeans who were experimenting with glider planes. The brothers were soon caught up in the dream of flying.

After trying out hundreds of designs, the Wright brothers tested their first "flying machine" on December 17, 1903, at Kitty Hawk, North Carolina. Orville made the first flight. The plane, powered by a small gasoline engine, stayed in the air for 12 seconds and flew a distance of 120 feet. Orville flew three more times that day. His longest flight lasted 59 seconds.

Improvements came quickly after the first flight. By 1905, the Wrights had built a plane that could turn, make figure-eights, and remain in the air for up to half an hour.

Surprisingly, the first flights did not attract much interest. No one could see any practical use for the flying machine.

It was the United States military that first saw a use for airplanes. In 1908, the Wrights demonstrated how planes could fly over battlefields to locate enemy positions. Then, they produced an airplane for the military that could reach the amazing speed of 40 miles per hour!

In time, the airplane would achieve its vast potential. It would change the world by making travel quicker and trade easier.

? IDENTIFY SUPPORTING DETAILS What details show the usefulness of the Wrights' "flying machine"?

>> In the years after the Wright Brothers' first flight, government and industry found many uses for airplanes. In this 1925 photo, pilot Charles Lindbergh (standing inside the plane, right) prepares to depart with the first-ever air mail delivery.

ASSESSMENT

1. **Describe** the major improvements in communication that occurred during the late 1800s.

2. **Generate Explanations** Explain how Thomas Edison changed industry and leisure in the United States.

3. **Identify Cause and Effect** Explain how refrigeration changed American eating habits.

4. **Identify Central Issues** Discuss Henry Ford's contributions to industry and American lifestyles.

5. **Generate Explanations** Explain how the invention of the airplane eventually became successful.

1. **Analyze Supply and Demand in the Cattle Business**
   Use the lessons in this topic to write a paragraph analyzing the impact of supply and demand on the cattle business in the 1800s. Be sure to describe the reasons for increased demand for meat, and how Texas ranchers supplied beef to meet that demand. In your paragraph, also describe how Texas ranchers got their beef to their customers.

2. **Draw Connections Between the Environment and Settlement of the Great Plains** Analyze how the physical characteristics of the environment of the Great Plains influenced economic activities, such as ranching and population distribution, and settlement patterns during the 1800s. Write a paragraph analyzing how the environment influenced ranching and settlement patterns during the 1800s. Analyze how cattle drives influenced the settlement of western towns, explain how new farm settlements affected the cattle boom, and analyze how the environment affected the cattle boom.

3. **Explain the Impact of the Homestead Act** Identify the effects of the Homestead Act and analyze how, paired with this legislation, the physical characteristics of the Great Plains influenced population distribution and settlement patterns during the 1800s. Write a paragraph analyzing how the Homestead Act and the physical characteristics of the Great Plains influenced population distribution and settlement patterns. Be sure to analyze the main effect of the Homestead Act and describe settlement patterns in Kansas, the Southwest, and Oklahoma.

4. **Describe the Impact of Physical Geography on the Great Plains** Describe the location of the Great Plains and analyze how the physical characteristics of the Great Plains influenced life on the plains, including population distribution, dependence on the physical environment, and economic challenges. Use the photo above and information from the lessons in this topic to write a paragraph describing how the physical characteristics of the Great Plains influenced life on the plains. Be sure to identify how the abundance of sod influenced life in the Great Plains, analyze environmental challenges and how settlers depended on the environment for their livelihood, and describe the economic challenges settlers on the Great Plains faced.

5. **Explain Plains Indian Ways of Life** Describe the way of life of the Plains Indians before the arrival of white settlers. Write a paragraph explaining the roles of farming and hunting, the use of horses, housing, governance, and gender roles. Explain the importance of the buffalo to the Plains Indians.

6. **Create a Timeline of Conflict in the West** Create a timeline of events showing conflict between American Indians and white settlers. Begin your timeline with settlers and traders first beginning to cross Plains Indians hunting grounds in the 1840s and end with the Dawes Act. Include at least six additional entries. Then write two or three sentences that draw a conclusion about the events you have noted on your timeline.

7. Identify the Effects of the Dawes Act Write a paragraph identifying the Dawes Act and describing its effects. Identify what the Dawes Act was, explain why it was enacted, describe what it was supposed to do, and describe its actual effects.

8. Analyze How Geographic Features Influenced Economic Activities Analyze how physical geographic features such as rich mineral deposits in the western mountains of the United States caused gold and silver rushes and influenced economic activities during the 1800s. Write a paragraph that describes how physical features in the western mountains of the United States influenced economic activities in the United States during the 1800s. Describe how physical features affected activity around the Comstock Lode, analyze how gold and silver strikes affected development of the West, and explain how towns developed on the mining frontier.

9. Explain How Physical Features Affected Transcontinental Railroad Construction Use information from the illustrations and the lessons in this topic to write a paragraph that explains how physical features affected construction of the first transcontinental railroad and analyzes why the completion of this railroad was a major event in American history. Be sure to identify the two companies that strived to complete a transcontinental railroad and the reasons they raced to finish, describe the physical features that made the building of the transcontinental railroad a challenging task, and analyze the impact that transcontinental railroads had on the settlement of the West.

10. Evaluate Contributions of Andrew Carnegie Write a paragraph describing the contributions of Andrew Carnegie. In your paragraph, evaluate why Carnegie is considered a captain of industry by reflecting on how he acquired wealth, how he controlled steel production through vertical integration, and how he used his money to help society.

11. Identify Points of View on Big Business Write a paragraph identifying the pros and cons expressed in the two points of view below. Identify each point expressed by the historians. Then relate each point to a specific positive or negative aspect of big business.

When Rockefeller founded Standard Oil, kerosene was 30 cents a gallon. Twenty years later, Rockefeller had almost a 90 percent market share and kerosene was only eight cents a gallon. Customers were the real winners here, because Rockefeller's size allowed him to cut costs. . . .

—Historian Burton W. Folsom, Jr.

To organize and exploit the resources of a nation upon a giant scale . . . and to do this only in the name of an uncontrolled appetite for private profit—here surely is . . . whence so much disaster, outrage, and misery has flowed.

—Historian Matthew Josephson

12. Explain Causes of the Growth of Labor Unions Write a paragraph explaining causes of the growth of labor unions in the late 1800s Include specific issues related to wages, hours, working conditions and child labor.

13. Identify Point of View on Labor Unions Write a paragraph identifying and explaining the point of view expressed by Samuel Gompers in the quotation below. Be sure to explain the points that Samuel Gompers makes in the quotation, why he believes that the best way to prevent strikes is to allow the right to strike, and what he thinks will happen if workers are denied the right to strike.

We recognize that peaceful industry is necessary to successful civilized life, but the right to strike and the preparation to strike is the greatest preventive to strikes. If the workmen were to make up their minds tomorrow that they would under no circumstances strike, the employers would do all the striking for them in the way of lesser wages and longer hours of labor.

—Samuel Gompers, Report on the (U.S.) Industrial Commission on Capital and Labor, 1890

14. Analyze How Inventions Improved People's Lives Write a paragraph analyzing how the development of new technologies improved people's lives in the late 1800s and early 1900s. Make sure to describe what new forms of technology emerged and analyze the specific effects of new technologies on people's lives.

15. **Explain the Impact of Mass Production**
    Use information from the lessons in this topic to write a paragraph discussing the use of mass production in automobile factories. Be sure to explain what the term *mass production* describes, how it can affect worker productivity, how it can benefit businesses, and how it can benefit consumers.

16. **Write About the Essential Question** **Write an Essay on the Essential Question: How should resources be distributed?** Use evidence from this topic to support your answer.

[**ESSENTIAL QUESTION**] What can individuals do to affect society?

11 The Progressive Era (1865–1920)

>> Newly arrived immigrants gaze at the Statue of Liberty

Topic 11 The Progressive Era (1865–1920)

Enduring Understandings

- A new wave of immigrants from different parts of the world came to the United States beginning in the late 1800s.

- Rapidly growing cities offered poor living conditions to many workers.

- Progressive reformers aimed to regulate big business and end corruption in politics, and the years around 1900 are known as the Progressive Era.

- Theodore Roosevelt, William Howard Taft, and Woodrow Wilson were Progressive presidents.

- While women gained new rights and opportunities in the early 1900s, minorities faced discrimination.

- Americans were drawn to new kinds of journalism, literature, art, and entertainment.

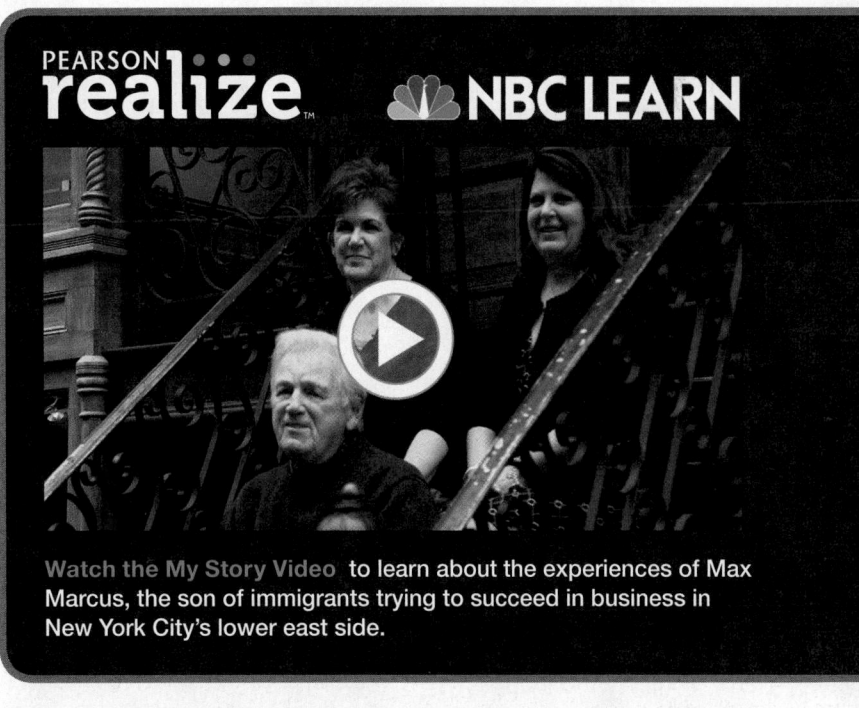

PEARSON realize™   NBC LEARN

Watch the My Story Video to learn about the experiences of Max Marcus, the son of immigrants trying to succeed in business in New York City's lower east side.

PEARSON realize™
www.PearsonRealize.com

Access your digital lessons including:
Topic Inquiry • Interactive Reading
Notepad • Interactivities • Assessments

A New Wave of Immigration

>> Beginning in the late 1800s, the Lower East Side of New York was overcrowded with immigrant families of many ethnic backgrounds. Although immigrants enjoyed the freedom of America, they endured a crowded and dirty environment.

▶ Interactive Flipped Video

>> Objectives

Explain why immigrants made the difficult journey to the United States.

Describe the problems "new immigrants" faced in adapting to life in the United States.

Explain the causes and effects of nativist opposition to immigration.

>> Key Terms

push factor
pull factor
pogrom
steerage
Statue of Liberty
acculturation
nativist
Chinese Exclusion
   Act

Between 1865 and 1915, more than 25 million immigrants poured into the United States. They came full of hope and excitement but also with anxiety, as this quote from a Norwegian immigrant shows.

Reasons for Immigration

> There was left the choice to stay home and wait for something to turn up, go out as a laborer or to learn a trade, or to sea, or to America! . . . Then west by train on road and route not known to us. We saw mountains, which must have been the Alleghenies, and felt much depressed. Was that America? Had we been fooled? We expected to see flat ground with no timber or boulders to clear. When we came far enough to see that kind of country our spirits rose again. . . .
>
> —Norwegian author Andreas Ueland, from *Recollections of an Immigrant*

Immigrants such as Ueland came to the United States for many reasons. **Push factors** are conditions that drive people from their homes. **Pull factors** are conditions that attract immigrants to a new area. For example, an industrial boom in the United States had created a huge need for workers that drew many immigrants.

Push Factors European immigrants were often small farmers or landless farmworkers. As European populations grew, land became scarce. Small farms could barely support the families that worked them. In some areas, new farm machines replaced farmworkers.

Political or religious persecution drove many people from their homes. In Russia, the government supported **pogroms** (POH grahmz), or organized attacks on Jewish villages. Persecution and violence also pushed Armenian Christians out of the Ottoman Empire (present-day Turkey).

Political unrest was another push factor. After 1910, a revolution erupted in Mexico. Thousands of Mexicans crossed the border into the southwestern United States.

Pull Factors Industrial jobs were the chief pull factor for immigrants. American factories needed labor. Factory owners sent agents to Europe and Asia to hire workers at low wages. Steamship companies offered low fares for the ocean crossing. Railroads posted notices in Europe advertising cheap land in the American West.

Often, one family member—usually a young, single male—made the trip. Once settled, he would send for family members to join him. As immigrants wrote home describing the "land of opportunity," they pulled other neighbors from the "old country." For example, one out of every ten Greeks immigrated to the United States in the late 1800s.

>> These immigrants are shown waiting at the arrivals hall at Ellis Island, which was the gateway for millions of immigrants entering the United States in the late 1800s and early 1900s.

The promise of freedom was another pull factor. Many immigrants were eager to live in a land where police could not arrest or imprison them without a reason and where freedom of religion was guaranteed to all by the Bill of Rights.

? LIST two push factors and two pull factors that brought immigrants to the United States.

A Challenging Journey Across an Ocean

Leaving home required great courage. The voyage across the Atlantic or Pacific was often miserable. Most immigrants could afford only the cheapest berths. Shipowners jammed up to 2,000 people in **steerage**, the airless rooms below deck. On the return voyage, cattle or cargo filled the same spaces.

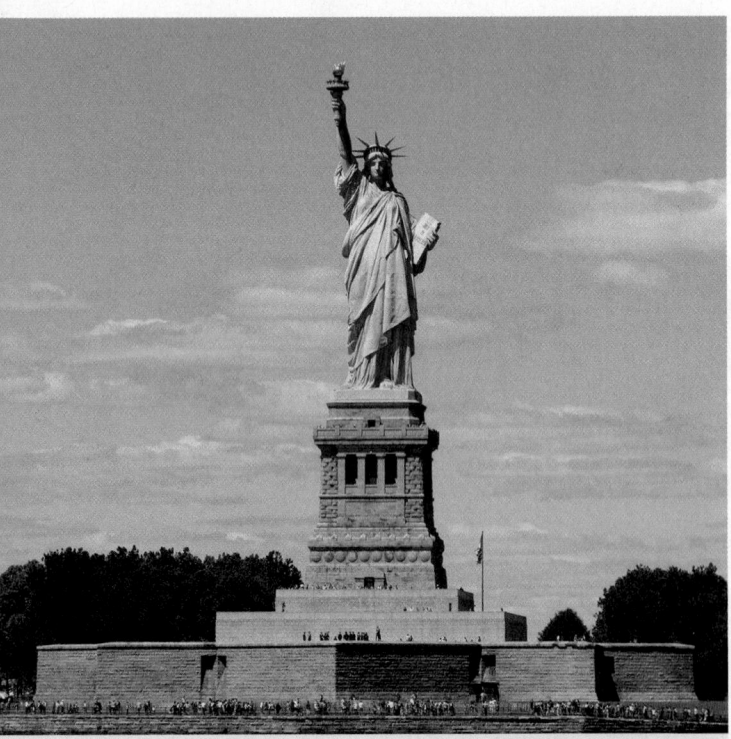

>> The Statue of Liberty was completed in 1886 and immediately became a beacon of hope and welcome for new immigrants. It remains one of our nation's enduring symbols of freedom.

In such close quarters, disease spread rapidly. An outbreak of measles infected every child on one German immigrant ship. The dead were thrown into the water "like cattle," reported a horrified passenger.

Ellis Island For most European immigrants, the voyage ended in New York City. Sailing into the harbor, they were greeted by the giant **Statue of Liberty**. Dedicated in 1886, it became a symbol of hope and freedom. A poem of welcome was carved on the base.

Give me your tired, your poor,
Your huddled masses yearning to breathe free,
The wretched refuse of your teeming shore.
Send these, the homeless, tempest-tossed to me:
I lift my lamp beside the golden door!

—Emma Lazarus, "The New Colossus"

In 1892, a new receiving station opened on Ellis Island. Here, immigrants had to face a dreaded medical inspection. Doctors watched newcomers climb a long flight of stairs. Anyone who limped or appeared out of breath might be stopped. Doctors also examined eyes, ears, and throats. The sick had to stay on Ellis Island until they got well. A small percentage who failed to regain full health were sent home.

With hundreds of immigrants to process each day, officials had only minutes to check each new arrival. To save time, they often changed names that they found hard to spell. Krzeznewski became Kramer. Smargiaso ended up as Smarga. Even the first name of one Italian immigrant was changed, from Bartolomeo to Bill.

Lucky immigrants went directly into the welcoming arms of friends and relatives. Many others stepped into a terrifying new land whose language and customs they did not know.

Angel Island After 1910, many Asian immigrants were processed on Angel Island in San Francisco Bay. Because Americans wanted to discourage Asian immigration, new arrivals often faced long delays. Many Asian immigrants scratched their feelings in poetry on the wall.

> Lin, upon arriving in America,
>
> Was arrested, put in a wooden building,
>
> And made a prisoner.
>
> I was here for one autumn.
>
> The Americans did not allow me to land.
>
> I was ordered to be deported.
>
> —*Taoist from the Town of Iron*

Despite such obstacles, many Asians were able to make a home in the United States. Many, however, faced a difficult adjustment.

>> This 1911 photo shows Asian immigrants arriving at Angel Island in San Francisco Bay.

❓ **DESCRIBE** What was the voyage to the United States like for most immigrants?

The Immigrant Experience in America

Many immigrants had heard stories that the streets in the United States were paved with gold. Once they arrived, they had to adjust to reality. "First," reported one immigrant, "the streets were not paved with gold. Second, they were not paved at all. Third, they expected me to pave them."

Newcomers immediately set out to find work. European peasants living off the land had had little need for money, but it took cash to survive in the United States. Through friends, relatives, labor contractors, and employment agencies, the new arrivals found jobs.

Immigrants often stayed in the cities where they landed. Cities were the seat of industrial work. City slums soon became packed with poor immigrants. By 1900, one neighborhood in New York's Lower East Side had become the most crowded place in the world.

A New Wave of Immigration Immigration patterns changed in the late 1800s. Most earlier immigrants had been Protestants from northern and western Europe. Those from England and some from Ireland already spoke English. The early wave of English, Irish, Germans, and Scandinavians became known as "old immigrants." At first, Irish Catholics and other groups faced discrimination. In time, they were drawn into American life.

After 1885, millions of "new immigrants" arrived from Southern and Eastern Europe. They included Italians, Poles, Greeks, Russians, and Hungarians. On the West Coast, a smaller but growing number of Asian immigrants arrived, mostly from China and, later, from Japan. There were also a few immigrants from Korea, India, and the Philippines.

Few of these new immigrants spoke English. Many of the Europeans were Catholic, Jewish, or Eastern Orthodox. Immigrants from Asia might be Buddhist or Daoist. Set apart by language and religion, they found it harder to adapt to a new life.

Home Away from Home Immigrants eased into their new lives by settling in their own neighborhoods. Large American cities became patchworks of Italian,

Irish, Polish, Hungarian, Greek, German, Jewish, and Chinese neighborhoods. Within these neighborhoods, newcomers spoke their own language, celebrated special holidays, and prepared foods as in the old country. Italians joined clubs such as the Sons of Italy. Hungarians bought and read Hungarian newspapers.

Religion stood at the center of immigrant family life. Houses of worship both united and separated ethnic groups. Catholics from Italy worshipped in Italian neighborhood parishes. Those from Poland worshipped in Polish parishes. Jewish communities divided into Orthodox, Reform, and Conservative branches.

Bridging Cultures As newcomers struggled to adjust, they were often torn between old traditions and American ways. The first generation to arrive went through a process of acculturation. **Acculturation** is the process of holding on to older

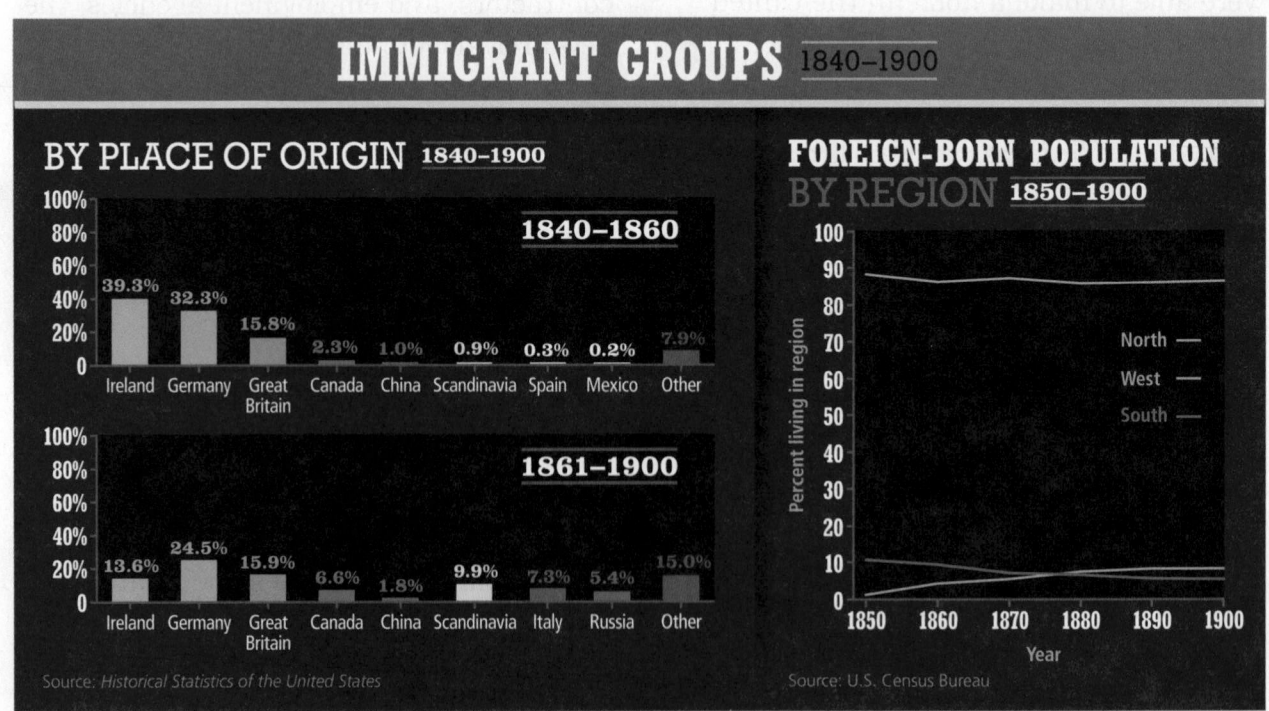

>> **Analyze Graphs** Compare the graphs showing the proportion of immigrants by place of origin. Summarize trends reflected in these graphs.

▶ **Interactive Chart**

traditions while adapting to a new culture. Immigrants learned how to use American institutions such as schools, factories, and the political system. At the same time, they tried to keep their traditional religions, family structures, and community life.

In their effort to adapt, immigrants blended old and new ways. For example, some newcomers mixed their native tongues with English. Italians called the Fourth of July "Il Forte Gelato," a phrase that actually means "the great freeze." In El Paso, Texas, Mexican immigrants developed *Chuco*, a blend of English and Spanish.

Children adapted to the new culture more quickly than their parents. They learned English in school and then helped their families to speak it. Because children wanted to be seen as Americans, they often gave up customs that their parents honored. They played American games and dressed in American-style clothes.

CHECK UNDERSTANDING What was one main difference between "old" and "new" immigrants?

Nativist Opposition

Even before the Civil War, Americans known as **nativists** sought to limit immigration and preserve the country for native-born, white Protestants. As immigration boomed in the late 1800s, nativist feelings reached a new peak.

Nativists argued that immigrants would not fit into American culture because their languages, religions, and customs were too different. Many workers resented the new immigrants because they took jobs for low pay. Others feared them because they were different. One magazine described all immigrants as "long-haired, wild-eyed, bad-smelling, atheistic, reckless foreign

>> This photo taken in the late 1800s shows Chinese laborers working on the Northwest Pacific Railway. Although they faced discrimination, Chinese immigrants helped build many railroads in the West.

▶ **Interactive Chart**

wretches, who never did an honest hour's work in their lives."

Wherever new immigrants settled, nativist pressure grew. Nativists targeted Jews and Italians in the Northeast and Mexicans in the Southwest. On the West Coast, nativists worked to end immigration from China.

Chinese Exclusion Since the California Gold Rush, Chinese immigrants had helped build the West. Most lived in cities in tight-knit communities called "Chinatowns." Others farmed for a living.

Most Americans did not understand Chinese customs. Also, some Chinese did not try to learn American ways. Like many other immigrants, they planned to stay only until they made a lot of money. They hoped to then return home to live out their lives as rich and respected members of

>> Grover Cleveland became the first of several U.S. Presidents to veto bills that banned illiterate immigrants from entering the United States.

from immigrating to the United States. Congress renewed the original 10-year ban several times. It was finally repealed in 1943.

Congress Limits Immigration In 1887, nativists formed the American Protective Association. The group campaigned for laws to restrict immigration. Congress responded by passing a bill that denied entry to people who could not read their own language.

President Grover Cleveland vetoed the bill. It was wrong, he said, to keep out peasants just because they had never gone to school. Three later Presidents vetoed similar bills. However, in 1917, Congress overrode President Woodrow Wilson's veto, and the bill became law.

? IDENTIFY CENTRAL IDEAS What was the main agenda of the nativists?

Chinese society. When that dream failed, many Chinese settled in the United States permanently.

As the numbers of Chinese grew, so did the prejudice and violence against them. Gangs attacked and sometimes killed Chinese people, especially during hard times. Congress responded to this anti-Chinese feeling by passing the **Chinese Exclusion Act** in 1882. It barred Chinese laborers from entering the country. In addition, no Chinese person who left the United States could return.

The Chinese Exclusion Act was the first law to exclude a specific national group

ASSESSMENT

1. **Draw Conclusions** Explain how many immigrants' experiences contrasted with their expectations about living in the United States.

2. **Identify Patterns** Explain how immigration patterns changed during the late 1800s.

3. **Generate Explanations** Describe the process of acculturation, and explain how immigrants adapted their own traditions to American culture.

4. **Determine Point of View** Summarize the beliefs of American nativists.

5. **Describe** the significance of the Chinese Exclusion Act.

Urbanization

>> Wealthy Americans used their wealth to build magnificent mansions that stood in stark contrast to the nearby slums. **Infer** How did these buildings reflect the status of their owners?

[Interactive Flipped Video]

"We cannot all live in cities," declared newspaper publisher Horace Greeley, "yet nearly all seem determined to do so." **Urbanization**, the movement of population from farms to urban areas, or cities, began slowly in the early 1800s. As the nation industrialized, the pace quickened. In 1860, only one American in five lived in an urban area. By 1890, one in three did.

>> **Objectives**

Explain why cities grew rapidly in the late 1800s.

Describe the relationship between social class and cities' geographies.

Describe the causes and effects of the settlement house and other urban reform movements.

>> **Key Terms**

urbanization
tenement
building code
Social Gospel
Salvation Army
Young Men's
   Hebrew
   Association
settlement house
Hull House
Young Men's
   Christian
   Association
Young Women's
   Christian
   Association
Jane Addams

PEARSON realize™   www.PearsonRealize.com
Access your Digital Lesson.

Cities Expand Rapidly

Jobs drew people to cities. As industries grew, so did the need for workers. New city dwellers took jobs in steel mills, meatpacking plants, and garment factories. Others worked as salesclerks, waiters, barbers, bank tellers, and secretaries.

Immigration and Domestic Migration

The flood of immigrants swelled city populations. So, too, did migrations from farm to city within the country. As the frontier closed, fewer pioneers went west to homestead. In fact, many Americans left farms and migrated to cities to find a better life. One young woman summed up the feelings of many farmers toward their backbreaking work.

> If I were offered a deed to the best farm . . . on the condition of going back to the country to live, I would not take it. I would rather face starvation in town.
>
> —quoted in *The Good Old Days—They Were Terrible!* (Bettmann)

African American Migration

African Americans, too, sought a better life in the cities. Most lived in the rural South. When hard times hit or prejudice led to violence, some headed to northern cities. By the 1890s, the south side of Chicago had a thriving African American community. Detroit, New York, Philadelphia, and other northern cities also had growing African American neighborhoods. The migration to the north began gradually, but increased rapidly after 1915.

As with overseas immigration, black migration usually began with one family member moving north. Later, relatives and friends followed. Like immigrants from rural areas in Europe, many African

THE GROWTH OF CITIES 1850–1920

POPULATION GROWTH IN 5 SELECT CITIES 1870–1920

- New York*
- St. Louis
- Chicago
- New Orleans
- San Francisco

* City limits expanded in 1900 and 1920 to include Manhattan, Brooklyn, Bronx, Queens, and Richmond.

Source: U.S. Census Bureau

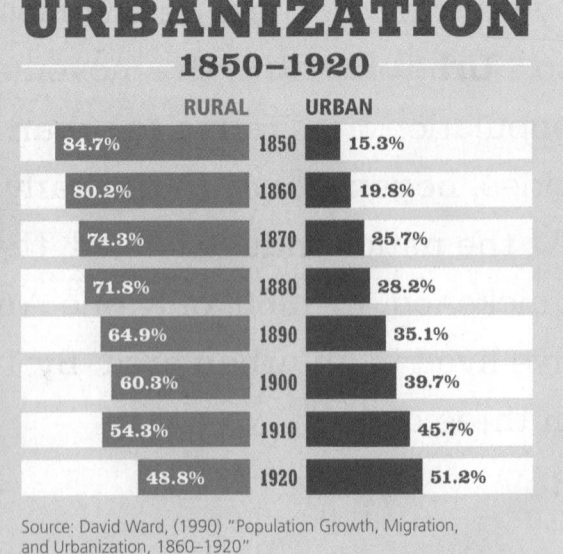

URBANIZATION 1850–1920

RURAL		URBAN
84.7%	1850	15.3%
80.2%	1860	19.8%
74.3%	1870	25.7%
71.8%	1880	28.2%
64.9%	1890	35.1%
60.3%	1900	39.7%
54.3%	1910	45.7%
48.8%	1920	51.2%

Source: David Ward, (1990) "Population Growth, Migration, and Urbanization, 1860–1920"

>> **Analyze Graphs** Explain how the percentage of Americans living in urban areas—or cities—and rural areas—or the countryside changed in the late 1800s and early 1900s.

▶ Interactive Chart

Americans faced the challenge of adjusting to urban life.

? RECALL What caused the rapid urbanization of the late 1800s?

City Neighborhoods Defined by Status

Cities grew outward from their old downtown sections. Before long, many cities took on a similar shape.

The Poor Poor families often clustered near the city's center, the oldest section. They struggled to survive in crowded slums. The streets were jammed with people, horses, pushcarts, and garbage.

Because space was so limited, builders devised a new kind of house to hold more people. They put up buildings six or seven stories high. They divided the buildings into small apartments, called **tenements**. Many tenements had no windows, heat, or indoor bathrooms. Often, 10 people shared a single room.

Crowding increased as businesses built factories near the city centers to take advantage of good rail connections and cheap labor. They forced more and more people into fewer and fewer apartments.

Typhoid and cholera raged through the tenements. Tuberculosis, a lung disease, was the biggest killer, accounting for thousands of deaths each year. Babies, especially, fell victim to disease. In one Chicago slum, around 1900, more than half of all babies died before they were one year old. Despite the poor conditions, the populations of slums grew rapidly.

The Middle Class Beyond the slums stood the homes of the new middle class, including doctors, lawyers, business

>> In big-city slums, lower-class families lived in cramped quarters with few conveniences. They also faced frequent outbreaks of disease.

managers, technicians, and office workers. Rows of neat, spacious houses lined tree-shaded streets. Here, disease broke out less frequently than in the slums.

Leisure activities gave middle-class people a sense of community and purpose. They joined clubs, singing societies, bowling leagues, and charitable organizations. As one writer said, the clubs "bring together many people who are striving upward, trying to uplift themselves."

The Wealthy Beyond the slums lay the mansions of the very rich protected by iron gates or brick walls. In New York, huge homes dotted upper Fifth Avenue, which was then on the outskirts of the city. In Chicago, 200 millionaires lived along the exclusive lakefront by the 1880s. In San Francisco, wealthy residents built their mansions nearer the center of the city in the exclusive Nob Hill area.

Rich Americans modeled their lives on those of European royalty. They filled their mansions with priceless artwork and gave lavish parties. At one banquet, the host handed out cigarettes rolled in hundred-dollar bills.

? DESCRIBE What was life like for the urban poor?

Effects of Rapid Urbanization

As more and more people crowded into cities, problems grew. Garbage rotted in the streets. Factories polluted the air. Crime flourished. Thieves and pickpockets haunted lonely alleys, especially at night.

Tenement buildings were deathtraps if a fire broke out. News reporter Jacob Riis

brought readers into the tenements in his startling exposé, *How the Other Half Lives.*

> Step carefully over this baby—it is a baby, spite of its rags and dirt—under these iron bridges called fire-escapes, but loaded down . . . with broken household goods, with washtubs and barrels, over which no man could climb from a fire.
>
> —Jacob Riis, *How the Other Half Lives*

Government Intervention By the 1880s, reformers pressured city governments for change. **Building codes** set standards for construction and safety. New buildings were required to have fire escapes and decent plumbing. Cities also hired workers to collect garbage and sweep the streets.

To reduce pollution, zoning laws kept factories out of neighborhoods where people lived. Safety improved when cities set up professional fire companies and police forces. Gas—and later electric—lights made streets less dangerous at night. As you will read, many cities built new systems of public transportation as well.

Pushed by reformers, city governments hired engineers and architects to design new water systems. New York City, for example, dug underground tunnels to the Catskill Mountains, 100 miles to the north. The tunnels brought a clean water supply to the city every day.

Religious Intervention Religious groups worked to ease the problems of the poor. The Catholic Church ministered to the needs of Irish, Polish, and Italian immigrants. An Italian-born nun, Mother Cabrini, helped found dozens of hospitals for the poor.

In cities, Protestant ministers began preaching a new **Social Gospel**. They

>> Rapid population growth in large cities such as New York brought with it many problems, such as streets filled with garbage.

▶ **Interactive Gallery**

called on their well-to-do members to do their duty as Christians by helping society's poor. One minister urged merchants and industrialists to pay their workers enough to enable them to marry and have families. He also proposed that they grant their workers a half day off on Saturdays in addition to their day off on Sunday.

In 1865, a Methodist minister named William Booth created the **Salvation Army** in London. It expanded to the United States by 1880. In addition to spreading Christian teachings, the Salvation Army offered food and shelter to the poor.

In Jewish neighborhoods, too, religious organizations provided community services. The first **Young Men's Hebrew Association** (YMHA) began in Baltimore in 1854. The YMHA provided social activities, encouraged good citizenship, and helped Jewish families preserve their culture. In the 1880s, the Young Women's Hebrew Association (YWHA) grew out of the YMHA.

Like the Salvation Army, the **Young Men's Christian Association** (YMCA) had its start in London and expanded to the United States later. In 1851 at the Old South Church in Boston, missionary Thomas Valentine established the first YMCA. By the 1860s, the YMCA became more than a meeting place and began offering to young men affordable rooms for rent, recreation activities, and gymnasiums.

At the time, the YMCA was exclusively for men. So, women formed their own association to meet the needs of female residents and factory workers. The first Ladies' Christian Association was formed in 1858 in New York City. In 1860, the association opened its first boarding house there. By 1866, the name had changed to the **Young Women's Christian**

>> Hull House in Chicago offered many activities to help immigrants feel more at home in their new surroundings. Here, an immigrant group sings in a Hull House choir.

▶ **Interactive 3-D Model**

Association (YWCA). It continued to provide assistance to young women in the form of low-cost housing, employment bureaus, and medical services.

? **IDENTIFY** What did the government do to improve the lives of city dwellers?

The Settlement House Movement

Some people looked for ways to help the poor. By the late 1800s, individuals began to organize **settlement houses**, community centers that offered services to the poor. The leading figure of the settlement house movement was a Chicago woman named **Jane Addams**.

A Social Leader Emerges Jane Addams came from a well-to-do family but had strong convictions about helping the poor.

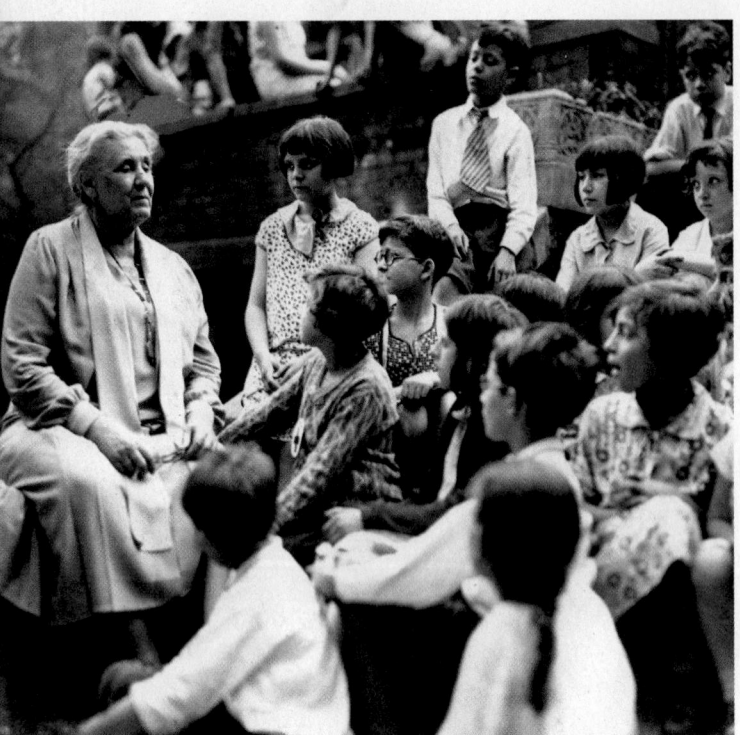
>> Hull House founder Jane Addams speaks to a group of children in 1935. Addams won the Nobel Peace Prize in 1931 for her efforts.

After college, she moved into one of the poorest slums in Chicago. There, in an old mansion, she opened a settlement house named **Hull House** in 1889.

Other idealistic young women soon joined Addams. They took up residence in Hull House so that they could experience firsthand some of the hardships of the slum community in which they worked. These women dedicated their lives to service and to sacrifice—"like the early Christians," in the words of one volunteer.

Hull House volunteers offered a wide variety of services. To help immigrants acculturate, they taught classes in American government and the English language. Other volunteers gave instruction in health care or operated day nurseries for children whose mothers worked outside the home. In addition, Hull House provided recreational activities for young people, such as sports, a choral group, and a theater.

The settlement house movement spread quickly. By 1900, about 100 such centers had opened in American cities.

Promoting Reform Addams and her staff helped bring about reform legislation. They studied the slum neighborhoods where they worked. They realized that the problems were too big for any one person or group, and they urged the government to act.

Alice Hamilton, a Hull House doctor, campaigned for better health laws. Florence Kelley worked to ban child labor. Jane Addams herself believed that reform legislation would be speeded if women were allowed to vote. She joined the continuing campaign for women's suffrage.

? DEFINE What was a settlement house?

ASSESSMENT

1. **Identify Central Issues** Describe the major factors that contributed to urbanization during the 1800s.

2. **Identify Cause and Effect** Explain how factories intensified problems for people in lower-class neighborhoods.

3. **Describe** the religious organizations that sought to improve urban communities during the 1800s.

4. **Generate Explanations** Describe Jane Addams' beliefs and explain how she contributed to reform movements.

5. **Summarize** the services that Hull House offered.

The Rise of Progressivism

>> In the early 1900s, Governor Robert La Follette of Wisconsin promoted a number of Progressive reforms known as the Wisconsin Idea.

▶ **Interactive Flipped Video**

The **Gilded Age** of the late 1800s got its name from an 1873 novel by Mark Twain and Charles Dudley Warner titled *The Gilded Age*. *Gilded* means coated with a thin layer of gold paint. It implies falseness beneath surface glitter. For many Americans, the novel, which poked fun at the era's greed and political corruption, captured the spirit of the time. In the words of one observer, it was government "of, by, and for the rich."

>> **Objectives**

Describe politics during the Gilded Age and efforts at political reform.

Identify efforts to regulate big business.

Explain how the muckrakers inspired reform.

Identify the Progressives and explain their reforms.

>> **Key Terms**

Gilded Age
patronage
merit
Civil Service
  Commission
civil service
interstate commerce
Interstate
  Commerce
  Commission
Sherman Antitrust
  Act
political boss
muckraker
Progressive
public interest
primary

initiative
referendum
recall
graduated income
  tax
William Tweed
Chester A. Arthur
Wisconsin Idea

Gilded Age Politics

The Gilded Age lasted from the 1870s through the 1890s. During this time, reformers struggled to clean up political corruption. Political power in the Gilded Age was split between the two major parties. Usually, the North and West voted Republican, and the South voted Democratic. Neither party controlled Congress for more than a term or two, although Republicans held the White House for nearly 25 years. However, Presidents generally had less power than Congress during the period.

For Americans of the Gilded Age, elections provided great entertainment. Campaigns featured brass bands, torchlight parades, picnics, and long speeches. Americans marched, ate, drank, and listened. The turnout of voters was never again as high—almost 80 percent of eligible voters.

Two concerns shaped politics. Many Americans worried about the power of the rich. They feared that bankers, industrialists, and other wealthy men were controlling politics at the expense of the public good. The other worry was corruption, especially bribery and voter fraud. Reformers blamed much of the problem on the spoils system, the practice of rewarding political supporters with government jobs.

How did city governments become so corrupt? As cities grew, they needed to expand services such as sewers, garbage collection, and roads. Often, politicians accepted money to give away these jobs. As a result, bribes and corruption became a way of life.

Corruption at the Top Powerful politicians called **political bosses** gained power in many cities. Political bosses also ruled county and state governments. Bosses controlled work done locally and demanded payoffs from businesses. City bosses were popular with the poor, especially with immigrants. They provided jobs and made loans to the needy. They handed out extra coal for heating in winter and turkeys at Thanksgiving. In exchange, the poor voted for the boss or his chosen candidate.

Boss Tweed In New York City, **Boss William Tweed** carried corruption to new extremes. During the 1860s and 1870s, he cheated the city out of more than $100 million. Journalists exposed Boss Tweed's wrongdoing. For example, cartoonist Thomas Nast pictured Tweed as a vulture feeding on the city. Nast's cartoons especially angered Tweed. His supporters might not be able to read, he said, but they could understand Nast's cartoons.

>> This cartoon by the artist Thomas Nast appeared in *Harper's Weekly* in the late 1800s. **Interpret Cartoons** How does this cartoon portray the rich?

Faced with prison, Tweed fled to Spain. There, local police arrested him when they recognized him from Nast's cartoons. When Tweed died in jail in 1878, thousands of poor New Yorkers mourned for him.

❓ CHECK UNDERSTANDING Why were political bosses popular with the poor?

Federal and Local Reform Efforts

The spoils system had grown since the days of Andrew Jackson. When a new President took office, job seekers swarmed into Washington. They demanded government jobs as rewards for their political support. Giving jobs to followers is called **patronage**.

Patronage often led to corruption. Some jobholders simply stole public money. Others had no skills for the jobs they were given. In New York, for example, one man was made court reporter even though he could neither read nor write.

Initial Reforms Calls for reform slowly brought change. In 1877, President Rutherford B. Hayes took steps toward ending the spoils system. He ordered an investigation of the New York customhouse. There, investigators found hundreds of appointed officials receiving high salaries but doing no work. Despite the protests of local Republican leaders, Hayes dismissed two customhouse officials.

In 1881, James Garfield entered the White House and was soon swamped with office seekers. He thought that government jobs should be awarded on the basis of **merit**, or ability, not politics.

That July, however, a disappointed office seeker, Charles Guiteau (gee TOH), shot the President. Garfield died two months later.

>> His rejection of the spoils system led to President James Garfield's assassination in 1881 at the age of 49.

The assassination sparked new efforts to end the spoils system.

Reform of Federal Jobs Vice President **Chester A. Arthur** succeeded Garfield. Arthur was a product of the spoils system. In fact, he was one of the New York customhouse officials dismissed by Hayes a few years earlier! Yet, as President, Arthur worked with Congress to reform the spoils system.

In 1883, Congress passed the Pendleton Act. It created the **Civil Service Commission** to conduct exams for federal jobs. The **civil service** includes all federal jobs except elected offices and the military. The aim of the Civil Service Commission was to fill jobs on the basis of merit. People who scored highest on the civil service exams earned the posts.

At first, the Civil Service Commission controlled only a few federal jobs. However, under pressure from reformers, later Presidents placed more jobs under the Civil Service Commission. By 1900, the commission controlled about 40 percent of all federal jobs.

Cities Encourage Honest Government

In many cities, reformers set up good-government leagues. Their goal was to replace corrupt officials with honest leaders. The leagues had some successes. In Minneapolis, a corrupt mayor was indicted. Cleveland reformers helped elect Tom Johnson mayor. Johnson gave out contracts honestly, improved garbage and sewerage systems, and set up services for the poor.

? **DESCRIBE** the role of the Civil Service Commission in political reform.

>> This bridge across a valley in California was built by the Central Pacific Railroad in 1877. That same year, Collis Huntington, the railroad's owner, tried to bribe Congress.

The Power of Big Business

In 1877, Collis Huntington, builder of the Central Pacific Railroad, tried to bribe members of Congress to kill a railroad bill that would be unfavorable to his interests. He gave large amounts of money to members of Congress. "It costs money to fix things," Huntington explained.

Government Regulation of Business

The behavior of men like Huntington convinced many Americans that big businesses controlled the government. They demanded that something be done to limit the power of big business.

In response, the government began to regulate railroads and other large businesses. Under the Constitution, the federal government had the power to regulate **interstate commerce**, or business that crossed state lines. In 1887, President Grover Cleveland signed the Interstate Commerce Act. It forbade practices such as pools and rebates. It also set up the **Interstate Commerce Commission** (ICC) to oversee the railroads.

At first, the ICC was weak. In court challenges, most judges ruled in favor of the railroads. Still, Congress had shown that it was ready to regulate big business. Later, Congress passed laws that made the ICC more effective.

Promoting Competition

In 1888, President Cleveland lost his bid for reelection. Benjamin Harrison became President. In 1890, Harrison signed the **Sherman Antitrust Act**. The act prohibited businesses from trying to limit or destroy competition.

The Sherman Antitrust Act sounded strong, but enforcing it proved difficult. At first, judges ruled in favor of trusts. They held that the law was an illegal attempt by the government to control private property.

Instead of regulating trusts, the Sherman Antitrust Act was often used against labor unions. The courts said union strikes blocked free trade and thus threatened competition. Later on, as the reform spirit spread, the courts began to use the Antitrust Act against monopolies.

❓ CHECK UNDERSTANDING How did the courts use the Sherman Antitrust Act to help big business?

The Muckrakers

Reformers used the press to turn public opinion against corruption. Newspaper reporters described how corruption led to inadequate fire and police protection and poor sanitation services. Jacob Riis (reess), a photographer and writer, provided shocking images of slum life.

Crusading journalists like Riis became known as **muckrakers**. People said they raked the dirt, or muck, and exposed it to public view. One muckraker, Ida Tarbell, targeted the unfair practices of big business. Her articles about the Standard Oil Company led to demands for more controls on trusts.

In 1906, Upton Sinclair's novel *The Jungle* shocked the nation. Although the book was fiction, it was based on facts. It revealed grisly details about the meatpacking industry, including descriptions of the horrid working conditions and the unsanitary practices in the plants. Sinclair told how the packers used meat from sick animals. He described how rats often got ground up in the meat, which was then dyed to make it seem healthy. He explained just how little thought was given to the health of the consumer.

>> Upton Sinclair's book *The Jungle* exposed conditions in the meatpacking industry in the early 1900s. The book caused an uproar that led to federal regulation of the industry.

▶ Interactive Timeline

There was never the least attention paid to what was cut up for sausage; there would come all the way back from Europe old sausage that had been rejected, and that was moldy and white—it would be dosed with borax and glycerin, and . . . made over again for home consumption.

—Upton Sinclair, *The Jungle*, 1906

Sinclair claimed that his purpose in writing *The Jungle* was to alert the public to the unfit working conditions of meatpackers. However, the public outrage focused on the contaminated food they were unknowingly being fed. Soon after the novel's publication, the federal government passed the Pure Food and Drug and Meat Inspection Act. Sinclair's writing did impact reform.

As magazines became affordable, muckrakers began publishing in them to reach a wider middle-class audience. *McClure's Magazine* was a popular forum for crusading journalists. Lincoln Steffens, who published with *McClure's Magazine*, eventually gathered his articles in a book about the political corruption that plagued cities across the nation.

> The [political bosses] control the whole process of voting, and practice fraud at every stage. The assessor's list is the voting list, and the assessor is the [boss's] man. . . . The assessor pads the list with the names of dead dogs, children, and non-existent persons.
>
> —Lincoln Steffens, *The Shame of the Cities*, 1904

Muckrakers helped change public opinion. For years, middle-class Americans had ignored the need for reform. When they saw how dishonest politicians and businesses corrupted the nation—and even the food they ate—they, too, demanded change.

? DEFINE What is a muckraker?

Progressive Reforms

By 1900, reformers were calling themselves **Progressives**. By that, they meant that they were forward-thinking people who wanted to improve American life. Progressives won many changes during the period from 1898 to 1917. As a result, this period is called the Progressive Era.

Progressives were never a single group with a single goal. Instead, they came from many backgrounds and backed different causes. They were united by a belief that the ills of society could be solved. Progressives wanted the government to act in the **public interest**, for the good of the people.

Both religion and science inspired Progressives. The Social Gospel movement of the late 1800s stressed the duty of Christians to improve society. At the same time, Progressives used scientific studies and statistics to find ways to solve society's problems.

Progressives valued education. John Dewey, a Progressive educator, wanted schools to promote reform. Schools must teach democratic values by example, he argued. He therefore urged students to ask questions and to work together to solve problems.

The Wisconsin Idea Among the leading Progressives was Robert La Follette of Wisconsin. "The will of the people shall be the law of the land," was his motto.

>> Lillian Wald was a leading Progressive. She was a nurse who established a settlement house to assist struggling immigrant families.

Progressive Political Reforms

Voters select their party's candidates	→ reducing the possibility of bribery or fraud
Voters can propose bills to the legislature	→ through petitions, requiring political bodies to deal with voter concerns
Voters can vote on bills directly	→ giving them the power to accept or reject laws that affect them
Voters can remove elected officials from office	→ thus making officials directly responsible to the people

SOURCE: Oakland Museum of California

>> In many states, Progressive reforms shifted political power to voters. **Draw Conclusions** What responsibilities does a citizen have when voting on a referendum?

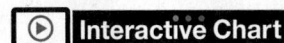

His fighting spirit won him the nickname "Battling Bob."

As governor of Wisconsin, La Follette introduced various Progressive reforms that became known as the **Wisconsin Idea**. For example, he lowered railroad rates. The result was increased rail traffic, which helped both railroad owners and customers.

Empowering Voters Progressives like La Follette wanted voters to participate more directly in government. Since Andrew Jackson's time, party leaders had picked candidates for local and state offices. Progressives called, instead, for primaries. In a **primary**, voters choose their party's candidate for the general election. In 1903, Wisconsin was the first state to adopt a primary run by state government officials. By 1917, all but four states had done so.

Other reforms gave voters more power. They included the **initiative**, which gave voters the right to put a bill before a state legislature. A certain number of qualified voters must sign initiative petitions to propose a law. The **referendum** allowed voters to put a bill on the ballot and vote it into law. The **recall** allowed voters to remove an elected official from office. That reform let voters get rid of corrupt officials.

Progressives from other states visited Wisconsin to study La Follette's reforms. A number of states elected Progressive governors eager for reforms.

Amending the Constitution Progressives fought for other changes, too. They favored lowering tariffs on imported goods. If American industry had to compete against foreign imports, they argued, consumers would benefit from lower prices.

Some reforms led to changes in the U.S. Constitution. Many reformers backed a **graduated income tax**, which taxes people at different rates. The wealthy pay taxes at a higher rate than the poor or the middle class.

>> **Interpret Cartoons** How is the Standard Oil Company depicted in this cartoon from 1904? What does the cartoon mean?

Because the Supreme Court had held that a federal income tax was unconstitutional, Progressives campaigned for a Sixteenth Amendment. It gave Congress the power to pass an income tax. By 1913, the states had ratified the amendment.

The states approved another amendment in 1913. Since 1789, state legislatures had elected senators. Powerful interest groups had sometimes bribed lawmakers to vote for certain candidates. Progressives wanted to end such abuses by having voters elect senators directly. In 1912, Congress approved the Seventeenth Amendment, which allowed for the direct election of senators. It was ratified a year later.

? IDENTIFY CENTRAL IDEAS What belief united the Progressive movement?

ASSESSMENT

1. **Identify Steps in a Process** Explain how city governments became corrupt over time.

2. **Describe** the relationship that often existed between political bosses and the poor.

3. **Generate Explanations** Describe the government's first attempts to limit the power of big businesses, and explain how they were ineffective at first.

4. **Identify Cause and Effect** Explain how muckrakers influenced public opinion.

5. **Draw Conclusions** Describe the significance of the Wisconsin Idea.

The Progressive Presidents

>> President Roosevelt spoke forcefully in favor of Progressive reforms during his presidency (1901–1909).

▶ Interactive Flipped Video

Theodore Roosevelt—also known as Teddy Roosevelt or "TR"—came from a wealthy New York family. As a child, he suffered from asthma and was often sick. To build his strength, he lifted weights, ran, and boxed.

>> Objectives

Identify Theodore Roosevelt's reform goals, including the Square Deal.

Compare and contrast William Howard Taft's policies with Theodore Roosevelt's.

Describe reforms under Woodrow Wilson.

>> Key Terms

trustbuster
Square Deal
Pure Food and Drug
   Act
conservation
national park
Bull Moose party
New Freedom
Federal Reserve Act
Federal Trade
   Commission
Theodore Roosevelt
William Howard Taft
Woodrow Wilson

Theodore Roosevelt's Path to the White House

A Life of Public Service Roosevelt could have enjoyed a life of ease. Instead, he decided to enter politics. He was determined to end corruption and work for the public interest.

Roosevelt's friends mocked his decision to devote his life to public service. They told him "that the men I met would be rough and brutal and unpleasant to deal with," he later recalled. He replied that he would not quit until he "found out whether I was really too weak to hold my own in the rough and tumble."

By age 26, Roosevelt was serving in the New York state legislature. Then, tragedy struck. In 1884, his mother and his young wife died on the same day. Overcome by grief, Roosevelt quit the legislature. He went west to work on a cattle ranch.

After two years, Roosevelt returned to the East and to politics. He served on the Civil Service Commission. He then headed New York City's police department and later became assistant secretary of the navy.

In 1898, the United States went to war against Spain. Roosevelt led a unit of troops in some daring exploits. He returned home to a hero's welcome and was elected governor of New York.

A Progressive Leader Since his days in the legislature, Roosevelt had pushed for reform. As governor, he continued to work for Progressive reforms. Other lawmakers called him a "goo goo," a mocking name for someone who wanted good government.

New York Republican bosses were relieved when Roosevelt resigned from the office of governor to become Vice President. Then, after President McKinley was shot in September 1901, Roosevelt became President. He was committed, he later wrote, to "making an old party Progressive."

> ❓ **TRACE** the major events in Theodore Roosevelt's life leading up to his presidency.

Encouraging Fair Business Practices

Roosevelt promised to continue McKinley's pro-business policies. He was not against big business. In fact, he believed business was a positive force and that giant corporations were here to stay.

Roosevelt saw a difference, however, between good trusts and bad trusts. Good trusts, he said, were efficient and fair and should be let alone. Bad ones took advantage of workers and cheated the

>> This photo shows state representative Theodore Roosevelt in 1884. Roosevelt would go on to become President of the United States and dedicate himself to furthering the public interest.

public. The government must either control them or break them up.

Regulating Trusts Roosevelt wanted to test the power of the government to break up bad trusts. In 1902, he asked the Attorney General, the government's chief lawyer, to bring a lawsuit against the Northern Securities Company. Northern Securities was a trust that had been formed to control competition among railroads. Roosevelt argued that the company used unfair business practices in violation of the Sherman Antitrust Act.

At news of the lawsuit, stock prices fell on Wall Street, New York's center of business and finance. "Wall Street is paralyzed at the thought that a President of the United States would sink so low as to try to enforce the law," one newspaper joked. While business leaders worried, many ordinary Americans cheered the President.

In 1904, the Supreme Court ruled that Northern Securities had violated the Sherman Antitrust Act. It ordered the trust to be broken up. The decision was a victory for Progressives. For the first time, the Sherman Antitrust Act had been used to break up trusts, not unions.

Next, Roosevelt had the Attorney General file suit against other trusts, including Standard Oil and the American Tobacco Company. In time, the courts ordered the breakup of both trusts because they blocked free trade.

Some business leaders called Roosevelt a **trustbuster**, a person who wanted to destroy all trusts. "Certainly not," replied Roosevelt, only those that "have done something we regard as wrong." He preferred to control or regulate trusts, not "bust" them.

>> A view of Wall Street in the early 1900s. The Wall Street district in New York City was the center of the U.S. financial sector.

A Pro-Labor President Roosevelt also clashed with mine owners. In 1902, Pennsylvania coal miners went on strike for better pay and a shorter workday. Mine owners refused to negotiate with the miners' union.

As winter approached, schools and hospitals ran out of coal. Furious at the mine owners, Roosevelt threatened to send in troops to run the mines. Finally, owners sat down with the union and reached an agreement. Roosevelt was the first President to side with labor.

? CHECK UNDERSTANDING How did Roosevelt feel about big business?

The Square Deal

Roosevelt ran for President in his own right in 1904. During the campaign, he promised Americans a **Square Deal**. By this, he meant that everyone from farmers and consumers to workers and owners should have the same opportunity to succeed. That promise helped Roosevelt win a huge victory.

Railroads were a main target of the Square Deal. The Interstate Commerce Act of 1887 had done little to end rebates and other abuses. Roosevelt therefore urged Congress to outlaw rebates. In 1906, Congress gave the ICC the power to set railroad rates.

Pushing for Regulations
Roosevelt wanted reforms to protect consumers. He had been shocked by Upton Sinclair's novel *The Jungle*. In response, he sent more government inspectors to meatpacking houses. The owners refused to let them in.

Roosevelt then gave the newspapers copies of a government report that exposed conditions in meatpacking plants. The public was outraged. This forced Congress to pass a law in 1906 allowing more inspectors to enter meatpacking houses.

Muckrakers had exposed drug companies for making false claims about medicines. They also showed how food companies added harmful chemicals to canned foods. In 1906, Congress passed the **Pure Food and Drug Act**, which required food and drug makers to list ingredients on packages. It also tried to end false advertising and the use of impure ingredients.

Resource Conservation
Roosevelt also took action to protect the nation's wilderness areas. To fuel industrial growth, lumber companies were cutting down whole forests. Miners were taking iron and coal from the earth at a frantic pace and leaving gaping holes.

Roosevelt loved the outdoors and worried about the destruction of the wilderness. He pressed for **conservation**, the protection of

>> A locomotive hauls timber in 1904. President Roosevelt fought for nature conservation at a time when forests were being cut down for construction and industry.

 Interactive Gallery

natural resources. "The rights of the public to natural resources outweigh private rights," he said.

Roosevelt wanted some forest areas left as wilderness. Others could supply needed resources. He wanted lumber companies to plant new trees in the forests they were clearing. Mining, too, should be controlled. In 1905, with the support of Congress, Roosevelt created the National Forest Service.

Under Roosevelt, the government also set aside about 194,000 acres for national parks. A **national park** is an area set aside for people to visit. It is run by the federal government.

? DEFINE What was Roosevelt's Square Deal?

President Taft

Roosevelt did not want to run for reelection in 1908. Instead, he backed **William Howard Taft**, his Secretary of War. Taft won easily. A confident Roosevelt said,

> [Taft's] policies, principles, purposes, and ideals are the same as mine. The Roosevelt policies will not go out with Roosevelt.
>
> —Theodore Roosevelt in a letter to George Trevelyan, November 6, 1908

Roosevelt then left to hunt big game in Africa. He left behind an impressive record as a reformer. He also left the presidency more powerful than it had been at any time since the Civil War.

Taft's approach to the presidency was far different from Roosevelt's. Unlike the hard-driving, energetic Roosevelt, Taft was quiet and careful. Roosevelt loved power. Taft feared it.

>> These Pennsylvania miners and many others worked in dirty and often dangerous conditions. President Taft improved mining safety by establishing the U.S. Bureau of Mines in 1910.

Nevertheless, Taft supported many Progressive causes. He broke up even more trusts than Roosevelt had. He favored the graduated income tax, approved new safety rules for mines, and signed laws giving government workers an eight-hour day. Under Taft, the Commerce Department set up an office to deal with the problems of child labor.

Despite such successes, Taft lost Progressive support. In 1909, he signed a bill that raised most tariffs. Progressives opposed the new law, arguing that tariffs raised prices for consumers. Also, Taft fired a high-level Forest Service official during a dispute over the sale of wilderness lands in Alaska. Progressives then accused the President of blocking conservation efforts.

? LIST some of the Progressive reforms that Taft supported.

Wilson Wins the Presidency

When Roosevelt returned from Africa, he found Taft under attack by reformers. In 1912, Roosevelt decided to run against Taft for the Republican nomination. Although Roosevelt had much public support, Taft controlled the Republican party leadership. At its convention, the party nominated Taft.

A Republican Split Progressive Republicans stormed out of the convention. They set up a new Progressive Party and chose Roosevelt as their candidate. He accepted saying, "I feel as strong as a bull moose." Roosevelt's supporters became known as the **Bull Moose party**.

The Democratic Nominee Democrats chose **Woodrow Wilson**, a Progressive, as their candidate. As a boy, Wilson made up his mind always to fight for what he thought was right. Wilson served as president of Princeton University and as governor of New Jersey. He was known as a brilliant scholar and a cautious reformer.

Together, Taft and Roosevelt won more votes than Wilson. However, they split the Republican vote. Their quarrel helped Wilson win the election of 1912 by beating Taft and Roosevelt in many states.

President Wilson's Inauguration
Woodrow Wilson's inaugural address reflected his strong sense of good and evil.

> The nation has been deeply stirred, stirred by a solemn passion, stirred by the knowledge of wrong, of ideals lost, of government too often . . . made an instrument of evil. The feelings with which we face this new age of right and opportunity sweep across our heart-strings like some air out of God's own presence.
>
> —Woodrow Wilson, Inaugural Address, March 1913

★ **THE ELECTION** OF **1912** ★

THE **PRESIDENTIAL CANDIDATES**

Sources: History.com; *The Public Purpose, Vol. III*

90 minutes
Length of time Teddy Roosevelt spoke after being shot during his campaign

46
Ballots necessary to select Woodrow Wilson as the Democratic candidate

"There are so many people in the country who don't like me."
—William Taft, statement made in a letter, 1912

THE **BATTLE** IN **KEY STATES**

NEW YORK 41.3% / 24.6% / 28.7% / 4.0%
ILLINOIS 35.3% / 33.7% / 22.1% / 7.1%
OHIO 41.0% / 22.2% / 26.9% / 8.7%
TEXAS 72.7% / 8.9% / 9.5% / 8.3%
CALIFORNIA 41.8% / 41.8% / 0.5% / 11.7%

Wilson / Roosevelt / Taft / Debs

DISTRIBUTION OF **VOTES**

% POPULAR VOTE — 42% / 27% / 23% / 8% Other

% ELECTORAL VOTE — 82% / 17% / 1%

WOODROW WILSON — Democratic Party
THEODORE ROOSEVELT — Bull Moose Party
WILLIAM TAFT — Republican Party

Sources: History.com; USElectionAtlas.org

Sources: USElectionAtlas.org

>> **Analyze Graphs** Based on the data showing the distribution of votes, was the 1912 election a close race or an easy victory? Explain your answer.

Wilson asked honest, forward-looking Americans to stand at his side. "I will not fail them," he said.

Increasing the Government's Role in the Economy At first, Wilson tried to break up trusts into smaller companies. By doing so, he hoped to increase competition in the American economy. "If America is not to have free enterprise, then she can have freedom of no sort whatever," he said. Wilson called his program the **New Freedom**.

To spur competition, Wilson asked Congress to lower tariffs on goods. A lower tariff would force U.S. producers to face foreign competition. After a struggle, Congress did lower tariffs. To make up for lost revenues, it then passed a graduated income tax.

To regulate banking, Congress passed the **Federal Reserve Act** in 1913. It set up the Federal Reserve System, an organization that controlled the supply of money to the U.S. financial system. The Federal Reserve also had the power to raise or lower interest rates.

Protecting Competition To ensure fair competition, President Wilson also persuaded Congress to create the **Federal Trade Commission** (FTC) in 1914. The FTC had the power to investigate companies and order them to stop using unfair practices to destroy competitors.

Wilson signed the Clayton Antitrust Act in 1914. He had wanted a much stronger law, but the new law did ban some business practices that limited free enterprise. In addition, it stopped antitrust laws from being used against unions, a major victory for labor.

Despite Wilson's successes, the Progressive movement slowed after 1914. By then, Progressives had achieved many

>> Under Wilson, Congress created the Federal Trade Commission (FTC) to promote competition. The FTC's present-day headquarters, in Washington, D.C., are shown here.

▶ **Interactive Chart**

of their goals. Also, the outbreak of war in Europe in 1914 drew Americans' attention. They worried that the war might soon affect them.

❓ **DEFINE** What was Wilson's New Freedom?

ASSESSMENT

1. **Draw Conclusions** Explain how experiences in Theodore Roosevelt's life contributed to his efforts as President.

2. **Summarize** President Roosevelt's position on trusts.

3. **Distinguish** between Roosevelt's expectations and the realities of Taft's presidency.

4. **Identify Cause and Effect** Describe the causes and effects of the split in the Republican Party.

5. **Generate Explanations** Explain how Woodrow Wilson's presidency affected the Progressive Movement.

Progress and Setbacks for Social Justice

>> Educator and reformer Booker T. Washington became the voice for many African Americans. He spoke out for racial equality in the early 1900s.

[▶] **Interactive Flipped Video**

>> Objectives

Describe women's efforts to win suffrage and improved opportunities.

Explain the campaign against alcohol.

Describe how African Americans confronted discrimination during the Progressive Era.

Identify the discrimination and hardships faced by Mexican Americans, Asian Americans, and American Indians during the Progressive Era.

>> Key Terms

National Woman
   Suffrage
   Association
suffragist
Nineteenth
   Amendment
Women's Christian
   Temperance
   Union
Eighteenth
   Amendment
lynch
NAACP
barrio

mutualista
"Gentlemen's
   Agreement"
Society of American
   Indians
prohibition
suffrage

The struggle of women for suffrage, or right to vote, went back many years. The Seneca Falls Convention in 1848 was the start of the organized women's rights movement. It called for many reforms, including women's suffrage.

The Path to Women's Suffrage

After the Civil War, Elizabeth Cady Stanton and Susan B. Anthony renewed calls for **suffrage**. They had opposed the Fifteenth Amendment because it gave the vote to African American men but not to women. In 1869, Stanton and Anthony set up the **National Woman Suffrage Association**, a group that worked for a constitutional amendment to give women the right to vote.

Beginnings in the West In most states, leading politicians opposed women's suffrage. Still, in the late 1800s, women won the right to vote in four western states: Wyoming, Utah, Colorado, and Idaho. Pioneer women had worked alongside men to build farms and cities. By giving women the vote, these states recognized the women's contributions.

When Wyoming applied for statehood in 1890, many members of Congress wanted it to change its law that gave women the vote. Wyoming lawmakers replied, "We may stay out of the Union for 100 years, but we will come in with our women." Wyoming barely won admission.

Women Gain Support In the early 1900s, the women's suffrage movement gained strength. More than 5 million women were earning wages outside the home. Although women were paid less than men, wages gave them some power. Many demanded a say in making the laws that affected them.

After Stanton and Anthony died, a new generation of leaders took up the cause.

Among the most outspoken was Carrie Chapman Catt. She had worked as a school principal and a reporter before she became a leader of the National Woman Suffrage Association.

Catt was a brilliant organizer. She created a detailed plan to fight for suffrage, state by state. Across the nation, **suffragists**, or people who worked for women's right to vote, followed her strategy.

Gradually, their efforts succeeded. One by one, states in the West and Midwest gave women the vote. Generally, women in these states could vote only in state elections. At the same time, more and more women were demanding a constitutional amendment to give them the right to vote in all elections.

? **DESCRIBE** What was Carrie Chapman Catt's main contribution to women's suffrage?

>> **Infer** What impact might this illustration of women voting in the early 1900s have had on people who saw it?

The Nineteenth Amendment

As the struggle dragged on, some suffragists, such as Alice Paul, took more radical steps to win the vote. Paul had marched with British suffragists in London. She had been jailed and gone on hunger strikes to help British women win the vote. When Paul returned home, she fought for suffrage for American women.

Taking the Fight to the Capital Soon after Wilson became President, he met with Paul and other suffragists. Wilson did not oppose women's suffrage, but he also did not back a constitutional amendment.

Paul told the President that suffragists wanted such an amendment. "And then," she recalled, "we sent him another delegation and another and another and another and another and another and another."

Early in 1917, Rose Winslow, Paul, and other women began to picket the White House. Within a few months, police started to arrest the silent protesters. Winslow and Paul were jailed for obstructing the sidewalk. A public outcry soon won their release. The women then resumed their picketing.

Women Win Suffrage By early 1918, the tide had finally turned in favor of suffrage. President Wilson agreed to support the suffrage amendment. In 1919, Congress passed the **Nineteenth Amendment**. It guaranteed women the right to vote. By August 1920, three fourths of the states had ratified the amendment, and it became part of the Constitution. The amendment doubled the number of eligible voters.

❓ CHECK UNDERSTANDING What was the purpose of the Nineteenth Amendment?

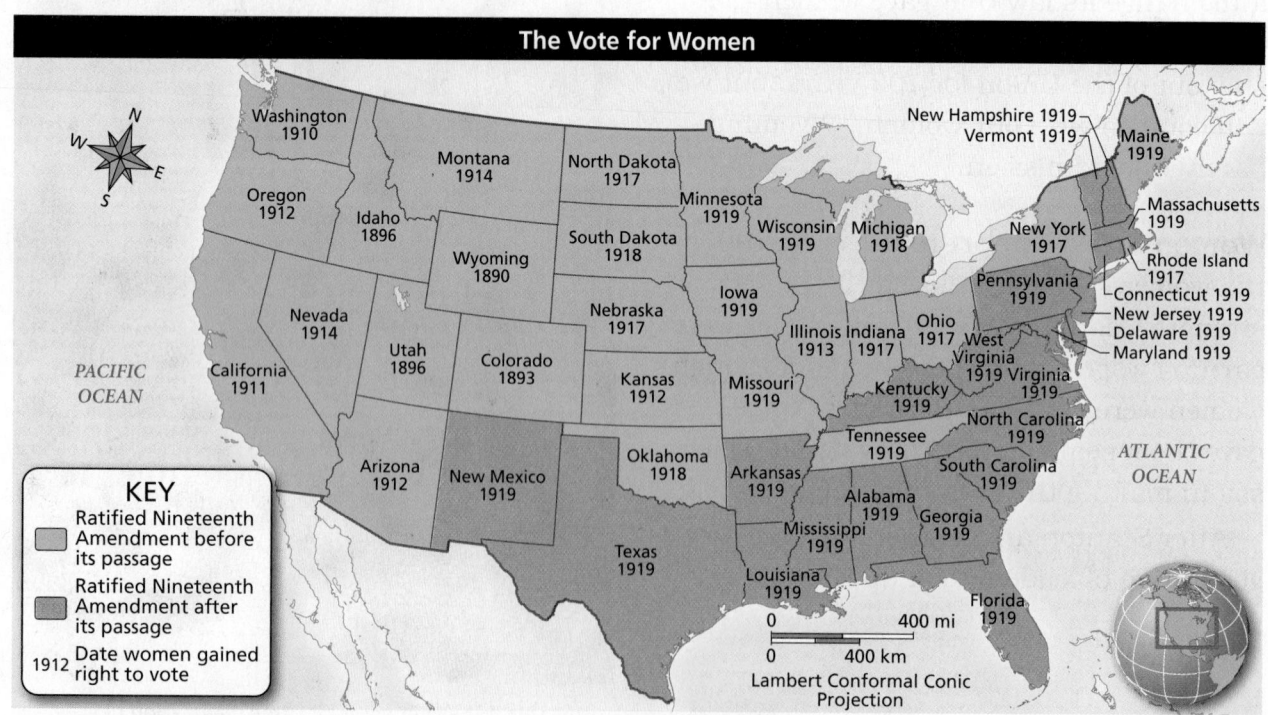

The Vote for Women

KEY
- Ratified Nineteenth Amendment before its passage
- Ratified Nineteenth Amendment after its passage
- 1912 Date women gained right to vote

Washington 1910
Oregon 1912
Idaho 1896
Montana 1914
North Dakota 1917
Minnesota 1919
Wisconsin 1919
Michigan 1918
New Hampshire 1919
Vermont 1919
Maine 1919
Massachusetts 1919
New York 1917
Rhode Island 1917
Connecticut 1919
New Jersey 1919
Delaware 1919
Maryland 1919
Nevada 1914
Utah 1896
Wyoming 1890
South Dakota 1918
Iowa 1919
Nebraska 1917
Illinois 1913
Indiana 1917
Ohio 1917
Pennsylvania 1919
West Virginia 1919
Virginia 1919
California 1911
Colorado 1893
Kansas 1912
Missouri 1919
Kentucky 1919
North Carolina 1919
Arizona 1912
New Mexico 1919
Oklahoma 1918
Arkansas 1919
Tennessee 1919
South Carolina 1919
Alabama 1919
Georgia 1919
Mississippi 1919
Texas 1919
Louisiana 1919
Florida 1919

PACIFIC OCEAN
ATLANTIC OCEAN

0   400 mi
0   400 km
Lambert Conformal Conic Projection

>> **Analyze Maps** In how many of the 48 states did women have the right to vote in 1918, the year before ratification of the 19th Amendment?

New Opportunities Arise

Besides working for the vote, women struggled to gain access to jobs and education. Most states refused to grant women licenses to practice law or medicine. Myra Bradwell taught herself law, just as Abraham Lincoln had done. Still, Illinois denied her a license in 1869 because she was a woman. In 1890, Illinois finally allowed her to practice law.

Access to Higher Education Despite obstacles, a few women managed to get the higher education needed to enter the professions. In 1877, Boston University granted the first Ph.D. to a woman. Slowly, more women entered graduate schools and earned advanced degrees. By 1900, the nation had about 1,000 women lawyers and 7,000 women doctors.

Forming Their Own Clubs During the late 1800s, middle-class women joined women's clubs. At first, most club women read books and sought other ways to improve their minds. In time, many became eager reformers. They raised money for libraries, schools, and parks. They pressed for laws to protect women and children, to ensure pure food and drugs, and to win the vote.

Faced with racial barriers, African American women formed their own clubs, such as the National Association of Colored Women. They battled to end racial injustice and worked for suffrage and other reforms.

Seeking Reform During the Progressive Era, many women became committed to reforming society. Some women entered the new profession of social work. Others campaigned to end social evils, such as child labor. Florence Kelley investigated conditions in sweatshops. In time, she was made the chief factory inspector for

>> Myra Bradwell was a lawyer who fought for women's legal rights as well as for her own right to practice law.

▶ Interactive Gallery

>> Members of the Federation of Colored Women's Clubs pose for a photo in Jacksonville, Florida, in the early 1900s.

the state of Illinois. Kelley's main concern, though, was child labor. She organized a boycott of goods produced by child labor. She helped publish a list of manufacturers whose factories met basic standards.

❓ IDENTIFY CENTRAL IDEAS Why did Illinois at first deny Myra Bradwell the right to practice law?

Fighting for Prohibition

The temperance movement to end the sale of alcoholic beverages began in the early 1800s. Many in the movement wanted the government to enact **prohibition**, or a ban on the manufacture and sale of alcoholic beverages. By 1900, the movement was gaining strength.

Women often led the temperance drive. Many wives and mothers recognized alcohol as a threat to their families. Drinking often caused violence and economic hardship at home.

>> Women in 1917 protest in favor of prohibition, or the banning of alcohol sales.

For political reasons, women also opposed saloons, where alcohol was served. In saloons, male political bosses made political decisions out of the reach of women. Most saloons refused entry to women.

The Crusade for Prohibition In 1874, a group of women organized the **Women's Christian Temperance Union** (WCTU). Frances Willard became its president in 1880. Willard recalled an incident at a Pittsburgh saloon.

> The tall, stately lady who led us placed her Bible on the bar and read a psalm. . . . Then we sang "Rock of Ages" as I thought I had never sung it before. . . . This was my Crusade baptism.
>
> —Frances E. Willard, *Glimpses of Fifty Years, the Autobiography of an American Woman*, 1889

Willard spoke tirelessly about the evils of alcohol. She called for state laws to ban the sale of liquor. She also worked to close saloons. In time, Willard joined the suffrage movement, bringing many WCTU members along with her.

Carrie Nation was a more radical temperance crusader. She dedicated her life to fighting "demon rum." After her husband died from heavy drinking, Nation often stormed into saloons. Swinging a hatchet, she smashed beer kegs and liquor bottles. Nation won publicity, but her actions embarrassed the WCTU.

Prohibition Becomes Law Temperance crusaders wanted a constitutional amendment banning the production and sale of liquor. Support for such an amendment grew after 1917, when the United States entered World War I. Temperance supporters argued that grain used to make liquor should be used instead to feed American soldiers.

Temperance leaders finally persuaded Congress to pass the **Eighteenth Amendment** in 1917. By 1919, three fourths of the states had ratified it. The amendment made it illegal to sell alcoholic drinks anywhere in the United States.

❓ IDENTIFY CENTRAL IDEAS What was the main purpose of the WCTU?

African Americans Face Discrimination

After Reconstruction, African Americans in the South lost many hard-won rights. Jim Crow laws led to segregation in schools, trains, and other public places. In the North, too, African Americans faced prejudice and discrimination. Landlords refused to rent homes in white areas to African Americans. Across the nation, African Americans were hired only for low-paying jobs.

The depression of 1893 made life even harder. In the South and elsewhere, jobless whites took out their anger on blacks. In the 1890s, more than 1,000 African Americans were **lynched**—murdered by mobs.

The murders outraged Ida B. Wells, an African American journalist. In her newspaper, *Free Speech*, Wells urged African Americans to protest the lynchings. She called for a boycott of streetcars and white-owned stores. Wells spoke out despite threats to her life.

A Moderate Approach to Gain Equality
During this period, Booker T. Washington spoke for many African Americans. He called on blacks and whites to live

>> African American suffragist and journalist Ida B. Wells used her newspaper *Free Speech* to speak out against the injustices African Americans faced in the late 1800s.

in harmony. In *Up From Slavery,* his autobiography, Washington told his own success story. Although born into slavery, he had taught himself to read. As a youth, he worked in coal mines, attending schools whenever he could. In 1872, he graduated from the newly founded Hampton Institute. Nine years later, he helped found the Tuskegee Institute in Alabama to offer higher education to blacks.

African Americans, said Washington, must work patiently to move up in society. First, he urged them to learn trades and earn money. Then, they would have the power to demand equality.

Business tycoons like Andrew Carnegie and John D. Rockefeller backed Washington. They helped him build trade schools for African Americans. Presidents also sought his advice on racial issues.

A More Radical Approach to Gain Equality Other African Americans, like W.E.B. Du Bois (doo BOYSS), took a different approach. Du Bois agreed with Booker T. Washington's view on the need for "thrift, patience, and industrial training." However, he added, "So far as Mr. Washington apologizes for injustice, . . . we must firmly oppose him." Instead of patiently accepting discrimination, Du Bois urged blacks to fight it actively.

In 1909, Du Bois, along with Jane Addams, Lincoln Steffens, and other reformers, organized the National Association for the Advancement of Colored People, or **NAACP**. Blacks and whites in the NAACP worked for equal rights for African Americans.

Successes Despite Discrimination
Most Progressives, though, gave little thought to the problems faced by African Americans. When black soldiers were accused of rioting in Brownsville, Texas, Teddy Roosevelt had their whole regiment dishonorably discharged. Later, President Wilson ordered the segregation of black and white government workers. When blacks protested, Wilson replied that "segregation is not humiliating, but a benefit."

Despite many obstacles, some African Americans succeeded. George Washington Carver discovered hundreds of new uses for peanuts and other crops grown in the South. His writings about crop rotation changed southern farming practices. Sarah Walker, better known as Madame C. J. Walker, created a line of hair care products for African American women. She became the first American woman to earn more than $1 million.

Black-owned insurance companies, banks, and other businesses served the needs of African Americans. Other businesses provided personal services that whites refused to offer African Americans. Among these were restaurants, beauty parlors and barber shops, and funeral parlors. Black colleges trained young people for the professions. Churches like the African Methodist Episcopal Church were training grounds for African American leaders.

? IDENTIFY Which African American leader called for fighting discrimination aggressively?

The Mexican-American Experience

Thousands of Americans of Mexican or Spanish descent lived in the United States, especially in the Southwest and West. They lived in areas acquired by the United States from Mexico under the

>> Writer and political activist W.E.B. Du Bois (standing at right) was a leader in the fight against racial discrimination in the early 1900s.

▶ **Interactive Timeline**

>> This image shows U.S. soldiers guarding refugees from the Mexican Revolution of 1910 in a camp in Texas. **Draw Conclusions** Besides the revolution, what other factors may have pushed Mexicans to immigrate to the United States?

Treaty of Guadalupe-Hidalgo and the Gadsden Purchase. In the early 1900s, however, large numbers of immigrants began arriving from Mexico.

In 1910, revolution and famine swept Mexico. Thousands of *Mexicanos*, or native-born Mexicans, fled their homeland into the United States. To them, it was *el norte* "the north." The immigrants came from all levels of Mexican society. Many were poor farmers, but some came from middle-class and upper-class families. Although many Mexicanos later returned home, some remained.

Life in the United States Mexican immigrants worked as field hands, built roads, and dug irrigation ditches. Some lived near the railroads they helped build. Still others worked in city factories, where they faced harsh conditions. They were paid less than white workers and were denied skilled jobs.

Like other immigrants, Mexicans created their own neighborhoods, or **barrios**. There, they preserved their language and culture, celebrated traditional festivals, and shared memories of Mexico. Los Angeles became home to the nation's largest barrio. Its population almost tripled between 1910 and 1920. Meanwhile, Mexican Americans moved to new parts of the United States. Seeking jobs, many moved to the Midwest and the Rocky Mountain region.

Mutual Aid Within the barrio, Mexican immigrants and Mexican Americans took many steps to help each other. Some formed **mutualistas**, or mutual aid groups. These groups worked like other immigrant aid societies. Members of mutualistas pooled money to buy insurance and pay for legal advice. They also collected money for the sick and needy.

❓ DEFINE What was a *mutualista*?

Blocking Asian Immigration

In the 1870s, whites on the West Coast pressed Congress to pass the Chinese Exclusion Act. The Act, passed in 1882, kept Chinese from settling in the United States. With no new immigration, the Chinese population declined.

Japanese Immigrants Still, the demand for cheap labor remained high. White employers on the West Coast and in Hawaii therefore got around the Chinese Exclusion Act by hiring workers from other Asian countries, mainly the Philippines and Japan. More than 100,000 Japanese

entered the United States in the early 1900s. Most had migrated to Hawaii to work on sugar plantations. When the United States annexed Hawaii in 1898, a number of Japanese saw the opportunity for a better life on the United States mainland.

Many newcomers from Japan were farmers. They settled on dry, barren land that Americans thought was useless. Through hard work and careful management of resources, the Japanese made their farms profitable. Soon, they were producing a large percentage of southern California's fruits and vegetables. Other newcomers worked in canneries, lumber mills, and mines.

Hawaiian planters brought workers from Japan, Korea, and the Philippines. They deliberately hired workers from diverse groups. They hoped this would keep workers from uniting to demand better wages or improved working conditions. Like Mexican immigrants, Asian workers

Asian Immigration to the United States.

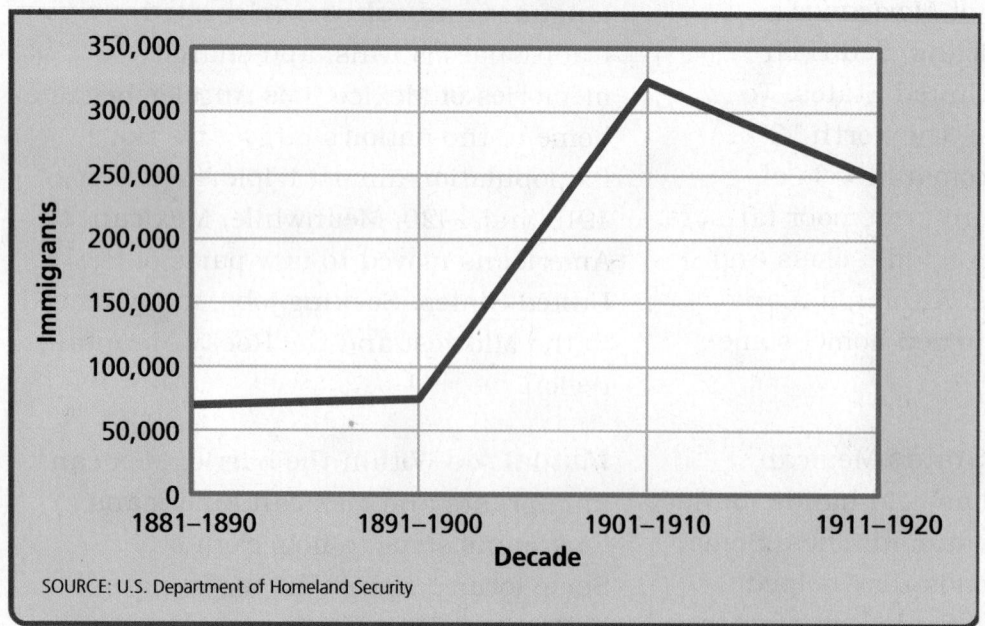

SOURCE: U.S. Department of Homeland Security

>> **Analyze Graphs** Summarize the trends in Asian immigration reflected in this graph.

were paid less than whites and were denied promotion to skilled jobs.

A "Gentlemen's Agreement" Prejudice against immigrants from Asia remained high. Many white farmers and factory workers resented the success of the Japanese. In California, the Japanese were barred from owning land and from many economic pursuits. In 1906, San Francisco forced all Asian students, including Japanese children, to attend separate schools. Japan protested the insult, and the issue threatened to cause an international crisis.

Unions and other groups also put pressure on President Roosevelt to limit immigration from Japan. Because Japan was a growing naval power in the Pacific, Roosevelt tried to soothe Japanese feelings. He condemned the segregated schools and offered his own solution. If San Francisco ended its segregation order, he would restrict further Japanese immigration.

In 1907, Roosevelt reached a **"Gentlemen's Agreement"** with Japan. Japan would stop any more workers from going to the United States. The United States, in exchange, would allow Japanese women to join their husbands who were already in this country. Anti-Japanese feeling did not decrease with the Gentlemen's Agreement. In 1913, California passed a law that banned Asians who were not American citizens from owning land. Before long, the United States would take more drastic steps to stop immigration from Asia.

❓ **CHECK UNDERSTANDING** What were the terms of Roosevelt's "Gentleman's Agreement" with Japan?

>> This photo shows people gathered at the general store in Ruidoso, New Mexico, in the late 1800s. The nearby Mescalero Apache Reservation was established here in 1883.

Discrimination Against American Indians

Though the Dawes Act was unmistakeably a failure, whites did not give up on their attempts to Americanize Native Americans, or American Indians. The discrimination against American Indian groups took many forms. They had been been robbed of their lands, forced to abandon their traditional ways of survival, and were being forced to adopt white American customs. The federal government established schools to teach American Indian children English. Attendance was mandatory. At these schools American Indians were given new names, haircuts, and clothing, according to white American practices.

American Indians who lived on reservations continued to rely on the federal government for assistance. On the

>> Members of the Society of American Indians attend a banquet in Philadelphia in 1914. **Explain** Based on clues from this image, why might members of this group have had different views than American Indians living on reservations?

Indians. It included artists, writers, Christian ministers, lawyers, and doctors from many different peoples. The Society worked for social justice and tried to educate white Americans about Indian life. However, it supported policies to force Indians into the American mainstream by abolishing reservations. This created so much opposition among American Indian groups that the Society went out of existence in 1925.

? IDENTIFY CENTRAL IDEAS What actions did the Society for American Indians support?

ASSESSMENT

1. **Identify Patterns** Explain how women's clubs changed over time.

2. **Generate Explanations** Explain why many women were opposed to saloons for political reasons.

3. **Compare and Contrast** the social and political ideas of Booker T. Washington and W.E.B. Du Bois.

4. **Identify Central Issues** Explain how whites in the government and big businesses responded to issues of racial discrimination.

5. **Generate Explanations** Explain the significance of the "Gentlemen's Agreement."

reservation many struggled with poverty, alcohol, and a lack of employment. Off of the reservation, many faced prejudice and discrimination.

In the early 1900s, a new generation of American Indian leaders emerged. One group set up the **Society of American**

>> Organized sports began as a way for factory employees to escape the drudgery of work but quickly became a national pastime. This photo shows the St. Louis Browns professional baseball team in 1883.

Interactive Flipped Video

A building boom changed the face of American cities. Cities such as Chicago and New York gradually began to run out of space in their downtown areas. Resourceful developers decided to build up instead of out.

>> **Objectives**

Describe how city life changed during the Progressive Era.

Identify forms of entertainment that Americans enjoyed during this period.

Describe how public education grew during the Progressive Era.

Identify changes in reading habits.

Explain the interest of Progressive Era writers and painters in subjects from everyday life.

>> **Key Terms**

skyscraper
suburb
department store
Vaudeville
Ragtime
compulsory
   education
parochial
Chautauqua Society
yellow journalism
dime novel
realist
local color

PEARSON realize. www.PearsonRealize.com Access your Digital Lesson.

Changes and Challenges in City Life

Touching the Sky After fire leveled downtown Chicago in 1871, planners tried out many new ideas as they rebuilt the city. Using new technology, they designed **skyscrapers**, tall buildings with many floors supported by a lightweight steel frame. The first skyscraper, only nine stories tall, was built in Chicago in 1885. As technology improved, builders competed to raise taller and taller skyscrapers.

Newly invented electric elevators, like those installed in larger apartment buildings, carried residents and workers to upper floors. Elevators moved so quickly, according to one rider, that "the passenger seems to feel his stomach pass into his shoes."

>> These New Yorkers are ice-skating in Central Park in 1900. Growing cities set aside land for parks, which gave people an opportunity to enjoy nature in the midst of the city.

Transportation Innovations As skyscrapers crowded more people into smaller spaces, they added to a growing problem: traffic. Downtown streets were jammed with horse-drawn buses, carriages, and carts.

Electricity offered one solution. Frank Sprague, an engineer from Richmond, Virginia, designed the first electric streetcar system in 1887. Streetcars, or trolleys, were fast, clean, and quiet. Many trolley lines ran from the center of a city to the outlying countryside, creating the first suburbs. A **suburb** is a residential area on or near the outskirts of a city.

Other cities built steam-driven passenger trains on overhead tracks. In 1897, Boston built the first American subway, or underground electric railway. Subways and elevated railroads carried workers rapidly to and from their jobs.

Some cities needed ways to move masses of people and goods across rivers. In 1874, James B. Eads designed and built a three-arched bridge across the Mississippi River at St. Louis. The Eads Bridge was more than a quarter of a mile long. Nine years later, New York City completed the Brooklyn Bridge linking Manhattan Island and Brooklyn. More than a mile long, it carried a footpath, roadways, and two railroad lines. The bridge was soon carrying 33 million people a year.

Places to Relax While cities grew up and out, some planners wanted to preserve open spaces. They believed that open land would calm busy city dwellers.

In the 1850s, landscape architect Frederick Law Olmsted planned spacious Central Park in New York City. Other cities followed this model. They set aside land for public parks that contained zoos and gardens so that city people could enjoy green grass and trees during their leisure time.

A New Pastime Shopping areas also got a new look. In the past, people had bought shoes in one store, socks in another, and dishes in a third. The new **department stores** sold all kinds of goods in different sections or departments. As the American economy was able to produce more goods at cheaper prices, American consumers were better able to afford them. Americans were therefore both producers and consumers of goods and services, encouraging new department stores to open across the country.

In New York, R. H. Macy opened a nine-story department store in 1902. Its motto stated, "We sell goods cheaper than any house in the world." Soon, other cities had department stores. Shopping became a popular pastime. People browsed through each floor, looking at clothes, furniture, and jewelry. On the street, "window-shoppers" paused to view elaborate displays behind enormous new plate-glass windows.

>> Large department stores such as Marshall Field & Company in Chicago offered customers a variety of items available for purchase all in a single location.

❓ **RECALL** How did developers respond to cities running out of space in their downtown areas?

More Americans Play Sports

The rise of the factory split the worlds of work and play more sharply than ever. With less chance to socialize on the job, there was more interest in leisure. Sports provided a great escape from the pressures of work.

"Play Ball!" Baseball was the most popular sport in the nation. Organized baseball was first played in New York. During the Civil War, New York soldiers showed other Union troops how to play. By the 1870s, several cities had professional baseball teams and the first professional league was organized.

Early baseball was somewhat different from today's game. Pitchers threw underhanded. Catchers caught the ball after one bounce. Fielders did not wear gloves. As a result, high scores were common. One championship baseball game ended with a score of 103 to 8!

At first, African Americans played professional baseball. In time, though, the major leagues barred black players. In 1885, Frank Thompson organized a group of waiters into one of the first African American professional teams, the Cuban Giants of Long Island. They took the name "Cuban," not because they were from Cuba, but in hopes that all-white teams might be willing to play them.

An Early Version of Football Football grew out of informal English games that also gave rise to rugby. Americans had played forms of football since colonial times. Early football called for lots of muscle and little skill. On every play, the opposing teams crashed into each other like fighting rams. The quarterback ran or jumped over the tangle of bodies.

Players did not wear helmets and were often hurt. In 1908 alone, 33 college football players died from injuries. Some colleges banned the sport or drew up stricter rules of play for the game.

Basketball Begins In 1891, James Naismith invented basketball. Naismith taught physical education at a Young Men's Christian Association (YMCA) in Springfield, Massachusetts. He wanted a sport that could be played indoors in winter. He nailed two bushel baskets to the gym walls. Players tried to throw a soccer ball into the baskets.

Basketball caught on quickly. It spread to other YMCAs and then to schools and colleges around the country.

? RECALL What was America's most popular sport in the late nineteenth century?

New Forms of Theater and Music

By the late 1800s, American cities supported a wide variety of cultural activities. Talented immigrants contributed to new forms of music and theater.

Music and other kinds of entertainment brought Americans together. People from different cultures sang the same songs and enjoyed the same shows. As railroads grew, circuses, acting companies, and "Wild West" shows toured the country. These traveling groups helped spread American

>> Children playing basketball on a New York City playground in 1911

▶ Interactive Gallery

culture beyond the cities to the small towns.

An Evening Out Many large cities organized symphony orchestras and opera companies. Generally, only the wealthy attended the symphony or the opera. For other city dwellers, an evening out often meant a trip to a vaudeville house. **Vaudeville** (VAWD vil) was a variety show that included comedians, song-and-dance routines, and acrobats.

Vaudeville provided opportunities for people from many ethnic backgrounds, such as Irish American dancer-singer George M. Cohan and Jewish comedians like the Marx Brothers. Will Rogers, a performer of Cherokee descent, was one of the best-loved entertainers in the nation. Wearing a cowboy hat and twirling a rope, Rogers used gentle wit to comment on American life. "Everybody is ignorant," he said, "only on different subjects."

Popular Music Songwriters produced many popular tunes, such as "Shine On, Harvest Moon." Later, Thomas Edison's phonograph sparked a new industry. By 1900, millions of phonograph records had been sold.

Ragtime was a new kind of music with a lively, rhythmic sound. Scott Joplin, an African American composer, helped make ragtime popular. His "Maple Leaf Rag" was a nationwide hit.

In towns and cities, marching bands played the military music of John Philip Sousa. Sousa wrote more than 100 marches, including "The Stars and Stripes Forever." His marches became favorites at Fourth of July celebrations.

❓ **CHECK UNDERSTANDING** How did Edison's phonograph affect the music industry?

>> African American composer and pianist Scott Joplin popularized ragtime music in the early 1900s and earned the nickname "King of Ragtime."

More Americans Attend School

Before 1870, fewer than half of American children went to school. Many who did attended one-room schoolhouses, with only one teacher. Often, several students shared a single book.

Government-Funded Schools As industry grew, the nation needed an educated work force. As a result, states improved public schools at all levels. By 1900, there were 4,000 kindergartens across the nation.

In the North, most states passed **compulsory education** laws that required children to attend school, usually through sixth grade. In the South, which had no tradition of public schools, the Freedmen's Bureau had built grade schools for both African American and white students.

By 1900, most southern schools were segregated.

In cities such as Boston and New York, public schools taught English to young immigrants. Children also learned about the duties and rights of citizens. In the 1880s, Catholics became worried that public schools stressed Protestant teachings. They opened their own **parochial**, or church-sponsored, schools.

A Typical School Day The typical school day lasted from 8:00 A.M. to 4:00 P.M. Pupils learned the "three Rs": reading, 'riting, and 'rithmetic. Students memorized and recited passages from the most widely used textbook, *McGuffey's Eclectic Reader.* With titles like "Waste Not, Want Not," the poems and stories taught not only reading but also religion, ethics, and values.

>> Reading, writing, and arithmetic were the focus of schools in the late 1800s. **Compare and Contrast** today's classrooms with those of the late 1800s such as the one shown here.

Schools emphasized discipline and obedience. Students had to sit upright in their seats, often with their hands folded in front of them. Punishment was swift and severe—a rap on the head for whispering or a paddling for arriving late.

Higher Learning After the Civil War, many cities and towns built public high schools. By 1900, there were 6,000 high schools in the country. Higher education also expanded. New private colleges for both women and men opened. Many states built universities that offered free or low-cost education.

To help meet the need for trained workers, the Chicago Manual Training School opened in 1884. It offered courses in "shop work," such as electricity and carpentry, as well as in a few academic subjects. Soon, most public schools in the nation had programs to prepare students for jobs in business and in industry.

Chautauqua In 1874, a Methodist minister opened a summer school for Bible teachers along Lake Chautauqua in New York. The next year, the camp was opened to the general public. Mostly middle-class men and women of all ages gathered at Chautauqua each summer. In addition to receiving spiritual guidance, they enjoyed lectures about art, politics, philosophy, and other subjects.

In 1903, the **Chautauqua Society** began to send out traveling companies. Before long, Chautauquas were reaching as many as 5 million people in 10,000 American towns every year.

? CHECK UNDERSTANDING How did public and parochial schools differ?

Education in the Progressive Era

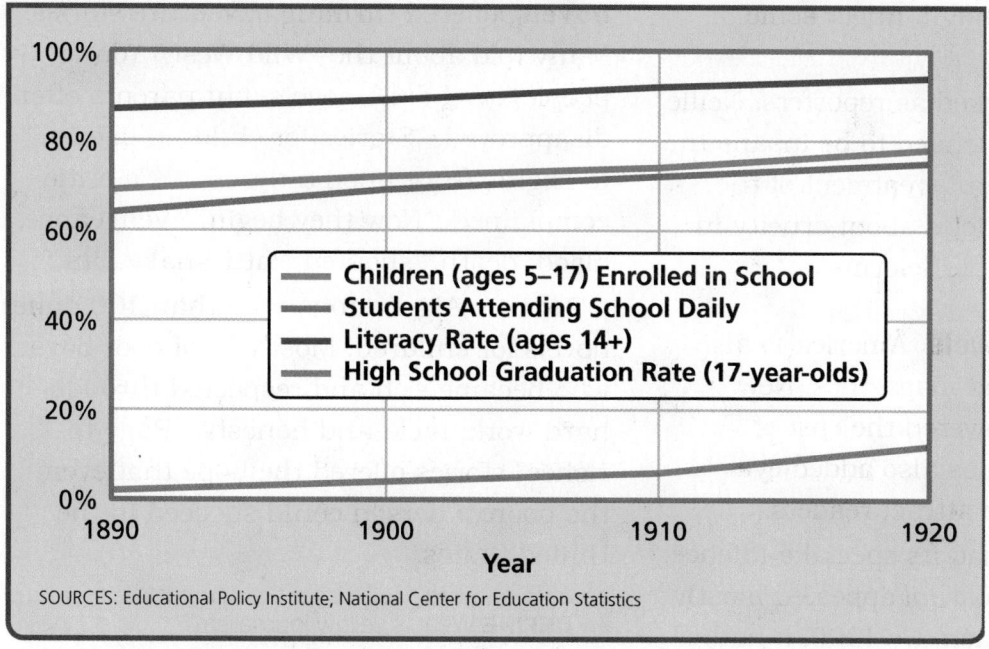

Children (ages 5–17) Enrolled in School
Students Attending School Daily
Literacy Rate (ages 14+)
High School Graduation Rate (17-year-olds)

SOURCES: Educational Policy Institute; National Center for Education Statistics

>> **Analyze Graphs** Draw conclusions about trends in the level of education, as shown in this graph.

News in Print

"Read all about it!" cried newsboys on city street corners. As education spread, people read more, especially newspapers. The number of newspapers grew dramatically. By 1900, half the newspapers in the world were printed in the United States.

The newspaper boom was linked to the growth of cities. In towns and villages, neighbors shared news face to face. In the crowded and busy cities, people needed newspapers to stay informed.

Newspapers reported on major events of the day. Most of them featured stories about local government, business, fashion, and sports. Many immigrants learned to read English by spelling their way through a daily paper. They also learned about American life.

Newspaper Publishers Joseph Pulitzer, a Hungarian immigrant, created the first modern, mass-circulation newspaper. In 1883, Pulitzer bought the New York *World*. He set out to make it lively and "truly democratic."

To win readers, Pulitzer slashed prices and added comic strips. Pictures and bold "scare" headlines attracted reader attention. The *World* splashed crimes and political scandals across its front page.

William Randolph Hearst challenged Pulitzer. Hearst's New York *Journal* began to outdo the *World* in presenting scandals, crime stories, and gossip. Critics complained that the papers offered less news and more scandal every day. They coined the term **yellow journalism** for the sensational reporting style of the *World* and the *Journal*.

The Female Readership Newspapers competed for women readers. They added special sections on fashion, social events, health, homemaking, and family matters. Newspapers rarely pushed for women's rights, however. Most were afraid to take bold positions that might anger some readers.

A few women worked as reporters. Nellie Bly of the *World* pretended to be insane in order to find out about treatment of the mentally ill. Her articles about cruelty in mental hospitals led to reforms.

Magazines and Novels Americans also read more books and magazines. New printing methods lowered the cost of magazines. Magazines also added eye-catching pictures to attract readers.

Each magazine had its special audience. *The Ladies' Home Journal* appealed mostly to middle-class women. By 1900, it had one million readers. Other magazines, such as *Harper's Monthly* and *The Nation*, specialized in politics or current events.

>> American novelist, poet, and short-story writer Stephen Crane described life in the slums and during the Civil War in his novels *Maggie: A Girl of the Streets* (1893) and *The Red Badge of Courage* (1895).

Low-priced paperbacks, known as **dime novels**, offered thrilling adventure stories. Many told about the "Wild West." Young people loved dime novels, but parents often disapproved. "Stories for children used to begin, 'Once upon a time . . . ,'"a critic complained. "Now they begin, '"Vengeance, blood, death," shouted Rattlesnake Jim.'"

Horatio Alger wrote more than 100 dime novels for children. Most told of poor boys who became rich and respected through hard work, luck, and honesty. "Rags-to-riches" stories offered the hope that even the poorest person could succeed in the United States.

? DEFINE What is yellow journalism?

American Writers and Artists Excel

In the 1880s, a new crop of American writers appeared. For the first time, Americans were reading more books by American authors than by British authors.

Depicting Reality One group of writers, called **realists**, tried to show the harsh side of life as it was. Many realists had worked as newspaper reporters. They had seen poverty and wanted to make people aware of the costs of urbanization and industrial growth.

Stephen Crane was best known for his Civil War novel, *The Red Badge of Courage*. Crane also wrote about the shattered lives of young city slum dwellers in novels such as *Maggie: A Girl of the Streets*. Jack London, born in California, wrote about miners and sailors on the West Coast who put their lives at risk in backbreaking jobs.

Kate Chopin found an audience in women's magazines for her short stories about New Orleans life. Chopin's stories showed women breaking out of traditional roles.

Paul Laurence Dunbar was the first African American to make a living as a writer. He wrote poems, such as "We Wear the Mask," in a serious, elegant style. In other poems, he used everyday language to express the feelings of African Americans of the time.

Mark Twain The most famous and popular author of this period was Mark Twain, the pen name of Samuel Clemens. Twain had his first success in 1865 with his comical short story "The Celebrated Jumping Frog of Calaveras County."

Like many other writers, Twain used local color to make his stories more realistic. **Local color** refers to the speech and habits of a particular region. Twain captured the speech patterns of southerners who lived and worked along the Mississippi River.

In novels like *Huckleberry Finn*, Twain used homespun characters to poke fun at serious issues. Huck, a country boy, and Jim, an escaped slave, raft down the Mississippi River together in the days before the Civil War. Huck comes to respect Jim and to view slavery as wrong. Here, Huck talks about Jim's love for his family.

> He was saying how the first thing he would do when he got to a free state he would go to saving up money, . . . and when he got enough he would buy his wife, which was owned on a farm close to where Miss Watson lived; and then they would both work to buy the two children, and if their master wouldn't sell them, they'd get an Ab'litionist to go and steal them.

—Mark Twain, *The Adventures of Huckleberry Finn*

>> American author Samuel Clemens, otherwise known as Mark Twain, gained national renown through his depiction of southern life in novels like *The Adventures of Huckleberry Finn* and *The Adventures of Tom Sawyer*.

>> Mark Twain's novel *The Adventures of Tom Sawyer* (1876) became a classic of American literature.

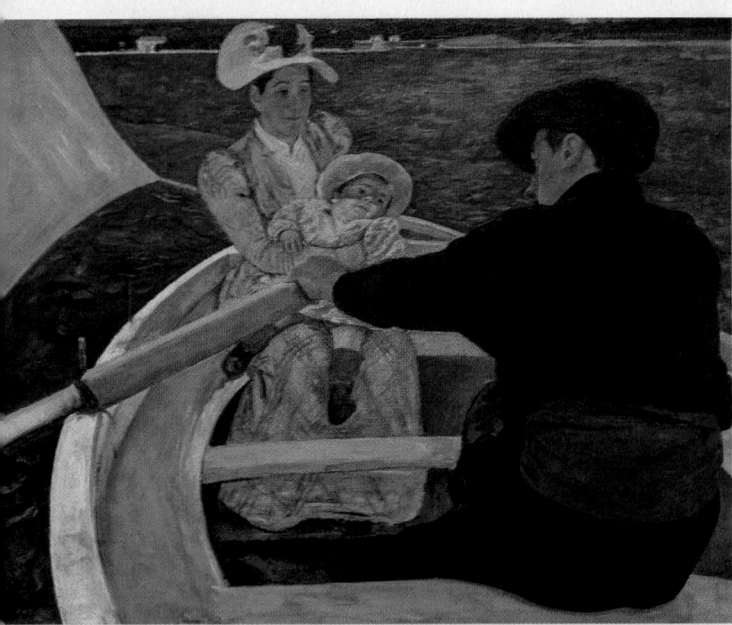

>> American artist Mary Cassatt used bold colors to paint scenes of everyday life, such as *The Boating Party* (1893).

▶ **Interactive Gallery**

Although *Huckleberry Finn* became a classic, some schools and libraries refused to buy the book. They claimed that Huck was a crude character who would have a bad influence on "our pure-minded lads and lasses."

Lifelike Art Like writers of the period, many artists sought to capture local color and the gritty side of modern life. In the late 1800s, leading artists painted realistic everyday scenes.

During the Civil War, Winslow Homer drew scenes of brutal battles for magazines. Later, he gained fame for realistic paintings of the New England coast. Thomas Eakins learned anatomy and dissected dead bodies to be able to portray the human form accurately. Many of his paintings depicted sports scenes or medical operations. Henry Tanner, an African American student of Eakins, won fame for pictures of black sharecroppers. Later, Tanner moved to Paris to enjoy greater freedom.

Other American artists preferred to work in Europe, too. James Whistler left Massachusetts for Paris and London. His use of color and light influenced young European artists. Mary Cassatt (kuh SAT) also carved out a place for herself in the French art world. Cassatt painted bright, colorful scenes of people in everyday situations, especially mothers with their children.

? **IDENTIFY CENTRAL ISSUES** What was the main goal of realists?

ASSESSMENT

1. **Generate Explanations** Explain how developers and engineers made use of space as cities grew.

2. **Describe** African American participation in early professional baseball.

3. **Describe** the ways in which education changed during the late 1800s.

4. **Connect** Explain how newspapers and dime novels related to American values of the time.

5. **Compare and Contrast** the work of realist artists with yellow journalism.

Foreign-Born Population in Major Cities

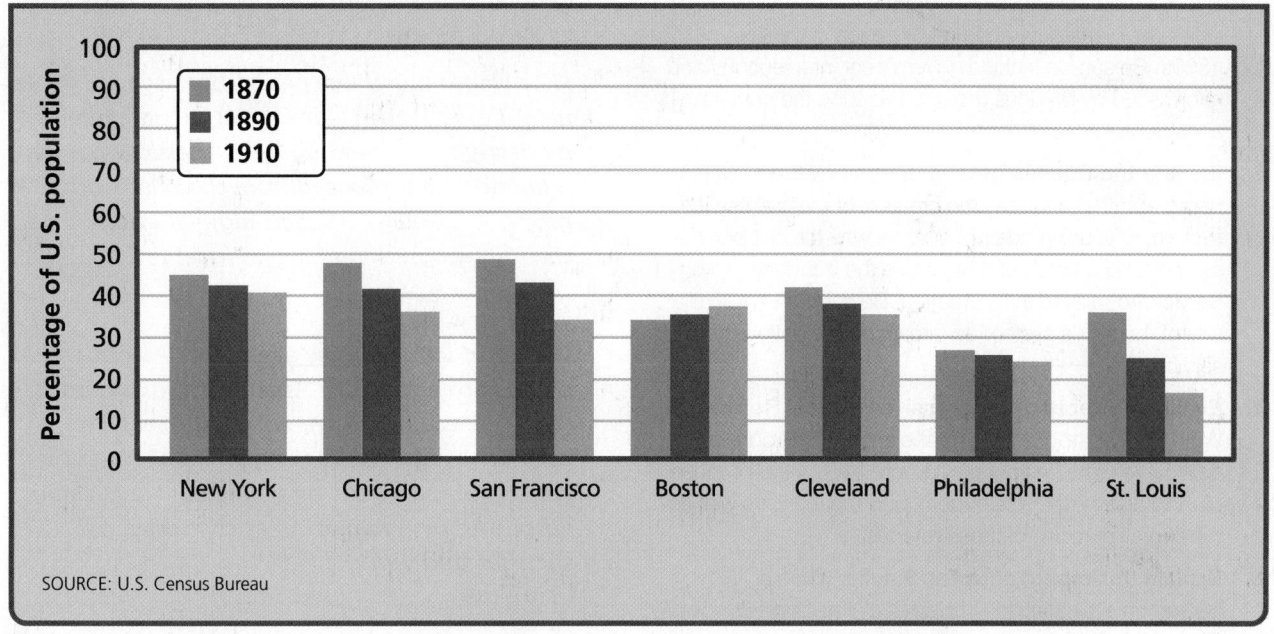

SOURCE: U.S. Census Bureau

1. **Analyze Changing Demographic Patterns in Cities**
   Use the graph above and information from the lessons in this topic to write a paragraph about how immigration changed the populations of cities in the late 1800s and early 1900s. Consider the following questions in your paragraph: What can you tell from the graph about the size of the immigrant population in the different cities? Why might immigrant populations be high in New York City and San Francisco? What factors might have contributed to the size of immigrant populations in cities?

2. **Describe Immigrant Optimism** Write a paragraph to describe how push and pull factors were related to immigration and immigrant optimism. Then use what you have learned to write a paragraph describing why the young woman in the quotation below might have felt so optimistic. Consider such things as the push factors that caused Russian and eastern European Jews to leave their countries and the pull factors that drew them to the United States.

America means for an immigrant a fairy promised land that came out true, a land that gives all they need for their work, a land which gives morality through her churches and education through her free schools and libraries.

—young Russian Jewish woman

3. **Explain the Effects of the Chinese Exclusion Act**
   Write a paragraph explaining the effect of the Chinese Exclusion Act of 1882 on Chinese immigrants. In your paragraph, make sure to identify what the act restricted and explain the negative effects on Chinese immigrants.

4. **Analyze Social Issues Affecting Urbanization**
   Write a paragraph analyzing the problems associated with living in a tenement in the late 1800s. Be sure to define the term *tenement* and discuss the living conditions inside tenements, and discuss the living conditions in the streets around tenements.

5. Describe Causes and Effects of Urban Reforms Describe the measures that reforms took to ease the problems created by rapid urbanization in the late 1800s. Be sure to include government interventions and reforms led by religious groups. Describe the causes and effects of these reforms.

6. Identify the Causes of Civil Service Reform Write a paragraph that analyzes the creation of the civil service system. In your paragraph, analyze why the civil service system was created and what role the Pendleton Civil Service Act played in its creation. Be sure to explain the role of the spoils system as a reason for creating the civil service.

7. Evaluate Effects of Progressive Political Reforms Write a paragraph evaluating the impact of Progressive political reforms. In your paragraph, explain the purpose of the initiative, the referendum, and the recall as well as the overall purpose of these reforms.

8. Explain the Impact of Upton Sinclair Write a paragraph evaluating the impact of Upton Sinclair's novel, *The Jungle*. Be sure to describe what *The Jungle* is about and evaluate the novel's short- and long-term impact on food safety.

9. Evaluate Effective Leadership Evaluate qualities of effective leadership by creating a chart that categorizes how President Theodore Roosevelt and Congress showed leadership by regulating business, public safety, and the environment. Be sure to include specific examples from each of these categories in your chart.

10. Analyze Roosevelt's Square Deal Use the quotation below to write a paragraph explaining what Roosevelt meant by a "Square Deal" for the American people. In your paragraph, consider what Roosevelt's Square Deal and the quotation indicate about his leadership qualities.

When I say I believe in a square deal, I do not mean to give every man the best hand. If good cards do not come to any man, or if they do come, and he has not got the power to play them, that is his affair. All I mean is that there shall be no crookedness in the dealing.

—Theodore Roosevelt, 1905

11. Compare W.E.B. Du Bois and Booker T. Washington Evaluate the impact of the writing and political work of W.E.B. Du Bois and Booker T. Washington on American society, and identify their points of view on a social studies issue or event. Write a paragraph comparing the points of view and the impact of these two men on African American civil rights. Be sure to consider how the views of Du Bois and Booker T.

Washington expressed in the quotations below differ and what led Du Bois to help found the National Association for the Advancement of Colored People (NAACP).

[The Negro must] live peaceably with his white neighbors . . . the Negro [must] deport himself modestly . . . depending upon the slow but sure influences that proceed from the possessions of property, intelligence, and high character for the full recognition of his political rights.

—Booker T. Washington

We claim for ourselves every single right that belongs to a freeborn American . . . and until we get these rights we will never cease to protest . . . How shall we get them? By voting where we may vote, by persistent, unceasing agitation, by hammering at the truth, by sacrifice and work.

—W.E.B. Du Bois

12. Explain the Importance of the Nineteenth Amendment Write a paragraph explaining the importance of the Nineteenth Amendment and the roles played by Carrie Chapman Catt and Alice Paul in its passage. In your paragraph, be sure to include important events leading to the passage of the Nineteenth Amendment, the importance of the Nineteenth Amendment, and the new opportunities for women that arose after the passage of the Nineteenth Amendment.

13. Analyze Challenges Faced by Mexican Americans During the Progressive Era Describe the experience of Mexican Americans during the Progressive Era. Be sure to include why many Mexicans came to the United States in the late 1800s, the challenges they faced, where many settled, and how they addressed challenges.

14. Identify the Effects of Urban Improvements Explain how life in cities improved in the late 1800s and early 1900s. Be sure to describe the effects of innovations in public transportation and travel as well as how technology helped solve some of the problems of crowding.

15. Compare American Writers and Artists in the Progressive Era Create a table in which you compare the work of at least four American writers during the Progressive Era. Then choose one of these writers and explain why you would be interested in reading his or her work.

16. Write About the Essential Question **Write an Essay on the Essential Question: What can individuals do to affect society?** Use evidence from this topic to support your answer.

Go online to PearsonRealize.com and use the texts, quizzes, interactivities, Interactive Reading Notepads, Flipped Videos, and other resources from this Topic to prepare for the Topic Test.

Texts

Quizzes

Interactivities

Interactive Reading Notepads

Flipped Videos

While online you can also check the progress you've made learning the topic and course content by viewing your grades, test scores, and assignment status.

12 Imperialism and World War I (1853–1919)

>> African American soldiers on the front during World War I

Enduring Understandings

- The United States expanded territories in the Pacific and increased influence abroad for economic and political reasons, continuing its shift from isolationist to expansionist.

- After a victory over Spain in the Spanish-American War, the United States gained additional territory in the Pacific and the Caribbean.

- Theodore Roosevelt adopted a policy of U.S. intervention in Latin American affairs.

- Mistrust among European nations caused many to form alliances for protection, and when crisis struck, a chain reaction of war declarations by allies started World War I.

- The United States, neutral during much of the war, joined the fighting to help the Allies, to protect American interests, and to defend democracy.

- After the Allies won the war, President Wilson wanted the United States to help secure the peace, but Congress chose a policy of isolation, or non-involvement in world affairs.

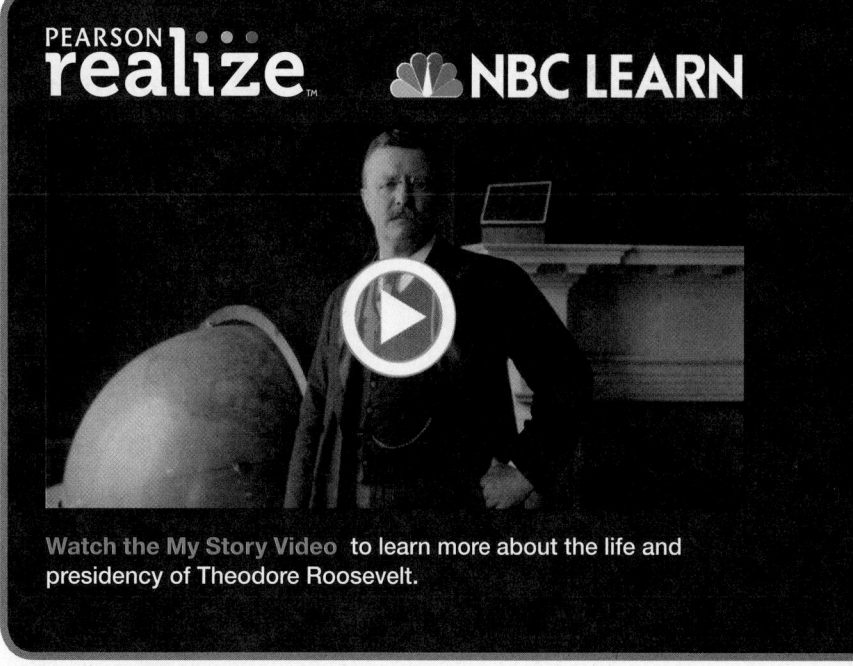

PEARSON realize™   NBC LEARN

Watch the My Story Video to learn more about the life and presidency of Theodore Roosevelt.

PEARSON realize™
www.PearsonRealize.com

Access your digital lessons including:
Topic Inquiry • Interactive Reading Notepad • Interactivities • Assessments

Expansion in the Pacific

>> This image shows Admiral Perry being greeted by Japanese officials in 1854. His visit led to the treaty that opened trade relations between Japan and the West.

Interactive Flipped Video

>> Objectives

Explain the early steps the United States took toward expansion in the Pacific.

Identify the meaning of imperialism and explain its causes.

Describe how the United States gained control of American Samoa and Hawaii.

Summarize how Americans protected their trade with China.

>> Key Terms

isolationism
expansionism
Treaty of Kanagawa
annex
Imperialism
racism
Great White Fleet
sphere of influence
Open Door Policy
Boxer Rebellion

In his Farewell Address, George Washington had advised the nation to have little to do with the political affairs of other nations. He had been concerned about forming dangerous alliances with other nations and had preferred that the United States be involved in international affairs only to protect its economic interests.

Expansion Leads to Trade With Japan

Washington's beliefs influenced the policy of **isolationism**. Later Presidents maintained this policy for over a hundred years. Americans had no wish to be dragged into Europe's frequent wars.

Expansion and Trade Yet, from its earliest existence, the American republic had also followed a policy of **expansionism**, or extending its national boundaries. Americans were constantly pressing westward across the continent.

At the same time, Americans conducted a lively foreign trade. Merchant ships carried American goods to Europe, as well as to Asian nations such as China. The island nation of Japan, however, refused to open its doors to American trade.

Overseas Trade With Japan Fearing outsiders, Japanese rulers had cut themselves off from the world in the 1600s. They expelled all westerners. Only a few Dutch merchants were permitted to trade once a year at the port of Nagasaki. Any foreign sailors who were shipwrecked on the shores of Japan were not allowed to leave.

Americans wanted Japan to open its ports to trade, as well as to help shipwrecked sailors. To achieve these goals, President Millard Fillmore sent Commodore Matthew Perry to Japan. Perry entered Tokyo Bay with four warships in July 1853. The Japanese had never seen steam-powered ships.

Japanese rulers ordered the Americans to leave. Before departing, though, Perry presented Japanese officials with a letter from President Fillmore. It asked the Japanese to open trading relations with the United States. Perry said he would return the following year for an answer.

Perry returned in February 1854, this time with nine warships. Impressed by this show of strength, the Japanese emperor signed the **Treaty of Kanagawa**. In the treaty, Japan accepted demands to help shipwrecked sailors. It also opened two ports to American trade.

Commodore Perry's Arrival in Japan

CAUSE	EFFECT
The United States wishes to begin trading with Japan.	President Fillmore sends Commodore Matthew Perry to Japan with four warships to pressure the Japanese to sign a trade agreement in July 1853.
Japan refuses to open its ports to American ships and orders the Americans to leave.	Perry presents Japanese officials with a letter from the President and says he will return the following year.
Perry returns to Japan early the following year with nine warships as a display of strength.	The Japanese enter into negotiations to sign the Treaty of Kanagawa, opening up ports to American trade.

SOURCES: PBS; Asia for Educators

>> Commodore Perry's visits to Japan proved to be a turning point in American relations with Asia. **Hypothesize** Why did the Japanese refuse to see Perry on his first visit?

>> This illustration shows an American ship off the coast of Japan in 1861. American ships were an increasingly common sight as trade developed between the two countries.

>> This photo shows the White Pass and Yukon Railroad near Skagway in Alaska, which was built after the U.S. purchased Alaska in 1867. **List** two advantages of purchasing Alaska.

Perry's visit launched trade between Japan and the West. It also made the Japanese aware of the power of the western industrial nations. Japan soon set out to become a modern industrial nation itself, with the United States as one of its models.

? CHECK UNDERSTANDING How did U.S. expansion and economic growth impact Japan?

U.S. Interest in the Pacific

American interest in Asia and the Pacific continued. In the 1860s, Secretary of State William Seward wanted the United States to dominate trade in the Pacific. In 1867, he persuaded Congress to **annex**, or take over, Midway Island, in the middle of the Pacific Ocean. The island became part of the United States. Seward also made a bold deal to buy the vast territory of Alaska from Russia.

A Late-Night Land Deal Seward saw Alaska as an important stepping stone for increasing U.S. trade in Asia and the Pacific. For their part, the Russians were eager to get rid of the territory, which was too far away to govern effectively.

One night in 1867, Seward was playing cards. Suddenly, he was interrupted by a message from the Russian ambassador. The czar, or emperor, of Russia was willing to sell Alaska to the United States for $7.2 million. Seward agreed to buy the land then and there.

"But your Department is closed," said the ambassador.

"Never mind that," Seward replied. "Before midnight you will find me at the Department, which will be open and ready for business."

Next morning, Seward completed the deal. The cost came to 2 cents an acre. The

World Imperialism, 1914

KEY
Home countries and their colonies

- United States
- Belgium
- United Kingdom
- China
- Denmark
- Netherlands
- France
- Germany
- Italy
- Japan
- Ottoman Empire
- Portugal
- Russian Empire
- Spain
- Independent

0   2000 mi
0   2000 km
Robinson Projection

>> **Analyze Maps** Based on the map, which nations held the most influence through their colonies around the world?

purchase of Alaska increased the area of the United States by almost one fifth.

"Seward's Folly" At the time, the purchase seemed foolish. Most Americans thought of Alaska as a barren land of icy mountains and frozen fish. They mockingly called the new territory "Seward's Ice Box" and referred to the purchase as "Seward's Folly."

Minds changed in the 1890s, after prospectors found gold in Alaska. Miners rushed to the new territory as they had once rushed to California. Since then, Seward's vision of Alaska as a valuable territory has proved correct. The lowlands of southern Alaska are well suited to farming. The land is also rich in timber, copper, petroleum, and natural gas. In 1959, Alaska became the forty-ninth state.

? RECALL Why did Seward buy Alaska?

The Age of Imperialism

The period between 1870 and 1914 has often been called the Age of Imperialism. **Imperialism** is the policy of powerful countries seeking to control the economic and political affairs of weaker countries or regions. Between 1870 and 1914, European nations, such as Britain, Germany, and France, seized control of almost the entire continent of Africa and much of southern Asia. During this period, the United States and Japan also became imperial powers.

Reasons for Imperialism There were several reasons for the growth of imperialism. First, the industrial nations of Europe needed raw materials and new markets. European factories used raw materials from Africa and Asia to manufacture goods. Some of these goods would then be sold in Africa and Asia.

A second factor that shaped imperialism was **racism**, or the belief that one race is superior to another. Many Europeans felt that they had a duty to spread their religion and culture to people whom they considered to be less civilized. British writer Rudyard Kipling called this responsibility "the white man's burden." Such thinking ignored that Africans and Asians already had rich cultures of their own.

A third cause was competition. When a European country colonized an area, it often closed markets of that area to other countries. A European nation might take over an area just to keep rival nations out.

American Expansionists Make Their Case Americans could not ignore Europe's race for colonies. By the 1890s, the United States was a world leader in industry and agriculture. American factories turned out huge amounts of steel and American

>> This photo shows British officers in India, one of the British Empire's largest colonies. Great Britain controlled markets and the export of raw materials throughout India.

farms grew surpluses of corn, wheat, and cotton. The nation was growing rapidly, and arguments in favor of expansion were popular.

Many people believed that the American economy would collapse unless the United States gained new foreign markets.

Today we are raising more than we can consume. Today we are making more than we can use. Today our industrial society is congested; there are more workers than there is work. . . . Therefore we must find new markets for our produce, new occupations for our capital, new work for our labor.

—Albert Beveridge, quoted in *Beveridge and the Progressive Era* (Bowers)

Expansionists also argued that Americans had a right and a duty to spread western culture. Josiah Strong, a Congregational minister, declared that Americans were "divinely commissioned" to bring democracy and Christianity "down upon Mexico, down upon Central and South America, out upon the islands of the sea."

Other expansionists stressed the need to make up for the vanishing frontier. For 100 years, the economy had boomed as Americans settled the West. The 1890 census said, however, that the frontier was gone. People in crowded eastern cities had no new land to settle. The solution, said some, was to take new land overseas.

Naval Power One leading supporter of American imperialism was naval captain Alfred Mahan. In an influential 1890 book, *The Influence of Sea Power Upon History*, Mahan argued that the prosperity of the United States depended on foreign trade. Furthermore, he said, a bigger navy was needed to protect American merchant

The United States Expands in the Pacific

KEY
United States and its possessions
(1857) Date of acquisition

RUSSIA

Alaska
(1867)

CANADA

CHINA

JAPAN

PACIFIC OCEAN

UNITED STATES

Midway Is.
(1867)

Hawaiian Is.
(1898)

Gulf of
Mexico

MEXICO

Philippine
Is.
(1898)

Wake I.
(1899)

Guam
(1898)

Johnston I.
(1858)

CENTRAL
AMERICA

Howland I.
Baker I.
(1857)

Palmyra Atoll
(1898)

Jarvis I.
(1858)

0   2,000 mi

American
Samoa
(1899)

0   2,000 km
Miller Cylindrical
Projection

AUSTRALIA

>> **Analyze Maps** Why would possession of the islands shown here be important to American trade with China and Japan?

 Interactive Map

ships. "When a question arises of control over distant regions," Mahan wrote, "it must ultimately be decided by naval power."

In Mahan's view, the United States could not expand its navy unless it controlled naval bases throughout the world. Mahan was especially interested in acquiring harbors in the Caribbean and the Pacific as links to Latin America and Asia.

Even before Mahan's appeal, Congress had begun to enlarge and modernize the navy. By 1900, a powerful American navy was ready for action. Its steam-powered ships were called the **Great White Fleet** because their steel hulls were all painted white.

? LIST the reasons for the increase in American expansionism.

American Influence in the Pacific

As naval power grew, the United States showed increasing interest in Samoa, a chain of islands in the South Pacific. Samoa had a fine harbor that could serve as a naval base and commercial port.

Germany and Great Britain also realized the value of the harbor. As the three nations competed for control, a military clash seemed likely. In 1889, German ships fired upon Samoan villages that were friendly to the Americans. For months, German and American sailors eyed each other nervously from their warships. Then, with tensions at their highest, a powerful storm sank ships of both countries. The disaster helped ease the crisis.

Later, the three nations arranged a peaceful settlement. The United States and Germany divided Samoa, while Britain received territories elsewhere in the Pacific.

The United States had demonstrated that it would assert its power in the Pacific Ocean.

Interest in Hawaii Another Pacific territory that had long interested the United States was Hawaii. Hawaii is a chain of eight large islands and more than 100 smaller islands. Hawaii's rich soil, warm climate, and plentiful rainfall allow farmers to grow crops all year round.

Westerners first learned about Hawaii in 1778. A British sea captain, James Cook, dropped anchor in the islands on his way to China. In the early 1800s, American ships bound for China began stopping in Hawaii, and a few American sailors and traders settled there.

Missions and Plantations In 1820, American missionaries began arriving

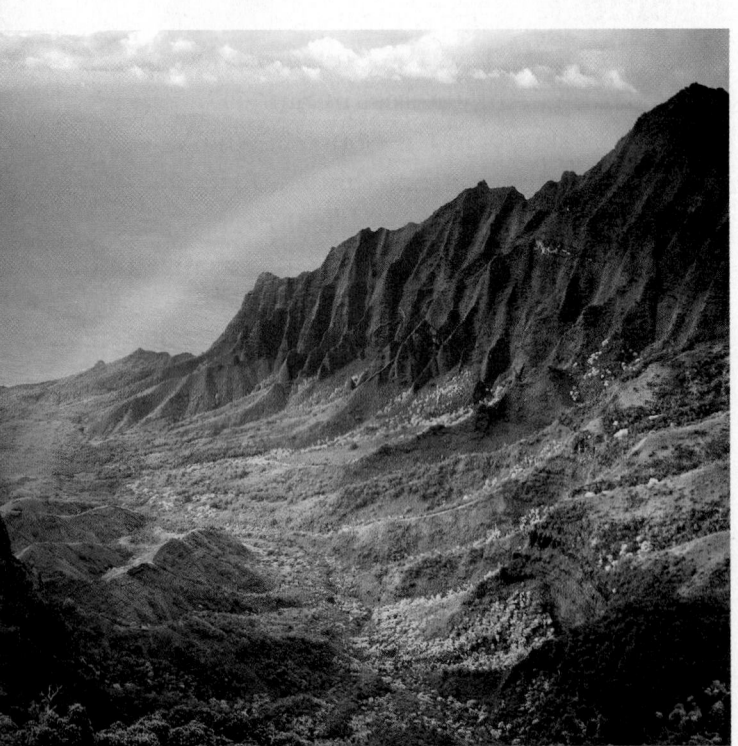

>> Seeking to increase its influence in the Pacific, the United States encouraged economic and political development in Hawaii, a string of islands in the Pacific.

in Hawaii. They were eager to convert the Hawaiians to Christianity. The missionaries and other Americans became valued advisers to the rulers of Hawaii. Americans helped write Hawaii's first constitution in 1840.

By the mid-1800s, Americans had set up large sugar plantations in Hawaii. Needing cheap labor, the planters imported thousands of workers from China, Korea, the Philippines, and Japan. By 1900, one fourth of Hawaii's population had been born in Japan.

As the sugar industry grew, so did the wealth and political power of American planters. In 1887, they forced the Hawaiian king, Kalakaua, to accept a new constitution. It reduced royal power and increased the planters' influence.

The Impact of American Involvement in Hawaii American influence in Hawaii significantly changed the social structure and cultural traditions of the native Hawaiian population. New rules outlawed Hawaiian traditions. The Hawaiian language could not be taught in schools, and dances such as the Hula were banned.

Imperialism also changed the relationship between the environment and Hawaii's people. Traditionally, land had been divided among the Hawaiian crown, the government, and the ruling elite. As American influence strengthened, control of much of Hawaii's land was given to American plantation owners instead.

Native forests were cleared and water was diverted for agricultural use. Foreigners further altered the environment by clearing native species and bringing in new animals and plants. Later efforts were introduced to reforest areas and change agricultural practices with exotic, non-native plants.

The Influence of American Plantation Owners Kalakaua died in 1891. The new queen, Liliuokalani (lih lee oo oh kah LAH nee), cherished Hawaiian independence. Rejecting the new constitution, she sought to reduce the influence and privileges of planters and foreign merchants.

In 1893, the American planters rebelled against the queen's attempt to limit their power. The American ambassador called for U.S. marines to land on Hawaii and protect American lives. In fact, the marines helped topple the queen. Faced with American guns, Liliuokalani gave up her throne.

> I yield to the superior force of the United States of America. . . . To avoid any collision of armed forces and perhaps the loss of life, I do this under protest, and impelled by said force, yield my authority.
>
> —Liliuokalani, letter to the United States government, 1893

Hawaii Is Annexed With Liliuokalani no longer in power, the planters quickly set up a republic and asked the United States to annex Hawaii. A debate raged in Congress for months. President Grover Cleveland blocked moves to take over the islands. "Our interference in the Hawaiian Revolution of 1893 was disgraceful," he later said.

Congress finally annexed Hawaii in 1898, after Cleveland left office. Two years later, Hawaii became a United States territory. In 1959, Hawaii became the fiftieth state.

❓ **IDENTIFY** one social, one economic, and one political impact of America's interest in Hawaii.

>> Queen Liliuokalani disagreed with the influence of foreign planters and merchants. **Deduce** Why do you think Liliuokalani was against foreign influence in Hawaii?

>> The United States annexed Hawaii in 1898 and Hawaii became a state in 1959. Pictured here is a U.S. flag being raised in place of the Hawaiian flag during the annexation ceremony.

Competition for Chinese Trade

Despite its new footholds in the Pacific, the United States was a latecomer to the race for Pacific and Asian territory. Britain, Germany, Japan, and other industrial nations were already competing for colonies in Asia. The rivalry was especially fierce in China.

Once the most advanced empire in the world, China had been weakened by years of civil war. In addition, China had refused to industrialize in the 1800s. It was unable to fight off industrial nations seeking profits from its vast resources and markets.

The Open Door Policy In the late 1800s, Britain, France, Germany, Russia, and Japan carved spheres of influence in China. A **sphere of influence** was an area, usually around a seaport, where a nation had special trading privileges. Each nation made laws for its own citizens in its own sphere.

The United States was eager to gain a share of the China trade. However, Secretary of State John Hay feared that the imperial powers would cut China off to American merchants. To prevent this, Hay sent a letter in 1899 to all the nations that had spheres of influence in China. He urged them to keep an "open door" in China permitting any nation to trade in the spheres of others. Reluctantly, the imperialist powers accepted the **Open Door Policy**.

The Boxer Rebellion Many Chinese resented foreign influence. Some formed a secret society called the Righteous Fists of Harmony, or Boxers. In 1900, the Boxers attacked westerners, whom they called "foreign devils," all over China. More than 200 foreigners were killed. Hundreds of others were trapped in Beijing, the Chinese capital.

Foreign governments quickly organized an international army that included 2,500 Americans. Armed with modern weapons, they fought their way into Beijing. They freed the trapped foreigners and crushed the uprising.

Several nations saw the **Boxer Rebellion** as an excuse to seize more land in China. Secretary of State Hay sent another Open Door letter, urging all nations to respect China's independence. Britain, France, and Germany officially accepted Hay's letter. Fearing war, Japan and Russia quietly observed Hay's policy. Hay's Open Door letters showed that, to

>> The Open Door Policy between imperial powers in China continued into the twentieth century. **Analyze Cartoons** How does this cartoon represent Chinese feelings about the Open Door Policy?

>> The Boxer Rebellion in 1900 was an attempt to expel all foreigners from China. This illustration shows Chinese forces battling British and Japanese troops.

Interactive Chart

defend its interests, the United States was ready to take a larger role in world affairs.

? CHECK UNDERSTANDING Why did the United States want an "open door" policy with China?

ASSESSMENT

1. **Generate Explanations** Determine how racism shaped imperialism, and explain why the racist logic of imperialism was flawed.

2. **Describe** the economic factors that influenced territorial expansion during the Age of Imperialism.

3. **Identify Cause and Effect** Explain how the U.S. sugar industry changed the physical and human geography of Hawaii.

4. **Connect** Explain how industrialization altered U.S. relations with both China and Japan.

5. **Draw Conclusions** Explain how imperialism affected relations among powerful western nations.

War and Empire

>> Colonel Theodore Roosevelt leads a charge in Cuba during the Spanish-American War.

▶ **Interactive Flipped Video**

>> Objectives

Summarize why tensions in Cuba led Americans to call for war with Spain.

Explain how Americans won a quick victory in the Spanish-American War.

Describe how the United States gained and ruled its new empire.

>> Key Terms

reconcentration
yellow journalism
Spanish-American
 War
Rough Riders
Buffalo Soldiers
Platt Amendment
protectorate
Foraker Act
atrocity
Theodore Roosevelt

President McKinley was worried about a looming war over Cuba, a Spanish-ruled island just 90 miles off the coast of Florida. Cuban patriots were in revolt against Spanish rule. Many Americans demanded that the President take action to help the Cubans. Almost every day, American newspapers reported stories of the cruelty and brutality of Spanish rule. The reports were often exaggerated, sometimes even made up. Nonetheless, they stirred American anger.

The Cuban Revolution

At first, the President resisted calls for war. But at 4 A.M. on April 25, 1898, a weary McKinley signed a declaration of war against Spain. The brief war that followed would launch the United States on its own age of imperialism in the Caribbean and the Pacific.

For many years, Americans had looked longingly at Cuba. As early as 1823, Secretary of State John Quincy Adams had compared Cuba to a ripe apple. A storm, he said, might tear that apple "from its native tree"—the Spanish empire—and drop it into the hands of the United States.

By the 1890s, Spain's once-vast empire in the Western Hemisphere had shrunk to two islands in the Caribbean: Cuba and Puerto Rico. Then, Cuban rebels created the storm that Adams had hoped for.

"Free Cuba!" In 1868, the Cuban people had rebelled against Spanish rule. The revolution was finally crushed after 10 years of fighting. Some of the revolutionaries fled to New York where they kept up the battle for freedom. Puerto Rican–born Lola Rodríguez de Tió wrote patriotic poems in support of Cuban independence. José Martí worked day and night raising funds and giving speeches in support of Cuban independence. He told sympathetic Americans of the Cuban struggle for freedom in his newspaper, *Patria*.

In 1895, Martí returned to Cuba. With cries of *Cuba Libre!*—"Free Cuba!"—rebels launched a new fight against Spain. Martí was killed early in the fighting, but the rebels continued the fight and won control of much of Cuba.

The rebels burned sugar cane fields and sugar mills all over Cuba. They hoped that

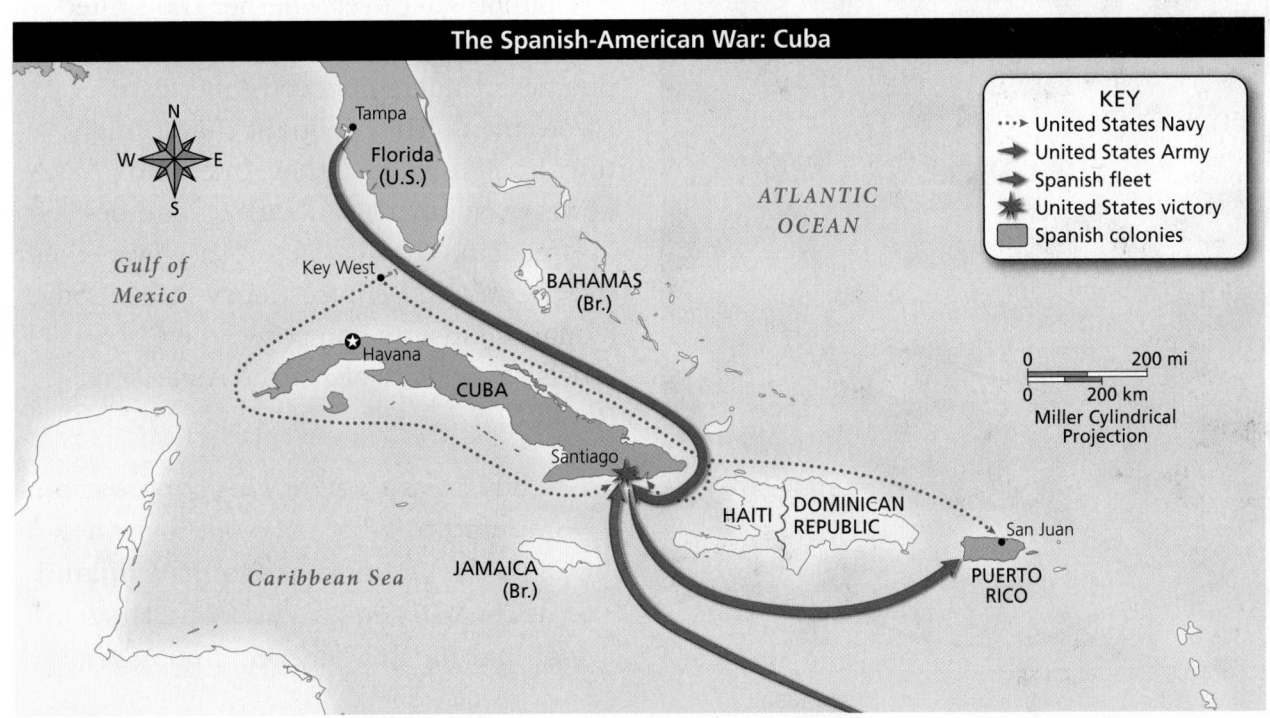

The Spanish-American War: Cuba

KEY
- ····▶ United States Navy
- ➤ United States Army
- ➤ Spanish fleet
- ✴ United States victory
- ▨ Spanish colonies

>> The United States hoped to avoid war, but was unable to stay out of war with Spain. Fighting in the Philippines and Cuba would follow. **Analyze Maps** Why did the United States have an interest in Cuba based on its location?

>> This photo shows a Cuban sugar planter with his staff and Spanish bodyguard in the 1890s. **Generate Explanations** Why might some Cubans have opposed the rebels?

>> This illustration shows Cuban rebels leading a charge against Spanish troops in the late 1890s.

this would make the island unprofitable for Spain and persuade the Spanish to leave. The rebels killed workers who opposed them. They even blew up some passenger trains.

In response, Spain sent a new governor to Cuba, General Valeriano Weyler (WAY ee lair). Weyler used brutal tactics to crush the revolt. In a policy known as **reconcentration**, his men moved about half a million Cubans into detention camps so that they could not aid the rebels. At least 100,000 Cubans in reconcentration camps died from starvation and disease.

Americans Are Divided In the United States, people watched the revolt in nearby Cuba with growing concern. The United States had vital economic links to the island. Americans had invested about $50 million in Cuban sugar and rice plantations, railroads, tobacco, and iron mines. American trade with Cuba was worth about $100 million a year.

Opinion split over whether the United States should intervene in Cuba. Many business leaders opposed American involvement. They thought that it might hurt foreign trade. Other Americans, however, sympathized with Cuban desires for freedom. They called on the government to take action. Senator Henry Cabot Lodge of Massachusetts compared the Cuban rebels to the Patriots in the American Revolution.

They have risen against oppression, compared to which the oppression which led us to rebel against England is as dust in the balance; and they feel that for this reason, if no other, they should have the sympathy of the people of the United States.

—Henry Cabot Lodge, Record of the 54th Congress, 1896

? CHECK UNDERSTANDING Why did the United States "look longingly" at Cuba?

War Fever

The press whipped up American sympathies for the people of Cuba. Two New York newspapers—Joseph Pulitzer's *World* and William Randolph Hearst's *Journal*—competed to print the most grisly stories about Spanish **atrocities**, or wartime acts of cruelty and brutality. The publishers knew that war with Spain would boost sales of their newspapers.

Sensational News To attract readers, Hearst and Pulitzer used **yellow journalism**, or reporting that relied on sensational stories and headlines. Often, these reports were biased or untrue. According to one story, a photographer bound for Cuba told Hearst that there was no war. "You supply the pictures," Hearst supposedly replied. "I'll supply the war." News stories described events in Cuba in graphic and horrifying detail.

Despite growing pressure, President Cleveland wanted to avoid war with Spain. He called the war fever in the United States an "epidemic of insanity." Stories in the press, he grumbled, were nonsense.

When William McKinley became President in 1897, he also tried to keep the country neutral. However, remaining neutral would soon become difficult.

The Battleship *Maine* In 1898, fighting broke out in Havana, the Cuban capital. Acting promptly, President McKinley sent

>> American publisher William Randolph Hearst's newspaper featured sensational stories about the Cuban struggle for independence to increase sales.

the battleship *Maine* to Havana to protect American citizens and property there.

On the night of February 15, the *Maine* lay at anchor in Havana harbor. Just after the bugler played taps, a huge explosion ripped through the ship. The explosion killed at least 260 of the 350 American sailors and officers on board.

The yellow press pounced on the tragedy. "DESTRUCTION OF THE WARSHIP *MAINE* WAS THE WORK OF AN ENEMY," screamed one New York newspaper. "THE WARSHIP *MAINE* SPLIT IN TWO BY AN ENEMY'S SECRET INFERNAL MACHINE?" blared the front page of another.

The real cause of the explosion remains a mystery. Most historians believe that a boiler blew up or that there was an accident in the ship's own ammunition hold. But Americans, urged on by Pulitzer and Hearst, clamored for war. "Remember the *Maine!*" they cried.

Still hoping to avoid war, McKinley tried to get Spain to talk with the Cuban rebels. In the end, however, he gave in to war fever. On April 25, 1898, Congress declared war on Spain.

❓ IDENTIFY MAIN IDEAS How did newspapers generate support for the war, and why?

The Spanish-American War

The **Spanish-American War** lasted only four months. The battlefront stretched from the nearby Caribbean to the distant Philippine Islands off the coast of Southeast Asia.

Capturing the Philippines Two months before the war started, Assistant Secretary of the Navy **Theodore Roosevelt** had begun making preparations for a possible war with Spain. Roosevelt quickly realized that a conflict with Spain would be fought not only in the Caribbean but wherever Spanish sea power lay. The Philippine Islands, a Spanish colony and Spain's main naval base in the Pacific, would be a major military objective.

Roosevelt believed it was important to attack the Spanish in the Philippines as soon as war began. He wired secret orders to Commodore George Dewey, commander of the Pacific fleet.

> Secret and confidential. Order the squadron . . . to Hong Kong. Keep full of coal. In the event of declaration of war Spain, your duty will be to see that the Spanish squadron does not leave the Asiatic coast, and then offensive operations in Philippine Islands.
>
> —Theodore Roosevelt, Telegram, February 25, 1898

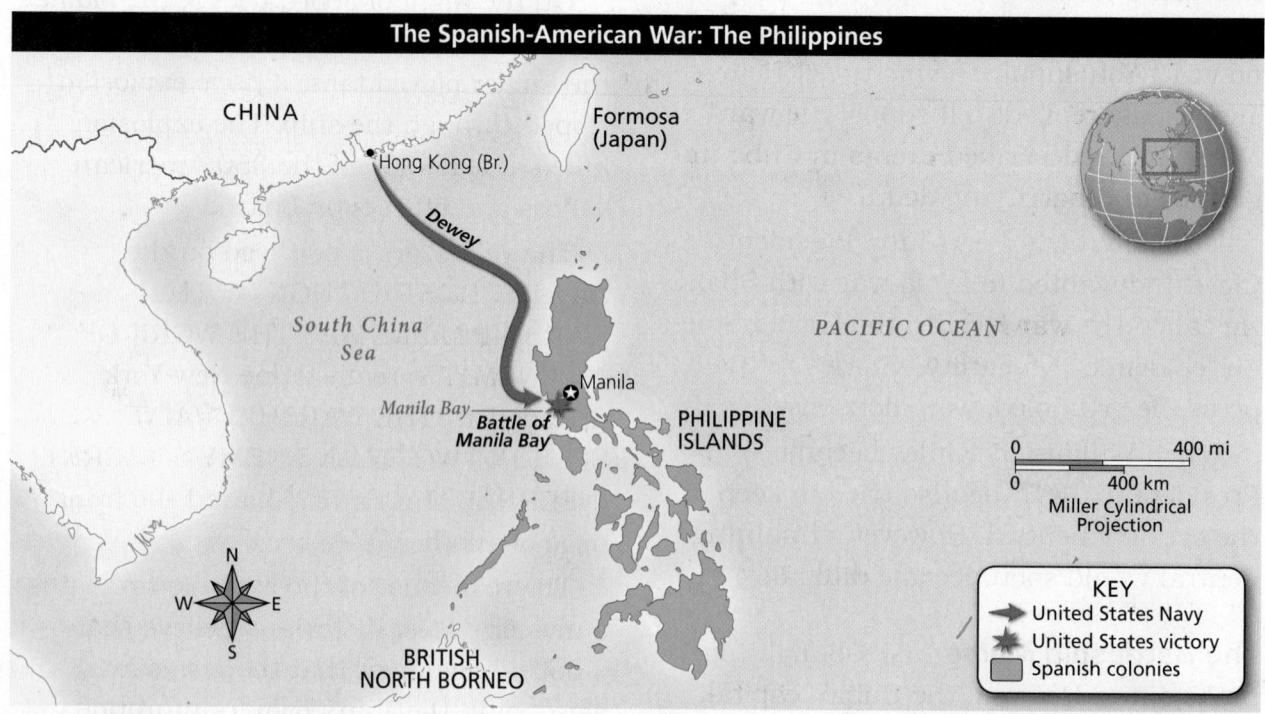

The Spanish-American War: The Philippines

CHINA
Formosa (Japan)
Hong Kong (Br.)
Dewey
South China Sea
PACIFIC OCEAN
Manila Bay
Manila
Battle of Manila Bay
PHILIPPINE ISLANDS
0   400 mi
0   400 km
Miller Cylindrical Projection
N W E S
BRITISH NORTH BORNEO

KEY
→ United States Navy
✶ United States victory
▢ Spanish colonies

>> **Analyze Maps** Describe the route that the United States Navy took to reach the Philippines.

▶ **Interactive Map**

Dewey followed Roosevelt's instructions. Immediately after war was declared, the Commodore sailed his fleet swiftly to Manila, the main city of the Philippines. On April 30, 1898, Dewey's ships slipped into Manila harbor under cover of darkness. There, the Spanish fleet lay at anchor.

At dawn, Dewey told his flagship commander, Charles Gridley, "You may fire when you are ready, Gridley." Taking their cue, the Americans bombarded the surprised Spanish ships. By noon, the Spanish fleet had been destroyed.

By July, American ground troops had landed in the Philippines. As in Cuba, local people there had been fighting for independence from Spain for years. With the help of these Filipino rebels, led by Emilio Aguinaldo (ah gwee NAHL doh), the American forces quickly captured Manila.

Victory in Cuba Meanwhile, American troops had also landed in Cuba. The expedition was badly organized. Soldiers wore heavy woolen uniforms in the tropical heat, and they often had to eat spoiled food. Yet, most were eager for battle.

None was more eager than Theodore Roosevelt. When the war broke out, Roosevelt resigned his position as Assistant Secretary of the Navy. He then organized the First Volunteer Cavalry Regiment, later called the **Rough Riders**. The Rough Riders were a mixed crew, ranging from cowboys to college students and adventurers.

The Rough Riders joined regular troops in the most notable land battle of the war. During the fight for the key Cuban city of Santiago, Americans had to gain control of the San Juan Heights overlooking the city. Under withering fire, charging American forces took two strategic hills.

>> This illustration shows the American navy defeating the Spanish fleet in the Battle of Manila, clearing the way for American ground forces to land in the Philippines soon after.

African American members of the 9th and 10th Cavalries, nicknamed **Buffalo Soldiers**, played a major role in the bloody victory. John J. Pershing, commander of the 10th Cavalry, later described how the troops united in what came to be called the Battle of San Juan Hill.

White regiments, black regiments, regulars and Rough Riders, representing the young manhood of the North and South, fought shoulder to shoulder, unmindful of race or color, . . . mindful of their common duty as Americans.

—John J. Pershing, quoted in *The Life of General Pershing* (MacAdam)

Two days later, the Americans destroyed the Spanish fleet in Santiago Bay. The Spanish army in Cuba surrendered.

American troops then landed on Puerto Rico and claimed the island.

Spanish Defeat Spain was defeated. On August 12, Spain and the United States agreed to end the fighting. American losses in battle were fairly light—379 killed. However, more than 5,000 Americans died of other causes, such as yellow fever, typhoid, and malaria.

John Hay, who was soon to become Secretary of State, summed up American enthusiasm for the war. "It's been a splendid little war," he wrote. A malaria-ridden veteran of the war had a different view: "I was lucky—I survived."

? **LOCATE** the areas of fighting in the Spanish-American War. Why did the war extend to so many regions?

Becoming a Colonial Power

In a peace treaty signed in Paris in December 1898, Spain agreed to grant Cuba its freedom. Spain also gave the United States two islands: Puerto Rico in the Caribbean and Guam in the Pacific. Finally, in return for $20 million, Spain handed over the Philippines to the United States.

Before the Senate approved the treaty, a great debate occurred. Many Americans objected to the treaty. They said it violated American principles of democracy by turning the United States into a colonial power.

Expansionists favored the treaty. They said that the navy needed bases in the Caribbean and the Pacific. They pointed out that the Philippines and Puerto Rico offered new territory for American businesses. Also, many Americans agreed

>> Spanish and American representatives signed the Treaty of Paris on December 10, 1898. The treaty concluded the Spanish-American War.

with President McKinley, who said that the United States would "uplift and civilize and Christianize [the Filipinos]." In fact, most Filipinos already were Christians.

Urged on by McKinley, the Senate narrowly approved the peace treaty in February 1899. At last, the United States had acquired a true overseas empire.

An American Protectorate in Cuba
Americans had to decide how to rule their new territories. When the war with Spain began, the United States pledged to "leave the government and control of [Cuba] to its people." That promise, however, was not kept. After the war, American soldiers remained in Cuba while the United States debated. Many in Congress believed that Cuba was not ready for independence. American business leaders feared that an independent Cuba might threaten their investments there.

In the end, the United States let the Cuban people write their own constitution. However, Cuba had to accept the **Platt Amendment**. The amendment allowed the United States to intervene in Cuba and gave the United States control of the naval base at Guantanamo Bay. In effect, the amendment made Cuba an American **protectorate**, a nation whose independence is limited by the control of a more powerful country.

The United States pulled its army out of Cuba in 1902. However, American soldiers would return to Cuba in 1906 and again in 1917.

New Government in Puerto Rico In Puerto Rico, the United States set up a new government under the **Foraker Act** of 1900. The act gave Puerto Ricans only a limited say in their own affairs. In 1917, Puerto Ricans were made citizens of the United States. Americans set up schools,

>> This 1902 political cartoon illustrated Cuba's lack of choices after it gained independence from Spain. All paths led to some form of U.S. control, none of which were appealing.

▶ **Interactive Chart**

improved healthcare, and built roads on the island. Even so, many Puerto Ricans wanted to be free of foreign rule.

Filipinos Revolt Filipino nationalists had begun fighting for independence long before the Spanish-American War. When the United States took over their land after the war, Filipinos felt betrayed. Led by Emilio Aguinaldo, they now fought for freedom against a new imperial power: the United States.

Aguinaldo, who had fought beside the Americans against Spain, accused the United States of forgetting its beginnings. The United States, he said, was using military force to keep the Filipinos from attaining "the same rights that the American people proclaimed more than a century ago."

>> Emilio Aguinaldo led Filipino nationalists in a war first against Spain and later against the United States.

The Philippine-American War was the first all-out Asian war in which the United States fought. It dragged on for years. At one point, about 60,000 American troops were fighting there. Finally, Aguinaldo was captured in 1901, and the war came to an end officially in 1902.

The Philippine-American War was longer and more costly than the Spanish-American War. More than 4,000 Americans died in the Philippines. Nearly 20,000 Filipino soldiers were killed. Another 200,000 civilians died from shelling, famine, and disease.

In 1902, the United States set up a government in the Philippines similar to the one in Puerto Rico. Filipinos, however, were not made American citizens because the United States planned to give them independence in the future. It was not until 1946, however, that the United States allowed Filipinos to govern themselves.

? **RECALL** How did the United States become a colonial power?

ASSESSMENT

1. **Generate Explanations** Explain how the rebellion in Cuba affected U.S. economic interests.

2. **Compare Points of View** Describe the contrasting points of view in the United States regarding intervention in Cuba.

3. **Identify Cause and Effect** Explain how yellow journalism influenced the Spanish-American War.

4. **Describe** the conditions of the peace treaty that ended the Spanish-American War, and explain why it was controversial.

5. **Identify Central Issues** Explain how the United States failed to keep its promise to Cuba after the Spanish-American War.

>> The USS *Nashville*'s 1903 arrival in Panama served to show U.S. support for the Panamanian rebellion against Colombia.

Interactive Flipped Video

When Theodore Roosevelt became President in 1901, he was determined to build a canal through Panama in Central America. Roosevelt knew that a canal would greatly benefit American commerce and military capability. By avoiding the long trip around South America, ships could shorten the journey from New York City to San Francisco by nearly 8,000 miles. Thus, a canal would reduce the cost of shipping goods. In addition, in the event of a war, the navy could quickly move ships back and forth between the Pacific Ocean and the Atlantic Ocean.

>> **Objectives**

Identify why and how the United States built the Panama Canal.

Explain Theodore Roosevelt's "big stick" policy in Latin America.

Summarize the crisis that erupted between the United States and Mexico.

>> **Key Terms**

isthmus
corollary
Roosevelt Corollary
dollar diplomacy
moral diplomacy
Woodrow Wilson

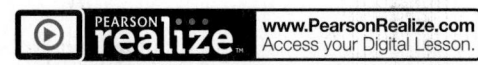
PEARSON
realize™
www.PearsonRealize.com
Access your Digital Lesson.

The Panama Canal

Roosevelt Makes an Offer A unique geographical feature, the Isthmus of Panama, provided an ideal location to build a canal. An **isthmus** is a narrow strip of land that has water on each side with the strip of land connecting two larger bodies of land. Only 50 miles of land separated the Caribbean Sea and the Pacific Ocean.

To build the canal, Roosevelt had to deal with Colombia, which owned the isthmus. Roosevelt asked Secretary of State John Hay to approach Colombia. Hay offered $10 million cash plus $250,000 a year to rent a strip of land across Panama.

Taking the Canal Zone When Colombia refused Roosevelt's offer, he was furious. "I do not think the [Colombian] lot of jack rabbits should be allowed permanently

>> This cartoon shows the increasing global influence of the American steel industry.

to bar one of the future highways of civilization," he exclaimed.

At times like this, Roosevelt was fond of quoting an African proverb: "Speak softly and carry a big stick, and you will go far." He meant that words should be supported by strong action. Roosevelt knew that some Panamanians wanted to break away from Colombia. He made it known that he would not help Colombia suppress the rebels. In fact, he might even support the rebellion.

On November 2, 1903, the American warship *Nashville* dropped anchor in the port of Colón, Panama. The next day, Panamanians rebelled against Colombia.

American forces stopped Colombian troops from crushing the revolt. Panama then declared itself an independent republic. The United States recognized the new nation at once. Panama in turn agreed to let the United States build a canal on terms similar to those it had offered to Colombia.

Roosevelt's action in Panama angered many Latin Americans. It also upset some members of Congress. The President, however, proudly stated, "I took the Canal Zone and let Congress debate."

❓ CHECK UNDERSTANDING Why did Roosevelt become involved in the Panamanian rebellion against Colombia?

Construction Proves Challenging

Roosevelt now had the right to build his canal. However, before work could begin, Americans had to conquer a deadly enemy: disease.

Preventing Tropical Disease With its tropical heat, heavy rainfall, and plentiful swamps, Panama was a

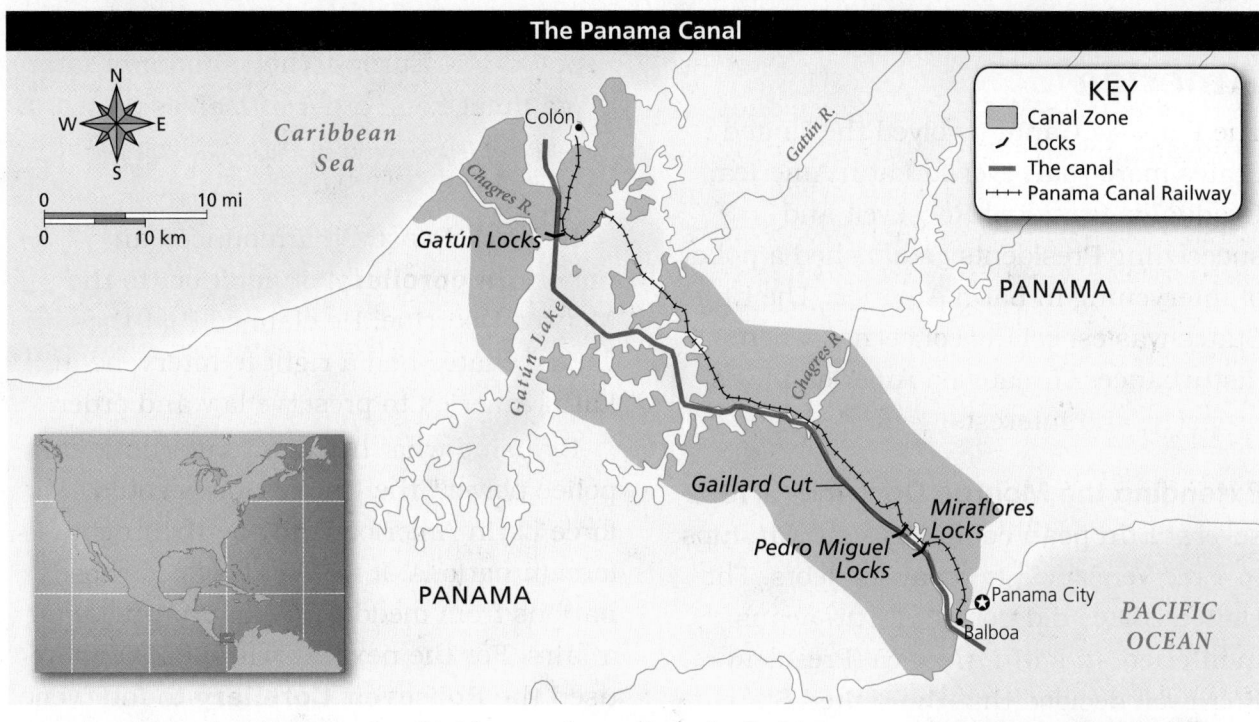

The Panama Canal

KEY
- Canal Zone
- Locks
- The canal
- Panama Canal Railway

Caribbean Sea

Colón

Gatún Locks

Chagres R.

Gatún R.

Gatún Lake

PANAMA

Chagres R.

Gaillard Cut

Pedro Miguel Locks

Miraflores Locks

Panama City

Balboa

PACIFIC OCEAN

PANAMA

>> **Analyze Maps** In which direction did ships travel to get from the Caribbean Sea to the Pacific Ocean?

Interactive Gallery

"mosquito paradise." This presented serious difficulties for the canal builders. Mosquitoes carry two of the deadliest tropical diseases: malaria and yellow fever.

Dr. William Gorgas, an army physician, arrived in Panama in 1905 to help control the mosquitoes and the spread of disease. He ordered workers to locate all pools of water, where mosquitoes laid their eggs. Day after day, the workers drained swamps, sprayed tons of insecticide, and spread oil on stagnant water to kill mosquito eggs.

By 1906, Gorgas had won his battle. Yellow fever disappeared from Panama. Malaria cases dropped dramatically. Work on the Panama Canal could proceed.

Difficult Work Under the supervision of army engineer Colonel George Goethals, more than 40,000 workers struggled to

dig the canal. Most were blacks from the West Indies. They blasted a path through mountains and carved out the largest artificial lake in the world at that time. In all, they removed more than 200 million cubic yards of earth. Then, they built gigantic locks to raise and lower ships as they passed through the canal. Finally, in 1914, the first ocean-going steamship traveled through the Panama Canal.

The new waterway helped the trade of many nations. American merchants and manufacturers benefited most. They could now ship goods cheaply to South America and Asia. However, many Latin American nations remained bitter about the way in which the United States had gained control of the canal.

? IDENTIFY SUPPORTING DETAILS What detail shows how the Panama Canal benefited American trade?

Intervention in Latin America

The Panama Canal involved the United States more than ever in Latin America. Gradually, President Roosevelt and succeeding Presidents established a policy of intervening in Latin America. The United States was especially concerned when disturbances threatened American lives, property, and interests.

Extending the Monroe Doctrine In 1902, several European countries sent warships to force Venezuela to repay its debts. The United States did not want Europeans to interfere in Latin America. President Roosevelt decided that the United States must step in to keep Europeans out. He declared:

> If we intend to say 'Hands off' to the powers of Europe, then sooner or later we must keep order ourselves.
>
> —Theodore Roosevelt, quoted in *T. R.: The Last Romantic* (Brands)

In 1904, Roosevelt announced an important **corollary**, or addition, to the Monroe Doctrine. He claimed that the United States had a right to intervene in Latin America to preserve law and order.

By using what he called "international police power," the United States could force Latin Americans to pay their debts to foreign nations. It would also keep those nations from meddling in Latin American affairs. For the next 20 years, Presidents used the **Roosevelt Corollary** to intervene in Latin America.

Dollar Diplomacy Roosevelt's successor, William Howard Taft, also favored a strong role in Latin America. However, he wanted to "substitute dollars for bullets." He urged American bankers to invest in Latin America. Taft's policy of building strong economic ties to Latin America became known as **dollar diplomacy**.

American investors responded eagerly. They helped build roads, railroads, and harbors in Latin America. These improvements increased trade, benefiting both the United States and local governments. The new railroads, for example, brought minerals and other resources to Latin American ports. From there, they were shipped all over the world.

Dollar diplomacy created problems, too. American businesses, such as the United Fruit Company, often meddled in the political affairs of host countries. Sometimes, the United States used military force to keep order. In 1912, when a revolution erupted in Nicaragua, the

>> President Roosevelt encouraged intervention in Latin America when U.S. interests were at stake.

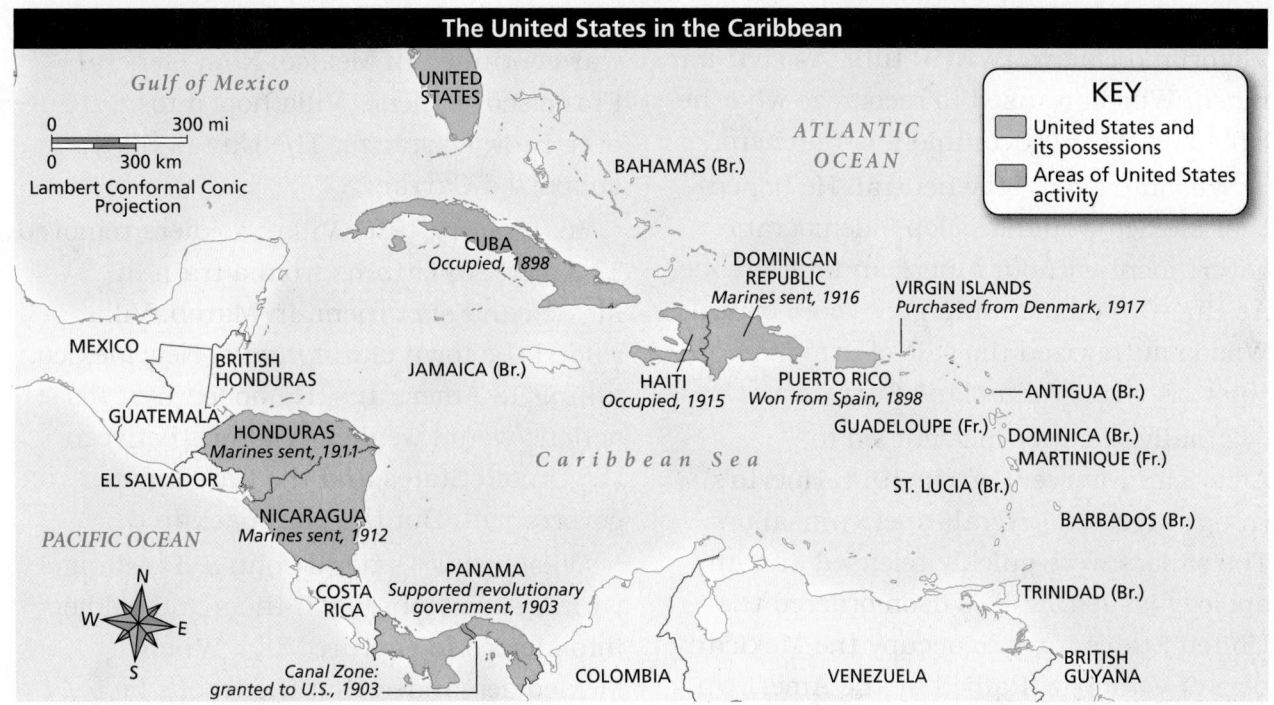

The United States in the Caribbean

KEY
- United States and its possessions
- Areas of United States activity

Gulf of Mexico

UNITED STATES

ATLANTIC OCEAN

BAHAMAS (Br.)

CUBA
Occupied, 1898

DOMINICAN REPUBLIC
Marines sent, 1916

VIRGIN ISLANDS
Purchased from Denmark, 1917

MEXICO

BRITISH HONDURAS

JAMAICA (Br.)

HAITI
Occupied, 1915

PUERTO RICO
Won from Spain, 1898

ANTIGUA (Br.)

GUATEMALA

HONDURAS
Marines sent, 1911

GUADELOUPE (Fr.)

DOMINICA (Br.)

MARTINIQUE (Fr.)

EL SALVADOR

Caribbean Sea

ST. LUCIA (Br.)

PACIFIC OCEAN

NICARAGUA
Marines sent, 1912

BARBADOS (Br.)

PANAMA
Supported revolutionary government, 1903

TRINIDAD (Br.)

COSTA RICA

Canal Zone:
granted to U.S., 1903

COLOMBIA

VENEZUELA

BRITISH GUYANA

0   300 mi
0   300 km
Lambert Conformal Conic Projection

>> **Analyze Maps** Which of the areas shown on the map were governed directly by the United States?

 Interactive Cartoon

United States sent in marines to protect American investments.

Moral Diplomacy The next President, **Woodrow Wilson**, condemned the heavy-handed foreign policy of earlier Presidents. "The force of America," he said, "is the force of moral principle." The goals of Wilson's **moral diplomacy** were to condemn imperialism, spread democracy, and promote peace.

Nevertheless, Wilson ordered military intervention in Latin America more than any prior President. He sent marines to quell disturbances in Haiti in 1915 and in the Dominican Republic in 1916. American troops remained in Haiti until 1934.

The United States declared that its troops were restoring order and guarding American lives and property. Still, many Latin Americans denounced the United

States for invading their countries and interfering in their internal affairs.

❓ **IDENTIFY MAIN IDEAS** How does dollar diplomacy differ from moral diplomacy?

U.S. Involvement in Mexico

Moral diplomacy faced its greatest test in Mexico. Porfirio Díaz, Mexico's president from 1884 to 1911, welcomed American investment. By 1912, Americans had invested about $1 billion to develop mines, oil wells, railroads, and ranches. Yet, most Mexicans remained poor. They worked the land of a few wealthy families, receiving very little for their labor.

Mexican Revolution Mexicans rebelled against Díaz in 1910. The new leader, Francisco Madero, promised democratic reform. Then, in 1913, Madero was himself overthrown and killed by General Victoriano Huerta (WEHR tuh). As civil war raged, Wilson refused to recognize what he called Huerta's "government of butchers."

Wilson tried to stay neutral. He hoped that Mexico would develop a democratic government without American interference. As Huerta's dictatorship grew more brutal, Wilson authorized the sale of arms to Huerta's rival, Venustiano Carranza.

Finally, a minor incident led to American intervention. In 1914, Huerta's troops arrested several American sailors. The sailors were quickly released and an apology issued. Still, Wilson ordered the United States Navy to occupy the Mexican port of Veracruz. Rallied by the American show of strength, Carranza's forces drove Huerta from power. The United States troops withdrew.

>> General Huerta's arrest of American sailors in 1914 prompted the U.S. Navy to take action. Here, American military members raise an American flag over the port of Veracruz.

The United States Invades Still, civil war continued in Mexico. Now, General Francisco "Pancho" Villa hoped to overthrow Carranza. The United States supported Carranza.

In January 1916, Villa's soldiers removed 17 American citizens from a train in Mexico and shot them. In March, Villa raided the town of Columbus, New Mexico, killing 18 Americans. He hoped that his actions would weaken relations between the United States and the Carranza government. But the plan backfired.

Wilson sent General John J. Pershing with an army of several thousand soldiers into Mexico to capture Villa. When Mexico demanded that the troops be withdrawn, Wilson refused. Still, both Wilson and Carranza resisted calls for war. After 11 months, Wilson ordered Pershing to withdraw without capturing Villa. The United States had again shown its willingness to use force to protect its interests. The incident strained relations with Mexico.

As United States troops headed home from Mexico, many Americans realized that their nation's role in world affairs had dramatically changed over the years. Now, the United States stationed troops and ships in both Asia and Latin America. American business interests spanned the globe. At the same time, an enormous war had begun in Europe in 1914. With its increased role in international affairs, the United States would find it impossible to stay out of the conflict.

🅿 **TRACE** how U.S. foreign policy toward Mexico changed over the course of Wilson's presidency.

>> Along with other revolutionaries, Mexican leader Pancho Villa (fifth from left) engaged in civil war to overthrow Carranza and rid Mexico of American influence.

ASSESSMENT

1. **Identify Steps in a Process** Explain how the United States gained the right to build the Panama Canal, and describe the effects of these actions.

2. **Generate Explanations** Explain why President Roosevelt extended the Monroe Doctrine with the Roosevelt Corollary.

3. **Draw Conclusions** Describe the advantages and disadvantages of dollar diplomacy.

4. **Compare and Contrast** Wilson's moral diplomacy with the policies of previous presidents.

5. **Analyze Context** Explain why the United States intervened in Mexico, and describe the results.

12.4 A European War

>> World War I was characterized by trench warfare, a brutal form of fighting that claimed many lives. This photo shows a British trench during the Battle of the Somme in France in 1916.

▶ **Interactive Flipped Video**

>> Objectives

Identify the causes of World War I.

Describe how war was fought in the trenches.

Explain how Germany's use of submarine warfare affected American neutrality.

>> Key Terms

nationalism
militarism
terrorist
kaiser
Central Powers
Allied Powers
stalemate
propaganda
Lusitania
neutral
trench warfare
U-boat

What caused the war in Europe? Tensions had been building there for years. When they erupted and war began in 1914, few Europeans were surprised.

The Buildup to War

Nationalism Creates Rivalries One cause of this tension came from the extreme feelings of **nationalism**, or pride in one's nation. In the 1870s, European nationalists demanded freedom and self-government. They believed that people with a common language and culture should throw off foreign rule and form their own countries.

While nationalism encouraged unity, it also created mistrust and bitter rivalry between nations. For example, France and Germany had gone to war in 1870. When France lost the war, it had to give Germany the iron-rich territory of Alsace-Lorraine. The French never forgot this blow to their national pride. They hoped for an opportunity to regain their lost territory.

In Eastern Europe, nationalism deepened hostility between Austria-Hungary and Russia. Russia encouraged Serbs and other minorities in Austria-Hungary to rise up against their rulers.

Imperialism and Militarism Another cause of problems in Europe came from imperialism. Between 1870 and 1914, rivalries expanded among powerful nations such as Britain, France, Germany, Italy, and Russia as they scrambled for colonies in Africa, Asia, and the Pacific. Often, several nations competed for power in the same region. This competition sometimes led to wars in places far from Europe.

Militarism was a third source of tension. **Militarism** is the policy of building up strong armed forces to prepare for war. European nations expanded their armies and navies, creating new stresses. For example, Germany built up its navy. Britain responded by adding more ships to its fleet. This race for naval dominance strained relations between the two nations.

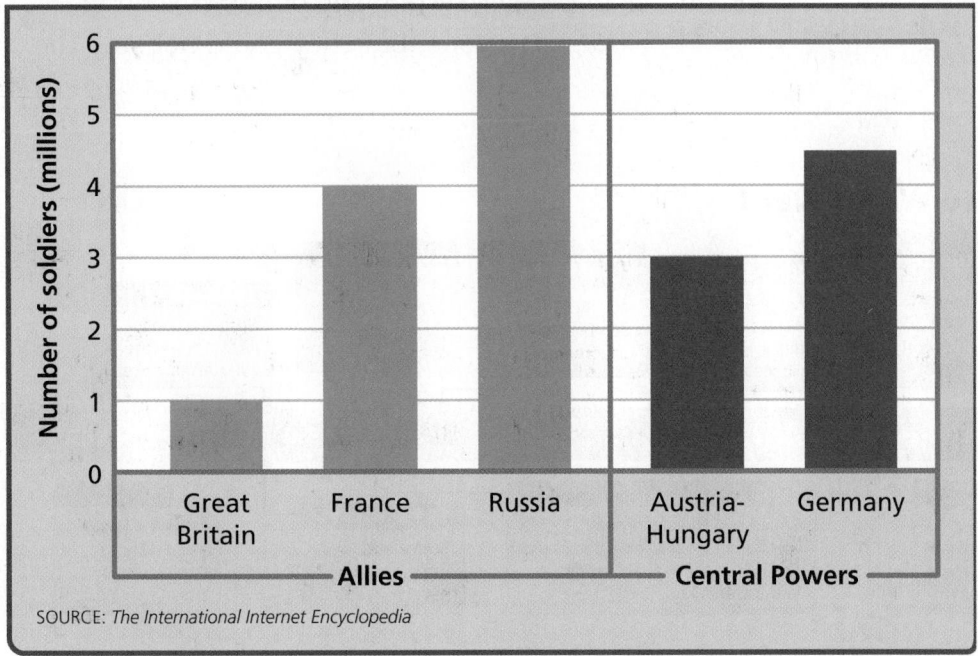

Standing Armies of Europe, 1914

SOURCE: *The International Internet Encyclopedia*

>> **Analyze Graphs** Based on the data in the graph, evaluate whether the Allies or Central Powers are more or less prepared for war.

The Alliance System To protect themselves, European powers formed rival alliances. Germany organized the Triple Alliance with Austria-Hungary and Italy. France responded by linking itself to Russia and Britain in the Triple Entente (ahn TAHNT).

The alliance system posed a new danger. Allies agreed to support one another in case of an attack. Thus, a crisis involving one member of an alliance also affected that nation's allies. This meant that a minor incident could spark a major war. On June 28, 1914, that incident took place.

? DEFINE What is militarism, and how did it contribute to World War I?

The Crisis Begins

For years, nationalism had caused turmoil in the Balkan peninsula in southeastern Europe. There, the rival nations of Albania, Bulgaria, Greece, Montenegro, Romania, and Serbia battled for territory. At the same time, Balkan nationalists called on related ethnic groups in Austria-Hungary to throw off Austrian rule.

The Archduke's Assassination In June 1914, a crisis that would have a devastating effect struck the region. Archduke Francis Ferdinand, heir to the throne of Austria-Hungary, was visiting Sarajevo, the capital of Bosnia. At the time, Bosnia was part of the Eastern European empire ruled by Austria-Hungary. Francis Ferdinand's visit angered members of the Black Hand, a Serbian terrorist group. A **terrorist** uses threats and violence to promote a cause. The Black Hand wanted Bosnia to break away from Austria-Hungary and join Serbia.

On June 28, the archduke and his wife, Sophie, rode through Sarajevo in an open car. Suddenly, a young terrorist named Gavrilo Princip stepped from the curb, waving a pistol. Taking aim, he fatally shot Francis Ferdinand and Sophie.

Alliances Declare War In the days that followed, Austria-Hungary accused the Serbian government of organizing the archduke's assassination. When Austria-Hungary threatened war, Russia moved to protect Serbia. Diplomats rushed to ease tensions, but they could not stop the

Events Leading to World War I

1871 France surrenders to Germany in the Franco-German War.

1882 Germany, Austria-Hungary, and Italy form a secret agreement called the Triple Alliance.

1894 France and Russia form the Franco-Russian Alliance.

1904 France and Britain sign the Entente Cordial to settle disagreements.

1904–1905 Japan defeats Russia in the Russo-Japanese War.

1912–1913 Serbia expands its territory in the two Balkan Wars.

1870   1880   1890   1900   1910   1920

1879 An alliance is formed between Austria-Hungary and Germany.

1907 Britain and Russia form an alliance, which leads to the formation of the Triple Entente between Britain, France, and Russia.

1912 Britain and France sign a naval agreement.

1914 Archduke Franz Ferdinand is assassinated by a Serbian nationalist, igniting World War I.

SOURCE: *Encyclopædia Britannica*

>> **Analyze Charts** How do the events in the timeline demonstrate the ease with which many European countries could fall into war?

Europe at War, 1914

KEY
- Allies
- Central Powers
- Neutral nations
- Neutral nations that later joined the Central Powers
- Neutral nations that later joined the Allies

>> **Analyze Maps** Identify the countries that comprised the Allies and the Central Powers at the start of the war in 1914.

Interactive Chart

system of alliances from running its fateful course.

On July 28, Austria-Hungary declared war on Serbia. The very next day, Russia ordered its forces to mobilize, or prepare for war. Austria-Hungary's ally, Germany, called on Russia to cancel the mobilization order. When it received no reply, Germany declared war on Russia on August 1.

On August 3, Germany declared war on Russia's ally France. The next day, when German armies sliced through neutral Belgium on their march to France, Britain declared war on Germany. Long before, Britain had promised to defend Belgium if it were attacked. Austria-Hungary declared war on Russia on August 6. In this way, what began as a local crisis in Bosnia exploded into a major war.

? IDENTIFY SUPPORTING DETAILS What details support the fact that the alliance system turned a local crisis into a world war?

Trench Warfare Leads to Stalemate

"You will be home before the leaves have fallen from the trees," the **kaiser**, or German emperor, promised his troops as they marched off to war. Europeans on both sides of the conflict thought the war would end soon. They were mistaken. The war dragged on for four blood-soaked years, from 1914 to 1918. At the time, the conflict was called the Great War. Later, it became known as the First World War or World War I.

The war pitted the **Central Powers**— Germany, Austria-Hungary, Bulgaria, and the Ottoman, or Turkish, Empire—against the **Allied Powers**, which were France, Britain, and Russia. In time, several other nations, including Italy, joined the Allies.

By November 1914, a German advance and an Allied counterattack had produced nothing but a deadly stalemate. A

stalemate is a deadlock in which neither side is strong enough to defeat the other. For three years, the two armies fought huge battles but with little to show for them.

Both sides dug in, creating a maze of trenches protected by barbed wire. Some trenches were shallow ditches. Others were elaborate tunnels that served as headquarters and first-aid stations. Between the frontline trenches of each side lay a "no man's land" of barbed wire.

In **trench warfare**, soldiers spent day after day shelling the enemy trenches. An attack would begin with hours of heavy artillery fire. Then, on orders from an officer, the troops charged "over the top" of the trenches. Armed with their rifles, soldiers raced across "no man's land" to attack the enemy. With luck, they might overrun a few trenches. Before long, the enemy would launch a counterattack, with similar results. In this way, the struggle went on, back and forth, over a few hundred yards of territory.

A new weapon used on both sides was gas—chlorine and mustard were two types. The clouds of gas floated into the trenches, choking and blinding the soldiers.

Because of the nature of trench warfare, most offensives were long and deadly. The Battle of Verdun lasted for 10 months in 1916. The Germans lost some 400,000 men trying to overrun French lines. The French lost even more lives defending their positions.

Meanwhile, in the East, the vast armies of Germany and Austria-Hungary faced off against those of Russia and Serbia. Stalemate and trench warfare brought deadly results there as well. By mid-1916, the Russians had lost more than one

>> During World War I, soldiers on both sides fought from trenches dug in the ground. The trenches were built as networked paths allowing armies to move men, supplies, and equipment over great distances without being exposed to enemy fire.

▶ **Interactive 3-D Model**

million soldiers. Yet, neither side could win a decisive victory.

? DESCRIBE the effects of trench warfare.

The United States Tries to Stay Neutral

When war broke out in Europe, the United States was determined to avoid being dragged into the conflict. The government adopted an official position of neutrality. **Neutral** means not taking sides in a conflict.

Public opinion, however, was divided, often along ethnic lines. Most Americans favored the Allies because of long-standing ties of language, history, and culture through Britain. Also, the United States and France had been allies in the American Revolution.

On the other hand, many of the 8 million Americans of German or Austrian descent favored the Central Powers. Millions of Irish Americans also sympathized with the Central Powers. They hated Britain, which had ruled Ireland for centuries. Many American Jews favored Germany over Russia. Some of them had fled persecution in Russia only a few years earlier.

Effects on the U.S. The war had several immediate effects on the United States. First, the economy boomed as American farmers and manufacturers rushed to fill orders for war goods. By 1917, trade with the Allies had greatly increased. Trade with the Central Powers also increased but by a much smaller amount. This trade imbalance meant that the United States was not strictly neutral.

Both sides waged a propaganda war in the United States. **Propaganda** is the

>> Gas was one of the most feared weapons of World War I. Soldiers wore gas masks such as this one to filter the poisoned air so they could breathe safely.

>> Although many Americans were in favor of the war, many others were against it. The pacifist position was shown in songs such as "I Didn't Raise My Boy To Be A Soldier" in 1915.

spreading of ideas that help a cause or hurt an opposing cause. Each side pictured the other as savage beasts who killed innocent civilians.

U-boats Attack As a neutral nation, the United States claimed the right to trade with either side in the conflict. Early in the war, however, Britain blockaded German ports, hoping to starve Germany into surrender. In response, Germany set up a blockade around Britain. To enforce the blockade, Germany used a powerful new weapon—a fleet of submarines known as **U-boats**. German U-boats attacked any ship that entered or left British ports. This meant that neutral ships would also be attacked.

U-boat attacks on neutral shipping raised a storm of protest. Under international law, a country at war could stop and search a neutral ship suspected of carrying war goods. However, German submarines were not equipped to conduct a search. After surfacing, they simply torpedoed enemy and neutral ships, often killing scores of civilians.

Germany warned the United States and other neutral nations to keep their ships out of the blockade zone. President Wilson responded by vowing to hold Germany responsible if its U-boats caused any loss of American life or property.

The Sinking of the _Lusitania_ Germany ignored Wilson's warning. On May 7, 1915, a German submarine torpedoed the _Lusitania_, a British passenger ship, off the coast of Ireland. Nearly 1,200 people died, including 128 Americans. An outraged Wilson threatened to break off diplomatic relations, or official ties, if Germany did not stop sinking passenger ships. Germany was not ready to strengthen the Allies by drawing the United States into the war. It agreed to restrict its submarine campaign.

German Blockade of Britain, 1915

KEY
☐ German War Zone

NORWAY

ATLANTIC
OCEAN

North
Sea

DENMARK

Scotland

UNITED
KINGDOM

Ireland _Irish
Sea_

Wales England NETH. GERMANY

London

BELGIUM

English Channel

FRANCE

0   200 mi
0   200 km
Equidistant Conic
Projection

>> **Analyze Maps** Based on information in the map, explain the German blockade strategy.

>> Nearly 1,200 people, including 128 American citizens, died when a German submarine sank the Lusitania in 1915.

Interactive Gallery

Before attacking any ship, U-boats would surface and give warning. This agreement, called the Sussex Pledge, kept the United States out of the war a little longer.

? **LIST** the difficulties the United States faced in staying neutral during World War I.

ASSESSMENT

1. **Draw Conclusions** Explain how nationalism increased tensions between European countries.

2. **Support Ideas With Evidence** Explain how World War I differed from previous wars.

3. **Compare Points of View** Describe American public opinion regarding World War I, and explain how this related to the United States' official position.

4. **Determine Cause and Effect** Explain how World War I affected the U.S. economy.

5. **Generate Explanations** Explain why Britain and Germany blockaded one another.

12.5 Entering the War

>> President Woodrow Wilson read his war message to Congress on April 2, 1917. Wilson signed the declaration of war four days later.

Interactive Flipped Video

>> **Objectives**

Summarize how President Wilson tried to bring about peace.

Explain why the United States chose to declare war.

Describe how the government prepared for and managed the war effort.

Identify the impact of the war on the home front.

>> **Key Terms**

warmonger
Zimmermann
  telegram
czar
Selective Service
  Act
draft
illiterate
bureaucracy
Liberty Bond
pacifist
Socialist

President Wilson tried to bring both sides to peace talks. He believed that the United States, as a neutral nation, could lead warring nations to a fair peace, a "peace without victory." But Wilson's peace efforts failed.

The U.S. Moves Toward War

Even as he was trying to make peace, Wilson knew that the United States might be drawn into the war. Thus, the President began to lobby for a stronger army and navy.

In 1916, Wilson ran for reelection against Republican Charles Evans Hughes. Although Hughes also favored neutrality, Democrats were able to portray him as a **warmonger**, or person who tries to stir up war. At the same time, they boosted Wilson's image with the slogan "He kept us out of war!"

The race was close. On election night, Hughes went to bed believing he had won. Just after midnight, his telephone rang. "The President cannot be disturbed," a friend told the caller. "Well, when he wakes up," the caller replied, "just tell him he isn't President." Late returns from California had given Wilson the election.

Diplomacy Ends In January 1917, Wilson issued what proved to be his final plea for peace. It was too late. In a desperate effort to break the Allied blockade, Germany had already decided to renew submarine warfare. Germany warned neutral nations that after February 1, 1917, its U-boats would have orders to sink any ship nearing Britain. German leaders knew that renewed U-boat attacks would probably bring the United States into the war. They gambled that they would defeat the Allies before American troops could reach Europe. To protest Germany's action, Wilson broke off diplomatic relations with Germany.

The Zimmermann Note A few weeks later, a startling discovery moved the United States closer to war. In February, Wilson learned that Arthur Zimmermann, Germany's foreign secretary, had sent a secret note to the German minister in Mexico. The **Zimmermann telegram**

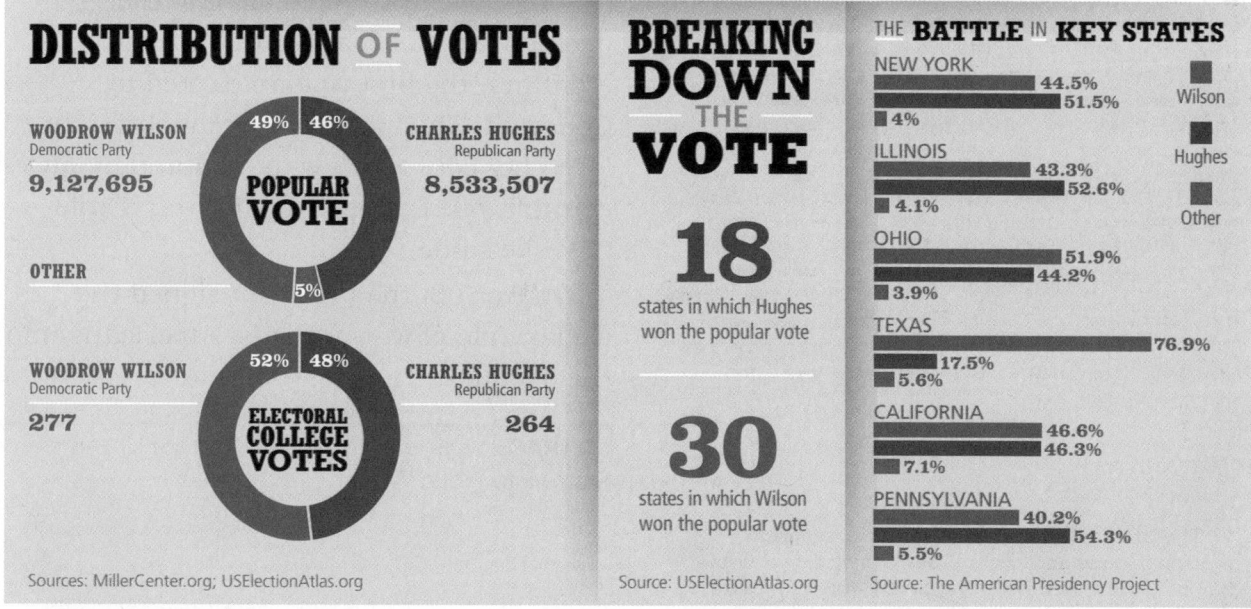

★ **THE ELECTION** OF **1916** ★

DISTRIBUTION OF **VOTES**

WOODROW WILSON
Democratic Party
9,127,695

POPULAR VOTE
49% | 46%
5%

CHARLES HUGHES
Republican Party
8,533,507

WOODROW WILSON
Democratic Party
277

ELECTORAL COLLEGE VOTES
52% | 48%

CHARLES HUGHES
Republican Party
264

Sources: MillerCenter.org; USElectionAtlas.org

BREAKING DOWN THE **VOTE**

18
states in which Hughes won the popular vote

30
states in which Wilson won the popular vote

Source: USElectionAtlas.org

THE **BATTLE** IN **KEY STATES**

■ Wilson
■ Hughes
■ Other

NEW YORK
44.5%
51.5%
4%

ILLINOIS
43.3%
52.6%
4.1%

OHIO
51.9%
44.2%
3.9%

TEXAS
76.9%
17.5%
5.6%

CALIFORNIA
46.6%
46.3%
7.1%

PENNSYLVANIA
40.2%
54.3%
5.5%

Source: The American Presidency Project

>> **Analyze Graphs** Analyze the distribution of popular votes and draw conclusions about the American public's opinion of Woodrow Wilson.

instructed the minister to urge Mexico to attack the United States if the United States declared war on Germany. In return, Germany would help Mexico win back its "lost provinces" in the American Southwest, which would include all of Texas, Arizona, and New Mexico. When Americans heard about the Zimmermann telegram, anti-German feeling soared.

The Russian Revolution Two other events in early 1917 pushed the United States still closer to war. First, German submarines sank several American merchant ships. Second, a revolution in Russia drove Czar Nicholas II from power.

For hundreds of years, **czars**, or Russian emperors, had ruled with absolute power. Several times in the 1800s and early

1900s, Russians revolted against czarist rule. Their efforts ended in failure.

When the war in Europe began in 1914, Russians united behind the czar. However, as the war brought heavy losses at the front and economic hardship at home, discontent resurfaced. In March 1917, riots protesting the shortage of food turned into a revolution. The czar was forced to step down. Revolutionaries then set up a Provisional Government and called for democratic reforms.

President Wilson welcomed the Russian Revolution. He was a firm believer in democracy, and it was against his principles to be an ally of an absolute ruler. Without the czar, it would be easier for Wilson to support the Allied cause.

Declaration of War Finally, President Wilson went before Congress on April 2, 1917, to ask for a declaration of war. "The world must be made safe for democracy," he declared. His war message assured the American people that entering the war was not only just; it was noble.

Congress voted for war 455 to 56. Among those who voted against the declaration was Jeannette Rankin of Montana, the first woman elected to Congress. She hated war as much as she loved her country. "I want to stand by my country, but I cannot vote for war. I vote no!" she said.

On April 6, the President signed the declaration of war. It thrust Americans into the deadliest war the world had yet seen.

? TRACE Outline the events that led the United States into World War I.

>> The United States intercepted this telegram, written in code and sent by Germany to Mexico on March 1, 1917. **Generate Explanations** What effect did the Zimmermann telegram have on the war?

▶ **Interactive Timeline**

★ BUILDING THE ARMED FORCES ★

THE U.S. MILITARY 1917–1918

4,281,800 WHITE

5,700 MEXICAN AMERICAN

4,700,000 U.S. DRAFTEES

400,000 AFRICAN AMERICAN

12,500 AMERICAN INDIAN

72% DRAFTED

28% ENLISTED

Source: National Center for Biotechnology Information

WOMEN'S JOBS IN THE MILITARY

- Clerk
- Nurse
- Driver
- Translator
- Cryptologist
- Telephone operator

30,000 WOMEN joined the United States military between 1917 and 1918

Source: National Women's History Museum

TRAINING THE RECRUITS

1,600% increase in size of U.S. Navy training facilities between 1917 to 1918

29,650 cadets trained as pilots from 1917–1918

500 colleges and universities establish Student Army Training Corps programs

Source: National Center for Biotechnology

MILITARY EXPENDITURES 1916–1918

Billions of current dollars (y-axis: 0, 2, 4, 6, 8, 10)

x-axis: 1916, 1917, 1918

3.5 MILLION rifles produced during the war

Source: EH.net

>> **Analyze Graphs** Based on the data showing the percentage of soldiers drafted (required to join) and those who enlisted on their own, what generalizations can you make about the popularity of the war among Americans?

Preparing for War

The day after Congress declared war, George M. Cohan wrote a new song. The patriotic tune swept the nation. Its opening lines expressed the confidence that Americans felt.

> Over there, over there, Send the word, send the word, over there, That the Yanks are coming . . .

—George M. Cohan, "Over There," 1917

Its closing message promised, "We'll be over, we're coming over, And we won't come back till it's over over there."

Americans had to do more than sing patriotic tunes, however. They had to prepare to fight—and quickly. The Allies needed everything from food to arms. Britain and France were on the verge of collapse. In Russia, soldiers were deserting to join the Russian Revolution.

The Military Expands Before it could fight, the United States needed to enlarge its armed forces. On May 18, 1917, Congress passed the **Selective Service Act**. It required all men from ages 21 to 30 to register for the military draft. A **draft** is a law requiring people of a certain age to serve in the military.

In the next 18 months, 4 million men and women joined the armed forces. People from every ethnic group enlisted. About 20,000 Puerto Ricans served in the armed forces, as did many Filipinos. Scores of soldiers were immigrants who had recently arrived in the United States.

Many American Indians were not citizens, so they could not be drafted. Large numbers of American Indians enlisted anyway. One family of Winnebago Indians provided 35 volunteers! They served together in the same unit.

At first, the armed forces did not allow African Americans in combat. When the government abandoned this policy, more than 2 million African Americans registered for the draft. Nearly 400,000 were accepted for duty. They were formed into segregated "black only" units that were commanded mostly by white officers. Still, African Americans rallied to the war effort.

Educating Recruits For many recruits, the Army offered several firsts. It was their first exposure to military authority and discipline. It was the first time most had ventured outside their farms and villages, let alone outside their country. Some had never taken regular baths or eaten regular meals before. Others had never used indoor plumbing. About 25 percent were **illiterate**, that is, unable to read or write. The army became a great educator. It taught millions of young Americans not only how to fight but also how to read, how to eat nutritious meals, and how to care for their daily health needs.

Shocking rates of illiteracy and other low test scores among recruits fueled a drive to reform public education. State and local school boards lengthened the school day and required students to spend more years in school. They raised teacher-training standards. More truancy officers patrolled the streets. By 1920, nearly 75 percent of all school-age children were enrolled in school.

❓ RECALL How did the United States expand its military?

Overseeing the War Effort

The United States reorganized its economy to produce food, arms, and other goods needed to fight the war. President Wilson set up government agencies to oversee the effort. A huge bureaucracy (byoo ROK ruh

>> This photo shows recruits at a military training camp in California. Military authority and discipline was strict in order to train troops for combat.

see) emerged to manage the war effort. A **bureaucracy** is a system of managing government through departments run by appointed officials.

Food Production Wilson chose Herbert Hoover to be head of the Food Administration. Hoover's job was to boost food production to feed American troops and send food to the Allies. In keeping with the nation's democratic traditions, Hoover relied on cooperation rather than force. He tried to win support for his programs with publicity campaigns that encouraged Americans to act voluntarily. "Food Will Win the War," proclaimed one Food Administration poster. Encouraged by rising food prices, farmers grew more crops. Citizens planted "victory gardens" to raise their own vegetables. People went without wheat on "wheatless Mondays" and without meat on "meatless Tuesdays." The food they saved helped the men in the trenches.

Industry War caught the nation short of supplies. The military had on hand only around 600,000 rifles, 2,000 machine guns, and fewer than 1,000 pieces of artillery. Disorder threatened as the military competed with private industry to buy scarce materials.

To meet this crisis, President Wilson set up a new government agency, the War Industries Board. It told factories what they had to produce. It also provided for the sharing of limited resources and decided what prices should be set.

Without the support of workers, industry could not mobilize. In 1918, Wilson created the War Labor Board. It settled disputes over working hours and wages and tried to prevent strikes. With workers in short supply, unions were able to win better pay and working conditions. Railroad workers, for example, gained a large wage increase

BOYS and GIRLS!
You can help your Uncle Sam Win the War

W.S.S.

Save your Quarters
Buy War Savings Stamps

>> In this propaganda poster from 1918, the U.S. government, represented by Uncle Sam, encourages children to support the war effort by purchasing War Savings Stamps.

and an 8-hour workday. With the President supporting workers, union membership rose sharply and labor unrest declined.

? CHECK UNDERSTANDING How did United States domestic policy boost production during the war?

Americans on the Home Front

Americans on the home front united behind the war effort. Movie stars, such as Charlie Chaplin and Mary Pickford, helped sell **Liberty Bonds**. By buying bonds, American citizens were lending money to the government to pay for the war. The sale of Liberty Bonds raised $21 billion, just over half of what the United States spent on the war.

To rally public support for the war, the government sent out 75,000 men known as "Four-Minute Men" to speak to the American people. The name reminded people of the heroic minutemen of 1776. It also referred to the four-minute speeches the men gave at public events, movies, and theatrical productions. The speakers urged Americans to make sacrifices for the goals of freedom and democracy.

Women Join the Work Force As men joined the armed forces, women stepped into men's jobs. Women received better pay in war industries than they had in peacetime. Still, they earned less than the men they replaced.

In factories, women assembled weapons and airplane parts. Some women drove trolley cars and delivered the mail. Others served as police officers, railroad engineers, or electric-lift truck drivers. By performing well in jobs once reserved for men, women helped change the view that they were fit only for "women's work." Unfortunately, most of the gains made by women later disappeared when the men returned to the workforce at the end of the war. Thousands of women lost jobs as army defense workers.

Anti-German Prejudice German Americans endured suspicion and intolerance during the war. Newspapers questioned their loyalty. Mobs attacked them on the streets. In 1918, a mob lynched Robert Prager, whose only crime was that he had been born in Germany. A jury later refused to convict the mob leaders.

Anti-German prejudice led some families to change their names. Schools stopped teaching the German language. Americans began referring to German measles as "liberty measles" and sauerkraut as "liberty cabbage."

>> This photo shows women working for an airplane manufacturing company in 1918. Many women worked in factories to support industrial production during the war.

Interactive Gallery

Urban Migration The war spurred migration within the nation. Immigration from abroad had stopped. The draft drained cities and factories of needed workers. Cities soon swelled with newcomers.

During the war, almost a half million African Americans and thousands of Mexican Americans embarked on a great migration from the South and Southwest to cities in the North.

In northern cities, many African Americans found better-paying jobs in war industries. As a result, African American migration continued after the war ended. At the same time, however, they ran into prejudice and even violence. Competition for housing and jobs sometimes led to race riots. Thirty-nine African Americans were killed during a 1917 riot in East St. Louis, Illinois. A New York parade protested the deaths. Marchers carried signs demanding, "Mr. President, Why Not Make AMERICA Safe for Democracy?"

In the Southwest, ranchers pressed the government to let more Mexicans cross the border. Almost 100,000 Mexicans entered the United States to work on farms, mostly in California and Texas.

By 1920, Mexicans were the leading foreign-born group in California. Some Mexicans moved on to northern cities to work in factories.

Throughout the war, Mexicans worked in cotton and beet fields, in copper mines, and in steel mills. All these jobs were important to the war effort. Yet after the war, when veterans returned and unemployment grew, the United States tried to force Mexican workers to return to Mexico.

Silencing Opposition Some Americans opposed the war. Among them were Progressives such as Jane Addams. Many

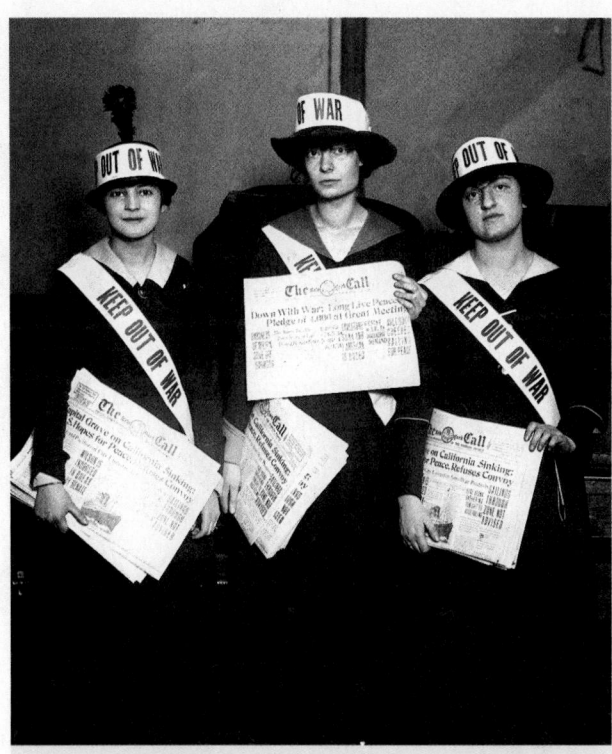

>> These women protested U.S. involvement in World War I by wearing sashes and hats that read "Keep Out of War." **Infer** What did this antiwar sentiment reveal about American support for the war?

of these critics were **pacifists**, people who refuse to fight in any war because they believe that war is evil.

Antiwar feeling also ran high among Socialists and radical labor groups. A **Socialist** believes that the people as a whole rather than private individuals should own all property and share the profits from all businesses. Socialists argued that the war benefited factory owners but not workers.

To encourage unity, Congress passed laws making it a crime to criticize the government or to interfere with the war effort. Nearly 1,600 men and women were arrested for breaking these laws. Eugene V. Debs, socialist candidate for President five times, was jailed for protesting the draft.

The government also jailed "Big Bill" Haywood, head of the Industrial Workers

>> This photo shows Eugene V. Debs giving a speech against the war in 1918. An outspoken protester, Debs was jailed for criticizing U.S. government draft policies.

of the World (IWW), a radical union. Using special powers granted under the wartime laws, government authorities ransacked the IWW's offices.

A few people questioned these laws. They argued that silencing critics violated the Constitution's guarantee of freedom of speech. Most Americans, however, felt that the laws were necessary in wartime.

? **RECALL** How did the United States raise money to pay for the war?

ASSESSMENT

1. **Identify Cause and Effect** Discuss the Zimmermann plot and its effects on the American public.

2. **Generate Explanations** Explain how the military draft led to social reforms.

3. **Describe** the ways in which U.S. citizens supported soldiers while supplies were scarce.

4. **Identify Patterns** Explain how migration patterns changed within the United States during World War I.

5. **Identify Central Issues** related to women's roles during wartime, and explain how they changed after the war ended.

12.6 Winning the War

>> An American gun crew advances on a German position during the Battle of Belleau Wood.

▶ **Interactive Flipped Video**

The outlook for the Allies grew even more bleak when Russia decided to withdraw from the war. In November 1917, a group known as the Bolsheviks seized power from Russia's Provisional Government. Led by Vladimir I. Lenin, the Bolsheviks wanted to stage a communist revolution in Russia.

>> **Objectives**

Identify the setbacks the allies suffered in 1917 and early 1918.

Explain how the American Expeditionary Force helped the Allies win the war.

Describe the toll on human life caused by the war.

>> **Key Terms**

Treaty of Brest-Litovsk
Harlem Hellfighters
Battle of Belleau Wood
Battle of the Argonne Forest
armistice
abdicate
epidemic
American Expeditionary Forces (AEF)
John J. Pershing
influenza

>> This photo shows Russian soldiers surrendering after a battle in World War I. Russia's withdrawal from the war reduced the Allies' chances of winning.

>> The signing of the treaty of Brest-Litovsk on March 3, 1918, between Germany and Russia marked the end of Russia's involvement in World War I.

Allied Setbacks

Lenin Withdraws Russia From War

Lenin embraced the ideas of Karl Marx, a German thinker of the 1800s. Marx had predicted that workers around the world would unite to overthrow the ruling class. After the workers revolted, they would do away with private property and set up a classless society. Lenin was determined to lead such a revolution in Russia.

Lenin opposed the war, arguing that it benefited only the ruling class. Once in power, he opened peace talks with Germany. In March 1918, Russia and Germany signed the **Treaty of Brest-Litovsk**, ending Russia's participation in the war. The treaty was harsh, requiring Russia to give up large amounts of land to Germany. Still, Lenin welcomed peace. With Russia out of the war, he could focus on the communist revolution.

The Allies saw the treaty as a betrayal. Through the treaty, Germany received coal mines and other valuable resources in Russia. More important, with Russia out of the struggle, Germany now moved its armies away from the Russian, or eastern, front to support its armies on the western front in France.

The German Offensive In early 1918, Germany mobilized its troops for an all-out attack on the Allies. By March 21, German forces had massed near the French town of Amiens. The Germans were preparing what they called a "peace offensive." They hoped that a final push would end the war.

The offensive opened with dozens of German divisions lined up against a small British force. Late at night, 6,000 German cannons began pounding the British troops camped at Amiens. Despite the heavy fire, the British held on. The battle lasted for two weeks. At last, on April 4, the Germans gave up their attack.

The Germans continued their offensive elsewhere. By late May, they had smashed through Allied lines along the Aisne (EHN) River.

On May 30, they reached the Marne River, just east of Château-Thierry (SHA toh tee ER ee). Paris lay only 50 miles away. At this point, American troops entered the war in force.

? IDENTIFY SUPPORTING DETAILS How did Russia's withdrawal from the war affect the Allies?

American Forces in France

By June 1918, American troops were reaching France in record numbers. More than one million American troops would arrive. Commanding the **American Expeditionary Forces (AEF)** was General **John J. Pershing**. Pershing was already well known at home. He had led American troops into Mexico in 1916 to hunt for Mexican rebel leader Francisco "Pancho" Villa.

Allied generals wanted the fresh troops to reinforce their own war-weary soldiers. Pershing refused. He insisted that American troops operate as separate units. The United States wanted to have an independent role in shaping the peace. Only by playing "a definite and distinct part" in the war would it win power at the peace table.

In the end, Pershing agreed to let some Americans fight with the British and French. At the same time, he set up an American operation to fight on its own.

African American Soldiers Among the first American units attached to the French Army was the 369th United States Infantry. This African American unit became known as the **Harlem**

Key Battles Involving Americans in World War I

KEY
- Allies, 1918
- Central Powers, 1918
- Neutral countries, 1918
- Allied front line, July 1918
- Armistice line, November 1918
- ★ Battle, 1918

>> **Analyze Maps** Based on the position of the Allied front line in July 1918, summarize Germany's position in the war at this time.

▶ **Interactive Map**

>> The African American soldiers known as Harlem Hellfighters served with distinction in the French army. **Infer** How do you think African American soldiers felt upon their return to the United States?

Interactive Gallery

Hellfighters. Although the United States allowed few African Americans to train for combat, the French respected the bravery of African American soldiers and were glad to fight side by side with them.

The Harlem Hellfighters spent more time under fire than any other American unit. For their bravery, the French awarded them the *Croix de Guerre*, their highest military honor, and numerous other decorations.

After the war, New Yorkers greeted the returning Hellfighters with a huge parade. "God bless you, boys!" they cheered. The unit commander felt a rush of joy. "They did not welcome us [as] a regiment of colored soldiers," he said, but as "a regiment of men who had done the work of men."

Battle of Belleau Wood Meanwhile, the Germans were continuing their "peace offensive." As Germans rolled across the Aisne River, the French prepared to evacuate Paris.

In June 1918, American troops plunged into their first major battle in Belleau (BEH loh) Wood, outside Paris. A French general sent General James Harbord of the United States a message: "Have your men prepare entrenchments some hundreds of yards to the rear in case of need." Harbord sent back a firm reply: "We dig no trenches to fall back on. The marines will hold where they stand."

The **Battle of Belleau Wood** raged for three weeks. During a series of attacks and counterattacks, the inexperienced but combat-ready Americans performed bravely. Expert marksmen hit their targets from hundreds of yards away. Individual soldiers charged German machine gun nests. When one man fell, another stepped in promptly to take his place. The

Americans suffered great casualties. But at last, on June 25, they emerged victorious from the woods. General Harbord passed along the good news: "Wood now exclusively U.S. Marine Corps."

? **CHECK UNDERSTANDING** Why did the American Expeditionary Force remain separate from other Allied forces?

Allied Victory

In mid-July, the Germans launched another drive to take Paris. They pushed the Allies back until they came up against American troops. Within three days, the Allies, with American help, had forced the Germans to retreat.

The Allies now took the offensive. French Marshal Ferdinand Foch (FOHSH), commander of the Allied forces, ordered attacks along a line from Verdun to the North Sea. American forces stormed the area between the Meuse (MYOOZ) River and the Argonne Forest.

The Final Offensive On September 26, 1918, in response to Foch's cry, "Everyone to battle!" more than one million American soldiers pushed into the Argonne Forest. This would be the final Allied offensive. Years of fierce fighting had left the land scarred with trenches and shell holes. The air still smelled of poison gas that had been used with deadly results against the men in the trenches in earlier battles.

At first, the Americans advanced despite heavy German fire. Then, rains and the thick woods slowed their movement. Small units drove forward to capture deadly German positions. Armed with a single rifle, Sergeant Alvin York of Tennessee wiped out a nest of German machine gunners. His brave act helped clear the way for advancing American troops. York

became the most decorated American soldier of the war.

Finally, after 47 days, the Americans broke through the German defense. They had won the **Battle of the Argonne Forest**. However, the cost was high. Americans had suffered more than 100,000 casualties in the battle.

British, French, and Belgian forces also smashed through the German lines in their areas. By November, German forces were in retreat. After more than four years of fighting, the Great War was finally nearing its end.

Armistice In September, German generals told the kaiser that the war could not be won. On October 4, Prince Max of Baden, head of the German cabinet, secretly cabled President Wilson.

>> American Alvin York did not want to go to war and asked to be excluded from the draft. But he eventually decided to serve in the army, and he won the Congressional Medal of Honor. **Infer** Why was York a reluctant hero?

To avoid further bloodshed, the German government requests the President to arrange the immediate conclusion of an armistice on land, by sea, and in the air.

—Max, Prince of Baden, Cable, October 4, 1918

An **armistice** is an agreement to stop fighting. President Wilson set two conditions for an armistice. First, Germany must accept his plan for peace. Second, the German emperor must **abdicate**, or give up power.

While German leaders debated a response, rebellion simmered in the ranks. Daily, the German army lost ground. Morale plunged among the troops. German sailors mutinied. People in several German cities threatened to revolt.

On November 9, the German emperor was forced to resign. He and his son fled to Holland, and Germany became a republic.

The new German leaders agreed to the armistice terms. At 11 A.M. on November 11, 1918—the eleventh hour of the eleventh day of the eleventh month—World War I ended at last.

? **RECALL** How did the Battle of Argonne Forest contribute to the end of the war?

The Costs of War

The costs of the war were staggering. A generation of young Europeans lost their lives. Between 8 million and 9 million people died in battle—more than had died in all the wars fought during the previous 100 years. Almost 4 million Russian, French, and British soldiers were killed. Germany alone lost close to 2 million men. The United States lost over 100,000 men. Many more died of diseases. More than 20 million soldiers on both sides were wounded.

Casualties of World War I

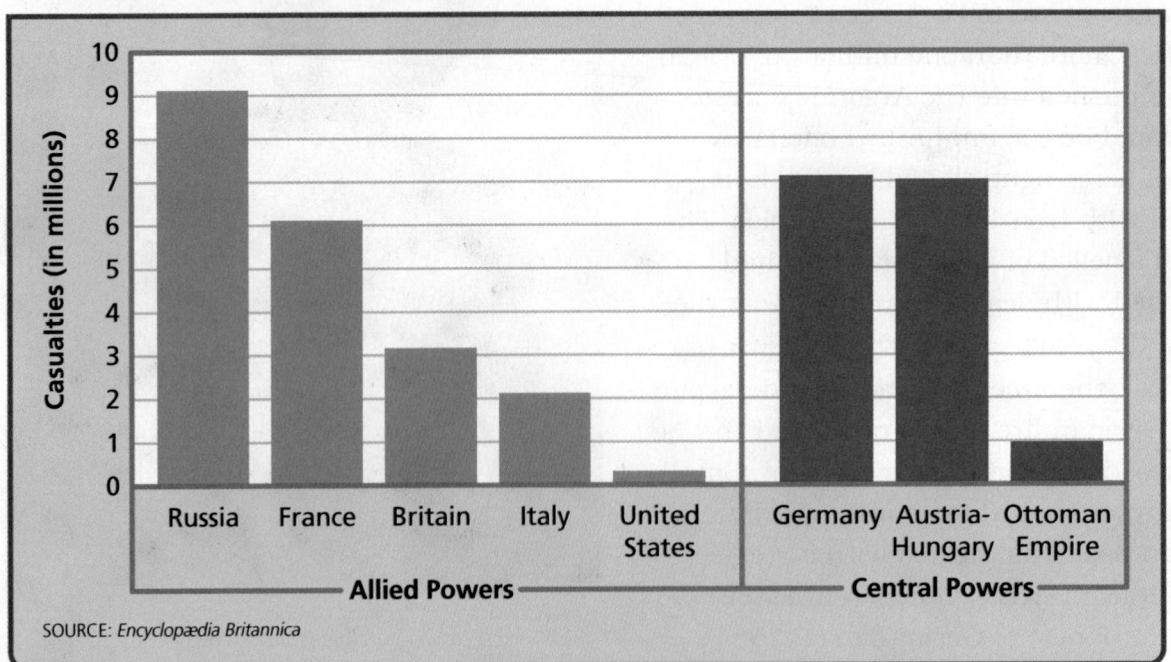

SOURCE: *Encyclopædia Britannica*

>> **Analyze Graphs** Compare the U.S. casualty total to those of other Allied nations and determine why U.S. casualties might have been different.

>> This 1914 photo shows what remained of Cambrai, France, after a German bombardment. World War I caused great destruction throughout Europe.

No one knows exactly how many civilians died of disease, starvation, and other war-related causes. Some historians believe as many civilians died as soldiers.

Much of northern France lay in ruins. Millions of Germans were near starvation. In France and other nations, many children were left orphaned and homeless.

In 1918, as the world was reeling from the war, a new disaster struck. A terrible **influenza** epidemic spread around the globe.

An **epidemic** is the rapid spread of a contagious disease among large numbers of people. Between 1918 and 1919, more than half a million Americans died in the flu epidemic. The death toll in other countries was even higher. All told, the epidemic killed more than 30 million people worldwide.

? **LIST** the costs of the war in addition to the number of soldiers killed in battle.

ASSESSMENT

1. **Identify Cause and Effect** Explain why Lenin chose to withdraw Russian troops from World War I.

2. **Identify Central Issues** Describe the achievements of the Harlem Hellfighters.

3. **Summarize** Explain how German civilians and soldiers reacted as they began to lose the war.

4. **Describe** the significance of the Battle of Belleau Wood.

5. **Generate Explanations** Explain why many civilians died during World War I in addition to soldiers.

12.7 Wilson and Isolationism

>> U.S. President Woodrow Wilson went to France with a list of ideas for a post-World War I peace settlement designed to prevent future wars.

Interactive Flipped Video

>> Objectives

Describe Wilson's fourteen-point peace plan.

Explain what Wilson achieved at the Paris Peace Conference.

Summarize why the Versailles Treaty and League of Nations failed to win support in the United States.

>> Key Terms

Fourteen Points
self-determination
League of Nations
Big Four
reparation
Treaty of Versailles
isolationist
mandate

On board the American naval ship *George Washington* were President Woodrow Wilson and his advisers. They were sailing to France in late 1918 to help the Allies set the terms of peace following World War I. As the ship passed the Statue of Liberty, a hopeful Wilson waved his hat to the crowd. At last, he would have a chance to keep his promise of making the world "safe for democracy."

688

PEARSON realize. www.PearsonRealize.com Access your Digital Lesson.

Wilson's Fourteen Points

Woodrow Wilson was the first American President to meet international leaders on foreign soil. He was determined to do whatever was needed to achieve his vision of a just and lasting peace. In the end, however, Wilson failed. The other Allied leaders, it turned out, did not share his vision or his hopes. Even the American people were in disagreement about how to approach the postwar world.

In Europe, Wilson visited Paris, London, Milan, and Rome. Everywhere, cheering crowds welcomed him. He thought that the crowds shared his goal of peace without victory. In fact, he was wrong. The Europeans who greeted Wilson so warmly scoffed at his high-minded proposals for peace. They and their leaders were determined to punish the Germans for the war.

In January 1918, even before the war ended, Wilson outlined his peace plan. Known as the **Fourteen Points**, it was meant to prevent international problems from causing another war.

The first point in Wilson's plan called for an end to secret agreements. Secrecy, Wilson felt, had encouraged the web of rival alliances that had helped lead to war. Next, he called for freedom of the seas, free trade, and a limit on arms. He urged peaceful settlement of disputes over colonies. He also supported the principle of national **self-determination**, that is, the right of national groups to have their own territory and forms of government.

For Wilson, however, the fourteenth point was the most important. It called for a "general association of nations," or **League of Nations**. Its job would be to protect the independence of all countries— large or small. His goals were clear.

> An evident principle runs through the whole program that I have outlined. It is the principle of justice to all peoples and nationalities, and their right to live on equal terms of liberty and safety with one another, whether weak or strong.
>
> —Woodrow Wilson, Speech, January 8, 1918

Selected Details From Wilson's Fourteen Points

All treaties between nations should be made public in order to avoid secret treaties such as the Triple Alliance.
All countries should be able to freely navigate the oceans and seas in times of peace.
Strengthening trade between countries will help create a lasting peace.
Nations should only keep enough weapons to be able to defend themselves against the possibility of attack.
An international organization of nations will help prevent the possibility of another world war.
Colonial claims must be settled with the involvement of local populations.

SOURCE: *Encyclopædia Britannica*

>> This chart summarizes several of the major points among Wilson's Fourteen Points. **Analyze Charts** Read the points and explain which you think is the most important point in terms of maintaining peace. Why?

 Interactive Gallery

>> The "Big Four" Allied leaders (from left, George, Orlando, Clemenceau, and Wilson) met in Paris in 1919 to negotiate a peace treaty after World War I.

Wilson persuaded the Allies to accept the Fourteen Points as the basis for making peace. However, the plan soon ran into trouble. Some goals were too vague. Others conflicted with reality. In Paris, Wilson faced a constant battle to save his Fourteen Points. He discovered that the Allies were more concerned with protecting their own interests than with forging a lasting peace.

? DESCRIBE What was the purpose of creating a League of Nations?

The Paris Peace Conference

Diplomats from more than 30 nations met in Paris and Versailles (vuhr SI) to negotiate five separate peace treaties known as the Peace of Paris. Key issues were decided by the leaders of the Allied nations known as the **Big Four**: Woodrow Wilson of the United States, David Lloyd George of Britain, Georges Clemenceau (kleh mahn SOH) of France, and Vittorio Orlando of Italy.

Allied Nations Disagree Each leader had his own aims. Wilson had called for "peace without victory." He opposed punishing the defeated powers.

The other Allies, however, ached for revenge. Germany must pay, they said. They insisted on large **reparations**, or cash payments, for the losses they had suffered during the war. Further, they wanted to include a "war guilt clause" that would force Germany to accept responsibility for the war.

The Allies were also determined to prevent Germany from rebuilding its military strength. In particular, Clemenceau wanted to weaken Germany so that it could never again threaten France. "Mr. Wilson bores me with his Fourteen Points," he complained. "Why, God Almighty has only ten!"

The haggling continued for months. In the end, Wilson had to compromise on his Fourteen Points in order to save his key goals, especially the League of Nations. However, he would not budge on the League. With the League in place, he believed, any mistakes made in Paris could later be corrected.

Humiliation for Germany By June 1919, the **Treaty of Versailles**, the most important treaty of the Peace of Paris, was ready. None of the Allies was satisfied with it. Germany, which had not even been allowed to send delegates to the peace talks, was shocked by the terms of the treaty. Still its representatives had no choice but to sign.

Under the treaty, Germany had to take full blame for the war. The treaty stated the following:

> The Allied and Associated Governments affirm, and Germany accepts, the responsibility of Germany and her allies for causing all the loss and damage to which the Allied and Associated Governments and their nationals have been subjected as a consequence of the war imposed on them by the aggression of Germany and her allies.
>
> —The Versailles Treaty, June 28, 1919, Article 231

Germany also had to pay the Allies huge reparations, including the cost of pensions for Allied soldiers or their widows and children. The total cost of German reparations would come to over $300 billion.

Other provisions of the Treaty of Versailles were aimed at weakening Germany. The treaty severely limited the size of the German military. It returned Alsace-Lorraine to France. In addition, the treaty stripped Germany of its overseas colonies, which were put under the control of Britain or France. The Germans, wrote one reporter, "suffered a horrible humiliation."

Britain and France were also given **mandates**, or authorization, by the League of Nations to govern territory in what was the Ottoman Empire. The purpose of the mandates was to govern these territories until they could function as independent nations. The British would control the former Turkish provinces of Iraq and Palestine, while the French would control Syria and Lebanon.

Wilson Keeps the League of Nations
Despite opposition to many of his Fourteen Points, Wilson succeeded in keeping some of them. In Eastern Europe, the

>> This modern photo shows the Hall of Mirrors in the palace of Versailles, where Germany signed the Treaty of Versailles. The treaty placed responsibility for the war on Germany.

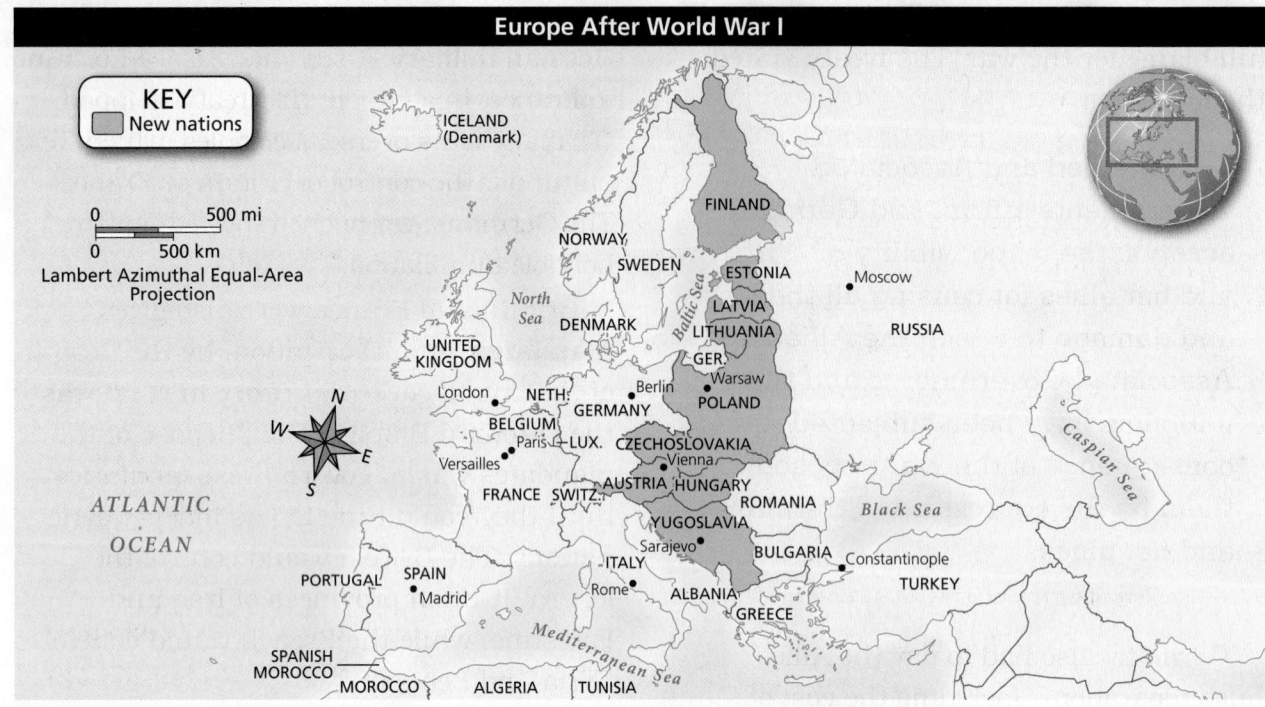

KEY
New nations

0   500 mi
0   500 km
Lambert Azimuthal Equal-Area Projection

ICELAND (Denmark)

North Sea

NORWAY
SWEDEN
FINLAND
ESTONIA
LATVIA
LITHUANIA
Moscow
RUSSIA

DENMARK
UNITED KINGDOM
London
NETH.
BELGIUM
Paris
LUX.
GER.
Berlin
Warsaw
POLAND
GERMANY
CZECHOSLOVAKIA
Vienna
AUSTRIA
HUNGARY
SWITZ.
FRANCE
Versailles

ATLANTIC OCEAN

PORTUGAL
SPAIN
Madrid

SPANISH MOROCCO
MOROCCO
ALGERIA
TUNISIA

Mediterranean Sea

ITALY
Rome
YUGOSLAVIA
Sarajevo
ALBANIA
GREECE
ROMANIA
BULGARIA
Black Sea
Constantinople
TURKEY

Caspian Sea

Baltic Sea

>> **Analyze Maps** Which new nations bordered Russia?

▶ **Interactive Map**

Allies provided for several new nations to be formed on the principle of self-determination, including Czechoslovakia and Yugoslavia. They were created out of lands once ruled by Germany, Russia, and Austria-Hungary. In addition, Poland regained its independence as a nation.

Some people were dissatisfied with the new boundaries. Many Germans, for example, had settled in Poland and Czechoslovakia. Before long, Germany would seek to regain control of German-speaking peoples in Eastern Europe.

To Wilson, however, his greatest achievement was persuading the Allies to include the League of Nations in the treaty. Wilson was certain that the League would prevent future wars by allowing nations to talk over their problems. If talk failed, members would join together to fight aggressors. "A living thing is born,"

he declared. The League "is definitely a guarantee of peace."

? **IDENTIFY CENTRAL IDEAS** Why was the Treaty of Versailles a humiliation for Germany?

Wilson Fights for the Treaty of Versailles

When President Wilson returned home, he faced a new battle. He had to persuade the Senate to approve the Versailles Treaty and to approve American participation in the League of Nations.

American Opposition Most Americans favored the treaty. A vocal minority opposed it, however. Some said that it was too soft on the defeated powers. Many German Americans felt that it was too harsh. Some Republicans hoped to embarrass President Wilson, a Democrat, by rewriting or defeating the treaty. **Isolationists**, people who wanted the

United States to stay out of world affairs, opposed the League of Nations. They were convinced that the League would lead to an "entangling alliance." Other people who were against the League felt that it did not have enough authority to solve any pressing economic problems. They thought that it could lead to another war.

Critics of the treaty found a leader in Henry Cabot Lodge of Massachusetts. Lodge, a Republican, was chairman of the powerful Senate Foreign Relations Committee. Lodge accepted the idea of the League of Nations. However, he wanted changes in some provisions relating to the League. He believed that Americans were being asked to "subject our own will to the will of others."

Specifically, Lodge objected to Article 10 of the treaty. It called for the League to protect any member whose independence or territory was threatened. Lodge argued that Article 10 could involve the United States in future European wars. He wanted changes in the treaty that would ensure that the United States remained independent of the League. He also wanted Congress to have the power to decide on a case-by-case basis whether the United States would follow League policy.

Wilson believed that Lodge's changes would weaken the League. Advisers urged the President to compromise, to give up some of his demands in order to save the League. Wilson replied, "Let Lodge compromise." He refused to make any changes.

The Senate Rejects the Treaty As the battle grew hotter, the President took his case to the people. In early September 1919, Wilson set out across the country. He traveled nearly 8,000 miles and made 37 speeches in 29 cities. He urged Americans to let their senators know that they supported the treaty.

>> President Wilson (center) led a march of peace in Washington, D.C., on his return from Paris in 1919.

>> President Wilson made many appearances in 1919 to rally public support for the League of Nations.

mourned, "[and] every morning I put flowers on its grave." Gone, too, was Wilson's cherished goal—American membership in the League of Nations.

The United States did not sign a peace treaty with Germany until 1921. Many nations had already joined the League of Nations. Without the United States, though, the League failed to live up to its goal of protecting members against aggression. Wilson's dream of a world "safe for democracy" would have to wait.

? CHECK UNDERSTANDING Why did Henry Cabot Lodge oppose the Treaty of Versailles?

Wilson kept up a relentless pace. On September 25, the exhausted President complained of a headache. His doctors canceled the rest of the trip. Wilson returned to Washington. A week later, his wife found him unconscious. He had suffered a stroke that left him bedridden for weeks.

In November 1919, the Senate rejected the Versailles Treaty. "It is dead," Wilson

ASSESSMENT

1. **Describe** the main components of President Wilson's Fourteen Points.

2. **Contrast** Identify the differences between Wilson and the other members of the Big Four at the Paris Peace Conference.

3. **Identify Central Issues** Explain why the Fourteen Points proved to be weak.

4. **Generate Explanations** Explain how the Treaty of Versailles changed the political geography of Europe.

5. **Compare and Contrast** different American opinions regarding the Treaty of Versailles.

1. **Explain the Motivation Behind Imperialism** Write a paragraph explaining why the United States entered the race for imperial expansion. Define *imperialism* and describe the reasons for the growth of this policy for industrial nations. Then, using the quotation below and your knowledge of the text, explain why American expansionists felt it was necessary to join in the imperial race and what nations were affected by this American policy.

   Today we are raising more [crops] than we can consume. Today we are making more than we can use. . . . Therefore we must find new markets for our produce, new occupation for our capital, new work for our labor.

   —Senator Albert J. Beveridge, "The March of the Flag," 1898

2. **Describe the Open Door Policy** Write a paragraph describing the Open Door Policy. Explain what spheres of influence are and what nations had spheres in China. Then explain why this was an issue for the United States and what the United States hoped to achieve through the policy.

3. **Identify the Economic Reasons That Drew the U.S. Into the Spanish-American War** Write a paragraph describing how economic considerations in Cuba drew the United States into the Spanish-American War. Consider what economic interests the United States had in Cuba and how the conflict between the Cuban rebels and the Spanish affected American economic interests. Then, describe how protecting American interests in Cuba helped lead the United States to war with Spain.

4. **Explain How the Spanish-American War Was a Turning Point** Write a paragraph explaining why its victory in the Spanish-American War was a turning point for the United States as a world power. Consider what the United States gained by winning the war, how that benefited Americans, and why the war could be considered a turning point.

5. **Analyze the Impact of Geographic Factors** Write a paragraph analyzing how physical geographic factors affected the construction of the Panama Canal. Describe how the physical characteristics of the land impacted the project and what effect the completion of the canal had on the United States.

6. **Explain Expansionist Policies** Write a paragraph explaining the presidential policies of Theodore Roosevelt, William Howard Taft, and Woodrow Wilson by answering the following questions: What was the Roosevelt Corollary? What was involved in Taft's dollar diplomacy? What did Wilson mean by "moral diplomacy"? What problems did these policies cause?

7. **Identify the Causes of World War I** Use your knowledge of the text to write a paragraph identifying the causes of World War I. Identify the roles played by nationalism, imperialism, militarism, alliances, and assassination.

8. **Sequence the Events Leading to World War I** Write a paragraph identifying how alliances caused a chain reaction that led to World War I. Identify the events that led to Austria-Hungary declaring war on Serbia and the events that brought other nations into the war. Then describe how the alliance system set off a sequence of events that eventually led to World War I.

9. **Analyze Issues of U.S. Involvement in World War I** Analyze major issues raised by U.S. involvement in World War I. Write a paragraph analyzing how Americans felt about World War I before the United States declared war. Answer the following questions: Why were Americans divided over which side to support in World War I? How did Americans react once the United States declared war?

10. **Identify Why the U.S. Entered World War I** Write a paragraph identifying the reasons the United States entered World War I. Take into consideration the German U-boat activity, the Zimmermann telegram, and the Russian Revolution.

11. **Describe the Economic Effects of World War I** Write a paragraph describing how the U.S. government managed the economy during World War I and the economic effects of that management. Consider the roles played by the Food Administration, the War Industries Board, and the War Labor Board.

12. **Identify the U.S. Entry Into World War I As Turning Point** Write a paragraph explaining why the entry of the United States into World War I was a turning point for the Allied forces. Consider the effect of Russia leaving the war and how the American troops made a difference.

TOPIC (12) ASSESSMENT

Wilson's Fourteen Points, 1918

1. Make no secret diplomatic agreements.

2. Allow freedom of the seas in peace and war.

3. Remove as many economic trade barriers as possible between countries.

4. Reduce stockpiles of military armaments to lowest point needed for domestic safety.

5. Adjust colonial claims, giving more weight to the views of the colonized peoples.

6. Evacuate and restore Russian territories seized during the war.

7. Restore and protect Belgium's sovereignty.

8. Restore French territory and settle the debate over Alsace-Lorraine.

9. Adjust Italy's boundaries according to the nationalities of populations living there.

10. Allow the peoples of the former Austro-Hungarian Empire to choose their own governments.

11. Redraw boundaries of Balkan states based on nationalities and historical allegiances.

12. Separate the Ottoman Empire into independent countries according to nationality; guarantee all nations access to the Dardanelles.

13. Restore and protect Poland as a sovereign state with access to the sea.

14. Establish an association of nations to provide collective security and to ensure peace.

---

13. Analyze the Battle of Argonne Forest Write a paragraph analyzing the significance of the Battle of the Argonne Forest. Answer the following questions: What was the Argonne Forest campaign? What part did the American Expeditionary Forces play in the campaign? Why was the Battle of the Argonne Forest significant?

14. Explain the United States As a World Power Write a paragraph explaining Henry Cabot Lodge's position on the United States as a world power. Consider what view Lodge is expressing in the quotation below and how this view differs from Wilson's view of America's place in the world.

I can never be anything else but an American, and I must think of the United States first, and when I think of the United States first. . . . I am thinking of what is best for the world, for if the United States fails, the best hopes of mankind fail with it.

—Henry Cabot Lodge, letter to President Woodrow Wilson, 1919

15. Analyze Woodrow Wilson's Fourteen Points Write a paragraph analyzing President Wilson's Fourteen Points. Describe the promise Wilson felt he was keeping with his Fourteen Points and what ideals the Fourteen Points represent. Use the chart above to analyze Wilson's point of view on how World War I and future wars should be resolved.

16. Evaluate the Pros and Cons of Participation in International Organizations Evaluate the pros and cons of U.S. participation in international organizations. Write a paragraph evaluating the arguments for and against the League of Nations. Consider the view of the opponents as well as supporters of the League of Nations.

17. Write About the Essential Question Write an essay on the Essential Question: What is America's role in the world? Use evidence from your study of this topic to support your answer.

Go online to PearsonRealize.com and use the texts, quizzes, interactivities, Interactive Reading Notepads, Flipped Videos, and other resources from this Topic to prepare for the Topic Test.

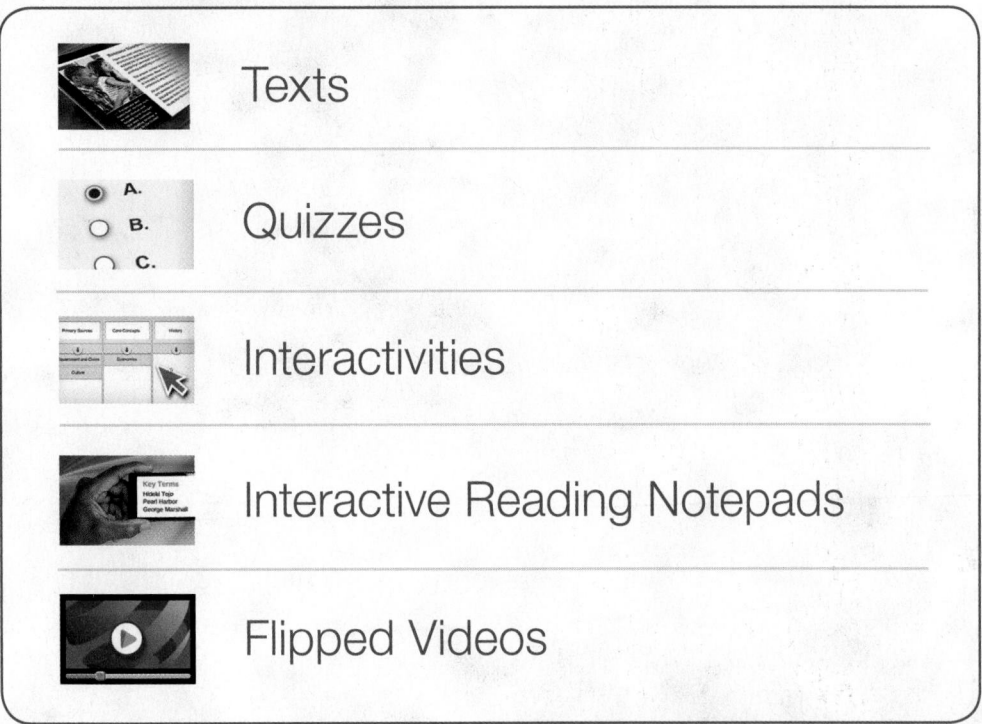

Texts

Quizzes

Interactivities

Interactive Reading Notepads

Flipped Videos

While online you can also check the progress you've made learning the topic and course content by viewing your grades, test scores, and assignment status.

[**ESSENTIAL QUESTION**] What Should Governments Do?

13 Prosperity and Depression (1919–1939)

>> A family leaving Texas during the Great Depression in search of work

Enduring Understandings

- During the 1920s there was prosperity at home and limited involvement overseas for the United States.

- The 1920s brought new freedom for women, widespread car ownership, and new cultural forms such as radio, movies, and jazz.

- Low pay for workers, economic hardship for farmers, and high levels of debt undermined prosperity led to a stock market crash and the Great Depression.

- Americans found Herbert Hoover's response to the Depression inadequate and elected Franklin Delano Roosevelt to replace him.

- Roosevelt's New Deal established the principle that the government should intervene to fight economic distress and unemployment, though it also faced criticism.

- The Depression brought special hardship to farmers on the Great Plains, women, and racial minorities but also inspired great works of art.

Watch the My Story Video to learn more about famed jazz singer Billie Holiday.

Access your digital lessons including:
Topic Inquiry • Interactive Reading
Notepad • Interactivities • Assessments

Harding and Coolidge

>> Following the sudden death of President Harding in 1923, Calvin Coolidge became President. He is shown here at his inauguration in 1925 after winning reelection.

▶ **Interactive Flipped Video**

>> Objectives

Describe how corruption hurt Harding's presidency.

Explain why the economy grew under Coolidge.

Identify the role the United States played in international politics during the 1920s.

>> Key Terms

recession
Teapot Dome
  Scandal
installment buying
stock
bull market
communism
disarmament
Kellogg-Briand Pact
interest
margin

World War I had helped the economy. Europeans ordered vast amounts of supplies from American factories. After the United States entered the war in 1917, American factories expanded rapidly to meet the demand for military supplies.

Republicans Regain the White House

When the war ended, more than 2 million soldiers came home and began to look for jobs. At the same time, factories stopped turning out war materials. The result was a sharp **recession**, or economic slump.

A Landslide Victory The recession fed voter discontent with the Democrats, who had held power for eight years. In the 1920 election, Warren Harding swamped his Democratic opponent.

For the top Cabinet posts, Harding chose able men who strongly followed pro-business policies. Andrew Mellon, a wealthy banker, became secretary of the treasury. Mellon balanced the budget and lowered taxes.

Herbert Hoover became the new secretary of commerce. During World War I, Hoover had earned the world's admiration by organizing efforts to supply food to millions of starving Belgians. As secretary of commerce, he worked to help American businesses expand overseas.

The Ohio Gang To fill most other Cabinet posts, however, Harding brought in his old friends. They became known as the "Ohio Gang." Harding himself was honest and hard-working, but the Ohio Gang saw government service as a way to enrich themselves. A series of scandals resulted. For example, Harding made Charles Forbes head of the Veterans Bureau. Forbes was later convicted of stealing millions of dollars from the bureau.

Harding looked upon Forbes's crime as a betrayal. When rumors of new scandals surfaced, he grew even more distressed. In August 1923, Harding died of a heart attack. Many believed that the scandals contributed to his sudden death.

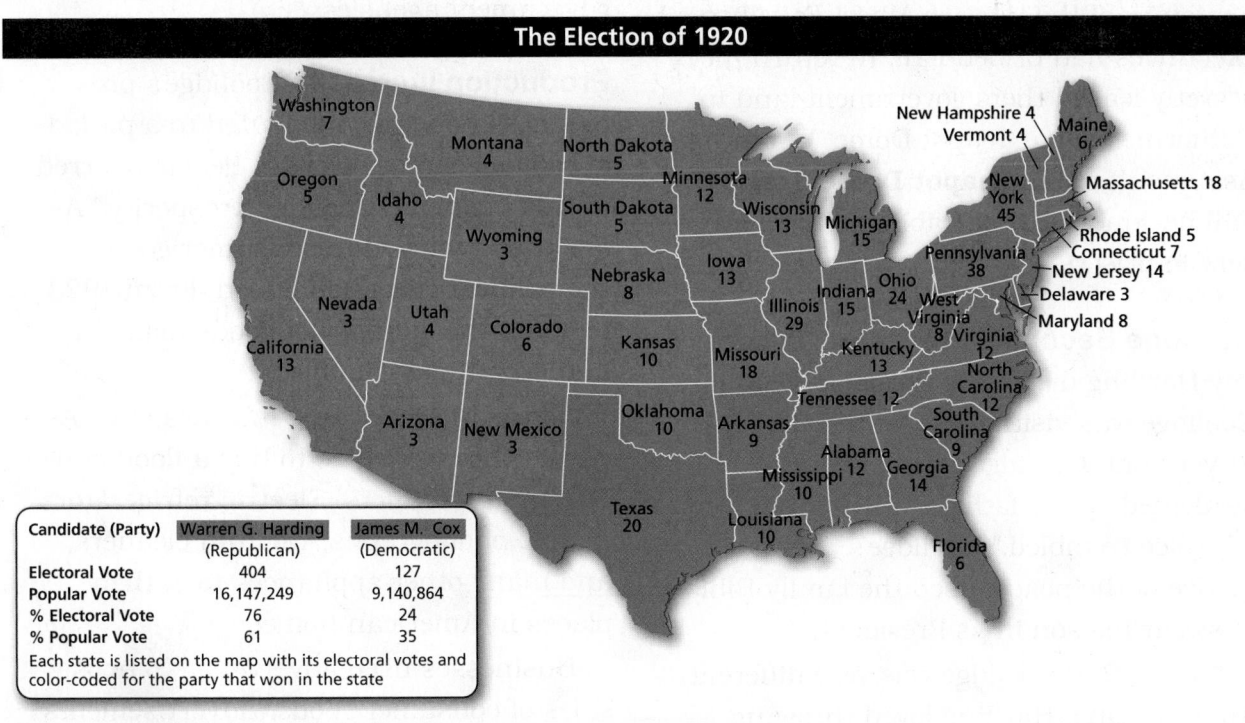

The Election of 1920

Candidate (Party)	Warren G. Harding (Republican)	James M. Cox (Democratic)
Electoral Vote	404	127
Popular Vote	16,147,249	9,140,864
% Electoral Vote	76	24
% Popular Vote	61	35

Each state is listed on the map with its electoral votes and color-coded for the party that won in the state

>> **Analyze Maps** Explain why the public's support for the presidential candidates might have been so clearly divided geographically.

>> This 1924 cartoon comments on the Teapot Dome Scandal during Warren Harding's administration. **Interpret Cartoons** Why is the teapot drawn to look like a steamroller?

After Harding died, new scandals came to light. The most serious involved Secretary of the Interior Albert Fall. Two oil executives had bribed Fall. In return, he secretly leased them government land in California and at Teapot Dome, Wyoming. As a result of the **Teapot Dome Scandal**, Fall became the first Cabinet official ever sent to prison.

Coolidge Becomes President On the day Harding died, Vice President Calvin Coolidge was visiting his father's farm in Vermont. Coolidge recalled, "I was awakened by my father. . . . I noticed that his voice trembled." Coolidge's father, a justice of the peace, used the family Bible to swear his son in as President.

"Silent Cal" Coolidge was very different from Harding. Harding loved throwing parties and making long speeches.

Coolidge was tight with both money and words. A woman reportedly told Coolidge she had bet that she could get him to say more than two words. "You lose," Coolidge replied.

Coolidge set out to repair the damage caused by the scandals. He forced the officials involved in scandals to resign. In 1924, Coolidge ran against Democrat John Davis and Progressive Robert La Follette. Voters chose to "Keep Cool With Coolidge" and returned the cautious New Englander to office.

? **IDENTIFY CENTRAL ISSUES** What fueled American discontent with Democrats?

Economic Growth Under President Coolidge

Like Harding, Coolidge believed that prosperity for all Americans depended on business prosperity. Coolidge cut regulations on business. He also named business leaders to head government agencies.

Production Increases Coolidge's pro-business policies contributed to a period of rapid economic growth. People referred to this boom as "Coolidge prosperity." As factories switched to consumer goods, the postwar recession ended. From 1923 to 1929, the quantity of goods made by industry almost doubled.

For most Americans, incomes rose. As a result, they were able to buy a flood of new consumer products. Electric refrigerators, radios, phonographs, vacuum cleaners, and many other appliances took their places in American homes.

Businesses used advertising to boost sales of consumer goods. Advertisements encouraged people to think that their happiness depended on owning a wealth of shiny, new products.

Faced with so many goods, people often wanted to buy things they could not afford. In response, businesses allowed **installment buying**, or buying on credit. For example, buyers could take home a new refrigerator by putting down just a few dollars. Each month, they paid an installment until they had paid the full price, plus **interest**, or a percentage of the price charged as a fee for the loan.

The new policy of "buy now, pay later" increased the demand for goods. At the same time, however, consumer debt jumped. By the end of the decade, consumers owed more than the amount of the federal budget.

The Stock Market Soars The economic boom of the 1920s gave the stock market a giant boost. Corporations sold **stocks**, or shares of ownership, to investors. Investors made or lost money depending upon whether the price of the shares went up or down.

By the late 1920s, more people were investing in the stock market than ever before. Stock prices rose so fast that some people made fortunes almost overnight. Stories of ordinary people becoming rich drew others into the stock market. Such a period of increased stock trading and rising stock prices is known as a **bull market**.

Many people bought stocks on **margin**. Under this system, an investor bought a stock for as little as a 10 percent downpayment, or margin. The buyer held the stock until the price rose and then sold it at a profit. Margin buying worked as long as stock prices kept going up.

In 1928 and 1929, however, the prices of many stocks rose faster than the value of

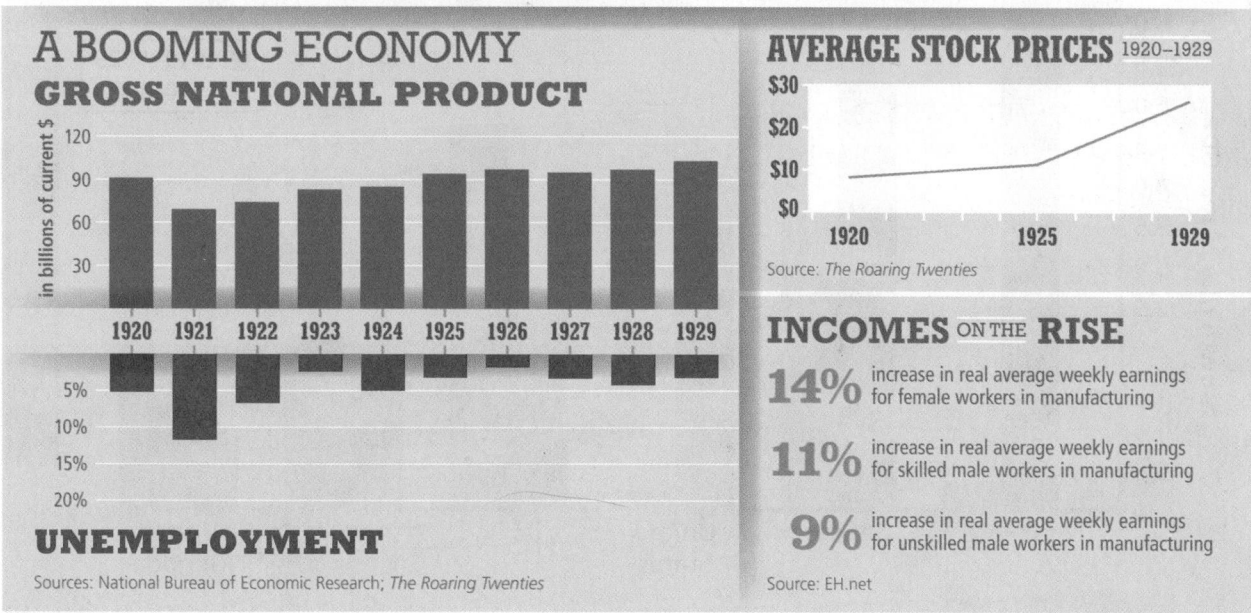

$ PROSPERITY IN THE **1920s $**

A BOOMING ECONOMY
GROSS NATIONAL PRODUCT

in billions of current $
120
90
60
30
1920 1921 1922 1923 1924 1925 1926 1927 1928 1929
5%
10%
15%
20%
UNEMPLOYMENT

Sources: National Bureau of Economic Research; *The Roaring Twenties*

AVERAGE STOCK PRICES 1920–1929
$30
$20
$10
$0
1920   1925   1929
Source: *The Roaring Twenties*

INCOMES ON THE **RISE**

14% increase in real average weekly earnings for female workers in manufacturing

11% increase in real average weekly earnings for skilled male workers in manufacturing

9% increase in real average weekly earnings for unskilled male workers in manufacturing

Source: EH.net

>> **Analyze Graphs** The gross national product (GNP) is the value of all the products and services that the nation produces. What do you notice about the relationship between changes in the GNP and the unemployment rate?

 Interactive Chart

the companies themselves. A few experts warned that the bull market could not last forever. Still, most investors ignored the warnings.

? LIST at least one example of Coolidge's pro-business policies.

A Return to Isolationism

After World War I, the United States was the world's leading economic power. Europeans expected the United States to take a major role in world affairs. Presidents Harding and Coolidge wanted to keep the hard-won peace in Europe. However, they did not want to commit the United States to the job of keeping world peace. The United States sent observers to the League of Nations but refused to join. Most Americans supported this return to prewar isolationism.

Latin American Investments During the war, Latin American nations had been cut off from Europe because of wartime threats to shipping. As a result, United States trade and investment in Latin America increased. This trend continued after the war. However, the United States limited its role abroad for fear that more involvement might push the country into another war.

At times, the United States intervened in Latin America. In 1926, for example, a revolution broke out in Nicaragua, where Americans owned plantations and railroads. Coolidge sent marines to oversee new elections.

In 1927, Mexico announced plans to take over foreign-owned oil and mining companies. American investors called on President Coolidge to send in troops. Instead, Coolidge sent a diplomat, Dwight Morrow, to Mexico. After much hard bargaining, Morrow was able to work out a compromise with the Mexican government.

World Economies After World War I

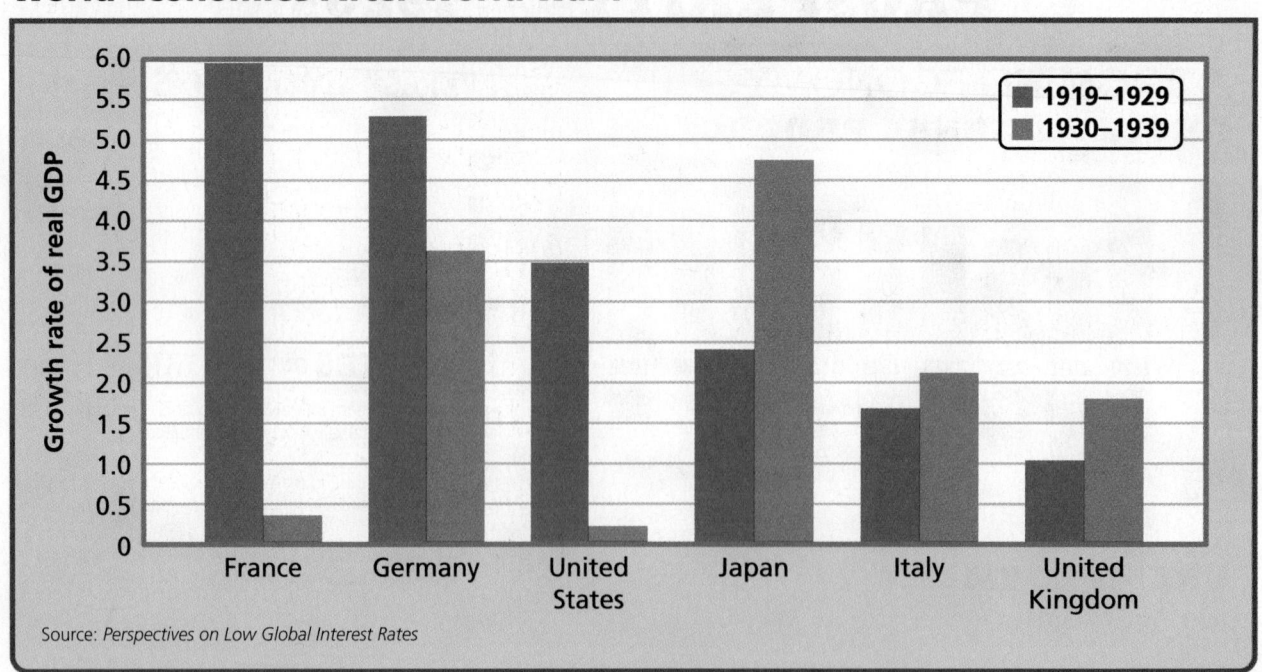

Source: *Perspectives on Low Global Interest Rates*

>> **Analyze Graphs** Compare the state of the U.S. economy in the 1920s to the American economy in the 1930s.

The First Communist State Meanwhile, the Soviet Union became the world's first communist state. **Communism**, as practiced in the Soviet Union, was an economic system in which all wealth and property were owned by the government.

The United States refused to recognize Lenin's government. Most Americans disliked communism. It shocked them when the Soviet government did away with private property and attacked religion. Still, Congress voted to provide $20 million in aid when famine threatened the Soviet Union in 1921. American aid may have saved as many as 10 million Soviet lives.

Pursuing Peace An arms race in Europe had helped cause World War I. For this reason, many people in the 1920s favored the reduction of armed forces and weapons of war, or **disarmament**. Pacifist groups such as the Women's International League for Peace and Freedom, founded by Jane Addams, led the call for disarmament in the United States and Europe.

Presidents Harding and Coolidge also backed peace efforts. At the Washington Conference of 1921, the United States, Britain, and Japan agreed to limit the size of their navies. Seven years later, the United States and 61 other nations signed the **Kellogg-Briand Pact**. This treaty outlawed war.

The treaty, however, had a fatal flaw. It did not set up any means for keeping the peace. One nation could still use force against another without fear of punishment. Still, many hailed the

>> At the 1921 Washington Naval Conference, the United States, Britain, and Japan agreed on a policy of disarmament to avert another war.

▶ **Interactive Chart**

Kellogg-Briand Pact as the beginning of a new age of peace.

? **CHECK UNDERSTANDING** Why did the United States intervene in Latin America?

ASSESSMENT

1. **Identify Cause and Effect** Explain how Herbert Hoover's actions affected the role of the United States in international politics in the 1920s.

2. **Compare** how Harding and Coolidge each tried to grow the economy.

3. **Interpret** How did advertising contribute to the bull market?

4. **Determine Point of View** Summarize the beliefs of American isolationists after World War I.

5. **Identify Central Issues** Why did many Americans dislike communism?

Social Change

>> This 1929 fashion magazine cover reflects the popularity of driving automobiles. **Interpret Images** What does this photo reveal about the changing role of women in the 1920s?

▶ **Interactive Flipped Video**

>> **Objectives**

Identify Prohibition.

Describe how life changed for women.

Explain the impact of the automobile and mass culture on American life.

>> **Key Terms**

Prohibition
bootlegger
repeal
League of Women
  Voters
Equal Rights
  Amendment
suburb
mass culture
organized crime

For nearly a century, reform groups such as the Woman's Christian Temperance Union had worked to ban alcoholic beverages. They finally achieved this when the states ratified the Eighteenth Amendment in January 1919. One year later, **Prohibition**, often referred to as the "noble experiment," went into effect. Prohibition was the legal ban of the manufacture, sale, or transportation of alcohol.

The Noble Experiment

In 1920, as today, alcohol abuse was a serious problem. Many Americans hoped the ban on liquor would improve American life. In fact, the ban did have some positive effects. Alcoholism declined during Prohibition. However, in the end, the ban did not work.

Going Underground One reason that Prohibition failed was that many Americans found ways to get around the law. Some people manufactured their own alcohol in homemade stills. Others smuggled in liquor from Canada and the Caribbean. Because these smugglers sometimes hid bottles of liquor in their boots, they became known as **bootleggers**.

Illegal bars, called speakeasies, opened in nearly every city and town. In some ways, speakeasies made drinking liquor more popular than ever. To enforce the ban, the government sent out federal Prohibition agents. These "g-men" traveled across the United States, shutting down speakeasies, breaking up illegal stills, and stopping smugglers.

Organized Crime Prohibition gave a huge boost to **organized crime**, or criminal activity organized as a business. Every speakeasy needed a steady supply of liquor. Professional criminals, or gangsters, took over the job of meeting this need. As bootleggers earned big profits, crime became a big business. Gangsters divided up cities and forced speakeasy owners in their "territories" to buy liquor from them. Sometimes, gangsters used some of their profits to bribe police officers, public officials, and judges.

The Experiment Ends Gradually, more Americans began to think that Prohibition was a mistake. The ban reduced drinking but never stopped it. Even worse, argued critics, Prohibition was undermining respect for the law. Every day, millions of Americans were buying liquor in

Prohibition and the Prison Population

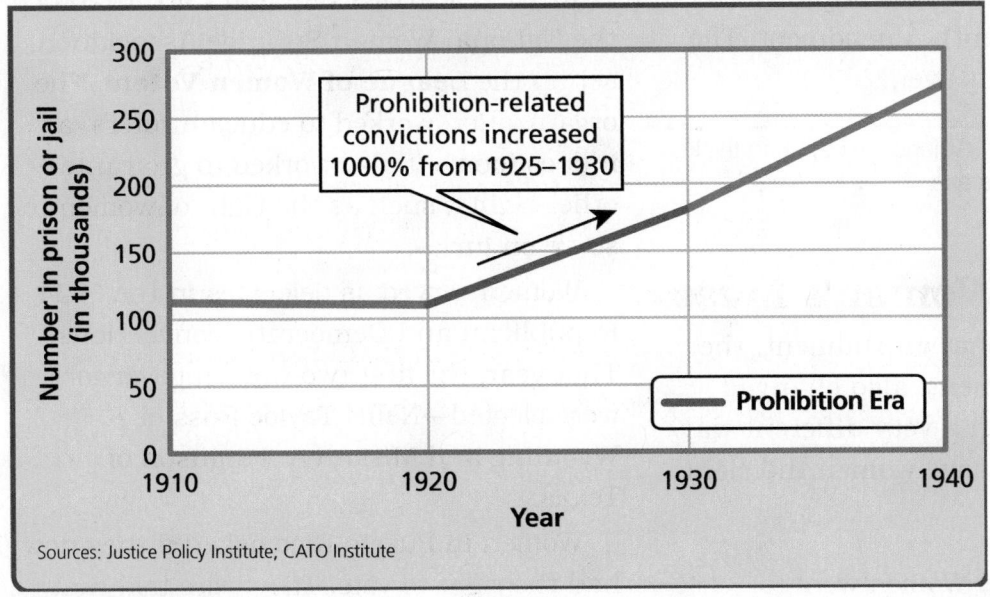

Sources: Justice Policy Institute; CATO Institute

>> **Analyze Graphs** Explain why prison populations rose so sharply during Prohibition.

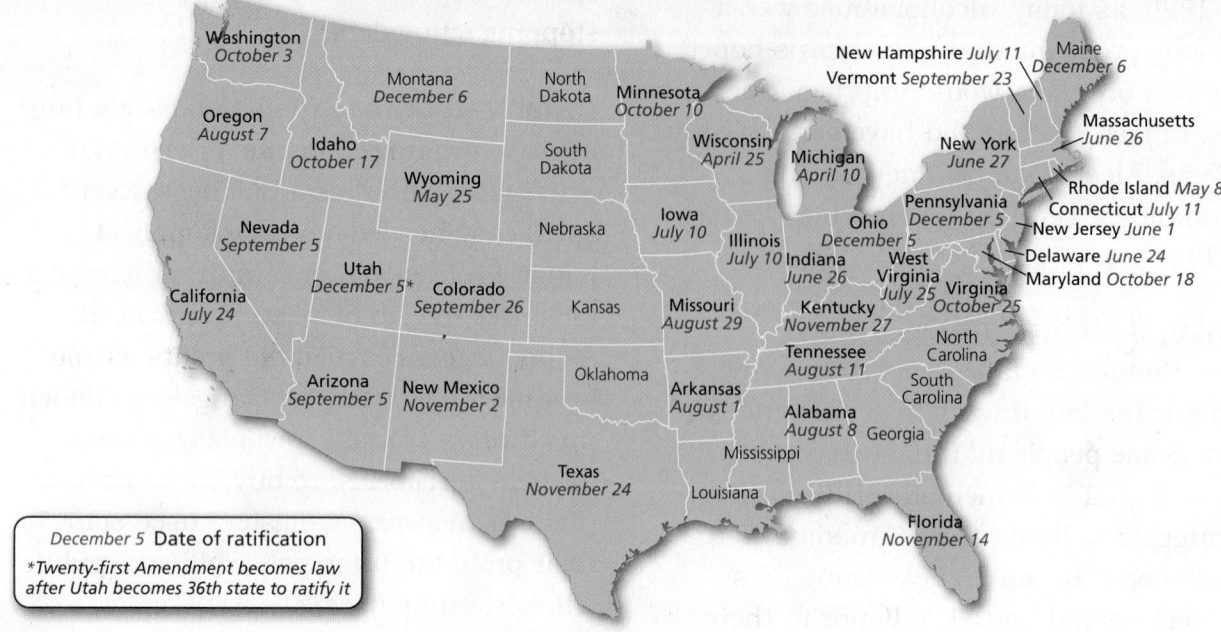

December 5 Date of ratification
*Twenty-first Amendment becomes law after Utah becomes 36th state to ratify it

>> Although Congress passed the Twenty-first Amendment, it still needed to be ratified, or approved, by three fourths of the states. **Infer** Why did many of the states take several months before ratifying the Twenty-first Amendment?

speakeasies. By the mid-1920s, almost half of all federal arrests were for Prohibition-related crimes.

By the end of the decade, many Americans were calling for the **repeal**, or ending, of Prohibition. In 1933, the states ratified the Twenty-first Amendment, which repealed the Eighteenth Amendment. The noble experiment was over.

? **LIST** two reasons why Americans began to think that Prohibition was a mistake.

Changes in Women's Lives

Another constitutional amendment, the Nineteenth Amendment, also changed American life, but in a very different way. Ratified in 1920, it gave women the right to vote.

Women Cast a Vote Women went to the polls nationwide for the first time in November 1920. Their votes helped elect Warren Harding President. Women did not vote as a group, however, as some people had predicted. Like men, some women voted for Republicans, and some for Democrats, and many did not vote at all.

In 1920, Carrie Chapman Catt, head of the National Woman Suffrage Association, set up the **League of Women Voters**. The organization worked to educate voters, as it does today. It also worked to guarantee other rights, such as the right of women to serve on juries.

Women served as delegates in the 1924 Republican and Democratic conventions. That year, the first two women governors were elected—Nellie Tayloe Ross of Wyoming and Miriam A. Ferguson of Texas.

Women in Puerto Rico asked if they now had the right to vote. They were told that they did not. Led by Ana Roqué de Duprey, an educator and writer, Puerto Rican women crusaded for the vote. In 1929, their crusade finally succeeded.

An Equal Rights Amendment Leaders in the suffrage movement began to work for new goals. Alice Paul, who had been a leading suffragist, pointed out that women still lacked many legal rights. For example, many professional schools still barred women, and many states gave husbands legal control over their wives' earnings. Paul called for a new constitutional amendment in 1923. Paul's proposed **Equal Rights Amendment** (ERA) stated that "equality of rights under the law shall not be denied or abridged by the United States or by any State on account of sex."

Many people feared that the ERA went too far. Some argued that women would lose legal safeguards, such as laws that protected them in factories. Paul worked hard for the ERA until her death in 1977.

The amendment passed in Congress but was never ratified by the states.

Women in the Workforce Women's lives changed in other ways in the 1920s. During World War I, thousands of women had worked outside the home for the first time. They filled the jobs of men who had gone off to war. When the troops came home, many women were forced to give up their jobs. Still, some remained in the workforce.

For some women, working outside the home was nothing new. Poor women and working-class women had been cooks, servants, and seamstresses for many years. In the 1920s, they were joined by middle-class women who worked as teachers, typists, secretaries, and store clerks. A few women even managed to become doctors and lawyers despite discrimination.

Women in the Workforce, 1890–1940

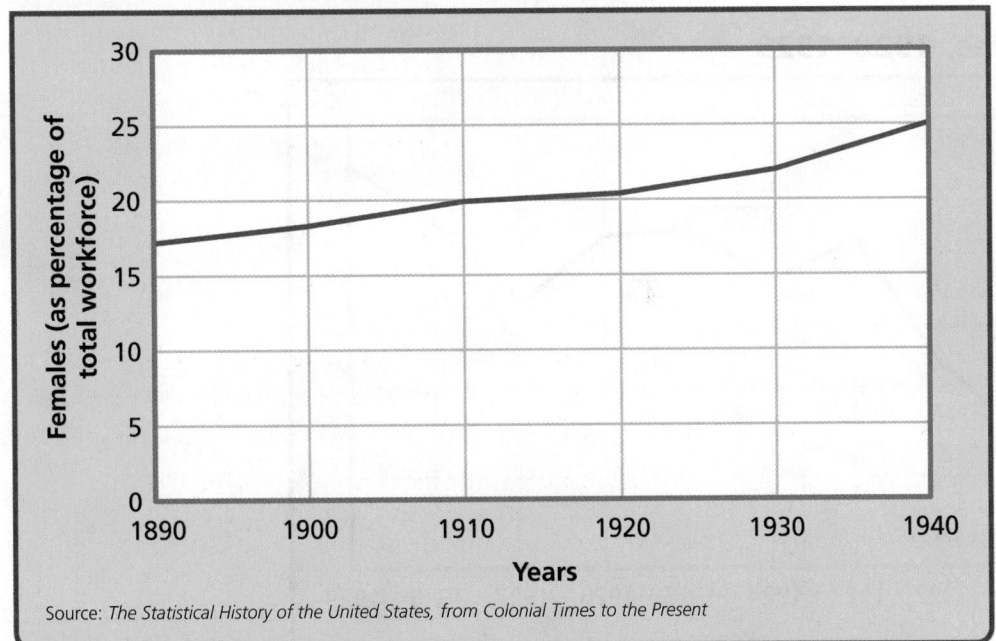

Source: *The Statistical History of the United States, from Colonial Times to the Present*

>> **Analyze Graphs** Explain why World War I would lead to an increase in women joining the workforce.

Life at home also changed for women. More of them bought ready-made clothes than sewed for the whole family as they had done in the past. Electric appliances such as refrigerators, washers, irons, and vacuum cleaners made housework easier. On the other hand, such conveniences also encouraged some women to spend even more time on housework. Women who worked outside the home found that they had to work a second shift when they came home. Most husbands expected their wives to cook, clean, and care for children even if they held full-time jobs.

? RECALL What was the main task of the League of Women Voters?

The Automobile Changes America

"Why on earth do you need to study what's changing this country?" one man asked the experts. "I can tell you what's happening in just four letters: A-U-T-O."

In the 1920s, Americans traveled to more places and moved more quickly than ever before—all because of the automobile.

The auto industry played a central role in the business boom of the 1920s. Car sales grew rapidly during the decade. The auto boom spurred growth in related industries such as steel and rubber.

Cars Become Affordable Lower prices sparked the auto boom. By 1924, the cost of a Model T had dropped from $850 to $290. As a result, an American did not have to be rich to buy a car. Car prices fell because factories became more efficient. As you have read, Henry Ford introduced the assembly line in his automobile factory in 1913. Before the assembly line, it took 14 hours to put together a Model T. In Ford's new factory, workers could assemble a Model T in 93 minutes. Other companies copied Ford's methods. In 1927, General Motors passed Ford as the top automaker. Unlike Ford, General Motors sold cars in a variety of models and colors.

Rise in Auto Sales, 1920–1929

>> **Analyze Graphs** Predict one reason for the rise in auto sales in 1927-1929.

>> Today, it is hard to imagine roads without any gas stations. In the 1920s, as cars became popular, entrepreneurs built many new filling stations, such as this one in Maryland in 1921.

Henry Ford had once boasted that people could have his cars in "any color so long as it's black." When General Motors introduced a low-priced car available in different colors, Ford lost many customers. Faced with the success of General Motors, he changed his mind. His next car, the Model A, came in different colors. Soon, car companies were offering new makes and models every year.

A Boost for the Economy Car sales spurred growth in other parts of the economy. By 1929, some four million Americans owed their jobs to the automobile, directly or indirectly. Tens of thousands of people worked in steel mills, producing metal used in cars. Others made tires, paint, and glass for cars. Some drilled for oil in the Southwest or worked in the oil refineries where crude petroleum was converted into usable gasoline.

The car boom had other effects. States and cities paved more roads and built new highways. In 1925, the Bronx River Parkway in New York was the first of many highways in parklike settings. Gas stations, car dealers, motels, and roadside restaurants sprang up across the country to serve the millions who traveled by car.

In 1920, there were only about 1,500 filling stations in the entire United States. By 1929, there were more than 120,000. Mechanic shops, or places to repair automobiles, also became a necessity.

Social Effects of Car Ownership Cars shaped life in the city and in the country. Many city dwellers wanted to escape crowded conditions. They moved to nearby towns in the country, which soon grew into suburbs. A **suburb** is a community located outside a city. With cars, suburban families could drive to the city even though it was many miles away. They could also drive to stores, schools, or work. No longer did people have to live where they could walk or take a trolley to work.

Another major shift came when suburban housewives refused to be confined to the passenger seat. Instead, they took their place behind the wheels of their own automobiles. As they did, they broke down still another barrier that separated the worlds of men and women.

In the country, cars brought people closer to towns, shops, and the movies. Such trips had taken several hours by horse and buggy. One farm woman bought a car before she got indoor plumbing. "You can't go to town in a bathtub," she explained.

? **DESCRIBE** how the automobile boosted the American economy.

A New National Culture

By making travel easier, cars helped Americans from different parts of the country learn more about one another. They played a role in creating a new national culture that crossed state lines.

New forms of entertainment also contributed to the rise of a **mass culture**. Mass culture is the set of values and practices that arise from watching the same movies, listening to the same music, and hearing the same news reports as others around the nation. In the 1920s, rising wages and labor-saving appliances gave families more money to spend and more leisure time in which to spend it.

Entertainment at Home Radio became very popular in the 1920s. The country's first commercial radio station, KDKA, started broadcasting in Pittsburgh in 1920.

>> These boys are listening to an early-model radio set in the 1920s. Radio was the first electronic device to bring entertainment and information directly into people's homes.

Interactive Gallery

By 1929, more than 10 million American families owned radios.

A new lifestyle emerged. Each night after dinner, families gathered around the radio to tune in to shows such as "Roxy and His Gang" or "Jack Frost's Melody Moments." Radio listeners enjoyed comedies and westerns, classical music and jazz, news reports and play-by-play sports broadcasts.

Going to the Movies In the 1920s, the movie industry came of age. Southern California's warm, sunny climate allowed filming all year round. Soon, Hollywood became the movie capital of the world.

Movies contributed to the new mass culture. Millions of Americans went to the movies at least once a week. They were thrilled to watch westerns, romances, adventures, and comedies. In small towns, theaters were bare rooms with hard chairs. In cities, they were huge palaces with red velvet seats.

The first movies had no sound. Audiences followed the plot by reading "title cards" that appeared on the screen. A pianist played music that went with the action.

Fans adored Hollywood movie stars. Cowboy stars like Tom Mix thrilled audiences with their heroic adventures. Clara Bow won fame playing restless, fun-seeking young women. The most popular star of all was comedian Charlie Chaplin, nicknamed "The Little Tramp." In his tiny derby hat and baggy pants, Chaplin presented a comical figure. His attempts to triumph over the problems of everyday life moved audiences to both laughter and tears.

In 1927, Hollywood caused a sensation when it produced *The Jazz Singer*. The film

>> Charlie Chaplin's fame as a silent film star began in the 1910s and continued through the 1920s and beyond. Chaplin continued to make popular silent films years after the shift to "talking pictures" in 1927.

was a "talkie"—a movie with a soundtrack. Soon, all new movies were talkies.

? DESCRIBE how radio contributed to a new national culture in America.

ASSESSMENT

1. **Integrate Information** Explain why Prohibition was eventually repealed.

2. **Hypothesize** several ways that life might be different today if the Equal Rights Amendment (ERA) had been ratified.

3. **Summarize** how life changed for women in the 1920s.

4. **Compare** the invention of the automobile to the invention of the telephone. How did they both change people's lives?

5. **Identify Cause and Effect** Which new inventions helped to unite Americans?

>> Young women known as flappers defied expectations and created new fashions by wearing short dresses and short hairstyles.

▶ **Interactive Flipped Video**

>> Objectives

Identify fads and fashions of the 1920s.

Explain the origins and effects of jazz music.

Identify new kinds of writing during the 1920s, including the Harlem Renaissance.

Identify heroes of the 1920s.

>> Key Terms

flapper
jazz
fad
expatriate

❝ Ev'ry morning, ev'ry evening, ain't we got fun?" went a hit song of 1921. During the "Era of Wonderful Nonsense"—yet another nickname for the 1920s—fun came in many forms.

Trends of the 1920s

Fun Fads Fads caught on, then quickly disappeared. A **fad** is an activity or a fashion that is taken up with great passion for a short time. Flagpole sitting was one fad of the 1920s. Young people would perch on top of flagpoles for hours, or even days. Another fad was the dance marathon, where couples danced for hundreds of hours at a time to see who could last the longest. Crossword puzzles and mah-jongg, a Chinese game, were other popular fads of the 1920s.

Dance crazes came and went rapidly. The most popular new dance was probably the Charleston. First performed by African Americans in southern cities such as Charleston, South Carolina, the dance became a national craze after 1923. Moving to a quick beat, dancers pivoted their feet while kicking out first one leg, and then the other, backward and forward.

Flapper Fashion Perhaps no one pursued the latest fads more intensely than the **flappers**. These young women rebelled against traditional ways of thinking and acting. Flappers wore their hair bobbed, or cut short. They wore their dresses short, too—shorter than Americans had ever seen. Flappers shocked their parents by wearing bright red lipstick.

To many older Americans, the way flappers behaved was even more shocking than the way they looked. Flappers smoked cigarettes in public, drank bootleg alcohol in speakeasies, and drove fast cars. "Is 'the old-fashioned girl,' with all that she stands for in sweetness, modesty, and innocence, in danger of becoming extinct?" wondered one magazine in 1921.

Only a few young women were flappers. Still, they set a style for others. Slowly, older women began to cut their hair and wear makeup and shorter skirts. For many Americans, the bold fashions pioneered by the flappers symbolized a new sense of freedom.

The Rise of Jazz Music Another innovation of the 1920s was **jazz**. Born in New Orleans, jazz combined West African rhythms, African American work songs and spirituals, and European harmonies and band music. Jazz also had roots in the ragtime rhythms of composers such as Scott Joplin.

Louis Armstrong was one of the brilliant young African American musicians who helped create jazz. Armstrong learned to play the trumpet in the New Orleans orphanage where he grew up. Armstrong had the ability to take a simple melody and experiment with the notes and the rhythm.

>> As dancing became popular in the 1920s, the fad of dance marathons grew. Young couples took part in dance marathons across the country to see who could dance the longest.

▶ **Interactive Gallery**

>> The Cotton Club in Harlem, New York, became a leading center of jazz music in the 1920s. Musicians such as Duke Ellington and Cab Calloway performed here regularly and gained nationwide fame.

This allowed his listeners to hear many different versions of the basic tune. Other great early jazz musicians included "Jelly Roll" Morton and singer Bessie Smith.

Jazz quickly spread from New Orleans to Chicago, Kansas City, and the mainly African American section of New York City known as Harlem. White musicians, such as trumpeter Bix Beiderbecke, also began to adopt the new style. Before long, the popularity of jazz spread to Europe as well.

Many older Americans worried that jazz and the new dances were a bad influence on the nation's young people. Despite their complaints, jazz continued to grow more popular. Today, jazz is recognized as an original art form developed by African Americans. It is considered one of the most important cultural contributions of the United States.

Athletic Heroes Radio, movies, and newspapers created celebrities known across the country. Americans followed the exploits of individuals whose achievements made them stand out from the crowd. Some of the best-loved heroes of the decade were athletes. Each sport had its stars. Bobby Jones won almost every golf championship. Bill Tilden and Helen Wills ruled the tennis courts. Jack Dempsey reigned as world heavyweight boxing champion for seven years. At the age of 19, Gertrude Ederle became the first woman to swim across the English Channel.

College football also drew huge crowds. Many Americans who had never attended college rooted for college teams. They were thrilled to watch the exploits of football stars like Red Grange, the "Galloping Ghost" of the University of Illinois.

Americans loved football, but baseball was their real passion. The most popular player of the 1920s was Babe Ruth. He became the star of the New York Yankees. Fans flocked to games to see "the Sultan of Swat" hit home runs. The 60 home runs he hit in one season set a record that lasted more than 30 years. His lifetime record of 714 home runs was not broken until 1974.

"Lucky Lindy" The greatest hero was Charles A. Lindbergh. On a gray morning in May 1927, he took off from an airport in New York to fly nonstop across the Atlantic Ocean—alone. His was the first solo, nonstop transatlantic flight.

For more than 33 hours, Lindbergh piloted his tiny single-engine plane, the *Spirit of St. Louis,* over the stormy Atlantic. He carried no map, no parachute, and no radio. At last, he landed in Paris, France. The cheering crowd carried him across the airfield. "Lucky Lindy" returned to the United States as the hero of the decade.

? **DEFINE** What was a flapper?

A New Generation of Writers

A new generation of American writers earned worldwide fame in the 1920s. Many of them were horrified by their experiences in World War I. They criticized Americans for caring too much about money and fun. Some became so unhappy with life in the United States that they moved to Paris, France. There, they lived as **expatriates**, people who leave their own country to live in a foreign land.

Hemingway and Fitzgerald Ernest Hemingway was one of the writers who lived for a time in Paris. Still a teenager at the outbreak of World War I, he traveled to Europe to drive an ambulance on the

Italian front. Hemingway drew on his war experiences in *A Farewell to Arms,* a novel about a young man's growing disgust with war. In *The Sun Also Rises,* he examines the lives of American expatriates in Europe.

Hemingway became one of the most popular writers of the 1920s. His simple but powerful style influenced many other writers.

The young writer who best captured the mood of the Roaring Twenties was Hemingway's friend F. Scott Fitzgerald. In *The Great Gatsby* and other novels, Fitzgerald examined the lives of wealthy young people who attended endless parties but could not find happiness. His characters included flappers, bootleggers, and moviemakers. Fitzgerald became a hero to college students and flappers, among others.

>> American author Ernest Hemingway became a prominent literary figure in the 1920s. His famous war novel *A Farewell to Arms* was based on his own experiences in Italy during World War I.

>> Edna St. Vincent Millay wrote poetry about youth, rebellion, and romantic ideals.

frantic pace of the 1920s in her verse, such as her short poem "First Fig."

My candle burns at both ends;

It will not last the night;

But ah, my foes, and oh, my friends—

It gives a lovely light.

—Edna St. Vincent Millay, "First Fig," 1920

Another writer, Eugene O'Neill, revolutionized the American theater. Most earlier playwrights had presented romantic, unrealistic stories. O'Neill shocked audiences with powerful, realistic dramas based on his years at sea. In other plays, he used experimental methods to expose the inner thoughts of tortured young people.

❓ IDENTIFY CENTRAL IDEAS Name an author who captured the boldness of Roaring Twenties culture in his writing.

Other Important Contributions

Sinclair Lewis grew up in a small town in Minnesota and later moved to New York City. In novels such as *Babbitt* and *Main Street,* he presented small-town Americans as dull and narrowminded. Lewis's attitude reflected that of many city dwellers toward rural Americans. In fact, the word *babbitt* became a popular nickname for a smug businessman uninterested in literature or the arts. In 1930, Lewis was the first American to win the Nobel Prize for literature.

Poet Edna St. Vincent Millay was enormously popular. She expressed the

The Harlem Renaissance

In the 1920s, large numbers of African American musicians, artists, and writers settled in Harlem, in New York City. "Harlem was like a great magnet for the Negro intellectual," said one African American writer. This gathering of African American artists and musicians led to the Harlem Renaissance, a rebirth of African American culture.

During the Harlem Renaissance, young black writers celebrated their African and American heritages. They also protested prejudice and racism. For the first time, too, a large number of white Americans took notice of the achievements of African American artists and writers.

Langston Hughes Probably the best-known poet of the Harlem Renaissance was Langston Hughes. He published his first poem, "The Negro Speaks of Rivers," soon after graduating from high school. The poem connected the experiences of African Americans living along the Mississippi River with those of ancient Africans living along the Nile and Niger rivers. Like other writers of the Harlem Renaissance, Hughes encouraged African Americans to be proud of their heritage.

In other poems, Hughes protested racism and acts of violence against African Americans. In addition to his poems, Hughes wrote plays, short stories, and essays about the African American experience.

Other Poets and Novelists Other poets such as Countee Cullen and Claude McKay also wrote of the experiences of African Americans. A graduate of New York University and Harvard, Cullen taught in a Harlem high school. In the 1920s, he won prizes for his books of poetry.

McKay came to the United States from Jamaica. In his poem "If We Must Die," he condemned the lynchings and other mob violence that African Americans suffered after World War I. The poem concludes with the lines "Like men we'll face the murderous, cowardly pack, / Pressed to the wall, dying but fighting back!"

THE **HARLEM RENAISSANCE**

THE GREAT MIGRATION: HARLEM

1,250,000
AFRICAN AMERICANS
MIGRATED TO
NORTHERN CITIES
— FROM —
SOUTHERN STATES
FROM 1910 TO 1930

1910   1930

Sources: *The New York Times*; *Manliness and Its Discontents*

■ Central Harlem's African American Population

75,000
copies of *American Mercury* sold per month in 1927

200
recordings made by Duke Ellington band at Cotton Club, 1927-1932

$8,000
weekly salary of Louis Armstrong by mid-1930s, 304 times average salary in the 1930s

Sources: University of Illinois; *Encyclopedia of the Harlem Renaissance*; Lone Star College

MAJOR EVENTS OF THE HARLEM RENAISSANCE

- 1915
- 1916 — **1917** Marcus Garvey founds the United Negro Improvement Association
- 1917
- 1918 — **1921** *Shuffle Along* opens on Broadway
- 1919
- 1920 — **1922** Claude McKay publishes *Harlem Shadows*
- 1921
- 1922 — **1922** Cotton Club (music club) opens
- 1923 — **1923** First book published by female Harlem Renaissance writer
- 1924
- 1925
- 1926 — **1926** Langston Hughes publishes *The Weary Blues*, a book of poems
- 1927
- 1928
- 1929 — **1928** First black history week is held
- 1930

Sources: Howard University; Yale University

>> **Analyze Graphs** Explain the relationship between the Great Migration and the Harlem Renaissance.

 Interactive Gallery

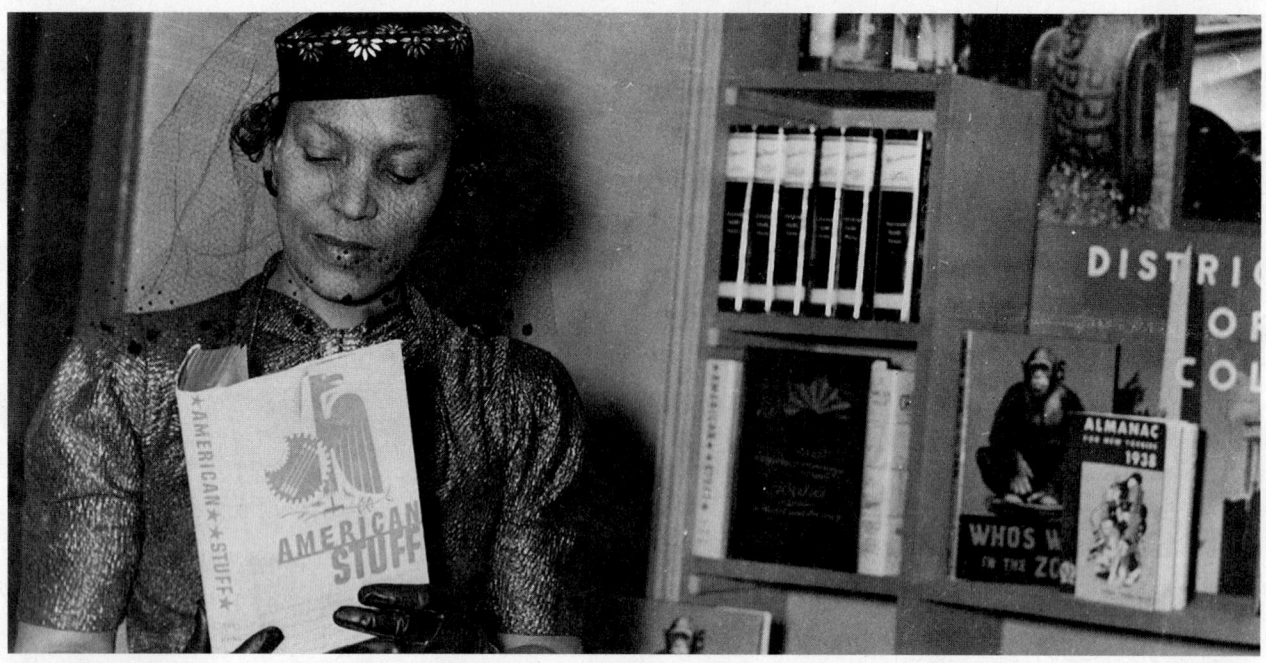

>> Author Zora Neale Hurston wrote of African Americans' experiences in the South in the early 1900s.

Zora Neale Hurston, who grew up in Florida, wrote novels, essays, and short stories. Hurston grew concerned that African American folklore "was disappearing without the world realizing it had ever been."

In 1928, she set out alone to travel through the South in a battered car. For two years, she collected the folk tales, songs, and prayers of African American southerners. She later published these in her book *Mules and Men*.

? DESCRIBE What did many Harlem Renaissance writers hope to achieve with their writing?

ASSESSMENT

1. **Determine Point of View** How did World War I affect the writing of Ernest Hemingway?

2. **Determine Point of View** How was F. Scott Fitzgerald's writing affected by the 1920s?

3. **Draw Conclusions** How did African American writers of the 1920s affect how white Americans related to African Americans in general?

4. **Determine Point of View** Based on the lines from one of Claude MacKay's poems ("Like men we'll face the murderous, cowardly pack, / Pressed to the wall, dying but fighting back!"), how would he probably have felt about the way in which equal rights should be achieved?

5. **Draw Conclusions** Why were many older Americans worried about jazz music?

>> The trial of Italian immigrants and anarchists Sacco and Vanzetti (center and right) and their 1927 execution divided the nation. List two reasons Americans feared foreigners in the 1920s.

▶ **Interactive Flipped Video**

Many Americans did not share in the boom of the 1920s. Workers in the clothing industry, for example, were hurt by changes in women's fashions. Shorter skirts meant that less cloth was needed to make dresses. Coal miners also faced hard times as oil replaced coal as a source of energy. Railroads slashed jobs because trains were losing business to cars and trucks.

>> **Objectives**

Identify Americans who faced economic hardship during the 1920s.

Explain the significance of the Scopes Trial and the Red Scare.

Describe the causes and effects of limits on immigration.

Identify the impact of racial tensions during the 1920s.

Describe the election of 1928.

>> **Key Terms**

company union
sabotage
anarchist
deport
nativism
quota system
Great Migration

PEARSON realize™
www.PearsonRealize.com
Access your Digital Lesson.

The Downside of the 1920s

Farmers Suffer Farmers were hit the hardest. During World War I, Europeans had bought American farm products, sending prices up. Farmers borrowed money to buy more land and tractors. They planned to pay off these loans with profits from increased production.

When the war ended, however, European farmers were again able to produce enough for their own needs. As a result, prices for American farm products dropped sharply throughout the 1920s. Farmers were unable to pay their debts. By the end of the decade, the farmers' share of national income had shrunk by almost half.

Labor Faces Losses For labor unions, too, the 1920s were a disaster. During the war, unions had worked with the government to keep production high. Labor's cooperation contributed to victory. In return, union leaders expected the government to support labor.

During the war, wages had not kept up with prices. Now, with the war over, workers demanded higher pay. When employers refused, unions launched a wave of strikes. Management moved quickly to crush the strikes. Because the government did not step in to help them, workers felt betrayed and management gained power.

The strikes turned much of the public against labor. One strike in particular angered many Americans. In 1919, the city of Boston fired 19 police officers who had tried to join the American Federation of Labor (AFL). Boston police struck in protest. The sight of police leaving their posts shocked the country.

The later 1920s saw even more setbacks for labor. In one court case after another, judges limited the rights of unions. At the same time, employers created **company unions**, labor organizations that were actually controlled by management. As a

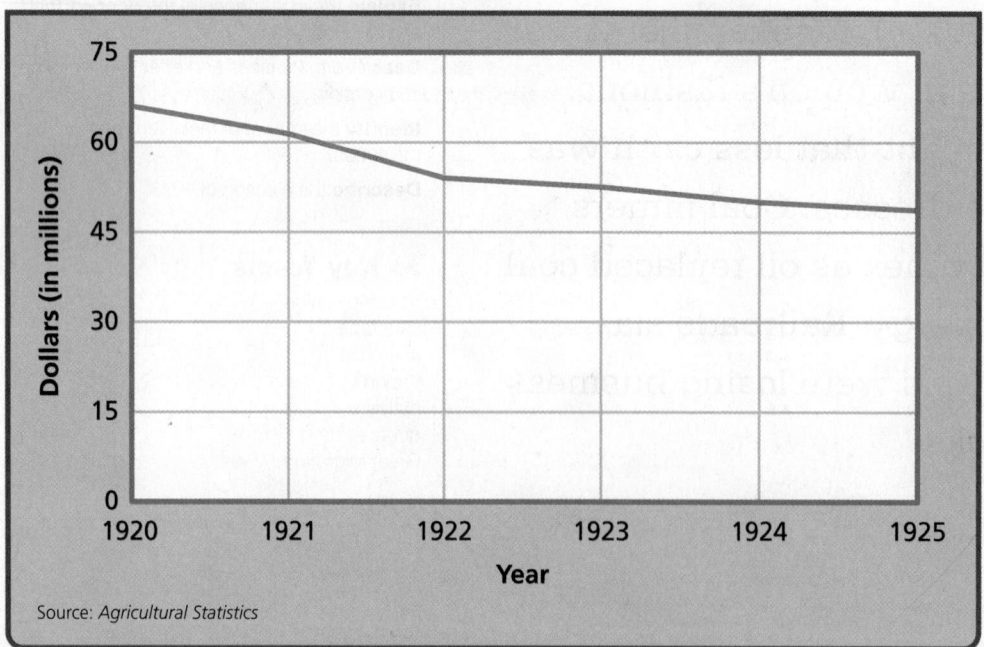

Value of Farmland, 1920–1925

Source: *Agricultural Statistics*

>> **Analyze Graphs** Explain what happened to the value of farmland in the 1920s.

result, membership in independent unions dropped from 5 million in 1920 to 3.4 million by 1929. Without strong unions, labor had little power to win higher wages.

? LIST several areas of the economy whose workers suffered economic losses during the 1920s.

Cultural Clashes

In the 1920s, cities drew thousands of people from farms and small towns. Those who stayed in rural areas often feared that new ways of life in the city were a threat to traditional values. Changes abroad also spurred nationwide worries about people with differing political views.

The Scopes Trial One clash between old and new values erupted in the small town of Dayton, Tennessee. At the center of the controversy was Charles Darwin's theory of evolution. Darwin, a British scientist, had claimed that all life had evolved, or developed, from simpler forms over a long period of time.

While biologists accepted Darwin's theory, some churches condemned it, saying it contradicted the teachings of the Bible. Tennessee, Mississippi, and Arkansas passed laws that banned the teaching of Darwin's theory. In 1925, John Scopes, a biology teacher in Dayton, taught evolution to his class. Scopes was arrested and tried.

Two of the nation's best-known figures opposed each other in the Scopes trial. William Jennings Bryan, who had run for President three times, argued the state's case against Scopes. Clarence Darrow, a Chicago lawyer who had helped unions and radicals, defended Scopes.

As the trial began, the nation's attention was riveted on Dayton. Reporters recorded

>> The Scopes "monkey trial" brought the teaching of evolution in public schools to national attention in 1925. High-school teacher John T. Scopes (center) was convicted and fined for teaching evolution to his students in the state of Tennessee.

every word of the battle between Darrow and Bryan. "Scopes isn't on trial," Darrow thundered at one point, "civilization is on trial." In the end, Scopes was convicted and fined. The laws against teaching evolution were defeated, or overruled, in later years.

Worries Cause a Red Scare During World War I, Americans had been on the alert for enemy spies and **sabotage**, or the secret destruction of property or interference with work in factories. These wartime worries led to a growing fear of foreigners.

The rise of communism in the Soviet Union fanned that fear. Lenin, the communist leader, called on workers everywhere to overthrow their governments. Many Americans saw the strikes that swept the nation as the start of a communist revolution.

Eliminating Extremists The actions of **anarchists**, or people who oppose organized government, added to the sense of danger. One group of anarchists plotted to kill well-known Americans, including John D. Rockefeller, the head of Standard Oil. Because many anarchists were foreign-born, their attacks led to an outcry against all foreigners.

The government took harsh actions against both anarchists and Communists, or "reds." During the red scare, thousands of radicals were arrested and jailed. Many foreigners were **deported**, or expelled from the country.

Sacco and Vanzetti The trial of two Italian immigrants in Massachusetts came to symbolize the antiforeign feeling of the 1920s. Nicola Sacco and Bartolomeo Vanzetti were arrested for robbery and murder in 1920. The two men admitted being anarchists but insisted they had committed no crime. A jury convicted them, however. Sacco and Vanzetti were then sentenced to death.

The Sacco and Vanzetti trial created a furor across the nation. The evidence against the two men was limited. The judge was openly prejudiced against the two immigrants. Many Americans thought that Sacco and Vanzetti were convicted, not because they were guilty, but because they were immigrants and radicals. The two men waited in jail during a six-year fight to overturn their convictions. Their appeals were turned down. In 1927, they were executed.

The issue of whether Sacco and Vanzetti received a fair trial has been debated ever since. In the meantime, some Americans felt the case proved that the United States had to keep out dangerous radicals.

? IDENTIFYING CENTRAL IDEAS What was the key issue in the Scopes trial?

The First Red Scare

November 1917 The Russian Revolution creates fear of communist infiltration in the United States.

November 1918 World War I ends, but many Americans continue to fear communists and radicals at home.

June 1919 Anarchists try to eliminate national leaders through bombs sent via mail.

January 1920 Government raids result in more than 4,000 arrests and 556 deportations of alleged communists across 33 cities.

May 1924 The Immigration Act imposes further restrictions on immigration.

May 1918 The Sedition Act prohibits people from criticizing the U.S. government.

March 1919 The Third Communist International is founded by Russian leader Vladimir Lenin to spread communism to other countries.

November 1919 Attorney General Mitchell Palmer orders raids resulting in 250 arrests of radicals across 11 cities.

December 1919 Groups such as the Industrial Workers of the World hold strikes and stage violent uprisings.

May 1921 The Emergency Quota Act restricts immigration.

1917   1919   1921   1923   1925

>> **Analyze Charts** Explain the relationship between immigration laws and Americans' fear of communists.

Tensions Divide Americans

In the end, the Red Scare died down. Yet, hostility toward foreigners led to a new move to limit immigration. As you recall, this kind of antiforeign feeling is known as **nativism**.

Immigration Quotas After the war, millions of Europeans hoped to find a better life in the United States. American workers feared that too many newcomers would force wages down. Others worried that communists and anarchists would flood in.

Congress responded by passing the Emergency Quota Act in 1921. The act set up a **quota system** that allowed only a certain number of people from each country to enter the United States. Only 3 percent of the people in any national group already living in the United States in 1910 could be admitted.

The quota system favored immigrants from northern Europe, especially Britain. In 1924, Congress passed new laws that further cut immigration, especially from eastern Europe, which was seen as a center of anarchism and communism. In addition, Japanese were added to the list of Asians denied entry to the country.

Hispanics Immigrate Latin Americans and Canadians were not included in the quota system. As a result, Mexican immigrants continued to move to the United States. Farms and factories in the Southwest depended on Mexican workers. The pay was low, and the housing was poor. Still, immigrants were drawn by the chance to earn more money than they could at home. By 1930, a million or more Mexicans had crossed the border.

The Jones Act of 1917 granted American citizenship to Puerto Ricans. Poverty on the island led to a great migration to the north. In 1910, about 1,500 Puerto Ricans lived on

>> This photo shows immigrants arriving at Ellis Island in the 1920s. At that time, a series of laws were passed to limit the number of immigrants entering the United States.

▶ **Interactive Chart**

the mainland. By 1930, there were about 53,000.

Racial Tensions Rise As African American soldiers returned from serving their country in the war, they began demanding equal rights. This, along with the large African American migration to northern cities, led to heightened racial tension and race riots. White racists formed a new Ku Klux Klan. Groups called the Universal Negro Improvement Association and the National Association for the Advancement of Colored People, or NAACP, organized to defend the rights of African Americans.

The New Klan Fear of change gave new life to an old organization. In 1915, a group of white men in Georgia declared the rebirth of the Ku Klux Klan. The original Klan had used terror to keep African Americans from voting after the Civil War. The new Klan had

>> At this 1926 march in Washington, D.C., Ku Klux Klan members demonstrated to preserve white supremacy in the United States. The Klan threatened violence against minorities, creating a state of fear, especially in the American South.

▶ **Interactive Gallery**

a broader aim: to preserve the United States for white, native-born Protestants.

The new Klan waged a campaign not only against African Americans, but also against immigrants, especially Catholics and Jews. Klan members burned crosses outside people's homes. They used whippings and lynchings to terrorize immigrants and African Americans. The Klan strongly supported efforts to limit immigration.

Because of its large membership, the Klan gained political influence. In the mid-1920s, however, many Americans became alarmed at the Klan's growing power. At the same time, scandals surfaced that showed Klan leaders had stolen money from members. Klan membership dropped sharply.

The Great Migration African Americans had hoped that their service during World War I would weaken racism at home.

However, returning African American soldiers found that the South was still a segregated society. In the North, too, racial prejudice was widespread.

Many African Americans moved north during and after the war. The large-scale movement north of African Americans during the early to mid-1900s is known as the **Great Migration**. African Americans took factory jobs in Chicago, Detroit, New York, Philadelphia, and other large cities. They often found that the only jobs open to them were low-paying ones. Also, due to discrimination, there were only a few neighborhoods where landlords would rent apartments to African Americans.

At the same time, many African Americans newly arrived from the South wanted to live near one another. As a result, areas with large African American populations grew up in many northern cities.

Many northern white workers felt threatened by the arrival of so many African Americans. Racial tension grew. In 1919, race riots broke out in several cities. The worst took place in Chicago, leaving 38 dead.

A Black Nationalist Leader Shocked by the racism they found, African Americans looked for new ways to cope. Marcus Garvey became one of the most popular African American leaders. He started the first widespread black nationalist movement in the United States. Garvey organized the Universal Negro Improvement Association. He hoped to promote unity and pride among African Americans. He believed that African Americans needed to rely on themselves rather than white people to get ahead. "I am the equal of any white man," Garvey said.

Garvey urged African Americans to seek their roots in Africa. Although few black Americans actually went to Africa, Garvey's "Back to Africa" movement built racial pride.

Election of 1928 By 1928, Republicans had led the nation for eight years. They pointed to prosperity as their outstanding achievement. Still, when asked about the upcoming election, President Coolidge said tersely, "I do not choose to run." Instead, Secretary of Commerce Herbert Hoover easily won the Republican nomination. The Democrats chose as their candidate Alfred E. Smith, the governor of New York.

The contrast between the candidates revealed the tensions lurking below the surface of American life. Smith, the grandson of Irish, Italian, and German immigrants, was the first Catholic to run for President. City dwellers, including many immigrants and Catholics, rallied around Smith. Hoover was a self-made millionaire from the Midwest who was respected for his management skill working to supply troops during World War I. He won votes from rural Americans and big business. Supporters of Prohibition also supported Hoover because Smith favored repeal.

In the election, Smith won the country's 12 largest cities. Rural and small-town voters supported Hoover. He won by a landslide. Americans hoped Hoover would keep the country prosperous. Less than a year after he took office, however, the economy would come crashing down.

? CHECK UNDERSTANDING Why did Congress cut immigration from eastern European countries more than from other countries?

ASSESSMENT

1. **Summarize** Why did many farmers suffer financial difficulties in the 1920s?

2. **Summarize** how World War I affected union workers in the 1920s.

3. **Compare** the Sacco and Vanzetti trial to the Scopes Trial. What was the significance of both trials to the culture of the 1920s?

4. **Cause and Effect** How did limits on immigration affect Mexicans coming to the United States?

5. **Determine Point of View** Why did calls for political and social equality of minorities increase after World War I?

★ **THE ELECTION** OF **1928** ★

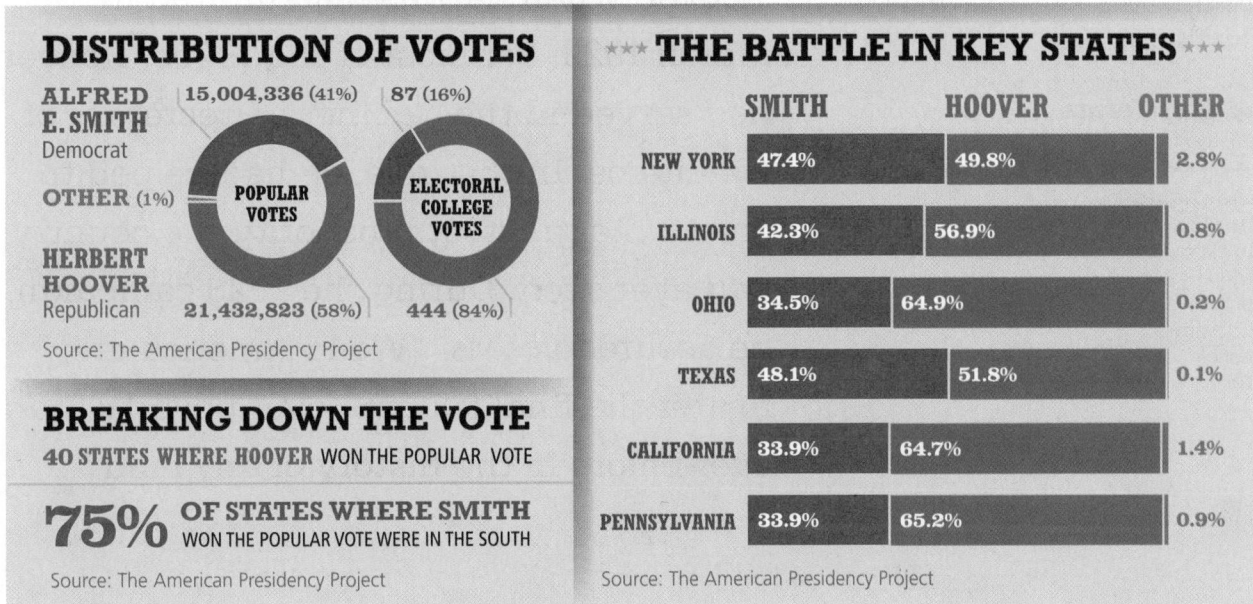

DISTRIBUTION OF VOTES

ALFRED E. SMITH Democrat — 15,004,336 (41%) | 87 (16%)

OTHER (1%)

POPULAR VOTES

ELECTORAL COLLEGE VOTES

HERBERT HOOVER Republican — 21,432,823 (58%) | 444 (84%)

Source: The American Presidency Project

BREAKING DOWN THE VOTE

40 STATES WHERE HOOVER WON THE POPULAR VOTE

75% OF STATES WHERE SMITH WON THE POPULAR VOTE WERE IN THE SOUTH

Source: The American Presidency Project

★★★ THE BATTLE IN KEY STATES ★★★

	SMITH	HOOVER	OTHER
NEW YORK	47.4%	49.8%	2.8%
ILLINOIS	42.3%	56.9%	0.8%
OHIO	34.5%	64.9%	0.2%
TEXAS	48.1%	51.8%	0.1%
CALIFORNIA	33.9%	64.7%	1.4%
PENNSYLVANIA	33.9%	65.2%	0.9%

Source: The American Presidency Project

>> **Analyze Graphs** In which key states did Smith win a higher share of the vote than he did nationally?

Entering the Great Depression

>> Unemployed Americans often lived in Hoovervilles such as this one in Seattle in 1937. The term *Hooverville* was an ironic joke based on the feeling that President Hoover was not doing enough to reverse the effects of the Depression.

Interactive Flipped Video

>> Objectives

Identify the causes of the stock market crash of 1929 and the Great Depression.

Explain how hard times affected Americans.

Describe and evaluate Hoover's response to the Depression.

>> Key Terms

on margin
Black Tuesday
Great Depression
bankrupt
relief program
soup kitchen
public works
Hooverville
bonus
Bonus Army

Most Americans had great confidence in their new President, Herbert Hoover, when he was inaugurated in March 1929. For most of the 1920s, Hoover had served in the Cabinet as secretary of commerce. In that role, he had helped to create the greatest prosperity the country had ever seen. During the 1928 campaign, he assured voters, "We in America are nearer the final triumph over poverty than ever before in the history of any land."

Causes of the Crash

Then, only seven months after Hoover's inauguration, the stock market crashed. The United States began a plunge into the worst economic depression in its history. Everywhere, stunned people asked: How could this have happened?

An Economic Slowdown When Hoover took office in 1929, he saw a growing economy. Along with most of the nation's leaders, he did not recognize the signs of trouble.

Hoover did realize that some Americans had not shared in the prosperity of the 1920s. As you have read, farmers already faced hardship in the 1920s. So did workers in the textile and coal industries. For workers in those industries, a booming economy was something they only read about in the newspapers. The words on a Pennsylvania mining town tombstone reflected their feelings of frustration.

> For forty years beneath the sod
>
> With pick and spade I did my task
>
> The coal king's slave, but now, thank God
>
> I'm free at last.
>
> —Tombstone inscription, Pennsylvania

In the mid-1920s, the overall economy began to slow down. No one noticed the slowdown because at that time the government did not keep detailed statistics.

The Crash By August 1929, some investors worried that the boom might soon end. They began selling their stocks. In September, more people decided to sell. The rash of selling caused stock prices to fall. Hoover reassured investors that the "business of the country . . . is on a sound and prosperous basis." Despite the President's calming words, the selling continued and stock prices tumbled.

Many investors had bought stocks on margin. Buyers of stocks **on margin** pay only part of the cost of the stock when they make the purchase. They borrow the rest from their stockbrokers. With prices falling, brokers asked investors to pay back what they owed. Investors sold their stock to repay their loans.

A panic quickly set in. Between October 24 and October 29, desperate people tried to unload millions of shares. As a result, stock prices dropped even further.

When the stock market opened on Tuesday, October 29, a wild stampede of selling hit the New York Stock Exchange. Prices plunged because there were no buyers. People who thought they

>> Worried people gather outside the New York Stock Exchange on October 24, 1929, the day the crash began, also known as Black Thursday.

owned valuable stocks were left with worthless paper.

After **Black Tuesday**, as it came to be called, business leaders tried to restore confidence in the economy. John D. Rockefeller told reporters, "My son and I have for some days been purchasing some common stocks." Replied comedian Eddie Cantor, "Sure, who else has any money left?"

? DEFINE What was Black Tuesday?

The Great Depression Sets In

The period of economic hard times that followed the crash is known as the **Great Depression**. It lasted from 1929 to 1941.

The stock market crash did not cause the Great Depression, but it did shake people's confidence in the economy. As the depression worsened, people tried to understand how the prosperity of the 1920s had vanished.

Causes of the Great Depression Among the chief causes of the Great Depression was overproduction. American factories and farms produced vast amounts of goods in the 1920s. Vast corporate profits made from increased production were not passed on to workers. As a result, the gap between rich and poor widened with the middle class slipping into poverty. In fact, over one third of American assets were owned by one percent of Americans—those with the most money.

Having such a small number of people in control of so much wealth contributed to an economic slump. First, the wealthy were more likely to save the money than spend it like those who were less wealthy. Second, those who were less wealthy saw their buying power fall.

THE **GREAT DEPRESSION**

1 DEFLATION*, 1928–1937

Inflation (percent change) / years 1928–1937

*The overproduction of goods created surpluses, which caused prices to decline.
Source: *Theory and Applications of Macroeconomics (v. 1.0)*

2 WAGES ON THE DECLINE

WEEKLY EARNINGS IN MANUFACTURING

1929 $27.36 (100%)
1932 $18.18 (66.5%)

Source: National Bureau of Economic Research

3 THE STOCK MARKET CRASHES

48% DECLINE IN THE DOW JONES INDUSTRIAL AVERAGE FROM SEPTEMBER TO NOVEMBER 1929

Source: *Theory and Applications of Macroeconomics (v. 1.0)*

4 UNEMPLOYMENT ON THE RISE

% of labor force

1929	1930	1931	1932	1933	1934	1935	1937
3.2	8.9	16.3	24.1	25.2	22.0	20.3	17.0	14.3

Source: *Theory and Applications of Macroeconomics (v. 1.0)*

>> American factories and farms increased production in the 1920s.
Analyze Graphs What effect did the overproduction of goods have on prices?

Interactive Chart

Events Leading to Global Economic Collapse, 1919–1930

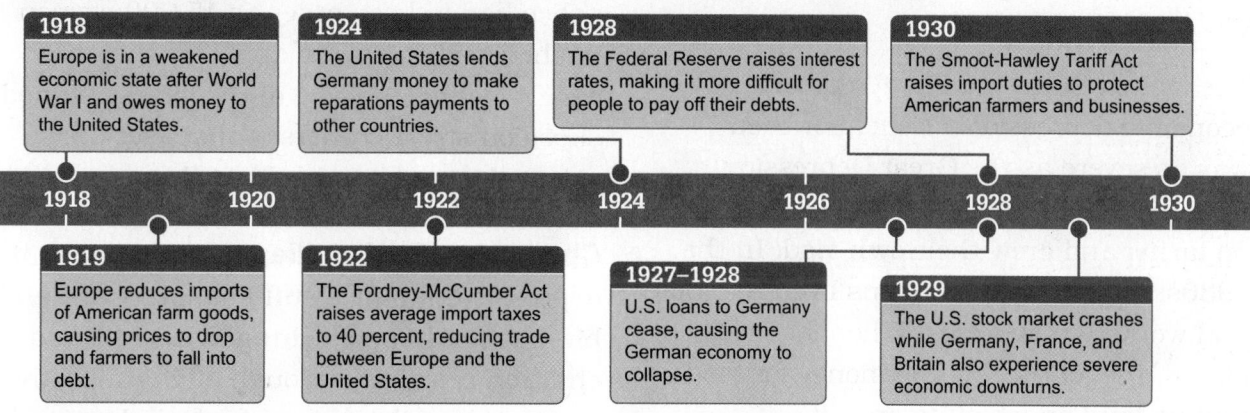

1918
Europe is in a weakened economic state after World War I and owes money to the United States.

1924
The United States lends Germany money to make reparations payments to other countries.

1928
The Federal Reserve raises interest rates, making it more difficult for people to pay off their debts.

1930
The Smoot-Hawley Tariff Act raises import duties to protect American farmers and businesses.

1919
Europe reduces imports of American farm goods, causing prices to drop and farmers to fall into debt.

1922
The Fordney-McCumber Act raises average import taxes to 40 percent, reducing trade between Europe and the United States.

1927–1928
U.S. loans to Germany cease, causing the German economy to collapse.

1929
The U.S. stock market crashes while Germany, France, and Britain also experience severe economic downturns.

Timeline: 1918 1920 1922 1924 1926 1928 1930

>> **Analyze Charts** How does the timeline show a relationship between the U.S. economy and the economies of other nations?

Because wages did not keep up with prices, workers could not afford to buy the goods that corporations continued to produce. Factories and farms were producing more goods than people were buying. As orders slowed, factories laid off workers.

Another cause of the depression was weakness in the banking system. During the 1920s, banks made unwise loans. For example, banks lent money to people who invested in the stock market. When the stock market crashed, borrowers could not repay their loans. Without the money from the loans, the banks could not give depositors their money when they asked for it. As a result, many banks were forced to close.

More than 5,000 banks closed between 1929 and 1932. When a bank closed, depositors lost their money. Often, a family's lifetime savings disappeared overnight.

A Series of Economic Problems After the stock market crash, the economy slid downhill at a fast pace. One disaster triggered another. The stock market crash, for example, ruined many investors. Without capital, or money, from investors, businesses could no longer grow and expand. Businesses could not turn to banks for capital because the banks were also in trouble.

As factories cut back on production, they cut wages and laid off workers. Unemployed workers, in turn, had little money to spend, so demand for goods fell further. In the end, many businesses went **bankrupt**—they were unable to pay their debts. As bankrupt businesses closed, even more people were thrown out of work.

The Great Depression led to a worldwide economic crisis. In the 1920s, the United States had loaned large sums to European nations. When American banks stopped making loans or demanded repayment of existing loans, European banks began to fail. The depression spread from nation to nation. By 1930, it had led to a worldwide economic collapse.

? IDENTIFY CENTRAL ISSUES What were two main causes of the Depression?

Life During the Great Depression

The United States had suffered earlier economic depressions. None, however, was as severe as the Great Depression. In earlier times, most Americans lived on farms and grew their own food. In the 1930s, millions of Americans lived in cities and worked in factories. When factories closed, the jobless had no money for food and no land on which to grow it.

The Jobless As the depression spread, the unemployment rate soared. By the early 1930s, one in every four workers was jobless. Millions more worked shortened hours or took pay cuts. Many of the jobless lost their homes. On city streets, people sold pencils and begged for money.

The chance of finding work was small. On an average day, one New York job agency had 5,000 people looking for work.

Only about 300 found jobs. In another city, police had to keep order as 15,000 women pushed and shoved to apply for six jobs cleaning offices. Some of the jobless shined shoes on street corners. Others set up sidewalk stands and sold apples.

Challenges for Families During the depression, families suffered. Marriage and birth rates dropped. Hungry parents and children searched through city dumps and restaurant garbage cans for food. In one school, a teacher ordered a thin girl to go home to eat. "I can't," replied the girl. "This is my sister's day to eat."

The pressure of hard times led some families to split up. The scarcity of food and work led to fathers and even children as young as 13 or 14 years old to leave home to hunt for work. Their leaving meant the family had fewer people to feed, but it also came at a cost: there were fewer

Unemployment, 1925–1935

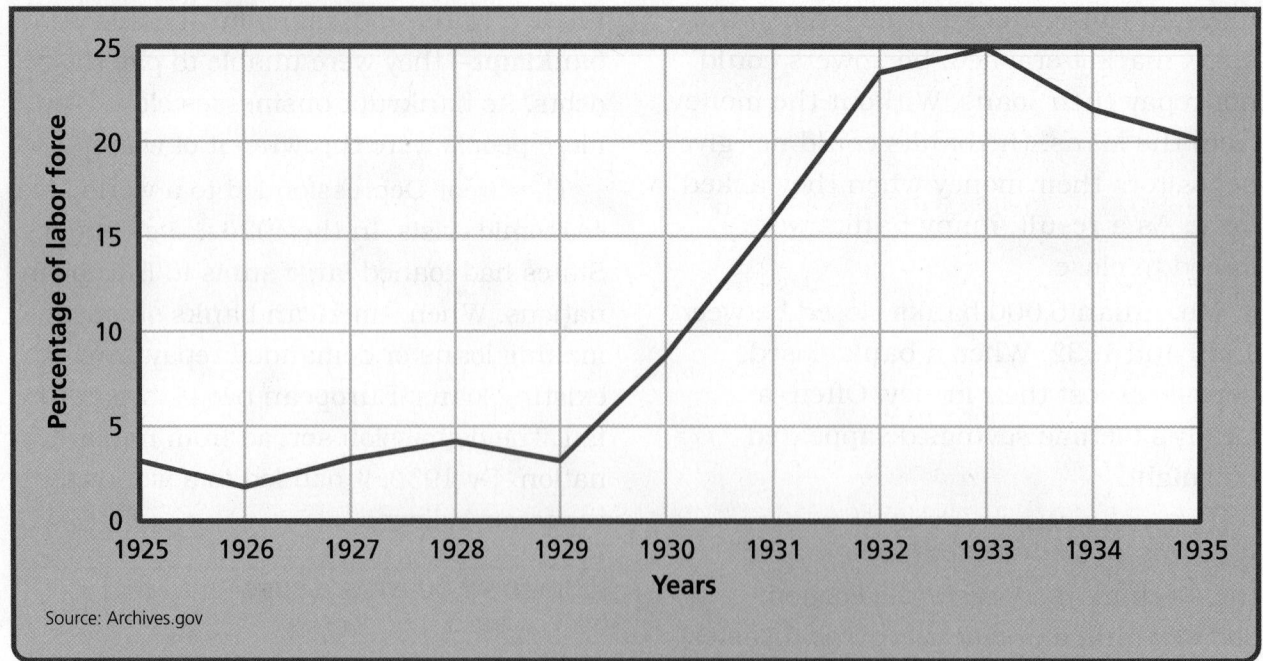

Source: Archives.gov

>> **Draw Conclusions** Identify at least one cause for the change in unemployment beginning in 1929 reflected in this graph.

people to care for any young children or elderly at home.

Jobless men and women drifted from town to town looking for work. Some "rode the rails," living in railroad cars and hitching rides on freight trains. Louis Banks, a young African American, later described what it was like to ride the rails.

> Twenty-five or thirty would be out on the side of the rail, white and colored. They didn't have no mothers or sisters, they didn't have no home, they were dirty, they had overalls on, they didn't have no food, they didn't have anything.
>
> — Louis Banks, Interview, 1970

Americans did their best to cope. They attempted to meet their basic needs by utilizing the scarce resources they possessed. Neighbors shared what little they had. Some families doubled up, taking in aunts, uncles, and cousins. Some families began to grow vegetables and can foods instead of shopping in stores.

The Great Depression shook Americans' belief in themselves. Many Americans defined their self worth partly on their ability to produce and consume goods and services. Without the opportunity to be productive members of the economy, many found their self worth diminished. "No matter that others suffered the same fate, the inner voice whispered, 'I'm a failure,'" one unemployed man wrote.

? CHECK UNDERSTANDING How did urbanization worsen the effects of the Depression?

The President Responds

President Hoover was deeply concerned about the suffering. However, Hoover did not believe that government should become

>> As joblessness multiplied during the Great Depression, an increasing number of people relied on the charity of soup kitchens for their meals.

▶ **Interactive Gallery**

directly involved in helping to end the business crisis. He feared that government might become too powerful. It was up to businesses, he felt, to work together to end the downslide.

Aid for the Needy At first, Hoover also opposed government **relief programs**—programs to help the needy. Instead, the President urged business leaders to keep workers employed and to maintain wages.

Hoover also called on private charities to help the needy. Churches set up **soup kitchens**, places where the hungry could get a free meal. Ethnic communities organized their own relief efforts. In San Francisco's Chinatown, fraternal societies gave out food and clothing. Father Divine, an African American religious leader in New York's Harlem, fed 3,000 hungry people a day. Mexican Americans and Puerto Ricans turned to aid societies.

Still, the numbers of the needy soon overwhelmed private charities.

President Hoover's strong belief in limited government affected his initial response to the economic crisis. Soon after taking office in 1930, he declared, "Prosperity cannot be restored by raids upon the public Treasury." However, as the Depression continued, he adopted some policies that he hoped would help people help themselves and stimulate the economy.

He set up public works programs. **Public works** are projects built by the government for public use. The government hired workers to build schools, construct dams, and pave highways. By providing jobs, these programs enabled people to earn money.

Hoover also asked Congress to approve the Reconstruction Finance Corporation, or RFC, in 1932. The RFC loaned money to banks, railroads, and insurance companies to help them stay in business.

Saving these businesses, Hoover hoped, would save thousands of jobs.

A Deepening Depression Hoover did more to reverse hard times than any previous President. However, his efforts were too little and came too late. In 1931, as the third winter of the depression approached, more and more people joined the ranks of the hungry and homeless. "Men are sitting in the parks all day long and all night long," wrote one man in Detroit.

Many people blamed the President for doing too little. He refused to establish a welfare system for those out of work, believing it would further devastate American morale. However, people were desperate for any help they could get. They gave the name **Hoovervilles** to the clusters of shacks where the homeless lived. People spoke of "Hoover blankets," the newspapers used by the homeless to keep warm when they slept outside. A cardboard patch that

>> President Herbert Hoover developed public works programs to provide Americans with jobs in the 1930s. The Hoover Dam on the Colorado River was one such project.

covered a hole in a shoe was called "Hoover leather." Men, women, and children lined up for "Hoover stew," the name they gave to the thin soup they received in soup kitchens.

The Bonus Army While people waited for the government to help, one group of Americans took action. After World War I, Congress had voted to give veterans a **bonus**, or additional sum of money, to be paid in 1945. In 1932, more than 20,000 jobless veterans marched to Washington to demand the bonus right away. For two months, the **Bonus Army**, as the group of veterans were called, camped in a tent city along the Potomac River.

The House of Representatives voted to give the veterans the bonus at once, but the Senate rejected the bill. Senators thought that the cost would prevent government action to aid the country's recovery. Many discouraged veterans then went home. However, thousands of others remained, vowing to stay until 1945 if necessary.

Local police tried to force the veterans to leave. Battles with police left four people dead. Hoover then ordered General Douglas MacArthur to clear out the veterans. Using cavalry, tanks, machine guns, and tear gas, MacArthur moved into the camp and burned it to the ground.

An editorial in the *Washington News* years later expressed the shock many Americans felt at the time.

> What a pitiful spectacle is that of the great American Government, mightiest in the world, chasing unarmed men, women, and children with Army tanks. . . . If the Army must be called out to make war on unarmed citizens, this is no longer America.

—*Washington News,* "The Summer of the BEF," November 23, 1932

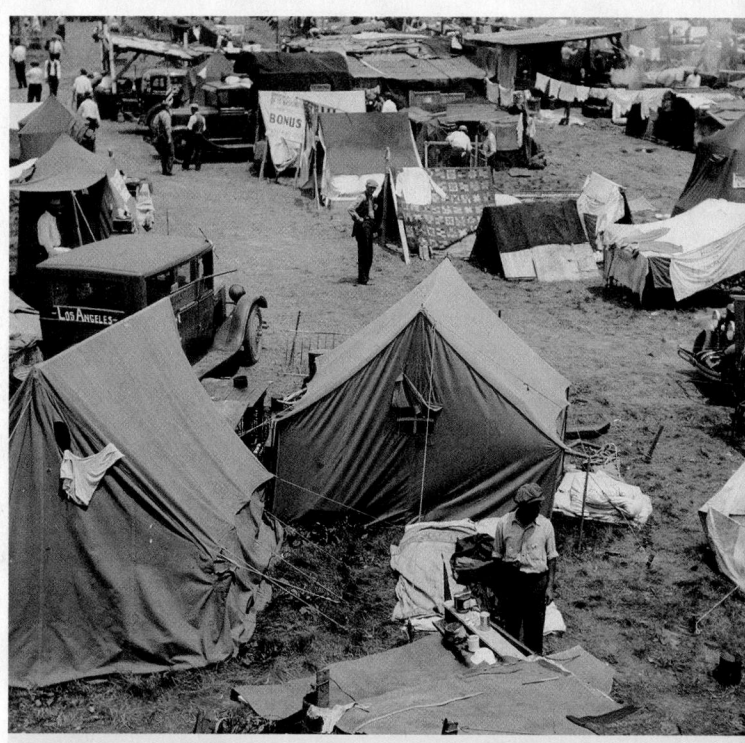

>> In 1932, Bonus Army members occupied a portion of Washington, D.C., in this camp.

After the attack on the Bonus Army, the President lost what little support he still had. Convinced that the country needed a change, many Americans looked for a new leader.

? **DEFINE** What are public works?

ASSESSMENT

1. **Summarize** how the Great Depression affected the world outside of the United States.

2. **Compare** family life before the Great Depression to family life during the Great Depression.

3. **Identify Cause and Effect** What was one effect of Hoover's reluctance to provide government aid programs?

4. **Cite Evidence** Why did popular support for President Hoover continue to fall after he ordered U.S. troops to clear the Bonus Army protests in Washington D.C.?

5. **Compare** how Americans felt about Herbert Hoover at the beginning of his presidency and at the end of his presidency.

Roosevelt's New Deal

>> This photo shows Roosevelt taking the oath of office at his first inauguration on March 4, 1933. Roosevelt eventually became the only president to serve more than two terms in office.

Interactive Flipped Video

>> Objectives

Explain why Roosevelt won the election in 1932.

Describe the impact of the New Deal, including the Hundred Days, jobless relief, labor reforms, Social Security, and other programs.

Explain why critics objected to the New Deal.

Describe Roosevelt's conflict with the Supreme Court.

Evaluate the effects of the New Deal.

>> Key Terms

polio
bank holiday
fireside chat
Hundred Days
New Deal
Civilian Conservation
    Corps
National Recovery
    Administration
Tennessee Valley
    Authority
pension

National Labor
    Relations Act
collective bargaining
Congress of
    Industrial
    Organizations
sit-down strike
Social Security Act
deficit spending
national debt

Franklin Delano Roosevelt, known as FDR, came from a wealthy, influential family. He attended Harvard University and Columbia Law School. In 1905, he married a distant cousin, Anna Eleanor Roosevelt.

Roosevelt's Path to the Presidency

During World War I, FDR served as assistant secretary of the navy. In 1920, he was the Democratic candidate for Vice President but lost in the Harding landslide.

Physical Challenges Then, in the summer of 1921, Roosevelt was stricken with a severe case of polio. A disease caused by a virus, **polio** has been almost totally wiped out in the United States today. However, before the development of a vaccine in the 1950s, polio was a devastating disease. FDR's legs were completely paralyzed. He struggled for years to rebuild his strength.

In time, Roosevelt returned to public life. In 1928, he was elected governor of New York. Then, in 1932, the Democrats made him their presidential candidate. The Republicans again nominated Herbert Hoover, even though they knew he had little chance of winning.

Winning the Election Roosevelt set a new tone right from the start. He broke with tradition by flying to the Democratic convention to accept the nomination in person. Standing before the delegates, he declared: "I pledge myself to a new deal for the American people."

Roosevelt did not spell out what he meant by "a new deal." Still, he sounded a hopeful note. In campaign speeches, he promised to help the jobless, poor farmers, and the elderly.

Voters responded to FDR's confident manner and personal charm. On election day, he won a landslide victory. Democrats also gained many seats in Congress. On inauguration day, the new President addressed the American people with optimism:

This great nation will endure as it has endured, will revive and will prosper. So, first of all, let me assert my firm belief that the only thing we have to fear is fear itself—nameless, unreasoning, unjustified terror which paralyzes needed efforts to convert retreat into advance.

—Franklin D. Roosevelt, Inaugural Address, March 4, 1933

President Roosevelt then issued a call to action. "This nation asks for action and action now," he said. Many Americans welcomed this energetic new President, especially since Hoover's more cautious approach had failed to end the nation's economic crisis.

? **TRACE** three major steps in Roosevelt's path to the presidency.

>> Franklin D. Roosevelt, a Democrat, became President of the United States in 1933 during one of the darkest periods of the country's history.

>> A key member of President Roosevelt's "brain trust," Secretary of Labor Frances Perkins—the woman in black standing just to the right of the president—looks on as he signs a bill into law in 1935.

Seeking Relief and Recovery

During his campaign for the presidency, FDR had sought advice on how to fight the Depression. He turned to a number of college professors who were experts on economic issues. These experts, nicknamed the Brain Trust, helped Roosevelt to plan bold new programs.

Once in office, President Roosevelt chose able advisers. Harold Ickes (IK eez), a Republican reformer from Chicago, became secretary of the interior. The President named social worker Frances Perkins the secretary of labor. Perkins was the first woman to hold a Cabinet post.

The new President moved forward on many fronts. He urged his staff to "take a method and try it. If it fails, admit it and try another. But above all try something."

Strengthening Banks Roosevelt's first challenge was the nation's crumbling banking system. Many banks had closed. Fearful depositors had withdrawn their savings from other banks. People hid their money under mattresses or buried it in their yards.

The President knew that without sound banks, the economy could not recover. On his second day in office, he declared a **bank holiday**. He closed every bank in the country for four days. He then asked Congress to pass the Emergency Banking Relief Act. Under this act, only those banks with enough funds to meet depositors' demands could reopen. Others had to stay closed.

A week after taking office, President Roosevelt spoke to Americans by radio. Under the new law, the President told the people, "it is safer to keep your money in a reopened bank than under your mattress."

>> Many banks, such as this one, closed during the Great Depression. Under the Emergency Banking Relief Act, the banks that did not have enough funds to meet depositors' demands were shut down permanently.

Selected Laws Passed During FDR's First Three Months

LAW	OBJECTIVE
Agricultural Adjustment Act	Establish production limits and provide federal subsidies to help farmers
Federal Unemployment Relief Act	Provide jobs that help to protect parks, forests, and public lands
National Industrial Recovery Act	Establish codes of fair practice for industries
Federal Emergency Relief Act	Grant funds to states to help them create their own relief projects
Emergency Railroad Transportation Act	Reorganize railroad administration to increase efficiency
Securities Act	Provide government oversight of stock trading to prevent fraud
Emergency Farm Mortgage Act	Provide loans to farmers facing foreclosures or debt defaults
Glass-Steagall Banking Reform Act	Prevent banks from making risky investments
Emergency Banking Act	Give the President power over banks
Tennessee Valley Authority Act	Provide electricity to poor areas in Tennessee and surrounding states

Sources: *Encyclopædia Britannica;* Archives.gov; Library of Congress; PBS

>> **Analyze Charts** This table lists examples of the laws put into place during Roosevelt's first hundred days. Which do you think was the most important to aid the struggling nation? Explain your answer.

 Interactive Cartoon

The radio broadcast worked. FDR explained things so clearly, said humorist Will Rogers, that even the bankers understood the situation. Reassured by the President, depositors returned their money to banks, and the banking system grew stronger.

FDR gave 30 radio speeches while in office. He called them **fireside chats** because he spoke from a chair near a fireplace in the White House. All across the nation, families gathered around their radios to listen to Roosevelt. Many felt the President understood their problems.

Laws for Recovery The bank bill was the first of many bills that FDR sent to Congress during his first three months in office. Between March 9 and June 16, 1933, Congress passed a record 15 major new laws. Even the President admitted he was "a bit shellshocked" by the **Hundred Days**, as this period was called.

The bills covered programs from job relief to planning for economic recovery. Together, they made up Roosevelt's New Deal. The **New Deal** laid out three main goals: relief for the jobless, plans for economic recovery, and reforms to prevent another depression.

Early Relief Programs In 1933, when Roosevelt took office, 13 million Americans were out of work. The President asked Congress for a variety of programs to help the jobless.

Among the earliest New Deal programs was the **Civilian Conservation Corps** (CCC). The CCC hired unemployed single men between the ages of 18 and 25. For $1 a day, they planted trees, built bridges, worked on flood-control projects, and developed new parks. The CCC served a double purpose. It conserved natural resources, and it gave jobs to young people. The Federal Emergency Relief Administration (FERA) gave federal money to state and local agencies. These agencies then distributed the money to the unemployed.

The WPA The Works Progress Administration (WPA) came into existence in 1935. The WPA put the jobless to work making clothes and building hospitals, schools, parks, playgrounds, and airports.

The WPA also hired artists, photographers, actors, writers, and composers. Artists painted murals on public buildings. The Federal Theatre put on new plays for adults and children, as well as classics by such writers as Shakespeare.

WPA writers collected information about American life, folklore, and traditions. Some WPA writers interviewed African Americans who had lived under slavery.

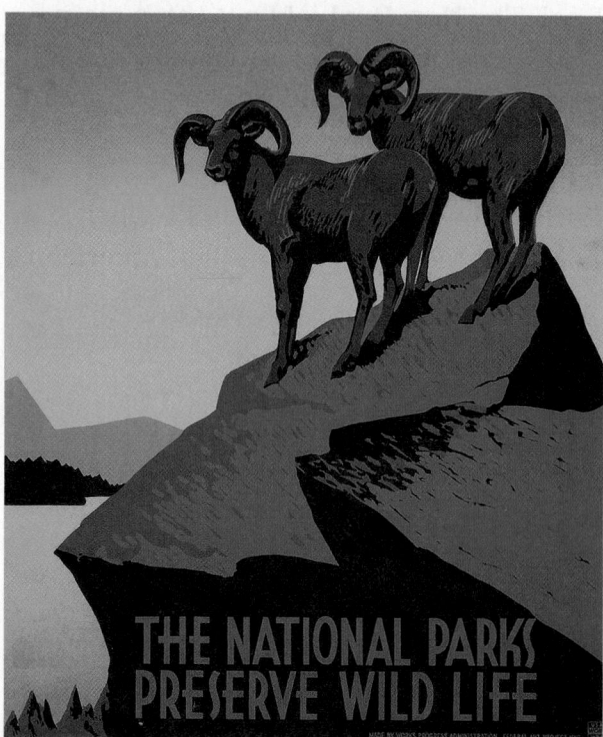

THE NATIONAL PARKS
PRESERVE WILD LIFE

MADE BY WORKS PROGRESS ADMINISTRATION · FEDERAL ART PROJECT NYC

>> This poster promoting the National Park Service was one of many created by the Works Progress Administration (WPA) during the Depression.

Today, scholars still use these interviews to learn firsthand about slave life.

Critics accused the WPA of creating make-work projects that did little to benefit the nation in the long run. "People don't eat in the long run," replied a New Dealer. "They eat every day."

? DEFINE What were the Hundred Days?

Reforming the Economy

To bring about recovery, the President had to boost both industry and farming. He developed programs that greatly expanded the government's role in the economy. With these and other programs, he hoped to prevent another depression.

Regulating Industry Overproduction and declining prices had been a major cause of the depression. Low prices during the depression had caused business to fail and created widespread unemployment. Aiming to boost the economy, New Dealers drew up plans to control production, stabilize prices, and keep workers on the job.

A key new law was the National Industrial Recovery Act (NIRA). Under this law, each industry wrote a code, or set of rules and standards, for production, wages, prices, and working conditions. The NIRA tried to end price cutting and worker layoffs.

To enforce the new codes, Congress set up the **National Recovery Administration** (NRA). Companies that followed the NRA codes stamped a blue eagle on their products.

The government encouraged people to do business only with companies displaying the NRA eagle. The NRA soon ran into trouble, however. Many companies ignored the codes. Also, small businesses felt that the codes favored the biggest firms.

The NIRA also set up the Public Works Administration (PWA). It promoted recovery by hiring workers for thousands of public works projects. PWA workers built projects such as the Grand Coulee Dam in Washington, public schools in Los Angeles, two aircraft carriers for the navy, and a deep-water port in Brownsville, Texas. Despite these efforts, the PWA did little to bring about recovery.

Subsidizing Farms On farms, overproduction remained the main problem. Surpluses kept prices and farmers' incomes low. A surplus occurs when farmers produce more than they can sell.

To help farmers, the President asked Congress to pass the Agricultural Adjustment Act (AAA). Under the AAA, the government paid farmers not to grow certain crops. Roosevelt hoped that with smaller harvests, the laws of supply and demand would force prices to rise.

The government also paid farmers to plow surplus crops under the soil and to destroy surplus cows and pigs. Many Americans were outraged that crops and livestock were being destroyed when people in the cities were going hungry. Yet, the plan seemed necessary to help farmers recover and keep them growing food.

The Rural Electrification Administration (REA) was created to help people in rural areas get the same electrical service as people in urban areas. The REA provided money to extend electric lines to rural areas. The number of farms with electricity rose from 10 percent to 25 percent. Electricity helped save many farms from ruin. For example, with refrigeration,

>> This 1936 photograph, "Migrant Mother" by Dorothea Lange, came to symbolize the struggles of migrant farm worker families during the Depression. **Interpret** how this photograph expresses the struggles of the family.

dairy farmers did not have to worry about milk going sour before it could be sent to market.

Tennessee Valley Authority Perhaps the boldest program of the Hundred Days was the **Tennessee Valley Authority** (TVA). It set out to remake the Tennessee River Valley. This vast region often suffered from terrible floods. Because the farmland was so poor, more than half the region's families were on relief.

The TVA was a daring experiment in regional planning. To control flooding, TVA engineers built 49 dams in seven states. The dams also produced cheap electric power. In addition to building dams, the TVA deepened river channels for shipping. It planted new forests to conserve soil and developed new fertilizers to improve farmland. The agency also set up schools and health centers.

The TVA sparked a furious debate. Critics argued that the government had no right to take business away from private companies in the region. Power companies in the Tennessee River Valley were especially outraged. They pointed out that the government, which did not have to make a profit for shareholders, could supply electrical power more cheaply than a private company could. Having to compete with the government, they said, might force them out of business.

Supporters replied that the TVA showed how the government could use its resources to help private enterprise. In the end, the program helped transform a region of desperate poverty into a prosperous and productive area.

Reforming the Economic System The third New Deal goal was to prevent another depression by reforming the economic system. During the Hundred Days, Congress passed laws regulating the stock market and the banking system. The Truth-in-Securities Act was designed to end the risky buying and selling of stocks in the hope of making a quick profit. Experts agreed that uncontrolled buying and selling was a leading cause of the 1929 crash.

Another law set up the Federal Deposit Insurance Corporation (FDIC). It insured depositors' accounts in banks approved by the government. If a bank insured by the FDIC failed, the government would make sure depositors received their money.

Later New Deal laws brought about other kinds of reforms. Laws regulated gas and electric companies. In 1938, a new law extended the Pure Food and Drug Act of 1906. It protected consumers by requiring manufacturers to list the ingredients in certain products. It also made sure that

Tennessee Valley Authority Dams Built, 1933–1939

KEY
Region served by TVA
— Hydroelectric dam

0   100 mi
0   100 km
Albers Conic Equal-Area Projection

>> **Analyze Maps** How many dams were constructed in Tennessee by the Tennessee Valley Authority?

Interactive Map

new medicines passed strict tests before they were put on the market.

? RECALL How did the Rural Electrification Act benefit farmers?

Supporting Workers and the Elderly

During the years of the New Deal, FDR supported programs to help workers and the elderly. Both groups faced particular hardship during the Great Depression.

Strengthening Unions In 1935, Congress passed the **National Labor Relations Act**, or Wagner Act. Senator Robert Wagner of New York, the act's sponsor, was a strong supporter of labor. The Wagner Act protected American workers from hostile management practices, such as firing a worker for joining a union. It also guaranteed workers the right to collective bargaining. **Collective bargaining** is the process by which a union representing a group of workers negotiates with management for a contract. Workers had fought for this right since the late 1800s.

The Wagner Act helped union membership grow from 3 million to 9 million during the 1930s. Union membership got a further boost when John L. Lewis set up the **Congress of Industrial Organizations** (CIO). The CIO represented workers in whole industries, such as steel, automobiles, and textiles.

With more members, unions increased their bargaining power. They also became a powerful force in politics.

Overcoming Obstacles Despite the Wagner Act, employers tried to stop workers from joining unions. Violent confrontations often resulted. Workers then tried a new strategy. At the Goodyear

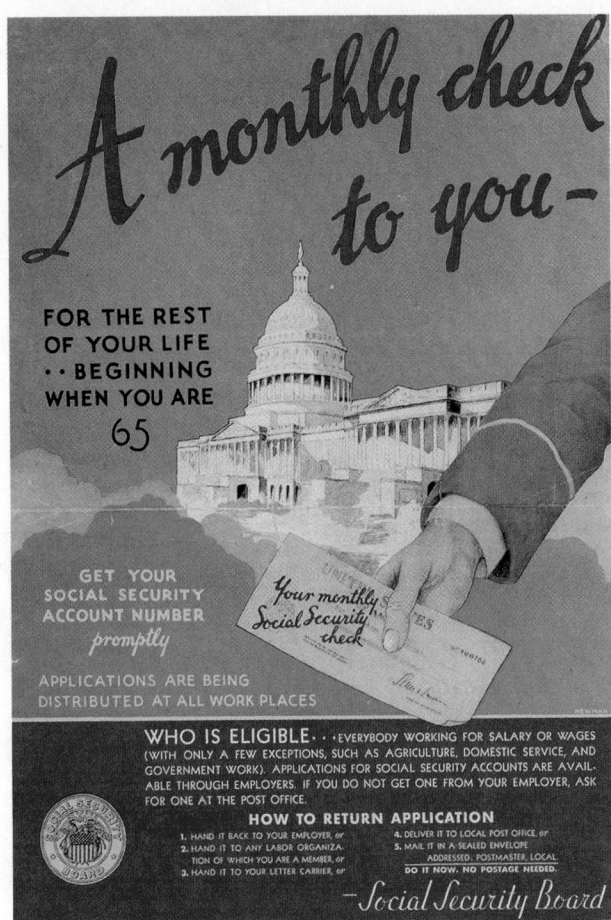

>> This 1935 poster promoted the newly established Social Security system, which gave financial assistance to the elderly, the unemployed, and the disabled.

Tire Factory in Akron, Ohio, workers staged a **sit-down strike**. They stopped all machines and refused to leave the factory until Goodyear recognized their union. The tactic worked. Workers at other factories made use of sit-down strikes until the Supreme Court outlawed them in 1939.

Social Security Meanwhile, the President sought to help the elderly. In the 1930s, the United States was the only major industrial nation that did not have a formal pension program. A **pension** is a sum of money paid to people on a regular basis after they retire. Roosevelt and Secretary of Labor Perkins pushed to enact an old-age pension program.

In September 1935, Congress passed the **Social Security Act**. The new law had three parts. First, it set up a system of pensions for older people. Payments from employers and employees supported this system.

Second, the new act set up the nation's first system of unemployment insurance. People who lost their jobs received small payments until they found work again. Third, the act gave states money to support dependent children and people with disabilities.

Criticism of Social Security Critics condemned the Social Security law. Some liberals pointed out that it did not include farm workers, domestic servants, or the self-employed—many of whom were women or members of minority groups. Some

conservatives, on the other hand, saw Social Security as another way for the government to take money away from people who had jobs. Others saw it as an unacceptable expansion of the role of government.

Despite these attacks, the Social Security system survived and expanded over the years. Today, it provides medical benefits and pensions to older Americans, as well as unemployment insurance to workers.

❓ **LIST** the three parts of Social Security.

Critics Attack the New Deal

Some of Roosevelt's most severe critics were people who had supported him in 1932. Among the most outspoken of these was Senator Huey Long of Louisiana. Long believed that the New Deal had not gone far enough to help the poor. Adopting the motto "Share Our Wealth," Long called for heavy taxes on the rich.

Reformer Francis Townsend, a California doctor, claimed the government had turned its back on older citizens. Townsend wanted everyone over age 60 to get a pension of $200 a month. People receiving the pension would have to retire, thus freeing up a job for someone else. They would also agree to spend the pension money at once to boost the economy.

On the other hand, many conservatives opposed the new government programs. They did not like the government intervention in business, banking, the stock market, or in the lives of individuals. Eventually, big names in industry and finance, including the DuPont family and Alfred P. Sloan of General Motors, formed

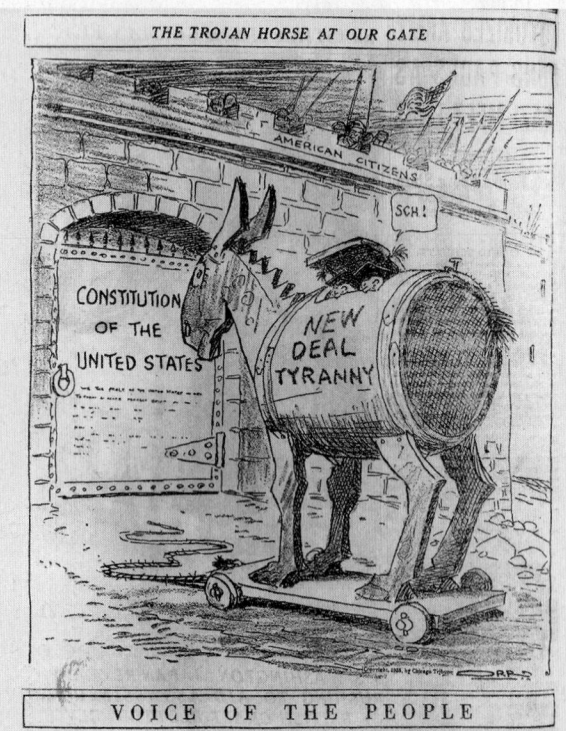

THE TROJAN HORSE AT OUR GATE

AMERICAN CITIZENS

CONSTITUTION OF THE UNITED STATES

NEW DEAL TYRANNY

VOICE OF THE PEOPLE

>> **Analyze Cartoons** The Trojan Horse refers to an ancient incident in which Greek soldiers hid inside a huge wooden horse given to Troy as a gift. Once inside Troy, the Greeks let the rest of their army into the kingdom. Why do you think the New Deal is portrayed as a Trojan Horse?

FDR's Plan to Change the Supreme Court

| In 1935, the Supreme Court works to quash many of President Roosevelt's New Deal programs. | In 1937, Roosevelt proposes increasing the number of Supreme Court Justices to more than nine. | If his plan is passed, Roosevelt could appoint one new Supreme Court Justice for every sitting Justice aged 70 or older who refused to retire, up to a maximum of 15. | Roosevelt's plan is viewed as a way to pack the Supreme Court full of his supporters, and the bill is struck down. |

Sources: *Encyclopædia Britannica; Archives.gov*

>> **Analyze Charts** Based on the information in the graphic, predict why Roosevelt's strategy would ultimately fail.

the Liberty League in an effort to combat the New Deal.

The League accused Roosevelt of abusing power and suggested that the New Deal was based on a socialist agenda. The government, they warned, was taking away basic American freedoms. In the end, the Liberty League lacked political savvy and ended up angering many Americans while alienating many of Roosevelt's other critics.

Facing Objections from the Supreme Court

In 1935, members of the Supreme Court began to attack the New Deal. In that year, the Supreme Court ruled that the National Industrial Recovery Act was unconstitutional. The NIRA, the Court ruled, gave too much power to the President and to the federal government. A year later, the Court struck down the Agricultural Adjustment Act. Then, it overturned eight other New Deal laws on constitutional grounds. To Roosevelt, the Supreme Court rulings threatened not only the New Deal but also his ability to lead the nation.

Roosevelt waited until after the 1936 election to take action. In that election, he easily beat his Republican opponent, Alf Landon of Kansas.

Soon after his inauguration in January 1937, Roosevelt put forward a plan to enlarge the federal courts. He called for raising the number of Justices on the Supreme Court from 9 to 15. The change would make it possible for him to appoint six new Justices who supported his programs.

"Court Packing" The President's move raised a loud outcry. Both supporters and critics of the New Deal accused him of trying to "pack" the Court with Justices who supported his views. They saw his move as a threat to the principle of separation of powers. For six months, the President fought for his plan. Even his allies in Congress deserted him. Finally, he withdrew his proposal.

Still, in the end, Roosevelt got the Supreme Court majority he wanted without a battle. One Justice who had voted against many New Deal laws changed his views. Another retired. Roosevelt filled his place with a new Justice who was favorable to his programs.

? IDENTIFY CENTRAL ISSUES What were the main liberal and conservative criticisms of the New Deal?

Evaluating the New Deal

The New Deal changed American government forever. Ever since, Americans have debated whether the change was good or bad for the country.

Criticism of the New Deal Before the 1930s, most Americans had little contact with the federal government. New Deal programs, however, touched almost every citizen. The federal government grew in size and power.

Many people worried about the increased power of government. They complained that the government was intruding in people's lives, threatening both individual freedoms and private property. These critics called for a return to the traditional policy of laissez faire—the idea that government should play as small a role as possible in the economy.

Critics also expressed alarm because the government was spending more than it took in. This practice of **deficit spending** was creating a huge increase in the **national debt**, or the total sum of money the government owes.

Finally, despite its vast spending, the New Deal had not achieved its major goal—ending the depression. In fact, full economic recovery did not come until 1941. This recovery was partly the result of increased U.S. production for nations fighting in World War II.

Support for the New Deal Supporters of the New Deal noted that FDR had steered the nation through the worst days of the depression. New Deal legislation had ended the banking crisis, protected farmers, and created work for millions of unemployed.

Supporters also argued that the government had a responsibility to use its power to help all of its citizens, not just businesses and the wealthy. Programs

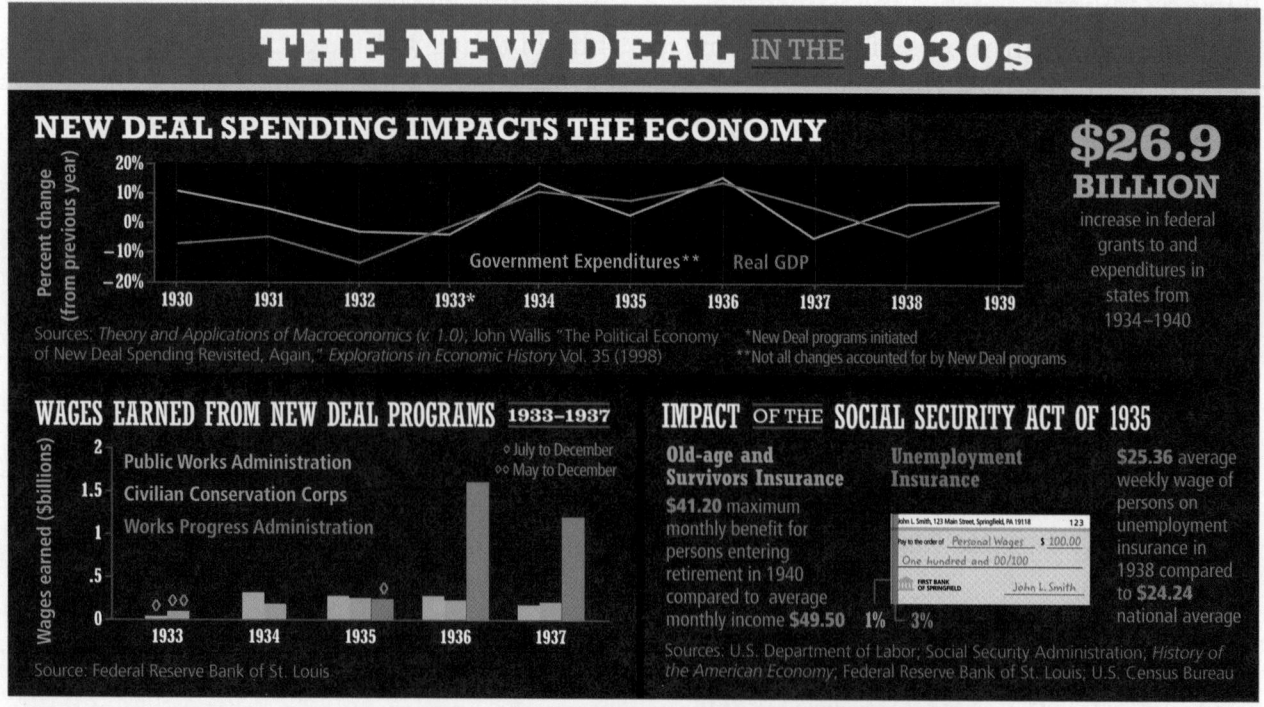

THE NEW DEAL IN THE 1930s

NEW DEAL SPENDING IMPACTS THE ECONOMY

Percent change (from previous year) — 20%, 10%, 0%, −10%, −20%
1930, 1931, 1932, 1933*, 1934, 1935, 1936, 1937, 1938, 1939

Government Expenditures**   Real GDP

Sources: *Theory and Applications of Macroeconomics (v. 1.0)*; John Wallis "The Political Economy of New Deal Spending Revisited, Again," *Explorations in Economic History* Vol. 35 (1998)
*New Deal programs initiated
**Not all changes accounted for by New Deal programs

$26.9 BILLION increase in federal grants to and expenditures in states from 1934–1940

WAGES EARNED FROM NEW DEAL PROGRAMS 1933–1937

Wages earned ($billions) — 2, 1.5, 1, .5, 0
◇ July to December
◇◇ May to December

Public Works Administration
Civilian Conservation Corps
Works Progress Administration

1933, 1934, 1935, 1936, 1937

Source: Federal Reserve Bank of St. Louis

IMPACT OF THE SOCIAL SECURITY ACT OF 1935

Old-age and Survivors Insurance
$41.20 maximum monthly benefit for persons entering retirement in 1940 compared to average monthly income $49.50   1%

Unemployment Insurance
3%

John L. Smith, 123 Main Street, Springfield, PA 19118   123
Pay to the order of Personal Wages $ 100.00
One hundred and 00/100
FIRST BANK OF SPRINGFIELD   John L. Smith

$25.36 average weekly wage of persons on unemployment insurance in 1938 compared to **$24.24** national average

Sources: U.S. Department of Labor; Social Security Administration; *History of the American Economy*; Federal Reserve Bank of St. Louis; U.S. Census Bureau

>> **Analyze Graphs** Based on the information provided about gross domestic product (GDP), which is a measure of an economy's size, describe the New Deal's impact on the economy.

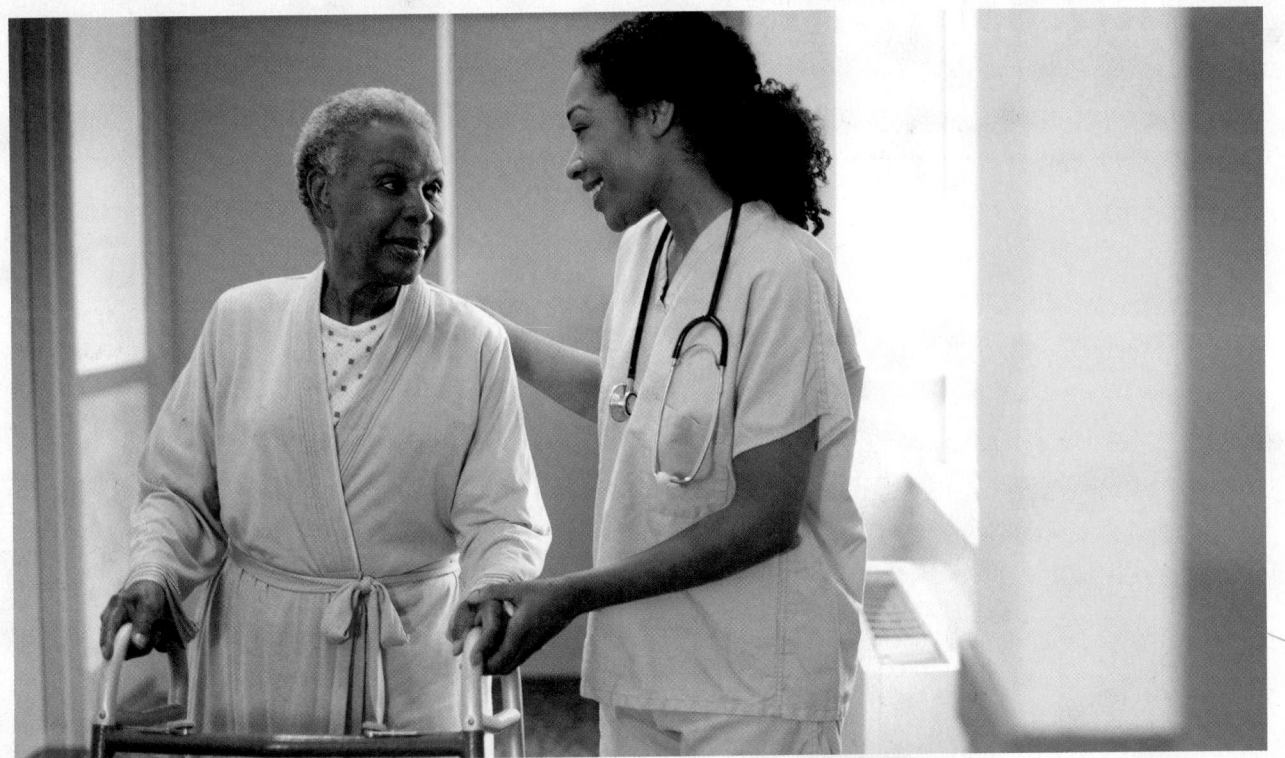

>> Today, many Americans rely on Medicare, Medicaid and other similar programs to defray their healthcare costs. New Deal programs established a precedent for the federal government to provide support for people who are poor, elderly, disabled, or unemployed.

such as Social Security, New Dealers said, were necessary for national survival.

Most important of all, supporters argued, the New Deal had saved the nation's democratic system. Elsewhere in the world, people were turning to dictators to lead them out of hard times. President Roosevelt, on the other hand, restored the nation to economic health while preserving its democracy.

Over the years, Americans have continued to debate the expanded role of government that began during the New Deal. The question whether government intervention in the economy helps or harms Americans' well-being remains a lively one today.

? **LIST** one argument for and one against the New Deal.

ASSESSMENT

1. **Summarize** why Americans felt confident about Roosevelt in the election of 1932.

2. **Identify Cause and Effect** What was the effect of Roosevelt's fireside chats?

3. **Generate Explanations** Explain why workers sought collective bargaining rights.

4. **Compare** life for families before and after the Social Security law set up a system of pensions for older people.

5. **Analyze Information** How was Roosevelt's attempt to change the Supreme Court a threat to the principles of checks and balances and separation of powers?

13.7 Life During the Depression

>> The Dust Bowl left thousands of American families homeless, forcing them to migrate to states on the West Coast.

[▶] **Interactive Flipped Video**

>> Objectives

Identify the causes and effects of the Dust Bowl.

Explain how the Depression affected women.

Describe the Depression's impact on African Americans and other groups.

Explain how the arts reflected life during the Depression.

>> Key Terms

Dust Bowl
migrant worker
Black Cabinet
civil rights
Indian New Deal

During much of the 1930s, states from Texas to the Dakotas suffered a severe drought. One region in the central Great Plains was especially hard hit. The topsoil dried out. High winds carried the soil away in blinding dust storms. As a result, this area became known as the **Dust Bowl**.

The Dust Bowl

Causes of the Dust Bowl Dust storms buried farmhouses, fences, and even trees over large areas of the plains. People put shutters over doors and windows, but the dust blew in anyway. Even food crunched when it was chewed. One storm blew dust from Oklahoma to Albany, New York. A Kansas farmer sadly reported that he sat by his window counting the farms going by.

What caused the disaster? Years of overgrazing by cattle and plowing by farmers destroyed the grasses that once held the soil in place. The drought of the 1930s and high winds did the rest.

Effects of the Dust Bowl Hardest hit by the drought and dust storms were poor farmers in Oklahoma and other Great Plains states. Hundreds of these "Okies" packed their belongings into cars and trucks and headed west. They became **migrant workers**—people who move from one region to another in search of work. They hoped to find jobs in the orchards and farms of California, Oregon, or Washington.

Once they reached the West Coast, the migrants faced a new hardship—they were not wanted. Local citizens feared that the newcomers would take away their jobs. Sometimes, angry crowds blocked the highways and forced the migrants to go elsewhere. Those migrants who did find work were paid little.

❓ IDENTIFY CAUSE AND EFFECT What caused the Dust Bowl?

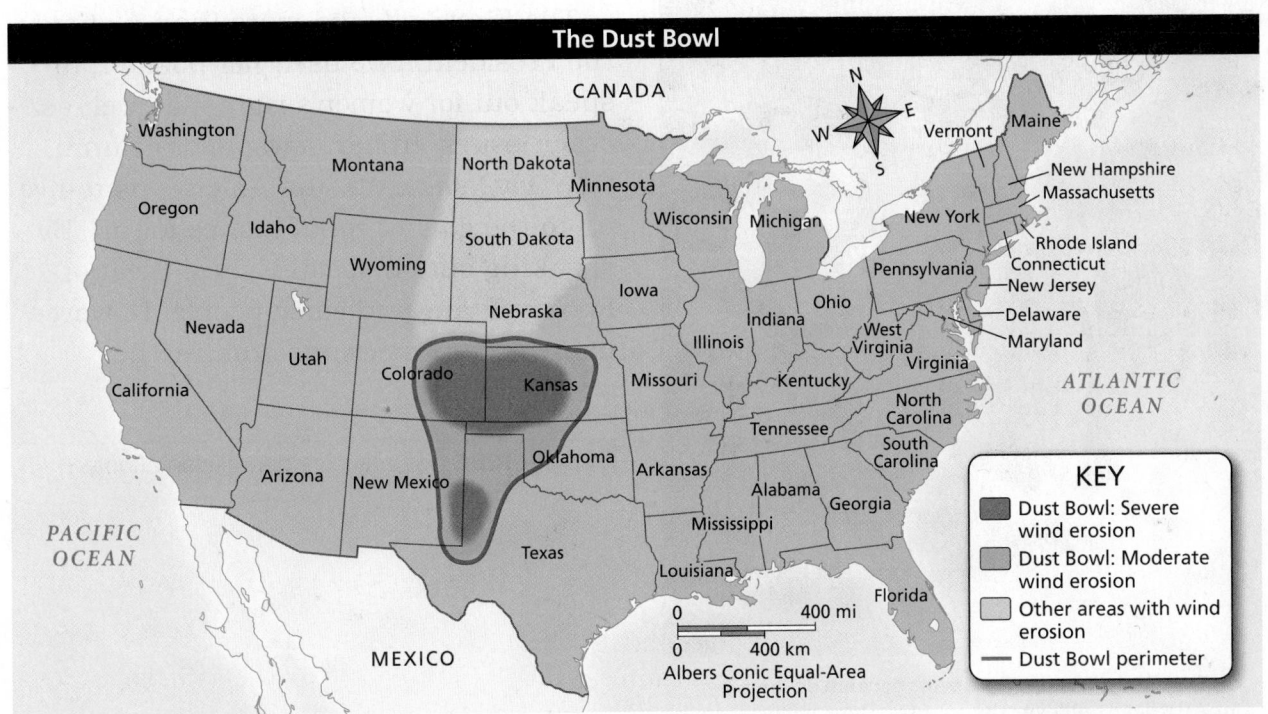

The Dust Bowl

KEY
- ■ Dust Bowl: Severe wind erosion
- ■ Dust Bowl: Moderate wind erosion
- □ Other areas with wind erosion
- — Dust Bowl perimeter

0   400 mi
0   400 km
Albers Conic Equal-Area Projection

>> **Analyze Maps** Identify the states most severely affected by the Dust Bowl during the depression.

▶ Interactive Gallery

The Depression Affects Women

Traditional roles took on added importance during the Depression. Homemakers had to stretch family budgets to make ends meet. Some women took in laundry to earn extra money. Others took in boarders to help pay the rent. Wives also found that unemployed husbands needed more nurturing to feel worthwhile.

Working women faced special problems during the Depression. If jobs were available, employers hired men before they would hire women. In order to spread jobs around, the federal government refused to hire a woman if her husband had a job.

Working Women Despite such obstacles, millions of women earned wages in order to support themselves and their families. During the 1930s, the number of married women in the work force increased by 52 percent. Educated women took jobs as secretaries, schoolteachers, and social workers. Other women earned livings as maids, factory workers, and seamstresses.

Some women workers struck for better pay. In San Antonio, Texas, at least 80 percent of the pecan shellers were Mexican American women. When employers lowered their pay, a young worker, Emma Tenayuca, organized the shellers and led them off the job. Tenayuca said later, "I had a basic faith in the American idea of freedom and fairness. I felt something had to be done."

The First Lady Takes a Stand Eleanor Roosevelt created a new role for the First Lady. Acting as the President's "eyes and ears," she toured the nation. She visited farms and Indian reservations and traveled deep into a coal mine. She talked to homemakers, studying the condition of their clothing on the washline to measure how well they were doing.

The First Lady did more than just aid the President. She used her position to speak out for women's rights, as well as other issues. In her newspaper column, "My Day," she called on Americans to live up to the goal of equal justice for all. By speaking out on social issues, Eleanor Roosevelt angered some people. However, many other Americans admired her strong stands.

? DESCRIBE two ways the depression affected women's lives.

>> First Lady Eleanor Roosevelt became an advocate for Americans all over the country. Here, she is seen walking at the center of a group on a visit to a job-training camp for unemployed women in 1933.

African Americans During the Depression

When the Great Depression hit, African American workers were often the first to lose their jobs. By 1934, black workers were suffering a 50 percent unemployment rate, more than twice the national average. Often, they were denied public works jobs. Some charities even refused to serve blacks at centers giving out food to the needy.

Eleanor Roosevelt and others close to the President urged him to improve the situation of African Americans. The President responded to their needs. For example, thousands of young African American men learned a trade through the CCC.

In aiding African Americans, FDR won their support for the Democratic party. The President invited African American leaders to the White House to advise him. These unofficial advisers became known as the **Black Cabinet**. They included Robert C. Weaver, a Harvard-educated economist, and Mary McLeod Bethune, a well-known Florida educator. Roosevelt appointed Bethune to head the National Youth Administration's Division of Negro Affairs. She was the first African American to head a government agency.

Often, Roosevelt followed the advice of the Black Cabinet. However, when African American leaders pressed the President to support an antilynching law, he refused. He feared that by doing so he would lose the support of southerners in Congress for his New Deal programs.

Many black leaders called on African Americans to unite to obtain their **civil rights**—the rights due to all citizens. African Americans used their votes, won higher-level government jobs, and kept up

>> The Civilian Conservation Corps gave an opportunity to work to African Americans, such as these men building a fence in Georgia during the depression.

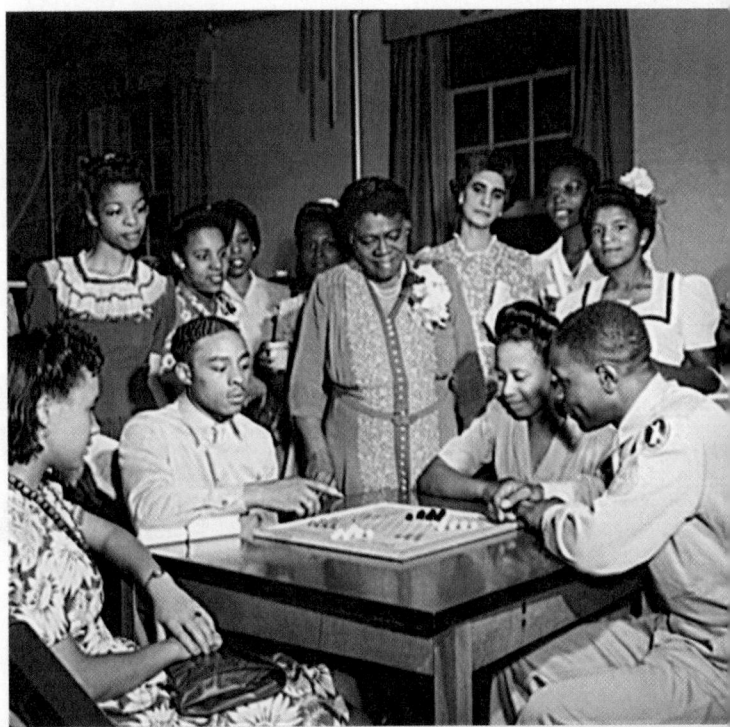

>> African American educator Mary McLeod Bethune, standing at the center of this photo, promoted the interests of African Americans across the country and served as advisor to President Roosevelt in the 1930s and 1940s.

pressure for equal treatment. Slowly, they made a few gains. However, the struggle for civil rights would take many more years.

? RECALL What was the purpose of Roosevelt's "Black Cabinet"?

Other Americans Weather the Depression

The hard times of the Great Depression created fear and insecurity among many Americans. These feelings sometimes erupted in discrimination and hostility toward Americans with different ethnic backgrounds.

Mexican Americans By the 1930s, Mexican Americans worked in many cities around the country. A large number, however, were farmworkers in the West and Southwest. There, they faced discrimination in education and jobs and at the polls.

In good times, employers had encouraged Mexicans to move north and take jobs in factories or on farms. When hard times struck, however, many Americans wanted Mexicans to be sent back to their original country. More than 400,000 people were rounded up and sent to Mexico. Some of them were American citizens.

Asian Americans Some Americans resented Chinese, Japanese, and Filipino workers who competed with them for scarce jobs. Sometimes, violence against Asians erupted. Responding to pressure, the government sought to reduce the number of Asians in the United States. In 1935, FDR signed a law that provided free transportation for Filipinos who agreed to return to the Philippines and not come back.

>> This photo shows the difficult living conditions of a Mexican American migrant farm family in 1937.

[▶] **Interactive Chart**

>> John Collier (center) was appointed commissioner of the Bureau of Indian Affairs. Here, he meets in 1938 with Sioux leaders who testified before Congress to demand rights for American Indians.

American Indians In 1924, Congress had granted all American Indians citizenship. Still, most Indians continued to live in deep poverty. President Roosevelt encouraged new policies toward American Indians.

In the 1930s, Congress passed a series of laws that have been called the **Indian New Deal**. The laws gave Indian nations greater control over their own affairs.

The President chose John Collier, a longtime defender of Indian rights, to head the Bureau of Indian Affairs. Collier ended the government policy of breaking up Indian landholdings. In 1934, Congress passed the Indian Reorganization Act (IRA). It protected and even expanded landholdings of Indian reservations. The Roosevelt administration also strengthened Indian governments by letting reservations organize corporations and develop their own business projects.

To provide jobs during the depression, the government set up the Indian Emergency Conservation Work Group. It employed American Indians in programs of soil-erosion control, irrigation, and land development.

? RECALL What was the purpose of the Indian New Deal?

Literature and Arts During the Depression

Creative artists powerfully portrayed the hardships of depression life. Many writers depicted the hard times Americans faced across the country. In his 1939 novel *The Grapes of Wrath*, John Steinbeck told the heartbreaking story of the Okies streaming over the mountains trying to build new lives in California.

Many painters turned to familiar themes. The huge murals of Thomas Hart Benton brought the history of the frontier to life. In *American Gothic*, Grant Wood painted an Iowa farmer and his daughter who look determined enough to survive any hardship.

The government sent out photographers to create a lasting record of American life during the Great Depression. The vivid photographs of Dorothea Lange showed the suffering of Dust Bowl farm families. Margaret Bourke-White photographed poor tenant farmers in the South.

>> Grant Wood completed his painting *American Gothic* in 1930. **Generate Explanations** for how the painting might have reflected the attitudes of people living through the depression.

Entertainment at Home Americans found ways to escape the hard times of the 1930s. Listening to the radio and going to the movies were among their favorite pastimes.

Every night, millions of Americans tuned in to their favorite radio programs. Comedians such as the husband-and-wife team, George Burns and Gracie Allen, made people forget their troubles for a time. With so many people out of work, daytime radio shows became popular. People listened to dramas like "Ma Perkins" that told the story of families weathering the depression. Because soap companies sponsored many of these serials, the programs became known as soap operas.

Perhaps the most famous broadcast took place in 1938. On Halloween night, actor Orson Welles presented a "newscast" based on a science fiction novel, *The War of the Worlds*. Welles grimly reported the landing of invaders from the planet Mars. People who tuned in late mistook the program for a real newscast. Thousands of terrified people ran into the streets, seeking ways to escape the Martian invasion.

Going to the Movies In the 1930s, moviemakers tried to restore Americans' faith in the future. Movies told optimistic stories about happy families or people finding love and success. Shirley Temple became a hugely popular star at the age of five. When Temple sang "On the Good Ship Lollipop," her upbeat spirit cheered up audiences.

One of the most popular movies was Walt Disney's *Snow White and the Seven Dwarfs*. It was the first full-length animated film. In 1939, Judy Garland won American hearts in *The Wizard of Oz*. The movie told of a young girl's escape from a

MASS ENTERTAINMENT IN THE 1930s ★

WEEKLY MOVIE ATTENDANCE
Percentage of Americans

50% IN 1925

73% IN 1930

76% IN 1939

In 2005, only **9%** of Americans attended movies weekly

25¢ average movie ticket price in 1933

Sources: Pautz, Michelle (2002) "The Decline in Average Weekly Cinema Attendance: 1930–2000"; *The 1930s*; *New York Daily News*; *Digital History*; *Industry and Firm Studies*

THE GOLDEN AGE OF HOLLYWOOD
Box Office Receipts

= $100 million

1932

1936

1940

1944

Sources: *Historical Statistics of the United States*; *Industry and Firm Studies*; *Digital History*

34% increase in number of movie theaters from 1932 to 1938

83% of every dollar Americans spent on amusement went to movies in the 1930s

THE GOLDEN AGE OF RADIO

Homes with radio sets (in millions)

30

20

0

1929 1930 1931 1932 1933 1934 1935 1936 1937 1938 1939

Sources: *Historical Statistics of the United States*, PBS

20 million average listeners for each episode of "The Lone Ranger" on the radio in 1939

Average cost of a radio in the 1930s was **$5**, down from $120 in the 1920s

>> **Infer** Generate an explanation for the overall increase in consumers spending money on entertainment during the depression.

bleak life in depression-era Kansas to the magical land of Oz.

The most expensively made and most popular movie of the 1930s was *Gone With the Wind*. It showed the Civil War in a romantic light. For more than three hours, many Americans forgot their worries as they watched the story of love and loss in the Old South. The movie also encouraged many Americans. They had survived hard times before. They would do so again.

❓ **CHECK UNDERSTANDING** What purposes did the arts serve during the Depression?

ASSESSMENT

1. **Identify Cause and Effect** How did the Great Depression affect the treatment of Dust Bowl migrants when they fled to the West Coast to find work?

2. **Summarize** how Eleanor Roosevelt's newspaper column helped influence both men and women's views on women's rights.

3. **Compare** how Roosevelt both helped and hurt the struggle for civil rights for African Americans.

4. **Compare and Contrast** how Asian and Mexican immigrants in the United States were treated in the 1930s.

5. **Summarize** how entertainment reflected American life in the 1930s.

TOPIC 13 ASSESSMENT

1. **Identify the Causes of the Great Depression**
Identify the causes of the Great Depression, including the growth of the use of the stock market in the 1920s. Write a paragraph describing buying behavior in the stock market during the 1920s. Identify what is a stock, a bull market, and buying on margin, and why buying on margin was risky.

2. **Analyze the Causes and Effects of the Changing Roles of Women** Write a paragraph analyzing the causes and effects of the changing role of women in the 1920s. Consider the 19th Amendment, women in the workforce, and how the role of women in society changed in the 1920s.

3. **Identify the Effects of Technological Innovations**
Write a paragraph analyzing the effects of technological innovations on American society and culture in the 1920s. Consider the effect the car industry's assembly line had on American society and the effect of radio and movies on American culture.

4. **Analyze the Causes and Effects of Cultural Change**
Explain new trends and changes in American culture during the 1920s. In a paragraph, identify causes and effects of those changes. Be sure to give examples from areas such as fashion, sports, and entertainment.

A great deal has been accomplished in this decade of 'renaissance'. . . . Today, one may see undesirable stories, but one may also read stories about Negro singers, Negro actors, Negro authors, Negro poets. The connotations [implied meanings] of the very word Negro have changed. A generation ago many Negroes were half or wholly [completely] ashamed of the term. Today, they have every reason to be proud of it.

— *James Weldon Johnson, article in* Harper's *magazine, 1928*

5. **Evaluate the Impact of the Harlem Renaissance**
Write a paragraph describing how the Harlem Renaissance affected American society. Describe what the Harlem Renaissance was, topics addressed by the writers of the Harlem Renaissance, and how the quotation from James Weldon Johnson expresses the impact of the Harlem Renaissance.

6. **Identify the Causes and Effects of the Red Scare**
Write a paragraph analyzing the causes and effects of the Red Scare. Define what the Red Scare was, consider the national and international events that contributed to the Red Scare, then consider its effects, such as the Sacco and Vanzetti case.

7. **Evaluate Nativism** Evaluate the historical roots and impact of nativism. Write a paragraph analyzing why nativists renewed their calls for restrictions on immigration following World War I and how Congress responded. Consider the social factors that contributed to nativist demands to limit immigration and the response of Congress to those demands.

8. **Draw Connections Between Literature and Society**
Describe new American writers and the kinds of writing that developed during the 1920s. Give specific examples of authors and their work. Explain how their work reflected American society in the 1920s.

9. **Explain the Significance of 1929** Write a paragraph explaining why 1929 was a significant date in American history. Explain what happened to the stock market in 1929, identify the timeline of the events, and explain why this was a turning point.

10. **Identify the Effects of Unemployment** Write a paragraph analyzing how the Great Depression led to increased rates of unemployment, and how this change affected people. Analyze how the stock market crash led to unemployment and what effect unemployment had on affected families.

11. **Compare Examples of Effective Leadership** Write a paragraph comparing the leadership qualities of Presidents Herbert Hoover and Franklin D. Roosevelt in dealing with the Great Depression. Describe each President's approach to resolving the problems created by the Great Depression and evaluate the two approaches in terms of effective leadership.

When Dorothea took that picture that was the ultimate. She never surpassed it. . . . She [the mother] has all the suffering of mankind in her but all the perseverance too. A restraint and a strange courage.

— Roy Stryker, FSA, on Dorothea Lange's "Migrant Mother"

12. **Explain Connections Between Art and Society** Use the photograph and quotation above, and at least two other Lange photographs and at least one secondary source about Lange's work to write a paragraph answering the following question: How did Dorothea Lange's photographs capture the characteristics and issues of the Great Depression?

13. **Identify the Continuing Effect of Social Security** Write a paragraph describing the effect of the Social Security Administration during the Great Depression and today. Describe why Congress passed the Social Security Act of 1935 and what the act provided for and how it was funded. Then, explain why Social Security is still important today.

14. **Identify the Causes of Migration** Analyze the causes of migration within the United States. Explain what caused farm families to leave rural areas in the Great Plains and migrate to other regions in the United States, and why they were drawn to those regions.

15. **Evaluate the Impact of New Deal Agencies** Write a paragraph analyzing how agencies such as the Civilian Conservation Corps (CCC), the Works Progress Administration (WPA), and the Social Security Administation provided economic support during the Great Depression. In your paragraph, identify the specific ways in which each agency supported workers and the economy during the Great Depression.

16. **Describe Connections Between Social Challenges and Film** Write a paragraph explaining why people were attracted to certain genres of films during the 1930s and how those genres reflected the social challenges of the time. Consider why people might have been attracted to certain genres of films and how the different genres reflected the social reality of the Great Depression.

17. **Write About the Essential Question** **Write an essay on the Essential Question: What should governments do?** Use evidence from your study of this topic to support your answer.

[**ESSENTIAL QUESTION**] When Is War Justified?

14 **World War II (1935–1945)**

>> American soldiers firing an artillery piece in battle during World War II

Enduring Understandings

- The United States government became more isolationist as totalitarian governments in Europe and Asia assumed power.

- World War II in Asia began with Japan attacking China, while war in Europe started when Germany invaded Poland.

- The United States, though neutral at the start of the war, joined the fighting after the Japanese attacked an American naval base at Pearl Harbor.

- On the home front, the U.S. economy and its industries were adapted to support the war effort, while women and minorities faced both opportunities and hardships.

- During the Holocaust, Nazi Germany systematically murdered millions of Jews and others they considered enemies.

- Germany and Japan surrendered to the Allies after years of intense fighting, ending the deadliest war in history.

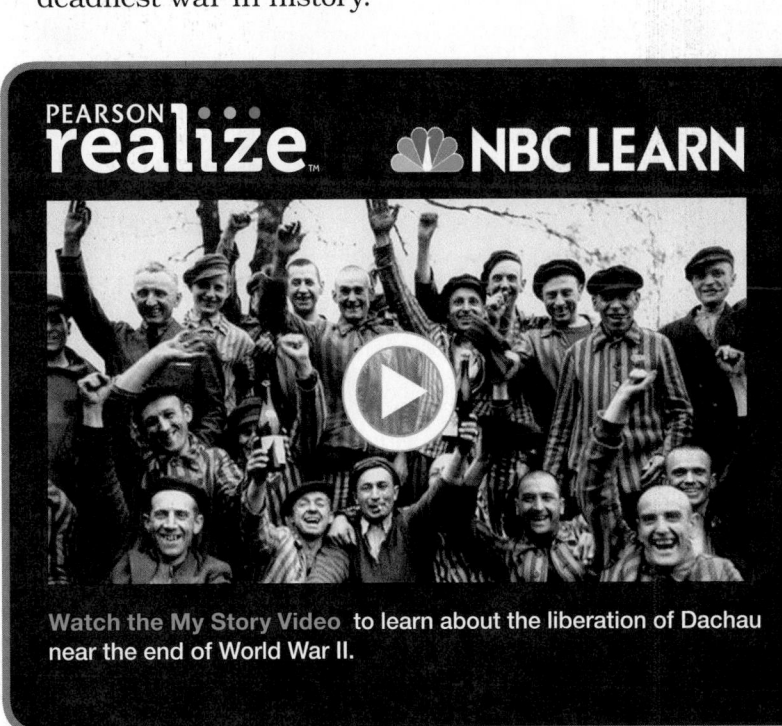

Watch the My Story Video to learn about the liberation of Dachau near the end of World War II.

PEARSON realize™
www.PearsonRealize.com

Access your digital lessons including:
Topic Inquiry • Interactive Reading Notepad • Interactivities • Assessments

Aggression Overseas and Isolationism at Home

>> Italy's Benito Mussolini (right) and Germany's Adolf Hitler (left) march in a 1937 military ceremony. Hitler and Mussolini were both fascist leaders.

▶ **Interactive Flipped Video**

>> **Objectives**

Explain how fascist governments came to power in Italy and Germany.

Identify the communist dictatorship Stalin set up in the Soviet Union.

Describe how military rulers took power in Japan.

Explain why the United States adopted a policy of isolationism as European and Asian nations moved toward war.

>> **Key Terms**

totalitarian state
fascism
aggression
Nazi
scapegoat
concentration camp
Neutrality Acts
Good Neighbor
    Policy

In the 1930s, a storm was gathering around the globe. New rulers had come to power in Europe and Asia. These leaders drew on resentment about their countries' fates after World War I. They also aimed to spread their influence. The competition among these rulers would change the lives of millions of people and cause mass destruction around the world.

Political Changes in Italy and Germany

In Italy and Germany, totalitarian leaders exerted complete control over the government and society. These dictators were fascists (FASH ists). **Fascism** was rooted in militarism, extreme nationalism, and blind loyalty to the state. Fascist dictators vowed to create new empires. While Communists drew much of their support from the working classes, fascists found allies among business leaders and landowners.

Fascist Italy In 1922, Benito Mussolini and his Fascist party seized power in Italy. He played on anger about the Versailles Treaty ending World War I. Many Italians felt cheated because the treaty did not grant Italy the territory it wanted.

Mussolini also used fear to gain power. Economic unrest and fears of a communist revolution plagued Italy, and many looked to Mussolini to stabilize the nation.

Once in power, Mussolini outlawed all political parties except his own. He controlled the press and banned criticism of the government. Critics were jailed or simply murdered. In schools, children recited the motto "Mussolini Is Always Right!"

Mussolini Conquers Ethiopia In the 1930s, Mussolini used foreign conquest to distract Italians from economic problems. Promising to restore the greatness of ancient Rome, he embarked on a program of military aggression. **Aggression** is a warlike act by one country against another without just cause.

Mussolini invaded the African nation of Ethiopia in 1935. The Ethiopians fought bravely. However, their cavalry and outdated rifles were no match for Italy's

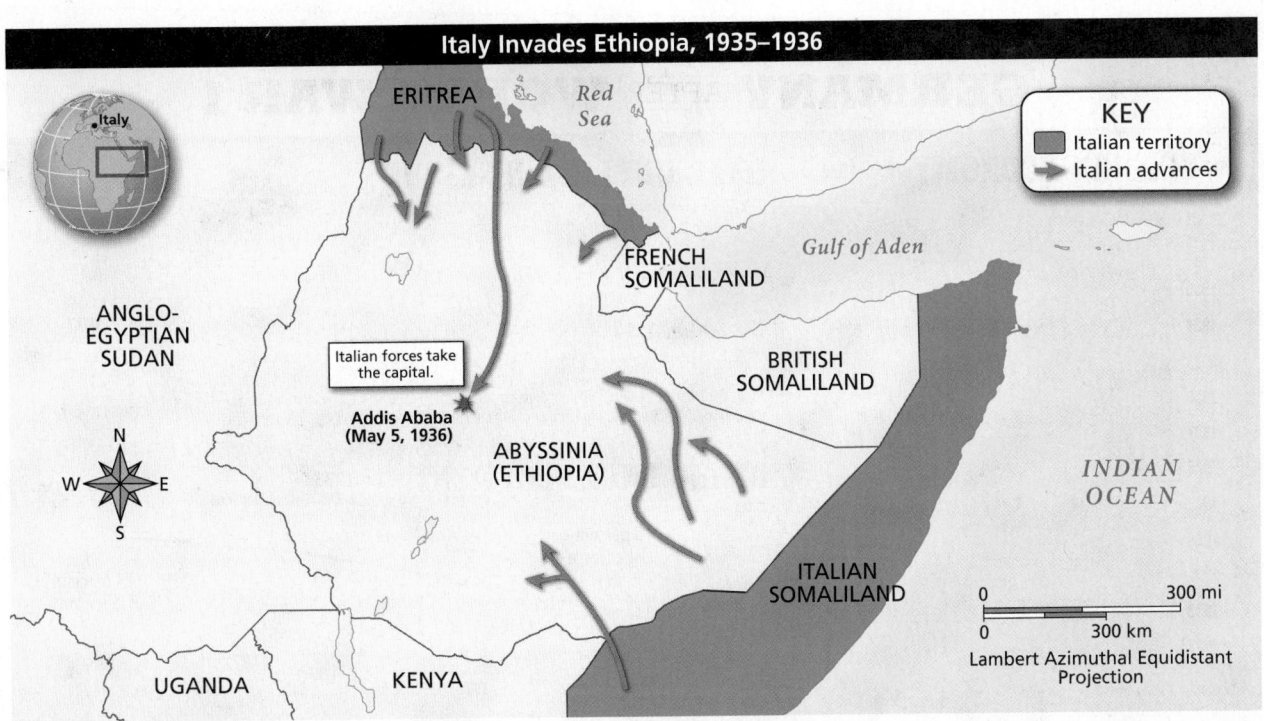

Italy Invades Ethiopia, 1935–1936

KEY
- Italian territory
- Italian advances

ERITREA
Red Sea
Italy
Gulf of Aden
FRENCH SOMALILAND
ANGLO-EGYPTIAN SUDAN
Italian forces take the capital.
BRITISH SOMALILAND
Addis Ababa (May 5, 1936)
ABYSSINIA (ETHIOPIA)
INDIAN OCEAN
ITALIAN SOMALILAND
0   300 mi
0   300 km
Lambert Azimuthal Equidistant Projection
UGANDA   KENYA

>> Ethiopia (also called Abyssinia at the time) is located in East Africa.
Analyze Maps What other nations' territory may have been at risk based on Italy's military aggression?

modern tanks and airplanes. Ethiopian emperor Haile Selassie (HI lee suh LAS ee) asked the League of Nations for aid. The League responded weakly. Britain and France were caught up in their own economic problems and unwilling to risk another war. Without help, Ethiopia fell.

Nazi Germany In Germany, Adolf Hitler brought the National Socialist German Workers' Party, or **Nazis**, to power. Like Mussolini, Hitler played on anger about the Versailles Treaty. Germans bitterly resented the treaty because it blamed their country for World War I and made them pay heavy war costs.

Hitler's Rise to Power Hitler assured Germans that they had not lost the war. Rather, he said, Jews and other traitors had "stabbed Germany in the back." The argument was false, but in troubled times people were eager to find a **scapegoat**—a person or group on whom to blame their problems.

Hitler was a powerful speaker and skillful politician. By the time depression struck, many Germans looked to him as a strong leader with answers to their problems.

In 1933, Hitler became chancellor, or head of the German government. Within two years, he ended democratic rule and created a militaristic totalitarian state. In Nazi Germany, the government controlled the press, the schools, and religion.

The following year, Hitler organized a week-long rally in Nuremberg. Crowds chanted slogans praising Hitler. Uniformed soldiers marched in endless parades and engaged in mock battles. American reporter William Shirer described the Nuremberg rally.

It is difficult to exaggerate the frenzy of the three hundred thousand

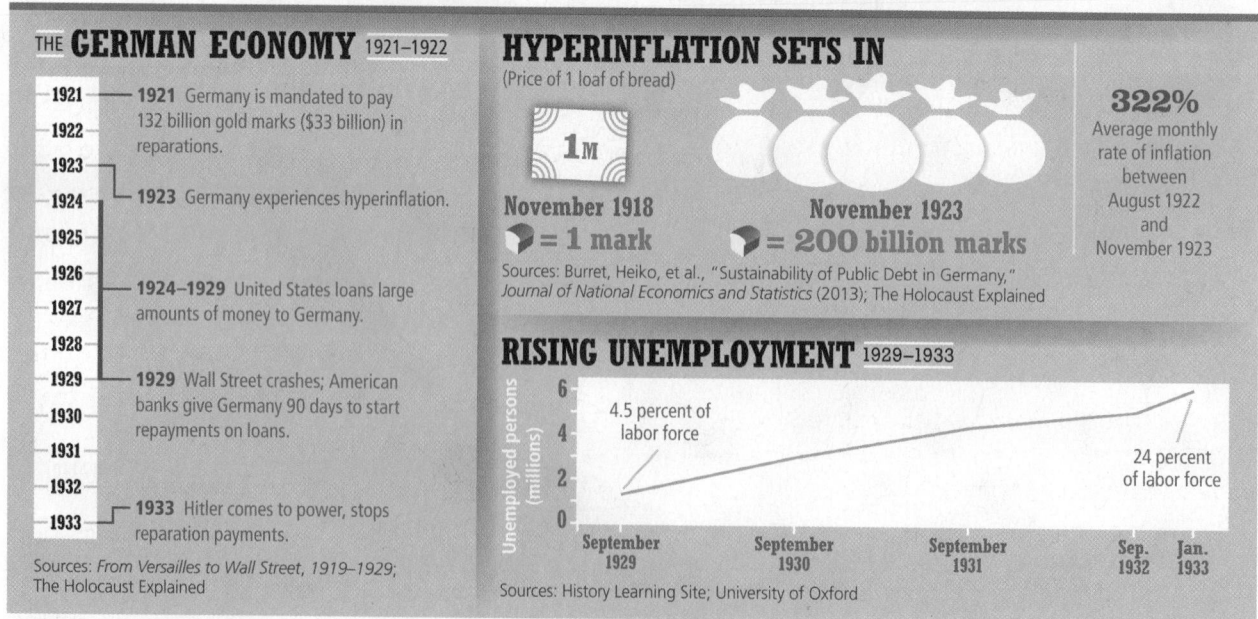

GERMANY AFTER WORLD WAR I

THE GERMAN ECONOMY 1921–1922

- 1921
- 1922
- 1923
- 1924
- 1925
- 1926
- 1927
- 1928
- 1929
- 1930
- 1931
- 1932
- 1933

1921 Germany is mandated to pay 132 billion gold marks ($33 billion) in reparations.

1923 Germany experiences hyperinflation.

1924–1929 United States loans large amounts of money to Germany.

1929 Wall Street crashes; American banks give Germany 90 days to start repayments on loans.

1933 Hitler comes to power, stops reparation payments.

Sources: *From Versailles to Wall Street, 1919–1929*; The Holocaust Explained

HYPERINFLATION SETS IN
(Price of 1 loaf of bread)

1M

November 1918
= 1 mark

November 1923
= 200 billion marks

Sources: Burret, Heiko, et al., "Sustainability of Public Debt in Germany," *Journal of National Economics and Statistics* (2013); The Holocaust Explained

322%
Average monthly rate of inflation between August 1922 and November 1923

RISING UNEMPLOYMENT 1929–1933

Unemployed persons (millions)

4.5 percent of labor force

24 percent of labor force

- September 1929
- September 1930
- September 1931
- Sep. 1932
- Jan. 1933

Sources: History Learning Site; University of Oxford

>> **Analyze Maps** What evidence from the graph titled "Rising Unemployment" partly explains why many Germans would support a change in government?

German spectators when they saw their soldiers go into action, heard the thunder of the guns, and smelt the powder.

—William L. Shirer, *Berlin Diary*

Persecution of Jews Hitler preached that Germans belonged to a race that was biologically superior to Jews, Gypsies, and other peoples. The Nazi government singled out the Jews for special persecution. Jews were deprived of their citizenship, forbidden to use public facilities, and driven out of almost every type of work. Later, Jews were rounded up and sent to **concentration camps**, prison camps for civilians who are considered enemies of the state. In time, Hitler would unleash a plan to kill all the Jews in Europe.

Germany Moves Toward War Hitler claimed that Germany had a right to expand to the east. In defiance of the Versailles treaty, he began to build up Germany's armed forces. Although the League of Nations condemned his actions, Hitler predicted that the rest of Europe would "never act. They'll just protest. And they will always be too late."

In 1936, German troops moved into the Rhineland, near the border with France and Belgium. The Versailles treaty had banned German troops from this region. France and Britain protested, but they took no other action.

? **IDENTIFY SUPPORTING DETAILS** How did political change in Germany result in military aggression in Europe?

ВПЕРЕД, ЗА РАЗГРОМ НЕМЕЦКИХ ЗАХВАТЧИКОВ И ИЗГНАНИЕ ИХ ИЗ ПРЕДЕЛОВ НАШЕЙ РОДИНЫ!

>> The Soviet totalitarian state was built on glorifying Joseph Stalin. This poster from the 1940s called on citizens to drive out the German invaders. **Evaluating Information** What emotions did this poster try to stir in the Soviet people?

▶ **Interactive Gallery**

Totalitarian Soviet Union and Militarist Japan

Totalitarian leaders also came to power in the Soviet Union and Japan. Unlike Italy and Germany, these leaders were not fascist. They did, however, seek complete control. They were unhappy with the terms of the Versailles Treaty and hoped to bring new glory to their nations. As in western Europe, the political changes underway in these regions drew the world closer to war.

Totalitarianism in the Soviet Union Vladimir Lenin set up a communist government in the Soviet Union. After Lenin's death in 1924, Joseph Stalin gained power. Stalin ruled as a totalitarian dictator. In a **totalitarian state**, a single party controls the government and every aspect of people's lives. Citizens must obey the government without question. Criticism of the government is severely punished.

Stalin took brutal measures to modernize Soviet industry and agriculture. He ordered peasants to hand over land and animals to government-run farms. Millions who resisted were executed or sent to labor camps.

Stalin also staged trials and executions of his political enemies. Many confessed to false charges under torture. Many millions of people were known to have perished by the hand of Stalin's ruthless dictatorship.

Military Rule in Japan Japan's economy suffered severely during the Great Depression. As many Japanese grew impatient with their democratic government, military leaders took power. Like Hitler, these leaders preached racial superiority. They believed that the Japanese were purer than, and superior to, other Asians as well as non-Asians.

The military rulers set out to expand into Asia. In 1931, Japanese forces seized a region in northeastern China known as Manchuria. The region was rich in coal and iron, two resources scarce in Japan. The Japanese set up a state in Manchuria called Manchukuo.

China called on the League of Nations for help. The League condemned Japanese aggression but did little else. The United States refused to recognize Manchukuo but took no action.

❓ **IDENTIFY SUPPORTING DETAILS** Why was the Soviet Union considered a totalitarian state?

Isolationism in the United States

In the United States, the strong isolationist mood of the 1920s continued. As war clouds gathered overseas, Americans were determined to keep from becoming involved. In 1935, Congress passed the first of a series of **Neutrality Acts**, which banned arms sales or loans to countries at war. Congress also warned Americans not to travel on ships of countries at war. By limiting economic ties with warring nations, isolationists hoped to stay out of any foreign conflict.

The Neutrality Acts, 1935–1939

YEAR	IMPACT
1935	Prohibited the sale and export of weapons to nations at war and required American weapons manufacturers to apply for an export license
1937	Prohibited U.S. citizens from traveling on ships of nations at war and banned American merchant ships from transporting weapons produced outside the United States to warring nations
1939	Lifted the ban on weapons but prohibited American ships from transporting goods to ports of nations at war

Source: United States Department of State

>> **Analyze Charts** What evidence from the 1939 Neutrality Act shows that the United States hoped to minimize involvement in any overseas war?

Relations with Latin America Closer to home, the United States tried to improve relations with Latin American nations. In 1930, President Hoover rejected the Roosevelt Corollary. The United States, he declared, no longer claimed the right to intervene in Latin American affairs.

Concerned about the problems in Asia and Europe, Franklin Roosevelt worked to build friendlier relations with Latin America. Under his **Good Neighbor Policy**, FDR withdrew American troops from Nicaragua and Haiti. The policy also emphasized trade and cooperation. Roosevelt also canceled the Platt Amendment, which had limited the independence of Cuba.

As world tensions increased, the need to strengthen ties in the Americas became more pressing. On a visit to Argentina, Roosevelt warned that any foreign aggressor "will find a hemisphere wholly prepared to consult together for our mutual safety."

Relations with the Soviet Union Roosevelt also improved relations with the Soviet Union. He restored diplomatic relations with the Soviet government in 1933, although he remained wary about allying too closely with the communist nation. In addition to benefiting the American economy, Roosevelt had hoped improved relations with the Soviet Union would decrease Japanese expansion in Asia.

? CHECK UNDERSTANDING Why did political changes in Europe and Asia lead the United States to develop a Good Neighbor Policy?

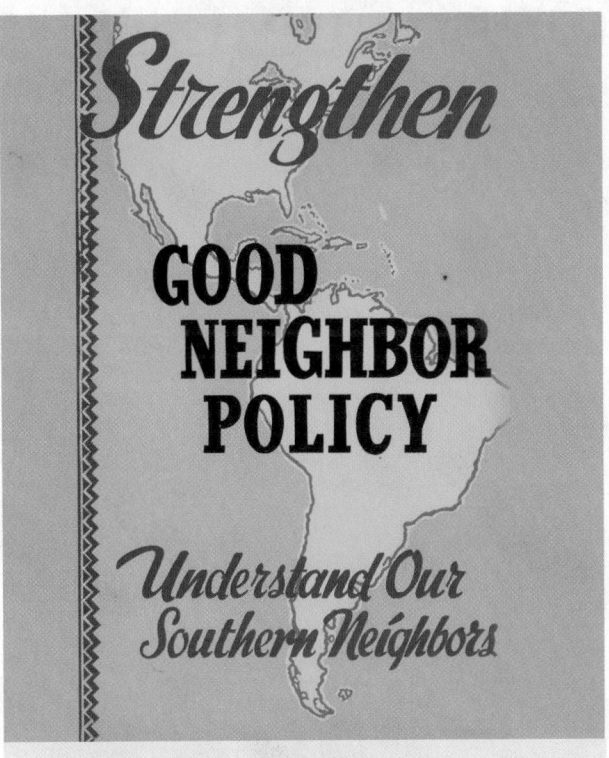

>> **Interpret Illustrations** What was the goal of this poster produced by the U.S. government in the 1930s?

ASSESSMENT

1. **Identify Steps in a Process** How did Mussolini seize power in Italy in 1922, and what actions did he take that led to a Fascist government in Italy?

2. **Draw Conclusions** How did the Nazi government justify its persecution of Jews during the early days of Hitler's rule?

3. **Identify Cause and Effect** How did Joseph Stalin's totalitarian rule affect the lives of Soviet citizens after Lenin's death in 1924?

4. **Identify Central Issues** What crisis allowed Japan's military leaders to take power, and what did the military leaders do after taking power?

5. **Identify Patterns** Discuss some of the actions the United States took during the 1930s that showed many preferred isolationism.

>> During the Battle of Britain in 1940, these and other squadrons of British planes were the first line of defense against Germany's relentless air attacks.

▶ **Interactive Flipped Video**

>> **Objectives**

Explain how aggression led to war in Asia and Europe.

Describe how the United States responded to the outbreak of World War II.

Explain why the United States finally entered the war.

>> **Key Terms**

Munich Conference
appeasement
Nazi-Soviet Pact
blitzkrieg
Axis
Allies
Battle of Britain
Lend-Lease Act
Atlantic Charter

The totalitarian governments that arose in Japan and Germany had strong imperial ambitions. They began advancing into surrounding territories. European leaders hoped to avoid war, and the United States was wary of getting involved. Yet the military aggression from these two nations would soon become impossible to ignore.

The Beginnings of War

Japan Invades China In 1937, Japan began an all-out war against China. Japanese planes bombed China's major cities. Thousands of people were killed. In the city of Nanjing alone, some 300,000 civilians and prisoners of war were murdered in a six-week massacre. Japanese troops defeated Chinese armies and occupied northern and central China.

The Japanese advance into China alarmed American leaders. They felt it undermined the Open Door Policy, which promised equal access to trade in China. It also threatened the Philippines, which the United States controlled. Nevertheless, isolationist feelings remained strong among the American people and kept the United States from taking a firm stand against the Japanese.

Americans React to Japanese Action in Asia Americans were angered by Japan's invasion of China. The United States did not want Japan to become an imperial power in Asia. However, the country did not support going to war against Japan. For many, the conflict in Asia was far away. It did not have a direct impact on their lives.

President Roosevelt reacted to the invasion with a speech denouncing Japan's "reign of terror and international lawlessness," but he maintained his neutral stance. As you will read, Roosevelt would eventually try to apply economic pressure to Japan to halt its military aggression. However, Japan sped up its attacks. Japan is an island nation with limited natural resources. It had its eye on British and Dutch colonies in Southeast Asia that were rich in oil, rubber, and other raw materials that its military could use.

>> The horror of war was expressed in this famous photo of a baby who somehow survived a 1937 Japanese bombing in China. **Drawing Conclusions** What effect do you think this photo had on Americans' attitudes toward the growing turmoil overseas?

Americans were concerned as the conflict in Asia spread. However, the United States would not go to war with Japan unless Japan attacked the United States directly.

German Expansion In Europe, Hitler continued his plans for German expansion. In 1938, just two years after occupying the Rhineland, Hitler annexed Austria. This action again violated the Treaty of Versailles. Once again, Britain and France took no action against Germany.

Later that year, Hitler claimed the Sudetenland, the western part of Czechoslovakia. He justified his demand by claiming that the Sudetenland contained many people of German heritage.

Appeasement Britain and France had signed treaties to protect Czechoslovakia but were reluctant to go to war. The two nations sought a peaceful solution. In September 1938, the leaders of Britain, France, Italy, and Germany met in Munich, Germany.

At the **Munich Conference**, Hitler promised that Germany would seek no further territory once it had acquired the Sudetenland. To preserve the peace, Britain and France agreed that Germany should have the Sudetenland. This practice of giving in to aggression in order to avoid war is known as **appeasement**.

The policy of appeasement failed. Nazi Germany seized the rest of Czechoslovakia the very next year. At last, Britain and France realized that they had to take a firm stand against Nazi aggression.

War Against Poland Hitler next eyed Poland. In August 1939, he signed the **Nazi-Soviet Pact** with Stalin. The two rival dictators agreed not to attack each other. Secretly, they also agreed to divide Poland and other parts of Eastern Europe.

German Advances, 1938–1939

KEY
- Germany (1938)
- Austria (1938)
- Sudetenland (September 1938)
- Protectorate of Bohemia and Moravia (March 1939)
- Protective zone (March 1939)
- Memel district (March 1939)
- Western Poland (September 1939)

>> **Analyze Maps** What evidence from the map shows that the German military aggressively expanded in the late 1930s?

▶ **Interactive Map**

Axis versus Allies World Map, July 1940

ATLANTIC
OCEAN

PACIFIC
OCEAN

PACIFIC
OCEAN

INDIAN
OCEAN

0   2000 mi

0   2000 km
Miller Cylindrical
Projection

KEY
- Axis territory
- Allied territory
- Neutral countries

>> **Analyze Maps** How would the balance of power between the Axis and Allied powers change after the United States and Soviet Union joined the Allies?

In September 1939, Hitler launched a **blitzkrieg**, or lightning war, against Poland. This new tactic involved rushing concentrated forces with superior firepower into a specific area to scatter the enemy and penetrate deeply into enemy territory. Unable to withstand modern German planes and tanks, the Poles soon surrendered.

Meanwhile, the Soviet Union seized eastern Poland. Stalin's forces also invaded Finland and later annexed Estonia, Lithuania, and Latvia. Stalin claimed that these steps were needed to build Soviet defenses.

? DEFINE What is appeasement and why was this policy not successful?

Germany Attacks France and Britain

Two days after Hitler's invasion of Poland, Britain and France declared war on Germany. A new world war had begun.

World War II was truly a global conflict. Military forces fought all over the world. Italy, Japan, and six other nations joined Germany to form the **Axis** powers. Opposing the Axis powers were the **Allies**. Before the war was over, the Allies would include Britain, France, the Soviet Union, the United States, China, and 45 other countries.

France Surrenders In the spring of 1940, Hitler's armies marched north and west. In April, they smashed through Denmark and Norway. In May, they overran Holland and Belgium and pushed into France. Hitler's ally, Italy, also attacked France.

Britain sent troops to help France resist the assault. The British and French, however, were quickly overpowered. By May, the Germans had forced them to retreat to Dunkirk, a French port on the English Channel. In a bold action, the British sent every available ship across the channel to rescue the trapped soldiers.

Unhindered, German armies entered France and marched on to Paris, the French capital. On June 22, 1940, barely six weeks later, France surrendered. The fall of France shocked the world.

Battle of Britain Britain now stood alone. Even so, the new prime minister, Winston Churchill, was confident.

> We shall fight on the beaches, we shall fight on the landing grounds, we shall fight in the fields and in the streets . . . we shall never surrender.
>
> —Winston Churchill, Speech to House of Commons, June 4, 1940

Hitler's plan to invade Britain, codenamed Operation Sea Lion, became a massive air battle. German planes dropped bombs on London and other British cities during the **Battle of Britain**. British fighter pilots fought back, gunning down nearly 2,000 German planes. By late 1940, after months of bombing, Hitler gave up his planned invasion of Britain.

In the United States, Americans listened to radio reports from London. Hearing of Britain's brave stand against Hitler, Americans wondered how much longer they could stay out of the war.

? RECALL Why did Britain and France declare war on Germany?

The United States Assists the Allies

After the invasion of Poland, President Roosevelt announced that the United States would remain neutral. He knew that most Americans favored the Allies but did not want to go to war.

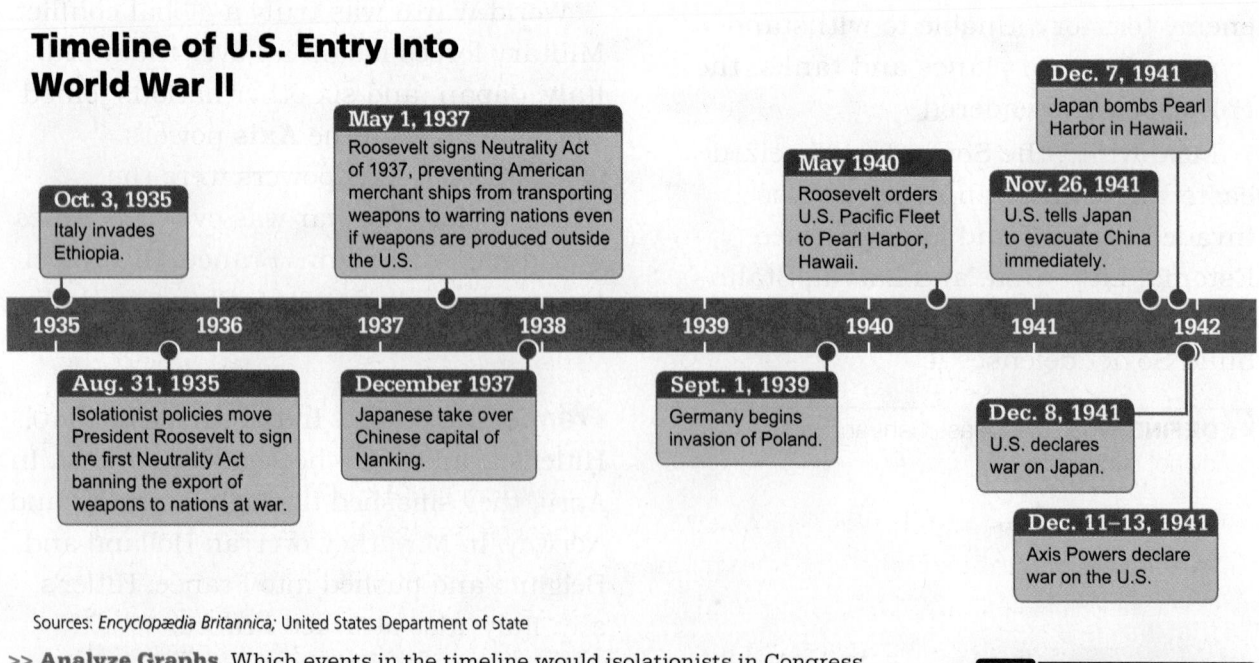

Timeline of U.S. Entry Into World War II

Oct. 3, 1935
Italy invades Ethiopia.

Aug. 31, 1935
Isolationist policies move President Roosevelt to sign the first Neutrality Act banning the export of weapons to nations at war.

May 1, 1937
Roosevelt signs Neutrality Act of 1937, preventing American merchant ships from transporting weapons to warring nations even if weapons are produced outside the U.S.

December 1937
Japanese take over Chinese capital of Nanking.

May 1940
Roosevelt orders U.S. Pacific Fleet to Pearl Harbor, Hawaii.

Sept. 1, 1939
Germany begins invasion of Poland.

Dec. 7, 1941
Japan bombs Pearl Harbor in Hawaii.

Nov. 26, 1941
U.S. tells Japan to evacuate China immediately.

Dec. 8, 1941
U.S. declares war on Japan.

Dec. 11–13, 1941
Axis Powers declare war on the U.S.

1935 1936 1937 1938 1939 1940 1941 1942

Sources: *Encyclopædia Britannica;* United States Department of State

>> **Analyze Graphs** Which events in the timeline would isolationists in Congress have supported?

▶ Interactive Chart

Aid for Allies At the same time, Roosevelt sought ways to help the Allies. He asked Congress to repeal the neutrality law that banned the sale of arms to warring nations. Isolationists blocked the move, but FDR won a compromise. The United States could sell arms to the Allies under a "cash-and-carry" plan. The Allies had to pay cash for the goods and carry them away in their own ships.

By 1940, German submarines had sunk many British ships. Roosevelt agreed to give Britain 50 old American destroyers. In exchange, Britain gave the United States 99-year leases on military bases in Newfoundland and the Caribbean.

New Policies The United States also took several steps to prepare for war. Congress approved greater spending for the army and navy and set up a military draft. It was the first time young men were required to serve in the army during peace.

Isolationists opposed these moves, especially aid for Britain. "I have been forced to the conclusion that we cannot win this war for England, regardless of how much assistance we extend," warned Charles Lindbergh, the hero pilot of the 1920s. Many other Americans, however, felt that the United States had no choice. If Britain fell, Hitler might control the Atlantic Ocean.

FDR Runs for Office Again The threat of war persuaded FDR to run for a third term in 1940. His decision broke the precedent set by George Washington of serving only two terms as President.

Republicans nominated Wendell Willkie, an Ohio businessman. Willkie was a strong critic of FDR's New Deal. Still, he agreed with Roosevelt on many issues, such as sending aid to Britain. Both candidates

"Ho hum! When he's finished pecking down that last tree he'll quite likely be tired."

>> Dr. Seuss drew this political cartoon for an American newspaper in 1941. **Interpret Cartoons** What do the two birds represent? What do the trees represent?

also pledged not to send Americans into any foreign wars.

Republicans—and some Democrats—criticized Roosevelt for breaking the two-term tradition. Still, the voters gave FDR a clear victory. After his defeat, Willkie worked to win Republican support for Roosevelt's war aims.

The Lend-Lease Act By late 1940, Britain was running out of cash. Roosevelt boldly suggested lending supplies to Britain. He proclaimed that Britain was defending democracy against totalitarian forces.

Despite opposition from isolationists, Congress passed the **Lend-Lease Act** in March 1941. It allowed sales or loans of war materials to "any country whose defense the President deems vital to the defense of the United States." Under Lend-

Lease, the United States sent airplanes, tanks, guns, and ammunition to Britain and other Allied nations. British merchant ships transported the goods, with escorts of American warships providing protection as far as Iceland.

Lend-Lease Extends to the Soviet Union

In June 1941, Hitler launched a surprise invasion of the Soviet Union. The attack, which took Soviet leadership off guard, was the largest invasion force in history. The invasion proved to be a vital turning point in the war, as it brought the Soviets over to the Allied side. It also meant that the Germans had to fight on two fronts instead of one.

Much of the American public remained anti-communist. President Roosevelt had condemned Stalin's totalitarian rule, but he decided to extend Lend-Lease aid to the Soviet Union. After much debate, Congress approved extending the aid to the Soviets.

Creating Postwar Goals

In August 1941, Roosevelt and Churchill issued the **Atlantic Charter**, which set goals for the postwar world. The two leaders agreed to seek no territory from the war. They pledged to support "the right of all peoples to choose the form of government under which they will live." The charter also called for a "permanent system of general security" similar to the League of Nations.

❓ IDENTIFY SUPPORTING DETAILS Although the United States didn't formally join the war, what details indicate its support for the Allies?

>> At the 1941 Atlantic Charter Conference, Roosevelt (left) and Churchill (right) agreed that: neither country would look to expand its territory; peoples' choice of government should be respected; and, all nations should feel secure against the threat of invasion.

The United States Declares War

To Roosevelt, Japanese aggressions in Asia were as alarming as Germany's advance through Europe. The Japanese had seized much of China. After Germany defeated France in 1940, Japan took control of French colonies in Southeast Asia. In September 1940, the Japanese signed an alliance with Germany and Italy.

Limiting Trade with Japan The United States tried to stop Japanese aggression by refusing to sell oil and scrap metal to Japan. This embargo angered the Japanese because they badly needed these resources. "Sparks will fly before long," predicted an American diplomat.

Japanese and American officials met in November 1941. Japan asked the United States to lift its trade embargo. The United States called on Japan to withdraw its armies from China and Southeast Asia. Neither side would compromise. As the talks limped along, Japan completed plans for a secret attack on the United States.

"A Date Which Will Live in Infamy" On Sunday morning, December 7, 1941, much of the American Pacific fleet was peacefully anchored at Pearl Harbor, Hawaii. Suddenly, Japanese planes swept through the sky. In less than two hours, they sank or seriously damaged 19 American ships, destroyed almost 200 planes, and killed about 2,400 people.

The attack was a desperate gamble by Japanese leaders. They knew they lacked the resources to win a long war with the United States. They believed, however, that Americans were weak and had no stomach for fighting. The Japanese thought the sneak attack would force the United States to beg for peace immediately. Instead,

>> In a photo taken by a Japanese pilot, the December 7, 1941, attack on Pearl Harbor is seen from the air. After the Japanese attack, the United States abandoned its policy of isolation and entered World War II.

Pearl Harbor united Americans in their determination to fight.

The Japanese made two other mistakes. First, they failed to sink the aircraft carriers stationed at Pearl Harbor. The carriers were at sea at the time of the attack. Second, the Japanese did not bomb the fuel oil tanks in Hawaii. Oil and aircraft carriers would become two keys to American victory in the war that followed.

The next day, a grave President Roosevelt addressed Congress. "Yesterday, December 7, 1941—a date which will live in infamy—the United States of America was suddenly and deliberately attacked by naval and air forces of the Empire of Japan," he began.

No matter how long it may take us to overcome this premeditated invasion, the American people, in their

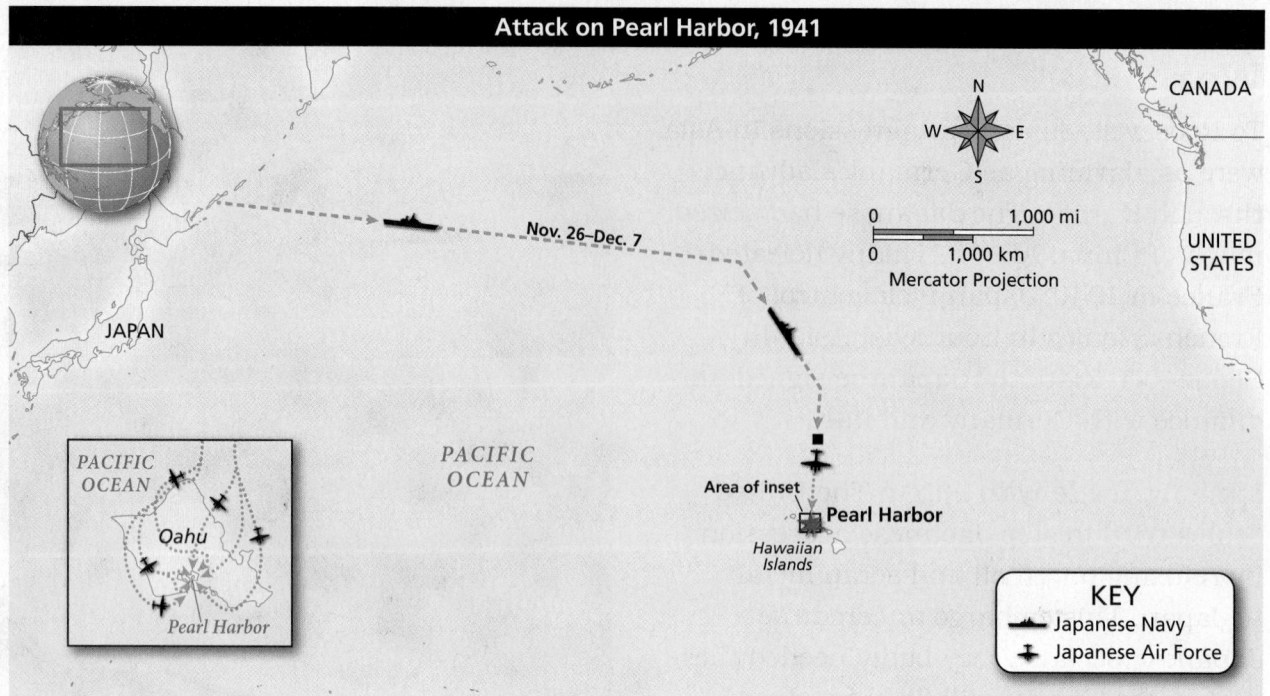

Attack on Pearl Harbor, 1941

Nov. 26–Dec. 7

JAPAN

PACIFIC OCEAN

PACIFIC OCEAN

Oahu

Pearl Harbor

Area of inset

Pearl Harbor

Hawaiian Islands

CANADA

UNITED STATES

0   1,000 mi
0   1,000 km
Mercator Projection

KEY
— Japanese Navy
✛ Japanese Air Force

>> **Analyze Maps** What evidence from the map indicates the attack on Pearl Harbor was carefully planned?

▶ **Interactive Map**

righteous might, will win through to absolute victory.

—Franklin D. Roosevelt, War Message to Congress, December 8, 1941

Congress declared war on Japan. In response, Germany and Italy declared war on the United States. Americans were now united in the cause of freedom. Even isolationists backed the war effort.

The attack on Pearl Harbor had an immediate affect on Americans' lives. Young men left schools and jobs to enter the war. The economy sped up to provide the necessary supplies. A new wartime society developed with a surge in patriotic feeling. For Japanese-, Italian-, and German-Americans, the war also brought difficulties. Many in the country viewed them with suspicion.

❓ DESCRIBE How did the attack on Pearl Harbor change the lives of many Americans?

ASSESSMENT

1. **Determine Point of View** What was the opinion of American leaders towards Japanese military action in China, and why did they feel this way?

2. **Summarize** Show how President Roosevelt was able to work with isolationists in Congress to support Britain while still keeping the United States officially neutral.

3. **Identify Steps in a Process** Describe how the United States began to prepare for war in the late 1930s.

4. **Draw Conclusions** What strategy led to the Japanese leaders' decision to attack Pearl Harbor, and was it successful?

5. **Identify Cause and Effect** How did the attack on Pearl Harbor immediately affect the lives of Americans?

WAR GARDENS FOR VICTORY

>> During World War II, the U.S. government used posters such as this to support the war effort in many ways, such as growing "victory" gardens.

▶ Interactive Flipped Video

During World War II, more than 15 million Americans served in the military. Many millions more spent the war years at home, far from the battlefields. Winning the war depended on mobilizing the home front to support and supply the armed forces.

>> **Objectives**

Describe how Americans mobilized the economy to provide materials and funds for World War II.

Summarize how women in the workforce helped the war effort.

Describe the impact the war had on African Americans.

Explain how and why Japanese Americans and other groups faced wartime restrictions.

>> **Key Terms**

War Production
  Board
rationing
victory garden
Rosie the Riveter
"Double V"
  campaign
Tuskegee Airmen
compensation
Bracero Program
internment

RAMPING UP PRODUCTION 1940–1944

Manufacturing output (percentage of 1930 level)

- Aircraft
- Munitions
- Shipbuilding
- Aluminum
- Steel

4,000 / 3,000 / 2,000 / 1,000 / 0

1940 — 1941 — 1942 — 1943 — 1944

Sources: Economic History Association; PBS

66% of Allied military equipment produced during the war made in the United States

$32.5 billion Value of goods exported to Allies through the Lend-Lease program

THE RATIONING OF FOOD

Each person was allowed **48** ration coupon points per month

- **Butter** (1 pound) – 16 points
- **Canned corn** (1.4 pounds) – 14 points
- **Bacon** (1 pound) – 11 points
- **Steak** (1 pound) – 5 to 8 points
- **Soup** (10.5 ounce can) – 6 points
- **Jam** (1 pound) – 6 points
- **Dried beans** (1 pound) – 2 points

Source: Ames Historical Society

FINANCING THE WAR

TAXES **45%** ($136.8 billion)

LIBERTY BONDS **55%** ($167.2 billion)

Source: Economic History Association

>> **Analyze Graph** What evidence shows that the United States supported the Allied war effort in the early 1940s?

Mobilizing For War

Training Recruits In 1941, the military's first task was to train forces for combat. Army, navy, and air bases were built all over the country. Recruits were trained to fight in the jungles of the Pacific, the deserts of North Africa, and the towns and farmlands of Europe.

Women joined all the armed services. Women pilots logged 60 million air miles ferrying bombers from base to base, towing targets, and teaching men to fly. Although women were not allowed in combat, many served close to the front lines.

A Wartime Economy Even more than in World War I, the government controlled the economy during World War II. Government agencies set the prices of goods, negotiated with labor unions, and decided what should be produced.

The **War Production Board** helped factories shift from making consumer goods to making guns, ships, aircraft, and other war materials. Automobile makers, for example, switched to producing tanks and trucks.

A Nazi leader once scoffed that "Americans can't build planes, only electric iceboxes and razor blades." He was wrong. In 1942 alone, American workers produced more than 48,000 planes and shipped more than 8 million tons of goods.

To control shortages and ensure that enough raw materials would be available for war production, the government imposed **rationing**, or limits on certain goods that people could buy. The government gave Americans ration coupons to purchase coffee, sugar, meat, gasoline, and other goods. When people ran out of coupons, they could not buy the items until new coupons were issued.

Consumer goods became scarce. To combat food shortages, many Americans planted **victory gardens**. At the height of the war, more than 20 million victory gardens produced 40 percent of all vegetables grown in the country.

To pay for the war, the government raised taxes. Also, as was the case in World War I, the U.S. government borrowed money from millions of American citizens by selling war bonds. Americans could buy a bond for a certain price with the expectation that they could redeem the bond from the government after ten years for a profit. In the meantime, the government would then use the money from bond sales to pay for the war. Movie stars took part in drives to sell bonds and boost patriotic spirit.

The war quickly ended the Great Depression. Unemployment fell as millions of jobs opened up in factories. Minority workers found jobs where they had been rejected in the past.

? **CHECK UNDERSTANDING** Why did America's entry into World War II end the Great Depression?

Women and African Americans Join the War Effort

"If you can drive a car, you can run a machine." Newspapers and magazines echoed this call to American women to work for victory. "Why do we need women workers?" asked a radio announcer. "You can't build ships, planes, and guns without them."

Women responded to the urgent demand for their labor. Almost five million women entered the work force. They replaced the men who joined the armed services.

Many women worked in offices. Millions more kept the nation's factories operating around the clock. Some welded, ran huge cranes, and tended blast furnaces. Others became bus drivers, police officers, and gas station attendants. The image of **Rosie the Riveter**, a fictional factory worker, became a symbol of American women's contribution to the war effort.

Because women were badly needed in industry, they were able to win better pay and working conditions. The government agreed that women and men should get the same pay for the same job. Many employers, however, found ways to avoid equal pay.

The war also changed fashions for women. Instead of wearing skirts on the job, many women dressed in trousers. They wore overalls and tied scarves around

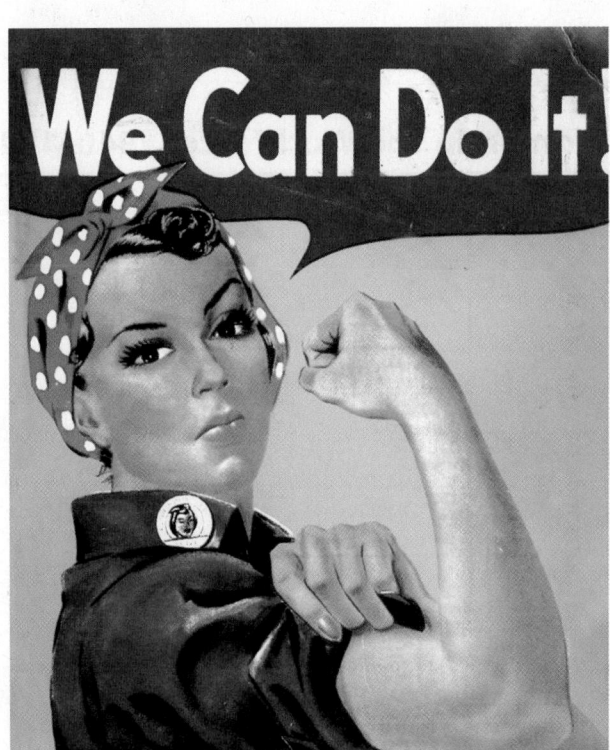

>> This World War II-era poster portrayed Rosie the Riveter. **Interpreting Images** What words describe the woman in this poster, and how do these words describe American feelings about the war effort?

their hair. More importantly, war work gave many women a new sense of confidence.

> I will never regret my two years or more in the shipyards. It gave me a good start in life. . . . I decided that if I could learn to weld like a man, I could do anything it took to make a living.
>
> —Nova Lee McGhee Holbrook, quoted in *A Mouthful of Rivets* (Wise)

Fighting a War Abroad and Discrimination at Home When the war began, African Americans rallied to their nation's cause, as they had during World War I. This time, however, African Americans decided to pursue a **"Double V" campaign**—victory over the enemy abroad and victory over discrimination at home.

As industry geared up for war, factories replaced "No Help Wanted" signs with "Help Wanted, White" signs. Such discrimination angered African Americans.

In 1941, A. Philip Randolph, head of the Brotherhood of Sleeping Car Porters, called for a protest march on Washington. The government, he said, "will never give the Negro justice until they see masses— ten, twenty, fifty thousand Negroes on the White House lawn."

Government officials worried that such a march would feed Hitler's propaganda machine. After meeting with Randolph, FDR ordered employers that did business with the government to end discrimination in hiring. As a result, the employment of skilled black workers doubled during the war.

However, as black employment increased, so did racial tension. Thousands of Americans—black and white—moved to cities to work in industry. Competition for scarce housing led to angry incidents. In 1943, race riots broke out in Detroit, New York, and other cities.

Women in the Workforce, 1940–1945

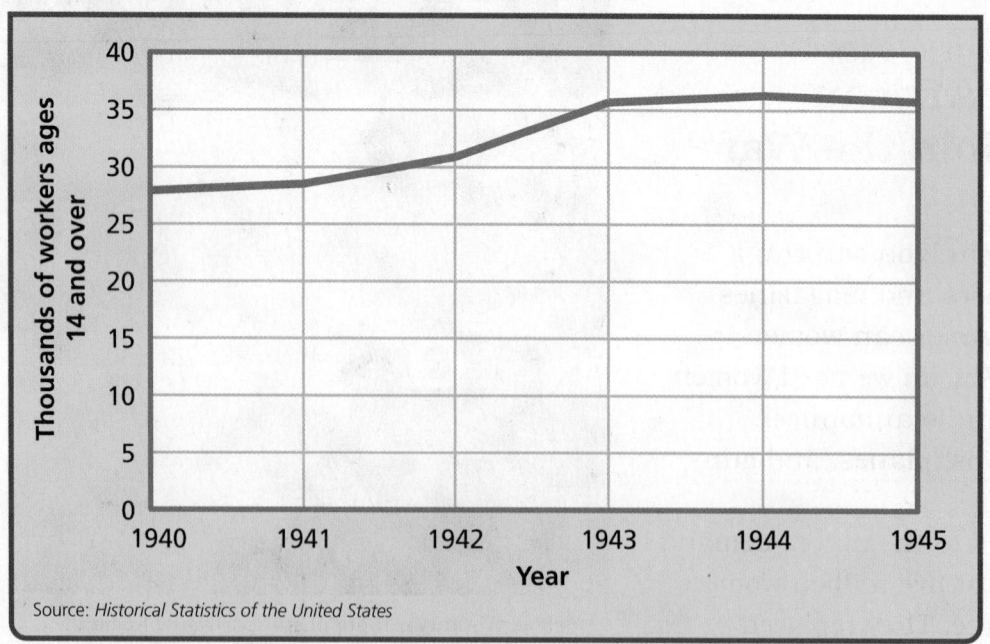

Source: *Historical Statistics of the United States*

>> **Analyze Graphs** Which year in the graph shows the most significant increase in the number of women in the U.S. workforce?

 Interactive Gallery

Heroism in the Military While FDR acted against discrimination in hiring, he refused to end segregation of the races in the military. Nearly a million African Americans enlisted or were drafted. They had to serve in all-black units commanded by white officers.

African Americans served heroically in all branches of the armed forces. One of the earliest heroes of the war was Dorie Miller, an African American sailor serving on the battleship *West Virginia.* During the attack on Pearl Harbor, Miller dragged his wounded captain to safety. Then, though he had no training as a gunner, Miller manned a machine gun to defend his ship against enemy planes. For heroism in action, Miller was awarded the Navy Cross.

In the army, African American soldiers formed artillery and tank units. African Americans in the navy served as gunners' mates and helped build bases in the Pacific. African American marines helped defend American posts against Japanese attacks.

The **Tuskegee Airmen** were African American fighter pilots who trained at Tuskegee, Alabama. By the end of the war, the Tuskegee airmen had destroyed or damaged about 400 enemy aircraft.

The contributions of African Americans to the war effort increased their determination to win justice at home. After the war, black veterans would be at the forefront of a renewed campaign for civil rights.

❓ **DEFINE** the "Double V" campaign and provide details showing its success and limitations.

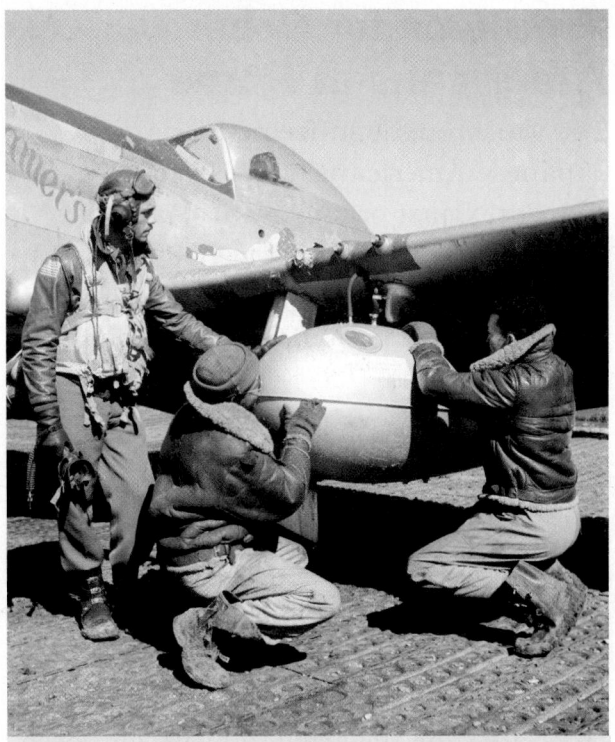

>> This photo shows some of the Tuskegee Airmen in 1945. The Tuskegee Airmen were a corps of African American pilots trained at Tuskegee, Alabama.

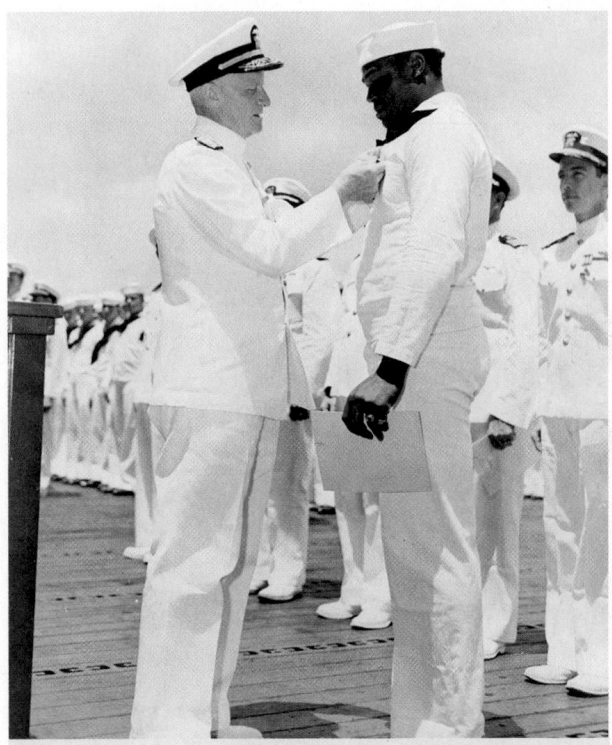

>> African American sailor Dorie Miller receives the Navy Cross for his bravery at Pearl Harbor on May 27, 1942.

Problems for Other Americans at Home

The war brought suffering to many Japanese Americans. Most lived on the West Coast or in Hawaii. Many of those on the West Coast were successful farmers and business people. For years, they had faced prejudice, in part because of their success.

Japanese American Relocation Camps

After the attack on Pearl Harbor, many Americans questioned the loyalty of Japanese Americans. Some thought they might act as spies and help Japan invade the United States. No evidence of disloyalty existed. Yet, President Roosevelt signed an order allowing the army to move Japanese Americans from their homes to "relocation camps." Many were American citizens by birth. Later, a court case challenged the

order, but the Supreme Court decided in *Korematsu* v. *United States* that such an order was constitutional in times of war.

About 110,000 Japanese Americans were forced to sell their homes, farms, or businesses at great loss. "We didn't know where we were going," recalled Peter Ota, who was 15 at the time. "We didn't know what to take. A toothbrush, toilet supplies, some clothes. Only what you could carry."

In the camps, Japanese Americans lived in crowded barracks behind barbed wire.

Japanese American Service and Compensation

Despite unfair treatment, thousands of Japanese American men served in the armed forces. Most were put in segregated units and sent to fight in Europe. There, they won many honors for bravery. The 442nd Nisei Regimental Combat Team became the most highly decorated military unit in United States history.

Years later, in 1988, Congress apologized to Japanese Americans who had suffered from **internment**, or temporary imprisonment, during World War II. Congress also approved **compensation**, or repayment for losses, in the amount of $20,000 to every survivor of the camps.

German Americans and Italian Americans

Japanese Americans were not the only group to face wartime restrictions. About 11,000 German Americans and several hundred Italian Americans were also held in government camps as "enemy aliens." Other German Americans and Italian Americans faced curfews or travel restrictions.

Mexican Americans

A growing Mexican American population also faced problems. Because of the need for workers, the United

>> American troops oversee the forced relocation of Japanese American families in April 1942. "Herd'em up, pack'em off" was the reaction of one newspaper columnist.

▶ **Interactive Gallery**

States signed a treaty with Mexico in 1942. It allowed the recruitment of Mexican laborers to work in the United States. Under this **Bracero Program**, many Mexicans moved north to work on farms and railroads.

In June 1943, a group of sailors on leave attacked some young Mexican Americans, beating them on the streets. The incident led to several days of rioting in Los Angeles. Newspapers blamed the violence on the Mexican Americans. But in her newspaper column, Eleanor Roosevelt argued that the riots were the result of "longstanding discrimination against the Mexicans in the Southwest."

Still, like other groups, Mexican Americans served bravely in the military during World War II. Despite lingering problems at home, Americans were united in their resolve to push on to victory in Europe and the Pacific.

>> In May 1943, these Mexican workers arrived to work in Stockton, California, as part of the Bracero Program. The agreement between Mexico and the United States temporarily filled the workforce openings left by Americans who were serving in the military.

? CHECK UNDERSTANDING Why did Japanese, German, and Italian Americans face unfair treatment during World War II?

ASSESSMENT

1. **Summarize** How did A. Philip Randolph impact the lives of African Americans during World War II?

2. **Identify Central Issues** What economic challenges did Americans on the home front face during World War II?

3. **Cite Evidence** How did Rosie the Riveter show the significant changes in American society during World War II?

4. **Identify Cause and Effect** How did America's entry into World War II affect the nation's economy?

5. **Identify Cause and Effect** How did World War II lead to heightened racial tensions in the United States?

14.4 Winning a Deadly War

>> The D-Day landing at Normandy was treacherous. Boats dropped Allied troops near the shore, where they had to slog through the surf and obstacles to advance up the beach. German gunners were perched on shore, firing at will.

Interactive Flipped Video

>> **Objectives**

Identify the early defeats and hardships the Allies suffered.

Explain how changes to Allied tactics later in the war turned the tide of the war in Europe.

Summarize how the war in Europe ended.

Explain why Japan finally surrendered.

Describe what made World War II the deadliest war in history.

>> **Key Terms**

Battle of Midway
Operation Overlord
Nuremberg Trials
Battle of the Bulge
island-hopping
Potsdam
   Declaration
Bataan Death March
kamikaze
Navajo code-talkers
Holocaust
concentration
   camps
death camps
D-Day

When Adolf Hitler learned of the Japanese attack on Pearl Harbor, he was delighted. "Now it is impossible for us to lose the war," he predicted. "We now have an ally who has never been vanquished in 3,000 years." Although Germany's alliance with Japan did not require it, Hitler promptly declared war on the United States.

The Allies Suffer Early Defeats

At first, Hitler's prediction looked as if it might come true. In early 1942, the situation looked bleak for the Allies. German armies occupied most of Europe and much of North Africa. The German war machine seemed unbeatable. German submarines were sinking ships faster than the Allies could replace them. Most of Europe was in Axis hands.

Meanwhile, Japan was sweeping across Asia and the Pacific. American forces were divided between two fronts. It was not until 1943 that the tide of battle turned. It took time for the Allies to develop new strategies, weapons, and forces to fight back Hitler and win the war in Japan.

Germany Invades the Soviet Union In the Soviet Union, German armies were closing in on Moscow, Leningrad, and Stalingrad during the summer of 1941. The Soviets resisted heroically. They burned crops and destroyed farm equipment so that the Germans could not use them. The harsh Russian winter that followed also greatly hindered the German advance.

Still, the German attack caused terrible hardships. During the 900-day siege of Leningrad that began in the fall of 1941, more than one million Russian men, women, and children died, mostly of starvation.

Japan Advances Across the Pacific
Meanwhile, Japanese forces were on the move in the Pacific. After the bombing of Pearl Harbor, they seized Guam, Wake Island, Hong Kong, and Singapore. General Douglas MacArthur commanded United States forces in the Southwest Pacific. With few troops, MacArthur had to defend a huge area. He directed American and Filipino troops in the defense of the

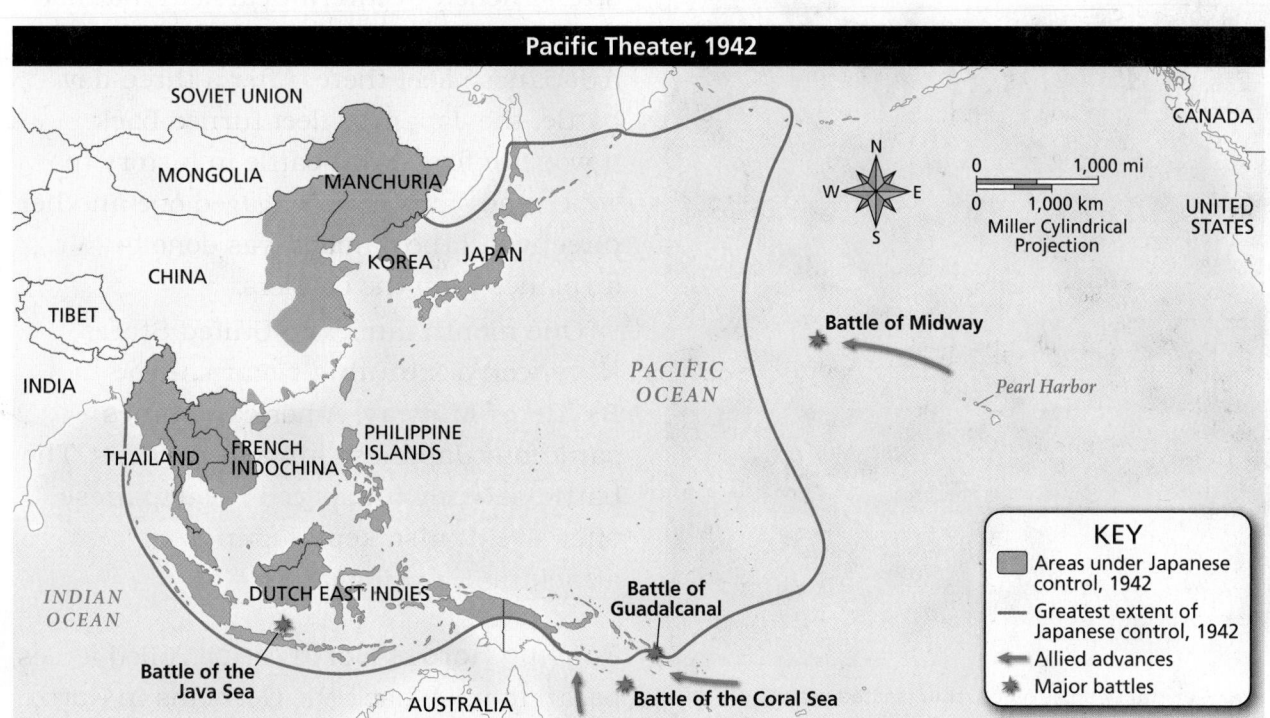

Pacific Theater, 1942

KEY
- Areas under Japanese control, 1942
- Greatest extent of Japanese control, 1942
- Allied advances
- Major battles

>> **Analyze Maps** Based on the map, what challenges did the U.S. military face in the Pacific Theater?

Philippines and the island of Bataan. They fought bravely against enormous odds.

> Besieged on land and blockaded by sea, cut off from all sources of help in the Philippines and in America, these intrepid fighters have done all that human endurance could bear. . . . Bataan has fallen, but the spirit that made it stand—a beacon to all liberty-loving peoples of the world—cannot fall!

—Norman Reyes, "Voice of Freedom" broadcast, 1942

In the end, MacArthur was forced to withdraw. However, about 75,000 American and Filipino troops left to defend Bataan were captured. Nonetheless, MacArthur announced from the safety of Australia: "I shall return."

The Japanese pressed on. They captured Malaya, Burma, and the Dutch East Indies. They threatened India to the west and Australia and New Zealand to the south.

>> General Douglas MacArthur (seated, left) observes American troops in the Philippines in 1944. MacArthur led the United States forces against Japan in the Southwest Pacific.

? IDENTIFY SUPPORTING DETAILS What details show the difficulties the United States faced in fighting a war in the Pacific?

The Allies Agree on a Strategy

To succeed against the Axis powers, the Allies had to agree on a strategy. Even before Pearl Harbor, American and British leaders had decided that the Allies must defeat Germany and Italy first. Then, they would send their combined forces to fight Japan.

Victories in Japan Adopting a "beat Hitler first" strategy did not mean abandoning the war in the Pacific. Chester Nimitz, commander of Allied forces in the Pacific, sent a naval task force into the Coral Sea near Java in May 1942. The task force, strengthened by aircraft carriers that had survived the attack on Pearl Harbor, met a Japanese fleet there. After a three-day battle, the Japanese fleet turned back. It was the first naval battle in history in which the ships never engaged one another directly. All the damage was done by airplanes from the carriers.

One month later, the United States Navy won a stunning victory at the **Battle of Midway**. American planes sank four Japanese aircraft carriers. The battle severely hampered the Japanese offensive. It also kept Japan from attacking Hawaii again.

Pushing Across North Africa Allied forces began to push back the Germans in North Africa. In October 1942, the British won an important victory at El Alamein in Egypt.

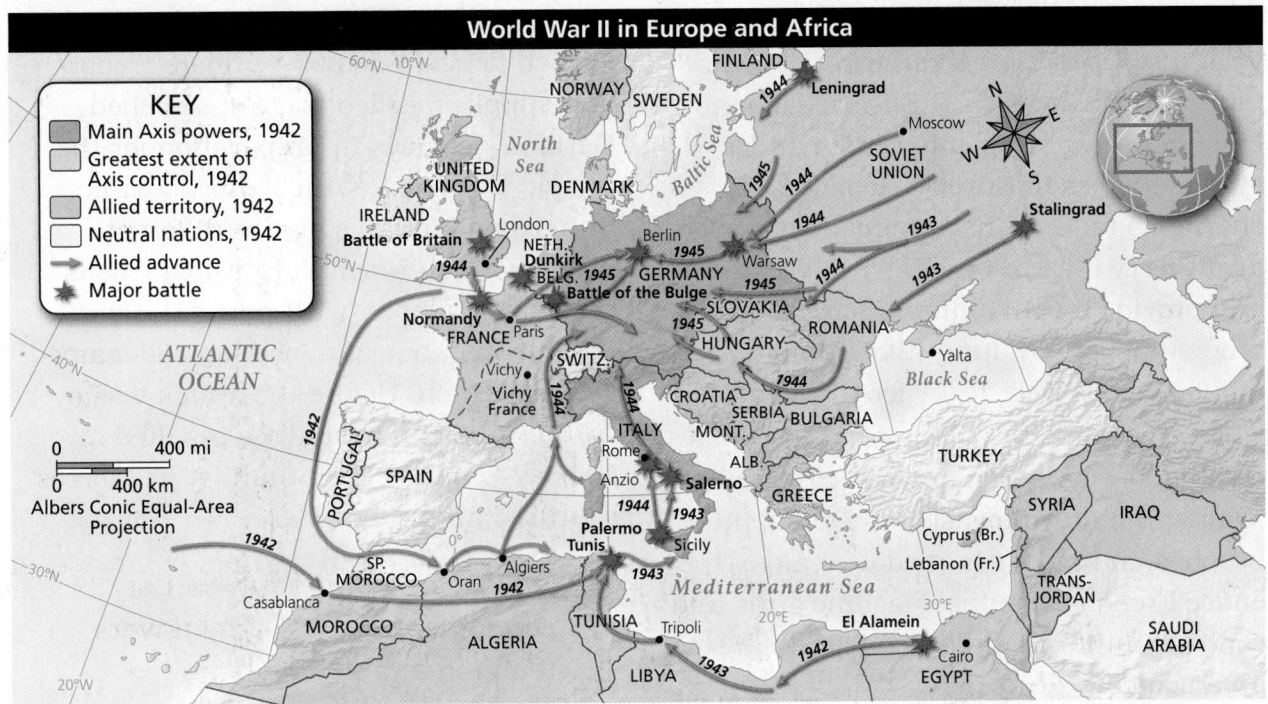

World War II in Europe and Africa

KEY
- Main Axis powers, 1942
- Greatest extent of Axis control, 1942
- Allied territory, 1942
- Neutral nations, 1942
- → Allied advance
- ✦ Major battle

0   400 mi
0   400 km
Albers Conic Equal-Area Projection

>> **Analyze Maps** What evidence from the map indicates that the Soviet Union gained territory previously taken by the Axis powers?

▶ **Interactive 3-D Model**

German forces under General Erwin Rommel were driven west into Tunisia.

Meanwhile, American troops under the command of Generals Dwight D. Eisenhower, Omar Bradley, and George S. Patton landed in Morocco and Algeria. They then pushed east. Allied armies trapped Rommel's forces in Tunisia. In May 1943, his army had to surrender.

The Allies Invade Italy From bases in North Africa, the Allies organized the invasion of Italy. They used paratroopers and soldiers brought by sea to capture the island of Sicily. In early September 1943, the Allies crossed from Sicily to the mainland of Italy.

By then, Mussolini had been overthrown as leader of Italy. The Germans, however, still occupied much of Italy. In a series of bloody battles, the Allies slowly fought their way up the peninsula. On June 4, 1944, Allied troops marched into Rome. It

was the first European capital to be freed from Nazi control.

The Eastern Front The Soviet army repelled the Germans from Leningrad in 1943. At Stalingrad, after months of fierce house-to-house fighting, Soviet soldiers forced the invading German army to surrender. Slowly, the Soviet army pushed the remaining German forces westward through Eastern Europe. Fighting in Russia and Eastern Europe was fierce. The Soviet Union would eventually lose some 9 million soldiers during the war, more than any other country.

For years, Stalin had urged Britain and the United States to send armies across the English Channel into France. Such an attack would create a second front in Western Europe and ease pressure in the East. However, not until 1944 were Churchill and Roosevelt prepared to attempt an invasion of Western Europe.

Operation Overlord Years of planning went into **Operation Overlord**, the code name for the invasion of Europe. General Eisenhower was appointed commander of Allied forces in Europe. He faced an enormous task. He had to organize a huge army, ferry it across the English Channel, and provide it with ammunition, food, and other supplies. By June 1944, almost 3 million troops were ready for the invasion.

The Germans knew that an attack was coming, but not when or where. To guard against the Allied invasion, they had mined beaches and strung barbed wire along the entire French coastline. Machine guns and concrete antitank walls stood ready to stop an advance.

D-Day in France In the early morning of June 6, 1944—**D-Day** as it was known—a fleet of 4,000 Allied ships carried the invasion force to France. Allied airplanes dropped thousands of paratroopers into occupied France. Gliders landed in the French fields to deliver yet more troops and supplies. Allied warships shelled German defenses in preparation for the attack. But most of the invasion came from troop landings on five different beaches along Normandy. Allied troops scrambled ashore, with particularly tough resistance at a location codenamed Omaha Beach. Before the attack was over, 2,400 American casualties resulted at "Bloody Omaha." Eventually Allied forces captured all five beaches.

> It all seemed unreal, a sort of dreaming while awake, men were screaming and dying all around me. . . . I honestly could have walked the full length of the beach without touching the ground, they were that thickly strewn about.
>
> —Melvin B. Farrell, *War Memories*

Despite intense German gunfire and heavy losses, Allied forces surged on to capture more territory along the coast of France. Every day, more soldiers landed at Normandy to reinforce the advance. However, fighting after D-Day was extremely slow and dangerous due to French farm fields that provided thick cover for the enemy. But the Allied ground troops fought stubbornly and pushed German forces back.

The Allied liberation of France continued with the capture of Cherbourg, an important French port, by the end of June. Then the Allies swept east and, on August 25, 1944, they entered Paris. After four years under Nazi rule, the Parisians greeted their liberators with joy. Within a month, all of France was free.

>> American soldiers march triumphantly through Paris after liberating the city on August 25, 1944.

? **DESCRIBE** the "beat Hitler first" strategy and give examples of its success.

TURNING POINTS IN WORLD WAR II

1 Battle of Midway, 1942
United States Navy sinks four Japanese aircraft carriers and destroys hundreds of airplanes. Major Japanese offensive is turned back.

2 Battle of Stalingrad, 1942–1943
Germans try to take Stalingrad. Russian troops and freezing weather force their surrender.

3 Battle of El Alamein, 1942
British drive back German advances. This leads to German surrender of African lands.

4 Invasion of Italy, 1943
British and American forces land in Sicily and go on into Italy. Hitler is forced to send troops to help Italy fight the Allies.

5 Invasion of Normandy (D-Day), 1944
Allied troops land on beaches of Normandy. They go on to free France from German control.

6 Battle of Guadalcanal, 1942–1943
Allied forces earn first major victory in Pacific, forcing the Japanese to withdraw.

>> **Analyze Graphs** What effect did the Battle of Stalingrad have on the war in Europe?

Germany's Defeat

By September, the Allies were moving east toward Germany. However, a shortage of truck fuel slowed the advance.

The German Counterattack On December 16, 1944, German forces began a fierce counterattack. They pushed the Allies back, creating a bulge in the front lines. During the **Battle of the Bulge**, as it was later called, the outnumbered American forces held the Germans back. Because of a fuel shortage, Germany was unable to power its tanks through the American defense. This hindered the German forces, allowing the Allies to maintain their ground.

The Battle of the Bulge slowed the Allies but did not stop them. While Allied armies advanced on the ground, Allied planes bombed Germany. At night, British airmen dropped tons of bombs on German cities. By day, the Americans bombed factories and oil refineries. The bombing caused severe fuel shortages in Germany and reduced the nation's ability to produce war goods.

Roosevelt's Death Stuns the Nation By mid-1944, the Allied advance in Europe shared headlines in American newspapers with the upcoming election. Breaking all tradition, President Roosevelt ran for a fourth term. His Republican opponent was Governor Thomas E. Dewey of New York.

Roosevelt was tired and ill. "All that is within me cries to go back to my home on the Hudson," he wrote. Still, he and his running mate, Senator Harry S. Truman of Missouri, campaigned strongly. Roosevelt won more than 54 percent of the vote.

In early April 1945, FDR was on vacation in Georgia. While he was sitting to have his portrait painted, the President complained of a headache. Within hours, he was dead.

>> President Roosevelt's funeral procession moves through Washington, D.C., on April 24, 1945. Roosevelt's death shook the nation and thrust Harry Truman into the role of commander in chief for the remainder of the war.

All over the world, people mourned Roosevelt. His death especially shocked Americans. After 12 years, many could hardly remember any other President. As for Truman, he was faced with taking over a country in the midst of war. "I felt like the moon, the stars, and all the planets had fallen on me," he later recalled.

Victory in Europe By April 1945, Germany was collapsing. American troops were closing in on Berlin from the west. Soviet troops were advancing from the east. On April 25, American and Soviet troops met at Torgau, 60 miles south of Berlin.

As Allied air raids pounded Berlin, Hitler hid in his underground bunker. Unwilling to accept defeat, he committed suicide. One week later, on May 7, 1945, Germany surrendered to the Allies. On May 8, the Allies celebrated the long-awaited V-E Day—Victory in Europe.

? **CHECK UNDERSTANDING** Why did the United States bomb German factories and oil refineries?

Japan Surrenders

While war raged in Europe, the Allies kept up pressure on Japan. The United States had two main goals in the Pacific war: to regain the Philippines and to invade Japan. Both tasks would prove difficult. American forces encountered stubborn resistance as they advanced into Japanese territories. Japanese soldiers were trained not to surrender, even if it was clear they were not going to win.

Capturing Japanese Islands To gain control of the Pacific Ocean, American forces used a strategy of capturing some Japanese-held islands and going around others. In this **island-hopping** campaign, each island that was won became another steppingstone to Japan.

A deadly routine developed. First, American ships and planes shelled and bombed an island. Next, troops waded ashore under heavy gunfire. Then, in hand-to-hand fighting, Americans overcame fierce Japanese resistance.

Navajo soldiers made a key contribution to American strategy in the Pacific. Using their own language, they radioed vital messages from island to island. The Japanese intercepted the messages but were unable to understand these **Navajo code-talkers**.

In October 1944, American forces under General MacArthur finally recaptured the Philippines. In hard-fought battles, other Pacific Allied forces then captured the islands of Iwo Jima (EE woh JEE muh) and Okinawa (oh kuh NAH wuh) from the Japanese. Capturing Iwo Jima was important because of the air base located there. Okinawa, just 340 miles from the mainland of Japan, was intended to be used as a launching point for the invasion of Japan.

For the Japanese, defending their homeland became a desperate struggle. Japanese leaders stressed an ancient code known as *Bushido*, or the Way of the Warrior. It emphasized loyalty, honor, and sacrifice. To surrender was to "lose face" or be dishonored. In suicide missions, **kamikaze** (kah muh KAH zee) pilots loaded old planes with bombs and then deliberately crashed them into Allied ships.

Plans to Invade By April 1945, American forces were close enough to launch attacks against the Japanese home islands. American bombers pounded factories and cities. American warships bombarded the coast and sank ships. The Japanese people suffered terribly. Yet, their leaders promised a glorious victory.

THE PACIFIC THEATER

THE ALLIED EFFORT

UNITED STATES   GREAT BRITAIN   NEW ZEALAND

AUSTRALIA   CANADA   FIJI

Source: In Their Words: AETN's World War II Oral History Project

U.S. CASUALTIES IN THE
PACIFIC
1941–1945

Navy   27,876
Marines   18,446
Army   211,528

Total Pacific Theater Casualties:
252,850

Sources: Naval History & Heritage Command; Association of the United States Army

U.S. NAVY VESSELS IN THE PACIFIC

Aircraft Carriers 575 ft.
Battleships 550 ft.
Heavy Cruisers 550 ft.
Destroyers 300 ft.
Gun Boats 300 ft.
Submarines 280 ft.
Torpedo Boats 70 ft.

Sources: PBS; Naval History & Heritage Command

MAJOR EVENTS IN THE PACIFIC THEATER

December 1941
Japan attacks Pearl Harbor

June 1942
Battle of Midway

June 1944
Battle of the Philippine Sea

February–March 1945
Battle of Iwo Jima

April–June 1945
Battle of Okinawa

August 1945
U.S. drops atomic bombs on Hiroshima and Nagasaki, Japan

August 14, 1945
Japan surrenders; World War II ends

Sources: The National WWII Museum; University of Virginia; PBS

>> **Analyze Graphs** Approximately how many casualties did the U.S. Army suffer in the Pacific theater during World War II?

United States military leaders made plans to invade Japan in the autumn. They warned that the invasion might cost between 150,000 and 250,000 American casualties.

A Secret Weapon Truman, Churchill, and Stalin met at Potsdam, Germany, in July 1945. While there, Truman received word that American scientists had successfully tested a secret new weapon, the atomic bomb. A single bomb was powerful enough to destroy an entire city. Some scientists believed that it was too dangerous to use.

From Potsdam, the Allied leaders sent a message warning Japan to surrender or face "prompt and utter destruction." Japanese leaders did not know about the destructive power of the atomic bomb. They ignored the **Potsdam Declaration**.

Atomic Bombs End the War With Japan
On August 6, 1945, the American bomber *Enola Gay* dropped an atomic bomb on Hiroshima, Japan. The blast destroyed most of the city, killing at least 70,000 people and injuring an equal number. On August 9, a second atomic bomb was dropped, on Nagasaki. About 40,000 residents died instantly. In both Nagasaki and Hiroshima, many more people later died from the effects of atomic radiation.

On August 14, 1945, the emperor of Japan announced that his nation would surrender. The formal surrender took place on September 2 aboard the USS *Missouri* in Tokyo Bay. The warship flew the same American flag that had waved over Washington, D.C., on the day that Japan bombed Pearl Harbor.

V-J ("Victory in Japan") Day sparked wild celebrations across the United States.

>> The United States dropped atomic bombs on Japan in August 1945, killing more than 100,000 people. This image shows the devastation of the bomb dropped on Hiroshima. **Hypothesize** Do you think it was right to drop the atomic bombs? Why or why not?

 Interactive Illustration

World War II Deaths

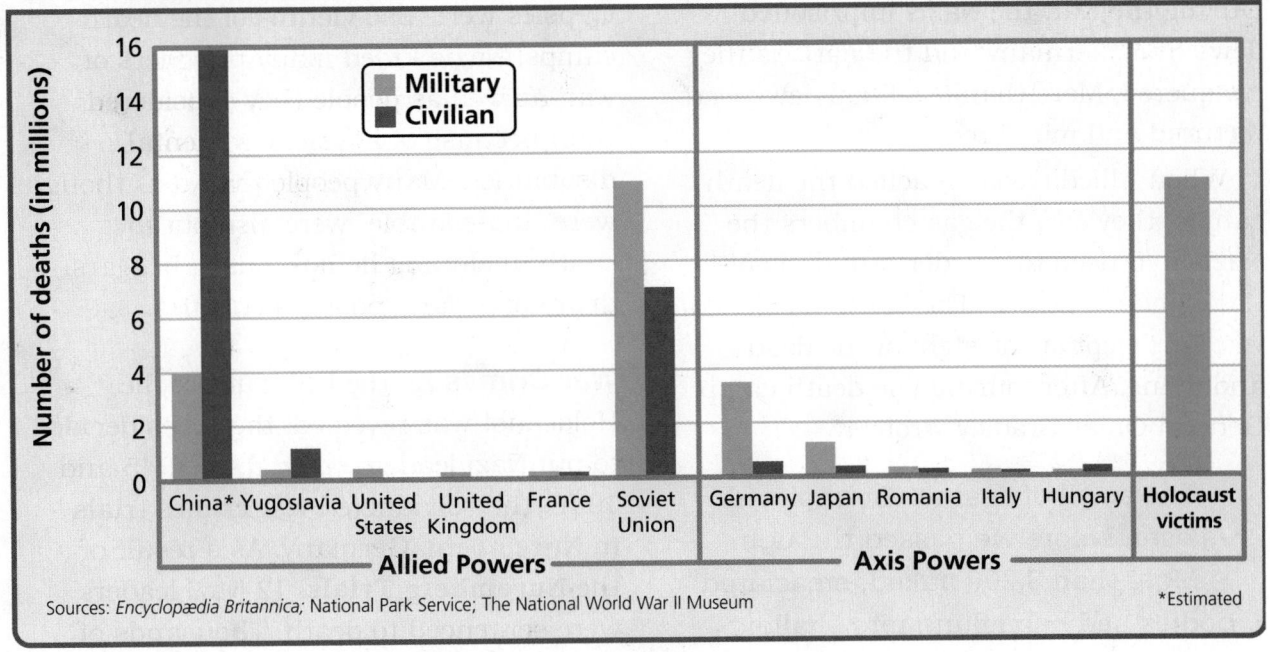

Sources: *Encyclopædia Britannica;* National Park Service; The National World War II Museum *Estimated

>> **Analyze Graphs** Approximately how many civilian casualties did the Allied Powers suffer in all?

People honked their car horns. Soldiers and sailors danced in victory parades. World War II was over at last.

? IDENTIFY MAIN IDEAS Why did Japan surrender in 1945?

The Devastation of World War II

World War II was the deadliest war in history. The exact number of casualties will probably never be known. However, historians estimate that between 30 million and 60 million people were killed.

World War I had been fought mainly in trenches in Europe. In World War II, fighting occurred on the land, sea, and air throughout many parts of the world. The war affected civilians more than any other war. Bombers destroyed houses, factories, and farms. By 1945, millions were homeless and had no way to earn a

living. Well over half of the deaths from the war were civilians.

After the war, Americans heard horrifying stories of the brutal mistreatment of prisoners of war. When the Japanese captured the Philippines in 1942, they forced about 75,000 American and Filipino prisoners to march 65 miles with little food or water. About 10,000 prisoners died or were killed during the **Bataan Death March**.

The Holocaust In the last months of the European war, Allied forces uncovered other horrors. The Allies had heard about Nazi **concentration camps**. These camps were areas where members of specially designated groups were confined. Some concentration camps were **death camps**, where people were systematically murdered. As they advanced into Germany and Eastern Europe, the Allies discovered the full extent of the **Holocaust**, the slaughter of Europe's Jews by the Nazis. During the war, the Nazis imprisoned Jews from Germany and the nations they conquered. More than 6 million Jews were tortured and murdered.

When Allied troops reached the death camps, they saw the gas chambers the Nazis had used to murder hundreds of thousands of people. The battle-hardened veterans wept at the sight of the dead and dying. After touring one death camp, General Omar Bradley wrote:

> The smell of death overwhelmed us even before we passed through. . . . More than 3,200 naked, emaciated bodies had been flung into shallow graves.
>
> —Omar N. Bradley, *A General's Life*

Nearly 6 million Poles, Slavs, and Gypsies were also victims of the death camps. Nazis killed many prisoners of war, as well as people they considered unfit because of physical or mental disabilities. Many people the Nazis thought were "undesirable" were also put to death, including homosexuals, beggars, drunkards, and political enemies.

War Crimes As the full truth of the Holocaust was revealed, the Allies decided to put Nazi leaders on trial. In 1945 and 1946, they conducted war crimes trials in Nuremberg, Germany. As a result of the **Nuremberg Trials**, 12 Nazi leaders were sentenced to death. Thousands of other Nazis were imprisoned. The Allies also tried and executed Japanese leaders accused of war crimes.

>> Prisoners of the Dachau concentration camp in Germany rejoice as the camp is liberated by American troops in 1945.

▶ Interactive Gallery

>> At the Nuremberg Trials (1945–46) the International Military Tribunal put on trial several Nazi leaders (seated in the two rows in front of the guards).

Postwar Challenges Americans looked ahead to life after such a devastating war. But more than ever before, the United States would have a critical influence on world affairs. The daunting task of moving on presented many challenges. How would Europe be rebuilt? What would happen to Germany? How would the emergence of the Soviet Union as a world power affect democracy around the world? In the wake of two terrible world wars, how could peace be maintained? World leaders struggled with these problems as a new modern era came to pass.

? **LIST** the reasons why World War II was so deadly.

1. **Identify the Rise of Italian Fascist Dictatorship**
Write a paragraph identifying what led to the rise of a fascist dictatorship in Italy after World War I. Identify what fascism is, the conditions in Italy following World War I that led to the rise of a dictatorship, and Benito Mussolini's role in establishing the dictatorship.

2. **Analyze and Interpret a Speech** Write a paragraph to describe Adolf Hitler's dictatorship in Germany during the 1930s. Then, analyze and interpret the excerpt below. Finally, write a paragraph identifying how the speech reflects the traits of a totalitarian dictatorship. Consider the characteristics of a totalitarian dictatorship and how Hitler's message reflects these characteristics.

"For everyone has to obey orders. We have obeyed orders. . . . And I must demand this of every German: You, too, must be able to obey orders, . . . We shall educate our People to do this and ignore the obstinacy [stubbornness] or stupidity of individuals. Bend or break—one or the other. We cannot permit this authority, the authority of the German People, to be challenged. . . ."

—Adolf Hitler, May 1, 1937

3. **Identify the Rise of Japanese Militarism** Write a paragraph identifying the impact of military leadership in Japan in the 1930s. Identify what conditions led to the military gaining power and what military leaders did once they were in power, both in Japan and in the region.

4. **Identify Dictatorship Aggression** Write a paragraph describing Germany's aggression during the 1930s and how the United States reacted to their actions. Identify what aggressive moves Germany made, how the United States reacted, and why the United States reacted in this way.

5. **Evaluate the International Leadership of Franklin D. Roosevelt** Write a paragraph evaluating how Franklin D. Roosevelt used his leadership skills to help Britain and the Allies before the United States entered World War II. Consider Roosevelt's challenges in working with Congress and his efforts to develop methods that allowed the United States to provide aid to the Allies.

6. **Identify the Attack on Pearl Harbor** Write a paragraph identifying the events surrounding the attack on Pearl Harbor. Consider why Japan attacked Pearl Harbor and what damage the attack inflicted. Explain what President Roosevelt did in response to the attack and why the attack was a turning point in World War II.

7. **Explain the Purchase of War Bonds** Explain how American patriotism inspired exceptional actions by citizens, including the purchase of war bonds. Write a paragraph explaining how buying war bonds allowed citizens to support the war effort. Explain how war bonds helped the war effort and how they benefited purchasers.

8. **Explain Rationing on the Home Front** Write a paragraph explaining rationing on the U.S. home front and describing its effects. Answer the following questions in your paragraph: What was rationing? How was rationing controlled? What kinds of goods and materials were rationed and why? How were victory gardens a response to the effects of rationing?

9. **Analyze the Internment of Americans** Analyze major issues of World War II, including the internment of German Americans, Italian Americans, and Japanese Americans. Write a paragraph analyzing why these groups were targeted, how they were treated, and what affect the presidential order had on Japanese Americans.

10. **Explain Constitutional Issues** Write a paragraph explaining the Supreme Court case that arose out of Japanese American internment during World War II. Identify the case, explain the Supreme Court's ruling, and describe what the government did in 1988.

11. **Describe Home Front Opportunities** Write a paragraph describing how employment opportunities on the home front changed for African Americans and Mexican Americans during the war and why. Consider the employment conditions African Americans faced in the United States, how A. Philip Randolph influenced those conditions, and what the Bracero Program was.

12. **Analyze the Normandy Invasion** Write a paragraph analyzing the Allied invasion of Normandy (Operation Overlord). Describe what the plan was, identify when the invasion began, and describe how the Allied troops finally broke through German defenses. Then, analyze why the invasion was a turning point in the war.

World War II in Europe, 1942–1945

KEY
- Greatest extent of Axis control, 1942
- Allied territory, 1942
- Neutral nations, 1942
- Allied advance
- Major battle

13. **Analyze Fighting on Multiple Fronts** Write a paragraph analyzing how the Allies fought on multiple fronts to defeat Italy and Germany. Use the map above and your knowledge of the text to analyze how the Allies advanced from several fronts toward Italy and Germany and how the advance from multiple fronts led to the Axis defeat.

14. **Evaluate the Effects of the Navajo Code Talkers** Evaluate how American patriotism inspired exceptional actions by military personnel. Write a paragraph explaining the role Navajo troops played in the Pacific island-hopping campaign during World War II. Explain what was the responsibility of the code talkers and evaluate how the Navajo language was so useful.

15. **Describe the Advancement Through the Pacific Islands** Write a paragraph describing the American strategy for advancing toward Japan. Explain what is meant by "island-hopping", and evaluate the success of the plan.

16. **Explain Turning Points in World War II** Write a paragraph explaining why the bombing of Hiroshima and Nagasaki in August 1945 was a turning point in World War II. Explain the significance of the following dates: August 6, 1945; August 9, 1945; August 14, 1945; and September 2, 1945.

17. **Write About the Essential Question** Write an essay on the Essential Question: When is war justified? Use evidence from your study of this topic to support your answer.

WE MARCH FOR JOBS FOR ALL NOW!

15 Postwar America (1945–1975)

>> Dr. Martin Luther King Jr. and others at the March on Washington in 1963

Enduring Understandings

- After World War II, the United States and the Soviet Union entered the Cold War, a rivalry between East and West that lasted nearly 50 years.

- The United States experienced great economic prosperity and lifestyle changes following World War II.

- The United States became involved in the Korean War to prevent communist expansion, but the war ended in a stalemate.

- Protests and political activities during the Civil Rights movement achieved greater rights for American minorities.

- The Cold War intensified during the Kennedy and Johnson administrations with the Cuban Missile Crisis and the Vietnam War, but calmed slightly during the Nixon administration.

PEARSON realize™   **NBC LEARN**

Watch the My Story Video to learn about the lessons that Minnijean Brown-Trickey teaches her students today about a historical event in which she participated.

PEARSON realize™
www.PearsonRealize.com

Access your digital lessons including:
Topic Inquiry • Interactive Reading
Notepad • Interactivities • Assessments

The Beginning of the Cold War

>> The Berlin Wall was a physical and symbolic barrier between West Berlin and East Germany. Many East Germans were killed trying to escape to the West.

▶ **Interactive Flipped Video**

>> **Objectives**

Explain why the United States took a leadership role in the world after World War II.

Summarize how the Cold War began.

Describe U.S. response to Soviet expansion.

Analyze how the crisis over Berlin led to new Cold War alliances.

Identify the events during 1949 that increased Cold War tensions.

>> **Key Terms**

Cold War
satellite nation
containment
Truman Doctrine
Marshall Plan
Berlin Airlift
Berlin Wall
North Atlantic Treaty
   Organization
Warsaw Pact
United Nations
iron curtain
United Nations

The devastation of World War II left a different world in its wake, leaving only the United States and the Soviet Union strong enough to exert global influence. However, the differences between the two countries led to a new kind of war. They did not clash directly in battle. Instead, they competed for power and influence around the world.

The Causes of the Cold War

This intense rivalry became known as the **Cold War**. It lasted for nearly 50 years. The Cold War pitted the West (the United States and its allies) against the East (the Soviet Union and its allies). The Cold War did not involve an actual armed conflict between the United States and the Soviet Union. However, the rivalry between the two countries led to conflict around the globe. The United States quickly assumed a leadership role in the post-World War II world as it attempted to stop the further spread of communism. Both nations moved to build up their military and weapons.

Distrust on Both Sides During World War II, the United States, Britain, and the Soviet Union had worked together. Yet, even before the war ended, tensions surfaced among the Allies.

The United States and Britain distrusted the Soviet Union. They disliked the communist rejection of religion and private property. They were angered by Soviet efforts to overthrow noncommunist governments. In fact, Soviet leaders boasted that communism would soon destroy free enterprise systems around the world.

The Soviets, in turn, distrusted the Western powers. They feared that the United States, now the world's most powerful nation, would use its military power to attack the Soviet Union. They feared that the United States would try to rebuild Germany in order to challenge the Soviet Union.

The Question of Eastern Europe Before World War II ended, Soviet armies drove German forces out of the Soviet Union and Eastern Europe and back into Germany. As a result, Soviet troops occupied much of Eastern Europe.

Stalin promised to hold free elections "as soon as possible" in these Eastern European nations. He soon broke that promise. "A freely elected government in any of the Eastern European countries would be anti-Soviet," he said, "and that we cannot allow."

By 1948, Communists controlled the government of every Eastern European country. Except for Yugoslavia, these countries became satellite nations of the Soviet Union.

A **satellite nation** is one that is dominated politically and economically by a more powerful nation. In each satellite nation, the Soviets backed harsh dictators. Citizens who protested were imprisoned or killed.

>> Joseph Stalin led the Soviet Union from 1922 to 1953. The Soviet Union was an ally of the United States during World War II, but became a rival.

Communism Gains Ground As early as 1946, the British statesman Winston Churchill had warned against Soviet expansion into Eastern Europe. Naming two cities that were located in the north and south of Europe, he said: "From Stettin in the Baltic to Trieste in the Adriatic, an iron curtain has descended across the Continent." The **iron curtain** cut off Soviet-run Eastern Europe from the democratic governments of the West.

Western fears of communism deepened as communist parties, backed by Stalin, achieved success in other parts of Europe. Italian Communists won many seats in the Italian parliament. In Greece, communist rebels waged a civil war to topple the Greek government. Communist-led unions conducted strikes that paralyzed the weak economies.

? **IDENTIFY CENTRAL ISSUES** What was the basic conflict that fueled the Cold War?

The Aftermath of War

President Harry S. Truman was determined to keep Soviet influence contained within existing boundaries. Thus, his Cold War policy was known as **containment**.

The Truman Doctrine In March 1947, President Truman asked Congress for $400 million in military and economic aid for Greece and Turkey. Eventually, with American aid, both countries held off communist threats.

This program to encourage nations to resist communist expansion became known as the **Truman Doctrine**.

> The free peoples of the world look to us for support in maintaining their freedoms. If we falter in our leadership, we may endanger the peace of the world—and we shall surely endanger the welfare of our own nation.
>
> —Harry Truman, Speech, March 12, 1947

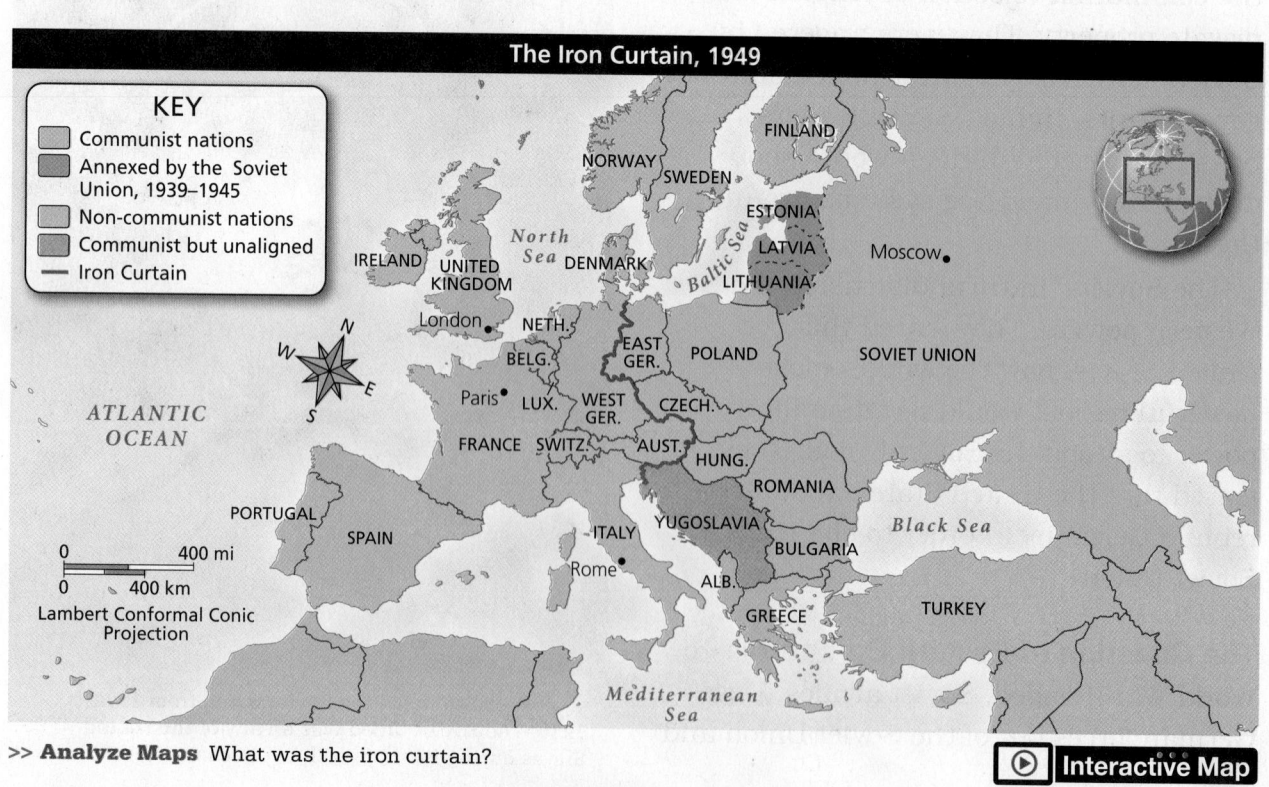

The Iron Curtain, 1949

KEY
- Communist nations
- Annexed by the Soviet Union, 1939–1945
- Non-communist nations
- Communist but unaligned
- Iron Curtain

>> **Analyze Maps** What was the iron curtain?

▶ **Interactive Map**

Germany Divided, 1945–1949

KEY
- Controlled by United States
- Controlled by Britain
- Controlled by France
- Controlled by Soviet Union

>> **Analyze Maps** What problems could occur by dividing the control of Germany and Berlin among four countries?

▶ **Interactive Chart**

The Marshall Plan Other European nations needed aid, too. The war had left Europe's homes, roads, and factories in ruins. When Secretary of State George Marshall toured Europe, he saw millions of homeless, hungry refugees.

Marshall feared that these conditions might encourage communist revolutions. So in June 1947, he proposed an ambitious plan to help Europe rebuild. The President and Congress accepted the **Marshall Plan**.

Between 1948 and 1952, the Marshall Plan provided more than $12 billion in aid to Western European countries. By helping these nations rebuild their economies, the Marshall Plan reduced the threat of communist revolutions in Western Europe.

A Divided City In 1948, a crisis developed in Berlin, Germany's largest city. After the war, the Allies had divided Germany into four zones. American, British, French, and Soviet troops each occupied a zone. Berlin, too, was divided among the four Allies, even though it lay inside the Soviet zone. By 1948, the United States, Britain, and France wanted to reunite their zones in Berlin and the rest of Germany.

Stalin opposed that plan. A reunited Germany, he felt, would again be a threat to the Soviet Union. To show his determination to prevent a united West Germany, Stalin closed all roads, railway lines, and river routes connecting West Berlin with West Germany. The blockade cut off West Berlin from American, British, and French aid.

Sending Supplies to West Berlin President Truman would not let West Berlin fall into Soviet hands. At the same time, he did not want to order American troops to open a path to West Berlin through the Soviet-occupied zone. That move could trigger war.

Instead, Truman approved a huge airlift. During the **Berlin Airlift**, hundreds of American and British planes carried tons of food, fuel, and other supplies to the two million West Berliners every day.

The airlift lasted for almost a year. Stalin finally saw that the West would not abandon West Berlin. In May 1949, he lifted the blockade. After the blockade, the United States, Britain, and France merged their zones in the west into the Federal Republic of Germany, or West Germany. They merged their zones in Berlin to form West Berlin, which was separate from but closely tied to West Germany.

The Berlin Wall Both Germany and Berlin remained divided throughout the 1950s. With American aid, West Germany rebuilt its economy and became a prosperous nation. In time, the Soviet zone became the German Democratic Republic, or East Germany.

East Germany was much poorer than West Germany, and it had a communist government. For years, East Germans fled communism by crossing into West Berlin. The flight of so many people embarrassed the communists.

In 1961, the East German government built a huge concrete wall topped with barbed wire. It sealed off East Germany from West Berlin. East Germans who tried to scale the wall were shot by East German border guards. The **Berlin Wall** cut off contact between families and friends. It became a bitter symbol of the Cold War that divided Europe and the world.

❓ **CHECK UNDERSTANDING** What did the Truman Doctrine and the Marshall Plan have in common?

Postwar Alliances

New military alliances emerged during the Cold War. A world peacekeeping organization was also established.

NATO and the Warsaw Pact To contain Soviet influences, the United States set up alliances with friendly nations. In 1949, it joined with many Western European countries to form the **North Atlantic Treaty Organization** (NATO). A key NATO goal was to defend Western Europe against any Soviet threat.

In 1955, the Soviet Union formed its own military alliance, the **Warsaw Pact**. The Soviet Union dominated its Warsaw Pact neighbors, forcing them to follow its policies.

The United Nations Many disputes were brought before a new world organization,

Post-World War II Military Alliances

NORTH ATLANTIC TREATY ORGANIZATION (1949)	WARSAW PACT MEMBERS (1955)
Belgium, Canada, Denmark, France, Iceland, Italy, Luxembourg, Netherlands, Norway, Portugal, United Kingdom, United States	Soviet Union, Albania, Bulgaria, Czechoslovakia, East Germany, Hungary, Poland, Romania

Source: *Encyclopædia Britannica*

>> **Recall** the nations that were part of the Allied and Axis powers during World War II. What similarities and differences do you notice in the list of NATO and Warsaw Pact members?

the **United Nations** (UN). Fifty-one nations ratified the UN charter in October 1945. Over time, membership in the United Nations expanded as new nations were admitted.

Under the UN charter, member nations agree to bring disputes before the body for peaceful settlement. Every member has a seat in the General Assembly, where problems can be discussed. A smaller Security Council also discusses conflicts that threaten peace.

Over the years, the UN has succeeded best in fighting hunger and disease and in improving education. UN relief programs have provided food, medicine, and supplies to victims of famine, war, and other disasters. Preserving peace has proved more difficult. Some nations have rejected UN resolutions, which are formal recommendations for courses of action. Still, UN negotiators and peacekeeping forces have sometimes eased dangerous crises.

Communist Advancements Until 1949, most Americans felt that they had the upper hand in the Cold War. After all, the United States was the only country with the atomic bomb. Then in September 1949, the United States learned that the Soviet Union had tested an atomic bomb.

A second shock followed. Communist forces, led by Mao Zedong (mow dzuh doong), gained power in China. The United States had long backed the Nationalists, led by Jiang Jieshi (jahng jeh shih), also known as Chiang Kai-shek. After a long civil war, Mao's forces triumphed. In October 1949, Mao set up the People's Republic of China. Jiang and his forces retreated to Taiwan, an island off the coast of China.

Communist leaders in China and the Soviet Union often disagreed with each other. Yet together, the two nations controlled

>> Many organizations delivered aid to countries after World War II. In this 1946 photo, a member of the United Nations Relief and Rehabilitation Administration provides food to hungry children in Greece.

almost a quarter of the globe. Many Americans feared that communism would spread still farther.

? RECALL What happened in 1949 that made Americans doubt their winning position in the Cold War?

ASSESSMENT

1. **Make Generalizations** Explain how the Cold War differed from prior wars.

2. **Support a Point of View with Evidence** Explain why the United States opposed the Soviet Union.

3. **Describe** the purpose of the Berlin Wall and identify its effects.

4. **Generate Explanations** Explain why the United Nations formed, and describe its strengths and weaknesses.

5. **Identify Cause and Effect** Describe the political changes that occurred in China during 1949, and explain how they affected the Cold War.

Korea and Other Postwar Conflicts

>> South Koreans flee south as the Communist North Korean army began its invasion of South Korea in 1950.

▶ Interactive Flipped Video

>> Objectives

Explain why the United States became involved in the conflict in Korea.

Summarize how the fighting in Korea ended.

Explain why the Cold War spread to Africa and other parts of Asia.

Explain why there were hunts for Communists at home and identify the results of the hunts.

>> Key Terms

38th parallel
demilitarized zone
perjury
censure
McCarthyism

Korea is a peninsula in East Asia. Russia and China border it to the north and the west. Japan lies to the east across the Sea of Japan (known in Korea as the East Sea). In the past, these powerful neighbors often competed to control Korea. From 1910 to 1945, Japan ruled Korea as a colony.

War on the Korean Peninsula

A Divided Nation As World War II ended, the United States and the Soviet Union agreed to a temporary division of Korea at the **38th parallel** of latitude. Both nations agreed that Korea would soon be reunited.

As the Cold War deepened, however, Korea remained divided. The United States backed a noncommunist government in South Korea. The Soviet Union supported the Communist government of North Korea. There was no agreement on when, or how, to reunite Korea.

Communist Aggression In June 1950, North Korean troops swept across the 38th parallel into South Korea. This marked the beginning of the Korean War. The South Korean army was quickly overwhelmed.

Within days, North Korean forces occupied Seoul (SOLE), the capital of South Korea.

President Truman responded forcefully to the attack. He asked the United Nations to send a military force to Korea. The UN Security Council voted to set up a force to be commanded by a general chosen by Truman. The President chose General Douglas MacArthur, who had commanded Allied forces in the Pacific during World War II. Although 16 nations joined the UN action in Korea, about 80 percent of the troops were American.

Strategic Advances At first, UN forces were outnumbered and poorly supplied. Armed with new Soviet tanks, the North Koreans pushed steadily southward. They soon occupied almost all of South Korea. MacArthur then launched a daring counterattack by sea. He landed United Nations forces at Inchon behind North

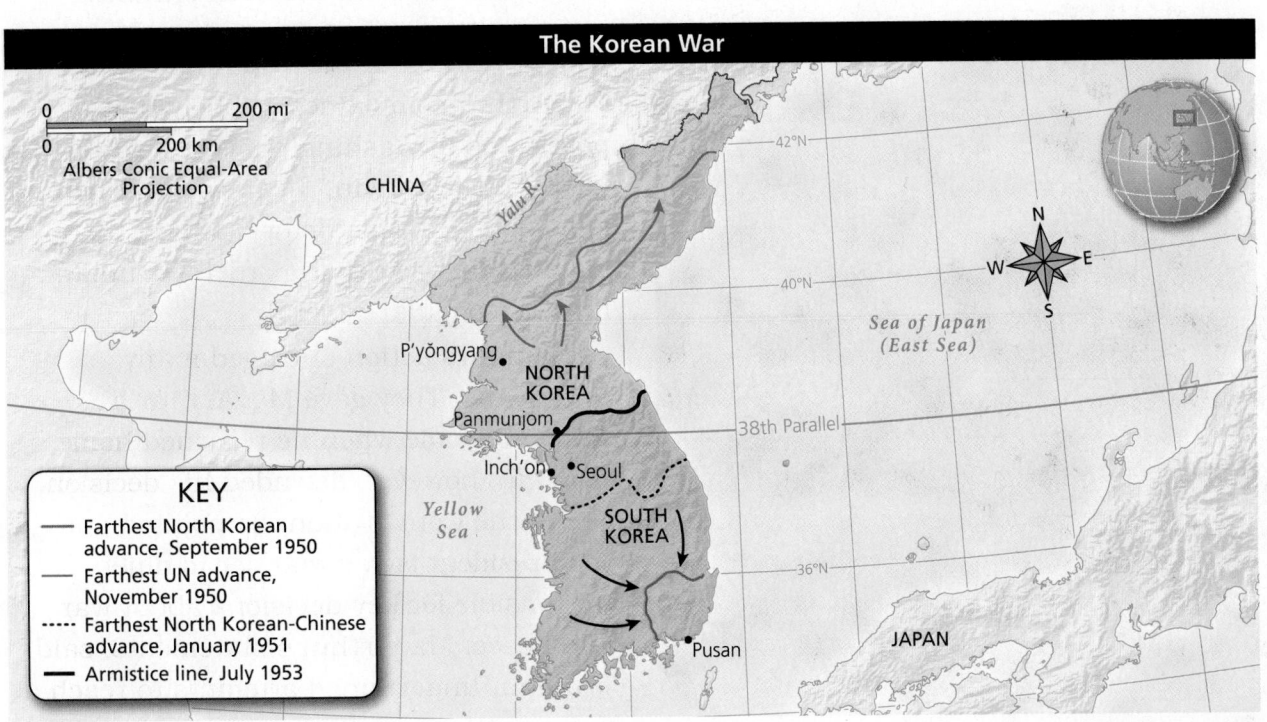

The Korean War

KEY
— Farthest North Korean advance, September 1950
— Farthest UN advance, November 1950
···· Farthest North Korean-Chinese advance, January 1951
▬ Armistice line, July 1953

>> **Analyze Maps** When the North Korean army made its deepest advance into South Korea in September 1950, was the South Korean capital of Seoul behind the enemy's line, or was it still in unoccupied South Korea?

Interactive Map

Korean lines. Caught by surprise, the North Koreans were forced back across the 38th parallel.

MacArthur's original orders called for him only to drive the invaders out of South Korea. Truman and his advisers, however, wanted to punish North Korea for its aggression. They also wanted to unite Korea. With these goals in mind, they won UN approval for MacArthur to cross into North Korea.

China Joins the Fight While MacArthur advanced northward, the Chinese government warned that it would not "sit back with folded hands" if the United States invaded North Korea. As UN forces neared the Chinese border, masses of Chinese troops crossed the Yalu River into North Korea. Communist China perceived the approach of Western forces, presumably there to contain communism,

as a threat to its own security. The Chinese were determined to fight off that threat.

Once again, the fighting seesawed. The Chinese overwhelmed the UN forces, pushing them back deep into South Korea. Then, the UN forces regrouped and pushed the Chinese back into North Korea. By March 1951, UN troops had regained control of the south. The war then turned into a bloody deadlock.

? IDENTIFY What is the best way to summarize American involvement in the Korean War?

The Fighting Ends

During the deadlock, a serious disagreement arose between General MacArthur and President Truman. MacArthur felt that to win the war, UN forces must attack China. Truman feared that an attack on China might lead to a world war. He hoped to limit the war and restore the border between North Korea and South Korea at the 38th parallel.

Disagreement at the Top A frustrated MacArthur complained publicly that politicians in Washington were holding him back. "We must win," he insisted. "There is no substitute for victory." Angry that MacArthur was defying orders, Truman fired the popular general.

Truman's action outraged many Americans. They gave MacArthur a hero's welcome when he returned home. Truman, however, defended his decision. Under the Constitution, he pointed out, the President is commander in chief, responsible for key decisions about war and peace. MacArthur's statements, said Truman, undermined attempts to reach a peace settlement.

>> General Douglas MacArthur (far right), a World War II veteran, assumed command of the UN forces in Korea at President Truman's request.

COSTS OF THE KOREAN WAR

THE HUMAN COST

Casualties

2,500,000	
2,000,000	
1,500,000	
1,000,000	
500,000	
0	

North Korea — 24% civilians
South Korea — 61% civilians
China
U.S. military

Source: *Encyclopædia Britannica*

A COSTLY WAR

United States

China — Includes $1.3 billion loan from Soviet Union

South Korea — Includes $0.5 billion in economic aid from United States

British Commonwealth

= $1 billion

Source: Congressional Research Service; FAS.org; History.navy.mil; *The Korean War*

FAMILIES BECOME SEPARATED

North Korea

South Korea

650,000 people moved from North Korea to South Korea

5,000 divided family members in South Korea allowed to meet relatives living in North Korea since 1953

Source: *Korea's Divided Families: Fifty Years of Separation*

>> **Analyze Graphs** Why do you think the graph shows civilian casualties for North Korea and South Korea but not for China and the United States?

Armistice Peace talks began in mid-1951. At first there was little progress. Meanwhile, the deadly fighting continued.

Republicans nominated Dwight Eisenhower, the popular World War II general, as their presidential candidate in 1952. During the campaign, Eisenhower pledged that if he were elected, he would personally go to Korea. At the same time, he would work to get the stalled peace talks going again.

Eisenhower won the election and visited Korea within a few weeks of his victory. By then, both sides were eager for a cease-fire. The only remaining problem was the return of prisoners of war. After long negotiations, the two sides finally agreed to turn this issue over to an international commission.

Finally, in July 1953, the two sides signed an armistice to end the fighting. It redrew the border between North Korea and South Korea near the 38th parallel, where it had been before the war.

Along the border, it also set up a **demilitarized zone** (DMZ), an area with no military forces. On either side of the DMZ, however, heavily armed troops dug in. They remain there today.

The Costs of the Korean War The human costs of the Korean War were staggering. Well over 30,000 Americans lost their lives in the war zone. Nearly 2 million Koreans and Chinese were also killed.

Politically, the Korean War changed nothing. Korea remained divided. (To this day, relations between North Korea and South Korea remain poor.) On the other hand, UN forces did push back North Korean forces during the war and kept communism out of South Korea. Through this action, the United States and its allies showed that they were ready to fight to prevent Communist expansion.

? DESCRIBE the terms of the Korean War armistice agreement.

A Cold War Around the Globe

The Korean War was not the only conflict resulting from the Cold War. Around the globe, rivalries sprang up between groups backed by the Soviet Union and United States respectively.

A Global Cold War In September 1959, the Soviet leader, Nikita Khrushchev (KROOSH chawf), arrived in New York to address the United Nations. Khrushchev, who had gained power a few years after Stalin died in 1953, spoke calmly at first. He expressed hopes that the Cold

War between the United States and the Soviet Union would end. Then, gradually his manner changed. Twice, he became so angry that he took off his shoe and pounded it on the table.

Khrushchev's trip to the UN symbolized the fact that the Cold War had become global. Although the Cold War had started in Europe, the United States and the Soviet Union now competed for allies and influence among the members of the United Nations.

Struggle for Power Over Colonies For years, many of the nations of Africa and Asia had been governed as colonies of European and other foreign powers. After World War II, many colonial people demanded and won independence. Some achieved independence peacefully. Others had to fight for it.

In the colonies, Communists often joined other groups to fight foreign control. Khrushchev called these struggles "wars of national liberation." Both openly and secretly, the Soviets gave economic and military aid to rebel forces.

The West tried to prevent the Soviets from expanding their influence. In their efforts, American leaders faced difficult choices. Should the United States provide aid to a colonial power? Should Americans use secret aid to counter the Soviets? Should they send troops into another nation to influence its internal affairs? In the end, the United States used all these tactics at one time or another to contain communism.

The Philippines The United States also had to deal with its own colony. In 1946, it withdrew from the Philippines, which it had acquired during the Spanish-American War. Crowds in Manila cheered

>> Soviet leader Nikita Khrushchev addresses the General Assembly at the United Nations in 1959.

Cold War Alliances, 1959

KEY
- United States and allied nations
- Soviet Union and allied nations

>> **Analyze Maps** What patterns can you find on the map regarding allies in Europe and Asia?

Interactive Chart

as the American flag was lowered and the Filipino flag was hoisted high.

Since then, the Philippines has struggled to preserve a democratic government. It has suffered from poverty, local uprisings, and dictatorships. Under the rule of Ferdinand Marcos, who was in power from 1965 to 1986, opposition parties were repressed. In the years that followed, the Philippines struggled to find a stable and honest government.

African Independence During the 1950s and 1960s, more than 30 African nations won freedom from European rule. Both the United States and the Soviet Union sought allies among these new nations.

After independence, some new nations faced civil wars among rival ethnic or tribal groups. Some fought border wars with their neighbors. The superpowers backed opposing sides in these struggles.

As a result, the Cold War turned local conflicts into international crises.

In East Africa, the United States and the Soviet Union took sides in a long war between Somalia and Ethiopia. The United States backed Somalia, while the Soviet Union supported Ethiopia. In southern Africa, the Cold War intensified a civil war in Angola.

South Asian Independence In 1947, India won independence from Britain. The Indian subcontinent was divided into two nations: India and Pakistan. Both the United States and the Soviet Union tried to win the support of these new nations.

Feeling threatened by the Soviet Union to its north, Pakistan became an ally of the United States. India accepted both American and Soviet aid but remained neutral in the Cold War.

French-ruled Indochina included present-day Laos, Cambodia, and Vietnam.

In each country, separate nationalist groups fought for independence. The wars lasted for almost 30 years and eventually drew in the United States, as you will read in Lesson 5.

? CHECK UNDERSTANDING How did the freedom of former colonies in Africa and Asia impact the Cold War?

Concern about Communism at Home

For many Americans, the Korean War increased worries about Communists at home. Communist sympathizers and spies, they feared, might be secretly working to overthrow the government. These concerns helped spark a hunt for Communists within American society.

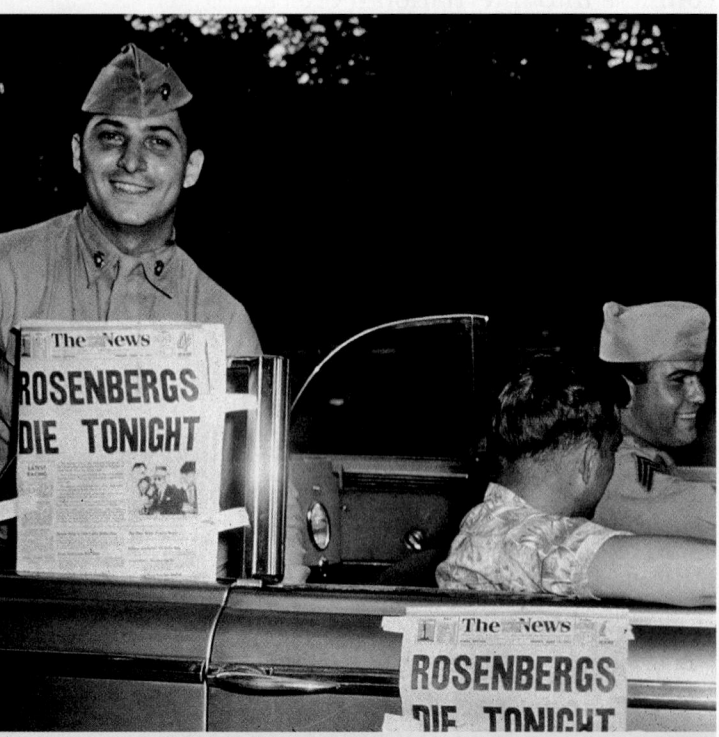

>> In 1953, some Americans celebrated the execution of Julius and Ethel Rosenberg—two Americans charged as spies working for the Soviets. **Generate Explanations** What does this say about the atmosphere in the United States in the 1950s?

During the Great Depression, some Americans had turned against democracy and free enterprise. They had rejected the efforts of the New Deal as ineffective. To them, communism offered the only solution to the nation's deep economic troubles. In time, however, many American Communists recognized that Soviet leader Joseph Stalin was a brutal dictator, and they left the party.

Hunting Spies Still, some remained avid Communists. Between 1946 and 1950, several people in the United States, Canada, and Britain were arrested as Soviet spies. In the United States, Ethel and Julius Rosenberg were sentenced to death for passing atomic secrets to the Soviets. Despite protests, both were executed in 1953. The Rosenberg case made many Americans wonder if other Soviet spies were living among them as ordinary citizens.

Americans also worried that there were Communists in high government positions. In 1950, Alger Hiss, a State Department official, was imprisoned for **perjury**, or lying under oath. Hiss had denied that he was part of a Soviet spy ring. Later evidence would suggest that Hiss and several other high government officials were passing secrets to the Soviet Union. It would also make it clear that Julius Rosenberg had indeed passed atomic secrets to the Soviets.

In 1947, President Truman ordered investigations of government workers to determine if they were loyal to the United States. Thousands of government employees were questioned. Some people were forced to resign. Many of those had done nothing disloyal to the United States.

The Second Red Scare

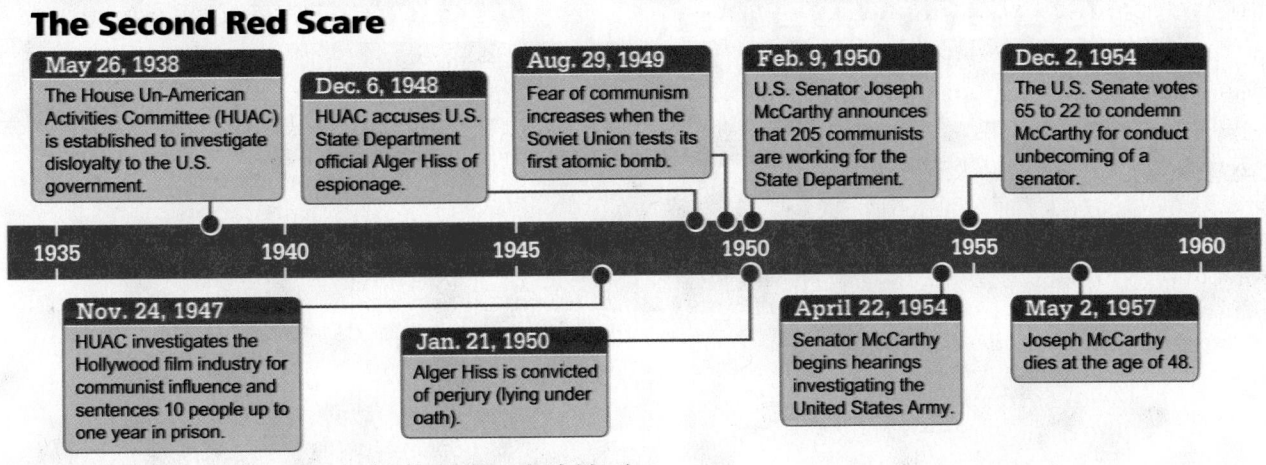

May 26, 1938
The House Un-American Activities Committee (HUAC) is established to investigate disloyalty to the U.S. government.

Dec. 6, 1948
HUAC accuses U.S. State Department official Alger Hiss of espionage.

Aug. 29, 1949
Fear of communism increases when the Soviet Union tests its first atomic bomb.

Feb. 9, 1950
U.S. Senator Joseph McCarthy announces that 205 communists are working for the State Department.

Dec. 2, 1954
The U.S. Senate votes 65 to 22 to condemn McCarthy for conduct unbecoming of a senator.

1935   1940   1945   1950   1955   1960

Nov. 24, 1947
HUAC investigates the Hollywood film industry for communist influence and sentences 10 people up to one year in prison.

Jan. 21, 1950
Alger Hiss is convicted of perjury (lying under oath).

April 22, 1954
Senator McCarthy begins hearings investigating the United States Army.

May 2, 1957
Joseph McCarthy dies at the age of 48.

Sources: *Encyclopædia Britannica*; U.S. National Archives and Records Administration

>> **Analyze Graphs** After McCarthy's censure, do you think the fear of communism in the United States faded permanently?

The McCarthy Era In 1950, Senator Joseph McCarthy of Wisconsin made a shocking announcement. He claimed to have a list of 205 State Department employees who were Communist party members. McCarthy was never able to prove his claims. Yet, McCarthy's dramatic charges won him national attention.

During the next four years, McCarthy's campaign spread suspicion across the nation. Businesses and colleges questioned employees. Many people were fired. The term **McCarthyism** came to be known as the use of reckless charges of disloyalty.

In 1954, the Senate held televised hearings to investigate a new McCarthy charge. He insisted that there were Communists in the United States Army. This time, McCarthy had gone too far. On national television, he came across as a bully, not a hero. His popularity plunged.

In December 1954, the Senate passed a resolution to **censure**, or officially condemn, McCarthy for "conduct unbecoming a member." As a result, McCarthy lost much of his support. By the time he died three years later, the Communist scare was mostly over.

? CHECK UNDERSTANDING How does the Rosenberg case demonstrate American attitudes toward communism during the Cold War?

ASSESSMENT

1. **Compare and Contrast** the viewpoints of General MacArthur and President Truman during the Korean War.

2. **Describe** the outcome of the Korean War.

3. **Generate Explanations** Explain how the Cold War turned regional conflicts into international crises around the world.

4. **Identify Central Issues** Describe the hunt for Communists that occurred within the United States.

5. **Identify Cause and Effect** Explain why Senator McCarthy eventually lost public support.

Eisenhower and Postwar America

>> As television brought entertainment to Americans in their homes, other entertainment industries felt threatened. The rise of television contributed to a sharp decline in movie-theater attendance in the 1950s.

▶ **Interactive Flipped Video**

>> Objectives

Discuss postwar problems in America.

Identify the factors that contributed to the economic and baby booms of the 1950s.

Explain how American lifestyles changed in the 1950s.

>> Key Terms

inflation
baby boom
productivity
standard of living
suburb
beatnik
Fair Deal
Sunbelt
GI Bill of Rights

In the decades after World War II, the United States experienced a boom like no other in its history. The population mushroomed, the economy prospered, and Americans enjoyed the highest standard of living any people had ever known.

Postwar Prosperity

When the war ended in 1945, two thirds of all American men between the ages of 18 and 34 were in uniform. Experts feared that without wartime production, many returning soldiers might not find jobs. Unemployment would rise, and the economy would tumble.

Addressing Economic Issues Even before the war ended, Congress passed the **GI Bill of Rights** to help returning veterans. Under this law, the government spent billions of dollars to help veterans set up farms and businesses. Many GIs received loans to pay for college or a new home. It also provided a full year of unemployment benefits for veterans who could not find work.

Inflation, or rising prices, was a major postwar problem. During the war, the government had controlled prices and wages. After the war, the controls ended. The price of goods rose. Workers demanded higher wages to pay for the price increases. When employers refused, labor unions called strikes. President Harry Truman was sympathetic to workers but feared that higher wages would only add to inflation. He urged strikers to return to work.

The Election of 1948 As the election of 1948 approached, President Truman and his Democratic party seemed doomed to defeat. Labor strikes and soaring prices had already helped Republicans win a majority in both the House and the Senate for the first time since the 1920s. Among Democrats, unhappy liberals and conservatives deserted Truman to form parties of their own. The Republicans confidently nominated Governor Thomas Dewey of New York for President.

Truman fought back. During his campaign, Truman traveled thousands of miles across the country by train. At every stop, he attacked the Republicans as "do-nothings" and "gluttons of privilege." When all the votes were counted, Truman won a surprise victory over Dewey.

The Fair Deal During his presidency, Truman proposed a new round of reform called the **Fair Deal**. He wanted to extend the liberal policies of his predecessor, Franklin D. Roosevelt.

In Congress, the Fair Deal faced heavy opposition from conservative Democrats and Republicans. Only a few of the proposals passed: a higher minimum wage, expanded Social Security benefits, and loans for buying low-cost houses. Congress rejected most of Truman's

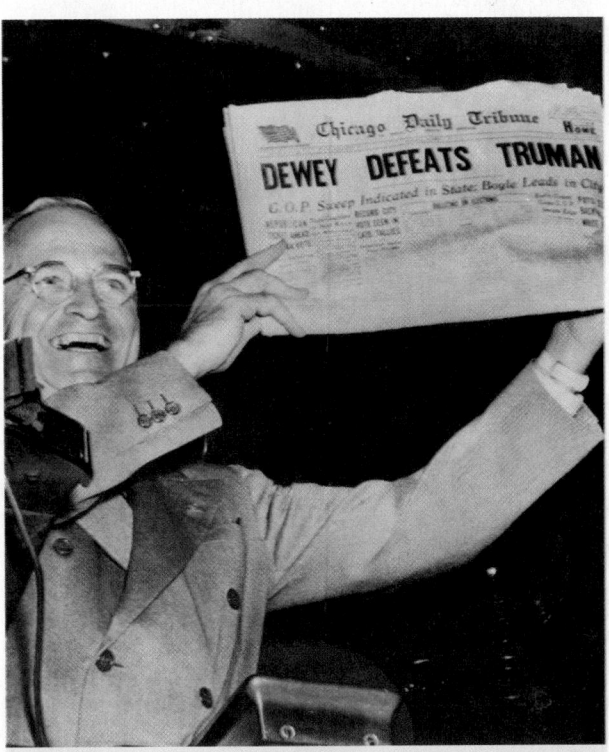

>> On November 3, 1948, Truman displayed the front page of the *Chicago Daily Tribune,* which incorrectly predicted his defeat by Republican Thomas E. Dewey. Although the odds were against him, Truman was elected back into office.

reforms, including a bold plan to provide government-financed health insurance.

A Moderate Takes Office In 1952, President Truman chose not to run for reelection. Democrats nominated Adlai Stevenson of Illinois. Republicans chose General Dwight D. Eisenhower, a hero of World War II. Eisenhower, known as "Ike," promised to end the conflict in Korea and lead Americans through the Cold War.

For the first time, television played a major role in a presidential campaign. Instead of long speeches, Republicans used 20-second TV "spots" of Ike responding to questions from hand-picked citizens. Complained one critic: "It was selling the President like toothpaste." Still, enough voters were impressed with Ike's military experience and foreign policy skills to give him a landslide victory.

>> The end of the war and the nation's newfound prosperity prompted many young Americans to start families. The result was a "baby boom" that significantly increased the U.S. population in the 1940s and 1950s.

▶ **Interactive Illustration**

Like most Republicans, President Eisenhower believed in limiting federal spending and reducing federal regulation of the economy. He called his political course the "straight road down the middle."

He favored cutting the federal budget but expanding Social Security benefits and some other New Deal programs. Most Americans supported Eisenhower's middle-of-the-road approach. In the 1956 presidential election, voters reelected Ike to a second term of office.

Baby Boom During the Great Depression and World War II, many Americans had put off having families. When the war ended and prosperity returned, the number of births soared.

Population experts called the phenomenon a **baby boom**. In the 1930s, the population of the United States had grown by only 9 million. In the 1940s it grew by 19 million and in the 1950s by an astounding 29 million! Most couples married young, had an average of three children, and completed their families by their late twenties.

Improvements in health care and nutrition contributed to the baby boom. Better care for pregnant women and newborn infants meant that more babies survived. Fewer children died from childhood diseases than had died in the past.

Prosperity Abounds In addition to the baby boom, there was an economic boom. The economy rapidly expanded in the postwar years. When an economy expands, more goods are produced and sold and more jobs are created.

Federal projects also increased factory production. The government spent more money to build new roads, houses, and

Homeownership, 1940–1960

*Estimated
†The first year for which Hawaii and Alaska are included
Source: *Historical Statistics of the United States*

>> **Analyze Graphs** Explain how the data on homeownership relates to standard of living.

schools. In the middle of the Cold War, government spending on military goods spurred the economy, too.

New technology added to the boom by promoting steady rises in **productivity**, or the average output per worker. Corporations began using computers to perform calculations and keep records.

High productivity allowed the United States to manufacture and consume, or use, more goods than any other country. Increased productivity also led to a workweek that averaged 40 hours. Americans now had more leisure time.

The good feeling produced by victory in World War II and the booming economy created a sense of public confidence in the United States. American citizens enjoyed a postwar prosperity that saw significant job growth throughout much of the nation.

? **LIST** factors that contributed to public confidence in the postwar United States.

Life in the 1950s

The economic boom raised Americans' **standard of living**, a measurement that determines how well people live based on the amount of goods, services, and leisure time people have. Americans bought washing machines, vacuum cleaners, televisions, automobiles, and many other consumer goods.

Public confidence in the United States replaced much of the financial worries associated with the Great Depression and World War II. Because so many of their purchases revolved around home and family, few Americans worried that they were saving little. Instead, most Americans enjoyed a life in which they had more money to spend. This consumer spending reshaped the country.

The New Suburbs With their newfound wealth, many people bought homes in the **suburbs**, or communities outside the cities.

The GI Bill encouraged home building in the suburbs by offering low-interest loans to veterans. During the 1950s, suburbs grew 40 times faster than cities.

Builder William Levitt pioneered a new way of building suburban houses. He bought large tracts of land and then divided them into small lots.

On each lot, he built a house identical to every other house in the tract. Because these houses were mass-produced, they cost much less to build than custom-made houses. They could also be constructed rapidly. Using preassembled materials, teams of carpenters, plumbers, and electricians could put up a Levitt house in 16 minutes.

Levitt began his first big project in 1947 on Long Island, where he put up 17,000 new homes. It was the largest housing development ever built by an American.

Levitt called the project Levittown. African Americans were barred from owning or renting in Levittown. Levitt feared that if he sold to blacks, whites would not buy.

Shopping centers with modern department stores sprang up near the suburban housing developments. There were eight shopping centers in 1946. By the end of the 1950s, there were 4,000. No longer did consumers have to travel to the city to buy what they wanted. Shiny new shopping centers were only a short drive away.

As millions flocked to the suburbs, central cities began a slow decline. Suburbs and shopping centers drained cities of businesses and taxes. Since most of those who moved were white, some critics complained that the United States was turning into a nation where African Americans lived in cities and whites lived in the suburbs.

>> Construction of new homes in the suburbs surged in the years after World War II. **Analyze Information** Why do you think more people chose to live in the suburbs?

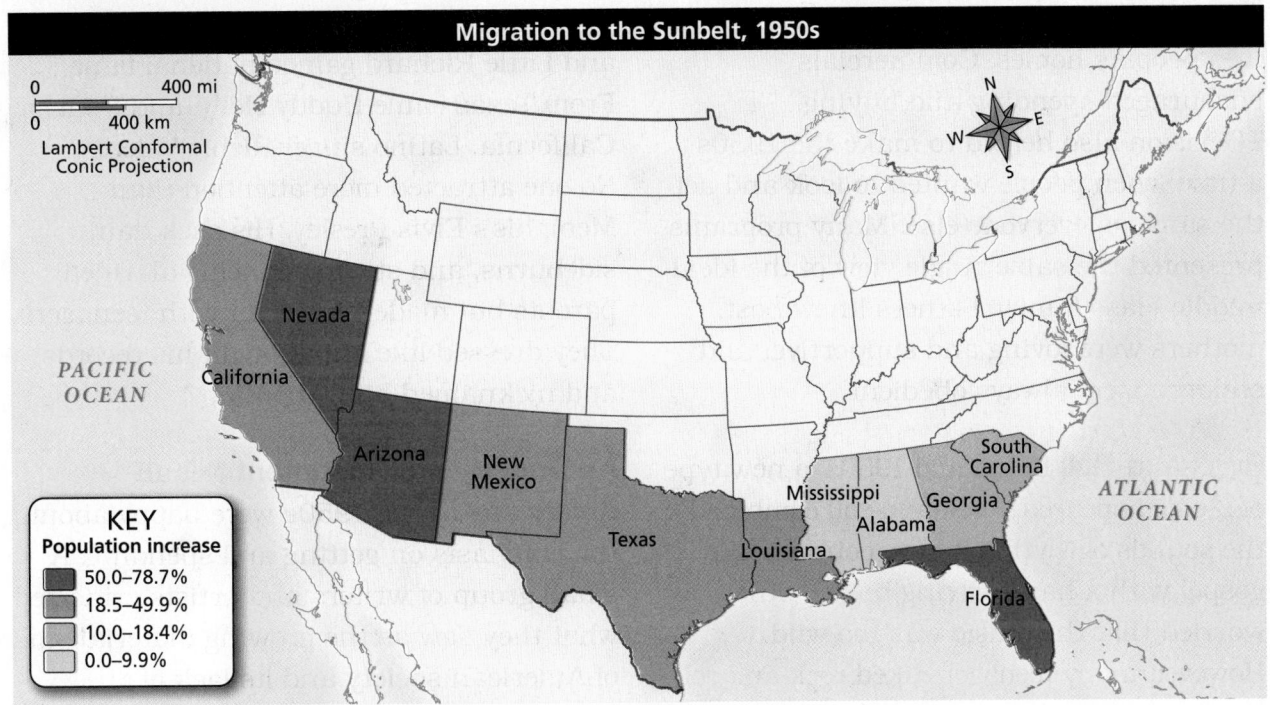

0   400 mi

0   400 km

Lambert Conformal
Conic Projection

PACIFIC
OCEAN

ATLANTIC
OCEAN

KEY
Population increase
- 50.0–78.7%
- 18.5–49.9%
- 10.0–18.4%
- 0.0–9.9%

Nevada

California

Arizona

New
Mexico

Texas

Louisiana

Mississippi

Alabama

Georgia

South
Carolina

Florida

>> **Analyze Maps** Why do you think these states were called the "Sunbelt"?

Moving South Americans also flocked to the **Sunbelt**, a region stretching across the southern rim of the country. States from Florida to Texas and California began to experience dramatic growth.

For Americans on the move, the Sunbelt, both then and now, had many lures: a warm climate; good jobs; a prosperous economy based on agriculture, oil, and electronics; and, national defense industries. Businesses still move to the region for its low taxes and growing workforce. The workforce included recent immigrants from Latin America and Asia. Like many ambitious newcomers, they were willing to work hard to establish new lives in the United States.

Taking to the Road During the 1950s, cars became more important to daily life. People living in the suburbs or the Sunbelt usually needed a car to drive to work. By 1960, 9 out of 10 families living in the suburbs owned a car. Since few people bought foreign cars, the American automobile companies, such as General Motors, profited greatly.

To accommodate the increase in automobiles, the federal government built thousands of miles of highways. In 1956, Congress passed the Federal-Aid Highway Act. This act called for a network of high-speed roads linking the nation. It set aside $41 billion to build 40,000 miles of highway.

The new highway system boosted the economy, especially the automobile and trucking industries. Americans could travel more easily for business or pleasure. As a result, a new roadside culture of motels and fast-food restaurants emerged.

Home Entertainment Television caught on slowly. At first, television screens displayed only in black and white, and they were very expensive. However, as TV sets shrank in price and grew in size, almost everybody wanted one. By 1960, 9 out of 10 households had at least 1 television.

Television brought news and entertainment into people's homes. Commercials encouraged spending and buying. Television also helped to make the 1950s a time when people wanted to look and act the same as everyone else. Many programs presented the same single view of the ideal middle-class family. Fathers knew best, mothers were loving and supportive, and children were always obedient.

Rock-and-Roll In the mid-1950s, a new type of music appeared. Rock-and-roll combined the sounds of rhythm, blues, country, and gospel with a hard-driving beat. Adults worried that the music was too wild. However, many teenagers liked rock-and-roll because it provided an opportunity for them to show their independence. *Teenager* was a word first used in the 1950s to describe someone between 13 and 19 years old.

>> A new style of music called rock-and-roll combined elements of country and blues and took the nation by storm in the 1950s. Elvis Presley was the biggest rock star of the era. **Infer** Why did some parents see rock-and-roll and stars like Elvis as a bad influence?

[▶] **Interactive Gallery**

African American singers Chuck Berry and Little Richard gained national fame. From Texas came Buddy Holly, and from California, Latino singer Richie Valens. No one attracted more attention than Memphis's Elvis Presley. His slick hair, sideburns, and steamy dancing alarmed parents but made Elvis a hit with teenagers. They dressed like him, bought his records, and nicknamed him "the King."

An Underlying Discontent Not all Americans in the 1950s were happy about the emphasis on getting and spending. A small group of writers and artists criticized what they saw as the growing materialism of American society and its lack of individuality. Novelist Jack Kerouac coined the term *beat*, meaning "weariness with all forms of the modern industrial state." Middle-class observers called Kerouac and others like him **beatniks**. Still, Kerouac's best-selling novel, *On the Road*, influenced many young Americans.

Most Americans paid little attention to these signs of discontent. Soon, however, a growing outcry could not be ignored.

[?] **CHECK UNDERSTANDING** How did the increase in the popularity of cars affect the United States?

ASSESSMENT

1. **Compare and Contrast** the policies of President Truman and President Eisenhower.

2. **Identify Cause and Effect** Describe the factors that contributed to the baby boom.

3. **Draw Conclusions** Explain how the average standard of living in the United States changed after World War II.

4. **Describe** William Levitt's contribution to suburban development.

5. **Generate Explanations** Explain how automobiles changed the lifestyles of many Americans.

>> Rosa Parks is shown in 1955, seated near the front of a Montgomery, Alabama, bus, an area usually reserved for white people.

[▶] Interactive Flipped Video

From the late 1940s to the 1970s, the United States witnessed profound changes in civil rights. Mass protests and coordinated demonstrations made it clear that discrimination against minorities would no longer be tolerated. But full equality would take time, and the struggle to get there would often be brutal.

>> Objectives

Explain how discrimination affected the lives of minorities in the United States.

Summarize how the courts, protests, and boycotts helped minority groups achieve greater rights.

Describe the role of Martin Luther King, Jr., in the Civil Rights Movement.

Compare how different groups tried to achieve equal rights.

>> Key Terms

segregation
integration
Civil Rights
  Movement
boycott
civil disobedience
sit-in
affirmative action
migrant worker
bilingual
Dr. Martin Luther
  King, Jr.
César Chávez

PEARSON
realize™ www.PearsonRealize.com
Access your Digital Lesson.

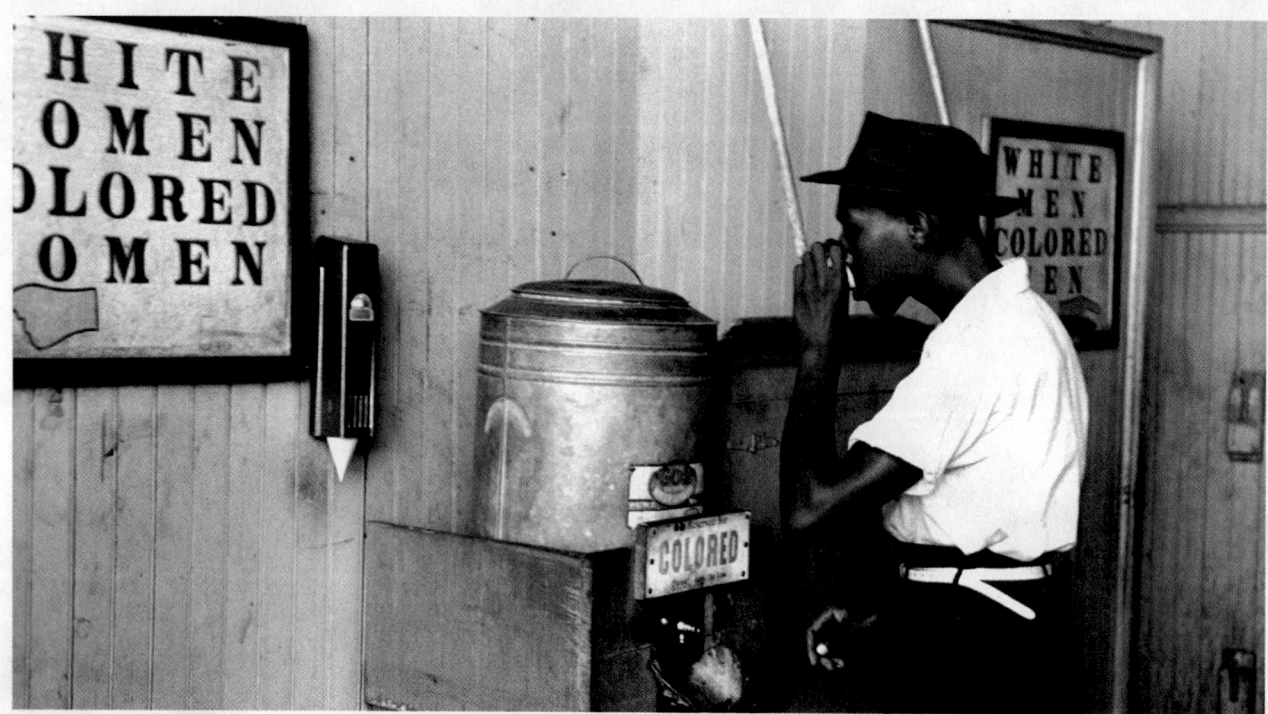

>> Racial discrimination took on many forms. African Americans were forced to use segregated bathrooms and water coolers as seen in this 1939 photo.

Discrimination Continues

Discrimination Against African Americans and Mexican Americans

Throughout the nation, discrimination limited the lives of millions of Americans. Qualified African Americans found themselves barred from good jobs and decent housing in the North. In the South, laws enforced strict **segregation**, or separation, of the races in schools, theaters, restaurants, and other public places. Facilities for blacks were inferior to those for whites.

Discrimination also limited Mexican Americans and other Latinos. They were not subject to strict segregation laws. However, other laws—as well as traditions—worked against them. In the Southwest, all-white schools closed their doors to Mexican American children. Instead, poorly equipped "Mexican schools" served them. Custom kept Mexican Americans from living in certain neighborhoods or using certain hotels or restaurants. Often, better-paying jobs were not open to them.

Fighting Segregation

For African Americans, the NAACP (National Association for the Advancement of Colored People) led the drive against discrimination. During World War II, NAACP membership rocketed from 50,000 to 500,000. Under Thurgood Marshall, its Legal Defense Fund mounted several court battles against segregation. It also helped blacks register to vote and fought for equal opportunity in housing and employment.

Legal Integration

There were two significant events in the 1940s in the fight against segregation. Jackie Robinson broke the color barrier in Major League Baseball in 1947 when he joined the Brooklyn Dodgers. He was even named rookie of the year. Not since Moses Fleetwood Walker had a black player joined the major leagues. Walker was the first African American player to join a major league team in 1884.

Under pressure from civil rights groups, President Truman ordered **integration**, or the mixing of different racial groups, in the armed forces in 1948. During the Korean War, black and white soldiers fought side by side.

After risking their lives abroad, veterans were unwilling to accept discrimination at home. Often they became leaders in the struggle for equal rights. "Veterans," explained an observer, "have acquired a new courage, and have become more vocal in protesting inequalities."

? DEFINE What did segregation suggest about American society at this time?

The Legal Struggle for Equality

During the 1950s, African Americans and Mexican Americans stepped up the struggle for equality. They took their cases to court but also protested in the streets. Their efforts became known as the **Civil Rights Movement**.

Equal Educational Opportunities The U.S. Supreme Court had decided in 1896 in *Plessy* v. *Ferguson* that "separate but equal" facilities for blacks and whites were constitutional. During the 1940s, the NAACP did not attack this idea head on. Instead, its lawyers argued that schools for African American students were not equal to white schools.

Such a legal strategy might improve black schools and other segregated facilities case by case, but those cases

did little to end segregation. By the early 1950s, laws in 21 states and the District of Columbia still enforced separate black and white public schools. Virtually all of the black schools were inferior to the white ones.

Oliver Brown of Topeka, Kansas, decided to challenge the Kansas school segregation law. He asked the local school board to let his daughter, Linda, attend a nearby white school rather than the distant black school to which she had been assigned. When board members refused, Brown filed a suit against the school board with the help of the NAACP. The case of *Brown* v. *Board of Education of Topeka* reached the Supreme Court.

To present the case in court, Brown hired lawyer Thurgood Marshall, who specialized in civil rights cases. Marshall

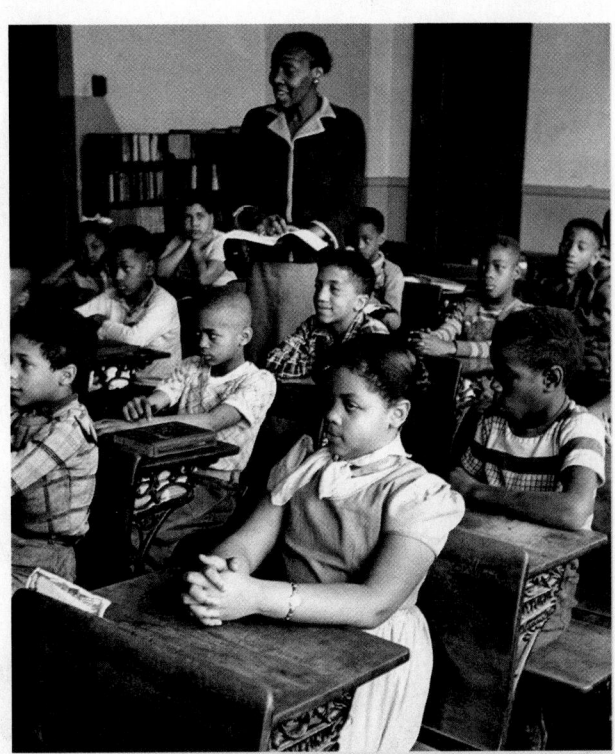

>> This photo shows student Linda Brown (front, center) in her segregated class in 1953. Brown's family sued the local school board to allow her to attend a different, all-white school. The case eventually went to the U.S. Supreme Court.

had served as legal director of the NAACP for more than ten years. He decided to challenge the whole idea of "separate but equal." Segregated schools, he argued, could never provide equal education. By their very nature, said Marshall, segregated schools violated the Fourteenth Amendment, which gave "equal protection" to all citizens.

The Supreme Court ruled in Brown's favor in 1954. Chief Justice Earl Warren noted that segregation affected the "hearts and minds" of black students "in a way unlikely ever to be undone."

> We conclude that in the field of public education, the doctrine of 'separate but equal' has no place. Separate educational facilities are always unequal.
>
> —Chief Justice Earl Warren, *Brown v. Board of Education of Topeka*

Desegregating Schools A year later, the Court ordered the schools to be desegregated "with all deliberate speed." In a few places, schools were integrated without much trouble. In many others, officials resisted. White politicians in these places decided that the phrase "with all deliberate speed" could mean they could take years to integrate their schools. Or, perhaps they would never obey the decision.

Arkansas Governor Orval Faubus called out the National Guard in 1957 in order to keep African American students from attending the all-white Central High School in Little Rock. President Eisenhower finally sent in federal troops because the Arkansas governor was defying a federal court order. Under their protection, black students entered Central High.

Eisenhower was the first President since Reconstruction to use armed troops in

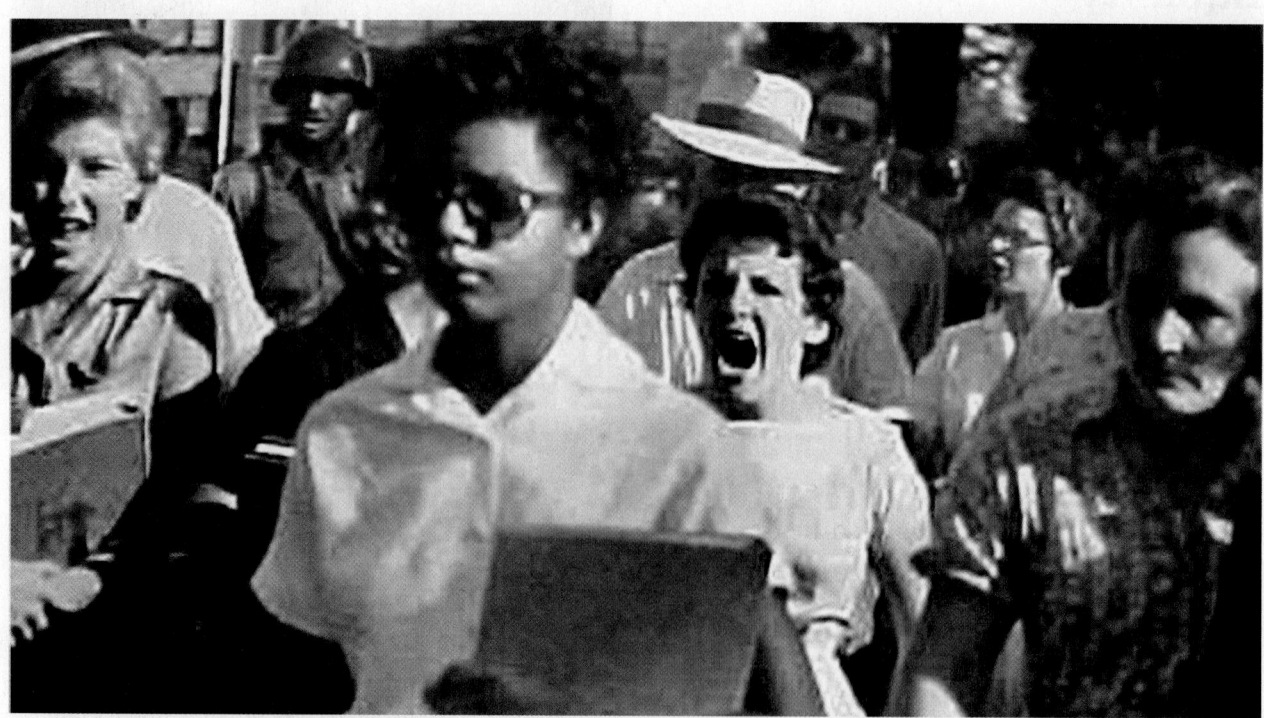

>> Elizabeth Eckford (front) makes her way into Little Rock High School on September 4, 1957, as white protesters taunt her. **Deduce** What does this photo reveal about Americans' attitudes toward desegregation in the 1950s?

Civil Rights and the Supreme Court

CASE	YEAR	SUMMARY
Brown v. Board of Education	1954	Ruled that racial segregation in public schools violated the Fourteenth Amendment; reversed the *Plessy* v. *Ferguson* ruling of 1896
Hernández v. Texas	1954	Ruled that discrimination based on class violated the Fourteenth Amendment, which guaranteed equal protection
Boynton v. Virginia	1960	Ruled that segregation of passengers on buses traveling across interstate lines was unconstitutional
Heart of Atlanta Motel, Inc. v. United States	1964	Ruled that refusing to rent rooms to African Americans was a violation of the Civil Rights Act of 1964, which prohibited racial discrimination in public places
Loving v. Virginia	1967	Ruled that state laws prohibiting interracial marriage were unconstitutional, forcing 16 states to revise their laws

Sources: *Encyclopædia Britannica;* United States Department of Education; City of Norman; National Criminal Justice Reference Service

>> This table lists selected important Supreme Court rulings that advanced civil rights in the United States. **Summarize** the purpose of bringing civil rights cases to the Supreme Court.

support of African American rights. The action showed that the federal government could play a key role in protecting civil rights.

A Jury of Peers Mexican Americans organized their own fight for civil rights. Mexican American veterans founded the American GI Forum of the United States (AGIF) in 1948 in order to campaign for equal rights. Similar to the NAACP, the AGIF supported legal challenges to discrimination.

In 1954, the same year as *Brown* v. *Board of Education*, Mexican Americans won an important legal battle when the Supreme Court ruled on the case of *Hernández* v. *Texas*.

Pete Hernández, a Mexican American, had been convicted of murder by an all-white jury in Texas. Among the lawyers who appealed his conviction was Gus Garcia, one of the leaders of the AGIF. Attorney James DeAnda, another Mexican

American, also helped. He had previously worked to desegregate areas of Corpus Christi, Texas, where Mexican Americans were not allowed to buy houses.

Hernández's lawyers argued that Mexican Americans in Texas were denied equality under the law because they were excluded from juries. The Supreme Court agreed. It overturned the conviction and ended the exclusion of Mexican Americans from Texas juries. In the future, other minority groups would use this decision to help win their civil rights.

? IDENTIFY CENTRAL IDEAS Why would a state governor refuse to follow a court order such as Orval Faubus did after the ruling of *Brown v. Board of Education?*

The Montgomery Bus Boycott

Court cases were not enough to end discrimination, as Rosa Parks discovered in December 1955. She was riding home from work on a crowded bus in Montgomery, Alabama. The driver ordered her to move to the back of the bus so that a white man could have her seat, as Alabama's segregation laws required. Parks, a well-known activist and a former secretary of the local chapter of the NAACP, refused to leave her seat. She was arrested and put in jail.

Rosa Parks's arrest angered African Americans in Montgomery. That night, several women from the NAACP composed a letter asking all African Americans to **boycott**, or refuse to use, the buses. The boycott, they hoped, would hurt the city financially and force an end to segregation on the buses. The women distributed thousands of copies of the letter to the African Americans in Montgomery.

To support the protest, Montgomery's black leaders formed a new organization, the Montgomery Improvement Association

(MIA). They chose **Dr. Martin Luther King, Jr.**, a Baptist minister, as its head.

Dr. King spoke at a meeting in the Holt Street Baptist Church. Hundreds packed the church. Thousands more stood outside. "We are here this evening . . . for serious business," King began. "Yes, yes!" the crowd shouted.

> You know, my friends, there comes a time when people get tired of being trampled over by the iron feet of oppression. . . . We are determined here in Montgomery . . . to work and fight until justice runs down like water, and righteousness like a mighty stream!
>
> —Martin Luther King, Jr., Speech, December 2, 1955

By December 5, 1955, most African Americans in Montgomery refused to travel by bus.

Civil Disobedience The boycott lasted from December 5 to December 20 of the next year. MIA carpools took some 20,000 African Americans to and from work each day. Many people simply walked. One elderly woman coined a phrase that became a motto of the boycott: "My feets is tired, but my soul is rested."

Angry whites fought back. Employers threatened to fire African Americans if they did not abandon the boycott. Police handed out traffic tickets to harass boycotters, and they frequently stopped African American drivers and demanded to see their licenses. They arrested King for speeding and kept him in jail for several days. King's house was bombed. Still, the boycott continued.

King insisted that his followers limit their actions to **civil disobedience**, or nonviolent protests against unjust laws. He said, "We must use the weapon of love. We must have compassion and understanding for those who hate us."

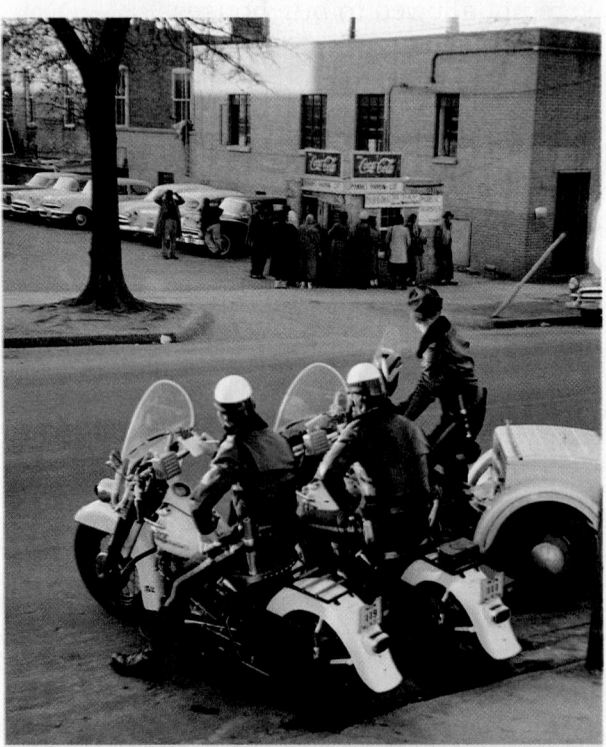

>> African Americans in Montgomery, Alabama, used carpools as a way to avoid taking buses during the boycott of 1955-56. Police are shown monitoring a group of African Americans waiting for a carpool lift.

Throughout the bus boycott, African American churches were vital to its success. Churches played a central role in the lives of African Americans across the country. In Montgomery, mass meetings were held in black churches. There, boycotters sang together, prayed together, and listened to stories of sacrifice. The churches kept morale high, provided leadership, and helped boycotters give each other courage and inspiration.

Finally, the MIA filed a federal lawsuit to end bus segregation in Montgomery. In 1956, almost a year after Rosa Parks had refused to move to the back of the bus, the Supreme Court ruled that segregation on Alabama buses was unconstitutional. The Montgomery bus company agreed to integrate the buses and to hire African American bus drivers.

Gaining National Attention The effects of the bus boycott reached far beyond Montgomery. The boycott brought national attention to the Civil Rights Movement. It launched nonviolent protest as a key tactic in the struggle for equality. Finally, the boycott introduced the nation to a new generation of African American leaders. Many were ministers from African American churches.

A Strong Leader One of the most important of these new national figures was boycott leader Martin Luther King, Jr. He was the son of a prominent Baptist minister. King had graduated from Morehouse College, a leading African American college. Later, he had earned a Ph.D. in religion and served as pastor of an African American church in Montgomery.

King had studied a wide range of philosophers and political thinkers. He had come to admire especially Mohandas

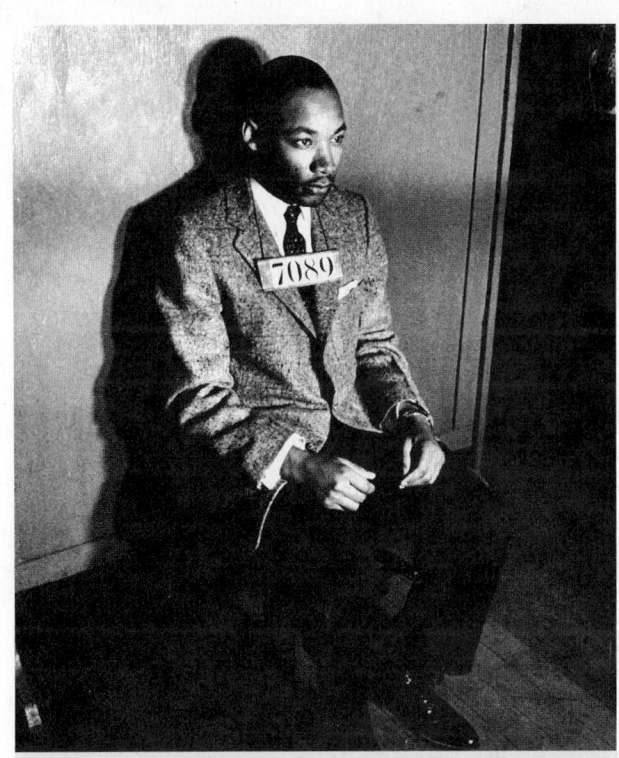

>> Martin Luther King, Jr., was arrested during the bus boycott in Alabama in the mid-1950s. A Baptist minister and civil rights activist, King promoted social change through peaceful means.

▶ **Interactive Illustration**

Gandhi, a political leader who had pioneered the use of nonviolence to end British rule in India.

Following the Montgomery victory, King and other African American leaders founded the Southern Christian Leadership Conference (SCLC) to carry on the crusade for civil rights. The group, consisting of nearly one hundred black ministers, elected King president and the Reverend Ralph Abernathy treasurer. The SCLC urged African Americans to fight injustice by using civil disobedience.

Understand that nonviolence is not a symbol of weakness or cowardice, but as . . . demonstrated, nonviolent resistance transforms weakness into strength and breeds courage in the face of danger.

— SCLC statement, January 10–11, 1957

Still, discrimination and segregation remained widespread. The Civil Rights Movement of the 1950s would soon grow into a howling wind of protest that would sweep across the country.

❓ **DEFINE** What makes civil disobedience an effective form of protest?

The Crusade for Equality Continues

In 1963, Anne Moody was a senior in college when she and two friends sat down at a "whites-only" lunch counter in Jackson, Mississippi. The waitress told them to move to the black section. Anne and her friends, all African Americans, stayed put. "We would like to be served," Anne said politely.

>> During this 1960 sit-in in Norfolk, Virginia, African American customers sit at a lunch counter, but the white waitresses turn their backs and refuse to serve them.

A crowd of whites pulled Anne and her friends from their seats. They beat one of Anne's friends, who was promptly arrested. When Anne and her other friend returned to their seats, they were joined by a white woman from her school. "Now there were three of us," Anne recalled, "and we were integrated." The crowd smeared them with ketchup and mustard and dragged them from the lunch counter.

Anne and her friends were using a form of protest called **sit-ins**, in which people sit and refuse to leave. The first sit-in took place at a lunch counter in Greensboro, North Carolina, in 1960. During the 1960s, thousands of blacks and whites were conducting sit-ins at public places across the South.

Segregation laws in the South limited the rights of African Americans not only at lunch counters but also in bus stations, restrooms, and other public facilities. In the 1960s, sit-ins and other forms of protest fanned the crusade for equality. The protests signaled a new determination to end segregation and discrimination.

Nonviolent Direct Action Civil rights groups planned the protests, but it was often young people like Anne Moody who carried them out. The Congress of Racial Equality (CORE), for example, organized "Freedom Rides." Busloads of young Freedom Riders— black and white— rode from town to town to integrate bus terminals in the South.

These early civil rights groups held firmly to the tactics of what Martin Luther King, Jr., called "nonviolent direct action." Sit-ins, boycotts, marches, and other peaceful methods were used to achieve their goals.

Police sometimes responded by using attack dogs or water hoses against

>> Peaceful demonstrators were frequently the victims of violence. Water hoses were sometimes used to disperse crowds at sit-ins as seen in this photo taken in Birmingham, Alabama, in 1963.

protesters. Houses and churches of black leaders were bombed. Civil rights workers—black and white—were sometimes injured or killed. By remaining nonviolent, protesters gained a moral advantage and the sympathy of many Americans.

In 1963, more than 200,000 Americans marched on Washington, D.C. They wanted Congress to pass laws to end discrimination and to help the poor. Among the speakers that day was Martin Luther King, Jr.

When we let freedom ring . . . we will be able to speed up that day when all of God's children, black men and white men, Jews and Gentiles, Protestants and Catholics, will be able to join hands and sing in the words of the old Negro spiritual, 'Free at last!

Free at last! Thank God Almighty, we are free at last!'

—Martin Luther King, Jr., Speech, August 28, 1963

The Federal Government Protects Civil Rights The demonstrations spurred Presidents Kennedy and Johnson to press for federal civil rights laws. Kennedy failed, but Johnson succeeded in pushing through the Civil Rights Act of 1964, which protected the right of all citizens to vote. It also outlawed discrimination in hiring and ended segregation in public places.

At the Democratic National Convention in 1964, Fannie Lou Hamer, an African American, told of her experiences while trying to register to vote in Mississippi. Her efforts, along with the help of others, were successful in gaining voting rights.

In 1965, the Voting Rights Act allowed federal officials to register voters in states practicing discrimination. It also ended literacy tests used to block African Americans from voting. As a result, tens of thousands of African Americans voted for the first time.

The new civil rights laws did not end all discrimination. In the North, no formal system of segregation existed. Informally, though, housing in certain neighborhoods and employment in many companies remained closed to African Americans.

Some Call for Separation Some African Americans believed that nonviolent protest had failed. The Black Panthers and other radical groups told African Americans to arm themselves. Blacks, they said, had to be ready to protect themselves and to fight for their rights.

Black Muslims, such as Malcolm X, argued that African Americans could succeed only if they separated from white society. Before being assassinated in 1965, Malcolm X began to change his views. He called for "a society in which there could exist honest white-black brotherhood."

Both moderates and radicals found common ground in talk of "black power." They urged African Americans to achieve economic independence by starting their own businesses and shopping in African American-owned stores. Leaders also called for "black pride," encouraging African Americans to learn more about their heritage and culture.

Race Riots In crowded city neighborhoods, many African Americans were angry about discrimination, lack of jobs, and poverty. Beginning in 1965, their anger boiled over into violence.

A confrontation between a white police officer and an African American man in Watts, an African America neighborhood in Los Angeles, triggered a riot there in August. During the next six days, rioters set fire to buildings and looted stores.

>> Mourners crowd the funeral procession route for Martin Luther King, Jr., in 1968. Anger over King's assassination triggered riots in cities across America.

AFRICAN AMERICANS IN GOVERNMENT

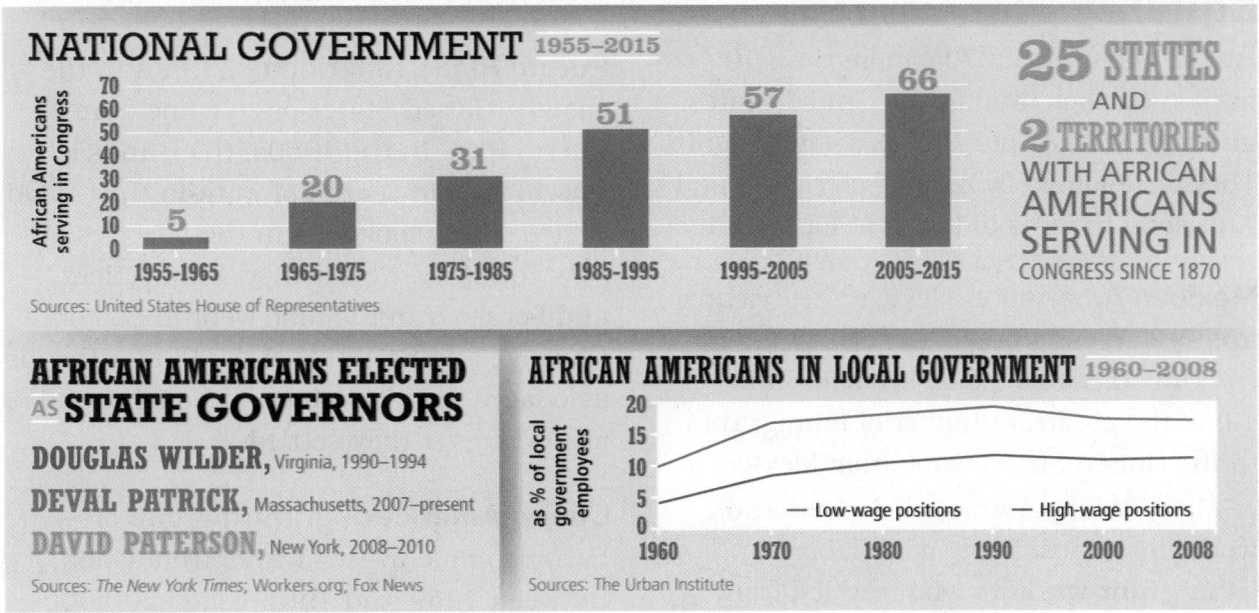

NATIONAL GOVERNMENT 1955–2015

African Americans serving in Congress

- 1955–1965: 5
- 1965–1975: 20
- 1975–1985: 31
- 1985–1995: 51
- 1995–2005: 57
- 2005–2015: 66

Sources: United States House of Representatives

25 STATES AND **2 TERRITORIES** WITH AFRICAN AMERICANS SERVING IN CONGRESS SINCE 1870

AFRICAN AMERICANS ELECTED AS STATE GOVERNORS

DOUGLAS WILDER, Virginia, 1990–1994
DEVAL PATRICK, Massachusetts, 2007–present
DAVID PATERSON, New York, 2008–2010

Sources: *The New York Times*; Workers.org; Fox News

AFRICAN AMERICANS IN LOCAL GOVERNMENT 1960–2008

as % of local government employees (1960, 1970, 1980, 1990, 2000, 2008)

— Low-wage positions   — High-wage positions

Sources: The Urban Institute

>> **Analyze Graphs** Based on the data in the graphs, what conclusions can you draw about the long-term effects of the Civil Rights Movement?

Some 4,000 people were arrested, 34 were killed, and 1,000 were injured. Over the next two years, Chicago, Detroit, and dozens of other cities exploded with violence, destruction, and death.

The Assassination of Dr. King Martin Luther King, Jr., continued to preach nonviolence. In April 1968, he went to Memphis, Tennessee, to support a strike of black sanitation workers. When he stepped outside his motel room, a white gunman killed him.

King's life has continued to inspire Americans to work for peaceful change. To honor his memory, his birthday was declared a national holiday in 1986.

Getting Results The Civil Rights Movement began to show some results in the 1970s. African Americans won public offices in small towns and large cities.

Atlanta, Cleveland, Detroit, New Orleans, and Los Angeles had all elected black mayors by 1979.

African Americans also made gains in the federal government. In 1967, Edward Brooke of Massachusetts became the first black senator since Reconstruction. A year later, President Johnson appointed Thurgood Marshall to the Supreme Court.

Many businesses and universities adopted **affirmative action** programs. These programs sought to hire and promote minorities, women, and others who had faced discrimination. By the 1970s, more African Americans were entering such professions as medicine and law. Yet, for all their efforts, African Americans still had to contend with bias in hiring, promotions, and pay.

? **LIST** three accomplishments of the 1964 Civil Rights Act.

Other Minorities Fight for Equality

By the end of the 1970s, more than 10 million Latinos lived in the United States, and they worked hard to gain equal rights. They were joined by Asian Americans and American Indians in the fight for equality.

Mexican Americans Mexican Americans are the largest group of Latinos living in the United States today. From 1960 to 1980, the greatest number of immigrants to the United States came from Mexico.

Many Mexican Americans lived and worked in cities. Many more labored as **migrant workers** who traveled from farm to farm looking for work. Low wages and harsh working conditions made life difficult for them. Discrimination made things worse. Mexican Americans were often barred from better-paying jobs and from better neighborhoods. Few schools offered programs for those whose first language was Spanish. Migrants moved so often that it was hard for their children to attend school regularly.

Puerto Rican Americans Latinos in the eastern United States often came from Puerto Rico. In the 1950s, thousands left Puerto Rico in search of work in the United States. Many took jobs in the factories of New York City, New Jersey, Connecticut, and Pennsylvania. Some went to Boston, Chicago, and San Francisco. Puerto Ricans also faced discrimination in housing and jobs wherever they settled.

Cuban Americans A third group of Latinos came in two waves from Cuba. Between 1959 and 1962, some 200,000 people fled to southern Florida when Fidel Castro set up a Communist government in Cuba. These immigrants were often middle class and well educated. They adapted quickly to their new home. A second wave of immigrants came in 1980 after Castro allowed thousands of people to leave the island. Many of the new

Cuban Immigration, 1959–1980

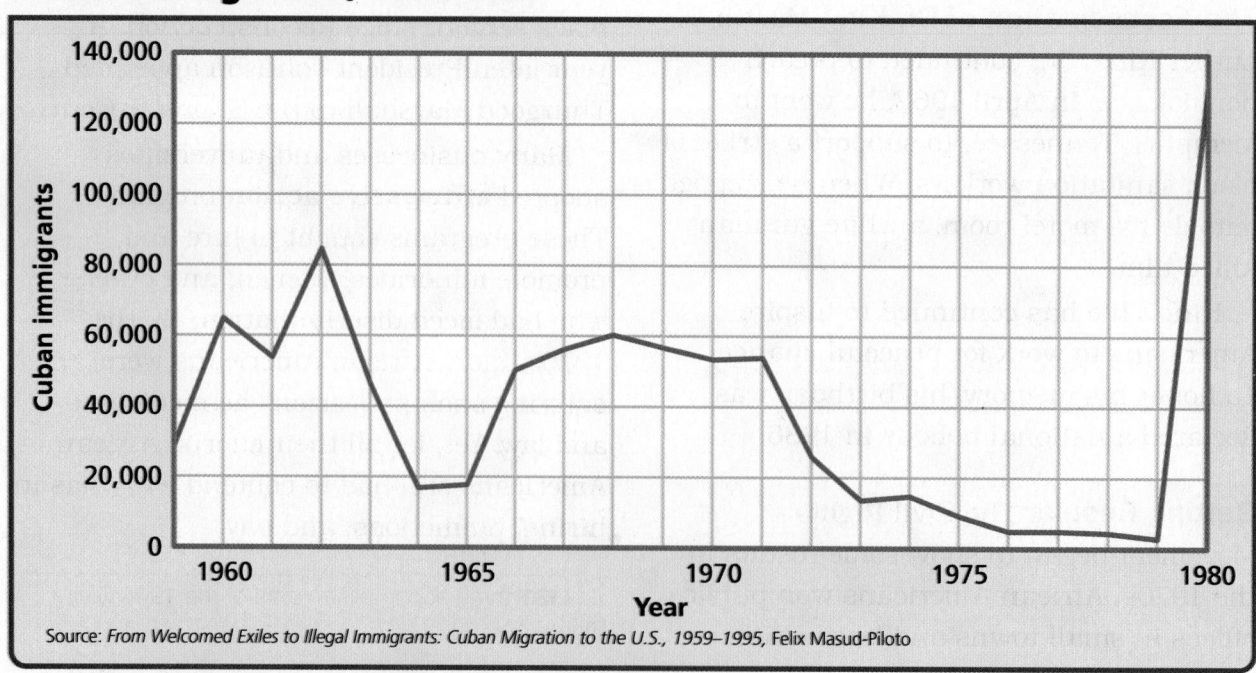

Source: *From Welcomed Exiles to Illegal Immigrants: Cuban Migration to the U.S., 1959–1995,* Felix Masud-Piloto

>> **Analyze Graphs** Cite evidence from what you have read that explains why Cuban immigration peaked in the early 1960s and again in 1980.

>> César Chávez (seen here in 1970) organized migrant farmworkers to rally for better working conditions and higher wages. **Applying Information** Why might it have been difficult to organize migrant farmworkers?

Interactive Gallery

refugees were unskilled. They had a hard time making a living.

As their numbers grew, Cuban Americans became a force in southern Florida. Miami took on a new look. Shop windows displayed signs in Spanish. Cuban restaurants and shops opened. Cubans published Spanish-language newspapers and operated radio and television stations. Cuban American politicians were soon elected.

Cooperation Yields Results In the 1960s, new Latino organizations sought change. **César Chávez** formed a union of migrant workers, the United Farm Workers. When farm owners refused to talk to the union, Chávez called for a nationwide boycott of farm products. In the end, the owners recognized the union, and workers won higher wages.

By the mid-1960s, Latinos began to publicly take pride in their history and culture. Mexican Americans called themselves *Chicanos,* a name that comes from the Spanish word *Mexicano.* Latino groups also registered voters and made sure that voting laws were enforced. These new voters helped to elect more Latino officials to represent their interests.

One result of these efforts was the Voting Rights Act of 1975. It required areas with many non-English-speaking citizens to hold bilingual elections. **Bilingual** means in two languages. In a bilingual election, information is provided in more than one language. With a ballot that was written in Spanish, it was easier for Latinos to vote.

The Bilingual Education Acts of 1968 and 1973 promoted bilingual programs in public schools with Spanish-speaking and Asian students.

>> In 1973, members of the American Indian Movement (AIM) staged the Wounded Knee protest to gain more rights for American Indian groups.

Asian Americans Asian Americans began their own fight against discrimination. In 1968, students at the University of California at Berkeley founded the Asian American Political Alliance (AAPA). Students of Chinese, Japanese, Filipino, and other Asian descent joined to promote the rights and culture of Asian Americans. As a result, between 1968 and 1973, universities across the nation created programs in Asian American studies.

American Indians American Indians also worked for their full rights. They claimed rights not only as individuals but also as members of tribal groups. Over the years, the federal government had recognized tribal governments by signing treaties with them.

During the late 1940s and the 1950s, the federal government tried to

break up tribal governments. They also encouraged American Indians to leave the reservations. By the late 1960s, more than half of all American Indians lived off the reservations, mainly in cities. Gradually, city life weakened traditional customs.

American Indians organized against these government policies. The National Congress of American Indians regularly sent delegations to Washington to defend Indian rights.

The American Indian Movement (AIM) protested the treatment of Indians. In 1973, AIM members occupied Wounded Knee, South Dakota, for several weeks. As you have read, the United States Army had killed nearly 300 American Indians at Wounded Knee in 1890. AIM wanted to remind people of the government's failure to deal fairly with American Indians. Protests and court cases have won sympathy for Indian causes and more rights for American Indians.

? **DRAW CONCLUSIONS** Why did rights of Latinos become a more prominent issue during the civil rights era?

The Women's and Gay Rights Movements

Women had long fought inequality. Since the 1960s, their drive for equal rights has been known as the Women's Rights Movement. Meanwhile, a movement for equal rights for homosexuals began to gain attention.

Inequality at Work In the workplace qualified women found that male employers were unwilling to hire them for certain jobs, and women were usually paid less than men, even for the same work. They were fired before men and promoted less quickly.

In 1966, writer Betty Friedan helped to set up the National Organization for Women (NOW), which worked for equal rights for women in jobs, pay, and education. It also helped women bring discrimination cases to court and campaigned for maternity leave and child-care centers. Urging women to be more politically active, NOW organized the Strike for Equality Parade down New York's Fifth Avenue in 1970. Some 50,000 women marched.

New laws helped women make some gains. The Equal Pay Act of 1963 required equal pay for equal work. The Civil Rights Act of 1964 outlawed discrimination in hiring based on gender and on race.

>> In 1963, Betty Friedan wrote *The Feminine Mystique*, a book that portrayed many American women's dissatisfaction with their place in society. Friedan then became a leader in the push for women's equality.

The Equal Rights Amendment In the 1970s, the women's movement suffered a major defeat. In 1972, Congress passed a proposal for the Equal Rights Amendment (ERA) to the Constitution. The amendment would ban discrimination based on gender. However, Phyllis Schlafly and other conservative women led a successful campaign against ratification of the amendment. They said the ERA would lead to women being drafted into the military and would harm the traditional family. Despite this defeat, the women's movement brought women more power and equality.

Gay and Lesbian Rights Movement Gay rights is one of the most strongly debated social issues of our time. In 1924, the first gay rights organization, The Society for Human Rights, was founded. However, the group received so much political pressure that it broke up shortly afterward.

Gays and lesbians continued to be exposed to discrimination, even by their own government. In 1953, President Dwight D. Eisenhower banned the hiring of gay men and lesbians for government jobs. Around the nation, gays and lesbians also suffered harassment by the police.

Gay and lesbian activists began to protest what they saw as unfair treatment. In 1950, Chuck Rowland and Harry Hay formed the Mattachine Society in Los Angeles. This was a gay rights group of mostly male members. In 1955, the Daughters of Bilitis, a lesbian group, was formed in San Francisco by Del Martin and Phyllis Lyon. Both groups started chapters around the nation. They also began to publish magazines promoting rights for gays and lesbians. In the 1960s, activists protested against employment discrimination in Washington, D.C., and San Francisco. At this time, homosexuality was against the law in most of the United States.

In 1969, police raided the Stonewall Inn in New York City—a known gathering place for homosexuals—aiming to arrest people just for being there. Police had been making such arrests for years. That night and for several days afterwards, homosexuals from around New York City rioted against the police. The events of Stonewall inspired gay men and lesbians elsewhere to fight for equal rights.

The next year, 5,000 gay men and women marked the first anniversary of the riots with a march in New York City. The event became a yearly celebration.

>> Women activists mirror the pose of the Statue of Liberty to show their support for the Equal Rights Amendment in 1970.

>> As this 1970 gay and lesbian pride march shows, gay men and lesbians began to be more open in their demand for equal treatment during this period.

Many Americans opposed gay men's and lesbians' growing demands for equal rights. Many condemned homosexuality because they considered it immoral for religious reasons. Due to this opposition, efforts to eliminate discrimination in jobs and housing had little success during the 1960s and 1970s. Gay and lesbian Americans continued to fight for equality.

❓ **DESCRIBE** the events at the Stonewall Inn in 1969 and explain their significance.

ASSESSMENT

1. **Generate Explanations** Explain the effect of the Korean War on integration efforts in the United States.

2. **Draw Conclusions** Describe the effects of the Montgomery Bus Boycott.

3. **Identify Cause and Effect** Explain how the Civil Rights Act of 1964 and affirmative action initiatives affected minorities.

4. **Identify Central Issues** Explain how the United States government affected American Indian groups during the 1950s.

5. **Describe** the emergence of the gay and lesbian rights movement.

Kennedy, Johnson, and Vietnam

>> This photograph shows American soldiers in Vietnam in 1965, fighting in the Battle of Ia Drang.

▶ Interactive Flipped Video

>> **Objectives**

Summarize the accomplishments of President Kennedy.

Summarize the accomplishments of President Johnson, including his "Great Society."

Explain why the United States became involved in the Vietnam War.

Describe the early years of the Vietnam War.

Describe American protests of the Vietnam War and explain the counterculture that developed during this era.

>> **Key Terms**

superpower	guerrilla
exile	domino theory
Bay of Pigs invasion	Gulf of Tonkin
Cuban missile crisis	Resolution
Alliance for Progress	escalate
Peace Corps	Tet Offensive
Organization of	draft
American States	counterculture
National Aeronautics	movement
and Space	Great Society
Administration	John F. Kennedy
Vietcong	Lyndon Johnson

The election of 1960 pitted Republican Vice President Richard Nixon against **John F. Kennedy**, a Democrat and Senator from Massachusetts.

A New President

Television Helps Kennedy Win The election was a close contest. Many Americans voted against John F. Kennedy because they felt he did not have enough experience to be President. Others worried about Kennedy's religion, Catholicism. No Roman Catholic had ever been President. Many Americans feared that Kennedy might be more loyal to the Roman Catholic Church than to the country. Kennedy reassured voters that he believed in the separation of church and state.

Television turned the tide for Kennedy. In the first televised debates ever held in a presidential campaign, Kennedy appeared youthful and confident. Nixon, recovering from a recent illness, looked tired and nervous. Kennedy won the election by a narrow margin.

Kennedy Inspires the Nation John F. Kennedy took the presidential oath of office on January 20, 1961. At 43, he was the youngest man ever elected President and the first to be born in the twentieth century. "Let the word go forth," he said, "that the torch has been passed to a new generation of Americans."

Kennedy's youth and idealism had inspired Americans during the campaign. Now he called them to service.

> The trumpet summons us again . . . to bear the burden of a long twilight struggle . . . against the common enemies of man: tyranny, poverty, disease, and war itself. . . . And so, my fellow Americans: ask not what your country can do for you—ask what you can do for your country.

—John F. Kennedy, Inaugural Address, January 20, 1961

For all his youth and high hopes, Kennedy and the Presidents who followed him faced tough challenges. The 1960s and 1970s were years of idealism. They also turned out to be a time of uncertainty, tragedy, and turmoil for Americans of all ages.

? **IDENTIFY CENTRAL ISSUES** What are two reasons people gave when they decided not to vote for Kennedy?

Communist Cuba

By the time Kennedy entered the White House, the United States and the Soviet Union had emerged as **superpowers**— nations with enough military, political, and economic strength to influence events worldwide. As leader of a superpower, President Kennedy was given the task of negotiating the country's way through Cold

>> John F. Kennedy (right) debates with Richard M. Nixon on television during the 1960 presidential election campaign. **Hypothesize** Why might Kennedy have outperformed Nixon on television?

>> This U.S. Defense Department photo shows the location of a missile base in Cuba in 1962, proving that missiles could be launched from Cuba.

>> Fidel Castro (center) was a revolutionary leader who turned Cuba into the first communist state in the western hemisphere. Here, Castro is seen giving a speech on January 8, 1959, after entering Havana to take control of the Cuban government.

War crises. In fact, the rivalry between the superpowers led to clashes in many places, including Cuba, an island in the Caribbean very close to the United States.

In 1959, Fidel Castro led a revolution that set up a communist state in Cuba. Castro's government took over private companies, including many owned by American businesses. Thousands of Cubans, especially those from the upper and middle classes, fled to the United States.

A Failed Invasion The Soviet Union began supplying Cuba with large amounts of aid. The growing ties between the Soviet Union and Castro's Cuba worried American officials. Cuba lies just 90 miles off the coast of Florida.

In 1961, President John F. Kennedy approved a plan to support Cuban exiles in an invasion of Cuba to overthrow Castro. **Exiles** are people who have been forced to leave their own country.

A force of about 1,400 Cuban exiles landed at the Bay of Pigs on Cuba's south coast. The invasion was badly planned. Castro's forces outnumbered the invaders and quickly rounded them up and jailed them, killing about 100 of the invaders. The **Bay of Pigs invasion** strengthened Castro in Cuba and embarrassed the United States.

Impending Crisis After the Bay of Pigs invasion, the Soviet Union gave Cuba more weapons. In October 1962, President Kennedy learned that the Soviets were secretly building missile bases on the island. If the bases were completed, atomic missiles could reach American cities within minutes.

As a result, Kennedy announced that American warships would be positioned

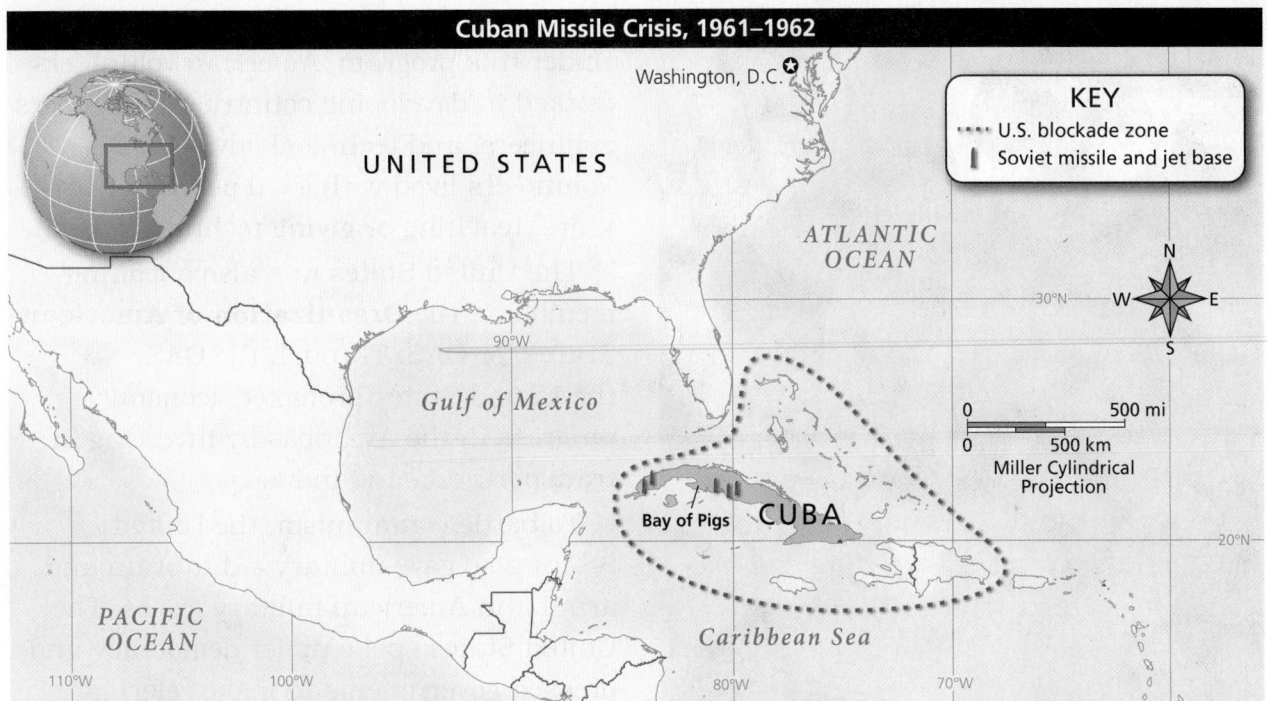

Cuban Missile Crisis, 1961–1962

Washington, D.C.

UNITED STATES

ATLANTIC OCEAN

KEY
···· U.S. blockade zone
⌐ Soviet missile and jet base

30°N

90°W

Gulf of Mexico

0   500 mi
0   500 km
Miller Cylindrical
Projection

Bay of Pigs   CUBA

20°N

PACIFIC
OCEAN

Caribbean Sea

110°W   100°W   80°W   70°W

>> **Analyze Maps** Explain the meaning of the dotted blue line on the map and its importance in the Cuban Missile Crisis.

▶ **Interactive Timeline**

around Cuba with orders to stop any Soviet ships carrying missiles. The world waited tensely as Soviet ships steamed toward Cuba. At the last minute, the Soviet ships turned back. "We're eyeball to eyeball," said Secretary of State Dean Rusk, "and I think the other fellow just blinked."

Kennedy's strong stand led the Soviets to compromise. Soviet leader Nikita Khrushchev agreed to remove Soviet missiles from Cuba. In turn, the United States promised not to invade the island. Still the **Cuban missile crisis** had shaken both American and Soviet officials. In all the years of the Cold War, the world never came closer to a full-scale nuclear war.

? IDENTIFY MAIN IDEAS What was the American government trying to accomplish with the Bay of Pigs invasion?

Reform and Progress

In the early 1900s, the United States had frequently intervened in the internal affairs of Latin American nations. Now, Cold War tensions led the United States under President Kennedy to resume its active role. A number of Presidents tried to contain communism in other Latin American nations.

Communism in Latin America Latin America had long faced severe social and economic problems. A huge gap existed between the wealthy few and the majority of people. In most countries, rural people lived in desperate poverty. When the poor migrated to cities seeking work, they were often forced to live in shacks without heat, light, or water.

Many poor Latin Americans saw communism as a solution to their

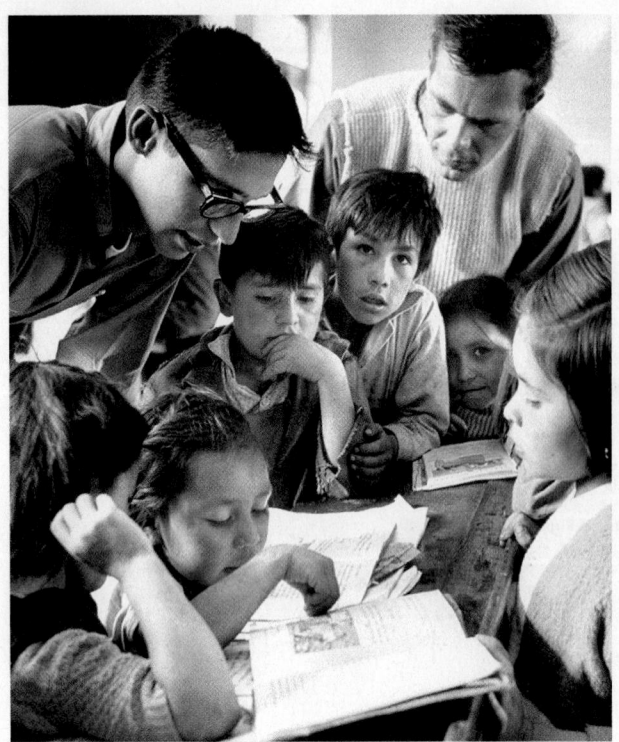

>> Peace Corps volunteers teach young Latin American children in the 1960s.

problems. Communists called for land to be distributed to the poor and for governments to take over foreign corporations. Some noncommunists also supported this view.

Kennedy Attempts Reform Many American leaders agreed with the need for reform. They hoped that American aid would help make Latin American nations more democratic, ease the lives of the people, and lessen communist influence.

In 1961, President Kennedy created an ambitious aid program called the **Alliance for Progress**. He urged Latin American countries to make reforms to improve the lives of their people. In return, the United States contributed aid to build schools and hospitals and to improve farming and sanitation services. The Alliance brought a few improvements, but it did not end the causes of poverty.

Kennedy also set up the **Peace Corps**. Under this program, American volunteers worked in developing countries as teachers, engineers, and technical advisers. Volunteers lived with local people for two years, teaching or giving technical advice.

The United States was also a leading member of the **Organization of American States**, or OAS. Through the OAS, the United States promoted economic progress in the Americas by investing in transportation and industry.

To battle communism, the United States also gave military aid to train and arm Latin American military forces. The United States spoke up for democracy and pressed governments to make reforms. Often, though, the United States ended up supporting military dictators because they opposed communism.

Kennedy Faces Challenges When Kennedy took office, he was handed the task of leading a country through the Cold War. In doing so, Kennedy took a hard line on many issues, responding directly to Soviet aggression in Cuba and Berlin. Luckily, in both instances, the Soviet Union backed off, but the American people remained worried about the outbreak of nuclear war.

Both the Soviet Union and the United States had developed large stocks of nuclear bombs and missiles. In fact, they had enough bombs to destroy civilization. When, in 1957, the Soviet Union launched *Sputnik I*, the world's first artificial satellite, Americans questioned whether Soviet rockets armed with atomic weapons could reach the United States.

As both superpowers raced to send larger satellites farther into space, the United States under President Kennedy's leadership set up the **National**

Aeronautics and Space Administration (NASA). Its mission was to direct an American space program to compete with that of the Soviets.

Many programs that began with the Kennedy administration are part of his legacy today. For example, NASA continues research today, sending more and more satellites into space and bettering Americans' lives with its technology. The Peace Corps works around the world, continuing to provide support to people in developing nations.

? **LIST** two aid programs established under President Kennedy's administration.

Johnson's Great Society

Nearly two years into his term, President Kennedy had achieved much, but he still had work to do. However, he never got a chance to continue it. Kennedy's life was cut short by an assassin.

The Kennedy Assassination On November 22, 1963, Kennedy traveled to Dallas, Texas, on a political tour. As his convertible passed cheering crowds, shots rang out. The President slumped in his seat. Later, John F. Kennedy died. That afternoon, Vice President **Lyndon Johnson** was sworn in as President.

A stunned American people reacted with grief and confusion, but more drama followed. Police caught Lee Harvey Oswald, the suspected gunman. However, after his arrest, Oswald himself was killed by another gunman.

Later a special government commission headed by Chief Justice Earl Warren concluded that a lone gunman, Lee Harvey Oswald, had murdered the President. Today, most historians agree with the conclusions of the Warren Commission.

President Johnson Carries On "Let us continue," said Johnson. He steered many

>> President John F. Kennedy greets a jubilant crowd in Forth Worth, Texas, on November 22, 1963. Hours later, he was assassinated in nearby Dallas, Texas.

>> As part of his Great Society program, President Lyndon B. Johnson signs the Medicare Bill on July 30, 1965. The law provided government funding for senior citizens' hospital expenses.

of Kennedy's proposals through Congress. In November 1964, voters returned him to the White House in a landslide victory. Johnson had his own program. He called it the **Great Society**. It boldly aimed at creating a decent living standard for every American. In a first step, Johnson declared a "war on poverty."

Congress had not supported Kennedy's poverty program. However, Johnson was more persuasive. He cornered members of Congress. Johnson successfully used his years of political experience to help get what he wanted. In just two years in office, Johnson pushed 50 new laws through Congress.

Johnson's Plan The Great Society had many programs. Under Medicare, the government helped pay hospital costs for senior citizens. Medicaid gave states money

to help poor citizens with medical bills. A new Office of Economic Opportunity created job-training programs for the unemployed. It gave loans to needy farmers and to businesses in poor sections of cities.

Programs to build housing for low-income and middle-income families were also part of the Great Society. To carry out these programs, Congress established the Department of Housing and Urban Development, or HUD. Robert Weaver headed the department. He was the first African American ever appointed to the Cabinet.

The Great Society had a mixed record. It aided the poor but at great cost to taxpayers. Government grew in size and intruded on people's lives as never before. Corruption sometimes plagued antipoverty programs. Still, Medicare, Medicaid, and other reforms helped millions and became permanent parts of American life.

? DESCRIBE President Johnson's Great Society.

The Vietnam War Begins

Vietnam is a narrow country that stretches about 1,000 miles along the South China Sea. Since the late 1800s, France ruled it as a colony. The United States became involved in a conflict there in the 1960s.

American involvement in Vietnam was very gradual. During the 1940s, Ho Chi Minh (hoh chee min), a Vietnamese nationalist and a Communist, had led the fight for independence. Ho's army finally defeated the French in 1954.

An international peace conference divided Vietnam into two countries. Ho Chi Minh led communist North Vietnam. Ngo Dinh Diem (noh din dyem) was the noncommunist leader of South Vietnam.

In the Cold War world, the Soviet Union supported North Vietnam. The United States backed Diem in the south.

The Vietcong Diem lost popular support during the 1950s. Many South Vietnamese thought that he favored wealthy landlords and was corrupt. He failed to help the nation's peasant majority and ruled with a heavy hand.

As discontent grew, many peasants joined the **Vietcong**—guerrillas who opposed Diem. **Guerrillas** (guh RIL uz) are fighters who make hit-and-run attacks on the enemy. They do not wear uniforms or fight in large battles. In time, the Vietcong became communist and were supported by North Vietnam. Vietcong influence quickly spread, especially in the villages.

The Domino Theory Vietcong successes worried American leaders. If South Vietnam fell to communism, they believed, other

The Vietnam War

>> **Analyze Maps** Recall information you learned about the Korean War. What similarities to the Korean War do you notice in this map, which shows political divisions during the Vietnam War?

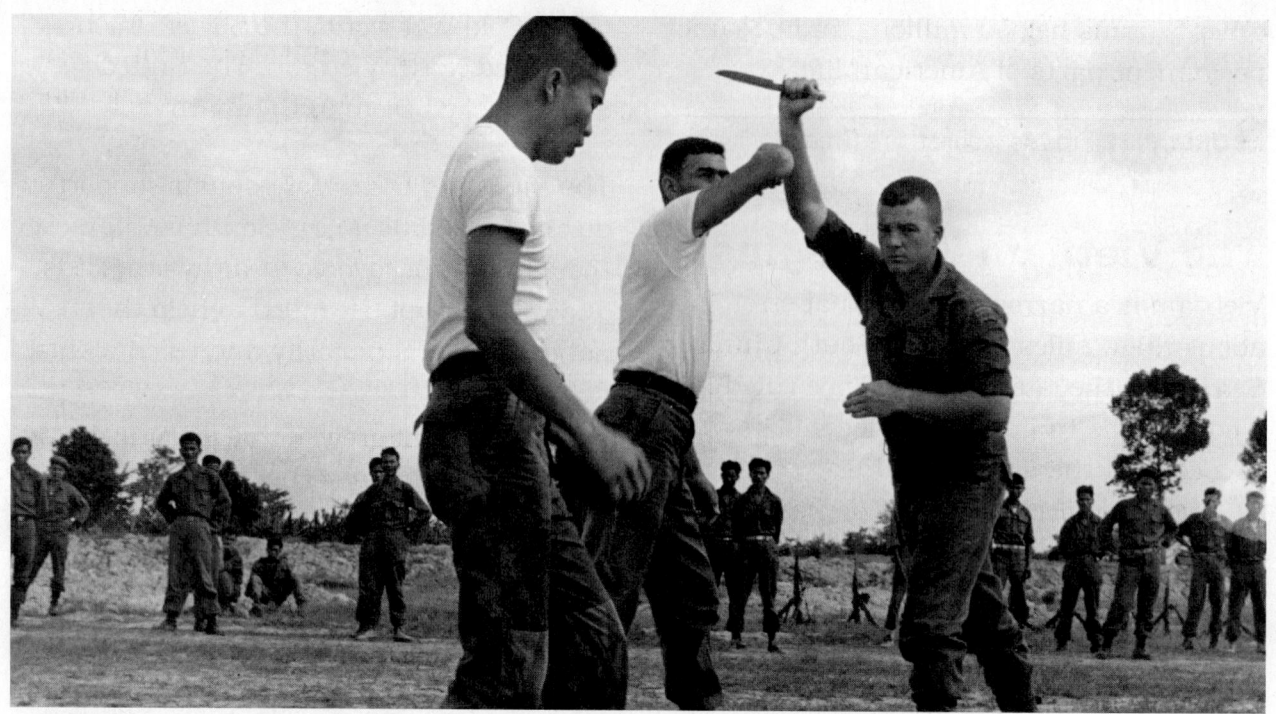

>> Two U.S. Army Rangers demonstrate a defense technique to a South Vietnamese soldier in 1962. Before fully entering the conflict in Vietnam, the U.S. military provided training to the South Vietnamese.

countries in the region would follow—like a row of falling dominoes. This idea became known as the **domino theory**. The United States decided that it must keep South Vietnam from becoming the first domino.

During the 1950s and 1960s, Presidents Eisenhower and Kennedy sent financial aid and military advisers to South Vietnam. The advisers went to help train the South Vietnamese army. They did not go to fight the Vietcong. Diem, however, continued to lose support. In November 1963, just a few weeks before President Kennedy's assassination, Diem was assassinated.

As the new President, Lyndon Johnson was also determined to keep South Vietnam from falling to the communists. He increased aid to South Vietnam, sending more arms and advisers. Still, the Vietcong continued to make gains.

Gulf of Tonkin Resolution In August 1964, President Johnson announced that North Vietnamese torpedo boats had attacked an American ship patrolling the Gulf of Tonkin off the coast of North Vietnam. At Johnson's urging, Congress passed the **Gulf of Tonkin Resolution**. It allowed the President "to take all necessary measures to repel any armed attack or to prevent further aggression." Johnson used the resolution to order the bombing of North Vietnam and Vietcong-held areas in the south.

With the Gulf of Tonkin Resolution, the role of Americans in Vietnam changed from military advisers to active fighters. The war in Vietnam **escalated**, or expanded. By 1968, President Johnson had sent more than 500,000 troops to fight in Vietnam.

Guerilla Warfare The Vietnam War differed from other wars that Americans had fought. Rather than trying to gain ground, Americans attempted to destroy enemy positions. However, the Vietcong were hard to pin down. When Americans found an enemy stronghold, the guerrillas disappeared into the jungle. When the Americans left, the Vietcong returned. As a result, Americans found themselves going back again and again to fight in the same areas.

Worse still, American soldiers often could not tell which villagers were Vietcong. The enemy might be the old woman cooking rice outside her hut or the man walking down a village path. "The farmer you waved to from your jeep in the day," explained an American soldier, "would be the guy with the gun out looking for you at night."

The Tet Offensive In January 1968, the Vietcong launched surprise attacks on cities throughout South Vietnam. Guerrillas even stormed the American embassy in Saigon, the capital of South Vietnam. The attack became known as the **Tet Offensive** because it took place during Tet, the Vietnamese New Year's holiday.

In the end, American and South Vietnamese forces pushed back the enemy. Still, the Vietcong had won a major political victory. The Tet Offensive showed that even with half a million American troops, no part of South Vietnam was safe from Vietcong attack. Many more Americans began to protest the war.

Hoping to restore calm to a nation rocked by protests, a weary President Johnson decided not to seek reelection in 1968. He told the American people that he needed to concentrate on his duties while in office rather than on winning reelection. He was also concerned about his health.

? DEFINE What is the domino theory?

>> A wounded American soldier is led to safety during the attack on the American embassy in Saigon, South Vietnam, as part of the Tet Offensive in January 1968. **Draw Conclusions** Why did the Tet Offensive affect Americans' opinion of the war?

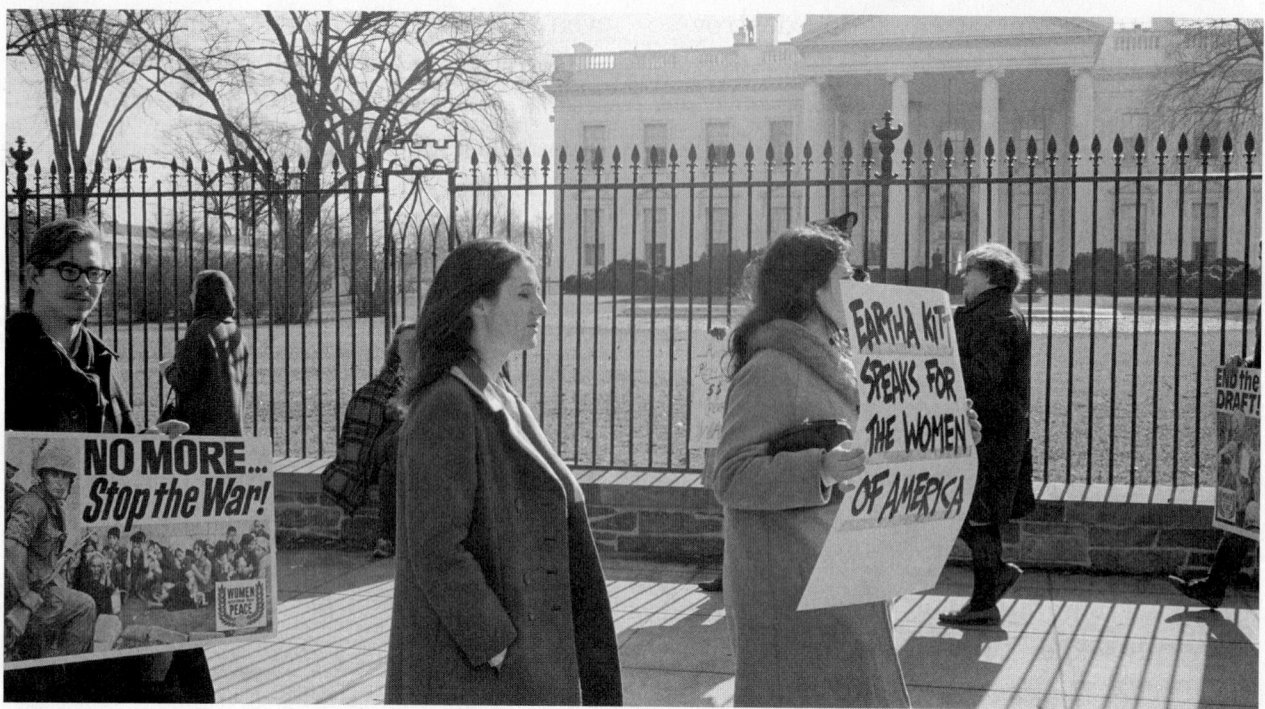

>> Young men and women protest the Vietnam War outside the White House in Washington, D.C., in January 1968. Views about American involvement in Vietnam were very mixed and divided the nation.

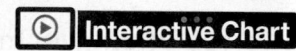
Interactive Chart

Protests at Home

Protest movements grew in the 1960s. The civil rights movement expanded. Some young people began to openly reject the values and lifestyles of their parents. Opposition to the war in Vietnam grew.

Protesting War As American casualties mounted, public support for the war faded. For the first time, Americans watched a war on television. They saw villages burned, children and old people caught in battle, and soldiers wounded and killed.

To build up troops, the United States expanded the **draft**, or system of mandatory enlistment into the armed forces. The draft affected American youth unequally. Many young middle-class men found ways to avoid the draft, such as attending college. As a result, many of the draftees sent to Vietnam were poor. A large number were African American and Latino.

As more and more young men were sent to fight in the Vietnam War, an antiwar movement gained strength. Protesters staged rallies, burned draft cards (notices that a person has been drafted), and refused to serve in the military. Many of the largest demonstrations took place on college campuses.

By the mid-1960s, the country split between "hawks" and "doves." Hawks supported the Vietnam War as a battle against communism. Doves opposed it. They saw it as a civil war involving the Vietnamese only.

Protesters charged that American lives and money were being wasted on an unjust war. The South Vietnamese government, they said, was corrupt and brutal, and the United States should not support it. They wanted the huge sums being spent on the war to be spent on social programs at home.

A Counterculture Emerges The antiwar protests fed a spirit of rebellion among young people. During the 1960s and early 1970s, many young people rejected traditional American values. Many young Americans joined the **counterculture movement**. They criticized competition and the drive for personal success. Instead of going to college, they "dropped out." Instead of traditional families, they lived together in groups or communes. Many listened to new forms of rock music. Some "turned on," or experimented with illegal drugs.

Inspired by the civil rights movement, counterculture protesters called for peace, justice, and social equality. They wore torn, faded jeans and work shirts to blur the differences between rich and poor. Men grew long hair and beards. Women refused to put on makeup. All wanted to look more natural and less like their parents.

Like the beatniks of the 1950s, members of the counterculture said American life was empty and materialistic. Some turned to eastern religions such as Buddhism in search of spiritual meaning.

>> Long hair and tattered clothing typified the counterculture movement of the late 1960s. The movement was based on the abandonment of traditional American values in favor of self-expression.

THE ELECTION OF 1968

DISTRIBUTION OF VOTES

Richard Nixon
Republican
31,785,480 (43%)

Hubert Humphrey
Democratic
31,275,166 (43%)

George Wallace
Independent
9,906,473 (14%)

Source: The American Presidency Project

1968 ELECTION POPULAR VOTE

1968 ELECTION ELECTORAL VOTE

Richard Nixon
Republican
301 (56%)

Hubert Humphrey
Democratic
191 (36%)

George Wallace
Independent
45 (8%)

BREAKING DOWN THE VOTE

5 States in which **Wallace** won the popular vote

13 States in which **Humphrey** won the popular vote

32 States in which **Nixon** won the popular vote

Source: The American Presidency Project

THE BATTLE IN KEY STATES

- Nixon
- Humphrey
- Wallace

State	Nixon	Humphrey	Wallace
NEW YORK	44.3	49.7	5.3
ILLINOIS	47.1	44.2	8.5
OHIO	45.2	42.9	11.8
TEXAS	39.9	41.1	19.0
CALIFORNIA	54.8	35.0	9.6
PENNSYLVANIA	44.0	47.6	8.0

Source: The American Presidency Project

>> **Analyze Graphs** The graph shows data concerning Richard Nixon's narrow victory in the 1968 election. Identify key states where Nixon lost the popular vote to Humphrey, and explain why he still won the election.

The Election of 1968 By 1968, the counterculture and antiwar movements were peaking. As a result, President Johnson's popularity plummeted. To avoid angry protesters, Johnson stayed in the White House more and more.

Johnson's decision not to run for reelection opened the way for other Democrats to seek their party's nomination in 1968. New York senator Robert Kennedy, brother of the late President, made a strong run. However, tragedy struck again for the Kennedy family. While campaigning in Los Angeles, Kennedy was shot and killed by a Palestinian who opposed the senator's support for Israel. The Democrats selected Vice President Hubert Humphrey as their candidate.

The Republicans again nominated former Vice President Richard Nixon. Nixon promised "peace with honor" in Vietnam and "law and order" at home. Alabama governor George Wallace entered the race as a third-party candidate. Helped by this and by divisions among Democrats over the Vietnam War, Nixon won a narrow victory.

? CONTRAST the hawks and the doves.

ASSESSMENT

1. **Identify Cause and Effect** Explain how television influenced the 1960 presidential election.

2. **Integrate Information** Explain how U.S. involvement in the Vietnam War compared to the Korean War.

3. **Generate Explanations** Explain why the United States intervened in Latin America, and describe the effects.

4. **Compare** the policies of President Kennedy and President Johnson.

5. **Identify Central Issues** Explain how the Vietnam War differed from prior wars.

The Nixon Years

>> President Richard Nixon promised to put an end to the Vietnam War and favored restrictions on government spending, as well as reforms in civil rights, the environment, and welfare.

Interactive Flipped Video

As President, Nixon tried to reduce government involvement in people's lives. He cut funds for many Great Society programs, including job training, education, and low-income housing. He also sought to return power to the states. He called this transfer of power the "New Federalism."

>> Objectives

Summarize the accomplishments of President Nixon.

Explain how the Vietnam War ended and identify the results of the war.

Explain the Watergate scandal and why Nixon resigned from office.

>> Key Terms

silent majority
stagflation
Khmer Rouge
boat people
détente
SALT Agreement
Watergate
Richard M. Nixon

The Nixon Years

The Silent Majority During his presidential campaign, **Richard M. Nixon** said that he wanted to help what he called the **silent majority**. These Americans were disturbed by the unrest of the 1960s but did not protest publicly. They were, Nixon explained, the "great majority of Americans, the nonshouters, the nondemonstraters."

True to his campaign promise, Nixon began a "law-and-order" program. Federal funds were used to help local police departments. Nixon also named four conservative justices to the Supreme Court. They tended to favor dealing harshly with lawbreakers.

The Moon Landing Nixon inherited the space program from Kennedy and Johnson. Its greatest triumph came in 1969 just as Nixon took office. In 1969, two astronauts landed a small craft on the moon's surface. With millions of television viewers around the world watching, Neil A. Armstrong became the first person to step onto the moon. "That's one small step for a man— one giant leap for mankind," he radioed back to Earth. American astronauts visited the moon five more times.

The Economy Suffers During the Nixon years, the economy suffered from **stagflation**, a combination of rising prices, high unemployment, and slow economic growth. To halt inflation, Nixon froze wages and prices. To stimulate economic growth, he increased federal spending.

Still, economic problems would not go away. Increased federal spending caused federal budget deficits; that is, the government spent more than it received in revenues. Early in Nixon's second term, an oil embargo put added pressure on the

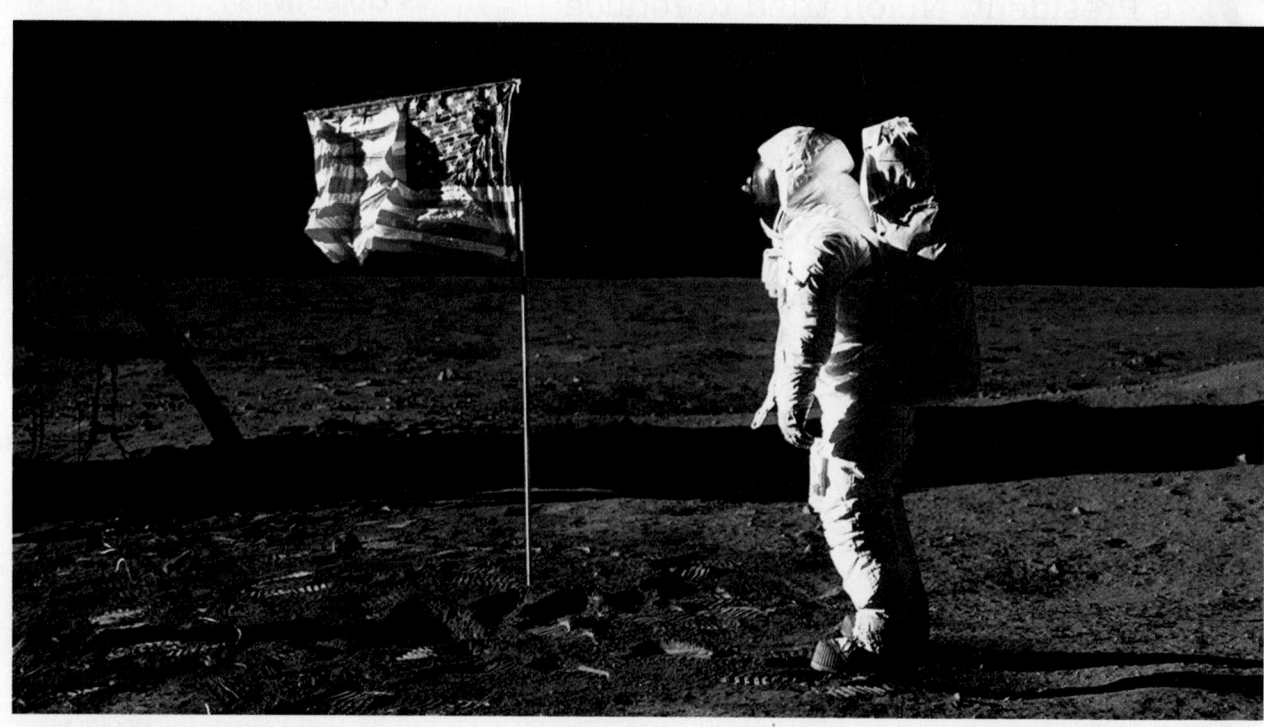

>> The space program begun during Kennedy's administration reached a peak with the 1969 moon landing by American astronauts.

▶ Interactive Gallery

economy. Higher energy prices caused the price of goods to rise even more.

❓ DRAW CONCLUSIONS Why do you think the moon landing was important?

Nixon Addresses Vietnam

At first President Nixon widened the war in Vietnam, hoping to weaken the enemy. For years, North Vietnam had used trails in nearby Cambodia to supply Vietcong soldiers in South Vietnam. The Vietcong also escaped to Cambodia when American and South Vietnamese units attacked.

In 1969, Nixon ordered the bombing of communist bases in Cambodia. Then, American and South Vietnamese forces invaded by land. These moves helped plunge Cambodia into its own civil war between communist and noncommunist forces.

Withdrawal of U.S. Troops Under pressure at home, President Nixon began to turn the war over to South Vietnam and withdraw American troops. Meanwhile, peace talks were held in Paris. In January 1973, the two sides reached a cease-fire agreement. The next year, the last American combat troops left Vietnam.

The United States continued to send large amounts of aid to South Vietnam. Even so, the South Vietnamese were unable to stop a North Vietnamese advance.

In April 1975, communist forces captured Saigon. They renamed it Ho Chi Minh City. Soon after, Vietnam was united under a communist government.

Communism in Cambodia That year, the communist **Khmer Rouge** (kuh MER ROOZH) won the civil war in Cambodia.

>> A Khmer Rouge soldier hides in the bush in Cambodia. Between 1975 and 1979, Cambodia suffered under the violent regime of the Khmer Rouge.

The Khmer Rouge imposed a brutal reign of terror on their own people. More than one million Cambodians starved to death or were killed.

In 1979, Vietnam invaded Cambodia and set up a new communist government. It was less harsh than the Khmer Rouge, but it could not end the fighting. Not until the 1990s would a shaky peace be restored in Cambodia.

The Aftermath The Vietnam War was a costly conflict. More than 58,000 American soldiers lost their lives. Over 150,000 American soldiers were wounded, and hundreds of thousands of soldiers suffered lingering effects from the psychological stress of the war. More than one million Vietnamese soldiers and perhaps half a million civilians died. The war shattered the Vietnamese economy.

After 1975, hundreds of thousands of people fled Vietnam and Cambodia. Refugees from Vietnam escaped in small boats. Many of these **boat people** drowned or died of hunger and thirst. Others made it to safety. Eventually, many were allowed to settle in the United States.

The Vietnam War was a painful episode in American history. Besides its huge cost, the war produced no victory and divided the nation. Some returning soldiers faced protests, and many others came home without a welcome, a much different experience than soldiers who had returned from previous wars to the admiration of the American people. Vietnam left Americans wondering about how far the nation should go to fight communism.

? **IDENTIFY CENTRAL IDEAS** Why did Nixon order attacks on Cambodia?

Foreign Policy Decreases Tension

In 1971, while Americans were still fighting in Vietnam, the Cold War showed signs of a thaw. President Nixon moved to ease world tensions. His first move was to seek improved relations with the People's Republic of China.

Recognizing Mao's China Since 1949, the United States had refused to recognize Mao Zedong's communist government in China. Instead, it recognized the Chinese Nationalists, now confined to the island of Taiwan. The United States gave arms and aid to the Nationalists and supported their claim to being the legitimate government of all China.

Richard Nixon had long been one of the most outspoken opponents of recognizing the communist government in China. As President, though, Nixon allowed secret

>> President Nixon and First Lady Pat Nixon visit the Great Wall of China in 1972.
Infer What was Nixon hoping to accomplish by visiting China?

Cold War Arms Buildup and SALT I and II

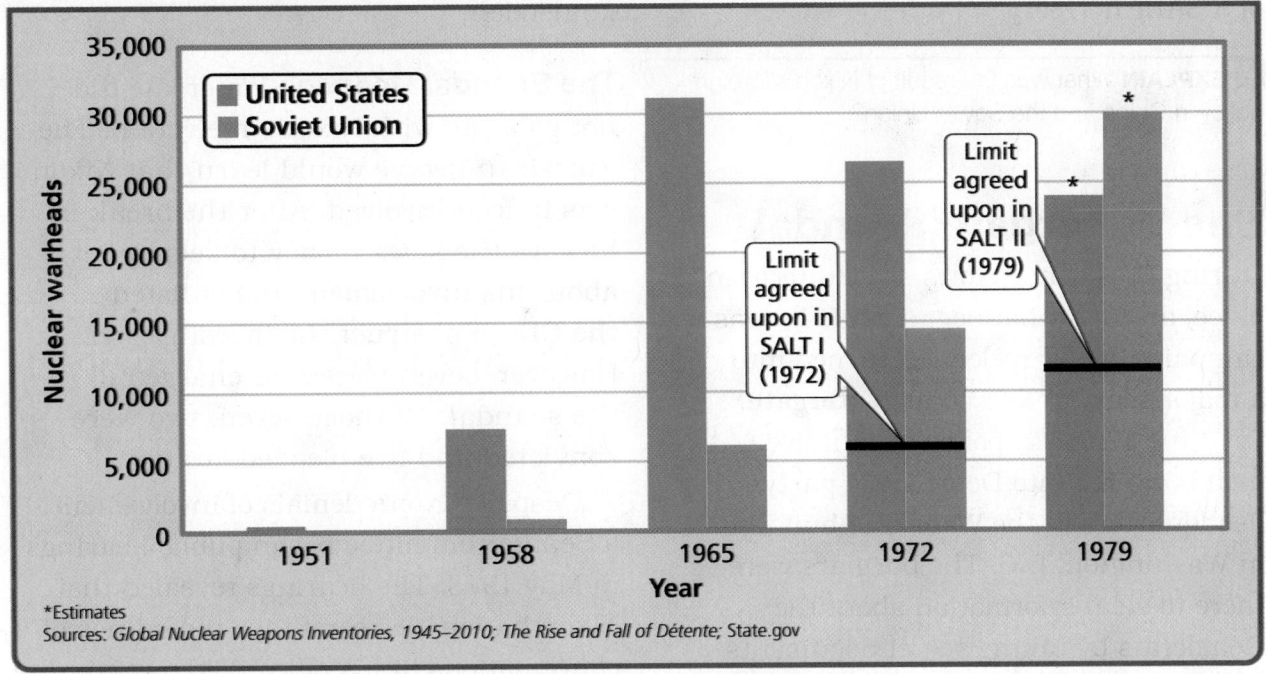

*Estimates
Sources: *Global Nuclear Weapons Inventories, 1945–2010; The Rise and Fall of Détente;* State.gov

>> **Analyze Graphs** Compare patterns you see in the levels of nuclear arms held by the two superpowers.

talks with Chinese officials that led to new openings for the two countries. To show its goodwill, China invited the American ping-pong team to a competition in Beijing.

To the surprise of many Americans, Nixon then visited the People's Republic of China in 1972. Television cameras captured the President walking along the Great Wall of China and attending state dinners with Chinese leaders. The visit was a triumph for Nixon and the start of a new era in relations with China. As tensions eased, the United States and China established formal diplomatic relations in 1979.

Détente President Nixon followed his visit to China with another historic trip. In May 1972, he became the first American President to visit the Soviet Union since the beginning of the Cold War. The trip was part of Nixon's effort to reduce tensions

between the superpowers. This policy was known as **détente** (day TAHNT). A French word meaning "loosening," détente represents an end to strained relations between countries.

Détente eased the tensions of the Cold War by establishing more trade and other contacts between the superpowers. It also led them to sign a treaty to limit the number of nuclear warheads and missiles. The treaty was known as the **SALT Agreement**. (SALT stands for Strategic Arms Limitation Talks.)

The next two Presidents, Gerald Ford and Jimmy Carter, continued the policy of détente. Trade between the United States and the Soviet Union increased. Under President Ford, Soviet and American astronauts conducted a joint space mission. In 1979, President Carter met with Soviet leader Leonid Brezhnev

(BREZH nef). They worked out the details of a SALT II Treaty.

? EXPLAIN What was the result of Nixon's foreign policy in China and the Soviet Union?

The Watergate Scandal

During President Nixon's second term in office, an event that began while he was campaigning for reelection turned into a major scandal known as **Watergate**. On June 17, 1972, police caught five men breaking into Democratic party headquarters in the Watergate building in Washington, D.C. The burglars were there to steal information about the Democrats by taking secret documents and wiretapping phones. Though it was suspected that the spies were linked to Nixon, no solid evidence was found at first. The President assured the public that no one in the White House was involved in the break-in. He won the election by a landslide.

The Scandal Deepens Watergate did not go away with Nixon's reelection. The American people would learn that Nixon was indeed involved. After the break-in, he gave the spies money to keep quiet about his involvement and enlisted the CIA to obstruct the investigation. However, seven men were charged in the scandal. Of those seven, two were convicted and five pleaded guilty.

Despite Nixon's denials of involvement, a Senate committee began public hearings in May 1973. The hearings revealed that Nixon had made secret tape recordings of conversations in his office. Nixon refused to give the committee the tapes, knowing that the tapes would prove his guilt.

In the fall of that same year, another unrelated scandal erupted. Vice President

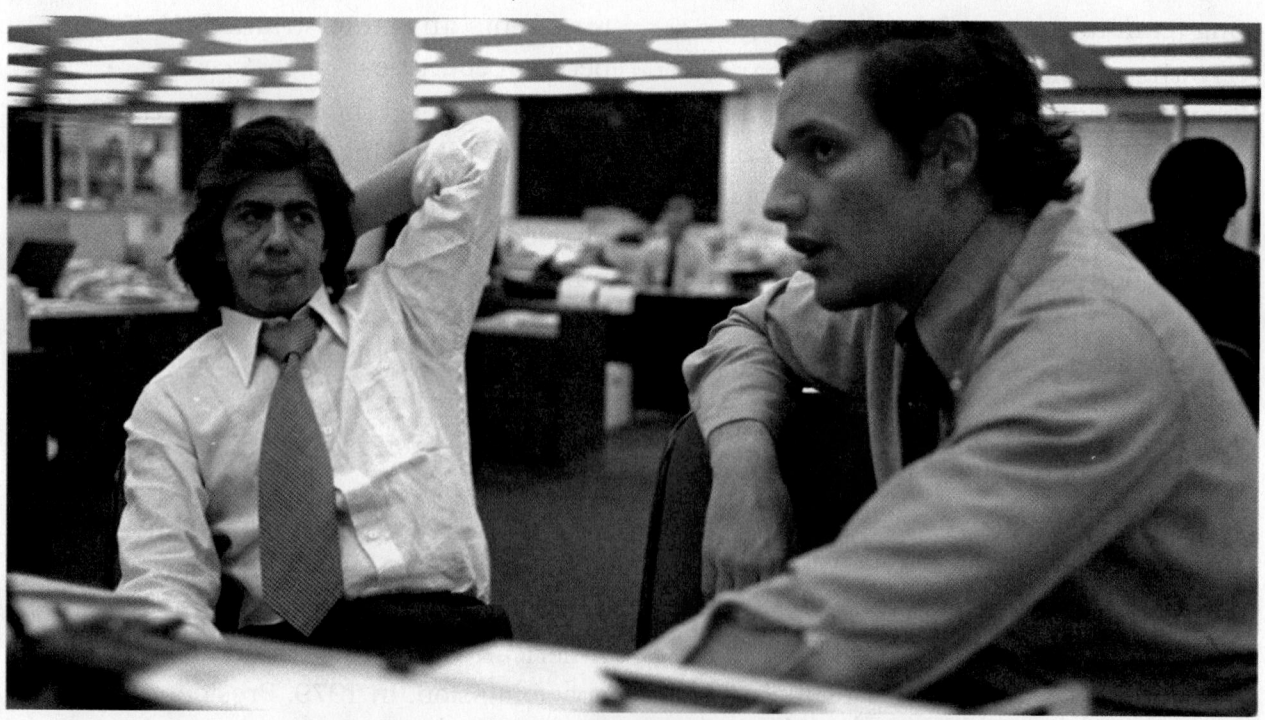

>> Carl Bernstein (left) and Bob Woodward, journalists for the *Washington Post*, reported on the Watergate scandal in 1973 that led to President Nixon's resignation.

Spiro Agnew was accused of taking bribes and evading taxes. He was forced to resign. The President chose Representative Gerald R. Ford of Michigan to replace him.

Nixon Resigns The following July 1974, Nixon was ordered by the Supreme Court to surrender the tapes. The Watergate crisis came to a head when Nixon continued to hold onto the tapes. A House of Representatives committee passed articles of impeachment against the President. One of several charges was obstructing, or blocking, justice.

A month later, on August 5, Nixon handed over the tapes that proved he and several close advisers had tried to cover up the truth about the Watergate break-in. Three days later, before an impeachment trial could begin, Richard Nixon became the first President to resign from office.

Ford Takes Office Gerald Ford, the new President, had a difficult job. He faced a troubled economy and the challenge of helping the nation emerge from a major political scandal. In response to the nation's troubled mood, President Ford granted Nixon a "full, free, and absolute pardon." He did so a month after Nixon resigned. Some felt that Nixon should have been brought to trial. Ford, however, wanted to save the country from a bitter debate over Watergate. Ford lost a great deal of public support because of that decision.

? **TRACE** the events that led to Nixon's resignation.

>> On October 17, 1974, President Gerald R. Ford explains to a subcommittee of the House of Representatives his reasons for granting a full pardon to former President Nixon.

 ▶ **Interactive Timeline**

ASSESSMENT

1. **Describe** the economic pressures that existed during Nixon's presidency.

2. **Identify Cause and Effect** Describe the effects of the Vietnam War.

3. **Identify Central Issues** Explain how relations between the United States and China changed during Nixon's presidency.

4. **Summarize** Describe the events of the Watergate scandal, and discuss its effects.

5. **Generate Explanations** Explain why President Ford pardoned Nixon.

The Berlin Airlift – Divided Germany

KEY
- Free
- Communist
- Flight path
- Airfield used by allies

Albers Conic Equal-Area Projection

1. **Describe Maps and the Berlin Airlift** Study the map above and the topic lessons to write a paragraph describing the importance of the Berlin airlift. Describe how Germany and Berlin were divided between East and West; why Stalin stopped all highway, railway, and waterway traffic from western Germany into West Berlin in June 1948; and how the United States and Britain responded.

2. **Describe the Marshall Plan** Use the information from the lessons in this topic and other sources to write a paragraph describing how the Marshall Plan provided aid to those in need and helped contain the expansion of communism. In your paragraph, be sure to describe why people in Western Europe needed help following the war; describe the type of aid the Marshall Plan provided; and describe how the Marshall Plan showed that aid could be used both as an economic policy and as a foreign policy to contain communism.

3. **Identify Bias** Write a paragraph identifying the bias in the excerpt of Joseph McCarthy's speech that appears after this question. In identifying the bias, be sure to consider what you know about the historical context of the time period, including what you know about McCarthy and McCarthyism; what you know about the language McCarthy used, as well as his frame of reference and point of view; and what you know about McCarthy's ability to provide evidence.

The reason why we find ourselves in a position of [weakness] is not because the enemy has sent men to invade our shores, but rather because of the traitorous actions of those who have had all the benefits that the wealthiest nation on earth has had to offer—the finest homes, the finest college educations, and the finest jobs in Government we can give. . . . I have here in my hand a list of 205 [individuals] that were known to the Secretary of State as being members of the Communist Party and who nevertheless are still working and shaping the policy of the State Department.

—Joseph McCarthy, speech in Wheeling, West Virginia, February 9, 1950

4. **Explain Outcomes** Use the information from the lessons in this topic and other sources to write a paragraph explaining the outcomes of U.S. involvement in the Korean War. In your paragraph, consider the short-term outcomes and the long-term outcomes.

5. **Analyze Migration Patterns** Write a paragraph analyzing the effects of the shift in population to the suburbs and Sunbelt. Consider the effects of the redistribution of population on the political power of the states and the effects of population growth and the redistribution of population on the environment of the suburbs and Sunbelt.

6. **Describe Pros and Cons** Write a paragraph describing the positive and negative impact of rock music. Describe the roots of rock-and-roll, explain how the popularity of rock added to American culture, and identify why some parents objected to Elvis Presley and other concerns people had about the growing influence of rock.

7. **Analyze Effects of *Brown* v. *Board of Education*** Write a paragraph analyzing the effects of *Brown* v. *Board of Education*. Identify when the Supreme Court heard the case, what the Court ruled, and the ruling's effect.

8. **Identify the Role of Nonviolent Protest in the Civil Rights Movement** Identify how Rosa Parks used nonviolent protest to expand the right to participate in the democratic process. Use the quotation below and the information from the lessons in this topic and other sources to write a paragraph identifying Rosa Parks and her contribution to nonviolent protest in the 1950s. Be sure to identify who Rosa Parks was; tell what form her nonviolent protest took; and describe the consequences of her action for Parks, the civil rights movement, and Montgomery.

The [policemen] asked if the driver had asked me to stand up, and I said yes, and they wanted to know why I didn't. I told them I didn't think I should have to stand up. After I had paid my fare and occupied a seat, I didn't think I should have to give it up.

—Rosa Parks

9. **Explain Outcomes** Write a paragraph explaining President Kennedy's political reasons for sending Peace Corps volunteers and sending aid through the Alliance for Progress to Latin American countries. Explain how the Cold War was a reason for starting the programs, the goals of each program, and the success of each program.

10. **Explain Turning Points** Write a paragraph explaining why the U.S. moon landing was a turning point. Explain and identify the "space race", the first person to land on the moon and when the landing occurred, and why the moon landing was a turning point in the space race.

11. **Analyze the Aftermath of the Vietnam War** Write a paragraph analyzing why President Nixon decided to withdraw American troops from Vietnam, what happened as a result, and how the aftermath of the Vietnam War affected Americans.

12. **Identify and Analyze Methods of Protest** Write a paragraph identifying and analyzing the nonviolent methods the United Farm Workers (UFW) used to bring about better conditions for migrant farmworkers. Identify the nonviolent methods the UFW used and analyze the effectiveness of these methods.

13. **Identify Leaders** Write a paragraph identifying the role Betty Friedan played in the women's rights movement. Answer the following questions in your paragraph: Who was Betty Friedan? How did she contribute to the women's rights movement?

14. **Explain Détente** Write a paragraph describing the effects of President Nixon's policy of détente. Be sure to define *détente*, explain why Nixon visited Moscow in May 1972, what SALT was and why it was important, and how détente affected the Cold War.

15. **Analyze the Effects of the Watergate Scandal** Use the information from the lessons in this topic to analyze and answer the following questions: What actions by the Nixon administration led to the Watergate scandal? How did President Nixon react when confronted with charges of wrongdoing? Why was the outcome of the Watergate scandal significant for the American government system?

16. **Reflect on the Essential Question** **Write an essay on the Essential Question: What is America's role in the world?** Use evidence from your study of this topic to support your answer.

16 A Global Superpower Facing Change (1975–2000)

Enduring Understandings

- Elected president in the late 1900s, Reagan called for a smaller role for government.

- Clinton's presidency brought economic prosperity but political controversy.

- The United States greeted the fall of communism in Russia and Eastern Europe, which ended the Cold War.

- After the Cold War, the United States played a key global role in promoting democracy and resolving regional conflicts.

>> President Ronald Reagan campaigning for re-election in 1984

PEARSON
realize ™   **NBC LEARN**

Watch the My Story Video to learn about a military officer's experiences in the Persian Gulf War.

PEARSON
realize ™
www.PearsonRealize.com

Access your digital lessons including:
Topic Inquiry • Interactive Reading
Notepad • Interactivities • Assessments

859

>> A campaign button for the 1980 Republican candidates for President and Vice President, Ronald Reagan and George H.W. Bush

[▶] **Interactive Flipped Video**

>> Objectives

Identify the challenges faced by the administration of Jimmy Carter.

Describe Ronald Reagan's conservative agenda.

Identify the challenges faced by the administration of George H. W. Bush.

Explain the issues that Bill Clinton faced as President.

>> Key Terms

Moral Majority
Reaganomics
deregulation
balanced budget
downsizing
recession
"Contract With America"
surplus
NAFTA

In 1976, Republicans nominated Ford for President. Democrats chose Jimmy Carter, the former governor of Georgia. Carter had no experience in Washington but used to his advantage the fact that he was a Washington outsider. He pointed out that "the vast majority of Americans . . . are also outsiders."

President Carter's Administration

After years of scandal in Washington, Carter's fresh face and promises of a new approach carried him to a narrow victory.

Carter's term began with a whirlwind of activity. In his first year, the new President sent Congress almost a dozen major bills. They included reforms in the Social Security system and in the tax code. But Carter's lack of experience in Washington hurt him. Congress refused to support his legislation.

The President did not fare much better with the problem of high inflation. When the government tried to slow inflation, prices only kept rising. Many families had trouble paying for food, clothing, and rent.

Although Carter was a Democrat, he adopted conservative solutions to the problem of high inflation. He cut government spending and appointed Paul Volcker as Chairman of the Federal Reserve. Volcker used monetary policy to attack inflation by reducing credit and raising interest rates.

Carter also adopted a conservative position when he took steps to deregulate the transportation industry. Reducing regulation increased free market competition. Policies such as the Airline Deregulation Act of 1978 brought lower prices for consumers.

In foreign affairs, Carter was a strong defender of human rights. The United States had signed the Helsinki Agreement just before he took office. Thirty-five nations pledged to respect basic rights such as religious freedom and freedom of speech. The United States, Carter said, should keep this pledge and not aid countries that violated human rights.

The Iranian Revolution and Hostage Crisis Even before Carter's presidency, the United States was deeply involved in conflicts in the Middle East. Iran was ruled

>> President Jimmy Carter, formerly governor of Georgia, attempted to use his position as a Washington "outsider" to bring change to the federal government.

>> Iranian demonstrators prepare to storm the U.S. embassy in 1979, carrying signs that picture their leader, Ayatollah Komeini.

>> During the energy crisis of 1979, gas was in short supply in the United States. American drivers found themselves waiting in long lines at gas stations.

▶ **Interactive Cartoon**

by a shah who had U.S. support. Then, in 1979, the Iranian Revolution forced the unpopular shah to flee. A religious leader, Ayatollah Khomeini (i yuh TOH luh koh MAYN ee), took control of Iran.

The shah had been a firm ally of the United States. The ayatollah was strongly anti-American. Where the shah had favored westernizing Iran, the new ruler wanted to enforce a strict, old-fashioned version of Islam. Neither, however, favored democracy.

In November 1979, President Carter let the shah enter the United States for medical treatment. In response, Iranian revolutionaries seized the American embassy and took 53 Americans hostage. The hostages were not freed until January 1981. The hostage crisis poisoned American relations with Iran for decades. It also affected domestic politics. During the 1980 presidential election campaign, conservatives and Republicans criticized Carter for not successfully defending the overseas interests of the United States.

An Energy Crisis The Iranian Revolution seriously disrupted oil production in Iran, which had been a major source of oil on the world market. Oil prices shot up, and Americans began to line up in cars at gas stations to buy gasoline, fearing that shortages would develop. Panic buying did lead to shortages in some places. Many Americans blamed President Carter's foreign policy for the gas lines and shortages.

After Iranians took Americans hostage in late 1979, Carter blocked any further oil imports from Iran. Then, in September 1980, war broke out between Iran and its neighbor, Iraq. Both countries had been major oil producers. The war further reduced world oil supplies and kept gas prices high.

The energy crisis undermined Americans' confidence and led many Americans to oppose Carter's reelection in 1980.

? **IDENTIFY** Give two examples of conservative policies that Carter adopted during his presidency to address economic instability.

The Conservative Movement Takes Hold

Ronald Reagan swept into office on a conservative tide. More Americans had come to agree with him that high taxes and "big government" were causing many national problems. "Government," he said, "is not the solution to our problems, government is the problem." These ideas contrasted sharply with the dominant ideas of the 1960s and 1970s.

Smaller Federal Government Since the 1930s, the federal government had grown steadily. President Franklin D. Roosevelt had begun this trend to help people through the Great Depression. Harry Truman, John Kennedy, and Lyndon Johnson continued the expansion. These liberal presidents believed that government should play a large role in managing the economy and providing social programs.

Beginning in the 1960s, a conservative movement warned against growing federal power. Arizona senator Barry Goldwater led the way. He argued for a smaller government nearer the people.

> Our towns and our cities, then our counties and our states, then our regional compacts—and only then the national government. That, let me remind you, is the ladder of liberty built by decentralized power.
>
> —Barry Goldwater, Speech at Republican National Convention, July 16, 1964

By the 1980s, conservatives dominated the Republican party. Led by Ronald Reagan, they believed that federal social programs had become too costly and that

The Conservative Movement

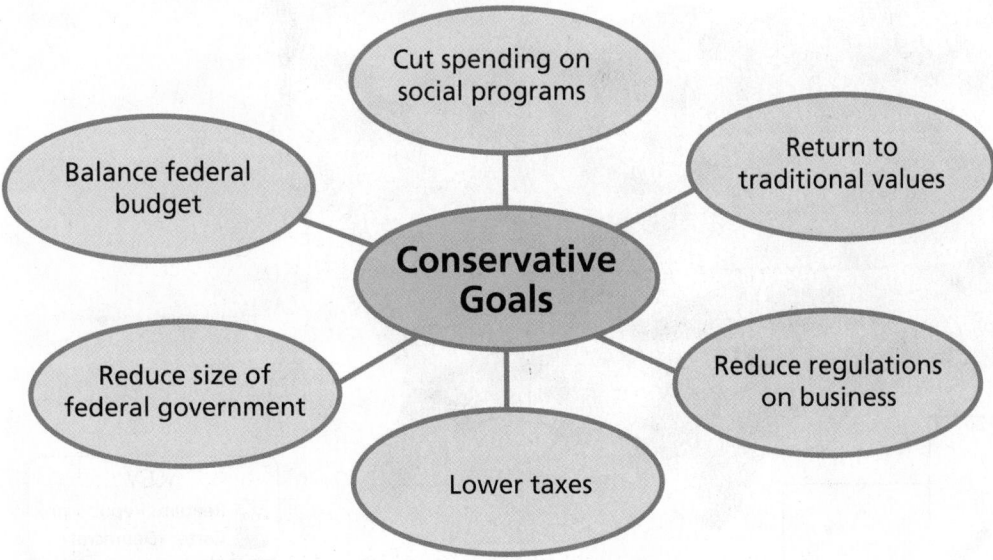

>> **Analyze Charts** One of the conservative goals listed was to reduce the size of the federal government. Choose one of the other goals in this chart that might also have reduced the size of government and explain how it might have done so.

federal regulations kept businesses from growing. State and local governments, they argued, were closest to the people and should decide what regulations were needed.

Social and Political Causes After decades of social change, many conservatives called for a return to traditional values. These included religion, family, and patriotism.

Reflecting the renewed emphasis on traditional values, evangelical Christian churches grew rapidly during the 1970s and 1980s. Evangelicals stressed personal conversion and sought to convert others. Evangelical ministers used television to widen their audience.

Many evangelicals took an active role in conservative political causes. In 1979, the Reverend Jerry Falwell founded the **Moral Majority**. The group aided political candidates who favored conservative religious goals, such as a constitutional amendment to allow organized prayer in public schools. In 1980, strong support

from the Moral Majority and the other conservative religious organizations helped put Ronald Reagan in the White House.

? **CHECK UNDERSTANDING** Why did conservatives support a more limited federal government?

The Reagan and Bush Presidencies

Reagan was a handsome man with a relaxed, friendly air. He had been a movie star before winning election as governor of California. His skill at presenting ideas in terms that ordinary people could understand earned him the nickname the Great Communicator.

.Reagan's Economic Program The new President's first priority was his economic program, often called **Reaganomics**. He persuaded Congress to cut taxes. Reagan hoped that taxpayers would use the extra money to buy more and save more. Buying

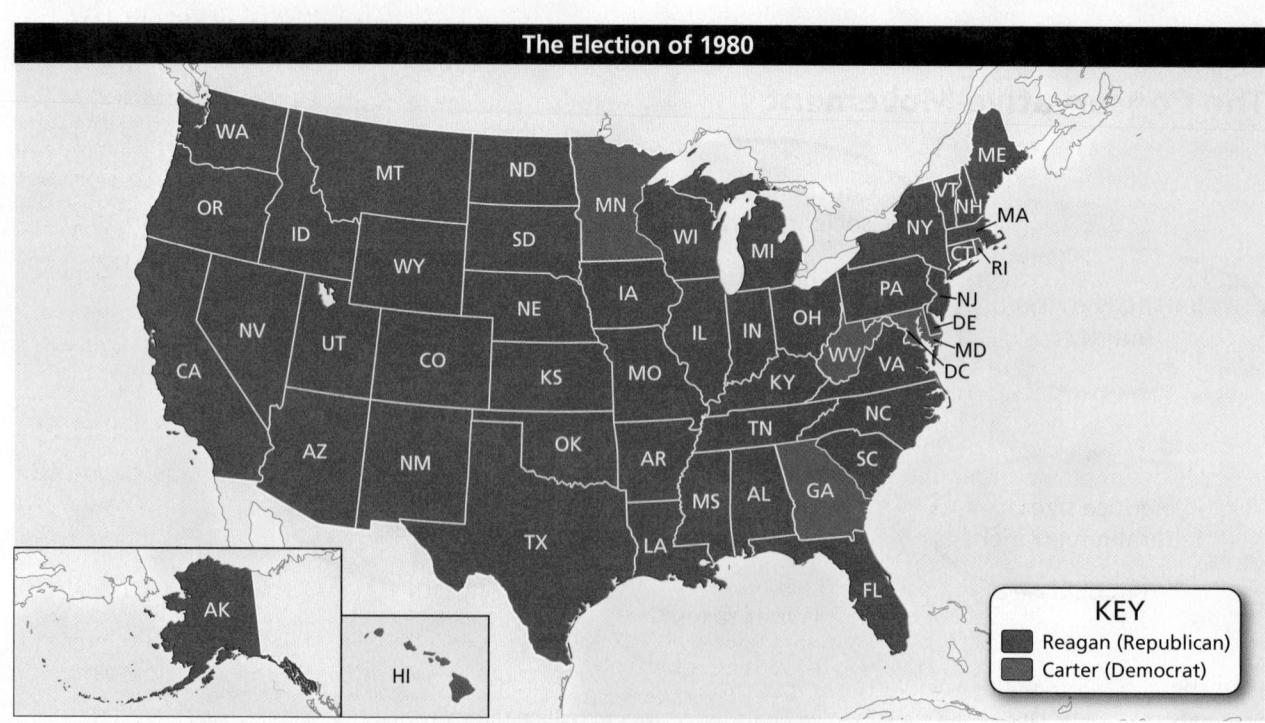

The Election of 1980

KEY
■ Reagan (Republican)
■ Carter (Democrat)

>> **Analyze Maps** Based on the information in the map, analyze the outcome of the election and how it reflected the political attitude of Americans in 1980.

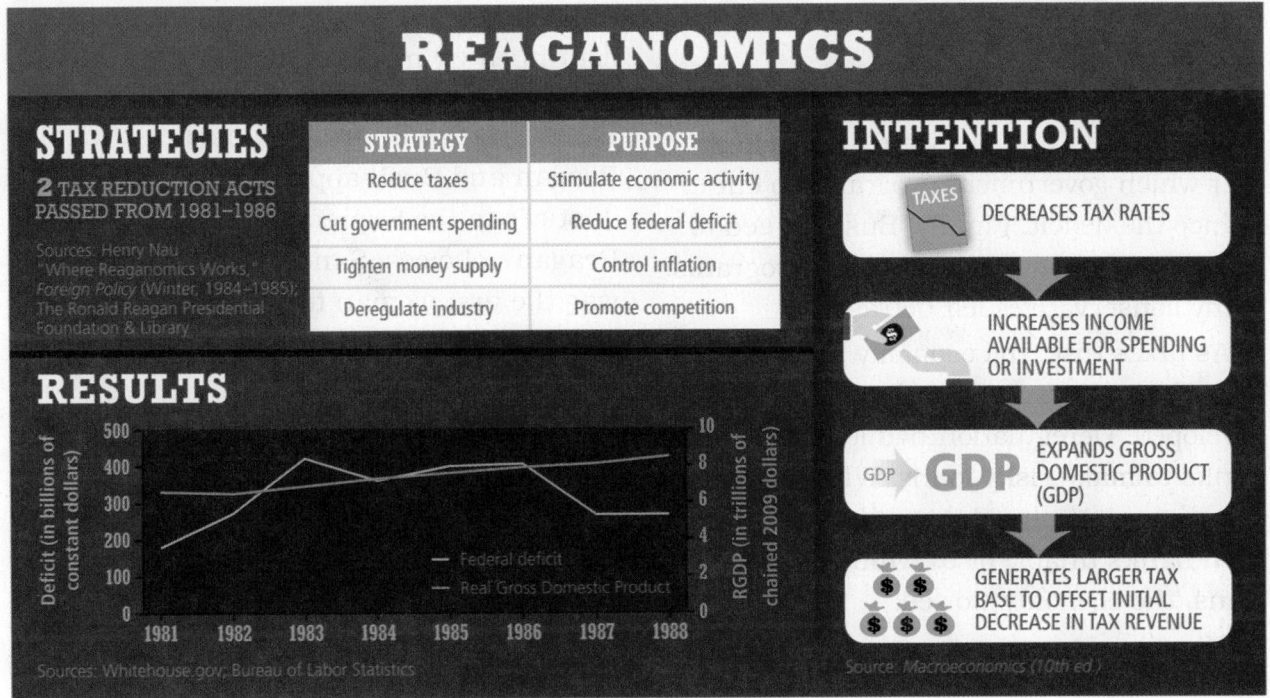

REAGANOMICS

STRATEGIES

2 TAX REDUCTION ACTS PASSED FROM 1981–1986

Sources: Henry Nau, "Where Reaganomics Works," *Foreign Policy* (Winter, 1984–1985); The Ronald Reagan Presidential Foundation & Library

STRATEGY	PURPOSE
Reduce taxes	Stimulate economic activity
Cut government spending	Reduce federal deficit
Tighten money supply	Control inflation
Deregulate industry	Promote competition

RESULTS

Deficit (in billions of constant dollars): 0, 100, 200, 300, 400, 500

RGDP (in trillions of chained 2009 dollars): 0, 2, 4, 6, 8, 10

Years: 1981, 1982, 1983, 1984, 1985, 1986, 1987, 1988

— Federal deficit
— Real Gross Domestic Product

Sources: Whitehouse.gov; Bureau of Labor Statistics

INTENTION

TAXES DECREASES TAX RATES

INCREASES INCOME AVAILABLE FOR SPENDING OR INVESTMENT

GDP EXPANDS GROSS DOMESTIC PRODUCT (GDP)

$$ $$ $$ GENERATES LARGER TAX BASE TO OFFSET INITIAL DECREASE IN TAX REVENUE

Source: *Macroeconomics* (10th ed.)

>> **Analyze Graphs** Based on the information in the graphs, explain how Reaganomics was intended to affect the federal deficit, and analyze if this result occurred.

more would spur business growth. Saving more would allow banks to invest in new business ventures. Reagan also promised to cut federal spending to reduce the size of government.

The President persuaded Congress to slow down spending increases on social programs, such as welfare, and aid to education. Critics charged that those cuts hurt the poor and children. Supporters responded that Reagan was just trimming programs that did not work.

A third goal of Reaganomics was **deregulation**, or reduction of restrictions on businesses. Reagan sped up an earlier trend toward deregulation. He opposed all laws, for example, that required industries to install expensive antipollution devices.

After a slow start, the economy was booming by 1984. When Reagan left office, there were 16 million more jobs, while inflation had been held in check.

The Budget Deficit Another of Reagan's goals—a balanced budget—proved harder to achieve. A **balanced budget** requires the government to spend only as much as it takes in. While Reagan cut social spending, he sharply increased military spending. As military spending rose and taxes fell, the budget deficit soared. For 1986, the deficit jumped to $240 billion, more than twice as high as under any previous President.

Still, the economy continued to expand, and Reagan remained popular. For many Americans, he had succeeded in restoring faith in the presidency, which had been so badly tarnished in recent years.

Bush's Economic Troubles Reagan's Vice President, George H. W. Bush, won a big victory in 1988. Bush vowed to continue Reagan's economic policies, cutting the deficit without raising taxes. "Read my lips," he pledged during the campaign. "No new taxes."

Bush could not keep his promise. By 1990, he and Congress were deadlocked over which government programs to cut to reduce the deficit. Finally, Bush agreed to raise taxes to save some popular programs. Many conservatives felt betrayed.

As taxes rose, the economy grew weaker. To make matters worse, a banking crisis developed. Deregulation had led some banks to make risky loans. When those loans were not repaid, many banks failed. With banks unable or unwilling to make loans, the economy slowed.

Many businesses cut costs by **downsizing**, or reducing their workforces. Downsizing increased business profits but also increased joblessness. These conditions soon produced a recession. A **recession** is an economic slump that is

milder than a depression. The recession continued for more than a year.

Conservative Supreme Court Justices
Reagan and Bush appointed a total of five Justices to the Supreme Court. (One of Reagan's choices, Sandra Day O'Connor, was the first woman to serve on the Court.) The new Justices were more conservative than those they replaced.

The more conservative Court placed new limits on the rights of suspected criminals, as well as on the right of prisoners to appeal convictions. The Court made it harder for workers to win job discrimination cases. It also reduced busing, which some school districts had used since the 1960s to achieve racial integration in public schools.

? **DESCRIBE** the three major ideas upon which Reaganomics was based.

>> Sandra Day O'Connor (right) became the first woman to serve as a Justice of the Supreme Court. Here, O'Connor is sworn in by Chief Justice Warren Burger (left) in 1981.

President Clinton Turns Toward the Center

Bush faced a stiff reelection challenge in 1992. Recession and unemployment continued. Bickering between Congress and the President left voters unhappy with Washington politics. The Democratic nominee, Arkansas governor Bill Clinton, promised more government involvement in areas ignored by Reagan and Bush.

On Election Day, voters signaled their dissatisfaction. Only 38 percent voted for Bush. Although he received less than half the popular vote—43 percent— Clinton won the highest number of votes. The remaining 19 percent went to Ross Perot, a Texas billionaire who ran as an independent candidate.

Improvements and Setbacks President Clinton followed a middle-of-the-road

Clinton and the Conservatives

ISSUE	CLINTON	CONSERVATIVES
Taxes	Asked Congress to increase taxes	Believed a tax increase would hurt the economy
Healthcare	Wanted to establish universal healthcare by requiring employers to offer insurance to all employees	Wanted to expand healthcare coverage by requiring individuals to purchase insurance
Medicare	Wanted to give early retirees access to Medicare	Believed Medicare was not financially stable enough to expand
Education	Proposed national testing in elementary and middle schools	Opposed expansion of federal control over education
Military	Opposed exclusion of homosexuals from the military	Supported exclusion of homosexuals from the military

Sources: U.S. National Archives and Records Administration; University of Virginia; Harvard University; The Office of Democratic Whip Steny Hoyer; Forbes

>> **Analyze Charts** Choose one of the issues listed in the chart and explain how Clinton's and conservatives' attitudes are consistent with what you know about liberal and conservative political values.

course. On the one hand, he moved cautiously when he persuaded Congress to increase some taxes and reduce spending. Yet this caution brought success. Under Clinton, for the first time in over 40 years, the federal deficit began a steady decline.

On the other hand, Clinton pushed for bold reform of the healthcare system. In 1994, some 37 million Americans had no health insurance. Clinton called for a national system of health insurance for almost all Americans. After heated debate, however, Congress defeated the plan. Many Americans worried that it would be too costly and involve the government too deeply in their lives.

To many Americans, the struggle over healthcare showed that Washington was paralyzed. Democrats controlled both Congress and the White House, yet the President could not get his own plan enacted.

Expanding Trade During the term of President Bush, the United States had negotiated with Mexico and Canada to conclude the North American Free Trade Agreement (**NAFTA**). Bush signed the agreement in October 1992, but he was unable to persuade Congress to ratify the agreement before he left the White House in January 1993.

In the United States, opponents argued that, by allowing free trade with Mexico, where pay was much lower and there were fewer laws protecting the environment, the agreement would result in American jobs leaving the country. Among those opposing NAFTA were much of the labor movement. Many U.S. business leaders, however, supported NAFTA, arguing that it would open up markets for U.S. products.

When Bush signed NAFTA in October 1992, he was in the midst of a presidential campaign against Bill Clinton. Clinton agreed to support NAFTA if provisions were added to the agreement protecting the environment and labor rights.

Even after Canada and Mexico agreed to those changes, however, opponents of the agreement put up a fight. They believed the changes did not go far enough. In the end,

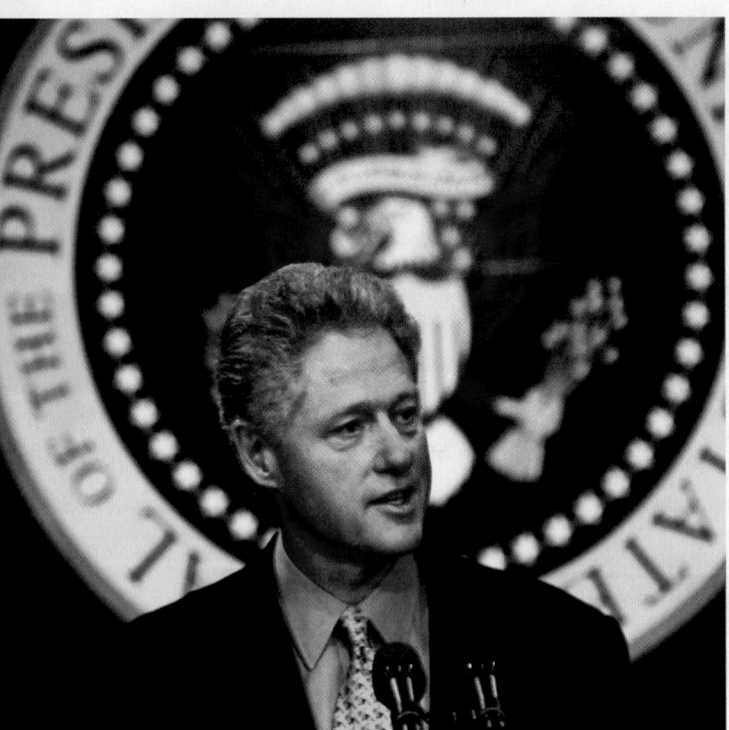

>> President Bill Clinton, a former governor of Arkansas, took office as President in January 1993. He was reelected to a second term in 1996.

strengthened the economy. Others point to sharply lower energy prices. Still others believe that economic growth was largely the result of using computers to make American workers more productive.

Clinton and the Conservatives Despite the improving economy, voter frustration with Clinton's healthcare plans helped Republicans win a resounding victory in the 1994 congressional elections. For the first time since the 1950s, Republicans held a majority in both the Senate and the House of Representatives.

Newt Gingrich of Georgia became Speaker of the House. Under his leadership, House Republicans drew up a **"Contract With America"**. This set of proposed laws included reducing social spending and environmental regulations and slashing taxes.

The President attacked many of the proposals as unfair to poor and middle-class Americans. After a bitter fight, he compromised with Congress on a plan to balance the federal budget by the year 2002. In fact, the economy grew so strongly that in 1998 the government reported a budget **surplus**, in which income exceeded spending. Over the next two years, the surplus grew even larger.

Congress and Clinton also compromised on welfare reform. The government limited the length of time a person could receive welfare benefits. In this way, it hoped to encourage unemployed Americans to find jobs.

though, Clinton convinced Congress to support the agreement.

NAFTA took effect on January 1, 1994. It opened the markets of all three North American countries to the free movement of trade and investment across borders. After the agreement took effect, trade among the three countries increased dramatically.

An Economic Boom After Clinton took office in 1993, the U.S. economy recovered strongly from recession. The economy continued to grow throughout Clinton's eight years in office, the longest uninterrupted period of economic growth in U.S. history. The economy's strong performance helped Clinton win reelection by a large margin in 1996.

Historians disagree on the reasons for the boom. Some believe that Clinton's effort to trim the federal budget deficit

Impeachment and Acquittal Controversy engulfed Clinton's second term. Federal prosecutors investigated Clinton for real estate dealings while he was governor of Arkansas. Prosecutors found no evidence of lawbreaking. However, they did accuse

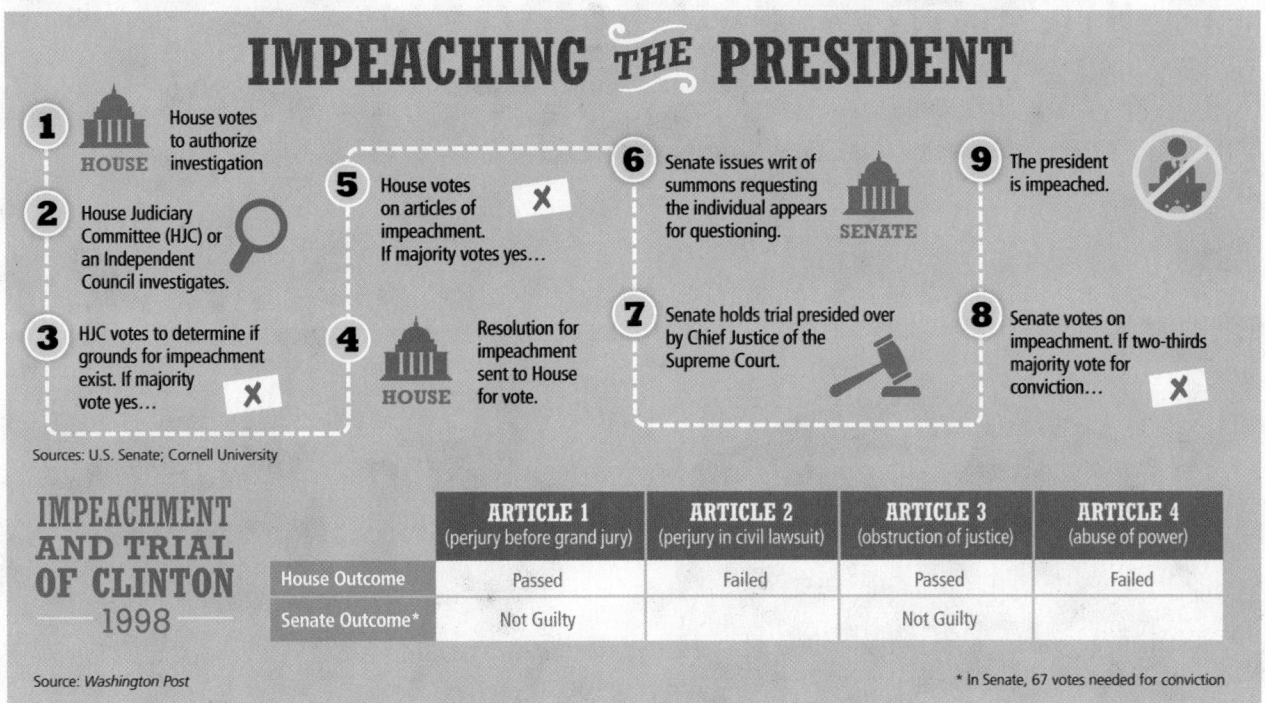

IMPEACHING THE PRESIDENT

1 HOUSE — House votes to authorize investigation

2 House Judiciary Committee (HJC) or an Independent Council investigates.

3 HJC votes to determine if grounds for impeachment exist. If majority vote yes…

4 HOUSE — Resolution for impeachment sent to House for vote.

5 House votes on articles of impeachment. If majority votes yes…

6 Senate issues writ of summons requesting the individual appears for questioning. SENATE

7 Senate holds trial presided over by Chief Justice of the Supreme Court.

8 Senate votes on impeachment. If two-thirds majority vote for conviction…

9 The president is impeached.

Sources: U.S. Senate; Cornell University

IMPEACHMENT AND TRIAL OF CLINTON — 1998

	ARTICLE 1 (perjury before grand jury)	ARTICLE 2 (perjury in civil lawsuit)	ARTICLE 3 (obstruction of justice)	ARTICLE 4 (abuse of power)
House Outcome	Passed	Failed	Passed	Failed
Senate Outcome*	Not Guilty		Not Guilty	

Source: Washington Post

* In Senate, 67 votes needed for conviction

>> **Analyze Graphs** Explain an example of checks and balances exhibited in the impeachment process illustrated in this graph.

the President of lying under oath about an improper relationship with a White House intern.

Amid heated debate, the House voted to impeach the President. For only the second time in history, the Senate tried a President. In February 1999, the Senate voted to acquit the President, and he continued in office until the end of his second term in 2001.

? IDENTIFY SUPPORTING DETAILS What factors encouraged economic growth during the Clinton administration?

ASSESSMENT

1. **Check Understanding** What was the Iran Hostage Crisis and how did it affect President Carter's political image?

2. **Draw Conclusions** What role did religion play in American politics in the 1980s?

3. **Contrast** Explain how Reagan and Bush's Supreme Court appointees were different from the Justices they replaced.

4. **Interpret** What was the "Contract with America," and how did President Clinton respond to it?

5. **Compare and Contrast** the policies of Ronald Reagan and Bill Clinton.

The End of the Cold War

>> Boris Yeltsin (left) became president of Russia after the Soviet Union broke apart. Here, Yeltsin meets with Bill Clinton in 1997.

▶ **Interactive Flipped Video**

>> Objectives

Describe the new Cold War tensions that developed after 1979.

Explain why communism fell in Eastern Europe and the Soviet Union.

Identify Americans' reaction to the end of the Cold War.

>> Key Terms

détente
Star Wars
Solidarity
martial law
glasnost
summit meeting

Efforts to reduce tensions during the Cold War had improved relations between the United States and the Soviet Union. However, this policy of détente ended suddenly in 1979. In December, Soviet troops invaded Afghanistan, a mountainous nation on the Soviet Union's southern border. Soviet troops were sent there to help a pro-Soviet government.

The End of Détente

Opposing the Soviet Union in Afghanistan

The United States condemned the Soviet invasion of Afghanistan. President Carter withdrew the SALT II Treaty from Senate approval hearings. The United States also refused to take part in the 1980 summer Olympic Games in Moscow.

Despite worldwide criticism, Soviet troops remained in Afghanistan for ten years. They suffered heavy losses as Afghan rebels, supplied by the United States, battled the communist government. The war in Afghanistan became so costly for the Soviets that it weakened the Soviet economy, and Soviet forces could not remain. In 1989, the Soviets were forced to pull all troops out of Afghanistan.

Reagan Reacts

Ronald Reagan declared that the Soviet Union was "the focus of evil in the modern world." He called on Americans to "oppose it with all our might." Reagan also took a tough anticommunist stand in Latin America.

Reagan wanted to deal with the Soviets from a position of strength. To achieve this, he persuaded Congress to increase military spending by more than $100 billion during his first five years in office. His Strategic Defense Initiative (SDI) also called for the development of a new weapons system that Reagan hoped could destroy Soviet missiles from space. SDI was nicknamed **Star Wars** after a popular movie of the time. Only the early stages of research were completed.

During Reagan's first term in office, the two superpowers continued to view each other with deep mistrust. In December 1981, with Soviet backing, Poland's communist government cracked down on **Solidarity**, an independent labor union. Solidarity members had gone on strike at Polish shipyards to demand labor reforms.

>> The Strategic Defense Initiative (SDI) was meant to detect and shoot down enemy missiles. Using mirrors, a ground-based laser would intercept missiles as they were detected. Space-based weapons were also planned that would disable or destroy missiles.

Under Soviet pressure, the Polish government imposed **martial law**, or emergency military rule, on the country. President Reagan condemned the move. He urged the Soviets to allow Poland to restore basic human rights. The United States also put economic pressure on Poland to end martial law.

❓ **IDENTIFY SUPPORTING DETAILS** Identify three details that support the claim that Reagan took a strong stand against the Soviet Union.

The Soviet Empire Crumbles

Cracks began to appear in the Soviet empire in the mid-1980s. Economic problems grew in part because of the huge sums the Soviets were spending on their military to try to keep up with the United States, whose free market economy was much stronger. The Soviets had little money left for producing consumer goods. Soviet citizens stood in line for hours waiting for poorly made products. The communist system was not working. The time was ripe for reform.

Gorbachev Breaks with the Past In 1985, a new Soviet leader, Mikhail Gorbachev (mee kah EEL GOR buh chawf), rose to power. He believed that only major reforms would allow the Soviet system to survive.

Gorbachev backed **glasnost**, the Russian term for speaking out openly. Glasnost, Gorbachev hoped, would lead citizens to find solutions to pressing economic and social problems. This new openness was a break with the past, when any criticism of government policies had been quickly silenced.

Improving Relations Gorbachev realized that he could not solve the Soviet Union's economic problems without cutting military spending sharply. To do so, he had to have better relations with the United States.

President Reagan and Gorbachev met at several summit meetings. A **summit meeting** is a conference between the highest-ranking officials of different nations. Reagan agreed to these meetings because he approved of Gorbachev's new policy of openness.

In 1987, the two leaders signed an arms control pact called the Intermediate Nuclear Force (INF) Treaty. In it, both nations agreed to get rid of their stockpiles of short and medium-range missiles. To prevent cheating, each side would have the right to inspect the other's missile sites. Two years later, Gorbachev withdrew Soviet troops from Afghanistan. This action

>> With a historic handshake, Reagan (right) and Gorbachev open their final summit meeting in Moscow in 1988. At the summit, the two leaders signed agreements on nuclear arms reduction, security, and human rights.

removed another barrier to cooperation between the superpowers.

Change Comes to Eastern Europe For more than 50 years, the communist governments of Eastern Europe had banned any open discussion of political issues. As in the Soviet Union, only one political party, the Communist party, was allowed to win elections. People were denied many basic rights, such as freedom of speech.

Now, in the late 1980s, Eastern European governments could no longer control the rising demands of their people for democratic and economic reforms. With opposition so widespread, most of those governments did not dare to use military force to oppose change. Furthermore, the Soviet Union did not have the power to suppress these protests. It was too busy trying to solve its own problems.

In 1989, Poland held its first free elections in 50 years. Polish voters rejected communist candidates in favor of those put up by the trade union, Solidarity. Solidarity leader, Lech Walesa (LEK vah WEN sah), had once been jailed by the Communists for almost a year. After the elections, he became head of a new Polish government.

One by one, communist governments fell in Czechoslovakia, Hungary, Bulgaria, and Albania. In Romania, a violent revolt toppled the country's longtime communist dictator.

In East Germany, protests in 1989 forced the communists from power. The government was forced to open gates in the Berlin Wall when citizens demanded to be let through. By 1990, Germany was reunited under a democratic government.

The Soviet Union Breaks Apart The Soviet Union was made up of 15 different republics held together by a strong central

>> In November 1989, the Berlin Wall fell. Here, jubilant East Germans rush past Checkpoint Charlie, the U.S. army's control point at the entrance to West Berlin.

▶ Interactive Illustration

Shifting Alliances

KEY
- NATO members, 1989
- Former Warsaw Pact members, 1989; admitted to NATO by 1999
- Other former Warsaw Pact members, 1989
- Neutral countries

UNITED STATES (NATO)

CANADA (NATO)

>> **Analyze Maps** Summarize the most important change in political alliances reflected in this map of Europe.

▶ Interactive Map

government in Moscow. Under Soviet rule, the republics had few powers. All important policy decisions were made in Moscow. Moscow was also the capital of the republic of Russia, containing most of the land and people of the Soviet Union.

By 1990, resentment of Moscow was high in the non-Russian republics. Some of their people demanded self-rule. Meanwhile, Gorbachev allowed political parties to form. For nearly 70 years, the Soviet Union had been a one-party communist state.

Hard-line communist officials were outraged. A group of them sent troops to oust Gorbachev. Their power grab did not last long. A Moscow politician who had rejected the Communist Party, Boris Yeltsin, led thousands of Russians in protest. They surrounded the Parliament building and forced troops to pull back.

As a Communist rejected by his own defeated party, Gorbachev was weakened.

In the months that followed, republic after republic declared its independence from the Soviet Union. In late 1991, Gorbachev resigned. By then, the Soviet Union had collapsed.

Fifteen new nations emerged from the old Soviet Union. Of these, Russia was the largest and most powerful. It began the difficult task of building a new economy based on a free-market system. In a free market, individuals decide what and how much to produce and sell. Under communism, the government had made such economic decisions.

Promoting Democracy in Eastern Europe The United States and Western European nations provided economic aid to Russia, the other former Soviet republics, and Eastern European nations. American experts offered advice to political and business leaders in Russia and Eastern Europe on the free-market system.

A Global Superpower Facing Change **874** 16.2 The End of the Cold War

The United States was eager to see stable, democratic governments emerge in the old communist world. It also hoped that the new nations would become trading partners.

Meanwhile, nations formerly under Soviet domination in Eastern Europe sought to protect their new freedom. Former East Germany became part of the North Atlantic Treaty Organization, or NATO, when Germany reunified in 1990. As a member of NATO, the United States promised to defend other members. In 1999, President Clinton welcomed Poland, the Czech Republic, and Hungary into NATO.

❓ **DESCRIBE** how the United States responded to the collapse of the Soviet Union.

The Aftermath of the Cold War

For almost 50 years, the Cold War deeply affected American life. Students in the 1950s and 60s practiced crouching under their desks in case of atomic attack. Hundreds of thousands of Americans went off to fight in the Korean and Vietnam wars. About 112,000 of them did not return.

The Costs of the Cold War Americans cheered the end of the Cold War and the emergence of democratic governments in Eastern Europe. Victory was costly, though. From 1946 to 1990, the United States spent over $6 trillion on national defense. The development of nuclear weapons and the arms race had created new dangers for the world. During and after the Cold War, other nations besides the superpowers worked to develop their own nuclear weapons.

The Cold War had divided Americans at times. The search for Communists in the 1950s had created an atmosphere of fear and suspicion. The Vietnam War had split the American public in an often bitter debate. Many Americans greeted the end of the Cold War with relief.

The Peace Dividend The collapse of the Soviet Union allowed President Clinton to cut military spending. Tens of thousands of U.S. troops stationed in Germany and other European countries to defend

Causes	Effects
• Soviet Union takes control of Eastern European nations. • Communism gains influence in developing nations. • Western powers fear Soviet expansion.	• Arms race between United States and Soviet Union results in heavy military spending. • Western powers and Soviet Union create separate military alliances. • Armed conflicts erupt in Korea and Vietnam. • United States and Soviet Union compete for influence in developing nations.

THE COLD WAR

>> **Analyze Charts** How did the Cold War affect U.S. military power?

>> U.S. soldiers attend a briefing at an American air base in Germany in 1999. Beginning in the 1990s, the number of U.S. troops stationed in Europe fell sharply.

against a possible Soviet attack were brought home. U.S. military bases were closed.

The money saved by reducing military spending, sometimes called a "peace dividend," helped Clinton to wipe out the federal budget deficit. Some economists believe that it contributed to the economic boom during the Clinton years.

There was another peace dividend that could not be measured in dollar terms. This was the feeling, after decades of living in fear of another world war, that the United States was free at last from serious external threats. This feeling of ease was short-lived, however. During the 1990s, the United States faced a number of new challenges around the world.

❓ IDENTIFY CENTRAL IDEAS What were the costs of fighting the Cold War?

ASSESSMENT

1. **Analyze Information** Explain how the Soviet Union dealt with the Solidarity movement in Poland. How did President Reagan respond?

2. **Identify Central Ideas** Discuss why Gorbachev believed in the concept of *glasnost*. How did it ease tensions between the United States and the Soviet Union?

3. **Compare and Contrast** How did Boris Yeltsin's Russia differ from Gorbachev's Soviet Union? How did their relationship with the United States differ?

4. **Identify Cause and Effect** Discuss the impact of the Cold War on the American public.

5. **Draw Conclusions** Explain why the emergence of democratic governments in Eastern Europe was so important. What effect did it have on U.S. relations with that region?

>> During the 1998-99 war in Kosovo, the United States provided humanitarian aid and assisted refugees. This family from Kosovo arrived at an air force base in New Jersey in 1999.

▶ **Interactive Flipped Video**

The Soviet Union split apart in 1991. The breakup brought an end to the Cold War. The United States remained the world's lone superpower.

>> **Objectives**

Describe how the end of the Cold War changed America's role in the world.

Explain why nuclear arms remained a threat.

Describe how the United States helped promote democracy.

Explain the role of the United States in conflicts in Russia and Eastern Europe, Latin America, the Middle East, and elsewhere.

>> **Key Terms**

mediator
apartheid
sanction
Strategic Arms
  Reduction Treaty
OPEC
Camp David
  Accords
PLO

PEARSON realize www.PearsonRealize.com Access your Digital Lesson.

A Post-Cold War World

Americans debated their function in the post–Cold War world. Some people wanted to reduce the role of the United States in world affairs. "In the post–Cold War world, we will no longer require our people to carry an unfair burden for the rest of humanity," said Representative Dana Rohrabacher.

Others argued that the nation must not retreat from the world. They thought that the United States had a responsibility to use its power wisely. "The United States must lead, period," declared Speaker of the House Newt Gingrich.

Neither President George H.W. Bush nor President Bill Clinton reduced U.S. engagement around the world. Both believed that fostering freedom and democracy abroad would only strengthen the United States at home.

>> Under arms-reduction agreements with the old Soviet Union, many nuclear weapons were dismantled. This disarmed Titan II missile is on display at a Tucson, Arizona, museum.

▶ **Interactive Illustration**

Disarmament As the former Soviet Union collapsed, the world faced a menacing challenge, the spread of nuclear weapons. The United States and Russia still had thousands of nuclear missiles in their possession. Other nations were developing nuclear weapons, too.

The United States and the old Soviet Union had already agreed to several treaties reducing nuclear arms. In 1991, they signed the most important agreement yet, the **Strategic Arms Reduction Treaty**, or START. Even more reductions followed in 1993.

Nuclear Proliferation Despite such progress, a new arms race loomed. In 1970, the Nuclear Nonproliferation Treaty came into force. Under the treaty, nuclear powers such as the United States promised to reduce their stock of nuclear weapons and not to spread nuclear weapon technology to other nations. Nations without nuclear weapons promised not to develop them.

A few countries, including Israel, India, and Pakistan, never agreed to this treaty. According to U.S. government sources, Israel developed nuclear weapons in the late 1960s, though Israel has never confirmed this.

In 1998, India confirmed the worst fears of other nations when it announced that it had conducted five nuclear tests. Two weeks later, Pakistan, its neighbor and deadly rival, exploded five nuclear devices of its own. World leaders saw the tests as the beginning of a dangerous new arms race.

President Clinton called for economic sanctions against both India and Pakistan but with little effect. Pakistan was later found to have shared nuclear weapons

Nuclear Proliferation, 1950–Present

July 16, 1945
United States tests the first atomic bomb in New Mexico.

February 13, 1960
First French atomic bomb is detonated in the Sahara desert.

May 1967
Israel builds its first atomic bomb just days before the Six-Day War.

March 5, 1970
The Nuclear Nonproliferation Treaty to limit the spread of nuclear weapons comes into force.

May 1998
Pakistan tests its first atomic bomb.

August 29, 1949
Russia tests its first atomic bomb using plutonium.

October 3, 1952
United Kingdom tests its first atomic bomb aboard the *HMS Plym*.

May 18, 1974
India tests its first atomic bomb in the Rajasthan Desert.

October 2006
North Korea tests its first atomic bomb.

October 16, 1964
China tests its first atomic bomb using uranium.

1940　1950　1960　1970　1980　1990　2000　2010

Sources: Encyclopædia Britannica; National Center for Biotechnology Information; U.S. Dept. of Energy; The Air University

>> Britain, France, and China joined the United States and Russia as nuclear powers, each with nuclear arms numbering in the hundreds. Each of the other countries in the "nuclear club" has fewer than 100 nuclear weapons.

technology with other countries, including North Korea.

? DEFINE What is nuclear proliferation?

Democratic Gains Around the Globe

The efforts of Presidents Bush and Clinton to promote global democracy supported a process that was already underway. Political freedom was spreading across the globe. With it came economic freedom, including the development of free markets with less interference from the state. In the last years of the 20th century, the United States encouraged both of these trends. American leadership met with both failures and successes.

American leadership took many forms. Sometimes the United States worked to influence foreign governments through quiet diplomacy or economic pressure. Sometimes it acted as a mediator.

A **mediator** is an agent that helps conflicting parties come to an agreement. Occasionally the United States used military force, often in cooperation with other nations.

Democracy in Asia In 1986, thousands of Filipinos protested the rule of dictator Ferdinand Marcos. They accused Marcos of fraud in a recent presidential election.

Proclaiming "people power," they refused to recognize Marcos as president. After weeks of demonstrations, the Philippine army joined the demonstrators. Marcos fled. The United States backed Corazon Aquino, the woman who had run against him. During the 1990s, the United States continued to provide economic aid for the young Filipino democracy.

Limited Reforms in China After President Nixon's historic visit to China, many hoped that the communist nation would begin to reform. During the 1980s, China did begin

>> Chai Ling (with microphone) delivers a speech to supporters in Tiananmen Square in Beijing, China, in 1989. Chai was one of the leaders of the student democracy movement in China, whose protests met with a violent crackdown.

>> In 1980, Cuban migrants depart from Mariel, Cuba, part of a massive movement of Cubans to the United States. At least 125,000 people made the journey in 1980 alone.

to build a free-market economy. However, Chinese leaders refused to accept political reforms.

In 1989, students and workers launched a bold campaign to bring democracy to China. Hundreds of thousands gathered at Tiananmen Square in the nation's capital, Beijing. However, the army crushed the demonstrations. Many people were killed or arrested.

President George H. W. Bush disapproved of the crackdown but took no strong action against the Chinese government. He hoped to influence China by keeping communication open. President Clinton followed a similar policy. On a 1998 visit to China, he pledged to strengthen ties between the two nations. At the same time, he publicly debated human rights issues with China's president.

Communism in Cuba and North Korea

Other communist nations refused to reform even when their people faced hard times. The fall of the Soviet Union deprived Cuba of its main source of trade and economic aid. As the Cuban economy spiraled downward, some 30,000 Cubans fled by boat to the United States. Still, after four decades, Cuba's communist dictatorship remained in power.

In 1994, the United States signed an agreement with Cuba to allow Cubans to emigrate more freely. At the same time, the United States continued to enforce a 40-year-old embargo aimed at toppling Castro.

On the Korean peninsula, the Cold War remained alive. There, the armies of communist North Korea and democratic South Korea faced each other along a tense border. In the 1990s, famine struck North Korea. The famine was worsened by the economic policies of the North Korean dictator, Kim Jong Il.

South Africa Ends Apartheid The cause of global democracy had its most dramatic success in South Africa. Since 1948, the government of South Africa had enforced a policy of **apartheid** (uh PAHRT hayt), or strict separation of races. The nation's nonwhite majority was segregated. By law, nonwhites and whites were required to use separate facilities. Nonwhites were allowed no voice in the government.

In 1986, Congress approved economic sanctions against South Africa to force an end to apartheid. **Sanctions** are measures aimed at making a country change its policy. American companies were forbidden to invest in South Africa or import South African products.

In the 1990s, in response to sanctions, South Africa moved to end minority rule. Under a new constitution, all races were permitted to vote for the first time in 1994. Nelson Mandela (mahn DEL uh), a black man who had spent 27 years in prison for opposing apartheid, was elected president. Mandela called for peace and reconciliation, or an agreement to come together, among South Africa's peoples. He helped establish democracy, racial equality, and freedom in South Africa.

? IDENTIFY SUPPORTING DETAILS How has the United States used economic pressure to promote the spread of democracy?

Challenges in Russia and Eastern Europe

After the Cold War, the nations that rejected communism struggled to adapt to their new freedoms. As the governments sold off state-run businesses to private enterprises, their economies were not able to adjust. The result was high unemployment and high inflation.

Russian president Boris Yeltsin sought to build a stable democracy. His efforts faltered when he failed to put down an

IMPACT OF U.S. SANCTIONS ON SOUTH AFRICA

COMPREHENSIVE ANTIAPARTHEID ACT, 1986
TO PRESSURE SOUTH AFRICA TO END APARTHEID

Banned U.S. businesses from making new investments in South Africa

Banned imports from South Africa (steel, coal, iron, etc.)

Cancelled landing rights for South African airlines

Stopped export of oil to South Africa

Source: Peterson Institute for International Economics

$40 million
in aid for victims of Apartheid
Source: *New York Times*

By the end of 1988, **23** states, **19** counties, and **79** cities adopted additional measures to limit U.S. investment in South Africa
Source: Peterson Institute for International Economics

IMPACT ON INVESTMENT
U.S. companies with direct investments in South Africa

Year	
1985	306
1986	266
1987	227
1988	136

Source: Peterson Institute for International Economics

IMPACT ON TRADE
South African Exports to U.S. (millions of current dollars)

(line graph showing values from 2,500 down to ~1,400 in 1987, rising to ~1,750 by 1992, years 1986–1992)

South Africa lost **$513 million** due to trade restrictions and oil embargo (estimated, 1985–94)
Source: Peterson Institute for International Economics

>> Analyze Graphs Predict how the sanctions imposed by the U.S. government on South Africa might have affected American businesses. How do you think American businesses reacted?

Interactive Chart

independence movement in the Russian province of Chechnya. The United States supported Yeltsin's democratic efforts and offered the Russian government advice on transitioning to a free-market economy.

Bosnian Civil War In Eastern Europe, Yugoslavia faced a civil war. Yugoslavia was made up of several republics, including Croatia, Serbia, and Bosnia-Herzegovina. In 1991, Croatia and Bosnia declared their independence. However, Serbs in Croatia and Bosnia wanted to remain part of Yugoslavia. With help from Serbia, they fought to prevent the new governments from splitting away. Fighting ended quickly in Croatia but continued in Bosnia. During four years of civil war, more than 250,000 people died, including many children and teenagers.

>> At the 1995 Dayton summit meeting in the United States, U.S. leaders mediated between Bosnian president Alija Izetbegovic (left), Croatian president Franjo Tudjman (center), and Serbian president Slobodan Milosevic (right).

To end the violence, the United States sponsored a meeting in Dayton, Ohio. There an agreement was hammered out. To help guarantee the peace agreement, President Clinton sent about 20,000 American troops to Bosnia. There, they joined NATO and Russian forces in a peacekeeping mission. The troops helped to restore order.

Kosovo Seeks Independence Kosovo, a province within Serbia, also sought greater independence. The Albanians living there were in the majority and resented Serbian rule.

In 1998, Serbs launched a series of attacks against Albanian rebels in Kosovo. Hundreds of thousands of Albanians fled the province. Many thousands of others were killed or wounded. President Clinton condemned the attacks as "feeding the flames of ethnic and religious division."

In March 1999, American air forces joined the air forces of other NATO nations in bombing Serbia. This forced Serbian troops to leave Kosovo. NATO peacekeeping forces then entered the province. The violence in Kosovo ended, and a slow process of rebuilding began.

? RECALL How did President Clinton aid peacekeeping efforts in Bosnia and Kosovo?

Intervention in Latin America, Africa, and Europe

In the early 1900s, the United States had frequently intervened in the internal affairs of Latin American nations. In the late 1900s, Cold War tensions led the United States to resume its active role.

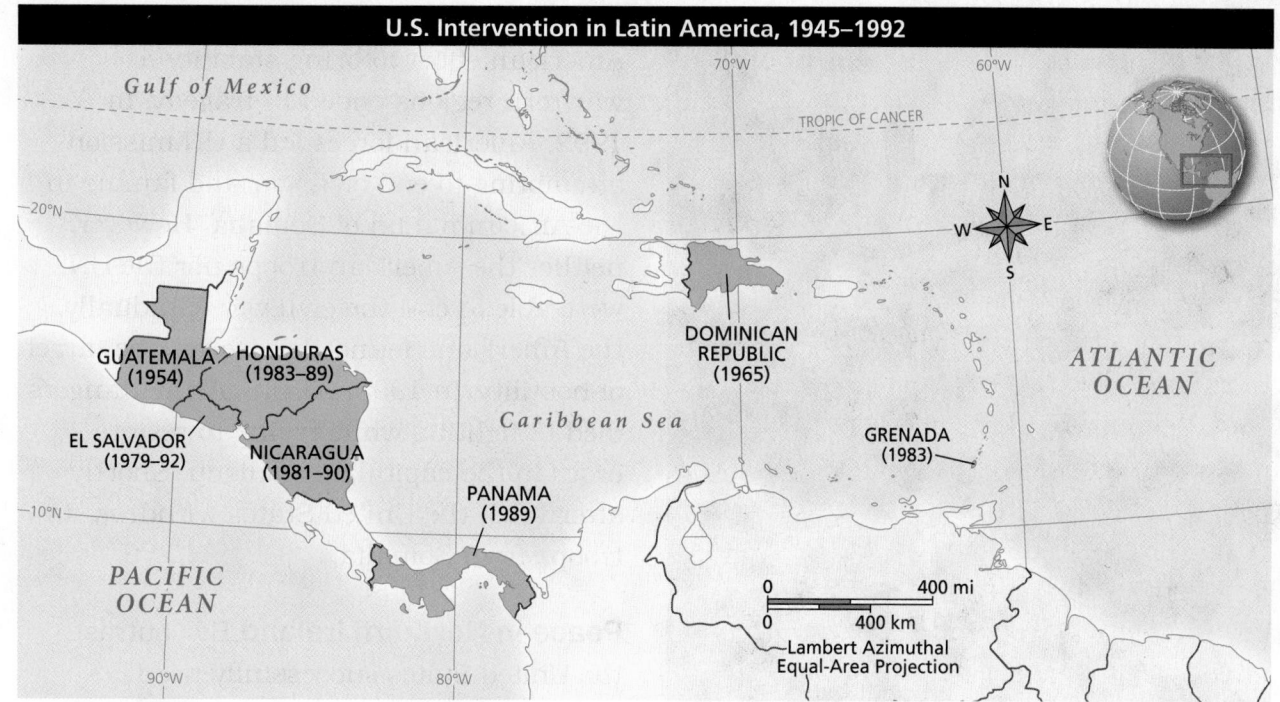

U.S. Intervention in Latin America, 1945–1992

>> **Analyze Maps** Of the nations on the map in which the United States intervened, which was the most recent intervention?

Civil Wars in Latin America During the Cold War, the United States returned to a policy of intervention in Latin American affairs. During the 1970s and 1980s, civil wars raged in several Central American countries. Rebels in El Salvador and Guatemala fought to overthrow harsh governments. The United States backed the governments because they were strongly anticommunist. The wars cost tens of thousands of lives. To escape the fighting, thousands of refugees fled to the United States.

In Nicaragua, a rebel group known as the Sandinistas overthrew a longtime dictator in 1979 and set up a socialist government. President Reagan, afraid that Nicaragua would become another Cuba, aided a group opposed to the Sandinistas. They were known as "Contras," from the Spanish word for "against."

Many members of Congress disagreed with President Reagan's policy in Nicaragua, especially after the Sandinistas won a democratic election in Nicaragua in 1984. They passed laws banning military aid to the Contras. Even so, some people on the President's staff arranged for military aid to the Contras secretly. They arranged to sell weapons to Iran in violation of an arms embargo against the country. The administration sent over half of the millions that Iran paid for the weapons straight to the Contras to aid in their fight.

When details of the "arms-for-hostages" deal became public, many Americans were outraged. The scandal became known as the Iran-Contra affair. Two Reagan officials were tried and convicted of lying to Congress, though the convictions were later successfully appealed. Finally, in 1990, Nicaragua held new elections. Nicaraguans rejected the Sandinistas and voted in new leaders.

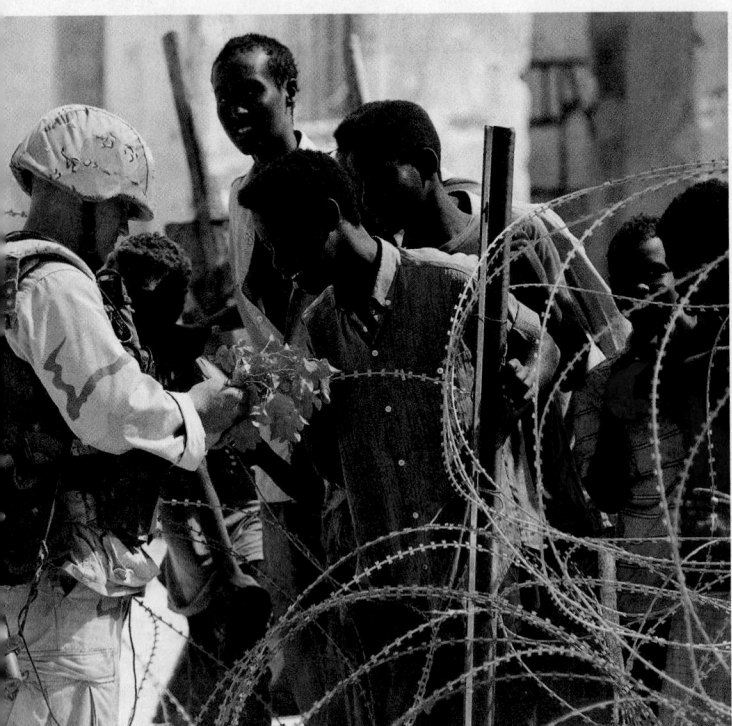

>> U.S. military was forced to return home when they failed to put an end to the civil war in Somalia in 1992. Here, a U.S. soldier is holding flowers given to him by a Somali girl.

>> As the conflict between Arab nations and Israel grew during the 1970s, Israel's Prime Minister Golda Meir (left) forged a strong alliance with the United States. Here, she meets with President Nixon (center) and U.S. Secretary of State Henry Kissinger (front, right) in 1979.

Tragedy in Somalia Sometimes the American effort to bring stability to war-torn regions ended in tragedy. In 1992, American forces led a UN mission attempting to end civil war and famine in the African nation of Somalia. However, neither the American troops nor the UN were able to end the civil war. Gradually, the Americans found themselves the target of hostility. In 1993, 18 U.S. Army Rangers died in fighting while trying to restore order in the capital, Mogadishu. Shortly afterward, the United States withdrew its troops from Somalia.

Peace in Northern Ireland By contrast, the United States successfully used diplomacy to ease conflict in Northern Ireland. Most members of the Catholic minority there wanted the region to be reunited with Ireland. Most of the Protestant majority wanted to remain under British rule. From 1969 to 1998, more than 3,000 people died in the fighting.

The United States sent former Senator George Mitchell of Maine to aid the Northern Ireland peace talks. He helped to produce an agreement in April 1998. Although the peace process was slow and often troubled, a lasting peace settlement seemed within reach.

? CHECK UNDERSTANDING Explain the Iran-Contra affair in your own words.

Conflict in the Middle East

Conflict had long troubled the Middle East, a region extending from southwestern Asia across North Africa. Over the centuries, friction among religious groups has led to discord and violence. European attempts to colonize the Middle East and competition for large oil reserves in the region added to tensions.

The Middle East Today

KEY
- Israel before 1967
- Area controlled by Israel since 1967
- Area controlled by Israel 1967-2005
- Members of OPEC
- Oil fields
- - - - Disputed border
- —— National border

>> **Analyze Maps** Name the areas that Israel controlled after 1967.

The United States had conflicting interests in the Middle East. It strongly supported the Jewish state of Israel. Yet, it also had ties to the Muslim Arab states that dominated the region. Arab nations such as Saudi Arabia supplied much of the oil used by Americans.

A Jewish State In the late 1800s, European Jews arrived in a region sometimes known as Palestine along the Mediterranean coast. They hoped to create a Jewish state in their ancient homeland. Jewish settlement grew in the 1930s as European Jews fled Nazi persecution.

In 1948, Arabs rejected a plan to divide the land into one Jewish and one Palestinian Arab state. Jews in the region announced the creation of the state of Israel. The United States and other nations quickly recognized the new nation.

Arab-Israeli Wars Neighboring Arab nations refused to recognize the Jewish

state. Instead, they attacked. But Israel won the 1948 war. More than 500,000 Palestinian Arabs fled to refugee camps in the region surrounding Israel. Most were not permitted to return after the war and were not paid for their lands and homes. Meanwhile, hundreds of thousands of Jewish refugees from Arab nations fled to Israel, leaving their lands and homes behind.

Arab nations fought Israel again in 1967 and 1973. Israel defeated its opponents in both wars. In 1967, it took control of territories neighboring Israel, including areas that were home to many Palestinian Arab refugees.

The United States sent aid to Israel in the 1973 war. Arab members of **OPEC**, the Organization of Petroleum Exporting Countries, retaliated. They cut off oil shipments to the United States and slowed down oil production. OPEC finally lifted the oil embargo in 1974.

A Move Toward Peace Egyptian president Anwar el-Sadat took a bold step toward peace in 1977. He became the first Arab head of state to visit Israel. When peace talks between the two nations broke down, President Jimmy Carter invited Sadat and Israeli Prime Minister Menachem Begin (muh NAHK um BAY gin) to Camp David, the President's retreat in Maryland.

In the **Camp David Accords** of 1978, Israel agreed to return the Sinai Peninsula to Egypt, and Egypt agreed to recognize Israel. The two nations signed a peace treaty in 1979.

The Palestinian Conflict Some Palestinian Arabs waged guerrilla war against Israel. Under Israeli rule, Palestinians in territories controlled by Israel had limited rights. Those living outside Israeli control wanted to return to their homeland under a Palestinian government. Many supported the Palestine Liberation Organization, or **PLO**. Its leader, Yasser Arafat, stated that the goal of the PLO was to destroy Israel.

In 1987, Palestinians in the Israeli-controlled West Bank and Gaza Strip took to the streets to protest Israeli rule. The unrest, called the *Intifada*, focused attention on the need to end the Israeli-Palestinian conflict.

After years of effort, the United States persuaded Israel and the PLO to come to the bargaining table. In 1993, the longtime enemies signed a pact in Washington, D.C. The PLO agreed to recognize Israel's right to exist and promised to give up violence. Israel agreed to limited self-rule for Palestinian parts of the Gaza Strip and West Bank. Despite this agreement, tensions persisted in the region.

The Iranian Revolution The United States was deeply involved in other Middle East conflicts. In 1953, the United States helped to overthrow the elected government of Iran and to return the dethroned Shah Muhammad Reza Pahlavi to power. Then, in 1979, a revolution forced the unpopular shah to flee. A religious leader, the Ayatollah Khomeini (i yuh TOH luh koh MAYN ee), took control of Iran.

The First Gulf War In August 1990, Saddam Hussein, the dictator of Iraq, sent 100,000 troops to invade oil-rich Kuwait. President George H.W. Bush feared that the invasion was the start of a larger plan to gain control of Middle East oil. Saddam Hussein ignored demands from the United States and the UN to withdraw from Kuwait. The UN then imposed a trade boycott on Iraq.

>> In September 1993, Israel and the PLO finally reached a peace agreement. Israeli Prime Minister Itzak Rabin (left) and PLO leader Yasser Arafat (right) shake hands in Washington, D.C., in front of President Clinton.

>> Kuwaiti troops such as these were trained by the United States and used U.S.-supplied equipment, such as this tank, during the 1990 Gulf War with Iraq.

When Saddam still refused to leave Kuwait, the United States and its UN allies launched an air attack on Iraq. This was followed by a massive attack on Iraqi troops in Kuwait and Iraq. Troops from 28 nations—including some Arab countries—joined the effort. It took only six weeks to defeat the Iraqis and free Kuwait.

Although the war was over, the UN boycott against Iraq continued. The goal was to force Saddam Hussein to stop his chemical and biological weapons programs. However, Hussein refused to cooperate with UN arms inspectors.

[?] **DESCRIBE** the role that the United States played in the Camp David Accords.

ASSESSMENT

1. **Analyze Information** Discuss the debate over the role of the United States in world affairs after the Cold War.

2. **Cite Evidence** What were the Tiananmen Square protests, and how did the United States respond to them?

3. **Express Ideas Clearly** How did apartheid affect nonwhites and whites in South Africa from the mid 1900s to the 1990s, and how did the United States push for an end to apartheid?

4. **Support Ideas with Evidence** What were some of the reasons for the conflict in Northern Ireland between 1969 and 1998, and what did the United States do to aid peacekeeping efforts?

5. **Generate Explanations** How did the conflict between Iraq and the United States and the UN develop in the early 1990s? How was it resolved?

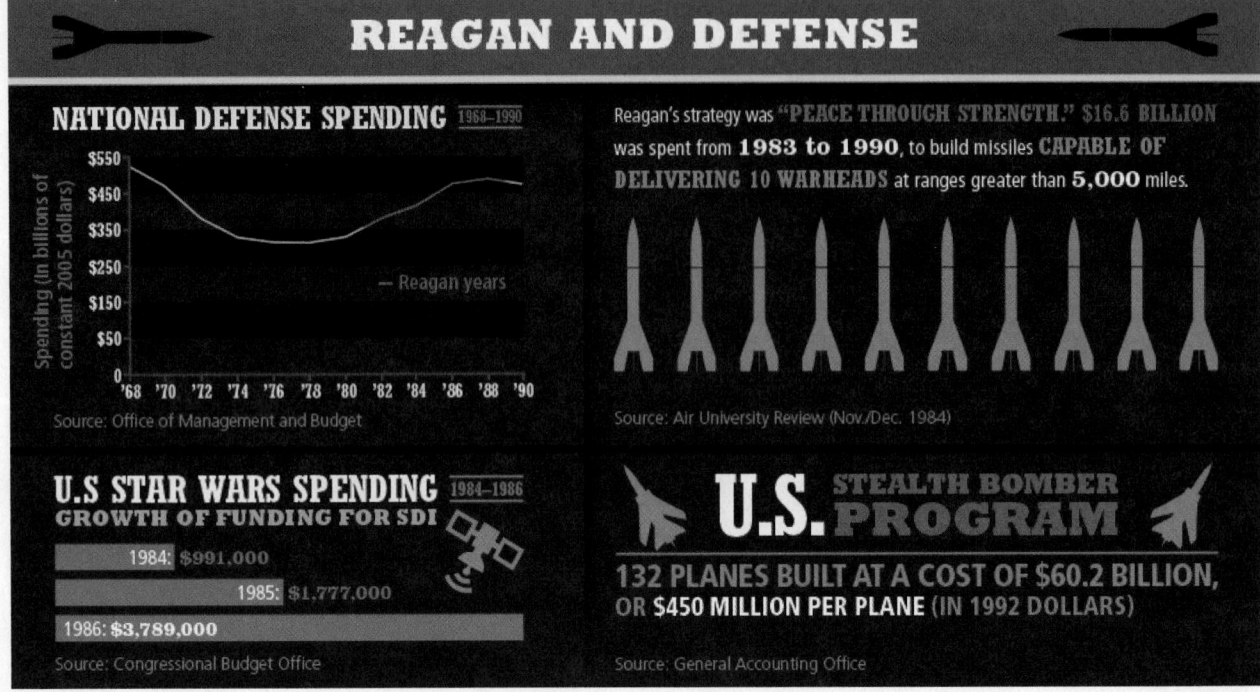

1. **Identify Cause and Effect** Use the graph above and the information from the lessons in this topic and other sources to write a paragraph describing President Reagan's approach to national defense and the relationship between his national defense strategy and foreign policy. In your paragraph, be sure to address the relationship between Reagan's defense strategy and the end of the Cold War.

2. **Analyze the Camp David Accords** Write a paragraph describing the Camp David Accords and the role that the United States played in the negotiations. Be sure to describe the conflict the Accords were meant to help resolve, the role the United States played in the Accords and the objective for which the Accords provided a framework.

3. **Evaluate International Treaties** Write a paragraph evaluating reasons why the United States signed the Strategic Arms Reduction Treaty, or START, in 1991. Then explain the possible pros and possible cons to U.S. agreement to this treaty.

4. **Explain the Goals of the Moral Majority** Write a paragraph explaining the Moral Majority's views and goals. Be sure to describe who founded the Moral Majority, what kind of organization it was, and what the quotation below and the text indicate about the concerns and goals of the Moral Majority.

We must reverse the trend America finds herself in today. Young people . . . have been born and reared in a different world than Americans of past worlds. . . . They have learned to disrespect the family as God has established it. . . . They have been taught that the Bible is just another book of literature. . . . They have been introduced to the drug culture.

—Reverend Jerry Falwell, *Listen America*, 1980

5. **Identify Viewpoints** Write a paragraph describing how the viewpoints of liberals and conservatives differed on significant issues in the 1980s. Describe each group's viewpoints.

6. **Evaluate Reaganomics** Write a paragraph describing President Reagan's economic theory as it was embodied in Reaganomics and how Reagan put the theory into practice. Be sure to explain why Reagan wanted to cut federal spending; evaluate how Congress worked with Reagan to implement his plan; and analyze how Reagan justified the effect of his plan on the wealthy.

7. **Explain the End of the Cold War** Write a paragraph describing how the Cold War came to an end. Explain the reforms Soviet President Gorbachev instituted and why, describe how these reforms affected U.S.-Soviet relations, and identify the historical events in the Soviet Union and Eastern Europe that led to the end of the Cold War.

8. **Identify Turning Points** Write a paragraph explaining why 1991 was a turning point in Cold War relations. Answer the following questions in your paragraph: What events occurred in the Soviet Union in 1991? How did these events affect U.S. foreign policy?

9. **Evaluate Dealings With Iran and the Contras** Explain how members of the Reagan administration acted illegally to sell arms to Iran and aid the Contras in Nicaragua. In a paragraph, give reasons for and against these actions, and evaluate their impact.

10. **Explain the Impact of Independent Candidates** Use the information in the topic and lessons to write a paragraph analyzing the impact of Ross Perot on the 1992 presidential campaign. Consider what percentage of the popular vote Perot received and explain how this statistic may have influenced the outcome of the election.

11. **Evaluate NAFTA** Use the information from the lessons in this topic and other sources to write a paragraph describing NAFTA. In your paragraph, be sure to describe what NAFTA is; what NAFTA's supporters claimed the pros of the agreement would be; what NAFTA's opponents claimed the cons of the agreement would be.

12. **Identify and Contrast Viewpoints on the Contract With America** Identify Newt Gingrich, and describe Gingrich's Contract With America. Be sure to describe who Gingrich was and why he launched the Contract With America. Identify what the Contract With America called for. Identify the viewpoints of Gingrich and other Republicans on Gingrich's proposals. Identify and contrast the viewpoints of Clinton and other Democrats on those proposals.

13. **Identify the Effects of Political Scandals** Write a paragraph describing the impact of scandals that President Clinton faced during his time in office. Be sure to identify the scandals; define *impeachment*; describe how one scandal led to impeachment proceedings, reactions to those proceedings, and the outcome of the proceedings. Finally, consider how scandals and political reactions to scandals might have affected the trust citizens had in the federal government and its leaders.

14. **Evaluate Pros and Cons** Use the lessons in this topic and other sources to write a paragraph describing the pros and cons of the United States participating in UN peacekeeping and relief missions. Draw historical evidence from U.S. participation in UN missions during the Bush and Clinton administrations; evaluate both the pros and cons of involvement; consider the effect of involvement and treaties on U.S. security.

15. **Identify the Causes and Effects of the Persian Gulf War** Use the information from the lessons in this topic and other sources to write a paragraph describing the causes and effects of the Persian Gulf War. In your paragraph, be sure to consider why Saddam Hussein invaded Kuwait; what actions President Bush took and why; what Operation Desert Storm did and did not accomplish.

16. **Reflect on the Essential Question** **Write an essay on the Essential Question: What is America's role in the world?** Use evidence from your study of this topic to support your answer.

17 Meeting New Challenges (1975–Present)

Enduring Understandings

- Terrorist attacks on the United States led to U.S. invasions of Iraq and Afghanistan.

- In a global economy, economic issues in other countries could affect the U.S. economy.

- The United States faced security threats in North Korea, Iran, and other parts of the Middle East and East Asia.

- New technologies improved communication, medical care, and U.S. energy security.

- The United States continued to face environmental challenges.

>> Advances in sciences and technology in the early 2000s included new uses for satellites.

PEARSON realize™   **NBC LEARN**

Watch the My Story Video, to learn how Steve Jobs transformed people's relationship to technology.

PEARSON realize™
www.PearsonRealize.com

Access your digital lessons including:
Topic Inquiry • Interactive Reading
Notepad • Interactivities • Assessments

Terrorism and Wars Overseas

>> The U.S. military worked with Afghans to hunt down terrorists in Afghanistan.

Interactive Flipped Video

>> **Objectives**

Describe the terrorist attacks of September 11, 2001, and their impact on the United States.

Explain why the United States went to war in Afghanistan and describe the course of that war.

Assess the impact of the U.S. intervention in Iraq.

Reflect on the treatment of prisoners following the September 11 attacks.

Identify the continuing challenges posed by jihadism.

>> **Key Terms**

jihadism
Islamic
  fundamentalist
terrorism
weapon of mass
  destruction
insurgency

On September 11, 2001, members of Al Qaeda, an international Islamist terrorist network, launched an attack against the United States. Osama bin Laden (oh SAH muh bin LAH dun) had founded Al Qaeda in 1988. Al Qaeda was based on the idea of **jihadism**.

The United States Responds to an Attack

Jihadism is an Islamic fundamentalist movement that supports violence in the struggle against those seen as enemies of the religion of Islam. Most **Islamic fundamentalists**—Muslims who believe that Islamic religious texts should be taken literally—are not jihadists. Jihadists, however, are generally Islamic fundamentalists. They are also Islamists, or Muslims who believe that society should be governed by religious, Islamic law.

With jihadism as its foundation, Al Qaeda pursued a strategy of **terrorism**, or the use of violence and cruelty to achieve political goals. Note that most Muslims, or people who follow Islam, are not fundamentalists and oppose both jihadism and terrorism.

Al Qaeda opposed American influence in the Muslim world and launched a number of attacks against American targets beginning in the 1990s, including U.S. embassies in Kenya and Tanzania. Hundreds of people died in these attacks, which led President Bill Clinton to order the bombing of bin Laden's headquarters in Afghanistan. The bombings were unsuccessful in stopping the terrorist network and in 2000, Al Qaeda attacked the *USS Cole*, an American Navy destroyer that was anchored at a port in Yemen on the coast of the Arabian Peninsula.

Al Qaeda Attacks the United States The East Coast's clear blue sky on the morning of September 11, 2001, gave no indication that the day would end far differently than it began. As Americans began their day, nineteen Al Qaeda terrorists prepared to seize four commercial airliners in an attack against the United States.

At 8:46 A.M., the hijackers crashed the first plane into one of the World Trade Center's twin towers, New York City's tallest buildings, a location later known as "ground zero." Another plane hit the second tower about 15 minutes later. Within the hour, a third plane crashed into the Pentagon, the American military headquarters in Arlington, Virginia. Brave passengers on a fourth plane bound for Washington, D.C., stormed the cockpit, leading the hijackers to crash the plane into a field in Shanksville, Pennsylvania.

Within two hours of the attack, the twin towers of the World Trade Center had collapsed. The September 11 attacks killed nearly 3,000 people and stunned Americans. President George W. Bush quickly blamed Osama bin Laden and Al Qaeda.

>> The September 11, 2001, terrorist attack shocked Americans. The World Trade Center towers in New York City were struck by hijacked aircraft, burned, and collapsed.

▶ **Interactive Gallery**

In response, the Bush administration launched what it called a global war on terrorism, far different from other wars America had fought. The enemy, less clearly defined, included terrorist groups that threatened the United States and its allies.

This effort to wipe out terrorism led the United States into wars in Iraq and Afghanistan. It also led to the creation of the Department of Homeland Security, which was given the job of safeguarding security within the United States. Meanwhile, Congress passed the USA PATRIOT Act, which allows officials to conduct surveillance on suspected terrorists at home and abroad.

The War in Afghanistan Shortly after the September 11 attacks, President Bush asked Afghanistan to surrender Osama bin Laden. The Taliban, the Islamic fundamentalist group that controlled Afghanistan, refused.

In October 2001, with authorization from Congress, American forces invaded Afghanistan. The war began with American-led bombing missions. By the end of 2001, the Northern Alliance, made up of Afghans who opposed the Taliban, had captured the capital city of Kabul. They established a new government that was friendly to the United States.

The United States provided money to support the new Afghan government, and American forces stayed in the country. In spite of this, the new government never gained full control of Afghanistan. During the war, bin Laden escaped to Pakistan. By 2007, the Taliban had regained some of its power in Afghanistan.

When Barack Obama became president in 2009, the war in Afghanistan was still underway. In 2009, Obama sent additional troops to Afghanistan to provide protection

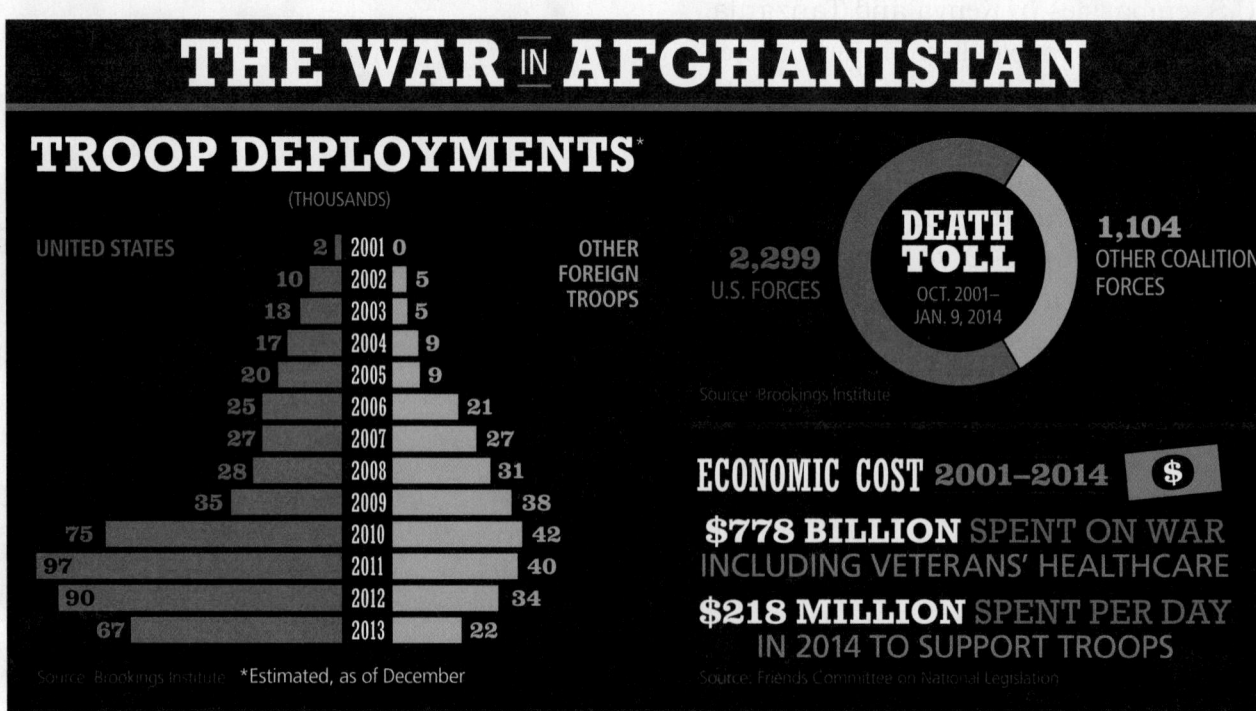

>> **Analyze Graphs** Based on the data in the bar graph on the left, summarize the role of the United States in the international coalition that fought in the war.

Iraq Regions and Ethnic Groups

KEY
- Kurd
- Sunni Arab
- Sunni Turkoman
- Shia Arab
- Sparsely populated

>> **Analyze Maps** Identify the areas in Iraq where ethnic conflicts might have been most likely to occur.

▶ Interactive Timeline

and to train Afghan forces. He promised to remove all American forces by the end of 2014.

When the United States entered Afghanistan in 2001, almost 90 percent of Americans supported the war. As the war dragged on, however, American support declined. When asked in 2012, 50 percent of Americans wanted the government to speed the removal of troops from Afghanistan. In 2014, a partial withdrawal of U.S. troops from Afghanistan began.

? IDENTIFY CAUSE AND EFFECT Why did the United States invade Afghanistan?

The Iraq War

In 2002 and 2003, tensions mounted between the United States and Iraq. Ever since the Gulf War of 1991, the United States and its allies had maintained a no-flight zone over parts of Iraq. They had also pushed for continued inspections of Iraqi military facilities to watch for the development of chemical, biological, or nuclear weapons, also known as **weapons of mass destruction**, or WMDs.

In his 2002 State of the Union Address, President Bush declared that Iraq formed an "axis of evil" with Iran and North Korea. Although none of the countries had a direct connection to the September 11 attacks, Bush accused them of protecting terrorists and hiding WMDs that threatened the United States. Iraq had repeatedly blocked inspections and refused to destroy weapons that violated rules set by the United Nations. In early 2003, the United States and Britain claimed to have evidence that Iraq in fact possessed WMDs.

War Breaks Out Based on this evidence, the Bush administration wanted UN approval to go to war but said it would act with or without that approval.

Congress approved a resolution that gave the President the power to use force, if necessary.

In March 2003, although Iraq had allowed UN officials to conduct inspections and had begun destroying weapons, U.S. officials said that Iraq had not done enough to address concerns. U.S. and British forces began bombing targets inside Iraq and then sent troops into the country. After a month, U.S. forces occupied the capital city of Baghdad. In May, Bush declared the war concluded. No working WMDs were ever found. In December, American forces captured Saddam Hussein and turned him over to an Iraqi court for trial. The court found him guilty and sentenced him to death in 2006.

In the meantime, the United States had transferred control to a temporary Iraqi government in 2004. The next year, Iraqis elected a national assembly that had the difficult job of organizing a government despite ongoing violent conflicts among the country's Sunni Muslim Arabs, Shia Muslim Arabs, and ethnic Kurds. Despite Bush's earlier claim, the Iraq War was not yet finished. U.S. forces faced the task of supporting the government and trying to end the violence. In fact, U.S. involvement in the war would continue until 2011.

Mixed Results and Withdrawal The United States paid a heavy price for the Iraq War. Almost 5,000 Americans and hundreds of thousands of Iraqis died. After eight years, the war cost more than a trillion dollars. Saddam Hussein was removed from power, but that did not bring peace to Iraq. Iraqis looted businesses and homes. Shiite and Sunni Arabs fought each other, and Arabs fought ethnic Kurds in the north. An **insurgency**, or armed rebellion, arose against American soldiers and the Iraqi government. The new Iraqi government was too weak to manage the country.

As the war continued, support for it decreased. By early 2007, polls showed that most Americans thought the war in Iraq was a mistake and was unwinnable. In spite of this, the Bush administration increased the number of American forces with a troop surge. The surge reduced ethnic and religious violence in the country for a time but did not end it.

In 2008, Iraqis demanded a plan for the withdrawal of American troops. In 2011, President Obama ordered the removal of American troops from Iraq. In December of that year, the last 500 soldiers left Iraq, with the exception of a few guarding the American embassy.

In 2014, a jihadist group based in Syria and calling itself the Islamic State gained

>> After the 2001 attacks on the United States, Osama bin Laden became a figurehead for jihadist terrorists. On May 2, 2011, U.S. Special Forces finally hunted him down and killed him.

control of much of western Iraq. Civil war resumed in Iraq, which threatened to split into separate territories dominated by the country's different ethnic and religious groups.

? **RECALL** How did the United States and Britain justify attacking Iraq?

The Continuing Challenges of Jihadism

In 2011, nearly 10 years after the September 11 attacks, American forces captured and killed Osama bin Laden at his compound in Pakistan. Bin Laden's death, however, did not signal the end of jihadism, Al Qaeda, or the threat of terrorism. Indeed, organizations linked to Al Qaeda seemed to be expanding after 2010. Meanwhile, the United States faced questions about how it had conducted the war on terrorism.

Policy Questions Following the September 11 attacks, Bush administration officials claimed that many areas of international law did not apply to the war on terrorism. They argued that this was especially true of laws on the treatment of prisoners, because members of Al Qaeda were not part of a regular national army. U.S. military officers worried that mistreatment would lead other countries to retaliate against American prisoners. Despite this concern, the Department of Defense approved methods of forcing prisoners to reveal information that some critics labeled as torture.

Mistreatment of prisoners at Abu Ghraib in Iraq received worldwide attention. The United States also faced criticism over the indefinite detention of prisoners at Guantanamo Bay in Cuba. Guantanamo Bay prison opened in 2002 to house

>> These jihadist protestors in Amman, Jordan, demonstrated against the United States in 2012. Most Muslims oppose jihadism.

detainees captured in Afghanistan, Iraq, Asia, and Africa through the war on terrorism. After 2002, the United States housed more than 700 detainees there. Many of the prisoners at Guantanamo have not been tried in court or proven to have acted illegally, though most are suspected of terrorism.

Relations with Afghanistan and neighboring Pakistan have also posed challenges. While the United States supported a new Afghan government led by Hamid Karzai during the early 2000s, his government faced widespread accusations of corruption. Karzai also grew increasingly hostile toward the United States.

Meanwhile, Pakistan, which received U.S. aid and provided an important supply route to Afghanistan, was accused of supporting the Taliban who were fighting the Afghan government. Members of

>> An Algerian soldier stands guard in the aftermath of a terrorist attack on an Algerian gas plant in January 2013. Islamist terrorism continued despite international anti-terrorist efforts.

Pakistan's military were also accused of sheltering Osama bin Laden, who lived for years near a major Pakistani military base.

The Roots of Jihadism Jihadism is a concept that is difficult for many non-Muslims to understand. Muslims define *jihad* as a struggle to achieve the goals of Islam. The struggle can take place inside a person, as that person struggles to accept and devote himself or herself to the requirements of Islam. The struggle can also take place externally, as a person battles individuals who are opposed to Islam. Jihadists emphasize this second definition, which they use to justify violent actions that most Muslims oppose.

Believing that Islam is under attack, the goal of jihadists is to fight those they see as opponents of Islam throughout the world, often using terrorist methods. They want to remove unfriendly governments in Muslim countries and wage war against countries that they see as enemies.

A Resilient Force By 2012, jihadist movements had taken root in Yemen, Pakistan, and Somalia, and the United States began attacking jihadists in these countries. Many of these jihadists were linked to Al Qaeda. Despite U.S. attacks, mainly by pilotless drone aircraft, jihadists seemed to remain strong in parts of these countries.

Meanwhile, jihadists groups had a growing presence in other parts of the Muslim world. In Syria, where a civil war was being fought, jihadist fighters linked to Al Qaeda gained territory. They also fought the government of Iraq after the U.S. withdrawal. Jihadist groups also launched violent attacks in Algeria, Mali, and Nigeria. U.S. policymakers were concerned about the spread of jihadists hostile to the United States and its allies but struggled to find an effective way to counter them.

? **EXPLAIN** What is jihadism?

ASSESSMENT

1. **Summarize** Why did the United States invade Afghanistan, and what was the outcome?

2. **Summarize** How did President George W. Bush and Congress respond to the September 11 attacks?

3. **Distinguish** Discuss the successes and failures of the U.S. war effort in Iraq.

4. **Summarize** Why did the United States face criticism about how it conducted the war on terrorism?

5. **Summarize** How did jihadists continue their mission after Osama bin Laden's death? How did the United States respond?

>> Unrest spread across the Arab world after the Arab Spring of 2011. This protest in Yemen took place in 2014.

▶ **Interactive Flipped Video**

The spread of nuclear weapons is known as **nuclear proliferation**. By the early 2000s, most countries in the world, including the United States, had signed the **Nuclear Non-Proliferation Treaty** (NPT). The NPT required countries that already had nuclear weapons to reduce their number of weapons. It also prohibited countries that did not have nuclear weapons from acquiring them. All countries, however, could use nuclear power for peaceful purposes. The goal of non-proliferation is to reduce the chance of nuclear war.

>> **Objectives**

Explain international concerns about nuclear proliferation in North Korea and Iran.

Describe the Israeli-Palestinian conflict and U.S. efforts to mediate it.

Identify U.S. responses to the Arab Spring and the Syrian Civil War.

Describe U.S. relationships with international allies.

>> **Key Terms**

Arab Spring
North Atlantic Treaty
  Organization
European Union
nuclear proliferation
Nuclear Non-
  Proliferation Treaty

Opposing the Spread of Nuclear Weapons

Nuclear Tensions With North Korea As the United States and the global community monitored nuclear proliferation, North Korea was one country that attracted attention. In 1985, North Korea joined the Nuclear Non-Proliferation Treaty. Since North Korea did not have nuclear weapons when it joined the NPT, it was prohibited from obtaining them.

International concern about its nuclear program led North Korea to use the program as a negotiating tool. In the 1990s, North Korea offered to end its nuclear program if the United States and other nations assisted North Korea with the construction of nuclear power plants.

Both sides reached an agreement in 1994. However, both sides accused each other of failing to live up to the agreement. In 2001, President George W. Bush announced that he would not negotiate with North Korea until it met a list of conditions.

In response, North Korea resumed its nuclear program. In 2003, the country withdrew from the NPT. In 2006, North Korea conducted its first nuclear weapon test, but many experts believed that the weapon had failed. In 2009, North Korea conducted its second nuclear weapon test. This time, most experts agree, the North Korean weapon successfully exploded.

The United States responded to North Korea's nuclear program through its own efforts and through international organizations such as the United Nations (UN). North Korea's nuclear program caused international concern because of the possibility of nuclear attacks or a nuclear disaster.

The UN Security Council, including the United States, condemned North Korea's nuclear testing and imposed sanctions, or restrictions, on trade with North Korea. Even China, North Korea's closest ally, supported UN Security Council resolutions requiring North Korea to end its nuclear program. In spite of this, North Korea

Pillars of the Nuclear Non-Proliferation Treaty

NON-PROLIFERATION	DISARMAMENT	PEACEFUL USES
• Countries that do not have nuclear capabilities agree not to produce or import nuclear weapons. • Countries that have nuclear capabilities agree not to sell or export nuclear weapons to countries that do not. • Groups of countries are allowed to establish zones that are free of nuclear weapons.	• All countries that have signed the treaty will no longer compete with other countries to produce nuclear weapons. • All countries that have signed the treaty will work toward eliminating their nuclear weapons inventory.	• All countries that have signed the treaty agree to share information and equipment to produce nuclear energy for peaceful uses, namely in the fields of energy and medicine.

Source: U.S. Department of State

>> **Analyze Charts** Based on the information in the chart, provide definitions for *non-proliferation* and *disarmament*.

continued constructing and testing nuclear weapons.

Iran's Nuclear Program Iran's nuclear program also alarmed the United States and other countries. Because Iranian governments expressed strong hostility to Israel, a U.S. ally, Israel voiced special concern. Iran began its nuclear program in the 1950s with American assistance. As an NPT member, Iran originally focused on developing nuclear power plants for peaceful purposes. In the late 1970s, however, evidence suggested that Iran was developing a nuclear weapons program. The United States and other countries worked to convince Iran to end that program.

The U.S. government asked other countries not to sell nuclear technology to Iran. It imposed sanctions that harmed Iran's economy. And, the United States partnered with other countries, as it had done in attempts to end North Korea's nuclear program. The **European Union** (EU) joined in imposing sanctions against Iran. Major Western powers moved to restrict Iran's access to the international financial system.

These efforts limited Iran's ability to sell oil, its most important export. This caused economic problems for Iran. In 2013, Iranians elected a new president, Hassan Rouhani, who was willing to negotiate with the United States and other powers over nuclear weapons. Negotiations to prevent Iran from developing nuclear weapons began in 2013, but mutual trust was difficult to establish, and the prospects for any deal were uncertain.

? RECALL What is the main purpose of the NPT?

>> U.S. Secretary of State John Kerry (right) met with Iranian Foreign Minister Mohammad Javad Zarif in 2013 to begin negotiations on limiting Iran's nuclear activities.

Unrest in Southwest Asia and North Africa

The United States had strong ties to North Africa and Southwest Asia. This region lies where the continents of Africa, Asia, and Europe meet. It is a region inhabited by Jews, Christians, and Muslims. As in past years, old conflicts in this region continued after 2000, and new conflicts emerged. The United States was a close ally of Israel, a mainly Jewish nation. At the same time, the U.S. economy relied on the oil production of Muslim nations, such as Saudi Arabia. The United States tried to resolve conflicts in this region. It remained committed to supporting democracy, its allies, and its own national interests.

Ongoing Arab-Israeli Tensions In 2003, President George W. Bush presented a "road map to peace" in the Israeli-Palestinian conflict. The goal was an independent Palestinian state and peaceful relations between Palestinians and Israelis.

Bush called for an end to the violence and for Israel to withdraw its troops permanently from Gaza and the West Bank, which Israel had occupied in 1967. However, resistance on both sides led to an abandonment of the "road map." Israeli Prime Minister Ariel Sharon, nonetheless, announced that he would withdraw Israeli forces from Gaza, home to more than 1.5 million Palestinians. Israel continued to control Gaza's boundaries, waters, and airspace. Israel also continued a policy of building Jewish settlements in the West Bank.

In 2006, missile attacks from an armed group had led Israel to invade Lebanon. The U.S. government supported Israel's action as defensive. The war only lasted a month but caused deaths and physical and economic damage. The UN negotiated an end to the war, but tensions between Arabs and Israelis remained.

In 2007, tensions between Israel and Gaza increased when Hamas, an organization labeled as terrorist by Israel and the United States, came to power in Gaza. When rockets launched from Gaza killed Israeli civilians, Israel attacked Gaza in late 2008 and early 2009. These attacks also resulted in deaths among Palestinian civilians.

Israel continued to restrict the flow of supplies and people across Gaza's borders. The U.S. government again supported Israel's actions as justified in terms of self-defense and continued to try to ease tensions between Israel and the Palestinians.

In 2014, another round of violence flared up between Hamas in Gaza and Israel. Hamas once again fired missiles into Israel, killing some civilians. Again Israel bombarded Gaza and sent troops into the territory, resulting in many civilian

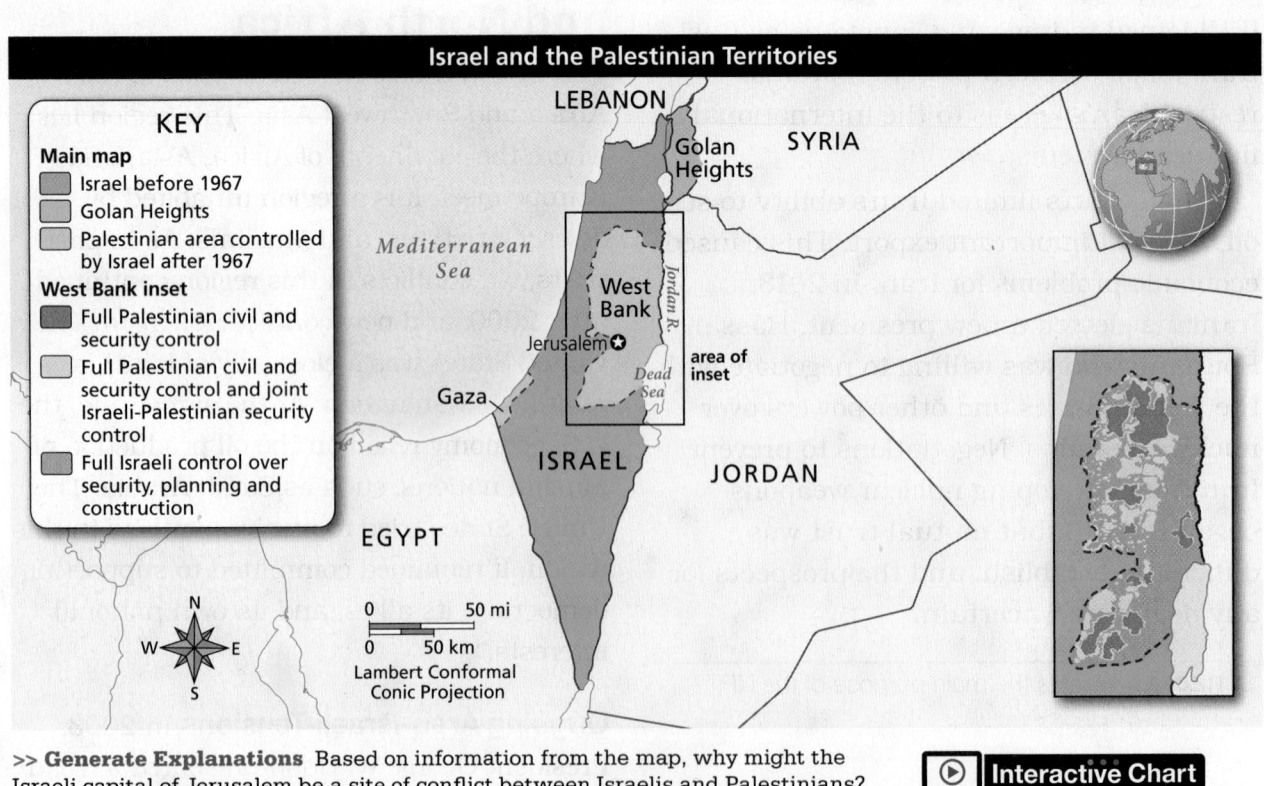

Israel and the Palestinian Territories

KEY

Main map
- Israel before 1967
- Golan Heights
- Palestinian area controlled by Israel after 1967

West Bank inset
- Full Palestinian civil and security control
- Full Palestinian civil and security control and joint Israeli-Palestinian security control
- Full Israeli control over security, planning and construction

0   50 mi
0   50 km
Lambert Conformal Conic Projection

>> **Generate Explanations** Based on information from the map, why might the Israeli capital of Jerusalem be a site of conflict between Israelis and Palestinians?

▶ **Interactive Chart**

deaths there. An end to the cycle of violence seemed far away.

An Uneasy Region Unrest within the Arab world extended beyond the Arab-Israeli conflict. In early 2010, protests against undemocratic governments began in Tunisia and spread to other Arab countries. Together, these pro-democracy protests became known as the **Arab Spring**. In Egypt, protestors called for President Hosni Mubarak to step down after almost three decades leading an undemocratic government. The United States agreed with the protestors, but the Obama administration moved cautiously in its support for the Arab Spring.

In Libya, protests led to a brutal response by the country's dictator, Muammar al-Qaddafi, that sparked a civil war. In March, the United Nations adopted a resolution that called for a truce and allowed a global force to protect civilians. The United States and other western forces bombed Qaddafi government targets in Libya. In October 2011, rebels captured and killed Qaddafi.

Pro-democracy movements spread to other Arab countries. In Syria, where the Arab Spring also triggered a civil war, the loss of life totaled 100,000 people or more. Meanwhile, in Egypt, the military overthrew the democratically elected government. The Obama administration expressed sympathy and gave limited support to democratic forces in both countries but worked to keep U.S. forces out of these conflicts.

? **DEFINE** What was the Arab Spring?

Assisting Other Nations

In 2005, President George W. Bush declared that the United States must "extend democracy throughout the world."

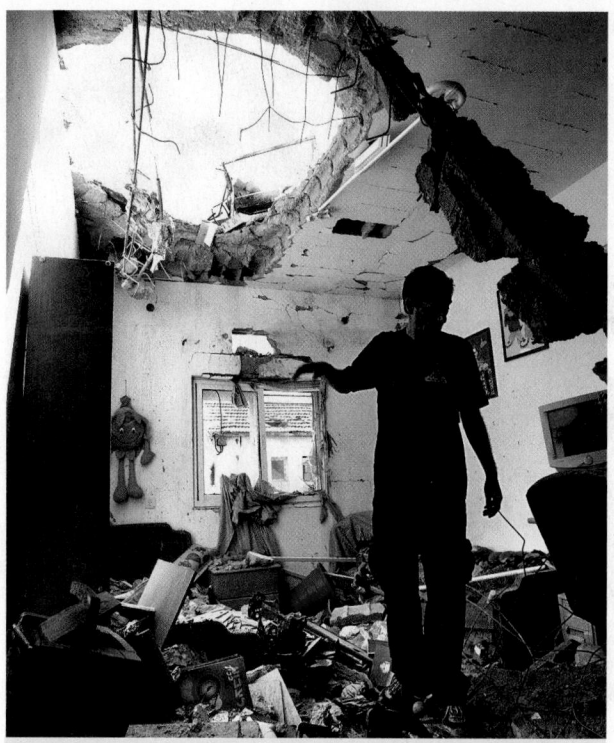

>> Throughout the 2000s, citizens of Israel lived under the threat of rocket attacks from their Arab neighbors. This Israeli home was struck by a rocket from the Lebanese militant group Hezbollah in 2006.

>> The 2006 fighting between Israel and Lebanon resulted in this scene of destruction in Tyre, Lebanon, after an Israeli air attack.

>> President Barack Obama worked to build stronger relationships with U.S. allies. His "pivot to Asia" was intended to strengthen relationships with Asian allies.

▶ **Interactive Gallery**

This commitment has led America to assist its allies and other nations.

The United States assisted efforts to end piracy off the coast of Somalia, in Africa. The capture of ships and their crews in the Indian Ocean threatened international shipping. Pirates demanded high ransom payments in exchange for the captured ships' crews and contents. The United Nations Security Council adopted resolutions to address Somali piracy. The United States, the **North Atlantic Treaty Organization** (NATO), the European Union, and other nations supplied naval patrols to protect waters off the coast of Somalia. These efforts reduced the number of pirate attacks.

As a member nation, the United States has supported the addition of Eastern European countries to the NATO alliance. Russia opposed the addition of countries that were under Soviet rule during the Cold War. The growth of NATO reinforced the U.S. goal of a free and peaceful Europe.

After Russia invaded Ukraine in 2014, NATO confirmed its commitment to protecting its easternmost members. The United States and the European Union imposed sanctions on Russia.

The United States also supported its allies through President Barack Obama's "pivot to Asia." This policy was an effort to give greater weight to East Asia in U.S. foreign policy. The "pivot to Asia" was important for domestic and international reasons. Through it, the United States aimed to strengthen its economic and diplomatic relationship with nations in the Pacific Rim.

At the same time, the United States could monitor China's moves in the region. China threatened the peace of the region by asserting claims to islands also claimed by Japan, the Philippines, Vietnam, and Malaysia. Besides protecting American interests in the Pacific, the "pivot to Asia" supported allies such as Japan.

? **DESCRIBE** the goals of the "pivot to Asia."

ASSESSMENT

1. **Generate Explanations** Why did tensions between the United States and North Korea increase in the 2000s?

2. **Summarize** How has the United States responded to Iran's nuclear weapon program?

3. **Distinguish** How have actions on both sides increased tensions between Israel and the Palestinian Arabs since 2007?

4. **Generate Explanations** Why has the "Arab Spring" that began in 2010 resulted in minimal democratic gains in the region?

5. **Summarize** How has the United States supported its allies in Europe, Africa, and Asia since 2005?

A Global Economy

>> A byproduct of globalization is that many products purchased by American consumers are manufactured in factories like this one in China.

▶ **Interactive Flipped Video**

hrough its financial and trade relationships, America became part of a global economy. In the 1990s and early 2000s, America's trade with other countries grew dramatically.

>> **Objectives**

Explain the connections between the U.S. economy and the global economy.

Describe the reasons for the 2007 recession.

Identify reasons for the U.S. economy's slow recovery after the 2007 recession.

>> **Key Terms**

globalization
bubble
mortgage
default
subprime mortgage
American Recovery
  and Reinvestment
  Act
debt ceiling

A Worldwide Economy Develops

Trade agreements with countries in the Americas and Asia strengthened U.S. relations and opened trade in new areas. American businesses benefited from lower production costs and the opening of new markets for trade. American consumers benefited from lower prices for goods and services.

Globalization, or the spread of a global economy, also posed potential problems, though. Some American workers suffered when companies moved work overseas. Also, when one country suffered an economic crisis, the entire global community was at risk.

A Crash and Recovery In the 1990s, the American economy grew strongly. This growth was partly due to the creation of new businesses and jobs in the technology industry.

Many Internet start-up companies, known as dot-coms, were founded during the decade. In some of these, owners and managers used risky business practices. They thought that if the number of customers increased, then profits would increase, too. This worked for some companies but not for all of them.

Investors saw the potential to make profits from dot-coms, so they bought stock in the companies. High demand for these stocks created a stock-market **bubble**. A bubble is an unstable condition of prices driven above the real value of an asset by buyers hoping that prices will rise further.

When many dot-coms failed to yield a profit, the bubble burst and stock prices plunged. Investment in these companies dried up. Between 1999 and 2001, many dot-com businesses had to close. Other

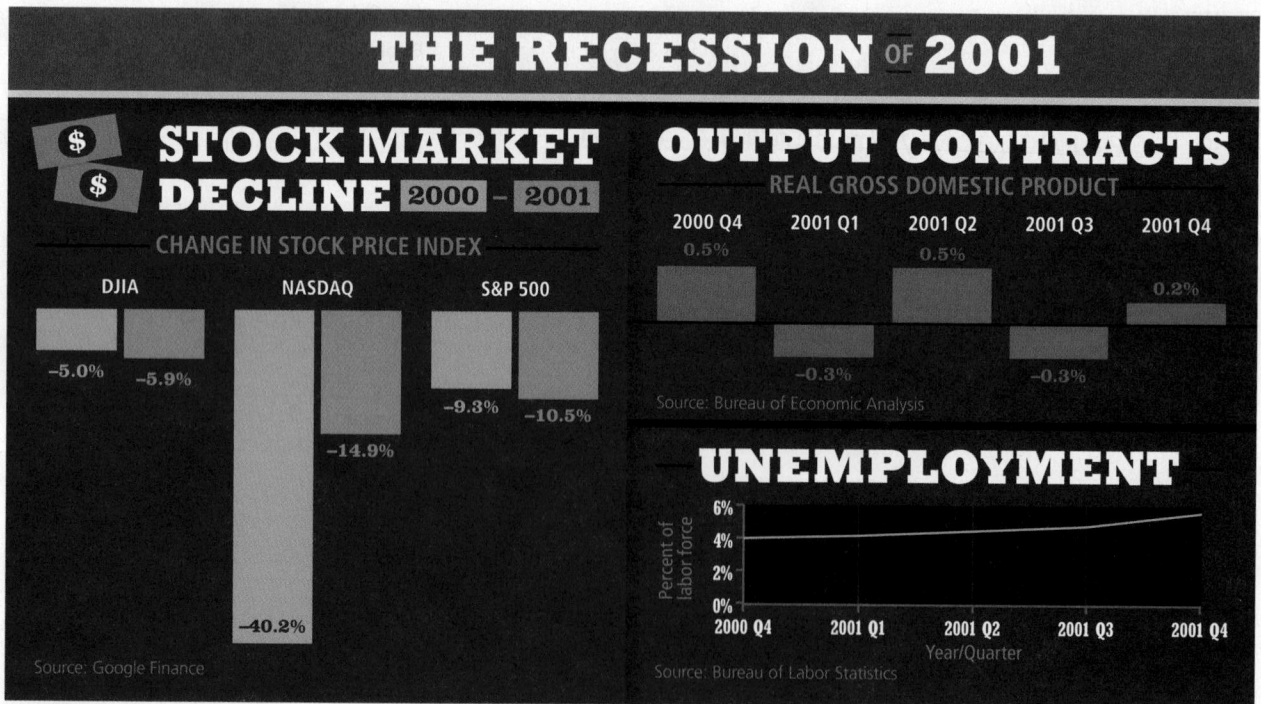

THE RECESSION OF 2001

STOCK MARKET DECLINE 2000 – 2001
CHANGE IN STOCK PRICE INDEX

DJIA: −5.0%, −5.9%
NASDAQ: −14.9%, −40.2%
S&P 500: −9.3%, −10.5%

Source: Google Finance

OUTPUT CONTRACTS
REAL GROSS DOMESTIC PRODUCT

2000 Q4: 0.5%
2001 Q1: −0.3%
2001 Q2: 0.5%
2001 Q3: −0.3%
2001 Q4: 0.2%

Source: Bureau of Economic Analysis

UNEMPLOYMENT
Percent of labor force: 0%, 2%, 4%, 6%
Year/Quarter: 2000 Q4, 2001 Q1, 2001 Q2, 2001 Q3, 2001 Q4

Source: Bureau of Labor Statistics

>> **Recall** causes and effects of the Great Depression of the 1930s. Compare the stock market and unemployment data in this graph about the 2001 recession to what you read about the depression.

U.S. Trade with Canada and Mexico, 1993–2013

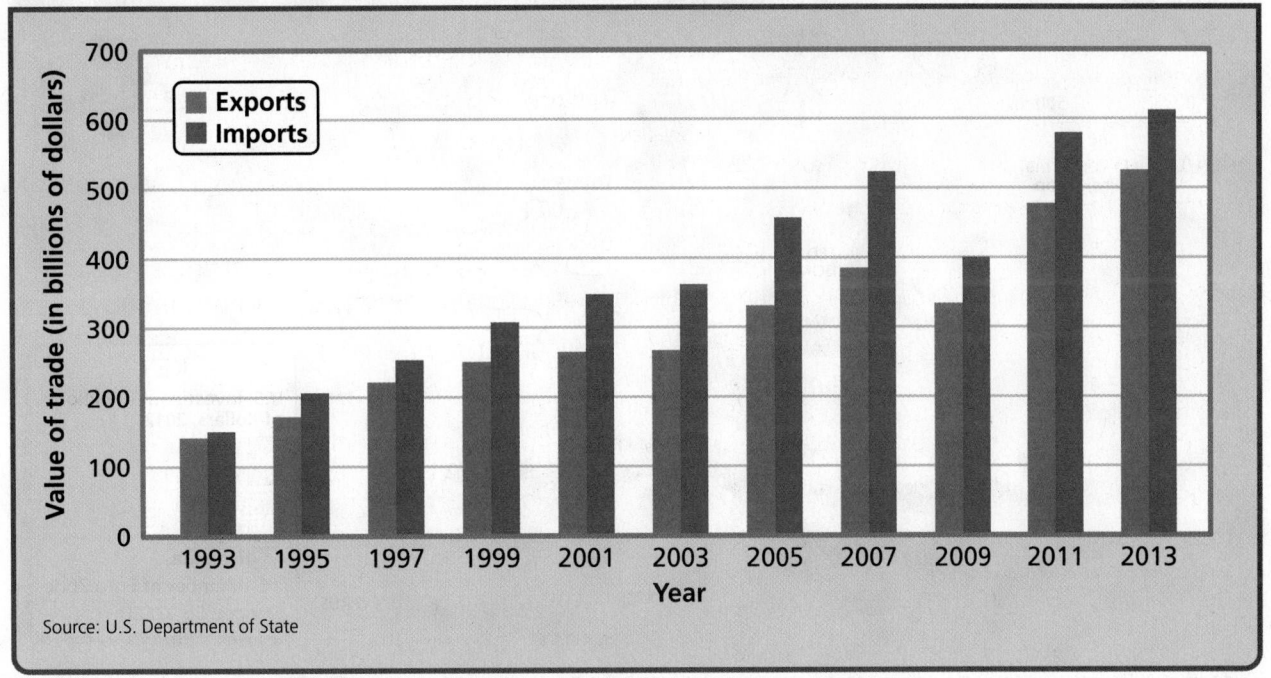

Source: U.S. Department of State

>> **Draw Conclusions** about the impact of NAFTA after 1993 based on the data in the graph.

companies, such as Google and Amazon, suffered losses but survived and eventually grew.

In 2001, the American economy entered a recession, partly as a result of the dot-com bubble bursting. A recession occurs when the economy shrinks instead of growing. The September 11 attacks also hurt the stock market, and the transfer of American manufacturing jobs to other countries deepened the recession.

The federal government responded to the economic crisis by lowering taxes, while the Federal Reserve System lowered interest rates to encourage people and businesses to borrow. The economy gradually recovered in 2003 and 2004.

Questions of Fraud When the stock market crashed in 2000, Americans realized that fraud had helped trigger the 1990s boom. Accounting firms and banks had increased stock prices by hiding the companies' real financial situation. Enron, a Houston energy company, exemplified this trend. Enron bought and sold electricity instead of producing it on its own. The company falsely reported billions of dollars in profits. A Texas jury convicted Enron executives of fraud, but it was too late to help investors. Fraud at Enron damaged Americans' trust of corporations in general.

Increasing Global Trade The North American Free Trade Agreement (NAFTA), established in 1993, linked the United States, Canada, and Mexico in a free trade zone. In 1995, the United States became a member of the World Trade Organization (WTO). The WTO works to remove barriers to and encourage trade and investment among countries.

NAFTA and the WTO encouraged the United States to negotiate similar

The European Union, 2014

0   500 mi
0   500 km
Lambert Conformal
Conic Projection

ATLANTIC
OCEAN

FINLAND €
SWEDEN
ESTONIA €
LATVIA €
LITHUANIA
UNITED KINGDOM
DENMARK
IRELAND €
NETHERLANDS €
POLAND
GERMANY €
CZECH REPUBLIC
SLOVAKIA €
BELGIUM €
LUXEMBOURG €
AUSTRIA €
HUNGARY
ROMANIA
FRANCE €
CROATIA
SLOVENIA €
BULGARIA
Black Sea
PORTUGAL €
SPAIN €
ITALY €
GREECE €
CYPRUS €
MALTA €   Mediterranean Sea

KEY
U.S. investment in billions
of dollars, 2012
■ $100+
■ $20–99.9
□ $5–19.9
□ $0–4.9
□ No data
€ Member of Euro Zone
Sources: EU, OECD

>> **List** the members of the European Union in which the United States has $20 billion or more invested.

▶ **Interactive 3-D Model**

agreements in other areas of the world. In 2005, the Central America Free Trade Agreement (CAFTA-DR) created a free-trade zone between the United States and several Latin American countries. The United States also negotiated a free-trade agreement with South Korea in 2007.

Each of these agreements allowed U.S. businesses to sell more goods and services overseas. Meanwhile, foreign businesses were able to increase sales in the United States.

These free-trade agreements increased global trade, but they were controversial. These agreements led some American businesses to move operations to other countries, where worker pay was lower and environmental regulations were weaker.

One of the world's main trading and investment alliances is the European Union (EU). The EU includes most European countries. In 2004, the EU expanded to include countries from Central and Eastern Europe and the Mediterranean.

Membership in the EU created new opportunities for these countries. It also attracted American investment. Many American banks and other firms opened branches within the EU to have access to its large market. In this way, what happened in the EU could affect the U.S. economy.

Growing Financial Ties Globalization brought benefits, like the expansion of trade opportunities. It could also present potential problems for the United States. The banking system throughout the world became closely connected. If the European banking system or the American banking system faced trouble, both sides would suffer the consequences.

In 1999, most countries in the European Union adopted a shared currency, known as the euro. The countries using the euro were known as the euro zone. The euro was the second most widely used currency in the world, behind the American dollar, by the 2010s. Euro-zone companies held large investments in the United States, and U.S. firms had large investments in the euro zone.

The EU was one of America's most important trade partners in the early 2000s. As a result, economic problems in Europe could hurt the United States. If euro-zone countries had less money to invest, Americans would have less money to grow new or existing businesses. If people and businesses in the euro zone had less money to spend, they would buy fewer products from American exporters.

? **RECALL** What was the purpose of the WTO?

A World Economic Crisis

As you read, to help the United States economy recover from the 2001 recession, the Federal Reserve System lowered interest rates. This enabled people to pay less to borrow money. Low interest rates encouraged Americans to increase the amount of money that they borrowed and spent.

It also allowed more Americans to buy homes, and low interest rates made larger **mortgages** affordable. Mortgages are loans to buy a piece of property that allow the lender to claim the property if the mortgage is not paid. As the demand for homes and mortgages increased, home prices also increased. This created a housing bubble much like the dot-com bubble that the stock market had experienced.

Banks and mortgage companies thought that home prices would keep increasing. As a result, they offered mortgages to people

The Housing Bubble, 2007-2009

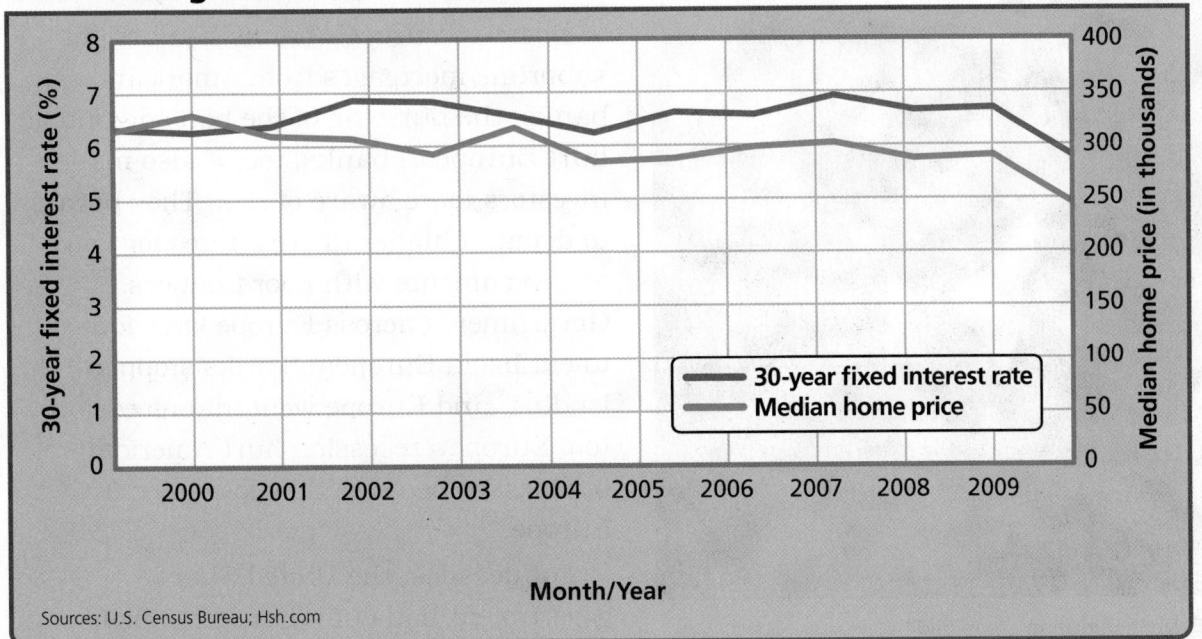

Sources: U.S. Census Bureau; Hsh.com

>> **Analyze Graphs** Describe how the housing bubble affected the prices of homes, and draw conclusions about how that might have affected the U.S. economy.

 Interactive Chart

who were considered lending risks because they could not easily afford the payments. These loans were known as **subprime mortgages**.

In the beginning, subprime mortgages had low interest rates, but the rates were often adjustable so that they could increase with market rates. When that happened, borrowers risked defaulting, or not being able to pay their mortgages.

In 2006 and 2007, overbuilding and a flood of sellers seeking to cash in on high prices for their homes caused American home prices to drop, which burst the housing bubble.

When prices dropped, many homeowners owed more on their mortgages than their homes were worth. When interest rates increased, some could not pay their mortgages. They also could not

>> Former chairman of the Federal Reserve Alan Greenspan testified before Congress in 2008. Greenspan admitted that poor regulation of the economy contributed to the late-2000s economic crisis.

sell and recover their investment because their homes had lost value.

Many of these borrowers defaulted on their mortgages, and banks repossessed, or foreclosed on the homes. Foreclosures left Americans without homes and left banks with massive financial losses. This triggered an economic crisis in which banks stopped making loans, businesses stopped expanding, and the stock market crashed. The United States entered another recession in 2007.

Global Repercussions The stock market crash and the mortgage crisis in 2007 led Americans to cut back on their spending. Reduced spending caused American businesses to fail, which increased unemployment. Consumers lost their jobs, their homes, their retirement savings, and their confidence in America.

Globalization, however, meant that the economic problems extended to the world. Decreases in American spending caused job losses for America's trade partners, such as China and Mexico.

Because Europe's banks had bought subprime mortgages from American banks, the bursting of the housing bubble hurt European banks, too. It also made investors more aware of risk. They began to demand higher interest rates for loans to governments with poor finances. Governments across Europe were forced to cut back, European banks stopped lending, and Europe went into recession, too. Europe's recession hurt American businesses because they lost sales in Europe.

For decades, the United States government had cut regulations, believing that government interference would damage banks. When the financial crisis resulted from what many saw as weak

Stock Fluctuations, 1999–2013

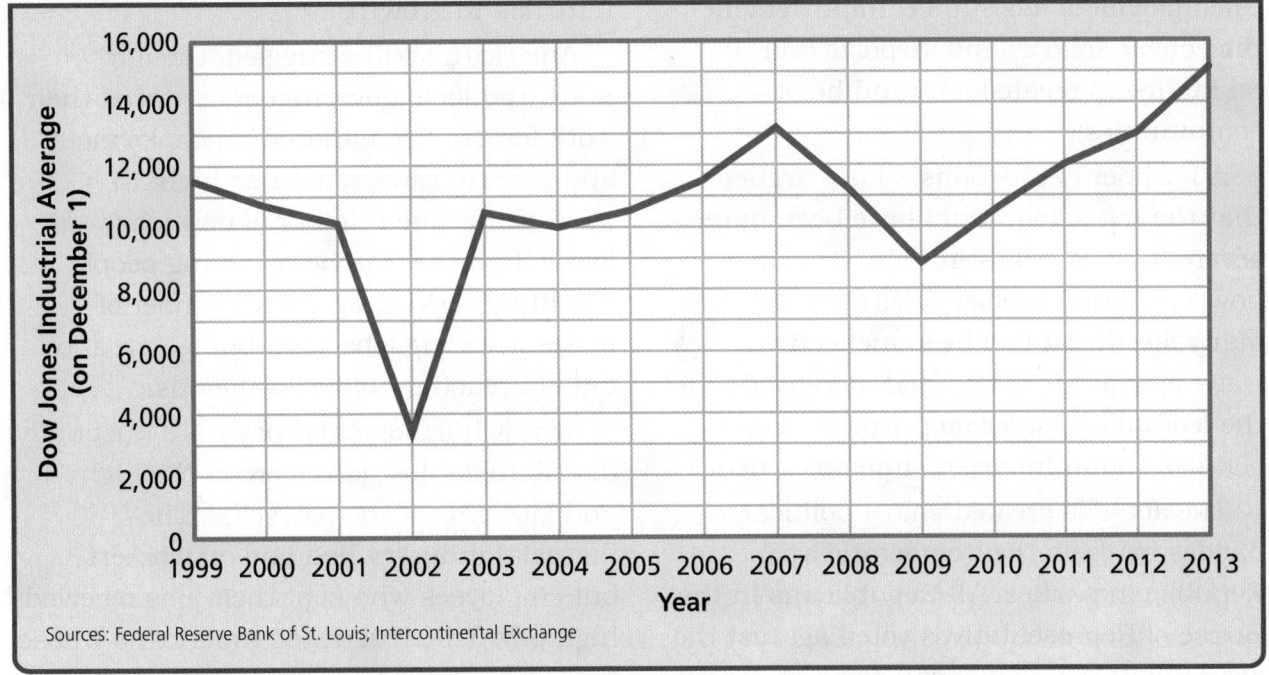

Sources: Federal Reserve Bank of St. Louis; Intercontinental Exchange

>> **Analyze Graphs** What evidence from the graph appears to contradict the view that recovery from the 2007-2009 recession was weak? Explain why.

regulation, the government reversed its policy. The Bush administration allowed a bank called Lehman Brothers to fail, but it worried about the national and global implications of additional banking failures.

In 2008, Congress provided money to bail out, or save, struggling insurance companies, banks, and financial institutions. The Bush administration thought that many large banks and financial firms were "too big to fail."

Administration officials believed that the connectedness of these companies to other businesses put the United States at risk of financial collapse and an economic depression. The bailout helped ensure the survival of these companies, but the economy remained weak.

? **DEFINE** What is a subprime mortgage?

A Weak Recovery

When President Barack Obama entered the White House in 2009, Americans were still experiencing the effects of the economic recession. The unemployment rate for the year averaged close to ten percent. Fourteen percent of Americans lived below the poverty line. Home prices continued to fall.

By 2011, little had changed. The unemployment rate hovered around nine percent and the poverty rate was close to 15 percent. The housing market had not yet recovered.

Stimulus Brings Controversy In 2009, President Obama signed into law the **American Recovery and Reinvestment Act**. The act aimed to stimulate the economy and reduce unemployment. Through it, Congress supplied funds to create jobs, increase unemployment and food stamp benefits, and reduce taxes.

Funds from the act also provided unemployment assistance. Improvement projects at schools and airports and on highways created jobs and helped communities.

A number of economists have argued that the recession would have been more severe without this stimulus. Critics, however, found problems with the act. Many felt that it had been ineffective, was too expensive, and had increased the federal deficit for no purpose. Some claimed that it increased unemployment.

The act also created sharp political divides between the Democratic and Republican parties. All Republicans in the House of Representatives voted against the act. Only three Republican senators voted in favor of it.

A Paper Recovery American recovery from the 2007 economic recession occurred slowly. The stock market rallied, and it appeared as if the recession had ended by 2010, in the sense that the economy returned to growth.

Americans still struggled, though. State and local governments reduced their work forces. The national unemployment and poverty rates remained high. In some years, the number of new jobs was lower than the number of young people reaching working age. The number of manufacturing jobs rose, but job creation did not reach pre-recession levels.

Meanwhile, jobs and pay were unequally distributed. Most jobs were at the high and low ends of the pay scale. The financial industry had laid off workers, but employees who kept their jobs received high pay. This frustrated Americans whose taxes were used to bail out the companies that were "too big to fail."

The largest number of job increases occurred in low-paying jobs. Workers with these jobs had difficulty supporting themselves and their families.

EMPLOYMENT TRENDS 2000–2014

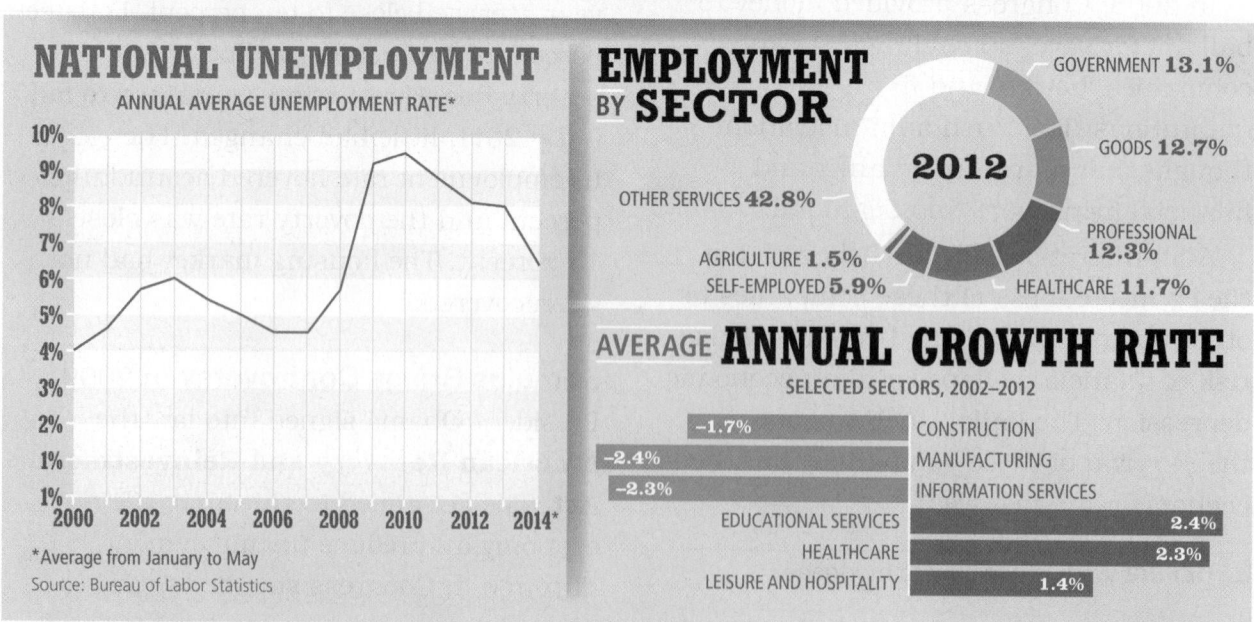

NATIONAL UNEMPLOYMENT
ANNUAL AVERAGE UNEMPLOYMENT RATE*

*Average from January to May
Source: Bureau of Labor Statistics

EMPLOYMENT BY SECTOR

2012

GOVERNMENT 13.1%
GOODS 12.7%
PROFESSIONAL 12.3%
HEALTHCARE 11.7%
SELF-EMPLOYED 5.9%
AGRICULTURE 1.5%
OTHER SERVICES 42.8%

AVERAGE ANNUAL GROWTH RATE
SELECTED SECTORS, 2002–2012

Sector	Rate
CONSTRUCTION	−1.7%
MANUFACTURING	−2.4%
INFORMATION SERVICES	−2.3%
EDUCATIONAL SERVICES	2.4%
HEALTHCARE	2.3%
LEISURE AND HOSPITALITY	1.4%

>> **Analyze Graphs** How do the data in the graph titled Annual Growth Rate support the idea that the early 2010s saw a "weak" recovery from the recession?

▶ **Interactive Chart**

Economic Dangers Persisted In the 2010s, debt crises in the United States and Europe threatened the economic stability of the world. When President Obama asked Congress to raise the **debt ceiling** in 2011 and 2013, Republicans refused unless the President agreed to a compromise.

The debt ceiling limits the amount of debt that the United States can owe. When the country nears the debt ceiling, Congress must vote to raise the limit, or the country risks **default**, or failure to repay a debt, and a possible financial crisis.

Tax cuts, wars in Iraq and Afghanistan, and slow economic growth had pushed America's debt to near its limit. Congress had to raise the debt ceiling to keep the country operating, but Republican members were only willing to do that if the President agreed to reduce the federal government's spending.

Meanwhile, a debt crisis occurred in Europe. Between 2009 and 2012, six euro-zone countries acknowledged that they were struggling to pay their debts and were facing default. Greece was the first country to show signs of problems.

This situation presented an economic problem for the world by putting into question government bonds. If banks are worried about money they have lent to governments, they are less likely to lend money to businesses and individuals. Recognizing this, European and international agencies all provided bailout money.

This bailout brought a temporary solution to the European debt crisis, but a number of countries continued to face heavy debts and a lack of economic growth. It was not clear that the debt problem had been corrected. A danger remained that one

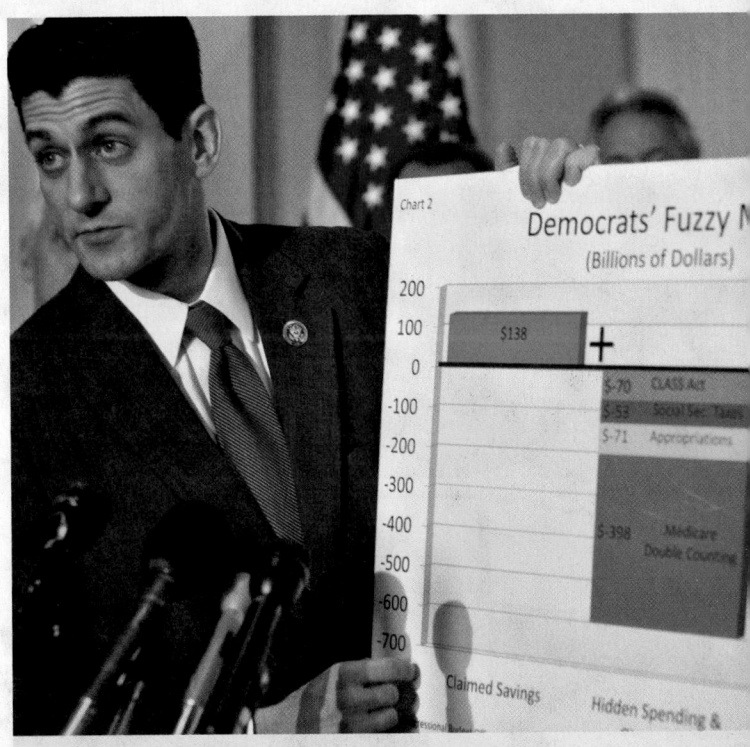

>> The debate over the economy divided Congress. Here, in 2010, outspoken Republican Representative Paul Ryan criticized Democrats' economic policy, calling their approach "fuzzy" math.

or more countries might default on its debt and cripple the global financial system.

? EXPLAIN What did the American Recovery and Reinvestment Act do?

ASSESSMENT

1. **Identify Cause and Effect** Discuss the dot-com boom and how it affected the American economy.

2. **Support Ideas with Evidence** What evidence from the text indicates that NAFTA faced significant criticism?

3. **Sequence Events** What events led to the United States' economic recession in 2007?

4. **Summarize** How did the Bush administration approach the financial crisis in 2008?

5. **Summarize** Why did the American Recovery and Reinvestment Act face criticism? How did it affect the political climate in the United States?

Advances in Science and Technology

>> By the early 2000s, many businesses, such as this financial firm, literally could not operate without extensive computer technology and a constant connection to the Internet.

▶ **Interactive Flipped Video**

>> Objectives

Describe the results of recent NASA research.

Identify environmental challenges and explain the ways in which those challenges are being addressed.

Describe the impact of advances in biotechnology and medicine.

Identify the effects of advances in digital technology and communication.

>> Key Terms

fossil fuel
pollution
climate change
drought
greenhouse gas
gene
biotechnology
HIV
AIDS
smart phone
Internet
Environmental
  Protection Agency
emission

During the early 2000s, the National Aeronautics and Space Administration (NASA) explored the solar system. Orbiters circled planets to gather information about each planet's chemical structure, magnetic field, and formation.

New Discoveries

These studies required planning and patience. It could take years from the time an orbiter is launched until it reached its destination. It took the *Messenger* orbiter seven years after its launch from Earth in 2004 to reach orbit around the planet Mercury. The *New Horizons* space probe needed a nine-year voyage after its launch in 2006 to reach Pluto, and the *Juno* orbiter needed five years after its launch in 2011 to reach Jupiter.

NASA gave special attention to Mars. Presidents George W. Bush and Barack Obama expressed support for the idea of sending astronauts to Mars in the future. To explore the planet, NASA sent orbiters to Mars during the 2000s. The *Mars Odyssey*, *Mars Express*, and *Mars Reconnaissance* orbiters circled Mars. They took photographs, recorded the weather, mapped the terrain, and sent the information back to Earth.

Beginning in 2004, NASA also sent scientific rovers to explore Mars. The *Opportunity* and *Spirit* rovers traveled across the planet's surface and sent images back to Earth. The *Curiosity* science laboratory collected and analyzed Martian soil and rocks. NASA's goal was to look for evidence of water and for fossils or organic materials to find out whether ancient life existed on Mars.

NASA also explored space beyond our solar system. Through the Kepler mission, NASA studied our Milky Way Galaxy in a search for new planets. Instead of using rovers and orbiters for this mission, NASA used a space-based telescope. The Kepler telescope collected images from the galaxy and sent them back to Earth. Scientists analyzing those images identified more

than 1,700 planets outside Earth's solar system.

❓ RECALL What was the purpose of the Kepler mission?

Responding to Environmental Challenges

As the global economy grew, it consumed growing amounts of energy. Most of that energy came from **fossil fuels**, such as oil, coal, and natural gas.

Fossil fuels are fuels formed in the distant past that have limited supplies and cannot be renewed. Once they are burned, they are gone and cannot be replaced. They also cause environmental damage by polluting the air when they are burned. **Pollution**, or harmful impurities added to the environment, is a worldwide problem.

>> In the 2000s, NASA focused on detailed exploration of our solar system. This artist's conception shows the *Juno* orbiter near the planet Jupiter.

>> Petroleum, or oil, extracted by oil wells such as this one in Texas, is one of Earth's most-used fossil fuels.

>> For more than forty years, Earth Day has provided citizens with an opportunity to celebrate and protect the environment. In this 2012 Earth Day parade in New Mexico, students created a "father sky" puppet.

Air or water pollution from other countries may affect the United States.

The Environmental Movement The modern environmental movement began in the 1960s with the publication of *Silent Spring*. In this book, Rachel Carson, a marine biologist, warned readers of the dangers of DDT. DDT is a chemical that farmers used to kill insects. Carson explained that DDT sprayed on crops did not just kill insects. It killed birds and fish and even threatened human food supplies.

Congress responded by passing a law to restrict the use of DDT. Soon environmental groups like the Sierra Club, the National Wildlife Foundation, and the Audubon Society lobbied Congress for additional protective laws. In 1970, President Richard Nixon created the **Environmental Protection Agency** (EPA). In the same year, environmentalists held the first Earth Day.

In the 2000s, environmentalists in the United States and throughout the world continued to address global environmental problems. They were concerned about such issues as groundwater contamination, chemical spills, depletion of the ozone layer in Earth's atmosphere, nuclear waste disposal, reliance on fossil fuels, the extinction of plants and animals, and the destruction of the rainforest.

The Issue of Climate Change **Climate change** is any measurable long-term change in climate. Climate change may affect precipitation, wind patterns, or temperature. Global warming, defined as an increase in average temperatures near Earth's surface, is one form of climate change.

According to the Environmental Protection Agency, during the 1900s, the

GLOBAL CLIMATE CHANGE

INCREASE IN CARBON DIOXIDE LEVELS SINCE THE INDUSTRIAL REVOLUTION

36%

GLOBAL SURFACE TEMPERATURE CHANGE
°F (RELATIVE TO 1960–1999 AVERAGE), DIFFERENT SCENARIOS

20th century actual	Year 2000 carbon dioxide levels hold steady	Some shift toward non-fossil fuels	Continued heavy use of fossil fuels
−1.1 +0.4	+0.4 +1.1	+0.4 +5.0	+0.4 +7.2
1900 2000	2000 2100	2000 2100	2000 2100

ARTIC SEA ICE COVER

1980   2011

Sources: National Climate Data Center; National Oceanic and Atmospheric Administration

>> **Identify** a consequence of climate change represented in the graph.

temperature near Earth's surface rose 1.4 degrees Fahrenheit. The EPA estimated that the temperature would increase another 2 to 11.5 degrees by 2100.

In the early 2000s, scientists expressed concern that climate change could affect farming, the water supply, personal health, and the weather. Scientific studies suggested that climate change had caused some areas, such as the eastern United States, to experience heavier rain and increased flooding.

Other areas, such as the western United States, had less precipitation and more frequent **droughts**. A drought is a shortage of water that affects plants and animals and energy production and increases the risk of wildfires.

Climate scientists concluded in the early 2000s that humans were the greatest contributors to climate change. Burning fossil fuels released carbon dioxide and other **greenhouse gases** into the atmosphere. Greenhouse gases, which blanket Earth, are gases that trap energy and cause the temperature to increase.

Some amount of greenhouse gases is needed for a stable climate, but too much will permanently change Earth's climate. The main greenhouse gas, carbon dioxide, remains in the atmosphere for almost 100 years, so past and present human action will affect future generations.

In the 2000s, the EPA collected information on pollution and greenhouse gas **emissions**, or gases released into the air. It also encouraged energy conservation and the development of cleaner energy. The EPA worked to reduce greenhouse gas emissions. Since both pollution and climate change were global issues, the EPA also worked with international partners.

Progress on Cleaner Energy To reduce greenhouse gas emissions, the U.S. government encouraged the use of renewable energy sources. Unlike fossil fuels, renewable energy sources have potentially unlimited supplies. Energy from the sun, wind, moving water, Earth's heat (geothermal energy), and organic plant and waste material (biomass) can restore itself.

Environmentalists preferred these energy sources to fossil fuels. They had the potential to decrease America's dependence on foreign oil, diminish greenhouse gas emissions, and reduce pollution. Critics argued, however, that these sources are often more expensive than fossil fuels and that relying on them could harm the economy.

Nuclear power and biofuels provided additional alternatives to fossil fuels. The dangers of nuclear power made it controversial, though. In 1979, the Three Mile Island nuclear power plant near Harrisburg, Pennsylvania, experienced a meltdown in its reactor. This accident caused radioactive material to leak and it forced people to evacuate the area. Radioactive material is harmful and can be deadly to people and other living things.

Nuclear power plants convert radioactive nuclear fuels into energy by capturing the force of splitting atoms. This process leaves behind nuclear waste, or radioactive material. Nuclear waste remains hazardous to people and other living things for hundreds of thousands of years. During the early 2000s, experts could not agree on a safe way to dispose of nuclear waste, so there was the risk that it could harm people for many generations to come.

Biofuels are alternative energy sources produced from converting biomass, plant, and waste material into liquid fuels. The most common forms of biofuels are ethanol and biodiesel. During the early 2000s, most ethanol in the United States was produced from corn. Beginning in 2005, federal law required a percentage of the gasoline sold in the United States to be mixed with at least small quantities of ethanol. Biodiesel is produced from oil crops such as soybeans. Both fuels can power automobiles.

Biofuels, however, were also controversial. Growing, processing, and transporting crops to create biofuels uses fossil fuels that contribute to pollution and consume energy. There were questions about whether the energy that biofuels produce was greater than the energy used to create the biofuels themselves. Critics also noted that using crops for fuel could increase food costs.

>> Wind turbines harness wind energy and convert it to electricity. They are one example of an alternative to fossil fuels.

▶ **Interactive Gallery**

? CHECK UNDERSTANDING Name two reasons why environmentalists preferred renewable energy sources to fossil fuels.

Advances in Biology and Medicine

In the years after 2000, scientists made progress identifying the building blocks of life, particularly **genes**. Genes are the hereditary material in organisms, including humans. Scientists, doctors, and other healthcare providers also made progress fighting disease.

The Biotech Revolution **Biotechnology** is technology based on biology. Advances in biotechnology helped feed, fuel, and heal the world. Biotechnology made rapid advances in the years after 2000. Not only did biotechnology improve medicine and agriculture, it also supported a growing industry based on creating products and services with biotechnology.

The medical field uses biotechnology to detect and fight disease. In 1990, the Human Genome Project brought the international scientific community together to map all the genes in the human body. The project was completed in 2003.

Scientists concluded that there are about 20,500 human genes. The complete set of genes in the human body is known as the human genome. Studying the human genome helped researchers understand human diseases. With this knowledge, they could develop new plans for the detection, treatment, and prevention of diseases.

Researchers also used biotechnology to make drugs to treat diseases. They learned to adjust the genes of microorganisms, such as bacteria, to make them produce useful drugs and other treatments. During the early 2000s, these efforts produced better and safer vaccines and brought down the cost of some medicines.

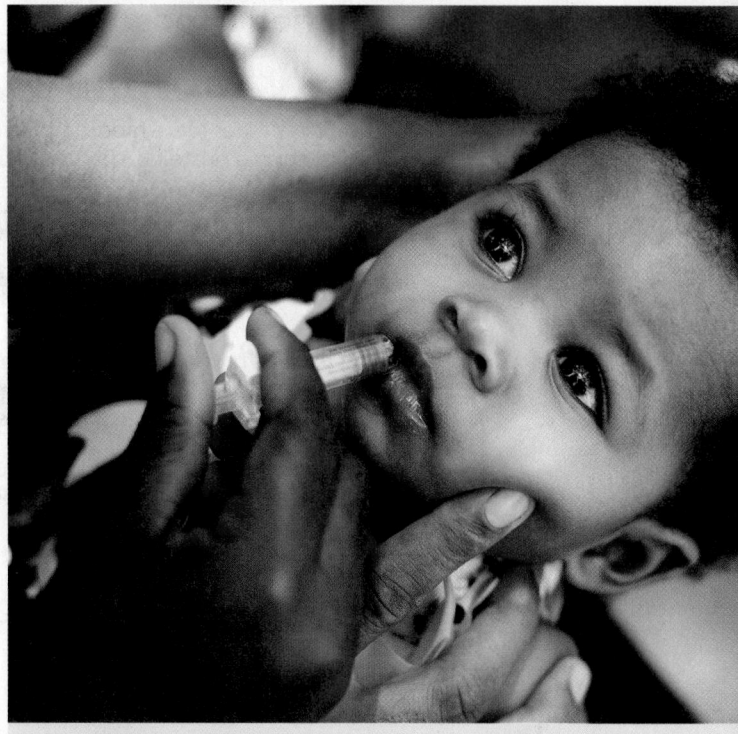

>> A healthcare worker administered the rotavirus vaccine to a child in Haiti in 2014. The vaccine is a biotechnology product that prevents illness in young children.

Farmers use biotechnology to increase crop production, develop crops that are resistant to insects, and enhance food nutrition. By adjusting the genes of crop plants, researchers were able to create varieties of crops that produced more food or that resisted drought, insects, and other agents that harmed crops. Ancient techniques of breeding also adjusted the genes of plants and livestock, but biotechnology does so in a targeted way using scientific methods. These advances helped many farmers and consumers.

Critics raised concerns about genetically modified organisms, including crops or livestock. These concerns include the rising dependence of farmers on biotechnology companies.

Researchers also expressed concern about possible dangers to the environment or human health from some uses of

Genetically Modified Foods

FOOD	GENETIC MODIFICATION
Sweet Potatoes	Sweet potatoes were modified to resist the *Sweet Potato Feathery Mottle Virus* (SPFMV) by injecting a protein from the virus that causes SPFMV.
Golden Rice	Golden rice was modified to produce nearly 20 times the amount of beta-carotene as other varieties of rice. Beta-carotene is changed into Vitamin A in the human body.
Papaya	Papaya was modified to resist the *Papaya Ringspot Virus* (PRSV) discovered in Hawaii in 1992.
Corn	The *Bacillus thuringiensis* (Bt) is a pesticide that was sprayed on plants. Scientists have found a way to incorporate Bt into the genetic material of corn so that the plant becomes naturally resistant to certain insects.
Milk	*Bovine somatotropin* (BST) is a growth hormone that cows produce naturally. Genetically modified bacteria are used to produce extra doses of BST fed to cows to boost their milk production.

Sources: Encyclopædia Britannica; U.S. Department of Agriculture, U.S. Environmental Protection Agency; U.S. Food and Drug Administration

>> **Analyze Charts** Based on the information in the chart, identify two purposes for creating genetically modified foods.

biotechnology in agriculture. However, scientists believed that genetically modified foods, as part of a healthy diet, posed no risk to human health.

Fighting Disease Globalization increased the impact and reach of illnesses and infectious diseases. The frequency of travel intensified the rate at which diseases could be transmitted throughout the world. This increased rate of transmission led to increased concern about health security.

The U.S. Centers for Disease Control and Prevention (CDC) worked with governments around the world to address this concern. The CDC helped other countries learn how to detect and prevent the spread of potential disease epidemics.

The CDC also supported HIV/AIDS programs in more than 70 countries. **HIV** stands for human immunodeficiency virus. HIV can cause **AIDS**, acquired immunodeficiency syndrome, an often fatal disease that attacks the human immune system. Although the human body cannot get rid of HIV, medication can prolong the lives of people infected with the virus.

During the 1990s, medications for AIDS improved. By the 2000s, nearly all Americans had access to effective AIDS treatments.

The United States has been a leader in medicine since the 1900s. During the years after 2000, the United States continued to develop better drugs and better ways of treating and preventing disease.

For example, beginning in the early 2000s, the National Cancer Institute began developing drugs and other treatments that targeted cancer cells. These treatments were safer and more effective than earlier treatments for cancer. Researchers have also developed improved surgical methods and new vaccines.

DEFINE What was a primary goal of the Human Genome Project?

A Networked World

Computers allow information to be saved, analyzed, and exchanged. The first computers in the world were mainframes, which were so large they could fill a room. In the 1950s and 1960s, only private businesses, the government, and universities could afford to own them. By the 1980s, affordability and smaller sizes made personal computers common in homes, small businesses, and schools.

By the early 2000s, new technology had made computers faster, less expensive, and more portable. Some computers could fit in a pocket.

The Internet In the 1960s, a scientist at the Massachusetts Institute of Technology worked to develop a system to connect computers worldwide. His ideas provided the basis for the **Internet**, a system of linking computers worldwide that gives users access to information. In 1969, the United States Department of Defense began linking its computers to computers at American universities. In the 1990s, private companies made the Internet available in homes and businesses.

The Internet makes email communication, instant messaging, Voice over Internet Protocol (VoIP) calls, video calls, and use of the World Wide Web, often simply known as the web, possible. The web was created in the 1980s using technology developed by the United States, Britain, and France.

Although sometimes lumped together, the web and the Internet are not the same. The web is one of many services that run on the Internet. It links documents through hypertext. Web browsers let people view those documents as images, texts, and multimedia on the Internet.

Personal computers and the Internet changed the world. They increased business productivity and efficiency. E-commerce expanded the marketplace to make it digital and global. People regularly bought products, paid bills, and managed their bank accounts online. Digital lessons, textbooks, and library resources transformed teaching and learning.

The Internet and the web introduced users to social networking. Social networks allow people with shared interests and backgrounds to connect digitally.

Social network sites can be used for personal and business connections. They allow people to set up profiles and manage who has access to the information that they share. Like the rest of the Internet, social networking sites presented risks when they did not adequately protect individual privacy or were vulnerable to data theft and viruses.

>> Early computers, such as this IBM "702" model from 1954, were so large they had to be housed in an entire room. Today, people use more powerful and much smaller computers daily in both business and at home.

The Mobile Revolution The first mobile phones, or cell phones, were developed in the 1970s, but they were awkward and expensive. Mobile phones came into wider use in the 1990s.

By the early 2000s, many Americans owned **smart phones**, or small, handheld phones with sophisticated computing capability and an ability to connect to the Internet via radio signals. Many individuals and families also owned tablet computers. Tablets are small mobile computers with touch screens that also connect to the Internet.

Mobile devices such as smartphones and tablets use application software, or apps, to operate. Originally, apps were used for simple tasks like sending and receiving email, managing a calendar, or collecting contact information.

Public demand led software engineers to develop apps for games, magazines and books, banking, and shopping. Today, Americans use apps for social networking, viewing videos, searching for information, and reading books.

In spite of their popularity, mobile devices raised some concerns. Phone use in cars led to accidents. Many states required people to use hands-free devices while driving.

People often found cell phone use disruptive in places such as restaurants, stores, and on public transportation. Smartphones contain chemicals that are toxic to humans and animals. The production and improper disposal of mobile devices damaged the environment.

Digital Security As use of the Internet and the web increased, concern over cybercrime increased with it. Cybercrime includes identity theft, or stealing identifying details from a person, usually to steal by charging purchases to that person. Cybercrime

GLOBAL MOBILE PHONE AND DATA USAGE 2000–2013

GLOBAL MOBILE PHONE SUBSCRIPTIONS, 2000 & 2010

Global mobile phone subscriptions (in billions)

■ DEVELOPING COUNTRIES
■ HIGH-INCOME COUNTRIES

Source: World Bank

CELL PHONE OWNERSHIP FOR SELECTED COUNTRIES, 2002–2013

■ 2002
■ 2013

*Estimated

Source: Pew Research Center

Percent of adults who own a cell phone

CHINA 50% / 95%
UNITED STATES* 65% / 90%
KENYA 9% / 82%
MEXICO 37% / 63%
PAKISTAN 5% / 53%

GLOBAL MOBILE DATA USAGE, 2011–2013

2011 ·)) 0.6
2012 ·)) ·)) ·) 2.4
2013 ·)) ·)) ·) ·)) ·)) ·)) ·)) 6.9

·)) = 1 quadrillion megabytes

Source: World Bank

>> **Analyze Graphs** Analyze the data in all three graphs and describe a general trend affecting mobile phone usage in the 2000s. Do all the graphs support this trend?

▶ **Interactive Gallery**

also includes fraud, espionage, and illegal intelligence gathering.

"Hackers," who tap into computers and threaten privacy, contribute to the spread of cybercrime. Today, most Internet attacks take place through computers based in the United States, China, and Russia.

Cyberwarfare is a digital form of warfare. It uses computers and other digital devices to attack an enemy's information system. It can be used in combination with military-based attacks, or it can be carried out on its own. Cyberwarfare can be directed toward businesses, agencies, organizations, and governments.

Politics or terrorism often motivate cyberattackers. If a cyberattack hit a country's power grid, it could cause traffic accidents, interrupt surgeries, and stop factory production.

During the 2000s, the Department of Defense's cyberwarfare unit and the National Security Agency (NSA) worked to protect the United States from cyberattacks. The NSA supported military operations, the intelligence community, government agencies, private industries, and America's allies. It collected and processed data to protect the security of the nation.

Some of the NSA's data collection methods were controversial. In 2013, NSA contractor Edward Snowden leaked NSA documents to the press. Snowden's actions were also controversial. The U.S. government charged that he had damaged the nation's security. The case raised questions about government surveillance of U.S. citizens and American allies and the balance between individual privacy and national security.

? CHECK UNDERSTANDING What concern do many people share about social networking sites?

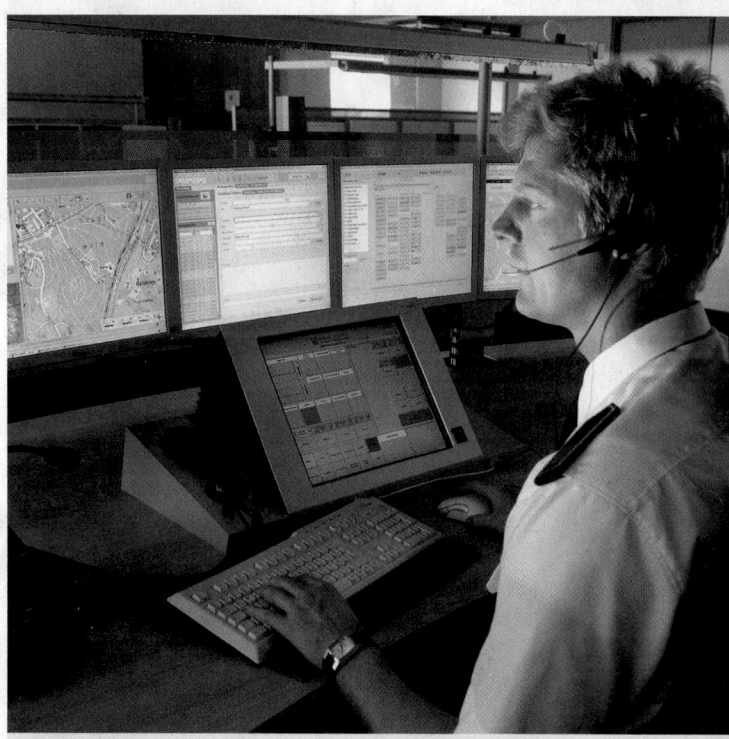

>> Air traffic controllers, police forces, and fire-safety dispatchers (seen here) relied on computer networks in the 2000s. The threat of cybercrime against these networks was a cause for concern.

ASSESSMENT

1. **Summarize** What steps did NASA take toward its goal of increasing our knowledge of the solar system?

2. **Generate Explanations** How was *Silent Spring* responsible for the creation of the modern environmental movement?

3. **Identify Cause and Effect** What causes climate change, and what efforts were made to address this issue?

4. **Support Ideas with Examples** What examples can you give to support the idea that advances in biotechnology helped to feed, fuel, and heal the world?

5. **Summarize** How did the increased use of the Internet and the web present new threats to its users?

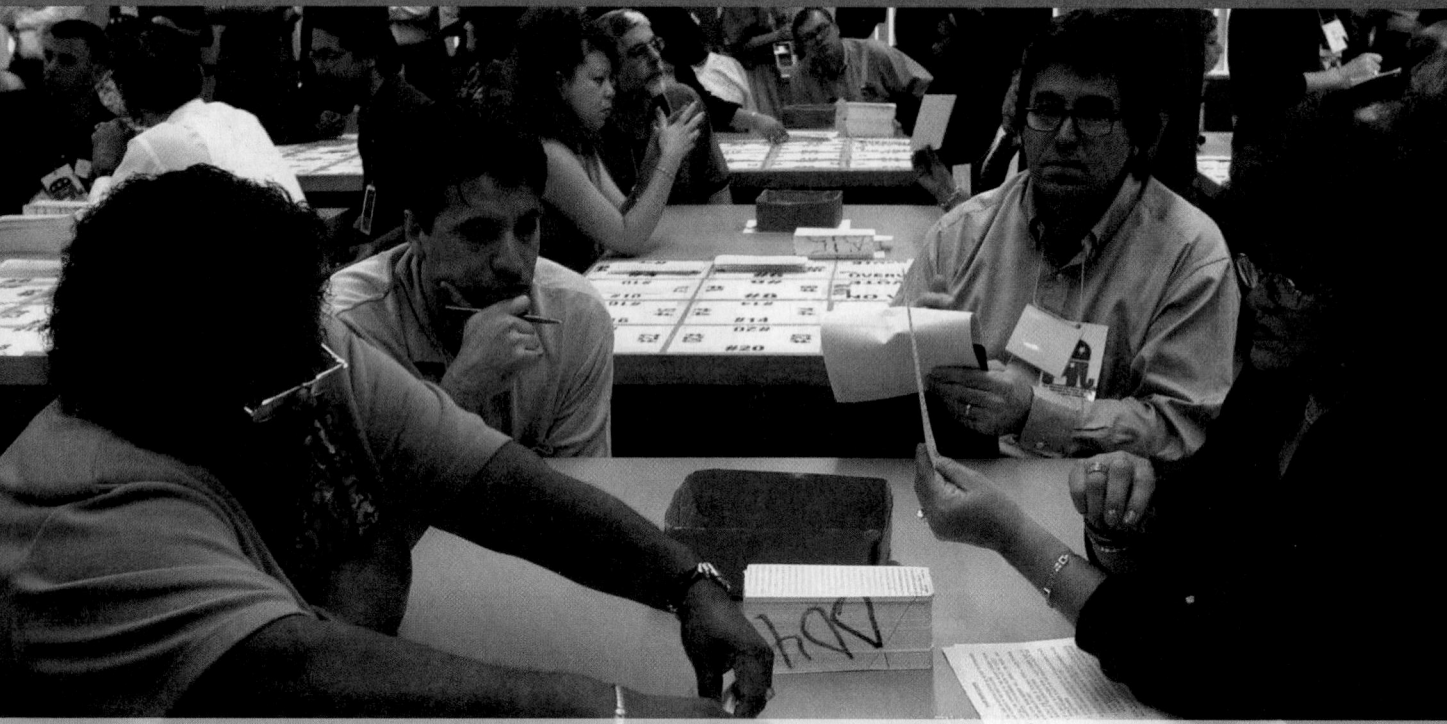

>> Florida election officials re-count ballots in the hotly contested presidential election of 2000.

▶ Interactive Flipped Video

>> **Objectives**

Describe significant events in George W. Bush's presidency.

Describe significant events in Barack Obama's presidency.

Describe the recent effects of immigration and expanded civil rights on American society.

Identify the domestic and foreign challenges Americans will face in the future.

>> **Key Terms**

affirmative action
deficit
Affordable Care Act

The election of 2000 was one of the most disputed in American history. The Republican candidate, Governor George W. Bush of Texas, was the son of former President George H.W. Bush. Bush faced Vice President Al Gore, the Democratic candidate. When the election ended, Gore had won the popular vote by a margin of about 540,000 votes, or one half of one percent. According to the U.S. Constitution, however, the electoral vote, or the vote of the Electoral College, determines who becomes President.

The Bush Era

With such a close election, the result rested on the electoral votes of one state: Florida. The initial results gave Bush a small lead, but winning Florida would have given Gore the votes he needed to win the election. Democrats expressed concern over confusion among Florida voters and problems with counting the ballots.

They asked the Florida Supreme Court to force a recount of the Florida votes. The recount began, but in December 2000, the United States Supreme Court ordered the recount to stop.

Bush, therefore, won the electoral votes of Florida and the presidential election of 2000. Al Gore conceded the election but voiced his disapproval of the Court's decision.

Standing Tall The election of 2000 showed sharp divisions within the country. Most Americans in the South and Mountain West voted for Bush. Most Americans in the Northeast, Upper Midwest, and on the West Coast voted for Gore. In the Senate, the Republican and Democratic parties were divided evenly with fifty seats each.

President Bush entered office in 2001 with plans for tax and education reform. The terrorist attacks on September 11, 2001, however, changed his presidency and the lives of Americans.

Bush led the nation as it fought back against the attacks. Americans showed an outpouring of patriotism in the months that followed. Bush benefited from that and from his strong response to the attacks, including the launch of a global war on terrorism. In September 2001, 90 percent of Americans approved of the job that Bush was doing as President.

In the same year, as the dot-com bubble burst, the United States slipped into an economic recession. Bush advocated for tax cuts to stimulate the economy. He argued

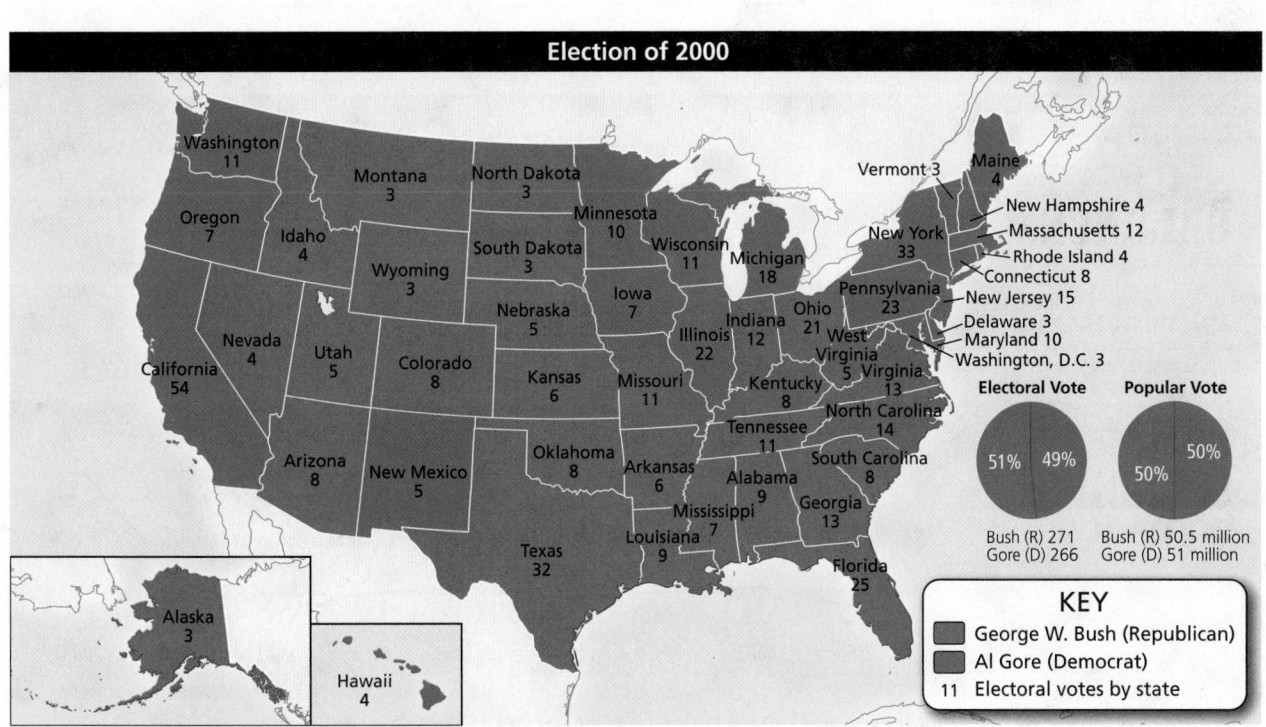

>> **Make Predictions** about how the political division shown in this map and these graphs might have affected government in the years after the 2000 election.

that if wealthy Americans and corporations paid lower taxes, they would be able to invest more money in the economy. Congress responded by passing the largest tax cuts in American history.

These tax cuts, when paired with the war on terrorism, increased the federal **deficit**, the amount of spending greater than income. The deficit added to the national debt.

Recovery from the 2001 recession occurred slowly. Still, when Bush ran for reelection in 2004, his popularity was high. Many Americans were reluctant to change leaders when the wars in Iraq and Afghanistan were still underway. Bush easily won reelection over his Democratic opponent, Senator John Kerry of Massachusetts. Unlike the election of 2000, Bush was the clear winner in 2004. He won the popular vote and received 286 electoral votes compared to Kerry's 251 votes.

Declining Popularity When Bush began his second term in 2005, more than half of Americans approved of the job he was doing as President. Over the next four years, however, Bush's popularity steadily declined. His average approval rating during his first term was 62 percent. During his second term, Bush's approval rating averaged 37 percent. It reached a low of 25 percent in November 2008.

Several factors caused President Bush's popularity to drop. The economy recovered from the 2001 recession by 2004, but not all Americans felt the recovery. Unemployment remained high and the percentage of people living in poverty increased.

Then, beginning in 2007, the country experienced another recession as the housing bubble burst and home values tumbled. The huge federal deficit that resulted from Bush's prior tax cuts and the wars in Iraq and Afghanistan added to the

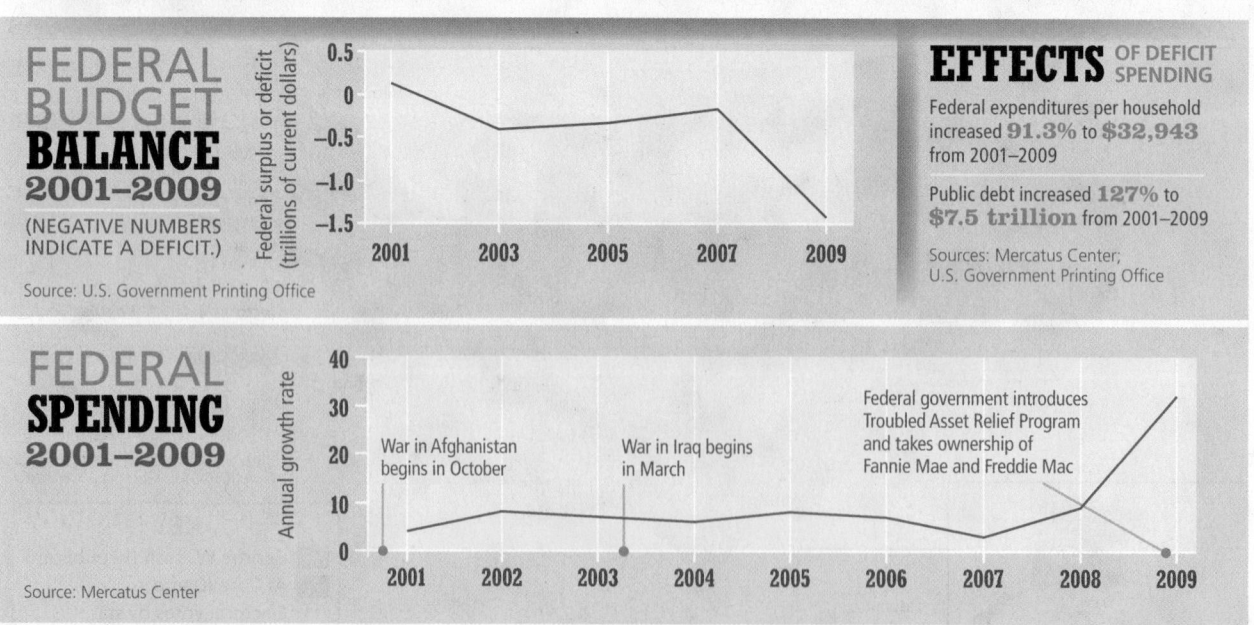

FEDERAL DEFICITS AND SPENDING 2001–2009

FEDERAL BUDGET BALANCE 2001–2009 (NEGATIVE NUMBERS INDICATE A DEFICIT.)

Federal surplus or deficit (trillions of current dollars)

Source: U.S. Government Printing Office

EFFECTS OF DEFICIT SPENDING

Federal expenditures per household increased **91.3%** to **$32,943** from 2001–2009

Public debt increased **127%** to **$7.5 trillion** from 2001–2009

Sources: Mercatus Center; U.S. Government Printing Office

FEDERAL SPENDING 2001–2009

Annual growth rate

War in Afghanistan begins in October

War in Iraq begins in March

Federal government introduces Troubled Asset Relief Program and takes ownership of Fannie Mae and Freddie Mac

Source: Mercatus Center

>> **Analyze Graphs** Describe how an increase in government spending might have affected the federal deficit. Then analyze the graphs. Do the data correspond to your prediction?

2006 Congressional Mid-Term Elections

SEATS GAINED/LOST		
	Republicans	**Democrats**
Senate	–6	+7
House of Representatives	–27	+32

Source: CNN

>> **Analyze Charts** Considering that a Republican, George W. Bush, was reelected as President in 2004, describe how the results of the 2006 congressional election were either a surprise or were to be expected.

problems. By 2008, the deficit totaled $455 million, the highest in history. Americans worried about their own economic future and the federal debt's effect on the next generation.

As Americans weathered the economic storm, residents of Louisiana and Mississippi weathered an actual storm. In August 2005, Hurricane Katrina made landfall in New Orleans, Louisiana. When the storm hit, the city flooded with water. About 1,500 people died. Two thirds of the city's residents were displaced from their homes. The Federal Emergency Management Agency (FEMA) was not prepared to deal with the results of Katrina.

President Bush, vacationing in Texas, seemed unaware of the disaster's extent, even though television broadcasts showed the horrifying scenes. The Bush administration received heavy criticism for its handling of Katrina. Bush's popularity rating dropped. During the 2006 midterm elections, Democrats took control of Congress for the first time since 1994.

? **RECALL** What are two factors that caused Bush's popularity to decline?

Obama's Presidency

In 2008, Americans struggled with a deepening economic recession, and the wars in Iraq and Afghanistan grew unpopular. A Democratic presidential victory seemed certain. Senator John McCain of Arizona was the Republican candidate. McCain was a U.S. Navy veteran who emphasized his foreign policy experience and support for the war in Iraq.

The Democratic candidate was Senator Barack Obama of Illinois. Obama expressed his opposition to the war in Iraq and promised voters that he would bring "hope" and "change" to Washington. Voters responded to his promises and handed him a clear victory. The son of a Kenyan father and an American mother, Barack Obama became the nation's first African American president.

A Challenging First Term President Obama entered office facing the economic recession and ongoing wars in Iraq and Afghanistan. In response to America's economic problems, he allowed some of the Bush-era tax cuts to expire and signed an economic stimulus bill.

The recession ended in 2010, in the technical sense that the economy resumed slow growth. Many Americans saw little economic improvement, though. Many faced foreclosure. Unemployment peaked at close to ten percent. The poverty rate remained high.

Obama campaigned on a promise to end the war in Iraq. In keeping with that promise, the last combat troops left Iraq in 2011. During his first term, however, Obama broadened the fight against terrorists. In 2012, Americans were involved in combat missions in Afghanistan, Yemen, Pakistan, and Somalia. Obama also extended the USA Patriot Act and gave up on his promise to close the Guantanamo Bay prison. He found that making promises as a candidate was different from enacting those changes as a president.

Beyond foreign policy and the economy, Obama devoted his first term to reorganizing the country's healthcare

>> Republican candidate Mitt Romney (left) failed to defeat President Barack Obama in the 2012 election. They engaged in a lively televised debate, shown here, on October 16, 2012.

system. In March 2010, Congress passed the **Affordable Care Act**, nicknamed "Obamacare."

The act required all Americans to purchase health insurance and provided funding to help lower-income Americans pay for insurance.

Support for the act was divided along party lines. All Republicans voted against it. In 2012, the Supreme Court upheld most provisions of the act, but it remained controversial. Critics argued that the act increased health insurance prices for some Americans who were already insured.

Government by Crisis In the 2010 elections, Republicans gained control of the House of Representatives. In the middle of his first term in office, Obama suddenly faced the challenge of working with a Republican-dominated House. Republicans also won seats in the Senate and several state governorships. Political gridlock resulted from the politically divided Congress. Republicans blocked passage of bills Obama supported. Republicans were limited in what they could accomplish since Democrats controlled the Senate. Congress experienced a political stalemate.

The congressional deadlock was apparent during debates about the federal budget and the debt ceiling from 2010 to 2012. Republicans wanted to cut spending and reduce taxes. Democrats wanted to protect federal programs and raise taxes on wealthy Americans to pay for them. They argued that economic hardship in America made support for existing federal programs essential.

In 2012, as President Obama ran for reelection, his approval rating hovered around 50 percent. Unemployment remained high, and economic recovery was still slow. Voters were frustrated by the

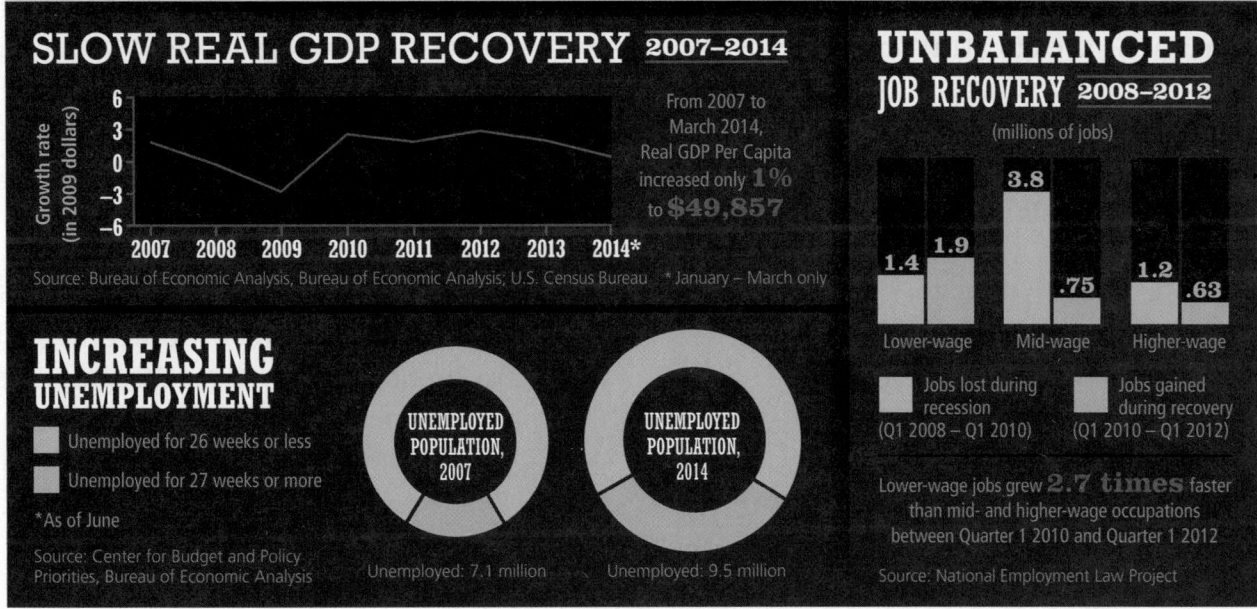

A WEAK RECOVERY

SLOW REAL GDP RECOVERY 2007–2014

Growth rate (in 2009 dollars)

6
3
0
-3
-6

2007 2008 2009 2010 2011 2012 2013 2014*

Source: Bureau of Economic Analysis, Bureau of Economic Analysis; U.S. Census Bureau   * January – March only

From 2007 to March 2014, Real GDP Per Capita increased only 1% to $49,857

INCREASING UNEMPLOYMENT

▪ Unemployed for 26 weeks or less

▪ Unemployed for 27 weeks or more

*As of June

Source: Center for Budget and Policy Priorities, Bureau of Economic Analysis

UNEMPLOYED POPULATION, 2007

UNEMPLOYED POPULATION, 2014

Unemployed: 7.1 million   Unemployed: 9.5 million

UNBALANCED JOB RECOVERY 2008–2012

(millions of jobs)

Lower-wage: 1.4 | 1.9
Mid-wage: 3.8 | .75
Higher-wage: 1.2 | .63

▪ Jobs lost during recession (Q1 2008 – Q1 2010)

▪ Jobs gained during recovery (Q1 2010 – Q1 2012)

Lower-wage jobs grew 2.7 times faster than mid- and higher-wage occupations between Quarter 1 2010 and Quarter 1 2012

Source: National Employment Law Project

>> **Analyze Graphs** How do the data about lower-, mid-, and higher-wage jobs reflect an unbalanced recovery?

political gridlock in Washington. American support for the war in Afghanistan had dwindled. In spite of these challenges, Obama won the election against his Republican opponent, Mitt Romney. Obama received 51 percent of the popular vote to Romney's 47 percent.

Economic Issues Unemployment was persistent after the recession of 2007 and 2008. Long-term unemployment reached record levels, and some Americans gave up on looking for work.

The movement of American jobs overseas contributed to these problems. Outsourcing of jobs lowered prices for consumers, but it resulted in job losses and global competition for American workers. Computers and robots also eliminated the need for many jobs.

The wealth of the richest Americans exploded during the 2000s. On the other hand, the financial situation for members of the middle and working classes worsened. These changes led to a growing gap between the wealthiest Americans and others and to a debate about income inequality.

? RECALL How did Republicans want to reduce the federal budget deficit?

Social Change

As the American population in the 2000s changed and grew, the country faced new challenges and revisited old ones. The United States saw increases in immigration, a changing ethnic makeup, and growing numbers of older Americans. Tensions over immigration echoed those the nation had faced during earlier waves of immigration.

Immigration Brings Changes and Challenges During the early 2000s, about one million immigrants entered the United States each year. Most of these immigrants came from Latin America and Asia. In

2010, just over half of the immigrants in the United States were Latino. *Latino* refers to people who were born in Latin America or are of Latin American descent. Latino immigrants came to the United States to escape political unrest and economic hardship and to seek opportunity. Asian immigrants came to the United States for many of the same reasons. In 2010, just over a quarter of the immigrants in the United States were Asian.

Americans' responses to immigrants varied. Some Americans valued immigrants' strong work ethic and the cultural diversity that they brought to the country. Other Americans worried about job competition and decreases in wages as the number of workers increased. They also worried about the cost of providing education, healthcare, and other services to immigrants. In response to these concerns, conservative politicians worked to restrict immigration and strengthen patrols of America's borders.

A Changing Mosaic Immigration made America more diverse. In 2010, a little more than one in eight Americans were born in foreign countries. Latinos were the largest minority group in the United States, outnumbering African Americans.

The United States population increased in number. Immigration contributed to this increase but so did longer lifespans. The "baby boomers," people who were born between the late 1940s and early 1960s, began to enter retirement. Older Americans made up 13 percent of the U.S. population in 2014. That figure was expected to increase to 20 percent by the year 2040. This meant that Americans were enjoying longer lives than they did in the past.

These changes raised concerns about healthcare costs and federal Social Security payments in the future.

Origins of U.S. Immigrants, 2010

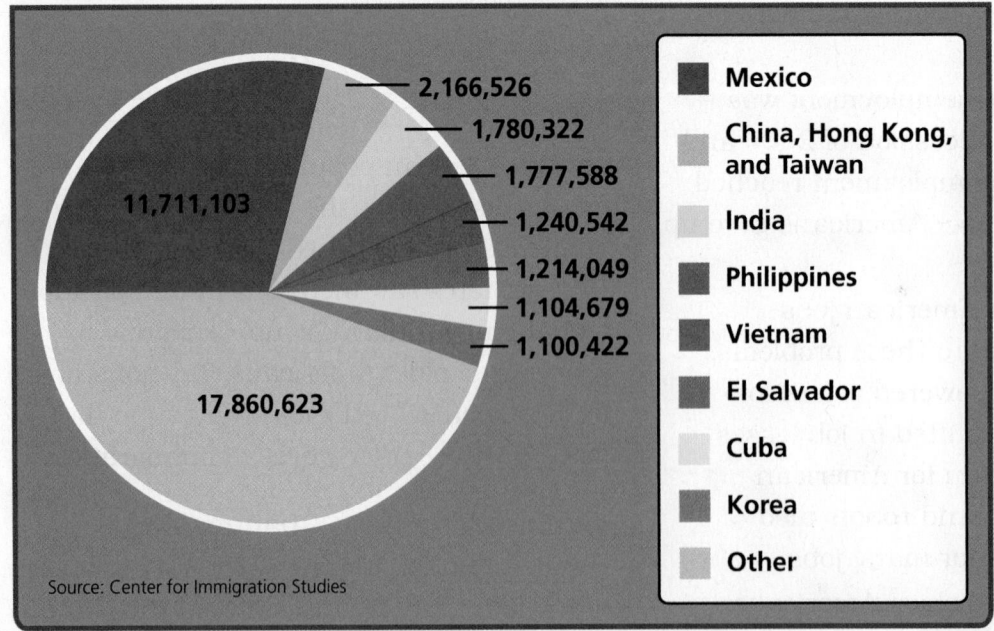

- 2,166,526
- 1,780,322
- 1,777,588
- 1,240,542
- 1,214,049
- 1,104,679
- 1,100,422
- 11,711,103
- 17,860,623

Mexico
China, Hong Kong, and Taiwan
India
Philippines
Vietnam
El Salvador
Cuba
Korea
Other

Source: Center for Immigration Studies

>> **Cite Evidence** in this graph to support the idea that immigration has made America more diverse.

▶ Interactive Chart

Affirmative Action Cases Heard by the U.S. Supreme Court

DATE	CASE	DETAILS
1978	*Regents of the University of California* v. *Bakke*	The Supreme Court ruled that affirmative action was constitutional but that racial quotas were not to be used in schools. Schools were not allowed to reserve a specific number of openings for minorities.
1995	*Adarand Constructors* v. *Pena*	The court stated that federal affirmative action programs were only constitutional if they fulfilled a governmental interest.
1996	*Hopwood* v. *University of Texas Law School*	The court ruled that an affirmative action program at the University of Texas was unconstitutional because factoring race into admissions decisions did not serve state interests.
2003	*Grutter* v. *Bollinger*	The Supreme Court ruled that the University of Michigan Law School's admissions process involving the consideration of minorities was not unconstitutional because the school had an interest in promoting racial diversity in its classrooms.

Sources: *Encyclopædia Britannica;* U.S. Department of Justice

>> **Compare** the Supreme Court rulings in the 1978 and 2003 cases. Explain similarities and differences you notice in the Court's approach to affirmative action.

As the American population increased in size, states also experienced demographic changes. In states such as California and New Mexico, and in the city of Washington, D.C., non-Latino whites were a minority of the population by the early 2000s. States in the South and Southwest were growing faster than the rest of the country. These Sunbelt states benefited from increases in population and more representation in Congress.

Family demographics also changed. In the early 2000s, families came in many varieties. In the 1960s, most families consisted of two parents and two or three children. This was no longer true. Single-parent families were increasingly common. More than one quarter of children lived in a single-parent household. Statistics projected that these trends would continue in future decades.

Questions over Rights In the 2000s, questions over affirmative action and same-sex marriage brought changes to the legal landscape. The U.S. Supreme Court played a significant role in these changes. In the 1960s, policymakers began to promote **affirmative action**, or a preference for hiring African Americans, women, or members of other groups that had faced discrimination. Eventually, local governments and universities adopted affirmative action policies to make sure that employees and students came from diverse ethnic backgrounds.

In 2003, the U.S. Supreme Court decided on two affirmative action cases from the University of Michigan. After hearing the arguments, the Court decided that colleges and universities had the right to consider race when deciding whether to admit a student. The justices concluded that globalization made it essential for college-educated military and business leaders to have racially and ethnically diverse backgrounds. The Court, however, ruled that universities could not use rigid formulas that gave preference to minority members over others.

In 2013, the Supreme Court again considered the question of minority rights. This time, the court ruled on the question of same-sex marriages. In its decision, the Court declared parts of the 1996 Defense of Marriage Act (DOMA) unconstitutional. DOMA required the federal government to deny recognition to same-sex marriages performed in states where those marriages were legal.

Through its decision, the Court ruled that married same-sex couples must receive federal benefits, such as health insurance, retirement funds, and tax refunds, just like other married couples. The Court's decision reflected society's growing acceptance of lesbian, gay, bisexual, and transgender people. Gays and lesbians served openly in the U.S. military after the Court's decision. The number of states that allowed same-sex marriages steadily increased.

? RECALL What did the Supreme Court rule in its 2013 decision on the Defense of Marriage Act?

America's Promise

During the 1900s, the United States experienced dramatic changes that transformed Americans' lives. Technological advances led to the development of the Internet, electric cars, cell phones, and personal computers. Astronauts walked on the moon, scientists explored the depths of the ocean, and researchers developed cures for diseases. Literacy rates in the United States increased from 25 percent to 86 percent. Life expectancy rose.

By the 2000s, the diversity of the American people had increased. Civil rights and political opportunities for minority groups had expanded. The African

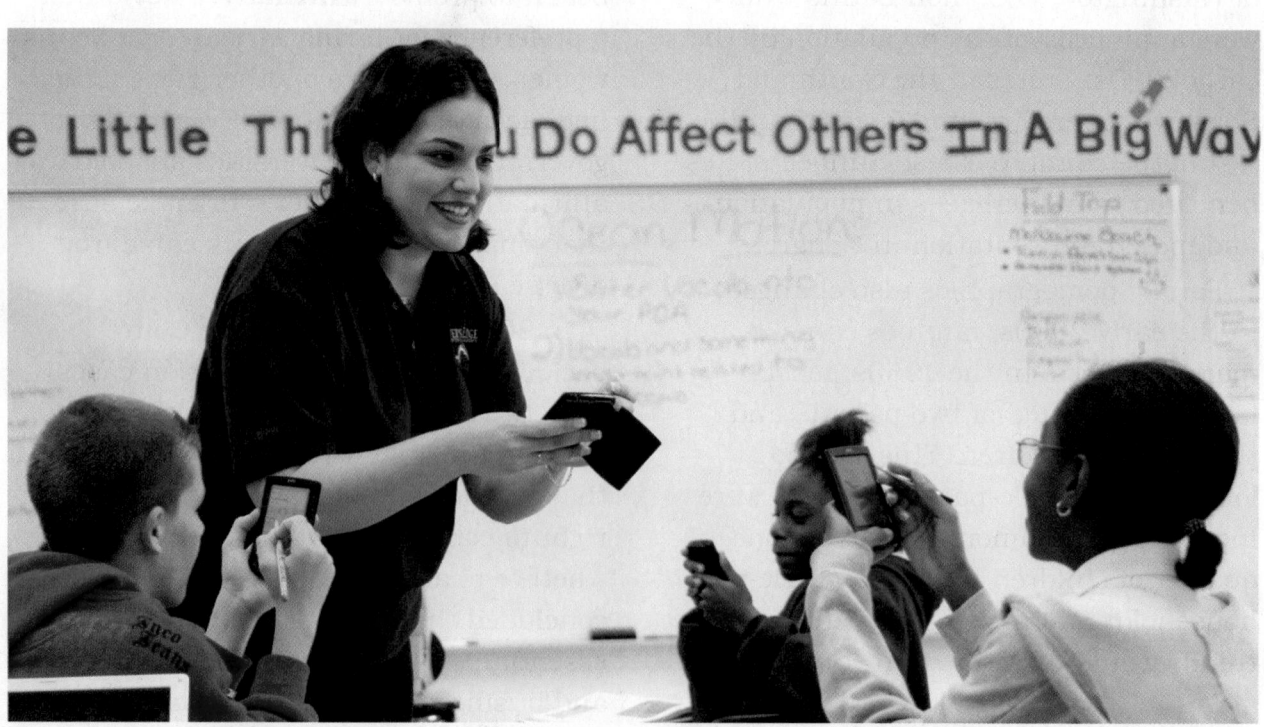

>> One impact of technology could be seen in many American classrooms, where handheld and other digital devices were commonly used.

Interactive Chart

American civil rights movement of the mid-1900s helped Thurgood Marshall become the first African American Supreme Court justice. It helped Colin Powell to become the first African American Secretary of State under George W. Bush and enabled Barack Obama to become the country's first African American President.

Rights for women also expanded. In the early 2000s, more than half of medical school and law school students were women. Women served as governors and on the Supreme Court. In the Clinton administration, Madeleine Albright served as the first female Secretary of State. In 2007, Nancy Pelosi became the first female speaker of the House of Representatives. The number of women serving in Congress continued to rise.

Americans still had questions to consider and solutions to find at home and abroad. The United States remained a world leader. Its role in world affairs continued to change. Globalization increased America's importance in the world, politically, economically, and militarily. It also increased Americans' responsibility to address worldwide problems, such as climate change, reliance on fossil fuels, economic crises, cyberwarfare, and the spread of infectious diseases.

At home, Americans faced the challenge of a changing demographic. The number of immigrants, people in nontraditional relationships, and people of different racial, ethnic, and religious backgrounds was likely to increase.

Traditionally, America has welcomed people of diverse backgrounds and beliefs. National pride, a commitment to economic opportunity, and a devotion to freedom have guided the United States since its founding.

>> In 2009, Sonia Sotomayor became the first Latino and the third woman Justice of the U.S. Supreme Court.

These three principles will continue to guide Americans in years to come.

? IDENTIFY CENTRAL IDEAS According to the text, what three principles guide Americans?

ASSESSMENT

1. **Generate Explanations** How did President Bush's response to the September 11 terrorist attacks influence the rest of his presidency?

2. **Generate Explanations** How did the recessions of 2001 and 2007 affect the American economy?

3. **Support Ideas with Examples** What evidence supports the idea that Congress was divided along party lines during Obama's presidency?

4. **Summarize** What effect did the Supreme Court's ruling on the question of same-sex marriage have on same-sex couples in American society?

5. **Summarize** What demographic changes affected the American population in the 2000s?

AMERICA'S CHANGING FAMILIES 1980 VS. 2010

AVERAGE LIFE EXPECTANCY
73.7 YEARS (1980)
78.7 YEARS (2010)

AVERAGE NUMBER OF PEOPLE PER HOUSEHOLD
1980 — 2.75
2010 — 2.58

AVERAGE FAMILY SIZE
1980 — 3.29
2010 — 3.14

MARRIED COUPLE FAMILY HOUSEHOLDS
1980 — 82.8%
2010 — 66.4%

UNMARRIED COUPLE HOUSEHOLDS
1980 — 3.0%
2010 — 5.2%

HEADS OF HOUSEHOLD UNDER 25
1980 — 8.3%
2010 — 4.1%

Sources: U.S. Census Bureau; National Center for Health Statistics, CDC

1. **Analyze Graphs** Use the graphs above and information from the lessons in the topic to write a paragraph identifying the family characteristics that distinguish the present era. Identify changes in life expectancy between 1980 and 2010; family size between 1980 and 2010; and the make up of households between 1980 and 2010.

2. **Identify the Causes and Effects of the War in Afghanistan** Use the information from the lessons in this topic and other sources to write a paragraph identifying the causes and effects of this war. In your paragraph, be sure to describe the reasons for the invasion of Afghanistan, the course of the war, and its effects.

3. **Explain the Significance of 2001 As a Turning Point** Use the information from the lessons in this topic and other sources to write a paragraph explaining the events of September 11, 2001, and how 2001 was a turning point for the United States. In your paragraph, be sure to explain how the United States was attacked; what group was responsible for the attacks; and why September 11, 2001, was a turning point for the United States.

4. **Evaluate U.S. Participation in International Organizations** Use the information from the lessons in this topic and other sources to write a paragraph evaluating the pros and cons of participating in the World Trade Organization. As part of your evaluation, consider the argument that global organizations undermine U.S. sovereignty. Also consider the argument that global organizations can enforce rules that benefit the United States. In your evaluation, consider such factors as the power of the World Trade Organization to negotiate and enforce trade agreements; how trade treaties might affect environmental efforts and worker's rights in the United States; and the opportunities for jobs and economic growth created by free trade.

5. **Identify the Impact of Globalization** Use the information from the lessons in this topic and other sources to write a paragraph identifying the economic impact of the rise of globalization. In your paragraph, be sure to identify what globalization is; the positive economic impact of globalization; and the negative economic impact of globalization.

6. **Identify the Causes and Effects of Financial Crisis** Identify the causes and effects of the financial crisis of 2007. Write a paragraph identifying both causes and effects of the crisis, including actions by bankers, homeowners, and employers. In your paragraph, be sure to identify what a "subprime" home mortgage loan is; why banks made subprime loans; what effect the collapse of the housing market had on banks, investment firms, and employment.

7. **Evaluate the American Recovery and Reinvestment Act of 2009** Use the lessons in this topic and other sources to write a paragraph evaluating the impact of the American Recovery and Reinvestment Act of 2009 on the public and the private sectors. In your paragraph, be sure to consider Obama's role in the act; the goal of the act; what the text and graphs indicate about the impact of the act.

8. **Identify Point of View** Use the lessons in the topic, the quote below, and other sources, to write a paragraph identifying the point of view expressed by Rachel Carson's book, *Silent Spring*. In your paragraph be sure to consider government response to *Silent Spring*; Carson's frame of reference and point of view in the quotation below and what the language of the quotation indicates about Carson's intent in writing *Silent Spring*.

Only in the moment of the time represented by the present century has one species— man—acquired significant power to alter the nature of his world. During the past quarter century this power has not only increased to one of disturbing magnitude but it has changed in character. The most alarming of all man's assaults upon the environment is the contamination of air, earth, rivers, and sea with dangerous and even lethal materials. This pollution is for the most part irrecoverable; the chain of evil it initiates not only in the world that must support life but in living tissues is for the most part irreversible. In this now universal contamination of the environment, chemicals . . . [are] changing the very nature of the world—the very nature of its life.

—Rachel Carson, *Silent Spring*

9. **Explain the Impact of Technological Innovations** Use the information from the lessons in this topic and other sources to write a paragraph describing how computers have transformed life in the United States. In your paragraph, be sure to explain how the Internet has transformed communication; discuss how personal computers have changed the workplace; describe how e-commerce has changed business transactions; and explain how social networking and cell phones have changed U.S. society.

10. **Identify the Causes and Effects of Innovations in Medicine** Write a paragraph explaining the causes and effects of new scientific discoveries and technological innovations in medicine. Consider the American emphasis on research and development,

how research leads to innovations in the treatment of diseases such as vaccines, and how technological innovations lead to a wider range of medical options.

11. **Explain 2008 As a Turning Point** Use the quotation below and the information from the lessons in this topic and other sources to write a paragraph explaining how the election of Barack Obama as President in 2008 was a turning point. In your paragraph, be sure to explain Obama's background before running for President; why the 2008 presidential race was a historical turning point; what Obama means in the quotation.

If there is anyone out there who still doubts that America is a place where all things are possible, who still wonders if the dream of our founders is alive in our time, who still questions the power of our democracy, tonight is your answer.

—Barack Obama, November 2008

12. **Identify the Effects of Debt** Explain the role that excessive debt played in the financial crisis beginning in 2007. In a paragraph, identify the effects of U.S. homeowner debt and the debts of European countries. Explain how debt affected the U.S. and world economies.

13. **Create Visual Presentations on Immigration** Use computer software and the information from the lessons in this topic and other sources to create a visual presentation about immigration to the United States since 2000. Use different means to convey information, including written, visual, or statistical means as appropriate. Be sure to use statistics from the lessons and other sources to create charts and graphs showing the characteristics of immigration and provide captions that explain what the charts and graphs show.

14. **Identify Significant Social and Political Issues** Use the information from the lessons in this topic and other sources to write a paragraph describing the social and political issues surrounding the Affordable Care Act. In your paragraph, be sure to identify what political issues surrounded the passage of the Affordable Care Act; the effects of the act; and why some people were opposed to the act.

15. Identify Causes and Effects of Political Gridlock
Use information from the lessons in this topic and other sources to write a paragraph identifying the causes and effects of political gridlock during the presidency of Barack Obama. How did control by Republicans and Democrats of different houses of Congress contribute to gridlock, and what were some of its effects?

16. Reflect on the Essential Question Write an essay on the Essential Question: **What can individuals do to affect society?** Use evidence from your study of this topic to support your answer.

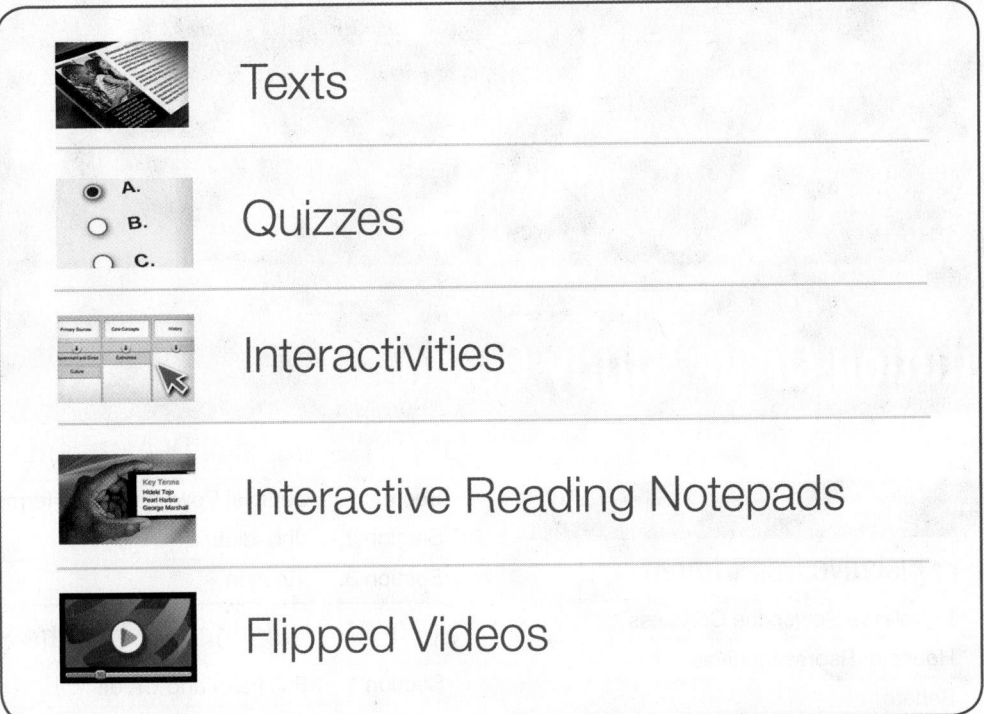

www.PearsonRealize.com
Access your Digital Lesson

Go online to PearsonRealize.com and use the texts, quizzes, interactivities, Interactive Reading Notepads, Flipped Videos, and other resources from this Topic to prepare for the Topic Test.

Texts

Quizzes

Interactivities

Interactive Reading Notepads

Flipped Videos

While online you can also check the progress you've made learning the topic and course content by viewing your grades, test scores, and assignment status.

Stock Connection Blue/Alamy

Constitution Quick Study Guide

Preamble

Articles

Article I. Legislative Department

Article II. Executive Department

Article III. Judicial Department

Article IV. Relations Among the States

Article V. Provisions for Amendment

Article VI. Public Debts; Supremacy of National Law; Oath

Article VII. Ratification of Constitution

The Preamble states the broad purposes the Constitution is intended to serve—to establish a government that provides for greater cooperation among the States, ensures justice and peace, provides for defense against foreign enemies, promotes the general well-being of the people, and secures liberty now and in the future. The phrase We the People emphasizes the twin concepts of popular sovereignty and of representative government.

Legislative Department

Section 1. Legislative power; Congress

Congress, the nation's lawmaking body, is bicameral in form; that is, it is composed of two houses: the Senate and the House of Representatives. The Framers of the Constitution purposely separated the lawmaking power from the power to enforce the laws (Article II, the Executive Branch) and the power to interpret them (Article III, the Judicial Branch). This system of separation of powers is supplemented by a system of checks and balances; that is, in several provisions the Constitution gives to each of the three branches various powers with which it may restrain the actions of the other two branches.

Section 2. House of Representatives

▶ **Clause 1. Election** Electors means voters. Members of the House of Representatives are elected every two years. Each State must permit the same persons to vote for United States representatives as it permits to vote for the members of the larger house of its own legislature. The 17th Amendment (1913) extends this requirement to the qualification of voters for United States senators.

▶ **Clause 2. Qualifications** A member of the House of Representatives must be at least 25 years old, an American citizen for seven years, and a resident of the State he or she represents. In addition, political custom requires that a representative also reside in the district from which he or she is elected.

▶ **Clause 3. Apportionment** The number of representatives each State is entitled to is based on its population, which is counted every 10 years in the census. Congress reapportions the seats among the States after each census. In the Reapportionment Act of 1929, Congress fixed the permanent size of the House at 435 members with each State having at least one representative. Today there is one House seat for approximately every 700,000 persons in the population.

The words "three-fifths of all other persons" referred to slaves and reflected the Three-Fifths Compromise reached by the Framers at Philadelphia in 1787; the phrase was made obsolete, was in effect repealed, by the 13th Amendment in 1865.

---

* The gray words indicate portions of the Constitution altered by subsequent amendments to the document.

▶ **Clause 4. Vacancies** The executive authority refers to the governor of a State. If a member leaves office or dies before the expiration of his or her term, the governor is to call a special election to fill the vacancy.

United States Constitution

PREAMBLE

We the People of the United States, in Order to form a more perfect Union, establish Justice, insure domestic Tranquility, provide for the common defence, promote the general Welfare, and secure the Blessings of Liberty to ourselves and our Posterity, do ordain and establish this Constitution for the United States of America.

Article I.

Section 1.

All legislative Powers herein granted shall be vested in a Congress of the United States, which shall consist of a Senate and House of Representatives.

Section 2.

▶ 1. The House of Representatives shall be composed of Members chosen every second Year by the People of the several States, and the Electors in each State shall have the Qualifications requisite for Electors of the most numerous Branch of the State Legislature.

▶ 2. No Person shall be a Representative who shall not have attained to the age of twenty-five Years, and been seven Years a Citizen of the United States, and who shall not, when elected, be an Inhabitant of that State in which he shall be chosen.

▶ 3. Representatives and direct Taxes* shall be apportioned among the several States which may be included within this Union, according to their respective Numbers, which shall be determined by adding to the whole Number of free Persons, including those bound to Service for a Term of Years and excluding Indians not taxed, three fifths of all other Persons. The actual Enumeration shall be made within three Years after the first Meeting of the Congress of the United States, and within every subsequent term of ten Years, in such Manner as they shall by Law direct. The Number of Representatives shall not exceed one for every thirty Thousand, but each State shall have at Least one Representative; and, until such enumeration shall be made, the State of New Hampshire shall be entitled to choose three, Massachusetts eight, Rhode Island and Providence Plantations one, Connecticut five, New York six, New Jersey four, Pennsylvania eight, Delaware one, Maryland six, Virginia ten, North Carolina five, South Carolina five, and Georgia three.

▶ 4. When vacancies happen in the Representation from any State, the Executive Authority thereof shall issue Writs of Election to fill such Vacancies.

5. The House of Representatives shall choose their Speaker and other Officers; and shall have the sole Power of Impeachment.

Section 3.

1. The Senate of the United States shall be composed of two Senators from each State chosen by the Legislature thereof for six Years; and each Senator shall have one Vote.

2. Immediately after they shall be assembled in Consequences of the first Election, they shall be divided, as equally as may be, into three Classes. The Seats of the Senators of the first Class shall be vacated at the Expiration of the second Year; of the second Class, at the Expiration of the fourth Year; and of the third Class, at the Expiration of the sixth Year; so that one-third may be chosen every second Year; and if Vacancies happen by Resignation, or otherwise, during the Recess of the Legislature of any State, the Executive thereof may make temporary Appointments until the next Meeting of the Legislature, which shall then fill such Vacancies.

3. No Person shall be a Senator who shall not have attained to the Age of thirty Years, and been nine Years a Citizen of the United States, and who shall not, when elected, be an Inhabitant of that State for which he shall be chosen.

4. The Vice President of the United States shall be President of the Senate but shall have no Vote, unless they be equally divided.

5. The Senate shall choose their other Officers, and also a President pro tempore, in the Absence of the Vice President, or when he shall exercise the Office of President of the United States.

6. The Senate shall have the sole Power to try all Impeachments. When sitting for that Purpose, they shall be on Oath or Affirmation. When the President of the United States is tried, the Chief Justice shall preside: And no Person shall be convicted without the Concurrence of two thirds of the Members present.

7. Judgment in Cases of Impeachment shall not extend further than to removal from Office, and disqualification to hold and enjoy any Office of honor, Trust, or Profit under the United States: but the Party convicted shall nevertheless be liable and subject to Indictment, Trial, Judgment and Punishment, according to Law.

▶ **Clause 5. Officers; impeachment** The House elects a Speaker, customarily chosen from the majority party in the House. Impeachment means accusation. The House has the exclusive power to impeach, or accuse, civil officers; the Senate (Article I, Section 3, Clause 6) has the exclusive power to try those impeached by the House.

Section 3. Senate

▶ **Clause 1. Composition, election, term** Each State has two senators. Each serves for six years and has one vote. Originally, senators were not elected directly by the people, but by each State's legislature. The 17th Amendment, added in 1913, provides for the popular election of senators.

▶ **Clause 2. Classification** The senators elected in 1788 were divided into three groups so that the Senate could become a "continuing body." One-third of the Senate's seats are up for election every two years.

   The 17th Amendment provides that a Senate vacancy is to be filled at a special election called by the governor; State law may also permit the governor to appoint a successor to serve until that election is held.

▶ **Clause 3. Qualifications** A senator must be at least 30 years old, a citizen for at least nine years, and must live in the State from which elected.

▶ **Clause 4. Presiding officer** The Vice President presides over the Senate, but may vote only to break a tie.

▶ **Clause 5. Other officers** The Senate chooses its own officers, including a president pro tempore to preside when the Vice President is not there.

▶ **Clause 6. Impeachment trials** The Senate conducts the trials of those officials impeached by the House. The Vice President presides unless the President is on trial, in which case the Chief Justice of the United States does so. A conviction requires the votes of two-thirds of the senators present.

   No President has ever been convicted. In 1868 the House voted eleven articles of impeachment against President Andrew Johnson, but the Senate fell one vote short of convicting him. In 1974 President Richard M. Nixon resigned the presidency in the face of almost certain impeachment by the House. The House brought two articles of impeachment against President Bill Clinton in late 1998. Neither charge was supported by even a simple majority vote in the Senate, on February 12, 1999.

▶ **Clause 7. Penalty on conviction** The punishment of an official convicted in an impeachment case has always been removal from office. The Senate can also bar a convicted person from ever holding any federal office, but it is not required to do so. A convicted person can also be tried and punished in a regular court for any crime involved in the impeachment case.

Section 4. Elections and Meetings

▶ **Clause 1.** **Election In 1842** Congress required that representatives be elected from districts within each State with more than one seat in the House. The districts in each State are drawn by that State's legislature. Seven States now have only one seat in the House: Alaska, Delaware, Montana, North Dakota, South Dakota, Vermont, and Wyoming. The 1842 law also directed that representatives be elected in each State on the same day: the Tuesday after the first Monday in November of every even-numbered year. In 1914 Congress also set that same date for the election of senators.

▶ **Clause 2.** **Sessions Congress** must meet at least once a year. The 20th Amendment (1933) changed the opening date to January 3.

Section 5. Legislative Proceedings

▶ **Clause 1.** **Admission of members; quorum** In 1969 the Supreme Court held that the House cannot exclude any member-elect who satisfies the qualifications set out in Article I, Section 2, Clause 2.

A majority in the House (218 members) or Senate (51) constitutes a quorum. In practice, both houses often proceed with less than a quorum present. However, any member may raise a point of order (demand a "quorum call"). If a roll call then reveals less than a majority of the members present, that chamber must either adjourn or the sergeant at arms must be ordered to round up absent members.

▶ **Clause 2.** **Rules** Each house has adopted detailed rules to guide its proceedings. Each house may discipline members for unacceptable conduct; expulsion requires a two-thirds vote.

▶ **Clause 3.** **Record** Each house must keep and publish a record of its meetings. The Congressional Record is published for every day that either house of Congress is in session, and provides a written record of all that is said and done on the floor of each house each session.

▶ **Clause 4.** **Adjournment** Once in session, neither house may suspend (recess) its work for more than three days without the approval of the other house. Both houses must always meet in the same location.

Section 4.

▶1. The Times, Places and Manner of holding Elections for Senators and Representatives, shall be prescribed in each State by the Legislature thereof; but the Congress may at any time by law make or alter such Regulations, except as to the Places of choosing Senators.

▶2. The Congress shall assemble at least once in every Year, and such Meeting shall be on the first Monday in December, unless they shall by Law appoint a different Day.

Section 5.

▶1. Each House shall be the Judge of the Elections, Returns and Qualifications of its own Members, and a Majority of each shall constitute a Quorum to do Business; but a smaller Number may adjourn from day to day, and may be authorized to compel the Attendance of absent Members, in such Manner, and under such Penalties, as each House may provide.

▶2. Each House may determine the Rules of its Proceedings, punish its Members for disorderly Behavior, and, with the Concurrence of two thirds, expel a Member.

▶3. Each House shall keep a Journal of its Proceedings, and from time to time publish the same, excepting such Parts as may in their Judgment require Secrecy; and the Yeas and Nays of the Members of either House on any question shall, at the Desire of one fifth of those Present, be entered on the Journal.

▶4. Neither House, during the Session of Congress, shall, without the Consent of the other, adjourn for more than three days, nor to any other Place than that in which the two Houses shall be sitting.

Section 6.

▶1. The Senators and Representatives shall receive a Compensation for their Services, to be ascertained by Law, and paid out of the Treasury of the United States. They shall in all Cases, except Treason, Felony, and Breach of the Peace, be privileged from Arrest during their Attendance at the Session of their respective Houses, and in going to and returning from the same; and for any Speech or Debate in either House, they shall not be questioned in any other Place.

▶2. No Senator or Representative shall, during the Time for which he was elected, be appointed to any civil Office under the Authority of the United States, which shall have been created, or the Emoluments whereof shall have been increased during such time; and no Person holding any Office under the United States, shall be a Member of either House during his Continuance in Office.

Section 7.

▶1. All Bills for raising Revenue shall originate in the House of Representatives; but the Senate may propose or concur with amendments as on other Bills.

▶2. Every Bill which shall have passed the House of Representatives and the Senate, shall, before it become a law, be presented to the President of the United States: If he approve, he shall sign it, but if not he shall return it, with his Objections to that House in which it shall have originated, who shall enter the Objections at large on their Journal, and proceed to reconsider it. If after such Reconsideration two thirds of the House shall agree to pass the Bill, it shall be sent, together with the Objections, to the other House, by which it shall likewise be reconsidered, and if approved by two thirds of that House, it shall become a Law. But in all such Cases the Votes of both Houses shall be determined by Yeas and Nays, and the Names of the Persons voting for and against the Bill shall be entered on the Journal of each House respectively. If any Bill shall not be returned by the President within ten Days (Sunday excepted) after it shall have been presented to him, the Same shall be a law, in like Manner as if he had signed it, unless the Congress by their Adjournment, prevent its Return, in which Case it shall not be a Law.

▶3. Every Order, Resolution, or Vote to which the Concurrence of the Senate and House of Representatives may be necessary (except on a question of adjournment) shall be presented to the President of the United States; and before the Same shall take Effect, shall be approved by him, or, being disapproved by him, shall be repassed by two thirds of the Senate and House of Representatives, according to the Rules and Limitations prescribed in the Case of a Bill.

Section 6. Compensation, Immunities, and Disabilities of Members

▶ **Clause 1. Salaries; immunities** Each house sets its members' salaries, paid by the United States; the 27th Amendment (1992) modified this pay-setting power. This provision establishes "legislative immunity." The purpose of this immunity is to allow members to speak and debate freely in Congress itself. Treason is strictly defined in Article III, Section 3. A felony is any serious crime. A breach of the peace is any indictable offense less than treason or a felony; this exemption from arrest is of little real importance today.

▶ **Clause 2. Restrictions on office holding** No sitting member of either house may be appointed to an office in the executive or in the judicial branch if that position was created or its salary was increased during that member's current elected term. The second part of this clause—forbidding any person serving in either the executive or the judicial branch from also serving in Congress—reinforces the principle of separation of powers.

Section 7. Revenue Bills, President's Veto

▶ **Clause 1. Revenue bills** All bills that raise money must originate in the House. However, the Senate has the power to amend any revenue bill sent to it from the lower house.

▶ **Clause 2. Enactment of laws; veto** Once both houses have passed a bill, it must be sent to the President. The President may (1) sign the bill, thus making it law; (2) veto the bill, whereupon it must be returned to the house in which it originated; or (3) allow the bill to become law without signature, by not acting upon it within 10 days of its receipt from Congress, not counting Sundays. The President has a fourth option at the end of a congressional session: If he does not act on a measure within 10 days, and Congress adjourns during that period, the bill dies; the "pocket veto" has been applied to it. A presidential veto may be overridden by a two-thirds vote in each house.

▶ **Clause 3. Other measures** This clause refers to joint resolutions, measures Congress often passes to deal with unusual, temporary, or ceremonial matters. A joint resolution passed by Congress and signed by the President has the force of law, just as a bill does. As a matter of custom, a joint resolution proposing an amendment to the Constitution is not submitted to the President for signature or veto. Concurrent and simple resolutions do not have the force of law and, therefore, are not submitted to the President.

Section 8. Powers of Congress

▶ **Clause 1.** The 18 separate clauses in this section set out 27 of the many expressed powers the Constitution grants to Congress. In this clause Congress is given the power to levy and provide for the collection of various kinds of taxes, in order to finance the operations of the government. All federal taxes must be levied at the same rates throughout the country.

▶ **Clause 2.** Congress has power to borrow money to help finance the government. Federal borrowing is most often done through the sale of bonds on which interest is paid. The Constitution does not limit the amount the government may borrow.

▶ **Clause 3.** This clause, the Commerce Clause, gives Congress the power to regulate both foreign and interstate trade. Much of what Congress does, it does on the basis of its commerce power.

▶ **Clause 4.** Congress has the exclusive power to determine how aliens may become citizens of the United States. Congress may also pass laws relating to bankruptcy.

▶ **Clause 5.** has the power to establish and require the use of uniform gauges of time, distance, weight, volume, area, and the like.

▶ **Clause 6.** Congress has the power to make it a federal crime to falsify the coins, paper money, bonds, stamps, and the like of the United States.

▶ **Clause 7.** Congress has the power to provide for and regulate the transportation and delivery of mail; "post offices" are those buildings and other places where mail is deposited for dispatch; "post roads" include all routes over or upon which mail is carried.

▶ **Clause 8.** Congress has the power to provide for copyrights and patents. A copyright gives an author or composer the exclusive right to control the reproduction, publication, and sale of literary, musical, or other creative work. A patent gives a person the exclusive right to control the manufacture or sale of his or her invention.

▶ **Clause 9.** Congress has the power to create the lower federal courts, all of the several federal courts that function beneath the Supreme Court.

▶ **Clause 10.** Congress has the power to prohibit, as a federal crime: (1) certain acts committed outside the territorial jurisdiction of the United States, and (2) the commission within the United States of any wrong against any nation with which we are at peace.

Section 8.

The Congress shall have Power

▶ 1. To lay and collect Taxes, Duties, Imposts and Excises to pay the Debts and provide for the common Defence and general Welfare of the United States; but all Duties, Imposts and Excises, shall be uniform throughout the United States;

▶ 2. To borrow Money on the credit of the United States;

▶ 3. To regulate Commerce with foreign Nations, and among the several States, and with the Indian Tribes;

▶ 4. To establish an uniform Rule of Naturalization, and uniform Laws on the subject of Bankruptcies throughout the United States;

▶ 5. To coin Money, regulate the Value thereof, and of foreign Coin, and fix the Standard of Weights and Measures;

▶ 6. To provide for the Punishment of counterfeiting the Securities and current Coin of the United States;

▶ 7. To establish Post Offices and post Roads;

▶ 8. To promote the Progress of Science and useful Arts, by securing, for limited Times to Authors and Inventors the exclusive Right to their respective Writings and Discoveries;

▶ 9. To constitute Tribunals inferior to the supreme Court;

▶ 10. To define and punish Piracies and Felonies committed on the high Seas, and Offences against the Law of nations;

11. To declare War, grant Letters of Marque and Reprisal, and make Rules concerning Captures on Land and Water;

12. To raise and support Armies; but no Appropriation of Money to that Use shall be for a longer Term than two Years;
13. To provide and maintain a Navy;

14. To make Rules for the Government and Regulation of the land and naval Forces;

15. To provide for calling forth the Militia to execute the Laws of the Union, suppress Insurrections and repel Invasions;
16. To provide for organizing, arming, and disciplining the Militia, and for governing such Part of them as may be employed in the Service of the United States, reserving to the States respectively the Appointment of the Officers, and the Authority of training the Militia according to the discipline prescribed by Congress;

17. To exercise exclusive Legislation in all Cases whatsoever, over such District (not exceeding ten Miles square) as may, by Cession of Particular States, and the Acceptance of Congress, become the Seat of the Government of the United States, and to exercise like Authority over all Places purchased by the Consent of the Legislature of the State in which the Same shall be, for the Erection of Forts, Magazines, Arsenals, Dockyards and other needful Buildings;—And

18. To make all Laws which shall be necessary and proper for carrying into Execution the foregoing Powers and all other Powers vested by this Constitution in the Government of the United States, or in any Department or Officer thereof.

Section 9.
1. The Migration or Importation of such Persons as any of the States now existing shall think proper to admit, shall not be prohibited by the Congress prior to the Year one thousand eight hundred and eight, but a Tax or duty may be imposed on such Importation, not exceeding ten dollars for each Person.

▶ **Clause 11.** Only Congress can declare war. However, the President, as commander in chief of the armed forces (Article II, Section 2, Clause 1), can make war without such a formal declaration. Letters of marque and reprisal are commissions authorizing private persons to outfit vessels (privateers) to capture and destroy enemy ships in time of war; they were forbidden in international law by the Declaration of Paris of 1856, and the United States has honored the ban since the Civil War.

▶ **Clauses 12 and 13.** Congress has the power to provide for and maintain the nation's armed forces. It established the air force as an independent element of the armed forces in 1947, an exercise of its inherent powers in foreign relations and national defense. The two-year limit on spending for the army insures civilian control of the military.

▶ **Clause 14.** Today these rules are set out in three principle statutes: the Uniform Code of Military Justice, passed by Congress in 1950, and the Military Justice Acts of 1958 and 1983.

▶ **Clauses 15 and 16.** In the National Defense Act of 1916, Congress made each State's militia (volunteer army) a part of the National Guard. Today, Congress and the States cooperate in its maintenance. Ordinarily, each State's National Guard is under the command of that State's governor; but Congress has given the President the power to call any or all of those units into federal service when necessary.

▶ **Clause 17.** In 1791 Congress accepted land grants from Maryland and Virginia and established the District of Columbia for the nation's capital. Assuming Virginia's grant would never be needed, Congress returned it in 1846. Today, the elected government of the District's 69 square miles operates under the authority of Congress. Congress also has the power to acquire other lands from the States for various federal purposes.

▶ **Clause 18.** This is the Necessary and Proper Clause, also often called the Elastic Clause. It is the constitutional basis for the many and far-reaching implied powers of the Federal Government.

Section 9. Powers Denied to Congress
▶ **Clause 1.** The phrase "such persons" referred to slaves. This provision was part of the Commerce Compromise, one of the bargains struck in the writing of the Constitution. Congress outlawed the slave trade in 1808.

Clause 2. A writ of habeas corpus, the "great writ of liberty," is a court order directing a sheriff, warden, or other public officer, or a private person, who is detaining another to "produce the body" of the one being held in order that the legality of the detention may be determined by the court.

Clause 3. A bill of attainder is a legislative act that inflicts punishment without a judicial trial. See Article I, Section 10, and Article III, Section 3, Clause 2. An ex post facto law is any criminal law that operates retroactively to the disadvantage of the accused. See Article I, Section 10.

Clause 4. A capitation tax is literally a "head tax," a tax levied on each person in the population. A direct tax is one paid directly to the government by the taxpayer—for example, an income or a property tax; an indirect tax is one paid to another private party who then pays it to the government—for example, a sales tax. This provision was modified by the 16th Amendment (1913), giving Congress the power to levy "taxes on incomes, from whatever source derived."

Clause 5. This provision was a part of the Commerce Compromise made by the Framers in 1787. Congress has the power to tax imported goods, however.

Clause 6. All ports within the United States must be treated alike by Congress as it exercises its taxing and commerce powers. Congress cannot tax goods sent by water from one State to another, nor may it give the ports of one State any legal advantage over those of another.

Clause 7. This clause gives Congress its vastly important "power of the purse," a major check on presidential power. Federal money can be spent only in those amounts and for those purposes expressly authorized by an act of Congress. All federal income and spending must be accounted for, regularly and publicly.

Clause 8. This provision, preventing the establishment of a nobility, reflects the principle that "all men are created equal." It was also intended to discourage foreign attempts to bribe or otherwise corrupt officers of the government.

Section 10. Powers Denied to the States

Clause 1. The States are not sovereign governments and so cannot make agreements or otherwise negotiate with foreign states; the power to conduct foreign relations is an exclusive power of the National Government. The power to coin money is also an exclusive power of the National Government. Several powers forbidden to the National Government are here also forbidden to the States.

Clause 2. This provision relates to foreign, not interstate, commerce. Only Congress, not the States, can tax imports; and the States are, like Congress, forbidden the power to tax exports.

▶2. The Privilege of the Writ of Habeas Corpus shall not be suspended, unless when in Cases of Rebellion or Invasion the public safety may require it.

▶3. No Bill of Attainder or ex post facto Law shall be passed.

▶4. No Capitation, or other direct, Tax shall be laid, unless in Proportion to the Census of Enumeration hereinbefore directed to be taken.

▶5. No Tax or Duty shall be laid on Articles exported from any State.

▶6. No Preference shall be given by any Regulation of Commerce or Revenue to the Ports of one State over those of another: nor shall Vessels bound to, or from, one State, be obliged to enter, clear or pay Duties in another.

▶7. No Money shall be drawn from the Treasury, but in Consequence of Appropriations made by Law; and a regular Statement and Account of the Receipts and Expenditures of all public Money shall be published from time to time.

▶8. No Title of Nobility shall be granted by the United States: And no Person holding any Office of Profit or Trust under them, shall, without the Consent of the Congress, accept of any present, Emolument, Office, or Title, of any kind whatever, from any King, Prince, or foreign State.

Section 10.

▶1. No State shall enter into any Treaty, Alliance, or Confederation; grant Letters of Marque and Reprisal; coin Money; emit Bills of Credit; make any Thing but gold and silver Coin a Tender in Payment of Debts; pass any Bill of Attainder, ex post facto Law, or Law impairing the Obligation of Contracts, or grant any Title of Nobility.

▶2. No State shall, without the Consent of the Congress, lay any Imposts or Duties on Imports or Exports, except what may be absolutely necessary for executing its inspection Laws; and the net Produce of all Duties and Imposts, laid by any State on Imports or Exports, shall be for the Use of the Treasury of the United States; and all such Laws shall be subject to the Revision and Control of the Congress.

▶ 3. No State shall, without the Consent of Congress, lay any Duty of Tonnage, keep Troops, or Ships of War in time of Peace, enter into any Agreement or Compact with another State, or with a foreign Power, or engage in War, unless actually invaded, or in such imminent Danger as will not admit of delay.

Article II
Section 1.

▶ 1. The executive Power shall be vested in a President of the United States of America. He shall hold his Office during the Term of four Years, and, together with the Vice President, chosen for the same Term, be elected as follows:

▶ 2. Each State shall appoint, in such Manner as the Legislature thereof may direct, a Number of Electors, equal to the whole Number of Senators and Representatives to which the State may be entitled in the Congress: but no Senator or Representative, or Person holding an Office of Trust or Profit, under the United States, shall be appointed an Elector.

▶ 3. The Electors shall meet in their respective States, and vote by Ballot for two Persons, of whom one at least shall not be an Inhabitant of the same State with themselves. And they shall make a List of all the Persons voted for, and of the Number of Votes for each; which List they shall sign and certify, and transmit sealed to the Seat of the Government of the United States, directed to the President of the Senate. The President of the Senate shall, in the Presence of the Senate and House of Representatives, open all the Certificates, and the Votes shall then be counted. The Person having the greatest Number of Votes shall be the President, if such Number be a majority of the whole Number of Electors appointed; and if there be more than one who have such Majority, and have an equal Number of Votes, then, the House of Representatives shall immediately choose by Ballot one of them for President; and if no Person have a Majority, then from the five highest on the List the said House shall in like Manner choose the President. But in choosing the President, the Votes shall be taken by States, the Representatives from each State having one Vote; a quorum for this Purpose shall consist of a Member or Members from two thirds of the States, and a Majority of all the States shall be necessary to a Choice. In every Case, after the Choice of the President, the Person having the greatest Number of Votes of the Electors shall be the Vice President. But if there should remain two or more who have equal Votes, the Senate shall choose from them by Ballot the Vice President.

▶ Clause 3. A duty of tonnage is a tax laid on ships according to their cargo capacity. Each State has a constitutional right to provide for and maintain a militia; but no State may keep a standing army or navy. The several restrictions here prevent the States from assuming powers that the Constitution elsewhere grants to the National Government.

Executive Department
Section 1. President and Vice President

▶ **Clause 1. Executive power, term** This clause gives to the President the very broad "executive power," the power to enforce the laws and otherwise administer the public policies of the United States. It also sets the length of the presidential (and vice-presidential) term of office; see the 22nd Amendment (1951), which places a limit on presidential (but not vice-presidential) tenure.

▶ **Clause 2. Electoral college** This clause establishes the "electoral college," although the Constitution does not use that term. It is a body of presidential electors chosen in each State, and it selects the President and Vice President every four years. The number of electors chosen in each State equals the number of senators and representatives that State has in Congress.

▶ **Clause 3. Election of President and Vice President** This clause was replaced by the 12th Amendment in 1804.

Clause 4. Date Congress has set the date for the choosing of electors as the Tuesday after the first Monday in November every fourth year, and for the casting of electoral votes as the Monday after the second Wednesday in December of that year.

Clause 5. Qualifications The President must have been born a citizen of the United States, be at least 35 years old, and have been a resident of the United States for at least 14 years.

Clause 6. Vacancy This clause was modified by the 25th Amendment (1967), which provides expressly for the succession of the Vice President, for the filling of a vacancy in the Vice Presidency, and for the determination of presidential inability.

Clause 7. Compensation The President now receives a salary of $400,000 and a taxable expense account of $50,000 a year. Those amounts cannot be changed during a presidential term; thus, Congress cannot use the President's compensation as a bargaining tool to influence executive decisions. The phrase "any other emolument" means, in effect, any valuable gift; it does not mean that the President cannot be provided with such benefits of office as the White House, extensive staff assistance, and much else.

Clause 8. Oath of office The Chief Justice of the United States regularly administers this oath or affirmation, but any judicial officer may do so. Thus, Calvin Coolidge was sworn into office in 1923 by his father, a justice of the peace in Vermont.

Section 2. President's Powers and Duties

Clause 1. Military, civil powers The President, a civilian, heads the nation's armed forces, a key element in the Constitution's insistence on civilian control of the military. The President's power to "require the opinion, in writing" provides the constitutional basis for the Cabinet. The President's power to grant reprieves and pardons, the power of clemency, extends only to federal cases.

4. The Congress may determine the Time of choosing the Electors, and the Day on which they shall give their Votes; which Day shall be the same throughout the United States.

5. No Person except a natural born Citizen, or a Citizen of the United States, at the time of the Adoption of this Constitution, shall be eligible to the Office of President; neither shall any person be eligible to that Office who shall not have attained to the Age of thirty-five Years, and been fourteen Years a Resident within the United States.

6. In Case of the Removal of the President from Office, or of his Death, Resignation, or Inability to discharge the Powers and Duties of the said Office, the Same shall devolve on the Vice President, and the Congress may by Law provide for the Case of Removal, Death, Resignation or Inability, both of the President and Vice President, declaring what Officer shall then act as President, and such Officer shall act accordingly, until the Disability be removed, or a President shall be elected.

7. The President shall, at stated Times, receive for his Services, a Compensation, which shall neither be increased nor diminished during the Period for which he shall have been elected, and he shall not receive within that Period any other Emolument from the United States, or any of them.

8. Before he enter on the Execution of his Office, he shall take the following Oath or Affirmation:
"I do solemnly swear (or affirm) that I will faithfully execute the Office of President of the United States, and will to the best of my Ability, preserve, protect and defend the Constitution of the United States."

Section 2.

1. The President shall be Commander in Chief of the Army and Navy of the United States, and of the Militia of the several States, when called into the actual Service of the United States; he may require the Opinion, in writing, of the principal Officer in each of the executive Departments, upon any Subject relating to the Duties of their respective Offices, and he shall have Power to Grant Reprieves and Pardons for Offences against the United States, except in Cases of Impeachment.

2. He shall have Power, by and with the Advice and Consent of the Senate, to make Treaties, provided two thirds of the Senators present concur; and he shall nominate, and by and with the Advice and Consent of the Senate, shall appoint Ambassadors, other public Ministers and Consuls, Judges of the supreme Court, and all other Officers of the United States, whose Appointments are not herein otherwise provided for, and which shall be established by Law: but the Congress may by Law vest the Appointment of such inferior Officers, as they think proper, in the President alone, in the Courts of Law, or in the Heads of Departments.

▶ **Clause 2. Treaties, appointments** The President has the sole power to make treaties; to become effective, a treaty must be approved by a two-thirds vote in the Senate. In practice, the President can also make executive agreements with foreign governments; these pacts, which are frequently made and usually deal with routine matters, do not require Senate consent. The President appoints the principal officers of the executive branch and all federal judges; the "inferior officers" are those who hold lesser posts.

3. The President shall have Power to fill up all Vacancies that may happen during the Recess of the Senate, by granting Commissions which shall expire at the End of their next Session.

▶ **Clause 3. Recess appointments** When the Senate is not in session, appointments that require Senate consent can be made by the President on a temporary basis, as "recess appointments." Recess appointments are valid only to the end of the congressional term in which they are made.

Section 3.
He shall from time to time give to the Congress Information of the State of the Union, and recommend to their Consideration such Measures as he shall judge necessary and expedient; he may, on extraordinary Occasions, convene both Houses, or either of them, and in Case of Disagreement between them, with Respect to the Time of Adjournment, he may adjourn them to such Time as he shall think proper; he shall receive Ambassadors and other public Ministers; he shall take Care that the Laws be faithfully executed, and shall Commission all the Officers of the United States.

Section 3. President's Powers and Duties
The President delivers a State of the Union Message to Congress soon after that body convenes each year. That message is delivered to the nation's lawmakers and, importantly, to the American people, as well. It is shortly followed by the proposed federal budget and an economic report; and the President may send special messages to Congress at any time. In all of these communications, Congress is urged to take those actions the Chief Executive finds to be in the national interest. The President also has the power: to call special sessions of Congress; to adjourn Congress if its two houses cannot agree for that purpose; to receive the diplomatic representatives of other governments; to insure the proper execution of all federal laws; and to empower federal officers to hold their posts and perform their duties.

Section 4.
The President, Vice President and all Civil Officers of the United States, shall be removed from Office on Impeachment for and Conviction of, Treason, Bribery, or other high Crimes and Misdemeanors.

Section 4. Impeachment
The Constitution outlines the impeachment process in Article I, Section 2, Clause 5 and in Section 3, Clauses 6 and 7.

Article III
Section 1.
The judicial Power of the United States, shall be vested in one supreme Court, and in such inferior Courts as the Congress may from time to time ordain and establish. The Judges, both of the supreme and inferior Courts, shall hold their Offices during good Behaviour, and shall, at stated Times, receive for their Services, a Compensation, which shall not be diminished during their Continuance in Office.

Judicial Department
Section 1. Judicial Power, Courts, Terms of Office
The judicial power conferred here is the power of federal courts to hear and decide cases, disputes between the government and individuals and between private persons (parties). The Constitution creates only the Supreme Court of the United States; it gives to Congress the power to establish other, lower federal courts (Article I, Section 8, Clause 9) and to fix the size of the Supreme Court. The words "during good Behaviour" mean, in effect, for life.

Section 2. Jurisdiction

▶ **Clause 1. Cases to be heard** This clause sets out the jurisdiction of the federal courts; that is, it identifies those cases that may be tried in those courts. The federal courts can hear and decide—have jurisdiction over—a case depending on either the subject matter or the parties involved in that case. The jurisdiction of the federal courts in cases involving States was substantially restricted by the 11th Amendment in 1795.

▶ **Clause 2. Supreme Court jurisdiction** Original jurisdiction refers to the power of a court to hear a case in the first instance, not on appeal from a lower court. Appellate jurisdiction refers to a court's power to hear a case on appeal from a lower court, from the court in which the case was originally tried. This clause gives the Supreme Court both original and appellate jurisdiction. However, nearly all of the cases the High Court hears are brought to it on appeal from the lower federal courts and the highest State courts.

▶ **Clause 3. Jury trial in criminal cases** A person accused of a federal crime is guaranteed the right to trial by jury in a federal court in the State where the crime was committed; see the 5th and 6th amendments. The right to trial by jury in serious criminal cases in the State courts is guaranteed by the 6th and 14th amendments.

Section 3. Treason

▶ **Clause 1. Definition** Treason is the only crime defined in the Constitution. The Framers intended the very specific definition here to prevent the loose use of the charge of treason—for example, against persons who criticize the government. Treason can be committed only in time of war and only by a citizen or a resident alien.

▶ **Clause 2. Punishment** Congress has provided that the punishment that a federal court may impose on a convicted traitor may range from a minimum of five years in prison and/or a $10,000 fine to a maximum of death; no person convicted of treason has ever been executed by the United States. No legal punishment can be imposed on the family or descendants of a convicted traitor. Congress has also made it a crime for any person (in either peace or wartime) to commit espionage or sabotage, to attempt to overthrow the government by force, or to conspire to do any of these things.

Section 2.

▶ 1. The judicial Power shall extend to all Cases, in Law and Equity, arising under this Constitution, the Laws of the United States, and Treaties made, or which shall be made, under their Authority;— to all Cases affecting Ambassadors, other public ministers, and Consuls;— to all Cases of Admiralty and maritime Jurisdiction;— to Controversies to which the United States shall be a Party;— to Controversies between two or more States;— between a State and Citizens of another State;— between Citizens of different States;— between Citizens of the same State claiming Lands under Grants of different States, and between a State, or the Citizens thereof, and foreign States, Citizens, or Subjects.

▶ 2. In all Cases affecting Ambassadors, other public Ministers and Consuls, and those in which a State shall be a Party, the supreme Court shall have original Jurisdiction. In all the other Cases before mentioned, the supreme Court shall have appellate Jurisdiction, both as to Law and Fact, with such Exceptions, and under such Regulations as the Congress shall make.

▶ 3. The trial of all Crimes, except in Cases of Impeachment, shall be by Jury; and such Trial shall be held in the State where the said Crimes shall have been committed; but when not committed within any State, the Trial shall be at such Place or Places as the Congress may by Law have directed.

Section 3.

▶ 1. Treason against the United States shall consist only in levying War against them, or in adhering to their Enemies, giving them Aid and Comfort. No Person shall be convicted of Treason unless on the Testimony of two Witnesses to the same overt Act, or on Confession in open Court.

▶ 2. The Congress shall have Power to declare the Punishment of Treason, but no Attainder of Treason shall work Corruption of Blood, or Forfeiture except during the Life of the Person attainted.

Article IV

Section 1.

Full Faith and Credit shall be given in each State to the public Acts, Records, and judicial Proceedings of every other State. And the Congress may by general Laws prescribe the Manner in which such Acts, Records and Proceedings shall be proved, and the Effect thereof.

Section 2.

▶ 1. The Citizens of each State shall be entitled to all Privileges and Immunities of Citizens in the several States.

▶ 2. A Person charged in any State with Treason, Felony, or other Crime, who shall flee from justice, and be found in another State, shall on Demand of the executive Authority of the State from which he fled, be delivered up, to be removed to the State having Jurisdiction of the Crime.

▶ 3. No Person held to Service or Labor in one State, under the Laws thereof, escaping into another, shall, in Consequence of any Law or Regulation therein, be discharged from Service or Labor, but shall be delivered up on Claim of the Party to whom such Service or Labor may be due.

Section 3.

▶ 1. New States may be admitted by the Congress into this Union; but no new State shall be formed or erected within the Jurisdiction of any other State; nor any State be formed by the Junction of two or more States, or Parts of States, without the Consent of the Legislatures of the States concerned as well as of the Congress.

▶ 2. The Congress shall have Power to dispose of and make all needful Rules and Regulations respecting the Territory or other Property belonging to the United States; and nothing in this Constitution shall be so construed as to Prejudice any Claims of the United States, or of any particular State.

Section 4.

The United States shall guarantee to every State in this Union a Republican Form of Government, and shall protect each of them against Invasion; and on Application of the Legislature, or of the Executive (when the Legislature cannot be convened) against domestic Violence.

Relations Among States

Section 1. Full Faith and Credit

Each State must recognize the validity of the laws, public records, and court decisions of every other State.

Section 2. Privileges and Immunities of Citizens

▶ **Clause 1. Residents of other States** In effect, this clause means that no State may discriminate against the residents of other States; that is, a State's laws cannot draw unreasonable distinctions between its own residents and those of any of the other States. See Section 1 of the 14th Amendment.

▶ **Clause 2. Extradition** The process of returning a fugitive to another State is known as "interstate rendition" or, more commonly, "extradition." Usually, that process works routinely; some extradition requests are contested however—especially in cases with racial or political overtones. A governor may refuse to extradite a fugitive; but the federal courts can compel an unwilling governor to obey this constitutional command.

▶ **Clause 3. Fugitive slaves** This clause was nullified by the 13th Amendment, which abolished slavery in 1865.

Section 3. New States; Territories

▶ **Clause 1. New States** Only Congress can admit new States to the Union. A new State may not be created by taking territory from an existing State without the consent of that State's legislature. Congress has admitted 37 States since the original 13 formed the Union. Five States—Vermont, Kentucky, Tennessee, Maine, and West Virginia—were created from parts of existing States. Texas was an independent republic before admission. California was admitted after being ceded to the United States by Mexico. Each of the other 30 States entered the Union only after a period of time as an organized territory of the United States.

▶ **Clause 2. Territory, property** Congress has the power to make laws concerning the territories, other public lands, and all other property of the United States.

Section 4. Protection Afforded to States by the Nation

The Constitution does not define "a republican form of government," but the phrase is generally understood to mean a representative government. The Federal Government must also defend each State against attacks from outside its border and, at the request of a State's legislature or its governor, aid its efforts to put down internal disorders.

Provisions for Amendment

This section provides for the methods by which formal changes can be made in the Constitution. An amendment may be proposed in one of two ways: by a two-thirds vote in each house of Congress, or by a national convention called by Congress at the request of two-thirds of the State legislatures. A proposed amendment may be ratified in one of two ways: by three-fourths of the State legislatures, or by three-fourths of the States in conventions called for that purpose. Congress has the power to determine the method by which a proposed amendment may be ratified. The amendment process cannot be used to deny any State its equal representation in the United States Senate. To this point, 27 amendments have been adopted. To date, all of the amendments except the 21st Amendment were proposed by Congress and ratified by the State legislatures. Only the 21st Amendment was ratified by the convention method.

National Debts, Supremacy of National Law, Oath

Section 1. Validity of Debts

Congress had borrowed large sums of money during the Revolution and later during the Critical Period of the 1780s. This provision, a pledge that the new government would honor those debts, did much to create confidence in that government.

Section 2. Supremacy of National Law

This section sets out the Supremacy Clause, a specific declaration of the supremacy of federal law over any and all forms of State law. No State, including its local governments, may make or enforce any law that conflicts with any provision in the Constitution, an act of Congress, a treaty, or an order, rule, or regulation properly issued by the President or his subordinates in the executive branch.

Section 3. Oaths of Office

This provision reinforces the Supremacy Clause; all public officers, at every level in the United States, owe their first allegiance to the Constitution of the United States. No religious qualification can be imposed as a condition for holding any public office.

Ratification of Constitution

The proposed Constitution was signed by George Washington and 37 of his fellow Framers on September 17, 1787. (George Read of Delaware signed for himself and also for his absent colleague, John Dickinson.)

Article V

The Congress, whenever two thirds of both Houses shall deem it necessary, shall propose Amendments to this Constitution, or, on the Application of the Legislatures of two thirds of the several States, shall call a Convention for proposing Amendments, which, in either Case, shall be valid to all Intents and Purposes, as Part of this Constitution, when ratified by the Legislatures of three fourths of the several States, or by Conventions in three fourths thereof, as the one or the other Mode of Ratification may be proposed by the Congress; Provided that no Amendment which may be made prior to the Year One thousand eight hundred and eight shall in any Manner affect the first and fourth Clauses in the Ninth section of the first Article; and that no State, without its Consent, shall be deprived of its equal Suffrage in the Senate.

Article VI

Section 1.

All Debts contracted and Engagements entered into, before the Adoption of this Constitution, shall be as valid against the United States under this Constitution, as under the Confederation.

Section 2.

This Constitution, and the Laws of the United States which shall be made in Pursuance thereof; and all Treaties made, or which shall be made, under the Authority of the United States, shall be the supreme Law of the Land; and the Judges in every State shall be bound thereby, anything in the constitution or Laws of any State to the Contrary notwithstanding.

Section 3.

The Senators and Representatives before mentioned, and the Members of the several State legislatures, and all executive and judicial Officers, both of the United States and of the several States, shall be bound by Oath or Affirmation, to support this Constitution; but no religious Test shall ever be required as a Qualification to any Office or public Trust under the United States.

Article VII

The ratification of the Conventions of nine States, shall be sufficient for the Establishment of this Constitution between the States so ratifying the same.

Done in Convention by the Unanimous Consent of the States present the Seventeenth Day of September in the Year of our Lord one thousand seven hundred and Eighty-seven and of the Independence of the United States of America the twelfth. In witness whereof We have hereunto subscribed our Names.

Attest:
William Jackson,
Secretary
George Washington,
President and Deputy
from Virginia

New Hampshire
John Langdon
Nicholas Gilman

Massachusetts
Nathaniel Gorham
Rufus King

Connecticut
William Samuel Johnson
Roger Sherman

New York
Alexander Hamilton

New Jersey
William Livingston
David Brearley
William Paterson
Jonathan Dayton

Pennsylvania
Benjamin Franklin
Thomas Mifflin
Robert Morris
George Clymer
Thomas Fitzsimons
Jared Ingersoll
James Wilson
Gouverneur Morris

Delaware
George Read
Gunning Bedford, Jr.
John Dickinson
Richard Bassett
Jacob Broom

Maryland
James McHenry
Dan of St. Thomas Jennifer
Daniel Carroll

Virginia
John Blair
James Madison, Jr.

North Carolina
William Blount
Richard Dobbs Spaight
Hugh Williamson

South Carolina
John Rutledge
Charles Cotesworth
  Pinckney
Charles Pinckney
Pierce Butler

Georgia
William Few
Abraham Baldwin

The first 10 amendments, the Bill of Rights, were each proposed by Congress on September 25, 1789, and ratified by the necessary three-fourths of the States on December 15, 1791. These amendments were originally intended to restrict the National Government—not the States. However, the Supreme Court has several times held that most of their provisions also apply to the States, through the 14th Amendment's Due Process Clause.

1st Amendment. Freedom of Religion, Speech, Press, Assembly, and Petition

The 1st Amendment sets out five basic liberties: The guarantee of freedom of religion is both a protection of religious thought and practice and a command of separation of church and state. The guarantees of freedom of speech and press assure to all persons a right to speak, publish, and otherwise express their views. The guarantees of the rights of assembly and petition protect the right to join with others in public meetings, political parties, interest groups, and other associations to discuss public affairs and influence public policy. None of these rights is guaranteed in absolute terms, however; like all other civil rights guarantees, each of them may be exercised only with regard to the rights of all other persons.

2nd Amendment. Bearing Arms

The right of the people to keep and bear arms was insured by the 2nd Amendment.

3rd Amendment. Quartering of Troops

This amendment was intended to prevent what had been common British practice in the colonial period; see the Declaration of Independence. This provision is of virtually no importance today.

4th Amendment. Searches and Seizures

The basic rule laid down by the 4th Amendment is this: Police officers have no general right to search for or seize evidence or seize (arrest) persons. Except in particular circumstances, they must have a proper warrant (a court order) obtained with probable cause (on reasonable grounds). This guarantee is reinforced by the exclusionary rule, developed by the Supreme Court: Evidence gained as the result of an unlawful search or seizure cannot be used at the court trial of the person from whom it was seized.

5th Amendment. Criminal Proceedings; Due Process; Eminent Domain

A person can be tried for a serious federal crime only if he or she has been indicted (charged, accused of that crime) by a grand jury. No one may be subjected to double jeopardy—that is, tried twice for the same crime. All persons are protected against self-incrimination; no person can be legally compelled to answer any question in any governmental proceeding if that answer could lead to that person's prosecution. The 5th Amendment's Due Process Clause prohibits unfair, arbitrary actions by the Federal Government; a like prohibition is set out against the States in the 14th Amendment. Government may take private property for a legitimate public purpose; but when it exercises that power of eminent domain, it must pay a fair price for the property seized.

1st Amendment

Congress shall make no law respecting an establishment of religion, or prohibiting the free exercise thereof, or abridging the freedom of speech, or of the press; or the right of the people peaceably to assemble, and to petition the Government for a redress of grievances.

2nd Amendment

A well-regulated Militia being necessary to the security of a free State, the right of the people to keep and bear Arms, shall not be infringed.

3rd Amendment.

No Soldier shall, in time of peace be quartered in any house, without the consent of the Owner, nor, in time of war, but in a manner to be prescribed by law.

4th Amendment.

The right of the people to be secure in their persons, houses, papers, and effects, against unreasonable searches and seizures, shall not be violated, and no Warrants shall issue, but upon probable cause, supported by Oath or affirmation, and particularly describing the place to be searched, and the persons or things to be seized.

5th Amendment.

No person shall be held to answer for a capital, or otherwise infamous crime, unless on a presentment or indictment of a Grand Jury, except in cases arising in the land or naval forces, or in the Militia, when in actual service in time of War, or public danger; nor shall any person be subject for the same offence to be twice put in jeopardy of life or limb; nor shall be compelled in any criminal case to be a witness against himself, nor be deprived of life, liberty, or property, without due process of law; nor shall private property be taken for public use, without just compensation.

6th Amendment

In all criminal prosecutions, the accused shall enjoy the right to a speedy and public trial, by an impartial jury of the State and district wherein the crime shall have been committed, which district shall have been previously ascertained by law, and to be informed of the nature and cause of the accusation; to be confronted with the witnesses against him; to have compulsory process for obtaining witnesses in his favor, and to have the Assistance of Counsel for his defence.

7th Amendment

In Suits at common law, where the value in controversy shall exceed twenty dollars, the right of trial by jury shall be preserved, and no fact tried by a jury, shall be otherwise re-examined in any Court of the United States, than according to the rules of the common law.

8th Amendment

Excessive bail shall not be required, nor excessive fines imposed, nor cruel and unusual punishment inflicted.

9th Amendment

The enumeration in the Constitution, of certain rights, shall not be construed to deny or disparage others retained by the people.

10th Amendment

The powers not delegated to the United States by the Constitution, nor prohibited by it to the States, are reserved to the States respectively, or to the people.

6th Amendment. Criminal Proceedings

A person accused of crime has the right to be tried in court without undue delay and by an impartial jury; see Article III, Section 2, Clause 3. The defendant must be informed of the charge upon which he or she is to be tried, has the right to cross-examine hostile witnesses, and has the right to require the testimony of favorable witnesses. The defendant also has the right to be represented by an attorney at every stage in the criminal process.

7th Amendment. Civil Trials

This amendment applies only to civil cases heard in federal courts. A civil case does not involve criminal matters; it is a dispute between private parties or between the government and a private party. The right to trial by jury is guaranteed in any civil case in a federal court if the amount of money involved in that case exceeds $20 (most cases today involve a much larger sum); that right may be waived (relinquished, put aside) if both parties agree to a bench trial (a trial by a judge, without a jury).

8th Amendment. Punishment for Crimes

Bail is the sum of money that a person accused of crime may be required to post (deposit with the court) as a guarantee that he or she will appear in court at the proper time. The amount of bail required and/or a fine imposed as punishment must bear a reasonable relationship to the seriousness of the crime involved in the case. The prohibition of cruel and unusual punishment forbids any punishment judged to be too harsh, too severe for the crime for which it is imposed.

9th Amendment. Unenumerated Rights

The fact that the Constitution sets out many civil rights guarantees, expressly provides for many protections against government, does not mean that there are not other rights also held by the people.

10th Amendment. Powers Reserved to the States

This amendment identifies the area of power that may be exercised by the States. All of those powers the Constitution does not grant to the National Government, and at the same time does not forbid to the States, belong to each of the States, or to the people of each State.

11th Amendment. Suits Against States

Proposed by Congress March 4, 1794; ratified February 7, 1795, but official announcement of the ratification was delayed until January 8, 1798. This amendment repealed part of Article III, Section 2, Clause 1. No State may be sued in a federal court by a resident of another State or of a foreign country; the Supreme Court has long held that this provision also means that a State cannot be sued in a federal court by a foreign country or, more importantly, even by one of its own residents.

12th Amendment. Election of President and Vice President

Proposed by Congress December 9, 1803; ratified June 15, 1804. This amendment replaced Article II, Section 1, Clause 3. Originally, each elector cast two ballots, each for a different person for President. The person with the largest number of electoral votes, provided that number was a majority of the electors, was to become President; the person with the second highest number was to become Vice President. This arrangement produced an electoral vote tie between Thomas Jefferson and Aaron Burr in 1800; the House finally chose Jefferson as President in 1801. The 12th Amendment separated the balloting for President and Vice President; each elector now casts one ballot for someone as President and a second ballot for another person as Vice President. Note that the 20th Amendment changed the date set here (March 4) to January 20, and that the 23rd Amendment (1961) provides for electors from the District of Columbia. This amendment also provides that the Vice President must meet the same qualifications as those set out for the President in Article II, Section 1, Clause 5.

13th Amendment. Slavery and Involuntary Servitude

Proposed by Congress January 31, 1865; ratified December 6, 1865. This amendment forbids slavery in the United States and in any area under its control. It also forbids other forms of forced labor, except punishments for crime; but some forms of compulsory service are not prohibited—for example, service on juries or in the armed forces. Section 2 gives to Congress the power to carry out the provisions of Section 1 of this amendment.

11th Amendment

The Judicial power of the United States shall not be construed to extend to any suit in law or equity, commenced or prosecuted against one of the United States by Citizens of another State, or by Citizens or Subjects of any Foreign State.

12th Amendment

The Electors shall meet in their respective States and vote by ballot for President and Vice President, one of whom, at least, shall not be an inhabitant of the same State with themselves; they shall name in their ballots the person voted for as President, and in distinct ballots the person voted for as Vice President, and they shall make distinct lists of all persons voted for as President, and of all persons voted for as Vice President, and of the number of votes for each, which lists they shall sign and certify, and transmit sealed to the seat of the government of the United States, directed to the President of the Senate;— The President of the Senate shall, in the presence of the Senate and the House of Representatives, open all the certificates and the votes shall then be counted;— the person having the greatest Number of votes for President shall be the President, if such number be a majority of the whole number of Electors appointed; and if no person have such a majority, then, from the persons having the highest numbers not exceeding three on the list of those voted for as President, the House of Representatives shall choose immediately, by ballot, the President. But in choosing the President, the votes shall be taken by States, the representation from each State having one vote; a quorum for this purpose shall consist of a member or members from two thirds of the States, and a majority of all the States shall be necessary to a choice. And if the House of Representatives shall not choose a President whenever the right of choice shall devolve upon them, before the fourth day of March next following, then the Vice President shall act as President, as in case of death or other constitutional disability of the President. The person having the greatest number of votes as Vice President, shall be the Vice President, if such number be a majority of the whole number of Electors appointed, and if no person have a majority, then from the two highest numbers on the list, the Senate shall choose the Vice President; a quorum for the purpose shall consist of two thirds of the whole number of Senators, a majority of the whole number shall be necessary to a choice. But no person constitutionally ineligible to the office of President shall be eligible to that of Vice-President of the United States.

13th Amendment

Section 1. Neither slavery nor involuntary servitude, except as a punishment for crime whereof the party shall have been duly convicted, shall exist within the United States, or any place subject to their jurisdiction.

Section 2. Congress shall have power to enforce this article by appropriate legislation.

14th Amendment

Section 1. All persons born or naturalized in the United States and subject to the jurisdiction thereof, are citizens of the United States and of the State wherein they reside. No State shall make or enforce any law which shall abridge the privileges or immunities of citizens of the United States; nor shall any State deprive any person of life, liberty, or property, without due process of law; nor deny to any person within its jurisdiction the equal protection of the laws.

Section 2. Representatives shall be apportioned among the several States according to their respective numbers, counting the whole number of persons in each State, excluding Indians not taxed. But when the right to vote at any election for the choice of electors for President and Vice President of the United States, Representatives in Congress, the Executive and Judicial officers of a State, or the members of the Legislature thereof, is denied to any of the male inhabitants of such State, being twenty-one years of age and citizens of the United States, or in any way abridged, except for participation in rebellion, or other crime, the basis of representation therein shall be reduced in the proportion which the number of such male citizens shall bear to the whole number of male citizens twenty-one years of age in such State.

Section 3. No person shall be a Senator or Representative in Congress, or elector of President and Vice President, or hold any office, civil or military, under the United States, or under any State, who, having previously taken an oath, as a member of Congress, or as an officer of the United States, or as a member of any State legislature, or as an executive or judicial officer of any State, to support the Constitution of the United States, shall have engaged in insurrection or rebellion against the same, or given aid or comfort to the enemies thereof. But Congress may, by a vote of two thirds of each House, remove such disability.

Section 4. The validity of the public debt of the United States, authorized by law, including debts incurred for payment of pensions and bounties for services in suppressing insurrection or rebellion, shall not be questioned. But neither the United States nor any State shall assume or pay any debt or obligation incurred in aid of insurrection or rebellion against the United States, or any claim for the loss or emancipation of any slave; but all such debts, obligations and claims shall be held illegal and void.

Section 5. The Congress shall have power to enforce, by appropriate legislation, the provisions of this article.

14th Amendment. Rights of Citizens

Proposed by Congress June 13, 1866; ratified July 9, 1868. Section 1 defines citizenship. It provides for the acquisition of United States citizenship by birth or by naturalization. Citizenship at birth is determined according to the principle of jus soli—"the law of the soil," where born; naturalization is the legal process by which one acquires a new citizenship at some time after birth. Under certain circumstances, citizenship can also be gained at birth abroad, according to the principle of jus sanguinis—"the law of the blood," to whom born. This section also contains two major civil rights provisions: the Due Process Clause forbids a State (and its local governments) to act in any unfair or arbitrary way; the Equal Protection Clause forbids a State (and its local governments) to discriminate against, draw unreasonable distinctions between, persons.

Most of the rights set out against the National Government in the first eight amendments have been extended against the States (and their local governments) through Supreme Court decisions involving the 14th Amendment's Due Process Clause.

The first sentence here replaced Article I, Section 2, Clause 3, the Three-Fifths Compromise provision. Essentially, all persons in the United States are counted in each decennial census, the basis for the distribution of House seats. The balance of this section has never been enforced and is generally thought to be obsolete.

This section limited the President's power to pardon those persons who had led the Confederacy during the Civil War. Congress finally removed this disability in 1898.

Section 4 also dealt with matters directly related to the Civil War. It reaffirmed the public debt of the United States; but it invalidated, prohibited payment of, any debt contracted by the Confederate States and also prohibited any compensation of former slave owners.

15th Amendment. Right to Vote— Race, Color, Servitude

Proposed by Congress February 26, 1869; ratified February 3, 1870. The phrase "previous condition of servitude" refers to slavery. Note that this amendment does not guarantee the right to vote to African Americans, or to anyone else. Instead, it forbids the States from discriminating against any person on the grounds of his "race, color, or previous condition of servitude" in the setting of suffrage qualifications.

16th Amendment. Income Tax

Proposed by Congress July 12, 1909; ratified February 3, 1913. This amendment modified two provisions in Article I, Section 2, Clause 3, and Section 9, Clause 4. It gives to Congress the power to levy an income tax, a direct tax, without regard to the populations of any of the States.

17th Amendment. Popular Election of Senators

Proposed by Congress May 13, 1912; ratified April 8, 1913. This amendment repealed those portions of Article I, Section 3, Clauses 1 and 2 relating to the election of senators. Senators are now elected by the voters in each State. If a vacancy occurs, the governor of the State involved must call an election to fill the seat; the governor may appoint a senator to serve until the next election, if the State's legislature has authorized that step.

18th Amendment. Prohibition of Intoxicating Liquors

Proposed by Congress December 18, 1917; ratified January 16, 1919. This amendment outlawed the making, selling, transporting, importing, or exporting of alcoholic beverages in the United States. It was repealed in its entirety by the 21st Amendment in 1933.

19th Amendment. Equal Suffrage—Sex

Proposed by Congress June 4, 1919; ratified August 18, 1920. No person can be denied the right to vote in any election in the United States on account of his or her sex.

15th Amendment

Section 1. The right of citizens of the United States to vote shall not be denied or abridged by the United States or by any State on account of race, color, or previous condition of servitude.

Section 2. The Congress shall have power to enforce this article by appropriate legislation.

16th Amendment

The Congress shall have power to lay and collect taxes on incomes, from whatever source derived, without apportionment among the several States, and without regard to any census or enumeration.

17th Amendment

The Senate of the United States shall be composed of two Senators from each State, elected by the people thereof, for six years; and each Senator shall have one vote. The electors in each State shall have the qualifications requisite for electors of the most numerous branch of the State legislatures.

When vacancies happen in the representation of any State in the Senate, the executive authority of such State shall issue writs of election to fill such vacancies: Provided, That the legislature of any State may empower the executive thereof to make temporary appointments until the people fill the vacancies by election as the legislature may direct.

This amendment shall not be so construed as to affect the election or term of any Senator chosen before it becomes valid as part of the Constitution.

18th Amendment.

Section 1. After one year from the ratification of this article the manufacture, sale, or transportation of intoxicating liquors within, the importation thereof into, or the exportation thereof from the United States and all territory subject to the jurisdiction thereof for beverage purposes is hereby prohibited.

Section 2. The Congress and the several States shall have concurrent power to enforce this article by appropriate legislation.

Section 3. This article shall be inoperative unless it shall have been ratified as an amendment to the Constitution by the legislatures of the several States, as provided in the Constitution, within seven years of the date of the submission hereof to the States by Congress.

19th Amendment

The right of citizens of the United States to vote shall not be denied or abridged by the United States or by any State on account of sex.

Congress shall have power to enforce this article by appropriate legislation.

20th Amendment

Section 1. The terms of the President and Vice President shall end at noon on the 20th day of January, and the terms of Senators and Representatives at noon on the 3d day of January, of the years in which such terms would have ended if this article had not been ratified; and the terms of their successors shall then begin.

Section 2. The Congress shall assemble at least once in every year, and such meeting shall begin at noon on the 3d day of January, unless they shall by law appoint a different day.

Section 3. If, at the time fixed for the beginning of the term of the President, the President elect shall have died, the Vice President elect shall become President. If a President shall not have been chosen before the time fixed for the beginning of his term, or if the President-elect shall have failed to qualify, then the Vice President elect shall act as President until a President shall have qualified; and the Congress may by law provide for the case wherein neither a President elect nor a Vice President elect shall have qualified, declaring who shall then act as President, or the manner in which one who is to act shall be selected, and such person shall act accordingly until a President or Vice President shall have qualified.

Section 4. The Congress may by law provide for the case of the death of any of the persons from whom the House of Representatives may choose a President whenever the right of choice shall have devolved upon them, and for the case of the death of any of the persons from whom the Senate may choose a Vice President whenever the right of choice shall have devolved upon them.

Section 5. Sections 1 and 2 shall take effect on the 15th day of October following the ratification of this article.

Section 6. This article shall be inoperative unless it shall have been ratified as an amendment to the Constitution by the legislatures of three fourths of the several States within seven years from the date of its submission.

21st Amendment

Section 1. The eighteenth article of amendment to the Constitution of the United States is hereby repealed.

Section 2. The transportation or importation into any State, Territory, or possession of the United States for delivery or use therein of intoxicating liquors, in violation of the laws thereof, is hereby prohibited.

Section 3. This article shall be inoperative unless it shall have been ratified as an amendment to the Constitution by conventions in the several States, as provided in the Constitution, within seven years from the date of the submission hereof to the States by the Congress.

20th Amendment. Commencement of Terms; Sessions of Congress; Death or Disqualification of President-Elect

Proposed by Congress March 2, 1932; ratified January 23, 1933. The provisions of Sections 1 and 2 relating to Congress modified Article I, Section 4, Clause 2, and those provisions relating to the President, the 12th Amendment. The date on which the President and Vice President now take office was moved from March 4 to January 20. Similarly, the members of Congress now begin their terms on January 3. The 20th Amendment is sometimes called the "Lame Duck Amendment" because it shortened the period of time a member of Congress who was defeated for reelection (a "lame duck") remains in office.

This section deals with certain possibilities that were not covered by the presidential selection provisions of either Article II or the 12th Amendment. To this point, none of these situations has occurred. Note that there is neither a President-elect nor a Vice President-elect until the electoral votes have been counted by Congress, or, if the electoral college cannot decide the matter, the House has chosen a President or the Senate has chosen a Vice President.

Congress has not in fact ever passed such a law. See Section 2 of the 25th Amendment, regarding a vacancy in the vice presidency; that provision could some day have an impact here.

Section 5 set the date on which this amendment came into force.

Section 6 placed a time limit on the ratification process; note that a similar provision was written into the 18th, 21st, and 22nd amendments.

21st Amendment. Repeal of 18th Amendment

Proposed by Congress February 20, 1933; ratified December 5, 1933. This amendment repealed all of the 18th Amendment. Section 2 modifies the scope of the Federal Government's commerce power set out in Article I, Section 8, Clause 3; it gives to each State the power to regulate the transportation or importation and the distribution or use of intoxicating liquors in ways that would be unconstitutional in the case of any other commodity. The 21st Amendment is the only amendment Congress has thus far submitted to the States for ratification by conventions.

22nd Amendment. Presidential Tenure

Proposed by Congress March 21, 1947; ratified February 27, 1951. This amendment modified Article II, Section I, Clause 1. It stipulates that no President may serve more than two elected terms. But a President who has succeeded to the office beyond the midpoint in a term to which another President was originally elected may serve for more than eight years. In any case, however, a President may not serve more than 10 years. Prior to Franklin Roosevelt, who was elected to four terms, no President had served more than two full terms in office.

23rd Amendment. Presidential Electors for the District of Columbia

Proposed by Congress June 16, 1960; ratified March 29, 1961. This amendment modified Article II, Section I, Clause 2 and the 12th Amendment. It included the voters of the District of Columbia in the presidential electorate; and provides that the District is to have the same number of electors as the least populous State—three electors—but no more than that number.

24th Amendment. Right to Vote in Federal Elections—Tax Payment

Proposed by Congress August 27, 1962; ratified January 23, 1964. This amendment outlawed the payment of any tax as a condition for taking part in the nomination or election of any federal officeholder.

25th Amendment. Presidential Succession, Vice Presidential Vacancy, Presidential Inability

Proposed by Congress July 6, 1965; ratified February 10, 1967. Section 1 revised the imprecise provision on presidential succession in Article II, Section 1, Clause 6. It affirmed the precedent set by Vice President John Tyler, who became President on the death of William Henry Harrison in 1841. Section 2 provides for the filling of a vacancy in the office of Vice President. The office had been vacant on 16 occasions and remained unfilled for the rest of each term involved. When Spiro Agnew resigned the office in 1973, President Nixon selected Gerald Ford per this provision; and, when President Nixon resigned in 1974, Gerald Ford became President and chose Nelson Rockefeller as Vice President.

22nd Amendment

Section 1. No person shall be elected to the office of the President more than twice, and no person who has held the office of President, or acted as President, for more than two years of a term to which some other person was elected President shall be elected to the office of the President more than once. But this Article shall not apply to any person holding the office of President, when this Article was proposed by the Congress, and shall not prevent any person who may be holding the office of President, or acting as President, during the term within which this Article becomes operative from holding the office of President or acting as President during the remainder of such term.

Section 2. This article shall be inoperative unless it shall have been ratified as an amendment to the Constitution by the legislatures of three fourths of the several states within seven years from the date of its submission to the States by the Congress.

23rd Amendment.

Section 1. The District constituting the seat of Government of the United States shall appoint in such manner as the Congress may direct:

A number of electors of President and Vice President equal to the whole number of Senators and Representatives in Congress to which the District would be entitled if it were a State, but in no event more than the least populous State; they shall be in addition to those appointed by the States, they shall be considered, for the purposes of the election of President and Vice President, to be electors appointed by a State; and they shall meet in the District and perform such duties as provided by the twelfth article of amendment.

24th Amendment.

Section 1. The right of citizens of the United States to vote in any primary or other election for President or Vice President, for electors for President or Vice President, or for Senator or Representative in Congress, shall not be denied or abridged by the United States or any State by reason of failure to pay any poll tax or other tax.

Section 2. The Congress shall have power to enforce this article by appropriate legislation.

25th Amendment.

Section 1. In case of the removal of the President from office or of his death or resignation, the Vice President shall become President.

Section 2. Whenever there is a vacancy in the office of the Vice President, the President shall nominate a Vice President who shall take office upon confirmation by a majority vote of both Houses of Congress.

Section 3. Whenever the President transmits to the President pro tempore of the Senate and the Speaker of the House of Representatives his written declaration that he is unable to discharge the powers and duties of his office, and until he transmits to them a written declaration to the contrary, such powers and duties shall be discharged by the Vice President as Acting President.

Section 4. Whenever the Vice President and a majority of either the principal officers of the executive departments or of such other body as Congress may by law provide, transmit to the President pro tempore of the Senate and the Speaker of the House of Representatives their written declaration that the President is unable to discharge the powers and duties of his office, the Vice President shall immediately assume the powers and duties of the office as Acting President.

Thereafter, when the President transmits to the President pro tempore of the Senate and the Speaker of the House of Representatives his written declaration that no inability exists, he shall resume the powers and duties of his office unless the Vice President and a majority of either the principal officers of the executive department or of such other body as Congress may by law provide, transmit within four days to the President pro tempore of the Senate and the Speaker of the House of Representatives their written declaration that the President is unable to discharge the powers and duties of his office. Thereupon Congress shall decide the issue, assembling within forty-eight hours for that purpose if not in session. If the Congress, within twenty-one days after receipt of the latter written declaration, or, if Congress is not in session, within twenty-one days after Congress is required to assemble, determines by two-thirds vote of both Houses that the President is unable to discharge the powers and duties of his office, the Vice President shall continue to discharge the same as Acting President; otherwise, the President shall resume the powers and duties of his office.

26th Amendment.

Section 1. The right of citizens of the United States, who are eighteen years of age or older, to vote shall not be denied or abridged by the United States or by any State on account of age.

Section 2. The Congress shall have the power to enforce this article by appropriate legislation.

27th Amendment.

No law varying the compensation for the services of the Senators and Representatives, shall take effect, until an election of Representatives shall have intervened.

This section created a procedure for determining if a President is so incapacitated that he cannot perform the powers and duties of his office.

Section 4 deals with the circumstance in which a President will not be able to determine the fact of incapacity. To this point, Congress has not established the "such other body" referred to here. This section contains the only typographical error in the Constitution; in its second paragraph, the word "department" should in fact read "departments."

26th Amendment. Right to Vote—Age
Proposed by Congress March 23, 1971; ratified July 1, 1971. This amendment provides that the minimum age for voting in any election in the United States cannot be more than 18 years. (A State may set a minimum voting age of less than 18, however.)

27th Amendment. Congressional Pay
Proposed by Congress September 25, 1789; ratified May 7, 1992. This amendment modified Article I, Section 6, Clause 1. It limits Congress's power to fix the salaries of its members—by delaying the effectiveness of any increase in that pay until after the next regular congressional election.

Name	Party	State [a]	Entered Office	Age On Taking Office	Vice President(s)
George Washington (1732–1799)	Federalist	Virginia	1789	57	John Adams
John Adams (1735–1826)	Federalist	Massachusetts	1797	61	Thomas Jefferson
Thomas Jefferson (1743–1826)	Dem-Rep[b]	Virginia	1801	57	Aaron Burr/George Clinton
James Madison (1751–1836)	Dem-Rep	Virginia	1809	57	George Clinton/Elbridge Gerry
James Monroe (1758–1831)	Dem-Rep	Virginia	1817	58	Daniel D. Tompkins
John Q. Adams (1767–1848)	Dem-Rep	Massachusetts	1825	57	John C. Calhoun
Andrew Jackson (1767–1845)	Democrat	Tennessee (SC)	1829	61	John C. Calhoun/Martin Van Buren
Martin Van Buren (1782–1862)	Democrat	New York	1837	54	Richard M. Johnson
William H. Harrison (1773–1841)	Whig	Ohio (VA)	1841	68	John Tyler
John Tyler (1790–1862)	Democrat	Virginia	1841	51	none
James K. Polk (1795–1849)	Democrat	Tennessee (NC)	1845	49	George M. Dallas
Zachary Taylor (1784–1850)	Whig	Louisiana (VA)	1849	64	Millard Fillmore
Millard Fillmore (1800–1874)	Whig	New York	1850	50	none
Franklin Pierce (1804–1869)	Democrat	New Hampshire	1853	48	William R. King
James Buchanan (1791–1868)	Democrat	Pennsylvania	1857	65	John C. Breckinridge
Abraham Lincoln (1809–1865)	Republican	Illinois (KY)	1861	52	Hannibal Hamlin/Andrew Johnson[c]
Andrew Johnson (1808–1875)	Democrat	Tennessee (NC)	1865	56	none
Ulysses S. Grant (1822–1885)	Republican	Illinois (OH)	1869	46	Schuyler Colfax/Henry Wilson
Rutherford B. Hayes (1822–1893)	Republican	Ohio	1877	54	William A. Wheeler
James A. Garfield (1831–1881)	Republican	Ohio	1881	49	Chester A. Arthur
Chester A. Arthur (1829–1896)	Republican	New York (VT)	1881	51	none
Grover Cleveland (1837–1908)	Democrat	New York (NJ)	1885	47	Thomas A. Hendricks
Benjamin Harrison (1833–1901)	Republican	Indiana (OH)	1889	55	Levi P. Morton
Grover Cleveland (1837–1908)	Democrat	New York (NJ)	1893	55	Adlai E. Stevenson

Name	Party	State [a]	Entered Office	Age On Taking Office	Vice President(s)
William McKinley (1843–1901)	Republican	Ohio	1897	54	Garret A. Hobart/ Theodore Roosevelt
Theodore Roosevelt (1858–1919)	Republican	New York	1901	42	Charles W. Fairbanks
William H. Taft (1857–1930)	Republican	Ohio	1909	51	James S. Sherman
Woodrow Wilson (1856–1924)	Democrat	New Jersey (VA)	1913	56	Thomas R. Marshall
Warren G. Harding (1865–1923)	Republican	Ohio	1921	55	Calvin Coolidge
Calvin Coolidge (1872–1933)	Republican	Massachusetts (VT)	1923	51	Charles G. Dawes
Herbert Hoover (1874–1964)	Republican	California (IA)	1929	54	Charles Curtis
Franklin Roosevelt (1882–1945)	Democrat	New York	1933	51	John N. Garner/ Henry A. Wallace/Harry S Truman
Harry S Truman (1884–1972)	Democrat	Missouri	1945	60	Alben W. Barkley
Dwight D. Eisenhower (1890–1969)	Republican	New York (TX)	1953	62	Richard M. Nixon
John F. Kennedy (1917–1963)	Democrat	Massachusetts	1961	43	Lyndon B. Johnson
Lyndon B. Johnson (1908–1973)	Democrat	Texas	1963	55	Hubert H. Humphrey
Richard M. Nixon (1913–1994)	Republican	New York (CA)	1969	56	Spiro T. Agnew [d]/Gerald R. Ford [e]
Gerald R. Ford (1913–2006)	Republican	Michigan (NE)	1974	61	Nelson A. Rockefeller [f]
James E. Carter (1924–)	Democrat	Georgia	1977	52	Walter F. Mondale
Ronald W. Reagan (1911–2004)	Republican	California (IL)	1981	69	George H. W. Bush
George H.W. Bush (1924–)	Republican	Texas (MA)	1989	64	J. Danforth Quayle
William J. Clinton (1946–)	Democrat	Arkansas	1993	46	Albert Gore, Jr.
George W. Bush (1946–)	Republican	Texas	2001	54	Richard B. Cheney
Barack Obama (1961–)	Democrat	Illinois (HI)	2009	47	Joseph R. Biden

[a] State of residence when elected; if born in another State, that State in parentheses.
[b] Democratic-Republican
[c] Johnson, a War Democrat, was elected Vice President on the coalition Union Party ticket.
[d] Resigned October 10, 1973.
[e] Nominated by Nixon, confirmed by Congress on December 6, 1973.
[f] Nominated by Ford, confirmed by Congress on December 19, 1974.

[Declaration of Independence]

Introduction

By signing the Declaration of Independence, members of the Continental Congress sent a clear message to Britain that the American colonies were free and independent states. Starting with its preamble, the document spells out all the reasons the people of the United States have the right to break away from Britain.

Primary Source

The Unanimous Declaration of the Thirteen United States of America

When in the Course of human events, it becomes necessary for one people to dissolve the political bands which have connected them with another, and to assume among the powers of the earth, the separate and equal station to which the Laws of Nature and of Nature's God entitle them, a decent respect to the opinions of mankind requires that they should declare the causes which impel [force] them to the separation.

We hold these truths to be self-evident, that all men are created equal, that they are endowed [gifted] by their Creator with certain unalienable [cannot be taken away] Rights, that among these are Life, Liberty and the pursuit of Happiness. That to secure these rights, Governments are instituted among Men, deriving their just powers from the consent of the governed. That whenever any Form of Government becomes destructive of these ends, it is the Right of the People to alter or to abolish it, and to institute new Government, laying its foundation on such principles and organizing its powers in such form, as to them shall seem most likely to effect their Safety and Happiness. Prudence [cautiousness], indeed, will dictate that Governments long established should not be changed for light and transient causes; and accordingly all experience hath shown that mankind are more disposed to suffer, while evils are sufferable, than to right themselves by abolishing the forms to which they are accustomed. But when a long train of abuses and usurpations [unjust uses of power], pursuing invariably the same Object evinces a design to reduce them under absolute Despotism [rule of absolute power], it is their right, it is their duty, to throw off such Government, and to provide new Guards for their future security.

Such has been the patient sufferance of these Colonies; and such is now the necessity which constrains them to alter their former Systems of Government. The history of the present King of Great Britain is a history of repeated injuries and usurpations, all having in direct object the establishment of an absolute Tyranny over these States. To prove this, let Facts be submitted to a candid world.

He has refused his Assent to Laws, the most wholesome and necessary for the public good.

He has forbidden his Governors to pass Laws of immediate and pressing importance, unless suspended in their operation till his Assent should be obtained; and when so suspended, he has utterly neglected to attend to them.

He has refused to pass other Laws for the accommodation of large districts of people, unless those people would relinquish [give up] the right of Representation in the Legislature, a right inestimable [priceless] to them and formidable to tyrants only.

He has called together legislative bodies at places unusual, uncomfortable, and distant from the depository of their public Records, for the sole purpose of fatiguing them into compliance with his measures.

He has dissolved Representative Houses repeatedly, for opposing with manly firmness his invasions on the rights of the people.

He has refused for a long time, after such dissolutions [closing down], to cause others to be elected; whereby the Legislative powers, incapable of Annihilation, have returned to the People at large for their exercise; the State remaining in the mean time exposed to all the dangers of invasion from without, and convulsions [riots] within.

He has endeavoured to prevent the population of these States; for that purpose obstructing the Laws for Naturalization of Foreigners; refusing to pass others to encourage their migrations hither, and raising the conditions of new Appropriations of Lands.

He has obstructed the Administration of Justice by refusing his Assent to Laws for establishing Judiciary powers.

He has made Judges dependent on his Will alone, for the tenure [term] of their offices, and the amount and payment of their salaries.

He has erected a multitude of New Offices, and sent hither swarms of Officers to harass our people, and eat out their substance.

He has kept among us, in times of peace, Standing Armies without the Consent of our legislatures.

He has affected to render the Military independent of and superior to the Civil power.

He has combined with others to subject us to a jurisdiction foreign to our constitution, and unacknowledged by our laws; giving his Assent to their Acts of pretended Legislation:

For quartering [lodging] large bodies of armed troops among us:

For protecting them, by a mock Trial, from punishment for any Murders which they should commit on the Inhabitants of these States:

For cutting off our Trade with all parts of the world:

For imposing Taxes on us without our Consent:

For depriving us in many cases, of the benefits of Trial by Jury:

For transporting us beyond Seas to be tried for pretended offences:

For abolishing the free System of English Laws in a neighbouring Province, establishing therein an Arbitrary government, and enlarging its Boundaries so as to render it at once an example and fit instrument for introducing the same absolute rule into these Colonies:

For taking away our Charters, abolishing our most valuable Laws, and altering fundamentally the Forms of our Governments:

For suspending our own Legislatures, and declaring themselves invested with power to legislate for us in all cases whatsoever.

He has abdicated Government here, by declaring us out of his Protection and waging War against us.

He has plundered our seas, ravaged our Coasts, burnt our towns, and destroyed the lives of our people.

He is at this time transporting large Armies of foreign Mercenaries [soldiers] to complete the works of death, desolation, and tyranny, already begun with circumstances of Cruelty and perfidy [dishonesty] scarcely paralleled in the most barbarous ages, and totally unworthy the Head of a civilized nation.

He has constrained our fellow Citizens taken Captive on the high Seas to bear Arms against their Country, to become the executioners of their friends and Brethren, or to fall themselves by their Hands.

He has excited domestic insurrections amongst us, and has endeavoured to bring on the inhabitants of our frontiers, the merciless Indian Savages whose known rule of warfare, is an undistinguished destruction of all ages, sexes and conditions.

In every stage of these Oppressions We have Petitioned for Redress [correction of wrongs] in the most humble terms: Our repeated Petitions have been answered only by repeated injury. A Prince, whose character is thus marked by every act which may define a Tyrant, is unfit to be the ruler of a free people.

Nor have We been wanting in attentions to our British brethren. We have warned them from time to time of attempts by their legislature to extend an unwarrantable jurisdiction over us. We have reminded them of the circumstances of our emigration and settlement here. We have appealed to their native justice and magnanimity [generosity], and we have conjured [begged] them by the ties of our common kindred, to disavow these usurpations, which would inevitably interrupt our connections and correspondence. They too have been deaf to the voice of justice and of consanguinity [relation by blood]. We must, therefore, acquiesce in the necessity, which denounces our Separation, and hold them, as we hold the rest of mankind, Enemies in War, in Peace Friends.

We, therefore, the Representatives of the United States of America, in General Congress, Assembled, appealing to the Supreme Judge of the world for the rectitude [justness] of our intentions, do, in the Name, and by Authority of the good People of these Colonies, solemnly publish and declare, That these United Colonies are, and of Right ought to be Free and Independent States; that they are Absolved from all Allegiance to the British Crown, and that all political connection between them and the State of Great Britain, is and ought to be totally dissolved; and that as Free and Independent States, they have full Power to levy War, conclude Peace, contract Alliances, establish Commerce, and to do all other Acts and Things which Independent States may of right do. And for the support of this Declaration, with a firm reliance on the protection of Divine Providence, we mutually pledge to each other our Lives, our Fortunes and our sacred Honor.

ASSESSMENT

1. **Identify Cause and Effect** How might the ideas about equality expressed in the Declaration of Independence have influenced later historical movements, such as the abolitionist movement and the women's suffrage movement?

2. **Identify Key Steps in a Process** Why was the Declaration of Independence a necessary document for the founding of the new nation?

3. **Draw Inferences** English philosopher John Locke wrote that government should protect "life, liberty,

and estate." How do you think Locke's writing influenced ideas about government put forth in the Declaration of Independence?

4. **Analyze Structure** How does the Declaration organize its key points from beginning to end?

[The Magna Carta]

Introduction

King John ruled England from 1199 to 1216. During his troubled reign, he found himself in conflict with England's feudal barons. The nobles especially resented John's attempts to tax them heavily. In 1215, the barons forced John to sign the Magna Carta, or Great Charter. Most of this document was intended to protect the rights of the barons. However, over time, the document came to guarantee some basic rights of English citizens. When English colonists came to North America, they brought these ideas with them. Eight of the 63 clauses of the Magna Carta are printed here.

Primary Source

12. No [tax] nor aid shall be imposed on our kingdom, unless by common counsel [consent] of our kingdom, except for ransoming our person, for making our eldest son a knight, and for once marrying our eldest daughter; and for these there shall not be levied more than a reasonable aid. . . .

30. No sheriff or bailiff [tax collector] of ours, or other person, shall take the horses or carts of any freeman for transport duty, against the will of the said freeman.

31. Neither we nor our bailiffs shall take, for our castles or for any other work of ours, wood which is not ours, against the will of the owner of that wood. . . .

38. No bailiff for the future shall, upon his own unsupported complaint, put any one to his "law," without credible [believable] witnesses brought for this purpose.

39. No freeman shall be taken or imprisoned . . . or exiled or in any way destroyed, nor will we go upon him nor send upon him, except by the lawful judgment of his peers [people of equal rank] or by the law of the land.

40. To no one will we sell, to no one will we refuse or delay, right or justice. . . .

45. We will appoint as justices, constables, sheriffs, or bailiffs only such as know the law of the realm [kingdom] and mean to observe it well. . . .

63. Wherefore it is our will, and we firmly enjoin [order], that the English Church be free, and that the men in our kingdom have and hold all the aforesaid liberties, rights, and concessions, well and peaceably, freely and quietly, fully and wholly, for themselves and their heirs, of us and our heirs, in all respects and in all places for ever, as is aforesaid.

ASSESSMENT

1. **Determine Author's Purpose** Why did the barons write the Magna Carta, and how did it affect the power of the king?
2. **Determine Central Ideas** What do you think is the most important right that this excerpt from the Magna Carta protects? Explain your answer.
3. **Identify Steps in a Process** How was the Magna Carta an important first step in the development of constitutional democracy?

[Mayflower Compact]

Introduction

The Pilgrims arrived at Massachusetts in 1620. Before disembarking, they signed a covenant that established a basis for self-government derived from the consent of the governed. Forty-one men signed the compact, agreeing to abide by the laws of the government. Women, who did not enjoy equal rights, were not asked to sign.

Primary Source

In the name of God, Amen. We, whose names are underwritten, the loyal subjects of our dread Sovereign Lord King James, by the grace of God, of Great Britain, France and Ireland king, defender of the faith, etc. Having undertaken, for the glory of God, and advancement of the Christian faith, and honor of our king and country, a voyage to plant the first colony in the Northern parts of Virginia, do by these presents solemnly and mutually in the presence of God and one of another, covenant [agree] and combine ourselves together into a civil body politick, for our better ordering and preservation, and furtherance [advancement] of the ends aforesaid; and by virtue hereof to enacte, constitute [establish], and frame such just and equal laws, ordinances, acts, constitutions and offices, from time to time, as shall be thought most meet [suitable] and convenient for the general good of the Colony unto which we promise all due submission and obedience. In witness whereof we have hereunder subscribed our names at Cape Cod the eleventh of November, in the year of the reign of our Sovereign Lord, King James, of England, France and Ireland, the eighteenth, and of Scotland the fifty-fourth. Anno Dom. 1620.

ASSESSMENT

1. **Identify Cause and Effect** How do you think that having this compact might have affected the Pilgrims once they arrived in North America?
2. **Analyze Interactions** What does the Mayflower Compact say about equality, and how might this view have influenced the system of government in the United States?
3. **Analyze Interactions** How do you think the organization of the Pilgrims "together into a civil body politick" influenced later ideas about government in the United States?

[Articles of Confederation]

Introduction

The Articles of Confederation were approved on November 15, 1777, and were in effect from March 1, 1781, when they were finally ratified by all 13 states, until March 4, 1789. They established a weak central government, which led to conflicts among the states. Demand soon grew for a stronger central government, leading to the creation of the United States Constitution.

Primary Source

To all to whom these Presents shall come, we the undersigned Delegates of the States affixed to our Names send greeting. Whereas the Delegates of the United States of America in Congress assembled did on the fifteenth day of November in the Year of our Lord One Thousand Seven Hundred and Seventy seven, and in the Second Year of the Independence of America agree to certain articles of Confederation [an alliance of states, usually for the purpose of defense] and perpetual [continuing forever] Union between the States of New Hampshire, Massachusetts Bay, Rhode Island and Providence Plantations, Connecticut, New York, New Jersey, Pennsylvania, Delaware, Maryland, Virginia, North Carolina, South Carolina and Georgia in the Words following, viz. [namely] "Articles of Confederation and perpetual Union between the states of New Hampshire, Massachusetts Bay, Rhode Island and Providence Plantations, Connecticut, New York, New Jersey, Pennsylvania, Delaware, Maryland, Virginia, North Carolina, South Carolina and Georgia."

[ART. I.] The Stile [style; name] of this confederacy shall be "The United States of America."

[ART. II.] Each state retains its sovereignty [the ability to make one's own laws and govern oneself], freedom and independence, and every Power, Jurisdiction and right, which is not by this confederation expressly delegated to the United States, in Congress assembled.

[ART. III.] The said states hereby severally enter into a firm league of friendship with each other, for their common defence, the security of their Liberties, and their mutual and general welfare, binding themselves to assist each other, against all force offered to, or attacks made upon them, or any of them, on account of religion, sovereignty, trade, or any other pretence whatever.

[ART. IV.] The better to secure and perpetuate mutual friendship and intercourse [communication and actions] among the people of the different states in this union, the free inhabitants of each of these states, paupers, vagabonds and fugitives from Justice excepted, shall be entitled to all privileges and immunities of free citizens in the several states; and the people of each state shall have free ingress [entrance] and regress [return] to and from any other state, and shall enjoy therein all the privileges of trade and commerce, subject to the same duties [taxes on imports or exports], impositions [taxes] and restrictions as the inhabitants thereof respectively, provided that such restriction shall not extend so far as to prevent the removal of property imported into any state, to any other state of which the Owner is an inhabitant; provided also that no imposition, duties or restriction shall be laid by any state, on the property of the united states, or either of them.

If any Person guilty of, or charged with treason, felony, or other high misdemeanor in any state, shall flee from Justice, and be found in any of the united states, he shall upon demand of the Governor or executive power, of the state from which he fled, be delivered up and removed to the state having jurisdiction of his offence.

Full faith and credit shall be given in each of these states to the records, acts and judicial proceedings of the courts and magistrates of every other state.

[ART. V.] For the more convenient management of the general interests of the united states, delegates shall be annually appointed in such manner as the legislature of each state shall direct, to meet in Congress on the first Monday in November, in every year, with a power reserved to each state, to recall its delegates, or any of them, at any time within the year, and to send others in their stead, for the remainder of the Year.

No state shall be represented in Congress by less than two, nor by more than seven Members; and no person shall be capable of being a delegate for more than three years in any term of six years; nor shall any person, being a delegate, be capable of holding any office under the united states, for which he, or another for his benefit receives any salary, fees or emolument [payment] of any kind.

Each state shall maintain its own delegates in a meeting of the states, and while they act as members of the committee of the states.

In determining questions in the united states, in Congress assembled, each state shall have one vote.

Freedom of speech and debate in Congress shall not be impeached or questioned in any Court, or place out of Congress, and the members of congress shall be protected in their persons from arrests and imprisonments, during the time of their going to and from, and attendance on congress, except for treason, felony, or breach of the peace.

[ART. VI.] No state without the Consent of the united states in congress assembled, shall send any embassy to, or receive any embassy from, or enter into any conference, agreement, or alliance or treaty with any King, prince or state; nor shall any person holding any office of profit or trust under the united states, or any of them, accept of any present, emolument, office or title of any kind whatever from any king, prince or foreign state;

nor shall the united states in congress assembled, or any of them, grant any title of nobility.

No two or more states shall enter into any treaty, confederation or alliance whatever between them, without the consent of the united states in congress assembled, specifying accurately the purposes for which the same is to be entered into, and how long it shall continue.

No state shall lay any imposts [taxes] or duties, which may interfere with any stipulations [conditions] in treaties, entered into by the united states in congress assembled, with any king, prince or state, in pursuance of any treaties already proposed by congress, to the courts of France and Spain.

No vessels of war shall be kept up in time of peace by any state, except such number only, as shall be deemed necessary by the united states in congress assembled, for the defence of such state, or its trade; nor shall any body of forces be kept up by any state, in time of peace, except such number only, as in the judgment of the united states, in congress assembled, shall be deemed requisite to garrison [assign troops to] the forts necessary for the defence of such state; but every state shall always keep up a well regulated and disciplined militia, sufficiently armed and accounted, and shall provide and constantly have ready for use, in public stores, a due number of field pieces and tents, and a proper quantity of arms, ammunition and camp equipage.

No state shall engage in any war without the consent of the united states in congress assembled, unless such state be actually invaded by enemies, or shall have received certain advice of a resolution being formed by some nation of Indians to invade such state and the danger is so imminent as not to admit of a delay, till the united states in congress assembled can be consulted: nor shall any state grant commissions to any ships or vessels of war, nor letters of marque [written permissions to cross a border] or reprisal, except it be after a declaration of war by the united states in congress assembled, and then only against the kingdom or state and the subjects thereof, against which war has been so declared, and under such regulations as shall be established by the united states in congress assembled, unless such state be infested by pirates, in which case vessels of war may be fitted out for that occasion, and kept so long as the danger shall continue, or until the united states in congress assembled shall determine otherwise.

[ART. VII.] When land-forces are raised by any state for the common defence, all officers of or under the rank of colonel, shall be appointed by the legislature of each state respectively by whom such forces shall be raised, or in such manner as such state shall direct, and all vacancies shall be filled up by the state which first made the appointment.

[ART. VIII.] All charges of war, and all other expences that shall be incurred for the common defence or general welfare, and allowed by the united states in congress assembled, shall be defrayed out of a common treasury, which shall be supplied by the several states, in proportion to the value of all land within each state, granted to or surveyed for any Person, as such land and the buildings and improvements thereon shall be estimated according to such mode as the united states in congress assembled, shall from time to time direct and appoint. The taxes for paying that proportion shall be laid and levied by the authority and direction of the legislatures of the several states within the time agreed upon by the united states in congress assembled.

[ART. IX.] The united states in congress assembled, shall have the sole and exclusive right and power of determining on peace and war, except in the cases mentioned in the sixth article—of sending and receiving ambassadors—entering into treaties and alliances, provided that no treaty of commerce shall be made whereby the legislative power of the respective states shall be restrained from imposing such imposts and duties on foreigners, as their own people are subjected to, or from prohibiting the exportation or importation of any species of goods or commodities whatsoever—of establishing rules for deciding in all cases, what captures on land or water shall be legal, and in what manner prizes taken by land or naval forces in the service of the united states shall be divided or appropriated—of granting letters of marque and reprisal in times of peace—appointing courts for the trial of piracies and felonies committed on the high seas and establishing courts for receiving and determining finally appeals in all cases of captures, provided that no member of congress shall be appointed a judge of any of the said courts.

The united states in congress assembled shall also be the last resort on appeal in all disputes and differences now subsisting [existing] or that hereafter may arise between two or more states concerning boundary, jurisdiction or any other cause whatever; which authority shall always be exercised in the manner following. Whenever the legislative or executive authority or lawful agent [of any] state in controversy with another shall present a petition to congress stating the matter in question and praying for a hearing, notice thereof shall be given by order of congress to the legislative or executive authority of the other state in controversy, and a day assigned for the appearance of the parties by their lawful agents, who shall then be directed to appoint by joint consent, commissioners or judges to constitute a court for hearing and determining the matter in question; but if they cannot agree, congress shall name three persons out of each of the united states, and from the list of such persons each party shall alternately strike out one, the petitioners beginning, until the number shall be reduced to thirteen; and from that number not less than seven, nor more than nine names as congress shall direct, shall in the presence of congress be drawn out by lot, and the persons whose names shall be so drawn or any five of them, shall be commissioners or judges, to hear and finally determine the controversy, so always as a major part of the judges who shall hear the cause shall agree in the determination: and if either party shall neglect to attend at the day appointed, without shewing [showing] reasons, which congress shall judge sufficient, or being present shall refuse to strike, the congress shall proceed to nominate three persons out of each state, and the secretary of congress shall strike in behalf of such party absent or refusing; and the judgment and sentence of the court to be appointed, in the manner before prescribed, shall be final and conclusive; and if any of the parties shall refuse to submit to the authority of such court, or to appear to defend their claim or cause, the court shall nevertheless proceed to pronounce sentence, or judgment, which shall in like manner be final and decisive, the judgment or sentence and other proceedings being in either case transmitted to congress, and lodged among the acts of congress for the security of the parties concerned: provided that every commissioner, before he sits in judgment, shall take an oath to be administered by one of the judges of the supreme or superior court of the state, where the cause shall be tried, "well and truly to hear and determine the matter in question, according to the best of his judgment, without favour, affection or hope of reward;" provided also that no state shall be deprived of territory for the benefit of the united states.

All controversies concerning the private right of soil claimed under different grants of two or more states, whose jurisdictions as they may respect such lands, and the states which passed such grants are adjusted, the said grants or either of them being at the same time claimed to have originated antecedent to such settlement of jurisdiction, shall on the petition of either party to the congress of the united states, be finally determined as near as may be in the same manner as is before prescribed for deciding disputes respecting territorial jurisdiction between different states.

The united states in congress assembled shall also have the sole and exclusive right and power of regulating the alloy and value of coin struck by their own authority, or by that of the respective states—fixing the standard of weights and measures throughout the united states—regulating the trade and managing all affairs with the Indians, not members of any of the states, provided that the legislative right of any state within its own limits be not infringed or violated—establishing and regulating post-offices from one state to another, throughout all the united states, and exacting such postage on the papers passing thro' [through] the same as may be requisite to defray [pay] the expences of the said office—appointing all officers of the land forces, in the service of the united states, excepting regimental officers—appointing all the officers of the naval forces, and commissioning all officers whatever in the service of the united states—making rules for the government and regulation of the said land and naval forces, and directing their operations.

The united states in congress assembled shall have authority to appoint a committee, to sit in the recess of congress, to be denominated "A Committee of the States," and to consist of one delegate from each state; and to appoint such other committees and civil officers as may be necessary for managing the general affairs of the united states under their direction—to appoint one of their number to preside, provided that no person be allowed to serve in the office of president more than one year in any term of three years; to ascertain the necessary sums of Money to be raised for the service of the united states, and to appropriate and apply the same for defraying the public expences—to borrow money, or emit bills on the credit of the united states, transmitting every half year to the respective states an account of the sums of money so borrowed or emitted—to build and equip a navy—to agree upon the number of land forces, and to make requisitions from each state for its quota, in proportion to the number of white inhabitants in such state; which requisition shall be binding, and thereupon the legislature of each state shall appoint the regimental officers, raise the men and clothe, arm and equip them in a soldier like manner, at the expence of the united states, and the officers and men so clothed, armed and equipped shall march to the place appointed, and within the time agreed on by the united states in congress assembled.

But if the united states in congress assembled shall, on consideration of circumstances judge proper that any state should not raise men, or should raise a smaller number than its quota, and that any other state should raise a greater number of men than the quota thereof, such extra number shall be raised, officered, clothed, armed and equipped in the same manner as the quota of such state, unless the legislature of such state shall judge that such extra number cannot be safely spared out of the same, in which case they shall raise, officer, clothe, arm and equip as many of such extra number as they judge can be safely spared. And the officers and men so clothed, armed and equipped, shall march to the place appointed, and within the time agreed on by the united states in congress assembled.

The united states in congress assembled shall never engage in a war, nor grant letters of marque and reprisal in time of peace, nor enter into any treaties or alliances, nor coin money, nor regulate the value thereof, nor ascertain the sums and expences necessary for the defence and welfare of the united states, or any of them, nor emit bills, nor borrow money on the credit of the united states, nor appropriate money, nor agree upon the number of vessels of war, to be built or purchased, or the number of land or sea forces to be raised, nor appoint a commander in chief of the army or navy, unless nine states assent to the same: nor shall a question on any other point, except for adjourning from day to day be determined, unless by the votes of a majority of the united states in congress assembled.

The congress of the united states shall have power to adjourn to any time within the year, and to any place within the united states, so that no period of adjournment be for a longer duration than the space of six Months, and shall publish the Journal of their proceedings monthly, except such parts thereof relating to treaties, alliances or military operations as in their judgment require secrecy; and the yeas and nays of the delegates of each state on any question shall be entered on the Journal, when it is desired by any delegate; and the delegates of a state, or any of them, at his or their request shall be furnished with a transcript of the said Journal, except such parts as are above excepted, to lay before the legislatures of the several states.

[ART. X.] The committee of the states, or any nine of them, shall be authorised to execute, in the recess of congress, such of the powers of congress as the united states in congress assembled, by the consent of nine states, shall from time to time think expedient to vest them with; provided that no power be delegated to the said committee, for the exercise of which, by the articles of confederation, the voice of nine states in the congress of the united states assembled is requisite.

[ART. XI.] Canada acceding to this confederation, and joining in the measures of the united states, shall be admitted into, and entitled to all the advantages of this union: but no other colony shall be admitted into the same, unless such admission be agreed to by nine states.

[ART. XII.] All bills of credit emitted, monies borrowed and debts contracted by, or under the authority of congress, before the assembling of the united states, in pursuance of the present confederation, shall be deemed and considered as a charge against the united states, for payment and satisfaction whereof the said united states, and the public faith are hereby solemnly pledged.

[ART. XIII.] Every state shall abide by [conform to; agree to] the determinations of the united states in congress assembled, on all questions which by this confederation are submitted to them. And the Articles of this confederation shall be inviolably observed by every state, and the union shall be perpetual; nor shall any alteration at any time hereafter be made in any of them; unless such alteration be agreed to in a congress of the united states, and be afterwards confirmed by the legislatures of every state.

And whereas it hath pleased the Great Governor of the World to incline [bend something in a certain direction] the hearts of the legislatures we respectively represent in congress, to approve of, and to authorize us to ratify the said articles of confederation and perpetual union. Know ye that we the undersigned delegates, by virtue of the power and authority to us given for that purpose, do by these presents, in the name and in behalf of our respective constituents, fully and entirely ratify and confirm each and every of the said articles of confederation and perpetual union, and all and singular the matters and things therein contained: And we do further solemnly plight [pledge] and engage the faith of our respective constituents, that they shall abide by the determinations of the united states in congress assembled, on all questions, which by the said confederation are submitted to them. And that the articles thereof shall be inviolably [without failure] observed by the states we respectively represent, and that the union shall be perpetual. In Witness whereof we have hereunto set our hands in Congress. Done at Philadelphia in the state of Pennsylvania the ninth Day of July in the Year of our Lord one Thousand seven Hundred and Seventy-eight, and in the third year of the independence of America.

Josiah Bartlett
John Wentworth Junr
August 8th 1778
On The Part & Behalf Of The State Of New Hampshire

John Hancock
Samuel Adams
Elbridge Gerry
Francis Dana
James Lovell
Samuel Holten
On The Part And Behalf Of
The State Of Massachusetts Bay

William Ellery
Henry Marchant
John Collins
On The Part And Behalf
Of The State Of Rhode Island
And Providence Plantations

Roger Sherman
Samuel Huntington
Oliver Wolcott
Titus Hosmer
Andrew Adams
On The Part And Behalf Of
The State Of Connecticut

Jas Duane
Fras Lewis
Wm Duer.
Gouv Morris
On The Part And Behalf Of
The State Of New York

Jno Witherspoon
Nathl Scudder
On The Part And In Behalf Of
The State Of New Jersey.
Novr 26, 1778.—

Robt Morris
Daniel Roberdeau
Jona Bayard Smith.
William Clingan
Joseph Reed
22d July 1778
On The Part And Behalf Of
The State Of Pennsylvania

Tho Mckean
Feby 12 1779
John Dickinson
May 5th 1779
Nicholas Van Dyke,
On The Part & Behalf Of
The State Of Delaware

John Hanson
March 1 1781
Daniel Carroll Do
On The Part And Behalf
Of The State Of Maryland

Richard Henry Lee
John Banister
Thomas Adams
Jno Harvie
Francis Lightfoot Lee
On The Part And Behalf Of
The State Of Virginia

John Penn
July 21st 1778
Corns Harnett
Jno Williams
On The Part And Behalf
Of The State Of No Carolina

Henry Laurens
William Henry Drayton
Jno Mathews
Richd Hutson.
Thos Heyward Junr
On The Part & Behalf Of
The State Of South Carolina

Jno Walton
24th July 1778
Edwd Telfair. Edwd Langworthy
On The Part And Behalf Of
The State Of Georgia

ASSESSMENT

1. **Draw Conclusions** As you have learned, a *confederation* is an alliance of states that typically forms for the purpose of defense. Why do you think the idea of a confederation was favored by the Framers at this point in American history?

How would the idea continue to influence the Framers in subsequent years?

2. **Determine Central Ideas** Historians commonly criticize the Articles of Confederation for setting up only a "loose" confederation of states. In what way was the confederation of states "loose"? Explain your answer with evidence from the text.

3. **Explain an Argument** Explain the argument that one weakness of the Articles of Confederation was that Congress was not granted the power to levy taxes.

4. **Draw Conclusions** Taken as a whole, the Articles of Confederation did not establish a strong national government, despite rules, such as those in Article VI, denying states certain powers. Give an example of a power granted to Congress that could have been strengthened, thereby creating a stronger national government.

[Northwest Ordinance]

Introduction
Adopted in 1787 by the Second Continental Congress, the Northwest Ordinance created a method for admitting new states to the Union. While the Articles of Confederation lacked a bill of rights, the Ordinance provided one that included many of the basic liberties that would later be included in the Constitution's Bill of Rights.

Primary Source
. . . **ART. 1.** No person, demeaning himself in a peaceable and orderly manner, shall ever be molested on account of his mode of worship or religious sentiments, in the said territory.

ART. 2. The inhabitants of the said territory shall always be entitled to the benefits of the writ of habeas corpus [a legal action that says an arrested person must be presented in court], and of the trial by jury. . . .

ART. 3. Religion, morality, and knowledge, being necessary to good government and the happiness of mankind, schools and the means of education shall forever be encouraged. . . .

ART. 6. There shall be neither slavery nor involuntary servitude in the said territory, otherwise than in the punishment of crimes whereof the party shall have been duly convicted: Provided, always, That any person escaping into the same, from whom labor or service is lawfully claimed in any one of the original States, such fugitive may be lawfully reclaimed and conveyed to the person claiming his or her labor or service as aforesaid.

ASSESSMENT

1. **Compare and Contrast** Which ideals expressed in this excerpt from the Northwest Ordinance became influential in other founding documents of the United States? Use specific examples in your response.
2. **Analyze Interactions** How do these excerpts from the Northwest Ordinance connect to the phrase "life, liberty, and the pursuit of happiness" from the Declaration of Independence?

[Anti-Federalist Papers]

Introduction

When the Constitutional Convention of 1787 produced the new constitution, many opposed its adoption. There were numerous men who made strong arguments on behalf on behalf of the opponents, known as the Anti-Federalists. The following excerpts provide a sampling of Anti-Federalist arguments. Richard Henry Lee, a Virginian, wrote the best-known Anti-Federalist essays of the time, "Letters from the Federal Farmer to the Republican." The first selection is from letters Lee wrote in October 1787. Luther Martin, the leading Anti-Federalist from Maryland, attended the Constitutional Convention as a delegate. The second selection is from a speech Martin gave on November 29, 1787. In it, he defends his decision to leave the Convention before its work was finished. Findley, Whitehill, and Smilie believed that they were prevented from expressing their

views because of the political maneuverings of the Federalists. The third selection is from "The Address and Reasons of Dissent of the Minority of the Convention of the State of Pennsylvania to their Constituents," which the three men published in the *Pennsylvania Packet and Daily Advertiser* on December 18, 1787.

Primary Sources

"Letters from the Federal Farmer to the Republican" by Richard Henry Lee

The present moment discovers a new face in our affairs. Our object has been all along to reform our federal system and to strengthen our governments to establish peace, order, and justice in the community—but a new object now presents. The plan of government now proposed is evidently calculated totally to change, in time, our condition as a people. Instead of being thirteen republics under a federal head, it is clearly designed to make us one consolidated government. . . . This consolidation of the states has been the object of several men in this country for some time past. Whether such a change can ever be effected, in any manner; whether it can be effected without convulsions and civil wars; whether such a change will not totally destroy the liberties of this country, time only can determine. . . .

The Confederation was formed when great confidence was placed in the voluntary exertions of individuals and of the respective states; and the framers of it, to guard against usurpation [an illegal grab of power, authority, or sovereignty], so limited and checked the powers that, in many respects, they are inadequate to the exigencies [requirements; demands] of the Union. We find, therefore, members of Congress urging alterations in the federal system almost as soon as it was adopted. . . .

We expected too much from the return of peace, and, of course, we have been disappointed. Our governments have been new and unsettled; and several legislature, [by their actions] . . . have given just cause of uneasiness. . . .

The conduct of several legislatures touching paper-money and tender [method of payment] laws has prepared many honest men for changes in government, which otherwise they would not have thought of—when by the evils, on the one hand, and by the secret instigations of artful men, on the other, the minds of men were become sufficiently uneasy, a bold step was taken, which is usually followed by a revolution or a civil war. A general convention for mere commercial purposes was moved for—the authors of this measure saw that the people's attention was turned solely to the amendment of the federal system; and that, had the idea of a total change been started, probably no state would have appointed members to the Convention. The idea of destroying, ultimately, the state government and forming one consolidated system could not have been admitted. A convention, therefore, merely for vesting in Congress power to regulate trade was proposed. . . .

The plan proposed appears to be partly federal, but principally, however, calculated ultimately to make the states one consolidated government.

The first interesting question therefore suggested is how far the states can be consolidated into one entire government on free principles. In considering this question, extensive objects are to be taken into view, and important changes in the forms of government to be carefully attended to in all their consequences. The happiness of the people at large must be the great object with every honest statesman, and he will direct every movement to this point. If we are so situated as a people as not to be able to enjoy equal happiness and advantages under one government, the consolidation of the states cannot be admitted.

There are certain unalienable and fundamental rights, which in forming the social compact ought to be explicitly ascertained and fixed. A free and enlightened people, in forming this compact, will not resign all their rights to those who govern, and they will fix limits [a bill of rights] to their legislators and rulers, which will soon be plainly seen by those who are governed, as well as by those who govern; and the latter will know they cannot be passed unperceived by the former and without giving a general alarm. These rights should be made the basis of every constitution; and if a people be so situated, or have such different opinions, that they cannot agree in ascertaining and fixing them, it is a very strong argument against their attempting to form one entire society, to live under one system of laws only.

It may also be worthy our examination how far the provision for amending this plan, when it shall be adopted, is of any importance. No measures can be taken toward amendments unless two-thirds of the Congress, or two-thirds of the legislature of the several states, shall agree. While power is in the hands of the people, or democratic part of the community, more especially as at present, it is easy, according to the general course of human affairs, for the few influential men

in the community to obtain conventions, alterations in government, and to persuade the common people that they may change for the better, and to get from them a part of the power. But when power is once transferred from the many to the few, all changes become extremely difficult; the government in this case being beneficial to the few, they will be exceedingly artful and adroit [skillful] in preventing any measures which may lead to a change; and nothing will produce it but great exertions and severe struggles on the part of the common people. Every man of reflection must see that the change now proposed is a transfer of power from the many to the few, and the probability is the artful and ever active aristocracy will prevent all peaceful measures for changes, unless when they shall discover some favorable moment to increase their own influence.

It is true there may be danger in delay; but there is danger in adopting the system in its present form. And I see the danger in either case will arise principally from the conduct and views of two very unprincipled parties in the United States—two fires, between which the honest and substantial people have long found themselves situated. One party is composed of little insurgents [people rising in opposition to a government], men in debt, who want no law and who want a share of the property of others—these are called levelers, Shaysites [opponents of the new Constitution], etc. The other party is composed of a few but more dangerous men, with their servile [submissive] dependents; these avariciously [greedily] grasp at all power and property. You may discover in all the actions of these men an evident dislike to free and equal government, and they will go systematically to work to change, essentially, the forms of government in this country—these are called aristocrats . . . . .

The fact is, these aristocrats support and hasten the adoption of the proposed Constitution merely because they think it is a stepping-stone to their favorite object. I think I am well-founded in this idea; I think the general politics of these men support it, as well as the common observation among them that the proffered plan is the best that can be got at present; it will do for a few years, and lead to something better. . . .

A speech given before the Maryland State legislature, November 29, 1787, by Luther Martin

It was the states as states, by their representatives in Congress, that formed the Articles of Confederation; it was the states as states, by their legislatures, who ratified those Articles; and it was there established and provided that the states as states (that is, by their legislatures) should agree to any alterations that should hereafter be proposed in the federal government, before they should be binding; and any alterations agreed to in any other manner cannot release the states from the obligation they are under to each other by virtue of the original Articles of Confederation. The people of the different states never made any objection to the manner in which the Articles of Confederation were formed or ratified, or to the mode by which alterations were to be made in that government—with the rights of their respective states they wished not to interfere. Nor do I believe the people, in their individual capacity, would ever have expected or desired to have been appealed to on the present occasion, in violation of the rights of their respective states, if the favorers of the proposed Constitution, imagining they had a better chance of forcing it to be adopted by a hasty appeal to the people at large (who could not be so good judges of the dangerous consequence), had not insisted upon this mode . . . .

It was also my opinion that, upon principles of sound policy, the agreement or disagreement to the proposed system ought to have been by the state legislatures; in which case, let the event have been what it would, there would have been but little prospect of the public peace being disturbed thereby; whereas the attempt to force down this system, although Congress and the respective state legislatures should disapprove, by appealing to the people and to procure [acquire] its establishment in a manner totally unconstitutional, has a tendency to set the state governments and their subjects at variance with each other, to lessen the obligations of government, to weaken the bands of society, to introduce anarchy and confusion, and to light the torch of discord and civil war throughout this continent. All these considerations weighed with me most forcibly against giving my assent to the mode by which it is resolved that this system is to be ratified, and were urged by me in opposition to the measure.

. . . [A] great portion of that time which ought to have been devoted calmly and impartially to consider what alterations in our federal government would be most likely to procure and preserve the happiness of the Union was employed in a violent struggle on the one side to obtain all power and dominion in their own hands, and on the other to prevent it; and that the aggrandizement of particular states, and particular individuals, appears to have been much more the subject sought after than the welfare of our country . . . .

When I took my seat in the Convention, I found them attempting to bring forward a system which, I was sure, never had entered into the contemplation of those I had

the honor to represent, and which, upon the fullest consideration, I considered not only injurious to the interest and rights of this state but also incompatible with the political happiness and freedom of the states in general. From that time until my business compelled me to leave the Convention, I gave it every possible opposition, in every stage of its progression. I opposed the system there with the same explicit frankness with which I have here given you a history of our proceedings, an account of my own conduct, which in a particular manner I consider you as having a right to know. While there, I endeavored to act as became a free man and the delegate of a free state. Should my conduct obtain the approbation [act of approval] of those who appointed me, I will not deny it would afford me satisfaction; but to me that approbation was at most no more than a secondary consideration—my first was to deserve it. Left to myself to act according to the best of my discretion, my conduct should have been the same had I been even sure your censure would have been my only reward, since I hold it sacredly my duty to dash the cup of poison, if possible, from the hand of a state or an individual, however anxious the one or the other might be to swallow it . . . .

"The Address and Reasons of Dissent of the Minority of the Convention of the State of Pennsylvania to their Constituents" by William Findley, Robert Whitehill, and John Smilie

Our objections are comprised under three general heads of dissent, viz. [namely]:

We dissent, first, because it is the opinion of the most celebrated writers on government, and confirmed by uniform experience, that a very extensive territory cannot be governed on the principles of freedom otherwise than by a confederation of republics, possessing all the powers of internal government but united in the management of their general and foreign concerns. . . .

We dissent, secondly, because the powers vested in Congress by this Constitution must necessarily annihilate and absorb the legislative, executive, and judicial powers of the several states, and produce from their ruins one consolidated government, which from the nature of things will be an iron-handed despotism, as nothing short of the supremacy of despotic sway could connect and govern these United States under one government.

As the truth of this position is of such decisive importance, it ought to be fully investigated, and if it is founded, to be clearly ascertained; for, should it be demonstrated that the powers vested by this Constitution in Congress will have such an effect as necessarily to produce one consolidated government, the question then will be reduced to this short issue, viz.: whether satiated [satisfied] with the blessings of liberty, whether repenting [regretting] of the folly of so recently asserting their unalienable rights against foreign despots at the expense of so much blood and treasure, and such painful and arduous struggles, the people of America are now willing to resign every privilege of freemen, and submit to the dominion of an absolute government that will embrace all America in one chain of despotism; or whether they will, with virtuous indignation, spurn at the shackles prepared for them, and confirm their liberties by a conduct becoming freemen. . . .

We dissent, thirdly, because if it were practicable to govern so extensive a territory as these United States include, on the plan of a consolidated government, consistent with the principles of liberty and the happiness of the people, yet the construction of this Constitution is not calculated to attain the object; for independent of the nature of the case, it would of itself necessarily produce a despotism, and that not by the usual gradations [small steps or changes] but with the celerity [speed] that has hitherto only attended revolutions effected by the sword.

To establish the truth of this position, a cursory [hasty] investigation of the principles and form of this Constitution will suffice.

The first consideration that this review suggests is the omission of a Bill of Rights ascertaining and fundamentally establishing those unalienable and personal rights of men, without the full, free, and secure enjoyment of which there can be no liberty, and over which it is not necessary for a good government to have the control—the principal of which are the rights of conscience, personal liberty by the clear and unequivocal establishment of the writ of habeas corpus, jury trial in criminal and civil cases, by an impartial jury of the vicinage [neighborhood] or county, with the common law proceedings for the safety of the accused in criminal prosecutions; and the liberty of the press, that scourge of tyrants, and the grand bulwark [safeguard] of every other liberty and privilege. The stipulations [conditions of agreement] heretofore made in favor of them in the state constitutions are entirely superseded by this Constitution. . . .

ASSESSMENT

1. **Compare and Contrast** How are the arguments of the Anti-Federalists represented in these excerpts similar and different?

2. **Assess an Argument** What do you think are the strongest and weakest parts of the Anti-Federalists' overall argument? Cite specific examples in the text.

3. **Analyze Interactions** How have Anti-Federalist viewpoints such as those expressed in the excerpts influenced the system of government of the United States? Consider the Bill of Rights and the final version of the U.S. Constitution as part of your answer.

[*Federalist* No. 10, James Madison]

Introduction

Of the 85 *Federalist Papers*, it is believed that 29 of them were written by James Madison. Among them was *Federalist* No. 10, which presents Madison's observations on dealing with the "mischiefs of faction" and the advantages of a republican (representative) form of government over that of a pure democracy. It was first published on November 23, 1787.

Primary Source

Among the numerous advantages promised by a well constructed Union, none deserves to be more accurately developed than its tendency to break and control the violence of faction [a group within a larger political group]. The friend of popular governments never finds himself so much alarmed for their character and fate, as when he contemplates their propensity [tendency] to this dangerous vice. He will not fail, therefore, to set a due value on any plan which, without violating the principles to which he is attached, provides a proper cure for it. The instability, injustice, and confusion introduced into the public councils, have, in truth, been the mortal diseases under which popular governments have everywhere perished; as they continue to be the favorite and fruitful topics from which the adversaries to liberty derive their most specious [seemingly true, but actually false] declamations.

The valuable improvements made by the American constitutions on the popular models, both ancient and modern, cannot certainly be too much admired; but it would be an unwarrantable partiality, to contend that they have as effectually obviated [made unnecessary] the danger on this side, as was wished and expected. Complaints are everywhere heard from our most considerate and virtuous citizens, equally the friends of public and private faith, and of public and personal liberty, that our governments are too unstable, that the public good is disregarded in the conflicts of rival parties, and that measures are too often decided, not according to the rules of justice and the rights of the minor party, but by the superior force of an interested and overbearing majority. However anxiously we may wish that these complaints had no foundation, the evidence, of known facts will not permit us to deny that they are in some degree true.

It will be found, indeed, on a candid review of our situation, that some of the distresses under which we labor have been erroneously charged on the operation of our governments; but it will be found, at the same time, that other causes will not alone account for many of our heaviest misfortunes; and, particularly, for that prevailing and increasing distrust of public engagements, and alarm for private rights, which are echoed from one end of the continent to the other. These must be chiefly, if not wholly, effects of the unsteadiness and injustice with which a factious spirit has tainted our public administrations.

By a faction, I understand a number of citizens, whether amounting to a majority or a minority of the whole, who are united and actuated [caused to do something] by some common impulse of passion, or of interest, adversed to the rights of other citizens, or to the permanent and aggregate interests of the community.

There are two methods of curing the mischiefs of faction: the one, by removing its causes; the other, by controlling its effects.

There are again two methods of removing the causes of faction: the one, by destroying the liberty which is essential to its existence; the other, by giving to every citizen the same opinions, the same passions, and the same interests.

It could never be more truly said than of the first remedy, that it was worse than the disease. Liberty is to faction what air is to fire, an aliment without which it instantly expires. But it could not be less folly to abolish liberty, which is essential to political life, because it nourishes faction, than it would be to wish the annihilation of air, which is essential to animal life, because it imparts to fire its destructive agency.

The second expedient [a way of achieving a result] is as impracticable as the first would be unwise. As long as the reason of man continues fallible [capable of being wrong], and he is at liberty to exercise it, different opinions will be formed. As long as the connection subsists [exists] between his reason and his self-love, his opinions and his passions will have a reciprocal influence on each other; and the former will be objects to which the latter will attach themselves. The diversity in the faculties of men, from which the rights of property originate, is not less an insuperable [uncontrollable] obstacle to a uniformity of interests. The protection of these faculties is the first object of government. From the protection of different and unequal faculties of acquiring property, the possession of different degrees and kinds of property immediately results; and from the influence of these on the sentiments and views of the respective proprietors, ensues a division of the society into different interests and parties.

The latent causes of faction are thus sown in the nature of man; and we see them everywhere brought into different degrees of activity, according to the different circumstances of civil society. A zeal for different opinions concerning religion, concerning government, and many other points, as well of speculation as of practice; an attachment to different leaders ambitiously contending for pre-eminence and power; or to persons of other descriptions whose fortunes have been interesting to the human passions, have, in turn, divided mankind into parties, inflamed them with mutual animosity, and rendered them much more disposed to vex and oppress each other than to co-operate for their common good. So strong is this propensity of mankind to fall into mutual animosities, that where no substantial occasion presents itself, the most frivolous and fanciful distinctions have been sufficient to kindle their unfriendly passions and excite their most violent conflicts. But the most common and durable source of factions has been the various and unequal distribution of property. Those who hold and those who are without property have ever formed distinct interests in society. Those who are creditors, and those who are debtors, fall under a like discrimination. A landed interest, a manufacturing interest, a mercantile interest, a moneyed interest, with many lesser interests, grow up of necessity in civilized nations, and divide them into different classes, actuated by different sentiments and views. The regulation of these various and interfering interests forms the principal task of modern legislation, and involves the spirit of party and faction in the necessary and ordinary operations of the government.

No man is allowed to be a judge in his own cause, because his interest would certainly bias his judgment, and, not improbably, corrupt his integrity. With equal, nay with greater reason, a body of men are unfit to be both judges and parties at the same time; yet what are many of the most important acts of legislation, but so many judicial determinations, not indeed concerning the rights of single persons, but concerning the rights of large bodies of citizens? And what are the different classes of legislators but advocates and parties to the causes which they determine? Is a law proposed concerning private debts? It is a question to which the creditors are parties on one side and the debtors on the other. Justice ought to hold the balance between them. Yet the parties are, and must be, themselves the judges; and the most numerous party, or, in other words, the most powerful faction must be expected to prevail.

Shall domestic manufactures be encouraged, and in what degree, by restrictions on foreign manufactures? These are questions which would be differently decided by the landed and the manufacturing classes, and probably by neither with a sole regard to justice and the public good. The apportionment of taxes on the various descriptions of property is an act which seems to require the most exact impartiality; yet there is, perhaps, no legislative act in which greater opportunity and temptation are given to a predominant party to trample on the rules of justice. Every shilling with which they overburden the inferior number, is a shilling saved to their own pockets.

It is in vain to say that enlightened statesmen will be able to adjust these clashing interests, and render them all subservient to the public good. Enlightened statesmen will not always be at the helm. Nor, in many cases, can such an adjustment be made at all without taking into view indirect and remote considerations, which will rarely prevail over the immediate interest which one party may find in disregarding the rights of another or the good of the whole.

The inference to which we are brought is, that the CAUSES of faction cannot be removed, and that relief is only to be sought in the means of controlling its EFFECTS.

If a faction consists of less than a majority, relief is supplied by the republican principle, which enables the majority to defeat its sinister views by regular vote. It may clog the administration, it may convulse the society; but it will be unable to execute and mask its violence under the forms of the Constitution. When a majority is included in a faction, the form of popular government, on the other hand, enables it to sacrifice to its ruling passion or interest both the public good and the rights of other citizens. To secure the public good and private rights against the danger of such a faction, and at the same time to preserve the spirit and the form of popular government, is then the great object to which our inquiries are directed. Let me add that it is the great desideratum [something wanted or needed] by which this form of government can be rescued from the opprobrium [disgrace; strong disapproval] under which it has so long labored, and be recommended to the esteem and adoption of mankind.

By what means is this object attainable? Evidently by one of two only. Either the existence of the same passion or interest in a majority at the same time must be prevented, or the majority, having such coexistent passion or interest, must be rendered, by their number and local situation, unable to concert and carry into effect schemes of oppression. If the impulse and the opportunity be suffered to coincide, we well know that neither moral nor religious motives can be relied on as an adequate control. They are not found to be such on the injustice and violence of individuals, and lose their efficacy in proportion to the number combined together, that is, in proportion as their efficacy becomes needful.

From this view of the subject it may be concluded that a pure democracy, by which I mean a society consisting of a small number of citizens, who assemble and administer the government in person, can admit of no cure for the mischiefs of faction. A common passion or interest will, in almost every case, be felt by a majority of the whole; a communication and concert result from the form of government itself; and there is nothing to check the inducements to sacrifice the weaker party or an obnoxious individual. Hence it is that such democracies have ever been spectacles of turbulence and contention; have ever been found incompatible with personal security or the rights of property; and have in general been as short in their lives as they have been violent in their deaths. Theoretic politicians, who have patronized this species of government, have erroneously supposed that by reducing mankind to a perfect equality in their political rights, they would, at the same time, be perfectly equalized and assimilated in their possessions, their opinions, and their passions.

A republic, by which I mean a government in which the scheme of representation takes place, opens a different prospect, and promises the cure for which we are seeking. Let us examine the points in which it varies from pure democracy, and we shall comprehend both the nature of the cure and the efficacy which it must derive from the Union.

The two great points of difference between a democracy and a republic are: first, the delegation of the government, in the latter, to a small number of citizens elected by the rest; secondly, the greater number of citizens, and greater sphere of country, over which the latter may be extended.

The effect of the first difference is, on the one hand, to refine and enlarge the public views, by passing them through the medium of a chosen body of citizens, whose wisdom may best discern the true interest of their country, and whose patriotism and love of justice will be least likely to sacrifice it to temporary or partial considerations. Under such a regulation, it may well happen that the public voice, pronounced by the representatives of the people, will be more consonant to the public good than if pronounced by the people themselves, convened for the purpose. On the other hand, the effect may be inverted. Men of factious [divisive] tempers, of local prejudices, or of sinister designs, may, by intrigue, by corruption, or by other means, first obtain the suffrages, and then betray the interests, of the people. The question resulting is, whether small or extensive republics are more favorable to the election of proper guardians of the public weal; and it is clearly decided in favor of the latter by two obvious considerations:

In the first place, it is to be remarked that, however small the republic may be, the representatives must be raised to a certain number, in order to guard against the cabals of a few; and that, however large it may be, they must be limited to a certain number, in order to guard against the confusion of a multitude. Hence, the number of representatives in the two cases not being in proportion to that of the two constituents, and being proportionally greater in the small republic, it follows that, if the proportion of fit characters be not less in the large than in the small republic, the former will present a greater option, and consequently a greater probability of a fit choice.

In the next place, as each representative will be chosen by a greater number of citizens in the large than in the small republic, it will be more difficult for unworthy candidates to practice with success the vicious arts by which elections are too often carried; and the suffrages of the people being more free, will be more likely to centre in men who possess the most attractive merit and the most diffusive and established character.

It must be confessed that in this, as in most other cases, there is a mean, on both sides of which inconveniences will be found to lie. By enlarging too much the number of electors, you render the representatives too little acquainted with all their local circumstances and lesser interests; as by reducing it too much, you render him unduly attached to these, and too little fit to comprehend and pursue great and national objects. The federal Constitution forms a happy combination in this respect; the great and aggregate interests being referred to the national, the local and particular to the State legislatures.

The other point of difference is, the greater number of citizens and extent of territory which may be brought within the compass of republican than of democratic government; and it is this circumstance principally which renders factious combinations less to be dreaded in the former than in the latter. The smaller the society, the fewer probably will be the distinct parties and interests composing it; the fewer the distinct parties and interests, the more frequently will a majority be found of the same party; and the smaller the number of individuals composing a majority, and the smaller the compass within which they are placed, the more easily will they concert and execute their plans of oppression. Extend the sphere, and you take in a greater variety of parties and interests; you make it less probable that a majority of the whole will have a common motive to invade the rights of other citizens; or if such a common motive exists, it will be more difficult for all who feel it to discover their own strength, and to act in unison with each other. Besides other impediments, it may be remarked that, where there is a consciousness of unjust or dishonorable purposes, communication is always checked by distrust in proportion to the number whose concurrence is necessary.

Hence, it clearly appears, that the same advantage which a republic has over a democracy, in controlling the effects of faction, is enjoyed by a large over a small republic,—is enjoyed by the Union over the States composing it. Does the advantage consist in the substitution of representatives whose enlightened views and virtuous sentiments render them superior to local prejudices and schemes of injustice? It will not be denied that the representation of the Union will be most likely to possess these requisite endowments. Does it consist in the greater security afforded by a greater variety of parties, against the event of any one party being able to outnumber and oppress the rest? In an equal degree does the increased variety of parties comprised within the Union, increase this security. Does it, in fine, consist in the greater obstacles opposed to the concert and accomplishment of the secret wishes of an unjust and interested majority? Here, again, the extent of the Union gives it the most palpable advantage.

The influence of factious leaders may kindle a flame within their particular States, but will be unable to spread a general conflagration [a large conflict] through the other States. A religious sect may degenerate into a political faction in a part of the Confederacy; but the variety of sects dispersed over the entire face of it must secure the national councils against any danger from that source. A rage for paper money, for an abolition of debts, for an equal division of property, or for any other improper or wicked project, will be less apt to pervade the whole body of the Union than a particular member of it; in the same proportion as such a malady is more likely to taint a particular county or district, than an entire State.

In the extent and proper structure of the Union, therefore, we behold a republican remedy for the diseases most incident to republican government. And according to the degree of pleasure and pride we feel in being republicans, ought to be our zeal in cherishing the spirit and supporting the character of Federalists.

ASSESSMENT

1. **Explain an Argument** Why does Madison say a republican form of government best suits the United States as it forms a new constitution?
2. **Assess an Argument** Do you agree with Madison's contention that a democratic republic is preferable to a pure democracy? Explain your position.
3. **Analyze Interactions** What do you think was the impact of *Federalist* No. 10 on the U.S. Constitution?

[*Federalist* No. 39, James Madison]

Introduction

In *Federalist* No. 39, James Madison takes on critics of the republican form of government favored by Madison and his allies. Those who opposed this form felt that the new government stripped individual states of their powers. They feared a federal government with too much power.

Madison rebuts this argument by saying that a republic is precisely the right form of government for the young nation and that the proposed constitution will establish a strong national government and preserve some powers of the states.

Primary Source

THE last paper having concluded the observations which were meant to introduce a candid survey of the plan of government reported by the convention, we now proceed to the execution of that part of our undertaking.

The first question that offers itself is, whether the general form and aspect of the government be strictly republican. It is evident that no other form would be reconcilable with the genius of the people of America; with the fundamental principles of the Revolution; or with that honorable determination which animates every votary [devotee] of freedom, to rest all our political experiments on the capacity of mankind for self-government. If the plan of the convention, therefore, be found to depart from the republican character, its advocates must abandon it as no longer defensible.

What, then, are the distinctive characters of the republican form? Were an answer to this question to be sought, not by recurring [referring back] to principles, but in the application of the term by political writers, to the constitution of different States, no satisfactory one would ever be found. Holland, in which no particle of the supreme authority is derived from the people, has passed almost universally under the denomination of a republic. The same title has been bestowed on Venice, where absolute power over the great body of the people is exercised, in the most absolute manner, by a small body of hereditary nobles. Poland, which is a mixture of aristocracy and of monarchy in their worst forms, has been dignified with the same appellation [designation]. The government of England, which has one republican branch only, combined with an hereditary aristocracy and monarchy, has, with equal impropriety, been frequently placed on the list of republics. These examples, which are nearly as dissimilar to each other as to a genuine republic, show the extreme inaccuracy with which the term has been used in political disquisitions.

If we resort for a criterion to the different principles on which different forms of government are established, we may define a republic to be, or at least may bestow that name on, a government which derives all its powers directly or indirectly from the great body of the people, and is administered by persons holding their offices during pleasure, for a limited period, or during good behavior. It is ESSENTIAL to such a government that it be derived from the great body of the society, not from an inconsiderable proportion, or a favored class of it; otherwise a handful of tyrannical nobles, exercising their oppressions by a delegation of their powers, might aspire to the rank of republicans, and claim for their government the honorable title of republic. It is SUFFICIENT for such a government that the persons administering it be appointed, either directly or indirectly, by the people; and that they hold their appointments by either of the tenures just specified; otherwise every government in the United States, as well as every other popular government that has been or can be well organized or well executed, would be degraded from the republican character. According to the constitution of every State in the Union, some or other of the officers of government are appointed indirectly only by the people. According to most of them, the chief magistrate himself is so appointed. And according to one, this mode of appointment is extended to one of the co-ordinate branches of the legislature. According to all the constitutions, also, the tenure of the highest offices is extended to a definite period, and in many instances, both within the legislative and executive departments, to a period of years. According to the provisions of most of the constitutions, again, as well as according to the most respectable and received opinions on the subject, the members of the judiciary department are to retain their offices by the firm tenure of good behavior.

On comparing the Constitution planned by the convention with the standard here fixed, we perceive at once that it is, in the most rigid sense, conformable to it. The House of Representatives, like that of one branch at least of all the State legislatures, is elected immediately by the great body of the people. The Senate, like the present Congress, and the Senate of Maryland, derives its appointment indirectly from the people. The President is indirectly derived from the choice of the people, according to the example in most of the States. Even the judges, with all other officers of the Union, will, as in the several States, be the choice, though a remote choice, of the people themselves, the duration of the appointments is equally conformable to the republican standard, and to the model of State constitutions The House of Representatives is periodically elective, as in all the States; and for the period of two years, as in the State of South Carolina. The Senate is elective, for the period of six years; which is but one year more than the period of the Senate of Maryland, and but two more than that of the Senates of New York

and Virginia. The President is to continue in office for the period of four years; as in New York and Delaware, the chief magistrate is elected for three years, and in South Carolina for two years. In the other States the election is annual. In several of the States, however, no constitutional provision is made for the impeachment of the chief magistrate. And in Delaware and Virginia he is not impeachable till out of office. The President of the United States is impeachable at any time during his continuance in office. The tenure by which the judges are to hold their places, is, as it unquestionably ought to be, that of good behavior. The tenure of the ministerial offices generally, will be a subject of legal regulation, conformably to the reason of the case and the example of the State constitutions.

Could any further proof be required of the republican complexion of this system, the most decisive one might be found in its absolute prohibition of titles of nobility, both under the federal and the State governments; and in its express guaranty of the republican form to each of the latter.

"But it was not sufficient," say the adversaries of the proposed Constitution, "for the convention to adhere to the republican form. They ought, with equal care, to have preserved the FEDERAL form, which regards the Union as a CONFEDERACY of sovereign states; instead of which, they have framed a NATIONAL government, which regards the Union as a CONSOLIDATION of the States." And it is asked by what authority this bold and radical innovation was undertaken? The handle which has been made of this objection requires that it should be examined with some precision.

Without inquiring into the accuracy of the distinction on which the objection is founded, it will be necessary to a just estimate of its force, first, to ascertain the real character of the government in question; secondly, to inquire how far the convention were authorized to propose such a government; and thirdly, how far the duty they owed to their country could supply any defect of regular authority.

First. In order to ascertain the real character of the government, it may be considered in relation to the foundation on which it is to be established; to the sources from which its ordinary powers are to be drawn; to the operation of those powers; to the extent of them; and to the authority by which future changes in the government are to be introduced.

On examining the first relation, it appears, on one hand, that the Constitution is to be founded on the assent and ratification of the people of America, given by deputies elected for the special purpose; but, on the other, that this assent and ratification is to be given by the people, not as individuals composing one entire nation, but as composing the distinct and independent States to which they respectively belong. It is to be the assent and ratification of the several States, derived from the supreme authority in each State, the authority of the people themselves. The act, therefore, establishing the Constitution, will not be a NATIONAL, but a FEDERAL act.

That it will be a federal and not a national act, as these terms are understood by the objectors; the act of the people, as forming so many independent States, not as forming one aggregate nation, is obvious from this single consideration, that it is to result neither from the decision of a MAJORITY of the people of the Union, nor from that of a MAJORITY of the States. It must result from the UNANIMOUS assent of the several States that are parties to it, differing no otherwise from their ordinary assent than in its being expressed, not by the legislative authority, but by that of the people themselves. Were the people regarded in this transaction as forming one nation, the will of the majority of the whole people of the United States would bind the minority, in the same manner as the majority in each State must bind the minority; and the will of the majority must be determined either by a comparison of the individual votes, or by considering the will of the majority of the States as evidence of the will of a majority of the people of the United States. Neither of these rules have been adopted. Each State, in ratifying the Constitution, is considered as a sovereign body, independent of all others, and only to be bound by its own voluntary act. In this relation, then, the new Constitution will, if established, be a FEDERAL, and not a NATIONAL constitution.

The next relation is, to the sources from which the ordinary powers of government are to be derived. The House of Representatives will derive its powers from the people of America; and the people will be represented in the same proportion, and on the same principle, as they are in the legislature of a particular State. So far the government is NATIONAL, not FEDERAL. The Senate, on the other hand, will derive its powers from the States, as political and coequal societies; and these will be represented on the principle of equality in the Senate, as they now are in the existing Congress. So far the government is FEDERAL, not NATIONAL. The executive power will be derived from a very compound source. The immediate election of the President is to be made by the States in their political characters. The

votes allotted to them are in a compound ratio, which considers them partly as distinct and coequal societies, partly as unequal members of the same society. The eventual election, again, is to be made by that branch of the legislature which consists of the national representatives; but in this particular act they are to be thrown into the form of individual delegations, from so many distinct and coequal bodies politic. From this aspect of the government it appears to be of a mixed character, presenting at least as many FEDERAL as NATIONAL features.

The difference between a federal and national government, as it relates to the OPERATION OF THE GOVERNMENT, is supposed to consist in this, that in the former the powers operate on the political bodies composing the Confederacy, in their political capacities; in the latter, on the individual citizens composing the nation, in their individual capacities. On trying the Constitution by this criterion, it falls under the NATIONAL, not the FEDERAL character; though perhaps not so completely as has been understood. In several cases, and particularly in the trial of controversies to which States may be parties, they must be viewed and proceeded against in their collective and political capacities only. So far the national countenance of the government on this side seems to be disfigured by a few federal features. But this blemish is perhaps unavoidable in any plan; and the operation of the government on the people, in their individual capacities, in its ordinary and most essential proceedings, may, on the whole, designate it, in this relation, a NATIONAL government.

But if the government be national with regard to the OPERATION of its powers, it changes its aspect again when we contemplate it in relation to the EXTENT of its powers. The idea of a national government involves in it, not only an authority over the individual citizens, but an indefinite supremacy over all persons and things, so far as they are objects of lawful government. Among a people consolidated into one nation, this supremacy is completely vested in the national legislature. Among communities united for particular purposes, it is vested partly in the general and partly in the municipal legislatures. In the former case, all local authorities are subordinate to the supreme; and may be controlled, directed, or abolished by it at pleasure. In the latter, the local or municipal authorities form distinct and independent portions of the supremacy, no more subject, within their respective spheres, to the general authority, than the general authority is subject to them, within its own sphere. In this relation, then, the proposed government cannot be deemed a NATIONAL one; since its jurisdiction extends to certain enumerated objects only, and leaves to the several States a residuary [residual; left over] and inviolable sovereignty over all other objects. It is true that in controversies relating to the boundary between the two jurisdictions, the tribunal which is ultimately to decide, is to be established under the general government. But this does not change the principle of the case. The decision is to be impartially made, according to the rules of the Constitution; and all the usual and most effectual precautions are taken to secure this impartiality. Some such tribunal is clearly essential to prevent an appeal to the sword and a dissolution of the compact; and that it ought to be established under the general rather than under the local governments, or, to speak more properly, that it could be safely established under the first alone, is a position not likely to be combated.

If we try the Constitution by its last relation to the authority by which amendments are to be made, we find it neither wholly NATIONAL nor wholly FEDERAL. Were it wholly national, the supreme and ultimate authority would reside in the MAJORITY of the people of the Union; and this authority would be competent at all times, like that of a majority of every national society, to alter or abolish its established government. Were it wholly federal, on the other hand, the concurrence of each State in the Union would be essential to every alteration that would be binding on all. The mode provided by the plan of the convention is not founded on either of these principles. In requiring more than a majority, and principles. In requiring more than a majority, and particularly in computing the proportion by STATES, not by CITIZENS, it departs from the NATIONAL and advances towards the FEDERAL character; in rendering the concurrence of less than the whole number of States sufficient, it loses again the FEDERAL and partakes of the NATIONAL character.

The proposed Constitution, therefore, is, in strictness, neither a national nor a federal Constitution, but a composition of both. In its foundation it is federal, not national; in the sources from which the ordinary powers of the government are drawn, it is partly federal and partly national; in the operation of these powers, it is national, not federal; in the extent of them, again, it is federal, not national; and, finally, in the authoritative mode of introducing amendments, it is neither wholly federal nor wholly national.

ASSESSMENT

1. **Summarize** How does Madison define a republic?
2. **Cite Evidence** What evidence does Madison offer to support his claim that the new government will be "neither wholly federal nor wholly national"?
3. **Analyze Interactions** How did *Federalist* No. 39 influence the U.S. Constitution?

[*Federalist* No. 51]

Introduction
Federalist No. 51 was first published on February 8, 1788, and was probably written by James Madison. It argues that the federal system and the separation of powers proposed in the Constitution provide a system of checks and balances that will protect the rights of the people.

Primary Source
TO WHAT expedient [resource], then, shall we finally resort, for maintaining in practice the necessary partition of power among the several departments, as laid down in the Constitution? The only answer that can be given is, that as all these exterior provisions are found to be inadequate, the defect must be supplied, by so contriving the interior structure of the government as that its several constituent parts may, by their mutual relations, be the means of keeping each other in their proper places. Without presuming to undertake a full development of this important idea, I will hazard a few general observations, which may perhaps place it in a clearer light, and enable us to form a more correct judgment of the principles and structure of the government planned by the convention.

In order to lay a due foundation for that separate and distinct exercise of the different powers of government, which to a certain extent is admitted on all hands to be essential to the preservation of liberty, it is evident that each department should have a will of its own; and consequently should be so constituted that the members of each should have as little agency as possible in the appointment of the members of the others. Were this principle rigorously adhered to, it would require that all the appointments for the supreme executive, legislative, and judiciary magistracies should be drawn from the same fountain of authority, the people, through channels having no communication whatever with one another. Perhaps such a plan of constructing the several departments would be less difficult in practice than it may in contemplation appear. Some difficulties, however, and some additional expense would attend the execution of it. Some deviations, therefore, from the principle must be admitted. In the constitution of the judiciary department in particular, it might be inexpedient to insist rigorously on the principle: first, because peculiar qualifications being essential in the members, the primary consideration ought to be to select that mode of choice which best secures these qualifications; secondly, because the permanent tenure by which the appointments are held in that department, must soon destroy all sense of dependence on the authority conferring them.

It is equally evident, that the members of each department should be as little dependent as possible on those of the others, for the emoluments [monetary payments] annexed to their offices. Were the executive magistrate, or the judges, not independent of the legislature in this particular, their independence in every other would be merely nominal.

But the great security against a gradual concentration of the several powers in the same department, consists in giving to those who administer each department the necessary constitutional means and personal motives to resist encroachments [intrusions; unwanted advances] of the others. The provision for defense must in this, as in all other cases, be made commensurate to the danger of attack. Ambition must be made to counteract ambition. The interest of the man must be connected with the constitutional rights of the place. It may be a reflection on human nature, that such devices should be necessary to control the abuses of government. But what is government itself, but the greatest of all reflections on human nature? If men were angels, no government would be necessary. If angels were to govern men, neither external nor internal controls on government would be necessary. In framing a government which is to be administered by men over men, the great difficulty lies in this: you must first enable the government to control the governed; and in the next place oblige it to control itself. A dependence on the people is, no doubt, the primary control on the government; but experience has taught mankind the necessity of auxiliary precautions.

This policy of supplying, by opposite and rival interests, the defect of better motives, might be traced through the whole system of human affairs, private as well as public. We see it particularly displayed in all the subordinate distributions of power, where the constant aim is to divide and arrange the several offices in such a manner as that each may be a check on the other—that the private interest of every individual may be a sentinel over the public rights. These inventions of prudence cannot be less requisite in the distribution of the supreme powers of the State.

But it is not possible to give to each department an equal power of self-defense. In republican government, the legislative authority necessarily predominates. The remedy for this inconveniency is to divide the legislature into different branches; and to render them, by different modes of election and different principles of action, as little connected with each other as the nature of their common functions and their common dependence on the society will admit. It may even be necessary to guard against dangerous encroachments by still further precautions. As the weight of the legislative authority requires that it should be thus divided, the weakness of the executive may require, on the other hand, that it should be fortified. An absolute negative on the legislature appears, at first view, to be the natural defense with which the executive magistrate should be armed. But perhaps it would be neither altogether safe nor alone sufficient. On ordinary occasions it might not be exerted with the requisite firmness, and on extraordinary occasions it might be perfidiously [traitorously; treachorously] abused. May not this defect of an absolute negative be supplied by some qualified connection between this weaker department and the weaker branch of the stronger department, by which the latter may be led to support the constitutional rights of the former, without being too much detached from the rights of its own department?

If the principles on which these observations are founded be just, as I persuade myself they are, and they be applied as a criterion to the several State constitutions, and to the federal Constitution it will be found that if the latter does not perfectly correspond with them, the former are infinitely less able to bear such a test.

There are, moreover, two considerations particularly applicable to the federal system of America, which place that system in a very interesting point of view.

First. In a single republic, all the power surrendered by the people is submitted to the administration of a single government; and the usurpations [illegal seizures of power] are guarded against by a division of the government into distinct and separate departments. In the compound republic of America, the power surrendered by the people is first divided between two distinct governments, and then the portion allotted to each subdivided among distinct and separate departments. Hence a double security arises to the rights of the people. The different governments will control each other, at the same time that each will be controlled by itself.

Second. It is of great importance in a republic not only to guard the society against the oppression of its rulers, but to guard one part of the society against the injustice of the other part. Different interests necessarily exist in different classes of citizens. If a majority be united by a common interest, the rights of the minority will be insecure. There are but two methods of providing against this evil: the one by creating a will in the community independent of the majority—that is, of the society itself; the other, by comprehending in the society so many separate descriptions of citizens as will render an unjust combination of a majority of the whole very improbable, if not impracticable. The first method prevails in all governments possessing an hereditary or self-appointed authority. This, at best, is but a precarious security; because a power independent of the society may as well espouse the unjust views of the major, as the rightful interests of the minor party, and may possibly be turned against both parties. The second method will be exemplified in the federal republic of the United States. Whilst all authority in it will be derived from and dependent on the society, the society itself will be broken into so many parts, interests, and classes of citizens, that the rights of individuals, or of the minority, will be in little danger from interested combinations of the majority.

In a free government the security for civil rights must be the same as that for religious rights. It consists in the one case in the multiplicity of interests, and in the other in the multiplicity of sects. The degree of security in both cases will depend on the number of interests and sects; and this may be presumed to depend on the extent of country and number of people comprehended under the same government. This view of the subject must particularly recommend a proper federal system to all the sincere and considerate friends of republican government, since it shows that in exact proportion as the territory of the Union may be formed into more circumscribed Confederacies, or States oppressive combinations of a majority will be facilitated: the best security, under the republican forms, for the rights of every class of citizens, will be diminished: and consequently the stability and independence of some member of the government, the only other security, must be proportionately increased. Justice is the end of government. It is the end of civil society. It ever has been and ever will be pursued until it be obtained, or until liberty be lost in the pursuit. In a society under the forms of which the stronger faction can readily unite and oppress the weaker, anarchy may as truly be said to reign as in a state of nature, where the weaker individual is not secured against the violence of the stronger; and as, in the latter state, even the stronger individuals are prompted, by the uncertainty of their condition, to submit to a government which may protect the weak as well as themselves; so, in the former state, will the more powerful factions or parties be gradually induced, by a like motive, to wish for a government which will protect all parties, the weaker as well as the more powerful. It can be little doubted that if the State of Rhode Island was separated from the Confederacy and left to itself, the insecurity of rights under the popular form of government within such narrow limits would be displayed by such reiterated oppressions of factious majorities that some power altogether independent of the people would soon be called for by the voice of the very factions whose misrule had proved the necessity of it.

In the extended republic of the United States, and among the great variety of interests, parties, and sects which it embraces, a coalition of a majority of the whole society could seldom take place on any other principles than those of justice and the general good; whilst there being thus less danger to a minor from the will of a major party, there must be less pretext, also, to provide for the security of the former, by introducing into the government a will not dependent on the latter, or, in other words, a will independent of the society itself. It is no less certain than it is important, notwithstanding the contrary opinions which have been entertained, that the larger the society, provided it lie within a practical sphere, the more duly capable it will be of self-government. And happily for the REPUBLICAN CAUSE, the practicable sphere may be carried to a very great extent, by a judicious modification and mixture of the FEDERAL PRINCIPLE.

ASSESSMENT

1. **Assess an Argument** Do you agree with Madison that, "In a free government the security for civil rights must be the same as that for religious rights"? Considering the history of the United States on the issue of civil rights for both women and racial minorities, in what way is Madison's remark ironic?

2. **Analyze Interactions** What effect did *Federalist* No. 51 have on the final U.S. Constitution?

3. **Explain an Argument** Why does Madison think it is important that the new government exercise a separation of powers?

[*Federalist* No. 78, Alexander Hamilton]

Introduction

The *Federalist Papers* were the brainchild of Alexander Hamilton, who conceived them and recruited James Madison and John Jay to the project. Hamilton is usually credited as the author of 51 of the 85 essays in the collection. Here, he discusses the national judiciary to be established by Article III in the proposed constitution. He emphasizes the vital need for an independent judiciary and its role in the interpretation of laws and the determination of their constitutionality. It was first published April 11, 1788.

Primary Source

WE PROCEED now to an examination of the judiciary department of the proposed government.

In unfolding the defects of the existing Confederation, the utility and necessity of a federal judicature [system of courts] have been clearly pointed out. It is the less necessary to recapitulate the considerations there urged, as the propriety of the institution in the abstract is not disputed; the only questions which have been raised being relative to the manner of constituting it, and to its extent. To these points, therefore, our observations shall be confined.

The manner of constituting it seems to embrace these several objects: 1st. The mode of appointing the judges. 2d. The tenure by which they are to hold their places. 3d. The partition of the judiciary authority between different courts, and their relations to each other.

First. As to the mode of appointing the judges; this is the same with that of appointing the officers of the Union in general, and has been so fully discussed in the

two last numbers, that nothing can be said here which would not be useless repetition.

Second. As to the tenure by which the judges are to hold their places; this chiefly concerns their duration in office; the provisions for their support; the precautions for their responsibility.

According to the plan of the convention, all judges who may be appointed by the United States are to hold their offices during good behavior; which is conformable to the most approved of the State constitutions and among the rest, to that of this State. Its propriety having been drawn into question by the adversaries of that plan, is no light symptom of the rage for objection, which disorders their imaginations and judgments. The standard of good behavior for the continuance in office of the judicial magistracy, is certainly one of the most valuable of the modern improvements in the practice of government. In a monarchy it is an excellent barrier to the despotism of the prince; in a republic it is a no less excellent barrier to the encroachments and oppressions of the representative body. And it is the best expedient which can be devised in any government, to secure a steady, upright, and impartial administration of the laws.

Whoever attentively considers the different departments of power must perceive, that, in a government in which they are separated from each other, the judiciary, from the nature of its functions, will always be the least dangerous to the political rights of the Constitution; because it will be least in a capacity to annoy or injure them. The Executive not only dispenses the honors, but holds the sword of the community. The legislature not only commands the purse, but prescribes the rules by which the duties and rights of every citizen are to be regulated. The judiciary, on the contrary, has no influence over either the sword or the purse; no direction either of the strength or of the wealth of the society; and can take no active resolution whatever. It may truly be said to have neither FORCE nor WILL, but merely judgment; and must ultimately depend upon the aid of the executive arm even for the efficacy of its judgments.

This simple view of the matter suggests several important consequences. It proves incontestably, that the judiciary is beyond comparison the weakest of the three departments of power; that it can never attack with success either of the other two; and that all possible care is requisite to enable it to defend itself against their attacks. It equally proves, that though individual oppression may now and then proceed from the courts of justice, the general liberty of the people can never be endangered from that quarter; I mean so long as the judiciary remains truly distinct from both the legislature and the Executive. For I agree, that "there is no liberty, if the power of judging be not separated from the legislative and executive powers." And it proves, in the last place, that as liberty can have nothing to fear from the judiciary alone, but would have every thing to fear from its union with either of the other departments; that as all the effects of such a union must ensue from a dependence of the former on the latter, notwithstanding a nominal and apparent separation; that as, from the natural feebleness of the judiciary, it is in continual jeopardy of being overpowered, awed, or influenced by its co-ordinate branches; and that as nothing can contribute so much to its firmness and independence as permanency in office, this quality may therefore be justly regarded as an indispensable ingredient in its constitution, and, in a great measure, as the citadel of the public justice and the public security.

The complete independence of the courts of justice is peculiarly essential in a limited Constitution. By a limited Constitution, I understand one which contains certain specified exceptions to the legislative authority; such, for instance, as that it shall pass no bills of attainder, no ex post facto laws, and the like. Limitations of this kind can be preserved in practice no other way than through the medium of courts of justice, whose duty it must be to declare all acts contrary to the manifest tenor of the Constitution void. Without this, all the reservations of particular rights or privileges would amount to nothing.

Some perplexity respecting the rights of the courts to pronounce legislative acts void, because contrary to the Constitution, has arisen from an imagination that the doctrine would imply a superiority of the judiciary to the legislative power. It is urged that the authority which can declare the acts of another void, must necessarily be superior to the one whose acts may be declared void. As this doctrine is of great importance in all the American constitutions, a brief discussion of the ground on which it rests cannot be unacceptable.

There is no position which depends on clearer principles, than that every act of a delegated authority, contrary to the tenor of the commission under which it is exercised, is void. No legislative act, therefore, contrary to the Constitution, can be valid. To deny this, would be to affirm, that the deputy is greater than his principal; that the servant is above his master; that the representatives of the people are superior to the people themselves; that men acting by virtue of powers, may do not

only what their powers do not authorize, but what they forbid.

If it be said that the legislative body are themselves the constitutional judges of their own powers, and that the construction they put upon them is conclusive upon the other departments, it may be answered, that this cannot be the natural presumption, where it is not to be collected from any particular provisions in the Constitution. It is not otherwise to be supposed, that the Constitution could intend to enable the representatives of the people to substitute their will to that of their constituents. It is far more rational to suppose, that the courts were designed to be an intermediate body between the people and the legislature, in order, among other things, to keep the latter within the limits assigned to their authority. The interpretation of the laws is the proper and peculiar [particular] province of the courts. A constitution is, in fact, and must be regarded by the judges, as a fundamental law. It therefore belongs to them to ascertain its meaning, as well as the meaning of any particular act proceeding from the legislative body. If there should happen to be an irreconcilable variance between the two, that which has the superior obligation and validity ought, of course, to be preferred; or, in other words, the Constitution ought to be preferred to the statute, the intention of the people to the intention of their agents.

Nor does this conclusion by any means suppose a superiority of the judicial to the legislative power. It only supposes that the power of the people is superior to both; and that where the will of the legislature, declared in its statutes, stands in opposition to that of the people, declared in the Constitution, the judges ought to be governed by the latter rather than the former. They ought to regulate their decisions by the fundamental laws, rather than by those which are not fundamental.

This exercise of judicial discretion, in determining between two contradictory laws, is exemplified in a familiar instance. It not uncommonly happens, that there are two statutes existing at one time, clashing in whole or in part with each other, and neither of them containing any repealing clause or expression. In such a case, it is the province of the courts to liquidate and fix their meaning and operation. So far as they can, by any fair construction, be reconciled to each other, reason and law conspire to dictate that this should be done; where this is impracticable, it becomes a matter of necessity to give effect to one, in exclusion of the other. The rule which has obtained in the courts for determining their relative validity is, that the last in order of time shall be preferred to the first. But this is a mere rule of construction, not derived from any positive law, but from the nature and reason of the thing. It is a rule not enjoined upon the courts by legislative provision, but adopted by themselves, as consonant to truth and propriety, for the direction of their conduct as interpreters of the law. They thought it reasonable, that between the interfering acts of an EQUAL authority, that which was the last indication of its will should have the preference.

But in regard to the interfering acts of a superior and subordinate authority, of an original and derivative power, the nature and reason of the thing indicate the converse of that rule as proper to be followed. They teach us that the prior act of a superior ought to be preferred to the subsequent act of an inferior and subordinate authority; and that accordingly, whenever a particular statute contravenes the Constitution, it will be the duty of the judicial tribunals to adhere to the latter and disregard the former.

It can be of no weight to say that the courts, on the pretense of a repugnancy [something that is offensive], may substitute their own pleasure to the constitutional intentions of the legislature. This might as well happen in the case of two contradictory statutes; or it might as well happen in every adjudication [judgment] upon any single statute. The courts must declare the sense of the law; and if they should be disposed to exercise WILL instead of JUDGMENT, the consequence would equally be the substitution of their pleasure to that of the legislative body. The observation, if it prove any thing, would prove that there ought to be no judges distinct from that body.

If, then, the courts of justice are to be considered as the bulwarks [defenders] of a limited Constitution against legislative encroachments, this consideration will afford a strong argument for the permanent tenure of judicial offices, since nothing will contribute so much as this to that independent spirit in the judges which must be essential to the faithful performance of so arduous a duty.

This independence of the judges is equally requisite to guard the Constitution and the rights of individuals from the effects of those ill humors, which the arts of designing men, or the influence of particular conjunctures, sometimes disseminate among the people themselves, and which, though they speedily give place to better information, and more deliberate reflection, have a tendency, in the meantime, to occasion dangerous innovations in the government, and serious oppressions

of the minor party in the community. Though I trust the friends of the proposed Constitution will never concur with its enemies, in questioning that fundamental principle of republican government, which admits the right of the people to alter or abolish the established Constitution, whenever they find it inconsistent with their happiness, yet it is not to be inferred from this principle, that the representatives of the people, whenever a momentary inclination happens to lay hold of a majority of their constituents, incompatible with the provisions in the existing Constitution, would, on that account, be justifiable in a violation of those provisions; or that the courts would be under a greater obligation to connive [secretly work to injure] at infractions in this shape, than when they had proceeded wholly from the cabals [secret political groups] of the representative body. Until the people have, by some solemn and authoritative act, annulled or changed the established form, it is binding upon themselves collectively, as well as individually; and no presumption, or even knowledge, of their sentiments, can warrant their representatives in a departure from it, prior to such an act. But it is easy to see, that it would require an uncommon portion of fortitude in the judges to do their duty as faithful guardians of the Constitution, where legislative invasions of it had been instigated by the major voice of the community.

But it is not with a view to infractions of the Constitution only, that the independence of the judges may be an essential safeguard against the effects of occasional ill humors in the society. These sometimes extend no farther than to the injury of the private rights of particular classes of citizens, by unjust and partial laws. Here also the firmness of the judicial magistracy is of vast importance in mitigating the severity and confining the operation of such laws. It not only serves to moderate the immediate mischiefs of those which may have been passed, but it operates as a check upon the legislative body in passing them; who, perceiving that obstacles to the success of iniquitous [wicked] intention are to be expected from the scruples [hesitations; doubts] of the courts, are in a manner compelled, by the very motives of the injustice they meditate, to qualify their attempts. This is a circumstance calculated to have more influence upon the character of our governments, than but few may be aware of. The benefits of the integrity and moderation of the judiciary have already been felt in more States than one; and though they may have displeased those whose sinister expectations they may have disappointed, they must have commanded the esteem and applause of all the virtuous and disinterested. Considerate men, of every description, ought to prize whatever will tend to beget or fortify that temper in the courts: as no man can be sure that he may not be to-morrow the victim of a spirit of injustice, by which he may be a gainer to-day. And every man must now feel, that the inevitable tendency of such a spirit is to sap the foundations of public and private confidence, and to introduce in its stead universal distrust and distress.

That inflexible and uniform adherence to the rights of the Constitution, and of individuals, which we perceive to be indispensable in the courts of justice, can certainly not be expected from judges who hold their offices by a temporary commission. Periodical appointments, however regulated, or by whomsoever made, would, in some way or other, be fatal to their necessary independence. If the power of making them was committed either to the Executive or legislature, there would be danger of an improper complaisance [willingness to please] to the branch which possessed it; if to both, there would be an unwillingness to hazard the displeasure of either; if to the people, or to persons chosen by them for the special purpose, there would be too great a disposition to consult popularity, to justify a reliance that nothing would be consulted but the Constitution and the laws.

There is yet a further and a weightier reason for the permanency of the judicial offices, which is deducible from the nature of the qualifications they require. It has been frequently remarked, with great propriety, that a voluminous code of laws is one of the inconveniences necessarily connected with the advantages of a free government. To avoid an arbitrary discretion in the courts, it is indispensable that they should be bound down by strict rules and precedents, which serve to define and point out their duty in every particular case that comes before them; and it will readily be conceived from the variety of controversies which grow out of the folly and wickedness of mankind, that the records of those precedents must unavoidably swell to a very considerable bulk, and must demand long and laborious study to acquire a competent knowledge of them. Hence it is, that there can be but few men in the society who will have sufficient skill in the laws to qualify them for the stations of judges. And making the proper deductions for the ordinary depravity [moral corruption] of human nature, the number must be still smaller of those who unite the requisite integrity with the requisite knowledge. These considerations apprise us, that the government can have no great option between fit character; and that a temporary duration in office,

which would naturally discourage such characters from quitting a lucrative line of practice to accept a seat on the bench, would have a tendency to throw the administration of justice into hands less able, and less well qualified, to conduct it with utility and dignity. In the present circumstances of this country, and in those in which it is likely to be for a long time to come, the disadvantages on this score would be greater than they may at first sight appear; but it must be confessed, that they are far inferior to those which present themselves under the other aspects of the subject.

Upon the whole, there can be no room to doubt that the convention acted wisely in copying from the models of those constitutions which have established good behavior as the tenure of their judicial offices, in point of duration; and that so far from being blamable on this account, their plan would have been inexcusably defective, if it had wanted this important feature of good government. The experience of Great Britain affords an illustrious comment on the excellence of the institution.

ASSESSMENT

1. **Summarize** What does Hamilton say is the role of judges?
2. **Analyze Interactions** How has *Federalist* No. 78 influenced the U.S. government?

[Farewell Address, George Washington]

Introduction

As he prepared to leave office in 1796, President George Washington made a speech describing his vision of the nation's future. The speech became known as Washington's Farewell Address. The speech deals with a wide range of topics, from the need to keep down the nation's debt to the importance of education. The two most enduring ideas from Washington's address were his caution against the dangers of forming political parties, and the issue of neutrality. Washington's ideas about foreign relations influenced American foreign policy for generations.

Primary Source

Let me now take a more comprehensive view, and warn you in the most solemn manner against the baneful [harmful, destructive] effects of the spirit of party generally.

This spirit, unfortunately, is inseparable from our nature, having its root in the strongest passions of the human mind. It exists under different shapes in all governments, more or less stifled, controlled, or repressed; but, in those of the popular form, it is seen in its greatest rankness [state of being excessive and unpleasant], and is truly their worst enemy. . . .

It agitates the community with ill-founded jealousies and false alarms, kindles the animosity of one part against another, foments [stirs up] occasionally riot and insurrection. It opens the door to foreign influence and corruption, which finds a facilitated [made easier] access to the government itself through the channels of party passions. Thus the policy and the will of one country are subjected to the policy and will of another. . . .

So likewise, a passionate attachment of one nation for another produces a variety of evils. Sympathy for the favorite nation, facilitating the illusion of an imaginary common interest in cases where no real common interest exists, and infusing into one the enmities [feelings of hostility] of the other, betrays the former into a participation in the quarrels and wars of the latter without adequate inducement or justification. It leads also to concessions to the favorite nation of privileges denied to others which is apt doubly to injure the nation making the concessions. . . .

The jealousy of a free people ought to be constantly awake, since history and experience prove that foreign influence is one of the most baneful foes of republican government. But that jealousy to be useful must be impartial [not favoring one side]. . . .

The great rule of conduct for us in regard to foreign nations is, in extending our commercial [relating to trade] relations, to have with them as little political connection as possible. So far as we have already formed engagements, let them be fulfilled with perfect good faith. Here let us stop. Europe has a set of primary interests which to us have none; or a very remote relation. Hence she must be engaged in frequent controversies, the causes of which are essentially foreign to our concerns. . . . Why, by interweaving our destiny with that of any part of Europe, entangle our peace and prosperity in the toils of European ambition, rivalship, interest, humor or caprice [sudden change]?

It is our true policy to steer clear of permanent alliances with any portion of the foreign world; so far, I mean, as we are now at liberty to do it; for let me not be understood as capable of patronizing [supporting] infidelity [disloyalty; unfaithfulness] to existing engagements. I hold the maxim [wise saying] no less applicable to public than to private affairs, that honesty is always the best policy. I repeat, therefore, let those engagements be observed in their genuine sense. But, in my opinion, it is unnecessary and would be unwise to extend them.

ASSESSMENT

1. **Determine Author's Purpose** What was Washington's purpose for writing this speech?
2. **Analyze Interactions** In his speech, Washington highlighted the problems with maintaining foreign alliances, but what are some ways that alliances can be constructive and useful?
3. **Assess an Argument** Washington cautions future generations against the nature of political parties and permanent foreign alliances. With the benefit of hindsight, which of these two warnings shows more foresight? Explain your answer.
4. **Draw Conclusions** In what way did Washington demonstrate presidential leadership by issuing his address?

[*Democracy in America, Alexis de Tocqueville*]

Introduction

Alexis de Tocqueville, a young French writer, visited the United States in 1831. During his travels, he observed firsthand the impact of Jacksonian democracy. After returning to France, Tocqueville began writing *Democracy in America*, a detailed look at American politics, society, economics, religion, and law. The first volume was published in 1835. The book is still studied and quoted by historians and politicians today. In these excerpts from *Democracy in America*, Tocqueville discusses the role of the American people in their government and gives his view of the American character.

Primary Source

The general principles which are the groundwork of modern constitutions–principles which were imperfectly known in Europe, and not completely triumphant even in Great Britain, in the seventeenth century–were all recognized and determined by the laws of New England: the intervention of the people in public affairs, the free voting of taxes, the responsibility of authorities, personal liberty, and trial by jury, were all positively established without discussion. From these fruitful principles consequences have been derived and applications have been made such as no nation in Europe has yet ventured to attempt.

. . . it is at least true that in the United States the county and the township are always based upon the same principle, namely, that everyone is the best judge of what concerns himself alone, and the most proper person to supply his private wants.

In America the people name those who make the law and those who execute it; they themselves form the jury that punishes infractions [violations] of the law. Not only are the institutions democratic in their principle, but also in all their developments; thus the people name their representatives directly and generally choose them every year in order to keep them more completely under their dependence. It is therefore really the people who direct. . . . This majority is composed principally of peaceful citizens who, either by taste or by interest, sincerely desire the good of the country. Around them parties constantly agitate. . . .

The American taken randomly [chosen without a plan] will therefore be a man ardent [intense] in his desires, enterprising [full of energy; willing to take on new projects], adventurous—above all, an innovator [a person who creates a new way of doing something]. This spirit is in fact found in all his works; he introduces it into his political laws, his religious doctrines, his theories of social economy, his private industry; he brings it with him everywhere, into the depths of the woods as into the heart of towns.

To evade the bondage of system and habit, of family maxims, class-opinions, and in some degree, of national prejudices; to accept tradition only as a means of information, and existing facts only as a lesson used in doing otherwise and doing better; to seek the reason of things for oneself, and in oneself alone; to tend to results without being bound to means, and to aim at the substance through the form;—such are the principle characteristics of what I shall call the philosophical method of the Americans. But if I go further, and if I seek among those characteristics the principle one which includes almost all the rest, I discover that, in most operations of the mind, each American appeals only to the individual effort of his own understanding.

ASSESSMENT

1. **Determine Central Ideas** In what way do the people "direct" the American democracy, according to Tocqueville?
2. **Summarize** What impressed Tocqueville during his time in America? Cite examples to support your answer.
3. **Draw Conclusions** In what way could Tocqueville's book be relevant today?

[Debate Over Nullification, Webster and Calhoun]

Introduction

The debates between Daniel Webster of Massachusetts and John C. Calhoun of South Carolina concerned the supremacy [highest power or authority] of the federal government over state governments. Many Southerners, in response to tariff laws that favored the North, supported the concept of "nullification." Nullification held that states had the right to disobey laws of Congress they thought were unconstitutional. Webster argued that nullification would destroy the Union. Calhoun supported nullification. In March 1833, they debated the issue on the floor of the United States Senate.

Primary Sources

The Constitution Not a Compact Between Sovereign States: Daniel Webster

I deny that any man can state accurately what was done by the people in establishing the present Constitution, and then state accurately what the people, or any part of them, must now do to get rid of its obligations, without stating an undeniable case of the overthrow of government. I admit, of course, that the people may, if they choose, overthrow the government. But, then, that is revolution.

The doctrine now contended for is, that, by nullification or secession, the obligations and authority of the government may be set aside or rejected, without revolution. . . .

The Constitution does not provide for events which must be preceded by its own destruction. SECESSION, therefore, since it must bring these consequences with it, is REVOUTIONARY, and NULLIFICATION is equally REVOLUTIONARY. What is revolution? Why, Sir, that is revolution which overturns, or controls, or successfully resists, the existing public authority; that which arrests the exercise of the supreme power; that which introduces a new paramount [ranking higher than any other] authority into the rule of the State.

Now, Sir, this is the precise object of nullification. It attempts to supersede [to cause to be set aside and replaced by something else] the supreme legislative authority. It arrests the arm of the executive magistrate. It interrupts the exercise of the accustomed judicial power. Under the name of an ordinance, it declares null and void, within the State, all the revenue laws of the United States. . . .

If Carolina now shall effectually resist the laws of Congress; if she shall be her own judge, take her remedy into her own hands, obey the laws of the Union when she pleases and disobey them when she pleases, she will relieve herself from a paramount power as distinctly as the American Colonies did the same thing in 1776. In other words, she will achieve, as to herself a revolution. . . .

To allow State resistance to the laws of Congress to be rightful and proper, to admit nullification in some States, and yet not expect to see a dismemberment [to divide up or mutilate] of the entire government, appears to me the wildest illusion, and the most extravagant folly.

"Speech in Reply to Daniel Webster on the Force Bill," John C. Calhoun

. . . Where does sovereignty reside? If I have succeeded in establishing the fact that ours is a federal system, as I conceive I conclusively have, that fact of itself determines the question which I have proposed. It is of the very essence of such a system, that the sovereignty [supreme and independent political authority] is in the parts, and not in the whole; . . . the parts are the units in such a system, and the whole is the multiple; and not the whole the unit and the parts the fractions.

Ours, then, is a government of twenty-four sovereignties, united by a constitutional compact, for the purpose of exercising certain powers through a common government as their joint agent, and not a union of the twenty-four sovereignties into one, which, according to the language of the Virginia Resolutions, already cited, would form a consolidation [a merger; union]. . . .

". . . There is no provision in the Constitution to authorize the General Government, through any of its departments, to control the action of the State within the sphere of its reserved powers; and that, of course, according to the principle laid down by the senator from Massachusetts himself, the government of the States, as well as the General Government, has the right to determine the extent of their respective powers, without the right of the part of either to control the other. The necessary result is the veto. . . ."

The States, unless deprived of it, possess the veto power, or what is another name for the same thing, the right of nullification. . . . It is the very shield of State rights, and the only power which that system of injustice against which we have contended for more than thirteen years can be arrested: a system of hostile legislation, of plundering by law, which must necessarily lead to a conflict of arms if not prevented.

ASSESSMENT

1. **Determine Central Ideas** What is Webster's central argument? Cite examples that Webster uses to support his argument.
2. **Determine Central Ideas** How would you summarize Calhoun's argument?
3. **Compare Points of View** How do both speakers use the Constitution in their speeches?
4. **Compare Points of View** With which Senator's argument do you think the Framers would agree?

[*Uncle Tom's Cabin*, Harriet Beecher Stowe]

Introduction

In Harriet Beecher Stowe's controversial story, a decent Kentucky slave owner is forced to sell his slave, Tom. Tom remains kind and gentle, despite losing his family and ending up in the possession of a cruel man named Simon Legree. For the first time, readers began to think of enslaved African Americans as people, rather than as possessions. In this excerpt, Tom is inspected and sold to Legree at an auction.

Primary Source

Various spectators, intending to purchase, or not intending, as the case might be, gathered around the group, handling, examining, and commenting on their various points and faces with the same freedom that a set of jockeys [riders] discuss the merits of a horse. . . .

Tom had been standing wistfully examining the multitude [large number] of faces thronging [filling in] around him, for one whom he would wish to call master. And if you should ever be under the necessity, sir, of selecting, out of two hundred men, one who was to become your absolute owner and disposer, you would, perhaps, realize, just as Tom did, how few there were that you would feel at all comfortable in being made over to. . . .

A little before the sale commenced [began], a short, broad, muscular man . . . elbowed his way through the crowd, like one who is going actively into business; and, coming up to the group, began to examine them systematically. From the moment that Tom saw him approaching, he felt an immediate and revolting horror at him, that increased as he came near. He was evidently, though short, of gigantic strength. His round, bullet head . . . and stiff, wiry, sunburned hair, were rather unprepossessing [unattractive] items. . . . This man proceeded to a very free personal examination of the lot. He seized Tom by the jaw, and pulled open his mouth to inspect his teeth; made him strip up his sleeve, to show his muscle; turned him round, made him jump and spring to show his paces. . . .

Tom stepped upon the block, gave a few anxious looks round; all seemed mingled [mixed] in a common, indistinct noise,—the clatter of the sales man crying off

his qualifications in French and English, the quick fire of French and English bids; and almost in a moment came the final thump of the hammer, and the clear ring of the last syllable of the word "*dollars*" as the auctioneer announced his price, and Tom was made over.—He had a master!

He was pushed from the block;—the short, bullet-headed man seizing him roughly by the shoulder, pushed him to one side, saying in a harsh voice, "Stand there, *you*!"

ASSESSMENT

1. **Compare and Contrast** How might readers who were proslavery and antislavery have responded to Stowe's novel?
2. **Explain an Argument** Why do you think Stowe decided to write a novel to voice her opinions about slavery?
3. **Determine Author's Point of View** In the twentieth and twenty-first centuries, *Uncle Tom's Cabin* has often been criticized for its stereotypical depictions of African Americans. What are some of the limitations to Stowe's perspective in this passage, and how might they affect how contemporary readers view the book?

["A House Divided," Abraham Lincoln]

Introduction

In 1858, two years before he was elected president, Abraham Lincoln ran for a U.S. Senate seat in Illinois. Lincoln was nominated by state Republicans to run against Democrat Stephen Douglas. Upon accepting the nomination, Lincoln addressed the increasingly incendiary issue of slavery. The U.S. Supreme Court had recently ruled that a slave who traveled to a free state remained the property of his or her owner. In his speech, "A House Divided," Lincoln took on this case, called the *Dred Scott* decision, as well as the policies of President James Buchanan, a Democrat.

Primary Source

Mr. President and Gentlemen of the Convention.

If we could first know *where* we are, *whither* we are tending, we could better judge *what* to do, and *how* to do it.

We are now far into the *fifth* year since a policy was initiated with the avowed [openly declared] object and *confident* promise of putting an end to slavery agitation.

Under the operation of that policy, that agitation has not only *not ceased*, but has *constantly augmented* [increased in size].

In *my* opinion it *will* not cease until a *crisis* shall have been reached and passed.

"A house divided against itself cannot stand."

I believe this government cannot endure permanently, half *slave* and half *free*.

I do not expect the Union to be *dissolved,*—I do not expect the house to *fall*; but I do expect it will cease to be divided.

It will become *all* one thing, or *all* the other.

Either the *opponents* of slavery will arrest the further spread of it, and place it where the public mind shall rest in the belief that it is in the course of ultimate extinction; or its *advocates* [people who support a policy] will push it forward till it shall become alike lawful in *all* the States, *old* as well as *new, North* as well as *South*.

ASSESSMENT

1. **Assess an Argument** Do you think Lincoln's argument was convincing? Explain your answer.
2. **Paraphrase** Rewrite this excerpt of Lincoln's speech in your own words.

[*First Inaugural Address, Abraham Lincoln*]

Introduction

When Abraham Lincoln took the oath of office on March 4, 1861, the country was on the brink of civil war. Lincoln used his first address to the nation as president to assure Southern states that he would not interfere with slavery, or prevent enforcement of the Fugitive Slave Act. However, he also made clear his intentions to uphold the Constitution and keep the Union together.

Primary Source

I have no purpose, directly or indirectly, to interfere with the institution of slavery in the States where it exists. I believe I have no lawful right to do so, and I have no inclination to do so.... Resolved, That the maintenance inviolate [safe from violation] of the rights of the States, and especially the right of each State to order and control its own domestic institutions according to its own judgment exclusively, is essential to that balance of power on which the perfection and endurance of our political fabric depend....

There is much controversy about the delivering up of fugitives from service or labor. It is scarcely questioned that this provision was intended by those who made it for the reclaiming of what we call fugitive slaves; and the intention of the lawgiver is the law. All members of Congress swear their support to the whole Constitution—to this provision as much as to any other. To the proposition, then, that slaves whose cases come within the terms of this clause "shall be delivered up" their oaths are unanimous.

I hold that in contemplation of universal law and of the Constitution the Union of these States is perpetual [never ending or changing]... [T]he Union is perpetual... The Union is much older than the Constitution.... But if destruction of the Union by one or by a part only of the States be lawfully possible, the Union is less perfect than before the Constitution, having lost the vital element of perpetuity. It follows from these views that no State upon its own mere motion can lawfully get out of the Union....

I shall take care, as the Constitution itself expressly enjoins upon me, that the laws of the Union be faithfully executed in all the States... [It is] the declared purpose of the Union that it will constitutionally defend and maintain itself. In doing this there needs to be no bloodshed or violence...

Plainly the central idea of secession is the essence of anarchy [society without government]. A majority held in restraint by constitutional checks and limitations, and always changing easily with deliberate changes of popular opinions and sentiments, is the only true sovereign of a free people. Whoever rejects it does of necessity fly to anarchy or to despotism [the rule of absolute power]. Unanimity [agreement by everyone] is impossible. The rule of a minority, as a permanent arrangement, is wholly inadmissible; so that, rejecting the majority principle, anarchy or despotism in some form is all that is left. . . .

In your hands, my dissatisfied fellow-countrymen, and not in mine, is the momentous issue of civil war. The Government will not assail [attack] you. You can have no conflict without being yourselves the aggressors. You have no oath registered in heaven to destroy the Government, while I shall have the most solemn one to "preserve, protect, and defend it."

I am loath [reluctant] to close. We are not enemies, but friends. We must not be enemies. Though passion may have strained it must not break our bonds of affection. The mystic chords of memory, stretching from every battlefield and patriot grave to every living heart and hearthstone all over this broad land, will yet swell the chorus of the Union, when again touched, as surely they will be, by the better angels of our nature.

ASSESSMENT

1. **Determine Author's Purpose** What does Lincoln hope to accomplish with his inaugural address?
2. **Analyze Style and Rhetoric** How would you describe Lincoln's tone toward the South?
3. **Assess an Argument** How do you think leaders of the Confederacy might have reacted to this speech?

[*Emancipation Proclamation, Abraham Lincoln*]

Introduction

Five days after the Union victory at Antietam, Abraham Lincoln issued the Emancipation Proclamation. The presidential decree freed all enslaved persons in states under Confederate control as of January 1, 1863. One of the most important documents in American history, it changed the nature of the Union cause and paved the way for the eventual abolition of slavery by the Thirteenth Amendment in 1865.

Primary Source

Whereas on the twenty-second day of September, in the year of our Lord one thousand eight hundred and sixty-two, a proclamation was issued by the President of the United States, containing, among other things, the following, to wit [namely]:

That on the first day of January, in the year of our Lord one thousand eight hundred and sixty-three, all persons held as slaves within any State or designated part of a State, the people whereof shall then be in rebellion against the United States, shall be then, thenceforward [from then on], and forever free; and the Executive Government of the United States, including the military and naval authority thereof, will recognize and maintain the freedom of such persons, and will do no act or acts to repress such persons, or any of them, in any efforts they may make for their actual freedom. . . .

And by virtue of the power, and for the purpose aforesaid, I do order and declare that all persons held as slaves within said designated States, and parts of States, are, and henceforward shall be free; and that the Executive government of the United States, including the military and naval authorities thereof, will recognize and maintain the freedom of said persons.

And I hereby enjoin [direct; order] upon the people so declared to be free to abstain from all violence, unless in necessary self-defence; and I recommend to them that, in all cases when allowed, they labor faithfully for reasonable wages.

And I further declare and make known, that such persons of suitable condition, will be received into the armed services of the United States to garrison [occupy with troops] forts, positions, stations, and other places, and to man vessels of all sorts in said service.

And upon this act, sincerely believed to be an act of justice, warranted [authorized; justified] by the Constitution, upon military necessity, I invoke the considerate judgment of mankind, and the gracious favor of Almighty God. . . .

ASSESSMENT

1. **Draw Conclusions** The number of enslaved people who were freed because of the Emancipation Proclamation increased gradually over time. Why do you think that was?
2. **Determine Author's Purpose** Why do you think President Lincoln issued the proclamation? Explain your answer.

3. **Explain an Argument** What justification does Lincoln give for issuing the proclamation?
4. **Assess an Argument** Do you agree with the justifications you cited in the previous answer? Why or why not?

[*Gettysburg Address, Abraham Lincoln*]

Introduction

At the Battle of Gettysburg, more than 51,000 Confederate and Union soldiers were listed as wounded, missing, or dead. President Lincoln gave this brief speech at the dedication of the Gettysburg National Cemetery on November 19, 1863. The five known manuscript copies of the speech differ slightly and historians debate which version Lincoln actually delivered. But the address is considered one of the most eloquent and moving speeches in American history. As Lincoln described the significance of the war, he invoked the Declaration of Independence and its principles of liberty and equality, and he spoke of "a new birth of freedom."

Primary Source

Four score [a group of twenty] and seven years ago our fathers brought forth on this continent, a new nation, conceived [planned] in Liberty, and dedicated to the proposition [judgment or opinion] that all men are created equal.

Now we are engaged in a great civil war, testing whether that nation, or any nation so conceived and so dedicated, can long endure. We are met on a great battle-field of that war. We have come to dedicate a portion of that field, as a final resting place for those who here gave their lives that the nation might live. It is altogether fitting and proper that we should do this.

But, in a larger sense, we can not dedicate—we can not consecrate [make sacred]—we can not hallow [honor as holy]—this ground. The brave men, living and dead, who struggled here, have consecrated it, far above our poor power to add or detract. The world will little note, nor long remember what we say here, but it can never forget what they did here. It is for us the living, rather, to be dedicated here to the unfinished work which they who fought here have thus far so nobly advanced. It is rather for us to be here dedicated to the great task remaining before us—that from these honored dead we take increased devotion to that cause for which they gave the last full measure of devotion—that we here highly resolve [decide] that these dead shall not have died in vain—that this nation, under God, shall have a new birth of freedom—and that government of the people, by the people, for the people, shall not perish from the earth.

ASSESSMENT

1. **Determine Author's Purpose** Why does Lincoln deliver this speech, and what effect does he hope it will have on the nation?
2. **Compare and Contrast** How might Northerners and Southerners have responded to this address by Lincoln?
3. **Draw Conclusions** What do you think makes this speech so powerful, and why is it considered so important to American history?

[*Second Inaugural Address, Abraham Lincoln*]

Introduction

Lincoln delivered his second inaugural address just over a month before his death. He spoke about the war, slavery, and the need "to bind up the nation's wounds." The speech's closing words of reconciliation and healing are today carved in the walls of the Lincoln Memorial.

Primary Source

. . . On the occasion corresponding to this four years ago all thoughts were anxiously directed to an impending civil war. All dreaded it, all sought to avert it. While the inaugural address was being delivered from this place, devoted altogether to saving the Union without war, insurgent [rebelling against authority or government] agents were in the city seeking to destroy it without war—seeking to dissolve the Union and divide effects by negotiation. Both parties deprecated [expressed disapproval of] war, but one of them would make war rather than let the nation survive, and the other would accept war rather than let it perish, and the war came.

One-eighth of the whole population were colored slaves, not distributed generally over the Union, but localized in the southern part of it. These slaves consti- tuted a peculiar [special] and powerful interest. All knew that this interest was somehow the cause of the war. To strengthen, perpetuate, and extend this interest was the object for which the insurgents would rend [tear apart] the Union even by war, while the Government claimed no right to do more than to restrict the territorial enlarge- ment of it. Neither party expected for the war the mag- nitude or the duration which it has already attained. Neither anticipated that the cause of the conflict might cease with or even before the conflict itself should cease. Each looked for an easier triumph, and a result less fun- damental and astounding. Both read the same Bible and pray to the same God, and each invokes His aid against the other. . . . Fondly [with trust] do we hope, fervently [with strong emotion] do we pray, that this mighty scourge of war may speedily pass away. Yet, if God wills that it continue until all the wealth piled by the bonds- man's two hundred and fifty years of unrequited [with nothing given in return] toil shall be sunk, and until every drop of blood drawn with the lash shall be paid by another drawn with the sword, as was said three thousand years ago, so still it must be said "the judgments of the Lord are true and righteous [morally correct] altogether."

With malice toward none, with charity for all, with firmness in the right as God gives us to see the right, let us strive on to finish the work we are in, to bind up the nation's wounds, to care for him who shall have borne the battle and for his widow and his orphan, to do all which may achieve and cherish a just and lasting peace among ourselves and with all nations.

["I Will Fight No More Forever," Chief Joseph]

Introduction
In 1877, the U.S. government ordered members of the Nez Percé Nation to move off their lands in western Oregon onto a reservation in Idaho. Instead, about 800 Nez Percés tried to escape to Canada. This group included Hin-mah-too-yah-latkekt, more commonly known as Chief Joseph. The Nez Percé traveled over 1,500 miles across Idaho and Montana, battling the U.S. Army along the way. Finally, with fewer than 500 of his people remaining and only 40 miles from Canada, Chief Joseph surrendered. On October 5, the exhausted survivors surrendered. Chief Joseph's speech has become a famous symbol of the resistance and conquest of Native Americans in the West.

Primary Source
I am tired of fighting. Our chiefs are killed. Looking Glass is dead. Toohulhulsote is dead. The old men are all dead. It is the young men who say yes or no. He who led the young men is dead.

It is cold and we have no blankets. The little children are freezing to death. My people, some of them, have run away to the hills and have no blankets, no food. No one knows where they are—perhaps freezing to death. I want to have time to look for my children and see how many I can find. Maybe I shall find them among the dead.

Hear me, my chiefs. I am tired. My heart is sick and sad. From where the sun now stands, I will fight no more forever.

ASSESSMENT

1. **Cite Evidence** In what part of the speech does Lincoln say that Southerners tried to secede without violence? Cite a specific example from the text.
2. **Draw Conclusions** Based on this address, how do you think Lincoln would have dealt with Southern states returning to the Union if he had lived to complete his second term? Explain your answer.

ASSESSMENT

1. **Draw Inferences** What does Chief Joseph's speech reveal about the treatment of Native American groups during this time period?
2. **Assess an Argument** Do you think you would have agreed with Chief Joseph if you were one of the chiefs to whom he was speaking? Why or why not?
3. **Evaluate Explanations** Why do you think this short speech has become so admired and famous?

[Preamble to the Platform of the Populist Party]

Introduction

The People's, or Populist, Party adopted its party platform in 1892 at its national convention in Omaha, Nebraska. The movement, which emerged from the Farmer's Alliance in the 1880s, sought political reforms and a redistribution of political and economic power.

Primary Source

The conditions which surround us best justify our co-operation; we meet in the midst of a nation brought to the verge of moral, political, and material [financial] ruin. Corruption dominates the ballot-box, the Legislatures, the Congress, and touches even the ermine of the bench. . . . The fruits of the toil [labor] of millions are boldly stolen to build up colossal fortunes for a few, unprecedented [never having happened or existed before] in the history of mankind; and the possessors of these, in turn, despise the Republic and endanger liberty. From the same prolific [producing a lot of something] womb of governmental injustice we breed the two great classes—tramps and millionaires. . . .

We have witnessed for more than a quarter of a century the struggles of the two great political parties for power and plunder [loot], while grievous [causing grief or suffering] wrongs have been inflicted upon the suffering people. We charge that the controlling influences dominating both these parties have permitted the existing dreadful conditions to develop without serious effort to prevent or restrain them. . . .

We believe that the power of government—in other words, of the people—should be expanded . . . to the end [result] that oppression, injustice, and poverty shall eventually cease in the land. . . .

ASSESSMENT

1. **Distinguish Among Fact, Opinion, and Reasoned Judgment** Which part(s), if any, of the first sentence in the platform are fact, which opinion, and which reasoned judgment?

2. **Identify Supporting Details** List three details from the platform that support the Populist Party's position.

3. **Draw Conclusions** What types of laws do you think the Populist Party might support? Give specific examples.

[*How the Other Half Lives: Jacob Riis*]

Introduction

Jacob Riis immigrated to the United States from Denmark in 1870. After living for several years in extreme poverty, he found a job as a police reporter for the *New York Tribune*. He became one of the leading muckrakers of the Progressive Era. Riis's writing and photographs helped expose the harsh living conditions in the crowded tenements of New York City. This excerpt is from Riis's 1890 book, *How the Other Half Lives*.

Primary Source

The problem of the children becomes, in these swarms, to the last degree perplexing. Their very number make one stand aghast [horrified]. I have already given instances of the packing of the child population in East Side tenements. They might be continued indefinitely until the array [orderly arrangement] would be enough to startle any community. For, be it remembered, these children with the training they receive—or do not receive—with the instincts they inherit and absorb in their growing up, are to be our future rulers, if our theory of government is worth anything. More than a working majority of our voters now register from the tenements.

I counted the other day the little ones, up to ten years or so, in a Bayard Street tenement that for a yard has a triangular space in the center with sides fourteen or fifteen feet long, just room enough for a row of ill-smelling closets [toilets] at the base of the triangle and a hydrant at the apex [highest point]. There was about as much light in this "yard" as in the average cellar. I gave up my self-imposed task in despair when I had counted one hundred and twenty-eight in forty families. . . .

Bodies of drowned children turn up in the rivers right along since summer whom no one seems to know anything about. When last spring some workmen, while moving a pile of lumber on a North River pier, found under the last plank the body of a little lad crushed to death, no one had missed a boy, though his parents afterward turned up. The truant [a pupil who misses school without permission] officer assuredly does not know, though he spends his life trying to find out, somewhat illogically, perhaps, since the department that employs him admits that thousands of poor children are crowded out of the schools year by year for want of room.

ASSESSMENT

1. **Identify Supporting Details** What details in this excerpt may have shocked readers of the time period? Why do you think muckrakers sought to shock their audience?
2. **Determine Meaning** To whom does the "Other Half" in the title refer? Why do you think Riis uses this phrase?
3. **Identify Cause and Effect** How do you think Riis's account might have contributed to social reforms for tenement housing?

[The Pledge of Allegiance]

Introduction
The Pledge of Allegiance was first written in 1892. It was revised twice before 1954, when the words "under God" were added, and it became the version that is still recited today.

Primary Source
I pledge allegiance [loyalty] to the Flag of the United States of America, and to the Republic for which it stands, one Nation under God, indivisible, with liberty and justice for all.

ASSESSMENT

1. **Determine Central Ideas** What is the main idea of the Pledge of Allegiance?

2. **Determine Author's Point of View** How do you think the author of the Pledge felt about the United States? Cite evidence from the pledge to support your answer.
3. **Analyze Style and Rhetoric** Why do you think the Pledge involves loyalty to the American flag as well as to the United States?
4. **Draw Conclusions** Why do you think we have a national pledge of loyalty to the country? What purpose does it serve?

["Atlanta Exposition Address": Booker T. Washington]

Introduction
In 1895, African American leader Booker T. Washington addressed a predominantly white audience in Atlanta. He urged fellow blacks to build friendly relations with whites and to start "at the bottom" by working at "the common occupations of life." Other black leaders rejected Washington's plan and called it the "Atlanta Compromise."

Primary Source
. . . Ignorant and inexperienced, it is not strange that in the first years of our new life we began at the top instead of at the bottom; that a seat in Congress or the state legislature was more sought than real estate or industrial skill; that the political convention or stump [political] speaking had more attractions than starting a dairy farm or truck garden [garden where vegetables are grown to be sold]. . . .

To those of my race who depend on bettering their condition in a foreign land or who underestimate the importance of cultivating [developing] friendly relations with the Southern white man, who is their next-door neighbor, I would say: "Cast down your bucket where you are" [make use of the resources that you don't realize are all around you]— cast it down in making friends in every manly way of the people of all races by whom we are surrounded.

Cast it down in agriculture, mechanics, in commerce, in domestic service [working as a servant in the employer's home], and in the professions [occupations that require special education, such as medicine or law]. And in this connection it is well to bear in mind that whatever other sins the South may be called to bear, when it comes to business, pure and simple, it is in the South that the Negro is given a man's chance in the commercial world. . . . Our greatest danger is that in the great leap from slavery to freedom we may overlook the fact that the masses of us are to live by the productions of our hands, and fail to keep in mind that we shall prosper in proportion as we learn to dignify and glorify common labour, and put brains and skill into the common occupations of life. . . . No race can prosper till it learns that there is as much dignity in tilling [plowing] a field as in writing a poem. It is at the bottom of life we must begin, and not at the top. Nor should we permit our grievances to overshadow our opportunities. . . .

ASSESSMENT

1. **Determine Central Ideas** What is the main idea of the speech as excerpted here?
2. **Draw Conclusions** Do you agree with the central idea expressed in the address? Cite examples to support your answer.
3. **Analyze Interactions** Why do you think some black leaders rejected the ideas Washington expressed in this address?

[*The Jungle*: Upton Sinclair]

Introduction

When Upton Sinclair published *The Jungle* in 1906, he meant to open America's eyes to the plight of workers in the filthy, dangerous Chicago stockyards. Instead, popular outrage focused on the wider-reaching threat of spoiled meat. Congress quickly passed the nation's first legislation regulating the meat, food, and drug industries. Sinclair, disappointed by his failure to provoke more sympathy for the overworked, underpaid workers, noted "I aimed at the public's heart, and by accident I hit it in the stomach."

Primary Source

There was never the least attention paid to what was cut up for sausage. . . . There would be meat that had tumbled out on the floor, in the dirt and sawdust, where the workers had tramped [walked heavily] and spit uncounted billions of consumption [tuberculosis] germs. There would be meat stored in great piles in rooms; and the water from leaky roofs would drip over it, and thousands of rats would race about on it. It was too dark in these storage places to see well, but a man could run his hand over these piles of meat and sweep off handfuls of the dried dung of rats. These rats were nuisances, and the packers would put poisoned bread out for them; they would die, and then rats, bread, and meat would go into the hoppers [containers] together.

This is no fairy story and no joke; the meat would be shoveled into carts, and the man who did the shoveling would not trouble to lift out a rat even when he saw one—there were things that went into the sausage in comparison with which a poisoned rat was a tidbit [small piece of food]. There was no place for the men to wash their hands before they ate their dinner, and so they made a practice of washing them in the water that was to be ladled into the sausage. There were the butt-ends of smoked meat, and the scraps of corned beef, and all the odds and ends of the waste of the plants, that would be dumped into old barrels in the cellar and left there. Under the system of rigid economy which the packers enforced, there were some jobs that it only paid to do once in a long time, and among these was the cleaning out of the waste barrels.

Every spring they did it; and in the barrels would be dirt and rust and old nails and stale water—and cartload after cartload of it would be taken up and dumped into the hoppers with fresh meat, and sent out to the public's breakfast.

ASSESSMENT

1. **Analyze Word Choice** Why do you think the use of the phrase "the public's breakfast" is so powerful in this passage?
2. **Draw Conclusions** What do you think it would have been like to work in this factory?
3. **Identify Cause and Effect** What effect do you think reading this selection from *The Jungle* would have had on Americans during this time period?
4. **Analyze Style and Rhetoric** How would you describe Sinclair's writing style, and how does it boost his credibility to readers?

[*The Fourteen Points:* Woodrow Wilson]

Introduction

In a speech to Congress on January 8, 1918, President Wilson laid out America's war aims and his vision for peace after the war. His speech included fourteen key points upon which he believed the peace following the war must be based. However, not all of Wilson's ideas were adopted at the Paris Peace Conference.

Primary Source

. . . What we demand in this war, therefore, is nothing peculiar [unique] to ourselves. It is that the world be made fit and safe to live in; and particularly that it be made safe for every peace-loving nation which, like our own, wishes to live its own life, [and] determine its own institutions [choose its own government]. . . . The program of the world's peace, therefore, is our only program; and that program, the only possible program as we see it, is this:

1. Open covenants [formal agreements] of peace, openly arrived at, after which there shall be no private international understandings of any kind but [instead] diplomacy shall proceed always frankly [openly and honestly] and in the public view.

2. Absolute freedom of navigation upon the seas, outside territorial waters, alike in peace and in war, except as the seas may be closed in whole or in part by international action for the enforcement of international covenants.

3. The removal, so far as possible, of all economic barriers and the establishment of an equality of trade conditions among all the nations consenting to the peace and associating themselves for its maintenance.

4. Adequate guarantees given and taken that national armaments will be reduced to the lowest point consistent with domestic safety.

5. A free, open-minded, and absolutely impartial adjustment of all colonial claims, based upon a strict observance of the principle that in determining all such questions of sovereignty the interests of the populations concerned must have equal weight with the equitable claims of the government whose title is to be determined. . . .

14. A general association [organization] of nations must be formed under specific covenants for the purpose of affording mutual guarantees of political independence and territorial integrity to great and small states alike.

ASSESSMENT

1. **Compare and Contrast** Points 6–13 deal with specific territorial issues, such as breaking up the Ottoman and Austro-Hungarian Empires and restoring sovereignty to Belgium and Poland. To an American in 1918, how would those points be different from the ones excerpted here?
2. **Draw Conclusions** Preventing war seems like an admirable goal. Why might a country reject some or all of Wilson's points?
3. **Integrate Information From Diverse Sources** Why might isolationists oppose some or all of Wilson's Fourteen Points?
4. **Draw Inferences** What political impact do you think Wilson's Fourteen Points had?

[Two Poems: Langston Hughes]

Introduction

Langston Hughes wrote about how it felt to be African American, from the pain of racial prejudice to his deep pride in his culture and heritage. The two poems below are among his most famous.

Primary Source

The Negro Speaks of Rivers

I've known rivers:
I've known rivers ancient as the world and older than the flow of human blood in human veins.

My soul has grown deep like the rivers.

I bathed in the Euphrates [river in the Middle East] when dawns were young.

I built my hut near the Congo [river in Central Africa] and it lulled me to sleep.
I looked upon the Nile [river in Egypt] and raised the pyramids above it.

I heard the singing of the Mississippi when Abe Lincoln went down to New Orleans, and I've seen its muddy bosom turn all golden in the sunset.

I've known rivers:
Ancient, dusky [dark] rivers.

My soul has grown deep like the rivers.

My People

The night is beautiful,
So the faces of my people.

The stars are beautiful,
So the eyes of my people.

Beautiful, also, is the sun.
Beautiful, also, are the souls of my people.

ASSESSMENT

1. **Analyze Style and Rhetoric** In both poems, Hughes repeats words and sentence structures. What effect does this style have?
2. **Determine Author's Point of View** What is the speaker's attitude toward being an African American?
3. **Identify Cause and Effect** Hughes was one of the important writers of the Harlem Renaissance, a 1920s creative movement of African American artists and writers. How do you think Hughes's poems might have affected other African Americans at this time?

["Four Freedoms": Franklin D. Roosevelt]

Introduction

In his State of the Union address to Congress on January 6, 1941, President Franklin D. Roosevelt stressed the danger that aggressive fascist powers presented to the United States. He urged the American people to support "those who are resisting aggression and are thereby keeping war away from our Hemisphere"—namely the Allies. At the end of his speech, Roosevelt sets out the ideals that he believed Americans should fight for: the Four Freedoms.

Primary Source

In the future days, which we seek to make secure, we look forward to a world founded upon four essential human freedoms.

The first is freedom of speech and expression—everywhere in the world.

The second is freedom of every person to worship God in his own way—everywhere in the world.

The third is freedom from want—which, translated into world terms, means economic understandings which will secure to every nation a healthy peacetime life for its inhabitants—everywhere in the world.

The fourth is freedom from fear—which, translated into world terms, means a world-wide reduction of armaments [weapons] to such a point and in such a thorough fashion that no nation will be in a position to commit an act of physical aggression against any neighbor— anywhere in the world. . . .

That is no vision of a distant millennium [thousand years]. It is a definite basis for a kind of world attainable in our own time and generation. That kind of world is the very antithesis of the so-called new order of tyranny which the dictators seek to create with the crash of a bomb.

To that new order we oppose the greater conception—the moral order. A good society is able to face schemes of world domination and foreign revolutions alike without fear.

Since the beginning of our American history, we have been engaged in change—in a perpetual [continuous, lasting] peaceful revolution—a revolution which goes on steadily, quietly adjusting itself to changing conditions—without the concentration camp or the quick- lime in the ditch. The world order which we seek is the cooperation of free countries, working together in a friendly, civilized society.

This nation has placed its destiny in the hands and heads and hearts of its millions of free men and women; and its faith in freedom under the guidance of God. Freedom means the supremacy of human rights everywhere. Our support goes to those who struggle to gain those rights or keep them. Our strength is our unity of purpose. To that high concept there can be no end save victory.

1. **Draw Inferences** What does Roosevelt believe America's role in the world should be?
2. **Analyze Structure** How does Roosevelt develop the concept of freedom over the course of his speech?
3. **Compare Points of View** How do you think an isolationist would respond to Roosevelt's speech?
4. **Determine Author's Purpose** Do you think Roosevelt highlighted the "Four Freedoms" during his 1941 State of the Union address to prepare the nation for war? Why or why not? Cite specific passages from his speech to support your answer.

[*The Diary of a Young Girl: Anne Frank*]

Introduction

In 1933, Adolf Hitler was elected Chancellor of Germany. During World War II, his Nazi Party rounded up European Jews, many of whom were transported to death camps. Anne Frank was a young Jewish girl who hid with her family in small concealed rooms in her father's office. Frank kept a diary from June 12, 1942 to August 1, 1944, when her family's hiding place was discovered. She died in a concentration camp in 1945. Frank's father survived and published her diary to share Anne's story with the world.

Primary Source

Saturday, June 20, 1942

My father was thirty-six when he married my mother, who was then twenty-five. My sister Margot was born in 1926 in Frankfort-on-Main. I followed on June 12, 1929, and, as we are Jewish, we emigrated to Holland in 1933, where my father was appointed Managing Director of Travies N.V. This firm is in close relationship with the firm of Kolen & Co. in the same building, of which my father is a partner.

The rest of our family, however, felt the full impact of Hitler's anti-Jewish laws, so life was filled with anxiety. In 1938 after the pogroms [organized killing and other persecution of Jews], my two uncles (my mother's brothers) escaped to the U.S.A. My old grandmother came to us, she was then seventy-three. After May 1940 good times rapidly fled: first the war, then the capitulation [surrender], followed by the arrival of the Germans, which is when the sufferings of us Jews really began.

Anti-Jewish decrees followed each other in quick succession. Jews must wear a yellow star. Jews must hand in their bicycles. Jews are banned from trains and are forbidden to drive. Jews are only allowed to do their shopping between three and five o'clock and then only in shops which bear the placard [sign] "Jewish shop." Jews must be indoors by eight o'clock and cannot even sit in their own gardens after that hour. Jews are forbidden to visit theaters, cinemas, and other places of entertainment. Jews may not take part in public sports. Swimming baths, tennis courts, hockey fields, and other sports grounds are all prohibited to them. Jews may not visit Christians. Jews must go to Jewish schools, and many more restrictions of a similar kind.

So we could not do this and were forbidden to do that. But life went on in spite of it all. Jopie [Jacqueline van Mearsen, Anne's best friend] used to say to me, "You're scared to do anything, because it may be forbidden." Our freedom was strictly limited. Yet things were still bearable.

Thursday, November 19, 1942

Countless friends and acquaintances have gone to a terrible fate. Evening after evening the green and gray army lorries [trucks] trundle [roll] past. The Germans ring at every front door to inquire if there are any Jews living in the house. If there are, then the whole family has to go at once. If they don't find any, they go on to the next house. No one has a chance of evading [avoiding] them unless one goes into hiding. Often they go around us with lists, and only ring when they know they can get a good haul. Sometimes they let them off for cash—so much per head, it seems like the slave hunts of olden times. But it's certainly no joke; it's much too tragic for that. In the evenings when it's dark, I often see rows of good, innocent people accompanied by crying children, walking on and on, in charge of a couple of these chaps, bullied and knocked about until they almost drop. No one is spared—old people, babies, expectant mothers, the sick—each and all join in the march of death.

How fortunate we are here, so well cared for and undisturbed. We wouldn't have to worry about all this misery were it not that we are so anxious about all those dear to us whom we can no longer help.

I feel wicked sleeping in a warm bed, while my dearest friends have been knocked down or have fallen into a gutter somewhere out in the cold night. I get frightened when I think of close friends who have now been delivered into the hands of the cruelest brutes that walk the earth. And all because they are Jews!

Wednesday, May 3, 1944

Why all this destruction? The question is very understandable, but no one has found a satisfactory answer to it so far. Yes, why do they make still more gigantic planes, still heavier bombs and, at the same time, prefabricated [mass-produced] houses for reconstruction? Why should millions be spent daily on the war and yet there's not a penny available for medical services, artists, or for poor people?

Why do some people have to starve, while there are surpluses [extra amounts] rotting in other parts of the world? Oh, why are people so crazy?

Saturday, July 15, 1944

In spite of everything I still believe that people are really good at heart. I simply can't build up my hopes on a foundation consisting of confusion, misery, and death. I see the world gradually being turned into a wilderness, I hear the ever approaching thunder, which will destroy us too, I can feel the sufferings of millions and yet, if I look up into the heavens, I think that it will all come right, that this cruelty too will end, and that peace and tranquility [calm] will return again.

ASSESSMENT

1. **Draw Inferences** What was the purpose of the restrictions the Nazis imposed on Jews? What were the effects of these laws?
2. **Analyze Style and Rhetoric** How would you describe the tone of Frank's diary? How does she relate to her subject matter?
3. **Determine Central Ideas** How does reading Frank's diary differ from reading a secondary source about the Holocaust? What might her diary teach readers today that other sources cannot?

[Charter of the United Nations]

Introduction

After World War I, more than 50 countries joined together to form the League of Nations. The League was supposed to prevent future wars by providing a forum for the peaceful settlement of international disputes. The United States never joined the League.

The idea of an international peacekeeping organization was revisited after World War II. In 1944, representatives from the United States, the Soviet Union, China, and the United Kingdom met for several months to work out the framework for the United Nations.

In 1945, representatives of 50 countries met in San Francisco to sign the United Nations charter, bringing the organization into being.

Here are the preamble and first two articles of that charter.

Primary Source

WE THE PEOPLES OF THE UNITED NATIONS DETERMINED

- to save succeeding [later] generations from the scourge of war, which twice in our lifetime has brought untold sorrow to mankind, and
- to reaffirm faith in fundamental human rights, in the dignity and worth of the human person, in the equal rights of men and women and of nations large and small, and
- to establish conditions under which justice and respect for the obligations arising from treaties and other sources of international law can be maintained, and
- to promote social progress and better standards of life in larger freedom,

AND FOR THESE ENDS

- to practice tolerance and live together in peace with one another as good neighbours, and
- to unite our strength to maintain international peace and security, and

- to ensure, by the acceptance of principles and the institution of methods, that armed force shall not be used, save in the common interest, and
- to employ international machinery for the promotion of the economic and social advancement of all peoples,

HAVE RESOLVED TO COMBINE OUR EFFORTS TO ACCOMPLISH THESE AIMS

- Accordingly, our respective Governments, through representatives assembled in the city of San Francisco, who have exhibited their full powers found to be in good and due form, have agreed to the present Charter of the United Nations and do hereby establish an international organization to be known as the United Nations.

CHAPTER I: PURPOSES AND PRINCIPLES
Article 1
The Purposes of the United Nations are:

1. To maintain international peace and security, and to that end: to take effective collective measures for the prevention and removal of threats to the peace, and for the suppression of acts of aggression or other breaches of the peace, and to bring about by peaceful means, and in conformity with the principles of justice and international law, adjustment or settlement of international disputes or situations which might lead to a breach of the peace;

2. To develop friendly relations among nations based on respect for the principle of equal rights and self-determination of peoples, and to take other appropriate measures to strengthen universal peace;

3. To achieve international co-operation in solving international problems of an economic, social, cultural, or humanitarian character, and in promoting and encouraging respect for human rights and for fundamental freedoms for all without distinction as to race, sex, language, or religion; and

4. To be a centre for harmonizing the actions of nations in the attainment of these common ends.

Article 2
The Organization and its Members, in pursuit of the Purposes stated in Article 1, shall act in accordance with the following Principles.

1. The Organization is based on the principle of the sovereign equality of all its Members.

2. All Members, in order to ensure to all of them the rights and benefits resulting from membership, shall fulfill in good faith the obligations assumed by them in accordance with the present Charter.

3. All Members shall settle their international disputes by peaceful means in such a manner that international peace and security, and justice, are not endangered.

4. All Members shall refrain in their international relations from the threat or use of force against the territorial integrity or political independence of any state, or in any other manner inconsistent with the Purposes of the United Nations.

5. All Members shall give the United Nations every assistance in any action it takes in accordance with the present Charter, and shall refrain from giving assistance to any state against which the United Nations is taking preventive or enforcement action.

6. The Organization shall ensure that states which are not Members of the United Nations act in accordance with these Principles so far as may be necessary for the maintenance of international peace and security.

7. Nothing contained in the present Charter shall authorize the United Nations to intervene in matters which are essentially within the domestic jurisdiction of any state or shall require the Members to submit such matters to settlement under the present Charter; but this principle shall not prejudice the application of enforcement measures under Chapter VII.

ASSESSMENT

1. **Cite Evidence** The government of a country is inflicting terrible human rights abuses on members of the opposition party. Based on the excerpt, can the United Nations intervene? Cite the part(s) of the charter that support your opinion.

2. **Explain an Argument** Several years of drought in western Asia have led to widespread famine. The UN arranges to bring convoys of food to starving people. One country, a member of the UN, does not want to let relief workers come inside its borders. Does any part of the charter cited here support or rebut the country's position? Explain your answer.

3. **Draw Conclusions** Has the United Nations been successful in its mission "to save succeeding generations from the scourge of war"? Explain your answer.

[Universal Declaration of Human Rights]

Introduction
The General Assembly of the United Nations adopted this declaration on December 10, 1948. The document sets forth the basic liberties and freedoms to which all people are entitled.

Primary Source
Article 1 All human beings are born free and equal in dignity [worthiness] and rights. They are endowed with reason and conscience and should act toward one another in a spirit of brotherhood.

Article 2 Everyone is entitled to all the rights and freedoms set forth in this Declaration, without distinction [difference] of any kind, such as race, colour, sex, language, religion, political or other opinion, national or social origin, property, birth or other status. . . .

Article 3 Everyone has the right to life, liberty and security of person.

Article 4 No one shall be held in slavery or servitude. . . .

Article 5 No one shall be subjected [forced to undergo] to torture or to cruel, inhuman or degrading [humiliating] treatment or punishment.

Article 9 No one shall be subjected to arbitrary arrest, detention or exile.

Article 13 Everyone has the right to freedom of movement. . . .

Article 18 Everyone has the right to freedom of thought, conscience and religion. . . .

Article 19 Everyone has the right to freedom of opinion and expression. . . .

Article 20 Everyone has the right to freedom of peaceful assembly and association. . . .

Article 23 Everyone has the right to work, to free choice of employment, to just and favourable conditions of work and to protection against unemployment . . .

Article 25 Everyone has the right to a standard of living adequate [satisfactory] for the health and well-being of himself and of his family, including food, clothing, housing and medical care and necessary social services, and the right to security in the event of unemployment, sickness, disability, widowhood, old age or other lack of livelihood in circumstances beyond his control.

Article 26 Everyone has the right to education. Education shall be free, at least in the elementary and fundamental stages. . . .

ASSESSMENT
1. **Analyze Interactions** How do you think the U.S. Bill of Rights might have influenced this declaration?
2. **Determine Author's Purpose** Why do you think the members of the United Nations wrote this declaration, and what did they hope it would accomplish?
3. **Determine Central Ideas** Based on this passage, how would you define the term "human rights"?

[Inaugural Address: John F. Kennedy]

Introduction
On January 20, 1961, President John F. Kennedy delivered his inaugural address. Kennedy projected youth and determination in his address. The speech was a call to action for all Americans.

Primary Source
. . . Let the word go forth from this time and place, to friend and foe alike, that the torch has been passed to a new generation of Americans—born in this century, tempered [toughened; strengthened] by war, disciplined by a hard and bitter peace, proud of our ancient heritage—and unwilling to witness or permit the slow undoing of those human rights to which this Nation has always been committed, and to which we are committed today at home and around the world.

Let every nation know, whether it wishes us well or ill, that we shall pay any price, bear any burden, meet any hardship, support any friend, oppose any foe, in order to assure the survival and the success of liberty. . . .

Now the trumpet summons us again—not as a call to bear arms, though arms we need; not as a call to battle, though embattled we are—but a call to bear the burden of a long twilight struggle, year in and year out, "rejoicing in hope, patient in tribulation [an experience that causes distress or suffering]"—a struggle against the common enemies of man: tyranny, poverty, disease, and war itself. . . .

In the long history of the world, only a few generations have been granted the role of defending freedom in its hour of maximum danger. I do not shrink from this responsibility—I welcome it. . . .

And so, my fellow Americans: ask not what your country can do for you—ask what you can do for your country.

My fellow citizens of the world: ask not what America will do for you, but what together we can do for the freedom of man. . . .

. . . unwilling to witness or permit the slow undoing of those human rights to which this Nation has always been committed, and to which we are committed today at home and around the world.

ASSESSMENT

1. **Determine Meaning** Why does Kennedy characterize the post-war period as "a hard and bitter peace"?
2. **Compare and Contrast** How does Kennedy address America's allies as compared to America's enemies? Cite examples from the speech to support your answer.

[*Silent Spring*: Rachel Carson]

Introduction
Rachel Carson was a marine biologist and conservationist who wrote extensively about ocean life. *Silent Spring*, published in 1962, examined how synthetic pesticides used by farmers and landowners were poisoning people and wildlife alike. The book issued a pointed critique against the ways human activities harmed the natural world.

Silent Spring help launched a movement of concerned consumers, which led to the creation of the Environmental Protection Agency and a ban on a number of pollutants.

Primary Source
There once was a town in the heart of America where all life seemed to live in harmony with its surroundings. . . . Then a strange blight [plant disease] crept over the area and everything began to change. Mysterious maladies [illnesses] swept across the flocks of chickens; the cattle and sheep sickened and died. . . . There was a strange stillness. The birds, for example—where had they gone? . . . On the mornings that had once throbbed with the dawn chorus of robins, catbirds, doves, jays, wrens, and scores of other bird voices there was now no sound; only silence lay over the fields and woods and marsh. . . . No witchcraft, no enemy action had silenced the rebirth of new life in this stricken [distressed] world. The people had done it to themselves.

. . . Only within the moment of time represented by the present century has one species—man—acquired significant power to alter the nature of his world.

During the past quarter century this power has not only increased to one of disturbing magnitude [great size] but it has changed in character. The most alarming of all man's assaults upon the environment is the contamination of air, earth, rivers, and sea with dangerous and even lethal [enough to cause death] materials. This pollution is for the most part irrecoverable [unable to be recovered]; the chain of evil it initiates not only in the world that must support life but in living tissues is for the most part irreversible. In this now universal contamination of the environment, chemicals . . . [are] changing the very nature of the world—the very nature of its life.

ASSESSMENT

1. **Draw Inferences** Why do you think Carson chose to write this book? What changes do you think she hoped to instigate?
2. **Analyze Style and Rhetoric** How would you describe Carson's writing style in this passage, and how do you think this style advances her argument?
3. **Assess an Argument** Why do you think *Silent Spring* was controversial when it was first published? Why do you think some readers might have objected to Carson's argument?

["I Have a Dream": Martin Luther King, Jr.]

Introduction
Martin Luther King, Jr., delivered the closing address at the March on Washington. For approximately 20 minutes, he mesmerized the crowd with one of the most powerful speeches ever delivered. In this excerpt, King speaks of his dream for America:

Primary Source
And so even though we face the difficulties of today and tomorrow, I still have a dream. It is a dream deeply rooted in the American dream.

I have a dream that one day this nation will rise up and live out the true meaning of its creed [set of fundamental beliefs or principles]: "We hold these truths to be self-evident; that all men are created equal."

I have a dream that one day on the red hills of Georgia, the sons of former slaves and the sons of former slave owners will be able to sit down together at the table of brotherhood.

I have a dream that one day even the state of Mississippi . . . will be transformed into an oasis of freedom and justice.

I have a dream that my four little children will one day live in a nation where they will not be judged by the color of their skin but by the content of their character.

I have a *dream* today.

I have a dream that one day, down in Alabama, . . . one day right there in Alabama little black boys and black girls will be able to join hands with little white boys and white girls as sister and brothers.

This is our hope and this is the faith with which I return to the South.

With this faith we will be able to hew [chop, cut, shape] out of the mountain of despair a stone of hope. With this faith we will be able to transform the jangling discords of our nation into a beautiful symphony of brotherhood . . . .

–this will be the day when all of God's children will be able to sing with new meaning: "My country 'tis of thee, sweet land of liberty, of thee I sing. Land where my father died, land of the Pilgrims' pride, From every mountainside, let freedom ring.". . .

When we allow freedom to ring—when we let it ring, when we let it ring from every village and every hamlet [small village], from every state and every city, we will be able to speed up that day when *all* of God's children, black men and white men, Jews and Gentiles [non-Jews], Protestants and Catholics, will be able to join hands and sing in the words of the old Negro spiritual: "Free at last! Free at last!

Thank God Almighty, we are free at last!"

ASSESSMENT

1. **Analyze Style and Rhetoric** Cite three examples of metaphors in King's speech.
2. **Draw Inferences** Why do you think King identifies three states in his speech? What effect does this have on his overall purpose?
3. **Draw Conclusions** What effect do you think this speech might have had on the civil rights movement?

["Letter from Birmingham Jail": Martin Luther King, Jr.]

Introduction
In 1963, Martin Luther King, Jr., led a campaign of nonviolent protest against segregation and discrimination in Birmingham, Alabama. Rather than obey a court order to desist, King went to jail. From there, he wrote a response to white Alabama clergymen who were urging King to be more moderate in his struggle. King responded that the wait for civil rights had been too long and that civil disobedience against unjust laws was needed to achieve social justice.

Primary Source
My Dear Fellow Clergymen,

While confined here in the Birmingham City Jail, I came across your recent statement calling our present activities "unwise and untimely." . . .

We have waited for more than 340 years for our constitutional and God-given rights. The nations of Asia and Africa are moving with jetlike speed toward the goal of political independence, and we still creep at horse and buggy pace toward the gaining of a cup of coffee at a lunch counter.

I guess it is easy for those who have never felt the stinging darts of segregation to say wait. But when you have seen vicious mobs lynch your mothers and fathers at will and drown your sisters and brothers at whim; when you have seen hate-filled policemen curse, kick, brutalize, and even kill your black brothers and sisters with impunity [without punishment]; when you see the vast majority of your 20 million Negro brothers smothering in an airtight cage of poverty in the midst of an affluent society; when you suddenly find your tongue twisted and your speech stammering as you seek to explain to your six-year-old daughter why she can't go to the public amusement park that has just been advertised on television, and see the tears welling up in her little eyes when she is told that Funtown is closed to colored children, . . . then you will understand why we find it difficult to wait. . . .

You express a great deal of anxiety over our willingness to break laws. . . .The answer is found in the fact that there are two types of laws: There are just and there are unjust laws. I would agree with Saint Augustine that "An unjust law is no law at all." . . .

All segregation statutes are unjust because segregation distorts the soul and damages the personality. It gives the segregator a false sense of superiority, and the segregated a false sense of inferiority. . . .

Let us all hope that the dark clouds of racial prejudice will soon pass away and the deep fog of misunderstanding will be lifted from our fear-drenched communities and in some not too distant tomorrow the radiant stars of love and brotherhood will shine over our great nation with all their scintillating beauty.

Yours for the cause of Peace and Brotherhood,

Martin Luther King, Jr.

ASSESSMENT

1. **Analyze Style and Rhetoric** How does King use rhetorical devices in his letter to support his argument against racial segregation? Cite specific examples from the text.
2. **Identify Supporting Details** What details does King offer to support his main point that racial segregation is unjust?
3. **Assess an Argument** What do you think is the most effective section of King's letter? Support your response.

4. **Draw Conclusions** How might have King's letter impacted the civil rights movement? Cite details from the text to support your answer.

["Tear Down This Wall": Ronald Reagan]

Introduction

On June 12, 1987, President Reagan spoke in West Berlin, near the Berlin Wall, not far from where the Brandenburg Gate stood in the eastern sector. His speech acknowledged the new Soviet leader Mikhail Gorbachev's efforts at reform in the Soviet Union. However, Reagan was not satisfied with Gorbachev's limited measures. He challenged the Soviet leader to show a real commitment to reform by tearing down the Berlin Wall that had stood between East and West Berlin since 1961. This wall symbolized the division between communism and democracy.

Primary Source

In the 1950s, Khrushchev predicted: "We will bury you." But in the West today, we see a free world that has achieved a level of prosperity and well-being unprecedented [never having happened or existed before] in all human history. In the Communist world, we see failure, technological backwardness, declining standards of health, even want of the most basic kind—too little food. Even today, the Soviet Union still cannot feed itself. After these four decades, then, there stands before the entire world one great and inescapable conclusion: Freedom leads to prosperity. Freedom replaces the ancient hatreds among the nations with comity [courtesy] and peace. Freedom is the victor [winner].

And now the Soviets themselves may, in a limited way, be coming to understand the importance of freedom. We hear much from Moscow about a new policy of reform and openness. Some political prisoners have been released. Certain foreign news broadcasts are no longer being jammed. Some economic enterprises have been permitted to operate with greater freedom from state control.

Are these the beginnings of profound changes in the Soviet state? Or are they token gestures, intended to raise false hopes in the West, or to strengthen the Soviet system without changing it? We welcome change and openness; for we believe that freedom and security go together, that the advance of human liberty can only strengthen the cause of world peace. There is one sign the Soviets can make that would be unmistakable, that would advance dramatically the cause of freedom and peace.

General Secretary Gorbachev, if you seek peace, if you seek prosperity for the Soviet Union and Eastern Europe, if you seek liberalization: Come here to this gate! Mr. Gorbachev, open this gate! Mr. Gorbachev, tear down this wall!

ASSESSMENT

1. **Determine Central Ideas** According to the first paragraph of this passage, why should Gorbachev tear down the Berlin Wall?
2. **Determine Author's Purpose** What was the purpose of Reagan's speech?
3. **Distinguish Among Fact, Opinion, and Reasoned Judgment** When Reagan says, "freedom is the victor," is that a fact, an opinion, or a reasoned judgment? Cite evidence from the speech to support your answer.

["Glory and Hope": Nelson Mandela]

Introduction
Nelson Mandela delivered this speech after having been elected president in South Africa's first multiracial election in 1994. Knowing that the injustices of apartheid would be hard to overcome, Mandela asked the people to work together for peace and justice.

Primary Source
Today, all of us do, by our presence here, and by our celebrations . . . confer [give] glory and hope to newborn liberty.

Out of the experience of an extraordinary human disaster that lasted too long must be born a society of which all humanity will be proud.

Our daily deeds as ordinary South Africans must produce an actual South African reality that will reinforce humanity's belief in justice, strengthen its confidence in the nobility of the human soul and sustain all our hopes for a glorious life for all. . . .

The time for the healing of the wounds has come. . . .

The time to build is upon us.

We have, at last, achieved our political emancipation [freedom from bondage or control by others]. We pledge ourselves to liberate all our people from the continuing bondage [slavery] of poverty, deprivation [lack of materials necessary for survival], suffering, gender and other discrimination. . . .

We have triumphed in the effort to implant [insert] hope in the breasts of the millions of our people. We enter into a covenant [binding agreement] that we shall build the society in which all South Africans, both black and white, will be able to walk tall, without any fear in their hearts, assured of their inalienable right to human dignity—a rainbow nation at peace with itself and the world. . . .

We understand it still that there is no easy road to freedom.

We know it well that none of us acting alone can achieve success.

We must therefore act together as a united people, for national reconciliation [a settling of differences that results in harmony], for nation building, for the birth of a new world.

Let there be justice for all. Let there be peace for all. Let there be work, bread, water, and salt for all. . . . The sun shall never set on so glorious a human achievement!

ASSESSMENT

1. **Explain an Argument** When apartheid ended, there was a danger of a backlash by blacks against whites who supported apartheid. How does Mandela's speech respond to that danger?
2. **Determine Author's Point of View** How would you describe the tone of Mandela's speech? How does this tone reflect Mandela's view of his country and its future?
3. **Determine Author's Purpose** Why do you think Mandela talks about building a new world, not just a new South Africa?

Sequence

Sequence means "order," and placing things in the correct order is very important. What would happen if you tried to put toppings on a pizza before you put down the dough for the crust? When studying history, you need to analyze the information by sequencing significant events, individuals, and time periods in order to understand them. Practice this skill by using the events listed on this page. Look for words that signal sequence.

- On April 18, 1775 about 700 British troops quietly left Boston in the darkness. Their goal was to seize the colonial arms.

- More than 60 years after the battles of Lexington and Concord, a well-known New England writer, Ralph Waldo Emerson, wrote a poem honoring the minutemen.

- George III was furious when he heard about the petition. The colonists, he raged, were trying to begin a war "for the purpose of establishing an independent empire!" The king vowed to bring the rebels to justice. He ordered 20,000 more troops to the colonies to crush the revolt. Congress did not learn of the king's response until months later.

[**1.**] Identify the topic and the main events that relate to the topic. Quickly skim titles and headings to determine the topic of the passage. As you read the passage, write a list of significant events, individuals, or time periods related to the topic.

[**2.**] Note any dates and time words such as "before" and "after" that indicate the chronological order of events. Look through your list of events, individuals, or time periods and write down the date for each. This will give you information to apply absolute chronology by sequencing the events, individuals, or time periods. Remember that some events may have taken place over a number of months or years. Is your date the time when the event started or ended? Make sure to note enough details that you can remember the importance of the information. If no date is given, look for words such as "before" or "after" that can tell you where to place this event, time period, or individual compared to others on your list. This will allow you to apply relative chronology by sequencing the events, individuals, or time periods.

[**3.**] Determine the time range of the events. Place the events in chronological order on a timeline. Look for the earliest and latest events, individuals, or time periods on your list. The span of time between the first and last entries gives you the time range. To apply absolute chronology, sequence the entries by writing the date of the first event on the left side of a piece of paper and the date of the last event on the right side. Draw a line connecting the two events. This will be your timeline. Once you have drawn your timeline, put the events in order by date along the line. Label their dates. To apply relative chronology, sequence the significant individuals, events, or time periods on an undated timeline, in the order that they happened. You now have a clear image of the important events related to this topic. You can organize and interpret information from visuals by analyzing the information and applying absolute or relative chronology to the events. This will help you understand the topic better when you can see how events caused or led to other events. You will also be able to analyze information by developing connections between historical events over time.

Categorize

When you analyze information by categorizing, you create a system that helps you sort items into categories, or groups with shared characteristics, so that you can understand the information. Categorizing helps you see what groups of items have in common. Practice this skill as you study the table on this page.

Comparing the New England and Middle Colonies

	NEW ENGLAND	MIDDLE COLONIES
MAIN REASON FOR SETTLEMENT	Avoid religious persecution	Economic gain
BUSINESS AND TRADE	Shipbuilding, shipping, fishing, forestry	Agriculture, skilled trades, shipping
AGRICULTURE	Mostly limited to the needs of the colonies	Fertile farmland produced export crops
ETHNIC DIVERSITY	Mainly English	English, Dutch, German, and Scotch-Irish
SETTLEMENT STRUCTURE	Close-knit towns	More scattered settlements
CULTURE AND SOCIETY	Religious uniformity; small family farms and businesses with few servants or slaves	Ethnic and religious diversity; larger farms and businesses need indentured servants

[**1.**] Identify similarities and differences among items you need to understand. You need to pay careful attention and sometimes do research to find the similarities and differences among the facts, topics, or objects that you need to understand. Scientists find groups, or categories, of related animals by analyzing the details of the animals' bodies. For example, insects with similar wings, legs, and mouth-parts probably belong in the same category. Gather similar information about all the things you need to understand. For example, if you know the location of one thing, try to find the locations of all the things you are studying. If you have different types of information about your topics, you will not be able to group them easily.

[**2.**] Create a system to group items with common characteristics. Once you have gathered similar kinds of information on the items you need to understand, look for items that share characteristics or features. Create categories based on a feature shared by all of the facts, topics, or objects you need to understand. For example, if you have gathered information on the population and political systems of several countries, you could categorize them by their population or their type of political system.

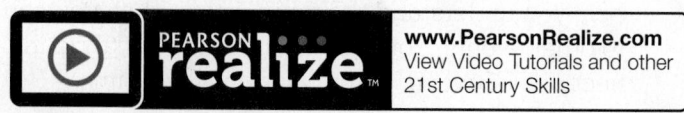

[3.] Form the groupings. Put each of the items that you are studying into one of the categories that you have created. If some items do not fit, you may need to make a new category or modify your categories. Label each category for the characteristic shared by its members. Examples of labels for categories might include "Countries with more than 100 million people," "Countries with fewer than 1 million people," "Democracies," or "Dictatorships."

Analyze Cause and Effect

When you analyze information by identifying cause-and-effect relationships, you find how one event leads to the next. It is important to find evidence that one event caused another. If one event happened earlier than another, it did not necessarily cause the later event. Understanding causes and effects can help you solve problems. Practice this skill as you study the cause and effect diagram on this page. By replacing the event in this diagram, you may use it to analyze the causes and effects of any event.

WAR OF 1812

Causes	Effects

[1.] Choose a starting point of observation. When trying to understand a historical event, choose the time of that event. If you are trying to understand a current event, you can work backward from a starting point in the present.

[2.] Consider earlier events to try to find connections to your starting point, including any language that signals causes. Put the evidence together to identify true causes. When reading, look for events that come before your starting point. Analyze whether these earlier events caused later events. Identify words that signal cause, such as "reason," "because," and "led to." Analyze the information by developing connections between historical events. Make sure that there is evidence showing that the earlier events caused the later events and did not just happen earlier.

[3.] Consider later events to try to find connections to your starting point, including any language that signals effects. Put the evidence together to determine true effects. Look for events that come after your starting point. Analyze the information in order to determine whether these later events are effects of earlier events. Identify words that signal effect, such as "led to," "so," and "therefore." Make sure that there is evidence showing that these later events were caused by earlier events and did not just happen later.

[4.] Summarize the cause-and-effect relationship and draw conclusions. Once you have identified the cause-and-effect relationships between different events, describe these relationships. Draw a diagram that develops the connections between the two historical events. Draw conclusions about any relationships that you see.

Compare and Contrast

When you analyze information by comparing and contrasting two or more things, you look for similarities and differences between them. This skill helps you understand the things that you are comparing and contrasting. It is also a skill that you can use in making choices. Practice this skill as you read the text excerpt on this page. What is the topic of the text? What is getting compared and contrasted?

> Despite Americans' common values, the United States struggled over issues of liberty and equality during the mid-1800s. The biggest point of difference was between northern and southern states over slavery. Many in the North opposed slavery while in the South slavery was a major part of the economy and culture.

[1.] Look for related topics and characteristics that describe them. When you are looking for similarities and differences between two things, it can help to start by identifying relationships between them. What do the two things have in common? If two things have nothing in common, such as a dog and a piece of pie, it will be difficult to find similarities or differences. On the other hand, you can compare and contrast two countries or political systems. Look through the information you have on the things or topics you want to compare and contrast, and identify the characteristics, or features, that describe those things or topics.

[2.] Look for words that signal comparison ("both," "similar to," "also") or contrast ("unlike," "different," "instead"). Look for words that show comparison, or similarity, and those that show contrast, or difference. Take notes on these similarities and differences. This will make it possible to analyze information more quickly.

[3.] Identify similarities and differences in the topics, and draw conclusions about them. Look through your notes and analyze the ways in which your topics are similar and different. Usually, topics have both similarities and differences. Try to find patterns in these similarities and differences. For example, all the similarities between two countries might be related to climate, and all the differences might be related to economics. Draw conclusions based on these patterns. In this example, you might conclude that a country's economy does not depend on its climate. Identifying similarities and differences by comparing and contrasting two topics lets you draw conclusions that help you analyze both topics as well as other topics like them.

Identify Main Ideas and Details

You can analyze information in a selection by finding the main idea. A main idea is the most important point in a selection. Identifying the main idea will help you remember details, such as names, dates, and events, which should support the main idea. Practice this skill by reading the text excerpt on this page.

> Despite Americans' common values, the United States struggled over issues of liberty and equality during the mid-1800s. The biggest point of difference was between northern and southern states over slavery. Many in the North opposed slavery while in the South slavery was a major part of the economy and culture.

[1.] Scan titles, headings, and visuals before reading to see what the selection is about. Often, important ideas are included in titles, headings, and other special text. Special text may be primary sources, words that are highlighted, or ideas listed with bullet points. Also, take a look at visuals and captions. By analyzing these parts of the text, you should quickly get a sense of the main idea of the article.

[2.] Read the selection and then identify the main point of the selection, the point that the rest of the selection supports: this is the main idea. Read through the selection to identify the main idea. Sometimes, the main idea will be the first or second sentence of one of the first few paragraphs. Sometimes, it will be the last sentence of the first paragraph. Other times, no single sentence will tell you the main idea. You will have to come up with your own sentence answering the question, "What is the main point of this selection?"

[3.] Find details or statements within the selection that support or build on the main idea. Once you have identified the main idea, look for details that support the main idea. Many or most of the details should be related to the main idea. If you find that many of the details are not related to what you think is the main idea, you may not have identified the main idea correctly. Identify the main idea that the details in the selection support. Analyze the information in the text by finding the main idea and supporting details.

Summarize

When you analyze information by summarizing, you restate the main points of a passage in your own words. Using your own words helps you understand the information. Summarizing will help you understand a text and prepare for tests or assignments based on the text. Practice this skill by reading the excerpt of text below. Then try to summarize it in one or two sentences.

> The authors of the Constitution wanted to prevent the creation of organized political parties or groups of people who seek to win elections and hold public office in order to reshape policy. They deemed these groups to be factions that were dangerous to the unity of a republic. Despite these intentions, practical politics resulted in the formation of two parties: the Federalists, led by Alexander Hamilton and John Adams, and the Democratic Republicans, led by Thomas Jefferson. During the 1790s, Americans were divided between the two parties. There was a tendency for northerners, especially merchants, to favor the Federalists. In contrast, southerners, especially farmers, voted mainly for Democratic Republicans.

[**1.**] Identify and write down the main point of each paragraph in your own words. You may identify the main idea right at the beginning of each paragraph. In other cases, you will have to figure out the main idea. As you read each paragraph, ask yourself, "What is the point this paragraph makes?" The point the paragraph makes is the main idea. Write this idea down in your own words.

[**2.**] Use these main points to write a general statement of the overall main idea of the passage in your own words. Once you have written down the main idea for each paragraph, write down the main idea of the passage. Write the main idea in your own words. If you have trouble identifying the main idea of the passage, review the titles and headings in the passage. Often, titles and headings relate to the main idea. Also, the writer may state the main idea in the first paragraph of the passage. The main idea of a passage should answer the question, "What is the point this passage makes?"

[**3.**] Use this general statement as a topic sentence for your summary. Then, write a paragraph tying together the main points of the passage. Leave out unimportant details. Analyze the information in the passage by summarizing. Use the main idea of the passage as a topic sentence for your summary paragraph. Use the main ideas that you identified for each paragraph of the passage to write sentences supporting the main idea of the passage. Leave out details that are not needed to understand the main idea of the passage. Your summary should be in your own words, and it should be much shorter than the original passage. Once your summary is written, review it to make sure that it contains all the main points of the passage. If any are missing, revise your summary to include them. If the summary includes unimportant details, remove them.

Generalize

One good way to analyze materials about a particular subject is to make generalizations and predictions. What are the patterns and connections that link the different materials? What can you say about the different materials that is true of all them? Practice this skill by reading the following statements and applying these steps. What generalization can you make about the relationship between Britain and the colonies?

- The Proclamation of 1763 forbade colonists to settle west of a boundary line established by the British. Colonists now had to pay for the additional British troops that had been sent to enforce the proclamation.

- The Seven Years' War, which included the French and Indian War, plunged Britain deeply into debt. The British prime minister, George Grenville, decided that colonists in North America should help share the burden.

- The Stamp Act of 1765 placed new duties (taxes) on legal documents. Stamp taxes were used in Britain and other countries to raise money, but had not required American colonists to pay such a tax until the Stamp Act.

[1.] Make a list. Listing all of the specific details and facts about a subject will help you find patterns and connections.

[2.] Generate a statement. From your list of facts and specific details, decide what most of the items listed have in common. Analyze your information by making generalizations and predictions.

[3.] Ensure your generalization is logical and well supported by facts. Generalizations can be valid or invalid. A generalization that is not logical or supported by facts is invalid.

Make Predictions

You can analyze information by making generalizations and predictions. Predictions are educated guesses about the future, based on clues you find in written material and information you already have. When you analyze information by making generalizations and predictions, you are thinking critically about the material you read. Practice this skill by analyzing the chart below and predicting which states would most likely object to the federal government taking over every state's debts.

State Debt Assumed by the New Federal Government, 1790

STATE	ASSUMED DEBT (IN DOLLARS)	STATE	ASSUMED DEBT (IN DOLLARS)
New Hampshire	300,000	Delaware	200,000
Massachusetts	4,000,000	Maryland	800,000
Rhode Island	200,000	Virginia	3,500,000
Connecticut	1,600,000	North Carolina	2,400,000
New York	1,200,000	South Carolina	4,000,000
New Jersey	800,000	Georgia	300,000
Pennsylvania	2,200,000		

SOURCE: Library of Congress

[**1.**] Review the content. Read your material carefully and research any terms or concepts that are new to you. It's important to understand the material before analyzing the information to make a prediction.

[**2.**] Look for clues. Gathering evidence is an important part of making predictions. Look for important words, statements, and evidence that seem to support the writer's point of view. Ask questions about what you are reading, including who, what, where, when, why, and how. Look for and analyze clues to help you generalize and predict.

[**3.**] Consider what you already know. Use related prior knowledge and/or connect to your own experiences to help you make an informed prediction. If you have experience with the subject matter, you have a much better chance of making an accurate prediction.

[**4.**] Generate a list of predictions. After studying the content, list the clues you've found. Then use these clues, plus your prior knowledge, to form your predictions. List as many possible outcomes as you can based on clues in the material and the questions you have considered.

Draw Inferences

What is the author trying to tell you? To make a determination about the author's message, you analyze information by drawing inferences and conclusions. You consider details and descriptions included in the text, compare and contrast the text to prior knowledge you have about the subject, and then form a conclusion about the author's intent. Practice this skill by analyzing the primary source report below to draw inferences about the feelings of the crew towards Magellan.

. . . Talking began amongst the crews about the old eternal hatred between the Portuguese and the Spaniards, and about Magellan's being a Portuguese. He, they said, could do nothing more glorious for his own country than to cast away this fleet, with so many men. Nor was it credible [believable] that he should wish to discover the Moluccas [a group of spice islands]. . . . Nor even had their course begun to turn towards those happy Moluccas, but rather to distant snow and ice, and to perpetual storms.

Magellan, very much enraged by these sayings, punished the men, but rather more harshly than was proper for a foreigner, especially when commanding in a distant country.
—Maximillianus Transylvanus, report to King Charles I of Spain

[**1.**] Study the image or text. Consider all of the details and descriptions included. What is the author trying to tell you? Look for context clues that hint at the topic and subject matter.

[**2.**] Make a connection. Use related prior knowledge to connect to the text or image. Analyze information by asking questions such as who, what, where, when, and how. Look for cause-and-effect relationships; compare and contrast. This strategy will help you think beyond the available surface details to understand what the author is suggesting or implying.

[**3.**] Form a conclusion. When you draw an inference, you combine your own ideas with evidence and details you found within the text or image to form a new conclusion. This action leads you to a new understanding of the material.

Draw Conclusions

When you analyze information by drawing inferences and conclusions, you connect the ideas in a text with what you already know in order to understand a topic better. Using this skill, you can "fill in the blanks" to see the implications or larger meaning of the information in a text. Practice this skill by reading the excerpt of text on this page. What conclusions can you draw based on the information in the paragraph? Is there enough information to draw a valid conclusion? What else might you need to know?

> Views on states' rights split the country into the North and South, just as slavery did. Yet the differences between the North and South went even further. The North was more urban, industrial, and business oriented than the South. It had many small farms. The South was more rural, agricultural, and steeped in tradition. Plantations were vital to its economy. In addition, northern Protestants had strict ideas about certain moral issues, especially slavery.

[**1.**] Identify the topic, main idea, and supporting details. Before reading, look at the titles and headings within a reading. This should give you a good idea of the topic, or the general subject, of a text. After reading, identify the main idea. The main idea falls within the topic and answers the question, "What is the main point of this text?" Find the details that the author presents to support the main idea.

[2.] Use what you know to make a judgment about the information. Think about what you know about this topic or a similar topic. For example, you may read that the English settlers of Jamestown suffered from starvation because many of them were not farmers and did not know how to grow food. Analyzing the information about their situation and what you know about people, you could draw the conclusion that these settlers must have had little idea, or the wrong idea, about the conditions that they would find in America.

[3.] Check and adjust your judgment until you can draw a well-supported conclusion. Look for details within the reading that support your judgment. Reading a little further, you find that these settlers thought that they would become rich after discovering gold or silver, or through trading with Native Americans for furs. You can use this information to support your conclusion that the settlers were mistaken about the conditions that they would find in America. By analyzing the information further, you might infer that the settlers had inaccurate information about America. To support your conclusions, you could look for reliable sources on what these settlers knew before they left England.

Interpret Sources

Outlines and reports are good sources of information. In order to interpret these sources, though, you'll need to identify the type of document you're reading, identify the main idea, organize the details of information, and evaluate the source for point of view and bias. Practice this skill by finding a newspaper or online report on a bill recently passed by Congress or a decision recently decided by the Supreme Court. What steps will you take to interpret this report?

[1.] Identify the type of document. Is the document a primary or secondary source? Determine when, where, and why it was written.

[2.] Examine the source to identify the main idea. After identifying the main idea, identify details or sections of text that support the main idea. If the source is an outline or report, identify the topic and subtopics; review the supporting details under each subtopic. Organize the information from the outline or report and think about how it connects back to the overall topic listed at the top of the outline or report.

[3.] Evaluate the source for point of view and bias. Primary sources often have a strong point of view or bias; it is important to analyze primary sources critically to determine their validity. Evaluating each source will help you interpret the information they contain.

Create Databases

Databases are organized collections of information which can be analyzed and interpreted. You decide on a topic, organize data, use a spreadsheet, and then pose questions which will help you to analyze and interpret your data. Practice this skill as you create a database of three northern and three southern states in 1850. You can find many kinds of state data for this year in the U.S. Census. (census.gov)

[1.] Decide on a topic. Identify the information that you will convert into a table. This information may come from various sources, including textbooks, reference works, and Internet sites.

[2.] Organize the data. Study the information and decide what to include in your table. Only include data that is pertinent and available. Based on the data you choose, organize your information. Identify how many columns there will be and what the column headings will be. Decide the order in which you are going to list the data in the rows.

[3.] Use a spreadsheet. A spreadsheet is a computer software tool that allows you to organize data so that it can be analyzed. Spreadsheets allow you to make calculations as well as input data. Use a spreadsheet to help you create summaries of your data. For instance, you can compute the sum, average, minimum, and maximum values of the data. Use the graphing features of your spreadsheet program to show the data visually.

[4.] Analyze the data. Once all of your data is entered and you have made any calculations you need, you are ready to pose questions to analyze and interpret your data. Organize the information from the database and use it to form conclusions. Be sure to draw conclusions that can be supported by the data available.

Analyze Data and Models

Data and models can provide useful information about geographic distributions and patterns. To make sense of that information, though, you need to pose and answer questions about data and models. What does the data say? What does it mean? What patterns can you find? Practice this skill as you study the data below.

State Populations, 1810–1840

STATE	POPULATION, 1810	POPULATION, 1840
New York	959,049	2,428,921
Ohio	230,760	1,519,467
Illinois	12,282	476,183
Louisiana	76,556	352,411
Tennessee	261,727	829,210

Source: U.S. Censuses of Population and Housing

[1.] Read the title to learn the geographic distributions represented by the data set, graph, or model.

[2.] Read the data given. When reviewing a graph, read the labels and the key to help you comprehend the data provided. Pose and answer questions to further understand the material. For example, you might ask "Who could use this data?" or "How could this data be used?" or even "Why is this data presented in this particular format?" Thinking critically about the data presented will help you make predictions and comprehend the data.

[3.] Study the numbers, lines, and/or colors to find out what the graphs or data represent. Next, find similarities and differences between multiple models of the same data. Do any additional research to find out more about why the information in the models differs.

[4.] Interpret the graph, data set, or model. Look for interesting geographic distributions and patterns in the data. Look at changes over time or compare information from different categories. Draw conclusions.

Read Charts, Graphs, and Tables

If you pose and answer questions about charts, graphs, or tables you find in books or online, you can find out all sorts of information, such as how many calories are in your favorite foods or what the value of a used car is. Analyzing and interpreting the information you find in thematic charts, graphs, and tables can help you make decisions in your life. Apply the steps of this skill as you study the infographic below.

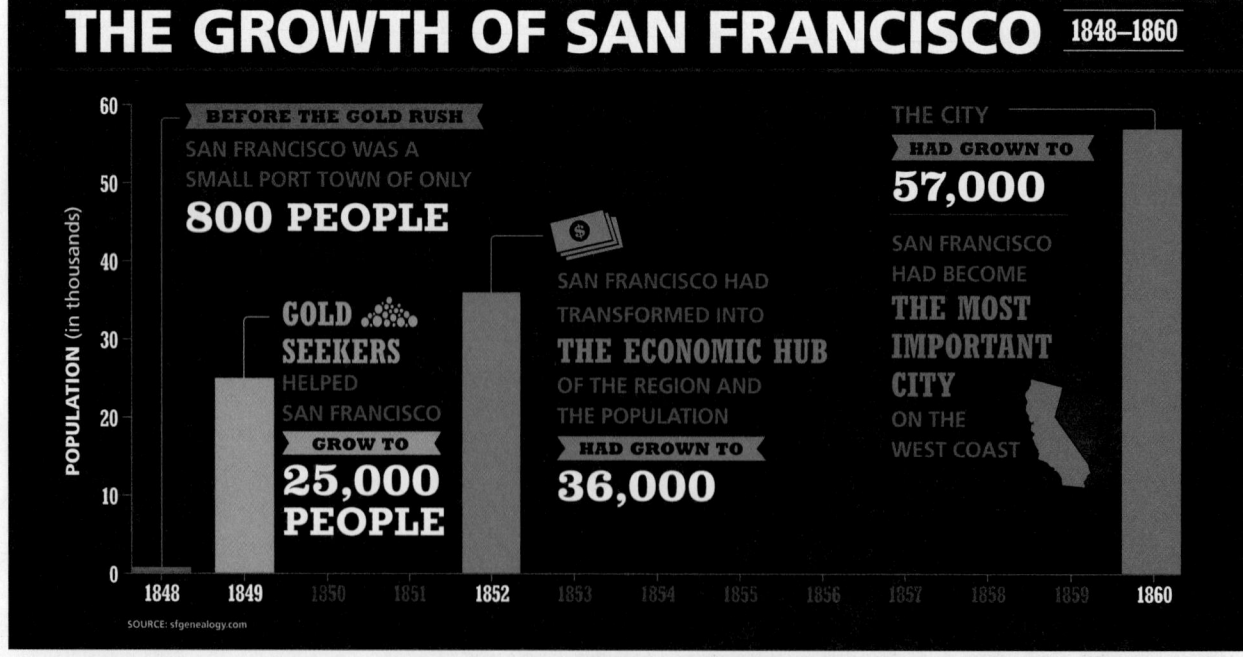

THE GROWTH OF SAN FRANCISCO 1848–1860

BEFORE THE GOLD RUSH
SAN FRANCISCO WAS A SMALL PORT TOWN OF ONLY
800 PEOPLE

GOLD SEEKERS HELPED SAN FRANCISCO GROW TO
25,000 PEOPLE

SAN FRANCISCO HAD TRANSFORMED INTO **THE ECONOMIC HUB** OF THE REGION AND THE POPULATION HAD GROWN TO
36,000

THE CITY HAD GROWN TO
57,000
SAN FRANCISCO HAD BECOME **THE MOST IMPORTANT CITY** ON THE WEST COAST

POPULATION (in thousands)

60 50 40 30 20 10 0

1848 1849 1850 1851 1852 1853 1854 1855 1856 1857 1858 1859 1860

SOURCE: sfgenealogy.com

[1.] Identify the title and labels of a chart, graph, or table, and read the key, if there is one, to understand the information presented. The title often tells you the topic of the chart, graph, or table, or the type of information you will find. Make sure you understand how the graph shows information. A key or legend often appears in a small box near the edge of the graph or chart. The key will tell you the meaning of lines, colors, or symbols used on the chart or graph. Notice also the column and row headings, and use your reading skills to figure out the meanings of any words you don't know.

[2.] Determine consistencies and inconsistencies, to see whether there is a trend in a graph, chart, or table. Organize information from visuals such as charts and graphs and decide whether or not there is a trend or pattern in the information that you see. Evaluate the data and determine whether the trend is consistent, or steady. Remember that there could be some inconsistencies, or exceptions to the pattern. Try not to miss the overall pattern because of a couple of exceptions.

[3.] Draw conclusions about the data in a chart, graph, or table. Once you understand the information, try to analyze and interpret the information and draw conclusions. If you see a pattern, does the pattern help you to understand the topic or predict future events?

[4.] Create a chart or graph to make the data more understandable or to view the data in a different way. Does the data in the chart or graph help you answer questions you have about the topic or see any causes or effects? For example, you could use your mathematical skills to create circle graphs or bar graphs that visually organize the data in a different way that allows you to interpret the data differently.

[5.] Use the data or information in charts and graphs to understand an issue or make decisions. Use your social studies skills to make inferences, draw conclusions, and take a stand on the issue.

Create Charts and Maps

Thematic charts, graphs, and maps are visual tools for representing information. When you create a thematic chart, graph, or map you will start by selecting the type of data you want to represent. Then you will find appropriate data to include, organize your data, and then create symbols and a key to help others understand your chart, graph, or map. Practice this skill by applying the steps below to chart the results of a poll you take of your classmates' favorite sports.

[1.] To create a chart or map, first select a region or set of data. Use a map to represent data pertaining to a specific region or location; use a chart to represent trends reflected in a set of data.

[2.] Research and find the data you would like to present in the chart or map. Your choice of data will be based on the theme you wish to explore. For example, a chart or map that explores the theme of changing demographics in Texas might include data about the location of different ethnic groups in Texas in the nineteenth, twentieth, and twenty-first centuries.

[3.] Organize the data according to the specific format of your chart or map.

[4.] Create symbols, a key (as needed), and a title. Create symbols to represent each piece of data you would like to highlight. Keep each symbol simple and easy to understand. After you have created the symbols, place them in a key. Add a title to your map or chart that summarizes the information presented. Your symbols and key will make it easier for others to interpret your charts and maps.

Analyze Political Cartoons

Political cartoons are visual commentaries about events or people. As you learn to analyze political cartoons, you will learn to identify bias in cartoons and interpret their meaning. You can start by carefully examining the cartoon and considering its possible meanings. Then you can draw conclusions based on your analysis. Practice this skill as you study the political cartoon below.

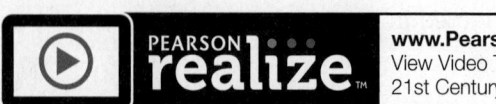

[1.] Fully examine the cartoon. Identify any symbols in the cartoon, read the text and title, and identify the main character or characters. Analyze the cartoon to identify bias and determine what each image or symbol represents. Conduct research if you need more information to decipher the cartoon.

[2.] Consider the meaning. Think about how the cartoonist uses the images and symbols in the cartoon to express his or her opinion about a subject. Try to interpret the artist's purpose in creating the image.

[3.] Draw conclusions. Use what you have gleaned from the image itself, plus any prior knowledge or research, to analyze, interpret, and form a conclusion about the artist's intentions.

Read Physical Maps

What mountain range is closest to where you live? What major rivers are closest to you? To find out, you would look at a physical map. You can use appropriate reading skills to interpret social studies information such as that found on different kinds of maps. Physical maps show physical features, such as elevation, mountains, valleys, oceans, rivers, deserts, and plains. Practice this skill as you study the map on this page.

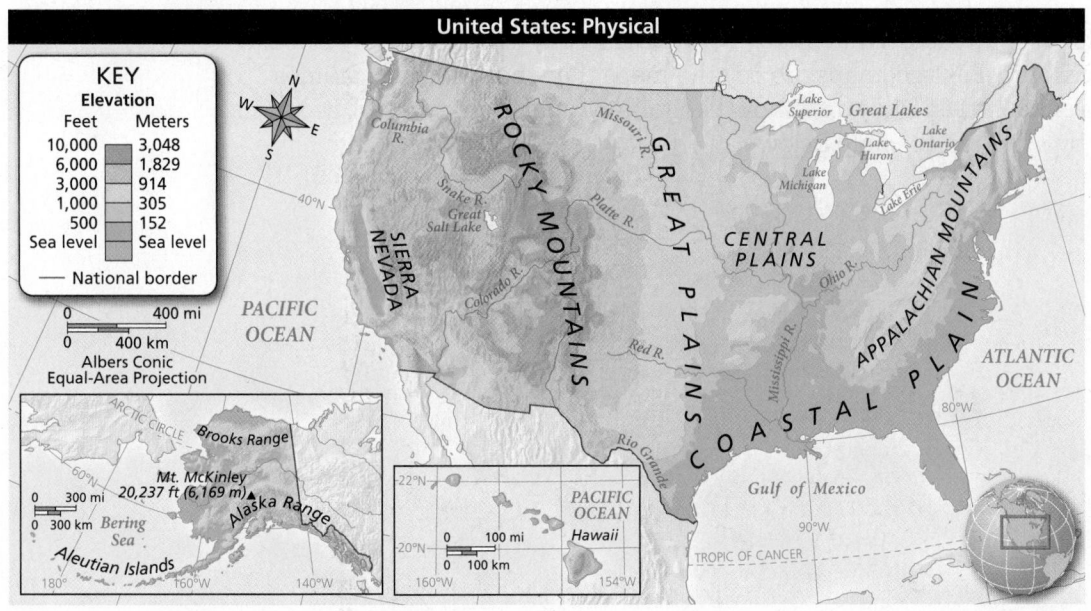

[1.] Identify the title and region shown on a map. A map's title can help you to identify the region covered by the map. The title may also tell you the type of information you will find on the map. If the map has no title, you can identify the region by reading the labels on the map.

[2.] Use the map key to interpret symbols and colors on a map. A key or legend often appears in a small box near the edge of the map. The legend will tell you the meaning of colors, symbols, or other patterns on the map. On a physical map, colors from the key often show elevation, or height above sea level, on the map.

[3.] Identify physical features, such as mountains, valleys, oceans, and rivers. Using labels on the map and colors and symbols from the key, identify the physical features on the map. The information in the key allows you to interpret the information from visuals such as a map. Rivers, oceans, lakes, and other bodies of water are usually colored blue. Colors from the key may indicate higher and lower elevation, or there may be shading on the map that shows mountains.

[4.] Draw conclusions about the region based on natural resources and physical features. Once you understand all the symbols and colors on the map, try to interpret the information from the map. Is it very mountainous or mostly flat? Does it have a coastline? Does the region have lots of lakes and rivers that suggest a good water supply? Pose and answer questions about geographic distributions and patterns shown on the map. Physical maps can give you an idea of lifestyle and economic activities of people in the region.

Read Political Maps

What is the capital of Mexico? What states border Baffin Bay? To find out, you could look at a political map. Political maps are colorful maps that show borders, or lines dividing states or countries. They also show capitals and major cities. Practice reading political maps by studying the map below.

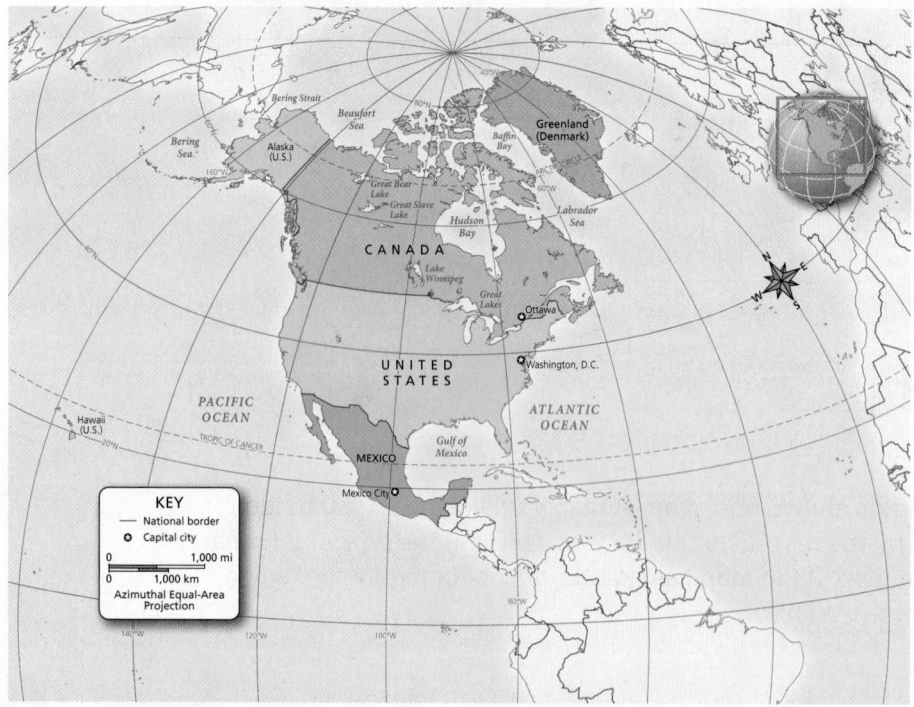

[1.] Identify the title of the political map and the region shown. A map's title can help you identify the region covered by the map. The title may also tell you the type of information you will find on the map. If the map has no title, you can identify the region by reading the labels on the map.

[2.] Use the map key to interpret symbols and colors on the map. A key or legend often appears in a small box near the edge of the map. The key will help you interpret information from visuals, including maps, by telling you the meaning of colors, symbols, or other patterns on the visual.

[3.] Identify boundaries between nations or states. Evaluate government data, such as borders, using the map. It is often easy to see borders, because each state or country will be a different color. If you cannot find the borders, check the key to find the lines used to mark borders on the map.

[4.] Locate capital cities. Look at the key to see how capital cities are shown on the map. They are often marked with a special symbol, such as a star.

[5.] Draw conclusions about the region based on the map. Once you understand all the symbols and colors on the map, use appropriate reading and mathematical skills to interpret social studies information, such as that shown on the map, in order to draw conclusions about the region. For example, are some countries very large with many cities? These countries are likely to be powerful and influential.

Read Special-Purpose Maps

Some maps show specific kinds of information. These special-purpose maps may show features such as climate zones, ancient trade routes, economic and government data, geographic patterns, or population. Locating and interpreting information from visuals, including special-purpose maps, is an important research skill. Practice this skill as you study the map on this page.

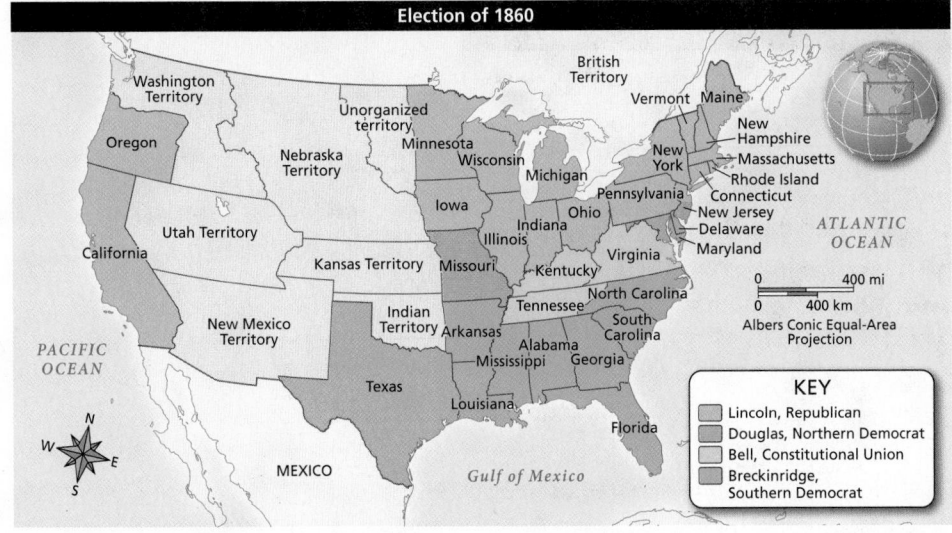

[1.] Identify the title and determine the purpose of a map. A map's title can help you identify the region covered by the map. The title may also tell you the purpose of the map. If the map has no title, see what information the map shows to determine its purpose.

[2.] Use the map key to make sense of symbols and colors on a map. A key or legend often appears in a small box near the edge of the map. The key will tell you the meaning of colors, symbols, or other patterns on the map. Special-purpose maps use these colors and symbols to present information.

[3.] Draw conclusions about the region shown on a map. Once you understand all the symbols and colors on the map, you can use appropriate skills, including reading and mathematical skills, to analyze and interpret social studies information such as maps. You can pose and answer questions about geographic patterns and distributions that are shown on maps. For example, a precipitation or climate map will show you which areas get lots of rainfall and which are very dry. You can evaluate government and economic data using maps. For example, a population map will show you which regions have lots of people and which have small, scattered populations. A historical map will show you the locations of ancient empires or trade routes. Thematic maps focus on a single theme or topic about a region. For example, you can interpret information from a thematic map representing various aspects of Texas during the nineteenth or twentieth century by studying the Great Military Map, which shows forts established in Texas during the nineteenth century, or by studying a map covering Texas during the Great Depression and World War II. By mapping this kind of detailed information, special-purpose maps can help you understand a region's history or geography.

Use Parts of a Map

If you understand how to organize and interpret information from visuals, including maps, you will be able to find the information you are looking for. Understanding how to use the parts of a map will help you find locations of specific places and estimate distances between different places. Practice this skill as you study the map on this page.

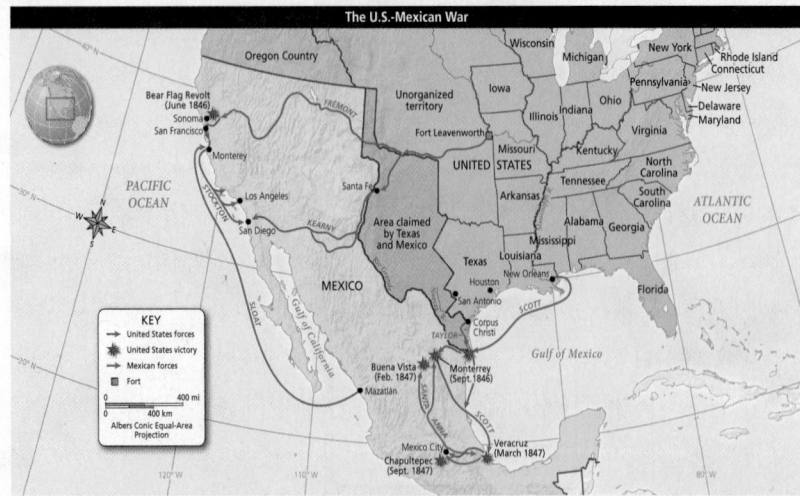

[**1.**] Identify the title and region of a map. Use appropriate reading skills to interpret social studies information such as map labels. A map's title can help you to identify the region covered by the map. The title may also tell you the type of information you will find on the map. If the map has no title, you can identify the region by reading the labels on the map.

[**2.**] Use the compass rose to determine direction. Although on most maps north is at the top of the map, you should always double check the compass rose. Often, on the compass rose, the first letter of each direction represents that direction. For example, "N" represents the direction "north." Some compass roses are as simple as an arrow pointing north.

[**3.**] Use the scale to estimate the distance between places. Use appropriate mathematical skills to interpret social studies information such as a map scale. The scale on a map shows how a measurement on the map compares to the distance on the ground. For example, if one inch on the map represents a mile, the number of inches between two places on the map is the distance in miles.

[**4.**] Use the key or legend on a map to find information about colors or symbols on a map. A key or legend often appears in a small box near the edge of the map. The legend will tell you the meaning of colors, symbols, or other patterns on the map.

[**5.**] Use the latitude and longitude grid to determine absolute locations. An absolute location is an exact description of a location on Earth's surface based on latitude and longitude. You can use the latitude and longitude lines on a map to find the absolute location of a place.

Analyze Primary and Secondary Sources

Primary sources are firsthand accounts of events. By contrast, secondary sources are secondhand accounts of events. Both sources are useful, but it is important to differentiate between valid primary and secondary sources. In this lesson, you'll learn how to locate and use primary and secondary sources to acquire information about the United States. Practice this skill by analyzing these two images to determine which is a primary source and which is a secondary source.

[1.] Determine who created the source as well as when and why it was created. Determine whether it is a primary or secondary source. Identify the author of the document. Next, look for the date the document was written or the date when the document was first published. Most primary sources are written close to the date of the events described. Secondary sources are often written well after the events described. Firsthand observers or participants in an event create primary sources. People who did not witness an event create secondary sources. Primary sources record an event. Secondary sources analyze or draw conclusions about events. Secondary sources rely on both primary and secondary sources. Good research requires you to analyze and evaluate the validity of information, arguments, and counterarguments from a primary or secondary source for frame of reference.

[2.] Identify the main idea and supporting details, and determine whether they are facts or opinions. Read the text carefully and ask yourself, "What point is this text making?" This point is the main idea. Then reread the text and list details that support this main idea. Decide whether these details are facts or opinions. If the details are facts, it should be possible to confirm them in other sources. If the author uses emotional language that shows feelings, the supporting details are probably opinions. Carefully analyze and evaluate the validity of information, arguments, and counterarguments from primary and secondary sources for point of view.

[3.] Decide whether the source's information is biased or if it is accurate and credible. Check statements in the text against reliable sources, such as encyclopedias or books written by experts on the topic. If reliable sources agree with the text, it is probably fairly accurate. If most of the text seems to be opinions rather than facts, it is not an accurate source of information. Still, these opinions can teach you about the author's world. A writer who observed an exciting or scary event may use emotional language to describe the event, but the source may still be a reliable account. An important part of research is analyzing and evaluating the validity of the information, arguments, and counterarguments from primary and secondary sources for bias or propaganda.

Compare Viewpoints

When people disagree about a topic, they have different viewpoints. Knowing how to analyze and evaluate the validity of information, arguments, and counterarguments from both primary and secondary sources for point of view can help you to learn more about a topic. Practice this skill by comparing the following viewpoints on the Compromise of 1850.

PEARSON
realize™

www.PearsonRealize.com
View Video Tutorials and other
21st Century Skills

"There are two descriptions of ties which bind this Union and this glorious people together. One is the political bond and tie which connects them, and the other is the fraternal [brotherly] commercial tie which binds them together. I want to see them both preserved."

–Henry Clay

"On the one hand our devotion to the Union—a devotion manifested in the confiding spirit with which we yielded many of the most important attributes of sovereignty for a connection with it…[O]n the other hand, a just sense of what is due to ourselves, will not permit us to submit to outrages and wrong from any quarter."

–Petre Hansborough Bell

[1.] Identify the authors of texts presenting different points of view and identify each author's frame of reference. Frame of reference is a term that describes the experiences, values, and ideas that influence a person's opinions and actions. It can also be referred to as *point of view*. First, identify the group or individual that wrote each text. Determine if the source is primary or secondary. As you read, take note of any information about the author's experiences or background. Also, look for any signs of what the author thinks is important. These types of statements can help you analyze and evaluate the validity of information, arguments, and counterarguments from both primary and secondary sources for point of view.

[2.] Recognize any similarities and differences between the authors' frames of reference and identify the opinion of each author. Pay attention to any similarities and differences between the two authors' experiences, values, and ideas. Read carefully to identify the opinion of each author. In an article about a rock band, an author who played guitar in a band for ten years argues that Band A is the best band today because of its great guitarist. In a second article, another author who sang for many years argues that Band B is the best because of its lead singer. Notice how authors' arguments and counterarguments are shaped by their frame of reference, or point of view.

[3.] Draw conclusions about similarities and differences between authors' points of view. With some information about the point of view of each author, you can understand why they have different opinions. This helps you to analyze and evaluate the validity of the information, arguments, and counterarguments. In the example of the two authors writing about rock bands, each author stresses his or her own areas of expertise. You might decide to listen to the band recommended by the singer if you share an interest in vocals. If you are more interested in instrumentals, you might choose the band recommended by the guitarist.

Identify Bias

Being able to analyze and evaluate the validity of information, arguments, and counterarguments for bias helps you to determine whether primary or secondary sources you find online, in books, or in the media are reliable. When you are able to identify bias in written, oral, and visual material, you can see when someone is presenting only one side of an issue or basing an argument on emotion instead of facts.

Practice this skill by applying the steps below whenever you read an editorial or an op-ed piece in the news media.

[**1.**] Identify the author of a source and the author's purpose. First, identify the author of the source. The author may be a group or an organization rather than a single person. The author may state his or her purpose very clearly in the source. If not, the type of source may give you an idea of the purpose. For example, the writer of an encyclopedia aims to summarize information about a subject. The author of a political Web site may want you to vote for a candidate.

[**2.**] Identify the main idea, and check whether the main idea is supported with facts or opinions. Read the document carefully and ask yourself, "What is the main point of this selection?" Your answer to this question is the main idea. Reread the document and list details that support this main idea. Decide whether these details are facts or opinions. To find out whether they are facts, check whether other reliable sources include the same information. If your source uses statements that shows feelings, those statements are probably opinions.

[**3.**] Look for the use of emotional language or one-sided opinions. Look for words that can show opinions such as "good" and "bad." Be aware of statements that make you feel angry, scared, or excited. Also, watch out for statements that only express one side of an issue. These are all signs of bias.

[**4.**] Draw conclusions about the author's bias, if any. Is the author using mostly emotional language with few facts to support his or her ideas? Are there insults or other very negative language in the source? If so, the source is probably biased. Similarly, if you notice that the author is presenting only one side of an issue, the source is probably not reliable. It is important to analyze and evaluate the information, arguments, and counterarguments in both primary and secondary sources for bias.

Evaluate Existing Arguments

When you evaluate existing arguments, you must evaluate and analyze the point of view and biases of your sources and their authors. Who is the author and what is he or she trying to accomplish? How valid are the arguments in your primary and secondary sources? If you master these skills, you will be able to analyze and interpret social studies information such as speeches. Practice this skill as you read and evaluate the excerpt on this page.

> There are two main ways in which those who have traveled to this part of the world pretending to be Christians have uprooted these pitiful peoples and wiped them from the face of the earth. First, they have waged war on them: unjust, cruel, bloody and tyrannical [using power unjustly] war. Second, they have murdered anyone and everyone who has shown the slightest sign of resistance. . . .
>
> The reason the [Spanish] have murdered on such a vast scale and killed anyone and everyone in their way is purely and simply greed. They have set out to line their pockets with gold. . . .

The Spaniards have shown not the slightest consideration for these people, treating them (and I speak from first-hand experience, having been there from the outset) not as brute animals— indeed, I would to God they had done and had shown them the consideration they afford their animals—so much as piles of dung in the middle of the road. They have had as little concern for their souls as for their bodies. . . .

—Bartolomé de Las Casas, *The Destruction of the Indies*, 1542

[**1.**] Identify the claim or thesis. What is the author or source claiming? The claim or thesis is usually found in the introduction and/or conclusion of a written or spoken argument.

[**2.**] Identify the reasons (claims to truth or facts) the author offers in support of his or her claim. What evidence does the author or source provide to support their claims? Make a list of the evidence provided to support each claim.

[**3.**] Evaluate the argument. Analyze and evaluate the validity of the evidence presented to support each claim. Use the appropriate skills to analyze and interpret social studies information, such as speeches. Research each claim to be sure that the author's statements are accurate. Carefully check for evidence of bias or propaganda. Be sure you understand the author's point of view and his or her frame of reference. Finally, check to be sure that the author's conclusions follow logically from the evidence presented. If the evidence is accurate, the author is free from bias, and conclusions follow logically from the evidence, the claims are probably valid.

Consider and Counter Opposing Arguments

Before you can effectively counter opposing arguments, you'll need to analyze possible counterarguments for frame of reference, bias, point of view, and propaganda. You'll plan your response ahead of time, collecting research and data. Then, you'll make a point of acknowledging the opposing view before presenting your counterarguments. To practice this skill, suppose you are a colonist debating whether to take up arms against the British. Choose a side of the debate to support. What arguments will you use to support your side of the debate? What counterarguments will you anticipate the other side using? Why is it useful to anticipate the other side's arguments?

[**1.**] Fully understand your argument and the potential counter points. Do research as needed to find out more about other opposing views. Analyze and evaluate the validity of possible counterarguments from primary and secondary sources for frame of reference, bias, point of view, and propaganda.

[**2.**] Make predictions and outline a response to several of the opposing views. Continue researching as needed. Researching, analyzing, and evaluating the validity of opposing arguments will help you support and strengthen your own. Opposing arguments can consist of any reasons, conclusions, or claims that oppose yours. Outline your response to each opposing reason, conclusion, or claim.

[3.] To counter an opposing argument, first acknowledge the opposing view. This strategy shows that you have heard the opposing argument and are responding accordingly. Consider using statements such as "I understand your point, but you should also consider the following..." You can also respond by refuting facts, logic, etc. Be sure to respond to each opposing argument. Ignoring or dismissing a counterargument shows that your response is weak and unsupported.

Participate in a Discussion or Debate

When you participate in a discussion or debate, your goal is to explain, analyze, and defend a point of view–often related to a current political or economic issue. To be a successful debater, you'll do your research, present your position, and defend your point of view in a courteous manner. Use the steps below to prepare for a discussion on this question: Do you think the United States should act as a "global policeman?" Why or why not?

[1.] Research. Before participating in a discussion or debate, do research to gain knowledge of your subject so that you may be an informed and prepared participant. Take notes as needed to help you prepare. Jot down main points and any questions you may have. As you research, decide where you might stand on the issue. Be sure to gather research and sources that will allow you to explain, analyze, and defend your point of view.

[2.] Present your position. After you have organized your thoughts and decided where you stand, explain and defend your point of view. Be sure to stay focused on the topic and your line of argument. Ask questions that challenge the accuracy, logic, or relevance of opposing views.

[3.] During the discussion or debate, be patient and courteous. Listen attentively, be respectful and supportive of peers, and speak only when instructed to do so by the moderator. Be sure to allow others to express their views; do not monopolize the debate or discussion. Speak clearly and slowly.

Give an Effective Presentation

When you create a written, visual, and oral presentation, you teach, convince, or share information with an audience. Effective presentations use both words and visuals to engage audiences. Delivery is also important. For example, you can use the way you move, speak, and look at the audience to keep people interested. Use the steps below to prepare and deliver a presentation on the Lewis and Clark Expedition.

[1.] Identify the purpose of your presentation and your audience. Think about the purpose of your written, visual, and oral presentation. If this is a research report, you will need facts and data to support your points. If you are trying to persuade your audience, look for powerful photos. Keep your audience in mind. Consider their interests and present your topic in a way that will engage them.

[2.] Write the text and find visual aids for your presentation. Look online and in books and magazines for information and images for your presentation. Organize the information and write it up carefully so that it is easy for your audience to under-stand. Diagrams can show complicated information in a clear way. Visuals also get people interested in the presentation. So choose large, colorful images that people in the back of the audience will be able to see.

[3.] Practice and work to improve your presentation. Keep practicing your oral presen-tation until you know the material well. Then, practice some more, focusing on improving your delivery.

[4.] Use body language, tone of voice, and eye contact to deliver an effective presen-tation. Answer questions if the audience has them. At the beginning of your oral presentation, take a breath, smile, and stand up tall. Speak more loudly and more clearly than you would in normal conversation. Also, try not to rush through the presentation. Glance at your notes but speak naturally, rather than reading. Look at people in the audience. If people are confused, pause to clarify. Finally, leave time for people in the audience to ask questions.

Write an Essay

There are four steps to writing an essay. You'll start by selecting a topic and research sources, then you'll write an outline and develop a thesis or point of view. After drafting your essay, you'll carefully proofread it to be sure you've used standard grammar, spelling, sentence structure, and punctuation. Finally, you'll revise and polish your work. To practice this skill, select a topic that interests you about the colonial period and develop a thesis. Then explain to a partner the steps you will take to write your essay.

[1.] Choose your topic and research sources. Check which types of sources you will need. Gather different types of reliable sources that support the argument you will be making.

[2.] Write an outline and generate a thesis. First write your topic at the top of the page then list all the points or arguments you want to make about the topic; also list the facts and examples that support these points. Your thesis statement will inform the reader of the point you are making and what question you will be answering about the topic. When writing your thesis, be as specific as possible and address one main idea.

[3.] Draft your essay. After finishing your research and outline, begin writing the body of your essay; start with the introduction then write a paragraph for each of your supporting points, followed by a conclusion. As you write, do your best to use standard grammar, spelling, sentence structure, and punctuation. Be sure any ter-minology is used correctly.

[4.] Revise. An important part of the writing process involves checking for areas in which information should be added, removed, or rewritten. Try to imagine that this paper belongs to someone else. Does the paper have a clear thesis? Do all of the ideas relate back to the thesis? Read your paper out loud and listen for awkward pauses and unclear ideas. Lastly, check for mistakes in standard grammar, spelling, sentence structure, punctuation, and usage.

Avoid Plagiarism

When you don't attribute ideas and information to source materials and authors, you are plagiarizing. Plagiarizing–claiming others' ideas and information as your own–is considered unethical. You can avoid plagiarizing by carefully noting down which authors and sources you'll be using, citing those authors and sources in your paper, and listing them in a bibliography. To practice this skill, suppose you have been assigned to write a research paper on American Indian cultures. Name three types of sources you might use to help you gather information. Explain how you will avoid plagiarism when you use these sources.

[1.] Keep a careful log of your notes. As you read sources to gain background information on your topic, keep track of ideas and information and the sources and authors they come from. Write down the name of each source next to your notes from that particular source so you can remember to cite it later on. Create a separate section in your notes where you keep your own thoughts and ideas so you know which ideas are your own. Using someone else's words or paraphrasing their ideas does not make them yours.

[2.] Cite sources in your paper. You must identify the source materials and authors you use to support your ideas. Whenever you use statistics, facts, direct quotations, or paraphrases of others' views, you need to attribute them to your source. Cite your sources within the body of your paper. Check your assignment to find out how they should be formatted.

[3.] List your sources in a bibliography at the end of your paper. List your source materials and authors cited in alphabetical order by author, using accepted formats. As you work, be sure to check your list of sources from your notes so that none are left out of the bibliography.

Solve Problems

Problem solving is a skill that you use every day. It is a process that requires an open mind, clear thinking, and action. Practice this skill by considering the lack of volunteers for a local project such as a food bank or park clean up and using these steps to solve the problem.

[1.] Understand the problem. Before trying to solve a problem, make sure that you gather as much information as possible in order to identify the problem. What are the causes and effects of the problem? Who is involved? You will want to make sure that you understand different perspectives on the problem. Try not to jump to conclusions or make assumptions. You might end up misunderstanding the problem.

[2.] Consider possible solutions and choose the best one. Once you have identified the problem and gathered some information, list and consider a number of possible options. Right away, one solution might seem like the right one, but try to think of other solutions. Be sure to consider carefully the advantages and disadvantages of each option. It can help to take notes listing benefits and drawbacks. Look for the solution whose benefits outweigh its drawbacks. After considering each option, choose the solution you think is best.

[3.] Make and implement a plan. Choose and implement a solution. Make a detailed, step-by-step plan to implement the solution that you choose. Write your plan down and assign yourself a deadline for each step. That will help you to stay on track toward completing your plan. Try to think of any problems that might come up and what you will do to address those problems. Of course, there are many things that you cannot predict. Stay flexible. Evaluate the effectiveness of the solution and adjust your plan as necessary.

Make Decisions

Everyone makes decisions. The trick is to learn how to make good decisions. How can you make good decisions? First, identify a situation that requires a decision and gather information. Then, identify possible options and predict the consequences of each option. Finally, choose the best option and take action to implement a decision. Practice this skill by considering the steps you should take when making a decision about which candidate you should vote for in a local, state, or national election.

[1.] Determine the options between which you must decide. In some cases, like ordering from a menu at a restaurant, our options may be clear. In other cases, you will need to identify a situation that requires a decision, gather information, and identify the options that are available to you. Spend some time thinking about the situation and brainstorm a number of options. If necessary, do a little research to find more options. Make a list of options that you might choose.

[2.] Review the costs and benefits of each option. Carefully predict the consequences of each option. You may want to make a cost-benefit list for each option. To do this, write down the option and then draw two columns underneath it. One column will be the "pro" or benefit list. The other column will be the "con" or cost list. Note the pros and cons for each of your options. Try not to rush through this process. For a very important decision, you may even want to show your list to someone you trust. This person can help you think of costs and benefits that you had not considered.

[3.] Determine the best option and act on it. Look through your cost-benefit lists. Note any especially serious costs. If an option has the possibility of an extremely negative consequence, you might want to cross it off your list right away. Look closely at the options with the most benefits and the fewest costs, and choose the one that you think is best. Once you have made a choice, take action to implement a decision. If necessary, make a detailed plan with clear steps. Set a deadline to complete the steps to keep yourself moving toward your goal.

Being an Informed Citizen

Informed citizens understand the responsibilities, duties, and obligations of citizenship. They are well informed about civic affairs, involved with their communities, and politically active. When it comes to issues they personally care about, they take a stand and reach out to others.

[1.] Learn the issues. A great way to begin to understand the responsibilities of citizenship is to first find topics of interest to you. Next, become well informed about civic affairs in your town, city, or country. Read newspapers, magazines, and articles you find online about events happening in your area or around the world. Analyze the information you read to come to your own conclusions. Radio programs, podcasts, and social media are also great ways to keep up with current events and interact with others about issues.

[2.] Get involved. Attend community events to speak with others who know the issues. Become well informed about how policies are made and changed. Find out who to speak to if you would like to take part in civic affairs and policy creation. There are government websites that can help direct you to the right person. These websites will also provide his or her contact details.

[3.] Take a stand and reach out. Write, call, or meet with your elected officials to become a better informed, more responsible citizen. Do research about candidates who are running for office to be an informed voter. Start your own blog or website to explore issues, interact with others, and be part of the community or national dialogue.

Political Participation

Political participation starts with an understanding of the responsibilities, duties and obligations of citizenship, such as serving the public good. When you understand your role as a political participant, you can get involved through volunteering for a political campaign, running for office, or interacting with others in person or online.

[1.] Volunteer for a political campaign. Political campaigns offer a wide variety of opportunities to help you become involved in the political process and become a responsible citizen by serving the public good. As a political campaign volunteer you may have the opportunity to attend events, make calls to voters, and explore your community while getting to know how other voters think about the responsibilities, duties, and obligations of citizenship.

[2.] Run for office in your school or community. A good way to become involved in your school or community is to run for office. Student council or community positions offer a great opportunity for you to become familiar with the campaign and election process.

[3.] Reach out to others. Start or join an interest group. Interest groups enable people to work together on common goals related to the political process. Write a letter or email to a public official. By contacting an elected official from your area, you can either support or oppose laws or policies. You can also ask for help or support regarding certain issues.

[4.] Interact online. Social networking sites and blogs offer a great way for people of all ages to interact and write about political issues. As you connect with others, you'll become more confident in your role as a citizen working for the public good.

Voting

Voting is not only a right. It is also one of the primary responsibilities, duties, and obligations of citizenship. Before you can legally vote, however, you must understand the voter registration process and the criteria for voting in elections. You should also understand the issues and know where different candidates stand on those issues.

[1.] Check eligibility and residency requirements. In order to vote in the United States, you must be a United States citizen who is 18 years or older, and you must be a resident of the place where you plan to vote.

[2.] Register to vote. You cannot vote until you understand the voter registration process. You can register at city or town election offices, or when you get a driver's license. You can also register by mail or online. You may also have the option of registering at the polls on Election Day, but this does not apply in all states. Make sure to find out what you need to do to register in your state, as well as the deadline for registering. You may have the option of declaring a political party when registering.

[3.] Learn the issues. As the election approaches, research the candidates and issues in order to be an informed voter. Watch televised debates, if there are any. You can also review the candidates' websites. By doing these things and thinking critically about what you learn, you will be prepared to exercise your responsibility, duty and obligation as a United States citizen.

[4.] Vote. Make sure to arrive at the correct polling place on Election Day to cast your ballot. Research to find out when the polls will be open. Advance voting, absentee voting, and voting by mail are also options in certain states for those who qualify.

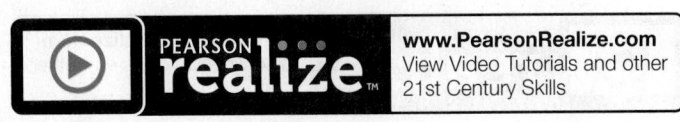

Serving on a Jury

As an American, you need to understand the duties, obligations and responsibilities of citizenship; among these is the expectation that you may be required to serve on a jury. You will receive a written notice when you are summoned to jury duty and you'll receive instruction on the special duties and obligations of a juror. You'll follow the American code of justice which assumes that a person is innocent until proven guilty, and you'll follow instructions about keeping trial information confidential.

[1.] Wait to receive notification. If you are summoned to serve as a juror, you will be first notified by mail. If you are chosen to move on to the jury selection phase, lawyers from both sides will ask you questions as they select the final jury members. It is an honor to serve as a juror, as it is a responsibility offered only to American citizens.

[2.] Follow the law and remain impartial. Your job is to determine whether or not someone broke the law. You may also be asked to sit on the jury for civil cases (as opposed to criminal cases); these cases involve lawsuits filed against individuals or businesses for any perceived wrong doing (such as broken contracts, trespassing, discrimination, etc.). Be sure to follow the law as it is explained to you, regardless of whether you approve of the law or not. Your decision about the trial should not be influenced by any personal bias or views you may have.

[3.] Remember that the defendant is presumed innocent. In a criminal trial, the defendant must be proven guilty "beyond a reasonable doubt" for the verdict to be guilty. If the trial team fails to prove the defendant to be guilty beyond a reasonable doubt, the jury verdict must be "not guilty."

[4.] During the trial, respect the court's right to privacy. As a juror, you have specific duties, obligations, and responsibilities under the law. Do not permit anyone to talk about the case with you or in your presence, except with the court's permission. Avoid media coverage once the trial has begun so as to prevent bias. Keep an open mind and do not form or state any opinions about the case until you have heard all of the evidence, the closing arguments from the lawyers, and the judge's instructions on the applicable law.

Paying Taxes

Paying taxes is one of the responsibilities of citizenship. How do you go about figuring out how much you've already paid in taxes and how much you still owe? It's your duty and obligation to find out, by determining how much has been deducted from your pay and filing your tax return.

[1.] Find out how taxes are deducted from your pay. In the United States, payroll taxes are imposed on employers and employees, and they are collected and paid by the employers. Check your pay stub to find out how much money was deducted for taxes. Be sure to also save the W-2 tax form your employer sends to you. You will need this form later on when filing your tax paperwork. Also save any interest income statements. All this information will help you fulfill your obligation as an American taxpayer.

[2.] Check the sales taxes in your state. All but five states impose sales and use taxes on retail sale, lease, and rental of many goods, as well as some services. Sales tax is calculated as the purchase price times the appropriate tax rate. Tax rates vary widely from less than one percent to over ten percent. Sales tax is collected by the seller at the time of sale.

[3.] File your tax return. Filing your tax return is more than an obligation: it's also a duty and responsibility of citizenship. You may receive tax forms in the mail, or pick them up at the local Post Office or library. Fill the forms in and then mail or electronically send completed tax forms and any necessary payments to the Internal Revenue Service (IRS) and your state's department of revenue. The IRS provides free resources to help people prepare and electronically file their tax returns; go to IRS.gov to learn more. Note: certain things such as charitable donations and business expenses are tax deductible.

[Africa: Political]

EUROPE

ASIA

Atlantic Ocean

Mediterranean Sea

Strait of Gibraltar

Madeira Islands (Portugal)

Algiers
Tunis
Rabat ⊛
Casablanca ○

MOROCCO

TUNISIA

Tripoli ⊛

Canary Islands (Spain)

ALGERIA

LIBYA

Alexandria ○
Cairo ⊛

EGYPT

Tropic of Cancer

Red Sea

Western Sahara (Morocco)

CAPE VERDE

MAURITANIA

Nouakchott ⊛

MALI

Tombouctou ○

NIGER

CHAD

Khartoum ⊛

SUDAN

ERITREA
Asmara ⊛

Gulf of Aden

DJIBOUTI
Djibouti ⊛

Dakar ⊛
Banjul ⊛

SENEGAL

GAMBIA

Bamako ⊛
Niamey ⊛

BURKINA FASO

Ouagadougou ⊛

Lake Chad

Kano ○
N'Djamena ⊛

Addis Ababa ⊛

GUINEA-BISSAU
Bissau ⊛

GUINEA

Conakry ⊛

SIERRA LEONE
Freetown ⊛

IVORY COAST

GHANA

BENIN

TOGO

NIGERIA
Abuja ⊛

CENTRAL AFRICAN REPUBLIC

SOUTH SUDAN

ETHIOPIA

Monrovia ⊛

LIBERIA

Yamoussoukro ○
Abidjan ○
Accra ⊛
Lomé ⊛
Porto-Novo ⊛
Lagos ○

CAMEROON

Bangui ⊛
Juba ⊛

Lake Turkana

SOMALIA

Malabo ⊛
Yaoundé ⊛

EQUATORIAL GUINEA

SÃO TOMÉ AND PRÍNCIPE

São Tomé ⊛

Libreville ⊛

GABON

CONGO

Kisangani ○

DEMOCRATIC REPUBLIC OF THE CONGO

Kampala ⊛
Kigali ⊛

UGANDA

KENYA

Lake Victoria

Nairobi ⊛

Mogadishu ⊛

Equator

Brazzaville ⊛

Bujumbura ⊛

RWANDA

BURUNDI

Dodoma ○

Mombasa ○

Indian Ocean

Cabinda (Angola)

Kinshasa ⊛

Lake Tanganyika

TANZANIA

Dar es Salaam ○

SEYCHELLES

Luanda ⊛

Atlantic Ocean

Lubumbashi ○

MALAWI

Lake Malawi

Moroni ⊛

COMOROS

Mayotte (France)

ANGOLA

ZAMBIA

Lilongwe ⊛

Lusaka ⊛

MOZAMBIQUE

Mozambique Channel

Harare ⊛

Antananarivo ⊛

ZIMBABWE

NAMIBIA

BOTSWANA

Windhoek ⊛

MADAGASCAR

Tropic of Capricorn

Gaborone ⊛

Pretoria ⊛
Maputo ⊛

Johannesburg ○
Mbabane ⊛
Lobamba ⊛

SWAZILAND

Bloemfontein ○
Maseru ⊛
Durban ○

LESOTHO

Cape of Good Hope

SOUTH AFRICA

Cape Town ⊛

Cape Agulhas

Legend
— National border
-- - Disputed border
⊛ National capital
○ Other city

Azimuthal Equidistant Projection

0   500   1000 miles

0   500   1000 kilometers

40°N · 30°N · 20°N · 10°N · 0° · 10°S · 20°S · 30°S · 40°S

20°W · 40°S · 10°W · 0° · 10°E · 20°E · 30°E · 40°E · 50°E

[Africa: Physical]

EUROPE

ASIA

Atlantic Ocean

Madeira Islands

Strait of Gibraltar

Mediterranean Sea

Canary Islands

of Cancer

ATLAS MOUNTAINS

Suez Canal

Sinai Peninsula

Qattara Depression

LIBYAN DESERT

Arabian Desert

Nile River

Lake Nasser

Red Sea

NUBIAN DESERT

S   A   H   A   R   A

Ahaggar Mountains

Tibesti Mountains

Gulf of Aden

S   A   H   E   L

Blue Nile R.

White Nile R.

Lake Tana

Senegal R.

Niger River

Lake Chad

10°N

Fouta Djallon

Volta R.

ETHIOPIAN HIGHLANDS

Lake Volta

Benue River

SUDD

Adamawa Highlands

GREAT RIFT VALLEY

Gulf of Guinea

Bioko

Ubangi R.

Congo R.

Lake Albert

Lake Turkana

Equator

São Tomé

CONGO BASIN

0°

Atlantic Ocean

N
W   E
S

Mt. Kilimanjaro
19,341 ft. (5,895 m)

Lake Victoria

Indian Ocean

Serengeti Plain

Lake Tanganyika

Zanzibar

10°S

Lake Malawi

Comoro Islands

Mozambique Channel

Zambezi R.

Madagascar

Elevation

Feet	Meters
More than 13,000	More than 3,960
6,500–13,000	1,980–3,960
1,600–6,500	480–1,980
650–1,600	200–480
0–650	0–200
Below sea level	Below sea level

—— National border

---- Disputed border

20°S

Okavango Basin

Limpopo R.

Tropic of Capricorn

NAMIB DESERT

KALAHARI DESERT

Azimuthal Equidistant Projection

0   500   1000 miles

0   500   1000 kilometers

Orange R.

Drakensberg

30°S

Cape of Good Hope

Cape Agulhas

20°W   40°S   10°W   0°   10°E   20°E   30°E   40°E   50°E   40°S

[Asia: Physical]

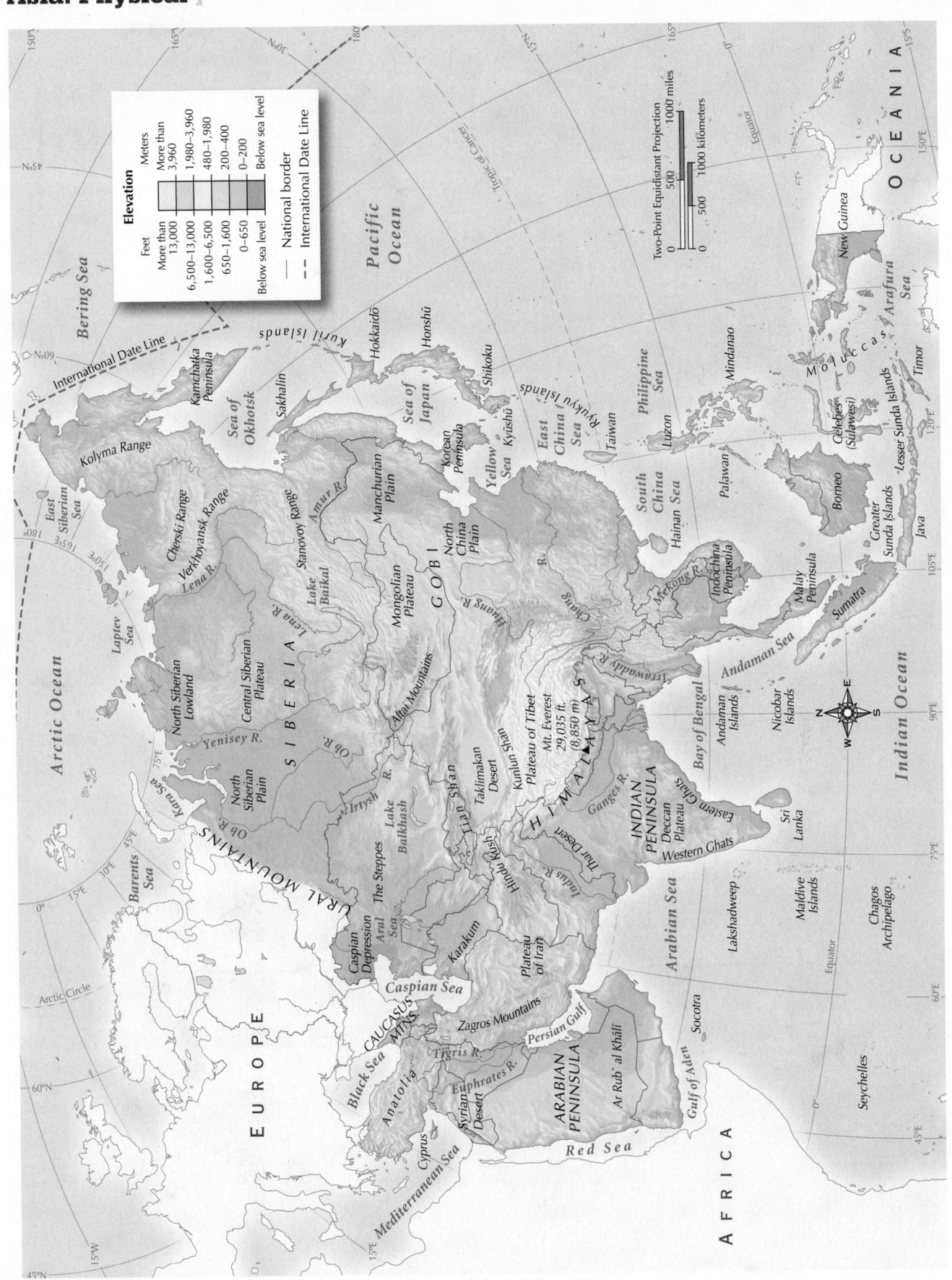

Elevation

Feet	Meters
More than 13,000	More than 3,960
6,500–13,000	1,980–3,960
1,600–6,500	480–1,980
650–1,600	200–400
0–650	0–200
Below sea level	Below sea level

—— National border

- - - International Date Line

Two-Point Equidistant Projection

1000 miles
1000 kilometers

Arctic Ocean

Bering Sea

Sea of Okhotsk

Pacific Ocean

Kamchatka Peninsula

Kolyma Range

Cherski Range

Verkhoyansk Range

Stanovoy Range

Sakhalin

Kuril Islands

Hokkaidō

Honshū

Sea of Japan

Shikoku

Kyūshū

Amur R.

Manchurian Plain

Korean Peninsula

Yellow Sea

East China Sea

Ryukyu Islands

Taiwan

Philippine Sea

Mindanao

OCEANIA

New Guinea

Moluccas

Arafura Sea

Timor

Celebes (Sulawesi)

Lesser Sunda Islands

Luzon

South China Sea

Hainan

Palawan

Borneo

Greater Sunda Islands

Java

Malay Peninsula

Sumatra

Indochina Peninsula

Mekong R.

Andaman Sea

Andaman Islands

Nicobar Islands

Bay of Bengal

Irrawaddy R.

Indian Ocean

East Siberian Sea

Laptev Sea

North Siberian Lowland

Lena R.

Lake Baikal

Mongolian Plateau

GOBI

North China Plain

Huang R.

Chang R.

Central Siberian Plateau

SIBERIA

Yenisey R.

Ob R.

North Siberian Plain

Irtysh

Lake Balkhash

Altai Mountains

Tian Shan

Taklimakan Desert

Kunlun Shan

Plateau of Tibet

Mt. Everest 29,035 ft. (8,850 m)

HIMALAYAS

Ganges R.

INDIAN PENINSULA

Deccan Plateau

Eastern Ghats

Western Ghats

Sri Lanka

Thar Desert

Indus R.

Hindu Kush

Karakum

Plateau of Iran

Aral Sea

Caspian Depression

The Steppes

URAL MOUNTAINS

Ob R.

Kara Sea

Barents Sea

EUROPE

Caspian Sea

CAUCASUS MTS.

Black Sea

Anatolia

Cyprus

Mediterranean Sea

Zagros Mountains

Tigris R.

Euphrates R.

Syrian Desert

Persian Gulf

ARABIAN PENINSULA

Ar Rub' al Khāli

Red Sea

Gulf of Aden

Socotra

Arabian Sea

Lakshadweep

Maldive Islands

Chagos Archipelago

Seychelles

AFRICA

International Date Line

Tropic of Cancer

Arctic Circle

Equator

National border
National capital
Other city

Caspian Sea

Perm'
Kazan'
Samara
Volgograd

RUSSIA

Nizhniy
Novgorod

Rostov-
on-Don
Donets'k
Sea of
Azov

Arkhangel'sk

White
Sea

Moscow

Black Sea

ASIA

Barents
Sea

St. Petersburg

Odessa

UKRAINE
Kiev

Chişinău
MOLDOVA

Constanţa

Istanbul
TURKEY

FINLAND

Tampere

Helsinki
Gulf of Finland
Tallinn
ESTONIA
Riga
LATVIA

Minsk
BELARUS

Bucharest
ROMANIA

BULGARIA
Sofia

Crete
(Greece)

LITHUANIA
Vilnius
RUSSIA

Belgrade
SERBIA
Skopje
MACEDONIA

Aegean
Sea

ARCTIC OCEAN

SWEDEN

Gulf of Bothnia

Stockholm

Göteborg

Baltic
Sea

POLAND
Warsaw
Łódź

Budapest
HUNGARY
Zagreb
CROATIA
BOSNIA AND
HERZEGOVINA
Sarajevo
MONTENEGRO
Podgorica
Tirane
ALBANIA

GREECE
Athens

Ionian
Sea

Mediterranean Sea

Arctic Circle

NORWAY

Oslo

DENMARK
Copenhagen

Hamburg

Berlin
GERMANY
Frankfurt

Prague
CZECH REPUBLIC
Munich
Vienna
AUSTRIA
LIECHTENSTEIN
Vaduz

Bratislava
SLOVAKIA

SLOVENIA
Ljubljana
Venice

Valletta
MALTA

Sicily
(Italy)

Tyrrhenian
Sea

North
Sea

Bergen

NETHERLANDS
Amsterdam

LUXEMBOURG
Luxembourg
SWITZERLAND
Bern
Milan

SAN
MARINO
VATICAN
CITY
Rome
Naples

Sardinia
(Italy)

Faeroe Islands
(Denmark)

Shetland
Islands
(U.K.)

Scotland
Glasgow
UNITED
KINGDOM
Manchester
England
London

BELGIUM
Brussels
Paris

FRANCE

Lyon

MONACO
Monaco
Marseille
Corsica
(France)

Andorra
la Vella
ANDORRA

Balearic Isands
(Spain)

English Channel

Northern
Ireland
IRELAND
Dublin

Wales

Bay of
Biscay

Toulouse

Barcelona

Valencia

ICELAND
Reykjavik

Lambert Conformal Conic
400 miles
200
0
400 kilometers
200
0

ATLANTIC
OCEAN

SPAIN
Madrid

Seville

Melilla
(Spain)

Ceuta
(Spain)

PORTUGAL
Lisbon

Gibraltar
(U.K.)

AFRICA

ITALY

Elevation

Feet	Meters	
More than 13,000	More than 3,960	
6,500–13,000	1,980–3,960	
1,600–6,500	480–1,980	
650–1,600	200–400	
0–650	0–200	
Below sea level	Below sea level	

—— National border

URAL MOUNTAINS

Pechora R.

Kama R.

Ural R.

Caspian Sea

Volga R.

Caspian Depression

Volga Upland

Don R.

CAUCASUS MTS.

Mt. Elbrus 18,510 ft. (5,642 m)

A S I A

Don R.

Sea of Azov

Central Russian Upland

Black Sea

Barents Sea

Kola Peninsula

White Sea

Lake Onega

Lake Ladoga

N. Dvina R.

Dnieper R.

Dniester R.

Bosporus

Sea of Marmara

Dardanelles

Gulf of Finland

NORTH EUROPEAN PLAIN

Vistula R.

Carpathian Mountains

Transylvanian Alps

Danube R.

Balkan Mountains

BALKAN PENINSULA

Aegean Sea

Crete

SCANDINAVIAN PENINSULA

Kjølen Mountains

Gulf of Bothnia

Gotland

Baltic Sea

Lake Vänern

Lake Vättern

Sjælland

Oder R.

Great Hungarian Plain

Dinaric Alps

Pindus Mts.

Ionian Sea

Mediterranean Sea

BARENTS Sea

ARCTIC OCEAN

Norwegian Sea

North Sea

Jutland

Elbe R.

Danube R.

Rhine R.

A L P S

Adriatic Sea

Apennines

ITALIAN PENINSULA

Tyrrhenian Sea

Sicily

Maltese Islands

Iceland

Jan Mayen

Arctic Circle

Faeroe Islands

Shetland Islands

Great Britain

Thames R.

English Channel

Seine R.

Loire R.

Lake Geneva

Mt. Blanc 15,775 ft. (4,808 m)

Massif Central

Garonne R.

Corsica

Sardinia

Balearic Islands

British Isles

Ireland

Bay of Biscay

Pyrenees

Ebro R.

Douro R.

Meseta

Tagus R.

Guadalquivir R.

IBERIAN PENINSULA

Strait of Gibraltar

A F R I C A

ATLANTIC OCEAN

Denmark Strait

Po R.

Lambert Conformal Conic

400 miles

400 kilometers

200

200

0

0

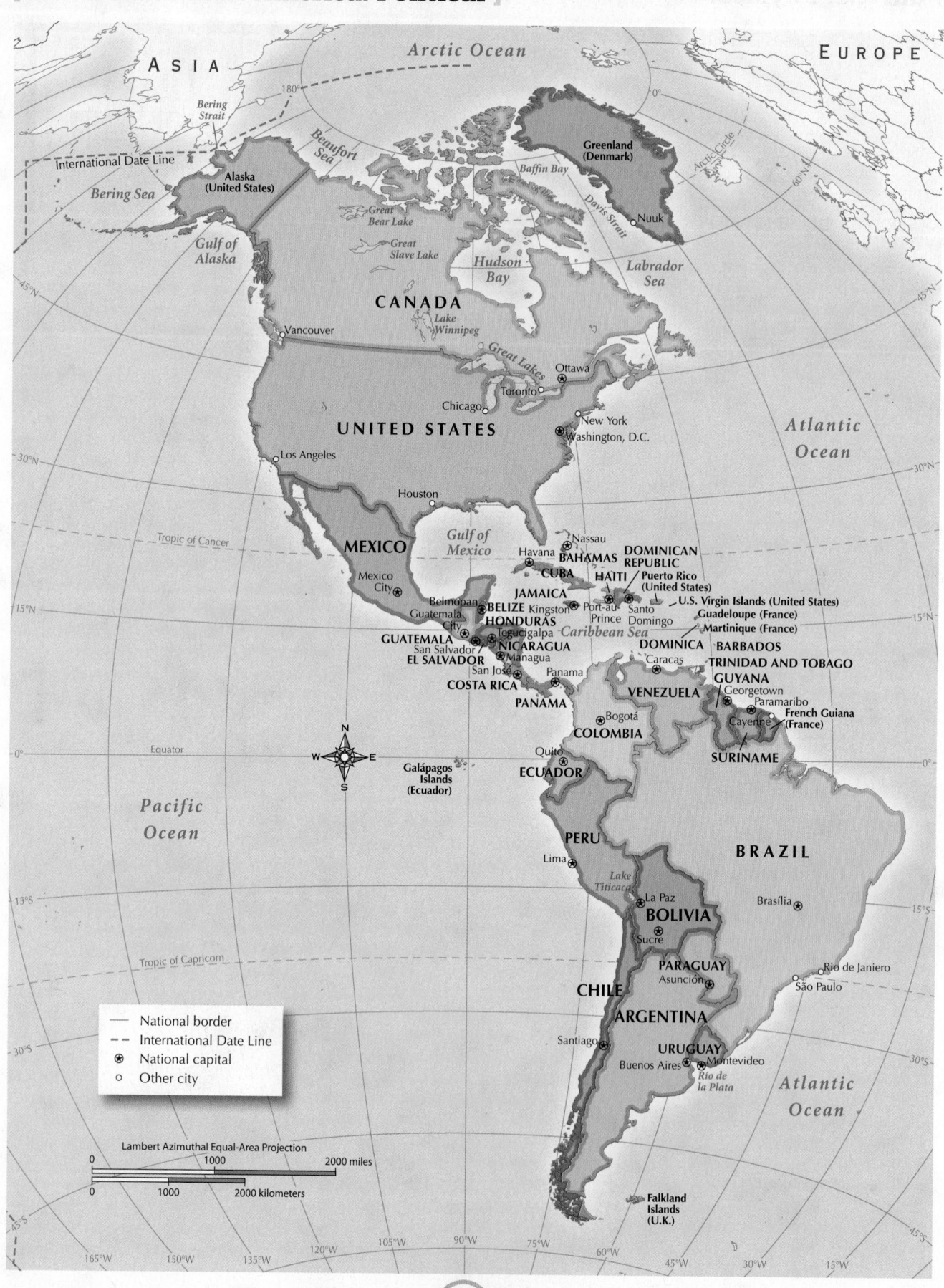

ASIA

Arctic Ocean

EUROPE

180°

0°

Bering Strait

International Date Line

Beaufort Sea

Baffin Bay

Greenland (Denmark)

Bering Sea

Alaska (United States)

Great Bear Lake

Davis Strait

Arctic Circle

60°N

Gulf of Alaska

Great Slave Lake

Hudson Bay

Labrador Sea

Nuuk

45°N

CANADA

Lake Winnipeg

45°N

Vancouver

Great Lakes

Ottawa

Toronto

Atlantic Ocean

Chicago

UNITED STATES

New York
Washington, D.C.

30°N

Los Angeles

30°N

Houston

Tropic of Cancer

Nassau

MEXICO

Gulf of Mexico

Havana

BAHAMAS

DOMINICAN REPUBLIC

Mexico City

CUBA

HAITI

Puerto Rico (United States)

15°N

Belmopan

JAMAICA

U.S. Virgin Islands (United States)

15°N

Guatemala City

BELIZE

Kingston

Santo Domingo

Guadeloupe (France)

GUATEMALA

HONDURAS

Port-au-Prince

Caribbean Sea

Martinique (France)

San Salvador

Tegucigalpa

DOMINICA

EL SALVADOR

NICARAGUA

BARBADOS

Managua

Caracas

TRINIDAD AND TOBAGO

San José

COSTA RICA

Panama

VENEZUELA

GUYANA

Georgetown

Paramaribo

PANAMA

Bogotá

Cayenne

French Guiana (France)

COLOMBIA

SURINAME

Equator

N

Galápagos Islands (Ecuador)

Quito

W   E

0°

ECUADOR

0°

S

Pacific Ocean

PERU

BRAZIL

Lima

Lake Titicaca

La Paz

Brasília

15°S

BOLIVIA

15°S

Sucre

Tropic of Capricorn

Rio de Janiero

PARAGUAY

São Paulo

Asunción

CHILE

ARGENTINA

Santiago

URUGUAY

30°S

Buenos Aires

Montevideo

30°S

Río de la Plata

Atlantic Ocean

___ National border
- - - International Date Line
⊛ National capital
○ Other city

Falkland Islands (U.K.)

Lambert Azimuthal Equal-Area Projection

0   1000   2000 miles

0   1000   2000 kilometers

45°S

45°S

165°W   150°W   135°W   120°W   105°W   90°W   75°W   60°W   45°W   30°W   15°W

North and South America: Physical

ASIA

EUROPE

Arctic Ocean

International Date Line

180°

Beaufort Sea

Ellesmere Island

Greenland

Arctic Circle

0°

Bering Strait

Mt. McKinley (Denali) 20,320 ft. (6,194 m)

Victoria Island

Baffin Bay

Baffin Island

Davis Strait

60°N

Bering Sea

Alaska Range

Mackenzie R.

Great Bear Lake

Labrador Sea

Aleutian Islands

Gulf of Alaska

Great Slave Lake

Hudson Bay

Island of Newfoundland

45°N

45°N

ROCKY MOUNTAINS

CANADIAN SHIELD

Yukon R.

Lake Winnipeg

Great Lakes

St. Lawrence R.

Cascades

Missouri R.

GREAT PLAINS

Atlantic Ocean

Sierra Nevada

Great Salt Lake

Colorado R.

Mississippi R.

Ohio R.

APPALACHIAN MTS.

30°N

30°N

Rio Grande

Tropic of Cancer

Baja California

Gulf of California

Sierra Madre Occidental

Sierra Madre Oriental

Gulf of Mexico

Cuba

Hispaniola

Lesser Antilles

15°N

15°N

Yucatán Peninsula

Jamaica

Greater Antilles

Caribbean Sea

Isthmus of Panama

Llanos

Orinoco R.

Guiana Highlands

Pacific Ocean

Galápagos Islands

Equator

0°

0°

N

W   E

S

Amazon R.

AMAZON BASIN

São Francisco R.

15°S

15°S

ANDES MOUNTAINS

Lake Titicaca

Brazilian Highlands

Elevation

Feet		Meters
More than 13,000		More than 3,960
6,500–13,000		1,980–3,960
1,600–6,500		480–1,980
650–1,600		200–400
0–650		0–200
Below sea level		Below sea level

—— National border

-- -- International Date Line

Tropic of Capricorn

Gran Chaco

Paraguay R.

Paraná R.

Aconcagua 22,834 ft. (6,960 m)

Pampas

Rio de la Plata

30°S

30°S

Atlantic Ocean

Patagonia

Lambert Azimuthal Equal-Area Projection

0   1000   2000 miles

0   1000   2000 kilometers

Tierra del Fuego

Falkland Islands

Cape Horn

45°S

45°S

165°W   150°W   135°W   120°W   105°W   90°W   75°W   60°W   45°W   30°W   15°W

Australia, New Zealand, and Oceania: Political-Physical

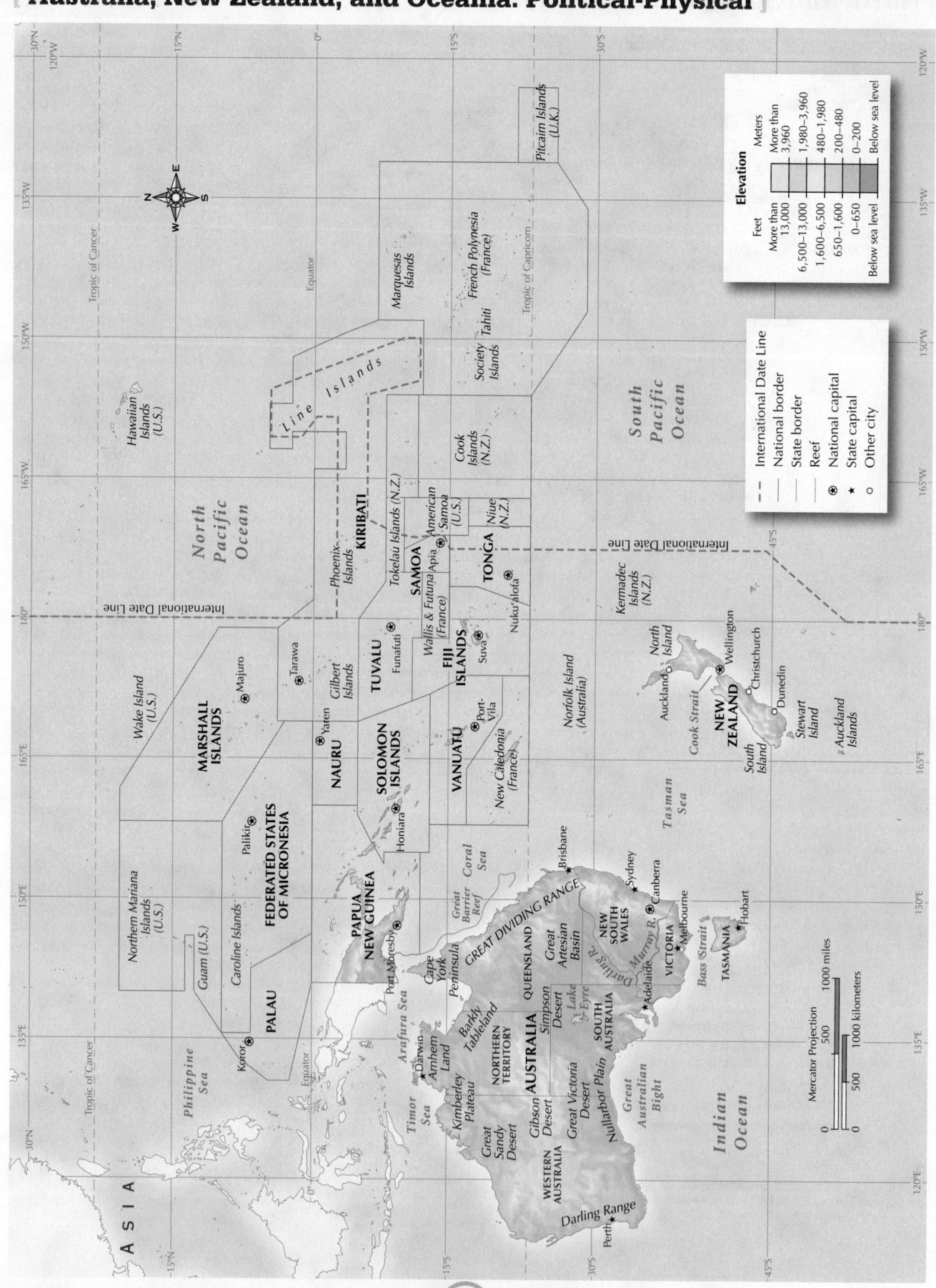

Elevation

Feet	Meters	
More than 13,000	More than 3,960	
6,500–13,000	1,980–3,960	
1,600–6,500	480–1,980	
650–1,600	200–480	
0–650	0–200	
Below sea level	Below sea level	

- - - International Date Line
— National border
— State border
Reef
⊛ National capital
★ State capital
○ Other city

PITCAIRN ISLANDS (U.K.)

Marquesas Islands

French Polynesia (France)

Society Islands

Tahiti

Tropic of Cancer

Equator

Tropic of Capricorn

South Pacific Ocean

Line Islands

Hawaiian Islands (U.S.)

North Pacific Ocean

Cook Islands (N.Z.)

KIRIBATI

Tokelau Islands (N.Z.)

American Samoa (U.S.)

Niue (N.Z.)

Phoenix Islands

SAMOA
Apia

TONGA
Nuku'alofa

Kermadec Islands (N.Z.)

International Date Line

Wake Island (U.S.)

Tarawa

Gilbert Islands

Majuro

TUVALU
Funafuti

Wallis & Futuna Islands (France)

FIJI ISLANDS
Suva

North Island
Wellington

Christchurch

MARSHALL ISLANDS

NAURU
Yaren

SOLOMON ISLANDS
Honiara

VANUATU
Port-Vila

New Caledonia (France)

Norfolk Island (Australia)

Auckland

NEW ZEALAND

Cook Strait

South Island

Dunedin

Stewart Island

Auckland Islands

Tasman Sea

Palikir

FEDERATED STATES OF MICRONESIA

Caroline Islands

Northern Mariana Islands (U.S.)

Guam (U.S.)

PALAU
Koror

PAPUA NEW GUINEA
Port Moresby

Coral Sea

Great Barrier Reef

Brisbane

GREAT DIVIDING RANGE

QUEENSLAND

Great Artesian Basin

NEW SOUTH WALES

Sydney

Canberra

VICTORIA

Melbourne

Murray R.

Darling R.

Bass Strait

TASMANIA
Hobart

Philippine Sea

Timor Sea

Arafura Sea

Cape York Peninsula

Darwin

Arnhem Land

NORTHERN TERRITORY

Barkly Tableland

AUSTRALIA

Simpson Desert

Lake Eyre

SOUTH AUSTRALIA

Adelaide

ASIA

Kimberley Plateau

Gibson Desert

Great Sandy Desert

WESTERN AUSTRALIA

Great Victoria Desert

Nullarbor Plain

Great Australian Bight

Indian Ocean

Darling Range

Perth

Mercator Projection
0   500   1000 miles
0   500   1000 kilometers

Sea of Okhotsk
Cherski Range
Kamchatka Peninsula
Kolyma Range
Kolyma R.
Laptev Sea
120°E
Severnaya Zemlya
Novosibirskiye Ostrova
90°E
East Siberian Sea
Kara Sea
60°E
Novaya Zemlya
Barents Sea
Franz Josef Land
30°E
Lake Ladoga
Kola Peninsula
EUROPE
Gulf of Bothnia
Baltic Sea
SCANDINAVIA

International Date Line
Aleutian Islands
180°
60°N
Bering Sea
St. Lawrence Island
Nunivak Island
Chukchi Peninsula
Wrangel Island
Chukchi Sea
Bering Strait
80°N
Arctic Ocean
North Pole
Svalbard
Norwegian Sea
Greenland
70°N
North Sea
0°
Shetland Islands
Arctic Circle
Jan Mayen
Faeroe Islands
British Isles
Ireland

North Magnetic Pole
90°W
Ellesmere Island
Denmark Str.
Greenland Sea
Iceland
Atlantic Ocean

Mt. McKinley (Denali) 20,320 ft. (6,194 m)
Alaska ▲
150°W
Beaufort Sea
120°W
Queen Elizabeth Islands
Greenland
60°N

Brooks Range
Alaska Range
Yukon River
Alaska Peninsula
Kodiak Island
Gulf of Alaska
Pacific Ocean
50°N
Amundsen Gulf
Banks Island
Victoria Island
Great Bear Lake
Mackenzie River
ROCKY MOUNTAINS
NORTH AMERICA
Baffin Bay
Baffin Island
Davis Strait
Foxe Basin
60°W
30°W
50°N

Lambert Azimuthal Equal Area Projection

0	400	800 miles
0	400	800 kilometers

Elevation

Feet	Meters
More than 13,000	More than 3,960
6,500–13,000	1,980–3,960
1,600–6,500	480–1,980
650–1,600	200–400
0–650	0–200
Below sea level	Below sea level

—— National border
- - - International Date Line

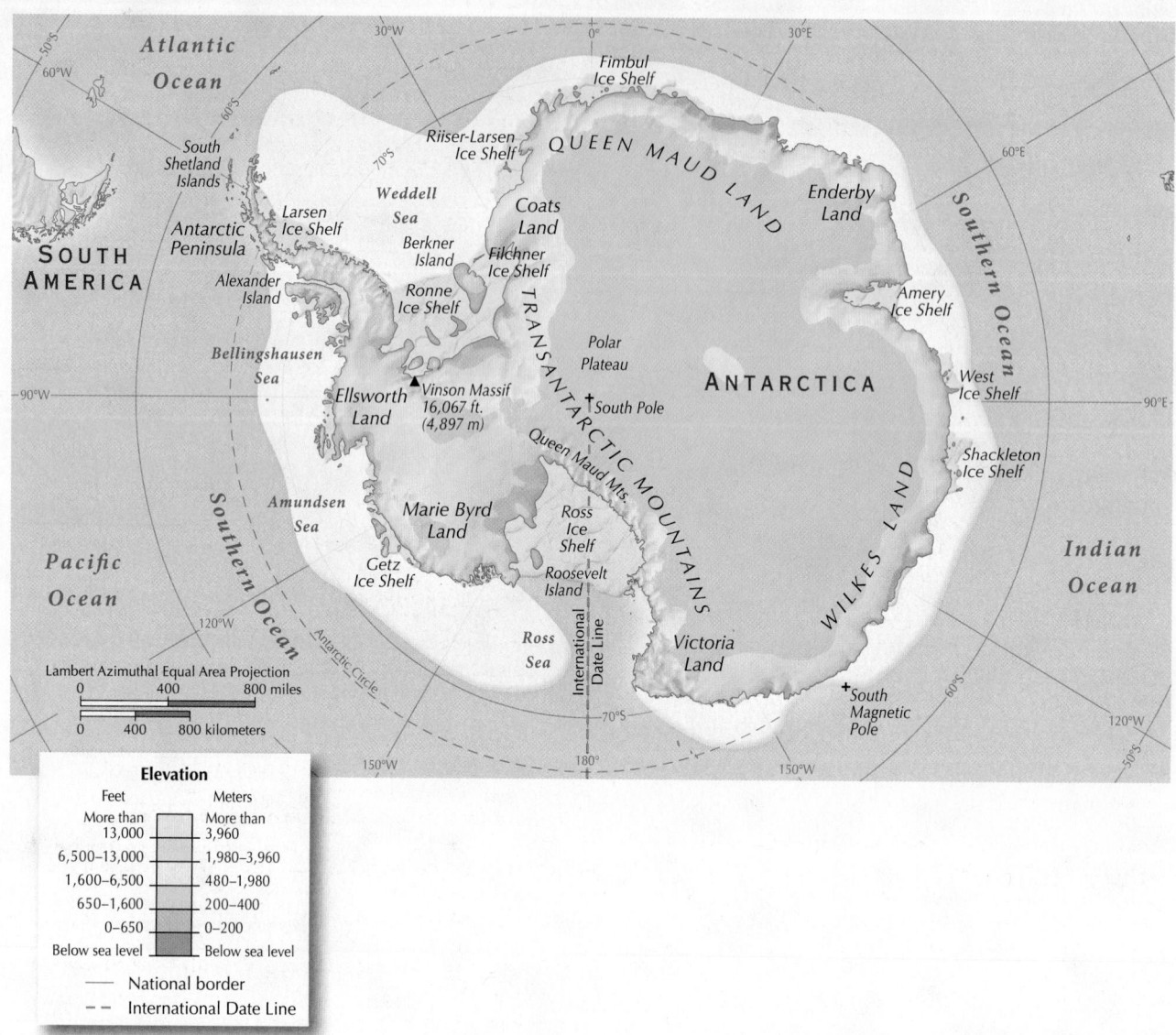

Atlantic Ocean

60°W

South Shetland Islands

SOUTH AMERICA

Antarctic Peninsula

Alexander Island

Larsen Ice Shelf

Weddell Sea

Berkner Island

Ronne Ice Shelf

Riiser-Larsen Ice Shelf

Fimbul Ice Shelf

QUEEN MAUD LAND

Coats Land

Filchner Ice Shelf

Enderby Land

Amery Ice Shelf

Bellingshausen Sea

Ellsworth Land

▲ Vinson Massif 16,067 ft. (4,897 m)

TRANSANTARCTIC MOUNTAINS

Polar Plateau

✝ South Pole

ANTARCTICA

West Ice Shelf

Southern Ocean

Shackleton Ice Shelf

90°W

Pacific Ocean

Southern Ocean

Amundsen Sea

Marie Byrd Land

Getz Ice Shelf

Queen Maud Mts.

Ross Ice Shelf

Roosevelt Island

Ross Sea

International Date Line

WILKES LAND

Victoria Land

+ South Magnetic Pole

90°E

120°W

Antarctic Circle

Lambert Azimuthal Equal Area Projection

0   400   800 miles

0   400   800 kilometers

Indian Ocean

120°W

70°S

150°W

180°

150°W

Elevation

Feet		Meters
More than 13,000		More than 3,960
6,500–13,000		1,980–3,960
1,600–6,500		480–1,980
650–1,600		200–400
0–650		0–200
Below sea level		Below sea level

—— National border

-- - International Date Line

Glossary

A

abdicate give up power

abolitionist person who wanted to end slavery

acculturation process of holding on to older traditions while adapting to a new culture

adobe sun-dried brick

affirmative action program to provide more job and education opportunities for people who faced discrimination in the past

AFL (American Federation of Labor) an organization of trade unions that represented skilled workers

aggression warlike act by one country without just cause alliance agreement between nations to aid and protect one another

Alliance for Progress economic aid program for Latin America developed by President Kennedy Allied Powers military alliance of France, Britain, Russia, Italy, and 20 other nations during World War I

Allies World War II military alliance of Britain, France, the Soviet Union, the United States, China, and 45 other countries

ally nation that works with another nation for a common purpose

altitude height above sea level

amend change

American Association of Retired Persons (AARP) organization that monitors issues of concern to older Americans

American Indian Religious Freedom Act a 1978 law that directed federal agencies not to interfere with Native American religious practices

Americans With Disabilities Act law passed in 1990 that prohibits discrimination in hiring people with physical or mental impairments

amnesty government pardon

anarchist person who opposes organized government

annex to add on or take over

anthropology the study of how people and cultures develop

Antifederalists people who opposed the Constitution and a strong national government

apartheid strict separation of races practiced in South Africa

appeal to ask that a decision be reviewed by a higher court

appeasement practice of giving in to aggression in order to avoid war

apprentice person who learns a trade or craft from a master

archaeology the study of evidence left by early peoples in order to find out about their way of life

armistice an agreement to stop fighting

arsenal place where guns are stored

Articles the main body of the Constitution, which establishes the framework for the United States government

Articles of Confederation first American constitution, passed in 1777, which created a loose alliance of 13 independent states

artifact object made by humans

artisan skilled worker

assembly line method of production in which workers stay in one place as products edge along past them on a moving belt

astrolabe navigational instrument used to determine latitude

Atlantic Charter a 1941 program developed by the United States and Britain that set goals for the postwar world

atrocity act of cruelty and brutality

authenticity the quality or condition of being genuine

Axis World War II military alliance of Germany, Italy, Japan, and six other nations

B

baby boom large increase in the birthrate from the late 1940s through the early 1960s

balanced budget condition that exists when the government spends only as much as it takes in

bank holiday closing of banks for four days during the Great Depression

bankrupt unable to pay debts

barrio Mexican neighborhood in the United States

Bataan Death March long trek across the Philippines that American and Filipino prisoners of war were forced to make by the Japanese in 1942

Battle of Belleau Wood hard-fought American victory over the Germans in France in 1918

Battle of Britain Germany's failed attempt to subdue Britain in 1940 in preparation for invasion

Battle of Midway a 1942 battle in the Pacific during which American planes sank four Japanese aircraft carriers

Battle of the Argonne Forest defeat of the Germans by French and American troops in France in October 1918

Battle of the Bulge German counterattack in December 1944 that temporarily slowed the Allied invasion of Germany

Battle of Verdun prolonged World War I battle in which more than 1 million died or were wounded

Bay of Pigs invasion failed invasion of Cuba in 1961 when a force of 1,200 Cuban exiles, backed by the United States, landed at the Bay of Pigs

beatnik 1950s person who criticized American culture for conformity and devotion to business

Berlin Airlift American and British relief effort to airlift supplies to West Berliners from 1948 to 1949

Berlin Wall wall built by the communist East German government in 1961 to seal off East Berlin from West Berlin

Bessemer process method developed in the 1850s to produce stronger steel at a lower cost

bias a leaning toward or against a certain person, group, or idea

Big Four leaders of Britain, France, the United States, and Italy after World War I

bilingual in two languages

bill proposed law

bill of rights written list of freedoms the government promises to protect

Bill of Rights first 10 amendments to the United States Constitution

Black Cabinet group of black leaders who unofficially advised President Franklin D. Roosevelt

black codes Southern laws that severely limited the rights of African Americans after the Civil War

Black Tuesday (October 29, 1929) day the stock market crashed, signaling start of the Great Depression

blitzkrieg the swift attacks launched by Germany in World War II

blockade the shutting of a port to keep people or supplies from moving in or out

boat people after the Vietnam War, refugees who escaped from Vietnam in small boats

bond certificate that promises to repay money loaned, plus interest, on a certain date

bonus additional sum of money

Bonus Army veterans who marched to Washington in 1932 to demand immediate payment of a World War I bonus boom period of swift economic growth

bootlegger person who smuggled liquor into the United States during Prohibition (p. 725)

border state slave state that remained in the Union during the Civil War

Boxer Rebellion uprising in China against westerners and Western influence in 1900

boycott to refuse to buy or use certain goods or services

bracero program recruitment of Mexican laborers to work in the United States during World War II

building code standards for construction and safety of buildings

bull market period of increased stock trading and rising stock prices

Bull Moose party Progressive Republicans who supported Theodore Roosevelt during the election of 1912

bureaucracy system of managing government through departments run by appointed officials

burgess representative to the colonial Virginia government

C

Cabinet group of officials who head government departments and advise the President

Camp David Accords 1979 peace treaty between Israel and Egypt in which Israel agreed to return the Sinai Peninsula to Egypt and Egypt agreed to recognize Israel

capital money raised for a business venture

capitalist person who invests in a business to make a profit

caravan group of people who travel together for safety

carpetbagger uncomplimentary nickname for a northerner who went to the South after the Civil War

cartographer person who makes maps

cash crop crop sold for money at market cash economy economy in which people exchange money for goods and services

cattle drive herding and moving herds of cattle, usually to railroad lines

caucus private meeting; often a political meeting

causeway raised road made of packed earth

cavalry troops on horseback

cede to give up

censure to officially condemn

Central Powers military alliance of Germany, Austria-Hungary, Bulgaria, and the Ottoman Empire during World War I

charter legal document giving certain rights to a person or company

checks and balances a principle of the United States Constitution that gives each branch of government the power to check the other branches

Chinese Exclusion Act 1882 law that barred Chinese laborers from entering the United States

chronology sequence of events over time

circumnavigate travel all the way around the Earth

citizen person who owes loyalty to a particular nation and is entitled to all its rights and protections

city-state large town that has its own government and controls the surrounding countryside

civic virtue the willingness to work for the good of the nation or community even at great sacrifice

civics the study of the rights and responsibilities of citizens

civil relating to lawsuits involving the private rights of individuals

civil disobedience idea that people have a right to disobey laws they consider to be unjust, if their consciences demand it

civil rights the rights due to all citizens

civil rights movement the efforts of African Americans to win equal rights

civil service all federal jobs except elected offices and those in the military

Civil Service Commission government agency created by the Pendleton Act of 1883 to fill federal jobs on the basis of merit

civil war war between people of the same country

Civil War amendments the Thirteenth, Fourteenth, and Fifteenth amendments to the United States Constitution

civilian nonmilitary (p. 249)

Civilian Conservation Corps New Deal program that hired unemployed men to work on natural conservation projects

clan group of two or more related families

climate average weather of a place over a period of 20 to 30 years

clipper ship fast-sailing ship of the mid-1800s

Cold War after World War II, long period of intense rivalry between the Soviet Union and the United States

collective bargaining process by which a union representing a group of workers negotiates with management for a contract

colony group of people who settle in a distant land but are still ruled by the government of their native land

Columbian Exchange the global exchange of goods and ideas resulting from the encounter between the peoples of the Eastern and Western hemispheres

committee of correspondence letter-writing campaign that became a major tool of protest in the colonies

communism economic system in which all wealth and property are owned by the state

company union labor organization that is actually controlled by management

compensation repayment for losses Comprehensive Test Ban Treaty agreement proposed in 1996 to end all testing of nuclear weapons

compromise settlement in which each side gives up some of its demands in order to reach an agreement

compulsory education requirement that children attend school to a certain grade or age

concentration camp prison camp for civilians who are considered enemies of the state

confederation league of independent states or nations

Congress of Industrial Organizations (CIO) labor organization founded in the 1930s to represent workers in basic mass-production industries

conquistador name for the Spanish explorers who claimed lands in the Americas for Spain

conservation protection of natural resources

Conservatives during Reconstruction, white southerners who resisted change

consolidate combine

constitution document that sets out the laws, principles, organization, and processes of a government

Constitutional Convention gathering of state representatives on May 25, 1787, to revise the Articles of Confederation

consumer user of goods and services

containment the policy of trying to prevent the spread of Soviet influence beyond where it already existed

continental divide mountain ridge that separates river systems flowing toward opposite sides of a continent

Contract With America 1994 legislative package that included trimming social welfare programs and slashing taxes

cooperative group of farmers who pool their money to buy seeds and tools wholesale

Copperhead northerner who opposed using force to keep the southern states in the Union

corduroy road road made of logs

corollary addition to an earlier stated principle

corporation business that is owned by investors

corral enclosure for animals

"cottonocracy" name for the wealthy planters who made their money from cotton in the mid-1800s

counterculture movement protest movement in the 1960s that rejected traditional values and culture

coureur de bois French colonist who lived in the woods as a fur trapper

cow town settlement that grew up at the end of a cattle trail

creole person born in Spain's American colonies to Spanish parents

Cuban missile crisis major Cold War confrontation in 1962

cultivate to prepare and use land for planting crops

culture entire way of life developed by a people

culture area region in which people share a similar way of life

currency money

czar Russian emperor

D

D-Day (June 6, 1944) day of the invasion of Western Europe by Allied forces

dame school school run by a woman, usually in her own home

Dayton Accord 1995 peace agreement negotiated among Bosnia, Croatia, and Serbia

debtor person who cannot pay money he or she owes

Declaration of Independence a 1776 document stating that the 13 English colonies were a free and independent nation

deficit spending government practice of spending more than is taken in from taxes

demilitarized zone (DMZ) area from which military forces are prohibited

democratic ensuring that all people have the same rights

department store large retail store offering a variety of goods organized in separate departments

deport expel from a country

depression period when business activity slows, prices and wages fall, and unemployment rises

deregulation reduction of restrictions on businesses

détente policy to reduce tensions between two countries

dictatorship government in which one person or a small group holds complete authority

diffusion process of spreading ideas from one culture to another

dime novel low-priced paperbacks offering adventure stories

direct democracy form of government in which ordinary citizens have the power to govern

disarmament reduction of armed forces and weapons of war

discrimination policy that denies equal rights to certain groups

dividend share of a corporation's profit

dollar diplomacy President Taft's policy of building strong economic ties to Latin America

domestic tranquillity peace and order at home

domino theory belief that if South Vietnam fell to communism, other countries in the region would follow

"Double V" campaign African American civil rights campaign during World War II

downsizing reducing a workforce

draft law that requires people of a certain age to enlist in the military

Dred Scott v. Sandford an 1857 Supreme Court case that brought into question the federal power over slavery in the territories

Dust Bowl region in the central Great Plains that was hit by a severe drought during the 1930s

E

e-commerce business and trade over the Internet

Earth Summit meeting of world leaders in 1992 to discuss key environmental issues

economics the study of how people manage limited resources to satisfy their wants and needs

Eighteenth Amendment a 1917 amendment to the United States Constitution that made it illegal to sell alcoholic drinks

electoral college group of electors from every state who meet every four years to vote for the President and Vice President of the United States

elevation height above sea level

emancipate to set free

Emancipation Proclamation Lincoln's 1863 declaration freeing slaves in the Confederacy

embargo ban on trade

encomienda land granted to Spanish settlers that included the right to demand labor or taxes from Native Americans

Environmental Protection Agency federal government agency that works to reduce pollution

environmentalist person who works to reduce pollution and protect the natural environment

epidemic rapid spread of a contagious disease

Equal Rights Amendment a 1923 proposed constitutional amendment intended to prohibit all discrimination based on sex; the amendment was never ratified

erosion gradual wearing away

escalate to expand

established church chosen religion of a state

executive branch branch of government that carries out laws

exile person who has been forced to leave his or her own country

expansionism policy of extending a nation's boundaries

expatriate person who renounces his or her own country and takes up residence in a foreign land

expedition long voyage of exploration

export trade product sent to markets outside a country

extended family family group that includes grandparents, parents, children, aunts, uncles, and cousins

F

faction opposing group within a party factory system method of producing goods that brought workers and machinery together in one place

fad activity or fashion that is taken up with great passion for a short time

famine severe food shortage

Fascism political system that is rooted in militarism, extreme nationalism, and blind loyalty to the state

Federal Reserve Act a 1913 law that set up a system of federal banks and gave government the power to control the money supply

Federal Trade Commission (FTC) government agency created in 1914 to ensure fair competition

federalism a principle of the United States Constitution that establishes the division of power between the federal government and the states

Federalist supporter of the Constitution who favored a strong federal government

Federalist Papers series of essays by Federalists James Madison, Alexander Hamilton, and John Jay in support of ratifying the Constitution

feudalism system of rule by lords who ruled their own lands but owed loyalty and military service to a monarch

Fifteenth Amendment an 1869 amendment to the United States Constitution that forbids any state to deny African Americans the right to vote because of race

54th Massachusetts Regiment African American unit in the Union Army

fireside chat radio speech given by President Franklin D. Roosevelt while in office

First Amendment amendment to the United States Constitution that safeguards basic individual liberties

first global age era at beginning of 1400s, when long-distance trade and travel increased dramatically

flapper young woman in the 1920s who rebelled against traditional ways of thinking and acting

flatboat boat with a flat bottom used for transporting heavy loads on inland waterways

Foraker Act law passed by Congress in 1900 under which the United States gave Puerto Ricans a limited say in government

foreign policy actions that a nation takes in relation to other nations

Fort Wagner fort in South Carolina that was the site of an attack by the African American 54th Massachusetts Regiment in 1863

forty-niner one of the more than 80,000 people who joined the gold rush to California in 1849

Founding Fathers leaders who laid the groundwork for the United States

Fourteen Points President Wilson's goals for peace after World War I Fourteenth Amendment an 1868 amendment to the United States Constitution that guarantees equal protection of the laws

free enterprise system economic system in which businesses are owned by private citizens who decide what to produce, how much to produce, and what prices to charge

free market economic system in which goods and services are exchanged with little regulation

Free-Soil party bipartisan antislavery party founded in the United States in 1848 to keep slavery out of the western territories

freedmen men and women who had been slaves

Freedmen's Bureau government agency founded during Reconstruction to help former slaves

French and Indian War a war that took place from 1754 to 1763 that led to the end of French power in North America

frigate fast-sailing ship with many guns

fugitive runaway

Fugitive Slave Act law passed in 1850 that required all citizens to aid in the capture of runaway slaves

G

gauge width of a train track

general welfare well-being of all the citizens of a nation

"Gentlemen's Agreement" a 1907 agreement between the United States and Japan to limit Japanese immigration

gentry highest social class in the 13 English colonies

geography the study of people, their environments, and their resources

Gettysburg Address speech made by President Lincoln in 1863 after the Battle of Gettysburg

Gilded Age the period in American history lasting from the 1870s to the 1890s, marked by political corruption and extravagant spending

glacier thick sheet of ice

glasnost policy in the Soviet Union of speaking openly about problems

global warming the slow but steady rise in the world's average temperature

Good Neighbor Policy President Franklin Roosevelt's policy intended to strengthen friendly relations with Latin America

graduated income tax tax on earnings that charges different rates for different income levels

grandfather clause law that excused a voter from a literacy test if his father or grandfather had been eligible to vote on January 1, 1867

Great Depression worst period of economic decline in United States history, beginning in 1929

Great White Fleet name for the steam-powered ships of the enlarged and modernized American navy of the early 1900s

guerrilla fighter who uses hit-and-run attacks

Gulf of Tonkin Resolution Congressional resolution passed in 1964 that authorized military action in Vietnam

H

habeas corpus the right not to be held in prison without first being charged with a specific crime

Harlem Hell Fighters the African American infantry unit that fought with the French Army in World War I

Haymarket Riot labor rally in Chicago in 1886 that ended in violence when a bomb exploded

Holocaust slaughter of Europe's Jews by the Nazis before and during World War II

Hooverville group of shacks in which the homeless lived during the Great Depression

House of Representatives the larger of the two bodies that make up the legislative branch of the United States government

Hull House settlement house founded by Progressive reformer Jane Addams in Chicago in 1889

Hundred Days first hundred days of President Franklin D. Roosevelt's presidency

I

ILGWU (International Ladies' Garment Workers Union) union of garment workers formed in 1900

illegal alien immigrant who enters a country without permission

illiterate unable to read or write

immigrant person who enters another country in order to settle there

Immigration Reform and Control Act law that allowed people who arrived illegally in the United States before 1982 to apply for citizenship

impeach to bring charges of serious wrongdoing against a public official

imperialism policy of powerful countries seeking to control the economic and political affairs of weaker countries or regions

import trade product brought into a country

impressment practice of forcing people into military service

inauguration ceremony in which the President officially takes the oath of office (p. 278)

income tax a tax on people's earnings

incriminate to give evidence against

indentured servant person who agreed to work without wages for a period of time in exchange for passage to the colonies

Indian New Deal series of laws passed in the 1930s that gave Native American nations greater control over their own affairs

indigo plant used to make a valuable blue dye

individualism concept that stresses the importance of each individual

Industrial Revolution gradual process by which machines replaced hand tools

inflation a rise in prices and a decrease in the value of money

infrastructure system of roads, bridges, and tunnels

initiative process by which voters can put a bill directly before the state legislature

installment buying buying on credit

integration mixing of different racial or ethnic groups

interchangeable parts identical, machine-made parts for a tool or an instrument

internal improvements improvements to roads, bridges, and canals

Internet series of interconnected computers that allow users to access and exchange computerized information

interstate commerce business that crosses state lines

Interstate Commerce Commission (ICC) government agency organized to oversee railroad commerce

intervention direct involvement

Intolerable Acts series of laws passed in 1774 to punish Boston for the Tea Party

irrigation bringing water to dry lands

Islam monotheistic religion founded by the prophet Muhammad in the early 600s

island hopping during World War II, Allied strategy of capturing Japanese-held islands to gain control of the Pacific Ocean

isolationist after World War I, American who wanted the United States to stay out of world affairs

isthmus narrow strip of land connecting two larger bodies of land

J

jazz music style that developed from blues, ragtime, and other earlier styles

jerky dried

Jim Crow laws laws that separated people of different races in public places in the South

judicial branch branch of government that decides if laws are carried out fairly

judicial review power of the Supreme Court to decide whether the acts of a President or laws passed by Congress are constitutional

Judiciary Act a 1789 law that created the structure of the Supreme Court and set up a system of district courts and circuit courts for the nation

jury duty the responsibility of every citizen to serve on a jury when called

K

kachina masked dancer at religious ceremonies of the Southwest Indians

kaiser title of the German emperor

kamikaze World War II Japanese pilot trained to make a suicidal crash attack, usually upon a ship

Kansas-Nebraska Act an 1854 law that established the territories of Nebraska and Kansas, giving the settlers the right of popular sovereignty to decide on the issue of slavery

Kellogg-Briand Pact a 1928 treaty outlawing war

Khmer Rouge communist party in Cambodia that imposed a reign of terror on Cambodian citizens

kinship sharing a common ancestor Knights of Labor an American labor organization founded in 1869 to protect the rights of workers (p. 591)

Ku Klux Klan secret society organized in the South after the Civil War to reassert white supremacy by means of violence

L

laissez faire idea that government should play as small a role as possible in economic affairs

latitude distance north or south from the equator

lawsuit legal case brought to settle a dispute between a person or group

League of Nations association of nations formed after World War I under Wilson's Fourteen Points plan

League of the Iroquois alliance of the five Iroquois nations

League of Women Voters organization established in 1920 to promote rights for women

legislative branch branch of government that passes laws

legislature group of people who have the power to make laws

Lend-Lease Act during World War II, the law that allowed the United States to sell arms and equipment to Britain

libel act of publishing a statement that may unjustly damage a person's reputation

liberty freedom

Liberty Bonds bonds sold by the United States government to raise money for World War I

limited government a principle of the United States Constitution that states that government has only the powers that the Constitution gives it

literacy test examination to see if a person can read and write; used in the past to restrict voting rights

local color speech and habits of a particular region

local government government on the county, parish, city, town, village, or district level

locomotive engine that pulls a railroad train

lode rich vein of gold, silver, or other valuable ore

longitude distance east or west from the Prime Meridian

Louisiana Purchase vast territory between the Mississippi River and Rocky Mountains, purchased from France in 1803

Lusitania British passenger ship that was torpedoed by a German U-boat in 1915; 1,200 people died, including 128 Americans

lynch for a mob to illegally seize and execute someone

M

Magna Carta signed in 1215, a British document that contained two basic ideas: monarchs themselves have to obey the laws, and citizens have basic rights

mainstreaming placing children with special needs in regular classes

majority more than half

Manifest Destiny 1800s belief that Americans had the right to spread across the continent

manor district ruled by a lord, including the lord's castle and the lands around it

map projection way of drawing Earth on a flat surface

Marbury v. Madison an 1803 court case in which the Supreme Court ruled that it had the power to decide whether laws passed by Congress were constitutional

Marshall Plan American plan to help European nations rebuild their economies after World War II

martial law rule by the army instead of the elected government

martyr person who dies for his or her beliefs

mass production process of making large quantities of a product quickly and cheaply

Mayflower Compact a 1620 agreement for ruling the Plymouth Colony

mediator agent who helps conflicting parties iron out their differences

mercantilism theory that a nation's economic strength came from keeping a strict control over its colonial trade

mercenary soldier who fights merely for pay, often for a foreign country

merit ability

mestizo in Spain's American colonies, person of mixed Spanish and Indian background

middle class in the 13 English colonies, a class that included skilled craftworkers, farmers, and some tradespeople

migrant worker person who moves from one region to another in search of work

militarism the policy of building up strong armed forces to prepare for war

militia army of citizens who serve as soldiers during an emergency

minuteman colonial militia volunteer who was prepared to fight at a minute's notice

mission religious settlement run by Catholic priests and friars

missionary person who tries to spread certain religious beliefs among a group of people

Missouri Compromise agreement, proposed in 1819 by Henry Clay, to keep the number of slave and free states equal

Monitor ironclad Union warship

monopoly a company or group having control of all or nearly all of the business of an industry

Monroe Doctrine President Monroe's foreign policy statement warning European nations not to interfere in Latin America

moral diplomacy President Wilson's policy of condemning imperialism, spreading democracy, and promoting peace

Moral Majority religious organization that backed conservative political causes in the 1980s

mountain man trapper who explored and hunted in Oregon Territory in the early 1800s

moving assembly line method of production by which workers stay in one place as products travel past on a moving belt

muckraker journalist who exposed corruption and other problems of the late 1800s and early 1900s

mudslinging the use of insults to attack an opponent's reputation

Munich Conference a 1938 meeting of the leaders of Britain, France, Italy, and Germany at which an agreement was signed giving part of Czechoslovakia to Hitler

mutualista Mexican American mutual aid group

N

NAACP (National Association for the Advancement of Colored People) organization founded in 1909 to work toward equal rights for African Americans

National Aeronautics and Space Administration (NASA) government agency that directs the American space program

national debt total sum of money that a government owes to others

National Labor Relations Act law passed in 1935 that protects American workers from unfair management practices

national park area set aside by the federal government for people to visit

National Recovery Administration government agency set up during the Great Depression to enforce new codes designed to stabilize industry

National Woman Suffrage Association group set up in 1869 to work for a constitutional amendment to give women the right to vote

nationalism excessive pride in one's nation

nativism antiforeign belief opposed to immigration

natural resources materials that humans can take from the environment to survive and satisfy their needs

natural rights rights that belong to all people from birth

naturalize to complete the official process for becoming a citizen

Navajo code-talkers during World War II, Navajo soldiers who used their own language to radio vital messages during the island-hopping campaign

Nazi member of the National Socialist German Workers' Party

Nazi-Soviet Pact agreement signed between Hitler and Stalin in 1939 in which the two dictators agreed not to attack each other

network system of connected railroad lines

neutral not taking sides in a conflict

Neutrality Acts series of laws passed by Congress in 1935 that banned arms sales or loans to countries at war

New Deal program of President Franklin D. Roosevelt to end the Great Depression

New Freedom President Wilson's program to break up trusts and restore American economic competition

"New South" term to describe the South in the late 1800s when efforts were made to expand the economy by building up industry

Nineteenth Amendment a 1919 amendment to the United States

Constitution that gives women the right to vote nominating convention meeting at which a political party chooses a candidate

North American Free Trade Agreement (NAFTA) treaty among the United States, Canada, and Mexico to gradually remove tariffs and other trade barriers

North Atlantic Treaty Organization (NATO) alliance formed in 1949 by the United States and Western European nations to fight Soviet aggression

northwest passage a waterway through or around North America

nullification idea that a state has the right to nullify, or cancel, a federal law that the state leaders consider to be unconstitutional

Nuremberg Trials Nazi war crimes trials held in 1945 and 1946

O

on margin practice that allows people to buy stock with a down payment of a portion of the full value

OPEC (Organization of Petroleum Exporting Countries) multinational organization that sets a common policy for the sale of petroleum

Open Door Policy policy issued by Secretary of State John Hay in 1899 that allowed a nation to trade in any other nation's sphere of influence in China

Operation Overlord code name for the Allied invasion of Europe in 1944

Organization of American States (OAS) international organization that promotes peace and economic progress in the Americas

override to overrule, as when Congress overrules a presidential veto

P

pacifist person who objects to any war; believes war is evil

Palestine Liberation Organization (PLO) Palestinian-Arab organization founded in 1964 to destroy Israel, mainly through the use of armed force

Parliament representative assembly in England

parochial church-sponsored; often used to refer to church-sponsored schools

patent license for a new invention

patriotism feeling of love and devotion toward one's country

patronage the practice of awarding government jobs to political supporters

patroon owner of a large estate in a Dutch colony

Peace Corps government organization that sends American volunteers to developing countries to teach or give technical advice

peninsulare person from Spain who held a position of power in a Spanish colony

pension sum of money paid to people on a regular basis after they retire

perjury to lie under oath

persecution mistreatment or punishment of a group of people because of their beliefs

Persian Gulf War a 1991 war in which the United States and its UN allies drove invading Iraqi forces out of neighboring Kuwait

petition formal written request to someone in authority that is signed by a group of people

Pickett's Charge failed Confederate charge at the Battle of Gettysburg

pit house house in the Arctic region dug into the ground and covered with wood and skins

plantation large estate farmed by many workers (p. 80)

Platt Amendment amendment to the 1902 Cuban constitution that allowed the United States to intervene in Cuba

Plessy v. Ferguson an 1896 court case in which the Supreme Court ruled that segregation in public facilities was legal as long as the facilities were equal

pogrom in Eastern Europe, an organized attack on a Jewish community

polio highly infectious disease that causes inflammation of the nerve cells of the brain stem and spinal cord, leading to paralysis

political boss powerful politician who controls work done locally and demands payoffs from businesses

political science the study of government

poll tax tax required before a person can vote

pool system in which several railroad companies agreed to divide up the business in an area

popular sovereignty in the mid-1800s, a term referring to the idea that each territory could decide for itself whether or not to allow slavery

potlatch ceremonial dinner held by some Native Americans of the Northwest Coast to show off their wealth

Potsdam Declaration message sent by the Allies in July 1945 calling for Japanese surrender

preamble introduction to a declaration, constitution, or other official document

precedent act or decision that sets an example for others to follow

precipitation water that falls in the form of rain, sleet, hail, or snow

predestination Protestant idea that God decided in advance which people would attain salvation after death

presidio fort where soldiers lived in the Spanish colonies

primary election in which voters choose their party's candidate for the general election

primary source firsthand information about people or events

productivity average output per worker

profiteer person who takes advantage of a crisis to make money

Progressive reformer in the late 1800s and early 1900s who wanted to improve American life

Prohibition ban on the manufacture, sale, and transportation of liquor anywhere in the United States from 1920 to 1933

propaganda spreading of ideas to help a cause or hurt an opposing cause

proprietary colony English colony in which the king gave land to proprietors in exchange for a yearly payment

protectorate nation whose independence is limited by the control of a more powerful country

Protestant Reformation movement to reform the Roman Catholic Church in the 1500s; led to the creation of many different Christian churches

psychology the study of how people think and behave

public interest the good of the people

public school school supported by taxes

public works projects built by the government for public use

pueblo a town in the Spanish colonies; Anasazi village

pull factor condition that attracts people to move to a new area

Pure Food and Drug Act a 1906 law that requires food and drug makers to list ingredients on packages

push factor condition that drives people from their homeland

Q

quipu device made of cord or string with knots that stood for quantities; used by the Incas to keep accounts and records

quota system system that limited immigration by allowing only a certain number of people from each country to immigrate to the United States

R

racism belief that one race is superior to another

radical person who wants to make drastic changes in society

Radical Reconstruction period beginning in 1867, when the Republicans, who had control in both houses of Congress, took charge of Reconstruction

Radical Republican member of Congress during Reconstruction who wanted to ensure that freedmen received the right to vote

ragtime popular music of the late 1800s that had a lively, rhythmic sound

ratify to approve

rationing limitations on the amount of certain goods that people can buy

Reaganomics President Reagan's economic program that cut taxes, cut federal spending on social programs, and increased military spending

realist writer or artist who shows life as it really is

rebate discount

recall process by which voters can remove an elected official from office

recession economic slump that is milder than a depression

reconcentration policy of moving large numbers of people into camps for political or military purposes

Reconstruction rebuilding of the South after the Civil War

Reconstruction Act an 1867 law that threw out the southern state governments that had refused to ratify the Fourteenth Amendment

referendum process by which people vote directly on a bill

refuge place where one is safe from persecution

refugee person who flees his or her homeland to seek safety elsewhere

relief program government program to help the needy

religious tolerance willingness to let others practice their own beliefs

rendezvous yearly meeting where mountain men traded furs (p. 382)

renewable resource resource that can be quickly replaced by nature

reparations cash payments made by a defeated nation to a victorious nation to pay for losses suffered during a war

repeal to cancel

representative government political system in which voters elect representatives to make laws for them

republic system of government in which citizens choose representatives to govern them

Republican party political party established in the United States in 1854 with the goal of keeping slavery out of the western territories

reservation limited area set aside for Native Americans

resident alien noncitizen living in the country

revival large outdoor religious meeting

Roosevelt Corollary statement by Theodore Roosevelt that the United States had a right to intervene in Latin America to preserve law and order

Rosie the Riveter fictional factory worker who became a symbol of working women during World War II

Rough Riders military unit organized by Theodore Roosevelt during the Spanish-American War

royal colony colony under the direct control of the English crown

rugged individualist person who follows his or her own independent course in life

S

sabotage secret destruction of property or interference with production in a factory or other workplace

sachem member of the tribal chief council in the League of the Iroquois

SALT Agreement (Strategic Arms Limitation Talks) treaty between the United States and the Soviet Union to limit the number of nuclear warheads and missiles

salvation everlasting life

Salvation Army an international charitable organization

sanctions measures designed to make a country change its policy

satellite nation nation that is dominated politically and economically by a more powerful nation

savanna region of grasslands scalawag white southerner who supported the Republicans during Reconstruction

scapegoat person or group who is made to bear the blame for others

secede to withdraw from membership in a group

Second Amendment amendment to the United States Constitution related to the right to bear arms

secondary source account provided after the fact by people who did not directly witness or participate in the event

sectionalism loyalty to a state or section rather than to the whole country sedition stirring up rebellion against a government

segregation legal separation of people based on racial, ethnic, or other differences

Selective Service Act law passed by Congress in 1917 that required all men from ages 21 to 30 to register for the military draft

self-determination right of national groups to have their own territory and forms of government

self-sufficient able to produce enough for one's own needs

Senate the smaller of the two bodies that make up the legislative branch of the United States government

Seneca Falls Convention an 1848 meeting at which leaders of the women's rights movement called for equal rights for women

separation of powers principle by which the powers of government are divided among separate branches

settlement house community center organized in the late 1800s to offer services to the poor

sharecropper person who rents a plot of land from another person and farms it in exchange for a share of the crop

Sherman Antitrust Act an 1890 law that banned the formation of trusts and monopolies in the United States

siege military blockade or bombardment of an enemy town or position in order to force it to surrender

silent majority term for Americans who were disturbed by unrest in the 1960s but did not protest publicly

sit-down strike strike in which workers refuse to leave the workplace until a settlement is reached

sit-in form of protest in which people sit and refuse to leave

skyscraper tall building with many floors supported by a lightweight steel frame

slave code laws that controlled the lives of enslaved African Americans and denied them basic rights

smuggling importing or exporting goods in violation of trade laws

Social Gospel movement within American Protestantism in the late 1800s that attempted to apply biblical teachings to society's problems (p. 609)

social reform an organized attempt to improve what is unjust or imperfect in society

social sciences studies that relate to human society and social behavior

Social Security Act a 1935 law that set up a system of pensions for older people and set up the nation's first system of unemployment insurance

Socialist person who supports community ownership of property and the sharing of all profits

Society of American Indians group that worked for social justice and tried to push Native Americans into the American mainstream

sociology the study of how people behave in groups

sod house house built of soil held together by grass roots

sodbuster farmer on the Great Plains in the late 1800s

Solidarity independent labor union that challenged Poland's communist government

soup kitchen place where food is provided to the needy at little or no charge

Spanish-American War war between Spain and the United States in 1898

speculator someone who invests in a risky venture in the hope of making a large profit

sphere of influence area where a nation had special trading privileges

spinning jenny machine developed in 1764 that could spin several threads at once

spoils system practice of rewarding supports with government jobs

Square Deal Theodore Roosevelt's campaign promise that all groups would have an equal opportunity to succeed

stagflation combination of rising prices, high unemployment, and slow economic growth

stalemate deadlock in which neither side is strong enough to defeat the other

standard of living index based on the amount of goods, services, and leisure time people have

Star Wars President Reagan's proposed weapons system to destroy Soviet missiles from space

states' rights the right of states to limit the power of the federal government

Statue of Liberty a large statue symbolizing hope and freedom on Liberty Island in New York Harbor

steerage on a ship, the cramped quarters for passengers paying the lowest fares

stock share of ownership in a corporation

Strategic Arms Reduction Treaty (START) a 1991 treaty signed by the United States and Soviet Union to reduce nuclear weapons

strike refusal by workers to do their jobs until their demands are met

strikebreaker replacement for a striking worker

subsidy financial aid or land grant from the government

suburb residential area on the outskirts of a city

suffrage the right to vote

suffragist person who worked for women's right to vote

summit meeting conference between the highest-ranking officials of different nations

superpower nation with the military, political, and economic strength to influence events worldwide

Supreme Court highest court in the United States established by the Constitution

surplus extra; condition that exists when income exceeds spending

sweatshop workplace where people labor long hours in poor conditions for low pay

T

tariff tax on foreign goods brought into a country

Teapot Dome Scandal, political scandal during President Harding's administration

telegraph communications device that sends electrical signals along a wire

temperance movement campaign against alcohol consumption

Ten Percent Plan Lincoln's plan that allowed a southern state to form a new government after 10 percent of its voters swore an oath of loyalty to the United States

tenement small apartment in a city slum building

Tennessee Valley Authority New Deal program that built dams to control flooding and produce cheap electric power

tepee tent made by stretching buffalo skins on tall poles

terrace wide shelf of land cut into a hillside

terrorism deliberate use of violence to spread fear and achieve political goals

Tet Offensive North Vietnamese and Vietcong surprise attack on American forces in Vietnam on the Vietnamese New Year's holiday in 1968

Thanksgiving day at the end of the harvest season set aside by the Pilgrims to give thanks to God

thematic map map that deals with a specific topic, such as population, natural resources, or elections

Thirteenth Amendment an 1865 amendment to the United States Constitution that bans slavery throughout the nation

38th parallel dividing line between South Korea and North Korea

total war all-out war that affects civilians at home as well as soldiers in combat

totalitarian state country where a single party controls the government and every aspect of people's lives

town meeting meeting in colonial New England where settlers discussed and voted on issues

trade deficit condition that exists when a nation buys more goods and services from foreign countries than it sells to them

trade union association of trade workers formed to gain higher wages and better working conditions

traitor person who betrays his or her country

transatlantic crossing or spanning the Atlantic Ocean

transcendentalists New England writers and thinkers who believed that the most important truths in life transcended, or went beyond, human reason

transcontinental railroad railroad that stretches across a continent from coast to coast

travois sled pulled by a dog or horse

treason actions against one's country

Treaty of Brest-Litovsk a 1918 treaty between Russia and Germany that ended Russia's involvement in World War I

Treaty of Kanagawa an 1854 treaty between Japan and the United States that opened up ports to American trade in Japan

Treaty of Versailles treaty signed on June 28, 1919, by Germany and the Allies; formally placed the responsibility for the war on Germany and its allies

Triangle Fire fire in 1911 at the Triangle Shirtwaist Factory in New York City that killed nearly 150 workers

triangular trade colonial trade route between New England, the West Indies, and Africa

tribe community of people that share common customs, language, and rituals

tributary stream or smaller river that flows into a larger one

tribute bribe

Truman Doctrine President Truman's policy of giving American aid to nations threatened by communist expansion

trust group of corporations run by a single board of directors

trustbuster person who wanted to break up all trusts

turning point moment in history that marks a decisive change

turnpike road built by a private company that charges a toll to use it

Tuskegee Airmen African American fighter pilots who trained in Tuskegee, Alabama, during World War II

tutor private teacher

Twenty-sixth Amendment amendment to the United States Constitution that lowered the minimum voting age from 21 to 18

U

U-boat German submarine used in World War I and World War II

unamendable unable to change

Uncle Tom's Cabin an 1852 novel by Harriet Beecher Stowe written to show the evils of slavery and the injustice of the Fugitive Slave Act

unconstitutional not permitted by the Constitution (pp. 257, 288)

Underground Railroad network of abolitionists who secretly helped slaves escape to freedom

United Nations world organization established in 1945 to provide peaceful resolutions to international conflicts

urbanization movement of population from farms to cities

V

vaquero Spanish or Mexican cowhand

vaudeville variety show made popular in the late 1800s that included comedians, song-and-dance routines, and acrobats

vertical integration practice in which a single manufacturer controls all of the steps used to change raw materials into finished products

veto to reject, as when the President rejects a law passed by Congress

victory garden during World War II, vegetable garden planted to combat food shortages in the United States

Vietcong Vietnamese guerrillas who opposed the noncommunist government of South Vietnam

vigilante self-appointed enforcer of the law

Virginia ironclad warship used by the Confederates to break the Union blockade

W

Wade-Davis Bill an 1864 plan for Reconstruction that denied the right to vote or hold office to anyone who had volunteered to fight for the Confederacy

War Production Board government agency created during World War II to help factories shift from making consumer goods to making war materials

warmonger person who tries to stir up war

Warsaw Pact military alliance, established in 1955, of the Soviet Union and other communist states in Europe

WCTU (Women's Christian Temperance Union) group organized in 1874 that worked to ban the sale of liquor in the United States

weather condition of the earth's atmosphere at a given time and place

wholesale buying or selling something in large quantities at lower prices

Wilmot Proviso law passed in 1846 that banned slavery in any territories won by the United States from Mexico

Wisconsin Idea series of Progressive reforms introduced in the early 1900s by Wisconsin governor Robert La Follette

women's rights movement organized campaign to win property, education, and other rights for women

writ of assistance legal document that allowed British customs officials to inspect a ship's cargo without giving a reason

Y

yellow journalism news reporting, often biased or untrue, that relies on sensational stories and headlines

Young Men's Hebrew Association (YMHA) organization founded in Baltimore in 1854 to provide community services to Jewish neighborhoods

Z

Zimmermann telegram a 1917 telegram sent from Germany's foreign secretary to the German minister in Mexico instructing the minister to urge Mexico to attack the United States if the United States declared war on Germany

A

abdicate/abdicar entregar el poder

abolitionist/abolicionista persona que quería acabar la esclavitud

acculturation/aculturación proceso por el cual se mantienen viejas tradiciones mientras se va adoptando otra cultura

Act of Toleration/Acta de Tolerancia ley aprobada por la asamblea de Maryland en 1649 que aseguraba la libertad religiosa para todos los cristianos

Adams-Onís Treaty/Tratado de Adams-Onís tratado de 1821 entre España y Estados Unidos según el cual España se comprometía a entregar Florida a Estados Unidos

adobe/adobe ladrillo secado al sol

affirmative action/acción afirmativa programa que proporciona más oportunidades de trabajo y educación a personas que sufrieron discriminación en el pasado

AFL/*AFL* organización de sindicatos que representaba a trabajadores cualificados

aggression/agresión acto similar a un acto de guerra de un país contra otro sin que haya una causa justa

Alamo/Álamo vieja misión española situada en Texas donde las fuerzas mexicanas bajo las órdenes de Santa Anna asediaron a los texanos en 1836

Albany Plan of Union/Plan de Unión de Albany propuesta de Benjamin Franklin que consistía en crear un solo gobierno para las 13 colonias

Alien and Sedition acts/Actas de Extranjería y de Sedición leyes apoyadas por los federalistas que permitían que el presidente expulsara a extranjeros o dificultara que obtuvieran la ciudadanía, y multara o encarcelara a ciudadanos por criticar al gobierno

alliance/alianza acuerdo entre naciones para ayudarse y protegerse mutuamente

Alliance for Progress/Alianza para el Progreso programa que desarrolló el presidente Kennedy para promover reformas sociales en América Latina

Allied Powers/potencias aliadas alianza militar entre Francia, Inglaterra, Rusia, Italia y 20 otras naciones durante la Primera Guerra Mundial

Allies/aliados alianza militar entre Inglaterra, Francia, la Unión Soviética, Estados Unidos, China y otros 45 países

ally/aliado nación que trabaja con otra nación hacia una meta común

altitude/altura elevación sobre el nivel del mar

amend/reformar cambiar

American Association of Retired Persons/Asociación Americana de Personas Jubiladas organización que lleva a cabo el seguimiento y control de los asuntos de interés para personas de edad más avanzada

American Colonization Society/Sociedad de Colonización Americana organización de principios del siglo XIX que proponía ayudar a los afroamericanos a que se mudaran a África

American Indian Religious Freedom Act/ Ley de Libertad Religiosa de los Indígenas Estadounidenses ley de 1978 que obligó a las agencias federales a no obstaculizar las prácticas religiosas de los indígenas

American System/sistema estadounidense programa para fomentar el crecimiento económico, promovido por Henry Clay a principios del siglo XIX; proponía imponer altas tasas a las importaciones

Americans With Disabilities Act/Ley de los Estadounidenses Discapacitados ley de 1990 que prohibe la discriminación al contratar a personas con dificultades físicas o mentales

amnesty/amnistía perdón del gobierno

anarchist/anarquista persona que se opone a todas las formas de gobierno organizado

annex/anexar agregar; incorporar un territorio

anthropology/antropología estudio de cómo se desarrollan las personas y las culturas

Antifederalists/antifederalistas personas que se oponían a la constitución y a un gobierno nacional fuerte

apartheid/apartheid separación estricta de las razas practicada anteriormente en Sudáfrica

appeal/apelar pedir a una corte de mayor autoridad que reconsidere una decisión

appeasement/apaciguamiento aceptación de agresiones para evitar una guerra

Appomattox Court House/Appomattox Court House ciudad de Virginia en donde la Confederación se rindió en 1865

apprentice/aprendiz persona que aprende un oficio o artesanía de un maestro

archaeology/arqueología estudio de las evidencias dejadas por culturas antiguas con el objeto de conocer su forma de vida

armistice/armisticio acuerdo para detener el combate

arsenal/arsenal depósito de armas

Articles/artículos parte principal de la constitución que establece la estructura del gobierno de Estados Unidos

Articles of Confederation/Artículos de la Confederación primera constitución de Estados Unidos; aprobada en 1777, creó una alianza tenue entre los 13 estados independientes

artifact/artefacto objeto hecho por seres humanos

artisan/artesano trabajador manual cualificado

assembly line/cadena de montaje método de producción según el cual los trabajadores permanecen en un lugar fijo mientras los productos pasan frente a ellos sobre una cinta transportadora

astrolabe/astrolabio instrumento de navegación que se usa para determinar la latitud

Atlantic Charter/Cédula del Atlántico programa creado por Estados Unidos e Inglaterra en 1941, que estableció objetivos para el mundo en la posguerra

atrocity/atrocidad acto de crueldad y brutalidad

authenticity/autenticidad condición de ser genuino

Axis/eje alianza militar durante la Segunda Guerra Mundial entre Alemania, Italia, Japón y otras seis naciones

B

baby boom/*baby boom* gran incremento de la tasa de natalidad en Estados Unidos desde finales de la década de1940 hasta principios de la década de 1960

Bacon's Rebellion/rebelión de Bacon revuelta liderada en 1676 por Nathaniel Bacon en contra del gobernador y de los indígenas de Virginia

balanced budget/presupuesto equilibrado condición que se da cuando el gobierno sólo gasta la cantidad que recibe

bank holiday/feriado bancario cierre de los bancos por cuatro días durante la Gran Depresión

Bank of the United States/Banco de Estados Unidos banco establecido en 1791 para retener los depósitos del gobierno y emitir papel moneda para el pago de las cuentas del gobierno y otorgar préstamos a granjeros y comerciantes

bankrupt/en bancarrota sin capacidad para pagar las deudas

barrio/barrio término que se refiere vecindarios de población mexicano-americana

Bataan Death March/marcha de la muerte de Bataan viaje largo y difícil a través de Filipinas que los japoneses obligaron a realizar a prisioneros de guerra estadounidenses y filipinos en 1942

Battle of Antietam/batalla de Antietam sangrienta batalla librada en Maryland en 1862 durante la Guerra Civil

Battle of Belleau Wood/batalla del bosque de Belleau difícil victoria de Estados Unidos sobre Alemania, en Francia en 1918

Battle of Britain/batalla de Inglaterra intento fracasado de Alemania de someter a Inglaterra en 1940, como preparación para una invasión

Battle of Bull Run/batalla de Bull Run primera gran batalla de la Guerra Civil, librada en Virginia en 1861

Battle of Bunker Hill/batalla de Bunker Hill primera gran batalla de la Revolución; librada en 1775

Battle of Chancellorsville/batalla de Chancellorsville batalla librada en Virginia en 1863 durante la Guerra Civil; fue una victoria importante para la Confederación

Battle of Cowpens/batalla de Cowpens batalla de 1781 librada en Carolina del Norte; fue una victoria importante de los colonos sobre los británicos

Battle of Fredericksburg/batalla de Fredericksburg batalla librada en Virginia en 1862 durante la Guerra Civil; fue una de las peores derrotas de la Unión

Battle of Gettysburg/batalla de Gettysburg batalla librada en Pennsylvania en 1863 durante la Guerra Civil; evitó que los Confederados invadieran el Norte

Battle of Lake Erie/batalla del lago Erie batalla de la guerra de 1812; las fuerzas de Estados Unidos, lideradas por Oliver Perry, vencieron a los británicos

Battle of Long Island/batalla de Long Island batalla de 1776 en Nueva York en la que más de 1,400 colonos murieron, resultaron heridos o fueron capturados

Battle of Midway/batalla de Midway batalla de 1942 en el Pacífico en la que aviones de Estados Unidos hundieron cuatro portaviones japoneses

Battle of New Orleans/batalla de Nueva Orleáns al final de la guerra de 1812, batalla en la que las fuerzas de Estados Unidos vencieron a los británicos

Battle of San Jacinto/batalla de San Jacinto batalla de 1836 entre texanos y mexicanos durante la guerra en la que Texas tretaba de independizarse de México

Battle of Saratoga/batalla de Saratoga en 1777, primera victoria importante de la Revolución

Battle of Shiloh/batalla de Shiloh batalla librada en 1862 en Tennessee, que terminó en una victoria de la Unión

Battle of the Argonne Forest/batalla del bosque de Argonne derrota de los alemanes en Francia en octubre de 1918 por las tropas francesas y estadounidenses

Battle of the Bulge/batalla de Bulge contraataque alemán en diciembre de 1944, que atrasó por un tiempo la invasión de los aliados a Alemania

Battle of Tippecanoe/batalla de Tippecanoe batalla de 1811 a propósito de las colonizaciones blancas en el territorio de Indiana

Battle of Trenton/batalla de Trenton batalla de 1776 librada en Nueva Jersey en la que las tropas de George Washington capturaron un campamento de Hessian

Battle of Verdun/batalla de Verdún batalla prolongada de la Primera Guerra Mundial en la que murieron o fueron heridas más de un millón de personas

Battle of Yorktown/batalla de Yorktown victoria de los colonos en Virginia en 1781 que obligó a los británicos a rendirse

battles of Lexington and Concord/ batallas de Lexington y Concord conflictos de 1775 entre colonos de Massachusetts y soldados británicos que dieron origen a la Revolución Americana

Bay of Pigs invasion/invasión de la bahía de los Cochinos intento fallido de invadir Cuba en 1961 por cubanos anticastristas

Bear Flag Republic/República de la Bandera del Oso sobrenombre de California después de declararse independiente de México en 1846

beatnik/*beatnik* en la década de 1950, persona que criticaba a la cultura estadounidense por su conformidad y devoción por los negocios

Berlin Airlift/puente aéreo de Berlín operación de ayuda llevada a cabo por aviones estadounidenses y británicos para transportar suministros a los habitantes de Berlín occidental durante el bloqueo soviético de 1948 a 1949

Berlin Wall/muro de Berlín muro construido por el gobierno comunista de Alemania oriental en 1961 para aislar Berlín oriental de Berlín occidental

Bessemer process/sistema Bessemer método inventado en la década de 1850 para producir un acero más resistente a un menor costo

bias/prejuicio inclinación a favor o en contra de cierta persona, grupo o idea

Big Four/los cuatro grandes los líderes de las naciones aliadas después de la Primera Guerra Mundial

bilingual/bilingüe en dos idiomas

bill/proyecto de ley ley que se propone para su aprobación

bill of rights/declaración de derechos lista escrita de las libertades que el gobierno promete proteger

Bill of Rights/Declaración de Derechos las primeras 10 enmiendas de la Constitución de Estados Unidos

Black Cabinet/Gabinete Negro líderes afroamericanos que asesoraban extraoficialmente al presidente Franklin D. Roosevelt en asuntos importantes para los afroamericanos

black codes/códigos de negros leyes aprobadas por los estados del Sur después de la Guerra Civil que limitaban con severidad los derechos de los afroamericanos

Black Tuesday/Martes Negro día en que calló el mercado de valores, marcando el comienzo de la Gran Depresión

blitzkrieg/*blitzkrieg* palabra alemana que significa guerra relámpago, los rápidos ataques lanzados por Alemania en la Segunda Guerra Mundial

blockade/bloqueo cierre de un puerto para que ni las personas ni las provisiones entren o salgan

boat people/balseros después de la guerra de Vietnam, refugiados que huyeron de Vietnam en pequeñas embarcaciones

bond/bono certificado que promete el pago de dinero que se ha prestado, más el interés, en una determinada fecha

bonus/bono cantidad adicional de dinero

Bonus Army/ejército del bono veteranos que marcharon hacia Washington en 1932 para exigir que se aprobara un proyecto de ley que proveía el pago inmediato del bono que les correspondía por la Primera Guerra Mundial

bootlegger/contrabandista persona que introducía de contrabando bebidas alcohólicas en Estados Unidos durante la época de la Ley Seca

Border Ruffians/rufianes de frontera bandas proesclavistas que a menudo combatían las fuerzas antiesclavistas en Kansas

border state/estado de frontera estado esclavista que permaneció en la Unión durante la Guerra Civil

Boston Massacre/masacre de Boston conflicto de 1770 entre colonos y tropas británicas en el que se dio muerte a cinco colonos

Boston Tea Party/Fiesta del Té de Boston protesta de 1773 en la que los colonos se vistieron de indígenas y lanzaron el té de los británicos a la bahía de Boston

Boxer Rebellion/rebelión de los Boxers revuelta contra Occidente y la influencia occidental en China en 1900

boycott/boicot rechazar la compra o el uso de ciertos bienes o servicios

bracero program/programa de braceros contratación de jornaleros mexicanos para trabajar en Estados Unidos durante la Segunda Guerra Mundial

Buffalo Soldiers/soldados búfalos sobrenombre de los afroamericanos integrantes de los batallones de caballería noveno y décimo durante la guerra Hispano-Americana

building code/código de construcción normas para la construcción y seguridad de los edificios

bull market/mercado alcista período en el cual la compraventa de acciones aumenta y suben los precios de las acciones

Bull Moose party/partido del alce republicanos progresistas que apoyaron a Theodore Roosevelt durante la elección de 1912

bureaucracy/burocracia sistema de administración del gobierno mediante departamentos dirigidos por funcionarios nombrados

burgess/burgués representante del gobierno colonial de Virginia

C

Cabinet/gabinete grupo de funcionarios que dirigen departamentos gubernamentales y aconsejan al presidente

Camp David Accords/acuerdos de Camp David tratado de paz firmado en 1997 entre Israel y Egipto en el que Israel accedió a devolver a Egipto la península de Sinaí y Egipto accedió a reconocer a Israel

capital/capital dinero con el que se inicia un negocio

capitalist/capitalista persona que invierte en un negocio con el fin de obtener beneficios

caravan/caravana grupo de personas que viajaban juntas por razones de seguridad

carpetbagger/*carpetbagger* sobrenombre despreciativo dado a los norteños que se mudaron al Sur después de la Guerra Civil

cartographer/cartógrafo persona que hace mapas

cash crop/cosecha de contado cosecha vendida por dinero en el mercado

cash economy/cultivo comercial economía en la que se intercambian dinero por mercancías y servicios

cattle drive/arreo de ganado conducir y llevar ganado, normalmente hacia las vías del ferrocarril

caucus/reunión encuentro privado, a menudo de carácter político

causeway/paso elevado camino elevado hecho con tierra comprimida

cavalry/caballería tropas a caballo

cede/ceder entregar censure/censurar condenar oficialmente

Central Powers/potencias centrales alianza militar entre Alemania, el Imperio Austro-Húngaro, Bulgaria y el Imperio Otomano durante la Primera Guerra Mundial

Chapultepec/Chapultepec fuerte en las afueras de Ciudad de México donde ocurrió una batalla entre Estados Unidos y México en 1847

charter/carta legal documento que da ciertos derechos a una persona o compañía

Chautauqua Society/sociedad chautauqua movimiento itinerante para la educación de adultos del siglo XIX

checks and balances/controlar y equilibrar principio de la Constitución de Estados Unidos que da a cada rama del gobierno el poder de vigilar las otras ramas

Chinese Exclusion Act/Ley de la Exclusión China ley aprobada por el Congreso en 1882 que prohibía a los trabajadores chinos entrar a Estados Unidos

chronology/cronología secuencia de sucesos a través del tiempo

circumnavigate/circunnavegar viajar alrededor de la Tierra

citizen/ciudadano persona que debe lealtad a una nación particular y se beneficia de la protección y de todos los derechos de dicha nación

city-state/ciudad estado ciudad grande que tiene su propio gobierno y controla el campo que la rodea

civic virtue/virtud cívica deseo de trabajar por el bien de una nación o comunidad aun a costa de grandes sacrificios

civics/educación cívica estudio de los derechos y responsabilidades de los ciudadanos

civil/civil se refiere a los juicios sobre derechos privados de los individuos

civil disobedience/desobediencia civil idea de que las personas tienen derecho a desobedecer las leyes que consideren injustas, si su conciencia lo exige

civil rights/derechos civiles los derechos que corresponden a todos los ciudadanos

civil rights movement/movimiento de los derechos civiles lucha de los afroamericanos para conseguir igualdad de derechos

civil service/servicio civil todos los puestos federales excepto los que se eligen por votación y los puestos militares

Civil Service Commission/Comisión de Servicio Civil agencia del gobierno creada en 1883 para asignar puestos federales basándose en el mérito de los candidatos

civil war/guerra civil guerra entre personas del mismo país

Civil War amendments/enmiendas de la Guerra Civil enmiendas Trece, Catorce y Quince de la Constitución de Estados Unidos

civilian/civil no militar

Civilian Conservation Corps/ Cuerpo de Conservación Civil programa del Nuevo Acuerdo que daba trabajo a hombres solteros y desempleados en proyectos de conservación de la naturaleza en todo el país

clan/clan grupo de dos o más familias emparentadas

Clermont/Clermont barco de vapor construido en 1807 por Robert Fulton; primero en obtener éxito comercial en aguas de Estados Unidos

climate/clima promedio del tiempo de un lugar en un período de 20 a 30 años

clipper ship/clíper barco de mediados del siglo XIX que navegaba velozmente

Cold War/Guerra Fría después de la Segunda Guerra Mundial, largo período de intensa rivalidad entre la Unión Soviética y Estados Unidos

collective bargaining/negociación colectiva proceso por el cual un sindicato que representa un grupo de trabajadores negociaba un contrato con la dirección de la empresa

colony/colonia grupo de personas que se establece en una tierra distante pero sigue bajo la dirección del gobierno de su tierra natal

Columbian Exchange/intercambio colombino intercambio global de bienes e ideas que resulta del encuentro entre los pueblos de los hemisferios occidental y oriental

committee of correspondence/comité de correspondencia campaña que consistió en escribir cartas y se convirtió en un importante instrumento de protesta en la colonia

Common Sense/Sentido común ensayo de Thomas Paine publicado en 1776 que instaba a las colonias a declarar la independencia

communism/comunismo sistema económico según el cual toda la propiedad y la riqueza pertenecen al Estado

company union/sindicato de empresa organización de trabajadores cuyo control recae realmente en la dirección de la empresa

compensation/compensación pago por pérdidas

Comprehensive Test Ban Treaty/Tratado de Prohibición de Ensayos Nucleares acuerdo propuesto en 1996 con el fin de terminar todas las pruebas de armas nucleares

compromise/compromiso documento en el que cada lado cede en algunas de sus posiciones para poder llegar a un acuerdo

Compromise of 1850/Compromiso de 1850 acuerdo con respecto a la esclavitud según el cual California se sumó a la Unión como estado libre, y se aprobó una estricta ley sobre esclavos fugitivos

compulsory education/educación obligatoria requisito de que los niños fueran a la escuela hasta un cierto grado o una cierta edad

concentration camp/campo de concentración campo de prisioneros civiles que se consideraban enemigos del Estado

confederation/confederación liga de estados o naciones independientes

Congress of Industrial Organizations/Congreso de Organizaciones Industriales organización de trabajadores fundada en la década de 1930 para representar a los trabajadores de las industrias básicas de producción en masa

conquistador/conquistador término que se refiere a los exploradores españoles que conquistaron en el nombre de España tierras en las Américas

conservation/conservación protección de los recursos naturales

Conservatives/conservadores durante la Reconstrucción, los blancos del Sur que se resistían al cambio

consolidate/consolidar reunir, juntar

constitution/constitución documento que establece las leyes, principios, organización y sistema de un gobierno

Constitutional Convention/Convención Constitucional reunión de los representantes de los estados realizada el 25 de mayo de 1787 para revisar los Artículos de la Confederación

consumer/consumidor el que usa bienes y servicios

containment/contención política que consistía en tratar de impedir la extensión de la influencia soviética más allá de donde ya existía

Continental Army/Ejército Continental ejército establecido por el Segundo Congreso Continental para luchar contra los británicos

continental divide/divisoria continental cadena de montañas que separa sistemas fluviales que corren en direcciones opuestas en un continente

Contract With America/contrato con América paquete legislativo aprobado en1994 por los republicanos de la Cámara de Representantes que incluía el recorte de los programas de asistencia social, la reducción de la normativa medioambiental y la bajada de impuestos

cooperative/cooperativa grupo de granjeros que contribuyen con dinero para comprar semillas o herramientas al por mayor

Copperhead/Copperhead norteño que oponía el uso de la fuerza para mantener los estados del Sur dentro de la Unión

corduroy road/camino de troncos camino hecho con troncos

corollary/corolario añadidura a un principio enunciado anteriormente

corporation/corporación negocio cuyos dueños son los inversionistas

corral/corral recinto para animales

"cottonocracy"/"algodocracia" sobrenombre dado a dueños de plantaciones ricos que hicieron su dinero con el algodón a mediados del siglo XIX

counterculture/contracultura movimiento de protesta de la década de 1960 que rechazaba los valores y la cultura estadounidenses tradicionales

coureur de bois/coureur de bois colonos franceses que cazaban animales por sus pieles

cow town/pueblo vaquero asentamiento formado al final de una ruta de ganado

creole/criollo persona de padres españoles nacida en las colonias españolas de América

Crusades/Cruzadas guerras en las que los cristianos lucharon por el control de la Tierra Santa entre 1100 y 1300

Cuban missile crisis/crisis de los misiles en Cuba enfrentamiento de gran importancia en 1962 en el que Estados Unidos bloqueó el intento soviético de poner misiles atómicos en Cuba

culture/cultura forma de vida de un pueblo

culture area/área cultural región en la que las personas tienen una forma de vida similar

currency/moneda dinero circulante

czar/zar emperador de Rusia

D

D-Day/Día D 6 de junio de 1944, día de la invasión de Europa occidental por las potencias aliadas

dame school/escuela de damas escuela privada dirigida por una mujer, generalmente en su propia casa

Dayton Accord/Acuerdo de Dayton acuerdo de paz negociado en 1995 entre Bosnia, Croacia y Serbia

debtor/deudor persona que no puede pagar el dinero que debe

Declaration of Independence/Declaración de Independencia documento de 1776 que declaraba que las 13 colonias formaban una nación independiente

deficit spending/gasto deficitario práctica del gobierno de gastar más de lo que se recauda por impuestos

demilitarized zone/zona desmilitarizada área en la que las fuerzas militares están prohibidas

democratic/democrático que asegura que todas las personas tengan los mismos derechos

Democratic Republican/republicano demócrata partidario de Thomas Jefferson

Democrats/demócratas quienes apoyaban a Andrew Jackson, incluyendo granjeros de frontera y trabajadores de fábrica

department store/gran almacén tienda que ofrece al por menor una variedad de artículos organizados en departamentos separados

deport/deportar expulsar de un país

depression/depresión período en que la actividad comercial disminuye, los precios y los salarios bajan, y aumenta el desempleo

deregulation/desregulación reducción al control de las empresas

détente/detente política de reducir las tensiones entre las superpotencias

dictator/dictador gobernante que tiene poder y autoridad absolutos

dime novel/novelas de diez centavos a finales del siglo XIX, libros de aventuras con tapa blanda y baratos

direct democracy/democracia directa forma de gobierno según la cual los ciudadanos comunes tienen el poder de gobernar

disarmament/desarme reducción de las fuerzas militares y el armamento

discrimination/discriminación política que niega derechos igualitarios a ciertos grupos de personas

dividend/dividendo parte de las ganancias de una corporación

dollar diplomacy/diplomacia del dólar política del presidente Taft que consistía en tratar de crear fuertes lazos económicos con Latinoamérica

domestic tranquility/tranquilidad interna orden y paz interna de una nación

domino theory/teoría del dominó convencimiento de que si Vietnam del Sur sucumbía al comunismo, otros países cercanos seguirían el mismo camino

"Double V" campaign/campaña "Doble V" campaña por los derechos civiles de los afroamericanos durante la Segunda Guerra Mundial

downsizing/reducción de plantilla reducir el número de trabajadores

draft/leva ley que obliga a las personas de cierta edad a alistarse en el servicio militar

Dred Scott v. Sandford/Dred Scott versus Sandford un caso que llegó a la Corte Suprema en 1857 y puso en duda el poder federal con respecto a la esclavitud en los territorios

Dust Bowl/Cuenca de Polvo región del centro de las Grandes Llanuras que sufrió una gran sequía en la década de 1930

E

e-commerce/comercio electrónico negocios y comercio por Internet

Earth Summit/Cumbre de la Tierra reunión de los líderes mundiales en 1992 para dialogar acerca de los principales asuntos medioambientales

economics/economía el estudio de cómo las personas manejan recursos limitados para satisfacer sus deseos y necesidades

Eighteenth Amendment/Enmienda Decimoctava enmienda a la Constitución de Estados Unidos aprobada en 1917 que declaraba ilegal la venta de bebidas en el país

electoral college/colegio electoral grupo de electores de cada estado que cada cuatro años vota para elegir al presidente y vicepresidente de Estados Unidos

elevation/elevación altura por encima del nivel del mar

emancipate/emancipar liberar

Emancipation Proclamation/ Proclama de Emancipación declaración de 1863 del presidente Lincoln que liberaba a los esclavos de la Confederación

embargo/embargo prohibición de comerciar

Embargo Act/Acta de Embargo ley de 1807 que impuso la prohibición total al comercio exterior

encomienda/encomienda tierra otorgada por el gobierno español a los colonos españoles; incluía el derecho a exigir trabajo o impuestos a los indígenas

English Bill of Rights/Declaración de Derechos Inglesa documento de 1689 que garantizaba los derechos de los ciudadanos ingleses

Enlightenment/Ilustración movimiento europeo de los siglos XVII y XVIII que enfatizaba el uso de la razón

Environmental Protection Agency/Agencia de Protección Medioambiental agencia del gobierno federal que tiene como cometido hacer cumplir la normativa medioambiental

environmentalist/ecologista persona que lucha por reducir la polución y proteger el medio ambiente

epidemic/epidemia dispersión rápida de una enfermedad contagiosa

Equal Rights Amendment/ Enmienda por la Igualdad de Derechos enmienda constitucional propuesta en 1923, que tenía como objetivo prohibir toda discriminación sexual; la enmienda nunca fue aprobada

Era of Good Feelings/era de los buenos sentimientos los ocho años de la presidencia de James Monroe, de 1817 a 1825

Erie Canal/canal de Erie canal artificial construido en 1825 que unía el lago Erie con el río Hudson

erosion/erosión desgaste gradual

escalate/extender intensificar

established church/iglesia oficial religión elegida por un Estado

execute/ejecutar llevar a cabo

executive branch/rama ejecutiva rama del gobierno que hace cumplir las leyes

exile/exiliado persona forzada a abandonar su propio país

expansionism/expansionismo política que consiste en extender los límites de una nación

expatriate/expatriado persona que renuncia a su propio país y pasa a residir en el extranjero

expedition/expedición largo viaje de exploración

export/producto de exportación artículo comercial que se envía a mercados extranjeros

extended family/familia extendida grupo familiar que incluye abuelos, padres, hijos, tías, tíos y primos

F

faction/facción grupo de oposición dentro de un partido

factory system/sistema de fábricas método de producción que reunió en un mismo lugar trabajadores y maquinaria

fad/novedad actividad o moda pasajera que se adopta con gran pasión por poco tiempo

famine/hambruna severa escasez de alimentos

Farewell Address/discurso de despedida el último discurso de los presidentes al expirar sus mandatos

Fascism/fascismo sistema político basado en el militarismo, el nacionalismo extremo y la lealtad ciega al Estado

Federal Reserve Act/Ley de la Reserva Federal ley de 1913 que estableció un sistema de bancos federales y dio al gobierno el poder de controlar el suministro de dinero

Federal Trade Commission/Comisión Federal de Comercio agencia del gobierno creada en 1914 para asegurar la competencia justa

federalism/federalismo principio de la Constitución de Estados Unidos que establece la división de poderes entre el gobierno federal y los estados

Federalist/federalista partidario de la Constitución quien estaba a favor de un gobierno federal o nacional fuerte

The Federalist Papers/Los Ensayos Federalistas ensayos escritos por los Federalistas James Madison, Alexander Hamilton y John Jay que apoyaban la ratificación de la Constitución

feudalism/feudalismo sistema de gobierno en el que los señores regían sus propias tierras pero debían lealtad y servicio militar a un monarca

Fifteenth Amendment/Enmienda Decimoquinta enmienda a la Constitución de Estados Unidos aprobada en 1869 que prohibe a los estados negar a los afroamericanos el derecho al voto por causa de su raza

54th Massachusetts Regiment/ regimiento 54° de Massachusetts unidad afroamericana del ejército de la Unión

fireside chat/charla alrededor del fuego discurso por radio del presidente Franklin D. Roosevelt durante su presidencia

First Amendment/Primera Enmienda enmienda a la Constitución de Estados Unidos que protege las libertades individuales básicas

First Continental Congress/Primer Congreso Continental reunión de delegados de 12 colonias en Filadelfia en 1774

first global age/primera era global época a comienzos del siglo XV en la que el comercio y los viajes aumentaron notablemente

flapper/*flapper* mujer joven que en la década de 1920 se revelaba contra los maneras tradicionales de pensar y actuar

flatboat/carguero de poco fondo embarcación que se usa para transportar carga pesada en rutas acuáticas de tierra adentro

Foraker Act/Ley de Foraker ley aprobada por el Congreso en 1900 bajo la cual Estados Unidos dio a los puertorriqueños una voz limitada en sus propios asuntos

foreign policy/política exterior acciones de una nación en relación con otras naciones

Fort Wagner/fuerte Wagner fuerte de Carolina del Sur objeto de un ataque en 1863 por parte del Regimiento 54° de Massachusetts

forty-niner/persona del cuarenta y nueve una de los más de 80,000 personas que en 1849 se unieron a la fiebre del oro

Founding Fathers/padres de la patria líderes que dieron los primeros pasos para la formación de Estados Unidos

Fourteen Points/los catorce puntos los objetivos del presidente Wilson para los tiempos de paz después de la Primera Guerra Mundial

Fourteenth Amendment/Enmienda Decimocuarta enmienda a la Constitución de Estados Unidos aprobada en 1868 que garantiza la protección igualitaria de las leyes

free enterprise system/sistema de libre empresa sistema económico en el cual los negocios son de los ciudadanos privados, y ellos deciden qué producir, cuánto producir, dónde vender los productos y qué precios cobrar

free market/mercado libre sistema económico en el cual los bienes y servicios se intercambian con pocas restricciones

Free-Soil party/partido del territorio libre partido antiesclavista fundado en 1848 en Estados Unidos, para mantener la esclavitud fuera de los territorios del oeste

freedmen/libertos hombres y mujeres que habían sido esclavos

Freedmen's Bureau/Oficina de Libertos agencia del gobierno de Estados Unidos fundada durante la Reconstrucción para ayudar a los libertos

French and Indian War/guerra Franco-Indígena guerra ocurrida de 1754 a 1763 que acabó con el poder francés en América del Norte

French Revolution/Revolución Francesa rebelión que tuvo lugar en Francia en 1789 y que acabó con la monarquía por un tiempo

frigate/fragata barco armado con muchos cañones que navega rápidamente

fugitive/fugitivo persona que huye

Fugitive Slave Act/Acta de los Esclavos Fugitivos ley de 1850 que exigía a todos los ciudadanos colaborar en la captura de esclavos fugitivos

Fundamental Orders of Connecticut/Órdenes Fundamentales de Connecticut plan de gobierno de la colonia puritana de Connecticut en 1639

G

Gadsden Purchase/Compra de Gadsden banda de tierra entre lo que es hoy Arizona y Nuevo México, por la cual Estados Unidos pagó a México $10 millones en 1853

gauge/entrevía distancia entre las vías del tren

General Court/Corte General asamblea representativa elegida de la colonia de la bahía de Massachusetts

general welfare/bienestar general bienestar de todos los ciudadanos de una nación

"Gentlemen's Agreement"/"acuerdo entre caballeros" acuerdo de 1907 entre Estados Unidos y Japón para limitar la inmigración japonesa

gentry/alta burguesía la clase social más alta en las 13 colonias inglesas

geography/geografía el estudio de las personas, su medio ambiente y sus recursos

Gettysburg Address/discurso de Gettysburg discurso pronunciado en 1863 por el presidente Lincoln después de la batalla de Gettysburg

Gibbons v. Ogden/Gibbons versus Ogden caso judicial de 1814 en el que la Corte Suprema confirmó el poder del gobierno federal para regular el comercio

Gilded Age/Época Dorada período en la historia estadounidense durante las últimas dos décadas del siglo XIX, marcado por la corrupción política y e derroche

glacier/glaciar capa gruesa de hielo

glasnost/*glasnost* política de hablar abiertamente de los problemas de la Unión Soviética

global warming/calentamiento global subida lenta pero ininterrumpida de la temperatura media de la Tierra

Glorious Revolution/Revolución Gloriosa movimiento de 1688 que llevó a William y a Mary al trono de Inglaterra y reforzó los derechos de los ciudadanos ingleses

Good Neighbor Policy/política de buena vecindad política del presidente Franklin Roosevelt que tenía como objetivo reforzar las relaciones de amistad con América Latina

graduated income tax/impuesto sobre la renta escalonado impuesto sobre las ganancias que aplica porcentajes distintos según los diferentes niveles de renta

grandfather clause/cláusula del abuelo ley que eximía a un votante de la prueba de alfabetización si su padre o su abuelo había sido elegible para votar el 1° de enero de 1867

Great Awakening/Gran Despertar movimiento religioso que tuvo lugar a principios del siglo XVIII en las colonias inglesas

Great Compromise/Gran Compromiso plan de la Convención Constitucional que resolvió los conflictos entre los estados grandes y los pequeños

Great Depression/Gran Depresión el peor período de decadencia económica de Estados Unidos; comenzó en 1929

Great White Fleet/Gran Flota Blanca nombre de los barcos de vapor de la marina de Estados Unidos, agrandados y modernizados, a principios del siglo XX

Green Mountain Boys/los muchachos de *Green Mountain* milicia colonial de Vermont liderada por Ethan Allen que llevó a cabo un ataque sorpresa al fuerte Ticonderoga

guerrilla warfare/guerrillero uso de tácticas militares de ataque y fuga inmediata

Gulf of Tonkin Resolution/ Resolución del Golfo de Tonkín resolución aprobada por el Congreso en 1964 que autorizó la intervención militar en Vietnam

Gullah/*Gullah* combinación del idioma inglés y de lenguas de África occidental que hablaban los afroamericanos en la colonia de Carolina de Sur

H

habeas corpus/habeas corpus derecho por el cual no puede encarcelarse a ninguna persona a menos que se le acuse de haber cometido un crimen específico

Harlem Hell Fighters/luchadores infernales de Harlem unidad de infantería compuesta por afroamericanos que luchó junto con el ejército francés en la Primera Guerra Mundial

Hartford Convention/Convención de Hartford reunión de delegados de Nueva Inglaterra durante la guerra de 1812 que amenazó con separarse de la Unión como protesta contra la guerra

Haymarket Riot/revuelta Haymarket mitin laboral que tuvo lugar en Chicago en 1886, encabezado por un grupo pequeño de anarquistas, terminó violentamente al explotar una bomba

Holocaust/Holocausto masacre de judíos europeos por parte de los nazis antes durante la Segunda Guerra Mundial

Hooverville/Hooverville conjunto de casuchas miserables donde vivían las personas que no tenían un hogar durante la Gran Depresión

House of Burgesses/Casa de los Burgueses asamblea de representantes de la Virginia colonial

House of Representatives/Cámara de Representantes el mayor de los dos cuerpos que forman la rama legislativa del gobierno de Estados Unidos

Hudson River School/escuela del río Hudson grupo de pintores estadounidenses que pintaban paisajes del valle del río Hudson en Nueva York, a mediados del siglo XIX

Hull House/casa Hull centro comunitario fundado en Chicago por la reformadora progresista Jane Addams en 1889

Hundred Days/los cien días los primeros 100 días de la presidencia de Franklin D. Roosevelt

I

ILGWU/*ILGWU* Sindicato Internacional de Trabajadoras de la Industria del Vestido, fundado en 1900

illegal alien/extranjero ilegal inmigrante que entra en un país sin autorización

illiterate/analfabeto que no sabe leer ni escribir

immigrant/inmigrante persona que se establece en otro país

Immigration Reform and Control Act/Ley de Reforma y Control de la Inmigración ley que permitía que las personas que llegaron de forma ilegal a Estados Unidos antes de 1982 pudieran quedarse en el país y solicitar la residencia

impeach/juicio político acusar formalmente de faltas serias a un representante político

imperialism/imperialismo política de los países poderosos que tratan de controlar los asuntos económicos y políticos de los países o regiones más débiles

import/producto de importación artículo comercial que se ha introducido a un país

impressment/leva práctica de forzar a las personas a que hagan el servicio militar

inauguration/toma de mando ceremonia en la cual el presidente jura su cargo

income tax/impuesto a los ingresos un impuesto al dinero que las personas ganan

incriminate/incriminar presentar evidencias en contra de alguien

indentured servant/sirviente por contrato persona que aceptaba trabajar sin pago por un tiempo a cambio de un pasaje a las colonias

Indian New Deal/Nuevo Acuerdo Indígena leyes aprobadas en 1930 que dieron a las naciones de los indígenas un mayor control en sus propios asuntos

Indian Removal Act/Acta de Reubicación de los Indígenas ley aprobada en 1830 que forzaba a muchos indígenas a mudarse hacia el oeste del río Mississippi

indigo/índigo planta usada para hacer una valiosa tintura azul

individualism/individualismo concepto que destaca la importancia de cada individuo

Industrial Revolution/Revolución Industrial proceso gradual en el que las máquinas reemplazaron a las herramientas manuales

inflation/inflación aumento de los precios y desvalorización del dinero

infrastructure/infraestructura sistema de caminos, puentes y túneles

initiative/iniciativa proceso por el cual los votantes pueden presentar un proyecto de ley directamente ante la legislación del estado

installment buying/compra a plazo comprar a crédito

integration/integración mezcla de diversos grupos raciales o étnicos

interchangeable parts/partes intercambiables partes o repuestos idénticos para herramientas o instrumentos hechos a máquina

internal improvements/mejoras internas mejoras hechas a caminos, puentes y canales

Internet/Internet ordenadores unidos de manera que los usuarios puedan acceder e intercambiar información

interstate commerce/comercio interestatal negocio que se lleva a cabo cruzando los límites de dos o más estados

Interstate Commerce Commission/Comisión de Comercio Interestatal agencia del gobierno que vigila el comercio ferroviario

intervention/intervención participación directa

Intolerable Acts/Actas Intolerables leyes aprobadas en 1774 para castigar a Boston por la Fiesta del Té

irrigation/irrigación riego de tierras áridas

Islam/islam religión monoteísta fundada por el profeta Mahoma a principios del siglo VII

island hopping/de isla en isla estrategia de los aliados durante la Segunda Guerra Mundial, que consistía en capturar islas ocupadas por los japoneses para obtener el control del Pacífico

isolationism/aislacionismo política que consiste en tener poca relación con los asuntos políticos de las naciones extranjeras

isthmus/istmo estrecha franja de tierra que une dos áreas de terreno más extensas

J

Jay's Treaty/Tratado de Jay acuerdo de 1795 entre Gran Bretaña y Estados Unidos que requería que Gran Bretaña pagara por los daños ocasionados por la captura de barcos estadounidenses, y devolviera los fuertes que aún ocupaba en el Oeste

jazz/*jazz* estilo musical que se desarrolló a partir del *blues*, el *ragtime* y otros estilos anteriores

jerky/tasajo carne secada

Jim Crow laws/leyes de Jim Crow leyes que separaban en los lugares públicos del Sur a las personas de diferentes razas

judicial branch/rama judicial rama del gobierno que decide si las leyes se practican de manera justa

judicial review/revisión judicial poder de la Corte Suprema para decidir si los actos de un presidente o las leyes aprobadas por el Congreso son constitucionales

Judiciary Act/Acta Judicial ley de 1789 que creó la estructura de la Corte Suprema y estableció un sistema de cortes de distrito y cortes de circuito a nivel nacional

jury duty/el deber de servir en un jurado obligación de todo ciudadano de servir en un jurado cuando se le llama

K

kachina/kachina bailarín enmascarado que participaba en ceremonias religiosas de los indígenas del Sudoeste

kaiser/*kaiser* título del emperador alemán entre 1871 y 1918

kamikaze/kamikaze piloto japonés entrenado durante la Segunda Guerra Mundial para estrellarse en un ataque suicida, generalmente contra un barco

Kansas-Nebraska Act/Acta de Kansas-Nebraska ley de 1854 que estableció los territorios de Kansas y Nebraska, dando a los colonos el derecho de soberanía popular para decidir con respecto a la esclavitud

Kellogg-Briand Pact/Pacto de Kellog-Briand tratado de 1928 que declaraba ilegal la guerra

Kentucky and Virginia resolutions/Acuerdos de Kentucky y Virginia declaraciones aprobadas en 1798 y 1799 que reivindicaban para los estados el derecho de decidir si una ley federal era constitucional

Khmer Rouge/Khmer Rojo partido comunista en Camboya que impuso un verdadero imperio de terror en los camboyanos

kinship/parentesco cuando se tienen antepasados en común

"kitchen cabinet"/"gabinete de cocina" grupo de consejeros extra oficiales de Andrew Jackson que se reunía con él en la cocina de la Casa Blanca

Knights of Labor/*Knights of Labor* organización laboral estadounidense fundada en 1869 para proteger los derechos de los trabajadores

Know-Nothing Party/partido Know-Nothing partido político de la década de 1850 que estaba en contra del catolicismo y de la inmigración

Ku Klux Klan/Ku Klux Klan sociedad secreta organizada en el Sur después de la Guerra Civil para afirmar la supremacía blanca por medio de la violencia

L

laissez faire/*laissez faire* idea de que el gobierno debería tener una función mínimo en los asuntos económicos

Lancaster Turnpike/carretera de peaje a Lancaster camino de peaje construido en la década de 1790 por una compañía privada; unía a Filadelfia con Lancaster, Pennsylvania

Land Ordinance of 1785/ Ordenanza de Tierras de 1785 ley que establecía un sistema para colonizar el Territorio del Noroeste

latitude/latitud distancia hacia el norte o el sur del ecuador

lawsuit/demanda caso legal iniciado para dirimir una disputa entre personas o grupos

League of Nations/Liga de las Naciones asociación de naciones formada después de la Primera Guerra Mundial bajo el plan de Los Catorce Puntos de Wilson

League of the Iroquois/Liga de los Iroquois alianza de las cinco naciones de los iroquois

League of Women Voters/Liga de Mujeres Votantes organización establecida en 1920 para garantizar los derechos de las mujeres

legislative branch/rama legislativa rama del gobierno que aprueba las leyes

legislature/legislatura grupo de personas que tiene el poder de hacer leyes

Lend-Lease Act/Ley de Préstamo Alquiler durante la Segunda Guerra Mundial, ley que permitió a Estados Unidos vender armas y equipamiento a Inglaterra

libel/libelo acto de publicar afirmaciones que pueden dañar injustamente la reputación de una persona

The Liberator/The Liberator el periódico antiesclavista más influyente, fundado por William Lloyd Garrison en 1831

liberty/libertad independencia

Liberty Bonds/bonos de la libertad bonos vendidos por el gobierno de Estados Unidos para recaudar dinero para la Primera Guerra Mundial

limited government/gobierno limitado principio de la Constitución de Estados Unidos que establece que el gobierno sólo tiene los poderes que la constitución le otorga

literacy test/prueba de alfabetización examen para determinar si una persona sabe leer y escribir; se usaba para restringir el derecho al voto

local color/color local habla y costumbres de una región determinada

local government/gobierno local gobierno del condado, distrito de condado, ciudad, pueblo, villa o distrito

locomotive/locomotora máquina que arrastra un tren

lode/filón veta rica en oro, plata u otro mineral valioso

Lone Star Republic/República de la Estrella Solitaria sobrenombre de Texas después que obtuvo su independencia de México en 1836

longitude/longitud distancia hacia el este o el oeste del primer meridiano

Louisiana Purchase/Compra de Luisiana vasto territorio entre el río Mississippi y las Montañas Rocosas que se le compró a Francia en 1803

Lowell girl/chica Lowell mujer joven que trabajaban en las fábricas de Lowell, Massachusetts durante la revolución industrial

Loyalist/*loyalist* colono que permaneció leal a Gran Bretaña

Lusitania/Lusitania barco de pasajeros inglés que fue torpedeado por un submarino alemán en 1915; 1,200 personas murieron incluyendo 128 estadounidenses

lynch/linchar captura y ejecución ilegal de una persona por parte de una multitud

M

Magna Carta/Carta Magna documento británico de 1215 cuyas dos ideas básicas sostienen que incluso los monarcas tienen que obedecer la ley y que los ciudadanos tienen derechos básicos

mainstreaming/mainstreaming integración de los niños con necesidades especiales en clases normales

majority/mayoría más de la mitad

Manifest Destiny/destino manifiesto creencia que se diseminó en el siglo XIX de que los estadounidenses tenían el derecho y la obligación de ocupar todo el continente, hasta el Pacífico

manor/señorío distrito regido por un Señor que incluía su castillo y las tierras que lo rodeaban

map projection/proyección cartográfica dibujo de la Tierra sobre una superficie plana

Marbury v. Madison/Marbury versus Madison caso judicial de 1803 en el cual la Corte Suprema dictaminó que tenía el poder de decidir si las leyes aprobadas por el Congreso eran constitucionales

Marshall Plan/plan Marshall plan estadounidense para ayudar a los países europeos a reconstruir sus economías después de la Segunda Guerra Mundial

martial law/ley marcial gobierno de militares en vez de un gobierno electo

martyr/mártir persona que muere por sus creencias

Mason-Dixon Line/línea de Mason-Dixon límite entre Pennsylvania y Maryland que dividía las colonias centrales de las colonias del sur

mass production/producción en masa proceso que consiste en hacer grandes cantidades de un producto, con gran rapidez y a bajo costo

Mayflower Compact/acuerdo Mayflower acuerdo de 1620 para gobernar la colonia de Plymouth

McCulloch v. Maryland/Mc Cullock versus Maryland caso judicial de 1819 en el que la Corte Suprema dictaminó que los estados no tenían derecho a interferir en las instituciones federales aunque estuvieran en su territorio

mediator/mediador agente que ayuda a las partes en conflicto a resolver sus diferencias

mercantilism/mercantilismo teoría de que el poder económico de una nación provenía de mantener un estricto control sobre el comercio de las colonias

mercenary/mercenario soldado que lucha exclusivamente por dinero, a menudo para un país extranjero

merit/mérito habilidad

mestizo/mestizo en las colonias españolas de las Américas, la persona que tiene mezcla indígena y española

Mexican Cession/cesión mexicana territorio mexicano de California y Nuevo México que se entregó a Estados Unidos en 1848

middle class/clase media en las 13 colonias inglesas, la clase social que incluía artesanos cualificados, granjeros y algunos comerciantes

migrant worker/trabajador itinerante persona que se traslada de una región a otra en busca de trabajo

militarism/militarismo política que consiste en reforzar las fuerzas armadas como preparación para la guerra

militia/milicia ejército de ciudadanos que sirven como soldados en una emergencia

minuteman/miliciano de la Guerra de Independencia voluntario de una milicia colonial que estaba siempre listo para luchar

mission/misión colonia religiosa administrada por frailes y monjas católicas

missionary/misionero persona que enseña sus creencias religiosas a otros

Missouri Compromise/compromiso de Missouri acuerdo, propuesto en 1819 por Henry Clay, para mantener igual el número de estados esclavistas y antiesclavistas

Monitor/Monitor buque de guerra blindado de la Unión

monopoly/monopolio compañía o agrupación que tiene control de toda o casi toda una industria

Monroe Doctrine/Doctrina Monroe política exterior del presidente Monroe que prevenía a las naciones europeas de no intervenir en América Latina

moral diplomacy/diplomacia moral política del presidente Wilson que consistía en condenar el imperialismo, extender la democracia y promover la paz

Moral Majority/Mayoría Moral organización religiosa que apoyaba causas políticas conservadoras en la década de 1980

Mormons/mormones miembros de la Iglesia de Jesucristo de los Santos de los Últimos Días fundada en 1830 por José Smith

Mound Builders/constructores de montículos nombre de varias culturas de América del Norte que construyeron grandes montículos de tierra, comenzando hace unos 3,000 años

mountain man/hombre de montaña cazador que exploraba Oregón a principios del siglo XIX

moving assembly line/cadena de ensamblaje en movimiento método de producción según el cual los trabajadores permanecen en un lugar mientras que los productos pasan frente a ellos en una cinta transportadora

muckraker/*muckraker* periodista que ponía en evidencia la corrupción y otros problemas a finales del siglo XIX y principios del siglo XX

mudslinging/detractar uso de insultos para atacar la reputación de un oponente

Munich Conference/Conferencia de Munich reunión en 1938 entre los líderes de Inglaterra, Francia, Italia y Alemania en la que se acordó entregar a Hitler parte de Checoslovaquia

mutualista/mutualista grupo de ayuda mutua de los estadounidenses de origen mexicano

N

NAACP/*NAACP* organización establecida para luchar por la igualdad de derechos de los afroamericanos

National Aeronautics and Space Administration/ Administración Nacional de la Aeronáutica y el Espacio agencia gubernamental que dirige el programa espacial estadounidense

national debt/deuda nacional cantidad total de dinero que un gobierno debe

National Labor Relations Act/Ley Nacional de Relaciones Laborales ley aprobada en 1935 que protege a los trabajadores de Estados Unidos de prácticas injustas por parte de sus patrones

national park/parque nacional área que el gobierno federal reserva para que las personas la visiten

National Recovery Administration/Administración para la Recuperación Nacional agencia gubernamental establecida durante la Gran Depresión para asegurar el cumplimiento de nuevos códigos diseñados para estabilizar la industria

National Road/Caminos Nacionales primer proyecto nacional de caminos financiado federalmente, que se inició en 1811

National Woman Suffrage Association/Asociación Nacional para el Sufragio de la Mujer grupo fundado en 1869 para luchar por una enmienda constitucional que concediera a las mujeres el derecho al voto

nationalism/nacionalismo orgullo excesivo en la propia nación

nativist/nativista persona a favor de que se limitara la immigración y Estados Unidos se reservara para los protestantes blancos nacidos en el país

natural resources/recursos naturales materiales que los seres humanos toman del medio ambiente para sobrevivir y satisfacer sus necesidades

natural rights/derechos naturales derechos que corresponden a todas las personas desde su nacimiento

naturalize/naturalizarse proceso oficial para convertirse en ciudadano

Nauvoo/Nauvoo comunidad mormona formada en la década de 1840 en los bancos del río Mississippi en Illinois

Navajo code-talkers/navajos que hablaban en código en la Segunda Guerra Mundial, soldados navajos que usaban su propio lenguaje para enviar por radio mensajes vitales para la campaña "de isla en isla"

Navigation Acts/Actas de Navegación leyes aprobadas por el parlamento inglés a finales del siglo XVII que regulaban el comercio entre Inglaterra y las colonias

Nazi/nazi miembro del partido Nacional Socialista de Trabajadores Alemanes liderado por Adolf Hitler

Nazi-Soviet Pact/pacto nazisoviético acuerdo firmado entre Hitler y Stalin en 1939 por el cual los dos dictadores se comprometieron a no atacarse mutuamente

Negro Fort/Fuerte de los Negros asentamiento de esclavos afroamericanos fugitivos en la colonia española de Florida

network/red sistema de vías de ferrocarril que se comunican

neutral/neutral que no toma partido en un conflicto

Neutrality Acts/Leyes de Neutralidad leyes aprobadas por el Congreso en 1935 que prohibían la venta o préstamo de armas a los países que estuvieran en guerra

Neutrality Proclamation/ Declaración de Neutralidad declaración de 1793 hecha por el presidente Washington que estipulaba que Estados Unidos no apoyaría ni ayudaría a Francia ni a Gran Bretaña en su conflicto europeo

New Deal/Nuevo Acuerdo programa del presidente Franklin D. Roosevelt para poner fin a la Gran Depresión

New Freedom/nueva libertad programa del presidente Wilson para acabar con los trusts y restituir la competencia económica en Estados Unidos

New Jersey Plan/Plan de Nueva Jersey plan de la Convención Constitucional apoyado por los estados pequeños que requería tres ramas del gobierno con una legislatura de cámara única

New Mexico Territory/Territorio de Nuevo México extensa región del suroeste que pertenecía a México en el siglo XIX

"New South"/"Nuevo Sur" término de fines de siglo XIX que describía el Sur cuando se esforzaba por expandir la economía a través de la industria

Nineteenth Amendment/Enmienda Decimonovena enmienda a la Constitución de Estados Unidos que da a las mujeres el derecho al voto

nominating convention/convencíon de postulaciones reuníon en la cual un partido político elige sus candidatos

Nonintercourse Act/Acta de No Intercambio ley de 1809 que permitía a los estadounidenses comerciar con todas las naciones excepto Francia y Gran Bretaña

North American Free Trade Agreement/Tratado de Libre Comercio Norteamericano tratado entre Estados Unidos, Canadá y México para eliminar gradualmente aranceles y otras barreras al comercio

North Atlantic Treaty Organization/Organización del Tratado del Atlántico Norte alianza constituida en 1949 por Estados Unidos y países de Europa occidental para combatir la agresión soviética

Northwest Ordinance/Ordenanza del Noroeste artículo de 1787 que establecía un gobierno para el Territorio del Noroeste

northwest passage/pasaje noroeste pasaje de agua a través o alrededor de América del Norte

nullification/anulación idea de que un estado tiene el derecho de anular o cancelar una ley federal que se considere inconstitucional

Nullification Act/Acta de Anulación acta aprobada por Carolina del Sur que declaraba ilegal la tasa de 1832

Nuremberg Trials/juicios de Nuremberg en 1945 y 1946, juicios a los crímenes de guerra de los nazis

O

Olive Branch Petition/Petición de la Rama de Olivo petición de paz enviada al rey George por los delegados coloniales después de las batallas de Lexington y Concord

on margin/con margen práctica que permite a las personas comprar acciones abonando una entrada del diez por ciento del valor total

OPEC/OPEP organización internacional que establece una política común para la venta de petróleo

Open Door Policy/política de puertas abiertas política promulgada por el Secretario de Estado John Hay en 1899 que permitía a una nación comerciar con China en la esfera de influencia de cualquier otra nación

Operation Overlord/operación Overlord nombre en código de la invasión de los aliados en Europa, ocurrida en 1944

Oregon Country/Territorio de Oregón término usado a principios del siglo XIX para designar lo que es hoy Oregón, Washington, Idaho y partes de Wyoming, Montana y Canadá

Oregon Trail/camino de Oregón ruta hasta Oregón usada por los trenes de carga en el siglo XIX

Organization of American States/Organización de Estados Americanos organización internacional que promueve la paz y el progreso económico en las Américas

override/invalidar no admitir, como cuando el Congreso decide no admitir el veto presidencial

P

pacifist/pacifista persona que se opone a todas las guerras porque cree que todas las guerras son malignas

Parliament/Parlamento en Inglaterra, asamblea representativa

parochial/parroquial de la iglesia; usado a menudo para referirse a las escuelas auspiciadas por la iglesia

patent/patente licencia para un nuevo invento

Patriot/patriota colono que estaba a favor de la guerra contra Gran Bretaña

patriotism/patriotismo sentimiento de amor y devoción hacia el propio país

patronage/patronato práctica de otorgar puestos gubernamentales a los partidarios políticos

patroon/patrón dueño de una gran propiedad en una colonia holandesa

Peace Corps/Cuerpo de Paz organización del gobierno que envía voluntarios estadounidenses a países en desarrollo para dar asistencia técnica

peninsulare/peninsular término que se refiere a un español que tenía una posición de poder en una colonia española

Pennsylvania Dutch/holandeses de Pennsylvania protestantes de lengua alemana que se establecieron en Pennsylvania

pension/pensión suma de dinero que se paga a las personas regularmente después de jubilarse

perjury/perjurio mentir bajo juramento

persecution/persecución maltrato o castigo a un grupo de personas a causa de sus creencias

Persian Gulf War/guerra del Golfo Pérsico guerra en 1991 en la que Estados Unidos y sus aliados en las Naciones Unidas expulsaron a las fuerzas invasoras de Iraq del contiguo territorio de Kuwait

petition/petición solicitud formal firmada por un grupo de personas dirigida a alguien de mayor autoridad

Pickett's Charge/ataque a Pickett ataque la Confederación como parte de la batalla de Gettysburg que fracasó

Pilgrims/peregrinos colonos ingleses que, en el siglo XVII, procuraron libertad religiosa en las Américas

Pinckney Treaty/Tratado de Pinckney acuerdo de 1795 con España que permitió a Estados Unidos transportar sus mercancías por el río Mississippi y almacenarlas en Nueva Orleáns

pit house/casa subterránea casa de la región ártica cavada en la tierra y cubierta con madera y pieles

Plains of Abraham/Planicies de Abraham campo cerca de Quebec donde en la guerra Franco-Indígena tuvo lugar una importante victoria de los británicos frente a los franceses

plantation/plantación gran propiedad cultivada por muchos trabajadores

Platt Amendment/Enmienda Platt enmienda de 1902 a la constitución cubana, que permitía a Estados Unidos intervenir en Cuba

Plessy* v. *Ferguson/Plessy versus Ferguson un caso legal de 1896 en el cual la Suprema Corte dictaminó que la segregación en las instalaciones públicas era legal si las instalaciones eran iguales

PLO/OPL organización palestino-árabe fundada en 1964 con el fin de destruir a Israel, principalmente a través del uso de fuerza armada

pogrom/*pogrom* en la Europa del este, ataque organizado a una comunidad judía

polio/polio enfermedad infecciosa que inflama las células nerviosas de la base del cerebro y la columna vertebral, produciendo parálisis

political boss/capo político político poderoso que controla el trabajo que se realiza localmente y exige sobornos a los negocios

political science/ciencias políticas el estudio del gobierno

poll tax/impuesto al voto impuesto que se requería antes de que las personas pudieran votar

Pontiac's War/guerra de Pontiac conflicto de 1763 entre indígenas y británicos sobre la colonización de tierras indígenas de los Grandes Lagos

pool/mancomunidad sistema por el cual varias compañías de ferrocarril se ponen de acuerdo en repartirse el negocio de cierta área

popular sovereignty/soberanía popular a mediados del siglo XIX, término que se refería a la idea de que cada territorio podía decidir por sí mismo si permitir la esclavitud

potlatch/*potlatch* cena ceremonial realizada por algunos indígenas de la costa noroeste para mostrar su riqueza

Potsdam Declaration/Declaración de Potsdam mensaje enviado por los aliados a los japoneses en julio de 1945 pidiéndoles que se rindieran

preamble/preámbulo introducción a una declaración, constitución u otro documento oficial

precedent/precedente acta o decisión que sirve de ejemplo a las que siguen

precipitation/precipitación agua que cae en forma de lluvia, cellisca, granizo o nieve

predestination/predestinación idea protestante según la cual Dios decidía de antemano quiénes, después de muertos, se salvarían

presidio/presidio fuerte de las colonias españolas donde vivían los soldados

primary election/elección primaria elección en la que los votantes eligen los candidatos de su partido para la elección general

primary source/fuente original información directa acerca de personas o sucesos

Proclamation of 1763/Proclama de 1763 ley que prohibía a los colonos ingleses establecerse al oeste de los montes Apalaches

productivity/productividad producción media por trabajador

profiteer/aprovechador persona que aprovecha una crisis para hacer dinero

Progressive/progresista reformista de finales del siglo XIX y principios del siglo XX que quería mejorar la calidad de vida en Estados Unidos

Prohibition/Ley Seca prohibición a la fabricación, venta y transporte de bebidas alcohólicas en todo el territorio de Estados Unidos entre 1920 y 1933

propaganda/propaganda difusión de ideas para apoyar una causa o perjudicar la causa opuesta

proprietary colony/colonia de propietarios colonia inglesa en la cual el rey daba tierras a propietarios a cambio de un pago anual

protectorate/protectorado nación cuya independencia está limitada por el control de un país más poderoso

Protestant Reformation/reforma protestante movimiento del siglo XVI para reformar la iglesia católica romana y que llevó a la creación de muchas iglesias cristianas

psychology/sicología el estudio del modo de pensar y comportarse de los seres humanos

public interest/interés público lo que es bueno para el pueblo

public school/escuela pública escuela financiada por los impuestos

public works/obras públicas proyectos construidos por el gobierno para uso público

pueblo/pueblo ciudad de las colonias españolas; aldea de los anazasi

pull factor/factor de atracción condiciones que atraen a la gente a mudarse a otra área

Pure Food and Drug Act/Ley de los Alimentos y Medicamentos Puros ley de 1906 que exige a los fabricantes de alimentos y medicamentos que indiquen los ingredientes en los envases

Puritans/puritanos grupo de protestantes ingleses que se establecieron en la colonia de la bahía de Massachusetts

push factor/factor de rechazo condiciones que hacen que la gente se vaya de sus lugares de origen

Q

Quakers/cuáqueros reformistas protestantes que creen en la igualdad de todas las personas

Quebec Act/Acta de Quebec ley que establecía un gobierno para Canadá y protegía los derechos de los católicos franceses

quipu/quipu artefacto hecho de cuerda o tiras con nudos que representaban cantidades; usado por los incas para sus registros y contabilidad

quota system/sistema de cupos sistema que limita la inmigración permitiendo que sólo un número determinado de personas de cada país entre a Estados Unidos

Quran/Corán libro sagrado del islam

R

racism/racismo creencia en la superioridad de una raza con respecto a otra

radical/radical persona que quiere realizar cambios drásticos en la sociedad

Radical Reconstruction/reconstrucción radical período que comenzó en 1867 cuando los Republicanos, que tenían el control de ambas cámaras, se hicieron cargo de la Reconstrucción

Radical Republican/republicano radical en la época de la Reconstrucción, miembro del Congreso que quería asegurarse de que los libertos recibieran el derecho a votar

ragtime/*ragtime* música popular de finales del siglo XIX, rítmica y alegre

ratify/ratificar aprobar

rationing/racionamiento limitación en la cantidad disponible para la venta al público de ciertos artículos

Reaganomics/*reaganomics* programa económico del presidente Reagan que bajó los impuestos, bajó los gastos federales en programas de asistencia social y aumentó los gastos militares

realist/realista escritor o pintor que muestra la vida tal como es

rebate/rebaja descuento

recall/impugnación proceso por el cual los votantes pueden destituir del cargo a un funcionario electo

recession/recesión disminución de la actividad económica que es más leve que una depresión

reconcentration/reconcentración política de trasladar grandes cantidades de personas a campos especiales con intención militar o política

Reconstruction/Reconstrucción reconstrucción del Sur después de la Guerra Civil

Reconstruction Act/Acta de la Reconstrucción ley de 1867 que anuló los gobiernos de los estados del Sur que se habían negado a ratificar la Enmienda Decimocuarta

referendum/referéndum proceso por el cual las personas votan directamente con respecto a un proyecto de ley

refuge/refugio lugar donde se está libre de persecuciones

refugee /refugiado persona que abandona su tierra natal en busca de seguridad en otro lugar

relief program/programa de ayudas programa del gobierno para ayudar a los necesitados

religious tolerance/tolerancia religiosa deseo de permitir que otros practiquen sus propias creencias

Renaissance/Renacimiento explosión europea de conocimientos que tuvo lugar desde finales del siglo XIV hasta el siglo XVI

rendezvous/*rendezvous* encuentro anual en el cual los hombres de montaña intercambiaban pieles

renewable resource/recurso renovable recurso que puede ser reemplazado rápidamente por la propia naturaleza

reparations/reparaciones después de una guerra, entregas de dinero por parte de una nación vencida a la nación vencedora para pagar por las pérdidas sufridas durante la guerra

repeal/revocar cancelar

representative government/ gobierno representativo sistema político según el cual los votantes eligen a los representantes que dictarán las leyes

republic/república sistema de gobierno en el cual los ciudadanos eligen representantes para que los gobiernen

Republic of Great Colombia/República de la Gran Colombia estado independiente fundado en 1819, compuesto por lo que hoy son Venezuela, Colombia, Ecuador

Republican party/partido republicano partido político establecido en 1854 en Estados Unidos, con el fin de mantener la esclavitud fuera de los territorios del oeste

resident alien/extranjero residente persona que vive en el país sin ser ciudadano

revival/reunión evangelista gran encuentro religioso al aire libre

Roosevelt Corollary/corolario de Roosevelt declaracíon del presidente Theodore Roosevelt según la cual Estados Unidos tenía el derecho a intervenir en Latinoamérica para preservar la ley y el orden

Rosie the Riveter/Rosie la Remachadora trabajadora de una fábrica ficticia que se convirtió en el símbolo de la contribución de las mujeres estadounidenses al esfuerzo que supuso la Segunda Guerra Mundial

Rough Riders/jinetes rudos sobrenombre de la unidad organizada por Theodore Roosevelt durante la guerra entre España y Estados Unidos

royal colony/colonia real colonia bajo el control directo de la corona inglesa

rugged individualist/individualista recalcitrante persona que sigue en la vida su propio camino independiente

S

Sabbath/sabbat día de descanso religioso

sabotage/sabotaje destrucción secreta de propiedades o interrupción de la producción en una fábrica u otro lugar de trabajo

sachem/*sachem* miembro del consejo tribal de jefes de la Liga de los Iroquois

SALT Agreement/Tratado *SALT* tratado firmado por Estados Unidos y la Unión Soviética para limitar el número de cabezas nucleares y misiles

salvation/salvación vida eterna

Salvation Army/Ejército de Salvación organización internacional de caridad

sanctions/sanciones medidas diseñadas para obligar a un país a cambiar su política

Santa Fe Trail/camino de Santa Fe ruta a Santa Fe, Nuevo México, que usaban los comerciantes en el siglo XIX

satellite nation/país satélite país dominado política y económicamente por otro más poderoso

savanna/sabana región de pastos

scalawag/*scalawag* blanco sureño que apoyaba a los Republicanos durante la Reconstrucción

scapegoat/chivo expiatorio persona o grupo sobre el que se descargan las culpas de otros

secede/separarse retirarse como miembro de un grupo

Second Amendment/Segunda Enmienda enmienda a la Constitución de Estados Unidos que se refiere al derecho a tener armas

Second Great Awakening/Segundo Gran Despertar extenso movimiento religioso en Estados Unidos a principios de siglo XIX

secondary source/fuente secundaria relato de los hechos proporcionado por personas que no participaron directamente o presenciaron los hechos ocurridos

sectionalism/seccionalismo lealtad a un estado o región antes que a todo el país

sedition/sedición rebelión en contra de un gobierno

segregation/segregación separación de las personas por razones de raza, etnia u otras características

Selective Service Act/Ley de Servicio Selectivo ley aprobada por el Congreso en 1917 que requería que todos los hombres de 21 a 30 años se inscribieran para el servicio militar

self-determination/autodeterminación derecho de los grupos nacionales a tener su propio territorio y formas de gobierno

self-sufficient/autosuficiente capaz de producir lo suficiente para satisfacer las necesidades propias

Seminole War/guerra de los Seminoles conflicto que se inició en Florida en 1817 cuando los indios seminoles resistieron ser trasladados

Senate/Senado el menor de los dos cuerpos que constituyen la rama legislativa del gobierno de Estados Unidos

Seneca Falls Convention/convención de Seneca Falls un encuentro de 1848 en el cual líderes del movimiento por los derechos femeninos reclamaron derechos igualitarios para la mujer

separation of powers/separación de poderes principio según el cual los poderes del gobierno se dividen en ramas separadas

settlement house/centro comunitario establecimiento organizado a finales del siglo XIX para ofrecer servicios a los pobres

sharecropper/aparcero persona que alquila un terreno de otra persona y lo trabaja a cambio de parte de la cosecha

Shays' Rebellion/rebelión de Shays revuelta de Massachussetts liderada por granjeros en 1786 en reacción a los altos impuestos

**Sherman Antitrust Act/Ley Antimonopolio de
Sherman** ley de 1890 que prohibía la formación de *trusts* y
monopolios en Estados Unidos

siege/sitio cerco por parte del ejército de una ciudad o
posición enemiga, seguido de bloqueo o bombardeo para
obligarla a que se rinda

silent majority/mayoría silenciosa término empleado para
referirse a los estadounidenses que estaban preocupados por
los disturbios de la década de 1960 pero no protestaban por
ello públicamente

Silk Road/Ruta de la Seda rutas terrestres que unían China
con el Oriente Medio

sit-down strike/huelga en el lugar de trabajo huelga en
la cual los obreros se niegan a salir del lugar donde trabajan
hasta que se llegue a un acuerdo

sit-in/sentada forma de protesta en la que la gente se sienta y
se resiste a marcharse

skyscraper/rascacielos edificio alto de muchos pisos
sostenido por un armazón de acero de poco peso

slave codes/códigos de la esclavitud leyes que controlaban
la vida de los esclavos afroamericanos y les negaban los
derechos básicos

smuggling/contrabando importar o exportar mercancías
violando las leyes de comercio

Social Gospel/evangelio social movimiento del
protestantismo estadounidense de finales del siglo XIX que
intentaba aplicar las enseñanzas de la Biblia a los problemas
sociales

social reform/reforma social intento organizado de mejorar
lo que es injusto o imperfecto en la sociedad

social sciences/ciencias sociales estudios que se refieren a
la sociedad y a la conducta social

Social Security Act/Ley de la Seguridad Social ley
de 1935 que estableció un sistema de pensiones para
personas mayores y el primer sistema nacional de seguro de
desempleo

Socialist/socialista persona que está a favor de que las
propiedades pertenezcan a la comunidad y se compartan
todas las ganancias

**Society of American Indians/ Sociedad de Indígenas
Estadounidenses** agrupación que luchaba por la justicia
social y la participación de indígenas en la corriente social
principal de Estados Unidos

sociology/sociología estudio del comportamiento de las
personas en grupos

sod house/casa de tepe casa construida con tierra sujetada
con raíces de hierbas

sodbuster/*sodbuster* granjero de las Grandes Llanuras de a
finales del siglo XIX

Solidarity/Solidaridad sindicato independiente que desafió
al gobierno comunista de Polonia

soup kitchen/olla popular lugar donde se proporciona
comida gratis o por un precio mínimo a los necesitados

Spanish-American War/guerra Hispano-Americana
guerra entre España y Estados Unidos en 1898, que tuvo
como resultado que España cediera Puerto Rico, Filipinas y
Guam a Estados Unidos, y otorgara la independencia a Cuba

speculator/especulador alguien que invierte dinero en un
negocio arriesgado con la esperanza de obtener grandes
ganancias

sphere of influence/esfera de influencia zona donde una
nación tenía privilegios comerciales especiales

spinning jenny/hiladora de varios husos máquina
inventada en 1764 que hilaba varios hilos al mismo tiempo

spoils system/sistema de sinecuras práctica que
recompensaba a los partidarios de un gobierno otorgándoles
empleos en dicho gobierno

Square Deal/acuerdo justo la promesa de Theodore
Roosevelt durante su campaña de que todos los grupos
tendrían las mismas oportunidades de éxito

stagflation/estagflación combinación de alza de precios,
alto desempleo y lento crecimiento económico

stalemate/punto muerto empate en el cual ninguno de los
lados es suficientemente fuerte como para derrotar al otro

Stamp Act/Acta de los Sellos ley de 1765 que imponía
nuevas obligaciones a los documentos legales y gravaba con
impuestos los periódicos, almanaques, naipes y dados

standard of living/nivel de vida índice basado en la
cantidad de bienes, servicios y tiempo libre que tienen las
personas

Star Wars/guerra de las galaxias sistema armamentístico
propuesto por el presidente Reagan con el objeto de destruir
los misiles soviéticos desde el espacio

states' rights/derechos de los estados el derecho de los
estados a limitar el poder del gobierno federal

Statue of Liberty/estatua de la Libertad estatua
monumental situada en la isla Liberty, en la bahía de Nueva
York, que simboliza la esperanza y la libertad

steerage/tercera clase en un barco, la zona hacinada en que
viajan los pasajeros con los billetes más baratos

stock/acción participación en la propiedad de una corporación

**Strategic Arms Reduction Treaty/Tratado de Reducción
de Armas Estratégicas** tratado firmado en 1991 por
Estados Unidos y la Unión Soviética para reducir las armas
nucleares

strike/huelga acción, por parte de los trabajadores, de
negarse a hacer su trabajo hasta que se acepten sus
condiciones

strikebreaker/rompehuelgas el que reemplaza a un
trabajador que está de huelga

subsidy/subsidio ayuda financiera o concesión de tierras por
parte del gobierno

suburb/suburbio área residencial en las afueras de una
ciudad

suffrage/sufragio derecho a votar

suffragist/sufragista persona que lucho por conseguir el
derecho al voto de las mujeres

summit meeting/cumbre reunión entre los gobernantes de
mayor rango de distintas naciones

superpower/superpotencia país con suficiente fuerza
militar, política y económica como para ejercer su influencia
por todo el mundo

Supreme Court/Corte Suprema corte de máxima autoridad
de Estados Unidos, establecida por la Constitución

surplus/superávit excedente; condición que se da cuando los
ingresos superan a los gastos

Sutter's Mill/Sutter's Mill lugar donde se descubrió oro en
1848, lo cual inició la fiebre del oro

Swahili/swahili idioma que mezcla palabras árabes con las
lenguas africanas locales, hablado en gran parte de África
oriental

sweatshop/taller del sudor fábrica donde la gente trabaja
muchas horas en malas condiciones y por poco dinero

T

tariff/tasa de importación impuesto que afecta a bienes extranjeros que se importan a un país

Tariff of Abominations/Tasa de Abominaciones tasa aprobada por el Congreso en 1828 que favorecía a la industria del Norte

Tea Act/Acta del Té ley de 1773 que permitía a la Compañia Británica de las Indias Orientales prescindir de los comerciantes de té y vender sus productos directamente a los colonos

Teapot Dome Scandal/escándalo *Teapot Dome* escándalo politico durante la administración del presidente Harding

Tejano/tejano person nacida en Texas de origen mexicano

telegraph/telégrafo mecanismo para comunicarse que envía señales eléctricas por un cable

temperance movement/movimiento por la temperancia campaña en contra del consumo de alcohol

Ten Percent Plan/Plan del Diez Por Ciento plan del Lincoln que permitía que un estado del Sur formara un nuevo gobierno después de que el diez por ciento de sus votantes juraran lealtad a Estados Unidos

tenement/apartamento de inquilinato pequeño apartamento en un barrio pobre de la ciudad

Tennessee Valley Authority/Autoridad del Valle del Tennessee programa del Nuevo Acuerdo para la construcción de diques que controlaban las inundaciones y producían energía eléctrica a un precio económico

tepee/tipi tienda construida con pieles de búfalo, estirada entre altos palos

terrace/terraza amplio escalón de tierra que se cava en la ladera de una colina

terrorism/terrorismo uso deliberado de actos arbitrarios de violencia con el fin de conseguir un determinado fin político

Tet Offensive/ofensiva *Tet* ataque orpresivo contra las fuerzas estadounidenses estacionadas en Vietnam en Año Nuevo vietnamita en 1968

Thanksgiving/Día de Acción de Gracias día al final de la temporada de cosecha que los peregrinos reservaban para dar gracias a Dios

thematic map/mapa temático mapa sobre un tema específico, como población, recursos naturales o elecciones

Thirteenth Amendment/Enmienda Decimotercera enmienda de 1865 a la Constitución de Estados Unidos que prohibe la esclavitud en toda la nación

38th parallel/paralelo 38 línea divisoria entre Corea del Sur y Corea del Norte

Three-Fifths Compromise/Compromiso de los Tres Quintos acuerdo logrado en la Convención Constitutional, según el cual las tres quintas partes de los esclavos de cada estado se contarían como parte de la población

total war/guerra total guerra absoluta que afecta tanto a los civiles en sus casas como a los soldados en combate

totalitarian state/estado totalitario país en el cual un único partido controla el gobierno y todos los aspectos de la vida de las personas

town meeting/cabildo abierto reunión en Nueva Inglaterra durante la colonia donde los colonos discutían y votaban

Townshend Acts/Actas de Townshend leyes aprobadas en 1767 que gravaban con impuestos bienes como vidrio, papel, pintura, plomo y té

trade deficit/déficit comercial condición que se da cuando un país compra a otros países más bienes y servicios de los que vende

trade union/gremio asociación de trabajadores de un mismo oficio formada para acceder a una paga mayor y a mejores condiciones de trabajo

Trail of Tears/Ruta de Lágrimas viaje forzado de los indígenas cheroquíes de Georgia hacia la región al oeste del Mississippi en el cual miles de indígenas murieron

traitor/traidor persona que traiciona a su país

transatlantic/transatlántico a través del Atlántico

transcendentalist/trascendentalista escritores de Nueva Inglaterra que creían que las verdades más importantes de la vida trascendían, o estaban más allá, de la razón humana

transcontinental railroad/ferrocaril transcontinental ferrocarril que cruza un continente de costa a costa

travois/*travois* trineo arrastrado por un perro o caballo

treason/traición acciones contra el propio país

Treaty of Brest-Litovsk/Tratado de Brest-Litovsk tratado de 1918 entre Rusia y Alemania que puso fin a la participación rusa en la Primera Guerra Mundial

Treaty of Ghent/Tratado de Gante tratado de paz firmado por Gran Bretaña y Estados Unidos a fines de la guerra de 1812

Treaty of Greenville/Tratado de Greenville tratado firmado por algunos indígenas en 1795, por el cual entregaron tierra que más tarde formaría parte de Ohio a cambio de dinero

Treaty of Guadalupe-Hidalgo/Tratado de Guadalupe-Hidalgo tratado de 1848 por el cual México entregó California y Nuevo México a Estados Unidos a cambio de $15 millones

Treaty of Kanagawa/Tratado de Kanagawa tratado de 1854 entre Japón y Estados Unidos que abrió los puertos para el comercio estadounidense con Japón

Treaty of Paris/Tratado de París acuerdo de 1763 entre Francia y Gran Bretaña que puso fin a la guerra FrancoIndígena, ; acuerdo de 1783 entre Estados Unidos y Gran Bretaña que reconoció a Estados Unidos como una nación independiente

Treaty of Versailles/Tratado de Versailles tratado firmado el 28 de junio de 1919 por Alemania y por los aliados; atribuía formalmente a Alemania y a sus aliados la responsabilidad por la guerra

Triangle Fire/incendio de Triangle incendio de 1911 en la fábrica *Triangle Shirtwaist* de Nueva York, donde murieron casi 150 trabajadores

triangular trade/comercio triangular ruta de comercio colonial entre Nueva Inglaterra, las Antillas y África

tribe/tribu comunidad de personas que tienen las mismas costumbres, lenguaje y rituales

tributary/tributario arroyo o río pequeño que desemboca en un río mayor

tribute/tributo contribución de dinero

Truman Doctrine/doctrina Truman política del presidente Truman de suministrar ayuda estadounidense a los países amenazados por la expansión comunista

trust/*trust* grupo de corporaciones gobernadas por un solo consejo administrativo

trustbuster/que lucha contra los *trusts* persona que desea destruir todos los *trust*

turning point/momento decisivo momento histórico que indica un cambio fundamental

turnpike/camino de peaje camino construido por una compañía privada que cobra un peaje por su uso

Tuskegee Airmen/aviadores de Tuskegee pilotos afroamericanos de aviones de guerra entrenados en Tuskegee, Alabama, en la Segunda Guerra Mundial

tutor/tutor maestro privado

Twenty-sixth Amendment/ Enmienda Vigesimosexta enmienda a la Constitución de Estados Unidos que redujo de 21 a 18 años la edad mínima requerida para votar

U

U-boat/submarinos *U-boat* submarinos alemanes usados en la Primera y Segunda Guerra Mundial

Uncle Tom's Cabin/La Cabaña del Tío Tom novela de Harriet Beecher Stowe en contra de la esclavitud y el Acta de Esclavos Fugitivos

unconstitutional/inconstitucional que no está permitido por la Constitución

Underground Railroad/Ruta Clandestina red de abolicionistas negros y blancos que ayudaban en secreto a huir a los esclavos hacia la libertad en el norte de Estados Unidos o Canadá

United Nations/Naciones Unidas organización mundial establecida en 1945 para proporcionar soluciones pacíficas a los conflictos internacionales

United Provinces of Central America/Provincias Unidas de América Central federación fundada en 1823 las actuales Guatemala, El Salvador, Honduras, Nicaragua y Costa Rica

urbanization/urbanización traslado de la población de las granjas a las ciudades

V

Valley Forge/Valley Forge lugar de Pennsylvania donde estaba el campamento del Ejército Continental comandado por Washington durante el invierno de 1777 y 1778

vaquero/vaquero término que se refiere a ganaderos mexicanos o hispanos

vaudeville/*vaudeville* espectáculo de variedades popularizado a finales del siglo XIX, que incluía comediantes, actuaciones de canto y baile, y acróbatas

vertical integration/integración vertical práctica por la cual un solo fabricante controla todos los pasos necesarios para transformar la materia prima en productos terminados

veto/veto rechazar, como cuando el presidente rechaza una ley que ha sido aprobada por el Congreso

victory garden/huerta de la victoria durante la Segunda Guerra Mundial, huerta que se plantaba para combatir la escasez de alimentos en Estados Unidos

Vietcong/*Vietcong* guerrilleros vietnamitas que se oponían al gobierno no comunista de Vietnam del Sur

vigilante/vigilante alguien que se designa a sí mismo para hacer cumplir la ley

Virginia/Virginia buque de guerra blindado que usaron los Confederados para quebrar el bloqueo de la Unión

Virginia Plan/Plan de Virginia plan de la Convención que recomendaba un gobierno nacional fuerte con tres ramas y una legislatura de dos cámaras

W

Wade-Davis Bill/Proyecto de Wade-Davis plan de 1864 para la Reconstrucción que negaba el derecho al voto o el acceso a la función pública a quienes se habían ofrecido a luchar por la Confederación

War Hawks/halcones de guerra miembros del Congreso que representaban al Oeste y al Sur y que instaban a la guerra contra Gran Bretaña antes de la guerra de 1812

War Production Board/Junta de Producción de Guerra agencia del gobierno creada durante la Segunda Guerra Mundial para ayudar a las fábricas a producir materiales de guerra en lugar de bienes de consumo

warmonger/belicista persona que fomenta la guerra

Warsaw Pact/Pacto de Varsovia alianza militar de la Unión Soviética con otros países comunistas de Europa establecida en 1955

WCTU/*WCTU* grupo organizado en 1874 que luchó por la prohibición de la venta de bebidas alcohólicas en Estados Unidos

weather/tiempo condición de la atmósfera terrestre en un lugar y momento determinado

Whigs/*Whigs* miembros del viejo Partido Republicano Nacional, liderado por John Quincy Adams

Whiskey Rebellion/rebelión del whisky protesta de 1794 con respecto a un impuesto aplicado a todas las bebidas alcohólicas producidas y vendidas en Estados Unidos

wholesale/venta al por mayor comprar o vender algo en grandes cantidades a precios reducidos

Wilmot Proviso/Cláusula de Wilmot ley aprobada en 1846 que proscribía la esclavitud en todos los territorios ganados a México por Estados Unidos

Wisconsin Idea/idea de Wisconsin serie de reformas progresistas introducidas a principios del siglo XX por el gobernador de Wisconsin Robert La Follette

women's rights movement/movimiento por los derechos femeninos campaña organizada para obtener el derecho a la propiedad, la educación y otros derechos para la mujer

writ of assistance/mandato de asistencia documento legal que permitía a los funcionarios de la aduana inglesa realizar la inspección de la carga de un barco sin tener que alegar razón alguna

X

XYZ Affair/*Affair XYZ* intento francés de 1797 de sobornar a Estados Unidos exigiendo pagos antes de que comenzaran las conversaciones sobre la captura por parte de los franceses de barcos estadounidenses neutrales

Y

Yankee/yankis sobrenombre de los comerciantes de Nueva Inglaterra que dominaban el comercio colonial

yellow journalism/periodismo amarillo periodismo que publica noticias a menudo falsas o mal intencionadas y se apoya en artículos y títulares sensacionalistas

Young Men's Hebrew Association/Asociación Hebrea de Jóvenes organización fundada en Baltimore en 1845 para ofrecer servicios comunitarios en los barrios judíos

Z

Zimmermann telegram/telegrama de Zimmermann
telegrama enviado en 1917 por el secretario de asuntos
exteriores de Alemania al ministro alemán en México,
dándole órdenes de instigar a México a que atacara a
Estados Unidos en caso de que éstos declarasen la guerra a
Alemania

Boston Massacre, 130, 138-140, 173-174

Boston News-Letter, 111

Boston Tea Party, 141-144, 174

Boston, Massachusetts, 81, 118

Boundaries,
  with Mexico, 325, 358

Bourke-White, Margaret, 754

Bowie, Jim, 347

Boxer Rebellion, 638, 646-647

boycotts,
  civil rights movement and, 819, 825
  of farm products, 831

Boyd, Henry, 388

Boynton v. Virginia, 823

bracero program, 775, 781, 794

Braddock, Edward, 127

Bradford, William, 70, 73, 77

Bradley, Omar, 785, 792

Brain Trust, 738

Branches of government, 187, 207, 214, 259-260, 295

Brant, Joseph, 124, 166

Brant, Molly, 124

Brazil,
  slavery in, 54

Breckinridge, John, 451

Brest-Litovsk, Treaty, 682

Brezhnev, Leonid, 853

Britain,
  allies, 274, 277, 355, 669, 769, 772, 794
  American Revolution, 121, 133, 140, 148, 173
  conflicts with, 121, 123, 128, 242, 324
  France and, 121-123, 128-129, 162, 173, 233, 242-243, 246, 248, 252, 267-269, 273, 277, 297, 641, 646, 665-667, 675, 686, 690-691, 731, 762-763, 768-770, 785, 801-802, 879, 921
  Industrial Revolution in, 369, 385
  War of 1812, 233, 273-275, 278, 285, 297, 324
  war with, 121, 129, 133, 149, 162, 167, 171, 233, 242, 252, 267, 274-275, 284, 297, 355, 476, 667, 670, 705, 762, 768-770

British East India Company, 142-143

British Guyana, 661

British troops, in colonies, 156, 160

Broadcasting, radio, 739

Brock, Isaac, 276

Brooke, Edward, 829

Brooklyn Dodgers, 820

Brooks, Preston, 442-443

Brotherhood of Sleeping Car Porters, 778

Brown v. Board of Education, 821-823, 857

Brown, John, 439
  abolitionist, 442, 448-449

Brown, Linda, 821

Brown, Moses, 370

Brown, Oliver,
  civil rights, 821

Brown, William Wells, 422

Brown-Trickey, Minnijean, 797

Browsers, Web, 921

Bruce, Blanche, 491, 507

Bryan, William Jennings, 546
  on evolution, 723
  Scopes Trial, 723

Buchanan, James, 445, 573

Budapest, 667

Budget,
  family, 750
  surplus, 860, 926

budget deficit, 850, 865, 868, 876

budget, federal, 257-258, 703, 814, 863, 868, 926, 928-929

Building boom, 623

bull market, 700, 703-705, 756

Bull Moose Party, 605, 610

Bull Run, 462-463
  Battle, 467

Bunker Hill, 151, 184
  Battle, 141, 161

Bureau of Indian Affairs, 753

Burger, Warren, 866

Burgoyne, John, 160, 162

Burning of Washington, 277

Burns, Anthony, 441

Burns, George, 754

Burnside, Ambrose, 465

Burr, Aaron, 248-250, 254-255

bus boycott,
  in Montgomery, 825

Bush, George H. W., 860, 880
  foreign policy under, 865

Bush, George W.,
  as President, 893, 898, 900-901, 903, 915, 924, 927, 933
  election of 2000, 924-925
  foreign policy of, 927

Business,
  contracts, 116, 195
  education, 210
  in South, 305, 518
  railroad, 531, 533-534, 561, 721, 734
  Roosevelt, Theodore, 634
  success in, 388

Businesspeople, 507

Butler, Andrew, 442

Buttonwood Agreement, 372

buying on margin, 756

C

Cabeza de Vaca, Álvar Núñez, 49

Cabinet,
  first, 702, 738, 842
  of Lincoln, 470

Cabot, John, 57, 68

Cahokia, 12, 167

Calhoun, John C., 282-283, 295, 322, 323
  on nullification, 363
  on slavery, 284, 430, 434-435, 437, 488
  on War of 1812, 435
  tariffs and, 315

California,
  Civil War, 456
  Compromise of 1850 and, 436
  congressmen, 434
  democrats, 727
  farming in, 353, 679, 749
  gold rush, 351, 360, 362
  independence of, 355
  Mexico and, 352, 354, 356, 537
  migration to, 361, 363
  missions in, 51, 351, 353
  Okies in, 754
  population, 362, 931
  revolt, 357
  settlement of, 352
  Spanish in, 351-353
  statehood for, 360
  whites, 931

California Gold Rush, 359, 363, 524, 589

California Trail, 355

Calloway, Cab, 716

Camden, South Carolina, battle at, 168

Camp David, 886

Camp David Accords, 877, 886-888

camp meetings, 403

Campaigns,
  in 1828, 308

Campbell, John, 111

Canada,
  border with, 268, 281
  British, 274, 338
  France and, 802
  French in, 128-129, 145
  Loyalists, 151
  NAFTA, 907

Canada West, 809

Canal Zone, 658-659, 661

canals,
  building, 287, 335, 364, 372
  Erie Canal, 336, 364
  Panama Canal, 658-659

Canary Islands, 35, 39

Capital,
  labor and, 580, 642, 695

Capital investment, 560

capitalism, 557, 562

capitalist, 368-370, 395

Capitol,
  building, 215, 288

Caribbean,
  Islands, 649, 652, 654, 838
  Spanish in, 652

Caribbean islands, 37, 39, 50
  Atlantic slave trade, 54-55

Carnegie Steel, 559-560, 564
Carnegie, Andrew, 558-559, 563, 580, 617
Carney, William, 468, 471
Carolina,
  Spain and, 332
Carranza, Venustiano, 662
Carson, Rachel, 916
Carter, Jimmy,
  as President, 853, 860-862, 871, 886
Cartier, Jacques, 58, 68
Carver, George Washington, 618
Casablanca,
  Morocco, 785
Cascade Mountains, 338
cash crop, 83, 89, 91, 98, 314, 325, 391-392
Cass, Lewis, 433
Castro, Fidel, 830, 838
Catholic Church,
  Protestant Reformation and, 57
Catholics,
  immigrants, 387
  in England, 57
  Irish, 727
Catlin, George, 420
Catt, Carrie Chapman, 613, 634, 708
Cattle,
  drives, 536-538, 546
Cattle trails, 529, 536
Cavalry Regiment, 653
Cayugas, 20
Cemetery Ridge, 480
Central America,
  dollar diplomacy and, 657
  Latin America, 290-291, 643, 657
  Spanish in, 290
Central High School, Little Rock, 822
Central Pacific Railroad, 527, 600
A Century of Dishonor, 556
Champlain, Samuel de, 58
Chaplin, Charlie, 677, 713
Chapultepec, 351, 356-357
Charles I, 74-75, 92
Charles II, 85, 87-88, 94
Charles Town, 93-94
Charleston,
  dance, 715
  in Revolutionary War, 161
  South Carolina, 104, 168, 393, 451, 471, 715
charter,
  for Jamestown, 63
Chautauqua, 623, 628
checks and balances, 203, 747, 869
  Constitution on, 177, 206, 213-214, 230
Cherokee Nation, 324-326
Cherokee Nation v. Georgia, 326
Chesapeake Bay, 64, 93, 161, 170, 277-278, 464
Chiang Kai-shek, 803

Cheswell, Wentworth, 158, 165
Chicago,
  Hull House, 595
  Illinois, 450, 531
  immigrants, 595
  railroads and, 576
  skyscrapers in, 624
  strikes, 567
Chicago Daily Tribune,
  on election of 1948, 813
child labor, 374-375, 566, 580, 596, 609, 615-616
children,
  enslaved, 9, 387, 399
  labor, 564
China,
  1949, 803, 852
  after Korean War, 805, 807, 843
  after World War I, 646-647
  communism, 806, 843
  imperialism, 641, 647
  Nixon, 852-853
  Open Door policy, 638, 646, 695, 767
  Portugal and, 34, 641, 809
  technological innovations from, 30
Chinampas,
  Aztec, 8
Chinese Americans, 362
Chinese Exclusion Act, 584, 633
  1882, 590, 620
Chinese immigrants,
  in California, 361
Chisholm Trail, 536, 538, 546
Chisholm, Jesse, 536
Chivington, John, 551
Choctaw, 324-325, 327-330
Christianity,
  enslaved African Americans and, 36-37
  Native Americans and, 3, 59, 340
  Renaissance and, 21
church and state, 75, 77
Church of England, 70, 74-75, 117
Church of Jesus Christ of Latter-Day Saints, 358
churches,
  African American, 618, 825
Churchill, Winston, 770
  on Iron Curtain, 800
Chávez, César, 819, 831
CIA, 854
Circuit courts, 236
cities,
  colonial, 111, 151
  conflicts within, 384, 387
  crisis in, 801
  Great Migration to, 679
  growth of, 247, 336, 360, 427, 592, 629
  immigrants in, 385-387, 473, 587-588, 592, 628, 633, 727
  immigration to, 592, 633
  industrial, 587

migration to, 592
problems in, 376, 393, 594
riots in, 570, 828
slums in, 587, 630
Southern, 393, 467, 492, 536, 715
urbanization, 376, 384, 386, 427, 591, 594
Cities and towns, 103, 115, 307, 379, 628, 707
  African Americans, 111
citizenship, 177, 225, 228-229
  African Americans and, 436, 501, 505, 516, 751
  Fourteenth Amendment and, 222, 501-502, 504, 519
  in Articles of Confederation, 179, 183
  in World War II, 746, 794, 815
City bosses, 598
civil disobedience, 141, 143, 173-174, 407, 411-412, 416, 424-425, 819, 824-826
Civil liberties, 248
civil rights, 53, 819, 831, 833-835, 849, 924, 932
  during Reconstruction, 519
  for Asian Americans, 752, 830, 832
  Fourteenth Amendment, 519, 822-823
  Great Depression, 751-752, 755
  of African Americans, 497, 519, 634, 748, 751, 755, 779, 820-829
  World War II, 779
Civil Rights Act of 1866, 501, 519, 829
Civil Rights Act of 1964, 823, 827, 829, 833, 835
Civil Rights Cases, 821, 823
civil rights movement, 846-847, 933
  1970s, 829
  effect, 825, 829, 857
  Freedom Rides, 826
  Johnson and, 797
  Kennedy and, 797
  March on Washington, 797
  Martin Luther King and, 797, 819, 825-826, 829
  Mexican Americans and, 821
  sit-ins, 819
civil service, 312, 597, 599-600, 634
Civil Service Commission, 597, 599-600, 606
Civil service reform, 634
Civil War,
  1861, 450, 453, 456, 458
  1863, 456, 463, 465
  African Americans, 367, 387-388, 391, 393-400, 405-406, 408-412, 420-423, 425, 427, 430, 432, 434-438, 440-441, 444, 447-448, 452-453, 458, 468-472, 474, 477, 482, 484, 487-488, 491, 493-494, 498, 505-506, 508, 510, 512, 518-519, 528, 540, 613, 625, 631-632, 725, 755, 846

Defense Department, 838
defense industry, 817
Defense of Marriage Act, 932
deficit spending, 746
Deficits,
    Bush, George W., 927
Delaware River, 61, 83, 85, 89-90, 121,
    158-160, 334
democracy,
    and Age of Jackson, 301, 303-304
Democratic National Convention,
    1964, 827
Democratic Party, 210, 317, 433, 486,
    610, 813, 854, 925
    election, 1860, 451
    elections, 451, 673
    ethnic groups, 387
    Great Depression, 751
    Jackson, Andrew, 302, 308, 311, 363
    Mexican-American War, 363
    on civil rights, 751
    on voting rights, 302
    presidential election of 1876, 515
    rise of Jacksonian, 311
Democratic Republicans, 245, 248-
    250, 252-255, 257-258, 262, 268-269,
    280-285, 298, 307
    on French Revolution, 256
Democratic Societies, 228
Dempsey, Jack, 716
Denver,
    Colorado, 536
Department of Agriculture,
    U.S., 544
Department of Defense, 897, 921
Department of Homeland Security,
    894
department store, 623, 625, 816
Depression,
    of 1870s, 570
deregulation, 860-861, 865-866
De Soto, Hernando, 49
desegregation, 822
détente, 849, 853, 857, 870-871
Dewey, George, 652
Dewey, John, 602
Dewey, Thomas E., 787, 813
Dias, Bartolomeu, 31-32
Díaz, Porfirio, 661
Dickinson, Emily, 421
dictatorships, 191, 193, 662, 760, 764,
    794, 809, 880
Digital technologies, 914
Dime novels, 623, 630, 632
Direct election, of senators, 604
disasters,
    nuclear, 900
discrimination,
    African Americans, 362, 387, 612,
        617-618, 726, 778, 820, 823, 828,
        931
    civil rights, 823, 828

in 1960s, 834-835
Progressive Era, 612
disease,
    epidemic of, 687, 920
    in camps, 468, 473, 650
    in Civil War, 473
    Native Americans, 39-40, 73, 353, 362
district courts, federal, 212-213
District of Columbia, 212, 238, 410,
    821
diversity,
    in cities, 386
    of immigrants, 386, 930
Dix, Dorothea, 404, 477
Dodge City,
    Kansas, 538
dollar diplomacy, 657, 660-661, 663,
    695
Domestic animals, 39, 551
Domestic servants, 744
Dominican Republic, 36, 54, 649, 661,
    883
domino theory, 836, 843-845
Dorchester Heights, 151-152
Dot-com bubble, 909, 925
Douglas, Stephen,
    Compromise of 1850, 436, 440
    election of 1860 and, 451
    Kansas-Nebraska Act, 440-441, 446,
        449
    Lincoln, Abraham, 446-447, 449, 451
Douglass, Frederick, 426, 445, 471,
    491
    as abolitionist, 407, 409, 444, 470
    Dred Scott decision, 444
    Emancipation Proclamation, 470
    Fugitive Slave Act, 444
    Narrative of the Life of Frederick Dou-
        glass, An American Slave, 398
Draft,
    in World War I, 679, 685
draft laws, 473-474
Draft riot, 473-474, 477, 488
Dred Scott v. Sandford, 439, 443-446,
    449, 488, 501
drought,
    1930s, 748-749
Drugs,
    illegal, 847
Du Bois, W.E.B., 634
Dunbar, Paul Laurence, 631
Duncanson, Robert S., 420
Durand, Asher, 419
Dust Bowl, 748-749, 754
Dutch East Indies, 783
Dutch Reformed church, 85
Dutch West India Company, 60

E

Eads, James B., 624
Eakins, Thomas, 632

Earth Day, 916
East Africa, 26-29, 31, 761, 809
East Berlin,
    Germany, 801, 856
East Germany, 798, 801-802, 809, 856,
    873, 875
East Indies, 31, 33, 35
Eastern religions, 847
Eckford, Elizabeth, 822
economic depression, 184, 320, 571,
    911
    Great Depression, 729, 732
Economic downturn, 533, 731
economic opportunity, 84-85, 301,
    358, 933
economic policy, 247, 250, 257-258,
    269, 856, 865, 880, 913
economic systems, 92, 99, 234, 236,
    239, 260, 497, 705, 742
economy,
    1920s, 703-704, 723
    1990s, 906
    after World War I, 671, 704, 776
    after World War II, 765, 775-776, 781,
        812, 815
    automobiles, 817
    Civil War, 393, 475, 519
    Clinton, 868
    colonial, 54, 98
    crisis, 909-910
    economic policy, 247
    Eisenhower, 814
    farming and, 90-91, 98, 286, 314, 362,
        544, 740
    global, 704
    government, 11, 86, 98, 237, 250, 289,
        301, 320, 426, 746-747, 776, 815,
        863, 868, 881-882
    Great Depression, 730, 764
    in cities, 368, 393, 402
    in Cold War, 815
    in England, 75
    industrial growth, 534
    national, 238, 289, 317, 392, 817
    Nixon, 850
    of South, 475, 519
    of West, 286
    recessions, 868, 905, 907, 909, 926-
        927, 933
    Reconstruction, 517
    slavery, 54, 284, 400, 408, 430
    Soviet, 871
Ederle, Gertrude, 716
Edison, Thomas, 572, 574, 578
education,
    aid to, 865
    cost of, 930
    discrimination in, 752
    for women, 416-417, 615, 833
    Great Society, 849
    Horace Mann, 405
    in Massachusetts, 108, 405, 626

installment buying, 700, 703
insurrection, 194
interchangeable parts, 368, 371
interest groups, 407, 412, 604
interest rates, 611, 704, 731, 861, 907, 909-910
International politics, 700, 705
Internet, 665, 906, 914, 921-923, 935
  development of, 932
internment, 775, 780, 794
Interracial marriages, 823
interstate commerce, 282, 289, 597, 600
Interstate Commerce Act, 600, 608
Interstate Commerce Commission (ICC), 597, 600, 608
Intervention,
  in Latin America, 294, 660-661, 882-883
Intolerable Acts, 141, 144-146, 148
Inuits, 12, 14
invasion of Iraq, 891
inventions,
  and business, 576
Iran, 809, 861, 883, 885-886, 889, 891, 895, 899, 901
  hostage crisis, 862, 869
Iran-contra affair, 883
Iranian Revolution, 861-862, 886
Iraq War, 862, 887, 894, 896, 898, 913, 926-928
  2003, 895
Ireland,
  famine in, 98
  immigrants from, 98, 386
Irish American, 627, 669
Irish Catholics, 587
Iron,
  workers, 513, 559
iron curtain, 798, 800
ironclads, 464-465
Iroquois, 12, 17-20, 42, 61-62, 122, 124-127, 129, 166, 173, 271, 297
Iroquois League, 4, 19-20, 40
irrigation, 11-13, 16, 28, 42, 352, 619, 753
  system, 359, 362, 391
Irving, Washington, 421-422
Islam, 21, 24, 28, 862, 893, 898
  in Africa, 25
Islamic fundamentalists, 892-893
isolationism, 639, 688-694, 704, 760-763, 765
  expansionism, 638
  in 1920s, 764
Israel, 23, 848, 878, 884, 895, 901, 903-904
  PLO, 886
  Six-Day War, 879, 885, 902
Italian Americans, 780-781, 794
Italian immigrants, 586, 594, 721, 724

Italy,
  Ethiopia, 761, 770
  World War I, 666-667, 686, 704, 717, 794
  World War II, 761, 768-770, 787, 791
Iwo Jima,
  Battle, 789

J

Jackson, Andrew, 270, 277, 307-308, 310-311, 313, 319, 349, 599
  as General, 281, 292, 295
  at New Orleans, 278-279, 297, 305
  Creek Indians, 305, 324
  election of 1824 and, 304-305
  election of 1828 and, 304, 309, 364
  Indian removal and, 330
  Mexico, 309, 364
  nullification crisis, 363-364
  Panic of 1837, 322, 363
  presidency of, 302, 330
Jackson, Helen Hunt, 556
Jackson, Stonewall, 462, 464, 466
Jackson, Thomas, 463
Jacksonian Democracy, 302, 309, 311, 364
Jacksonians, 311
James II, 116
Jamestown,
  Virginia, 63, 66, 103
Jamestown Colonists, 64-65, 70
Japan,
  after Korean War, 805
  after World War I, 639, 704
  after WWII, 789
  atomic bomb and, 789-790
  attacks Pearl Harbor, 774, 789, 794
  China, 34, 588, 641, 643-644, 647, 652, 759, 767, 770, 773, 783, 791, 809, 904
  economy, 764
  immigration from, 621
  in Age of Imperialism, 647
  Korea, 620, 644, 783, 804
  Russia and, 643, 646, 666
  trade with, 34, 638-640, 643, 773
  Washington Naval Conference, 705
Japanese American internment, 794
Japanese Americans,
  in World War II, 775, 780, 794
Japanese immigrants, 620
Jay, John, 171, 198, 236, 243
jazz music, 423, 699, 713-716, 720
Jefferson, Thomas, 138, 169-170, 181, 226, 229, 241, 246, 335
  as Democratic Republican, 245, 248-250, 253-257, 298
  as President, 249, 254-256
  as secretary of state, 235, 295
  as Vice President, 249-250, 254-255
  committees of correspondence and,

145
  Declaration of Independence, 155-156, 174, 256, 407
  election of 1796 and, 245, 250
  election of 1800 and, 253-255
  foreign policy of, 234, 248
  inauguration, 234, 257
  Louisiana Purchase, 256
  on Constitution, 192
  on Monroe Doctrine, 295
  on religious freedom, 145
  on slavery, 426
  on Whiskey Rebellion, 234, 295
  presidency of, 253, 256
  Second Continental Congress and, 141, 155, 174
Jeffersonian Republicans, 249
Jerusalem, 23, 885, 902
Jewish immigrants, 159
Jews, European, 633, 885
Jiang Jieshi, 803
Jim Crow, 519
Jim Crow law, 513, 516, 518-519, 617
jobs, outsourcing, 929
Jobs, Steve, 891
Johnson, Andrew, 496-497, 505
  impeachment of, 503
Johnson, Anthony, 68, 99
Johnson, James Weldon, 756
Johnson, Lyndon B., 836, 863
  and Great Society, 842
  as President, 841-844
Johnson, Tom, 600
Johnson, William, 124
Joint Committee on Reconstruction, 498, 500
Joliet, Louis, 59
Jones Act, 725
Jones, Absalom,
  War of 1812, 279
Jones, Bobby, 716
Jones, John Paul, 158, 167
Joplin, Scott, 627, 715
Joseph, Chief, 553-554, 556
Josephson, Matthew, 580
journalists,
  on Watergate scandal, 854
Judaism, 23, 25
judicial branch, 185, 187, 203, 206-207
judicial review, 203, 213-214, 231, 256, 260, 269, 295, 501
Judicial system, 213
Judiciary Act, 212, 234-236, 244, 258-259
Jungle, The,
  Sinclair, 601
jury, right to trial by, 194, 202, 207, 229

religion, freedom of, 78, 183, 207, 221
    and government, 179, 199
    in Bill of Rights, 179, 199, 220, 586
Religious freedom, 45, 69-73, 77-78,
    87-88, 94, 118, 145, 202, 220, 231, 301,
    358, 861
religious movements, 106, 402
Religious tolerance, 69, 77, 111
Religious wars, 70
Relocation camps, 780
reparations, 688, 690-691, 731, 762
representation,
    by the South, 230
    of enslaved African Americans, 189
Republic of Texas, 330, 347, 349-350
Republican National Convention,
    450
    1964, 863
Republican Party, 209-210, 248, 611,
    673, 863, 912
    African Americans and, 304, 503
    Civil War and, 445-446, 449
    election of 1856 and, 449
    election of 1896 and, 546
    election of 1912 and, 610
    Fifteenth Amendment, 503
    founding of, 439
    New Right and, 503
    Roosevelt and, 610
republicanism, 206
Republicans,
    Party, 701
Research and development, 935
reservation, Indian, 622, 753
resources,
    for Civil War, 458
Revels, Hiram R., 491, 507
Revenue,
    Tax, 865
revenue, federal, 850
Revere, Paul, 139, 146-147, 165
Revolutionary War, 148, 150, 161, 175,
    183, 242, 246, 283
    Native Americans in, 324, 420
Revolutions,
    French, 240
    in Cuba, 838
Rhode Island, 78-79, 81, 84, 89, 114,
    118, 168, 180, 185, 200-202, 212, 237,
    250, 254, 262, 278, 309, 325, 332, 356,
    364, 370, 382, 410, 417, 431, 434, 440,
    451, 456, 469, 529, 614, 701, 708, 749,
    925
    colony of, 75, 77, 132
Rights,
    African American, 100, 116, 223, 304,
        362, 395, 398, 452-453, 491, 501,
        505, 513, 515, 519, 617, 725, 751,
        823, 826
    colonial, 116
    constitutional, 221, 260, 364, 489, 613
    gay and lesbian, 834

Human, 202
in Bill of Rights, 1, 116, 179, 199, 202,
    219-220, 222-223
in Magna Carta, 116, 194
Latino, 833
Native American, 53, 116, 133
of women, 116, 138, 164, 223, 367,
    402, 414-415, 418, 426, 509, 612-
    614, 708-709, 933
Riis, Jacob, 594, 601
Rio Grande, 356-357
Roaring Twenties, 703, 714-720
Robinson, Jackie, 820
rock-and-roll, 818, 857
Rockefeller, John D., 561, 617, 724,
730
Rocky Mountains, 16, 58, 81, 265, 340,
    345, 359, 528, 547, 561, 570, 619
    Western Canada, 338
Rogers, Will, 627, 739
Rolfe, John, 65
Roman Catholic Church, 22, 56, 74,
346, 837
Roman Catholics, 57, 70, 85, 92, 837
    Native Americans as, 353
Rommel, Erwin, 785
Roosevelt Corollary, 657, 765
    World War I, 660, 663, 695
Roosevelt, Eleanor, 736, 750-751, 781
Roosevelt, Franklin D., 794, 813
    as President, 737, 757, 774, 863
    effect of, 757
    inaugural address by, 737
    on New Deal, 737, 757
    World War II and, 765
Roosevelt, Theodore, 583, 657
    as governor of New York, 606
    as Vice President, 606
    conservation and, 605
    election of 1912 and, 610
    in Spanish-American War, 637, 648,
        652, 695
    navy, 652
    on Progressive Party, 610
    on Square Deal, 605, 634
    Washington, Booker T., 634
    with Rough Riders, 648, 653
Rosebud Reservation, 556
Rosenberg, Julius, 810
Rosie the Riveter, 775, 777, 781
Ross, Betsy, 164
Ross, John, 326
Rough Riders, 648, 653
royal colonies, 83, 86, 91
Royal government, 53, 150
Royal governors, 145
Runaways,
    from slavery, 166, 436
Rural Electrification Administra-
    tion, 741
Rush, Benjamin, 201
Rusk, Dean, 839

Russia, 129, 263, 266, 293, 296, 530, 585,
    588, 646, 665-669, 674-675, 681-682,
    686, 692, 695, 785, 804, 859, 877-879,
    881, 904, 923
    Alaska, 338, 640, 643
    Soviet Union, 870, 874, 876
Russian Revolution,
    in World War I, 674-675, 695, 724
Russo-Japanese War, 666
Russwurm, John, 388, 409
Ruth, Babe, 717

S

St. Augustine,
    Florida, 51
St. Lawrence River, 58, 123, 128
St. Louis,
    Missouri, 263, 266, 296, 355, 536
Sacco and Vanzetti, 721, 724, 727, 756
Sacco, Nicola, 724
Saddam Hussein, 886-889, 896
Sahara Desert, 879
Saigon, 845, 851
    Vietnam war, 843
Salem,
    Massachusetts, 81
SALT I, 853
SALT II, 853, 854, 871
Salt Lake City, 355
    Utah, 359
Salvation Army, 591, 595
Same-sex marriage, 931-933
Samoa,
    American, 638, 643
San Antonio,
    Alamo in, 344, 347, 349
    Texas, 344, 356, 536, 750
San Diego,
    California, 51, 353, 355
San Francisco,
    California, 51, 355, 362, 536
San Jacinto, 348-349
San Juan,
    Puerto Rico, 649
sanctions, 877-878, 881, 900-901, 904
Sand Creek Massacre, 551
Sandburg, Carl, 488
Sandinistas, 883
Sanford, John, 443
sanitation, 393, 468, 601, 829, 840
Santa Anna, Antonio López de, 344,
    347-349, 357
Santa Fe,
    New Mexico, 49, 51, 266, 352, 356-357
Santa Fe Trail, 351-352, 355
Santo Domingo, Hispaniola, 36, 49
Sarajevo, 666-667
    Yugoslavia, 692
Saratoga,
    battle at, 158, 161
Saudi Arabia, 785, 885, 901

Acknowledgments

[Photography]

v, Monkey Business/Fotolia; **vii,** Monkey Business/Fotolia; **x,** MarclSchauer/Shutterstock; **xi,** Pictorial Press Ltd / Alamy; **xii,** North Wind / North Wind Picture Archives - All rights reserved.; **xiii,** trekkerimages / Alamy; **xiv,** Everett Collection Inc / Alamy; **xix,** Steidle Art Collection/SuperStock; **xv,** nik wheeler / Alamy; **xvi,** North Wind Picture Archives / Alamy; **xvii,** Dbimages/Alamy; **xviii,** Everett Collection Historical/Alamy; **xx,** FPG/Getty Images; **xxi,** Underwood Archives / Getty Images; **xxii,** US National Archives/Roger-Viollet/The Image Works; **xxiii,** Photo Researchers, Inc.; **xxiv,** Robert W. Kelley/Getty Images; **xxv,** Dirck Halstead/The LIFE Images Collection/Getty Images; **xxvi,** PF-(space1)/Alamy; **xxxii,** Michael Flippo/Fotolia; **001,** Richard G. Bingham II / Alamy; **002,** MarclSchauer/Shutterstock; **004,** Yvan/Shutterstock; **006,** Zbiq/Shutterstock.com; **007,** Tom Salyer Stock Connection Worldwide/Newscom; **010,** Yaro/Shutterstock.com; **011,** MarclSchauer/Shutterstock; **014T,** Danita Delimont/Alamy; **014B,** The Trustees of the British Museum/Art Resource, NY; **015,** Brooklyn Museum/Corbis; **016T,** Phillip Augustavo/Alamy; **016B,** Phillip Augustavo/Alamy; **017,** North Wind/North Wind Picture Archives; **018,** Corbis; **019,** North Wind/North Wind Picture Archives; **020,** Akg-Images; **021,** North Wind/North Wind Picture Archives; **023,** Ancient Art and Architecture/Alamy; **024T,** Bridgeman Art Library; **024B,** Dorling Kindersley/Getty Images; **027,** A. Gmez/Flickr/Getty Images; **030,** SSPL/Getty Images; **031,** National Gallery, London / Art Resource, NY; **034,** Viking, (9th century)/The Art Gallery Collection / Alamy; **035T,** Christopher Columbus (mosaic), Salviati, Antonio (1816–90) / Palazzo Tursi, Genoa, Italy / Peter Newark American Pictures / The Bridgeman Art Library; **035B,** Mikael Utterstrm/Alamy; **036,** Scala/White Images/Art Resource, NY; **038,** Art Resource, NY; **044,** Pictorial Press Ltd / Alamy; **046,** Look and Learn/Bridgeman Art Library; **047,** Library of Congress Prints and Photographs Division Washington, D.C. [LC-USZC4-741]; **048,** Gianni Dagli Orti/The Art Archive / Alamy; **051,** North Wind Picture Archives/Alamy; **052,** Schalkwijk / Art Resource, NY; **053,** North Wind Picture Archives/Alamy; **056,** North Wind/North Wind Picture Archives; **057,** Alfredo Dagli Orti/The Art Archive/Art Resource, Inc.; **059,** North Wind Picture Archives / Alamy; **060,** North Wind Picture Archives/Alamy; **061,** North Wind Picture Archives / Alamy; **062,** North Wind Picture Archives; **063T,** Hulton Archive/Getty Images; **063B,** North Wind/North Wind Picture; **064,** spiritofamerica/Fotolia; **065,** North Wind Picture Archives/Alamy; **066,** MPI/Getty Images; **069,** The Signing of the Mayflower Compact, c.1900 (oil on canvas), Moran, Edward Percy (1862–1935)/Pilgrim Hall Museum, Plymouth, Massachusetts/The Bridgeman Art Library; **070,** Picture History/Newscom; **071T,** North Wind Picture Archives; **071B,** Suchan/Shutterstock; **073,** North Wind Picture Archives / Alamy; **074,** Pilgrim Fathers and Squanto, the friendly Indian, after an illustration by C. W. Jefferys, 1926 (colour litho), American School, (20th century)/Private Collection/Peter Newark Pictures/The Bridgeman Art Library; **076T,** Pantheon/SuperStock; **076B,** North Wind/North Wind Picture Archives; **077,** Universal Images Group Limited/Alamy; **078,** North Wind Picture Archives/Alamy; **079,** North Wind Picture Archives/Alamy; **080,** North Wind Picture Archives / Alamy; **083,** Niday Picture Library/Alamy; **085,** ClassicStock / SuperStock; **086,** North Wind/North Wind Picture Archives; **087,** SNS Group/Alamy; **088,** SuperStock/Alamy; **089,** North Wind Picture Archives/Alamy; **090,** The Art Gallery Collection / Alamy; **092,** North Wind / North Wind Picture Archives; **094,** North Wind / North Wind Picture Archives; **095,** North Wind Picture Archives; **096,** North Wind Picture Archives/Alamy; **099,** Hulton Archive/Getty Images; **101,** North Wind Picture Archives; **102T,** North Wind/North Wind Picture Archives; **102B,** MPI/Archive Photos/Getty Images; **103,** MPI/Archive Photos/Getty Images; **104,** North Wind Picture Archives; **105,** Art Resource, NY; **106,** Corbis; **107,** Lebrecht Music and Arts Photo Library/Alamy; **108,** North Wind Picture Archives/Alamy; **109,** North Wind Picture Archives/Alamy; **110,** North Wind Picture Archives; **111,** North Wind Picture Archives; **112,** North Wind Picture Archives/Alamy; **113,** World History Archive/Image Asset Management Ltd. / Alamy; **120,** North Wind / North Wind Picture Archives - All rights reserved.; **122,** North Wind Picture Archives/Alamy; **124,** Library of Congress Prints and Photographs Division Washington, D.C. 20540 USA[LC-DIG-pga-00861]; **127,** North Wind Picture Archives/Alamy; **128,** Timewatch Images/Alamy; **131,** North Wind Picture Archives/Alamy; **133,** George Grenville (1712–70) (litho), Houston, Richard (1721–75) / Leeds Museums and Galleries (Leeds Art Gallery) U.K. / The Bridgeman Art Library; **134,** Historical/Corbis; **135,** North Wind/North Wind Picture Archives; **136,** DeAgostini/SuperStock; **137,** Image Asset Management Ltd. / Alamy; **138,** North Wind/North Wind Picture Archives; **139,** North Wind Picture Archives/Alamy; **141,** Library of Congress; **142,** North Wind / North Wind Picture Archives; **143,** North Wind/North Wind Picture Archives; **144,** Revere, Paul (1735–1818) (after) / Private Collection / The Bridgeman Art Library; **146,** North Wind Picture Archives/Alamy; **148,** Apic/Hulton Archive/Getty Images; **149T,** SuperStock; **149 B,** North Wind Picture Archives/Alamy; **151,** SuperStock/Glow Images; **152,** George Schaub/SuperStock; **153,** North Wind Picture Archives/Alamy; **154,** lawcain/Fotolia; **155,** lawcain/Fotolia; **156T,** North Wind/North Wind Picture Archives; **156B,** Ivy Close Images / Alamy; **157,** Universal Images Group Limited/Alamy; **158,** Painting/Alamy; **160,** North Wind Picture Archives / Alamy; **162T,** North Wind/North Wind Picture Archives; **162B,** Library of Congress Prints and Photographs Division[LC-USZC4-6877]; **163,** Tompkins Harrison (1813–84) / Private Collection / Photo Christie's Images / The Bridgeman Art Library; **164,** North Wind Picture Archives/ Alamy; **165,** Virginia Historical Society, Richmond, Virginia, USA / The Bridgeman Art Library; **166,** Christie's Images/Corbis; **167,** New York Public Library, USA / The Bridgeman Art Library; **168,** Kean Collection/Getty Images; **169,** North Wind Picture Archives/Alamy; **171,** North Wind Picture Archives/Alamy; **172,** Universal History Archive/UIG / The Bridgeman Art Library; **176,** trekkerimages / Alamy; **178,** ClassicStock/Alamy; **179,** State of Massachusetts in Convention, State Constitution, 16th June 1780 (litho), American School, (18th century)/Gilder Lehrman Collection, New York, USA/The Bridgeman Art Library; **181,** H -D Falkenstein/ima /AGE Fotostock; **183,** North Wind Picture Archives/Alamy; **184,** North Wind Picture Archives/Alamy; **185,** Virginia Constitutional Convention of 1829–30 (oil on panel), Catlin, George (1794–1872) / Virginia Historical Society, Richmond, Virginia, USA / The Bridgeman Art Library; **187,** Constitutional Convention (w/c on paper), Ferris, Jean Leon Gerome (1863–1930) / Private Collection / The Bridgeman Art Library; **188,** Image Asset Management/Alamy; **190,** SuperStock/Glow Images; **191,** SuperStock / SuperStock; **192T,** Culture Club/Hulton Archive/Getty Images; **192B,** Classic Image / Alamy; **193,** Bettmann/CORBIS; **195,** World History Archive/Image Asset Management Ltd. / Alamy; **196,** Akg-Images/Newscom; **197,** Library of Congress Prints and Photographs Division[LC-USZC2-2452]; **198,** North Wind Picture Archives; **199,** Manuel Balce Ceneta/AP Images; **201,** North Wind/North Wind Picture Archives; **202,** Jackson, Peter (1922–2003) / Private Collection / © Look and Learn / Bridgeman Images; **203,** Kumar Sriskandan/Alamy; **204,** ANAM Collection / Alamy; **205,** Pablo Martinez Monsivais/AP Images; **206,** Manuel Balce Ceneta/AP Images; **208,** Cristina Ciochina/Shutterstock; **209,** U.S. Senate, 111th Congress, Senate Photo Studio; **210,** Cbp/Alamy; **211T,** Orhan am/Fotolia; **211B,** DOD Photo/Alamy; **214,** Artley Cartoons; **215T,** Stephen Saks Photography/Alamy; **215B,** Ross D. Franklin/AP Images; **217,** ZUMA Press, Inc./Alamy; **218,** AZP Worldwide/Fotolia; **219,** Jim West/Alamy; **221,** North Wind Picture Archives/Alamy; **222,** LHB Photo/Alamy; **224,** D. Hurst / Alamy; **225,** Jim West / Alamy; **226,** Eddie Ledesma/ZUMA Press/Newscom; **227,** Jeff Greenberg 3 of 6 / Alamy; **229,** Sam Dao/Alamy; **232,** Everett Collection Inc / Alamy; **234,** Photo Researchers, Inc./Science Source; **235,** Everett Collection Inc./AGE Fotostock; **238,** Joshua Roberts / Alamy; **239,** Matt Rourke/AP Images; **240,** Kean Collection/Hulton Archive/Getty Images; **241T,** DeAgostini / SuperStock; **241 B,** Everett Collection/Newscom; **244,** The Print Collector/Glow Images; **245,** North Wind Picture Archives / Alamy; **246,** C Inger/Corbis; **247,** Robert Salmon/Bettmann/Corbis; **249,** Library of Congress; **251,** Photos.com / Getty Images Plus/Getty Images; **252,** American School, (18th century) / Archives du Ministere des Affaires Etrangeres, Paris, France / Archives Charmet / Bridgeman Images; **253,** Hulton Archive/Getty Images; **255,** Bettmann/Corbis; **256,** GL Archive / Alamy; **257 T,** The Art Archive at Art Resource, NY; **257 B,** aisa/World Illustrated/Photoshot; **259,** North Wind Picture Archives/Alamy; **260,** Currier, N. (1813–88) & Ives, J.M.(1824–95) (after) / Private Collection / Bridgeman Images; **261,** Bettmann/Corbis; **264 T,** mpi/Archive Photos/Getty Images; **264B,** mpi/Archive Photos/Getty Images; **265,** Washington State Historical Society / Art Resource, NY; **267,** The Hongs at Canton, before 1820 (oil on ivory), Chinnery, George (1774–1852) (follower of) / Ferens Art Gallery, Hull Museums, UK / The Bridgeman Art Library; **268,** North Wind Picture Archives/Alamy; **270,** Everett Collection/Newscom; **272,** North Wind Picture Archives / Alamy; **273T,** Library of congress; **273B,** World Pictures/Alamy; **274 T,** North Wind / North Wind Picture Archives; **274 B,** The Trustees of the British Museum / Art Resource, NY; **276,** Niday Picture Library/Alamy; **277,** North Wind / North Wind Picture Archives; **279,** Library of Congress Prints and Photographs Division, [LC-DIG-highsm-09904]; **280,** The Art Archive / Alamy; **281,** The Art Archive / Alamy; **282,** North Wind Picture Archives; **283,** North Wind Picture Archives / Alamy; **285 T,** ArtPix /

Alamy; **285 B,** Thomas Allom/ The Bridgeman Art Library /Getty Images; **287T,** Lebrecht Music and Arts Photo Library/Alamy; **287B,** North Wind / North Wind Picture Archives; **288 T,** Library of Congress Prints and Photographs Division [LC-DIG-highsm-16698]; **288 B,** North Wind Picture Archives / Alamy; **289,** Interfoto/Alamy; **291,** Gianni Dagli Orti/The Art Archive / Alamy; **293,** Picture History/Newscom; **294,** Dalrymple/Bettmann/ Corbis; **300,** nik wheeler / Alamy; **302,** Everett Collection Inc /Alamy; **304,** North Wind /North Wind Picture Archives; **307T,** SuperStock/Getty Images; **307 B,** Getty Images; **308,** Kennedy Galleries, New York, USA / The Bridgeman Art Library; **310,** North Wind /North Wind Picture Archives; **311,** North Wind /North Wind Picture Archives; **312,** North Wind /North Wind Picture Archives; **313,** Corbis; **314,** The Print Collector / Alamy; **315,** Audio & Moving Image Rights notgranted under NAPPA terms; **318,** Private Collection / PeterNewark American Pictures /The Bridgeman Art Library; **319,** Herbert Orth/Time Life Pictures/Getty Images; **320 T,** Bettmann/Corbis; **320 B,** Corbis; **321,** North Wind / North Wind Picture Archives; **322,** Antman Archives / The Image Works; **323,** The New York Public Library /Art Resource, NY; **324,** North Wind / North Wind Picture Archives; **326,** Newberry Library / SuperStock; **327,** Universal Images Group / Art Resource, NY; **329T,** zerega / Alamy; **329 B,** SuperStock / SuperStock; **331,** North Wind Picture Archives / Alamy; **333,** Harper Collins Publishers / The Art Archive at Art Resource, NY; **335,** North Wind Picture Archives; **336,** Private Collection / Look and Learn /The Bridgeman Art Library; **337,** Science Photo Library / Alamy; **339,** North Wind Picture Archives / North Wind; **340,** Getty Images; **341,** Private Collection / PeterNewark American Pictures /The Bridgeman Art Library; **342,** Getty Images; **344,** fotogal/Fotolia; **346T,** Anne Rippy / Alamy; **346B,** INTERFOTO / Alamy; **347,** World History Archive /Alamy; **348,** Bettmann/Corbis; **350,** Fotolia; **351,** Huntington Library /SuperStock; **353T,** North Wind /Nancy Carter\North Wind Picture Archive; **353B,** North Wind / North Wind Picture Archives; **357,** David R. Frazier/Photolibrary, Inc. / Alamy; **359,** Lordprice Collection / Alamy; **361,** Underwood Archives/Getty Images); **362,** Archive Images / Alamy; **366,** North Wind Picture Archives / Alamy; **368,** Mary Evans Picture Library/Alamy; **369,** North Wind/North Wind Picture Archives; **370,** North Wind/North Wind Picture Archives; **371,** North Wind / North Wind Picture Archives; **372,** Bettmann/Corbis; **373,** Library of Congress; **374,** Edward Gooch/Hulton Archive/Getty Images; **376,** Niday Picture Library/Alamy; **377,** Elizabeth Whiting & Associates/Corbis; **378,** SSPL/The Image Works; **379 T,** Chronicle / Alamy; **379 B,** Everett Collection Inc / Alamy; **380,** Chronicle/Getty Images; **381,** ClassicStock/Alamy; **383,** Stock Montage/Archive Photos/Getty Images; **384,** Everett Collection/ Newscom; **385,** North Wind Picture Archives/Alamy; **386,** Corbis; **387,** Susan Van Etten/Photo Edit; **388,** TopFoto/The Image Works; **389,** John Elk III/ Alamy; **390T,** Darryl Vest/Shutterstock; **390B,** North Wind Picture Archives/ Alamy; **391,** North Wind Picture Archives/Alamy; **394,** North Wind/North Wind Picture Archives; **395,** North Wind/North Wind Picture Archives; **396,** Tarker/Corbis; **397,** North Wind Picture Archives/AP Images; **398,** American Photographer, (19th century)/Private Collection/Peter Newark American Pictures/The Bridgeman Art Library; **399,** North Wind Picture Archives / The Image Works; **400,** North Wind Picture Archives; **401,** Universal Images Group Limited/Alamy; **403,** Library of Congress Prints and Photographs Division; **404,** Library of Congress Prints and Photographs Division; **405,** North Wind/North Wind Picture Archives; **406,** Library of Congress Prints and Photographs Division; **407,** Lebrecht Music and Arts Photo Library/Alamy; **408,** Library of Congress Prints and Photographs Division[LC-USZC4-5321]; **409T,** Samuel Cornish (engraving), American School, (19th century) / Collection of the New-York Historical Society, USA / The Bridgeman Art Library; **409B,** North Wind Picture Archives/Alamy; **411,** North Wind Picture Archives/North Wind Pictures; **413,** Bettmann/Corbis; **414,** Bettmann/Corbis; **415,** Historical/Corbis; **416,** Art Resource, NY; **418,** Kean Collection/Archive Photos/Getty Images; **419,** Tomas Abad/Alamy; **420,** Akg-Images/Newscom; **421 T,** The Print Collector/Alamy; **421B,** Lebrecht Music and Arts Photo Library/Alamy; **422T,** Bettmann/Corbis; **422B,** Bettmann/Corbis; **423,** Vereshchagin Dmitry/Shutterstock; **424,** Bettmann/Corbis; **425,** Kim Grant/ Lonely Planet Images/Getty Images; **428,** Dbimages/Alamy; **430,** Bettmann/ Corbis; **432,** North Wind Picture Archives/The Image Works; **435T,** Picture History/Newscom; **435B,** Picture History/Newscom; **437,** Topham/The Image Works; **439,** North Wind Picture Archives/Alamy; **441,** Bettmann/Corbis; **442,** North Wind Picture Archives / Alamy; **443,** Bettmann/Corbis; **444T,** Everett Collection/Newscom; **444B,** Photo Researchers, Inc/Science Source; **445,** Library of Congress Prints and Photographs Division; **446,** North Wind Picture Archives / Alamy; **447T,** Kean Collection/Hulton Archive/Getty Images;

447B, Everett Collection Historical / Alamy; **449,** Peter Horree/Alamy; **450,** Pictorial Press Ltd/Alamy; **452T,** Corbis; **452B,** The New York Historical Society/Archive Photos/Getty Images; **453,** Library of Congress Prints and Photographs[LC-DIG-pga-01584]; **454,** Niday Picture Library/Alamy; **455,** Niday Picture Library/Alamy; **457,** North Wind Picture Archives/Alamy; **459,** Archive Pics/Alamy; **460,** Library of Congress Prints and PhotographsDivision[LC-USZ62-6958]; **461,** Niday Picture Library/Alamy; **462,** Library of Congress Prints and Photographs Division[LC-USZ62-86311]; **464,** Interfoto/Travel / Alamy; **465,** Library of Congress Prints and Photographs Division[LC-DIG-stereo-1s02827]; **466,** Library of Congress Prints and Photographs Division[LC-USZC4-3365]; **467,** Stapleton Historical Collection/ Heritage Image Partnership Ltd/Alamy; **468,** Library of Congress Prints and Photographs Division[LC-DIG-ppmsca-08047]; **470,** The First Reading of the Emancipation Proclamation (oil on canvas), Carpenter, Francis Bicknell (1830–1900) / Library of Congress, Washington D.C., USA / The Bridgeman Art Library; **471,** Library of Congress Prints and Photographs Division; **473,** Library of Congress Prints and Photographs Division; **474,** Bettmann/Corbis; **477,** The Art Archive/Alamy; **478,** North Wind Picture Archives/Alamy; **479,** MPI/Getty Images; **480,** Library of Congress Prints and Photographs Division; **481,** North Wind Picture Archives/Alamy; **483,** Bettmann/Corbis; **484,** Everett Collection Inc/Alamy; **485,** North Wind / North Wind Picture Archives; **486,** Niday Picture Library / Alamy; **490,** Everett Collection Historical/Alamy; **492,** National Archives and Records Administration / Alamy; **493,** Image Asset Management Ltd. / Alamy; **494,** Library of Congress Prints and Photographs Division [LC-USZ62-107637]; **495,** Library of Congress Prints and Photographs Division[LC-USZ62-117666]; **496T,** Proscenium Box in which Lincoln sat in which he was assassinated 1865 (photo), . / Universal History Archive/UIG / The Bridgeman Art Library; **496B,** The Art Archive/Alamy; **497,** North Wind Picture Archives/Alamy; **498,** PF/ NA/Alamy; **499,** The Art Archive/Alamy; **500,** North Wind Picture Archives / Alamy; **501,** Library of Congress Prints and Photographs Division Washington, D.C.[LC-DIG-ppmsca-11312]; **502,** Niday Picture Library/Alamy; **504,** North Wind Picture Archives / Alamy; **505,** MPI/Archive Photos/Getty Images; **506,** North Wind Picture Archives/Alamy; **507,** Library of Congress Prints and Photographs Division Washington, D.C.[LC-DIG-cwpbh-00554]; **508,** Library of Congress prints and Photographs division [LC-USZ62-105555]; **509,** GL Archive/Alamy; **510,** Bettmann/Corbis; **511,** Bettmann/Corbis; **512,** The Metropolitan Museum of Art. Image source: Art Resource, NY; **513,** Archive Photos/Getty Images; **515,** North Wind Picture Archives/Alamy; **516,** North Wind Picture Archives/Alamy; **518,** North Wind Picture Archives/Alamy; **522,** Steidle Art Collection/SuperStock; **524,** ClassicStock/Alamy; **525,** Timothy H. O'Sullivan/George Eastman House/Gettty Images; **526,** Hulton Archive/Getty Images; **527,** Southern Pacific News Bureau/AP Images; **528,** PF-usna/Alamy; **530,** Minnesota Historical Society/Corbis; **531,** North Wind Picture Archives/ Alamy; **533,** Kean Collection/Archive Photos/Getty Images; **535,** Cattle Drive 2, c.1877 (oil on canvas), Walker, James (1818–89) / California Historical Society Collections at the Autry / Gift of Mr and Mrs Reginald F. Walker / The Bridgeman Art Library; **537,** Bill Manns / The Art Archive at Art Resource, NY; **538,** North Wind Picture Archives/Alamy; **539,** age fotostock/Alamy; **540,** Bettmann/Corbis; **541,** Library of Congress Prints and Photographs Division [LC-USZ62-103813]; **542,** mpi/Getty Images; **543T,** SuperStock/SuperStock; **543B,** North Wind/North Wind Picture Archives; **545,** Niday Picture Library/ Alamy; **547,** Library of Congress Prints and Photographs Division Washington, D.C[LC-USZC4-12466]; **548,** The Buffalo Hunt, c.1832 (coloured engraving), Catlin, George (1794–1872) / Bibliotheque Nationale, Paris, France/Giraudon/ The Bridgeman Art Library; **549,** North Wind Picture Archives/Alamy; **550T,** Smithsonian American Art Museum, Washington, DC/Art Resource, NY; **551,** North Wind Picture Archives/Alamy; **553,** Archive Photos/Alamy; **554T,** Niday Picture Library/Alamy; **554B,** Library of Congress Prints and Photographs Division[LC-USZ62-68504]; **555,** National Geographic Image Collection / Alamy; **557,** North Wind Picture Archives/Alamy; **558,** Everett Collection Historical/Alamy; **560,** FPG/Getty Images; **561T,** Library of Congress Prints and Photographs Division[LC-USZ62-11724]; **561B,** Photo by Time Life Pictures/Mansell/Time Life Pictures/Getty Images; **562,** Chicago History Museum/Getty Images; **563,** Library of Congress Prints and Photographs Division[LC-USZC4-494]; **565,** Glasshouse Images/Alamy; **566,** Jacob August Riis/Corbis; **567,** North Wind Picture Archives/ Alamy; **568T,** Everett Collection Historical/Alamy; **568B,** Everett Collection/Newscom; **569,** Franklin D. Roosevelt Library Photographs, 1870 - 2004/National Archives and Records Administration; **570,** Everett Collection/Newscom; **572,** Akg-Images/ NASA/Newscom; **573T,** Library of Congress Prints and Photographs

Division[LC-USZ6-166]; **573B**, Roger Viollet/Getty Images; **574**, Library of Congress Prints and Photographs Division[LC-USZ62-57001]; **575T**, Stapleton Historical Collection/Heritage Image Partnership Ltd/Alamy; **575B**, Everett Collection/SuperStock; **576**, Byron Company (fl.1890–1942)/© Museum of the City of New York, USA/The Bridgeman Art Library; **577**, Everett Collection Inc/Alamy; **578**, Time Life Pictures/Getty Images; **582**, FPG/Getty Images; **584**, Historic Collection/Alamy; **585**, Library of Congress Prints and Photographs Division [LC-B201-5202-13]; **586**, mbuild/Fotolia; **587**, Fotosearch/Archive Photos/Getty Images; **589**, Bettmann/Corbis; **590**, Library of Congress Prints and Photographs Division[LC-USZ62-124416]; **591**, Library of Congress Prints and Photographs Division[LC-USZ62-105032]; **594**, Bettmann/Corbis; **595**, Lewis W. Hine/Premium Archive/Getty Images; **596**, AP Images; **597**, Library of Congress Prints and Photographs Division[LC-USZ62-75157]; **598**, Copyright © North Wind Picture Archives - All rights reserved.; **599**, Library of Congress Prints and Photographs Division[LC-USZ62-7622]; **600**, PhotoQuest/Getty Images; **601**, Historical/Corbis; **602**, Historical/Corbis; **604**, Library of Congress Prints and Photographs Division[LC-DIG-ppmsca-25884]; **605**, Akg-Images/Newscom; **606**, Library of Congress Prints and Photographs Division[LC-DIG-ppmsca-37557]; **607**, B.J. Falk/Corbis; **608**, E.S. Bruce/Corbis; **609**, Corbis; **611**, Library of Congress Prints and Photographs Division[LC-DIG-pplot-13734-01527]; **612**, KEYSTONE Pictures USA/Alamy; **613**, Library of Congress Prints and Photographs Division; **615T**, ZUMA Press, Inc./Alamy; **615B**, Eartha M. M. White Collection/University of North Florida; **616**, Minnesota Historical Society/CORBIS; **617**, © Pictorial Press Ltd / Alamy; **618**, Hulton Archive/Archive Photos/Getty Images; **619**, Corbis; **621**, Getty images; **622**, MPI/Getty Images; **623**, Mark Rucker/Transcendental Graphics/Getty Images; **624**, Detroit Publishing Company/Interim Archives/Getty Images; **625**, Library of Congress Prints and Photographs Division; **627**, Pictorial Press Ltd/Alamy; **628**, Picture History/Newscom; **630**, Lebrecht Music and Arts Photo Library/Alamy; **631T**, Library of Congress Prints and Photographs Division Washington, D.C.; **631B**, Library of Congress Prints and Photographs Division Washington, D.C; **632**, Active Museum/Alamy; **636**, Underwood Archives / Getty Images; **638**, Charles Phelps Cushing/ClassicStock/Alamy; **640T**, American naval vessel in a Japanese harbour, 1861 (colour woodcut), Japanese School, (19th century) / Private Collection / The Bridgeman Art Library; **640B**, Reinhard Tiburzy/Alamy; **642**, Sean Sexton Collection/Corbis; **644**, Katrina Brown/Fotolia; **645T**, Akg-Images/Newscom; **645B**, Hawaii State Archive/AP Images; **646**, Bettmann/Corbis; **647**, Library of Congress Prints and Photographs Division Washington, D.C; **648**, Photo Art Collection (PAC)/Alamy; **650B**, Chronicle/Alamy; **651**, Library of Congress Prints and Photographs Division Washington; **654**, Library of Congress Prints and Photographs Division; **655**, Library of Congress Prints and Photographs Division; **656**, Library of Congress Prints and Photographs Division[LC-DIG-hec-12736]; **657**, U.S. Naval Historical Center; **658**, North Wind/North Wind Picture Archives; **660**, Corbis; **662**, "Formal raising of first flag of U.S. Veracruz 2 P.M. April 27, 1914" Photograph by Hadsell taken during the U.S. occupation of Veracruz, 1914. Spanish American War / Universal History Archive/UIG / The Bridgeman Art Library; **663**, Library of Congress Prints and Photographs Division; **664**, GL Archive/Alamy; **669T**, Daniel Templeton/Alamy; **669B**, Pictorial Press Ltd/Alamy; **671**, Classic Image/Alamy; **672**, Library of Congress Prints and Photographs Division[LC-USZ62-113662]; **674**, National Archives and Records Administration; **676**, American Stock Photography/ClassicStock/Alamy; **677**, MPI/Getty Images; **678**, Akg-Images/Newscom; **679**, Bettmann/Corbis; **680**, Bettmann/Corbis; **681**, Photo Researchers/Alamy; **682T**, Hulton-Deutsch Collection/Corbis; **682B**, Berliner Verlag/Archiv/picture alliance / ZB/Newscom; **684**, National Archives and Records Administrations; **685**, Department of U.S. Army/AP Images; **688**, Library of Congress Prints and Photographs Division Washington, D.C; **691**, Jose Ignacio Soto/Shutterstock; **693**, Mondadori Collection/UIG Universal Images Group/Newscom; **694**, Picture History/Newscom; **698**, US National Archives/Roger-Viollet/The Image Works; **700**, SZ Photo/Scherl/DIZ Muenchen GmbH, Sueddeutsche Zeitung Photo/Alamy; **702**, Library of Congress Prints and Photographs Division[LC-DIG-npcc-03674]; **705**, Library of Congress Prints and Photographs Division; **706**, ClassicStock/Alamy; **711**, Library of Congress Prints and Photographs Division; **712**, Bettmann/Corbis; **713**, Library of Congress Prints and Photographs Division[LC-USZ62-125864]; **714**, Bettmann/Corbis; **715**, DIZ Muenchen GmbH, Sueddeutsche Zeitung Photo/Alamy; **716**, Hulton Archive/Getty Images; **717**, Library of Congress Prints and Photographs Division [LC-USZ61-1100]; **718**, Underwood & Underwood/Historical/Corbis; **720**, Library of Congress Prints and Photographs Division; **721**, Bettmann/Corbis; **723**, Everett Collection/Newscom; **725**, Library of Congress Prints and Photographs Division; **726**, Everett Collection Historical/Alamy; **728**, World History Archive/Image Asset Management Ltd./Alamy; **729**, World History Archive/Image Asset Management/Alamy; **733**, FPG/Staff/Hulton Archive/Getty Images; **734**, Uwe Pillat/Shutterstock; **735**, Heritage Image Partnership Ltd/Alamy; **736**, KEYSTONE Pictures USA/ZUMAPRESS/Newscom; **737**, Library of Congress Prints and Photographs Division[LC-DIG-hec-17355]; **738T**, Everett Collection/Newscom; **738B**, Everett Collection/Newscom; **740**, Library of Congress Prints and Photographs Division [LC-DIG-ppmsca-23061]; **741**, Library of Congress Prints and Photographs Division/Lange, Dorothea[LC-DIG-fsa-8b29516]; **743**, Library of Congress Prints and Photographs Division[LC-DIG-ppmsca-07216]; **744**, Fotosearch/Archive Photos/Getty Images; **748**, Library of Congress Prints and Photographs Division[LC-USF34-018214-E]; **750**, Everett Collection Historical/Alamy; **751T**, pf / Alamy; **751B**, Library of Congress Prints and Photographs Division[LC-USW3-034740-C]; **752**, Library of Congress Prints and Photographs Division[LC-USF34-030714-D]; **753**, AP Images; **754**, Danita Delimont/Alamy; **758**, Photo Researchers, Inc.; **760**, DIZ Muenchen GmbH/Sueddeutsche Zeitung Photo/Alamy; **763**, Akg-Images/Alamy; **765**, Library of Congress Prints and Photographs Division[LC-DIG-ppmsca-18560]; **766**, World History Archive / Alamy; **767**, Everett Collection/Newscom; **771**, Dr. Seuss Collection, MSS 230. Mandeville Special Collections Library, UC San Diego; **772**, DIZ Muenchen GmbH/Sueddeutsche Zeitung Photo/Alamy; **773**, Library of Congress Prints and Photographs Division[LC-USZ62-129812]; **775**, Library of Congress Prints and Photographs Division[LC-USZC4-4436]; **777**, World History Archive/Image Asset Management Ltd./Alamy; **779T**, Library of Congress Prints and Photographs Division[LC-F9-02-4503-330]; **779B**, Library of Congress Prints and Photographs Division[LC-USZ62-131712]; **780**, Library of Congress Prints and Photographs Division[LC-USZ62-44093]; **781**, Everett Collection/Newscom; **782**, Bettmann/Corbis; **784**, Bettmann/Corbis; **786**, AP Images; **788**, Library of Congress Prints and Photographs Division[LC-USZ62-67439]; **790**, Everett Collection Historical/Alamy; **792**, Stanislav Krasilnikov/ZUMA Press/Newscom; **793**, Interfoto/ History/Alamy; **796**, Robert W. Kelley/Getty Images; **798**, World History Archive/Alamy; **799**, Library of Congress Prints and Photographs Division[LC-USZ62-127379]; **803**, AP Images; **804**, Archive Image / Alamy; **806**, Library of Congress Prints and Photographs Division[LC-USZ62-70920]; **808**, AP Images; **810**, Hulton Archive/Getty Images; **812**, Lambert/Archive Photos/Getty Images; **813**, Library of Congress Prints and Photographs Division[LC-DIG-ppmsca-33570]; **814**, Yale Joel; **816**, FPG/Staff; **818**, Everett Collection/Newscom; **819**, Underwood Photo Archives / Underwood Photo Archives; **820**, Everett Collection / SuperStock; **821**, Carl Iwasaki//Time Life Pictures/Getty Images; **822**, St Petersburg Times/ZUMAPRESS/Newscom; **824**, Don Cravens/The LIFE Images Collection/Getty Images; **825**, Don Cravens/Time & Life Pictures/Getty Images; **826**, Perry Breon/Virginian-Pilot/AP Images; **827**, Charles Moore/Black Star/Alamy; **828**, Keystone Pictures USA/Alamy; **831**, Everett Collection/Newscom; **832**, Kevin McKiernan/ZUMA Press/Newscom; **833**, AP Images; **834**, stf/AP Images; **835**, Spencer Grant/Archive Photos/Getty Images; **836**, US Army Photo / Alamy; **837**, Pictorial Press Ltd / Alamy; **838T**, U.S. Defense Department/AP Images; **838B**, Tor Eigeland/Alamy; **840**, Donald Uhrbrock//Time Life Pictures/Getty Images; **841**, AP Images; **842**, AP Images; **844**, AP Images; **845**, Hong Seong-Chan/AP Images; **846**, Library of Congress Prints and Photographs Division[LC-DIG-ppmsca-24360]; **847**, INTERFOTO / Alamy; **849**, Library of Congress Prints and Photographs Division[LC-DIG-ppmsca-03411]; **850**, Amiko Kauderer/NASA Images; **851**, Keystone/Getty Images; **852**, AP Images; **854**, AP Images; **855**, Benjamin E. "Gene" Forte - CNP/Newscom; **858**, Dirck Halstead/The LIFE Images Collection/Getty Images; **860**, Fotosearch/Archive Photos/Getty Images; **861**, Arthur Grace/ZUMAPRESS/Newscom; **862T**, Mohammad Sayad/Ap Images; **862B**, Universal Images Group Limited/Alamy; **866**, PF-(usna) / Alamy; **868**, Ellisphotos/Alamy; **870**, HEIKKI SAUKKOMAA/Getty Images; **872**, AFP/Getty Images; **873**, Thomas Kienzle/AP Images; **876**, U.S. Air Force/Staff Sergeant Chris Steffen/AP Images; **877**, Tom Mihalek/Getty Images; **878**, Weird NJ/Splash News/Newscom; **880B**, File photo/KRT/Newscom; **882**, Joe Marquette/POOL/AFP/Getty Images/Newscom; **884T**, Tannen Maury/AP Images; **884B**, PhotoQuest/Getty Images; **886**, Cynthia Johnson/The LIFE Images Collection/Getty Images; **887**, Thomas Hartwell/Time & Life Pictures/Getty Images; **890**, PF-(space1)/Alamy; **892**, US Army Photo/Alamy; **893**, PCN Photography/Alamy; **896**, World History Archive/ Alamy; **897**, Jamal Nasrallah/EPA/Newscom; **898**, Yomiuri Shimbun /AP Images; **899**, Xinhua/

Sipa USA/Newscom; **901,** Carolyn Kaster/Pool/AP Images; **903T,** DAVID FURST/Getty Images; **903B,** Trinity Mirror / Mirrorpix / Alamy; **904,** Kristoffer Tripplaar/Alamy; **905,** Lucas Schifres/Getty Images; **910,** Bloomberg/Getty Images; **913,** US House / Alamy; **914,** Kaiser/Caro/Alamy; **915,** Stocktrek Images/Getty Images; **916T,** Jim Parkin/Shutterstock; **916B,** ZUMA Press, Inc / Alamy; **918,** pedrosala/Shutterstock; **919,** Hector Retamal/Getty Images; **921,** Everett Collection/Newscom; **923,** Jochen Tack/Alamy; **924,** Marta Lavandier/AP Images; **928,** Mike Segar/Reuters/Newscom; **932,** Chuck Mason/Alamy; **933,** Jim Young/Reuters/Corbis; **938,** Stock Connection Blue / Alamy; **n/a,** Bill Manns/The Art Archive/Art Resource, NY; **n/a,** Bettmann/Corbis; **n/a,** Niday Picture Library/Alamy; **n/a,** Library of Congress Prints and Photographs Division[LC-USZC4-12466]; **n/a,** North Wind Picture Archives/Alamy; **n/a,** Return of the Warriors, 1906 (w/c on paper), Russell, Charles Marion (1865–1926) / Private Collection / Peter Newark Western Americana / The Bridgeman Art Library; **n/a,** Niday Picture Library/Alamy; **n/a,** National Geographic Image Collection / Alamy; **n/a,** Southern Pacific News Bureau/AP Images; **n/a,** PF-usna/Alamy; **n/a,** Culver Pictures / The Art Archive at Art Resource, NY; **n/a,** William Henry Vanderbilt (1821–1885), who greatly extended his father Cornelius's railroad interests, standing as a Colossus, puppet-master over the American railroad. The smaller figures are Jay Gould (1836–1892) American financier and speculator, right; **n/a,** Image Asset Management Ltd./Alamy

[Text Acknowledgments]

Al Jazeera, Transcript of bin Laden's Full Speech, November 2004. Copyright © Al Jazeera.; **Alfred A. Knopf,** The Negro Speaks of Rivers," and "My People" from THE COLLECTED POEMS OF LANGSTON HUGHES by Langston Hughes, edited by Arnold Rampersad with David Roessel, Associate Editor, copyright © 1994 by the Estate of Langston Hughes. Used by permission of Alfred A. Knopf, an imprint of the Knopf Doubleday Publishing Group, a division of Random House LLC. All rights reserved; **Alfred A. Knopf,** Of Plymouth Plantation by William Bradford. Copyright © 1981 Alfred A. Knopf.; **BiblioLife,** The Jesuits in North America by Francis Parkman. Copyright © 2010. BiblioLife.; **Bridges, Roger,** The Betrayal of the Freedmen? Rutherford B. Hayes and the End of Reconstruction? Copyright © Roger D. Bridges. Used by permission.; **CBS Corporation,** In Our Own Words: Extraordinary Speeches of the American Century by Orson Welles . Copyright © CBS Corporation; **Center for Instructional Development and Educational Research,** Inaugural Address by Bill Clinton, January 20, 1993. Copyright © Center for Instructional Development and Educational Research.; **Cesar E. Chavez Foundation,** Cesar Chavez, "Education of the Heart- Quotes by Cesar Chavez." United Farm Workers. Copyright © Cesar E. Chavez Foundation. http://www.ufw.org/_page.php?menu=research&inc=history/09.html.; **CNN,** Riled About Rail: Why All the Anger Over High Speed Trains? Copyright © CNN. Used by permission.; **Cornell University Law School,** Militarism in a Global Age: Naval Ambitions in Germany and the United States Before World War I by Dirk Bonker, 2012. Copyright © Cornell University Law School.; **Cuomo, Mario,** Democratic National Convention Keynote Address, 1984. Copyright © Mario Cuomo.; **Doubleday,** Excerpts from "Diary of a Young Girl: The Definitive Edition" by Anne Frank, edited by Otto H. Frank and Mirjam Pressler, translated by Susan Massotty, translation copyright © 1995 by Doubleday, a division of Random House LLC. Used by permission of Doubleday, an imprint of the Knopf Doubleday Publishing Group, a division of Random House LLC. All rights reserved.; **Dover Publications,** How the Other Half Lives by Jacob Riis. Copyright © Dover Publications.; **Encyclopedia Britannica, Inc.,** Sketches of American Policy by Noah Webster from The Lawbook Exchange, Ltd, 1785. Copyright © Encyclopedia Britannica, Inc.; **Encyclopedia Britannica, Inc.,** Allan Nevis and Henry Graff, "George Washington: President of United States." Reprinted with permission from Encyclopædia Britannica, © 2014 by Encyclopædia Britannica, Inc.; **Foner, Eric,** The Supreme Court and the History of Reconstruction - and Vice-Versa by Eric Foner from Columbia Law Review, November 2012. Copyright © Eric Foner.; **Fordham University Press,** Lincoln on Democracy by Abraham Lincoln, G. S. Boritt. Copyright © 2004 by Fordham University Press.; **George Eastman House,** George Eastman Educational Packet. Copyright © George Eastman House.; **George Mason University,** Annual Report of the Secretary of the Interior for the Fiscal Year Ended June 30, 1938. Copyright © George Mason University; **George Washington University,** The Secret History of the Great Asian War. Copyright © George Washington University.; **Google Inc.,** Debate Between Republican Presidential Candidates, George H. Bush and Ronald Reagan, 1980. Copyright © Google, Inc.; **Google Inc.,** TV interview with David Frost, May 20, 1977. Copyright © Google Inc.; **Greenwood Press, Inc.,** History of Mexico by Burton Corkwood. Copyright © Greenwood Press.; **Hackett Publishing Company,** True History of the Conquest of New Spain by Bernal Diaz del Castillo. Copyright © 2012 Hackett Publishing Company.; **Harold Ober Associates,** The Collected Poems of Langston Hughes by Langston Hughes edited by Arnold Rampersad with David Roessel, Associate Editor. Copyright © 1994 by the Estate of Langston Hughes. Used by permission of Harold Ober Associates Incorporated.; **Harper Collins Publishers,** You Learn by Living: Eleven Keys for a More Fulfilling Life by Eleanor Roosevelt. Copyright © Harper Collins Publishers.; **Harvard University Press,** "Dissertation on the Canon and Feudal Law" from Papers of John Adams, vol. 1 by John Adams and Robert Joseph Taylor (ed.). Copyright © 2010 Harvard University Press.; **Houghton Mifflin Harcourt Publishing Company,** Silent Spring by Rachel Carson. Copyright © Houghton Mifflin Harcourt.; **Independent Living Institute,** The Story of a Sweatshop Girl: Sadie Frowne Independent, LIV, September 25, 1902. Copyright © Independent Living Institute; **Information Age Publishing,** Assessing Discussion of Public Issues: A Scoring Guide by Ronald W. Evans from The Handbook on Teaching Social Issues. Copyright © Information Age Publishing. Used by permission.; **Institute of Islamic Knowledge,** English Translation of the Meaning of Al-Qur'an: The Guidance for Mankind translated by Muhammad Farooq-i-Azam Malik. Copyright © 1997 The Institute of Islamic Knowledge. Used by permission.; **Kent State University Press,** The Use of Military Force to Protect the Gains of Reconstruction by William Blair from Civil War History, Vol. 51, Issue 4, December 2005. Copyright © Kent State University Press.; **KERA,** The Borderlands on the Eve of War: A Conversation with David J. Weber. Copyright © KERA. Used by permission.; **Ludwig Von Mises Institute,** Democracy's False Prophet by David Gordon from The Mises Review, September 2002. Copyright © Ludwig von Mises Institute.; **M.E. Sharpe, Inc., Publisher,** "The Antecedents: World Trade Before the Discovery of America" from A Financial History of the United States, Vol. 1: From Christopher Columbus to the Robber Barons (1492–1900) by Jerry Markham. Copyright © 2001 M.E. Sharpe.; **Marcus Garvey People's Political Party,** A Tree Without Roots. Copyright © Marcus Garvey People's Political Party.; **McFarland & Company, Inc. Publishers,** "Ulysses S. Grant, 1861–1864: His Rise from Obscurity to Military Greatness", My Bondage and Freedom by Frederick Douglass. Copyright © 1855 by NEW YORK AND AUBURN: MILLER, ORTON & MULLIGAN.; **McFarland & Company, Inc. Publishers,** Ulysses S. Grant, 1861–1864: His Rise from Obscurity to Military Greatness by William Farina. Copyright © McFarland & Company, Inc. Publishers.; **Mobile Reference,** Life and Times of Frederick Douglass by Frederick Douglass. Copyright © 2010 by Mobile Reference; **National Council of Churches,** "I Corinthians, Chapter 13" from Holy Bible: With the Apocryphal. Copyright © 1989 National Council of Churches of Christ.; **Native American Aid,** Unknown, "Living Conditions." Native American Aid, 2014. http://www.nrcprograms.org/site/PageServer?pagename=naa_livingconditions; **Navajivan Trust,** "Chapter XVI, Passive Resistance" from Indian Home Rule by Mahatma Gandhi. Copyright © Navajivan Trust. Used by permission.; **Neville Chamberlain,** Peace for Our Time by Neville Chamberlain, September 30, 1938. Copyright © Neville Chamberlain.; **New York Times,** Interview with Charles A. Lindbergh from The New York Times, May 23, 1927. Copyright © The New York Times.; **Next Decade Entertainment, Inc.,** Source: "Brother, Can You Spare a Dime," by E.Y. "Yip" Harburg and Jay Gorney. Published by Gorney Music(ASCAP). Gorney Music Administered by Next Decade Entertainment, Inc. All Rights Reserved. Use by Permission.; **Nobel Media AB,** Speech upon accepting the Nobel Peace Prize by Frank B. Kellogg, December 10, 1929. Copyright © Nobel Media AB.; **Octopus Publishing Group Limited,** The Sinews of Peace by Winston Churchill, 1948. Copyright © Octopus Publishing Group Limited.; **Oxford University Press (UK) - Journals,** Harriet Beecher Stowe : A Life by Joan D. Hedrick. Copyright © 1994 by Oxford University Press.; **Penguin Books, Ltd. (UK),** "Freedom from Fear" from FREEDOM FROM FEAR AND OTHER WRITINGS, REVISED EDITION by Aung San Suu Kyi, edited by Michael Aris, copyright © 1991, 1995 by Aung San Suu Kyi. Used by permission of Viking Penguin, a division of Penguin Group (USA) LLC.; **Penguin Group,** "Freedom from Fear" from FREEDOM FROM FEAR AND OTHER WRITINGS, REVISED EDITION by Aung San Suu Kyi, edited by Michael Aris, copyright © 1991, 1995 by Aung San Suu Kyi. Used by permission of Viking Penguin, a division